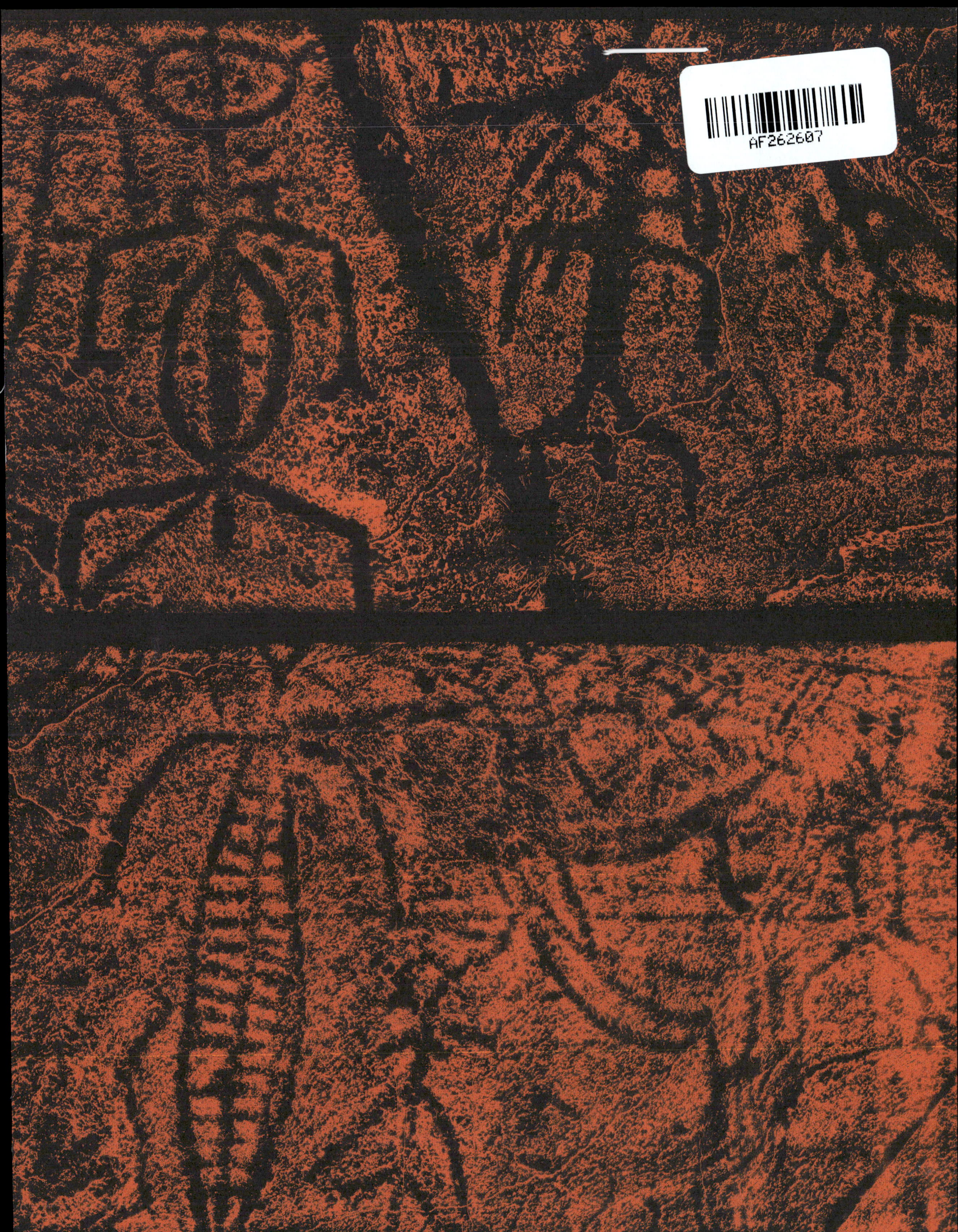
AF262607

ROCK ART

and its Legacy in Myth and Art

ROCK ART

and its Legacy in Myth and Art

PETROGLYPHS FROM EURASIA, ARABIA AND NORTHERN AFRICA

**CHRISTOPH BAUMER
& THERESE WEBER**

BLOOMSBURY ACADEMIC

LONDON · NEW YORK · OXFORD · NEW DELHI · SYDNEY

BLOOMSBURY ACADEMIC
Bloomsbury Publishing Plc
50 Bedford Square, London, WC1B 3DP, UK
1385 Broadway, New York, NY 10018, USA
29 Earlsfort Terrace, Dublin 2, Ireland

BLOOMSBURY, BLOOMSBURY ACADEMIC and the Diana logo are trademarks of Bloomsbury Publishing Plc

First published in Great Britain 2025

Cover design: Christopher Bromley
Cover image © Christoph Baumer
Front endpaper: Rubbing of petroglyphs at Amtmannsnes, Norway.
Back endpaper: Rubbing of petroglyphs from Saimaluu Tash, Kyrgyzstan.

ISBN: HB: 978-0-7556-5044-6
          ePDF: 978-0-7556-5046-0
          eBook: 978-0-7556-5045-3

Copyedited by Henry Howard
Book design by Christopher Bromley
Project Manager Carolann Young, ITS
Printed and bound in Italy

For product safety related questions contact productsafety@bloomsbury.com

To find out more about our authors and books visit www.bloomsbury.com and sign up for our newsletters.

Contents

3.

The Influence of Rock Art on Contemporary Art   361

By Therese Weber

Appendices

Indexes

1

Definitions and Methods

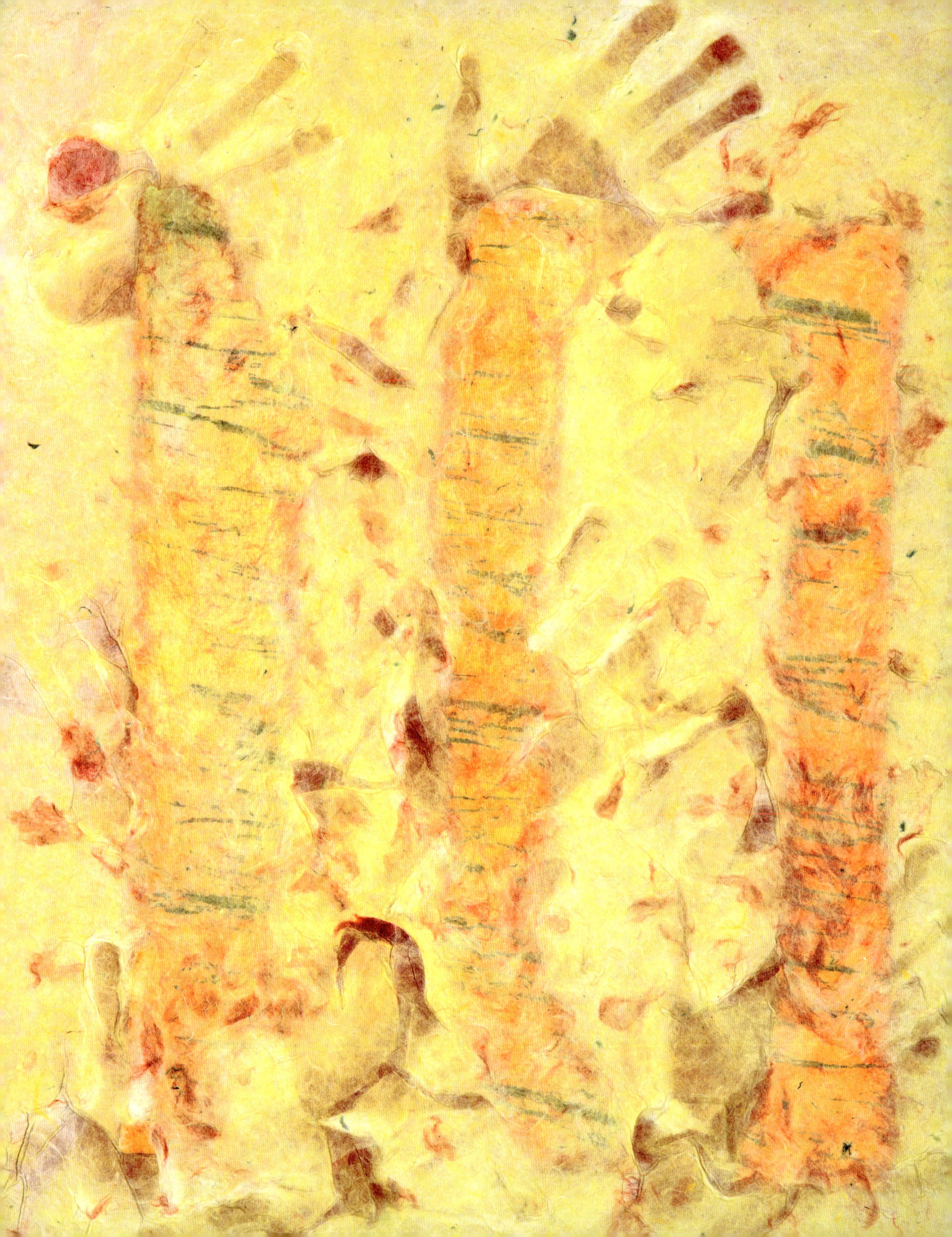

I. Defining Rock Art and Contextualizing Petroglyphs

After attracting the interest of the public and some famous artists in Europe and the USA in the 1920s and 1930s, rock art subsequently fell somewhat out of the focus of both science and art, but since the turn of the third millennium it has enjoyed renewed attention. Rock art is defined as markings applied by humans to natural and non-portable stone surfaces; in some cases, these markings were placed on softer surfaces such as mud that later dried and hardened. Unlike portable art such as body ornamentations, amulets and figurines, rock art is fixed to the landscape. Rock art is a universal cultural and social phenomenon, found on all continents but Antarctica.

1. Petroglyphs and other forms of rock art

Five main types of rock art can be distinguished, according to the technology of production. **1) Petroglyphs**, a term derived from the Greek *pétros* (πέτρος), 'stone', and *glúphein* (γλύφειν), 'to carve, engrave', are created by removing more or less of the surface of a rock by pecking, gouging, engraving, incising or edging.[1] **2) Pictoglyphs**, also called **pictographs** or **rock paintings**, are made by applying to rock surfaces ground minerals such as ochre (a mixture of ferric oxide) for yellow and red colours, manganese oxide for black and kaolin clay or chalk for white; as a binder, water was used, and sometimes also blood, animal or vegetable oils and egg white.[2] Manganese oxide was often replaced by charcoal, which from the perspective of today's scientists has the advantage that it can be radiocarbon dated, as can the organic binders. Pictoglyphs are made by painting, drawing, printing or stencilling. Except in hyper-arid climates, rock paintings only survive in places protected from precipitation, such as caves or rock shelters (rock faces lying under a promontory).[3] The term **cave art** or **parietal art** comprises pictographs and petroglyphs located in caves and shelters dating from the Upper Palaeolithic (*ca.* 50–12 ka BP).[4] Whereas the golden age of West European and Uralian parietal art falls within the Last Glacial Period, also called Last Ice Age, which in those regions ended *ca.* 11.7 ka BP, most petroglyphs were created in the post-glacial epoch, that is the succeeding Holocene.[5]

The major exceptions, that is rock engravings dating from the late Upper Palaeolithic, are found in a number of French caves such as Les Trois-Frères (fig. 10), Cussac (fig. 3), Niaux, Gabillou, Gorge d'Enfer, Les Combarelles, Saint-Cirq-du-Bugue, Grotte du Cheval at Arcy-sur-Cure, La Mouthe, Pair-non-Pair, La Croze-à-Gontran, Bara-Bahau and Bourdeilles (Bernous).[6] An exception to the location of Palaeolithic petroglyphs inside caves are the two flat sandstone fragments discovered in 2016 near Piechegu, southern France, which are engraved with the profiles of four horses. These petroglyphs were not located in a cave or by a shelter, but were part of a large slab that stood at the edge

---

1. ← Therese Weber, *Hand into the Future I*. As an essential tool for performing actions, the hand here symbolizes all eras. It is just as relevant today as it was in prehistoric times. 64 × 49 cm. Washi, coloured and cast mulberry fibre; pulp painting on both sides, 2023.

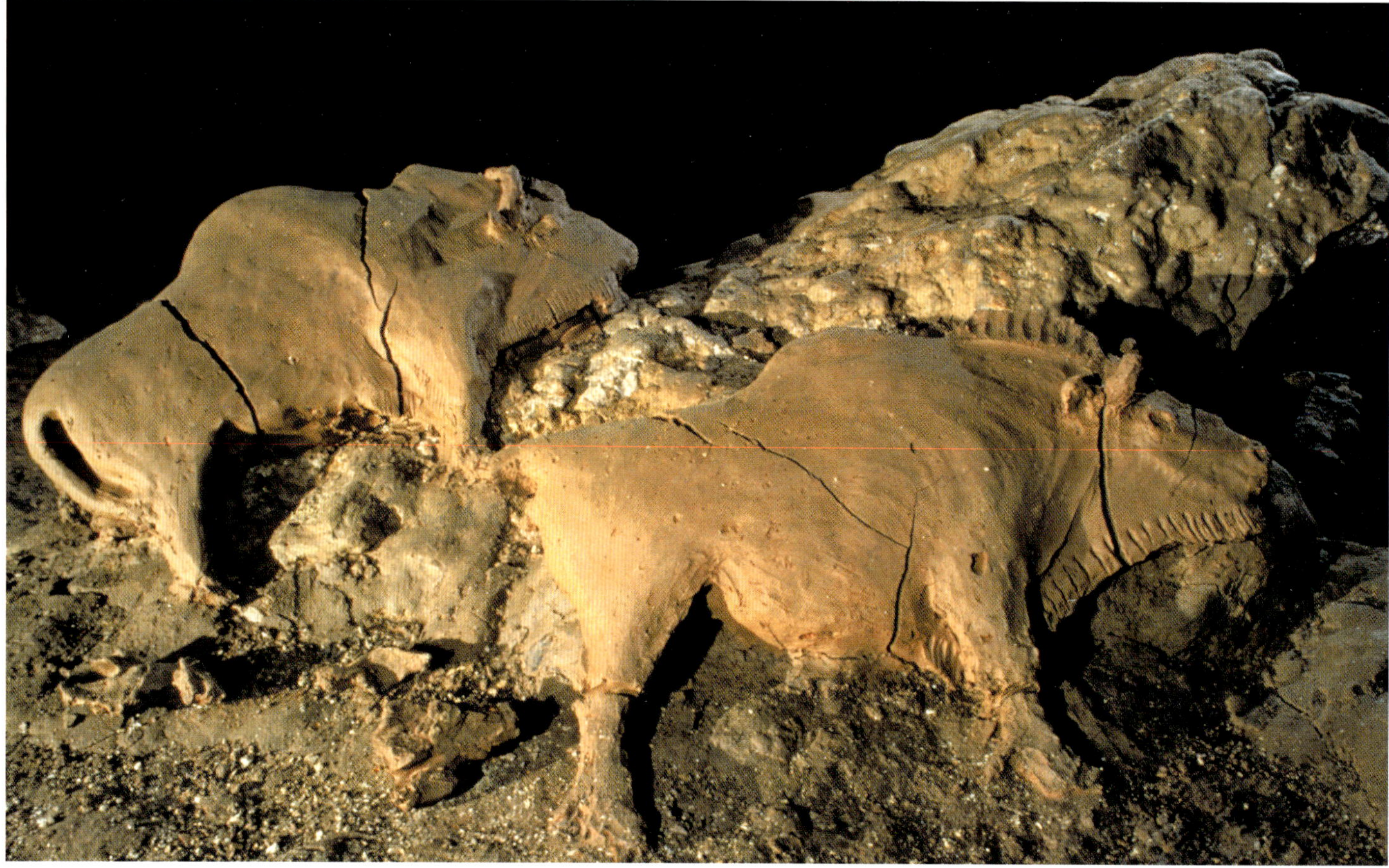

2. Clay high-relief of two bison from the Upper Palaeolithic in the cave of Tuc d'Audoubert, French Pyrenees. The figures are located in the deepest and darkest hall of the cave complex, 588 m from the entrance. © Association Louis Bégouën, France.

of a settlement and was therefore visible to everyone. The site is dated to the early Magdalenian (20–14 ka BP); the function of these petroglyphs remains unknown.[7] Outside France, rock engravings from the Upper Palaeolithic can be found (inter alia) among the oldest petroglyphs of the Côa Valley in north-eastern Portugal; in the Parpalló Cave, Spain, where *ca.* 5,000 painted and engraved limestone plaques featuring animals and plants have been found; in the neighbouring Cova Dones Cave;[8] in Italy in the Addaura cave;[9] in western Mongolia; possibly in Siberia; and at Qurta in Egypt.

3) **Geoglyphs**, in turn, are larger abstract or figurative images made on horizontal ground using stones or earth. Positive geoglyphs are built by arranging stones on the ground while a negative geoglyph is produced by removing material from the ground surface in order to make a differently coloured lower layer visible, an approach similar to making petroglyphs. Geoglyphs, like those in Nazca, Peru, have huge dimensions, sometimes more than a hundred metres long, so that they can only be identified from an elevated viewpoint. The next category of rock art comprises non-portable, carved **4) rock reliefs** which remain in their landscape attached to the living rock. The most famous ones

from the Upper Palaeolithic are the high reliefs of two bison made from clay in the cave of Tuc d'Audoubert located in the foothills of the French Pyrenees (fig. 2) which are dated 16.5 ka cal. BP.[10] It is striking that these two high reliefs were made in the deepest part of the cave complex; the effort required of the artists seems to be related to the importance of bison as a major supplier of meat.[11] The various contemporaneous footprints, probably of adolescents, made in the clay floor of this cave which was difficult and dangerous to access suggest that it served as a site of rituals of passage from youth to adulthood.[12] Mention must be made of the high reliefs of the Venus of Laussel from *ca.* 25 ka BP, the aurochs from Le Fourneau du Diable near Bourdeilles dated to *ca.* 20 ka BP, and the horses at Cap Blanc from 15 ka BP, one of which is more than two metres long.[13]

Related to petroglyphs from a technical point of view are **5) graffiti**, an ambiguous term referring to different forms of visual communication: in archaeology, the very thinly incised rock figures from the Central Asian Turkic (*ca.* 5th–9th century CE) and Kazakh (15th–19th century CE) epochs are called graffiti; so too are ancient inscriptions or scribbles edged into monuments without the consent of the owners. Famous examples are the thousands of personal epigrams, greetings, notices and obscene texts engraved on public and private monuments from Roman antiquity.[14] Also found widely spread are the names and epigrams inscribed by early Christians in catacombs, by medieval prisoners on the walls of their gaols and the politico-satirical declarations painted or engraved during the Middle Ages on public monuments. The term graffiti takes on a definite pejorative connotation when applied to the recent pecking, engraving or spraying of names or political statements on existing ancient rock art or other monuments. This kind of graffiti amounts to the defacement of cultural heritage, since they are incompatible with the original petroglyphs or pictographs.[15] Finally, in the 1970s the trend arose of drawing images with spray paint on the exterior of buildings, on the walls of subways or on trains. These graffiti are judged to be either vandalism, a punishable offence, or valuable street art. At present, the pseudonymous artist and political activist Banksy is the most famous representative of such graffiti-based street art.

Finally, free-standing **stone steles** with engraved patterns or figures are also related to petroglyphs, provided at any rate that the engraved motifs show similarities with petroglyphs from the same culture and region. Steles are usually taller than they are wide.[16] In particular, the so-called **deer stones** from Bronze Age Mongolia and

3. ↓ Petroglyphs of horses and bison in the Great Panel in the cave of Cussac, Dordogne, south-eastern France. Although the first archaeological investigations of the cave, which is tubular and 1,600 m long, took place as early as 1950, its monumental engravings were only discovered in September 2000 after the removal of a rockslide. The Great Panel is located 310 m from the entry. Alongside horses and bison, there are also images of ibexes, rhinoceroses and mammoths, which are sometimes associated with human females, as well as scratches made by bear claws. The petroglyphs, which are stylistically very homogenous, date to the middle Gravettian period around 29 to 28 ka BP. Cussac is one of the very few sites where human remains have been found in a cave bearing Palaeolithic rock art. At Cussac, the bones of at least six humans, among them one complete male skeleton, were found in two places 150 and 230 m from the entry. The human bones have also been dated to the middle Gravettian which means the rock art and burials date from the same period; the bones of bears also found in the cave are 10 to 18 millennia older than the human ones. It seems that soon after 28 ka BP the cave was closed off, either naturally or intentionally.[1] © Centre National de la Préhistoire, Périgueux, France.

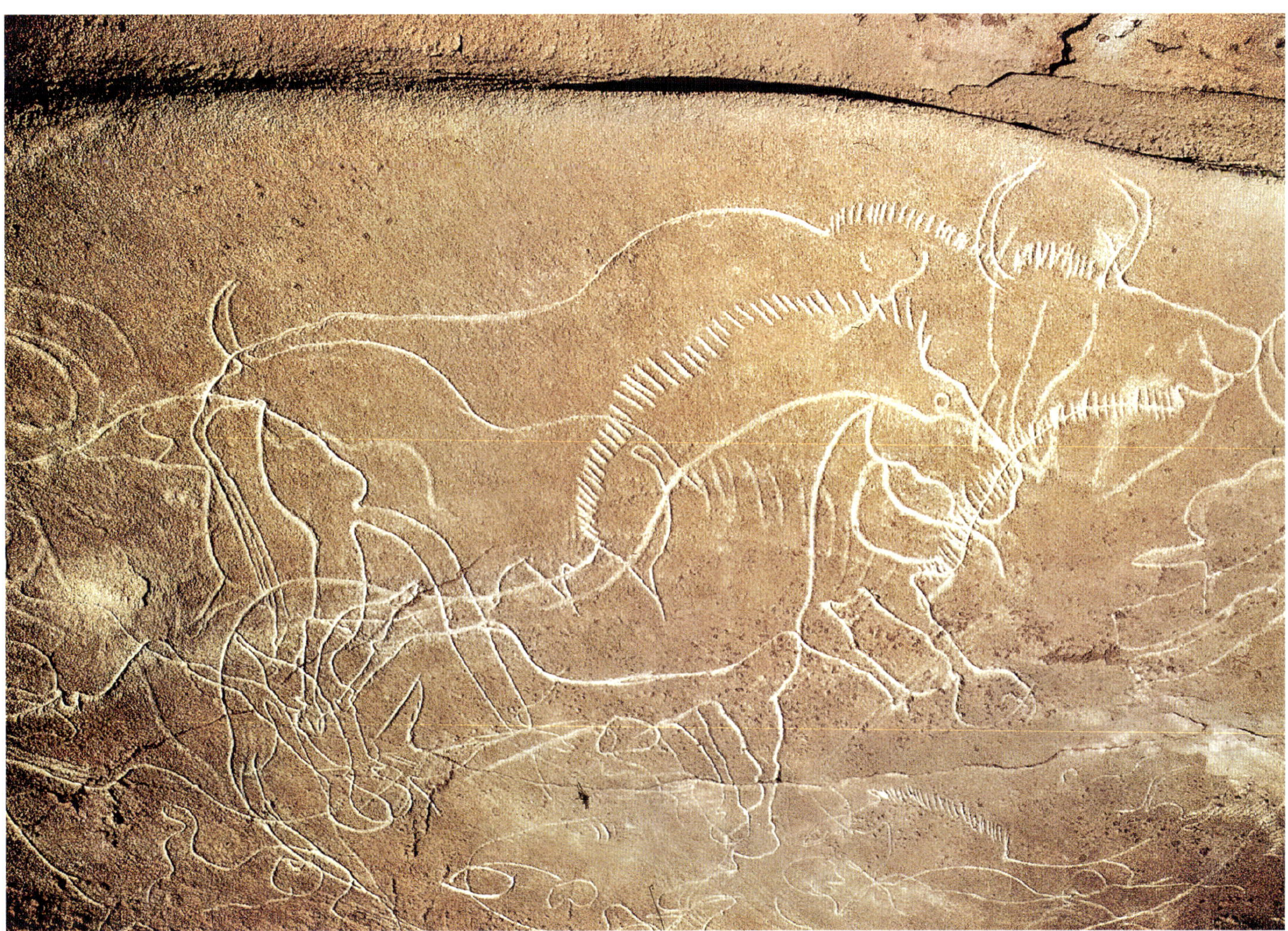

the Sayan-Altai region, whose entire surface is covered with figurative images ground into the stone, are comparable to the contemporary petroglyphs to which their images are often virtually identical.

This book concentrates on outdoor petroglyphs and will leave the subject of cave engravings untouched.[17] It addresses the other forms of rock art only marginally, in order to place the development of petroglyphs in a broader cultural context.[18] In terms of geography, the focus will lie on the Afro-Eurasian cultural realm, that is the vast area stretching from Mongolia in the east to the Sahara in the west. Although the space under consideration is immense, various kinds of contacts existed between individual regions, such as between the individual focal points of Central Asia as well as between them and the Himalayan region and Siberia; between Siberia, Karelia and Arctic Scandinavia; between southern Scandinavia and the Alpine region and the Mediterranean area; and between the latter, Arabia and North Africa. Therefore, cultural regions with little or no connection to the Afro-Eurasian realm, such as Australia, South East Asia, central China and both Americas are not addressed. As the number of petroglyph sites within this huge realm runs into the thousands, with millions of individual images, a selection of sites had to be made with the aim of presenting those that are most typical, and those that are unique, within each region. The present authors have, in 19 expeditions and journeys over the course of the last 26 years, personally studied and documented more than 90 per cent of the sites described. This focus on petroglyphs means that certain regions, such as Eastern Europe, which have a rich prehistoric heritage in terms of portable art but largely lack petroglyphs, will not be discussed.[19]

In the face of innumerable specialized contributions to the subject dedicated to a single area, epoch or topic, the present book aims at offering a broad and well-illustrated overview of petroglyphs within the Afro-Eurasian realm as a whole. Where applicable, it will attempt to connect rock art motifs to the mythological heritage of their respective cultures. The final chapter will show how rock art in general and petroglyphs in particular are not only a cultural relic from the distant past, but have, since the early twentieth century, provided inspiration for leading visual artists.

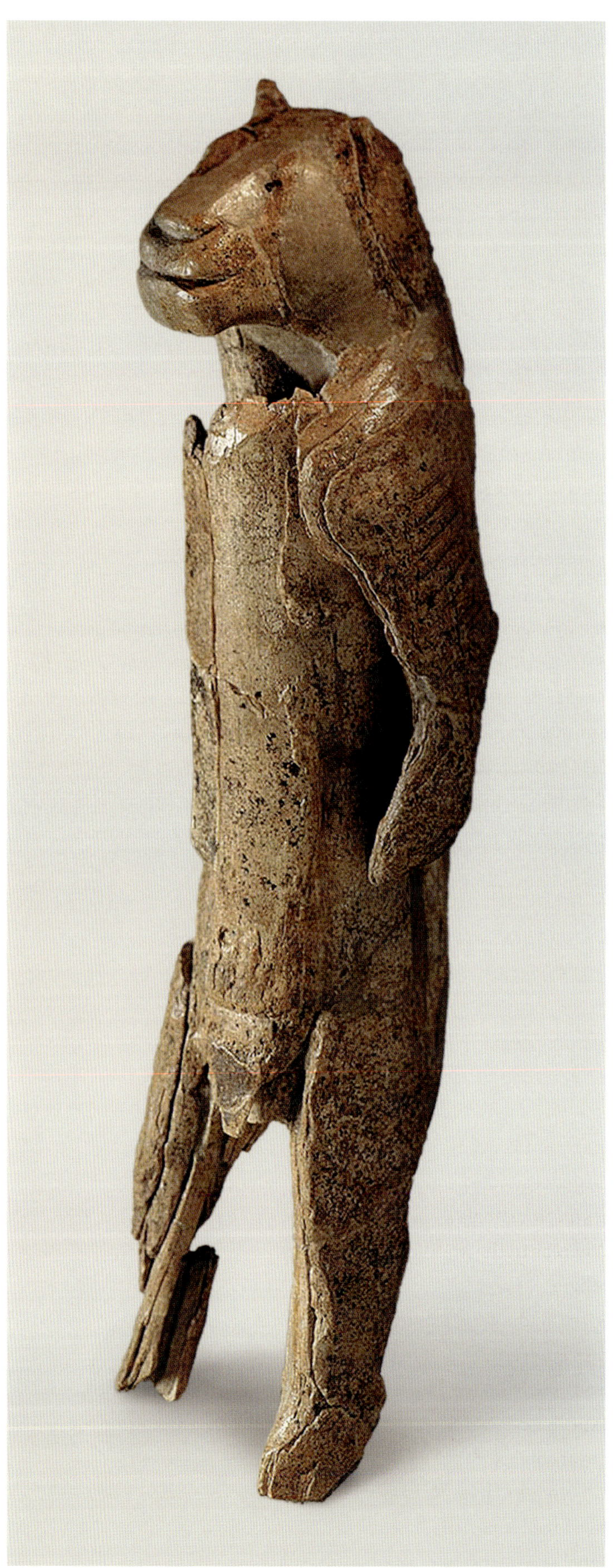

4. Figurine of a hybrid being with a male human body and the head of a lion or a bear. The figurine, made from mammoth ivory, is 35,000 to 40,000 years old and was excavated in the Hohlenstein-Stadel Cave, southern Germany. It has been reconstructed three times, most recently in 2013, from more than 200 pieces excavated in 1939. Museum Ulm, Ulm, Germany.

2. Is rock art 'art'?

Do petroglyphs represent 'art', as the term 'rock art' implies? The understanding of 'art', specifically of visual art, experienced a dramatic break with the appearance of Marcel Duchamp's first readymade sculpture – a porcelain urinal – in 1917. From then on, conceptual criteria increasingly pushed aesthetic ones into the background, and almost into insignificance. In conceptual art, ideas, and often socio-political concepts, become dominant, allowing such works to ignore the values of aesthetics and aesthetic pleasure. 'Art' is no longer a creation which is perceptually attractive and pleasing, but is what the artist himself or herself, a curator or an art critic declares to be 'art'. Such an arbitrary definition is hardly applicable to rock art.

In the history of European philosophy, Plato and Aristotle saw the essence of art, be it verbal, musical or visual, in *mímesis*, the imitation of nature. However, Plato denied that art could encapsulate the 'truth', that is the essence of things, and quoted Socrates' allegory of the three beds: the first is the ideal of a bed, Kant's 'thing-in-itself'; the second a human-made bed which imitates the ideal; and the third a painting of a bed which imitates the first imitation.[20] A similar hypothesis was advanced by Pliny the Elder in his *Natural History*, stating that 'the art of painting … originated in tracing lines round the human shadow'.[21] The aspiration to reproduce nature as exactly as possible is encapsulated in the story of the painting contest between Zeuxis and Parrhasius told by Pliny: whereas Zeuxis painted some grapes so naturally that the birds flew towards the painted fruits, Parrhasius painted a curtain with such singular truthfulness that Zeuxis, proud of his achievement, haughtily demanded that the curtain should be drawn aside so he could see his adversary's picture. Upon discovering his mistake, he admitted defeat, for he had only deceived birds, but Parrhasius had deceived him, a human.[22] Besides these rather restricted conceptions, art was defined by parameters of aesthetic criteria such as beauty, grace and formal perfection. Whereas in the Middle Ages visual art was chiefly in the service of religion, that is Christianity and its message (as was also the case with Buddhist art), in the later Middle Ages and in the Renaissance the representation of nature or of a celestial world as the aim of art was now joined by that of expression: artists conveying personal experiences, feelings or messages through the visual medium of the art object.[23]

In his *Critique of Judgement* from 1790, Immanuel Kant developed a concept of beauty related to art by starting from the beholder, the perceiving subject. What is judged as beautiful in art is that which creates a feeling of pleasure in the subject, even though it is neither useful nor purposeful nor morally good: the beautiful triggers a 'disinterested pleasure'.[24] Contrary to Kant, Georg W.F. Hegel, who emphasized the indispensable importance of art within human cultures, argued that art had to be more than just a formal imitation of what exists, and pleasant to the eye. Art must also stimulate reflection on what it expresses and conveys. Like philosophy or the sciences, art also encompasses understanding. The main purpose of art is to present, or rather stimulate, an understanding that can only be gained through sensual perception. Hegel insisted, however, that its content is by no means the only criterion for judging art, which otherwise drifts into didacticism. Art must be meaningful, but also satisfy aesthetic criteria of beauty.[25] Since art has always conveyed an underlying idea, it has always existed in a particular cultural context.

Insofar as petroglyphs were embedded in their respective cultures and, depending on the era, reflected animate nature, rituals and myths as well as social and historical processes, they can be included within the concept of 'art'; all the more so in that many petroglyphs masterfully combine both artistic expression and closeness to nature while at the same time presenting aspirational role models and social visions. Concerning rock art, however, Hegel was mistaken on one point. As will be explained below in this chapter, there was no gradual development within rock art, no ladder of progress, but a sudden outburst of creative and masterful two- and three-dimensional artworks in both Central and Western Europe as well as in South East Asia more than 40,000 years ago. Allegedly, Pablo Picasso himself consecrated rock art, especially parietal art, as true art, declaring that 'we [the famous artists] haven't invented anything', adding in a stance sceptical of artistic evolution, 'In art there is neither past nor future.'[26] And in 1984, Joseph Beuys claimed: 'Maybe I am a reborn cave artist.'[27]

From an anthropological point of view, Howard Murphy formulated a definition of art that also fits petroglyphs: 'Art objects are ones with aesthetic and/or semantic attributes … that are used for representational or presentational purposes.'[28] Especially in pre-literate cultures, that is prehistoric societies without written records, rock art was one of the most important visual media for the communication of ideas, beliefs and values as well as for the transmission of knowledge concerning rituals and their performance. Insofar as archaeology is the science of researching past cultures and societies by studying their material relics, often deeply buried in the soil and – for example in the case of imported grave goods – located far from their places of origin, the exploration and study of rock art, which has remained *in situ* for millennia and

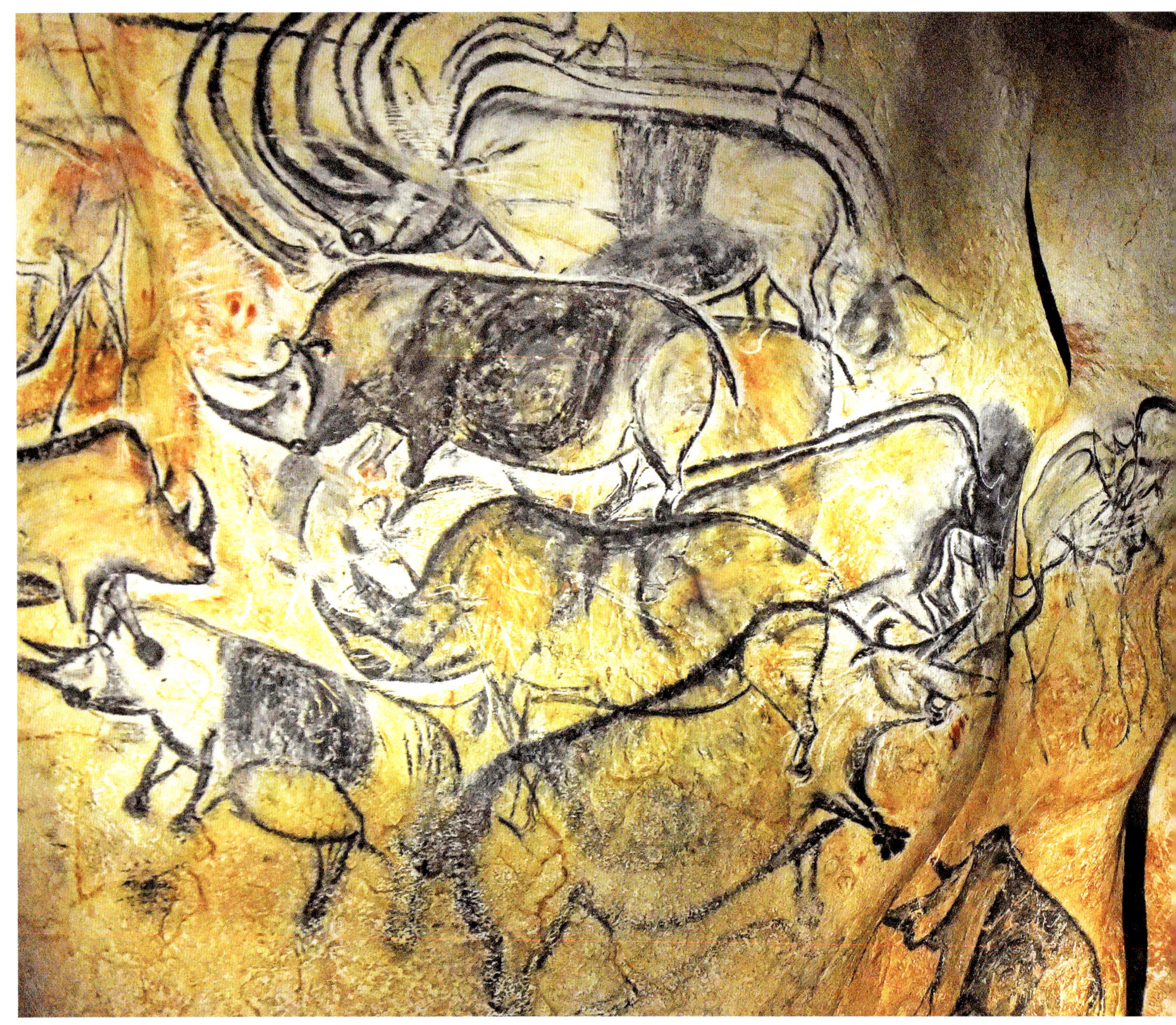

5. Parietal paintings from the Aurignacian period, 37–36.2 ka cal. BP, in the Hall of the Lions, the deepest hall of the Chauvet cave. From right to left: a pack of lions attacks a group of bison, then a young mammoth with ball-shaped paws and a group of running rhinoceroses; the horn of the upper rhinoceros seems to be multiplied to represent successive snapshots of movement.

has mostly stayed intact thanks to the durability of the material, can serve as an essential supplement to our understanding of prehistoric mankind. However, as has been emphasized by Sven Ouzman, 'rock art images are not like signifiers and have no necessary and sufficient relation of relevance with a signified.'

Petroglyphs do not have the unambiguity of text. In his words, 'images are often things in themselves and not something standing for something else,'[29] and the meaning of a certain petroglyph, for instance a ship, a chariot or a hunting scene may vary depending on the cultural context. Occasionally, ethnology can contribute to clarify the meaning of petroglyphs by the study of long-established myths and thus open a window into the vanished world of the distant past. Archaeology, rock art studies and ethnology complement each other since the archaeology of prehistoric cultures is often restricted to information from burials and grave goods that

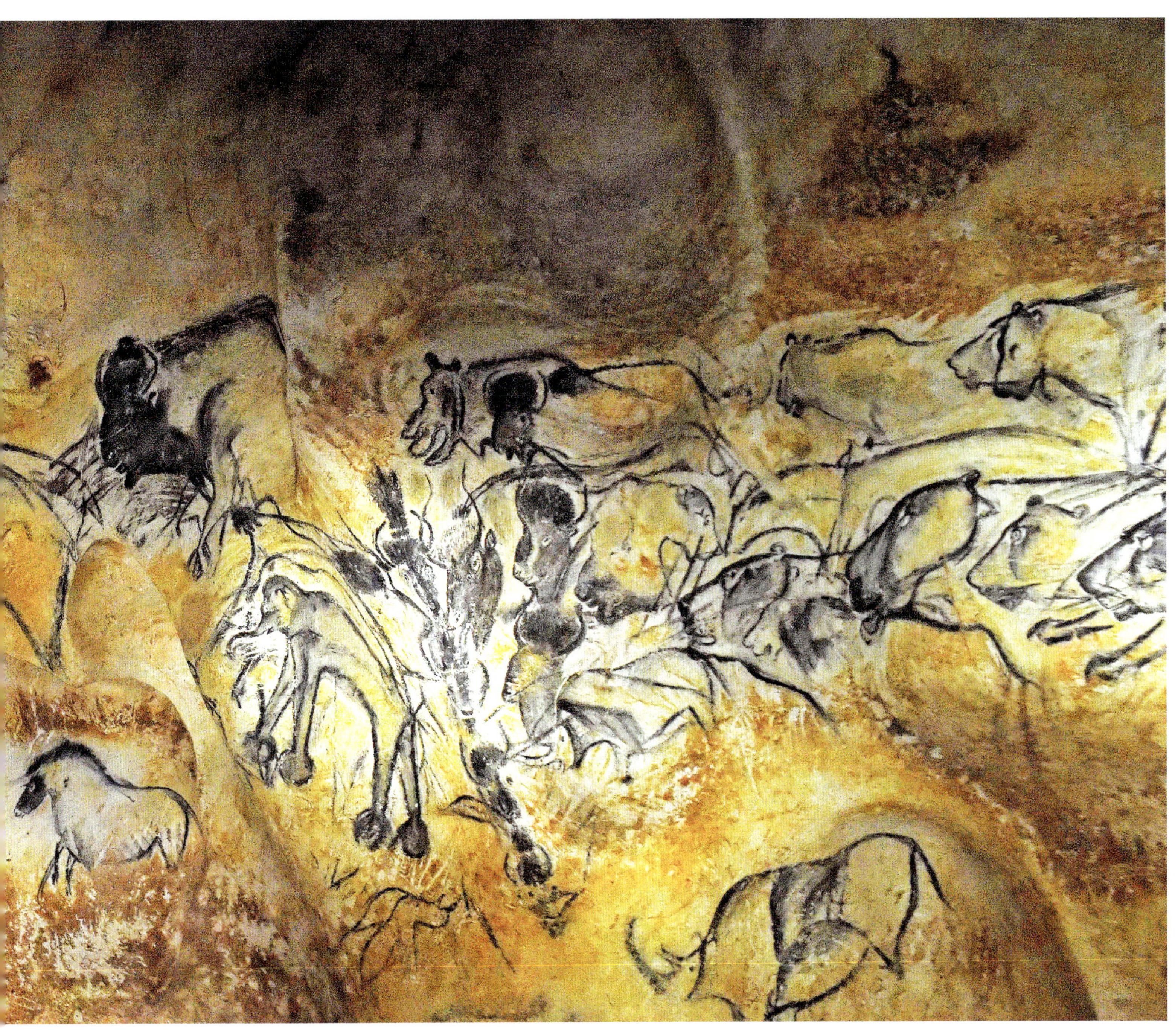

supply insights into funeral customs, social norms and the material culture. Petroglyphs, by contrast, inform us about the ways of life of peoples, their activities, economies and, studied in tandem with comparative ethnology, their ideas. At some petroglyph sites of Central Asia, especially in Kazakhstan and Mongolia, there are spatial and temporal connections between petroglyphs and graveyards, i.e. between the world of the living and that of the dead. Therefore the investigation of petroglyphs and the archaeological excavation of adjacent tombs will ideally go hand-in-hand in order to obtain a comprehensive trove of information allowing

for a meaningful understanding of the historical and cultural background of the petroglyphs.

Rock art, together with portable figurines and musical instruments made from bone or ivory, is not only humanity's oldest artistic expression, but also, metaphorically speaking, an illustrated, open-air archive recording bygone cultures, including the prevailing ecologies and economies of those times. Rock art is a gateway to the exploration of the material and conceptual worlds of ancient peoples. Although rock art gradually lost its importance with the advent of writing, petroglyphs remained a lively means of expression in several cultures, either with petroglyphs and inscriptions juxtaposed, in the Arabian Peninsula, in the Upper Indus Valley of northern Pakistan and in the Sahara, or, in the form of cave paintings, as part of important rituals in sub-Saharan Africa and Australia. However, although petroglyphs have been a global cultural phenomenon, they have not been a universal medium. In many regions with adequate rock surfaces, petroglyphs are absent. In those cultures, portable art made from perishable or imperishable materials took the place of petroglyphs.

3. The 'invention' of rock art

For *ca.* 2.7 million years, hominins (early humans) produced only purely functional objects such as stone and possibly bone tools. As regards art, the question arises of when, by whom and in what form non-utilitarian, artistic objects first emerged. The benefit of a utilitarian object is practical; the benefit of a non-utilitarian one is mental or emotional. From the moment humans expressed themselves by transforming raw materials such as rocks, bones or ivory, they not only modified their environment but immortalized the products of their striving for articulation, which would become accessible to the interpretation of future generations. These issues have been the subject of controversial debates for more than a century. For a long time, the axiom of a stylistic evolution of rock art as formulated by Abbé Henri Breuil (1877-1961) held that Middle Palaeolithic artists developed increasingly sophisticated skills, culminating in the realistic and dynamic cave paintings of Altamira;[30] these most impressive paintings date to around 17.5-15 ka BP.[31] Yet as early as the 1930s, the German ethnologist and pioneer of African rock art research Leo Frobenius (1873-1938) had questioned the theory of a gradual evolution of art from the simple or childish to the sophisticated and accomplished.[32] The age of the paintings of Lascaux, discovered in 1940, is estimated at 19-17 ka BP; like those of Altamira they belong to the Magdalenian cultural period (20-14 ka cal. BP). Until the 1980s and 1990s it was believed that the early, rather simple examples of parietal art stemming from pre-Magdalenian periods had been made by the anatomically modern human *Homo sapiens*, who had reached Western Europe and the region located north of the Alpine ice shield in today's Swabian Jura, migrating from the east, around 43000 BP, at a time when Neanderthals still existed in Europe.[33]

Regarding the timing of the appearance of art, the discovery in the 1990s of pieces of ochre in the South African cave of Blombos which were engraved with intersecting lines dating from *ca.* cal.

77 ka BP (or according to some, 72 ka BP) suggested that rock art first appeared in that time frame.[34] However, these incisions were most probably mere graphic marks or, at best, signs.[35] They hardly qualify as art, nor as symbols since we have no idea what these lines could have been a symbol of. Neither the incised objects from Blombos nor similar ones from other African sites, nor rudimentarily decorated fragments of ostrich eggshells of a similar age seriously questioned the then prevailing view whereby rock art appeared for the first time in French cave art towards the end of the Aurignacian cultural period (*ca.* 43-32/31 ka cal. BP).[36] The oldest parietal art found in Africa which is comparable to that in France comes from the Apollo 11 Cave in Namibia, discovered in 1969. It consists of seven mobile schist plaques bearing animal figures drawn with red, black and white pigments and dated to *ca.* 30000 cal. BP.[37] In the Levant, which was associated with *H. sapiens* since its earliest migrations out of Africa, very few figurative objects dating to the Levantine Aurignacian were found; it was only in the late Pleistocene Natufian cultural period (*ca.* 13-10 ka BP) that works of art became frequent.[38] Also in Australia, which was populated by *H. sapiens* around 65-50 ka BP, the earliest securely dated painting, featuring a kangaroo, dates from 17.5-17 ka cal. BP.[39]

In December 1994, the discovery of the parietal paintings and engravings in the Chauvet Cave in southern France shook previous beliefs about the beginning of cave art. The paintings feature almost 300 animals belonging to thirteen different species, herbivores such as woolly rhinoceroses, mammoths, bison, aurochs, wild horses and reindeer as well as carnivores – cave lions and hyenas, leopards and bears – and also an owl. These paintings appear as perfect masterpieces in their naturalistic and dynamic rendering of moving animals, the attention to spatial perspective, the application of light and dark surfaces to create shadows, and the use of the natural shape of the rock surfaces as a design element of the images. Particularly impressive are a pack of lions attacking a herd of bison, and the rendering of a running rhinoceros where, like in a stroboscopic image, the back and the horn of the rhinoceros are multiplied to represent successive snapshots of movement (fig. 5), and also a duel between two rhinoceroses. The depiction of the lioness chasing the bison looks like a composed scene, not the outcome of an additive process extending over a longer period of time. Furthermore, the cave artists had smoothed the face of the rock prior to painting. When most of the paintings were dated in 1996 to 32-30 ka cal. BP, that is to the final phase of the Aurignacian (a dating confirmed in 2012), these findings not only proved that the earliest cave paintings were more than 10,000 years older than previously assumed, they also refuted the theory of a gradual evolution of parietal art from simple to sophisticated.[40] The representations of animals in the Chauvet Cave, and the Cosquer Cave[41] dating mainly to the Solutrean (26–20 ka cal. BP), are at the same time the oldest extant and the anatomically most precise of all parietal art. More recent research has pushed the earliest black zoomorphic Chauvet paintings, featuring groups of lions and rhinoceroses, back even as far as 37–36.2 ka cal. BP.[42] The Chauvet paintings furthermore reveal that the Aurignacian artists, who were basically hunter-gatherers, possessed exceptional powers of observation.[43] Producing such artistic and expressive art in the darkness of caves[44] demanded several highly developed mental competences, such as sharp observational skills, an accurate memory, a strong power of imagination to mentally visualize the remembered animal and, finally, the capability to reduce three- to two-dimensionality. The level of skills these people from the Aurignacian were equipped with went far beyond those of Neanderthals, and their works of art surpassed a mere copying of nature.[45] The interplay of these art-related skills with the acquisition of a sufficiently complex language to formulate imaginary stories allowed for the visual expression of concepts, beliefs and myths. The cave paintings from the Ice Age seem to follow distinct conventions and styles that changed over time, whereby 'style' is defined as a specific way of making something which is characteristic for a group of makers at a certain period and place, in which the canon of their design of forms is encoded. Parietal works of art were not the random products of individuals but the outcome of a social iconography guided by a collective mindscape.

In the 1980s and 1990s it became obvious that a second focus of the earliest art from the Ice Age existed in the Swabian Jura, southern Germany. Between the 1930s and 2008, thirty-three more or less well-preserved three-dimensional figures made from bone or ivory were discovered in six different caves. They feature, among other things, nine mammoths, eight lions, two horses, two bison, two fishes, two women and, most remarkably, three hybrids consisting of an upright standing human with the head of a lion or bear (fig. 4).[46] In particular, the therianthrope[47] dating to 40–35 ka cal. BP found in the Hohlenstein-Stadel Cave, 31.7 cm tall, made from mammoth ivory and featuring a man-lion or man-bear, indicates that at the beginning of the Aurignacian *sapiens* humans already possessed impressive capabilities of abstraction and imaginative powers.[48] By emphasizing individual aspects of selected animals or humans, these artists went beyond the mere reproduction of nature. Other highlights are the so-called Venus of Hohle Fels from mammoth ivory, dated 40000–35000 cal. BP, and at least eight flutes made from the bones of vultures, swans and mammoths from the same period which are the oldest musical instruments ever found.[49] The 'Venus'-figure of Hohle Fels and the man-lion (or man-bear) from Hohlenstein-Stadel are the two oldest safely dated human figures worldwide; both were incised with lines suggesting body decorations. In contrast to the cave paintings of Spain and France, the Swabian figures also focused on humans, as some of the figures also feature humans or human–animal hybrids. It is clear that the people from this culture were not only concerned with the surrounding animal world, but also with

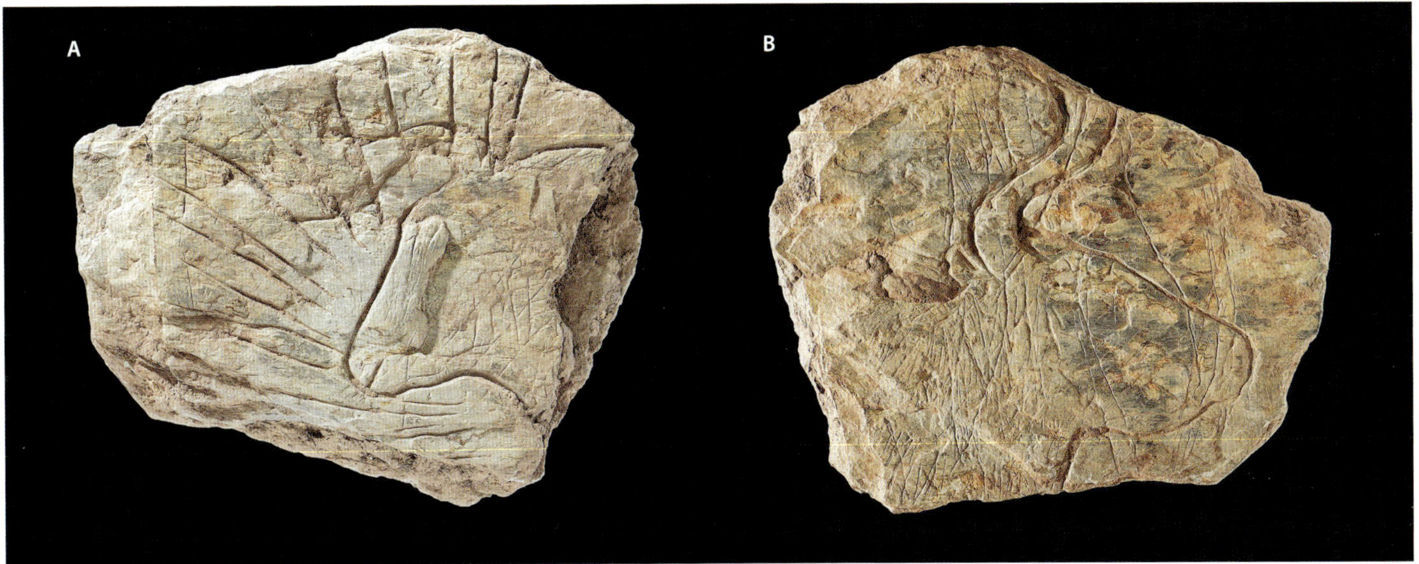

6. Slate slab engraved on both sides dating from the Early Azilian period. On the left, the head of an aurochs is surrounded by rays and its horns are directed forward. On the right, the head of an aurochs has been superimposed on the back of a horse; its horns are directed upwards. Shelter, Rocher de l'Impératrice, Finistère, western France. 10.8 × 10.2 cm. Fouilles Nicholas Naudinot, 2013. Rennes, DRAC-SRA Bretagne, propriété CD Finistère, 317.

themselves, that is with their position in a human–animal world perceived as fluid. About 40,000 to 35,000 years ago both figurative art and music were part of the material culture of Aurignacian humans. The question remains open whether this community in the Swabian Jura invented and developed figurative art and musical instruments locally or whether their forefathers brought them from somewhere else, probably a region further east. It is also remarkable that these figurines have no equal in Western Europe. The recent find in the cave of Gorges in the French Jura of an alleged small animal head crudely carved from a fragment of an ammonite dated to *ca*. 36200 BP is hardly comparable to the figurines from Swabia which are accomplished works of art; at best, it represents an awkward attempt.[50]

In 2014, the record held by Chauvet for the oldest cave paintings and by the Swabian Jura for the oldest figurative artwork worldwide was seriously challenged by discoveries on the Indonesian islands of Sulawesi and Kalimantan. First, hand prints and hand stencils made by spreading a mixture of red ochre and water over hands placed against a cave wall, as well as a painting of a red deer-pig (babirusa), were dated to 39.9 to 35.4 ka BP.[51] Within the next few years several even more ancient discoveries were reported, namely in 2018 the naturalistic painting of a wild bovid from Kalimantan dated to 40 ka BP and, in 2019, a painted hunting scene from the cave Leang Bulu Sipong 4 on Sulawesi. It represents eight small humanoids with animal characteristics such as animal faces, possibly therianthropes or humans wearing masks, chasing two warty pigs and four dwarf buffaloes. This is not only the oldest known hunting scene, but also the oldest visual rendering of a scene including action, in other words a story. The animals were scientifically dated to 43 ka BP for one pig and to 41 ka and 40.9 ka BP for two dwarf buffaloes, but no date has been established for the hunters.[52] However, the lack of dates for the hunters cannot exclude the possibility that they are later additions. In 2021, finally, a 45,500-year-old painting of a warty pig was published, which had been discovered in the cave Leang Tedongnge within the same karst region as Leang Bulu Sipong.[53] According to current knowledge, the paintings from these two latter caves are not only the oldest preserved visual representations of animals and humans but the oldest known figurative artworks. This allows the hypothesis that South Asian *Homo sapiens*, who probably reached Sulawesi between 69 ka and 59 ka BP, was the first to create figurative art.[54] What is also striking about the cave paintings of the Indonesian islands is the depictions of humans, in contrast to Western Europe where animal images dominated in the Upper Palaeolithic and human figures only really appeared in the Neolithic. Presumably the

hunters of Western Europe remained in a quasi-symbiotic psychological relationship with fauna for longer than the people of South East Asia, where tropical flora played a more important role than in cold Europe.

On the other hand, claims from 2012 that non-figurative rock paintings from three Spanish caves may have been 'symbolic expressions of the Neanderthals',[55] and a subsequent claim from 2018 that these paintings dated as far back as at least 65 ka BP and 'implied Neanderthal authorship'[56] were quickly disputed and had been proven untenable by 2020. As was shown, both studies had only used the very oldest date of dozens of dates obtained by analysing calcite deposits overlying paintings using the uranium-thorium (U–Th) method.[57] Since this method is prone to overestimation of ages, such results should be cross-checked with dates obtained by other methods, which both studies had omitted to do. In the words of the palaeoanthropologist Randall White, there is 'no proof that Neanderthal society needed a long-lasting means of communication to consolidate its values and beliefs. [...] In short, there is still no convincing archaeological evidence that Neanderthals created Iberian cave art.'[58]

Yet a publication from June 2023 suggested at first glance that Neanderthal people could have reached an intermediate stage towards rock art. In the cave complex of La Roche-Cotard in central France, which was rediscovered in 1846 and excavated in 1912 and the 1970s, more extensive research has been conducted since 2008. Besides artefacts of the Mousterian type,[59] about 400 non-figurative markings such as lines, dots and patterns, organized into groups, were identified on the walls of Cave III. The researchers claim that these markings are deliberately grouped in spatial terms and are human-made, and can be clearly distinguished from accidental scratch-marks made by animals. Since the cave was sealed shut by flood sediments from the nearby Loire River around 54,000–60,000 years ago, long before *Homo sapiens* had reached central France,[60] and since all excavated artefacts belonged to the Mousterian industry which in Western Europe is only associated with *H. neanderthalensis*, these marks may be attributed to Neanderthals.[61] However, these markings are somewhat similar to the incisions found on pieces of ochre from the Blombos cave. They are signs, neither symbols nor works of art, and do not represent an intermediate step towards rock art.

Present knowledge leads to the conclusion that it was *H. sapiens* who achieved the quantum leap of creating artworks, first in South East Asia, and, a few millennia later and 12,000 kilometres away, in Central and Western Europe. It is striking that it took the anatomically modern *H. sapiens ca*. 270,000 years to take the step from producing purely utilitarian objects to radically non-utilitarian art. Therefore, the emergence of art cannot be solely attributed to the new neurological capabilities of anatomically modern humans, who first emerged around 315 ka BP in Northern Africa.[62] Genetic evolution in terms of brain morphology and connectivity continued till modern brain organization was established at the transition from the Middle to the Upper Palaeolithic around 55,000 to 45,000 years ago. This development went in parallel with the emergence of modern behavioural patterns as observed from archaeology.[63] This collateral development of behavioural modernity was at the same time a cultural phenomenon; culture being defined as the most important non-genetic agent shaping humans through socialization processes. It encompasses, among other things, behavioural norms, customs, beliefs and art. This means that genetic and cultural evolution interact to produce human behaviours.[64]

Almost as suddenly as accomplished parietal art appeared in South-Western and Central Europe *ca.* 40,000 years ago, so did it vanish abruptly in its accomplished form during the transition from the terminal Ice Age to the Holocene. At that time, with an acceleration in climate warming, the remaining Ice Age fauna such as mammoth, bison,[65] giant deer and reindeer, unable to adapt fast enough to the rapid return and expansion of forests, migrated back to their former northern habitats following the receding tundra.[66] When the Ice Age fauna left, the hunter-gatherers of Western and Central Europe had to adapt, which meant either following big game northwards or hunting steppe and woodland animals such as aurochs, red deer and wild boar. Since the latter did not live in large groups or undertake massive seasonal migrations, the hunters abandoned their shelters, became more mobile in their patterns of hunting and scattered. At the same time, bows and arrows gradually replaced spears as the main hunting tool.

As a consequence of these environmental changes, the beliefs and needs that supported elaborate parietal art changed too, and cave art gradually became obsolete. Interestingly, at the end of the Magdalenian, around 14300 cal. BP, there was not only an exchange of fauna in Europe, but also a change in human genetics. According to the palaeogeneticists Wolfgang Haak and Johannes Krause, 'a large-scale genetic turnover [took place] as early as 14 ka in central and western European hunter-gatherers associated with multiple techno-complexes – [the] Federmesser, Azilian [lithic industries] ...' The expanding population, which spread from today's Italy northwards, had reached the area south of the Alps 3,000 to 4,000 years earlier; they came from the east, probably from the Levant and Anatolia. 'From at least 14,000 years ago, an ancestry related to this culture [located in Italy] spread from the south across the rest of Europe, largely replacing the Magdalenian associated gene pool.'[67] The immigrant population was most probably better adapted to the warmer conditions than the Magdalenians.

The end of sophisticated parietal painting illustrates how climate change impacted fauna and also humans, who had to adapt their economic and social organization, which led to shifts in beliefs and, in turn, in art production. During the transitional archaeological periods of the Epipalaeolithic and Mesolithic, rock art continued, but only with more rudimentary and sometimes highly schematized execution. Examples are the paintings in the Spanish Levante (Eastern Iberia), petroglyphs at the site of Fariseu in the Côa Valley, and the figurative carvings on schist plaques from the early phases of the Azilian (*ca.* 14.3–13.5 ka cal. BP) in the Franco-Cantabrian region (north-eastern Spain and south-western France).[68] However, the discovery of 45 deeply engraved schist tablets from the Rocher de l'Impératrice shelter in Brittany (north-western France) which date from the early Azilian show that the changes in visual art lagged somewhat behind the techno-logical transformations (fig. 6). Whereas the lithic tools belonged fully to the technology of the Azilian, the naturalistic rendering of bulls and horses displays a continuation of final Magdalenian iconography.[69]

In retrospect it should be noted that works of parietal art, and to a lesser degree also weaponry, showed a remarkable homogeneity over a period of 25,000 years, despite regional variations.[70] On the other hand, burial practices were regionally more distinctive.[71] The relative unity in the art is all the more astonishing in view of the extremely low population density: in the Aurignacian, an average of 1,500 humans lived at any one time in Western and Central Europe; in the early Gravettian 2,800 and in the late Gravettian only 1,000, rising to 3,100 during the Last Glacial Maximum and 7,700 in the Magdalenian.[72] In spite of the large distances between the small groups of humans spread through Western and Central Europe, they must have been frequent contacts during which technological innovations were shared and a common mythological heritage was nurtured.

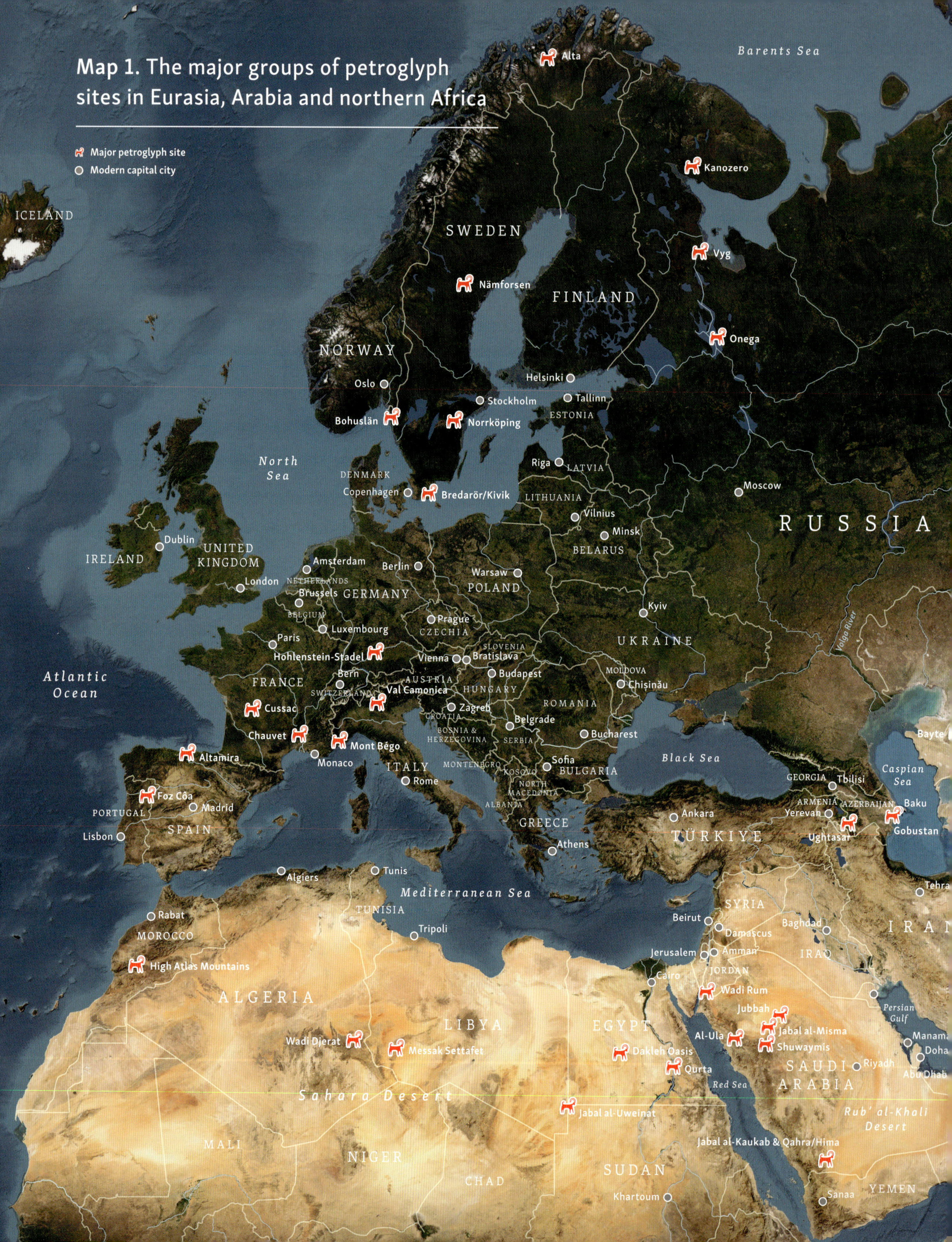

Map 1. The major groups of petroglyph sites in Eurasia, Arabia and northern Africa
Major petroglyph site
Modern capital city
Barents Sea
Alta
ICELAND
Kanozero
SWEDEN
Vyg
Nämforsen
FINLAND
Onega
NORWAY
Helsinki
Oslo
Stockholm
Tallinn
ESTONIA
Bohuslän
Norrköping
North Sea
Riga
LATVIA
DENMARK
Moscow
Copenhagen
Bredarör/Kivik
LITHUANIA
Vilnius
RUSSIA
Dublin
Minsk
IRELAND
UNITED KINGDOM
Amsterdam
Berlin
BELARUS
Warsaw
London
NETHERLANDS
Brussels
GERMANY
POLAND
BELGIUM
Luxembourg
Kyiv
Paris
Prague
Hohlenstein-Stadel
CZECHIA
UKRAINE
Vienna
Bratislava
Bern
SLOVENIA
MOLDOVA
Cussac
Val Camonica
AUSTRIA
Budapest
Chișinău
FRANCE
SWITZERLAND
HUNGARY
Volga River
Chauvet
Mont Bégo
Zagreb
ROMANIA
Altamira
Monaco
ITALY
CROATIA
Belgrade
Bucharest
BOSNIA & HERZEGOVINA
SERBIA
Foz Côa
Madrid
MONTENEGRO
Sofia
Black Sea
Bayte
PORTUGAL
Rome
KOSOVO
BULGARIA
GEORGIA
Tbilisi
Caspian Sea
SPAIN
NORTH MACEDONIA
ARMENIA
AZERBAIJAN
Baku
Lisbon
ALBANIA
Yerevan
Ughtasar
Gobustan
GREECE
TÜRKIYE
Algiers
Tunis
Athens
Ankara
Tehra
Atlantic Ocean
Mediterranean Sea
SYRIA
IRA
Rabat
TUNISIA
Beirut
Baghdad
MOROCCO
Tripoli
Damascus
High Atlas Mountains
Jerusalem
Amman
IRAQ
Cairo
JORDAN
ALGERIA
LIBYA
EGYPT
Wadi Rum
Persian Gulf
Jubbah
Manam
Al-Ula
Jabal al-Misma
Doha
Wadi Djerat
Messak Settafet
Dakleh Oasis
Shuwaymis
Abu Dhab
Qurta
SAUDI ARABIA
Riyadh
Red Sea
Sahara Desert
Jabal al-Uweinat
Rub' al-Khali Desert
Jabal al-Kaukab & Qahra/Hima
MALI
NIGER
SUDAN
Sanaa
YEMEN
CHAD
Khartoum

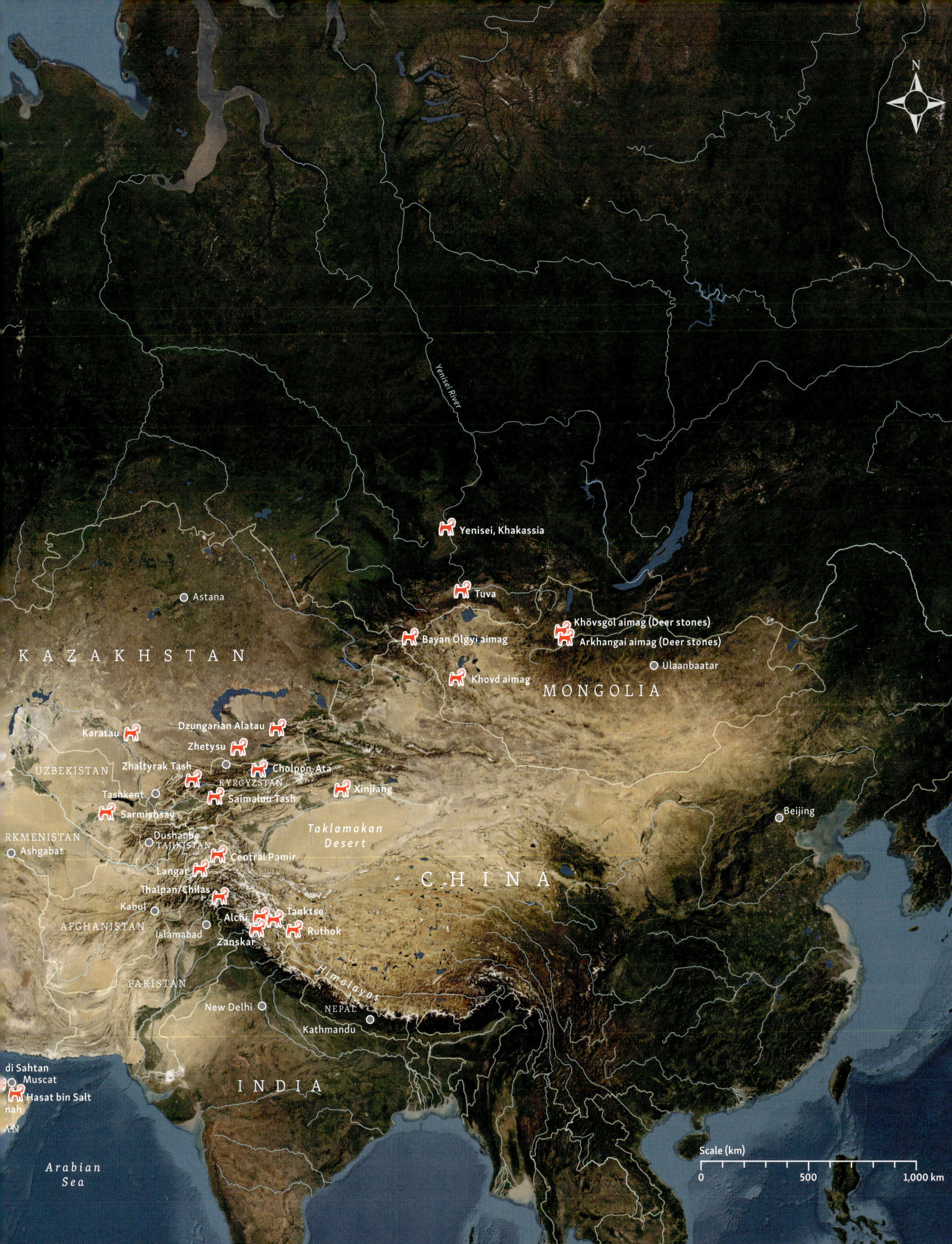

N
Yenisei River
Yenisei, Khakassia
Tuva
Khövsgöl aimag (Deer stones)
Bayan Ölgyi aimag
Arkhangai aimag (Deer stones)
Khovd aimag
Astana
KAZAKHSTAN
MONGOLIA
Ulaanbaatar
Karatau
Dzungarian Alatau
Zhetysu
Zhaltyrak Tash
UZBEKISTAN
Cholpon-Ata
KYRGYZSTAN
Tashkent
Saimaluu Tash
Xinjiang
Sarmishsay
RKMENISTAN
Dushanbe
TAJIKISTAN
Taklamakan
Desert
Beijing
Ashgabat
Central Pamir
CHINA
Langar
Thalpan/Chilas
Kabul
Alchi
Tanktse
AFGHANISTAN
Islamabad
Ruthok
Zanskar
PAKISTAN
Himalayas
New Delhi
NEPAL
Kathmandu
di Sahtan
Muscat
Hasat bin Salt
nah
AN
INDIA
Arabian
Sea
Scale (km)
0
500
1,000 km

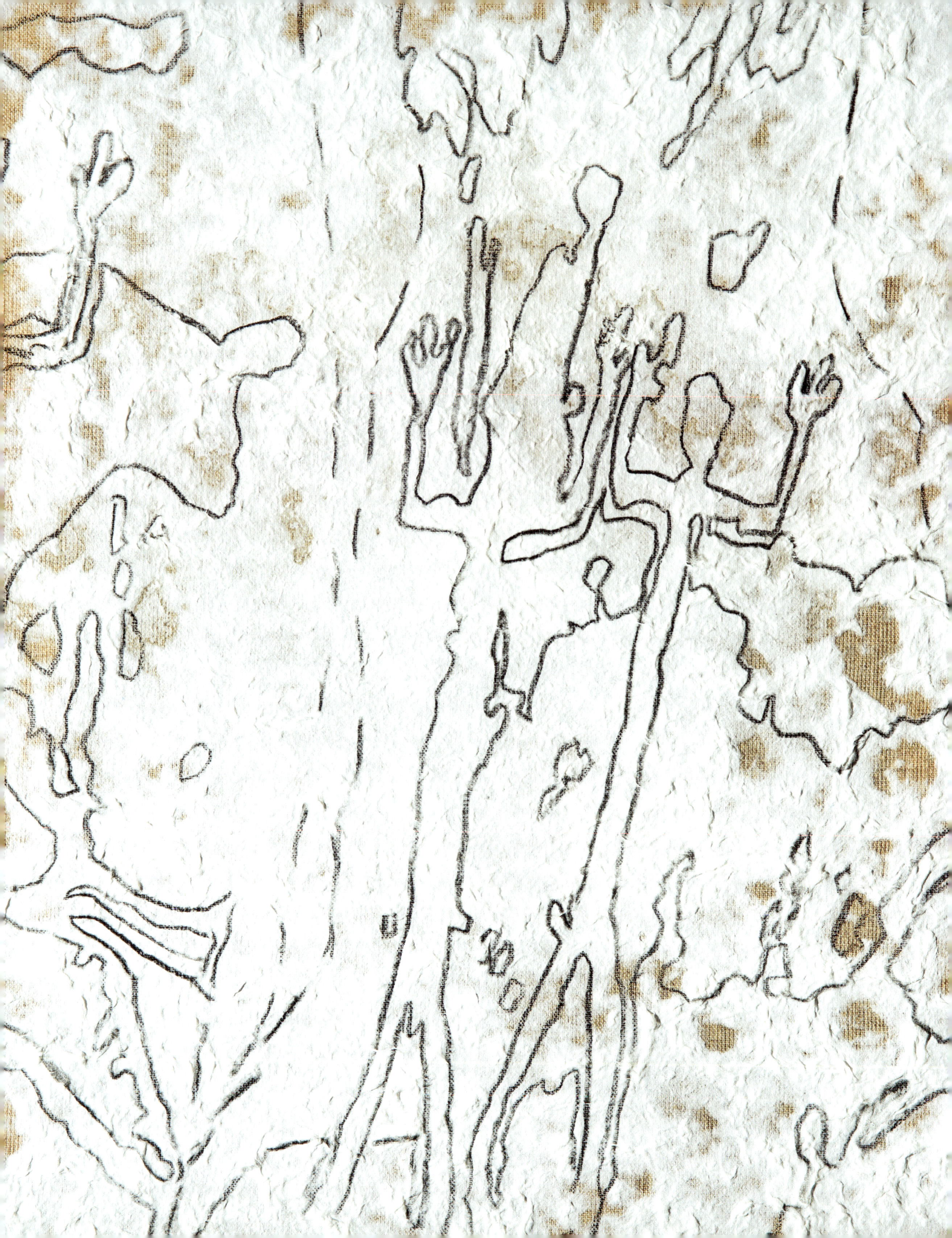

II. Petroglyphs as a Mirror of Climate Changes, Economic Transformations and Beliefs

Before presenting the rock art of Afro-Eurasia, some fundamental aspects of dealing with petroglyphs need to be addressed. They concern the conceptual approach, as well as the dating and interpretation of petroglyphs.

1. The conceptual grid

Petroglyphs did not arise in a vacuum. They were made by hunter-gatherers, mobile pastoralists or farmers and, in the case of southern Scandinavia and Arabia, also by travelling merchants. All these people spent their working time outdoors in nature, in more or less intimate contact with the surrounding wildlife. In non-urban, prehistoric times, the human and animal worlds were closely intertwined. However, which animal species lived in a particular region was a function of the prevailing climate and, as far as herbivores were concerned, of the existing vegetation. As described in the previous chapter regarding the end of parietal art at the transition from the Last Ice Age to the Holocene, animals adapted to climate changes by moving in parallel with their preferred vegetation, and humans either followed their prey or adapted by inventing new strategies. For whatever reason

people created petroglyphs, they reflected their economic activities, guiding principles and mental concepts such as myths. Myths are defined here as stories about the origin of humans and animals and their position within the cosmos; they are an explanation and justification for the way the world is.[1] Labelled by the anthropologist Claude Lévi-Strauss as 'bricolage intellectuel', that is 'intellectual Do-It-Yourself', myths are intellectual constructs without a material basis.[2] Regularly held rituals formed an initiation into the myths and updated them, thus consolidating the social order. Since the makers of rock art reflected their own environment, be it real or mental, in their works, petroglyphs (and rock paintings) correlate with their surroundings, the existing fauna of the time, their culture's economic and social organization as well as its prevailing worldview and myths.[3] Moreover, to quote Kieran D. O'Hara's dictum, 'climate change was the metronome that paced' rock art throughout the Afro-Eurasian realm.[4] This interconnection of petroglyphs with climate, fauna and economy will be outlined in this book in each of the regions under discussion.

The rising temperatures and increased precipitation at the onset of the Holocene not only prompted major alterations in vegetation and movement, and even replacements of fauna, but also a reshaping of the landscape. The relatively rapid melting of immense ice masses led to both glacioeustasy, that is a rise in sea levels of up to 120 metres, and glacioisostasy, a rebound of landmasses in places where the ice shields had vanished.[5] The consequences were on the one hand the inundation of vast areas of land, and on the other the emergence of coastal land which had previously been under water. In turn, river systems were

7. ← Therese Weber, *Signs of the Moment V.* Transformation of petroglyphs from areas of Kazakhstan. They are integrated into the structured, rock-like surface of the picture, as if on natural stone appearing in an unfamiliar environment. 50 × 40 cm. Pulp from mulberry tree fibre on linen fabric, chalk drawing, 2011.

remodelled and rivers changed their courses. In Europe, the most dramatic changes in landscape occurred in Doggerland, the landmass connecting Western Europe with Britain, which was flooded during the seventh millennium BCE, and in Scandinavia during the sixth and second millennia BCE, where, once the three-kilometre-thick ice shield had melted, coastal land masses that had previously been underwater rose above sea level by 30 or more metres.[6] These new landmasses repeatedly became favoured sites for the creation of petroglyphs.[7]

Pronounced climate and temperature changes, as well as oscillations in atmospheric carbon dioxide (CO_2) concentrations, are not a recent phenomenon, but have been taking place for millions of years. Just to name two extreme cases, during the Triassic (251–199.6 million years BP), when dinosaurs flourished on the Pangaea supercontinent, the average temperature at the equator was 40 °C, there were no polar ice caps and the atmospheric CO_2 concentrations were, at 1,750 ppm, more than four times higher than today's 412 ppm;[8] while during the Palaeocene–Eocene Thermal Maximum (PETM), *ca.* 55.8 million years ago, there were no ice caps and a very high CO_2 concentration, surpassing 1,500 ppm; yet it was in this period that modern mammal taxonomic orders, including primates, appeared in Europe and North America.[9] Obviously anthropogenic factors cannot have triggered these spectacular climate changes; they represent only a minority of such agents. There are at least eleven such factors impacting climate.

The first four are astronomical and orbital. 1) The obliquity (axial tilt) of the Earth, that is the inclination of the Earth's axis relative to the equatorial plane of the orbit, is not stable, but oscillates between *ca.* 22° and 25° within a cycle of approx. 44,000 years. 2) The Earth's orbit around the Sun is not circular but elliptical, with the radius of this ellipse changing continuously. This change, known as eccentricity, has a cycle of 100,000 years. 3) Precession is caused by the gravitational forces of some celestial bodies on the rotating Earth. Due to the fact that the Earth's radius is larger at the equator than at the poles, these tidal forces cause a rotational torque that attempts to turn the Earth's axis of rotation perpendicular to the ecliptic; as a result, the Earth's axis is wobbling in a cycle of *ca.* 26,000 years. These three factors mean that the amount of solar radiation reaching the Earth is variable over time.[10] 4) The sun's radiation is in itself fluctuating, depending on its degree of activity and variations in its magnetic field.

Further agents impacting climate are: 5) continental drift, that is the slow movement of tectonic plates which can have fundamental impacts on 6) the currents in the oceans such as the Gulf Stream and 7) the global wind circulation, that is the jet streams. 8) Volcanic mega-eruptions, which release huge amounts of aerosols such as sulphur dioxide into the atmosphere, can provoke short-term climate cooling. If they occur in the tropics, they can influence the global climate, since aerosols trapped in the stratosphere reflect sunlight and thus less solar energy reaches the Earth, temporarily cooling the climate.[11] In the case of the Hunga Tonga submarine volcano eruption in January 2022, the enormous amount of water vapour injected into the stratosphere had a major 'greenhouse gas' effect, significantly contributing to global warming over the next five to six years.[12] 9) The ice albedo feedback in turn is a positive feedback that amplifies a trend towards either warming or cooling. Albedo measures the reflectivity of non-self-illuminating surfaces, which depends on their properties of absorbing or reflecting radiation. A black body absorbs incoming radiation and has no albedo (value 0), ice reflects all incoming radiation and has full albedo (value 1). A global warming trend leads to a reduction of ice and snow surfaces triggering an additional absorption of solar radiation and rising temperatures, while a global cooling causes the expansion of ice and snow surfaces and thus an increased reflection of radiation, leading to additional cooling.

The final two climate-changing agents are in part anthropogenic. 10) Human landscape transformation, such as deforestation for agricultural purposes, salinization of soils due to overirrigation or massive overgrazing of pastures can impact on regional climate characteristics. 11) Greenhouse gases amplify the impact of solar radiation. Most of the penetrating, short-wave solar radiation that reaches the Earth's surface and cloud layers gets reflected into the atmosphere as long-wave terrestrial radiation. There, greenhouse gases such as water vapour, carbon dioxide, ozone, nitrous oxide and methane absorb this radiation and return half of it to the Earth. Without the greenhouse effect, there would be hardly any life on our planet, for its current effect is estimated to amount to about 36 °C; without greenhouse gases, the average temperature on Earth would fall from +15 °C to −21 °C.[13] However, the accelerated increase in carbon dioxide and methane since the Industrial Revolution is mainly man-made.

That these various factors continued throughout history to have a strong impact on tropical and subtropical monsoon activities and on changes of landscape due to land rise is reflected in petroglyphs, especially in Arabia and the Sahara with their fragile climates, as well as in Scandinavia.

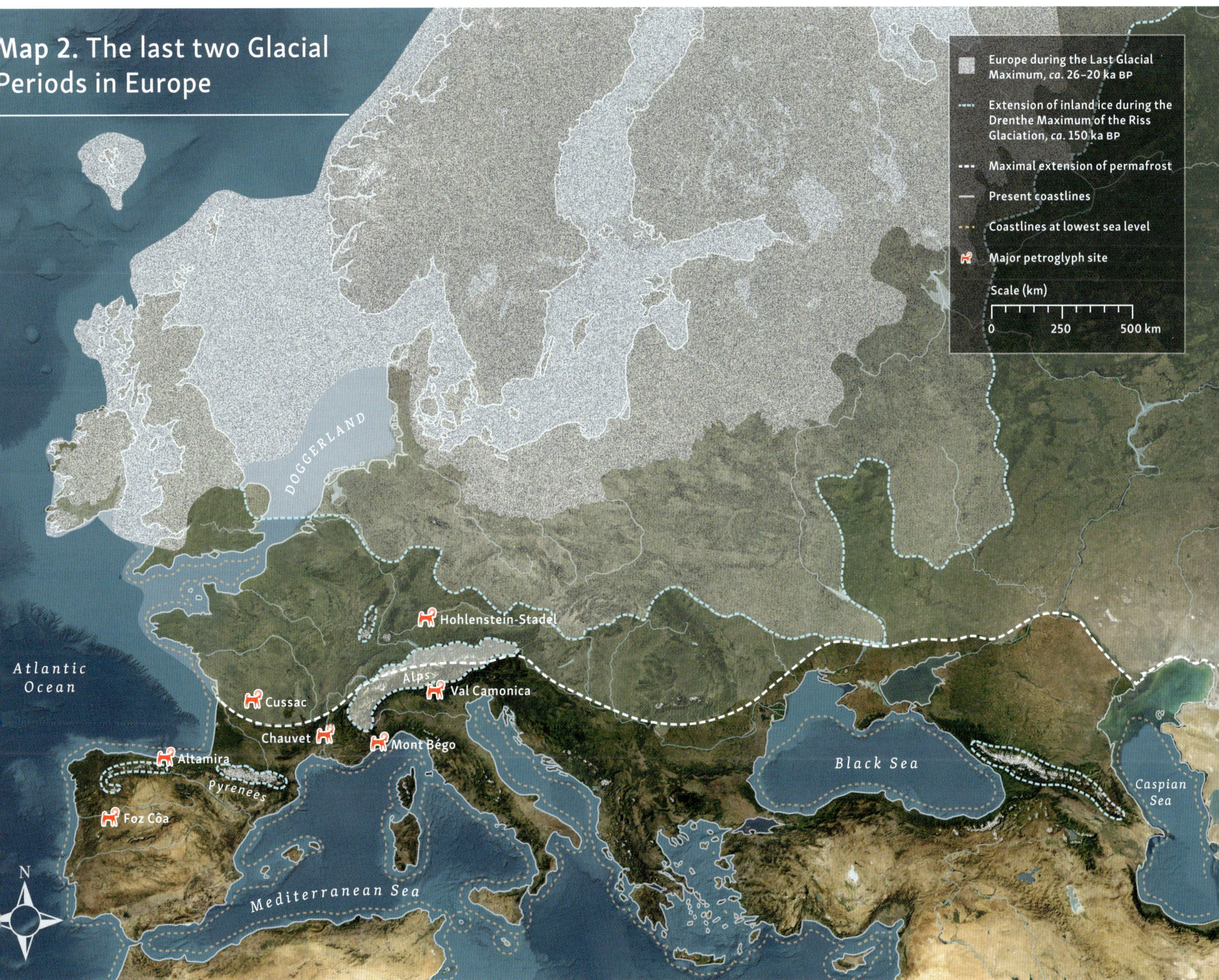

2. Dating petroglyphs

In the past, research into petroglyphs has been treated with scepticism by archaeology, since the main tools for obtaining dates for the material relics of past cultures are excavation and stratigraphy, whereas petroglyphs cannot be excavated, nor do they exist in stratigraphic contexts. Furthermore, petroglyphs were afflicted with the stigmas both of being art and of having emerged from a proto-religious environment, two fields that apparently cannot be rationally understood from a traditional scientific perspective.

Rock art, especially petroglyphs which lack organic material, is indeed difficult to date, except when it is precisely dated by a related inscription. In general, one can distinguish between two types of dating, direct and indirect. Indirect dating methods either establish relative chronologies or deduce the age of petroglyphs from another dated object. A **relative chronology** can be drawn up when the same stone surface has been worked on several times over a longer period with newer images superimposed each time on older ones to create banks of overlaid imagery dating to different periods. Such palimpsests make it possible to sketch relative chronologies.

In environments which experienced major climatic changes and changes of fauna, figures of animals can offer a rough indication of age. Thus, the petroglyph of an extinct animal suggests a **date *ante quem***, provided the date of its extinction or disappearance from the respective region is known. Conversely, the image of a domesticated animal offers a **date *post quem.*** Other time-related markers are weapons, vehicles such as carts and light chariots, inscriptions and, occasionally, religious symbols. Another, unreliable, method is to scientifically date organic matter which *seems* to be related to the petroglyph, such as charcoal or bones found in a shelter in close proximity to rock art.[14] A much more reliable indicator of different epochs over time is the oscillation of sea levels. Where there have been marine transgressions, the sea will have left layers of sediment on the ground which would appear above sea level during an ensuing marine regression. This means that petroglyphs found below the level of these sediments must be older than the beginning of the marine transgression and, conversely, those petroglyphs located above the level of the marine sediments will have been carved after the transgression had ended. Such layers formed by fluctuations in sea levels are found at the shores of the Caspian Sea. A similar indicator is provided by the glacioisostasy in Scandinavia, mentioned above. Since the petroglyphs were usually located near maritime or fluvial coasts, the date for the land's rebound provides reliable *post quem* dating. **Stylistic attributes** represent another basis for constructing chronologies. Style denominates a distinctive manner in which something is made which is specific to a certain timespan and territory. The concept of style makes it possible to group and classify works of art, which allows for rough indications of dating. The prerequisite is that the rock art style in question has unique and unmistakable characteristics, as was the case with the Iron Age Saka style in Central Asia or the Neolithic Messak style in the Eastern Sahara.

As for direct dating methods, their scope of application varies. **Radiocarbon (^{14}C) dating** is only applicable to pictographs since it analyses organic material; this method was first published in 1949. Radiocarbon is naturally produced in the upper atmosphere by the impact of cosmic rays on atmospheric nitrogen. The resultant ^{14}C mixes with oxygen, building radioactive carbon dioxide which is absorbed by plants via photosynthesis and by animals and humans via nutritional consumption. The proportion of ^{14}C is constant in all living organisms but starts to decay upon death with a half-life period of 5,730 years. This means that the maximum age the ^{14}C method can gauge is *ca.* 51,600 years by which time only 0.21% of the original ^{14}C remains undecayed. However, radiocarbon dating

had an inherent source of error, namely the assumption that the concentration of atmospheric ^{14}C has remained constant, at least for the last 5,730 years. This is not the case, since oscillations in solar activity and the terrestrial magnetic field impact the atmospheric ^{14}C concentration. In order to correct the non-linear time scale of radiocarbon dates, they were calibrated by correlating them with dendrochronological dates or maritime or lacustrine varves (the annual layers of sediment left by seas or lakes). Since the 1980s, Accelerator Mass Spectrometry (AMS) has been applied, which has a thousand times higher sensitivity than classical decay measurements and requires only a minute fraction of a sample in the range of thousandths of a gramme.[15]

Uranium–thorium dating is another type of radiometric dating. It is based on the radioactive decay of uranium isotopes (^{238}U), which turn into thorium (^{230}Th) as they decay. Whereas ^{238}U is water-soluble, ^{230}Th is not. If water runs over a cave painting, calcium carbonate is deposited on its surface in the course of time, and ^{238}U is incorporated into the lime. The uranium isotope ^{238}U now begins to decay. Via intermediate stages, ^{238}U turns into the uranium isotope ^{234}U, which has a half-life of 246,000 years. This in turn transforms into the radioactive thorium with a half-life of 76,000 years. In samples of limestone deposits, the ratio of uranium isotopes to thorium can be measured and the time when the limestone layer was formed can be calculated, allowing dating up to around 500,000 years ago.[16]

Dating rock varnish is a method of assessing the age of petroglyphs in arid regions. Rock varnish, also called desert varnish, is a dark, sometimes shiny coating less than a millimetre thick, consisting of mainly clay minerals derived from windblown mineral dust and held together by iron and manganese oxides and hydroxides that occur mainly on sandstone in deserts or on basaltic stones. The geochemical process requires heating of the stone surface by the sun and wetting by dew. Desert varnish only forms on physically stable rocks not exposed to strong erosion. Manganese-rich varnish correlates with humid climatic conditions and appears dark brown to black, whereas iron-rich varnish is orange-coloured and correlates with arid conditions. In regions where rocks are covered with desert varnish, petroglyphs were made by removing the dark varnish layer, which exposed the underlying light sandstone and made the desired figure stand out against the dark surroundings. If the varnish regrowth rate is known for a specific type of rock within a certain region with similar weather patterns, it is possible to estimate the age of petroglyphs by measuring the degree of revarnishing.[17] Once the varnish has grown back to 100 per cent, it is hardly possible to distinguish petroglyphs from their natural environment, and measurements become impossible.[18] However, since the rate of revarnishing may be influenced by several factors,[19] such rock varnish measurements need to be corroborated by dates obtained by other means.[20] Similar restrictions apply to **lichenometry** which attempts, mainly in polar and high mountain environments, to provide *ante quem* data for rock surfaces covered by lichen.[21]

Luminescence dating methods measure the time elapsed since certain minerals were last exposed to sunlight or significant heat. The results convey rough *ante quem* dates. **Thermoluminescence (TL)** dating measures when heat was last applied to a mineral, while **Optically Stimulated Luminescence (OSL)** measures the last previous solar light exposure. These methods have been used sporadically for dating paintings and petroglyphs covered by sediment.[22] Finally, it should be noted that at present none of the listed methods can reliably date individual petroglyphs without being correlated with results obtained by other methods.

3. Early records of rock art

Interest in rock art in Europe began relatively late, when in 1627 the Norwegian university teacher and doctor Peder Alfsön made a couple of ink-and-watercolour drawings of petroglyphs at Backa Brastad, Bohuslän, which then still belonged to Norway, itself part of the Danish–Norwegian Union.[23] Yet the earliest mention of rock art was made by the Chinese philosopher Han Fei (*ca.* 280–233 BCE), followed by a more detailed description of petroglyphs from Inner Mongolia in the book *Shui Jing Zhu* by the Chinese geographer Li Daoyuan (466 or 472–527 CE).[24] He obtained his knowledge about rock art sites in the year 494 during a lengthy inspection tour through several Chinese provinces. In his book, Li Daoyuan not only mentioned about twenty rock art sites spread over thirteen provinces, but also described the various figures. Based on his precise indications, archaeologists in the twentieth century were able to rediscover most of the sites he had described.[25] In Europe, the traveller Pierre de Montfort visited the Vallée des Merveilles in the Alps in 1460 and described it as 'a hellish place with figures of devils and a thousand demons carved everywhere in the rocks'.[26] More than a hundred years later in 1575, the French writer François de Belleforest mentioned some paintings and footprints of large and small animals in a cave near Miramont in the Périgord in southern France which can only be the cave of Rouffignac.[27] Another century later, the Savoyard historian Pietro Gioffredo described the

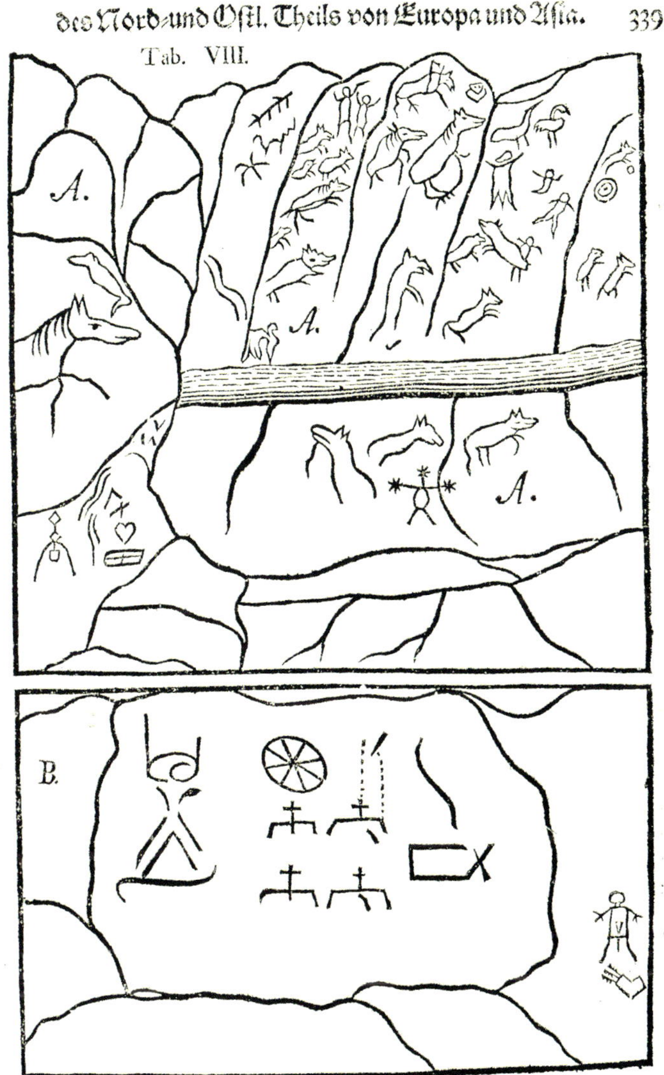

8. One of the oldest renderings of petroglyphs made by Philipp Johann von Strahlenberg in 1721 or 1722. Strahlenberg, Philipp Johann von, *Das Nord- und Östliche Theil von Europa und Asia, in so weit solches das gantze russische Reich mit Siberien und der grossen Tartarey in sich begreiffet* (Stockholm: published by the author, 1730), p. 339.

Vallée des Merveilles in more detail than his predecessor Pierre de Montfort, and recognized that the petroglyphs were several centuries old.[28]

Rock art research really began in Russia and Sweden. In Russia, the ambassador Nikolai M. Spafary first described petroglyphs in the Yenisei Valley which he had seen during his journey to China in 1675, and in 1692 the Dutch traveller and politician Nicolas Witsen, who had visited Russia in 1664–65, published his *Noord en Oost Tartarije* with descriptions and sketches of petroglyphs from the Urals. Then in 1721, Tsar Peter I (r. 1682–1725), who knew Witsen from his 1697 stay in

Amsterdam, dispatched the German naturalist Daniel Gottlieb Messerschmidt (1685–1735) to research in Siberia.[29] In 1722 Messerschmidt met the former Swedish officer Philipp Johann Tabbert von Strahlenberg, who had lived as a prisoner of war in Siberia. Together they undertook several surveys and excavations of ancient monuments, made drawings of petroglyphs and discovered runic inscriptions which were published in Strahlenberg's *Das Nord- und Östliche Theil von Europa und Asia* in 1730 (fig. 8).[30] In Sweden, interest in rock art was sparked in 1756 when carved images were discovered on the inner side of the Bronze Age stone cist of Bredarör near Kivik in eastern Skåne (figs 191–93).[31] Several drawings of these eight slabs were made by G.F. Feldt in 1756 (on behalf of Niels Wessman), in 1764 by Nils Reinhold Brocman and in 1775 by Carl Gustav Hilfeling.[32] The latter's research and drawings of the petroglyphs of Litsleby in Bohuslän in 1792 marks the start of the professional recording of petroglyphs in Sweden, which was continued by the scholars Carl Georg Brunius and Axel Emanuel Holmberg.[33]

Greater advances were made in the discovery (from a European point of view) and reporting of rock art in the distant, unknown continents than in Old Europe, as a result of the exploration of Africa and the Americas by European scholars, travellers and missionaries. In the course of the eighteenth century, about a dozen travellers reported rock art from Africa (mainly paintings), and in South East Asia the Dutch trader J. Keyts was the first to mention rock paintings in New Guinea.[34] In North America, mapping and recording of rock art began in 1711 while in South America the Jesuit ethnographer Pedro Lozano (1697–1752) described numerous petroglyph and pictoglyph sites in Colombia, Brazil, Paraguay and Peru.[35] Later, the Prussian explorer and polymath Alexander von Humboldt surveyed petroglyphs in the basin of the Orinoco in 1800 and paved the way for the analysis of rock varnish.[36] However, it was to be decades before the true age of Palaeolithic rock art was recognized. This came about in 1865 with the publication of a mammoth ivory plaque with an engraved mammoth dating to the Magdalenian that had been discovered

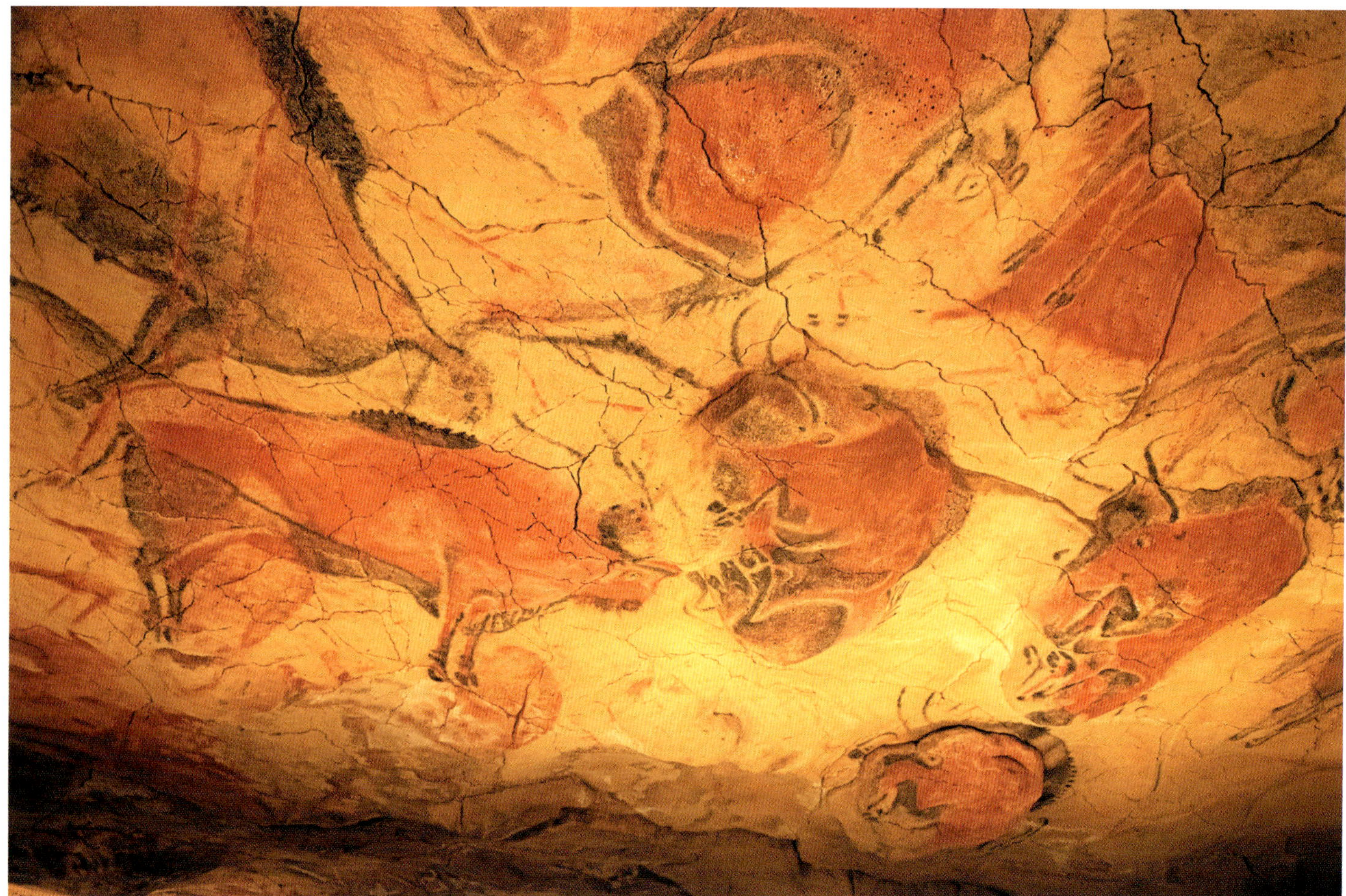

9. Paintings of bison in the cave of Altamira, north-eastern Spain, from *ca.* 17.5–15 ka BP. Their authenticity was doubted for more than twenty years, mainly for ideological reasons.

in 1864 in the shelter of La Madeleine in the Dordogne (France). Since the mammoth disappeared from France towards the end of the Pleistocene, this find proved that humans had coexisted with mammoths and had created portable art more than 10,000 years ago.[37] Nevertheless, when in 1880 Marcelino Sanz de Sautuola published his discoveries of parietal paintings in the cave of Altamira, northern Spain, and attributed them to the Palaeolithic, he was fiercely attacked by the leading French scientists and accused of forgery (fig. 9).[38] It is an irony of history that de Sautuola's dating was accepted more by conservative clerical circles than by atheist adepts of evolutionism. In the view of the former, the beautifully and masterfully created paintings could well have been made by very early humans since God's creation was perfect from its very beginning, whereas for the latter it was inconceivable that 'primitives' could produce perfect artworks.[39] According to some evolutionists, the paintings at Altamira were a fake which had been organized by a group of clerics to discredit Darwin's theory of evolution.[40] The community of prehistorians recognized the authenticity of the Altamira parietal art only in 1902 after three recently discovered French caves were authenticated.[41]

4. Interpreting rock art

To see and identify rock art is one thing, to understand and interpret it is another. The need to attempt interpretations stems from the fact that in all major rock art regions there are numerous petroglyphs or compositions of petroglyphs that mean something above and beyond the mere depiction of everyday life. Until the 1960s, prehistoric petroglyphs and paintings were interpreted in a rather casual manner. On the one hand, monolithic explanations of a global pretension were advanced, such as hunting magic or shamanism; on the other, rock art was connected to historic events or traditional religious texts and legends, without questioning whether these texts were relevant at the time of the creation of the petroglyphs. Finally, the existence of vaguely defined universal archetypes was supposed.

Initially, parietal paintings were believed to be meaningless **'art for art's sake'** – but why should prehistoric people creep into dark caves of difficult access to accomplish beautiful paintings nobody would see? Most probably, in Palaeolithic times the act of painting was not an end in itself. In 1903 the French archaeologist Salomon Reinach sketched out the concept that cave paintings were part of **hunting magic**, an approach which was picked up by Abbé Breuil and expanded to include petroglyphs.[42] The magic

is supposed to work in two ways; first to secure a successful hunt and second to appease the supreme spirit of that animal species, in order to ensure that the supreme spirit will again send animals and not remove its species from the region where the hunters live. According to this interpretation, cave art was made by hunters solely for hunters. Such rituals of hunting magic were observed by Leo Frobenius at the beginning of the twentieth century on an expedition with the southern African San people (Bushmen). Before a hunt, a hunter drew an image of an antelope on the floor and shot an arrow at it. After the successful hunt, he returned to the image and smeared it with blood from the killed prey.[43] Such preparatory rituals were also practised by aboriginal peoples in Australia.[44] In such cases, the act of creating an ephemeral figure is obviously more important than the image itself. But while there are many thousands of hunting scenes in petroglyphs, the concept of hunting magic is questionable when applied to parietal paintings where clearly identifiable hunting scenes are extremely rare, and the animals depicted hardly correspond to those that were mainly consumed. Nevertheless, 86 per cent of the species featured in parietal cave painting were regularly hunted, 10 per cent sporadically and only 4 per cent were never hunted.[45] Hunting definitely played an important role in parietal art, as it did in everyday life at that time. In some cases, Breuil and the ethnologist Louis Capitan applied a **totemist**[46] interpretation to parietal art, which may occasionally be applicable to petroglyphs, but not to cave paintings which mostly depict large varieties of different animal species within the same cave. On the other hand, to use the anthropological concept of **animism**[47] differentiates insufficiently between various traditions and types of rock art.

Finally, in the 1950s, attempts were made to connect certain parietal paintings to **shamanism**, defined as the altering of the state of consciousness to allow the performing shaman to enter in contact with spirits for a huge variety of purposes such as healing, soothsaying or hunting. Shamanism was first recorded in the late seventeenth century to describe rituals observed among the Tungus (Evenki) native Siberians.[48] Several facts question the adequacy of shamanism as an explanatory approach for rock art. First, shamanism was never the universal religion of prehistoric hunter-gatherers, a kind of primordial religion from the Stone Ages as was postulated by the influential, esoterically inclined religious scholar Mircea Eliade (1907–1986), who never carried out field research himself.[49] Also, those people living in Siberia, Australia or South Africa who still practise shamanistic hunting, healing or soothsaying rituals are in no way 'living fossils' from the Stone Age from whom one could draw conclusions about the worldviews of

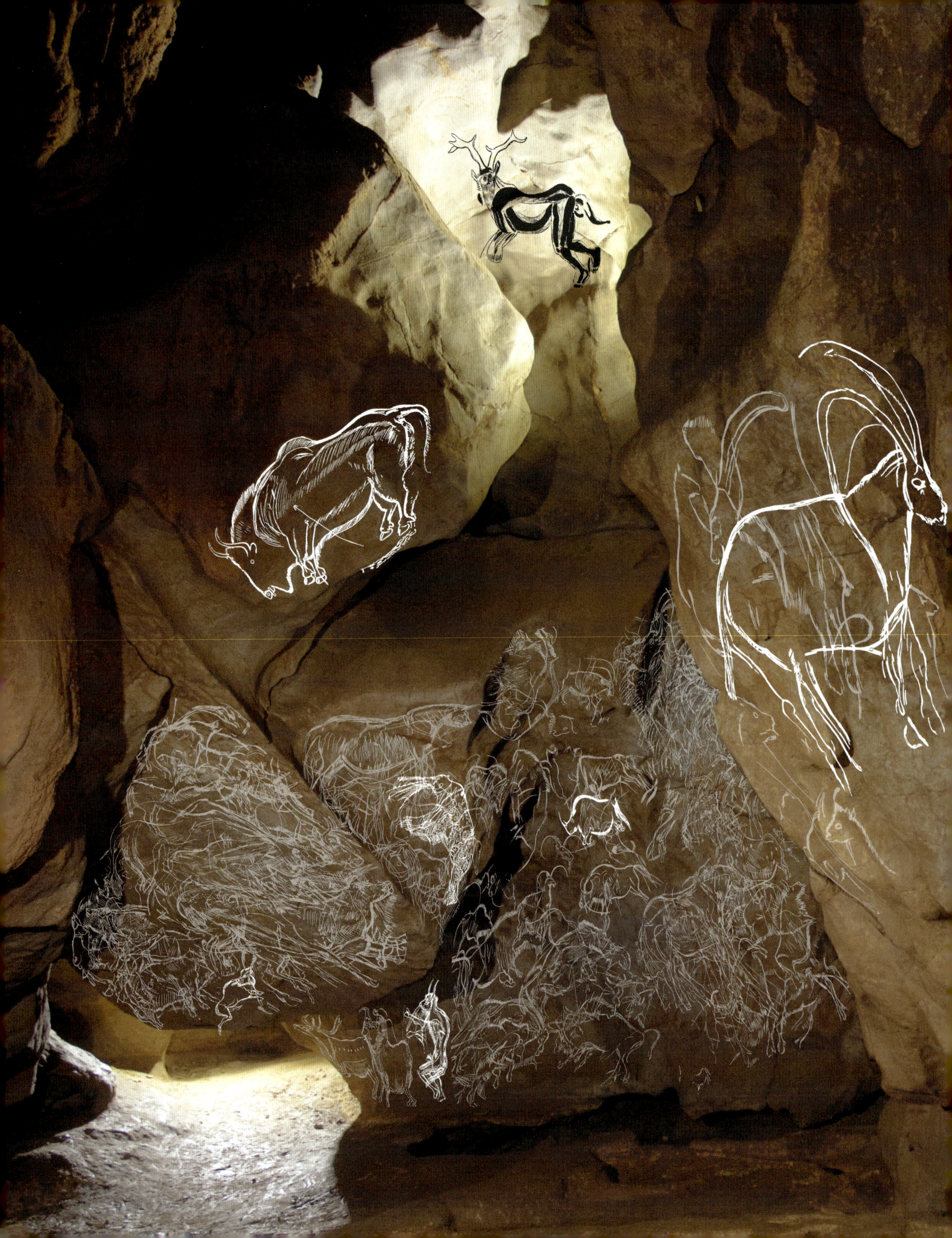

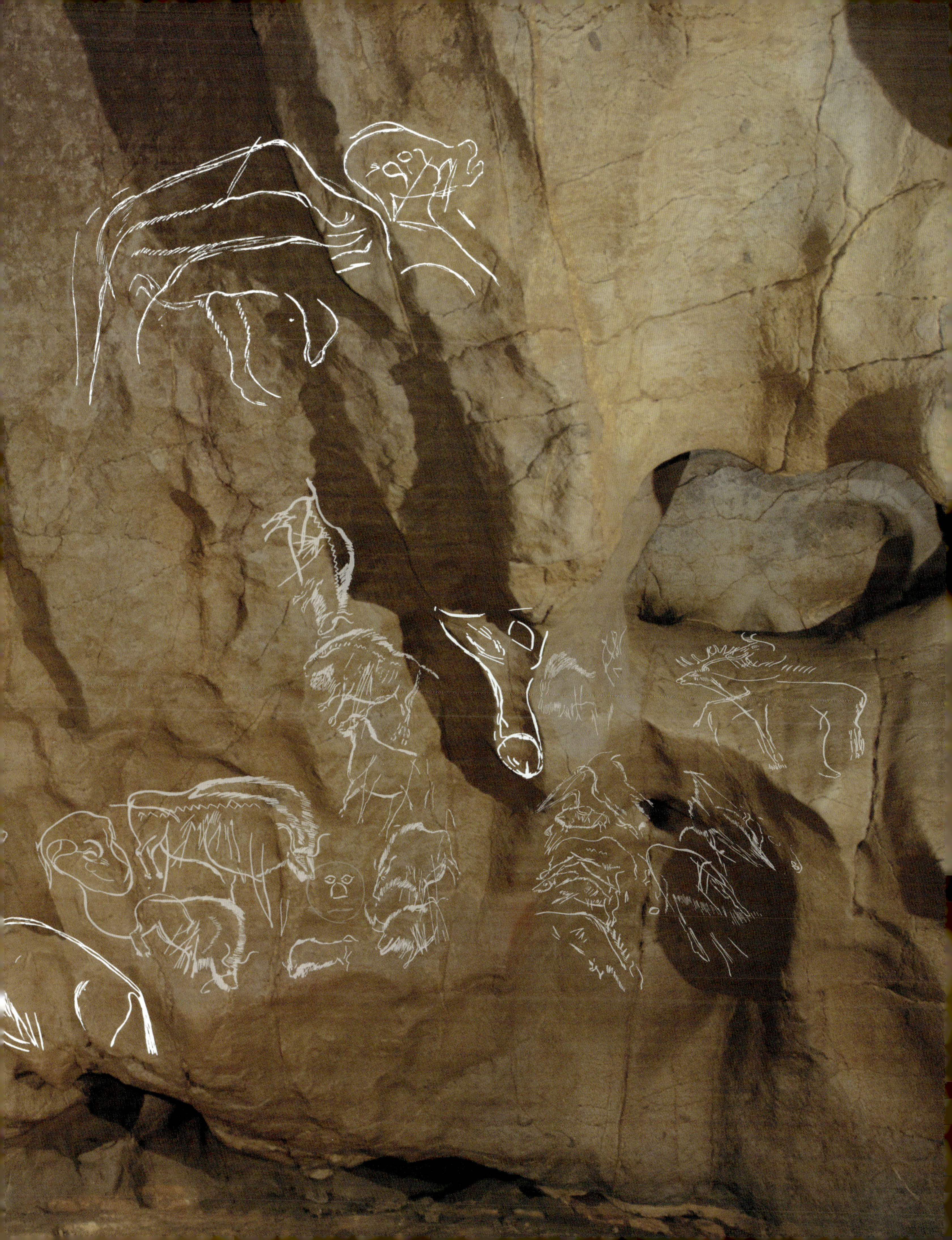

ancient hunter-gatherers and the intended meanings of the rock art they created.[50] Such a type of comparative ethnology which associates cultures separated from each other by thousands of years and kilometres is an unacceptable simplification; comparative ethnology needs to be plausible and reconstructable. It is such speculations which have discredited comparative studies in general and reduced rock art research to mere classification.

Next, shamanism is not a religion understood as a codified set of beliefs relating to transcendental, holy, divine and spiritual powers combined with strictly normed behaviour, moral and practices. Shamanism and its corresponding myths have neither priests nor sacred places nor a dividing barrier between this material world and the supranatural other worlds. In shamanism, as in some other ancient worldviews, the realms of humans, animals and spirits are not strictly segregated but form a permeable continuum. Shamanism is a practice dedicated to worldly goals of everyday life; like religious rituals, shamanism is a strategy that attempts to master reality. Furthermore, proponents of a shamanistic interpretation of rock art often associated shamanistic performances with hallucinogenic drugs (which is indeed the case in Central and South America) and attributed the use of such agents to shamanist practices in Mongolia and Central Asia. There, petroglyph scenes have been interpreted as depictions of shamanistic rituals performed after the ingestion of hallucinogenic fly agaric (*Amanita muscaria*) without clarifying whether the ingestion of such mushrooms was practised in the culture of that time and whether the plant grew in that region.[51]

Finally, as Andrzej Rozwadowski reminds us, 'a close look at the rock art indicates that images of shamans are not common in Northern Asia and largely absent in Central Asia. Rather, and

---

10. ↵ The hall called the Sanctuaire (sanctuary) in the Cave Les Trois-Frères, French Pyrenees. The hall, 8 m long, is located deep inside the cave system and was discovered on 21 July 1914 by the three Bégouën brothers, Max, Jacques and Louis, from whom the name of the cave is derived. The hall contains more than 500 engravings and one painted engraving, the so-called 'Sorcerer' at the top left. Bison, reindeer and horses predominate among the engravings, followed by mammoths, wild asses, rhinoceroses, bears, two therianthropes and one large phallus. The smaller therianthrope, known as the 'Petit-Sorcier à l'arc musical' (little wizard with a musical bow) at the bottom left has a human body with a bison's head. Whether the figure plays a musical instrument remains debatable. The partly painted engraving of the larger therianthrope at the top left is 3 m above ground level. It is a composite creature with human legs, short front legs or arms, the tail of a horse, antlers of a reindeer, the beak of an eagle, eyes of an owl, and a long human beard.[2] This therianthrope has been interpreted as a magician performing a rite, an animal deity or, much less likely, a dancing shaman or disguised hunter. Other engravings of therianthropes from the Upper Palaeolithic exist at Gabillou and Mas d'Azil, France. The engravings are executed in the naturalistic style of the Upper Palaeolithic Magdalenian. Photo and tracing based on tracings made by Abbé Breuil. © Éric Bégouën / Association Louis Bégouën, France.

consistently with the ethnographic record, shamanic rock art appears to be relatively recent in the region.'[52] There certainly exist petroglyphs associated with shamanistic practices and beliefs in Siberia and Northern Central Asia,[53] but the oft-repeated claim is untenable that 'the caves [with parietal art] were passages that led to the lower level of the shamanic cosmos. … Shamans visited the lower world during their hallucinations. During the Upper Palaeolithic, they went there not only during their visions but also literally'.[54] By this claim, Jean Clottes and David Lewis-Williams treat European and African rock art as representations of shamanistic visions experienced in trance under the effect of hallucinogenic agents. That such a reductionist quasi-dogma is hardly universally applicable and not relevant for outdoor petroglyphs is already apparent when studying rock art from western Mongolia. Since it predates shamanism in the region, the shamanistic theory necessarily fails to explain it. The earliest petroglyphs which may represent shamans and their paraphernalia date from the second half of the first millennium BCE.[55] Of course, this does not exclude the possibility that some shamanistic beliefs had much more ancient roots.

From the 1960s onwards, the pendulum swung in the opposite direction with a rejection of all interpretative attempts based on the alleged impossibility of connecting prehistoric art to the minds of those prehistoric people who made it. This latter approach limits the study of rock art to description and quantifiable research. However, since a piece of rock art is not only the representation of a real thing but at times also conveys a meaning that varies depending on its cultural context, it remains the mission of rock art research not just to describe, but also to interpret and explain. To postulate that every piece of rock art is polysemantic, that is has several meanings, and that this fundamental and inherent ambiguity precludes one from distinguishing a plausible interpretation from a wrong one, is nothing other than the denial of the possibility of knowledge. As succinctly formulated by David Lewis-Williams, 'by advocating theoretical and epistemological nihilism those who propagate it are relieved of the need to produce any original thought or research'. Lewis-Williams continues that it is the task of researchers to 'steer a safe passage between reductionist monolithism and unbridled polysemy, between Scylla and Charybdis'.[56]

As early as the 1960s, the palaeoanthropologist André Leroi-Gourhan and the prehistorian Annette Laming-Emperaire sought a way out of the impasse created by the rejection of interpretations. They believed they had found a solution in **structuralism**, more exactly by analysing rock art using concepts of structural linguistics. Basically, these two structuralist palaeoethnologists aimed to find a system within rock art without bothering with interpretative theories. They analysed the positions of single parietal figures in relation to each other and to the topography of the caves and processed the data statistically. This resulted in a bizarre 'sexualization' of art since all abstract signs and images of animals were interpreted as masculine or feminine and the caves were interpreted as prehistoric sanctuaries.[57] The questionability of such simplistic categorizations became quickly apparent when, for example, Leroi-Gourhan claimed that the horse symbolized masculinity and the bison femininity, while Laming-Emperaire asserted the contrary.[58] Such a reductionist approach is hardly helpful in understanding prehistoric rock art; it also negates the creativity of prehistoric artists.

The South African archaeologist David Lewis-Williams attempted in the 1980s to revive the **shamanistic** interpretation of rock art, now based on neuropsychological concepts, which led to the collaboration with the French prehistorian Jean Clottes already mentioned. Having conducted research on the rock art of the southern African San, Lewis-Williams postulated that the artists were actually shamans working in trance in the frame of specific rituals such as rain-making ceremonies, and that the altered states of consciousness provoked visions which the shaman-artists reproduced in their cave and shelter paintings. He claimed that this type of trance developed in three stages leading to visions starting with simple forms and culminating in complex figures.[59] Lewis-Williams summarized as follows:

At the beginning of the 'intensified trajectory' people see iridescent geometric precepts that derive from the wiring of the brain … known as entopic phenomena. Their forms are independent of their cultural context [sic!]. Next, subjects feel as if they are passing through a tunnel or vortex. Finally, … subjects see full-blown hallucinations of animals, people, monsters, and compound images.

The author continues:

The fully modern people of the Upper Palaeolithic could not have avoided experiencing the normal spectrum of human consciousness, and … would have experienced hallucinations projected onto rock surfaces … with paint or engravings.

Then he concludes: 'Here, wired into the human brain, is a possible explanation for the origin of religion.'[60] According to this shamanistic hypothesis, rock art (and possibly religion) on a global level is the result of altered neuropsychological processes triggered by some hallucinogenic agent.

Critics were quick to notice that the ethnographic material used to explain the ritualistic behaviour of the San was based on evidence collected in the nineteenth and twentieth centuries among peoples from the Kalahari savanna 'who do not (and never did) make rock art – not least because the Kalahari is largely devoid of rock surfaces'.[61] This approach, which blends a shamanistic explanation with structuralist concepts, overlooks the fact that there is no way to substantiate the hypothesis that prehistoric Africans, Central Asians, Mongols, Scandinavians, Karelians or Palaeolithic people used hallucinogenic drugs as is the case in Central and South America where mescaline or psylocibin were used in rituals. Also, the hypothesis that parietal art was triggered by a lack of oxygen within deep caves is simply wrong, for carbon monoxide and dioxide do not produce hallucinations, but rather dizziness, nausea and ultimately death.[62] Finally, this mechanistic theory degrades rock art to the reproduction of visions triggered by a drug-induced trance – there is room neither for any creativity of the artist nor for any correlation between rock art and ecological, economic and societal developments. It is a fundamentally ahistorical perspective reducing art to determinism.

In order to bridge the gap between adherents of interpretative approaches to rock art and their opponents who focussed on quantitative data, the archaeologist Christopher Chippindale and the ethnologist Paul S.C. Taçon sought a way to enhance the strict archaeological approach. In their seminal publication *The Archaeology of Rock-Art* (1998) they proposed to supplement the **formal methods** such as dating, visual and descriptive renderings, investigations of spatial arrangements among images and within the landscape, and statistical analyses, with **informed methods**.

By informed methods we mean those that depend on some sort of insight passed on directly or indirectly from those who made and used rock-art – through ethnography, through ethnohistory, through the historical record, or through modern understanding known with good cause to perpetuate ancient knowledge.[63]

Claude Lévi-Strauss, the founder of structuralist ethnology, had already written in 1958, referring to pre-Columbian art: 'We can no longer doubt that the key to many heretofore incomprehensible motifs is directly accessible in myths and tales that are still current.'[64] Ethnology is relatively safe to apply in cultures where the tradition of making rock art is still alive and knowledge regarding its meaning is kept vivid, as for example among aboriginal communities of Australia. There, to create rock art and to 'refresh' them by repainting or re-engraving them are meaningful acts which are embedded in their worldview and myths. Even so the mythological framework of rock art as it is understood today by knowledgeable Indigenous Australians and their immediate ancestors may have experienced changes over time, so that the present meaning of a certain figure or composition may be different from its significance five millennia ago. When **palaeoethnology** or comparative ethnology is used to link **mythical heritage**, for example ancient Indo-European or Nordic myths, to rock art, the suggested cultural connections have to be contextually plausible in geographical and chronological terms, as must be the line of transmission from the rock paintings to the surviving oral or written source. As mentioned above, all myths and mythical notions, even though they may often be slow to change, are embedded in a certain culture or in a plurality of cultures sharing a common heritage.[65] There are neither so-called universal archetypes nor global myths nor global interpretations.[66]

Given the fact that in the third and second millennia BCE the steppes of Eastern Europe and Central Asia were populated by speakers of Indo-European languages who expanded southwards to Iran, south-eastwards to the Indian subcontinent and westward to Europe, there existed during the Bronze and Iron Ages a vast interconnected realm of languages sharing a common source. Linguistic and palaeoethnological research has demonstrated that these Indo-European cultures, especially their largest branch, of Indo-Iranian language-speakers, shared common cultural elements, especially in the areas of mythology, beliefs and rituals. Parts of this shared heritage were created orally during the second half of the second millennium BCE, first in the shape of the *Vedas*, especially the oldest, the *Rig Veda*, and slightly later of the *Avesta*, the venerated book of the ancient Iranians.[67] Most likely, the *Rig Veda* and *Avesta* are two versions of a shared archaic heritage. These sacred books do not present an urban world but a rural one, primarily of stockbreeders and to a lesser extent farmers.[68] Since a major proportion of Central Asian petroglyphs date to the Bronze and Iron Ages, it makes sense to explore possible correlations between these petroglyphs and the Indo-Iranian cultural heritage. In the words of Andrzej Rozwandowski, 'the Indo-Iranian mythology is one of the possible sources for interpreting petroglyphs'.[69] This means that petroglyphs from different cultures related to the Indo-Iranian linguistic realm may reasonably have been inspired by the same mythical heritage. A connection between cultures is most likely to be inferred in the case of complex mythical ideas or special

petroglyphs, but not in the case of simple, ubiquitous items such as circles, cup marks, sexuality or widespread animals such as ibexes. As the research on Central Asian petroglyphs by the French archaeologist Henri-Paul Francfort has shown, the two approaches of palaeoethnology and shamanism do not have to compete, but may in fact complement each other.[70] As will be discussed in the following chapters, there exist between rock art regions great differences in terms of mythological heritage: whereas it is rich for Central Asia and more modest for southern Scandinavia, it is poor for the Sahara and nearly non-existent for Arabia. In any case, one has to remain alert to the risk of retro-projecting medieval or antique myths onto prehistoric epochs. Another question is when and on what occasions petroglyphs were carved. The question arises in view of the fact that petroglyphs were made on the same site over long periods of as much as one or two millennia. Even in the case of a very large number of petroglyphs such as Tsagaan Salaa (Mongolia) or Saimaluu Tash (Kyrgyzstan) which number tens of thousands of images, the average production is as low as ten to twenty images a year.

Finally, the question must be asked whether rock art was also associated with burial rituals. Although burials sometimes occurred in a spatial correlation with petroglyphs, their making was usually centuries or even millennia apart which rules out a contextual relation between rock art and burial rites. However, there are some examples where rock art appeared in the context of funerals, for example inside the above-mentioned cave of Cussac, where the burials and the creation of the petroglyphs took place in a comparable time frame (fig. 3). Even if there were a couple of generations between the burials and the carving of the petroglyphs, the latter group could not ignore the earlier one. Other spectacular examples for a contextual relation between rock art and funeral rituals are the burials at Bredarör at Kivik, southern Sweden, the burial sites of Khar Chuluut, Hulagash and Chuluut Bulak in Mongolia, and the burials at Karakol in the Russian Altai. If the Bronze Age engravings on the more than one thousand deer steles in Mongolia are also classified as petroglyphs, these too are directly related to burial and sacrificial rituals. The engraved deer stones were part of ritual sites where horses were sacrificed and buried and where people were occasionally laid to rest. In all these instances, the petroglyphs possibly expressed mythological contents that were significant in the frame of funeral rites.

To conclude, it should be noted that the question of the meaning of the numerous Palaeolithic signs remains unanswered. They appear as dots, lines or geometric shapes, isolated or in groups. As with the cup mark petroglyphs, the simplicity of the painted Palaeolithic signs makes it impossible to unambiguously interpret their meaning.

2

Rock Art by Major Region

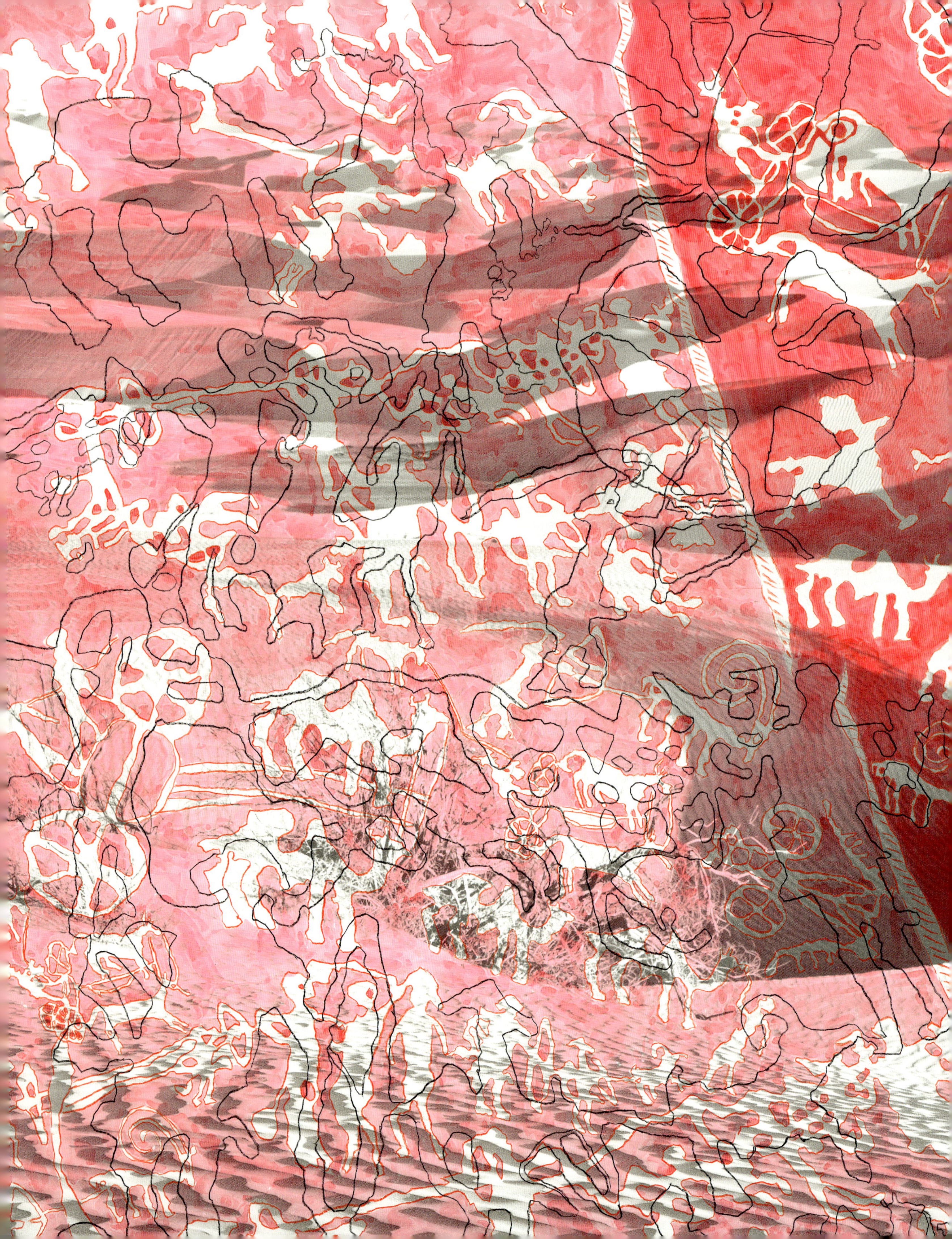

III. Central Asia

Central Asia is defined here in geographic terms as the region that lies between the Caspian Sea to the west, central Mongolia to the east, the southern Siberian steppe to the north, and the Hindu Kush and Kunlun mountain chains to the south. It stretches from roughly longitude 50° to 108° east and latitude 33° to 55° north and encompasses the five former Soviet republics of Kazakhstan, Kyrgyzstan, Tajikistan, Turkmenistan and Uzbekistan, along with southern Russia from Lake Baikal to the Volga, northern Afghanistan, the Xinjiang and Inner Mongolia autonomous regions in northern China, and the independent Republic of Mongolia. The maximum distance along the east–west axis is approximately 4,500 kilometres and along the north–south axis approximately 2,400 kilometres.

1. Geography, climate and migrations

Geographic and climatic peculiarities have decisively shaped the development of Central Asia. Due to its particular position as a northern inland region, the compensatory mechanisms of maritime climates play only a minor role, which leads to a distinctive continental climate with pronounced temperature differences between cold and hot seasons. Photosynthesis, vital to the

growth of plants, is directly related to the amount of daylight, which is drastically reduced in northern zones during the long winter season. In addition, the prevailing west winds from the Atlantic and Mediterranean lose much of their moisture and compensating effect when they encounter the Urals and sweep eastward as dry winds. As a consequence, the climatic differences between summer and winter, as well as the relative aridity, markedly increase toward the east. In south-eastern Central Asia the trend toward aridity increases still further because the Hindu Kush, Pamir, Kunlun and Himalaya mountain chains on its southern edge force the moist summer monsoon clouds that stream from south to north to rise and release their moisture as rain before reaching Central Asia.

The Central Asian landmass forms an enormous rectangle that falls into several climatic zones, whose main axes run east-west. North of Central Asia proper extend the barren polar desert and the treeless permafrost of the tundra steppe, north of the Arctic Circle.[1] South of the tundra lies the taiga with its immense coniferous forests, which are interspersed in its southern part with deciduous forests, for example of birch. These forests appeared at the end of the last Ice Age, 12,000 to 10,000 years ago; they stand on permafrost whose surface thaws in early summer, leading to marshy conditions. On the southern edge of the taiga, the forests merge with a narrow zone of temperate steppe forests, which marks the northernmost band of Central Asia proper. The forest is followed by steppe entirely of grass, becoming more desert-like to the south. The Central Asian steppe is part of the Eurasian steppe, which extends from the lower Danube plain in the west over 7,600 kilometres almost to the Pacific Ocean, partially interrupted only by the Altai Mountains. The

11. ← Therese Weber, *Metamorphoses III*. The inhospitable, empty desert is juxtaposed with a living society. In this palimpsest, the representation of animals and people with their carts and tools illustrates their early presence and mobility in a fascinating landscape. 220 × 135 cm. Detail: 180 × 135 cm. Chinese ink painting and drawing over a photograph of the Taklamakan Desert, China (2003 expedition) on handmade paper, 2018.

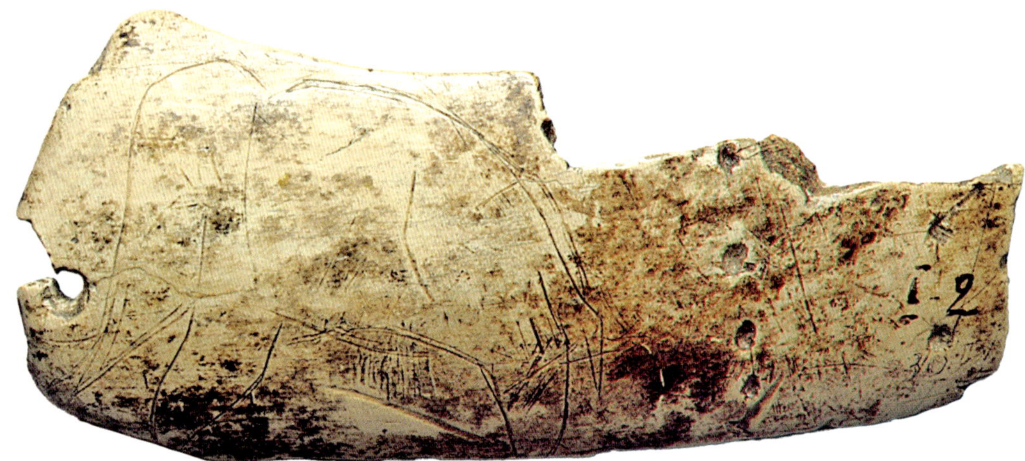

12. Plaque from mammoth tusk with engraved mammoth from the Mal'ta–Buret' culture, *ca.* 23 ka BP. Mal'ta, Irkutsk oblast, Russian Federation. The State Hermitage Museum, Saint Petersburg, Russian Federation.

climate of the grass steppe is semi-arid; it is not humid enough to allow the growth of forests and is largely unsuitable for agricultural use. Hunting and pastoralism were the main sources of subsistence; only sophisticated irrigation systems could overcome these obstacles. Further south stretches a huge desert belt encompassing the Gobi, Dzungarian, Taklamakan, Kyzyl Kum and Karakum deserts as well as the desertic Ustyurt Plateau.

As in Europe, during the late Pleistocene Central Asia witnessed changes in its ecosystems. During the Last Glacial Maximum (26 ka–19 ka BP), major parts of the tundra turned into cold barren steppe while the tundra advanced southwards, reducing the taiga ecosystem. As a consequence, the northern areas of Central Asia were depopulated as the hunter-gatherer communities migrated south and west for survival. From this cold period stem some of the oldest artworks of Central Asia, namely the more than two dozen small ivory, bone and antler figurines which were found at Mal'ta and Buret' north of Irkutsk on the western bank of the Angara River. They feature either extremely slim, clothed women or plump naked women with pronounced breasts and hips as well as various animals. The grave goods of the Mal'ta–Buret' culture, dated to *ca.* 23 ka BP, also included plaques made from mammoth tusk which were engraved with figures of mammoths – predecessors of the petroglyphs (fig. 12). In those days, the region of the Mal'ta–Buret' culture consisted of tundra steppe through which herds of reindeer would migrate seasonally. Mal'ta probably served as a temporary camp from which hunters ambushed migrating reindeer.[2] The culture of Mal'ta existed at the same time as that of Kostenki-Avdeevo-Gagarino west of the Ural Mountains and the European hunter-gatherer culture of the Epigravettian; possibly these three cultures formed a wide-ranging shared cultural horizon, including social networks.

Towards the end of the Pleistocene, during the Bølling–Allerød interstadial (14.7–12.9 ka BP), the cooling trend reversed and the tundra once more advanced northwards, as did the forested taiga which caused the gradual extinction of the glacial megafauna.[3] Subsequently the northern regions were slowly resettled. This interglacial trend towards higher temperatures was, in the northern hemisphere, suddenly interrupted by the Younger Dryas (12.9–11.7 ka BP) which was caused by the relatively rapid melting of major parts of the Laurentide Ice Sheet that covered much of North America.[4] This caused the North Atlantic's surface temperature to cool, in turn preventing the warm Gulf Stream from reaching the west of the Eurasian continent, and giving rise there to a renewed cooling to almost glacial conditions. With the start of the Holocene at 11.7 ka BP (*ca.* 9700 BCE), temperature and humidity rose again during the Preboreal (9700–8700 BCE) ushering in the warm Boreal (8700–7300 BCE) and Atlantic (7300–3700 BCE) periods; during the latter, forests significantly expanded, which formed favoured habitats for deer, bears and boar.[5] The following Subboreal (3700–500 BCE) heralded a renewed cooler, drier period that lasted until the onset of anthropogenic warming in the 1960s. In the regions discussed, the impact of climate oscillations will be apparent in the development of rock art.

This topography determined the regions in which rock art was at all possible, namely mountainous areas and larger valleys. Particularly rich in petroglyphs are today's western Mongolia, Khakassia in southern Siberia, southern Kazakhstan, Kyrgyzstan, southern Tajikistan and, to a lesser degree, Uzbekistan. In this chapter, the petroglyphs will be discussed in chronological order by country. In southern Siberia there is a major issue: in many regions, petroglyphs are mostly situated near mighty rivers and lakes, where the prehistoric settlements were located; in the impenetrable south Siberian taiga, as in Karelia (shared between modern Russia and Finland), there was no other means of communication than waterways. In Khakassia, however, rock art has been lost due to the construction of the Sayano-Shushenskaya Dam (1963–78). As a result, a section of the Yenisei River area which was particularly rich in petroglyphs was completely flooded and their only remnants are their documentation in the form of black-and-white ink drawings of single figures, which often disregard the links between the images and the general context.[6] Planning errors even led to the destruction of petroglyph sites lying outside the submerged area.[7]

Due to their huge open spaces, the Central Asian steppes acted as a corridor for migrating peoples. At first, during the Neolithic and Bronze Ages, the direction of migration of Indo-European speakers was primarily from north-west to east and south-east, but in the Iron Age the direction reversed, from north-east to south-west, starting with the migrations of the Xiongnu and Hunnic peoples. It was the westward Hunnic migration that set in motion the ethno-linguistic transformation of the Eurasian steppe from Indo-European to Turkic groups of primarily East Asian ancestry.[8] The use of the horse as a mount from the last centuries of the second millennium BCE multiplied the mobility of the steppe pastoralists and their military potential, as is reflected in petroglyphs. Of the huge number of trans-Eurasian migrations, among the most important, whose traces are also found in Bronze

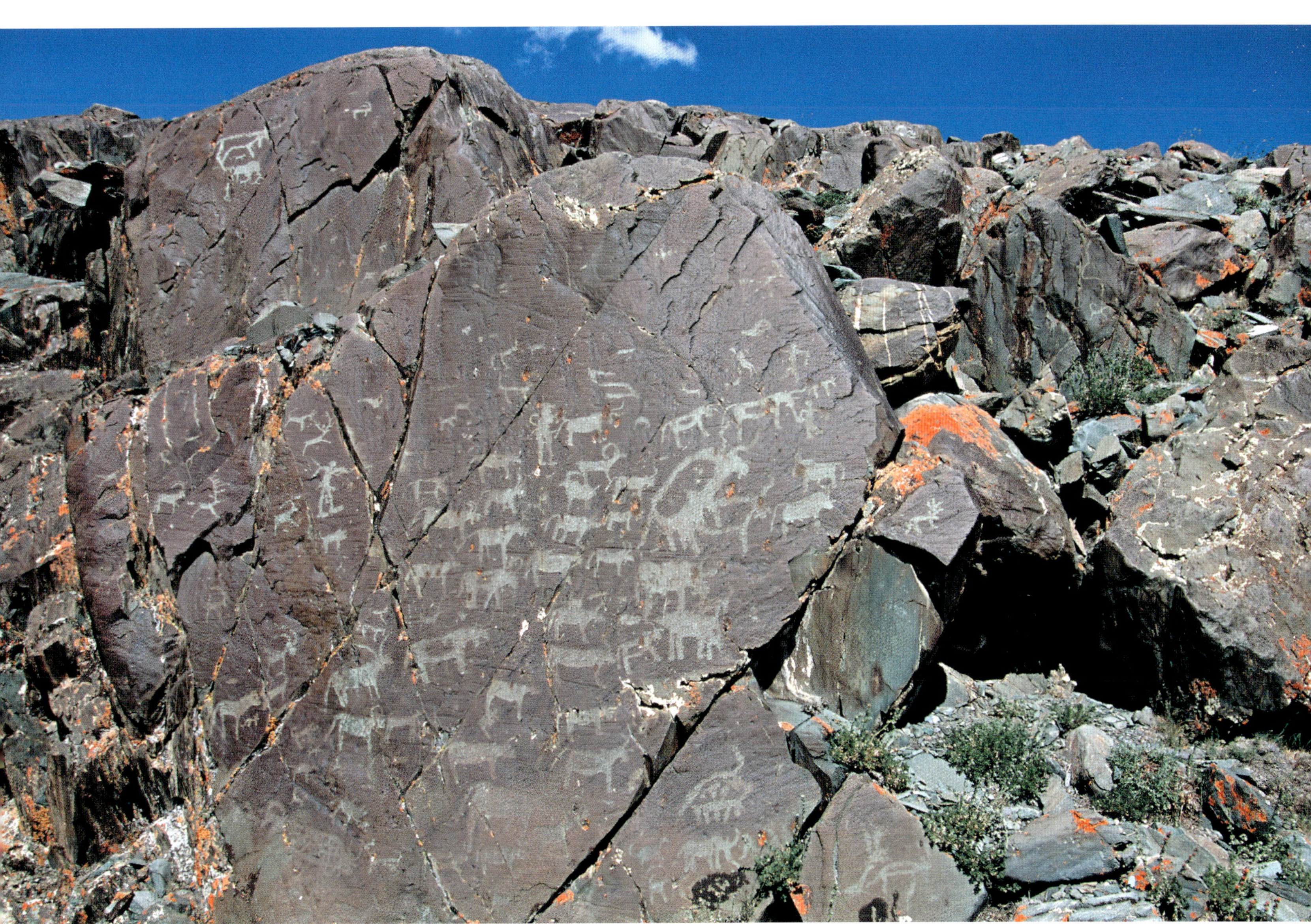

13. A cattle herd with a few ibexes and pastoralists from the Bronze Age. Since virtually all the animals are moving in the same direction and a human leads a large bull on a leash, the scene illustrates a herd on its march, possibly moving to new pastures. A second human, probably a man, spurs another bull to advance, and a third controls the herd from behind. Tsagaan Salaa–Baga Oigor, Bayan Ölgyi Aimag, western Mongolia. Photo 2002.

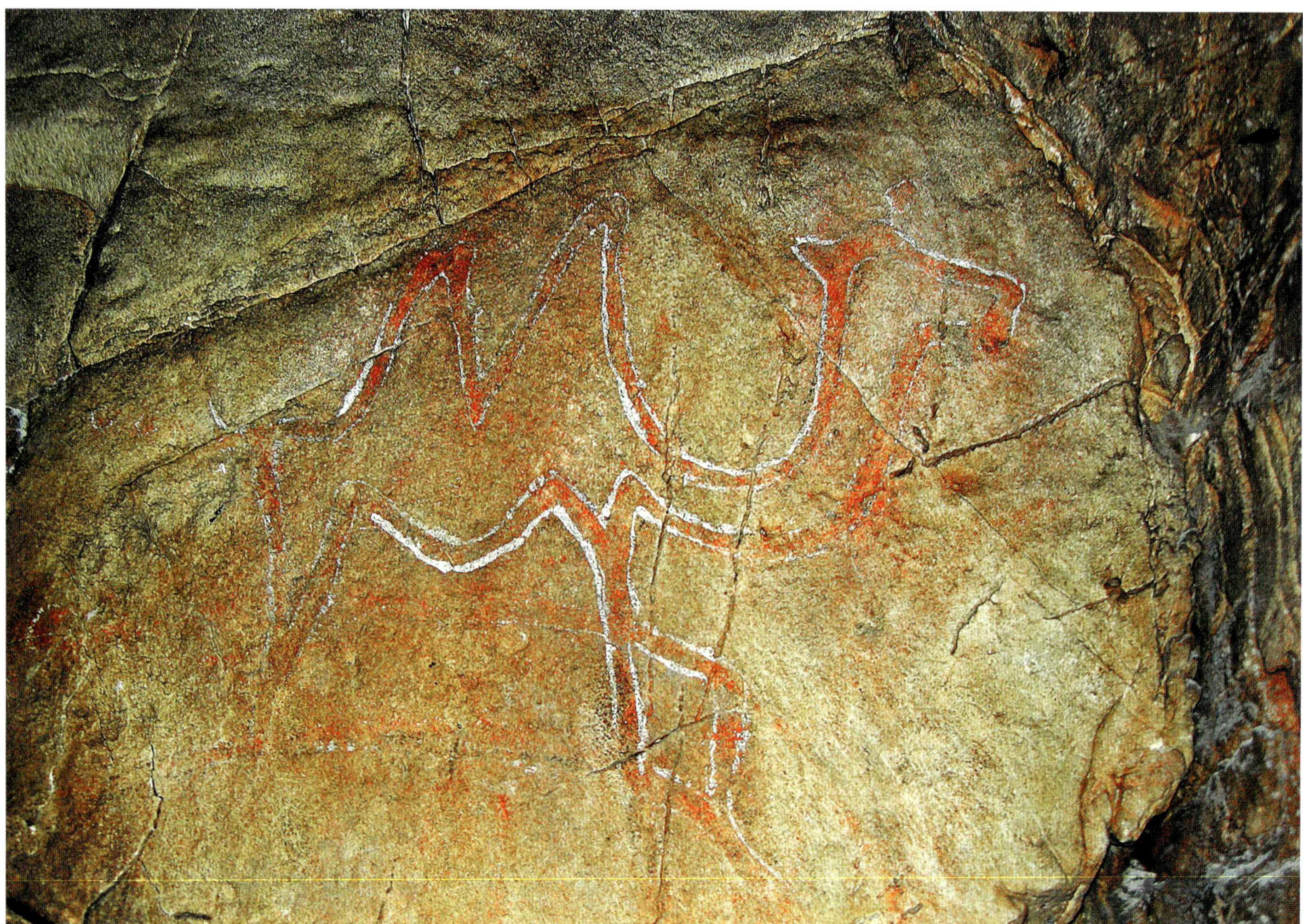

14. Rock painting from the Upper Palaeolithic of a Bactrian camel in the cave of Khoid Tsenkeriin Agui, Khovd aimag, western Mongolia. This painting of a camel and the one in Shulgan-Tash, southern Siberia, are probably the oldest representation of a camel worldwide. Photo 2002.

Age petroglyphs, was the multidirectional spread of the speakers of Indo-European languages from the later fourth millennium BCE. The likely homeland of the Proto-Indo-European (PIE) speakers was the Pontic Steppe located between the Dnieper, the northern Caucasus and the Urals.[9] Out of this environment, in the fourth millennium BCE there emerged in the steppe west of the Ural the Yamnaya culture (3300–2250 BCE) and east of the Ural its counterpart the Afanasievo culture (3300–2350 BCE) which stretched over the Minusinsk Basin in Khakassia as far as the Altai, and almost to today's central Mongolia.[10] In terms of genetics, the carriers of the Yamnaya culture were steppe pastoralists descended from eastern European hunter-gatherers who shared ancestry with hunter-gatherers from the South and North Caucasus as well as from the Near East.[11] This means that a major part of the Indo-European languages had a steppe origin.

From the late fourth to the early third millennium BCE, Indo-European speakers spread both westwards and south-eastwards. In the middle of the Holocene, Europe witnessed two mass-migrations, namely first the Neolithic spread of agriculture from the Levant and Anatolia from the early seventh millennium BCE, followed by the arrival of the Yamnaya, Indo-European speaking steppe pastoralists. As Amy Goldberg has observed, 'the Neolithic transition was driven by mass migration of both males and females in roughly equal numbers, … whereas the Later Bronze Age migration and cultural shift were instead driven by male migration, potentially connected to new technology and conquest.'[12] This migration from the steppe over a distance of 2,500 kilometres occurred in successive waves and was probably supported by the recent introduction of the wheel and the domestication of the horse, at this point used for draught.[13] The magnitude of the migration, that is the gene flow, can be gauged from the fact that Corded Ware People – a culture flourishing from *ca.* 3000 to 2350 BCE in Northern and Central Europe – had 75 per cent Yamnaya ancestry. In other words, the steppe migrants replaced three-quarters of

the genetic make-up of Central Europeans.[14] This migration of
Yamnaya people was not only very impactful, it was also exceptionally fast, in Volker Heyd's words 'a leapfrog rather than wave-of-
advance migrations'.[15] In fact, as Heyd has highlighted, the
transmission of the Yamnaya steppe ancestry from the Dnieper to
the Rhine, a distance of 1,500 kilometres, took about 150 years. For
a comparable distance, the early Neolithic agricultural migration
from the Aegean to the Rhine was spread over 1,000 years.[16] The
Yamnaya migrants brought to Europe not only elements of their
material culture, such as metallurgical technologies, but also their
virile ideology, as is reflected in the Bronze Age petroglyphs of
Scandinavia and Central Asia.

In the course of the third millennium BCE, Indo-Europeans of
the Afanasievo culture migrated south, reaching the Tarim Basin
in today's Xinjiang (north-western China) around 2000 BCE. These
migrants, who spoke a proto-Tocharian language, had possibly
come under pressure from Mongolid groups of the northern

Siberian type. These Mongolid people had advanced to the west
and in the Minusinsk Basin had developed the Okunev culture
(2400–1750 BCE).[17] The domestication of the horse occurred east of
the Urals during the earlier Afanasievo period, around 3000 BCE,
whereas the horse-drawn light chariot was introduced around
2000 BCE during the subsequent Sintashta culture (2200–1700 BCE)
which was part of the Andronovo cultural complex (2200–1250
BCE).[18] The Andronovo cultures were multiethnic, but shared
a homogenous material culture and an Indo-Iranian mythical
heritage. A couple of centuries after the introduction of the light
chariot, horse riding developed, first for purposes of herding,
which would have a far-reaching impact on the size of herds and
the organization of societies, leading to a higher potential for
conflicts. In terms of languages, the Indo-Iranian group separated
from the Indo-European family during the Afanasievo period and
split in turn into the Iranian and Indo-Aryan families during the
early Andronovo period,[19] presumably as individual groups from

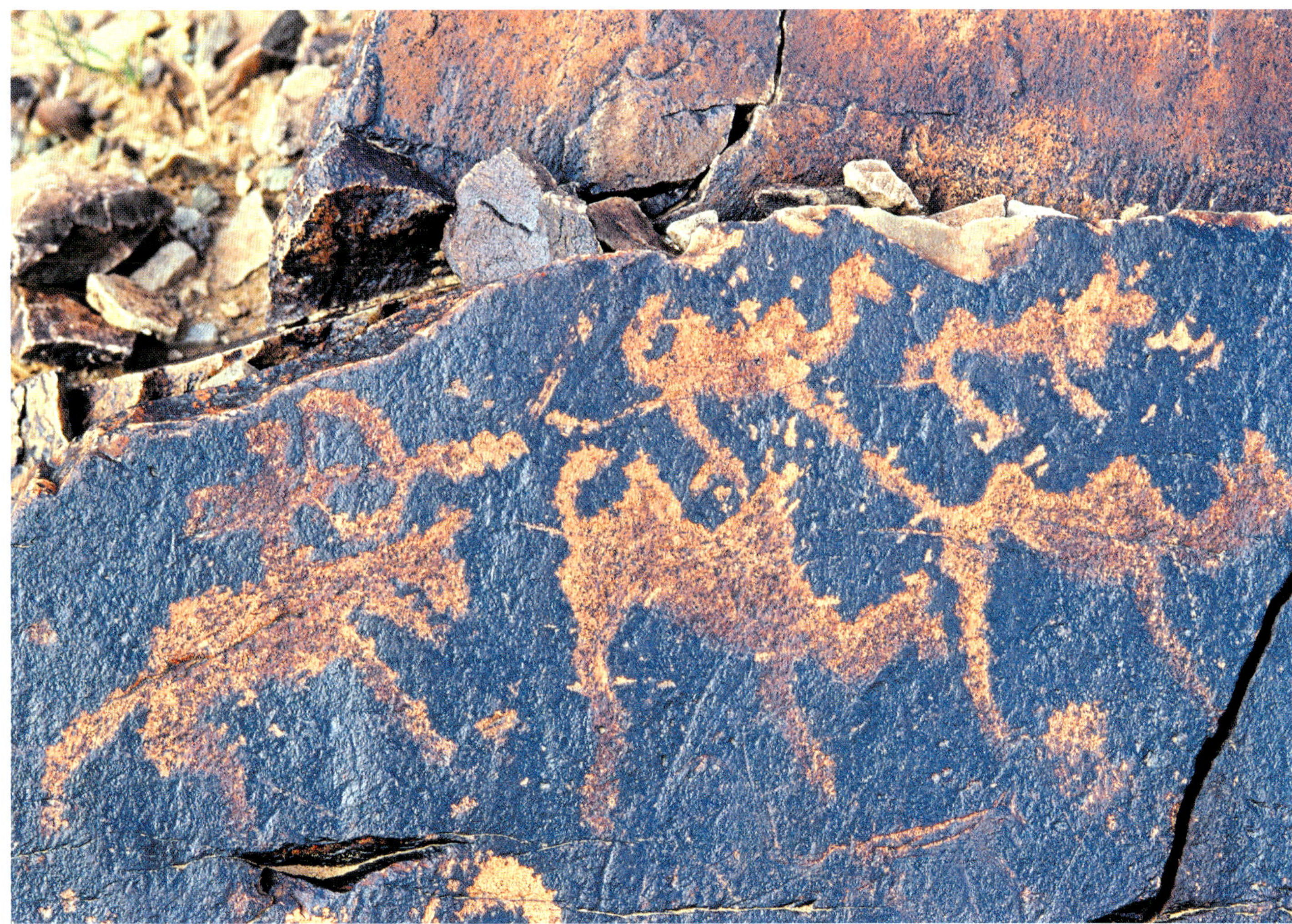

15. A mounted archer hunts camels. Bronze Age, Sirven foothills, Ömnögov aimag, south-western Mongolia. Photo 2001.

the Andronovo cultural complex began to leave their homeland between the Volga and the Yenisei. From about 1800 BCE or a little later, one group set out in successive waves to the south, towards Margiana, Bactria and the Pamir Mountains, where the mythical homeland of the Aryans, called Airyana Vaeja, is presumed to have been;[20] the other headed south-west to the Iranian high plateau. From the Pamirs, the Indo-Aryan groups descended into the plain of the Indus where they possibly contributed to the collapse of the Indus civilization. As suggested by genetics, these newcomers of Andronovian Indo-Aryan speakers were a 'major contributor to the Ancestral North Indian component found in the Indian subcontinent'.[21]

2. Mongolia, Tuva and Siberia

While in Europe the earliest cave paintings are about 37,000 to 30,000 years old, the earliest rock paintings of Central Asia (including Mongolia) were possibly painted *ca.* 15,000 years ago. They are located in the cave of **Khoid Tsenkeriin** in the province of Khovd in western Mongolia, and were first published by the Soviet archaeologist A.P. Okladnikov in 1966. An account by Eleonora Novgorodova followed in 1969.[22] In the depths of the cave, where semi-darkness prevails, contour drawings of animals are recognizable on a pinkish-yellow limestone background, as well as arrows and dots, drawn in brown and reddish ochre tones. All the animals are shown in profile and consist at most of an outline. They represent wild sheep, ibexes, antelopes, a wild, two-humped camel, giant ostriches and certain unidentifiable figures and marks, as well as two mammoths or, according to Okladnikov, two small elephants of the species *Elephas namadicus* (fig. 14).[23] These last two animals provide evidence of the age of the paintings, since the mammoth and *E. namadicus* died out in Mongolia *ca.* 15,000 years ago at the latest, which is thus the lower limit of the dating.[24] At that time a warm interim period, the Bølling–Allerød interstadial, forced both species to migrate north into colder Siberia. Simultaneously with the mammoth, or shortly thereafter, the ostrich also died out in Mongolia; its petrified eggshells bear witness to its earlier widespread range. The portrayal of the camel is likewise notable, since it is, together with the painting of a camel in the Shulgan-Tash Cave, possibly the oldest worldwide representation a two-humped, Bactrian camel.[25] Only slightly younger are the carvings of two pairs of Bactrian camels on a mammoth tusk discovered near Tomsk, western Siberia, which date to around 13000 cal. BP.[26] A slightly curved line drawn under the camel of Khoid Tsenkeriin indicates

a sand dune and a second line above it shows the horizon, lending the drawing a hint of three-dimensionality. As on a palimpsest, somewhat later portrayals of Siberian deer, antelope, Siberian ibex, horses and arrows overlay the Palaeolithic paintings; it appears that the original pictures were reinterpreted as a hunting scene. Possibly, the paintings in the Khoid Tsenkeriin cave were created by those people from the late Upper Palaeolithic whose worked stone tools Okladnikov had discovered in the immediate vicinity of the cave.[27] Unfortunately, the paintings have been damaged since the cave was long known to pastoralists and Okladnikov had the images redrawn to enhance their visibility.

Unexpectedly, another rock painting of a Bactrian camel also dating from the Upper Palaeolithic was found in 2017 in the **Shulgan-Tash** karst cave, also called Kapova Cave. It is located on a western foothill of the Urals in southern Siberia, about 3,000 kilometres west of Khoid Tsenkeriin. Discovered in 1959, the red paintings in the cave made from haematite- and goethite-based ochre[28] feature 46 zoomorphs, among them ten horses, seven mammoths, two woolly rhinoceroses and one bison as well as four anthropomorphic figures. The analysis of a fallen fragment of paint gave a date around 16–14 ka BP.[29] Some of the paintings were covered with calcite. When in 2017 this calcite was removed, a strange figure which had been interpreted as the legs of an anthropomorph turned out to be the rear legs of a large Bactrian camel measuring 60 by 55 centimetres.[30] According to some scholars, these paintings, 4,000 kilometres east of Franco-Cantabria, represent the eastern-most extension of European parietal art.[31] The deep interior of the **Yamazy-Tash** Cave (Ignat'evskaya Cave), located about 150 kilometres north of Shulgan-Tash, was also decorated with 13,000- to 14,000-year-old paintings; unfortunately, they are not as well preserved, due to vandalism. One can make out a few mammoths, horses, a rhinoceros, an aurochs, and possibly a two-humped camel, along with a couple of anthropomorphic figures and a human-animal hybrid made up of a human body and a bird's head and legs.[32] The very poorly preserved paintings of **Serpievka 2** presumably date from the late Upper Palaeolithic; those of **Muradymovka** are from a more recent time.[33]

Among the oldest petroglyphs of Central Asia are those that include portrayals of mammoths, woolly rhinoceroses or ostriches. Since petroglyphs are notoriously difficult to date, the temporal attribution of early petroglyphs remains debated. The rich sites of **Oglakhty** and **Tepsei** in the valley of the Yenisei in southern Siberia, which allegedly also included petroglyphs of the late Upper Palaeolithic or Mesolithic, have been flooded by the artificial Sayano-Shushenskaya Lake and their attributed

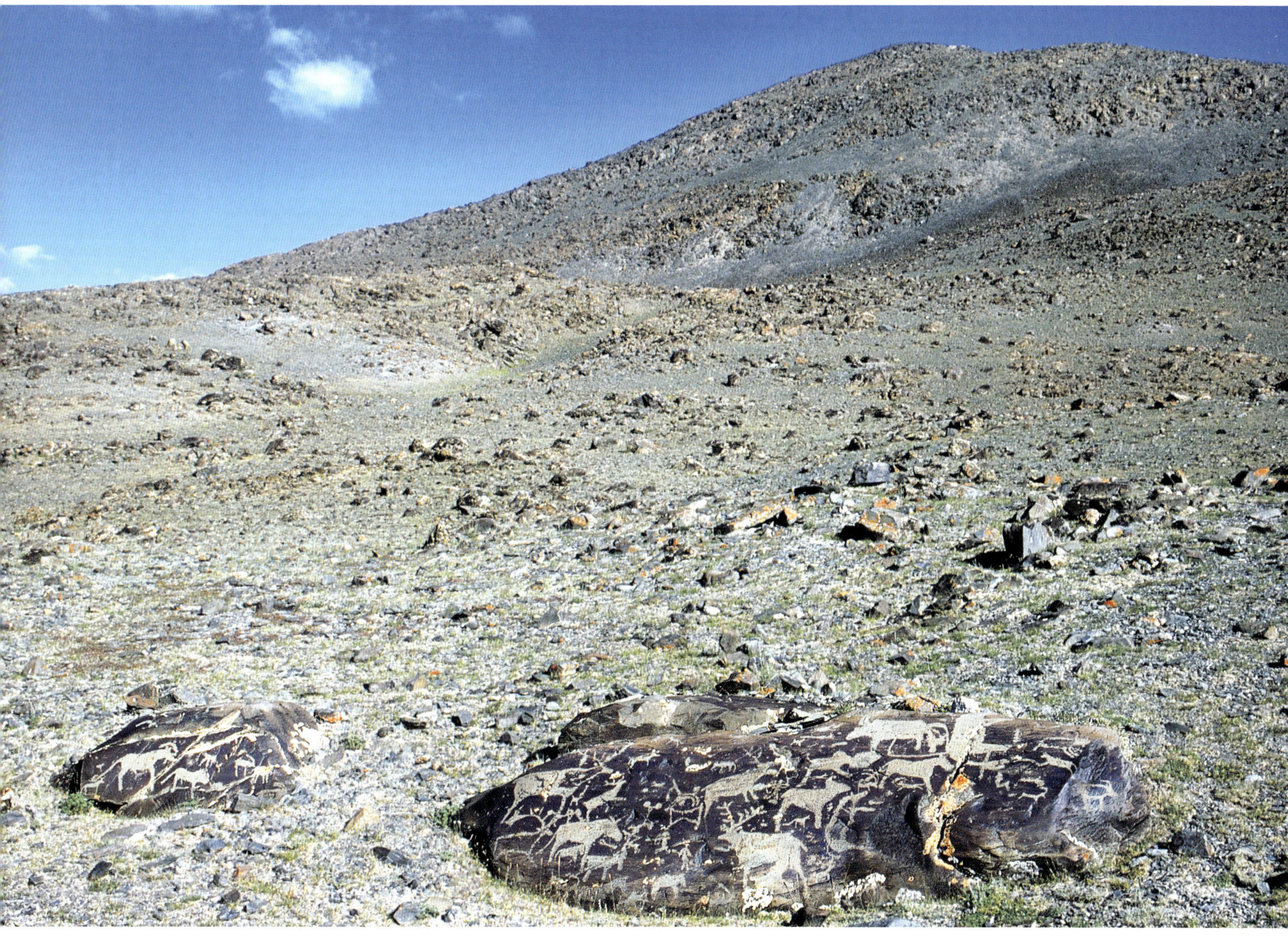

16. Boulder with images of stags, does, bulls, an equid and possibly a boar. Bronze Age, Tsagaan Salaa–Baga Oigor, Bayan Ölgyi aimag, western Mongolia. Photo 2002.

ages can no longer be verified.[34] The dating of the oldest petroglyphs at the site of **Rashan Khad**, Khentii aimag (province) in eastern Mongolia, which was used over several millennia, is also disputed. Next to medieval inscriptions in Old Mongolian, Chinese, Arabic and more recent Buddhist epigrams in Tibetan script, there are numerous non-figurative signs of indeterminate meaning which Novgorodova dates to the Mesolithic.[35] As to the three petroglyphs of massive and static standing animals, their dating depends on their identification: if they represent rhinoceroses, they would come from the Upper Palaeolithic; if they represent aurochs thrusting forward with their heads down, they are from the Neolithic or rather the early Bronze Age as

surmised by Jacobson-Tepfer.[36] Concerning the oldest petroglyphs at the smaller site of **Aral Tolgoi**, near the Khoton Nuur (Lake), Bayan Ölgyi aimag, western Mongolia, they have been differently dated within the Mongolian–American–Russian research team. Whereas Jacobson-Tepfer dates the oldest images, among others of a rhinoceros, to the late Pleistocene, that is the Upper Palaeolithic, Tseveendorj assigns them to the Mesolithic and Kubarev to the Neolithic to early Bronze Age, not least because he interprets the supposed rhinoceros as a boar.[37]

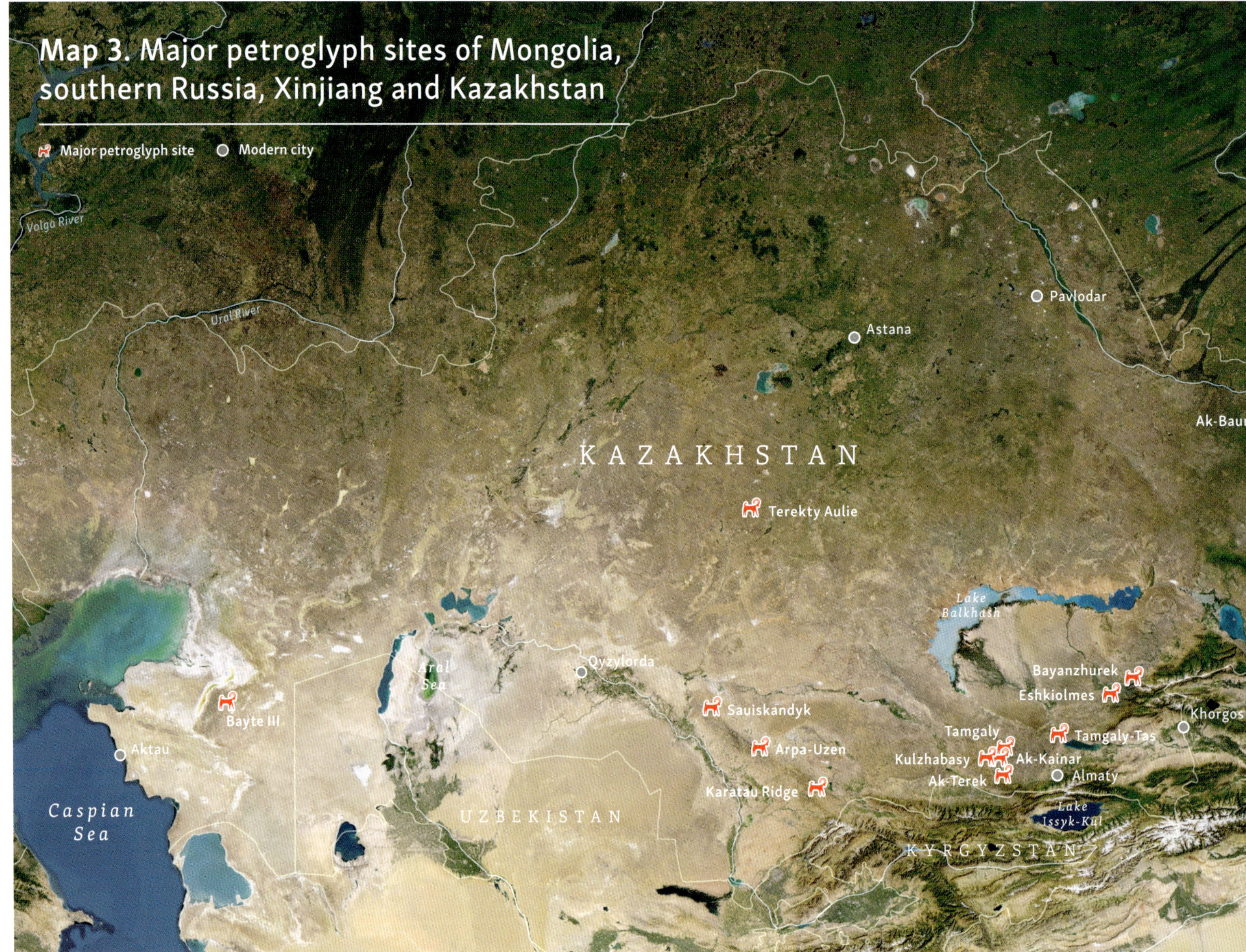

The major rock art sites within Mongolia[38] are, in an approximate chronological order, as follows:

- **Khoid Tsenkeriin** in the province (aimag) of Khovd in western Mongolia is famous for its cave paintings from the Upper Palaeolithic.

- **Aral Tolgoi** is located *ca*. 40 km south of Tsagaan Gol on the western shore of Khoton Nuur. Some of the heavily weathered petroglyphs most probably date to the Upper Palaeolithic.

- **Tsagaan Salaa–Baga Oigor** in north-western Mongolia is, together with the site of Upper Tsagaan Gol, the largest petroglyph complex in the country. The petroglyphs date from the Upper Palaeolithic to the earlier Iron Age.

- **Upper Tsagaan Gol** is situated *ca*. 35 km south of Tsagaan Salaa–Baga Oigor. This rich complex has petroglyphs mainly from the Mesolithic or Neolithic up to the late Bronze Age.

- **Biluut** is also situated at Khoton Nuur, *ca*. 20 km south-east of Aral Tolgoi. Its petroglyphs are mainly from the Bronze and Iron Ages with some spectacular images of giant horses from the Turkic period.

- **Khar Chuluut**, **Hulagash** and **Chuluut Bulak** are located in the basin of the upper Khovd River, Bayan Ölgyi aimag. These sites have walled enclosures whose stone slabs are decorated with petroglyphs from the Bronze Age.

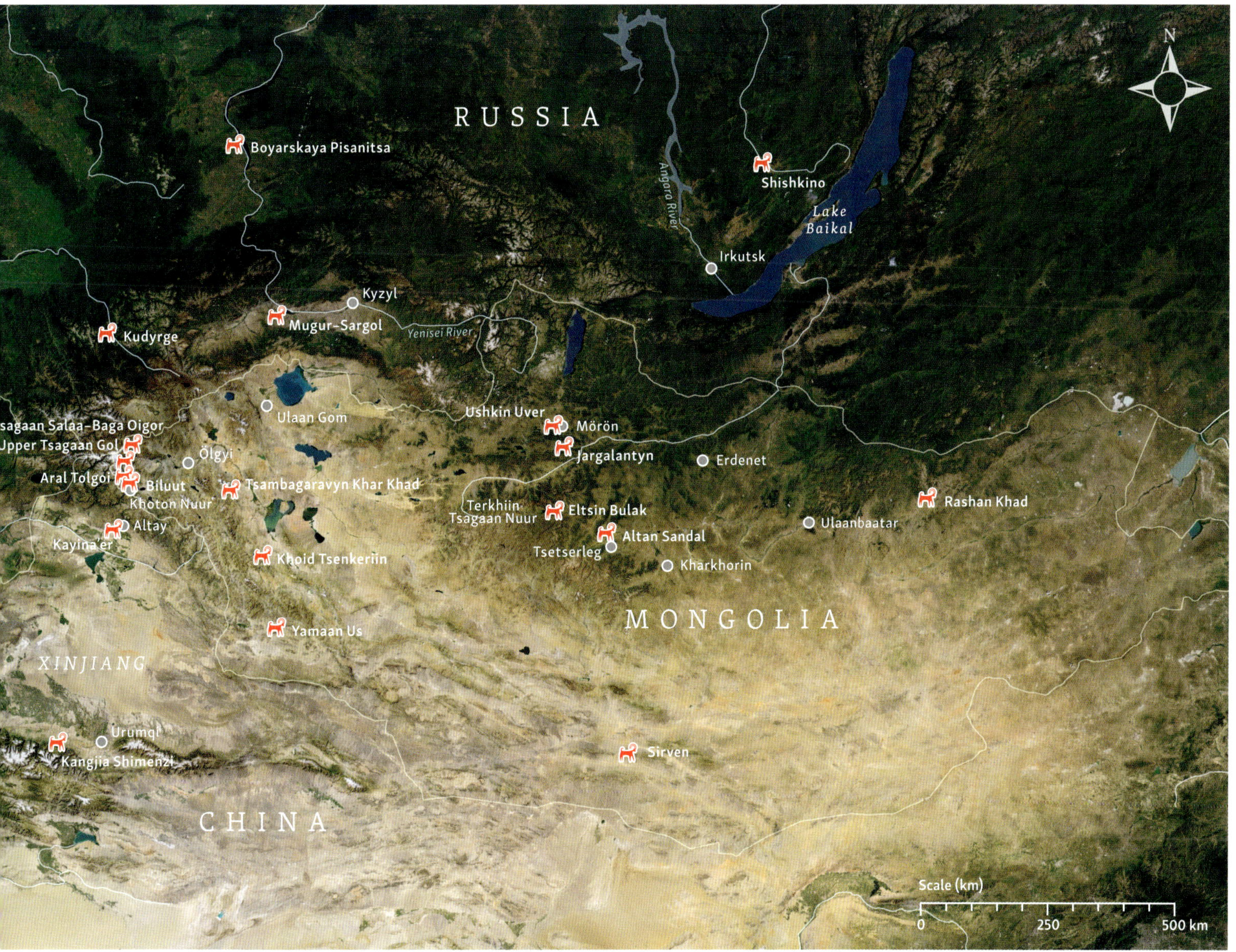

- **Chadaman Uul**, Khovd aimag, has petroglyphs from the late Neolithic to the Iron Age.

- **Rashan Khad**, Khentii aimag in eastern Mongolia. The dating of archaic-looking animals to the Mesolithic is disputed. There are numerous short inscriptions in Old Mongolian, Chinese, Arabic and Tibetan script.

- **Nüchen Ütüg**, Khovd aimag, has petroglyphs of several combat scenes and many ibexes and deer from the late Bronze Age and the Iron Age.

- **Sirven** lies near the Khongoryn Els dune complex in the Gobi Desert. Its petroglyphs date mainly from the late Bronze and Iron Age.

- **Eltsin Bulak** in the Khorgo National Park, Arkhangai aimag has some outstanding late Bronze Age/early Iron Age petroglyphs.

- **Yamaan Us**, Khovd aimag. Its petroglyphs range from the Bronze Age to the Xiongnu Iron Age.

- **Tsambagaravyn Khar Khad** in Khovd aimag is famous for its Saka Iron Age and Turkic petroglyphs.

Mongolia underwent a similar climatic development to Western and Central Europe, though without the balancing effect that comes from proximity to the ocean. During winter, Mongolia is impacted by the Siberian high-pressure circulations leading to intense cold and aridity, while the Altai and Sayan mountains shield the country from the westerlies.[39] Its climate is markedly continental. As outlined in table 1, when the Last Glacial Maximum ended around 19 ka BP, it was followed by a moderate, gradual warming which allowed for the growth of grass and forest steppes where mammoths, rhinoceros and wild horses roamed.[40] Then the interruption of the Younger Dryas (*ca.* 12.9–11.7 ka BP) resulted in renewed glacial conditions, and forests retreated in favour of dry steppe. With the onset of the Holocene, warmer and more humid conditions prevailed which led to the disappearance of the large Ice Age animals such as mammoth and rhinoceros. At the same time, the grass steppes and low-density forests with boreal trees provided an ideal environment for aurochs, elk and bears. After about five millennia of warm climate, a slow, moderate cooling began around 6500 BP. At first, larch and pine replaced spruce, but in the course of continued cooling during the Bronze Age (4400–2900 BP) forests in general retreated. During this period, people complemented hunting with herding, which soon developed into mobile pastoralism. The beginning of the Iron Age witnessed a period of moderate warming and humidity from *ca.* 2900 BP to 2000 BP, that is the turn of the first millennium, whereupon temperatures and humidity again decreased to present conditions. It was in this period that the anthropogenic impact on nature began to be noticeable, in the shape of deforestation and overgrazing.[41] From now on, the widespread use of the horse as a mount decisively shaped the region's economy and the social organization.

Table 1: Chronological correlation between climate, fauna, flora and economy in north-western and western Mongolia and its reflection in rock art[42]

Cultural Period	Date	Climate	Flora	Fauna	Economy	Typical Images
Upper Palaeolithic	26–19 ka BP	Late Glacial Maximum, peak *ca.* 21000 BP, extreme cold	steppe / desert tundra	mammoth, woolly rhinoceros, ostrich	hunter-gatherers	
	19–14.7 ka BP	Late Ice Age hyper-arid in west Mongolia	gradual transition from tundra to steppe	mammoth, woolly rhinoceros, ostrich	hunter-gatherers	mammoth, woolly rhinoceros, ostrich
	14.7–12.9 ka BP	Bølling–Allerød interstadial	grass and forest steppe	mammoth, woolly rhinoceros, ostrich	hunter-gatherers	mammoth, woolly rhinoceros, ostrich
	12.9–11.7 ka BP	Younger Dryas, renewed cooling	retreat of forests, dry steppe	mammoth, woolly rhinoceros, ostrich, wild camel	hunter-gatherers	mammoth, woolly rhinoceros, ostrich, camel
Mesolithic	11.7 ka–6500 BP	warm, humid	low-density forest of boreal trees followed by dense forests	aurochs, elk, argali, ibex, bear, wild horse, wolf	hunter-gatherers	aurochs, elk, argali, ibex, bear, Siberian ibex
Neolithic	6500–4400 BP	slow, gradual cooling and drying	larch and pine replace spruce, start of forest retreat	aurochs, elk, bear, wild horse, moose, wolf	hunter-gatherers	hunters with clubs, birthing women, bell-shaped figures

Bronze Age
  Khirigsuurs
  Deer stones
	4400–2900 BP (900 BCE)	continued cooling and drying	forest retreat	wild yak, domesticated yak, deer, bear, ibex, horse, Bactrian camel, wolf, snow leopard	hunters, herders, mobile pastoralists	hunter with bow, combat, cart, chariot, cattle herd, stable, camel, stylized deer

Iron Age
  Warmer interval
  Xiongnu Period
	900 BCE–550 CE
	900–1 BCE
	244 BCE–155 CE
		present conditions	start of anthropogenic impact on environment (deforestation, overgrazing); grass steppe	bear, deer, domesticated yak, ibex, boar, horse, camel	mobile pastoralists, warrior horsemen, traders	horsemen, camel rider, recurve bow, cattle herd, combat, stylized deer, 'Animal Style', ceremonial chariot with baldachin

Turkic Empires	550–750 CE	present conditions	grass steppe	bear, deer, domesticated yak, ibex, boar, horse, camel	mobile pastoralists, warrior horsemen, traders	riders, armoured horsemen, mounted falconer, *tamga*

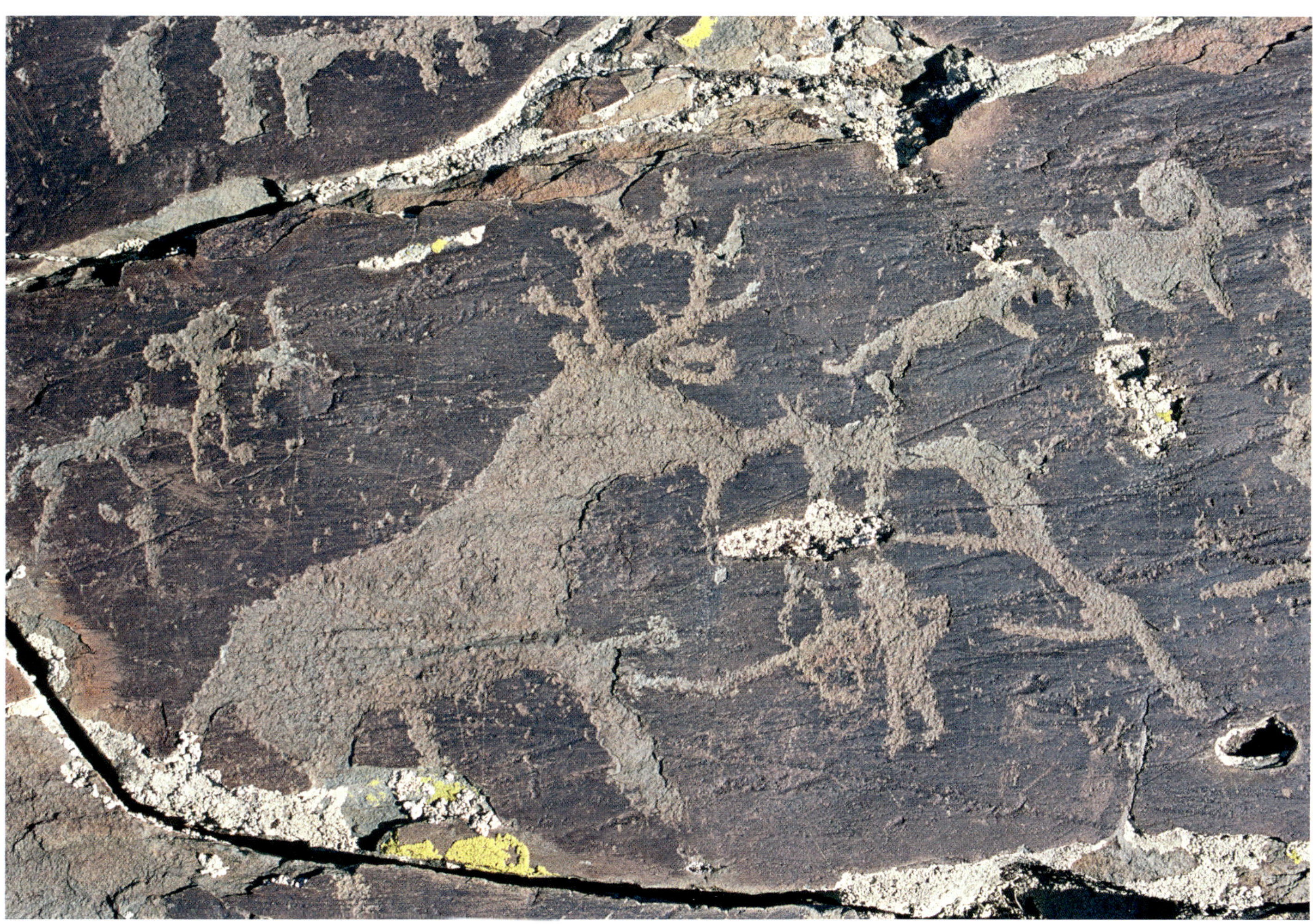

17. Two hunters supported by dogs shoot arrows at a large stag. Bronze Age, Tsagaan Salaa–Baga Oigor, Bayan Ölgyi aimag, western Mongolia. Photo 2002.

The climate-induced changes in fauna and economy can be vividly tracked in the petroglyphs of the huge site of **Tsagaan Salaa–Baga Oigor** (Tsagaan Salaa for short) in Bayan Ölgyi aimag. The preferred rock for creating petroglyphs was metamorphosed sandstone (metagreywacke)[43] which had been formed during the creation of the mountains by high pressure and heat and which was subsequently abraded and polished by advancing and retreating glaciers in the course of the later Pleistocene. In this rough mountain steppe landscape tens of thousands of petroglyphs are spread out mainly along the left banks of the rivers Tsagaan Salaa and Baga Oigor; the lowest are about twenty metres above the valley floor at a height of 2,240 metres above sea level, the highest are at 2,630 metres (fig. 16). The petroglyphs are landmarks of life over the course of climate fluctuations and the corresponding development of a hunter-gatherer society into one of semi-mobile stockbreeders and finally nomadic pastoralists.[44] The earliest figures were made by direct pecking of the image outlines by using a hard stone which removed the varnish and allowed the brightly coloured bedrock to become apparent. The figures are accordingly rough and static-looking. The few petroglyphs of mammoths, possibly a rhinoceros and a couple of animals executed in a similar style suggest a date in the late Upper Palaeolithic.[45] Following the Younger Dryas interlude, mammoths and rhinoceroses disappeared and in rock art aurochs (*Bos primigenius*), elk, moose and red deer predominated. The petroglyphs of these animals, as well as of argalis (wild mountain sheep) and horses, were usually portrayed in the style of a monumental, somewhat static idealized realism; and all appear in profile. Toward the end of the Mesolithic, they are joined by pictures of bears and Siberian ibexes; the latter suggest the start of a retreat of the forests.[46]

Towards the end of the subsequent Neolithic, the first human figures appear in the petroglyphs; before this, rock art was dominated by animals. Now, however, not only was the relationship between human and animal reflected in the petroglyphs, but also essential aspects of human existence. Animals no longer stood alone at the centre of the picture; the human being moved

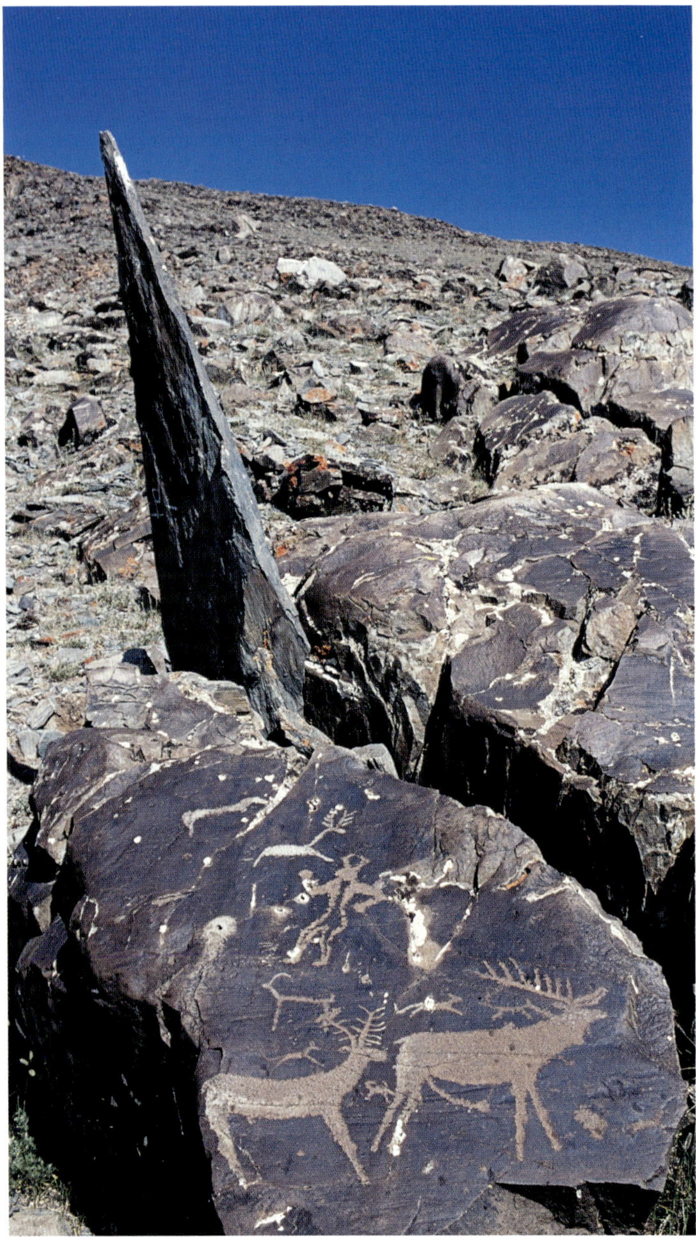

18. Two stags and a human wearing a horned mask; he is possibly a hunter disguised as a deer. Bronze Age, Tsagaan Salaa–Baga Oigor, Bayan Ölgyi aimag, western Mongolia. Photo 2002.

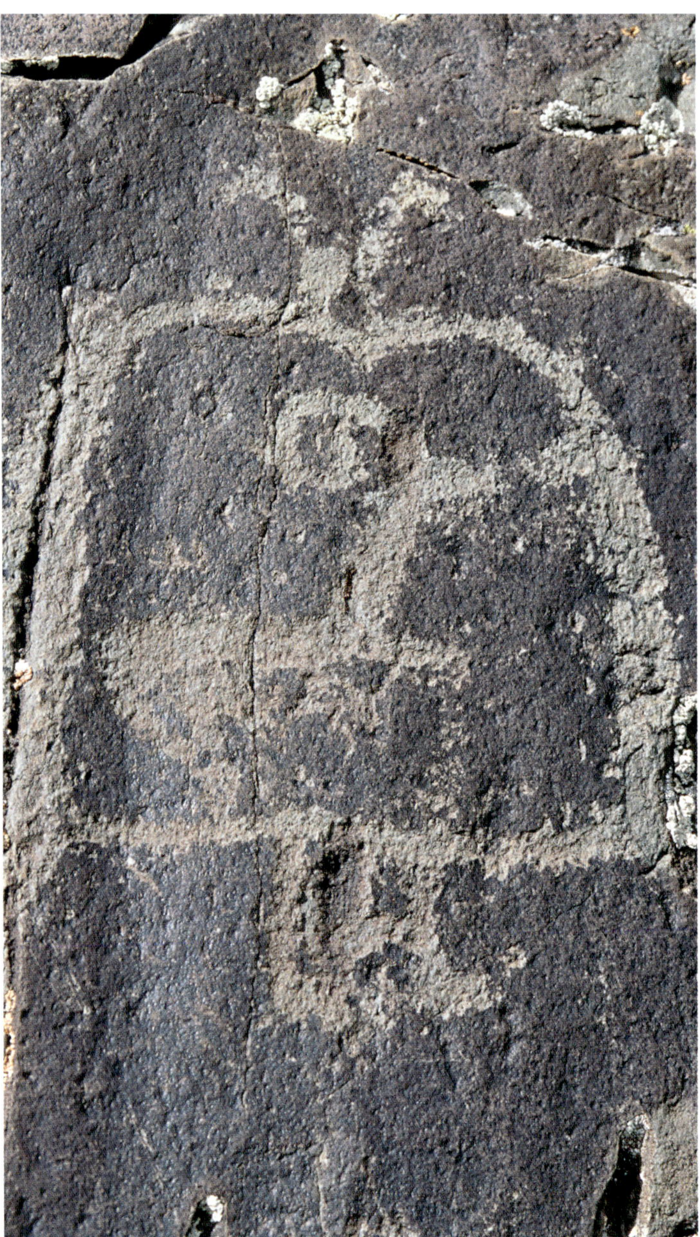

19. Horned and faceless bell-shaped anthropomorph with a small argali inside its belly. Bronze Age, Tsagaan Salaa–Baga Oigor, Bayan Ölgyi aimag, western Mongolia. Photo 2002.

there as well. In Tsagaan Salaa, three theme cycles can be seen: the hunt, human reproduction, and perhaps also a first step into the world of the supernatural. Neolithic hunters, usually large figures armed with a club or spear, were mostly portrayed frontally, as were birthing women. These latter figures possibly not only symbolized human fecundity, but also evoked the fertility of the hunted animal species. As in the preceding periods, people lived by hunting and gathering; hunters now used the long (or self) bow made from a single piece of wood. The third type of human portrayal is mysterious. It shows a bell-shaped figure with short

legs, whose faceless head wears a pair of horns, and inside the body there occasionally appears an infant or an animal like a small argali (fig. 19).

The ongoing cooling and drying trend that had begun in Central Asia in the Neolithic accelerated, affecting western Mongolia and the Altai in particular and heralding the start of the Bronze Age. As a consequence of the climatic disruption, forests shrank and grasslands rapidly expanded. In the petroglyphs, aurochs and moose have disappeared and hunters, assisted by dogs, prey on deer, wild yaks, horses, argali and ibexes; they use composite bows with a higher draw weight. In contrast to the Upper Palaeolithic parietal cave paintings in Europe where clearly recognizable hunting scenes are rare, they are widespread in Central Asian Holocene rock art. From now on, petroglyphs were realized by indirect pecking: the artist used an impact stone as hammer to hit a strong, sharp stone chisel and so cut the varnish from the rock. Indirect pecking allowed for more precise work and thus finer figures. The bulk of the petroglyphs of Tsagaan Salaa date from the Bronze Age; and, as noted by Jacobson-Tepfer, men are mostly featured in profile or three-quarter view, women frontally.[47] Animals appear now less static, but rather in motion. Sometimes hunters are featured wearing animal skins and having animal heads and horns; these images hardly represent shamans transforming themselves into animals as is sometimes claimed; rather the animal skin and mask are worn by a hunter to disguise himself as an animal in order not to raise the suspicion of his prey (fig. 18).[48] Another strange-looking figure consists of an armed man wearing a mushroom-shaped head covering and on the back of his hips something that looks like a ball-shaped tail. This motif appears in the entire eastern half of Central Asia, in Mongolia and Inner Mongolia, southern Siberia, Kazakhstan and Kyrgyzstan, which suggests interregional cultural ties (figs 25, 74). It is scarcely plausible that this image illustrates a shaman under the influence of fly agaric and wearing a false tail. The mushroom-shaped headgear could rather symbolize the vault of the sky or, if the petroglyph dates to the late Bronze Age, a bronze helmet decorated with feathers.[49] As to the alleged tail, it represents either part of a fur jacket worn in those times, a mace or a ball flail.[50]

During the Bronze Age, several innovations reached western Mongolia which had their origin first in the Afanasievo culture, and later in the Sintashta culture (a part of the Andronovo complex) from which they had been transmitted to the Okunev culture and subsequently to the Altai. These innovations were first, the wheel, originally with only four massive spokes, then fully spoked; second, the domestication of the horse for purposes other than consumption; and third, developments in metallurgy. There were several steps involved in exploiting the potential of these innovations. The wheel was first used in heavy two-axle carts, and later in light single-axle chariots, while the horse was first used as a draught animal, and later as a mount. Finally, there were improvements in bronze horse bridles and, around 900 BCE, iron began to replace bronze in utility objects for use as opposed to decoration. The new metal led to dramatic changes in mobility and weaponry, with the introduction of iron horse gear and iron arrowheads, battle axes and swords. The impact of these innovations was all the greater as the climate became harsher, colder and drier, and new, adapted survival strategies became necessary. The retreat of the forests and the consequent reduction in wild game triggered a step-by-step shift from hunting and sedentary herding to semi-mobile pastoralism supported by the use of carts. A very rare petroglyph scene illustrating the daily life of pastoralists is located at **Boyarskaya Pisanitsa** on the left bank of the River Yenisei in Khakassia, Russia. Forming a strip more than ten metres long and 80 centimetres high, this petroglyph from the Tagar culture (1000–200 BCE) shows a settlement of yurt-like dwellings and winter log-houses (not in the image), herders, hunters, masks, cattle, deer, sheep, dogs and typical bronze cauldrons (fig. 20). Unfortunately, this unique petroglyph site was lost beneath the deep waters of the Sayano-Shushenskaya reservoir.[51]

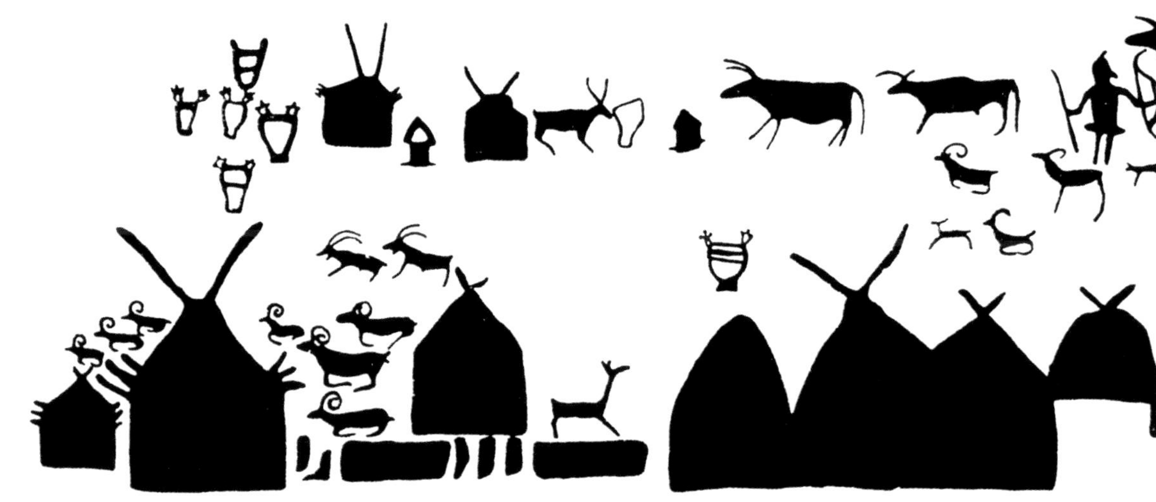

20. Ink drawing of a detail from the petroglyphs of Boyarskaya Pisanitsa in Khakassia, Russian Federation. It shows yurt-like dwellings of stockbreeders from the Tagar culture (1000–200 BCE). After Kšica, Miroslav and Kšicová, Olga, *Felsbilder zwischen Schwarzem Meer und Beringstrasse* (Brno: *PREH-ART-EXPO*, 1994), pp. 177f.

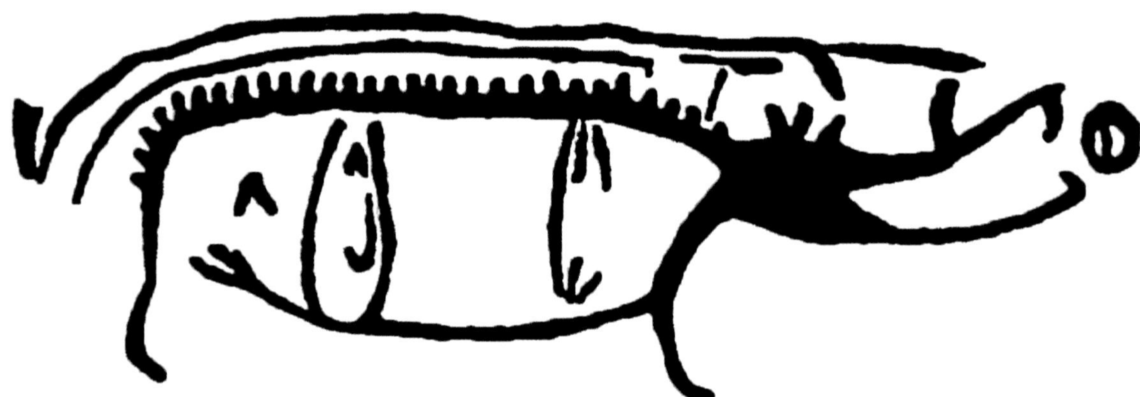

21. A monstrous animal capturing the sun. Ink drawing of a probably Bronze Age petroglyph at Shishkino, Perm krai, Russian Federation. After Shvets, Irina, *Studien zur Felsbildkunst Kasachstans* (Darmstadt: Philipp von Zabern, 2012), pl. 82.

Also lost is a rare image of a hunter on skis pursuing a deer or an elk located at **Kamenny Ostrov**, the 'Stone Island' in the river Angara, a tributary of the Yenisei;[52] a similar petroglyph exists at Tsagaan Salaa.[53] It remains doubtful if these two similar scenes really illustrate a myth of the Evenki, according to which the giant elk Kheglen stole the sun, impaled it on its horns, and carried it to the north, causing eternal night and cold to threaten humanity. In order to save it, the divine hero Ma'en (Main) pursued the elk and tore the sun away from it, returning it to the people at dawn. The Evenki believed that this cosmic drama played out every night. According to this interpretation, the engraved skier would represent Ma'en, who is pursuing Kheglen.[54] Both scenes could just as well represent a real elk hunt, since this rather simple scene is also featured in petroglyphs of Karelia and northern Scandinavia.[55]

However, another rock art scene which has also disappeared into the waters of the artificial Sayano-Shushenskaya lake, 200 metres deep, may well be connected to an ancient Siberian myth. The rock painting of **Kantegir**, in red and dating from the Bronze Age, shows a hybrid monster with the stout body and open jaws of a bear but walking on four human legs, pursuing a star.[56] A similar petroglyph exists at **Shishkino** at a bank of the upper Lena River, north of Lake Baikal. It represents a mythical creature 160 centimetres long with an elongated body with a serrated back, the snout of a crocodile and a horn on the upper jaw. The monster is about to capture and devour an astral body, probably the sun or the moon (fig. 21).[57] This piece of rock art, probably dating from the Bronze Age, illustrates the ancient myth of the cosmic pursuit of the sun which was widespread in Siberia, among the Evenki, Chukchi and other peoples. This myth is about the eternal vanishing and rebirth of the sun, the fight between light and darkness. It tells of a ferocious monster, symbolizing the forces of death and everlasting darkness, chasing the sun, symbol of life and abundance, in order to devour it.[58] When the sun escapes into the west, transforming itself into the underground and nocturnal sun, darkness covers the earth. But when the sun has completed its nocturnal journey through the underworld, it reappears in the east, bringing light again.[59] It was in a later version of this ancient myth that the sun is abducted by the aforementioned giant elk Kheglen and is rescued by the heroic hunter Ma'en who pursues the elk in its subterranean, nocturnal flight and kills it at midnight, whereupon the remains of the elk transform into the constellations of Orion and Ursa Major (the 'Big Dipper').[60] Among the ancient Samoyedic peoples, it was a bear who chased the elk which carried the sun on its antlers. The bear rescues the sun and brings it to the underworld so that it can rise the next morning. The day when the bear kills the fleeing elk will be doomsday.[61] In another variant of this myth, the hunter who rescues the sun from the elk is a therianthrope consisting of a powerful human body with the head of bear (or other carnivore) with open jaws. In the petroglyph at Mount Ozernoye, in the middle Yenisei, which illustrates this version, the therianthrope pursues an elk from whose back radiate rays, indicating that the elk carries the sun away.[62] As observed by Okladnikov, in the imaginations of ancient hunters, 'world events unfolded like a dramatic hunt'.[63] These myths reflected the frightening fact that in northern, especially Arctic, climes, the sun disappears from the sky in winter for weeks or even months at a time. In other petroglyphs from the Sayan Valley and the Altai, an elk or deer is shown carrying not one sun on his antlers, but two, three or even five.[64] The latter petroglyphs probably illustrated another myth, possibly one known from the Nenets people, which explained the origin of the petroglyphs in a particular way: in a distant past there were three suns in the sky. It was so hot on earth that rocks melted like wax, and the demigods drew petroglyphs into the molten stones with their fingers.[65] Two of the three suns had to be shot down with arrows.

Furthermore, the cosmic pursuit of the sun was not part of the mythological heritage of Bronze Age and Iron Age Siberian peoples only: the myth also spread to Scandinavia where it was recorded in the Norse *Edda*. There, the mythical wolf Fenrir pursues the sun in order to devour it. To save the sun from the all-powerful Fenrir, Tyr, the patron-god of warriors, binds Fenrir with an unbreakable chain. However, at Ragnarök, the cataclysmic doom of the gods, Fenrir succeeds in breaking his chain and finally catches the sun, prompting the destruction of creation.[66] The motif of the wolf threatening the sun is also found on Celtic coins from the first century BCE.[67] These myths involving a pursuit of the sun are part of a wider corpus of Siberian and North American myths whose common denominator is a cosmic hunt with the final transformation of the animals involved (and the hunter) into stars and constellations.[68] Assuming a Eurasian origin, the myth was probably spread when people crossed some 15,000 to 14,000 years ago from easternmost Siberia over frozen Beringia to the North American continent.[69]

Such monsters threatening to catch the sun were also engraved on the monumental stone steles from the Okunev culture (2400–1750 BCE) located in the Minusinsk Basin of Khakassia and Krasnoyarsk krai (district). These steles made from granite or greywacke are up to six metres high and slightly bent forward, like a sabre (fig. 31).[70] The front is formed not by the wide side, but the narrow side where one or two human masks, various kinds of solar symbols, herbivores such as ibexes, deer and bulls, and geometric marks are engraved. The carnivores are usually portrayed on both wider sides, but sometimes they also extend to the front side. The steles in most cases were sited in connection to burial sites, though in later periods they also stood alone. In virtually all cases the steles were oriented to the rising sun and were associated with a nearby altar. The exact function of these anthropomorphic monuments remains unknown, but they were definitely part of a set-up used for specific rituals such as the veneration of ancestors which would be

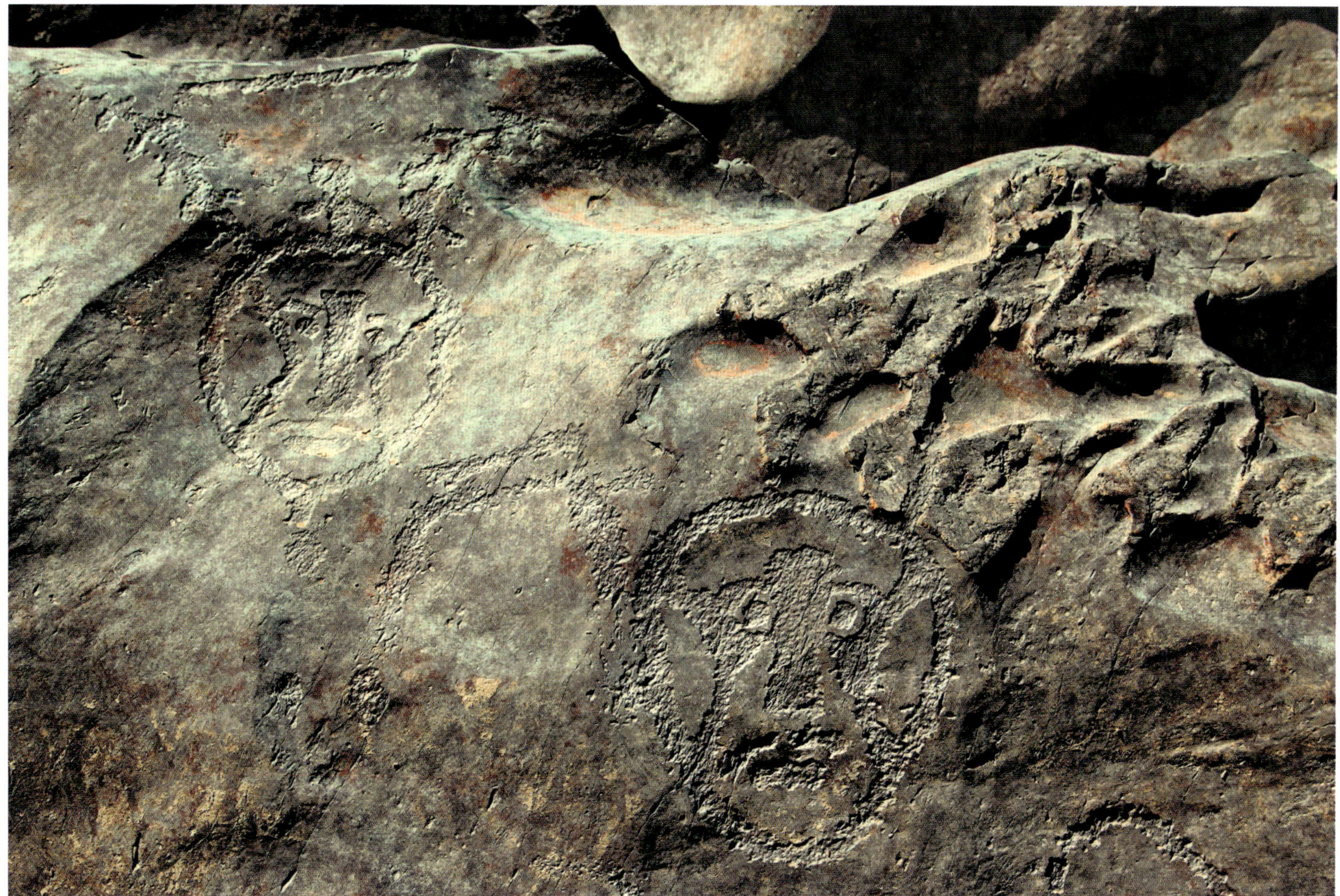

22. Two Bronze Age masks from Mugur–Sargol, Tuva, Russian Federation. The cheeks of both masks have similar geometric decorations to the anthropomorphic steles of the Chemurchek (Qie'muerqieke) culture (fig. 23); two curved fir trees stand above the rear mask. Photo 2019 by Pavel Leus.

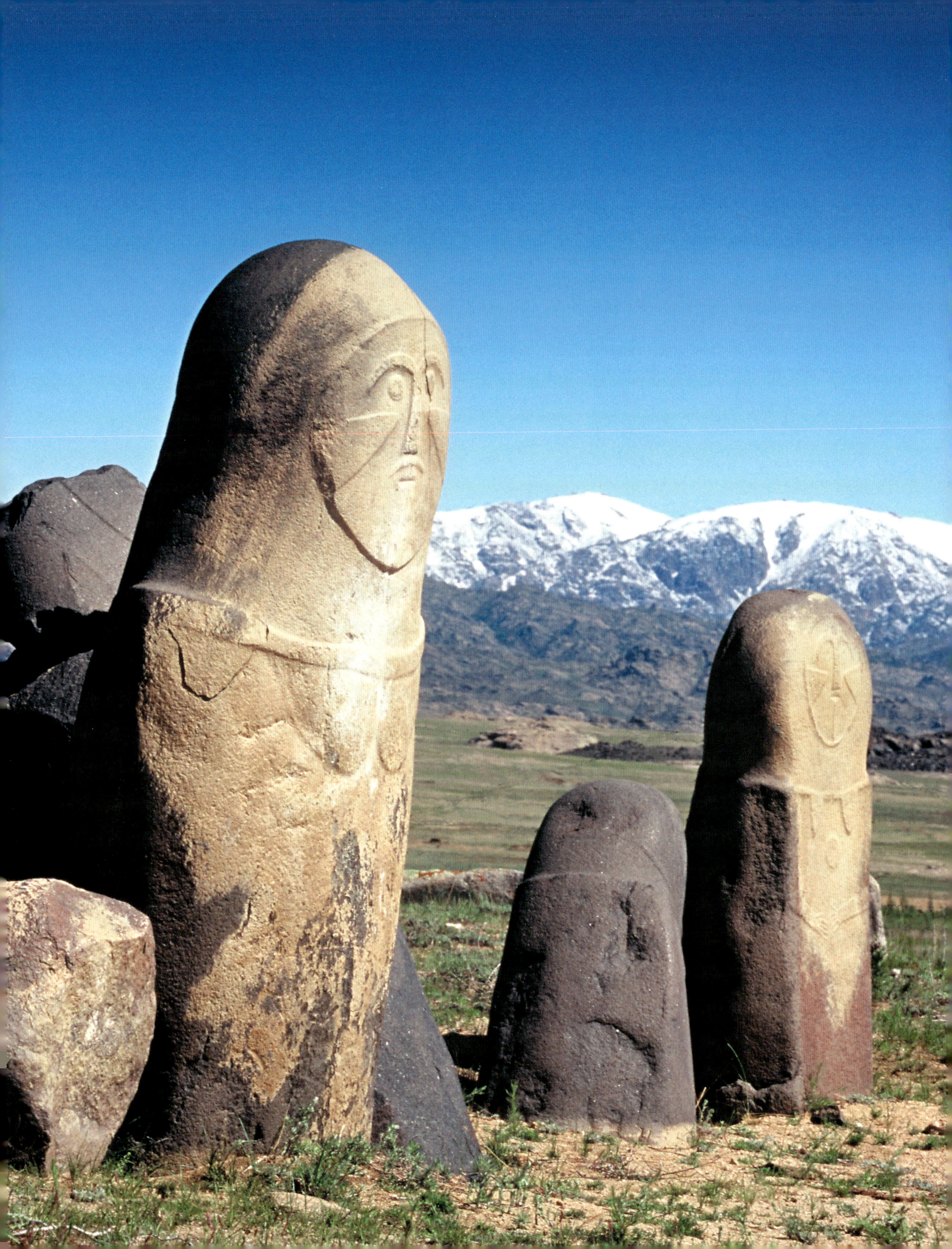

combined with a solar cult. The latter aspect is suggested by those free-standing, rectangular stone monuments that prominently feature a human face adorned with solar rays.[71] Distantly related petroglyphs of anthropomorphized suns showing slight similarities are also found in the later Bronze Age sites of Tamgaly (Kazakhstan) and Saimaluu Tash (Kyrgyzstan).

The motif of human or quasi-human masks must have been of high importance for the Okunev culture, since they appear in petroglyphs of various sizes. At a lonely place called Chortcha Kho (near Kazanovka in Khakassia) there is a petroglyph of a life-size human face with distinct eyes and an open mouth formed of a natural crack. As the authors observed in 2002, people were still bringing food offerings such as bread, fat and vodka.[72] Throughout Khakassia, Tuva, southern Siberia and northern Central Asia, hundreds of smaller petroglyphs feature human-like masks (or faces). One of the most interesting collection of masks is the Bronze Age site of **Mugur–Sargol**, located in Tuva on the left bank of the river Yenisei. On quite a few masks, a short handle is visible below the chin, with which the mask could be held in front of the face. Some masks render a human face more or less naturalistically, others are quite simple while others subtly mix traits of an animal into the anthropoid face. Numerous other masks have lines sticking out of their heads looking like antennae or horns. Especially in east Siberian regions, in the basins of the rivers Ussuri and Amur, these horns are quite large, suggesting the antlers of a cervid. The latter could perhaps symbolize Ulgen, the main deity of the Samoyedic Nenets.[73] On a mask from Mugur–Sargol, a small figure stands on the top of the mask, flanked by two outwardly bent fir trees; the small standing figure could represent the *ongon* of a 'shaman', that is a representation of the spirit which protects the performer of rituals (fig. 22). The cheeks of the mask are decorated with very similar triangular patterns to those carved on some anthropomorphic stone steles from the Chemurchek culture (fig. 23). On some masks from Mugur–Sargol, there is no outline and only the mouth, nose and eyes are shown. On another mask (or face), the pointed ears of an animal are added, possibly a fox or a wolf. It was often reported by explorers of the eighteenth and nineteenth centuries that during ceremonies Siberian shamans used to wear either antlers or a mask with antlers. Finally, other masks from the Amur-Ussuri region resemble later carved and painted wooden masks as worn by east Siberian shamans in the eighteenth and

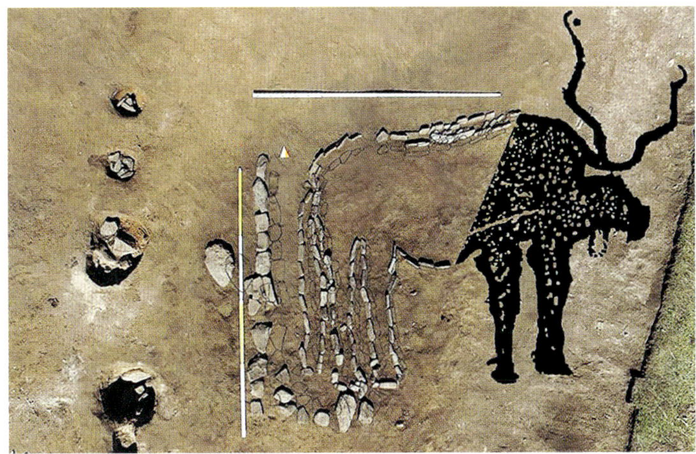

24. Geoglyph in the shape of a bull from Khondergey, Tuva, Russian Federation. This bull-shaped geoglyph is unique for Central Asia. Photo 2021 by M.E. Kilunovskaya.

nineteenth centuries.[74] Whether the petroglyphs of masks made three or four thousand years ago can be connected with masks worn during rituals such as the initiation of youths into adulthood or whether they represented deities and spirits remains unknown. In Tuva, a unique discovery was made in 2021 when the geoglyph of a bull was found within a Bronze Age burial complex. The bull was formed of a careful arrangement of local pebbles (fig. 24). It originally measured *ca.* four by three metres, and only its rear part is preserved, its front legs and head having been disturbed by road construction work. This animal-shaped geoglyph seems to be unique for Central Asia.[75]

In the Bronze Age petroglyphs were not only engraved on rocks, but also on funeral constructions. At the sites of Khar Chuluut, Hulagash and Chuluut Bulak, in Bayan Ölgyi aimag, Mongolia, several burials were surrounded by rectangular enclosures, up to three metres long and two metres wide, which consisted of stone slabs inserted vertically into the ground. These slabs were engraved with the images of humanoids with rectangular or bell-shaped bodies with sometimes just two antennae instead of a head.[76] Other anthropomorphs seem to have three heads and anticipate the double-headed humanoids of Kangjia Shimenzi in the Tian Shan.[77] Also singular are the petroglyphs of male anthropomorphs girded with a dagger and seemingly standing on a single foot, like the monopod at Besovy Sledki, near Vyg in Russian Karelia.[78] Then there are images of humans with bi-triangular bodies and masks. All these petroglyphs date to the later third millennium BCE. Of a later date are images of deer, boars, felines, horses, a raptor and camels, which are from the Iron Age.[79]

Returning to Tsagaan Salaa, the use of horses, and in semi-desert steppes of camels, for riding turned sedentary and pedestrian herding into fully mobile mounted pastoralism, which

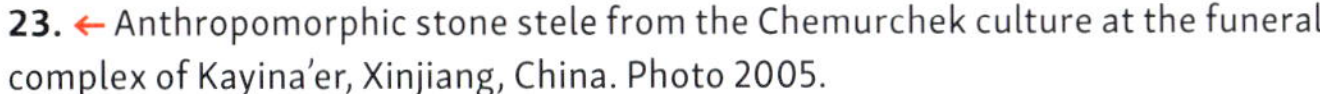

23. ← Anthropomorphic stone stele from the Chemurchek culture at the funeral complex of Kayina'er, Xinjiang, China. Photo 2005.

represented not only a technological change but also a cultural one. Mounted pastoralism not only allowed the increasingly meagre pastures to be rotated more quickly, but also made possible the control of larger herds of big herbivores. The spread of horse riding in turn required adaptions in weaponry, since the long bow was unusable by riders, and so came to be replaced in the Iron Age by a shorter recurve bow. The supply of arrows was kept in a combined quiver and bow case made from leather, called a *gorytós* by the Greeks when they encountered the Scythians, who originated in Tuva in southern Siberia, on the Black Sea coasts.[80] All these changes in turn increased competition among social groups for pastures and access to water sources, which led to an increase in the level of organization of society and the need for leadership. Whereas the heavy biaxial cart was of great use for moving nomadic camps, the light battle chariot remained of limited utility in the mountainous and semi-mountainous steppes. However, during the Bronze Age and early Iron Age it remained highly valued within the Andronovian worldview as an object of prestige and an attribute of divinities.

All these material and cultural changes are reflected in the petroglyphs at Tsagaan Salaa, which are no longer static, but show scenes with action. Hunting scenes decrease markedly in number and portrayals of domesticated cattle herds become more widespread. Images of laden oxen or yaks and biaxial carriages led by herders on foot or on horseback and guarded by dogs illustrate how stockbreeders moved from pasture to pasture.[81] But they also had settled winter residences, as suggested by the stone engravings showing outlines of huts and stables with cattle standing inside them. All this implies that the concept of property rapidly gained currency. Among hunter-gatherers, the idea of property was presumably not widespread, and would have been dangerous for the community. But insofar as herder families or groups identified available pastures and protected winter camps with secure access to water as 'their own', they became owners of a particular territory, which they had to defend. This development led to the emergence of geometric marks, called *tamga* in Turkic, which were applied to horses, cattle and monuments as well as on rocks to

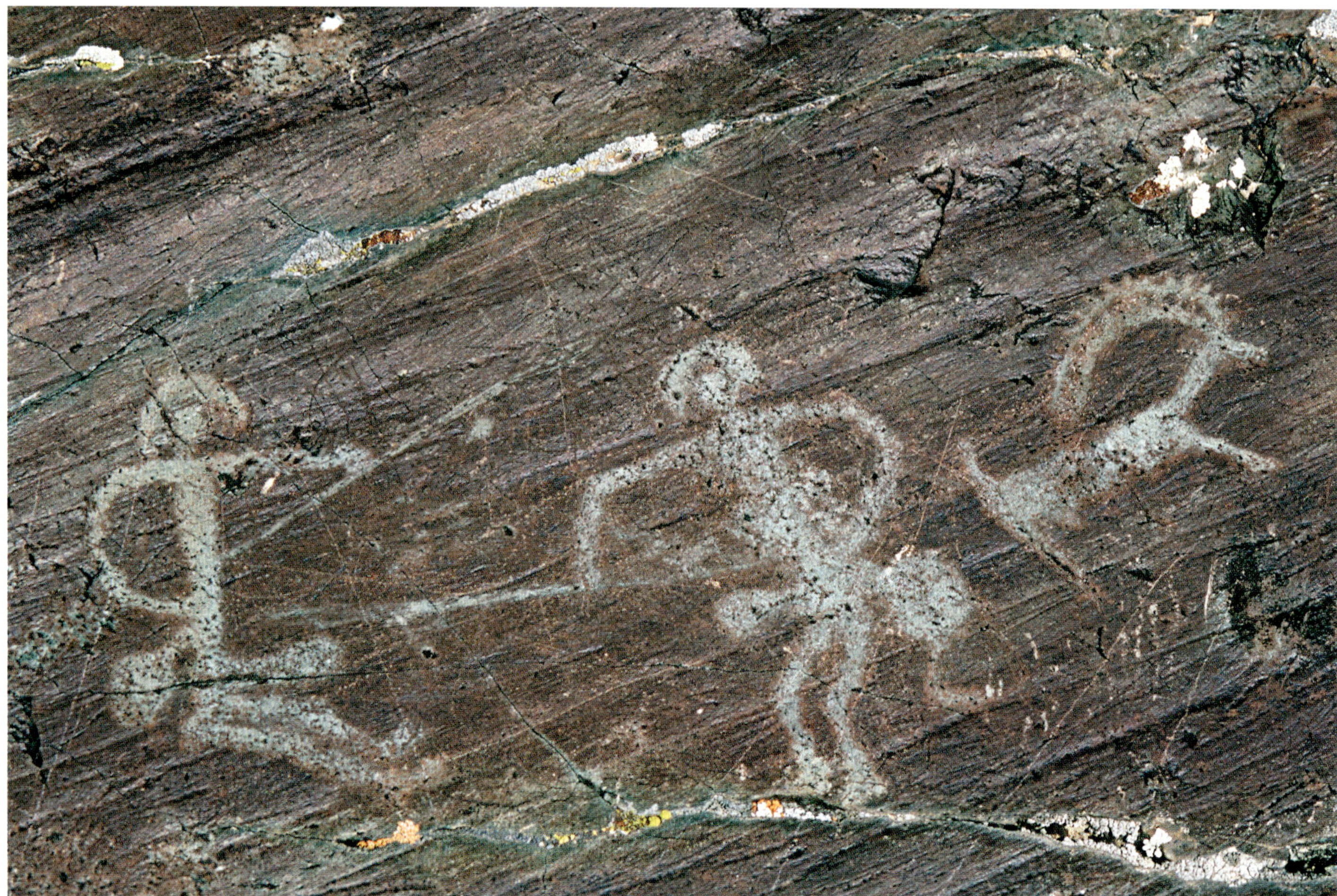

25. Duel between two men with short lances wearing mushroom-shaped headdresses. Later Bronze Age, Tsagaan Salaa–Baga Oigor, Bayan Ölgyi aimag, western Mongolia. Photo 2002.

26. Ink drawing of a petroglyph scene from Baga Oigor III, Bayan Ölgyi aimag, western Mongolia, Late Bronze Age. On the left, a man leads two horses on a leash, in the centre a man holding a long stick stands at the entrance of a rectangular space, and on the right two horses lie back-to-back within this rectangular space, attached to a drawbar; next to them a human lies on the ground. The scene probably illustrates a burial and horse sacrifices. Ink drawing by V.D. Kubarev, permission of Esther Jacobson-Tepfer. Sher, Jakov and Francfort, Henri-Paul (eds), *Répertoire des pétroglyphes d'Asie centrale*, fasc. 6, vol. 1: Kubarev, Vladimir, Jacobson, Esther and Tseevendorj, Damdensurenjin, *Mongolie du nord-ouest. Tsagaan Salaa/Baga Oigor* (Paris: De Boccard, 2001), p. 386, fig. 983.

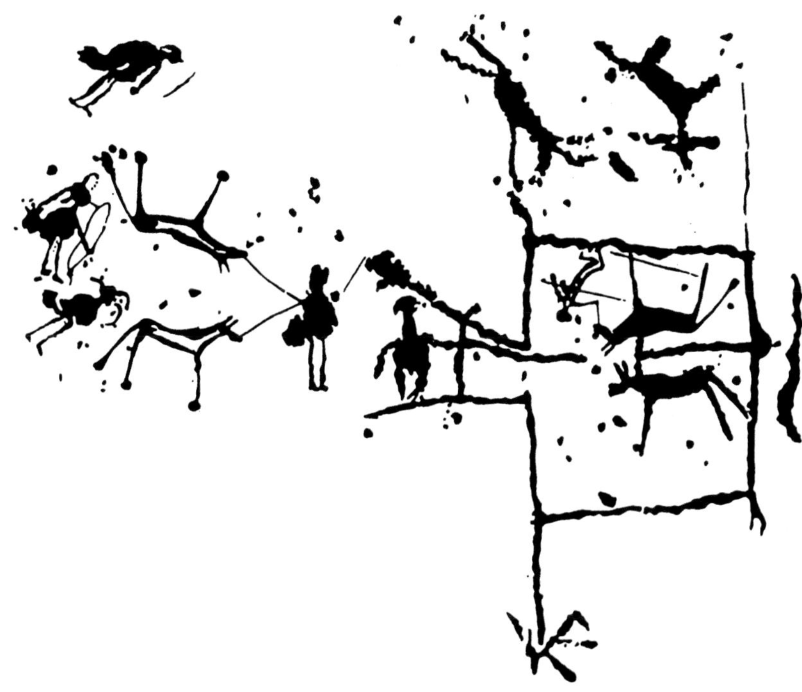

express ownership by a clan or tribe. In more desert environments than Tsagaan Salaa, such as the Gobi, camels now appear as mounts or draught animals.[82]

The meaning of the single-axle chariots pulled by horses, oxen or even deer remains mysterious. Do they merely show a prestige object? Or were they possibly connected with solar concepts as in the rock art of Kazakhstan and Kyrgyzstan? More probably they were associated with specific mortuary rituals which were customary for high-ranking members of society in several Eurasian steppe cultures. The chariots were rendered in petroglyphs in a special way, as a mixture of aerial and side views. The floor of the wagon was depicted from above, but the wheels were shown as if they were lying flat on the floor. The harnessed draught animals were depicted in profile as if lying on their sides with their backs turned towards the drawbar, and the driver was shown from above as if lying flat behind the chariot. Perhaps this view illustrated a chariot burial in which the deceased was driven to the grave on a chariot, whereupon the horses were sacrificed and the chariot was placed in the burial chamber with the wheels removed. Two unique and very similar petroglyph scenes engraved on the same large boulder at Baga Oigor III from the Late Bronze Age may confirm such an interpretation (fig. 26).[83] In one scene two horses lie within a rectangular bounded space, possibly a tomb, back-to-back, attached what is probably a drawbar; next to them lies a person with bent legs. In front of the narrow entrance stands a human holding a long stick, maybe a lance, who acts as a guardian. The interpretation

of Esther Jacobson-Tepfer whereby this image represents a burial seen from the upper rim of the pit is enhanced by two other horses lying, seemingly dead, next to the pit and another human leading two further horses to sacrifice.[84] In the second petroglyph scene, two horses and a human in a crouching position also lie within an enclosure and at least four people lead three additional horses to the funeral paddock. One of these people wears a horned headdress or mask and seems to hit the head of a stallion with a pick; this latter scene is reminiscent of the famous scene of a horse sacrifice at the petroglyph site of Tamgaly in southern Kazakhstan (fig. 53). Both scenes illustrate the late Bronze Age ritual of sacrificing horses at important burials and burying them in the same pit as the deceased. The evidence of the two burial and horse sacrifice scenes at Baga Oigor III, indicating that horse burials were already taking place in the Late Bronze Age, is corroborated by various Late Bronze Age khirigsuur arrangements (for khirigsuurs see the excursus below). An interesting exception to this conventional rendering of chariots as seen from above was found in 2011 at the complex of **Biluut** near Lake Khoton, about 70 kilometres south of Tsagaan Salaa. In that scene from the Iron Age, the two horses pulling a chariot with its driver are shown in profile, galloping, which conveys an unusual impression of speed.[85]

In the **Sirven** foothills in the Gobi Desert, and also at Tsagaan Salaa, there is a very distinct scene from the late Bronze Age: it shows a man who stands wide-legged between two standing bulls positioned in mirror image; he holds the bulls by their snouts

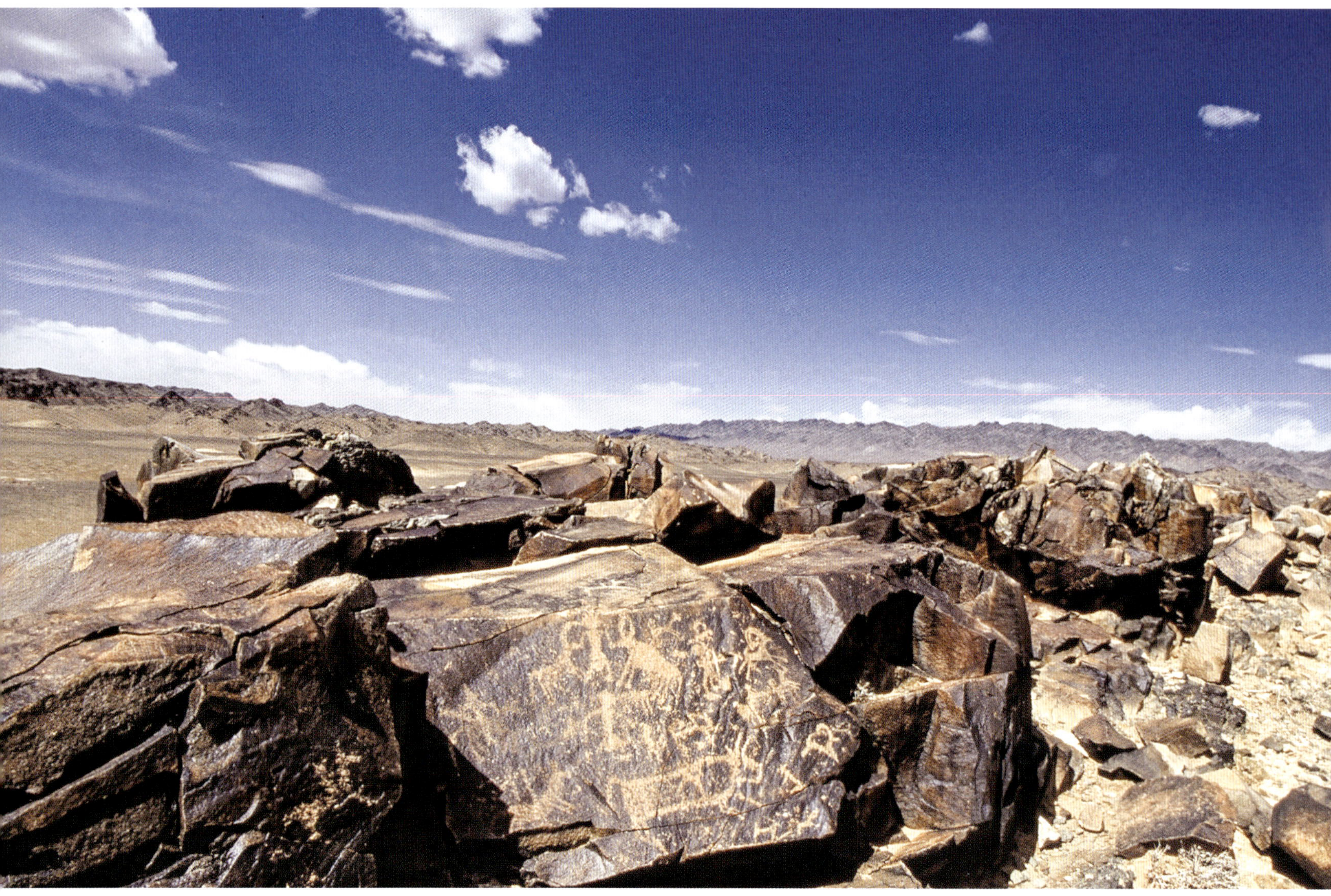

27. The petroglyphs on the central rock show a man standing between two bulls and other cattle. He represents the Lord of Animals, a widespread mythological concept in prehistoric Eurasia. Bronze Age, Sirven foothills, Ömnögov aimag, south-western Mongolia. Photo 2001.

or throats (fig. 27). Similar petroglyphs exist at Shimaily I in the Tarbagatai Mountains[86] and at Ak-Terek,[87] both in eastern Kazakhstan.[88] In the former, the man holds two horses, in the latter two bulls. This image represents the Lord of Animals, a mythical concept which was widespread, first in Iran and the Middle East from the fifth millennium BCE, and later throughout the Eurasian continent.[89] The concept appeared often in a female form as Mistress of Animals: for example in ancient Greece, Artemis, the goddess of hunt and wilderness, is sometimes described as *pótnia therôn*, 'mistress of wild animals'.[90] This mythical concept has been documented, inter alia, on clay statues from Neolithic Çatalhöyük (Anatolia), on Sumerian, proto-Elamite, Bactrian, Harappan, Minoan, Assyrian, Achaemenid and Sasanian seals as well as on a silver ceremonial axe from Bactria

Margiana dating to *ca*. 2000 BCE. This motif also appeared on the ivory handle of a Neolithic knife from Upper Egypt and on an ivory plaque from the Bull-Headed Lyre from Ur (Mesopotamia) as well as on stone vessels from Jiroft (Iran), and on Etruscan and Attic ceramics. This concept, it is also found on metalwork from Luristan (Iran), Urartu, the Scythians, Greeks and Bulgars, as well as on Saka jewellery discovered in northern Afghanistan, and even on bronze plaques from Benin in West Africa. This mythical concept probably originated in the realm of Iran and Mesopotamia from where it spread north-east and westward.[91] Its meaning was likely twofold: it symbolized in sedentary, agrarian societies the taming of wild nature by mankind, but in hunting and pastoral societies the spirit of animals, or of a species of animals, which had to be appeased in order to allow humans to continue hunting, for it was believed that the Lord or Mistress of Animals could grant or deny game to humans.

After this comes another innovation in rock art. Whereas in pre-Bronze Age petroglyphs weapons were shown only aimed at animals being hunted, they are now turned against other humans as well, in duel or even battle scenes where men confront each other with lances and bows (fig. 25).[92] In many scenes of duels between archers in Central Asia, the archers seem to use overlong arrows, almost like lances, which are depicted as a straight line running from the bow to the target. However, it is not lances that are shown, but the arrows' trajectory. Other scenes illustrate archers attacking a small caravan of herders moving camp or trying to steal animals which are isolated from the herd. Then, in what is clearly a battle scene in the Upper Tsagaan Gol, two hostile groups of archers are represented shooting at each other. The two parties are divided by a natural crack in the rock; the one on the left numbers ten archers, the one on the right five. Of the fifteen archers involved, thirteen are probably from the early Iron Age, with two added in the Turkic period.[93] This sudden appearance of combat scenes should not be interpreted as implying that pre-Bronze Ages societies were free of violence, but that violence was now an admired value. As in several Andronovian cultures and also in other more distant Indo-European cultures which were predominantly male-dominated, such as southern Scandinavia and the Alpine

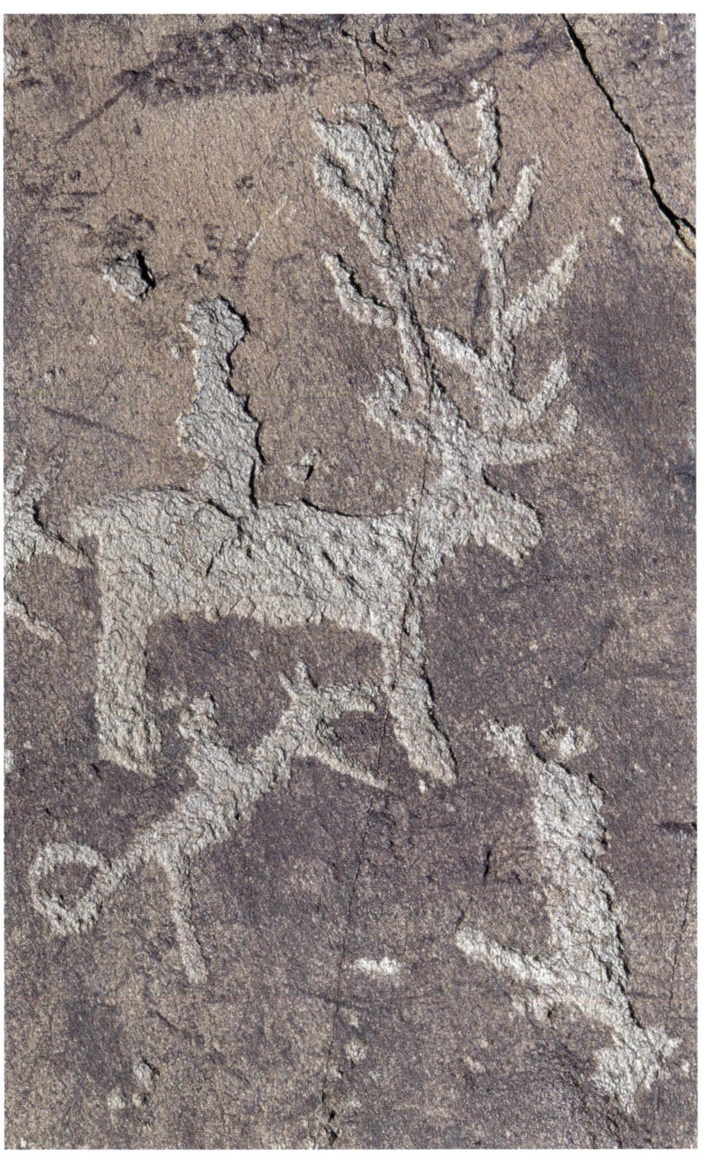

28. A human riding a stag or reindeer with huge antlers. Bronze Age, Tsagaan Salaa–Baga Oigor, Bayan Ölgyi aimag, western Mongolia. Mongol Tsaatan reindeer pastoralists continue to mount their animals to this day. Photo 2002.

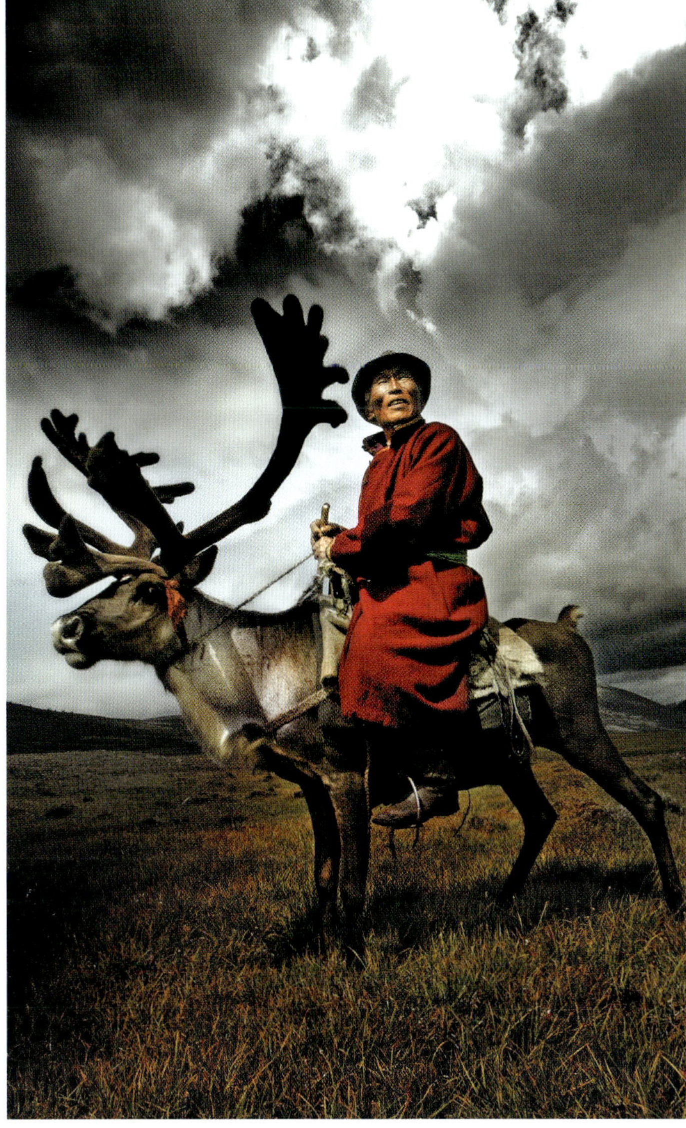

29. A Tsaatan reindeer herdsman north-east of Lake Khövsgöl, Khövsgöl aimag, Mongolia. Photo by Donna Todd, 2004.

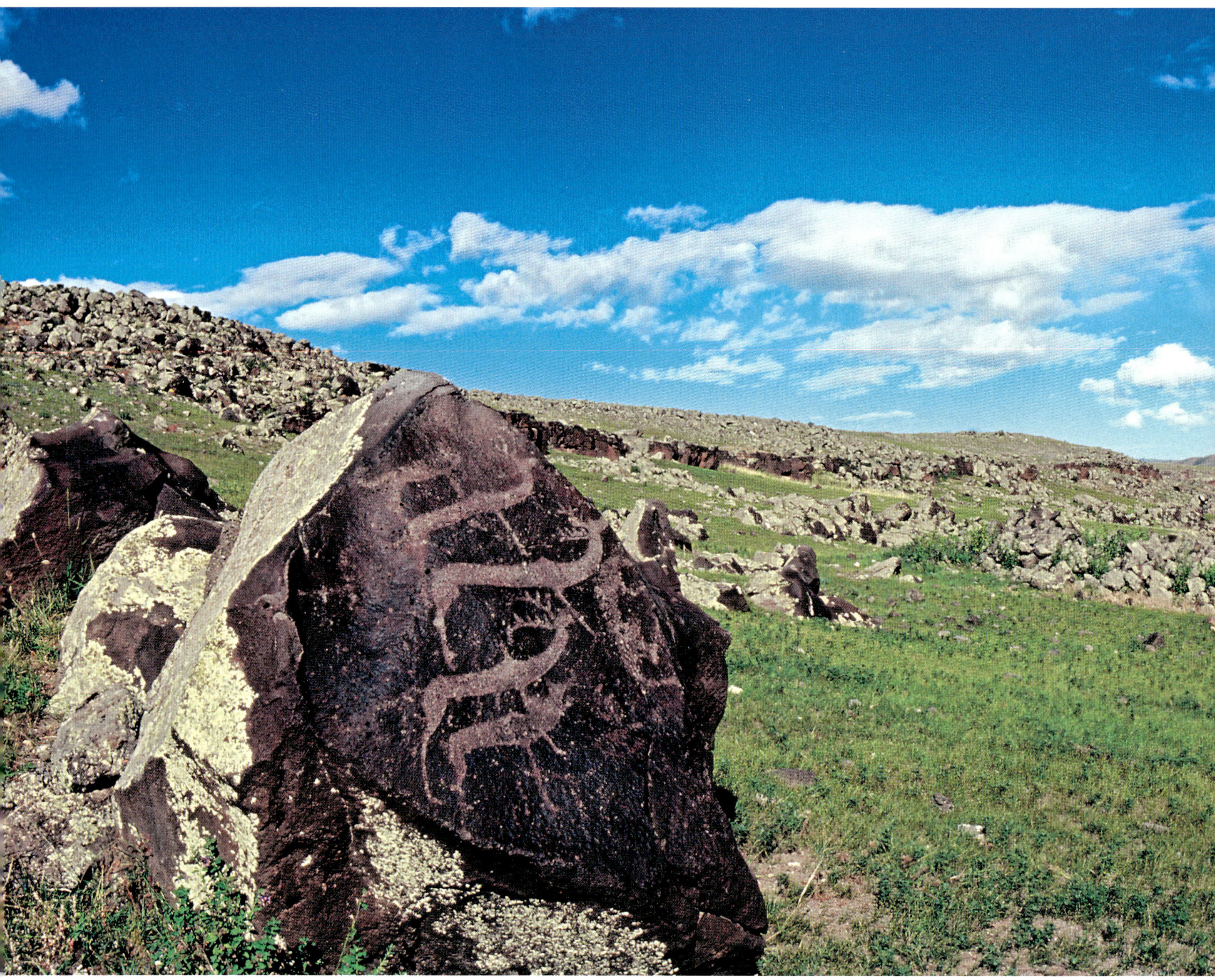

30. Petroglyphs of stylized deer at Eltsin Bulak. Early first millennium BCE. Arkhangai aimag, central Mongolia. Photo 2001.

regions, combat was now an aspirational value – the erstwhile hunter had been transformed into a warrior. This new belligerent spirit articulated itself in a few non-literate cultures in rock art, in others in epic tales celebrating warfare and the valiant hero.[94] However, in western Mongolia as well as most of Central Asia, there are no stand-alone petroglyphs of weapons such as battle axes, halberds and swords such as are found in Scandinavia and the Alpine regions of Mont Bégo (France) and Val Camonica (Italy). Instead, stand-alone figures of weapons were often engraved on the

so-called deer stones from the Bronze Age, especially on those of the Sayan type (see the excursus below).

In the transitional period from the Bronze to the Iron Age the rendering of a few animals, above all of stags, becomes distinctively stylized. In one type, the antlers of stags assume the shape of a tree; they become a metaphor for the Tree of Life. In this context the stag with the tree-like antlers also symbolizes fertility (fig. 28). Its antlers, shed and regrown each year, stand for the cycle of life and death; they symbolize the reproduction of humans and

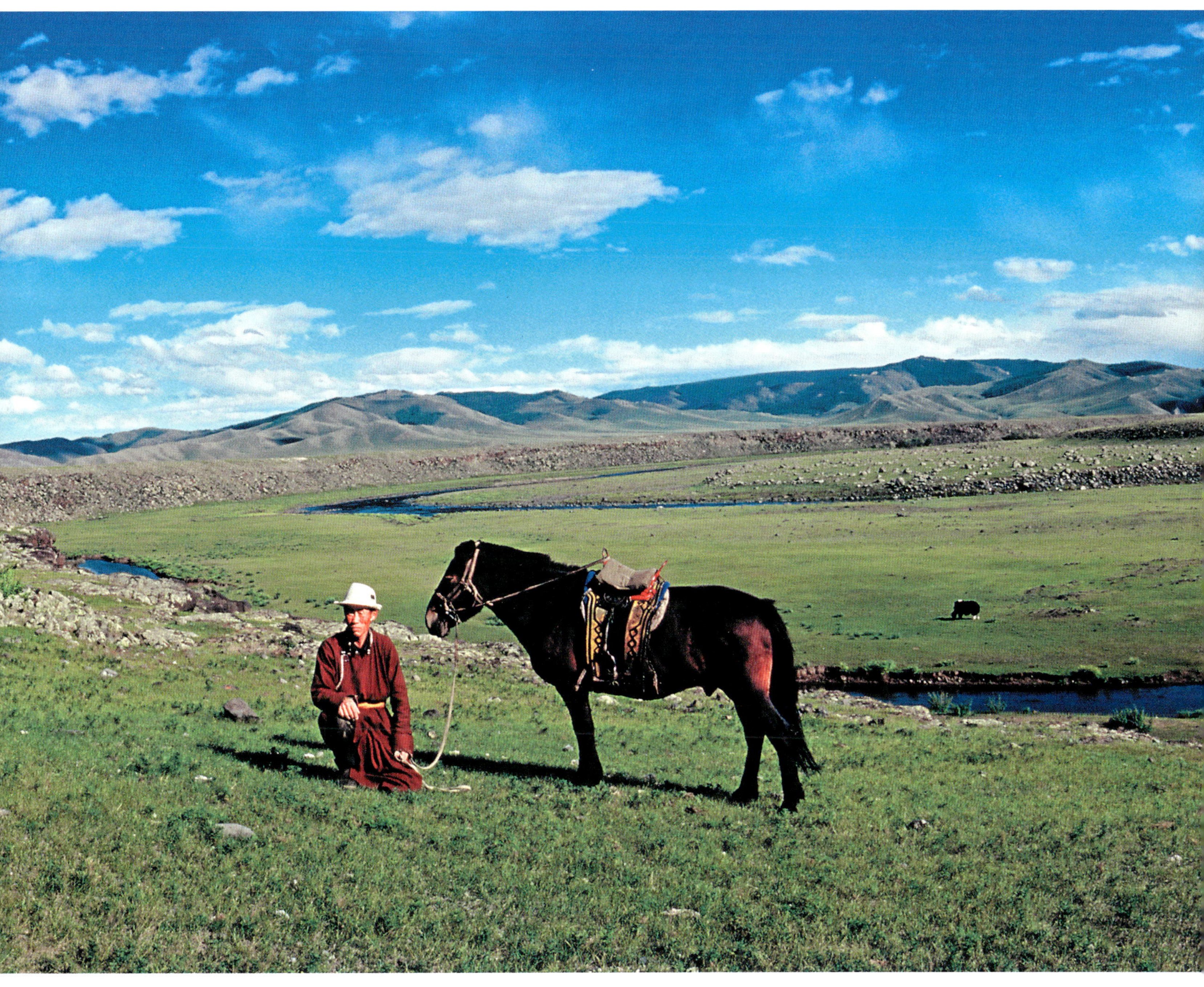

animals as well as the rebirth of nature after winter. This motif recalls an archaic myth of the Siberian and northern Mongolian Evenki, in which the Tree of Life grew out of the head of a female deer lying on the ground.[95] In the other type, deer are portrayed with elongated bodies, short legs, highly elongated snouts like birds' beaks and their antlers stretched in waves over their long back (figs 32, 34). The same types of deer figures are found on the deer stones of central Mongolia. The deer steles were in turn one of the forerunners of the Animal Style widespread among the Saka and Scythians, which extended from the Altai to the Black Sea and the Pamirs. The final significant period of petroglyphic art, that of the Turkic empires, is represented only sparingly in Tsagaan Salaa; outstanding examples of it are found at Tsambagaravyn Khar Khad (fig. 43).

Deer stones and anthropomorphic stone figures

In the course of the middle to later Bronze Age, that is simultaneously with the beginning of horse riding, two new kinds of monuments
emerged: *khirigsuurs* and *deer stones*. A khirigsuur consists of a huge
stone mound built over a stone cist. It is either surrounded by one or
two circular or rectangular stone arrangements or by straight stone
lines laid radially like spokes as far as the outermost stone perimeter.
Larger khirigsuurs are often surrounded by smaller, round cairns; the
whole monument may reach a diameter of 100 metres. The satellite
cairns occasionally cover a shallow pit containing skulls, vertebrae
or hooves of sacrificed horses, ceramics, beads and bronze objects.
Khirigsuurs served as burial grounds or as cenotaphs[96] where horse
sacrifices were offered – again a distinctive feature of the Indo-Iranian
Andronovian culture where the horse was associated with the sun.

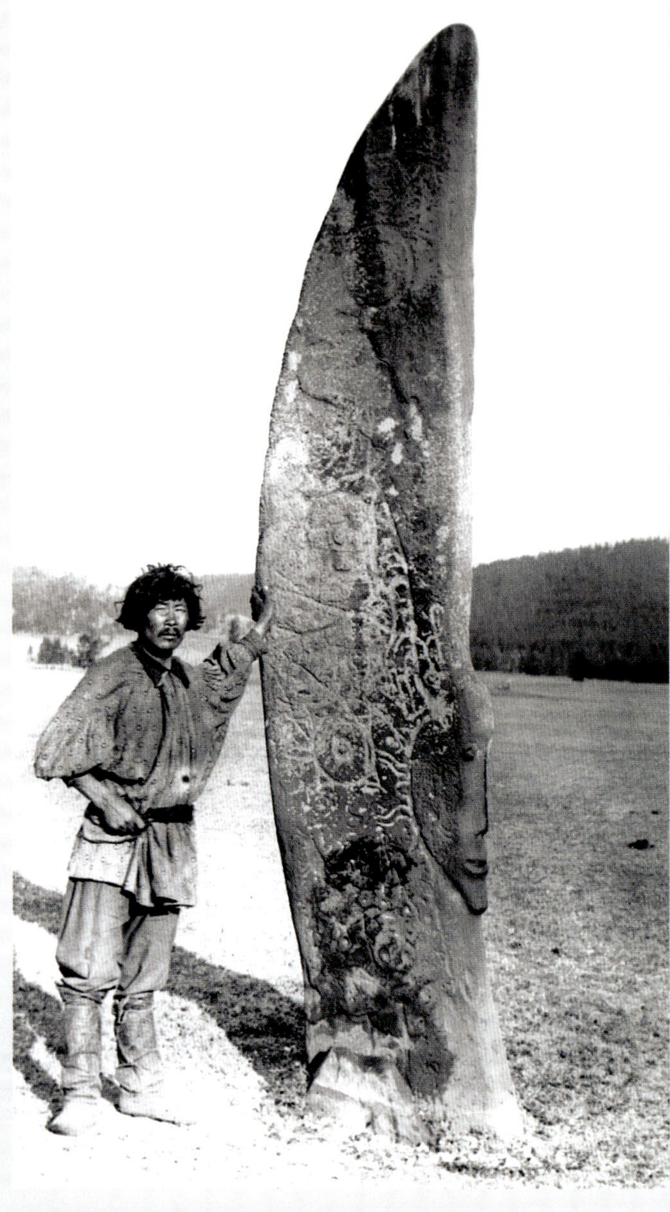

Sometimes deer stones stand next to khirigsuurs. The coincidence of
horse riding, horse sacrifice, khirigsuurs, deer stones and the increasingly important motif of the stag, along with stylized petroglyphs and
an ideology upholding virile values of combat, indicate a new culture
and possibly suggest the arrival of different people coming from the
western Altai.

Western and central Mongolia is a land not only of petroglyphs
but also of deer stones. The latter are free-standing stone steles, up
to four metres tall, with low-relief peckings followed by polishing, in
which the dominant motifs are initially deer and weapons, with later a
few horses, big cats and boars added. Of more than one thousand deer
stones known, 85 per cent are found in Mongolia, with the remainder
in the Altai, Tuva, Xinjiang and the Eurasian steppes.[97] Continuing the
tradition of carved cultic stone steles of earlier steppe cultures, such
as those of the neighbouring Okunev culture already mentioned[98] and
the Chemurchek culture (2600–1800 BCE),[99] these steles often carried
petroglyphs on the front and sides (figs 33–36). After the deer stones,
the tradition of anthropomorphic stone steles was carried on in the
second half of the first millennium BCE in by the Pontic Scythians
and the Sarmatians on the Mangyshlak Peninsula (Kazakhstan). A
few centuries later in the regions of Mongolia and the Altai came the
stone statues of the Turkish and Uyghur empires and finally the stone
portrayals of both warriors and women by the Kipchak (Cuman) people,
who roamed the steppe stretching from Kazakhstan to Ukraine in the
eleventh to thirteenth centuries. As with deer stones, the lower parts of
these stone statues are sometimes engraved with a belt complete with
weapons and a whetstone, as well as with horses and warriors.[100] Stone
statues still enjoy veneration today as Mongolians and Tuvans tie blue
scarves around their necks, rub fat into their hands and bellies, and bring
flasks of vodka as offerings, after which they ask for the blessing of
their ancestors. This veneration impressed the German explorer Daniel
Gottlieb Messerschmidt when he visited the Minusinsk Basin. Writing in
1722, he described how

*The heathen Tatars [of Abakan] showed much reverence for these
[statues] and rode three times around each one, after which ceremonies
they offered them some of their own provisions or placed these on
the pedestal under the grass so they [the statues] could eat from it
according to their appetite.*[101]

A long block of granite, greywacke or slate served as the material
for the deer stones. The artists first polished the surface, before they
carved figures on all four sides, according to a defined iconographic
canon. All the stones were divided into three parts. The top represented the head, which was portrayed three-dimensionally only in very
rare cases and was usually represented simply by a necklace, two or

31. Monumental stele with an anthropomorphic face. Okunev culture
(2400–1750 BCE). Khakassia, Russian Federation. Historic photograph from the
early twentieth century. Leont'ev, Nikolaj V. and Kapel'ko, Vladimir F., *Steinstelen
der Okunev-Kultur* (Mainz: Philipp von Zabern, 2002), p. 56.

three slash marks which possibly rendered tattoos, and earrings. The 318-centimetre-high, well-preserved stele no. 14 from the cultic site of Ushkin Uver in northern Mongolia, with its human face oriented toward the rising sun in the east, makes clear that the deer stones were anthropomorphic representations, even if, unlike the Old Turkic statues, they have no arms (fig. 33). The weapon belt that divides the upper from the lower section supports this interpretation. On this belt are found the typical weaponry of steppe horsemen of the late Bronze Age such as a sheathed bow, an axe, a decorated dagger, a knife and a whetstone, so that the deer stone may be understood as a codified portrayal of an armed warrior from the late Bronze Age and early Iron Age. In addition to the weapons, five-pointed shields sometimes adorned the lower third of the deer stones, as did small deer. In the centre section stylized red male deer (Altai maral) with elongated bodies, short legs or legs folded under their bellies, long, bird-like snouts and antlers that cover their spine, seem to fly heavenward (fig. 32). On a few cigar-shaped steles, the deer circle around all the sides, moving dynamically upward. On other steles of the later Sayan type are carved horses, gazelles, boars or hunting scenes, in which predatory cats attack a horse. Sometimes on the narrow sides sun symbols replace the earrings, and a sun symbol occasionally tops the upper section of the front side. There are indications that the images of flying deer and weapons, which were gouged into the deer stones, were sometimes painted in red, as is the case with some Okunev steles. It remains unknown whether the paint was applied originally or at a later time.[102]

The deer stones may be divided into three chronologically sequential groups.[103]

The **Mongol–Altai group** (1400–850 BCE): in the earliest group, stylized deer, knives and daggers with animal protomes predominate, which are typical of the Karasuk culture (1450–1000 BCE). These motifs suggest a date in the later Bronze Age. The fifteen steles of the cultic site at Ushkin Uver date from this early time, as typical Karasuk weapons are engraved on several of them. The motif of deer flying heavenward is also found on contemporaneous petroglyphs and on later tattoos of Scythian warriors of the Altai. A further indication that the rock art on the deer stones was influenced by the Karasuk culture is the fact that the elongated trunks of the stylized deer have exactly the same shape as typical Karasuk daggers.

The **Sayan group** (900–700 BCE): in this group both the dynamism of movement and the stylized deer have disappeared and the weapons lack any decoration. Deer, standing stiffly on tiptoe, boars, leopards, horses, and kulans (wild asses) are now depicted realistically, and they are joined by coiled-up predatory cats. Petroglyphs of deer and boars standing on tiptoe are also widespread in Tuva, in north-eastern Xinjiang, in southern Kazakhstan and Kyrgyzstan.

The **Eurasian group** (700–500 BCE): on the stones of this final, numerically small group the tendency toward simplification reached its austere high point. Animals have practically disappeared, while simply sketched weapons in the lower section and slashes and circles in the upper part remain.

Carved deer stones were sometimes parts of large khirigsuur complexes, as in **Ushkin Uver** in the Khövsgöl aimag, northern Mongolia (fig. 33). This measures about 950 by 400 metres and was part of a sacred site of approximately 25 square kilometres with more

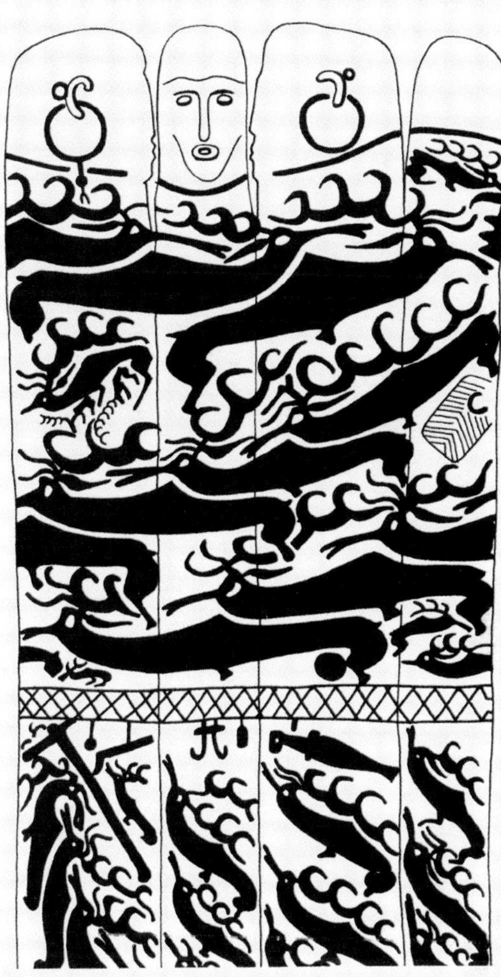

32. Rubbing traced with Indian ink of deer stone no. 14 at Ushkin Uver. *ca.* 1400–850 BCE. Khövsgöl aimag, northern Mongolia. After Nowgorodowa, Eleonora, *Alte Kunst der Mongolei* (Leipzig: VEB E.A. Seemann, 1979), p. 146.

than 200 stone structures. In the northern half of the complex a slab grave, a stone platform and fifteen khirigsuurs along with numerous satellite mounds are found in an enclosure, and in the southern half stand fifteen deer stones made of granite, arranged in two rows and oriented with their front sides facing east.[104] Small stone circles lie between the steles. Since many of the steles, which are often carved on all four sides, lay fallen beneath the ground until the 1970s, they are very well preserved. Stele no. 14, with its top shaped into a human face of uncertain gender, is especially outstanding.[105] In the centre and lower sections at least 27 deer are crowding against one another, and on the weapon-belt are found on the front a yoke-shaped fastener; on the right side, an axe and a whetstone; and on the left, a dagger with an animal-shaped handle in the classical style of the Karasuk culture (fig. 32). The figure has a pentagonal shield on the back at shoulder height. Partial excavations carried out in 2003 brought to light human burials in only two of the fifteen khirigsuurs, although five horse burials were found at each group of khirigsuurs and deer stones. The sacrificed horses were always buried in the same way: the skulls were laid with

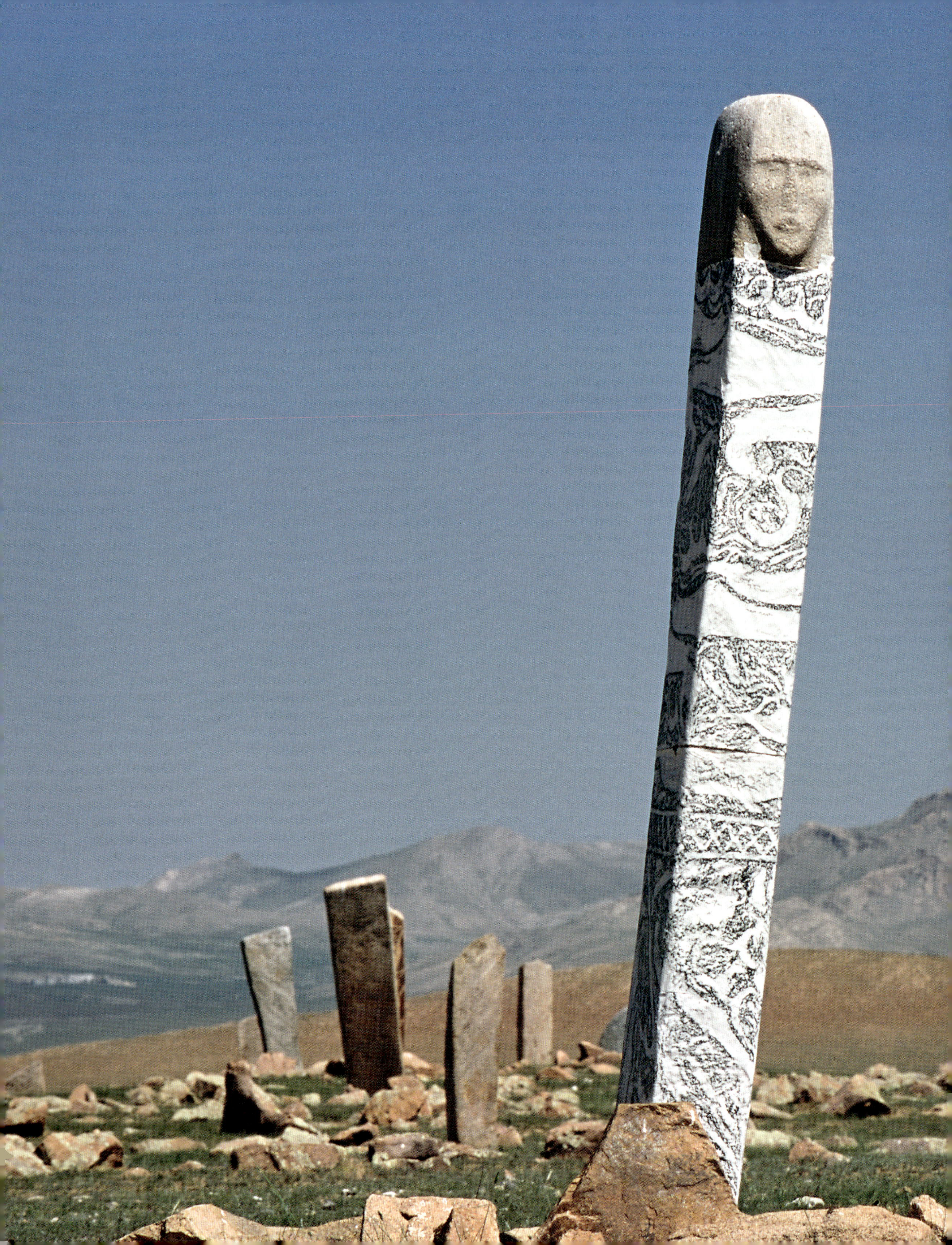

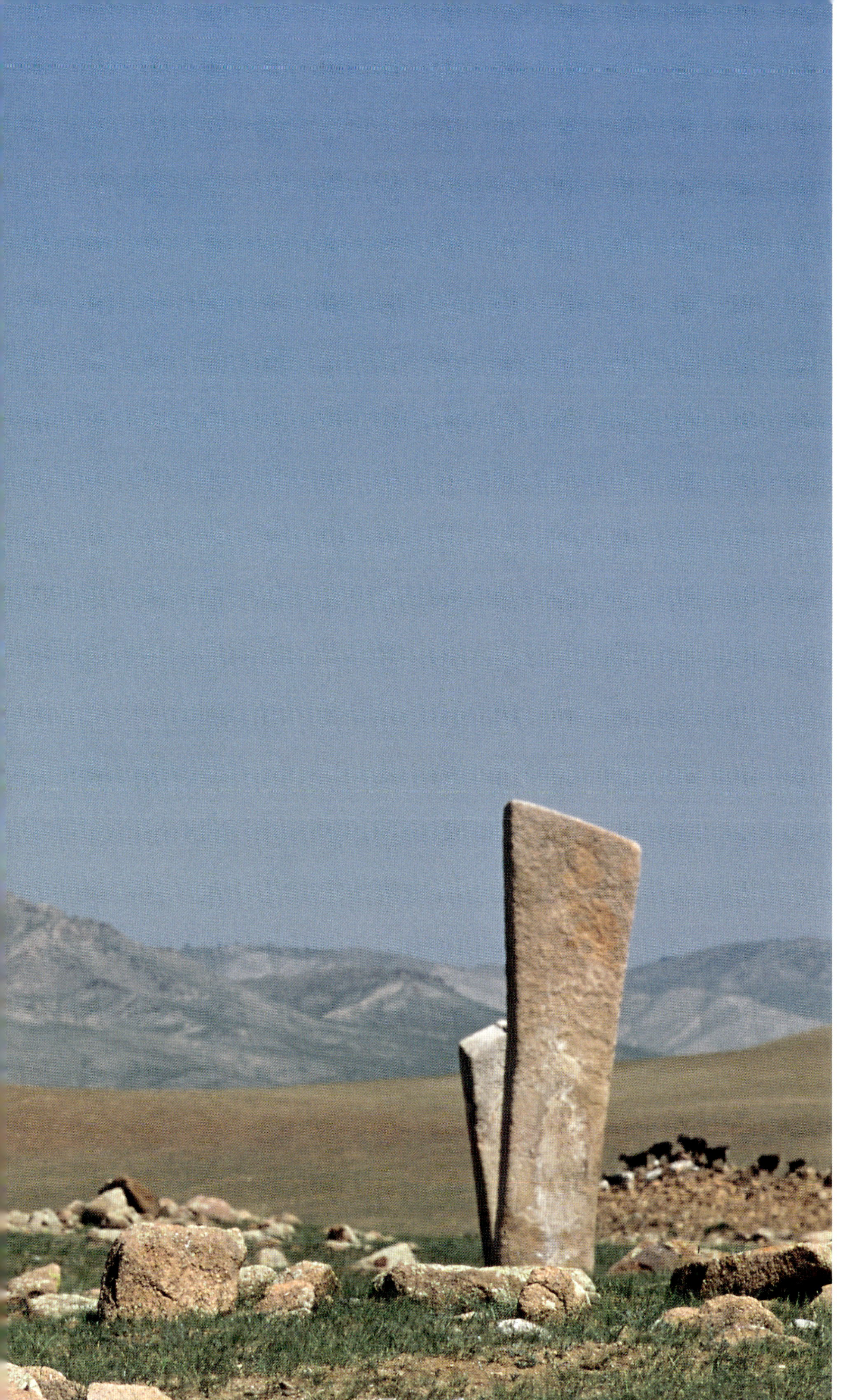

33. The anthropomorphic deer stone no. 14 from the sacrificial and burial site of Ushkin Uver. *ca.* 1400–850 BCE. Khövsgöl aimag, northern Mongolia. Photo 2002.

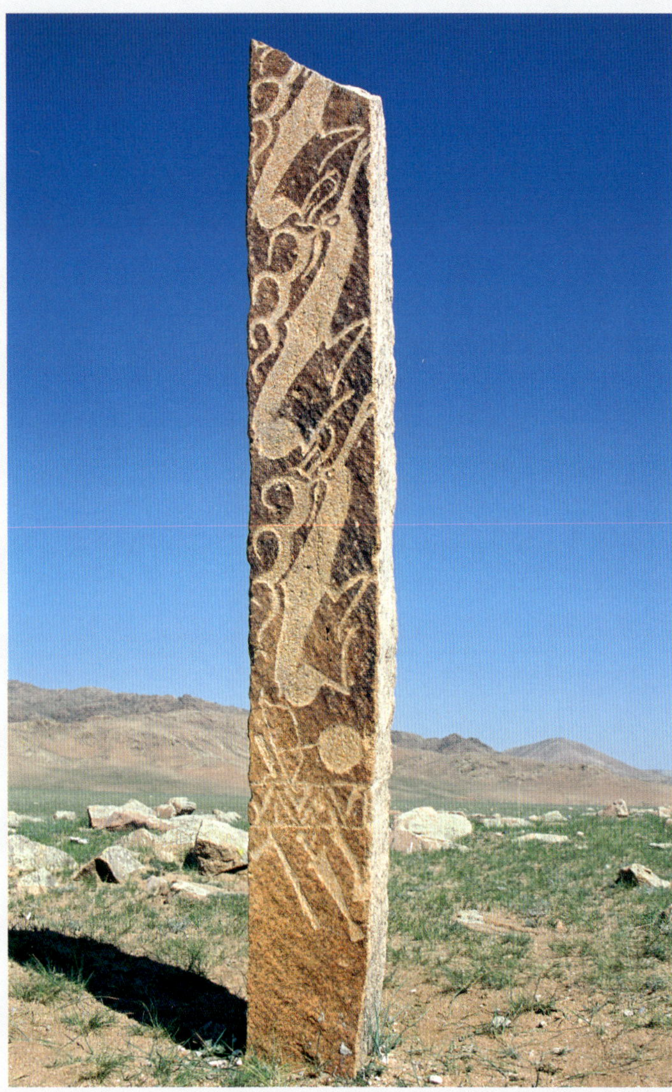

34. Deer stone no. 9 at Ushkin Uver. In the upper part, stylized deer seem to fly heavenward, in the lower weapons are engraved, such as a quiver and a bow, a battle axe and daggers. *ca.* 1400–850 BCE. Khövsgöl aimag, northern Mongolia. Photo 2002.

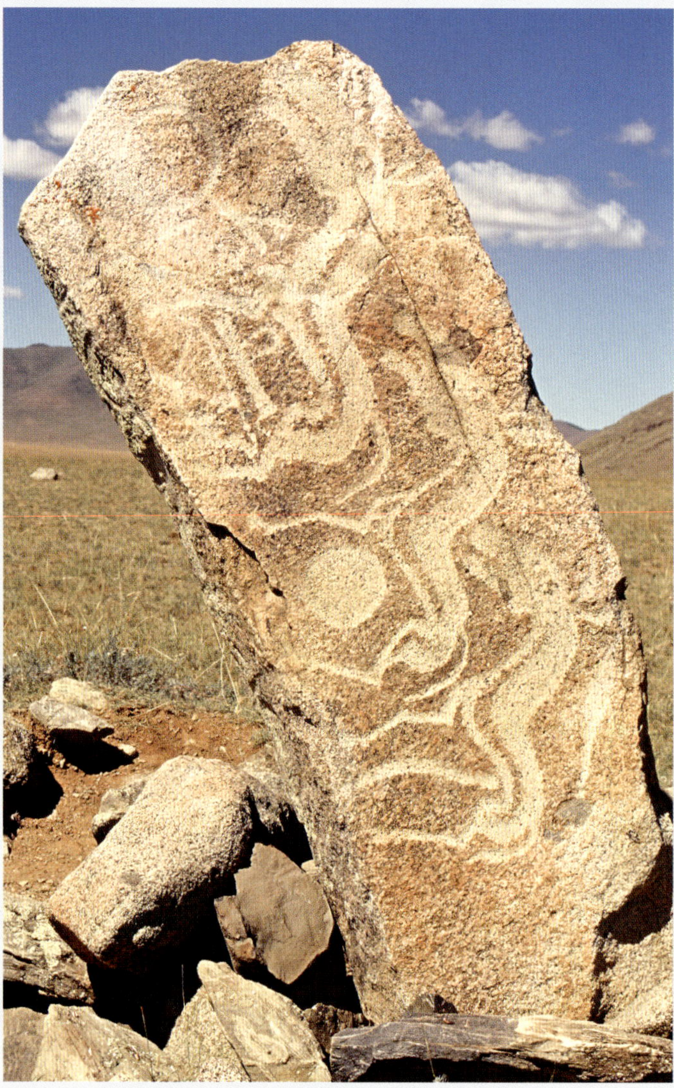

35. Deer stone with three engraved horses from *ca.* 900–700 BCE, Altan Sandal. An excavation conducted in 2021 brought to light some 400 satellite horse burials. Arkhangai aimag, central Mongolia. Photo 2002.

noses pointing east and accompanied by neck vertebrae and hooves.[106] Ushkin Uver was primarily a sacrifice site, where horse sacrifices were performed in the context of an ancestor cult. Similar sacrifice sites were also found at the later Iron Age slab grave complexes of **Jargalantyn Am** and **Altan Sandal** in Arkhangai aimag, central Mongolia, where most of the deer stones were taken down and reappropriated for the construction of slab grave enclosures. At Jargalantyn Am, the deer stones were used to form the sides of the grave, or re-erected at its four corners.[107] At the site of Altan Sandal, excavations conducted by a Mongolian–French expedition in 2021 identified remains of slaughtered or sacrificed horses in about 400 satellite tumuli. As at Ushkin Uver, the noses of the horses' skulls were always oriented towards the rising sun. Assuming that the horse heads represented a *pars pro toto* for a living horse, they possibly symbolized the mount which carried the deceased to the realm of the rising sun.[108] A similar reuse of existing, ancient monuments took place in the fifth century BCE in neighbouring

Khakassia, where the carriers of the Tagar culture (1000–200 BCE) used Okunev steles to build their princely tombs.[109]

As suggested by the myth of the Evenki relating to an elk mentioned above, the recumbent deer with huge upright antlers connects the earth, which is also the realm of death, with the sky and the sun, symbolizing life. Excavations of the graveyards of Pazyryk and Tuekta in the Russian Altai and at Berel in the Kazakh Altai, dating from the sixth to fourth centuries BCE, provide evidence that deer, together with ibex, accompanied the dead into the afterlife. In the tombs archaeologists discovered sacrificed horses wearing masks made of felt, leather and wood which represented stags or ibexes (fig. 54). In some instances, a tiny figurine of a feline predator or a bird of prey sat on top of the mask suggesting its attack on the stag or ibex. In some cases, gold leaf covered the antlers and horns.[110] The small winged horse figurines, covered in gold leaf and bearing ibex horns or deer antlers, which adorned the felt caps of the dead, belong in the same context.[111] Thanks to these grave goods, the horse acquired the attributes of the deer and its regenerative power, or that of the ibex, which was venerated as an 'inhabitant of heaven'[112] and a symbol of fertility. It appears that the horse, symbolically transformed into a deer or ibex, served as guide and mount for the deceased in entering the afterlife. This singular concept is not only found in the burials mentioned, but was also rendered in petroglyphs of the Tsagaan Gol Valley.[113] This idea was also present earlier in the Caucasus, for archaeologists found in a grave from the fifteenth or fourteenth century BCE in present-day northern Azerbaijan that the deceased had been placed on a sled to which two deer were harnessed; a horse had also been sacrificed.[114] This burial recalls a petroglyph from Baga Oigor in which a deer is harnessed to a chariot. It is thus conceivable that on the deer stones the deer with bird-like snouts galloping or flying toward heaven are symbolically accompanying into the afterlife the deceased person to whom the stele is dedicated.

One other fact is noteworthy: most khirigsuur complexes have satellite mounds with horse burials, and the bigger ones count hundreds of horse mounds, but the horse is not present on the classical deer stones of the Mongol–Altai group, whereas the deer is omnipresent on the steles but hardly found in satellite mounds. As a

hypothesis it is suggested that the horse, a steppe animal, together with the bull, the paramount animal of the Andronovians,[115] represented an inheritance from the Andronovian migrants, while the deer, which is at home in forests and steppes alike, was revered by the local people of the Altai and south Siberia. Regardless of the interpretation, the mere fact that hundreds of khirigsuur complexes with associated deer stones were built, following strict rules, over a major part of Mongolia implies a cultural uniformity and a surprising social cohesion among nomadic tribes and clans.

Distant descendants of the anthropomorphic deer stones are the large stone figures of the ancient Turks and Uyghurs dating from the seventh to tenth centuries CE, which interestingly can be found in the same distribution area as the deer stones. The male figures have a head, arms and wear a belt. Turkic stone men usually hold a goblet with their right hand, the Uyghur ones a flask with both hands (fig. 37). In the eighth to eleventh centuries, the Turkic Karluks brought the concept of male stone figures to Semirech'e (south-eastern Kazakhstan and northern Kyrgyzstan).[116] One of the few locations where Turkic anthropomorphic figures still stand in their original places in the context of sanctuaries and burials are those in the Kyrgyz Alatau Mountains south of the city of Merke in southern Kazakhstan.

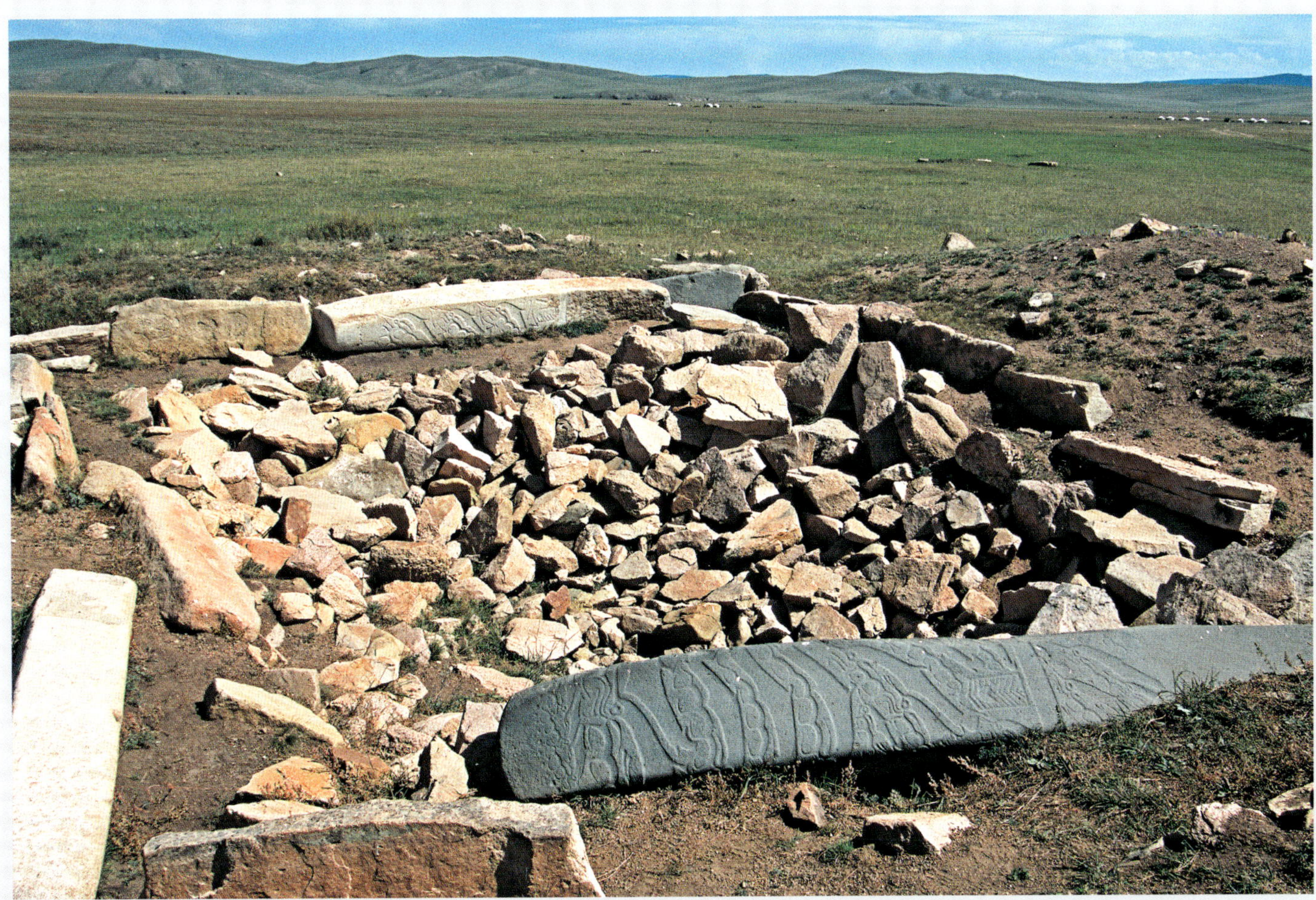

36. At the sacrificial and burial complex of Jargalantyn Am (*ca.* 1250–1100 BCE), older deer stones were taken down and reused in the later Iron Age to create an enclosure for a slab grave. Arkhangai aimag, central Mongolia. Photo 2001; since then, the deer stones got reinstalled.

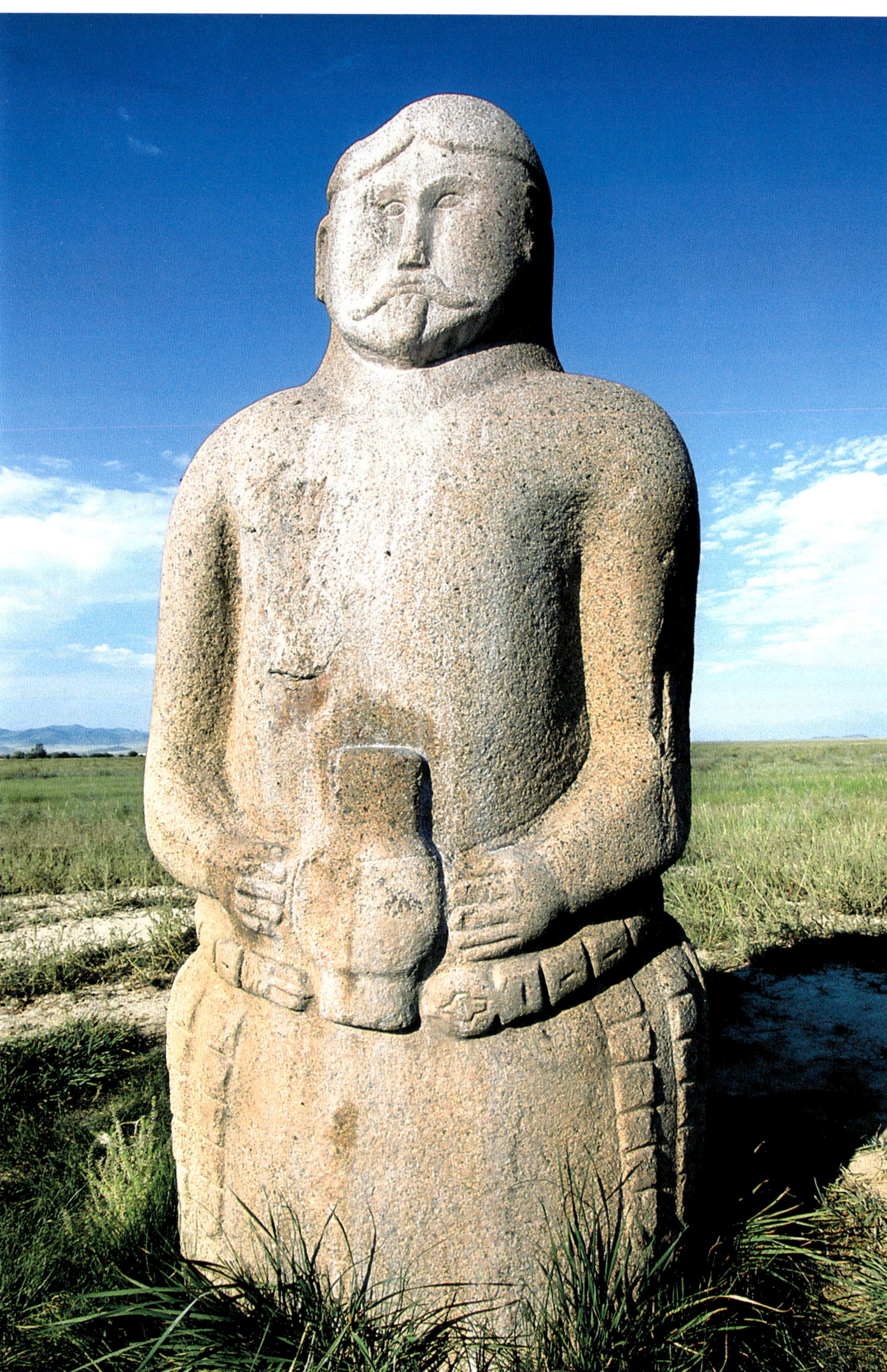

37. Stone statue of a Turkic-Uyghur man holding a vessel in both hands, 150 cm tall. Eighth–ninth century CE. Kyzyl-Mazhalyk, Tuva, Russian Federation. Photo 2002.

The pronounced cultural homogeneity in Mongolia and the Altai during the late Bronze Age and the early Iron Age had a lasting influence on the ensuing **Scythian (Saka) culture** from the middle Iron Age (*ca.* 850 BCE–250 BCE), namely on the so-called **Scytho-Siberian Animal Style** which emerged in today's region of Tuva at the second half of the ninth century BCE.[117] In this strictly canonized style, the animals initially preferred by the Saka such as snow leopards, raptors and deer were rendered in such a way that emphasized those features of the animal that had a particular meaning in the Saka's hierarchy of value.[118] The similarity of the images of maral on deer stones and petroglyphs with cast objects made in bronze or gold such as belt buckles and decorative plaques, wooden objects, jewellery, horse harnesses, saddle bags, textiles, felt appliqué and even tattoos indicates that the specific virile value system that had emerged in the middle Bronze Age continued in intensified form among the Saka. Based on the subsequent westward migration of the Scythians to Central Asia, the Pamirs, the Caucasus, Assyria, the Pontic Steppe and the shores of the Black Sea, the Scytho-Siberian Animal Style evolved, picking up other cultural influences on the way, and culminated in the artworks of the Graeco-Scythian style.[119] Particularly spectacular are the colourful tapestry bands discovered in three Saka graveyards at Shanpula, Khotan (Hetian) district in Xinjiang, China. These are the coloured hems of women's skirts, knotted from woollen yarn. The motifs depict stylized winged stags or reindeer sporting fantastic antlers, winged goats, camels, birds of prey, horsemen and stylized mountains. Out of the back of some stags, the neck and head of a bird of prey seem to grow. All the animals and horsemen walk to the right. In one scene, a mounted hunter holding a drawn bow pursues a winged quadruped animal which has a bearded human head decorated with peacock feathers. A falcon accompanies the hunter (fig. 40). This motif is of Iranian origin and is reminiscent of depictions of Mithra, who, accompanied by a raven, pursues a mythical creature.[120] Unlike the therianthropes in Saharan rock art that consist of a human body and an animal's head, on this Saka textile they are mythical animals with human heads. Whereas some concepts like the hybrid animals hark back to the burial goods from Pazyryk in the Altai, the elaborate and extravagant antlers display some similarities with the wooden figures of deer covered with gold foil from Filippovka in the southern Urals, dated to the early fourth century BCE.[121] The Shanpula textiles have been radiocarbon-dated to a unusually long period, the third century BCE to fourth century CE.[122] It is noteworthy that at Shanpula, motifs which were usually associated with the symbolic world of male values are applied to the ornaments of female clothes.

Besides the clear parallels between the expression of the Animal Style in stone engravings and portable objects, there are also significant differences. In contrast to portable objects such as weapons or jewellery, in contemporaneous petroglyphs there are only a few scenes showing a carnivore killing a herbivore or a fight between two predators; an exception are the petroglyphs of the Karatau Ridge in southern Kazakhstan (see below). On the other hand, the petroglyphs show an increase in the representation of horsemen and a decrease in hunting scenes. At the same time, a new trend of Animal Style developed in the petroglyphs such that the animals now stand motionless on tiptoe, and volute designs placed on the shoulders and thighs of deer, and later also of bears or boar, form a transition from the body to the forelegs and rear legs. In some petroglyphs, volutes were designed in a way to suggest a solar symbol. Such a return to more static rendering of animals is detectable from the early Saka kurgan of Arzhan 1, Tuva, dating from the early eighth century BCE, where a deer stone with such an engraving of a deer had been reused in the construction of the kurgan.[123] This specific style later spread from Tuva, the Altai and Mongolia to Xinjiang in north-western China and

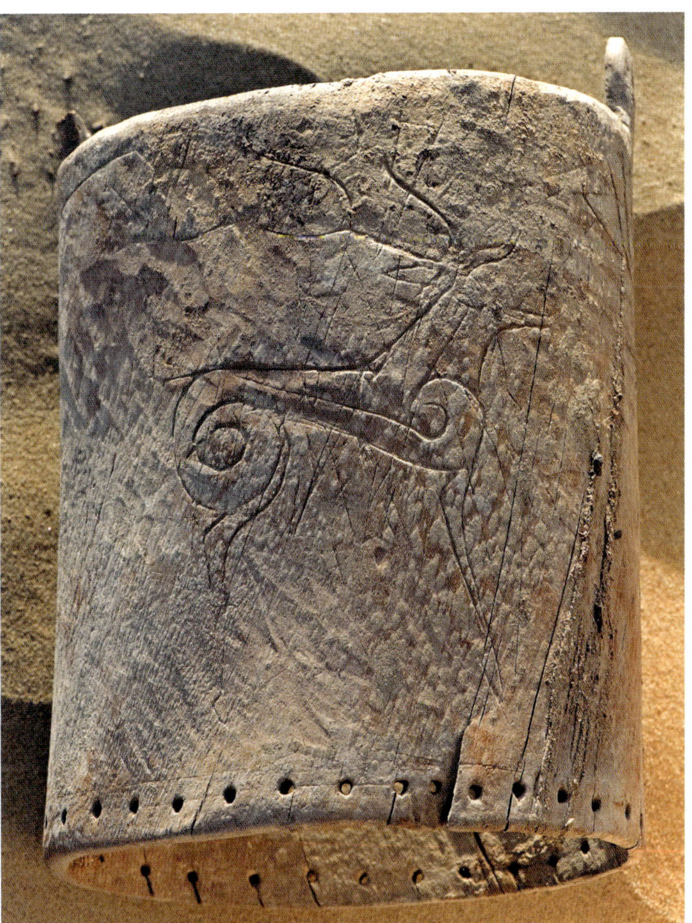

38. Deer on tiptoe and with spiral-shaped body engraved in the Scytho-Siberian Animal Style on a wooden tub from the cemetery of Satma Mazar. *ca.* 390–200 BCE. Xinjiang, China. Photo 2002.

west and south-westward to Kazakhstan Kyrgyzstan, Tajikistan and Uzbekistan. In general, during the Saka period the quantity of petroglyphs produced declined within Mongolia, Tuva, Kazakhstan and Kyrgyzstan compared to portable objects. This happened in parallel with the increased mobility of the Iron Age pastoralists.

With the rise in Mongolia in the third century BCE of the multiethnic tribal confederation of the Xiongnu (244 BCE–155 CE), which rapidly expanded into northern China, the Altai, Xinjiang and eastern Kazakhstan, a new style arose in petroglyphs. The various facets of Xiongnu rock art reflected the multiethnicity of the federation. Xiongnu visual art on rocks and metal objects superficially adopted the Animal Style, but the animals were rendered in a more realistic way. Yaks, bulls and camels were added to the repertoire of fauna and, especially in petroglyphs, animals were again shown in dynamic movement. This renewed realism also represented the wilder attributes of predators such as ferocity and aggression (fig. 41). Moreover, on metalworks, fights between animals arranged in a symmetric way become dominant and reveal a Chinese influence. One of the most impressive petroglyph

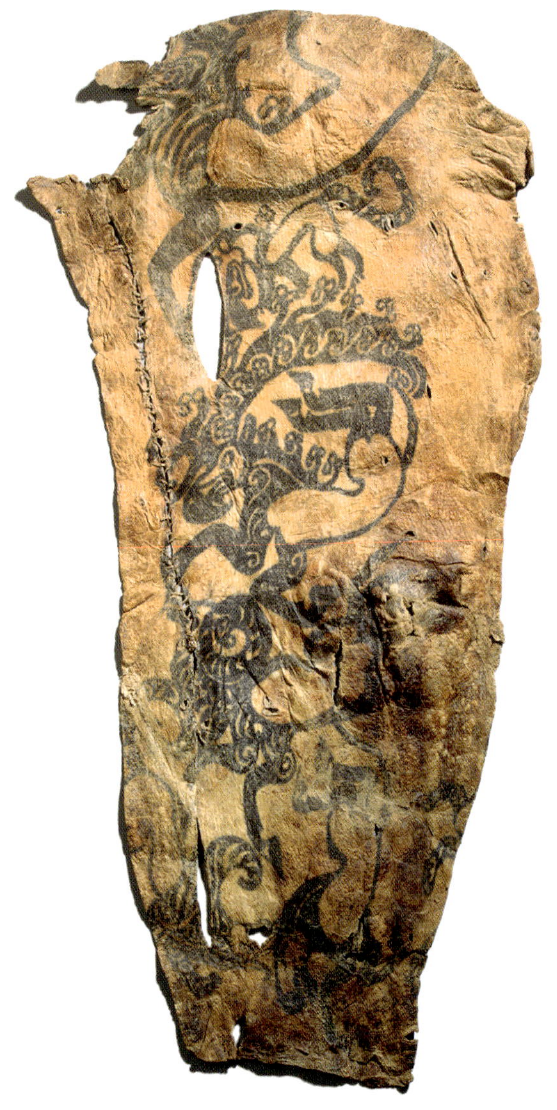

39. ← Tattoos in the Scytho-Siberian Animal Style on the skin of the arm of a warrior buried in kurgan no. 2 at Pazyryk, Altai, Russian Federation, *ca.* 300 BCE. At the top is a predator, probably a wolf or a panther, with a long, curled tail, and in the centre a hybrid animal consisting of the twisted body of a horse, the antlers of a stag with raptors' heads growing out of the tips of the antlers, and the beak of a raptor. The State Hermitage Museum, Saint Petersburg, Russian Federation.

40. ↙ A rider accompanied by a hunting falcon pursues a composite winged, four-legged creature with a bearded head. Fragment from a woollen skirt edging, slit woven, *ca.* first two centuries CE, probably from the graveyard of Shanpula, Xinjiang, China. © Abegg-Stiftung, CH-3132 Riggisberg, inv. no. 5138.

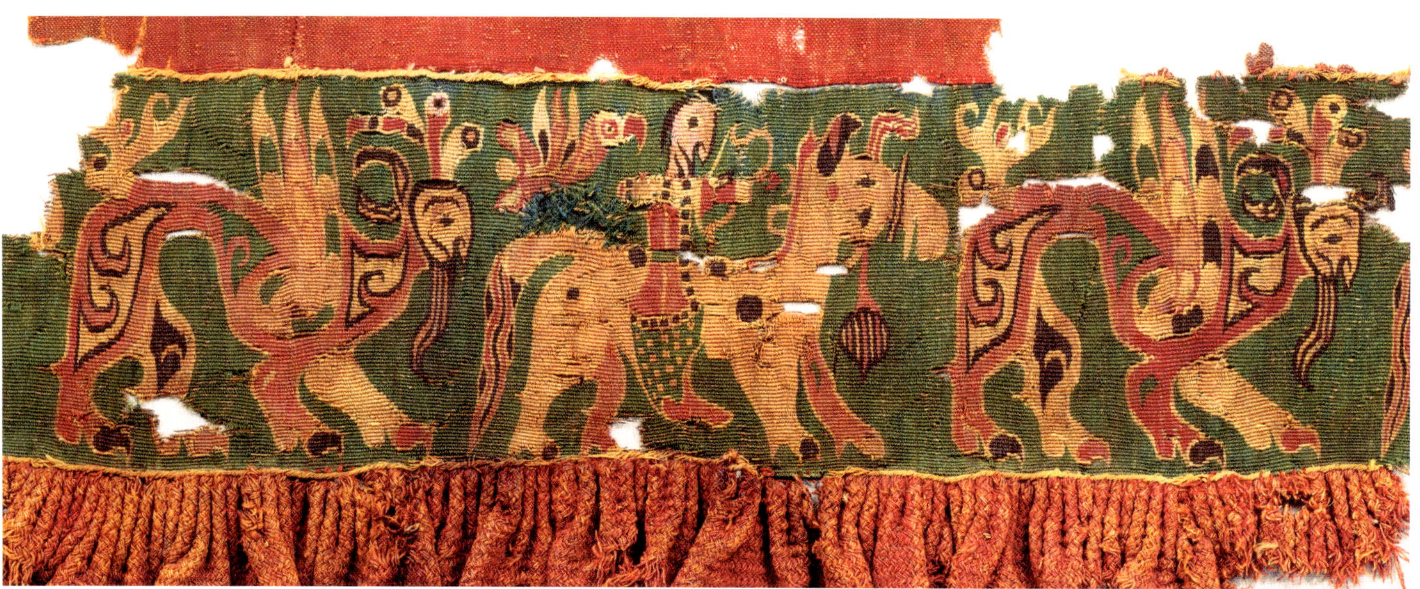

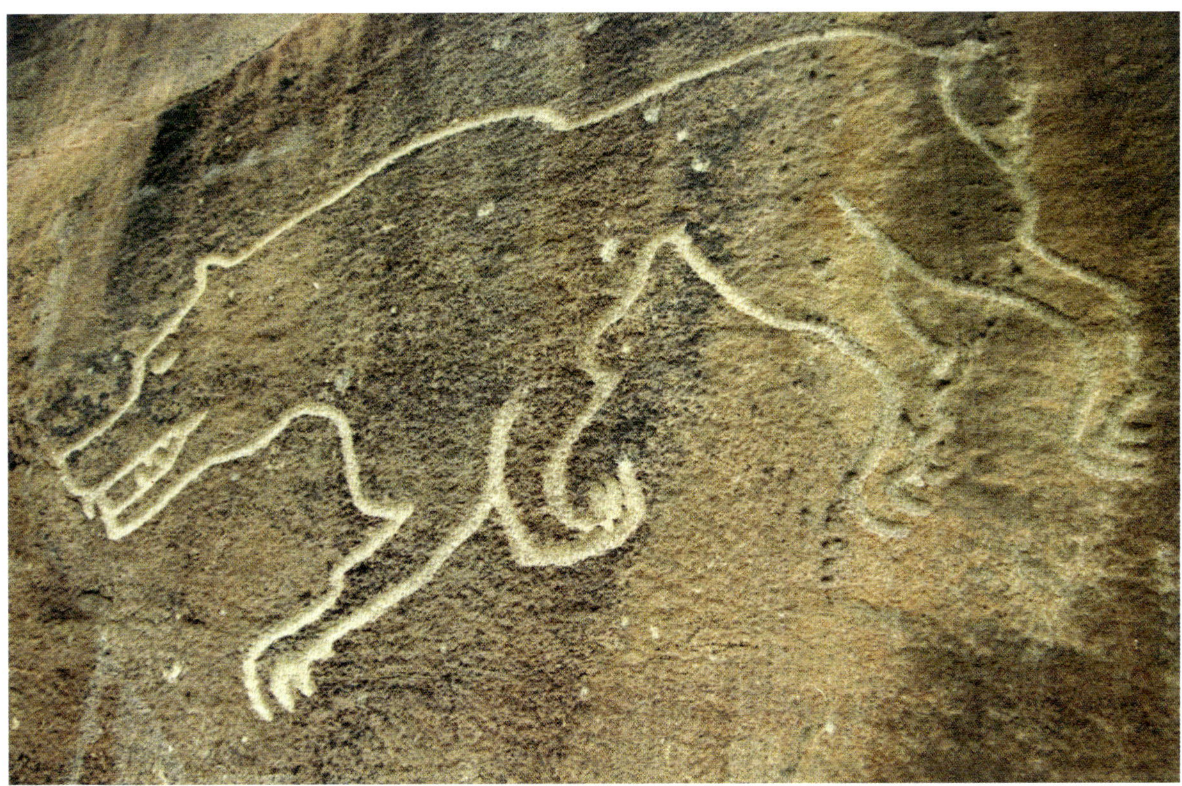

41. Petroglyph of a running bear 150 cm long from Maly Bayan-Kol near Kyzyl, Tuva, Russian Federation. Engraved in the Tashtyk Style in the Hunno-Sarmatian period, beginning of the first millennium CE. Photo by Pavel Leus.

sites of the Xiongnu is located in Khovd province in Mongolia, in the **Yamaan Us** Valley. On a greywacke surface twenty by twelve metres in size are two concentrations of petroglyphs dating from the Bronze Age to the Turkic period (fig. 42). From the Bronze Age there are a battle scene with bow and arrows as well as battle axes, a four-horse chariot with eight spokes and an unharnessed chariot shown in aerial view; then there are dogs or wolves and numerous stags from the Bronze and Iron Ages, the latter being rendered as on classical deer stones.

Most remarkable at Yamaan Us, however, are the depictions in profile of two Chinese ceremonial chariots with baldachin-like roofs. The first chariot, engraved about ten metres above the stream bed, is pulled by a horse, with a rider riding ahead; inside the chariot sits most probably a woman wearing a headdress or diadem. The second chariot, carved about four metres above the ground, is pulled by three horses; one rider goes in front and one behind, and in it likely again a female person is seated. The horses are shown in a swift trot. But whereas these are typical, small Mongol steppe horses, the purely ceremonial chariots with baldachins look Chinese. These two scenes can be interpreted in two ways: in one, a dead person was symbolically or even actually driven to her or his final resting place in such a chariot. There, the chariot was dismantled and given to the dead for the journey to the afterlife. Such burial chariots with parasols were excavated at the huge princely Xiongnu

graveyard of Gol Mod, Arkhangai aimag, Mongolia.[124] More likely, however, the scenes illustrate the travel of a Chinese princess to the court of the chanyu, the Xiongnu supreme ruler. The Chinese emperors used to give Chinese princesses and ceremonial chariots as an indirect tribute to the chanyu, who passed them on to his viceroys. Noteworthy, finally, are the petroglyphs of tree-tiered *tamga* tribal marks and signs of authority; such sophisticated *tamgas* are only found among the Xiongnu.

A few hundred years later, in the period of the Göktürk khaganates (552–745 CE),[125] another, very distinct petroglyph style appeared which led to a brief resurgence of petroglyph-making. Most of the depictions were scratched into the rock with a pointed metal object, both as finely contoured incised drawings and as deeper, groove-shaped images. They usually represent armed horsemen, hunts and single animals. There is a striking site of Turkic petroglyphs at **Tsambagaravyn Khar Khad** in the Khovd province of Mongolia (fig. 43). Besides a few stylized deer, two camels and a large horse with a curled tail, are engraved at least five Turkic horsemen wearing full-body scale armour dating from the sixth to seventh century CE.[126] It is well known from archaeological finds and Chinese sources that the ancient Turkic armies not only included light cavalry, but also heavy cavalry made up of cataphracts, that is riders fighting with lances on fully armoured horses. The cataphracts used stirrups, wore helmets adorned with

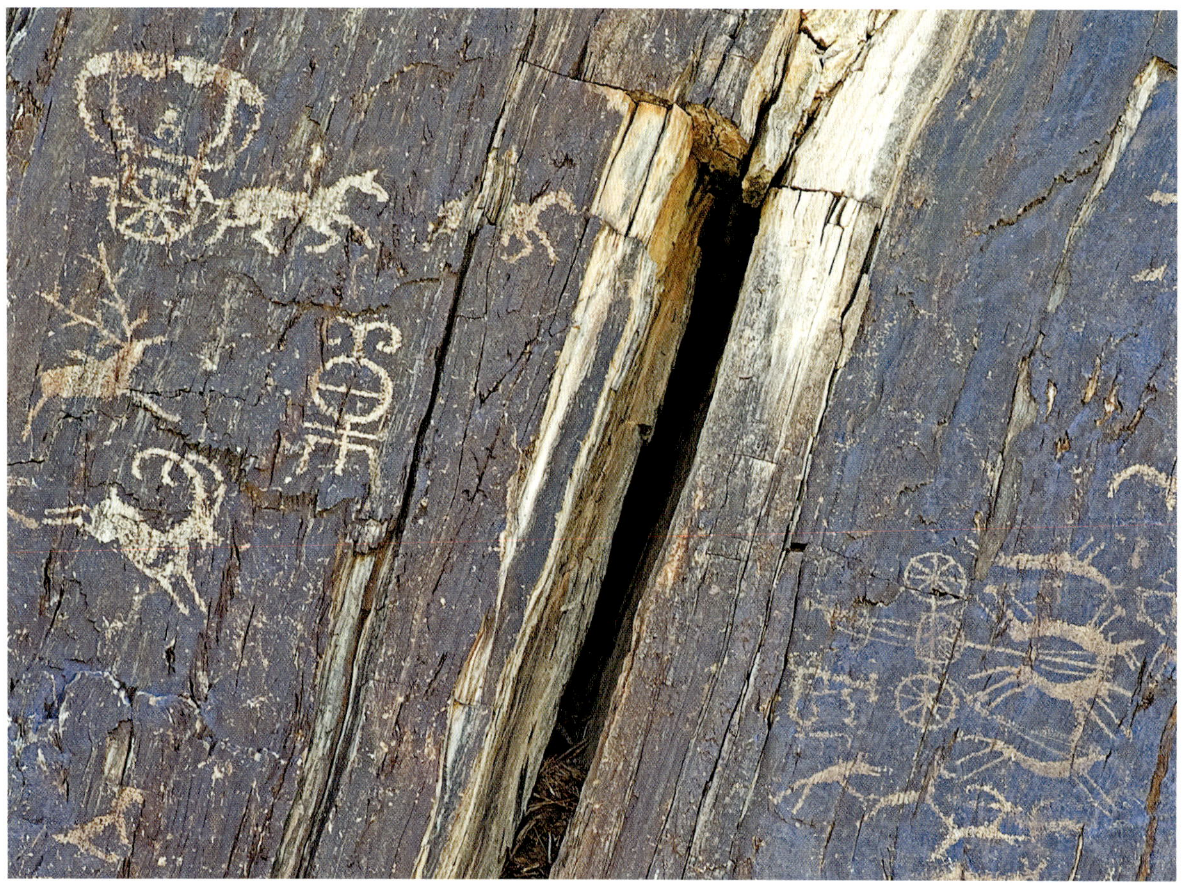

42. At the lower right, a *quadriga* shown in top view from the Bronze Age; on the upper left, a single-axle ceremonial chariot with canopy from the Xiongnu period (244 BCE–155 CE). Yamaan Us, Khovd aimag, western Mongolia. Photo 2012.

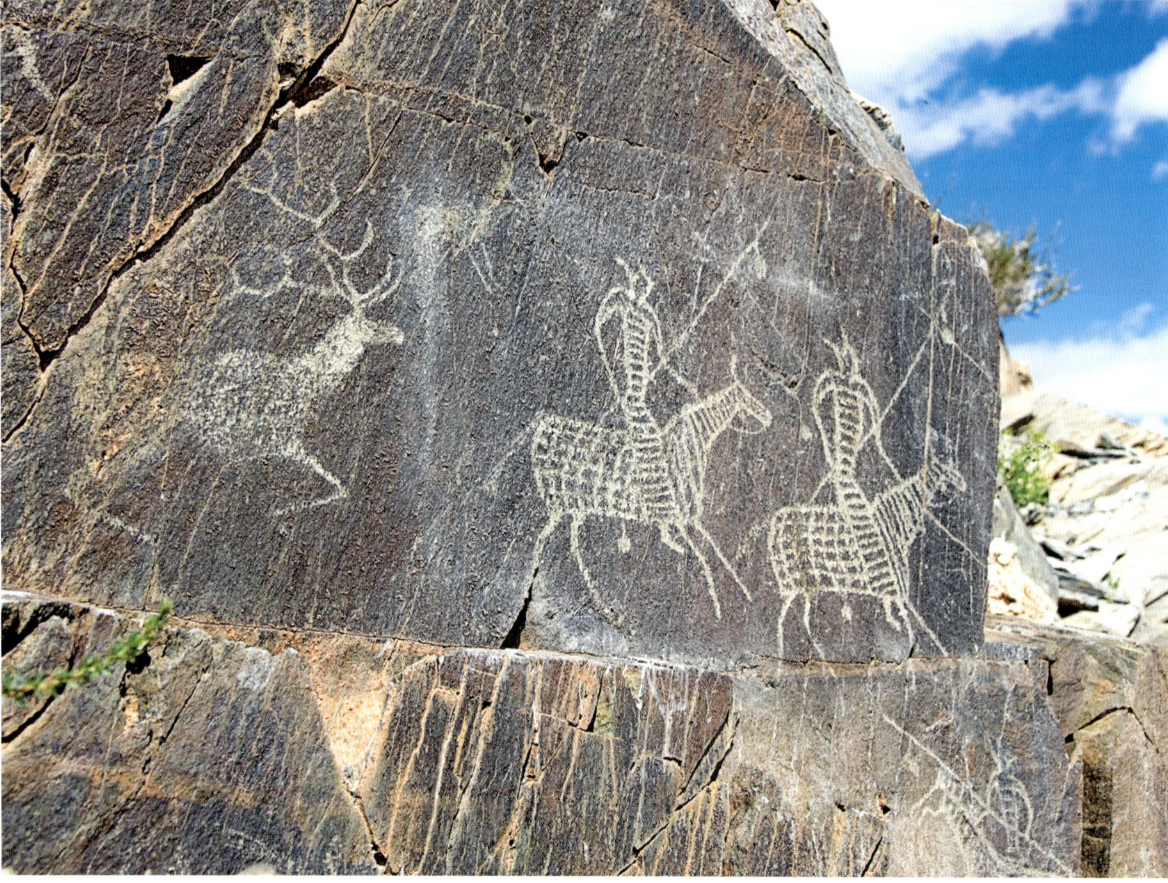

43. Petroglyphs of heavily armoured Göktürk horsemen and a stag at Tsambagaravyn Khar Khad. Sixth–seventh century CE. Khovd aimag, western Mongolia. Photo 2012.

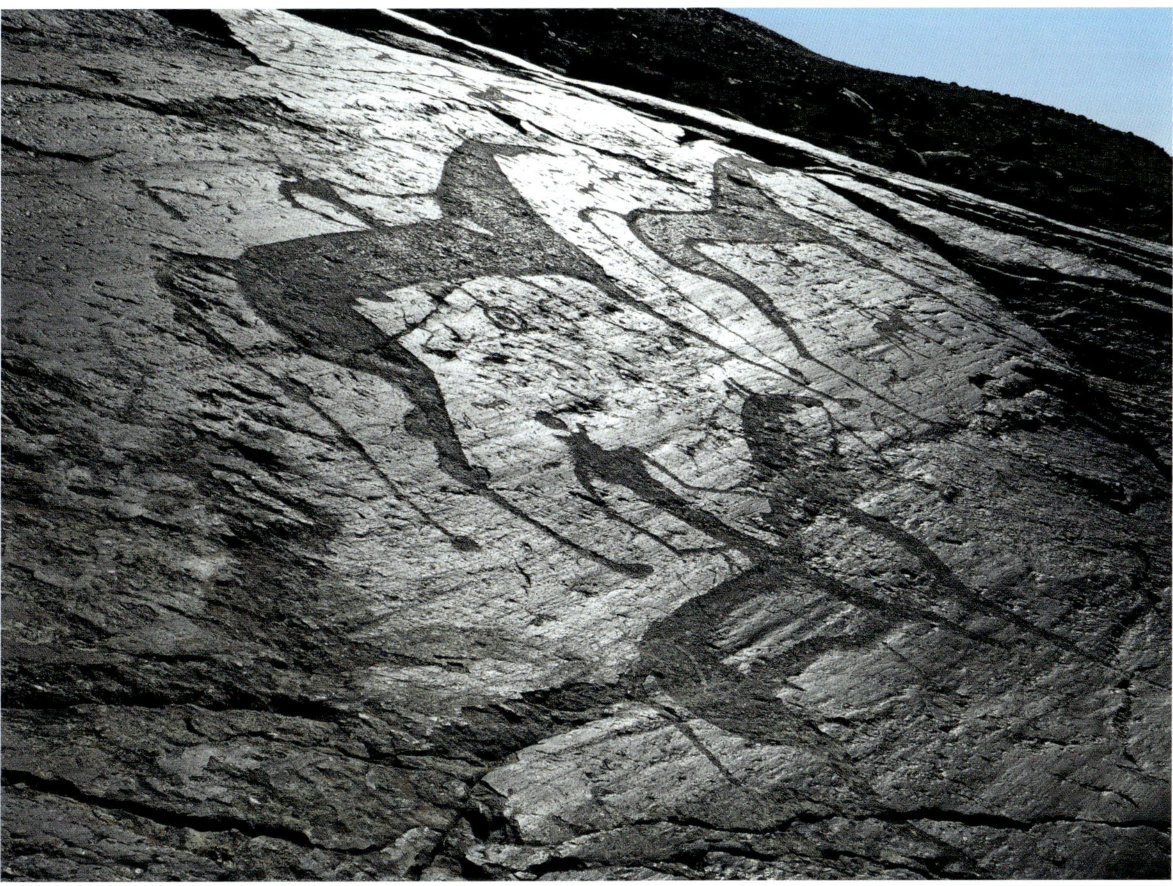

44. Horsemen at Biluut II. Late Iron Age, Bayan Ölgyi aimag, western Mongolia. Photo 2019 by Johannes Reckel, Germany.

feathers and fixed tiny bells to the tip of their lances. In general, such petroglyphs from the Turkic period follow the then prevailing tradition of glorifying successful warriors in epics and myths. Finely incised, almost graffiti-like petroglyphs of ancient Turkic horsemen are also found along the foothills of the Yuzhno-Chuysky Ridge in Russian Altai,[127] in eastern Kazakhstan and on the Ustyurt Plateau, in western Kazakhstan.

A different kind of petroglyph was discovered by Sergei Rudenko and Alexei Glukhov in 1924–25 when they excavated an early medieval Turkic graveyard at **Kudyrge** in the Chulysman Valley, in the eastern Russian Altai, which was dated to the First Turkic Khaganate (552–603 CE) (fig. 45). At one of the tombs a stone figure *ca.* 40 centimetres high was excavated which bore engravings on three sides. Unfortunately, the original figure with the petroglyphs has disappeared and only Rudenko's sketch has survived.[128] On the front a male face (or mask) with moustache and beard is engraved. On the back a seated woman is featured dressed in rich robes with a three-pointed crown and ear pendants; next to her sits a smaller woman, possibly a girl, also richly dressed. On the third side three dismounted horsemen are kneeling, faced towards the two women. The kneeling person in the middle also wears a crown, the one at the

top a mask of a horse.[129] The main figure is usually interpreted as the mother goddess, protectress of children and possibly also the earth.[130] Whether the kneeling horsemen are shamans remains a guess.[131]

As soon as the ancient Turkic people introduced their runic script during the Second Khaganate (682–745 CE), stone steles also served as a canvas for lengthy proclamations, of which the two memorial steles for the Göktürk general and statesman Tonyukuk (*ca.* 646–725 CE) are among the most famous. On the steles, which stand in the **Tuul Valley** south-east of Ulaan Baatar, Tonyukuk lists his main victories and diplomatic successes. Later, in the period of the Genghis Khanids and subsequent principalities, political and religious Buddhist texts were carved on rocks, but the carving of figurative petroglyphs had come to an end during the eighth century CE. As to the question of why petroglyph engraving largely ceased, as in other regions, there is only conjecture. The introduction of writing certainly provided more reliable ways to record and communicate ideologies, myths and cultural heritage, although the majority of the world's populations remained illiterate for many centuries after the introduction of writing. It is possible that oral epics replaced petroglyphs as a means of communication, which now went out of fashion and were forgotten. Most of the later,

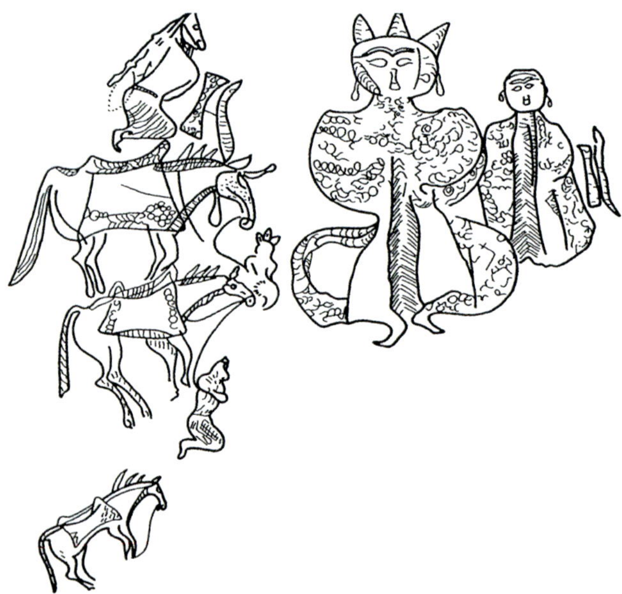

of the second millennium BCE. The Russian archaeologist Alexey Kovalev conjectures that these anthropomorphic steles were influenced by a very late Neolithic culture flourishing in the Swiss and French valley of the Rhône 6,000 kilometres away. Against this bold hypothesis it should be considered that whereas the eastward migration of Yamnaya and Andronovo peoples is attested, there is no indication that late Neolithic people from the Rhône Valley ever migrated to the homeland of the Yamnaya people. Only a genetic analysis could possibly support such a hypothesis.[132]

About 460 kilometres south of Kayina'er and 105 kilometres south-west of Ürümqi is the petroglyph site of **Kangjia Shimenzi** near Quergou in Hutubi district. On a northern foothill of the Tian Shan Mountains, some 300 mostly anthropomorphic figures are spread over a fourteen-metre-long frieze five metres above the ground. The size of the figures varies from a few centimetres to more than two metres, and they date from different periods. The foot of

post-Turkic and post-Uyghur petroglyphs look like mere scribbles, made without deeper meaning.

South of the Altai lies Xinjiang whose northern part was impacted by the Bronze Age steppe cultures further north, since its lush pastures offered ideal living conditions for stockbreeding nomads. Three types of Bronze Age gravesites have been identified: large khirigsuurs with deer stones of the Sayan type (900–700 BCE); simple pit graves; and the mysterious graves of the Chemurchek (Qie'muerqieke) culture (2600–1800 BCE). These consist of one or more cist graves, which are surrounded usually by a rectangular, or more rarely by a circular, stone enclosure made of upright stone slabs. Next to some of these graves stand anthropomorphic stone steles with heights from 60 to over 150 centimetres. From the shoulders of the plump figures the neck moves seamlessly into the broad head. The faces are schematic and the figures often wear a neck ring, and the cheeks are sometimes marked with sculpted triangular patterns. Petroglyphs are carved into the sides. Exemplary for such figures is the complex of **Kayina'er** about 40 kilometres west of the district capital of Altay (fig. 23). On the evidence of the grave goods excavated, they date to the beginning

---

45. ↑ Ink drawing of a ceremonial scene on a boulder next to a Turkic burial near Kudyrge, Altai, Russian Federation. Three dismounted horsemen kneel in front of a richly dressed woman, possibly a female deity. After a drawing from Rudenko, Sergey I. and Glukhov, Alexey N., 'Kudyrge burial ground in Altai', in: *Materials on Ethnography*, vol. 3, no. 2 (Leningrad: State Publisher of Russian Museums, 1927).

46. → Memorial stele inscribed in Old Turkic runes commemorating the Göktürk general Tonyukuk (*ca.* 646–725), a leading politician of the Second Turkic Khaganate. Tuul Valley in the Nailakh district of Ulaan Baatar, central Mongolia. Photo 2001.

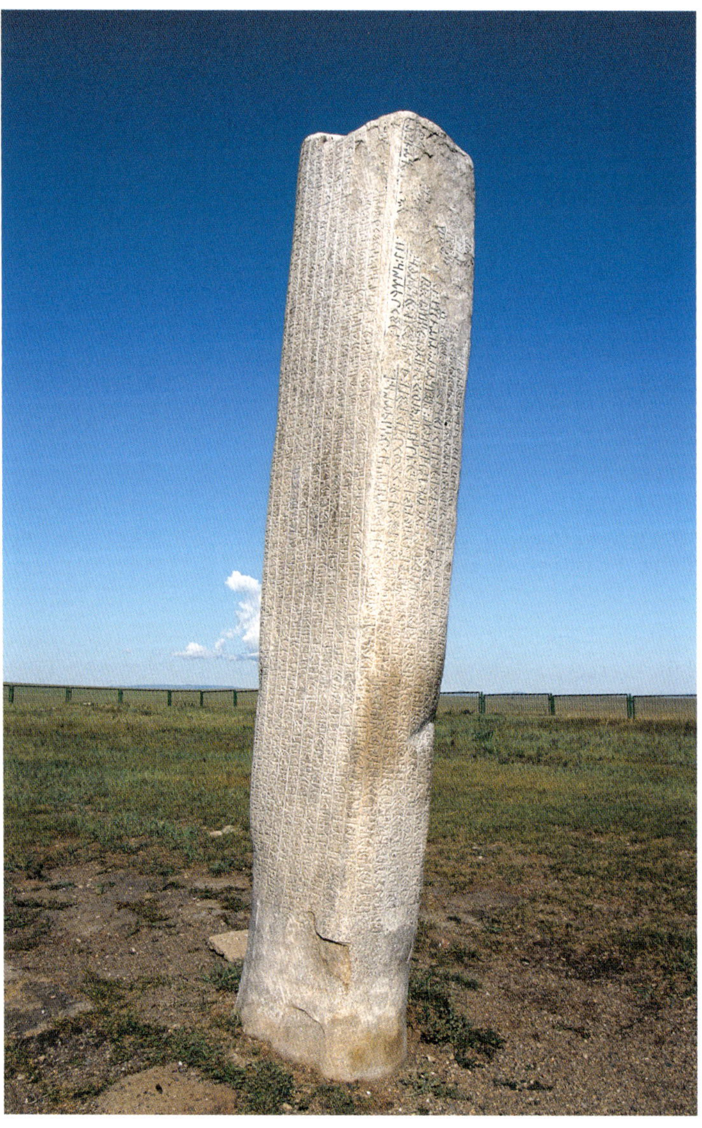

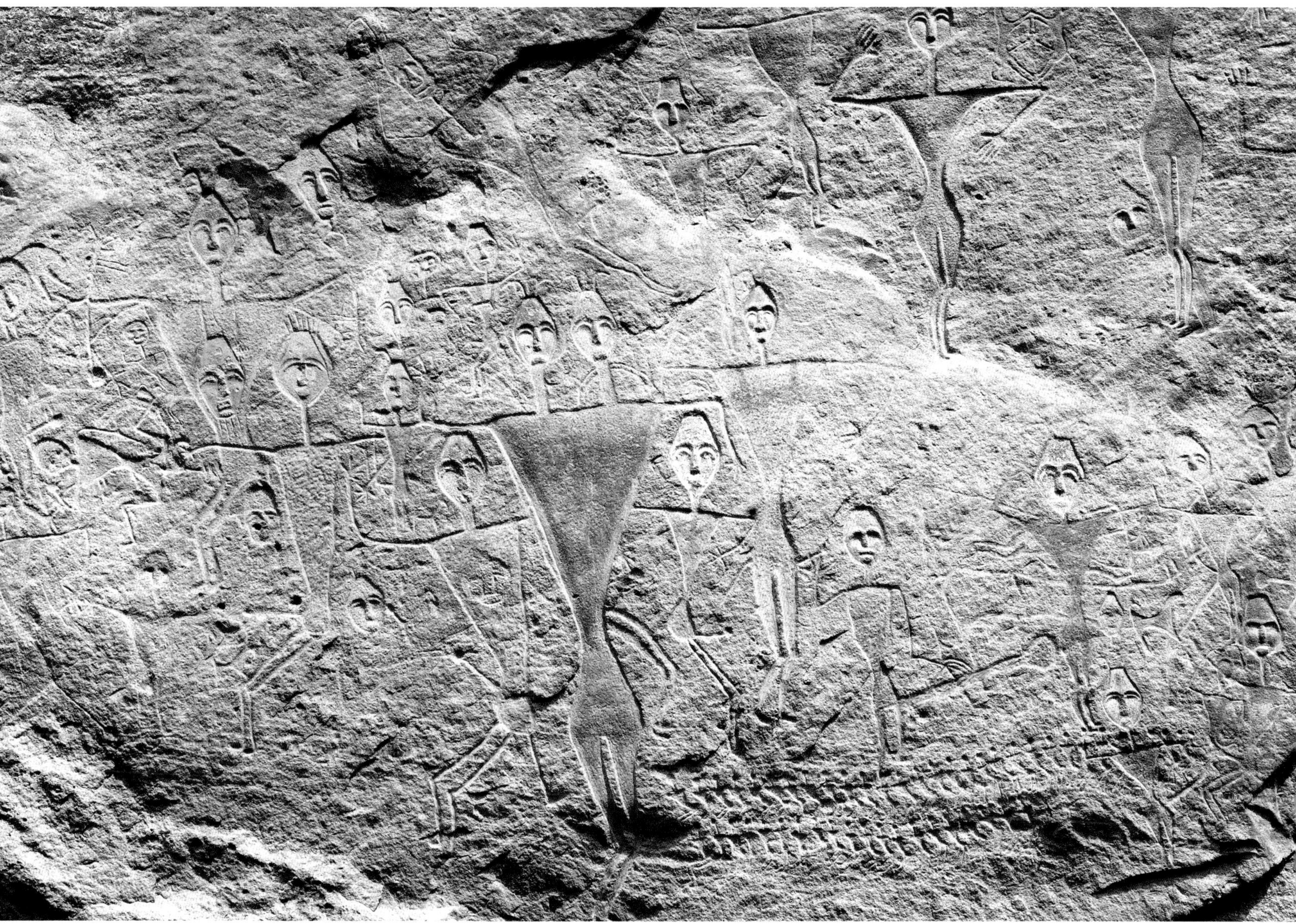

47. A section of the deeply engraved petroglyphs at Kangjia Shimenzi, Xinjiang, China, *ca.* 1250–1000 BCE. Most figures have triangular torsos, some are ithyphallic and one has two heads; the traces of red and white paint are original. Photo 2005.

the rock face, beneath this band, is decorated with a few archaic hunting scenes, ibexes and wave patterns from the late Neolithic. The dominant, large composition looks stylistically unified and consists of seven or eight scenes (fig. 47). Dance scenes predominate, sprinkled with depictions of sexual acts, men with large penises, masks, and two-headed women or hermaphrodites. Most of the figures have a triangular upper body with broad shoulders and a narrow waist, and oval heads; a few of them wear a kind of mask with two antenna-like attachments, probably feathers. The narrow, small faces with prominent noses and brow ridges suggest Europid people. Between the figures are engraved dozens of masks, with a few also on the chests of the dancers. In the uppermost scene, only women dance beside an ithyphallic man; in two lower registers small figures, each a few centimetres tall, dance in front of a standing ithyphallic man. The large figures are deeply chiselled and polished; a few retain traces of red and white paint. The sight of this painted composition must have made an overwhelming impression; perhaps corresponding fertility rites once took place here. While this composition is unique, similar human figures have been found at the Bronze Age site of **Sagan-Zaba** located on the western shore of Lake Baikal.[133] The main scenes at Kangjia Shimenzi probably date to the last quarter of the second millennium BCE, with the two pairs of horses standing on their hind legs across from each other and the two tigers, depicted in the Scytho-Siberian Animal Style, dating from the middle of the first millennium BCE.

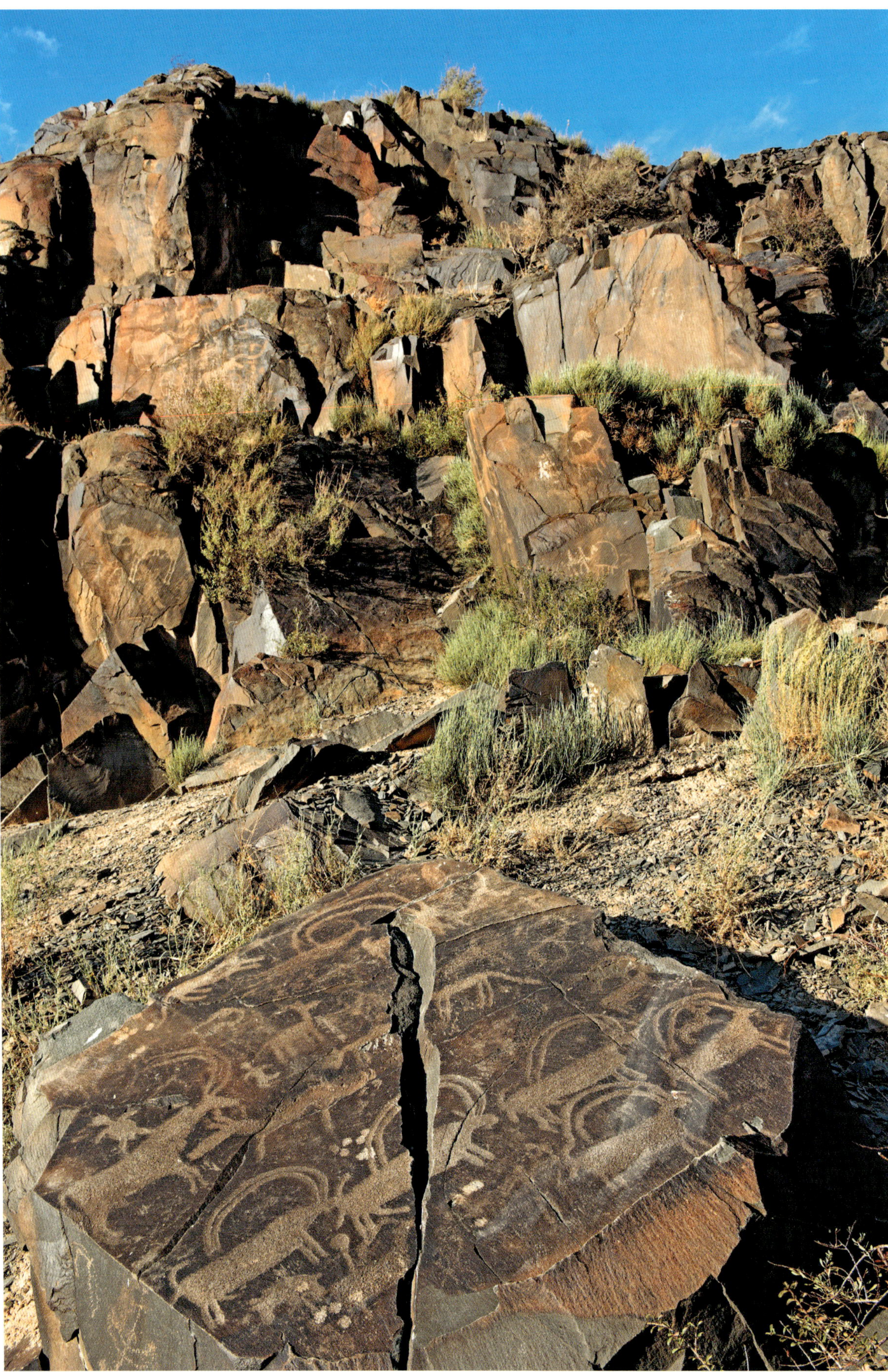

48. In the front, below, ibexes, a horned horse and normal horses; at the back, above, the sacrifice of a horned horse. Bronze Age, Tamgaly III, southern Kazakhstan. Photo 2018.

3. Kazakhstan

With a surface of 2,724,900 square kilometres Kazakhstan is the world's largest landlocked country, and consequently has a continental climate. However, its topographical diversity results in different climate zones. Whereas the climate in northern and eastern Kazakhstan is more or less comparable to that in Khakassia, Tuva and western Mongolia, the region called Zhetysu (Semirech'e, that is 'Seven Rivers') which comprises southern Kazakhstan and north-west Kyrgyzstan and lies along the northern foothills of the Tian Shan Mountain Range enjoys a more humid climate. It contrasts to the desertic Betpak-Dala, the 'Hungry Steppe' and, further west, to the Ustyurt Plateau to which belongs the peninsula of Mangyshlak.

Petroglyph sites are located in the rocky and mountainous regions of eastern and southern Kazakhstan. In these regions, the warm and moist Atlantic Climate Optimum was followed around 2500 BCE by a period of aridity which lasted until about the middle of the second millennium BCE. Then colder and more pluvial conditions set in, lasting until about 100 BCE, which were especially pronounced in the foothills of the Tian Shan. As a result of increased moisture, desert and semi-desert steppes gradually turned into grass steppes.[134] This change in landscape was one of the main factors which motivated the Andronovian people to increasingly migrate into Zhetysu and eastern Kazakhstan.[135] The arrival

of the pastoralist Andronovians, the spread of horse riding and the expansion of pastures triggered a conversion from modest agriculture and settled herding of cattle to mobile pastoralism focusing on horse breeding and to a renewed increase in hunting. There were two kinds of mobile pastoralism: in the flat steppes, mobility was horizontal, with herds moving between places of similar altitude, while in the foothills, mobility was vertical: herds were kept on the valley floor during winter, but in spring were moved uphill till they reached high-altitude pastures located 3,000 metres above sea level or more, such as Saimaluu Tash in Kyrgyzstan. These economic changes and the arrival of a new population which brought different worldviews and myths are reflected in the petroglyphs of Kazakhstan. Whereas the bull dominated in petroglyphs from the early Bronze Age, from the late Bronze Age it was replaced by the horse and, to a lesser degree, by the camel. In terms of climatic changes, the northern Tian Shan foothills enjoyed a moderately moist climate during the first millennium CE which allowed for renewed agricultural activities, a partial return to settled lifestyles and, in Zhetysu, the emergence of urbanization. As of 1200 CE, a repeated cooling trend triggered a return to increased mobile pastoralism. Agriculture rebounded and re-urbanization began in the second half of the nineteenth century with a renewed trend to warmer conditions and the region's integration into the Russian Empire.

The petroglyphs in Kazakhstan are usually divided into the following periods:[136]

- Pre-Bronze Age (before the 22nd century BCE).

- Early-middle Bronze Age (22nd–14th century BCE).

- Late Bronze Age (13th–9th century BCE).

- Early Iron Age, Saka period (9th/8th–4th century BCE).

- Late Iron Age, Hun period (3rd century BCE–5th century CE).

- Turkic period (6th–9th century CE).

- Medieval period (10th–18th century CE).

- Ethnographic period (19th–21st century CE).

Kazakhstan counts the following major rock art sites,[137] listed in chronological order:

- **Shatyrtas** in south Kazakhstan is a complex of more than 25 rock shelters and caves decorated with geometric paintings mostly dating from the Chalcolithic[138] and early Bronze Age.

- **Ak-Baur** is a cave in east Kazakhstan containing paintings of signs allegedly dating from the Bronze Age.

- **Khulzhabasy** in the southern Kazakh Chu-Ili Mountains is the only site with Neolithic and Chalcolithic petroglyphs, that predates the twenty-second century BCE. All periods are present at Khulzhabasy down to the medieval Turkic epoch.

- **Arpa-Uzen** in the southern Kazakh Karatau Range has petroglyphs mainly from the middle and late Bronze Ages as well as the Saka period, little from the Xiongnu–Hunnic and Turkic periods and quite a few from the Kazakh epoch (fifteenth–nineteenth centuries).

- **Ak-Kainar** is located in Zhetysu (Semirech'e), south-eastern Kazakhstan, 70 km west of Almaty. Its earliest petroglyphs date from the middle Bronze Age to the early Iron Age. There are also inscriptions in the Tibetan and Mongolic Oirat languages as well as petroglyphs from the Ethnographic period, that is the nineteenth and twentieth centuries.

- **Tamgaly** also lies in Zhetysu, 110 km north-west of Almaty; it is the most interesting site in Kazakhstan. Its oldest petroglyphs are slightly later than the earliest at Ak-Kainar, and date from the fifteenth century BCE. Most famous are the Bronze Age petroglyphs featuring sun-headed anthro-pomorphs and hybrid horses with long horns. Tamgaly's petroglyphs from the Saka and Turkic periods, though fewer, are also of high quality.

- **Bayanzhurek** lies to the north of the Dzungarian Alatau Range in south-eastern Kazakhstan. It includes petroglyphs from the whole of the Bronze Age, and later examples from the Turkic period.[139]

- **Eshkiolmes** lies in the north-western foothills of the Dzungarian Alatau. It consists of a rich collection of petroglyphs from the middle Bronze Age to the Turkic period. The site consists of 24 canyons spread over a distance of 25 km. At the mouths of canyons 8 to 10 – at a place called Talapty – settlements and graveyards from the late Bronze Age have been excavated.[140]

- **Sauiskandyk,** in south Kazakhstan, is on a northern foothill of the Karatau Range. The majority of petroglyphs date from the Bronze Age, but the most interesting ones are from the Saka and Xiongnu periods: the latter feature wheeled wagons with baldachin-like roofs, similar to those in Yamaan Us, Mongolia. There are also dozens of Arabic inscriptions and Kazakh *tamgas.*

- **Moldazhar** in eastern Kazakhstan is noteworthy for its petroglyphs of horses dating from the late Bronze Age and Iron Age.

- **Terekty Aulie** is in central Kazakhstan. The site is unique for two reasons: whereas most petroglyph sites are sandstone, the petroglyphs at Terekty Aulie were engraved into three granite hills, much harder than sandstone. As a consequence, the pecking of the images had to be deeper and they were polished on completion. Moreover, the vast majority of petroglyphs feature horses shown in profile. They are dated to the middle Bronze Age, the epoch when the Andronovo complex spread in eastern Central Asia, in which culture the horse played a crucial role. It is tempting to associate the petroglyphs with the neighbouring graveyard which is related to the Alakul culture, belonging to the Andronovo complex.[141]

- **Karatau Ridge** lies in the district of Taraz in south Kazakhstan, close to the Kyrgyz border. It comprises the sites of **Karasay**, **Maymak** and **Gabayevka** and consists of a vast selection of images from the Bronze Age to the Xiongnu–Hunnic period. Unique among the petroglyphs of the Karatau Ridge are the scenes of predators attacking and killing herbivores and the images of large felid carnivores.[142]

- **Ak-Terek** is about 100 km west of Almaty; while the site counts some Bronze Age petroglyphs, the majority are from the Saka Iron Age period.

- **Bayte III** in the Mangyshlak peninsula, western Kazakhstan, is not actually a petroglyph site but an Alano-Sarmatian sanctuary dating from the third to second century BCE whose walls were covered with engraved *tamgas* from no fewer than 273 different clans, and figurative graffiti of high symbolic importance.

- **Tamgaly-Tas** lies 90 km north of Almaty on the right bank of the River Ili. The site features four Buddhist deities, a Buddhist teacher and Buddhist inscriptions in Oirat, Tibetan and Manchu.

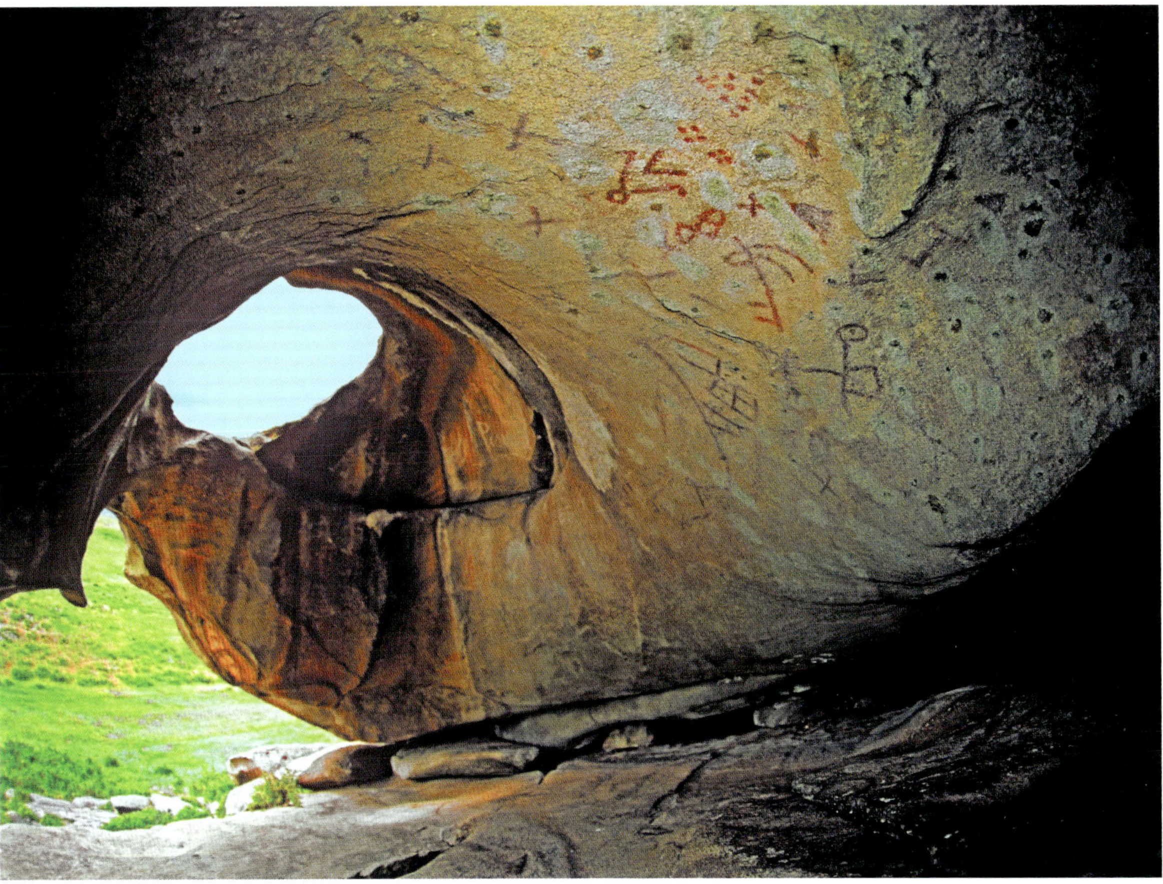

49. Interior of the Ak-Baur Cave in eastern Kazakhstan with paintings allegedly from the Bronze Age. Photo 2009.

A detailed description of all these sites would go beyond the framework of this book and sometimes seem repetitive. Instead, a chronological overview of the most important petroglyph motifs follows, and in particular those images that are unique to Kazakhstan. But before that, two sites with rock paintings need to be introduced.

Probably the oldest rock art site in Kazakhstan is the complex of **Shatyrtas**, meaning 'stone tents', which is located in the Sarybulak Gorge in the southern district of Zhambyl. Although known to the local people, these shelters were first researched only in 2019 by Alexey Rogozhinsky when he surveyed the Kindyktas Mountains. The shelters and caves are ornamented with paintings in various reddish tones mainly representing geometric motifs, possibly vessels, as well as anthropomorphs and zoomorphs. According to Rogozhinsky, there are clear similarities between the painted geometric figures at Shatyrtas and painted ceramics from Geoksyur (south-east Turkmenistan) and Sarazm (north-west Tajikistan) which are dated to the periods Namazga II–III (3500–2500 BCE for Geoksyur) and Sarazm I–II (3500–2900 BCE for Sarazm). This hypothesis is supported by hand-painted ceramic sherds with similar patterns which were excavated in the immediate vicinity of three painted shelters. Assuming that these observations are correct, these finds suggest a migration of people from the proto-urban, agricultural regions of Geoksyur and Sarazm to the Kindyktas Mountains about five millennia ago. This is plausible since the Kindyktas Mountains have rich copper deposits for which Geoksyur and Sarazm had a high demand.[143] The intriguing cave of **Ak-Baur** is in east Kazakhstan about twenty kilometres west of River Irtysh. The cave is located in a small granite hill of pyramidal shape and has a circular opening in its arched ceiling, like the smoke-hole of a yurt. Opposite the entrance, on the cave's northern wall and on the adjoining section of the dome, about 80 signs are painted with red-brown ochre which comprise around 40 more or less different patterns. Over the course of the day, the sunlight would have lit up the paintings section by section. The purpose of this allegedly Bronze Age monument remains unknown; possibly it served as a kind of observatory or as a place to perform certain rituals.[144]

Most of the Early Bronze Age petroglyphs dating to the beginning of the second millennium BCE are located at **Kulzhabasy**; among other things, they show large wild aurochs (*Bos primigenius*) with huge, long horns; their bodies are marked by diagonally

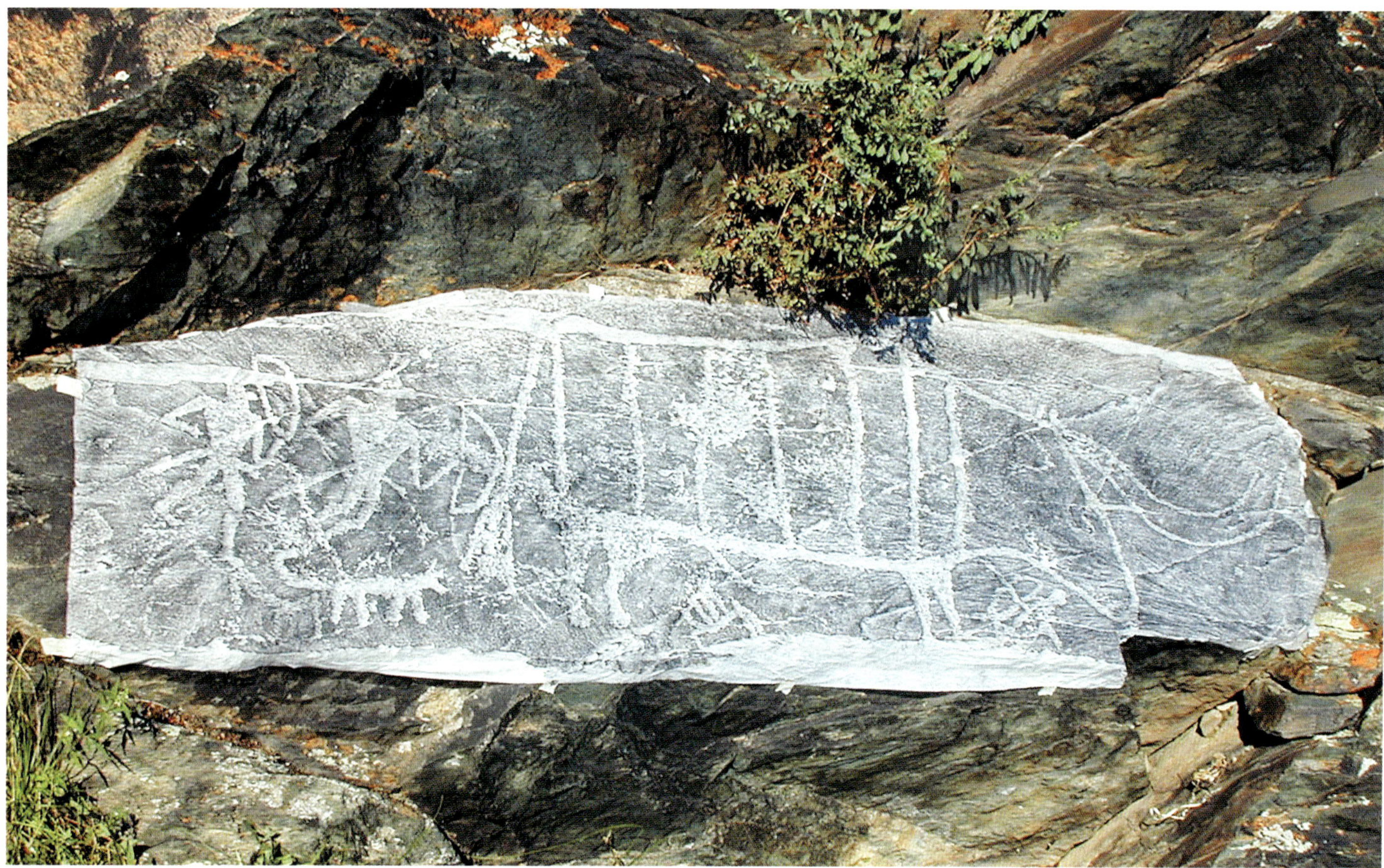

50. A large aurochs is attacked by two hunters wearing wolf masks. *In situ* rubbing. Early Bronze Age, Kulzhabasy III, southern Kazakhstan. Photo Alexey Rogozhinsky.

intersecting lines. In a spectacular scene, a huge bull is attacked by hunters who wear a carnivore's mask, possibly that of a wolf (fig. 50).[145] Several of the most iconic petroglyph figures and scenes in Kazakhstan are to be found at **Tamgaly**, whose name means 'place of tribal signs' (*tamgas*). It was first researched by Anna Maksimova in 1957 and later by Alexey Maryashev and Alexey Rogozhinsky.[146] The dating of the older petroglyphs based on stylistic criteria has been confirmed by the excavations of Rogozhinsky, who discovered slabs engraved with petroglyphs in some middle Bronze Age tombs, located about one kilometre from the main petroglyph site.[147] Whereas he thought that these petroglyphs had been created at the time of the burials, that is the fourteenth or thirteenth century BCE, Karl Baipakov and Alexey Maryashev were convinced that they were older, since they had originally been engraved at the main site; they dated probably from the fifteenth century BCE and had been removed later for use as building material in the burial cists.[148] In any case, all the Bronze Age burials are clearly related to the Andronovo cultural complex which had been brought to south Kazakhstan by the migration of the Andronovian pastoralists. Since a Bronze Age settlement was also discovered in the vicinity

of the cemeteries and petroglyphs, one can hypothesize that this complex reflects the material relics of Andronovians' daily life as well as their funeral rites and mythical beliefs, which had amalgamated with those of the local inhabitants. At a later date, during the Iron Age and Turkic periods, the pecking of petroglyphs was concentrated at the smaller, peripherical Site VI.

The archaeological complex is divided into eight sites, of which the five main ones are situated on both sides of a narrow canyon. It seems that the central Site IV was the centre of this sanctuary-like place, for it is only here that all the major figures and scenes such as bulls, bull–horse hybrids, sun-headed figures and chariots are incorporated into one single composition.[149] The bull was an important animal in societies which practised settled pastoralism, as was the case not only in the local cultures of south Kazakhstan, but also among the early Andronovians before they began their migration southward. The bull, or rather the mythical concept of the bull, was venerated and sacrifices were offered. As in several other early-to-middle Bronze Age sites, petroglyphs of huge bulls with long wavy horns dwarf all the other figures. An intriguing scene from **Zevakino** in eastern Kazakhstan seems to illustrate an unequal fight between four bulls and five unarmed men. Two bulls trample over two (probably dead) men stretched out on the ground, a third bull throws a human from his horns to the ground and the fourth one has impaled another man; the fifth man, holding a cudgel, also lies on the ground with outstretched legs and arms.[150] In this scene, it is not the bulls that are sacrificed, but the men. In another singular scene at Tamgaly, a sun-headed anthropomorph, or rather deity, stands on the back of a bull with huge upward-curving horns.[151] One interpretation sees in this scene the supremacy of the forces of light over those of darkness.[152] Another, in an Andronovian context more relevant, interpretation links this scene with those ancient Indo-Iranian deities who had a symbolic zoomorphic incarnation in the shape of a venerated animal.[153] For example, the all-powerful Indian god of war, Indra or the Iranian god of light and justice, Mithra were both associated with bulls. A further striking representation of an aurochs is at **Ak-Kainar**. The bull has two pairs of horns; the shorter ones have a recurved shape while four humans holding each other by the hand cling to the tip of the extremely long, straighter horns (fig. 51). This scene could possibly evoke the Zoroastrian mythical bull Srisok whose horns were so long that they bridged ravines and rivers and people could walk on them to overcome these obstacles.[154]

After the Andronovians had mastered horse riding and started their migrations, the bull was gradually supplemented by the horse as the most revered animal, which was associated with the sun. The symbolic ascendence of the horse during the first half of the second millennium BCE went hand in hand with the spread of burials including light chariots and horse sacrifice. However, the bull was not completely pushed aside, as one of his main characteristics, the elongated horns, was kept and transferred to the horse. In at least two scenes at Tamgaly, an anthropomorphic figure kills a horned horse with a typical Bronze Age axe (fig. 53); several other horses with long horns are rendered standing alone.[155] In one particular petroglyph, a long-horned horse is shown inside a large cow, as if the cow is pregnant with a baby horse–bull (fig. 52). In the scene of the horse–bull sacrifice, the anthropomorph has a bird's head or wears a bird's mask, and in his belt he carries a mace. The small

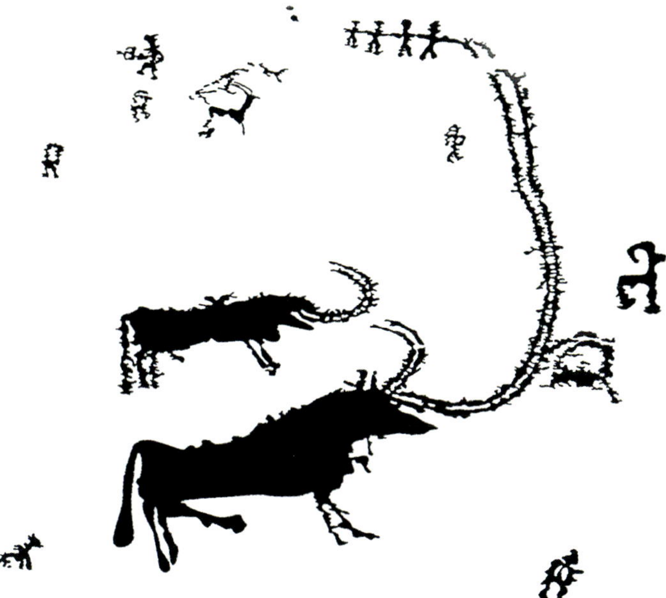

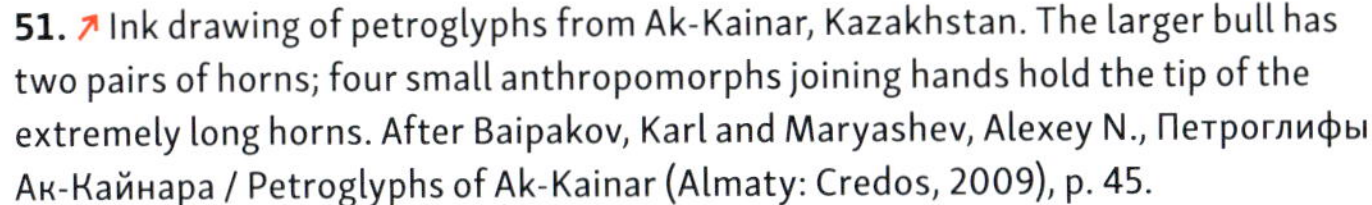

51. ↗ Ink drawing of petroglyphs from Ak-Kainar, Kazakhstan. The larger bull has two pairs of horns; four small anthropomorphs joining hands hold the tip of the extremely long horns. After Baipakov, Karl and Maryashev, Alexey N., Петроглифы Ак-Кайнара / Petroglyphs of Ak-Kainar (Almaty: Credos, 2009), p. 45.

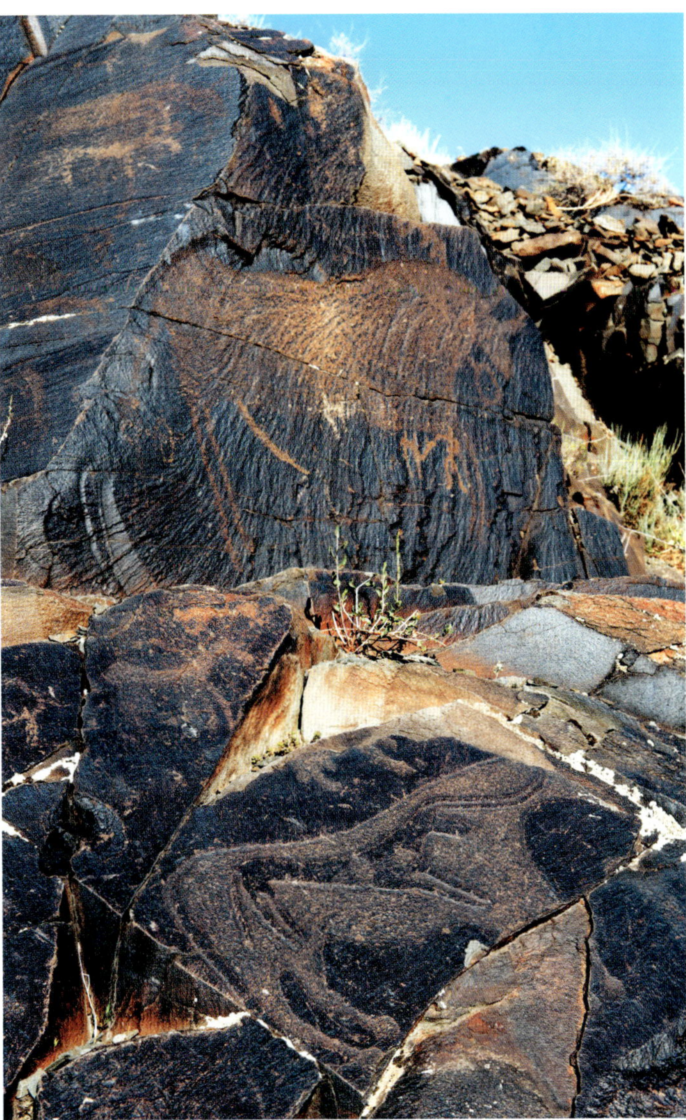

52. Above, a huge bull; below, a long-horned horse has been engraved inside a cow, as if implying that the cow is pregnant with the horned horse. Bronze Age, Tamgaly III, southern Kazakhstan. Photo 2018.

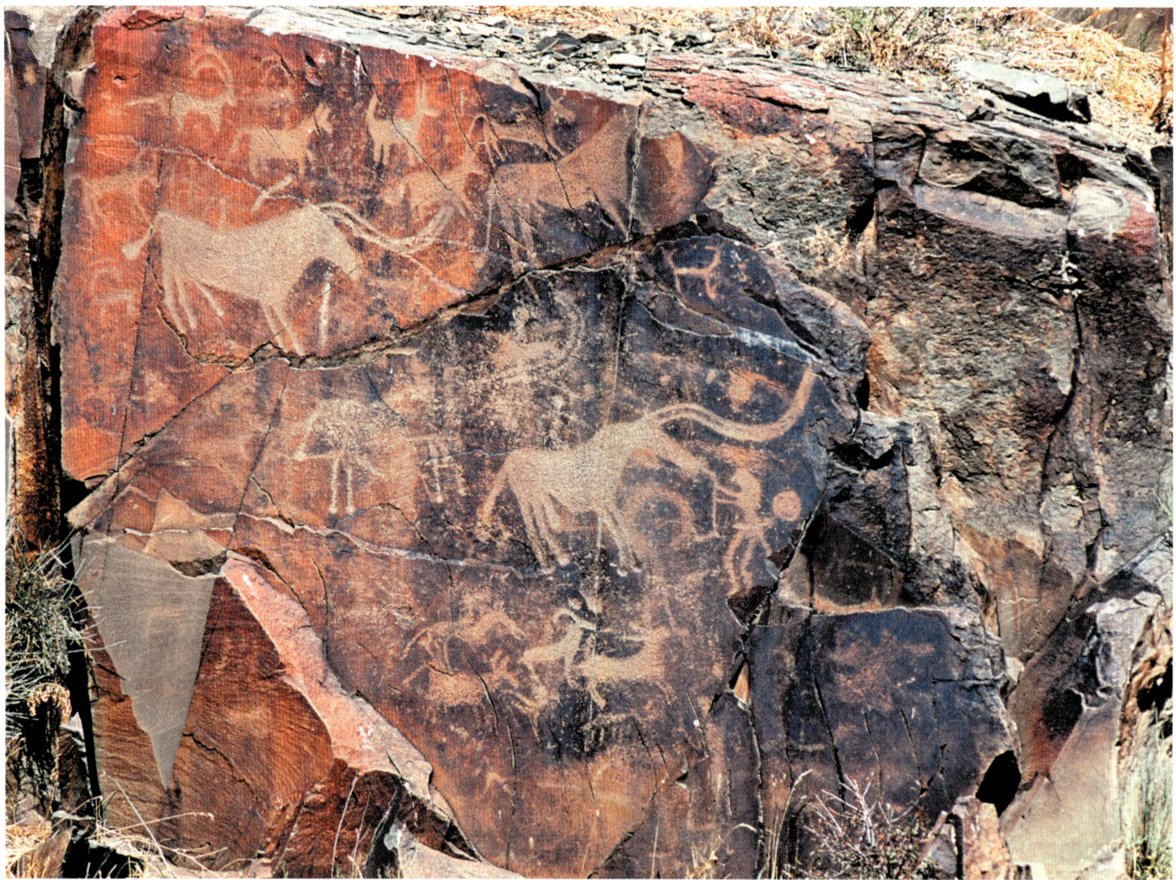

53. In the centre of the scene, a man wearing a bird mask and a small mace hits a horned stallion on the head with a Bronze Age axe. The tiny rider on the sacrificial horse has been added later. Bronze Age, Tamgaly III, southern Kazakhstan. Photo 2018.

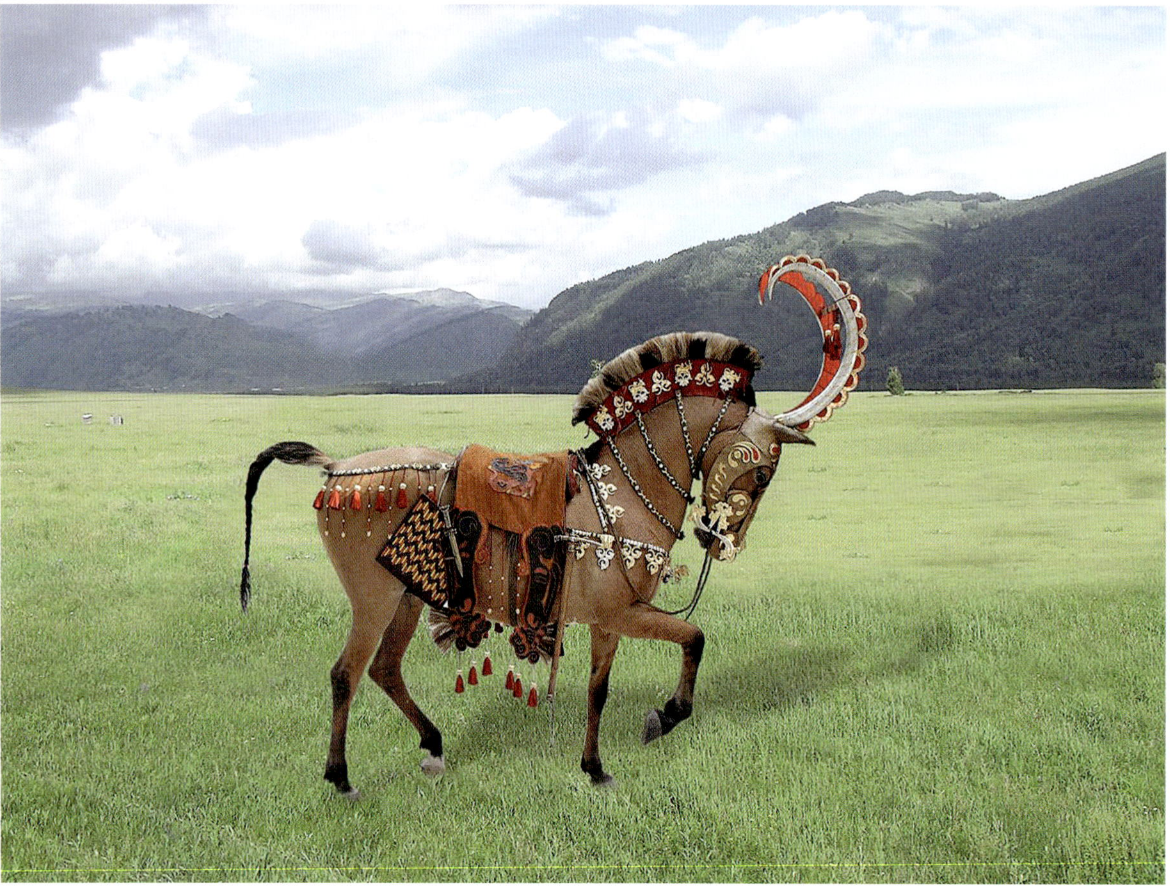

54. Illustration based on archaeological findings dating from the Saka Pazyryk culture of a horse prepared for a burial ceremony. The State Hermitage Museum, Saint Petersburg, Russian Federation.

rider sitting on the horse has been added later. It remains a matter for debate in which order this scene was composed: Baipakov and Maryashev believe, as does Rogozhinsky, that the Bronze Age longhorn bulls were transformed in the later Iron Age, in the time of the Saka Pazyryk culture (fourth to second centuries BCE), into horses to be ritually sacrificed.[156] Henri-Paul Francfort, however, thinks that the long horns were added at the time of the Pazyryk culture to an original horse dating from the earlier Iron Age. This interpretation aligns with Pazyryk burials where the dead were accompanied by sacrificed horses decorated with stag or ibex antlers made out of leather, silver or gold sheets.[157] Finally, based on stereoscopic macro-photographs, Irina Shvets believes that these scenes, including the bull–horses and the sacrificing anthropomorph, were created at the same time.[158] The present author follows Francfort's argument, since the horns do indeed look like later additions to an older horse image. The sacrificed horses at Pazyryk were also killed by an axe directed against their skulls, as in the petroglyphs at Tamgaly; they were meant to symbolically carry the buried warrior or noble person to the netherworld. At Tamgaly, there is also a petroglyph of a horse wearing deer antlers, exactly like the sacrificed horses in the Pazyryk burials.[159]

Horse sacrifices on the occasion of elite burials have been performed for millennia in various steppe cultures, and in a developed form since the culture of Sintashta at the latest. Herodotus (*ca.* 484–424 BCE) also described such horse sacrifices at burials among the Iron Age Scythians and Saka as well as the Massagetae, who lived east of the Caspian Sea. While archaeological finds in dozens of kurgans between the Altai and the Black Sea have confirmed Herodotus' detailed accounts of the burial rites of Scythian kings, with regard to the Massagetae he directly relates the sun cult to the horse sacrifices. 'The only god they worship is the sun, to which they sacrifice horses: the idea behind this is to offer the swiftest of mortal creatures to the swiftest of the gods.'[160] Such horse sacrifices are also mentioned in the *Rig Veda*; but they were not made at the occasion of a burial but rather performed by a living ruler to acquire power and glory.[161]

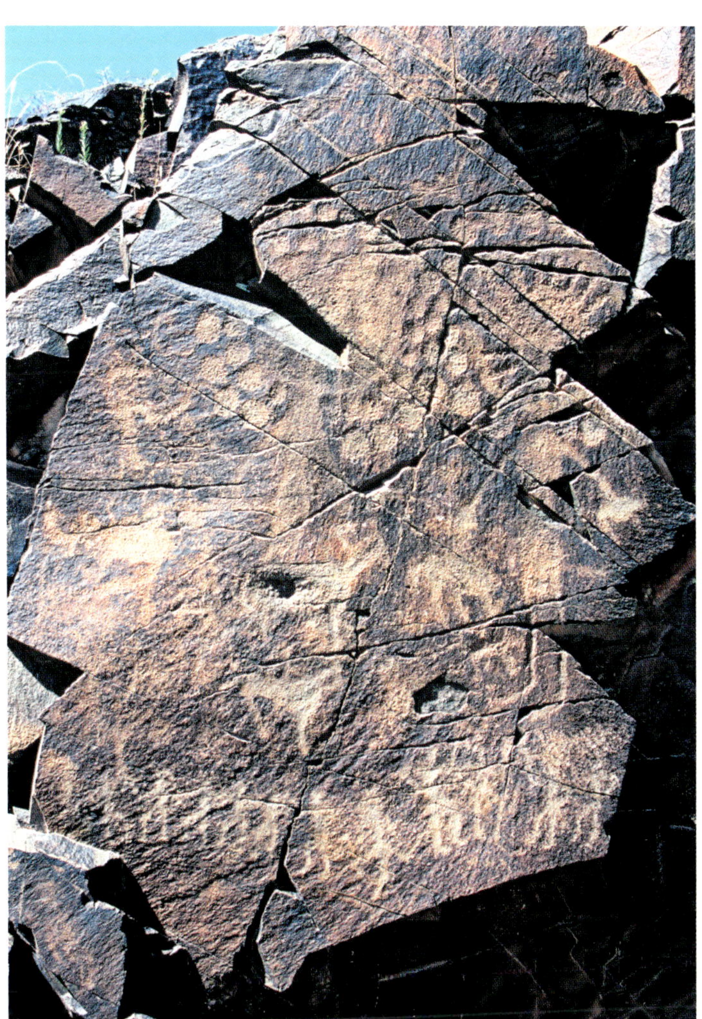

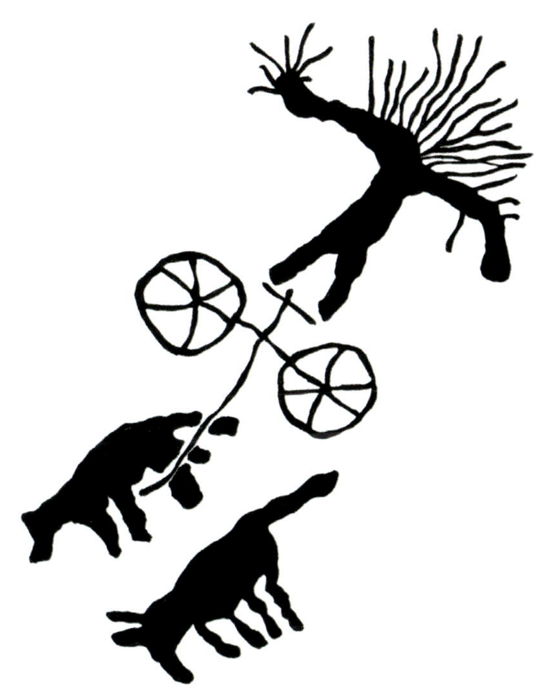

---

55. ↗ Twelve small humans dance beneath two sun-headed anthropomorphic figures. Bronze Age, Tamgaly IV, southern Kazakhstan. Photo 2005.

56. Ink drawing of a sun-headed anthropomorph driving a single-axle chariot. Bronze Age petroglyph at Eshkiolmes, eastern Kazakhstan. After Baipakov, Karl, Maryashev, Alexey N. et al., *Петроглифы в горах Ешкиольмес / The Eshkiolmes Rock's Petroglyphs* (Almaty: OST-XXI Vek, 2005), p. 118, fig. 26. Sher, Jakov and Francfort, Henri-Paul (eds), *Répertoire des pétroglyphes d'Asie*, fasc. 5: Mar'yashev, A.N., Goryashev, A.A. and Potapov, S.A., *Kazakhstan I : Choix de Pétroglyphes du Semirech'e* (1998), p. 32.

The main petroglyph scene at Tamgaly is located in Site IV. It features seven sun-headed anthropomorphic figures standing in a row, their heads surrounded by a halo of rays, which in turn is circled by a dotted wreath (fig. 55). Under two of them, eleven Lilliputian people armed with small maces are shown dancing; a twelfth human lifts his arms towards the sun-headed figures in a devotional gesture.[162] Based on the pronounced size difference between the sun-headed figures and the dancing humans, one can suppose that the former represent not human mortals but solar deities. This scene was composed in two stages, since the sun-deities date from the middle or later Bronze Age, the dancing humans from the early Iron Age.[163] At Tamgaly as well as Ak-Kainar[164] and Saimaluu Tash (Kyrgyzstan), and also at Sarmishsay (Uzbekistan), we find petroglyphs of single standing figures that are probably sun-headed deities.[165] Moreover, at Eshkiolmes[166] and at Yelangash[167]

(Russian Altai) petroglyphs of sun figures driving a chariot suggest associations with the Indian sun god Surya (fig. 56). A possible source for such sun-headed figures may be identified in stone slabs from Karakol, Altai, which date to around 2400 BCE and thus belong to the transitional period from Afanasievo to Okunev. These engraved or painted slabs featured anthropomorphs whose heads are surrounded by a halo of rays which, however, could also represent a feathered headdress. They were later reused to build the cists of graves belonging to the Okunev culture. On a slab painted with red, black and white colours are portrayed anthropomorphic and theriomorphic standing figures, whose heads are decorated with sunbeams and feathers.[168] Since the paintings were found on the inside of the cists, they were turned toward the dead. Several stand-alone stone steles of the Okunev culture also feature sun-headed figures.[169] Petroglyphs of two-axle carts and single-axle

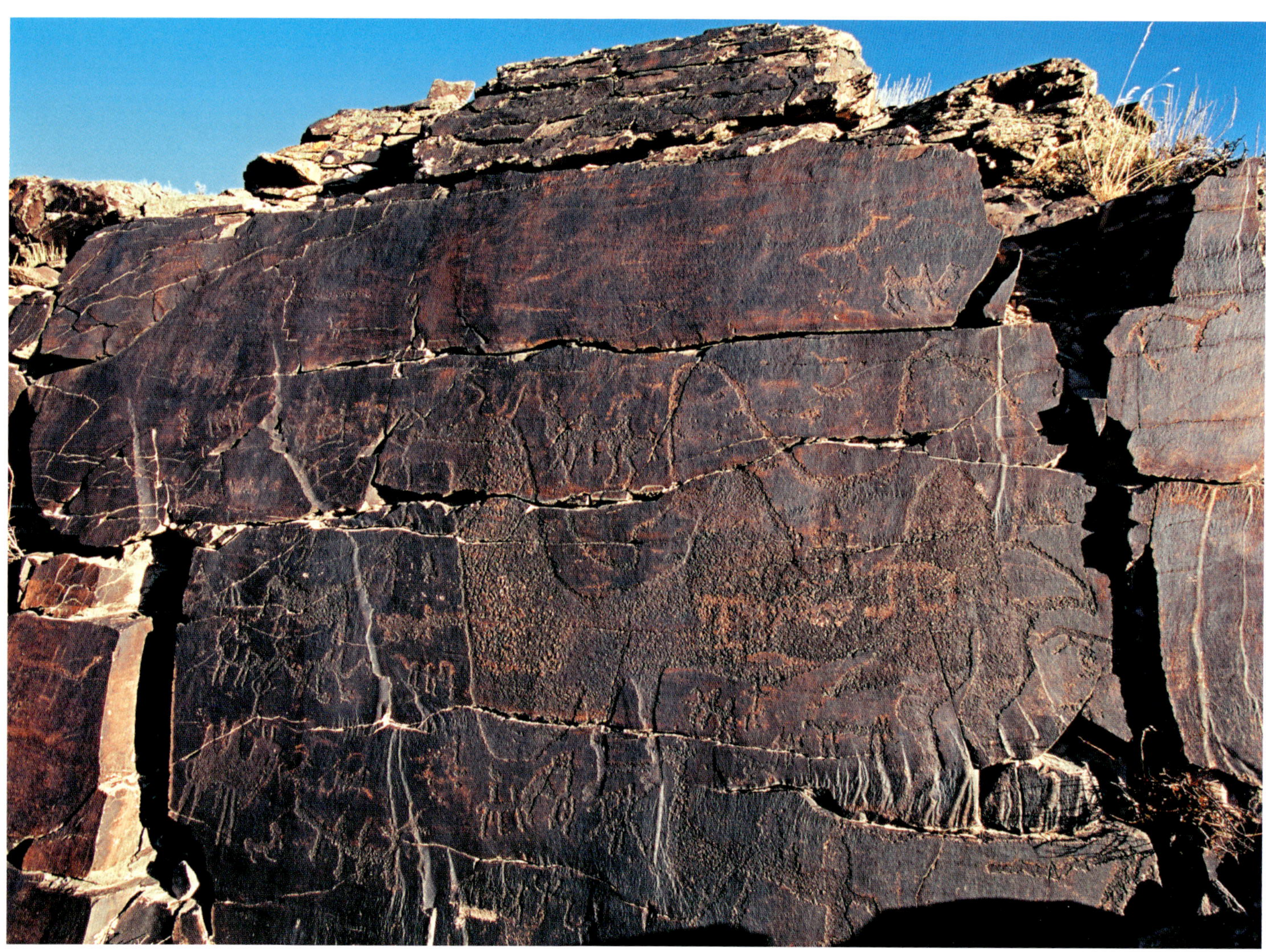

57. Palimpsest from the Bronze Age of two large Bactrian camels; the bigger one is almost two metres long. Arpa-Uzen, Karatau Mountains, southern Kazakhstan. Photo 2005.

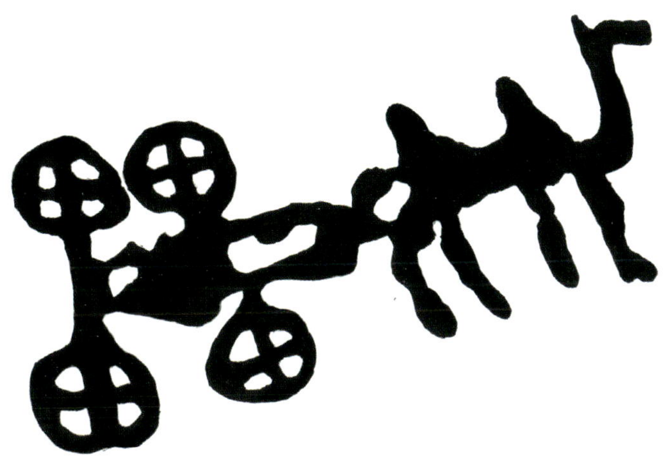

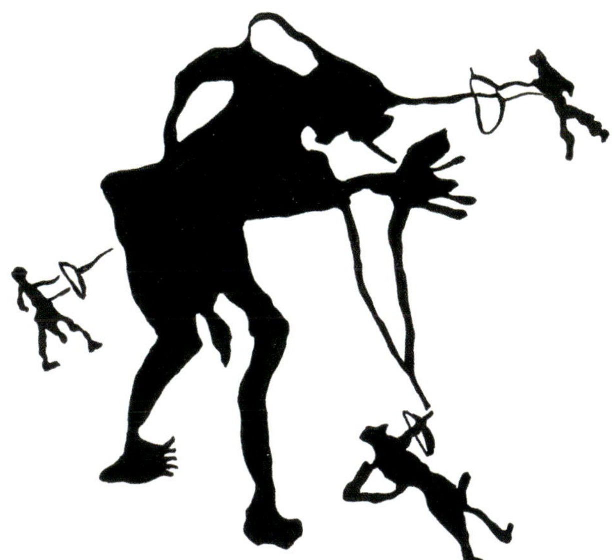

chariots without drivers or with a 'normal' human without a halo of rays are abundant in several sites of in Kazakhstan.[170]

The veneration of sun-headed deities was part of the mythological heritage of the early Indo-Iranians of the Afanasievo and Andronovo cultures. Further traces of such a cult practised by Indo-Europeans can be found in the eastern and southern Tarim Basin in north-western China: for example, in the necropolis of Gumugou in the Lop Nor desert, dating from around 1800 to 1600 BCE, which featured six spectacular tomb arrangements. Above each burial chamber stood a ring of wooden poles tightly placed next to each other and standing four to seven deep. These formed a kind of hub around which stood seven to nine concentric circles of thicker wooden poles, placed farther apart. Seen from above, the trunks look like rays streaming outward from the ring-shaped centre – the sun symbolism is obvious. At another site, Zaghunluq, located in the southern Tarim Basin, Europids were buried in around 800 BCE with a sun symbol drawn with ochre on the temples of the naturally mummified horsemen.[171]

The probable sun deities at Tamgaly and other sites may be associated with deities from the ancient Indo-Iranian pantheon, above all with Mithra. In the *Vedas*, Mithra brings forth the morning light and is correspondingly invoked at dawn in the *Rig Veda*. The god of fire, Agni and the sun god, Surya are also represented with radiant crowns; like the Greek Helios the latter crosses the sky with a horse-drawn chariot.[172] In the Zoroastrian scriptures, Mithra is not identified with the sun god but rather venerated as the god of truth and contracts, but later, at the time of the Iranian Parthians (247 BCE–224 CE) and the Sasanids (224–651 CE), he was also worshipped as the

58. Ink drawing of a petroglyph illustrating a two-humped camel pulling a four-wheeled chariot. Later Bronze Age, Arpa-Uzen, Karatau Mountains, southern Kazakhstan. After Novozhenov, Victor A., *Communications and the Earliest Wheeled Transport of Eurasia* (Moscow: TAUS Publishing, 2012), p. 95, fig. 42.

59. Three small archers attack an unarmed giant as he tumbles. Ink drawing of a Bronze Age petroglyph scene from Eshkiolmes, eastern Kazakhstan. After Baipakov, Karl, Maryashev, Alexey N. et al., Петроглифы в горах Ешкиольмес / The Eshkiolmes Rock's Petroglyphs (Almaty: OST-XXI Vek, 2005), p. 112, fig. 9.

sun god. In images he drives a chariot pulled by white horses or wears a crown of sunbeams. In the *Avesta* he is glorified as the 'lord of wide pastures', who drives a 'high-wheeled chariot', 'drawn by fiery horses', which indicates an origin in a stockbreeding culture that used horse-drawn vehicles.[173] The concept of horses pulling the sun through the sky is also present in Bronze Age petroglyphs and pieces of portable art from southern Scandinavia (for which see below).

As suggested by Luc Hermann, there may have existed two complementary 'sanctuaries' near Tamgaly dedicated to moon-headed deities, namely at **Karakyr**, located seven kilometres north-west of Tamgaly, and at **Gorny**, situated 25 kilometres to the south.[174] At these two sites, a crescent moon was chiselled over the heads of anthropomorphs. In Hermann's words, 'Tamgaly was a place of worship of the sun, whereas Karakyr and Gorny were sanctuaries for the moon in the same micro-regional cultic area.'[175] A further petroglyph of such a moon-headed figure is at Ak-Kainar. These moon-headed deities look different from the typical mushroom-headed anthropomorphs present at Ak-Kainar and Saimaluu Tash (see fig. 83). A rare petroglyph associated with the sun is the swastika found on Andronovian ceramics.

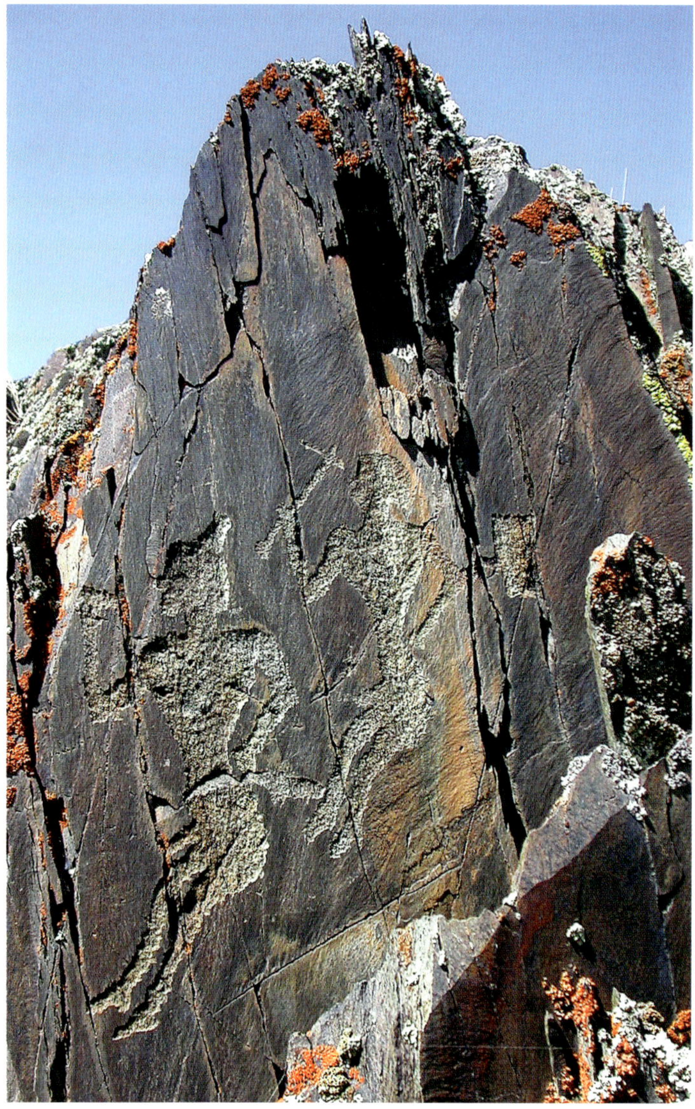

60. Two men brandishing a battle axe. Early Iron Age, Kulzhabasy V, southern Kazakhstan. Photo Alexey Rogozhinsky.

A peculiar variant of the swastika was discovered in **Zavkhan** aimag, north-western Mongolia, whose four arms, oriented clockwise, have the shape of horse heads.[176] A similar zoomorph swastika at **Mayemyr** in eastern Kazakhstan is formed by six goats' heads oriented anticlockwise.[177] Other intriguing figures of Tamgaly dating from the Bronze Age show humans holding in one or both hands a crosier-shaped crook; they have a tail and short protruding outcrops on their back, legs and front. Possibly they are wearing an animal skin. The meaning of these figures is difficult to grasp. Since they are unarmed, they can hardly represent disguised hunters. Andrzej Rozwadowski draws a parallel with the staves of shamans, carefully interpreting these figures wearing animal skins as shamans;[178] in any case, a connection with a ritual is probable.

During the later Bronze Age not only the horse but also the Bactrian camel grew in economic importance, since this strong and resilient animal was ideal for transporting heavy loads in harsh and cold environments; furthermore, it was a source of meat, milk and wool. Nevertheless, it never enjoyed a comparable veneration to that of the horse. The petroglyph of a large Bactrian camel, almost two metres long, at **Arpa-Uzen** which is surrounded by small humans lifting their arms might possibly visualize a veneration of the camel (fig. 57).[179] This hypothesis is further supported by the fact that at no other site in Kazakhstan is there such a high proportion of camel images. In another petroglyph, there is a Bactrian camel 130 centimetres long. At Arpa-Uzen there are also hunting scenes of ibexes, chariots, several duels between archers and a heraldic scene of two horses rearing up in mirror image. In other scenes two humans facing each other hold their arms up high, and are possibly dancing. Another relatively large camel, mounted by a small human, was chiselled at the site of **Karatau** where it stands under the petroglyphs showing a duel between two archers; it is dated to the Bronze Age.[180] The three images of a defeated giant at **Eshkiolmes** likewise represent another striking motif from the later Bronze Age. In two petroglyphs, the giant is surrounded by archers. In one scene, he is tumbling, in the other he raises his hands in an act of surrender. In the third scene the giant is attacked by horsemen; in all three scenes he is unarmed.[181] In a fourth petroglyph scene archers attack a smaller giant who is standing upright.[182] Insofar as in Indo-European mythologies giants and titans often represent a group of former dominant gods who ruled over chaos and who had been defeated and evicted by the present gods who in turn had transformed chaos into order, these petroglyphs may either represent the victory of the present gods over the titans or, in an allegorical sense, the victory of mankind over the chaos of nature.

In the course of the first millennium BCE, bulls, sun-headed figures, chariots and ithyphallic men disappear from petroglyphs, while ibexes, camels, hunting scenes, horsemen and conflict scenes significantly increase. In addition, stags in the style of the Mongol deer stones and the ensuing Animal Style appear at sites such as Tamgaly, Eshkiolmes, Bayanzhurek and Zhyngylshak.[183] The hunters chase their prey with bow and arrows; they are either on foot or mounted on horses and camels, or shoot from a light chariot.[184] Later, in the Iron Age and Turkic period, petroglyphs visualizing duels and combats become prominent, reflecting the militaristic ethic and worldview of that time. Scenes of combat dating from the early Iron Age to the Turkic period are present in particular at Eshkiolmes, Sagyr, Bayanzhurek and Oy-Dzhaylau.[185]

They illustrate combats between foot warriors, between foot warriors and horsemen, and between horsemen. In terms of duels, the petroglyphs show mortal combats between archers as well as men on foot fighting with battle clubs, battle axes and battle picks, and also duels between horsemen armed with lances or with sword and shield.[186] Interestingly, the duellers who fight with picks or pointed battle hammers in the petroglyphs of **Sagyr** carry a *gorytós* on their belts; they probably represent dismounted horsemen.[187] A typical motif of the Turkic period features a horseman with a standard which designated the rider's tribal affiliation and symbolized tribal unity. Some of the flags have the shape of a wolf's head which was the principal totem animal of the ancient Turkic peoples. According to Turkic mythology, a she-wolf saved a mutilated boy, the sole survivor of his tribe. The youth later impregnated the wolf who bore ten sons, the future founders of the ten leading Turkic tribes. Their leader was Ashina, from whom the Turkic khagans claimed descent.[188] Several horsemen holding standards are chiselled at Tamgaly site VI (fig. 61).

About twelve kilometres north of Tamgaly, at a place called **Kogaly Bastal**, which means 'Reeds at the source', there is a tiny, highly interesting petroglyph site from the Turkic period. It was discovered in 2007 by Alexey Rogozhinsky.[189] The main scene, 95 cm wide and 50.5 cm high, features typical Turco-Sogdian motifs as are known from wall-paintings from Panjikent as well as from Sino-Sogdian stone funeral beds and sarcophagi dating from the sixth to eighth century CE (fig. 62). In the upper centre, a man wearing a long kaftan holds a smaller, kneeling man (also wearing a kaftan) by the neck and threatens him with a ball-and-chain flail. Behind the standing man figures a bird, possibly a cock. Above this large central figure, a human seems to fly; this is probably a heavenly messenger, similar to a Chinese *apsara*. If we interpret this scene within a mythical Sogdian–Zoroastrian context, the main figure could represent the Zoroastrian *yazata* (divinity) Sraosha whose attribute is a cock and who oversees how believers follow the obligation of right thought, speech and actions. He also confronts the dead in the netherworld with their past deeds. Accordingly, in this scene Sraosha is threatening a culprit. The figure flying over his head underscores his divinity. Sraosha is however confronted on the right-hand side of the scene by an attacking mounted archer with drawn arrow.

To the left of Sraosha a second horseman gallops towards him, holding in his right hand a staff ending in a human head.

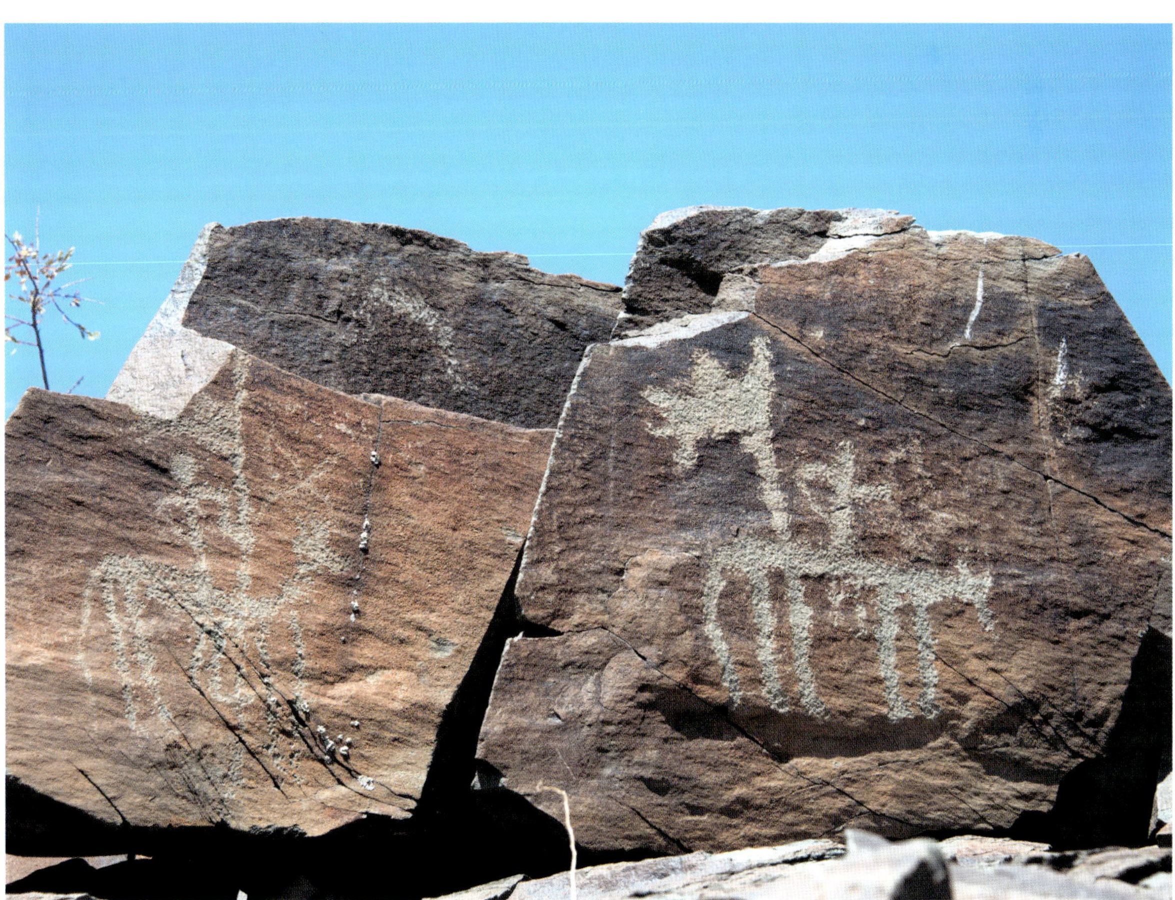

61. Two horsemen, each holding a banner. Turkic period, Tamgaly VI, southern Kazakhstan. Photo 2018.

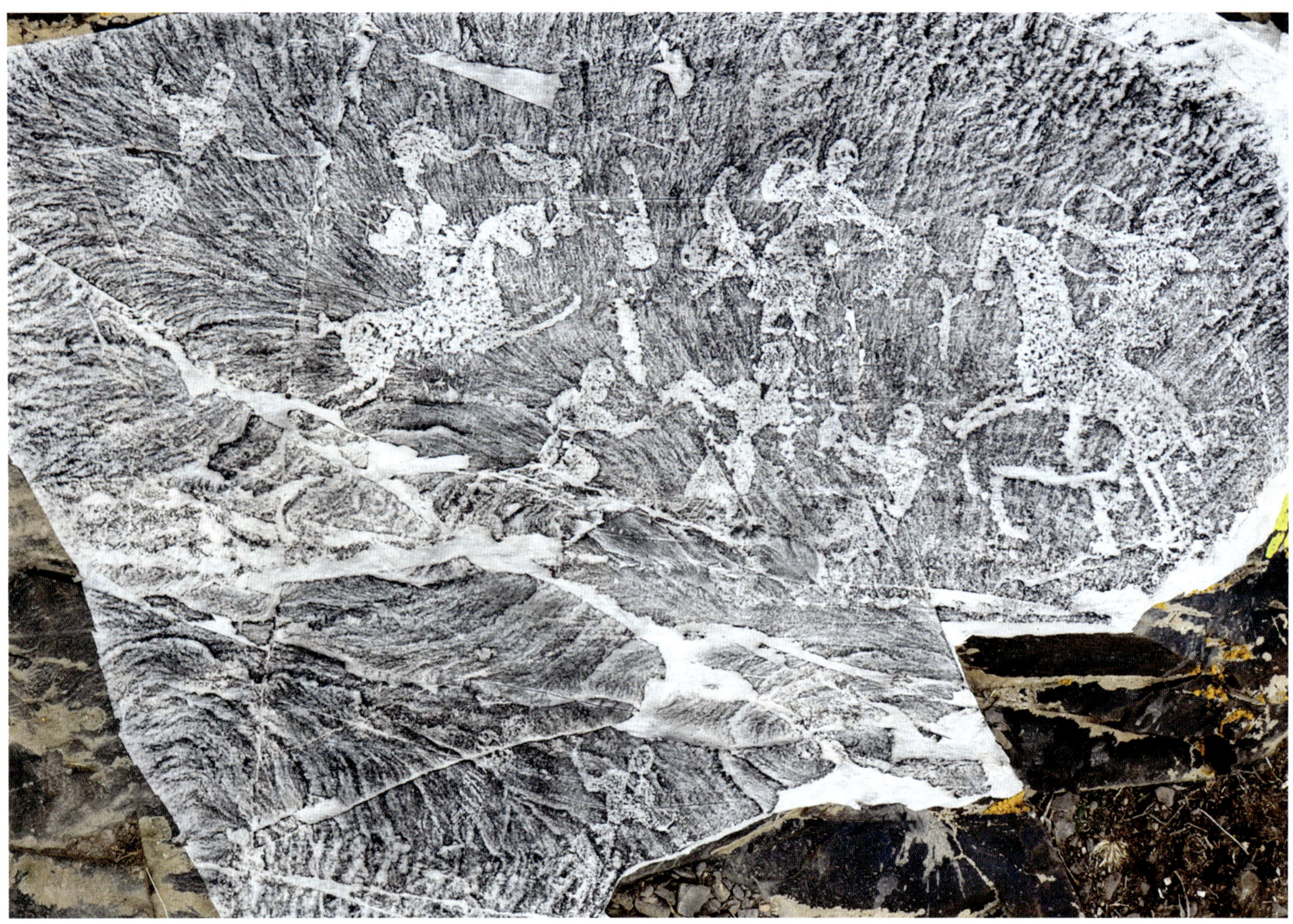

62. ↑ Rubbing taken *in situ* of a complex petroglyph scene from the Turkic period. From left to right in the upper part: a standing man holds a falcon on his right arm; a rider holding a mace rides on a galloping horse which seems to have two heads; above him two figures hold a wreath. To the right, a man wearing a long kaftan holds a smaller, kneeling man by the neck and threatens him with a ball-and-chain flail. Behind the standing man a bird is seen. Above this large central figure, a human seems to fly. From the right edge a mounted archer approaches with drawn arrow. In the middle part of the scene, a sitting man holds a drinking vessel, and in front of him stands a man wearing a long straight sword who fills the cup with a jug. Behind him stands a second man wearing a long straight sword and holding an elongated pitcher. At the bottom stand two other men; the one on the left seems to wear a coat of mail, while the other one raises a drinking cup in his right arm. The upper scene probably illustrates Sogdian–Zoroastrian lore, the central one strongly resembles banquet scenes on Sogdian paintings and stone carvings. (For an interpretation see the main text.) Kogaly Bastal, south Kazakhstan. Photo Alexey Rogozhinsky.

63. → Buddhist petroglyphs from the Dzungar period around 1710 CE. From left to right: Buddha Shakyamuni, Bodhisattva Avalokitesvara, the medicine Buddha Bhaishajyaguru. The petroglyph has been vandalized since 2005. Tamgaly-Tas, right bank of the Ili River, southern Kazakhstan. Photo 2005.

Such ceremonial staffs were a sign of nobility as seen in Sogdian murals from Panjikent dating from the seventh to eighth century CE.[190] Strangely, the horse seems to have two heads – or it may be the head of an unfinished second horse. The eminent character of this horseman is underscored by the two figures above his head who seem to hold a wreath over the horseman. Behind the mounted mace holder stands a man with outstretched arms who seems to be holding a falcon on his right lower arm, possibly the falcon of the seated khagan in the lower register. Under Sraosha are three people: to the left a man sits in a relaxed position and holds a drinking vessel; in front of him stands another man wearing a long straight sword, who fills the cup of the sitting man with a jug; behind him stands a third man wearing a long straight sword and holding an elongated pitcher. This scene is very similar to representations on Sino-Sogdian stone funeral beds and sarcophagi from the sixth to seventh century CE which feature a seated khagan and his respectful attendants.[191] Below this scene stand two further men: the smaller standing on the left might be wearing a coat of

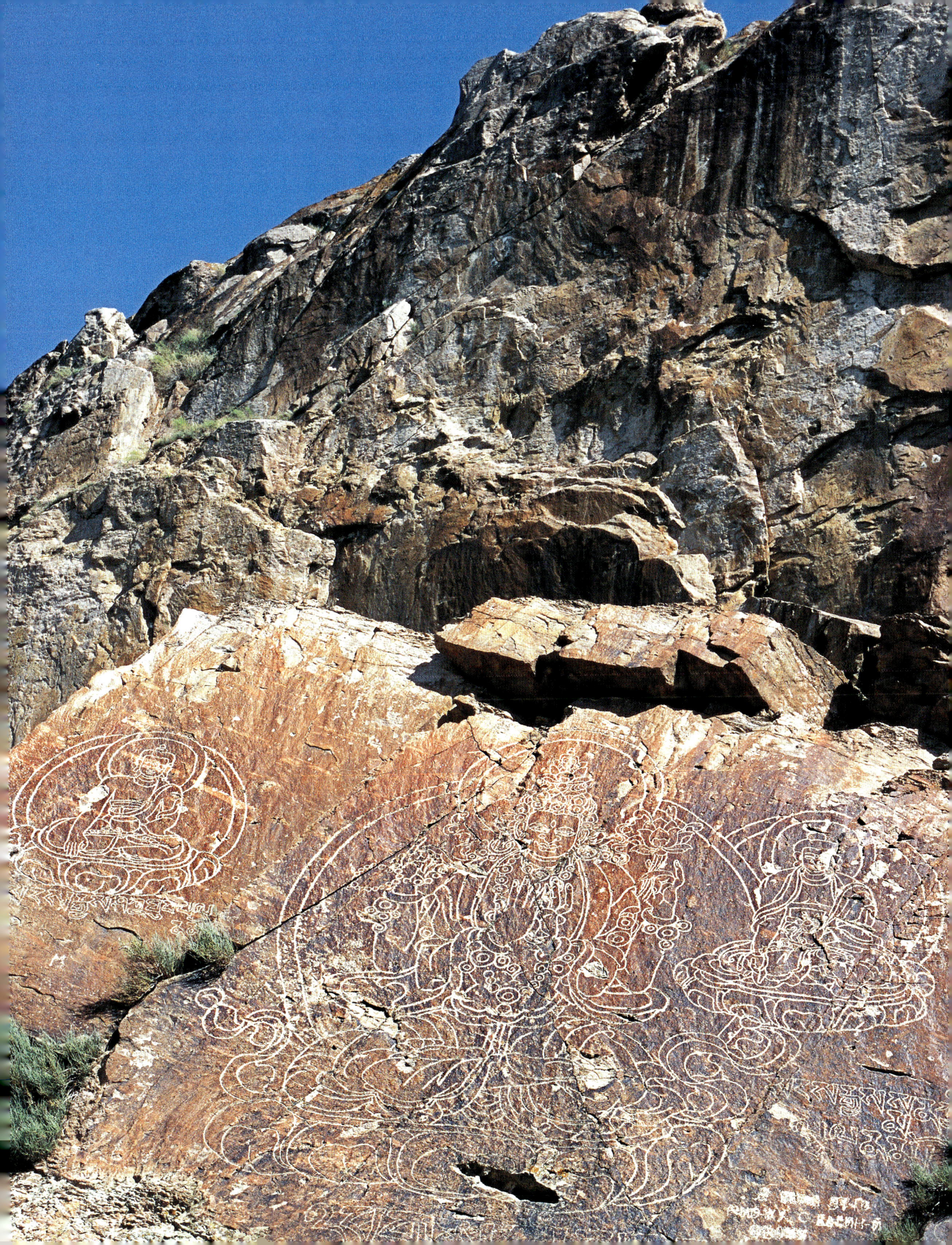

mail, while the larger figure at the right raises a drinking cup in his right hand. As explained by Alexey Rogozhinsky, all the figures, as well as their clothes and the style of the representations, strongly resemble Sogdian paintings and funeral stone carvings illustrating scenes derived from Sogdian Zoroastrianism and Turkic courtly life. From the same period dates a particular runic inscription at Tamgaly which is interpreted as a brief Manichaean prayer.[192]

On the Ustyurt Plateau in western Kazakhstan stands the sanctuary of **Bayte III** dating from the third to second century BCE, the epoch of the Saka Massagetae. It consisted of a temple with an overall circular floor plan of ten metres diameter surmounted by a two-tier domed cupola. A ditch surrounded the temple and behind the ditch stood an arc of 35 stone statues of warriors. The floor within was in the shape of an equilateral cross. Soon after its construction, the temple was damaged by an earthquake, after which local pastoralists and travellers chiselled hundreds of *tamgas* into its walls.[193] The Turkic term *tamga* (in Persian *nishan*) denotes, within the realm of Central Asia and Mongolia, a kind of legal mark regulating property, tribal affiliation and dynastic sovereignty. These signs were introduced by steppe people and identified private or communal property, the authorship of craftsmen such as potters, tribal allegiance, and, on coins, the ruling dynasty. In total, 273 different types of *tamgas* have been identified on the walls of the Bayte sanctuary which could indicate up to 273 different clans or groups. Also among them are the royal *tamgas* seen on Chorasmian coins minted between the first century BCE and the fourth century CE.[194] Numerous *tamgas* found at Bayte are identical to those used by the Alano-Sarmatians living in the Pontic Steppe from the early first century BCE to their eviction by the Huns before 375 CE.[195] These parallels are not surprising since the ancestors of the Sarmatians had migrated from the Ustyurt Plateau to the Pontic Steppe; the westward migration of *tamgas* illustrates the corresponding migration of the later Sarmatian horsemen.

On the walls of the temple figures and scenes combined with *tamgas* were also engraved. The following petroglyphs are especially revealing: a horseman with a lowered standard facing the entrance to a labyrinth; a mounted archer drawing an arrow on an already wounded ibex; a single-axle chariot next to a dead person lying on the ground, with a crawling snake just below it; another chariot beside two corpses; a horse standing in front of a standard fixed in the ground. Based on the clear association between the *tamgas* of Bayte and those of Alano-Sarmatians, Sergey Yatsenko and Jangar Ilyasov deciphered these petroglyphs by reference to the ancient Alano-Sarmatian mythology as it has been transmitted in Ossetian tradition.[196] The horseman with the lowered standard

shows the owner of the tomb as he prepares himself to enter the labyrinth that is the netherworld; the mounted archer symbolizes a mythical hunter pursuing an ungulate which was really a disguised female spirit enticing the hunter to follow her into the otherworld; one chariot carries the owner of the tomb to the realm of death while the snake suggests hope, since it can find the magic bead which can bring (temporal) resurrection. The other two corpses are possibly sacrificed servants; the horse and the standard indicate the favourite horse of the dead warrior and his burial standard. At the festivities held one year after the man's death, the standard would be burnt and his horse sacrificed. This interpretation is the more plausible since the grave of a young noble warrior had been dug next to the temple briefly after its construction.[197] The petroglyphs at Bayte III are an excellent example of how mythological records can help in deciphering rock art.

Occasionally, *tamgas* were made as huge geoglyphs. One exists at **Amangeldi**, Kazakhstan, another at **Chash-tepe**, Turkmenistan; both are located within ancient graveyards of the Hunnic Chionite people from the third to fourth century CE. The former has a diameter of 94 metres and a height of 80 centimetres and is in the shape of a three-legged swastika, the latter has a diameter of more than 40 metres and is in the shape of a four-legged swastika with crooked ends. The function of such huge *tamgas* remains unknown, seeing as they could only be recognized from a high viewpoint which is impossible in these plains. Yatsenko and Ilyasov surmise that these geoglyphs were a 'visual symbol of a joint efforts of different units of the same clan'.[198]

In Kazakhstan, the latest significant petroglyph site is **Tamgaly-Tas** with its Buddhist figures and inscriptions in Mongolic Oirat, Tibetan and Manchu. They were engraved by the Buddhist Oirats around 1710. The large images, up to two metres high, represent the historical Buddha Shakyamuni, Bodhisattva Avalokitesvara (in Tibetan, Chenrezig), the Dhyani Buddha Akshobhya (Mikyöpa), the medicine Buddha Bhaisajyaguru (Sangyé Menla) and the Buddhist master and proponent of Mahayana Buddhism, Nagarjuna.[199] Some of the inscriptions were added later in the course of the eighteenth century. Unfortunately, after the authors' visit in 2005 the Buddha figures were victims of deliberate vandalism; they were partly painted over and were the target of gunfire. Finally, the tradition of engraving petroglyphs continued in the so-called Ethnographic period, that is from the nineteenth century to the present. At several rock art sites within the former Soviet Union, portraits of Lenin, of pilots, tank drivers or ordinary soldiers as well as naked women were engraved.[200] In Kazakhstan, the tradition of rock art has remained especially alive up to the

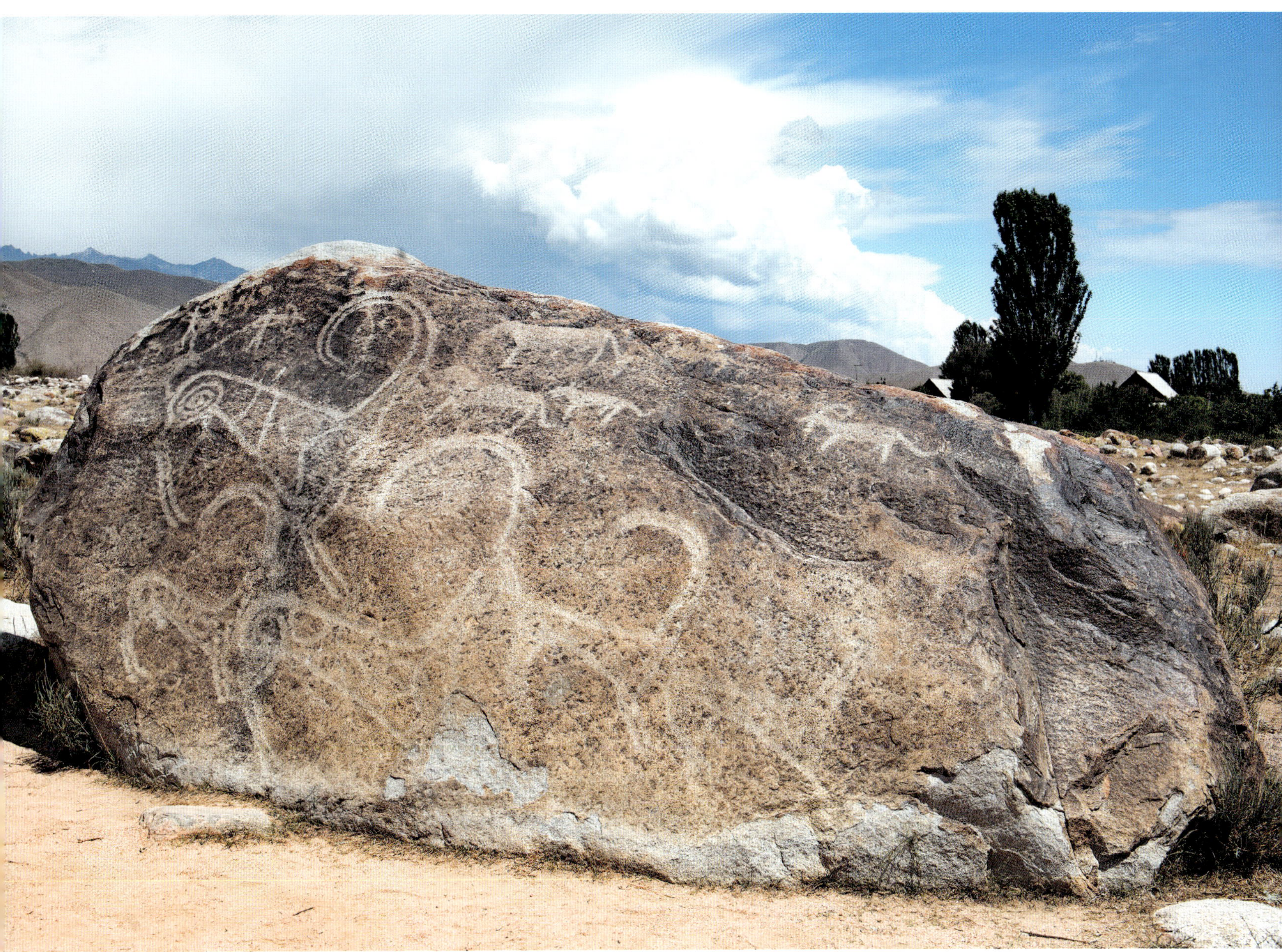

64. Ibexes in the Animal Style at Cholpon-Ata near the northern shore of Lake Issyk-Kul, north-eastern Kyrgyzstan. Iron Age. Photo 2017.

present day in the necropolises of the Ustyurt Plateau. Here, not only are the traditional stone statues of a ram which stands next to a tomb engraved with images of horses, battle axes, sabres and inscriptions,[201] but the mausolea themselves also bear rock art. On the outside walls, petroglyphs of camels, horses, ibexes, weapons and ships are engraved, while inside the walls are painted with things that were important for the deceased, such as a car, camels, guns or oil rigs and production plants. Such decoration of the inside walls of a mausoleum continues a tradition among Turkic people as described in a Chinese chronicle from the Tang Dynasty (618–907 CE): 'They [the Turks] built a house on the grave, draw his picture on the interior walls and specify the wars he fought ...'[202]

4. Kyrgyzstan

Like Kazakhstan and Tajikistan, Kyrgyzstan is fully landlocked. The landscape of Kyrgyzstan is more than 80 per cent mountainous; it is dominated by the Tian Shan and Pamir-Alay mountain ranges which account for two-thirds of Kyrgyzstan's territory. Due to its many high mountains which act as moisture catchers, Kyrgyzstan is relatively well watered. Climatic development in the larger part of Kyrgyzstan, dominated by the Tian Shan Mountains, was similar to that in southern Kazakhstan. The climate in the region of the Alay Range in the south-east of Kyrgyzstan underwent a more arid development and tends to be drier.

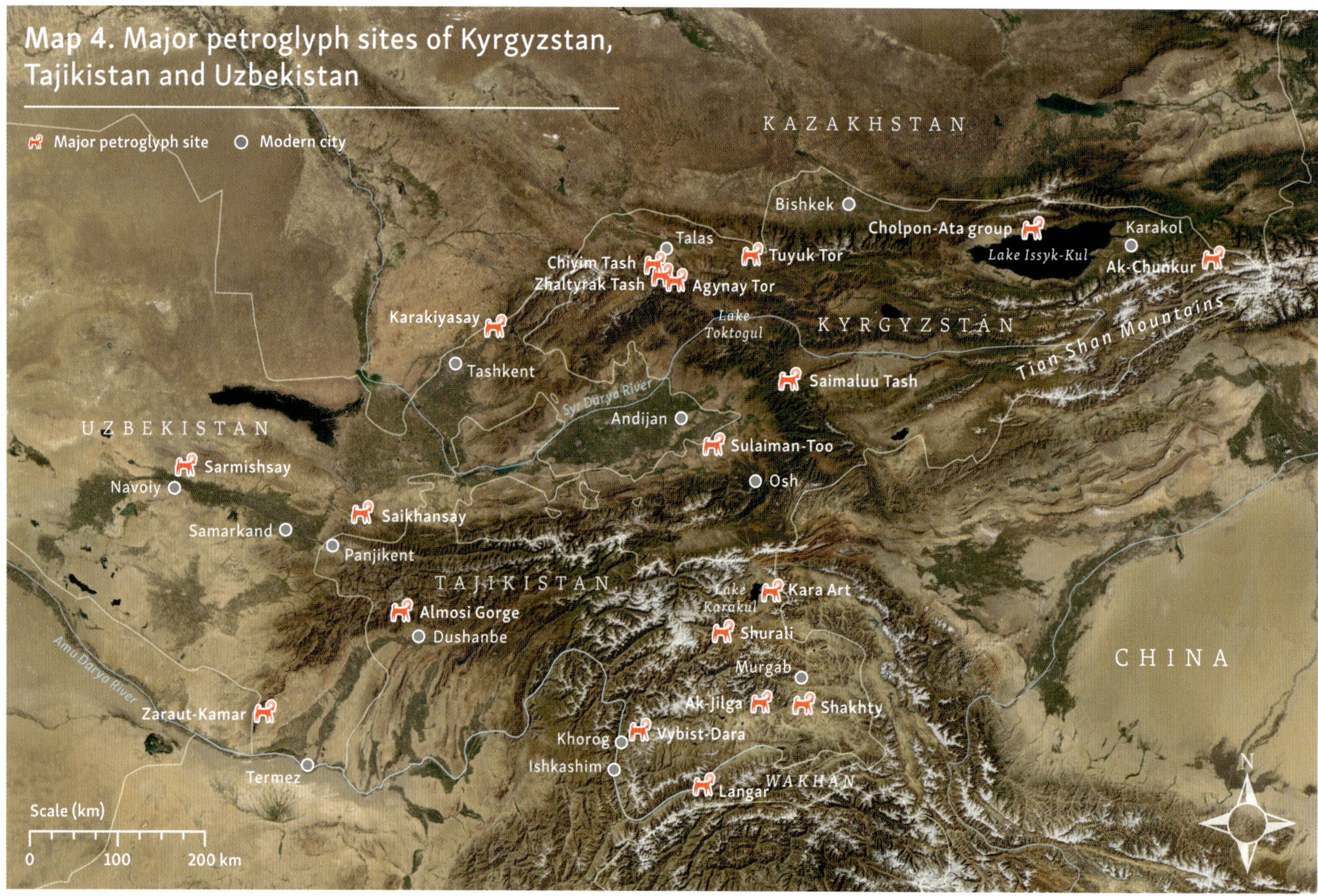

Some of the most important sites are, in chronological order:

- **Ak-Chunkur** is a cave located in the Tian Shan Mountains at an altitude of 3,151 m asl in north-eastern Kyrgyzstan. The red paintings, made with ochre, probably date from the later Neolithic, sixth to fifth millennium BCE; they represent humans, ibexes and geometric symbols. Unfortunately, they are covered by soot from torches lit by tourists and from fires made by local shepherds.

- **Saimaluu Tash** is a high-altitude site that is situated above 3,000 m asl and is one of the richest and largest petroglyph sites of Central Asia. It is located in the eastern Fergana Range, part of the Tian Shan. The petroglyphs date mainly from the Bronze Age and early Iron Age.

- **Zhaltyrak Tash** is another alpine site located 50 km south of Talas in north-western Kyrgyzstan. It is famous for its petroglyphs from the later Bronze Age and especially for its early Iron Age Saka images made in the typical Saka Animal Style.

- **Agynay Tor** is about three km north of Zhaltyrak Tash; this small site features petroglyphs from the Bronze and Iron Age.

- **Sulaiman-Too**, 'Solomon's throne', is a mountain in the city of Osh, south-western Kyrgyzstan. Its petroglyphs date from the later Bronze Age to the Turkic period. Although it is a UNESCO World Heritage site, numerous petroglyphs have been vandalized by spray paint.

- **Cholpon-Ata**, **Ornok**, **Kara-Oy** and **Baetovo** are four connected sites at the northern shore of Lake Issyk-Kul. They are especially rich in petroglyphs from the Saka and Wusun[203] Iron Age periods.

- **Tuyuk Tor** at the Karakol River, Talas oblast, north-western Kyrgyzstan. This smaller site contains a wide selection of motifs dating from the Bronze Age to the Middle Ages.

- **Chiyim Tash** is situated 24 km north-west of Zhaltyrak Tash at an altitude of *ca*. 2,900 m asl, with a second site 200 m higher. Besides Bronze Age petroglyphs of animals, humans and vehicles, its interest lies in its various Turkic *tamgas*.

The more or less connected sites of **Cholpon-Ata**, **Ornok**, **Kara-Oy** and **Baetovo** are located on the northern shore of Lake Issyk-Kul and form an elongated rectangle of approximately twenty square kilometres. The petroglyphs were pecked and carved into the dark patina of granite and granitoid boulders which came down millennia ago from the Küngöy Ala-Too Range to the north. Although the region has been settled at least since the Neolithic, most of the petroglyphs date from the Saka and Wusun Iron Ages (ninth to third century BCE and second century BCE to fifth century CE respectively). Unfortunately, parts of the complex were destroyed in the 1930s and 1970s when the airport of Cholpon-Ata was built and later enlarged. A second calamity struck in the year 2002 when some of Cholpon-Ata's most impressive petroglyphs were treated with Paraloid B-72, a thermoplastic resin used in fossil preparation, without sufficient testing. As the author noticed in 2004, the result was very unsatisfactory since the petroglyphs were now covered by a greyish film. Furthermore, Paraloid B-72 changes characteristics of the rock and its patina. In the 2010s, this acrylic fixative was removed from some of the boulders.[204]

Besides numerous petroglyphs of ibexes, deer with pronounced antlers, wolves and dogs attacking deer, bulls, snow leopards, camels, hunting scenes, horsemen and camel riders duelling with lances or javelins, there are some notable petroglyphs outside Cholpon-Ata proper. For example, on the so-called 'Five Shamans' stone at Ornok it is in fact not shamans that are depicted but dismounted steppe horsemen who wear a kind of kaftan and are armed with swords (fig. 65). Another scene at Kara-Oy illustrates a horseman catching a deer with a sling attached to a long pole, as is still practised today in Mongolia for catching horses. Also at Kara-Oy is an image of two unusually large deer from the Saka period (fig. 66).[205] On another boulder at Kara-Oy, a fantastic animal has feet of an almost circular shape and a head surrounded by a kind of unfinished, double halo of rays. Again at Kara-Oy, on a boulder one metre high, two men stand next to each other armed with battle axes; one of them holds a smaller, unarmed human by a sling fixed to his neck. Possibly this scene hints at an execution or human sacrifice.

The large site of **Saimaluu Tash** lies in the eastern part of the Fergana Mountain Range, about 115 kilometres north-east of the city of Osh. Due to its altitude – which ranges from 2,860 to 3,350 metres above sea level – the site is covered by snow for ten to eleven months of the year and is only accessible in peak summer. Since the snow protects the stones from rapid temperature fluctuations, they are exceptionally well preserved. The difficult access, involving a strenuous ascent and crossing a small glacier, further protects the

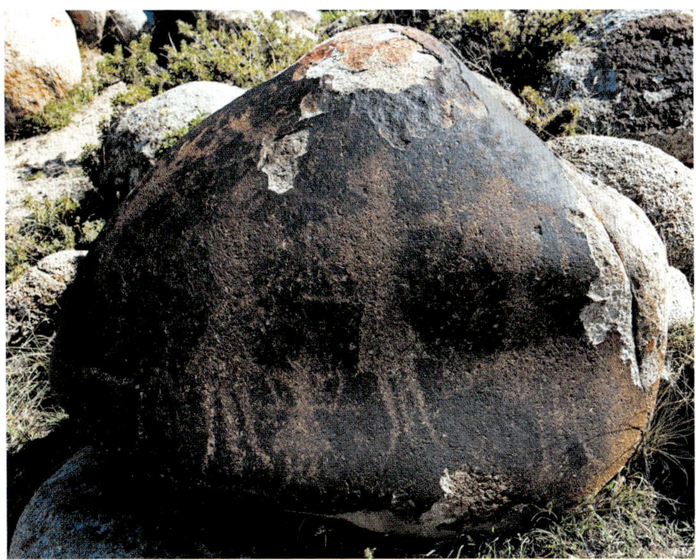

65. One juvenile and four adult men wearing kaftans and armed with swords. Ornok, near the northern shore of Lake Issyk-Kul. Iron Age, north-eastern Kyrgyzstan. Photo 2017.

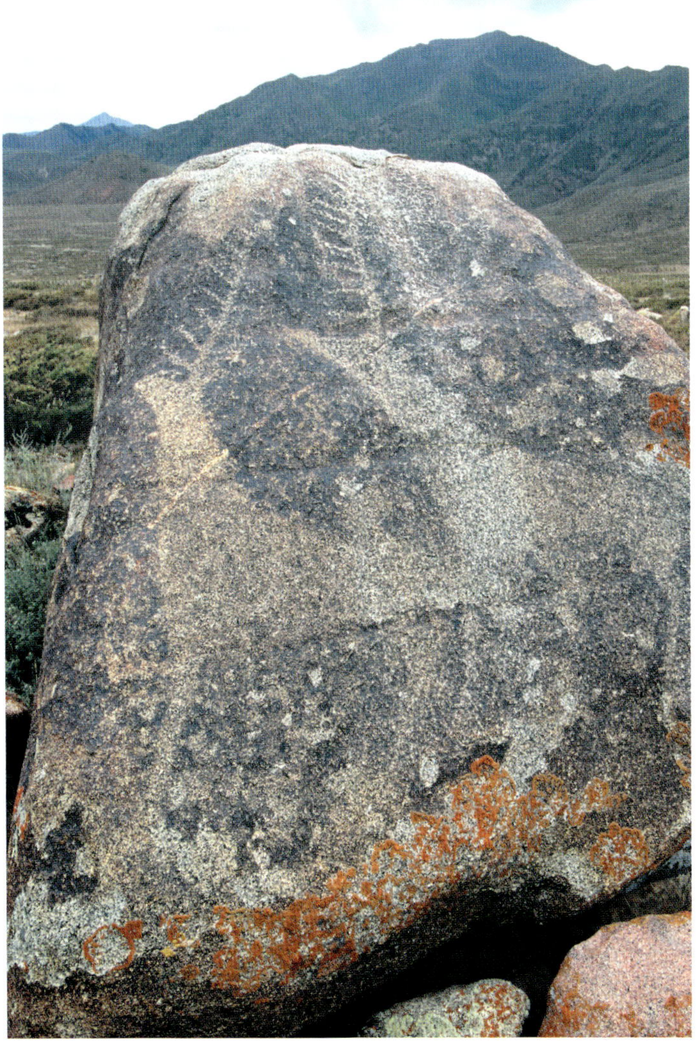

66. Two-metre-high deer with upright, fir tree-like antlers. Kara-Oy, near the northern shore of Lake Issyk-Kul. Iron Age, north-eastern Kyrgyzstan. Photo 2005.

petroglyphs from vandalism.[206] Although most of the petroglyphs at Saimaluu Tash are quite small, they were deeply pecked and great attention was given to details. They date mainly from the Bronze Age (2200–900 BCE) and the Iron Age (900 BCE–450 CE); a few belong to the Turkic period (450–900 CE). The locations of the petroglyphs extend over two valleys, divided by a steep ridge. Saimaluu Tash I represents the most important site and lies in the western valley, while the smaller and slightly less ancient Saimaluu Tash II is located along the upper edges of the neighbouring eastern valley. Here some Iron Age kurgans were excavated, but no traces of settlements were identified.[207] The former, larger site is located in a glacial corrie containing several moraine deposits; it stretches over a length of 1,800 metres; its maximum width is just over one kilometre, resulting in a total area of about 1.9 square kilometres. The majority of petroglyphs are to be found along a stretch of moraine 496 metres long (figs 68, 69). The second, smaller site measures a little under one square kilometre. In total, there are about 5,000 to 6,000 basaltic stones, covered with a relatively thick crust of shiny dark grey varnish, which are adorned with petroglyphs, amounting to between 30,000 and 35,000 individual images.[208]

The name of the site provides a strong clue to its nature, as 'Saimaluu Tash' means 'stones with drawings' in Kyrgyz. It was officially rediscovered by the military topographer Nikolai G. Khludov in 1902. He was followed by General I.T. Poslavsky who visited the site only briefly yet confirmed its importance. Nevertheless, it was more than 40 years till B.M. Zima resumed research in 1946. One of the reasons for this neglect was the fact that in the earlier 1920s the Fergana Mountain Range, and hence also Saimaluu Tash, were a refuge for the Muslim anti-Soviet Basmachi fighters. Then in the following decades the Stalinist Great Terror and World War II paralysed most archaeological work. After Zima, A.N. Bernshtam conducted major research in 1950; he erroneously assumed that the petroglyphs in the moraine of Saimaluu I had originally been pecked into cliff faces which were later destroyed by a huge earthquake.[209]

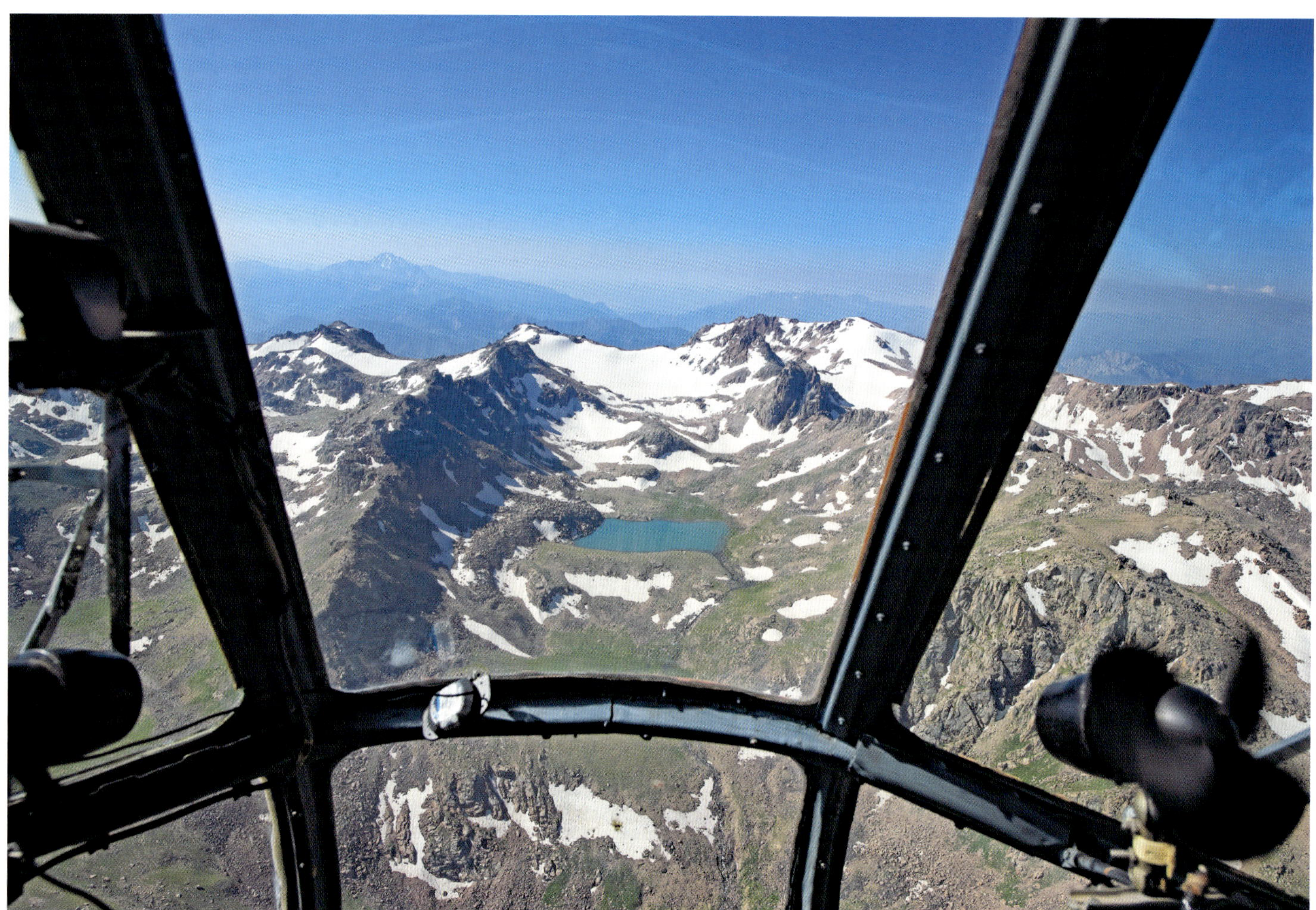

67. Approaching by helicopter the Fergana Mountain range towards Saimaluu Tash, Kyrgyzstan. Photo 2017.

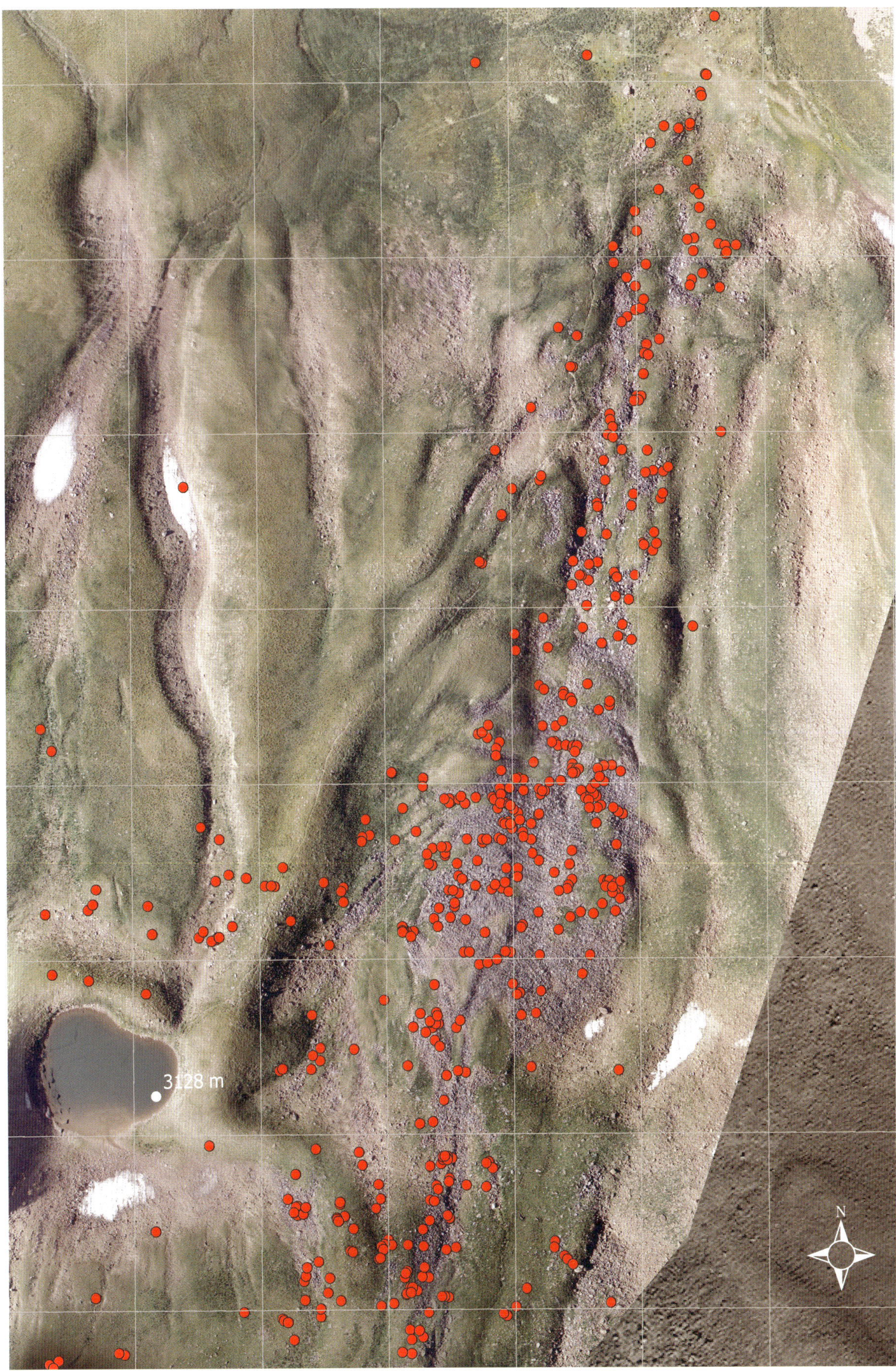

68. Aerial map showing the distribution of petroglyph sites in the main moraine of Saimaluu Tash I, Kyrgyzstan. Lateral moraines have additional petroglyphs which are not featured in this map. The location of the petroglyphs was surveyed using Global Navigation Satellite System (GNSS) receivers with decimetre accuracy. Made by Matthias Schenker and Thomas Koblet. © Christoph Baumer and ESRI, Zurich.

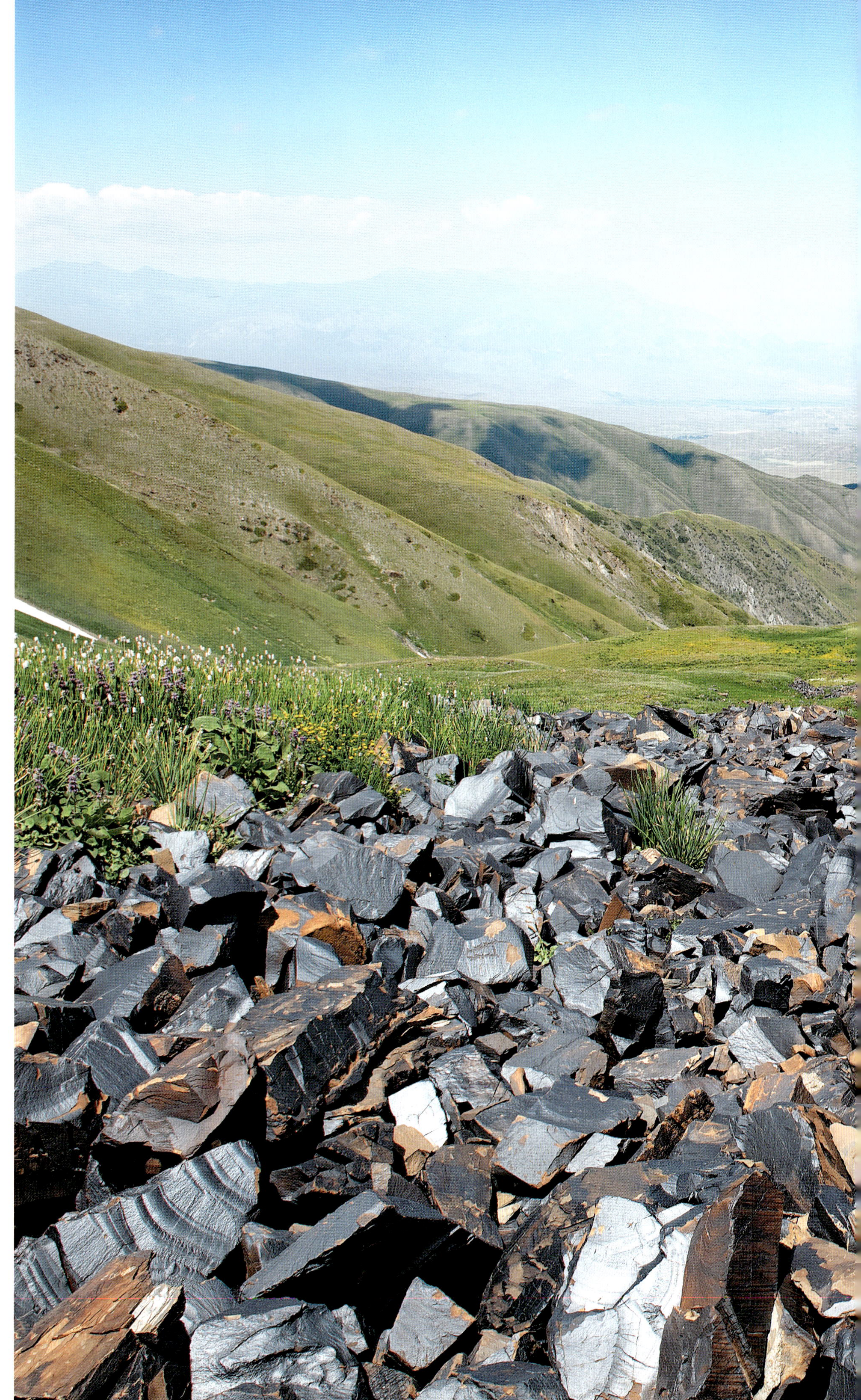

69. The main moraine at Saimaluu Tash I looking north. A mountain path is engraved in the rock at the right. Photograph taken at 3,140 m asl. Kyrgyzstan. Photo 2017.

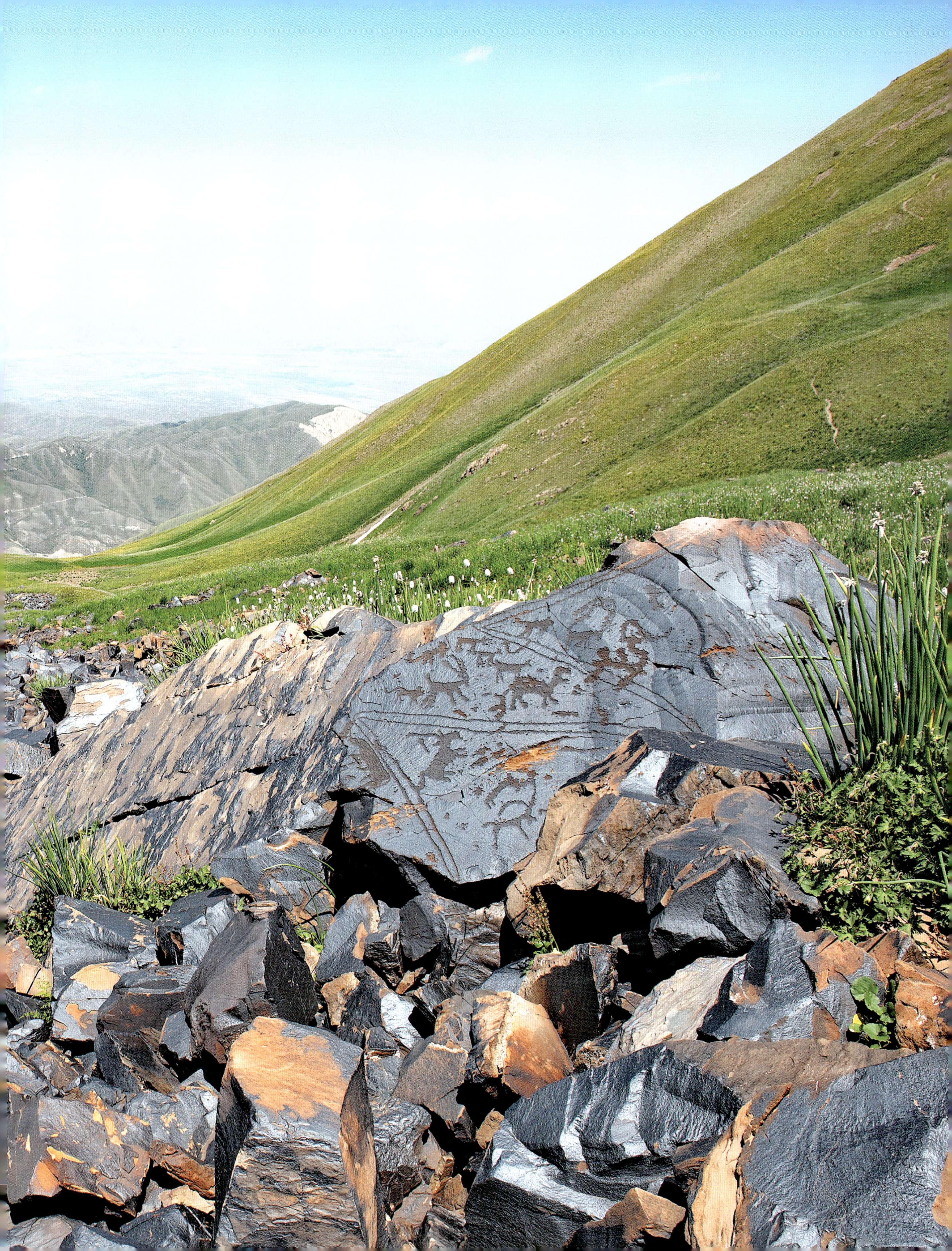

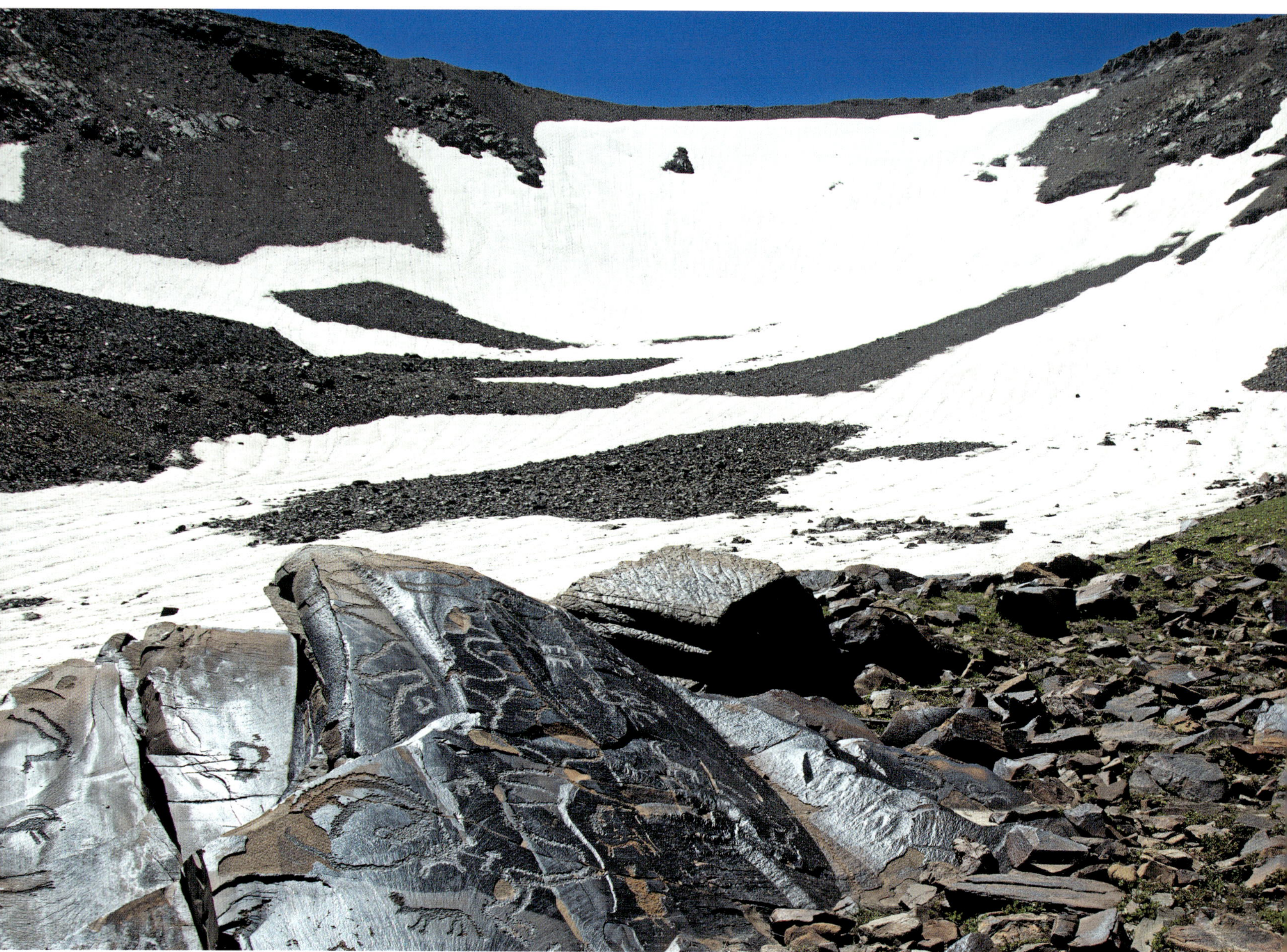

70. On the boulder in the foreground are petroglyphs of two ibexes with extremely long horns, behind are two wavy lines which represent either mountain paths or rivers. Saimaluu Tash II, Kyrgyzstan. Photo 2017.

Pecking of petroglyphs began at Saimaluu Tash in the earlier Bronze Age, around 2000 BCE, when the climate in the alpine regions of the Kyrgyz Tian Shan became warmer and moister. Alpine glaciers were retreating and the tree line was advancing upwards, creating favourable conditions for an expansion of agriculture into the foothills. While crop cultivation flourished in the lower valleys, a semi-mobile pastoral economy thrived in the uplands. These pastoralists practised seasonal vertical migration that led them all the way to the steep grass slopes of Saimaluu Tash, which in those days were free of snow for several months. Images from this period include both arable and pastoral scenes, such as ploughing and simple carts being pulled by oxen. Erotic representations and sun symbols also occur; an analysis of their distribution revealed that they occasionally appear in the vicinity of ploughing scenes. In one scene, 18 humans are copulating in groups of two and three, and a snake stands in the centre of the scene (fig. 80).[210] The clustering of these symbols would fit with the presence of a fertility cult. By the middle to later Bronze Age, the climate became warmer and more arid, bringing a reduction in crop growing in favour of cattle breeding. This trend was accelerated by the arrival of migrating Andronovian pastoralists from the north.[211]

By the advent of the Iron Age (*ca.* 900 BCE), semi-mobile pastoralism was the dominant way of life in Fergana. This coincided with the disappearance of ploughing scenes, solar symbols and figures with arms raised (presumably in devotion or dancing) from the petroglyph repertoire.[212] Instead, the dominant motifs were now stylized archers, deer and ibexes shown in the Steppe Animal Style, as well as horses, wolves and snow leopards attacking herbivores. Ithyphallic figures also vanished, with virility now expressed by the bearing of weapons. Finally, earlier representations of carts with plain wheels drawn by oxen were replaced by light chariots with spoked wheels pulled by horses. As in north-western Mongolia and Kazakhstan, the mastering of horse riding and the introduction of iron led to the emergence of a martial culture. This new worldview is reflected in an increasing number of petroglyphs featuring horsemen and duels between mounted archers as well as archers fighting on foot. Around 2,000 years ago, the glaciers were advancing once more in the alpine regions. Very cold and dry winters alongside cold summers led to a regression of grass meadows and a drop in the tree line, which today lies around 2,300 to 2,400 metres above sea level. Only a very few petroglyphs belong to this period. Finally, from around 500 CE, the climate warmed once again. In the valleys, crop cultivation regained its importance. Alpine pastures, though, were still used during the summer months, as witnessed by petroglyphs dating to the Turkic period, including a few *tamgas*. Whereas petroglyphs of *tamgas* are usually found at lower altitudes, they occasionally also occur in alpine regions, for example at the above named site of Chiyim Tash. In the lowlands, pastures were probably often marked as the property of individual families or clans, whereas in the high mountains there were collective rights of use.

It is a characteristic of the Saimaluu Tash petroglyphs that they often stand in relation to each other and depict scenes involving hunting, ploughing, carnivores chasing herbivores, duelling archers, and mountain landscapes intersected by paths or rivers and dotted with animals, humans and solar figures.

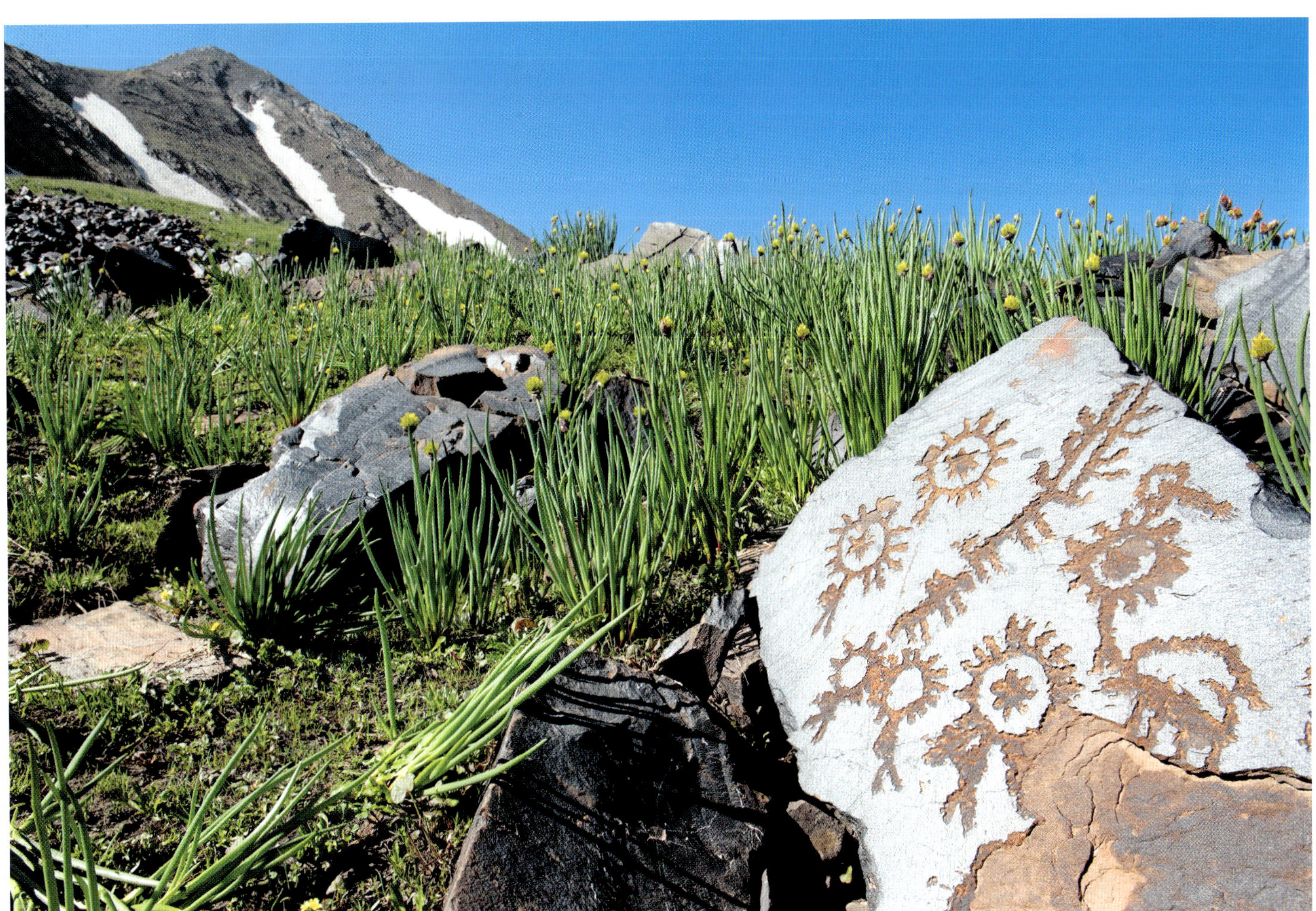

71. Solar figures and a deer with huge antlers. Bronze Age, Saimaluu Tash I, Kyrgyzstan. Photo 2017.

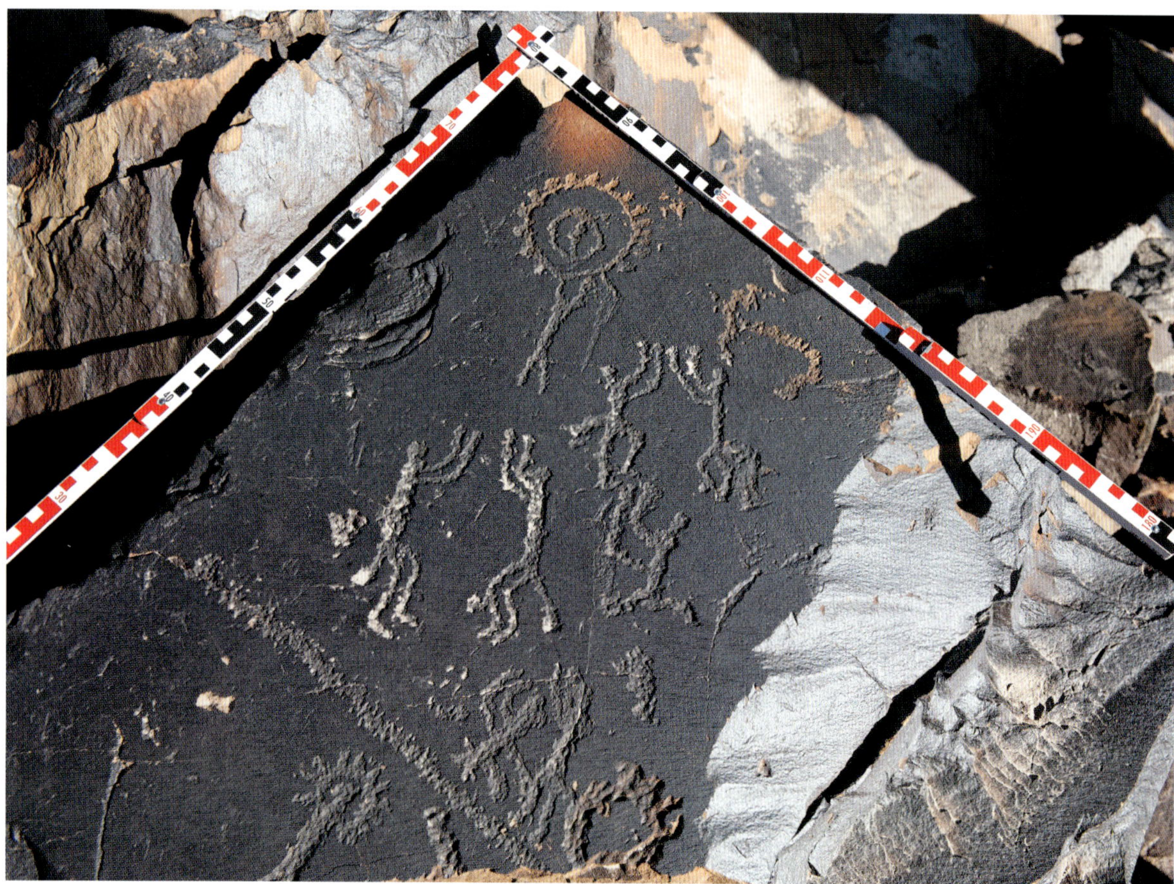

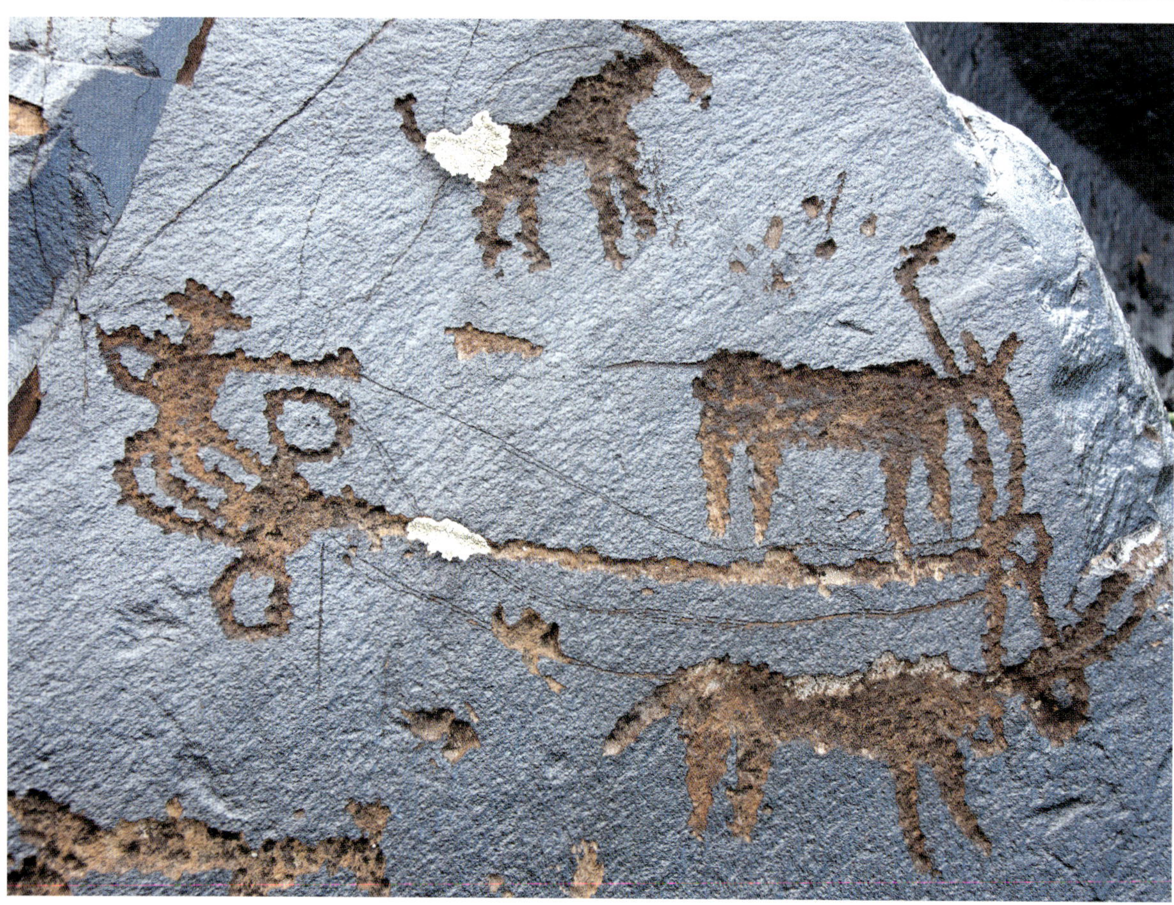

72. ← Above, a human holds a solar disc; below, orants lift their arms towards the sun. Bronze Age, Saimaluu Tash I, Kyrgyzstan. Photo 2017.

73. ↙ A charioteer standing on the floor of a light chariot. The front horse wears a pair of horns. Bronze Age, Saimaluu Tash I, Kyrgyzstan. Photo 2017.

74. → Three complete and one fragmentary ploughing scene with mixed draught animals. Bronze Age, Saimaluu Tash I, Kyrgyzstan. Photo 2017.

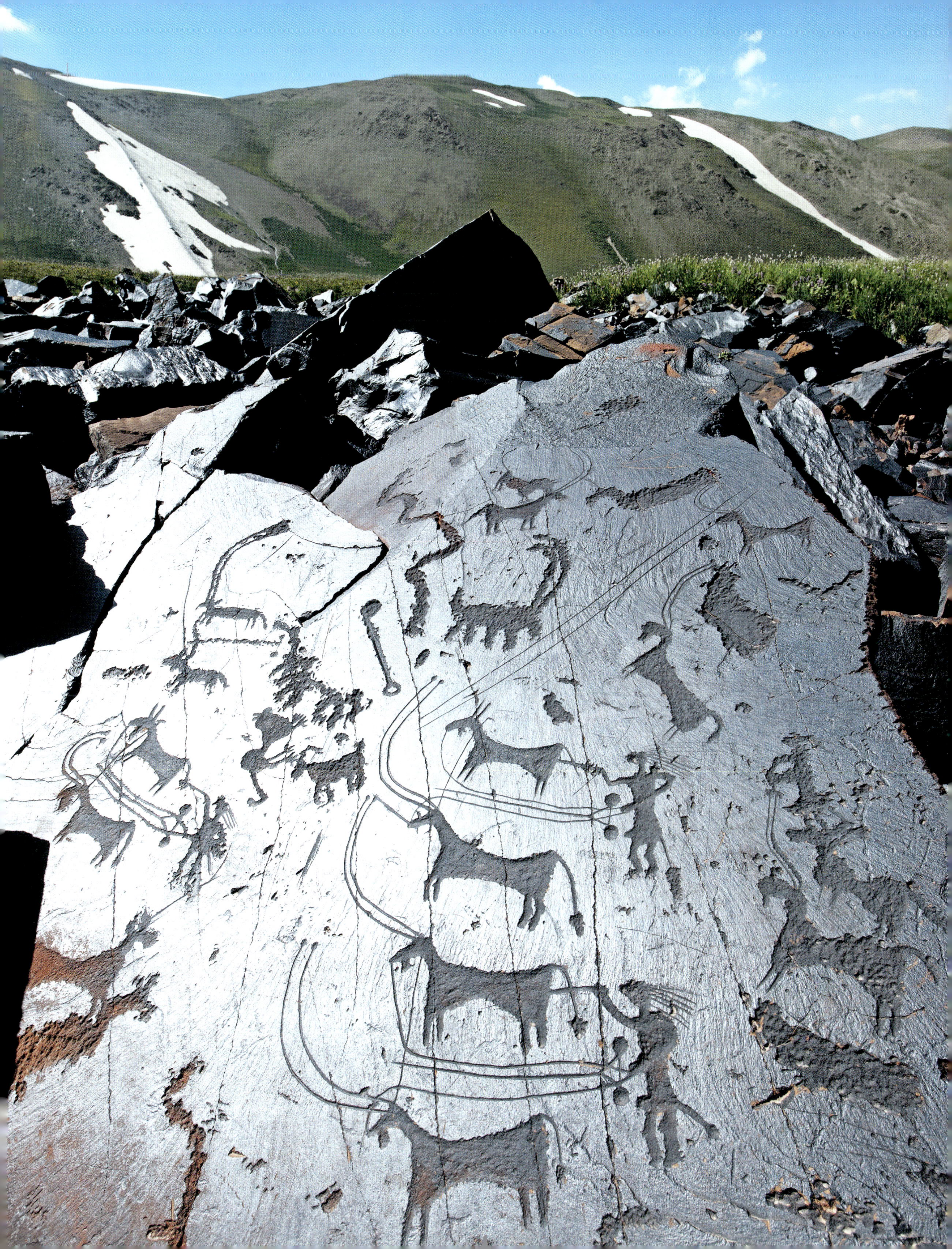

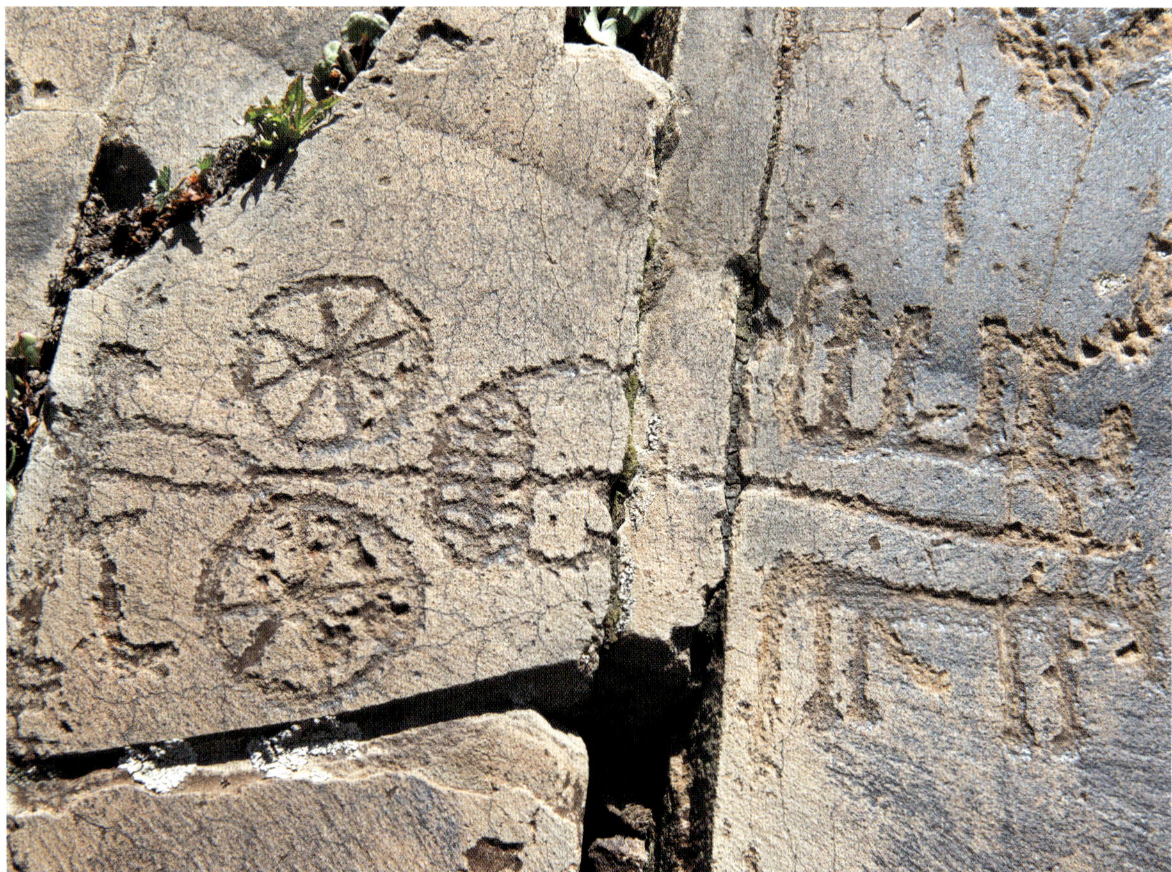

75. An ithyphallic man walking behind a light chariot with spoked wheels. Bronze Age, Saimaluu Tash I, Kyrgyzstan. Photo 2017.

A few motifs at Saimaluu Tash deserve special attention. In particular, there is a unique group of roughly 50 depictions of wheeled vehicles and tools. These range from early two-wheel frame ploughs with tiny (or even no) wheels, to double-axle wagons and, finally, more than two dozen light chariots. As Bernshtam hypothesized, the Bronze Age petroglyphs of a (sometimes ithyphallic) man with braided hair walking behind a harnessed pair of animals probably represent ploughing scenes involving a frame plough with miniature wheels – although the possibility that they depict a driver following his cart on foot, as postulated by Yakov Sher, cannot be entirely excluded (fig. 74).[213] It is striking that the plough drivers' braided hair is shown stretched out straight like rays of the sun. A solar reference is all the more likely as figures on neighbouring stones either lift sun discs above their heads or represent some kind of sun-headed anthropomorphs. Conceptually similar sun-headed figures from the same period are found in Kazakhstan, especially at Tamgaly, in Khakassia and on older stone steles of the Okunev culture (2400–1750 BCE). The tails visible on some figures evoke the fur jackets worn at that time, or maces or ball flails. That ball flails were part of Bronze Age weaponry is shown in another scene where at least twelve men are fighting, or performing a mock fight, with ball flails and bows and arrows.

Ploughing images are unusual within the wider corpus of Central Asian petroglyphs, and so too is the pairing of different harnessed draft animals, such as a bull and a horse, a bull and a donkey, or a bull and a goat. Given that combining different animals in a single harness is possible but not really practical, these petroglyphs surely have a mythological significance.[214] This interpretation fits with some petroglyphs of 'bulls', identified by their long horns, that have the body of a horse like at the above-mentioned site of Tamgaly in Kazakhstan. A pairing of different draft animals appears in the mythologies of at least three cultures speaking Indo-European languages.[215] First, a text from Hattusa, once the capital of the Hittite Empire, describes the ritual harnessing of a horse and a mule to a chariot. Then, in Greek mythology, Apollo pairs two lions with two boars to the chariot of Admetus who had to drive it to King Pelias, while Dionysus is represented driving a chariot pulled by a team of various beasts, such as a bull, a griffin and a lion.[216] Finally, in the hymns of the Indian *Rig Veda*,[217] the youthful twin divine horsemen known as the Ashvins harness not only winged horses to their chariot, but also a bull and a porpoise.[218] Indeed, a scene featuring a chariot team consisting of two horses and a bull is also found on an Indian

76. Two horses pull a solar disc behind them. Bronze Age, Saimaluu Tash II, Kyrgyzstan. Photo 2017.

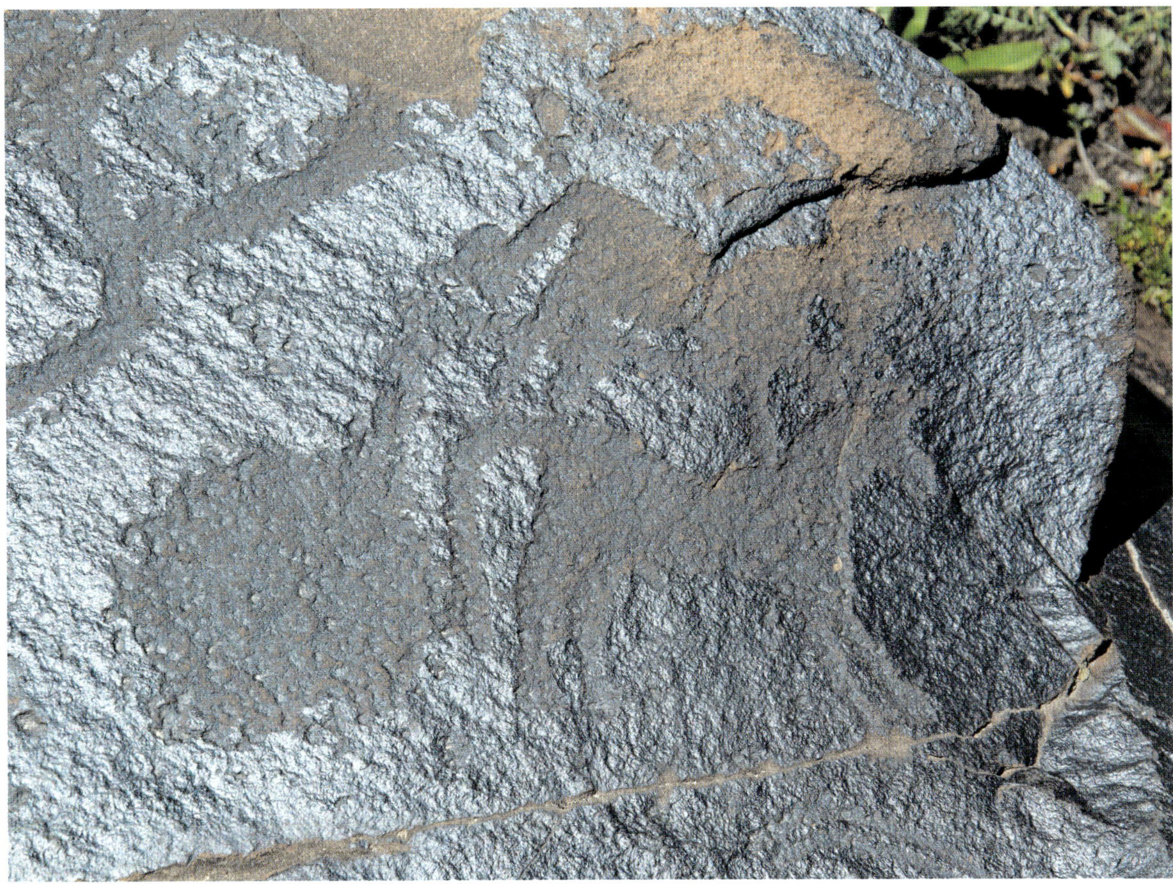

77. A bull charges a solar disc. Bronze Age, Saimaluu Tash I. Bronze Age, Saimaluu Tash I, Kyrgyzstan. Photo 2017.

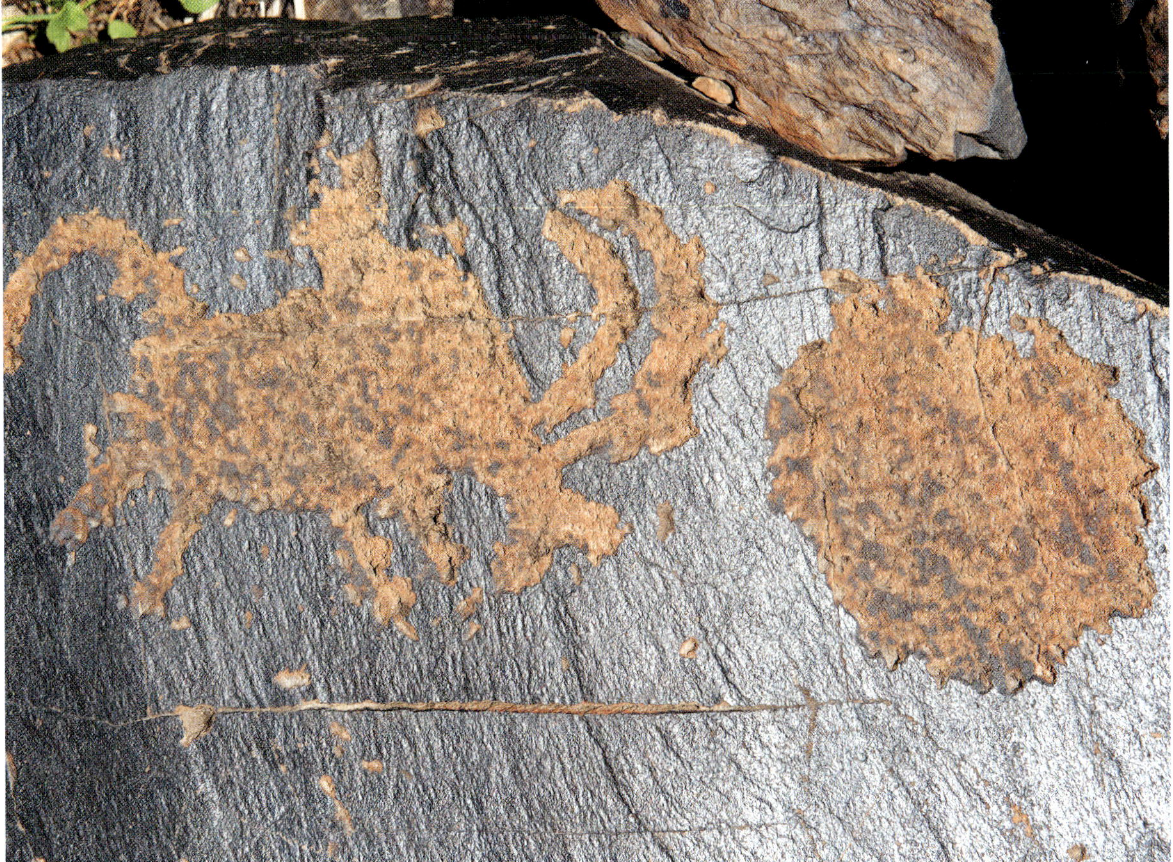

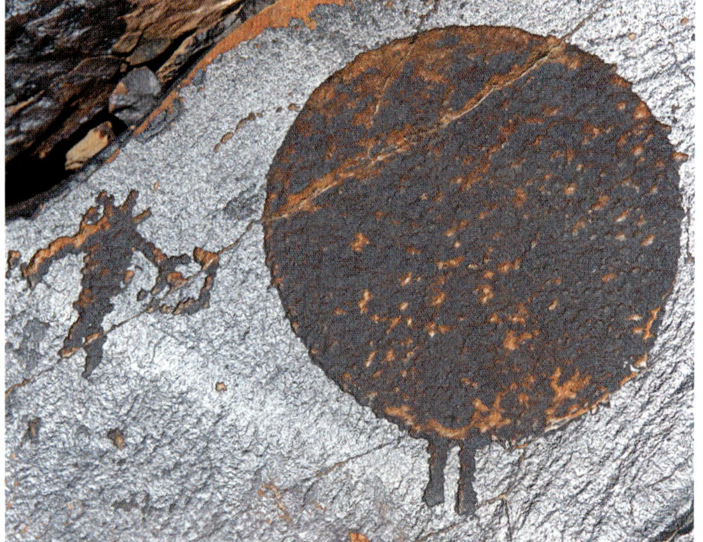

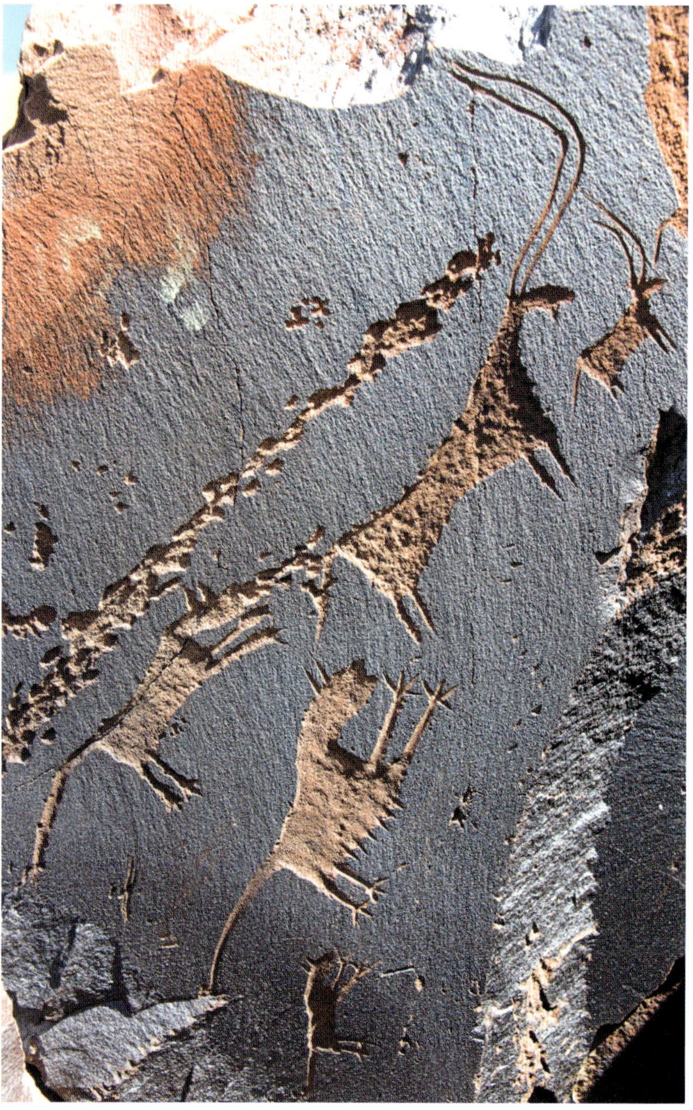

bronze libation cup from the Maurya Period, dating 235–185 BCE and now in the Cleveland Museum of Art.[219] It is probable that the Andronovian Indo-European immigrants shared their mythological worldview with the inhabitants of the Fergana region, from which a combined agrarian fertility and solar cult arose. The ploughing scenes at Saimaluu Tash may, then, be interpreted as the visualization of a cultic enactment of a ritual believed to ensure fertility. Yet the pairing of different animals can also be viewed as a magical attempt to combine the venerated attributes of different animals into a single team under human control. By harnessing two different animals on the same yoke, the commanding figure symbolically magnifies the power at his disposal. A similar mythological mechanism was observed in the petroglyphs of Tamgaly mentioned above, showing horses with bull horns, and the burial custom encountered in the Altai and Kazakhstan where sacrificed horses were adorned with bovines' and caprines' horns made from leather. The juxtaposition of ploughs and chariots in a confined space indicates that the Saimaluu Tash petroglyphs were inspired by an agrarian as well as a nomadic worldview.

It is striking that petroglyphs featuring single-axle battle chariots are also plentiful within this mountainous landscape. These chariots are clearly distinguished from the two-wheel frame ploughs by the light, eight-spoke wheels and the platform on which the charioteer stands. Such a prominent presence at Saimaluu Tash within the rugged Fergana Range – where chariots obviously had no practical use – is once again best understood within a mythological framework. Its source can again be traced to the early Andronovians, who came from the cultural realm of Sintashta, in the eastern Ural region, where the origins of the light battle chariot can be found around 2000 BCE. Chariots are often mentioned in the *Rig Veda* and in the Iranian Avesta as the vehicles of gods, mainly deities associated with the sun, such as Surya, Agni, Indra or Mithra. Intriguingly, in some scenes at Saimaluu Tash the charioteer does not stand in the chariot but walks behind it while holding the reins, or even pushes the chariot harnessed to horses, which might also serve to emphasize the sacred character

---

78. ⬉ An archer stands in front of a solar disc with tiny legs. Bronze Age, Saimaluu Tash I, Kyrgyzstan. Photo 2017.

79. ⬅ A male and a female predator, probably wolves, attack a hybrid animal with the body of a horse and disproportionately long bull's horns. Bronze Age, Saimaluu Tash I, Kyrgyzstan. Photo 2017.

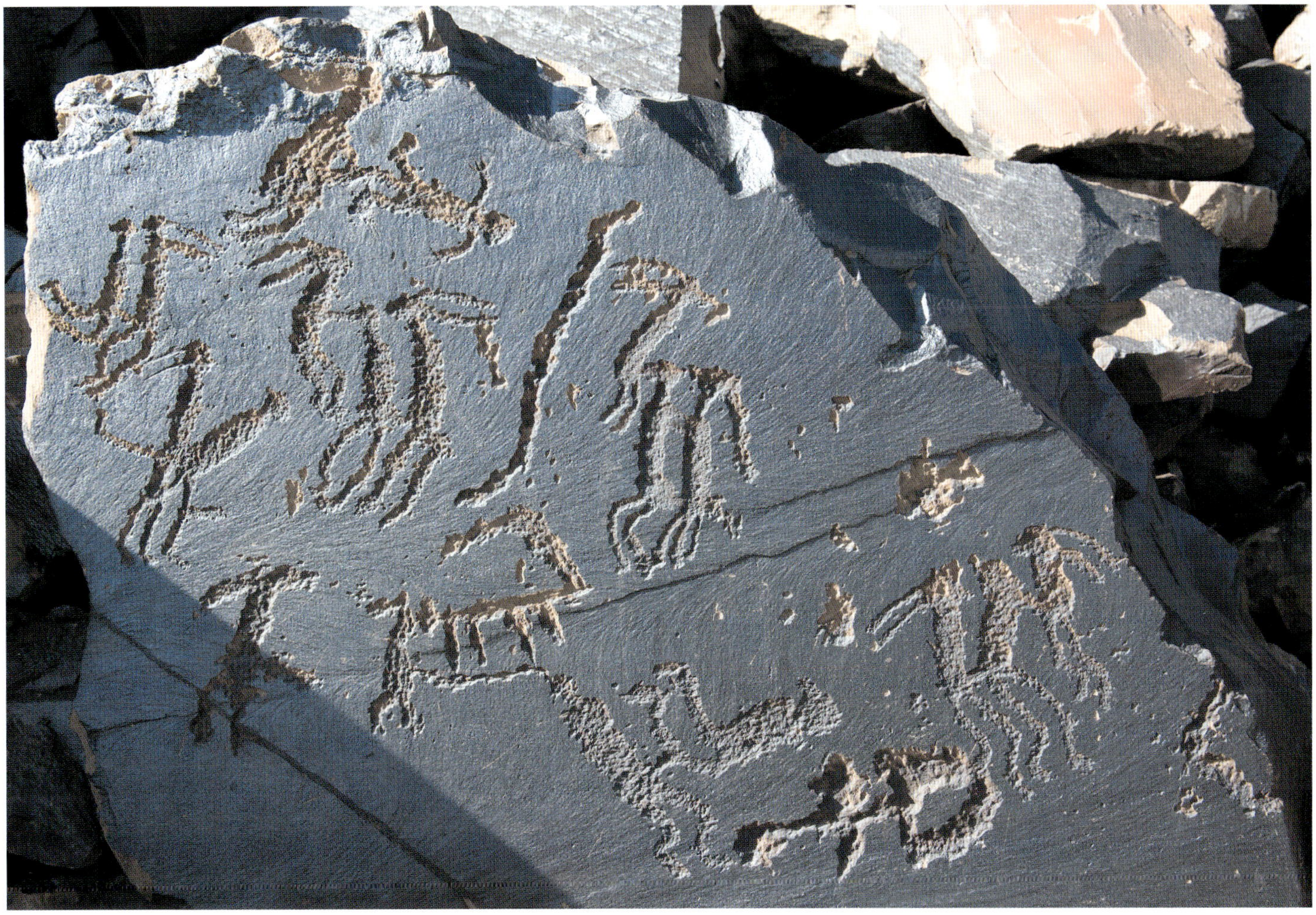

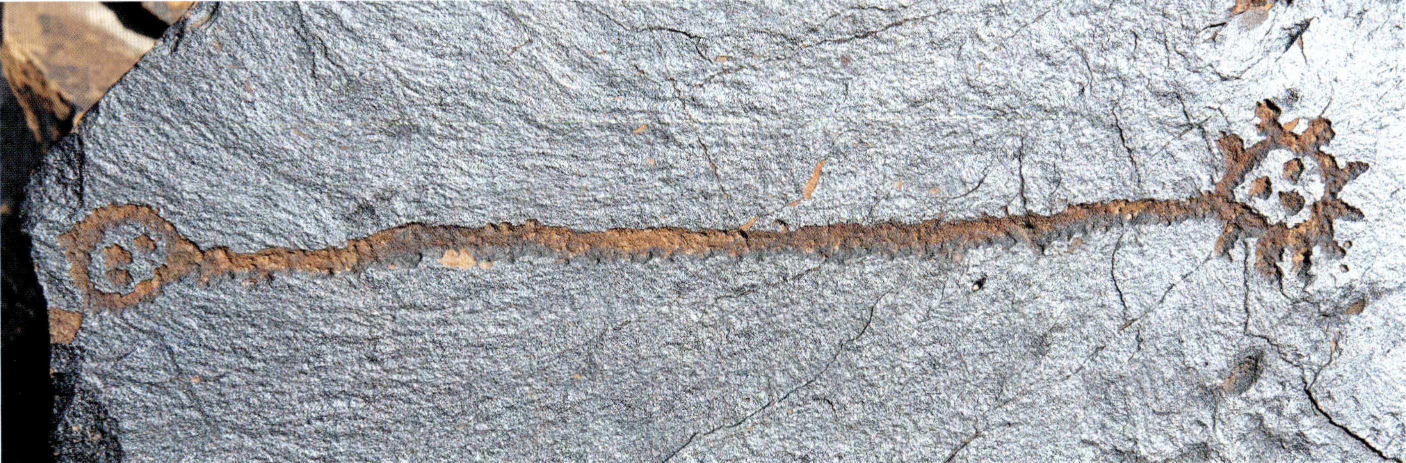

80. ↑ Erotic scene with 18 copulating humans and, in the centre, a snake. Bronze Age, Saimaluu Tash I, Kyrgyzstan. Photo 2017.

81. A so-called 'dumbbell' probably representing sun and moon or the sun by day and night. Bronze Age, Saimaluu Tash I, Kyrgyzstan. Photo 2017.

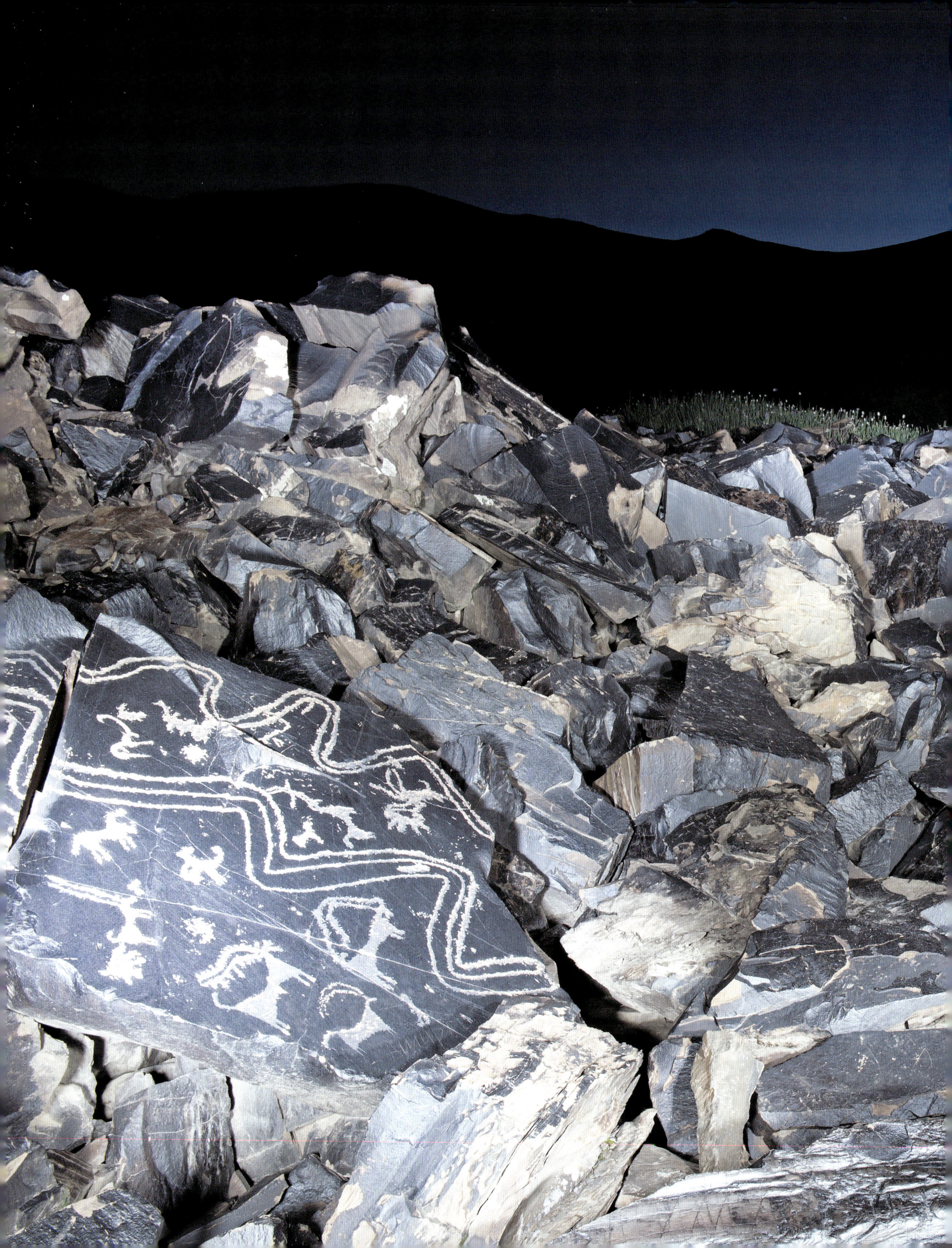

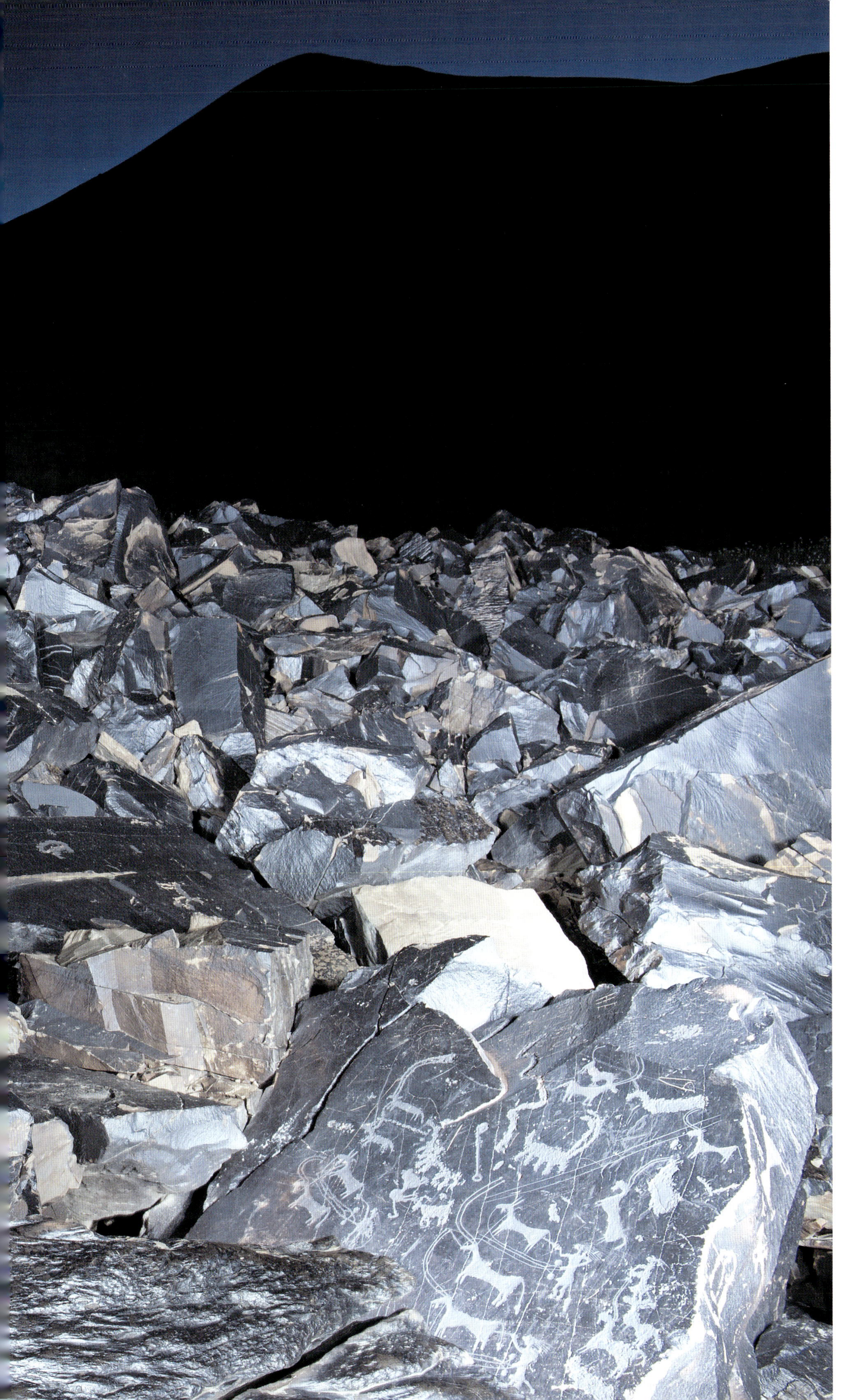

82. On the left an engraved mountain landscape with two rivers (or two additional mountains) and ibexes, on the right ploughing scenes. Bronze Age, Saimaluu Tash I, Kyrgyzstan.
Night photo 2017.

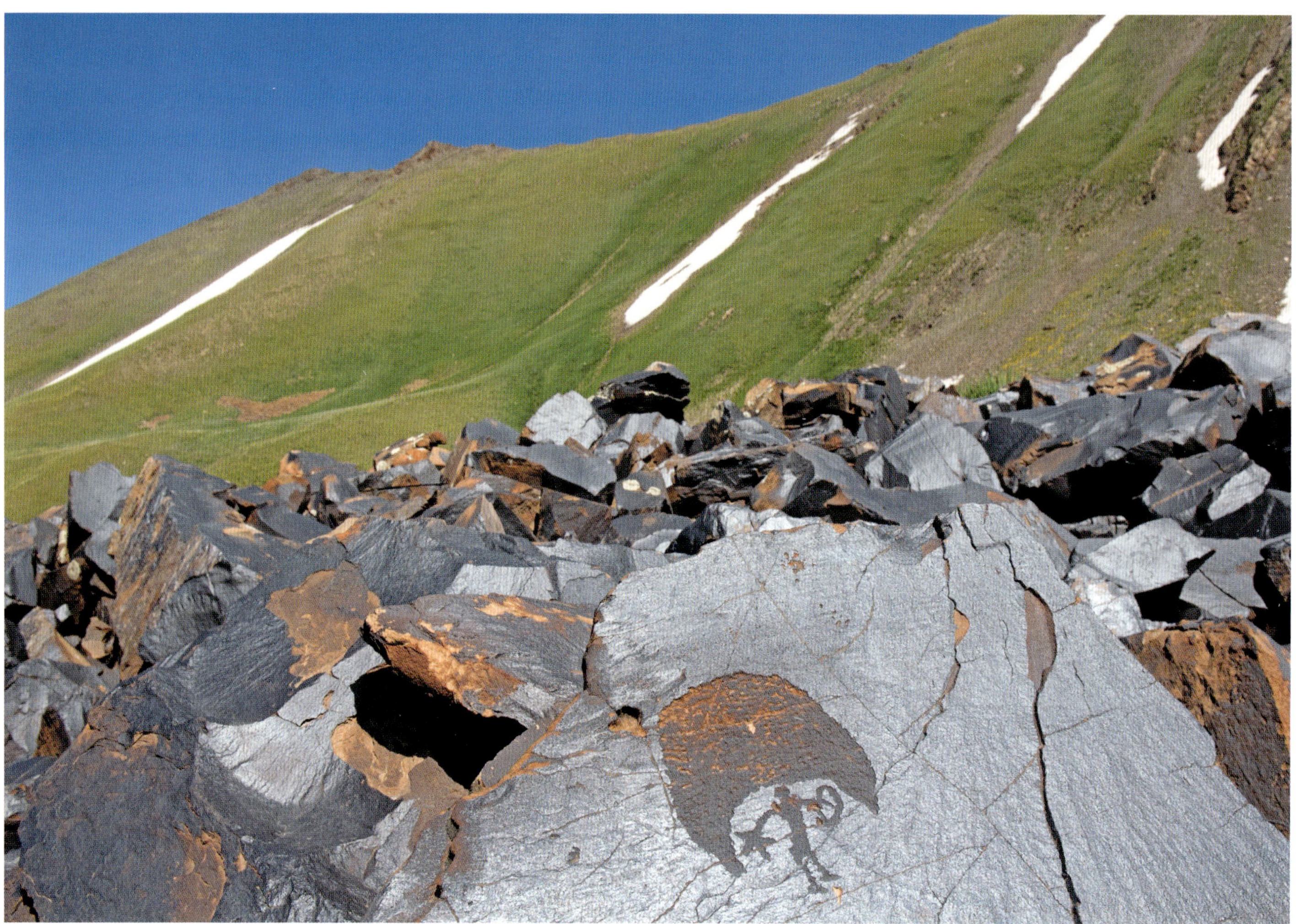

83. A tiny human stands under the vault of the sky. The object he holds in his right hand might be a flat drum or a bow. The steep slope in the background leads to Saimaluu Tash II. Bronze Age, Saimaluu Tash I, Kyrgyzstan. Photo 2017.

of a divine chariot (fig. 75). In the *Histories*, Herodotus narrates an army review by the Iranian King of Kings Xerxes. There, the sacred horses 'were followed by the holy chariot of Zeus [that is Ahura Mazda] drawn by eight white horses, with a charioteer on foot behind them holding the reins – for no mortal man may mount into the chariot's seat.'[220] Given that the ancient Iranians drew on the same mythological heritage as the Andronovians, we may suspect that this concept is reflected in the rock art scenes. Possibly they visualize ritual chariot drives. Since the chariot petroglyphs were made at Saimaluu Tash in areas without tombs, the present author interprets them as the vehicles of Indo-Iranian divinities or as solar symbols rather than an allegory of a dead person's journey to the netherworld.

An intriguing variant on the chariot motif can be found at Saimaluu Tash II, where two horses are pictured pulling a large disc or sphere, which is attached to the vehicle's drawbar (fig. 76). This image might allude to the myth of one or two divine horses drawing the sun across the sky during daytime. The mythological concept of solar horses pulling the sun is found not only in the Indian *Rig Veda*,[221] but also in Nordic mythology and rock art, for example at Balken in southern Sweden (fig. 181). Another intriguing notion relating to solar mythology is an attack on the sun disc or a star by a monster or a wild bull (fig. 77). This petroglyph probably relates to the myth discussed above of a fabulous animal eager to devour the sun or other celestial bodies. With that in mind, the chase of a mythical hybrid animal in the shape of a deer (or horse) with huge antlers by predators such as wolves may be understood not only as an allegory of life being dogged by inescapable death, but also of animals associated with the sun being pursued by primeval predators (fig. 79). In another scene, an archer with three rays protruding from his head prepares to shoot at a large sun disc standing on two tiny feet (fig. 78). This image is possibly an allusion to the aforementioned myth about the shooting down of the two redundant and harmful suns.

Two other motifs may also be understood in the context of astral bodies. The first resembles a kind of dumbbell, which consists of a straight rod between 15 and 90 centimetres in length, with a disc or ring fixed at each end. In some instances, one of the two discs is shaped like a sun, which suggests an interpretation of these 'dumbbell' objects as either the sun and moon, or, perhaps, the sun during the day and at night (fig. 81). The second motif with a possible astral connection features a small human who seems to wear a giant headdress in the shape of a mushroom (fig. 83). Some authors have interpreted this widespread image as a shaman and the mushroom fly agaric that produces trances and hallucinations when consumed. However, it should rather be understood as a human standing under the infinite vault of the sky; in a single petroglyph at Saimaluu Tash, the figure seems to hold a flat drum. To conclude the interpretation of Saimaluu Tash's petroglyphs with the help of mythology, it is clear that they reflect a mixture of non-Indo-European and Indo-Iranian cultural heritage. Saimaluu Tash retained its status as a special place where rituals were performed into the twentieth century; local hunters informed the author that a few decades ago local people still used to climb to the site in August bringing lambs, which they would ritually slaughter next to the tiny lake near the main moraine.

Another characteristic of the Saimaluu Tash petroglyphs are various animals such as horses, goats, wolves and snow leopards with bodies that consist of two triangles connected at the top. A similar bi-triangular style of body has recently been found on a petroglyph of the same age at Kayrit Oasis and on a painted pottery sherd from Dzharkutan, both sites located in south-eastern Uzbekistan, 650 kilometres south-west of Saimaluu Tash. These finds confirm, *contra* Martynov et al.,[222] Bernshtam's opinion that there existed a cultural connection between the Chust culture and the Saimaluu Tash petroglyphs, for two painted potsherds found in Osh which belonged to the Chust cultural realm display obvious similarities with petroglyphs at Saimaluu Tash. One decoration shows a bull with bi-triangular body and extremely long horns, the other a bi-triangular animal body.[223] On the other hand, the hypothesis formulated by Bernshtam, Masson and Ploskhikh making a connection between the bi-triangular figures at Saimaluu Tash and similar renderings of ibexes on painted ceramics from Susa I, Tepe Sialk, and Namazga III, all dating from the fourth millennium BCE,[224] is highly unlikely due to a time gap of more than a millennium and the huge geographical distances. To date the Saimaluu petroglyphs to 4000–3000 BCE is also impossible.

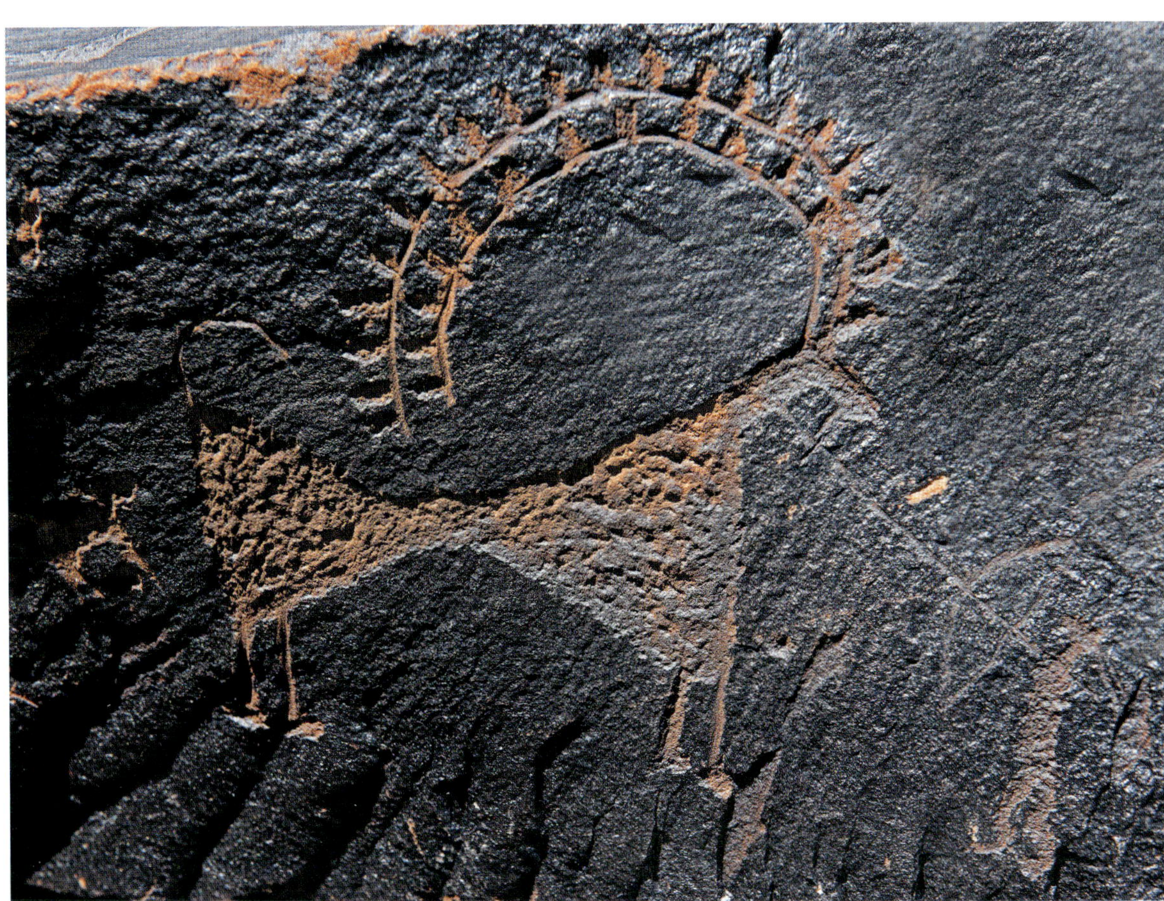

84. An ibex with body in bi-triangular style. The archer shooting at the ibex's neck was possibly added later. Late Bronze Age, Saimaluu Tash I, Kyrgyzstan. Photo 2017.

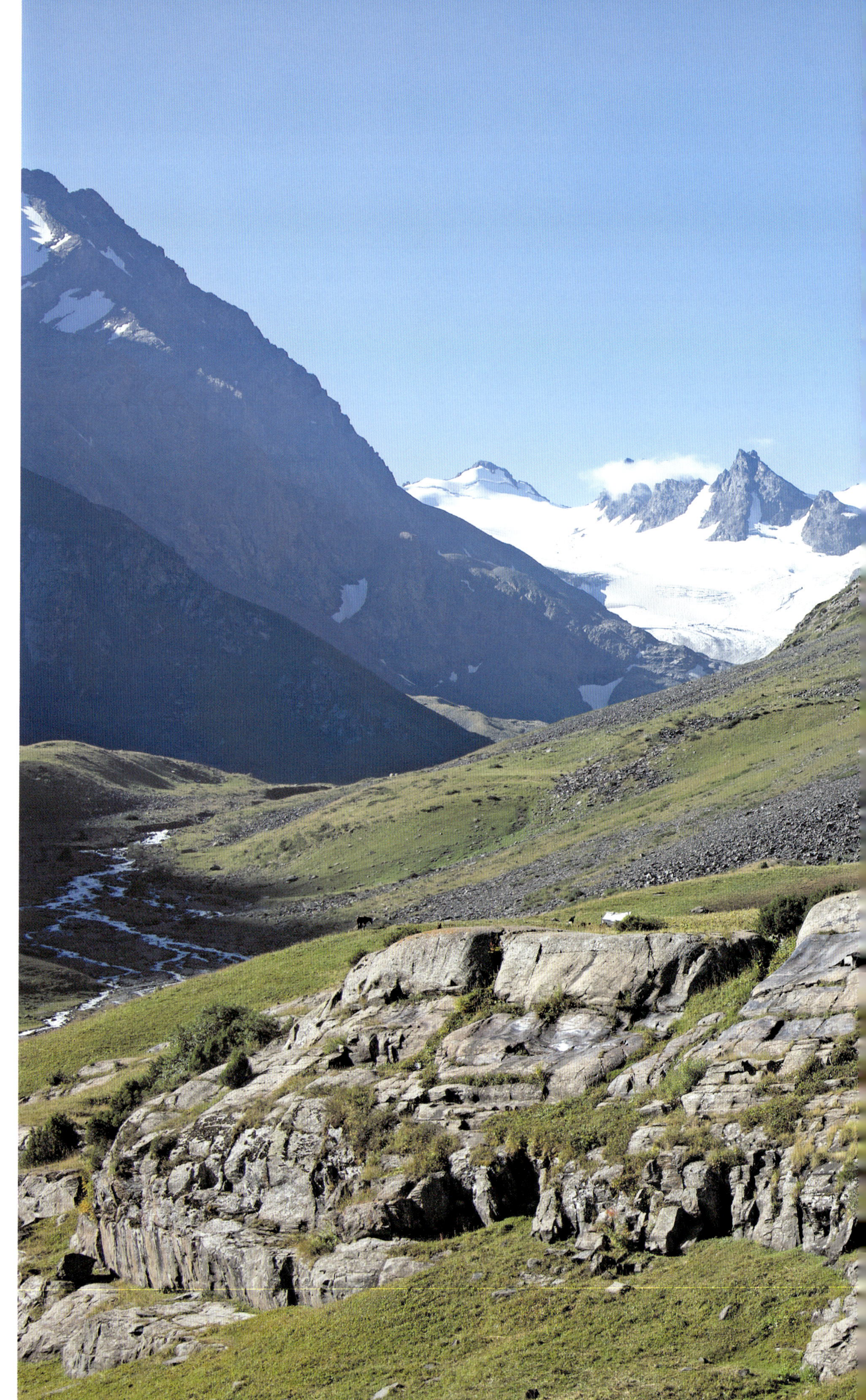

85. The site of Zhaltyrak Tash is situated at the confluence of the Kandybay River (at the left) and the Agynay river (not visible) which form the Kaman-Suu river in the Talas Alatau mountain range, north-western Kyrgyzstan. Photo 2017.

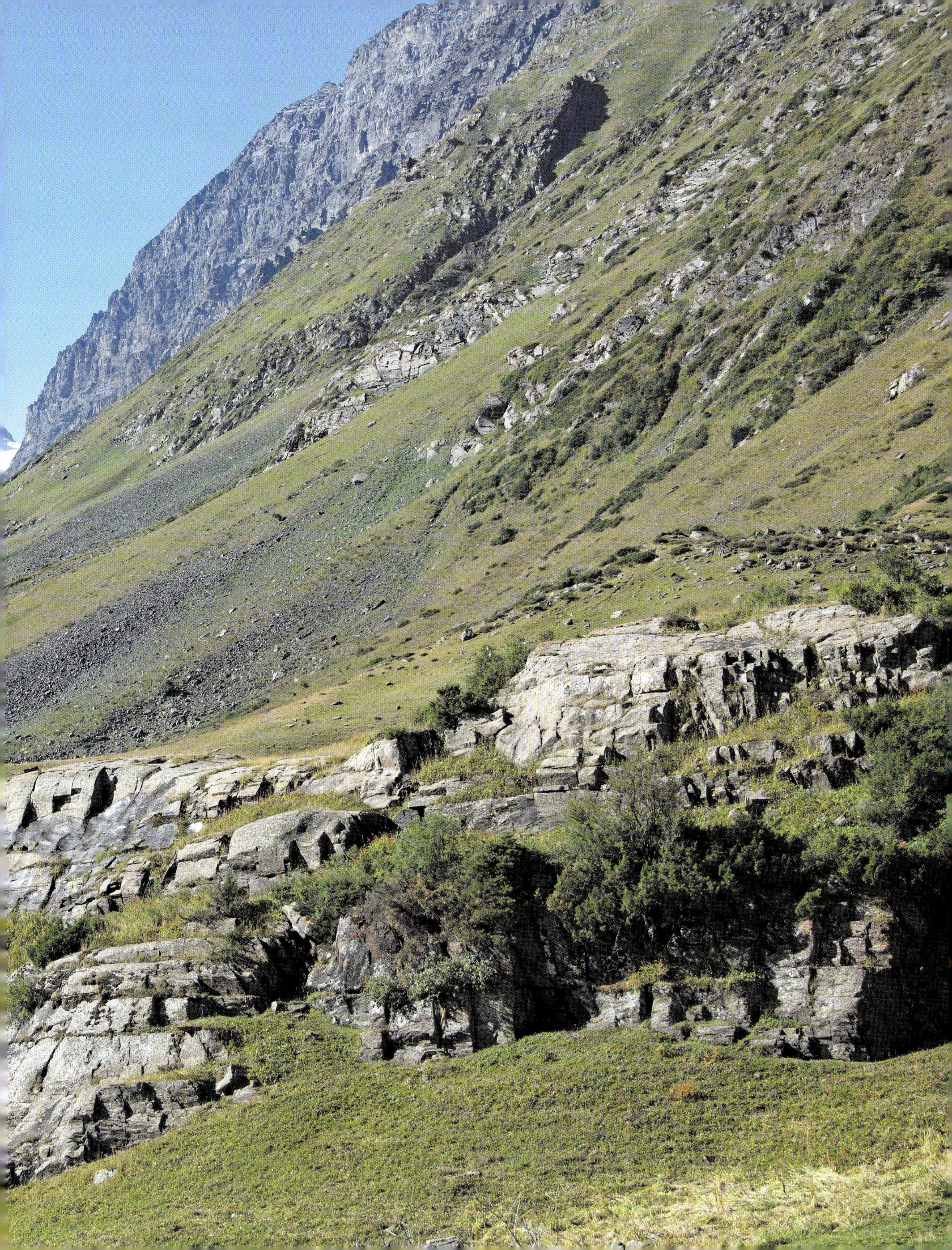

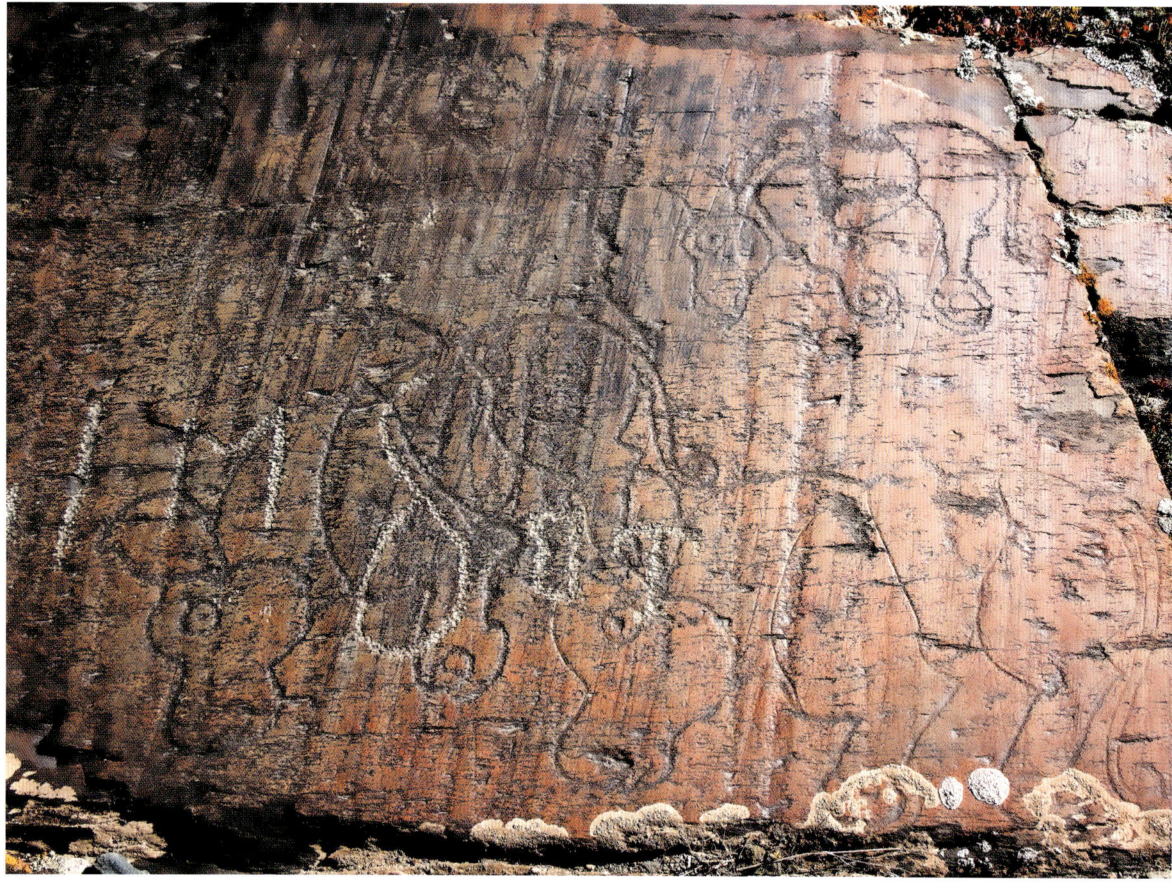

86. Petroglyphs of three hybrid animals with the heads and bodies of bears and curved tails like a panther. Saka Iron Age, Zhaltyrak Tash, north-western Kyrgyzstan. Photo 2017.

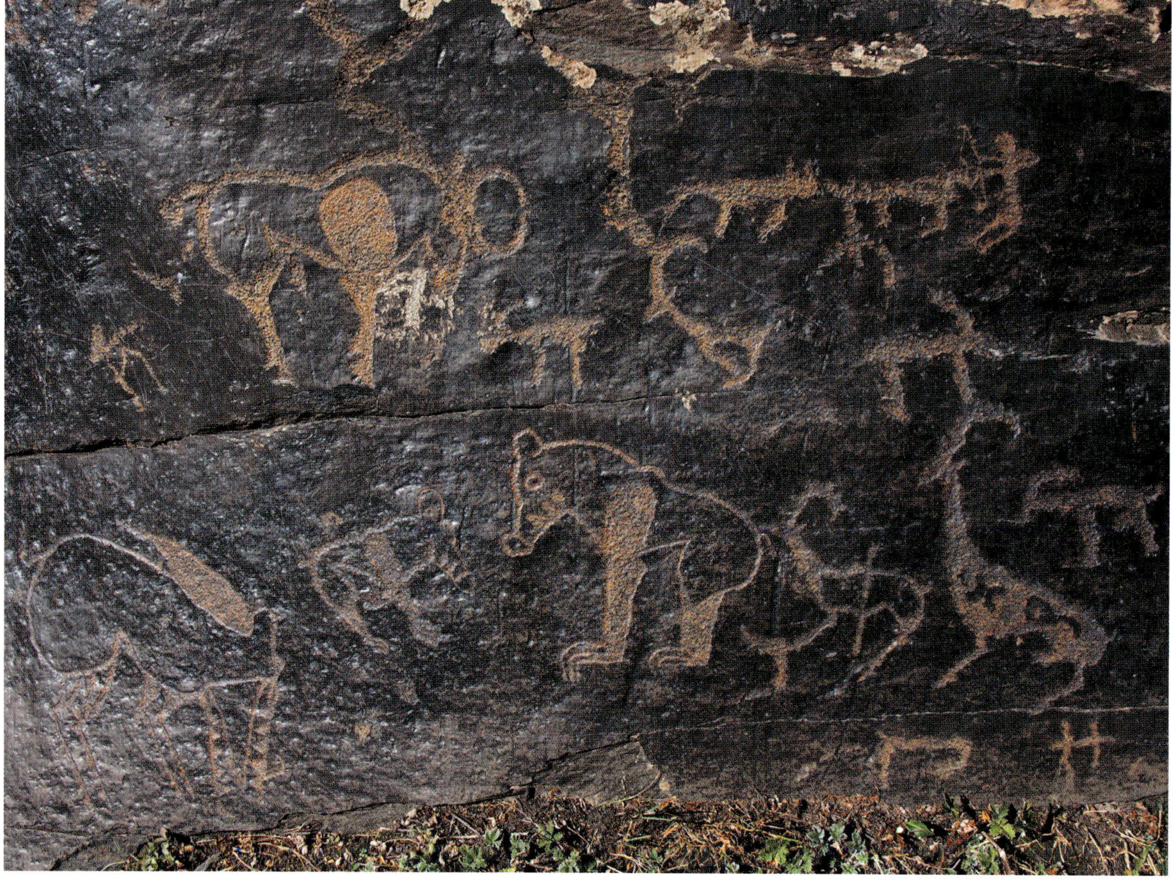

87. Petroglyphs in the Saka Iron Age style of a bull and a hunting scene above, and below of a winged fantastic animal with bared teeth, two bears and two mountain goats. Zhaltyrak Tash, north-western Kyrgyzstan. Photo 2017.

Contrary to Tashbayeva who claims an absence of palimpsests at Saimaluu Tash, there are in fact quite a few, among others the image of a hybrid human-ibex, in which a standing human was transformed into the front legs of a stylized ibex. Finally, the rock art of Saimaluu Tash does not include indoor domestic activities, with the exception of enclosures or compartmented dwellings seen from above. Moreover, there are no children or humans clearly portrayed as women, with the exception of erotic images and some birthing scenes. On the other hand, certain predators are clearly identified as female by their teats (fig. 79).

The alpine site of **Zhaltyrak Tash** can only be reached on foot by following the Tabylgaty River or by crossing the 3,004-metre-high Agynay Tor Pass. The name Zhaltyrak Tash means 'shining stone', as the dark brown varnish of the basaltic rocks shines in the sun. The site was supposedly rediscovered in 1956 by the local explorer V.M. Gaponenko who first called it Ur-Maral.[225] It is situated on the left bank of the Kaman-Suu River, a tributary of the Tabylgaty River, itself a tributary of the Ur-Maral River. Later, in 1985–86, the site was investigated by Jakov Sher who named it Zhaltyrak Tash in order to differentiate it from the several other petroglyph sites within the Ur-Maral valley system.[226] The petroglyphs are concentrated on two surfaces of a huge cliff 180 metres long at the bottom and 140 metres at the top; the height varies from around eight to thirteen metres. The petroglyphs are engraved in the upper horizontal surface, where they are quite weathered and in parts covered by lichen, and on the slanted eastern side; they date from the Bronze Age to the medieval Turkic period. At Zhaltyrak Tash many petroglyphs were created by deeply stamping points very close to each other, following the contour lines; occasionally, on parts of larger images such as the legs of bears or bulls, the varnish was removed from the entire surface inside the contour. Later, in the Turkic period, a different method was applied and the petroglyphs were thinly carved.

Besides several Bronze Age images of single-axle chariots and single wheels, Zhaltyrak Tash has one of the richest collection of petroglyphs from the Saka Iron Age. There is a bear more than one metre long, a group of three hybrid animals consisting of heads and bodies of bears and long tails curved at their tips like predators' tails (fig. 86), and in another group a small bear is facing a larger one, while to their left stands a winged fantasy animal with a strongly toothed muzzle, with two gazelles to their right and a bull above (fig. 87). The image of the wild boar strongly resembles similar petroglyphs at Sauiskandyk (Kazakhstan), at Chuy-Oozy in the Russian Altai, and on the stele of Arzhan 1 (Mongolia) more than 2,000 kilometres away as the crow flies.[227]

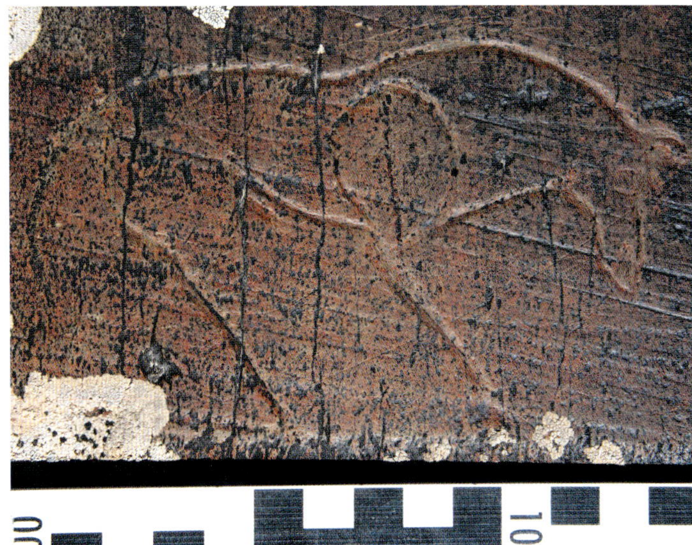

88. Petroglyph showing a kind of snow leopard or horse. Saka Iron Age, Zhaltyrak Tash, north-western Kyrgyzstan. Photo 2017.

This similarity shows that it is correct to refer to a specific Saka style of petroglyphs. Then there are several deer and stags standing on tiptoe and with their antlers stretching straight upwards, and two small reclining caprines chiselled inside the body of a larger deer. From the same period date the petroglyphs of a wolf, another predator attacking a man and his cow, and a large camel.

Zhaltyrak Tash has also some interesting petroglyphs from the Hunnic and Turkic periods. Very unusual are the heavily weathered images of a centaur shooting an arrow and of dragons or winged dogs.[228] Then there are engravings, again heavily weathered, of Hunnic warriors fighting on foot with lances, which look very similar to the warriors engraved in the famous bone plate of Orlat found north of Samarkand in Uzbekistan more than 500 kilometres to the north-west.[229] Then, on an isolated small boulder, is a petroglyph of a standing archer carrying a recurved bow in his *gorytós*; this petroglyph from the Turkic period has probably been reworked. Close to the petroglyphs there also a couple of kurgans from the Saka period. These burial tumuli suggest the hypothesis that this place, located at the confluence of two rivers flowing from two glaciers, was formerly perceived as a sacred site. As in the case of Saimaluu Tash, the pastoralists leading their sheep and goats to the meadows located near Zhaltyrak Tash still use this place as a high-altitude summer pasturage.

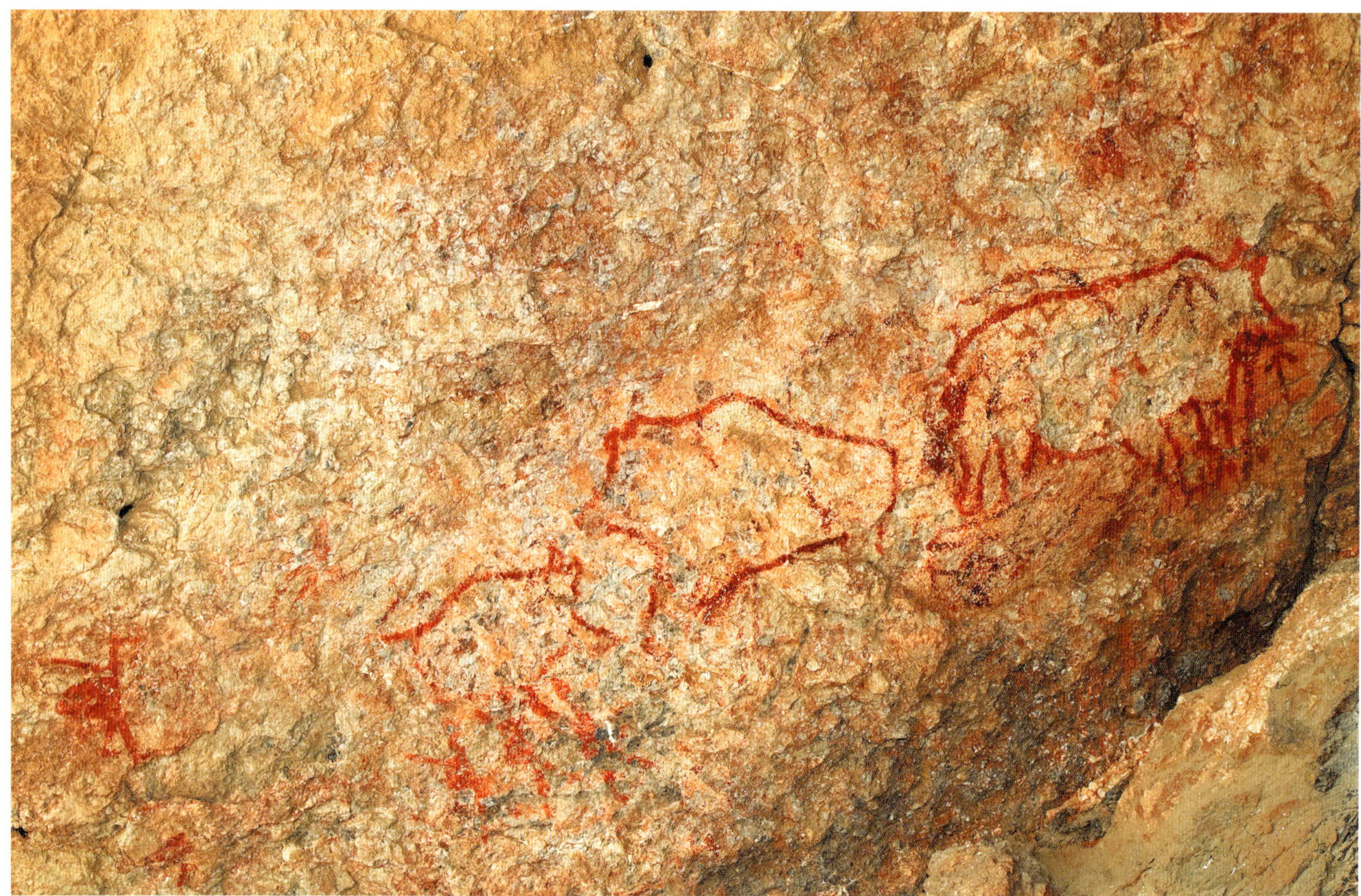

89. Mesolithic rock painting of a bear hunt. A small hunter wearing a bird mask and a bird-like costume approaches a boar (or small bear) and two bears; the larger bear on the right is hit by arrows. *ca.* 5000 BCE. Shakhty shelter in the Pamir mountains, Gorno-Badakhshan, eastern Tajikistan. Photo 2008.

5. Tajikistan

Most of the ancient rock art of Tajikistan lies in its eastern and south-eastern parts, in the Badakhshan Mountainous Autonomous Region, also called Gorno-Badakhshan. The region's landscape is shaped by the desertic high plateau of the Pamir Mountains, and it has a harsh, strictly continental climate. The palaeoclimatic history of Badakhshan, which shares its border in the north with southern Kyrgyzstan and in the east with Xinjiang, is part of a supraregional system extending to western Xinjiang, northern Pakistan and north-eastern Afghanistan. Following an initial retreat of glaciers at the beginning of the Holocene, the Pamir Uplands were for the first time briefly populated, but a depopulation soon followed during a subsequent arid, cold period (12 ka–8000 BP) until the climate became milder and more humid. This renewed retreat of the glaciers allowed for a nomadic resettlement of the central Tajik Pamirs by people arriving from the west. Between *ca.* 2300 and 1500 BCE, climatic conditions again became arid, followed

by a trend to a cooler and more humid climate which lasted until *ca.* 350 BCE, though the cooler period was interrupted by a brief, warmer hiatus from *ca.* 1000 to 650 BCE. After a peak in moist and cool conditions around 450 BCE, the trend reversed with a moderate return to a drier and warmer climate until 50 CE, coinciding with the so-called Roman Warm Period. After two further changes in trend, the Little Ice Age set in around 550 CE, lasting till the end of the nineteenth century.[230] A population came and went in the Pamir Uplands following the rhythm of the climate changes. During wetter periods, mobile pastoralists would migrate in summer with their herds from the lower valleys to the Uplands and leave again in autumn. During desertic periods the central Pamirs remained virtually depopulated but for caravan traffic.

90. → One of the 26 geoglyphs located at the Iron Age burial site of Shurali at an altitude of 3,783 m asl in the Pamir mountains, Gorno-Badakhshan, eastern Tajikistan. Photo 2008.

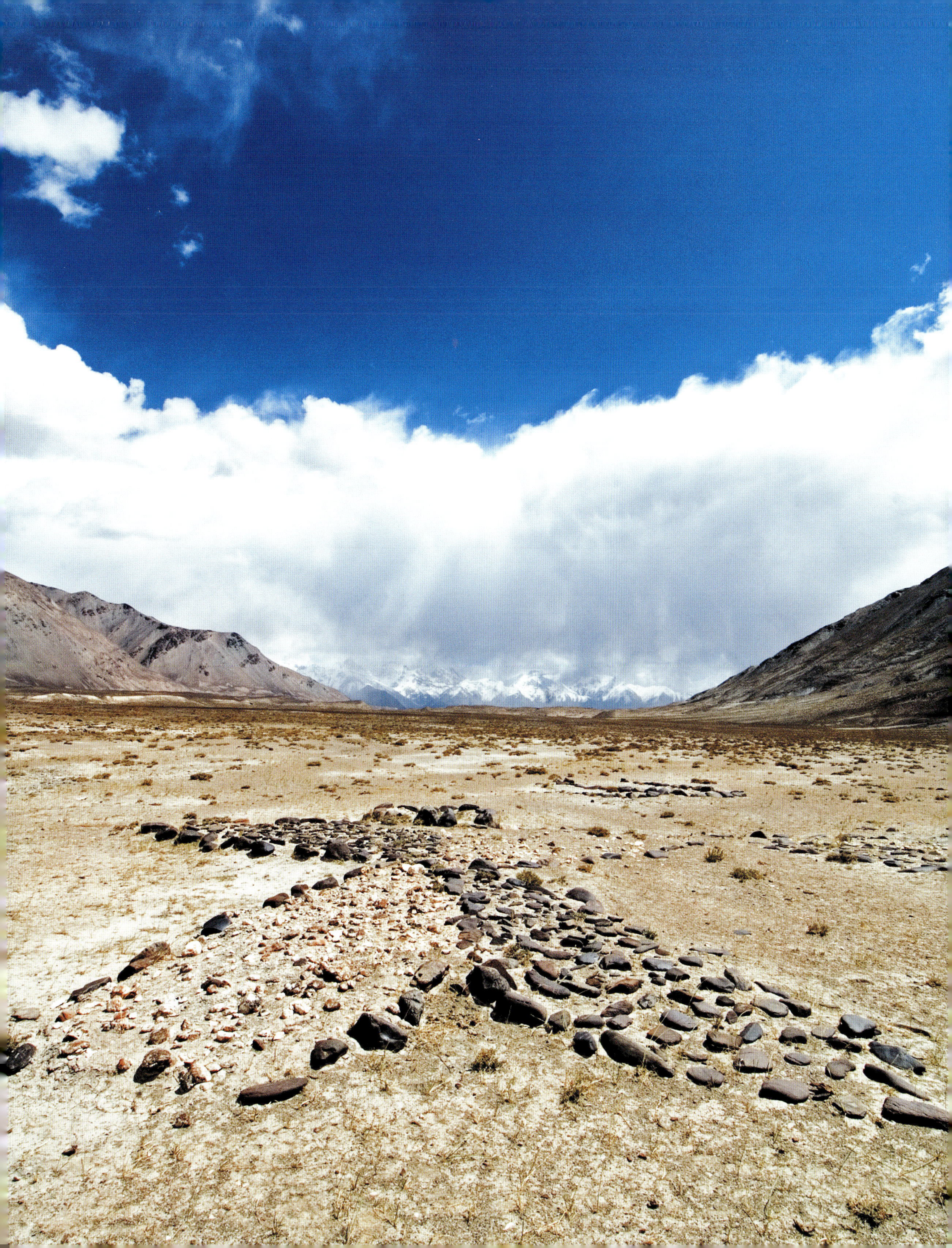

The most important rock art sites in Tajikistan are, in a chronological order:[231]

- **Shakhty** is a rock shelter with well-preserved paintings from the Mesolithic. Six other rock shelters exist in the vicinity of Shakhty with poorly preserved paintings.

- **Vybist-Dara** is located east of Khorog and has petroglyphs from the late Bronze Age or early Iron Age up till the Middle Ages.

- **Soy Sabagh** lies in Sughd province, north-western Tajikistan. Most petroglyphs date from the Bronze Age and feature bulls, ibexes, turs, chariots, archers, hunting scenes and wave-like lines.

- **Ak-Jilga** is a small high alpine site with several interesting petroglyphs of chariots from the Saka Iron Age.

- **Kara Art**, located near the shore of Lake Kara-Kul at an altitude of 4,040 m asl, consists of almost twenty large geoglyphs from the Saka Iron Age.

- **Shurali**, situated 40 km south-west of Lake Kara-Kul has 26 geoglyphs from the Saka Iron Age.

- **Langar** is the largest Tajik petroglyph site with images mainly from the Kushan and Hunnic–Hephtalites periods (first to fifth century CE) as well as from the middle and late Middle Ages.

- The central part of the **Hissar–Alay** as well as of the **Kurama** and **Mogoltau** mountain ranges contain a few smaller rock art sites.

- **Almosi Gorge**. The site located near Tajikistan's capital Dushanbe contains an ancient bilingual inscription which made possible the decipherment in 2023 of the hitherto unknown Kushan script.

The rock shelter of **Shakhty** lies in the Kurteke-Say Valley in the central Pamir Uplands, 35 kilometres south-east of the village of Murgab. The shelter is located around 40 metres above the floor of the valley at an altitude of 4,199 metres above sea level. The paintings are drawn in ochre pigments of various shades. Based on the dating of stone tools excavated near the shelter, the paintings have been assigned a date in the Mesolithic around 5000 BCE. At that epoch, the glaciers had retreated and the relatively mild climate provided a livelihood for seasonal herders; there would have been grass steppe and possibly also shrubs. The abri of Shakhty was discovered by chance in 1958, by archaeologists seeking refuge from the weather. The cave-like shelter, oriented to the north, has an opening about six and a half metres wide and eight metres high; its depth measures less than four metres, but it nonetheless offers protection from sun and rain.[232] The paintings on limestone are arranged on the southern side of the cave on a frieze 250 centimetres long, about 160 to 200 centimetres above the ground. Of the seven remaining figures, four are clearly recognizable: to the far left an ornitho-anthropomorph 23 centimetres tall, holding a club, approaches three rather large animals. The anthropomorph represents a hunter wearing a bird mask and a bird-like costume as camouflage (fig. 89). To his right stands the figure of a wild boar, 40 centimetres long, turned away from the hunter; it has either fallen into a trap or is surrounded by highly stylized hunters. To the right of the boar a bear, 60 centimetres long, is ready to jump to the left, as if to attack the boar; below the bear one or two spears are stuck in the ground, with which it has possibly been injured. To the far right stands a bear 85 centimetres long, looking to the right, toward which three arrows fly from different directions; the scene portrays a bear hunt. These rock paintings are part of the Markansu culture of the eastern Pamirs, to which the Mesolithic site at Oshkhona also belongs.[233] Just two kilometres from Shakhty is the shelter of **Kurtek** 4,020 metres above sea level, with traces of badly preserved Neolithic images; one of them has been interpreted by Vadim Ranov as a 'dancing anthropomorph'.[234] East of Shakhty, near the **Naiza-Tash** pass, 4,137 metres above sea level, there is another shelter with poorly preserved paintings of three anthropomorphs and geometric patterns.[235] In 2018 and 2019, a Tajik–Russian expedition discovered traces of additional paintings in the vicinity of Shakhty at the shelters and caves named **Shakhty II**, **Shakarak**, **Madian** and **Zhukov**, which the researchers tentatively dated to the Mesolithic or even to the Upper Palaeolithic.[236] In contrast to the rock paintings of Khoid Tsenkeriin in Mongolia, in those of Shakhty human figures clearly appear in the context of a hunt. Presumably these rock paintings had a magical function within such a context.

In the region of Lake Kara-Kul there are two sites with large geometric geoglyphs, up to twenty metres long and seven metres wide; they are parts of two graveyards from the Saka Iron Age period. They are **Kara Art**, located one kilometre from the eastern

shore of the lake, and **Shurali** 40 kilometres south-west of the lake.
They were made by first outlining the border of the geometric
figure with large pebbles, after which the earth within the
delimited area was removed to a depth of 20 centimetres and
then filled with small stones to build a foundation. Finally, dark
stones and white quartzite stones were placed onto the foundation
in such a way that they protruded around 10 centimetres above the
ground level and formed a black-and-white pattern (fig. 90).
At Kara Art, there are 19 geoglyphs and 25 kurgans; at the three
sites at Shurali, 26 geoglyphs and at least seven kurgans. At both
sites, nearly all the geoglyphs are oriented toward the south-east.
At Shurali, two geoglyphs, one of them shaped like an arrow,
mark the summer and winter solstices and another the spring and
autumn equinoxes, while at Kara Art, three mark the spring and
autumn equinoxes, and another the summer and winter solstices.[237]
The shapes of a few other geoglyphs are similar to those of *tamgas*.
During excavations conducted in 2003, cists made from slate slabs
were examined. In one tomb the bones of two women were found

along with glass, lapis lazuli and turquoise beads as well as two
brass bracelets; in another tomb the remains of a man, with a knife
and an arrowhead.[238] Most probably the kurgans and the geoglyphs
were interrelated.

About 60 kilometres west of Shakhty is the small, high-altitude
petroglyph site of **Ak-Jilga** at 3,800 metres above sea level, where
the petroglyphs are concentrated on a boulder of black schist 24
metres long and 19 metres wide. All the figures were engraved in
a fine style and feature hunting scenes of ibexes, horsemen, bulls,
humans and skeletons. Peculiar to Ak-Jilga is a kind of parade of
four chariots each drawn by two horses. Whereas on most Central
Asian petroglyphs of chariots viewed from above, the driver
standing on the vehicle is shown as if folded down to the rear, at
Ak-Jilga the standing driver is shown from behind, which gives
the impression that he is lifting the chariot and the horses with
outstretched arms. These petroglyphs, as well as other archaeological traces, can be dated to the period of transition from the Bronze
to the Iron Age.[239]

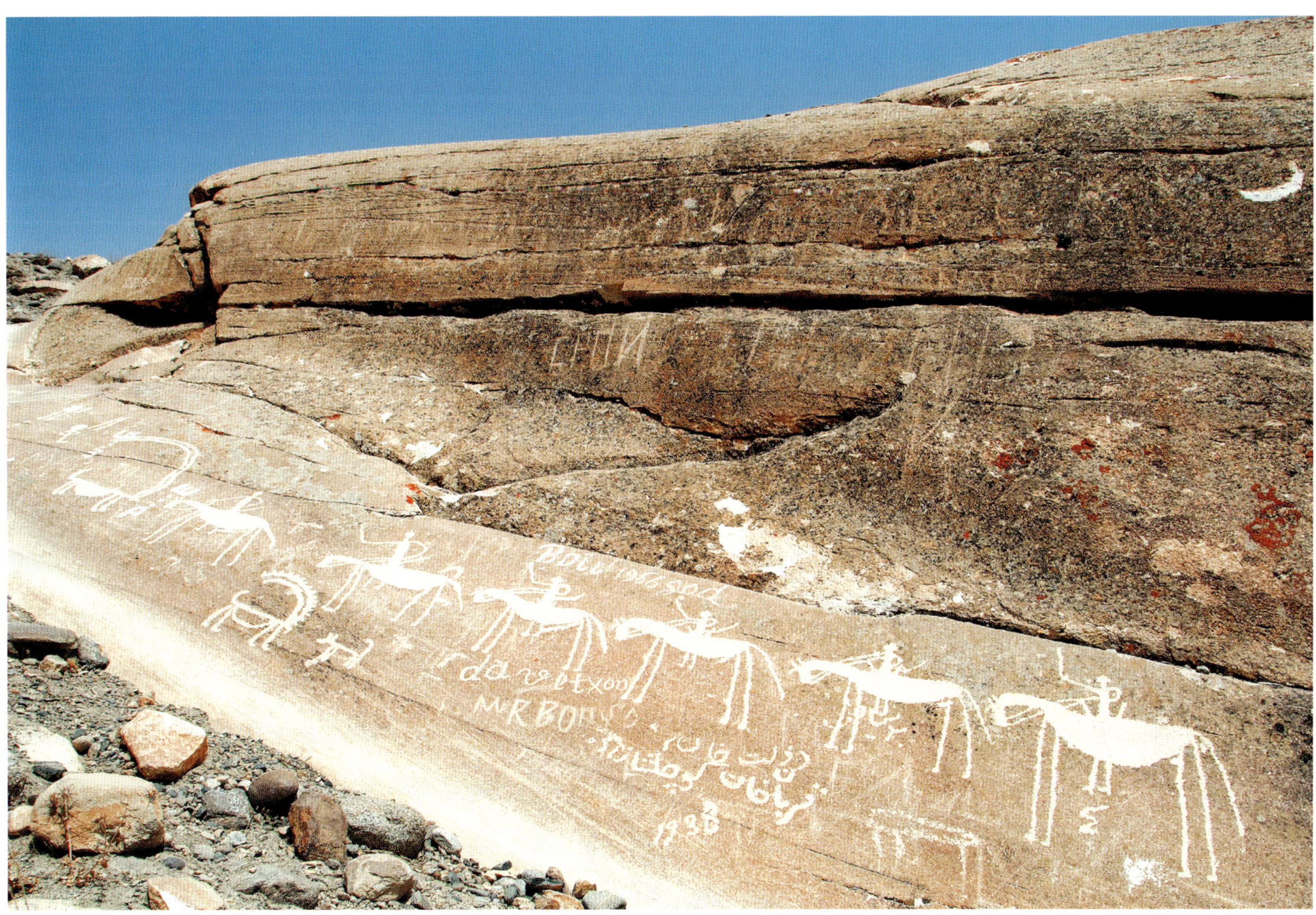

91. Petroglyphs from the late Middle Ages of sabre-brandishing horsemen and ibexes at Langar, Gorno-Badakhshan, southern Tajikistan. Photo 2008.

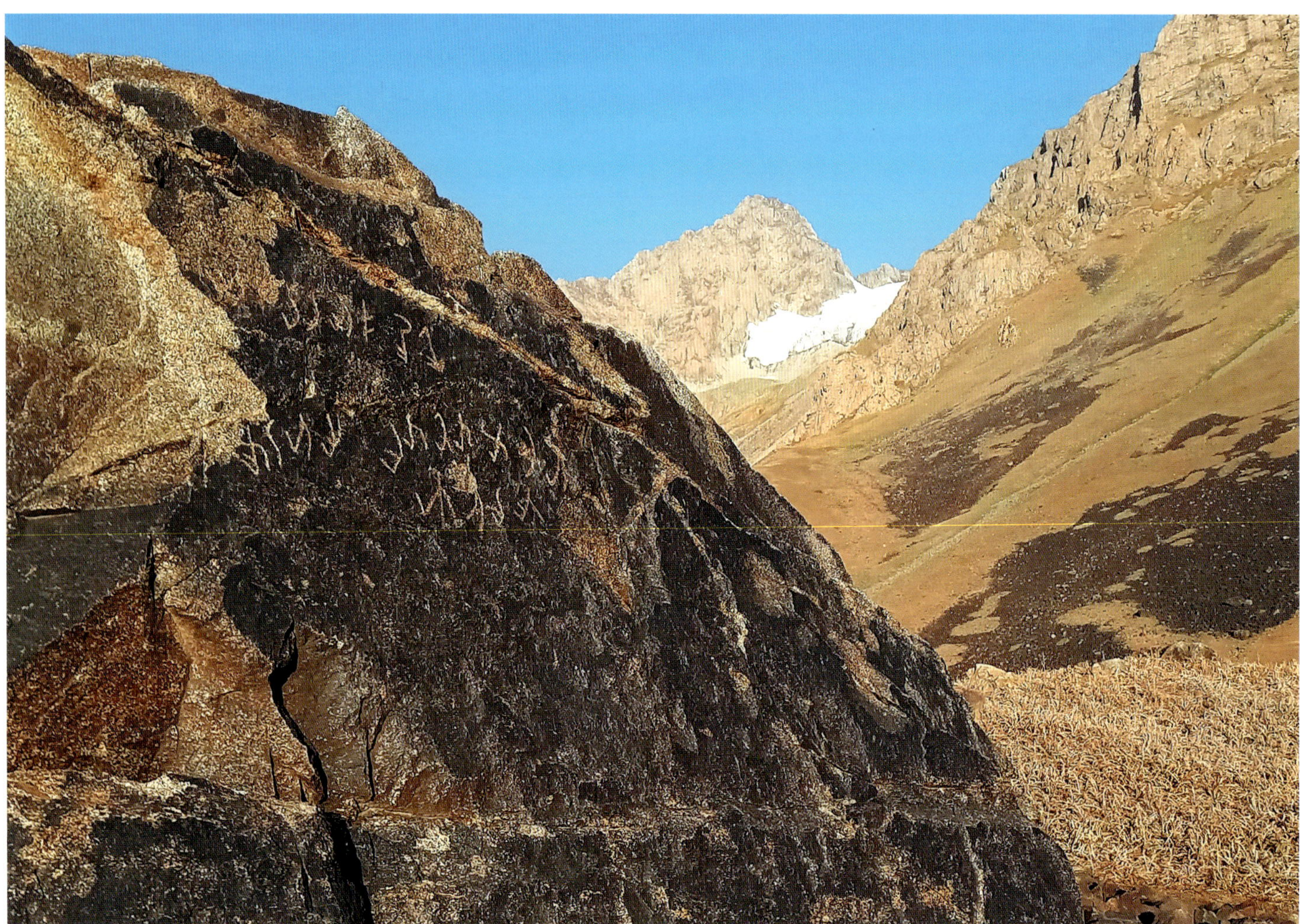

92. The rock inscription in the Issyk-Kushan script discovered at an altitude of 2,950 m asl in summer 2022 in the Almosi gorge of the Hissar mountain range, Tajikistan. Photo 2022. © Bobomullo Bobomulloev, Tajikistan.

The site of **Langar** is situated near the confluence of the rivers Wakhan and Pamir on the border with modern Afghanistan. Most of the roughly 6,000 petroglyphs are spread over a steep granite slope lying between 2,910 and 3,216 metres above sea level. In the past, one of the numerous branches of the Silk Road passed through the Wakhan Corridor and thus also through Langar. The rock art shows a broad variety of motifs, ranging from ibexes, either alone and in herds or hunted by humans and snow leopards, to images of bulls, deer, Buddhist stupas, *tamgas*, a large standard, solar signs, an archer 180 centimetres tall and a *rubab*, a musical stringed instrument resembling a lute. While there are quite a few petroglyphs from the late Bronze Age and from the Iron Age, the majority date from the later Middle Ages to the nineteenth century. From these latter two periods are images of horsemen and hunters on foot armed with bow and sabres or with guns (fig. 91). Unfortunately, since the site is easily accessible from the village of Langar, many of the rock art surfaces have been disfigured with recent inscriptions of personal names.

Another high-altitude site is **Vybist-Dara**, situated 30 kilometres to the east of the city of Khorog, the capital of Badakhshan. The town spreads along the right bank of the river Panj which forms the border with Afghanistan. At Vybist-Dara, the moraine of granite rocks and pebbles is located at an altitude of 3,500 metres above sea level and is reached by a nine-kilometre-long ascent. There are numerous petroglyphs of horsemen, among them many mounted archers, hunters on foot, ibexes, humans holding each other by the hand, combat scenes and single spoked wheels or solar signs, as well as *tamgas*. Finally, there are petroglyphs featuring an open right palm called *hamsa* or *Fatima's hand*. The *hamsa* is a Muslim symbol of protection and is often worn as an amulet made from silver or jet; it is especially popular among the Pamiri Naziri Ismailis, a small branch of the Shiites.[240] The petroglyphs are dated to the Iron Age and the Islamic Middle Ages. About 70 kilometres east of Khorog is the tiny site of **Chartem** which numbers a dozen engraved rocks. The petroglyphs feature recent inscriptions in Arabic as well as horsemen brandishing a sabre, a hunter with a gun, ibexes, a dog and several *hamsa* symbols. They date from the late Middle Ages and the nineteenth to twentieth centuries.

Scientifically important petroglyphs were very recently identified in the **Almosi Gorge** in north-western Tajikistan at an altitude of 2,950 metres above sea level, since a bilingual rock inscription around 2,000 years old provided the key to the partial decipherment of the 'unknown Kushan script' which has superficial similarities with the Indo-Iranian Kharosthi (Gandari) script. This previously undeciphered Kushan script has been identified since the 1950s in more than 30 inscriptions discovered in today's Afghanistan, Tajikistan, Uzbekistan and Kazakhstan; most of them are dated from the second century BCE to the third century CE, with a couple as late as the seventh century CE. Famous among them are the trilingual rock inscription of Dasht-i Nawur in the Gandhari, Bactrian and Kushan scripts, which was discovered in Afghanistan at an altitude of 4,320 metres above sea level, and an inscribed silver bowl from the Issyk kurgan, Kazakhstan.[241] The bilingual rock inscription of Almosi consisted of a text in the unknown Kushan script and of a Bactrian text written in Greek script (fig. 92). Together with the trilingual inscription from Dasht-i Nawur, the Almosi inscription served to decipher the Kushan script, in the same way that the Rosetta Stone previously made it possible to decrypt the Egyptian hieroglyphs. The starting points in the deciphering process were the name of the Kushan emperor Vima Takto (Vema Takhtu, r. *ca*. 80–102 CE), his title 'King of Kings' and various epithets. Subsequently, fifteen consonants, two ligatures and four vowel diacritics of the unknown Kushan script, comprising approximately 23 to 30 signs, were able to be deciphered. Surprisingly, this new script was derived from Imperial Aramaic which was used in the Achaemenid Empire.[242] It seems that it was used to record a previously unknown Middle Iranian language which held a middle position between the Bactrian and the Khotanese Saka languages. On the basis of current knowledge, it is believed that this newly identified language was native to northern Bactria from where the nomadic Yuezhi, the future founders of the Kushan Empire, picked it up on their migration southward.[243] Alternatively, should further research reveal that this language was closely related to Khotanese Saka, it may have been the original language of the Yuezhi who originated from Gansu in north-western China.[244] The authors of the decipherment propose to call the new script the 'Issyk-Kushan Script' and the corresponding language 'Eteo-Tocharian'.[245] The high-altitude rock inscriptions of Almosi and Dasht-i Nawur exemplify the cultural relevance of petroglyphs.

6. Uzbekistan

The rock art sites of Uzbekistan are mainly located in the mountainous eastern part of the country, bordering Tajikistan in the south-east, Kyrgyzstan in the east and Kazakhstan in the north-east. Only the important site of Sarmishsay in the Karatau Mountain Range, which is the westernmost spur of the Alay-Hissar Range, lies in central Uzbekistan. The Uzbek regions that contain rock art went through similar climatic developments to those to their east.

The most important rock art sites in Uzbekistan are, in a chronological order:

- **Zaraut-Kamar** in southern Uzbekistan, 80 kilometres north-west of Termez, a border city with Afghanistan. The cave complex contains paintings allegedly from the Mesolithic, but most likely rather from the last two or three centuries.

- **Sarmishsay** is in central Uzbekistan in the Nuratau Mountain Range, 130 kilometres north-west of Samarkand.

- **Saikhansay** is located 220 kilometres south-east of Sarmishsay and 30 kilometres south of Jizzakh in the northern foothills of the Morguzar Mountain Range.

- **Beldersay** and **Karakiyasay** are two small sites located 60 and 54 kilometres north-east of Tashkent respectively. The images date from the Bronze and Saka Iron Ages; several others are from the Ethnographic period.[246] The petroglyphs of Karakiyasay are spread over a steep slope ranging from 2,100 to 2,300 m asl.

The cave paintings of **Zaraut-Kamar** are situated in the Karautsay Gorge in the Kugitangtau Mountains, a south-western spur of the Hissar Mountain Range. Although they are famous, the authenticity and age of these paintings are debated and doubtful. They were discovered in 1912 by the Russian topographer Fyodorov who made some sketches. In 1939, the archaeologist G.V. Parfyonov explored the various caves and dated the paintings, based on lithic finds made in the surroundings and on style, to the Upper Palaeolithic. A member of Parfyonov's expedition, the artist A.Yu. Roginskaya, made watercolour sketches of the figures, 291 images in total, which were published in 1950. These watercolour copies show a bull hit by an arrow and some smaller bulls, a group of small archers measuring five to seven centimetres and several equally small ornitho-anthropomorphic figures who may represent hunters disguised as birds.[247] Other images, as well as the inscriptions, were attributed to the Islamic Middle Ages. A further survey in 1964 by A.A. Formozov revealed, however, that many figures allegedly found by Parfyonov did not exist or were stains formed naturally by the oxidation of ferrous minerals within the rock. Furthermore, the copies made by Roginskaya turned out to be not only erroneous,

but they also omitted the medieval figures and inscriptions in Arabic. Nevertheless, these sketches have remained to this day the main documentation of this site and are still used in publications. Concerning the estimated age of these paintings, Formozov excluded a Palaeolithic date and suggested one in the Mesolithic or Neolithic–Chalcolithic.[248] Furthermore, recent research has revealed a probable link with a Tajik tradition of adorning houses with paintings at the feast of Nawruz, celebrating spring equinox.[249] Today the paintings have still barely been examined scientifically. All these circumstances mean that a prehistoric dating of the Zaraut-Kamar paintings is highly problematic; many of them, if not all, are probably just a couple of centuries old.

With *ca.* 4,000 images, **Sarmishsay** is the largest rock art site of Uzbekistan. The gorge with the petroglyphs is located 30 kilometres north of Navoiy in the Nuratau Mountain Range, a western buttress of the Hissar Range. The rocks are the result of long shaping, crushing and folding processes dating from the Silurian period (443.7–419.2 mya[250]). The stratified layers are about 600 metres thick and consist mainly of sandstones, as well as aleurolite (siltstone), limestone and shale.[251] The petroglyphs were almost always carved on slate, though occasionally on patinated sandstone. The narrow valley is oriented north–south. The majority of the rock art, which is subdivided into fifteen groups, is situated on both the eastern and western sides of the gorge over a distance of four kilometres. They were first studied in 1959 by the archaeologist Kh. Mukhamedov, and later, from 1993, by a Polish–Uzbek expedition led by Mukhiddin Khujanazarov. The earliest petroglyphs date from the Eneolithic or early Bronze Age, the latest from the late Middle Ages.[252] The earlier petroglyphs date to the fourth millennium BCE and were created by mostly sedentary hunters belonging to the later Kelteminar culture (*ca.* 5200–2500 BCE). Their petroglyphs were made using stone hammers and chisels. In the early third millennium BCE, the Kelteminar people began to adopt agriculture, yet they remained an Eneolithic culture. The step forward into the Bronze Age was made by the people of the succeeding Zamanbaba culture (*ca.* 2500–1400 BCE) who practised agriculture and pastoralism; their rock art was made using metallic chisels.[253] Then, around the middle of the second millennium BCE, nomads from the Andronovo cultural complex migrated into the region from the north-east, bringing with them their own mythological heritage. In at least two aspects some of the Bronze Age petroglyphs of Sarmishsay show similarities in terms of specific content to the Indo-Iranian mythological worldview as known from the rock art sites of Tamgaly and Saimaluu Tash. No prehistoric tombs were found in the valley, but there are several *mazars*, places associated

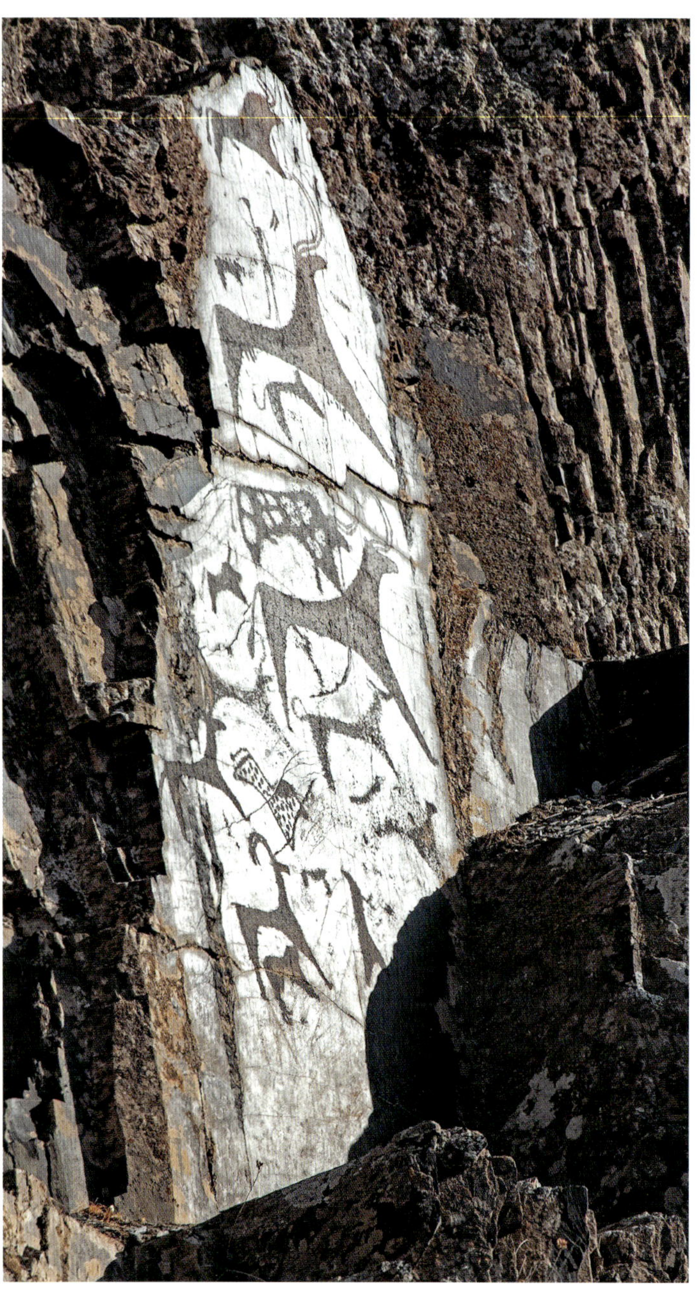

93. Petroglyphs of bulls, ibexes and hybrid animals such as ibexes with bulls' horns. Second millennium BCE. Sarmishsay, group III, central Uzbekistan. Photo 2023.

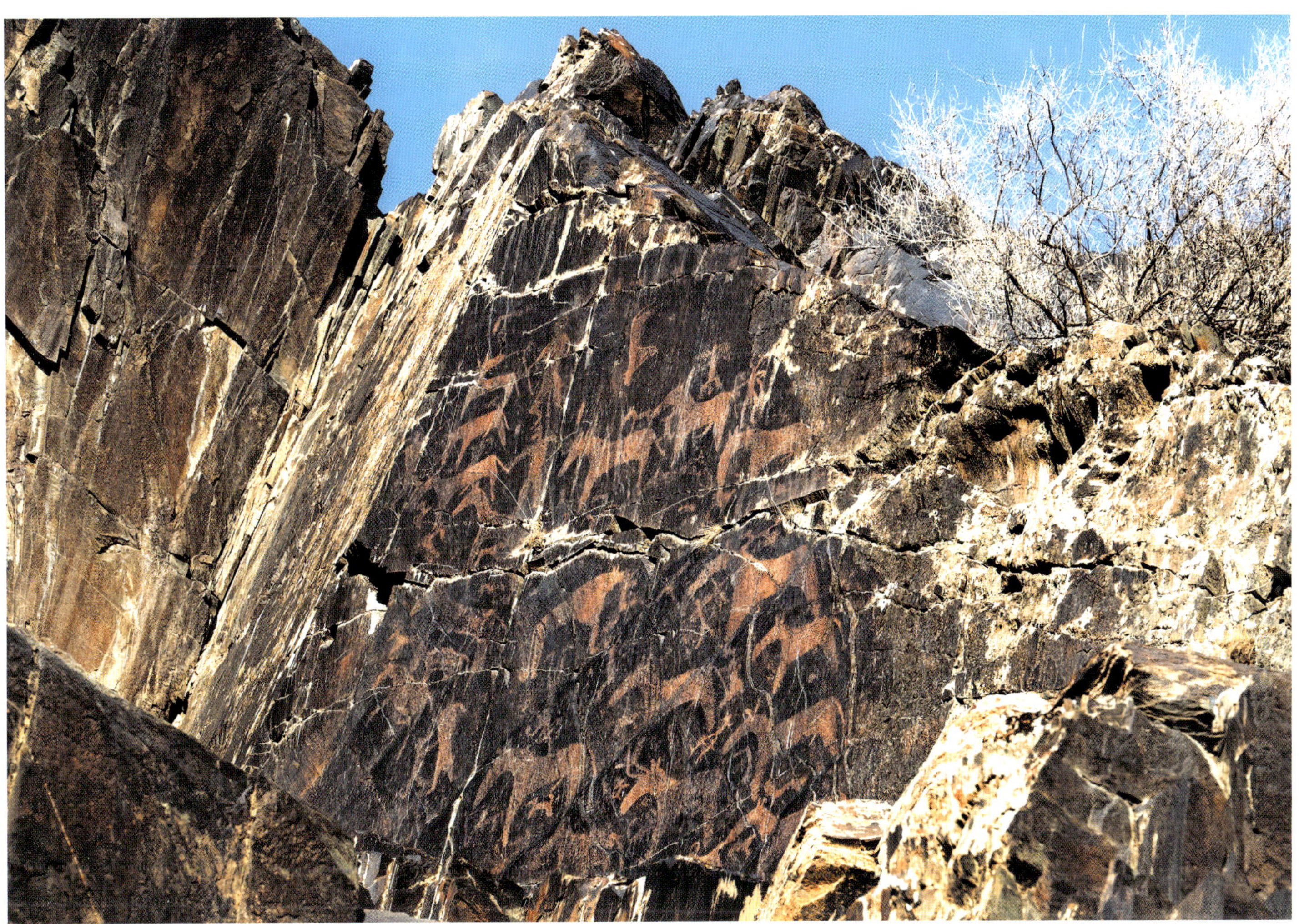

94. Petroglyph panel with 16 kulans, a lion, dogs and humans. Second millennium BCE. Sarmishsay, group III, central Uzbekistan. Photo 2023.

with the burial of a venerated Muslim. Starting at the northern entry into the gorge, the most important groups are as follows:

- **Group III** lies on the eastern bank of the River Sarmishsay. High above the floor of the gorge there are images from the Bronze Age of a few bulls and ibexes placed one above the other (fig. 93). It is striking that a couple of bulls really look like bulls, whereas others seem to rather represent composite animals consisting of the body of an ibex or a boar with bulls' horns. Noteworthy also are the petroglyphs of two sturdy men, respectively 70 and 50 centimetres high, the second of which has broad, female-like hips and is drawing a bow. Nearby can be seen two dancing men with crossed forearms held above their heads, a few kulans, another bull and a feline, probably a panther or cheetah. In addition, there is a unique image of a ladder or staircase which leads to a rectangular figure divided into compartments; this singular composition may represent a house. About 60 metres further north, a large panel, 250 centimetres wide, features at least 16 kulans, a large lion, dogs and a few hunters (fig. 94).

- **Group IV** is on the western bank of the river. Spread over a distance of *ca*. 300 metres can be found petroglyphs of a sow with her piglets, and two mysterious elliptical figures with short rays placed on top of each other and enclosed by a cartouche. Then, further south, are two pairs of adorants facing each other, quite similar to the petroglyphs of adorants at Saimaluu Tash; above them stand two Bactrian camels. These petroglyphs of the adorants and camels are from the early Iron Age (fig. 98). It is unclear whether the adorants and the Bactrian camels are related to each other or not. If they were, it would be a tempting speculation to associate the camels with the mount epitomizing the ancient Iranian deity Verethragna, god of victory.[254] Next to these images is a group consisting of three Bactrian camels, two horsemen and a standing man 70 centimetres tall, and a second group comprising a bull, an ibex, a

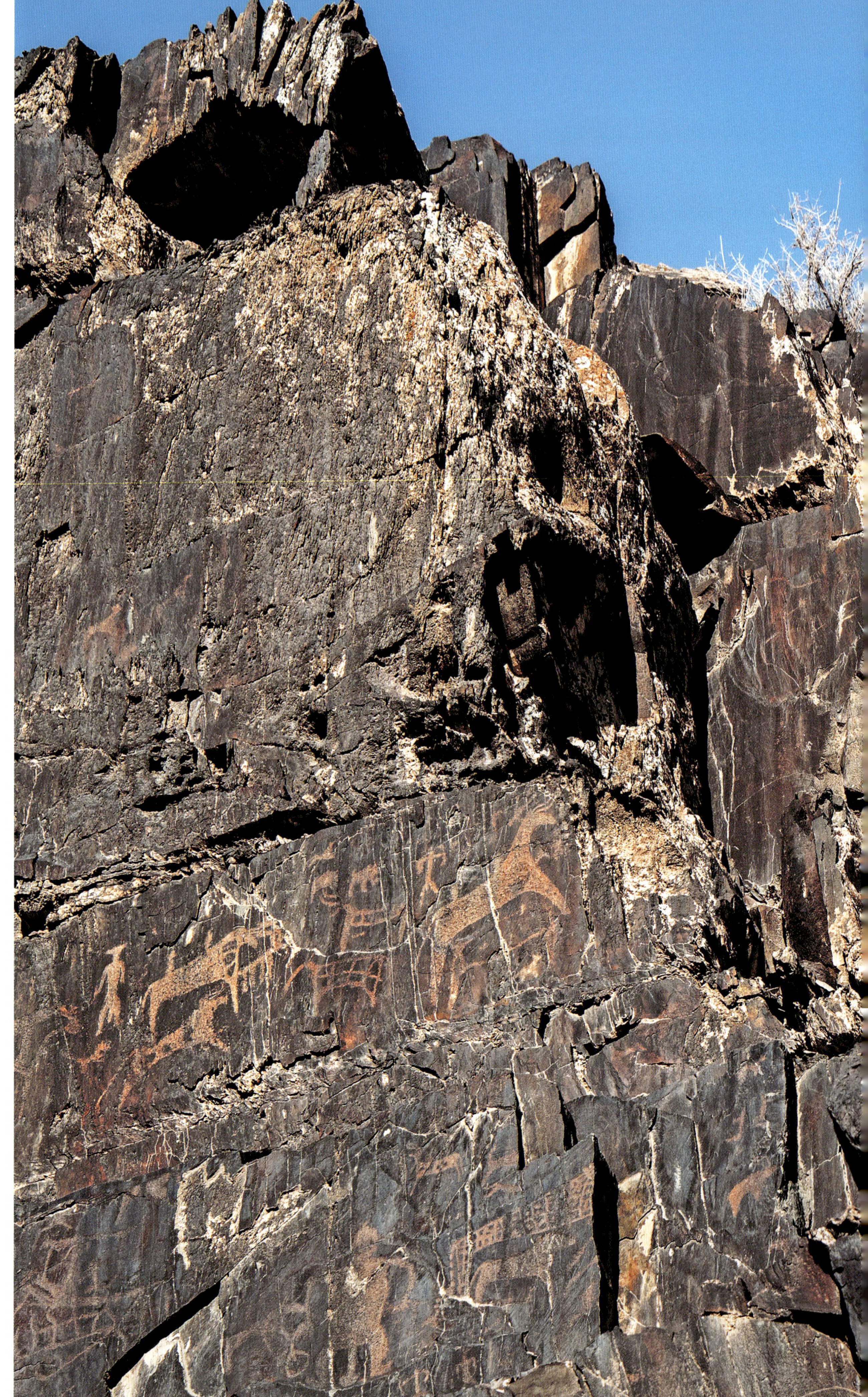

95. Northern part of the large group VI at Sarmishsay. The petroglyphs show aurochs and bulls or hybrid horse–bulls with long horns; a few of them have their bodies divided into compartments which probably illustrates the ancient habit of painting patterns on domesticated cattle. Bronze Age, central Uzbekistan. Photo 2023.

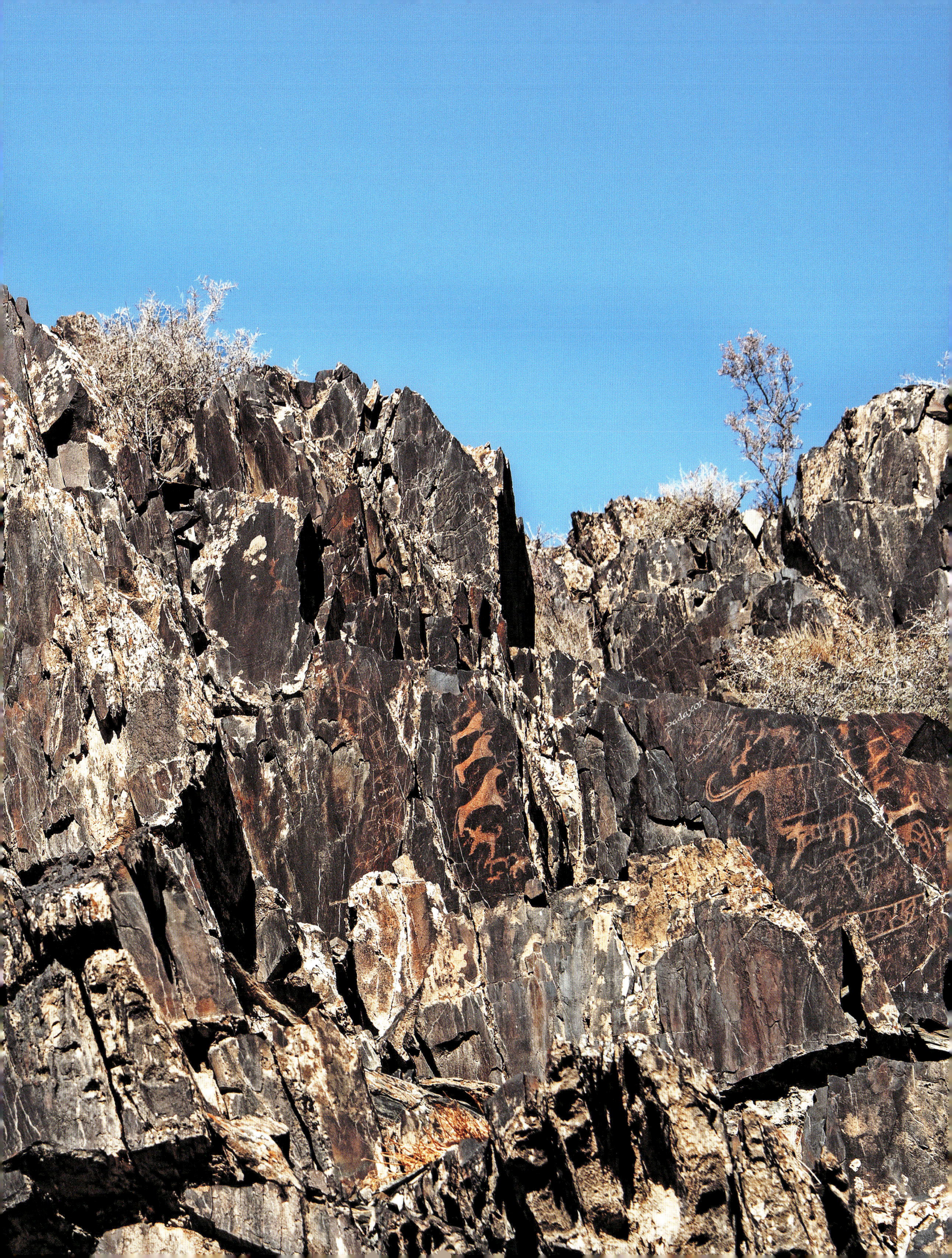

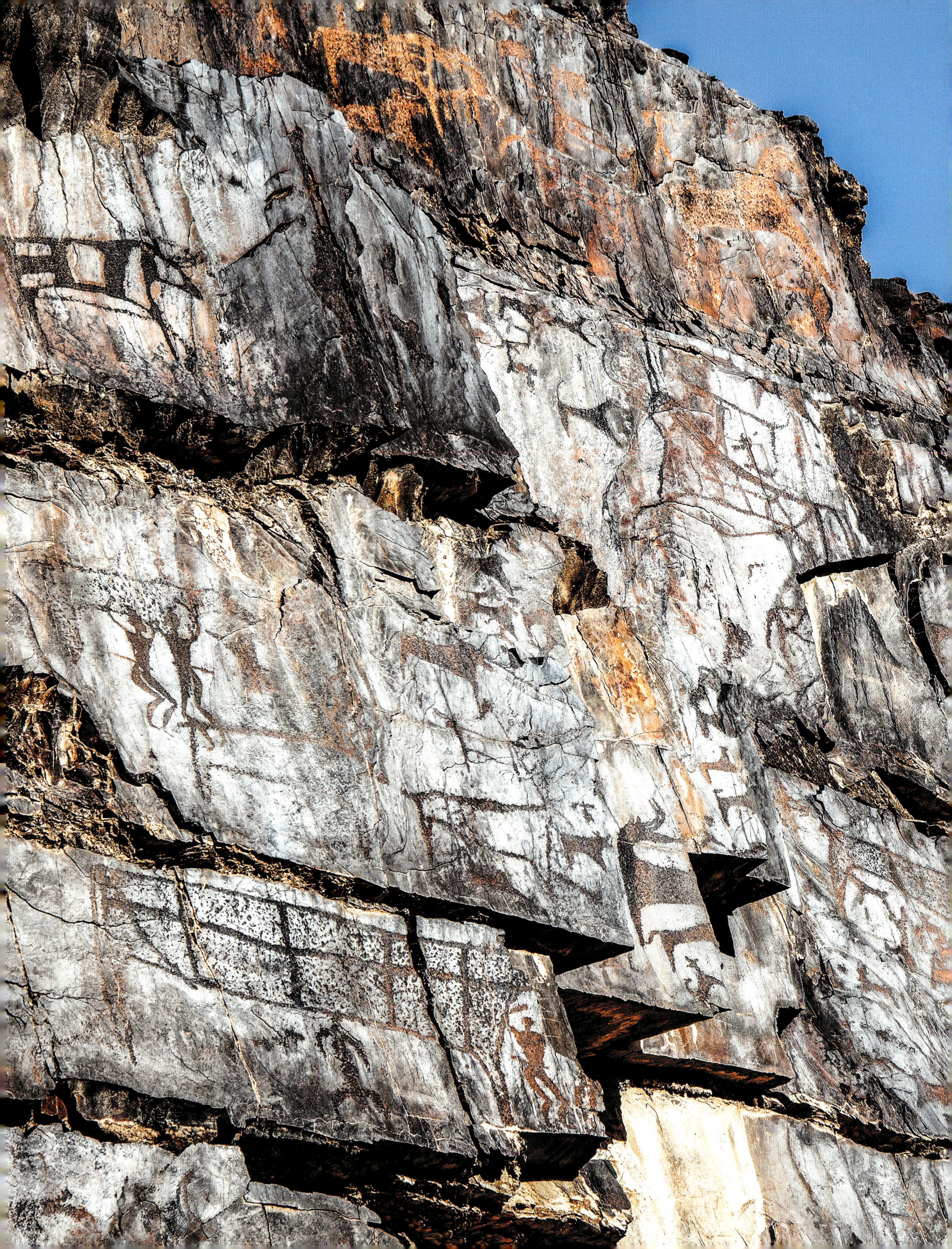

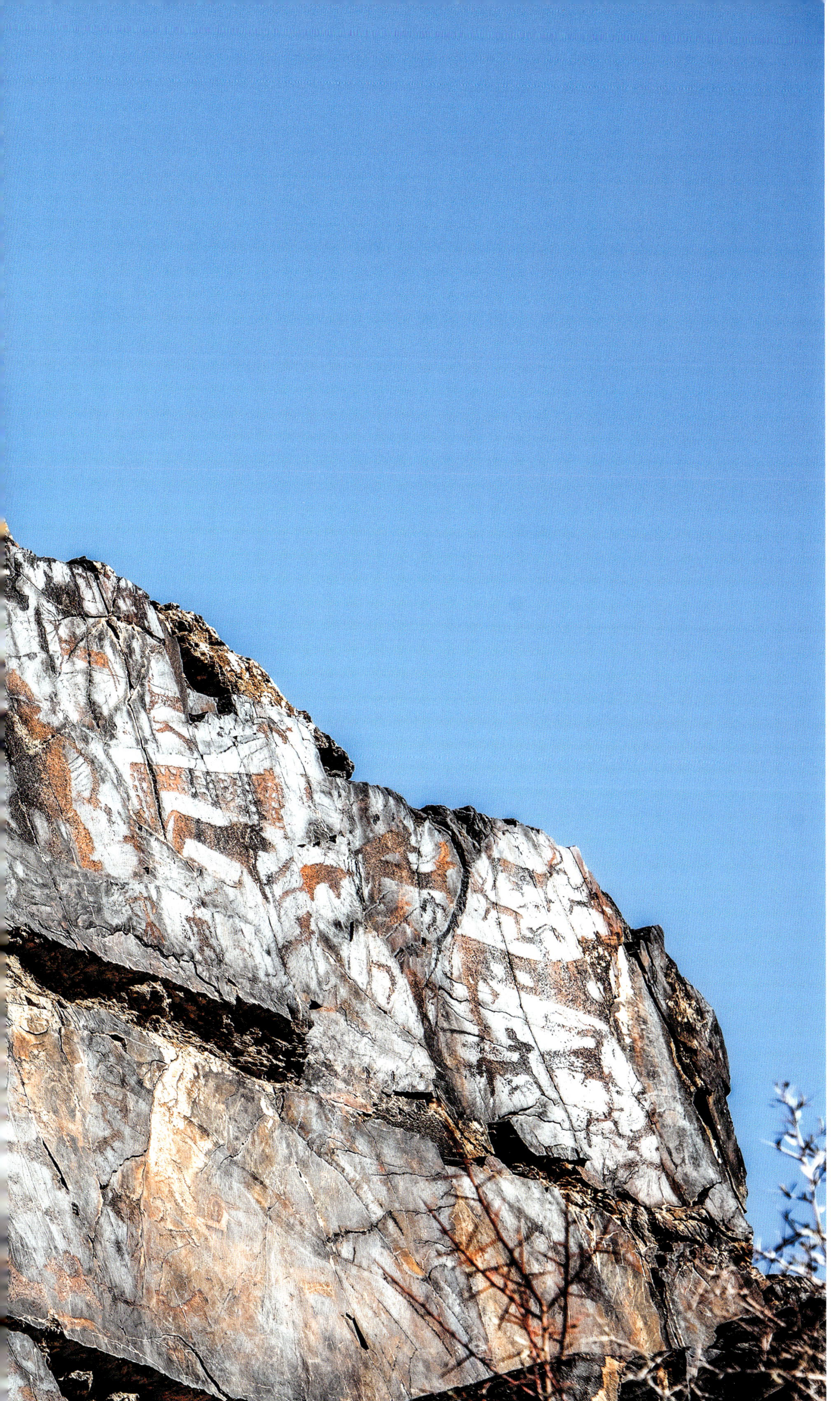

96. Southern part of the large group VI at Sarmishsay with aurochs, bulls, predators, dogs, a camel and humans. To the left, two armed men are dancing with bent knees. Bronze and early Iron Age, central Uzbekistan. Photo 2023.

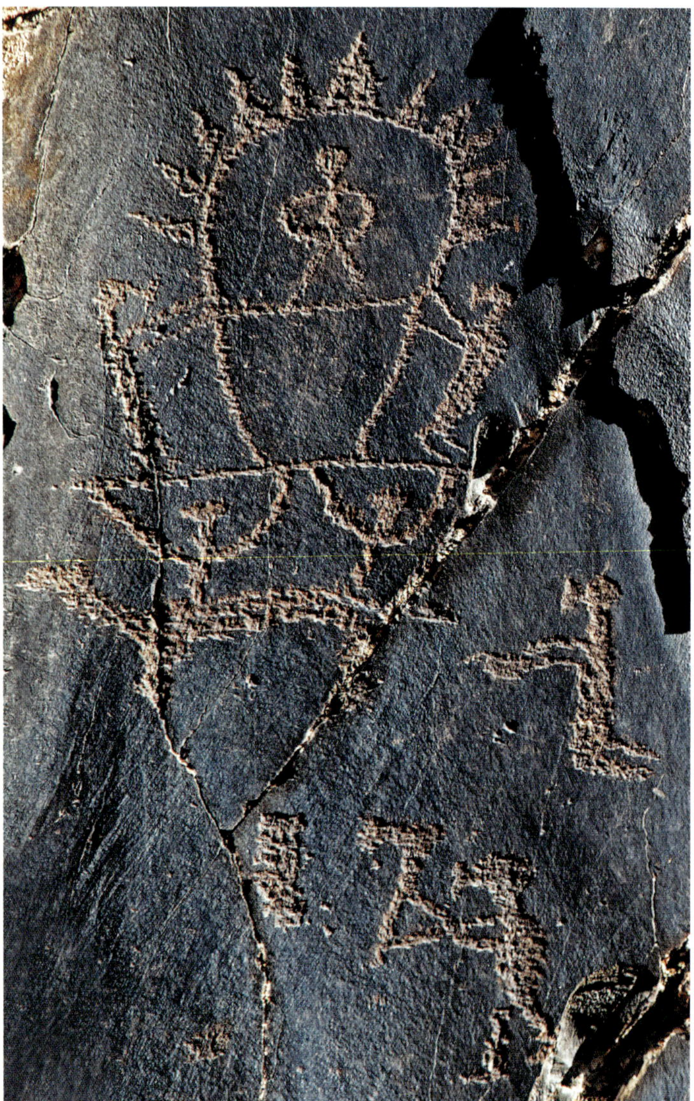

97. A scene with rich mythological content from group X at Sarmishsay, from the later Bronze Age or earlier Iron Age. At the top stands a solar figure, possibly the ancient Iranian solar god Mithra, on a bar which is held by two Zoroastrian priests wearing a *padam*, that is a face mask. They in turn stand on a platform or bar held by two other men standing on an animal, probably a horse. At the bottom right are two further priests with face masks. Central Uzbekistan. Photo 2023.

also seen in Mongolia, Kazakhstan and Kyrgyzstan. It probably represents either a special garment or a ball flail. Next can be seen a peaceful-looking wolf standing next to a man and a fabulous animal composed of the body and head of a horse, a bushy tail like a cow's or a yak's, and circular-shaped horns. About 200 metres southward, a hunter shoots an arrow at a deer which is being pursued by a dog. To the left stands a large bull from the Bronze Age, whose body is divided into segments, one of which could represent its intestines.

- **Group VI** is on the western bank. In this large group there are several scenes involving small humans with large bulls. Some have their bodies divided into compartments, others have long horns as seen at Tamgaly (Kazakhstan); they probably represent aurochs and date from the early Bronze Age (figs 95, 96). The relation between bulls and humans is also reminiscent of scenes at Tamgaly. On another rock higher up, an archer wearing a headdress looking like a ribbon curved backwards shoots an arrow at a distant bull; in front of him a snake rises up. On another panel, two bulls from the Iron Age are attacked by a large dog and a hunter; one of the horned bulls has a slim body like a horse which again suggests a composite animal. Hybrid animals consisting of the body of a horse and bull's horns were one of the characteristics of the rock art at Tamgaly. Such concepts belonged to the imaginary world of the later Bronze Age Andronovians and the Iron Age Sakas of Pazyryk. In the southern, lower part of this group, two men armed with daggers are dancing with bent knees (fig. 96). At the top of a steep cliff about 150 metres north of Group VI are the only four petroglyphs featuring vehicles; they are heavily weathered and feature two single-axe chariots and two double-axle carts.

wolf, a feline and a boar. Then follows a panel featuring at least three carnivores, possibly panthers or cheetahs, chasing more than a dozen kulans. Finally, there is a striking petroglyph of a standing man with his feet turned fully outwards, which was the typical posture of Kushan rulers on coins and in statues. Southern and western Uzbekistan belonged to the Kushan zone of influence in the first and second centuries CE.

- **Group IX** lies on the eastern bank. Noteworthy in this smaller group are, first, three standing men armed with daggers. One of them seems to have a tail ending in a ball – a characteristic

- **Group X** is situated on the eastern bank about 300 metres south of Group IX. In the lower part of this complex are petroglyphs featuring a sex scene between humans, and figures of a camel, ibexes and two deer in the Saka Iron Age style. A little higher up is a group of slender caprines or mountain gazelles, also from the Iron Age. Then follows a singular scene: a man, surrounded by a flaming, elongated halo, stands wide-legged on a central bar which is held by two attendants who clearly wear face masks. These two attendants stand on a second, longer bar, which is held by two other men with arms upraised. These two men stand in turn on an animal which has the body of a horse but a long neck and head of a camel. At the lower right of this composition, a kneeling human with outstretched arms offers a bowl, while below him a standing man wields an axe; both of them wear face masks (fig. 97). The upper figure with the radiant halo suggests a solar deity from the Indo-Iranian mythological realm as at Saimaluu Tash, Tamgaly and Ak-Kainar. This scene, unique in rock art, may thus be interpreted as follows: at the top stands the ancient solar god Mithra, who was also venerated as god of treaties and truth.[255] Mithra and the two upper Zoroastrian priests are in turn held up by two lower-ranking priests standing on the back of a mythical animal which carries the sun; the animal is one of the helpers of the sun – a topic also found in Vedic mythology and,

surprisingly, in ancient Scandinavian rock art (see below). The two Zoroastrian priests at the bottom right assist in a ceremony. These images of solar motifs at Sarmishsay, Tamgaly, Ak-Kainar and Saimaluu Tash not only suggest the existence of a common, supra-regional Indo-Iranian mythological heritage stretching from southern Kazakhstan to Kyrgyzstan and central Uzbekistan, but also highlight the relevance of rock art for our understanding of the culture of that time.

- **Group XIII** lies on the eastern bank. This smaller complex features at its bottom a large, humped bull with short horns and above it another bull with long horns which is threatened by a cheetah and an archer. A little higher come other petroglyphs from the Bronze Age, namely an ithyphallic man armed with a dagger, a kulan, a dog and another man with a triangular-shaped torso, resembling those at Saimaluu Tash. Then, a few metres higher up, there are the petroglyphs of a bull and a camel rider girded with a sword and holding a bow; he follows a man on foot. This scene is from the Middle Ages. The camel rider was afterwards turned into a ruler, since his crown was added later as can be judged from its brighter, that is more recent, repatination. The petroglyphs at Sarmishsay reveal a variety of subjects, several of which belong to the wider Indo-Iranian mythological realm, while others are local in origin.

- **Saikhansay** is a small site situated in the northern foothills of the Morguzar Mountain Range. Noteworthy are the petroglyphs of two men facing each other in lively positions, as if dancing. Both wear a mask with a long beak. There are also several hunting scenes of long-horned aurochs and of ibexes as well as of domestic bulls, horses, wild boar and four-spoked wheels or solar symbols. These images date from the late Bronze Age; later petroglyphs illustrate Bactrian camels and hunters armed with a gun resting on a bipod.[256]

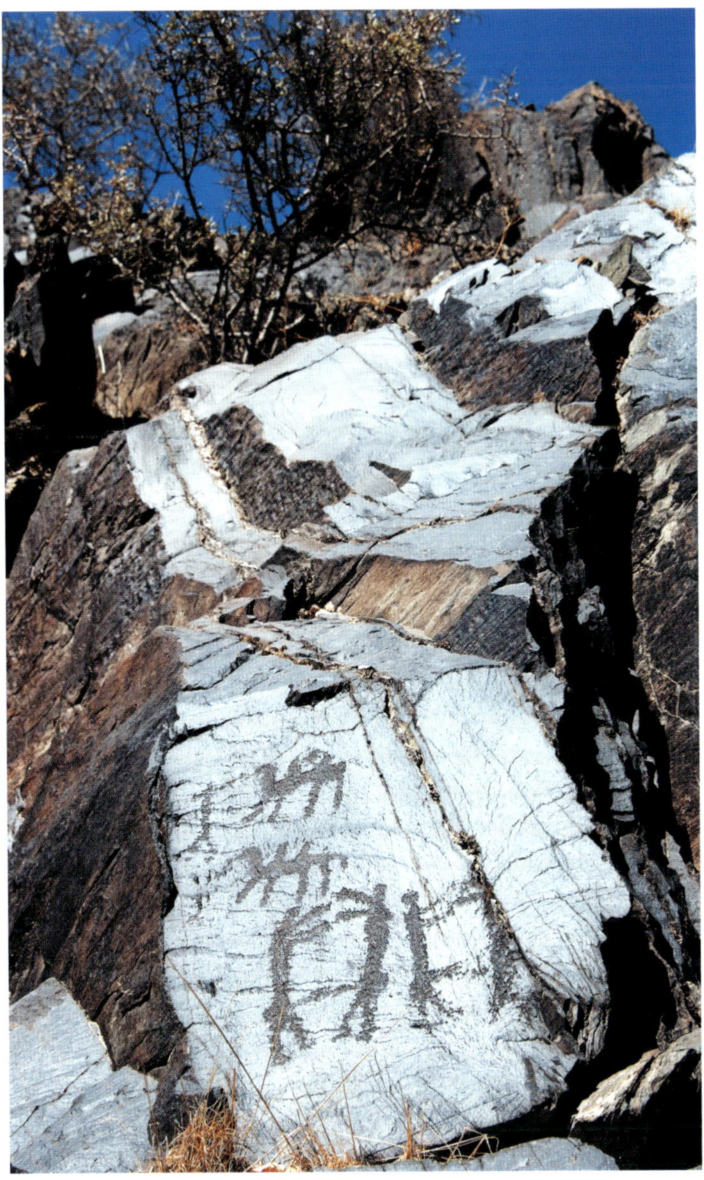

98. Two pairs of men face each other with arms raised, and above, two Bactrian camels. Bronze Age, Sarmishsay, group IV, central Uzbekistan. Photo 2023.

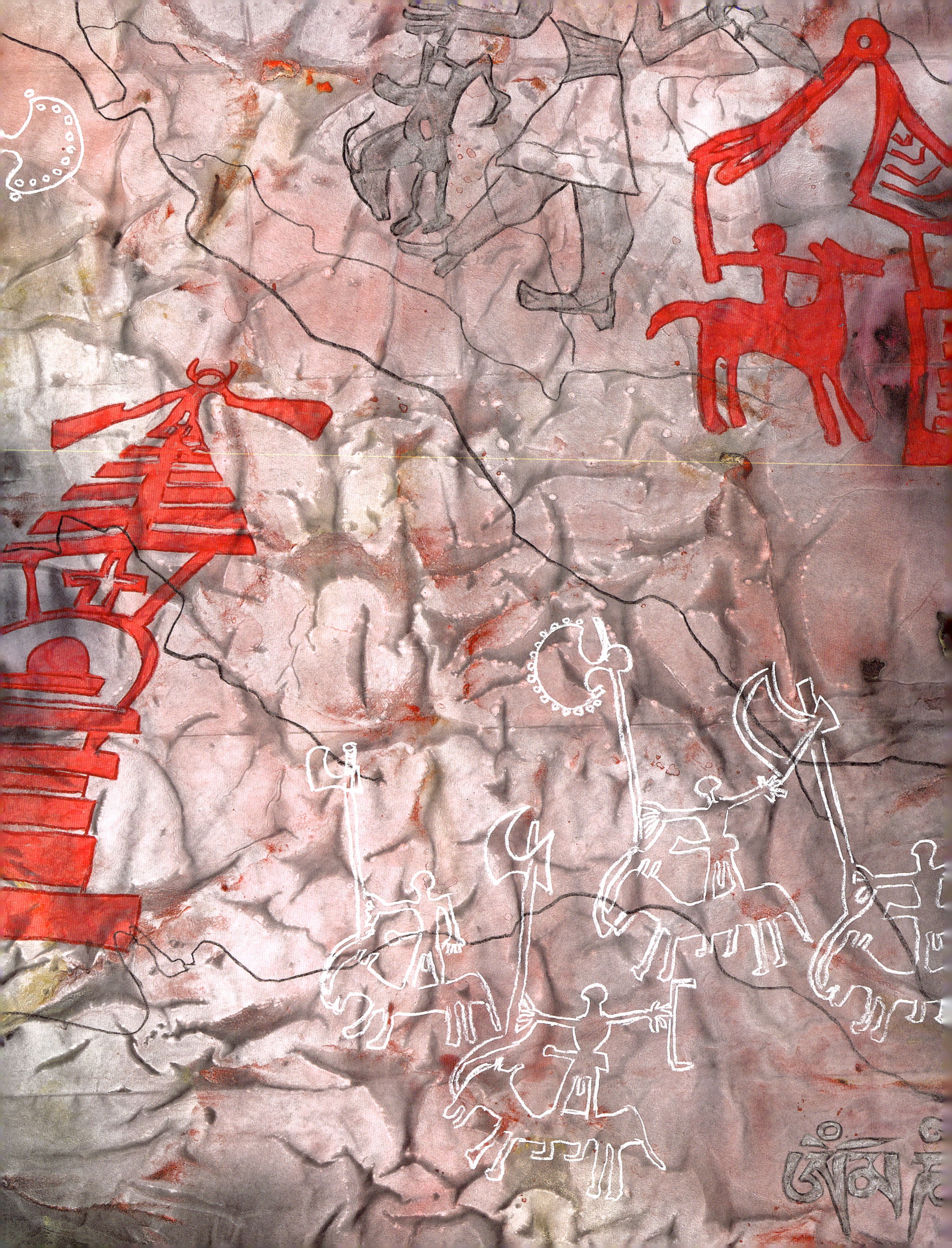

IV. Himalaya, Transhimalaya and Karakoram

The mighty mountain ranges of the Pamirs in the north-west, the Hindu Kush in the south-west, the Karakorams in the centre, the Kunlun in the north-east and the Himalayas in the south-east separate Central Asia from the Indian subcontinent, but they were not insurmountable obstacles. Extremely high passes, such as the Karakoram Pass 5,540 metres above sea level, have connected the Tarim Basin with Ladakh for thousands of years; and in the west, the Hindu Kush can be bypassed via Merv (Turkmenistan), Herat and Kandahar (Afghanistan) to reach the Indian plains. As a result, it is not really surprising to find traces of Central Asian cultures and peoples within these mountain ranges and to the south of them, wherever the carriers of those cultures held onto their identity and the tradition of making rock art. As will be shown, Buddhism appropriated not only the practice of rock engraving, but also the already engraved surfaces onto which new symbols and inscriptions were added and superimposed. Regions showing an influence from Central Asia in their petroglyphs are the western Tibetan high plateau, Ladakh and Zanskar, as well as Gilgit-Baltistan in northern Pakistan.

Western pioneers who explored and described petroglyphs in Ladakh include the Austro-Hungarian ethnographer and linguist Károly Jenő Ujfalvy de Mezőkövesd (1842–1904) who travelled through the western Himalayas in 1881, Martin Conway (1856–1937) and, above all, the Moravian missionary and Tibetologist August Hermann Francke (1870–1930) who lived in Ladakh from 1896 to 1908, before being commissioned in 1909–1910 by the British-Indian government to explore and document the historic monuments of Ladakh, including petroglyphs and rock inscriptions.[1] Francke identified the following scripts in rock inscriptions: three types of Brahmi, Takri, Kharosthi, Sarada, Devanagari, Lantsa (Ranjana), Tibetan and Arabic.[2] Concerning the highly important petroglyph site of Tanktse (Drangtse), F.E. Shaw had already noted in 1906 its various inscriptions and surprising Maltese crosses.[3] As for the Tibetan high plateau, the Swedish explorer Sven Hedin (1865–1952) was, in October 1900, probably the first who noticed and carefully described petroglyphs featuring humans, mounted and on foot, hunting antelopes, kulans, wild yaks and a tiger. From the image of a tiger on the Tibetan plateau Hedin deduced that these petroglyphs had been pecked by people who were familiar with tigers. Hedin suggested that they were hunters coming from the Lop Nor region in the eastern Tarim Basin where tigers had roamed in the past.[4]

Concerning the Gilgit-Baltistan region, Ujfalvy de Mezőkövesd was again the first to take note of the rock art, this time in Baltistan. He published his findings in 1884.[5] The next pioneer was Ghulam Mohammad, chief clerk in the Political Office of Gilgit, who published some information on Buddhist petroglyphs featuring stupas and Brahmi inscriptions in 1905.[6] Eight years later, Sir Aurel Stein (1862–1943) noticed Buddhist petroglyphs on some boulders when travelling through the Hodar Valley to Yasin in August 1913.[7]

99. ← Therese Weber, *Emergence of Powers I.* Traditions, communication and armed conflicts meet in the terrain with border regions, mountains and rivers. Buildings engraved in stone testify to the worship of the deities in the Himalayan regions. 84 × 68 cm. Chinese ink painting and chalk drawing on mulberry paper, 2024.

Then, in 1942, Stein explored a few Buddhist rock inscriptions and petroglyphs near the village of Chilas situated on the left bank of the Upper Indus. At that time, he followed indications given by Captains A.W. Redpath and C.D. Murphy, assistant political agents, Gilgit, and by G.H. Emerson of the Imperial Civil Service.[8] The petroglyphs and inscriptions of Gilgit-Baltistan, especially those in the region of Chilas, were later thoroughly researched between 1979 and 2012 by a Pakistani–German team headed by Ahmad Hasan Dani and Karl Jettmar, and from 1989 by Harald Hauptmann. The results were published in the monumental, eleven-volume monograph *Materialien zur Archäologie der Nordgebiete Pakistans* (1994–2013).[9] As in Ladakh, large-scale Buddhist stone reliefs like those of Kargah near Gilgit and of Manthal near Skardu were already known in the nineteenth century.

1. Western Tibet, Ladakh and Zanskar

Although the petroglyphs in western Tibet on the one hand and in Ladakh and Zanskar on the other show some differences, these three regions are discussed together. The reason for this is the fact that communication routes linking these regions have existed since the Bronze Age. Moreover, parts of western Tibet and Ladakh formed a cultural and religious community from about the sixth century CE until the nineteenth century, and (with an interruption from *ca.* 842 to 912) in political terms until 1684 when the Treaty of Tingmosgang fixed the boundary between Tibet and Ladakh, which was reduced to the status of a vassal of the Indian Mughal Empire.

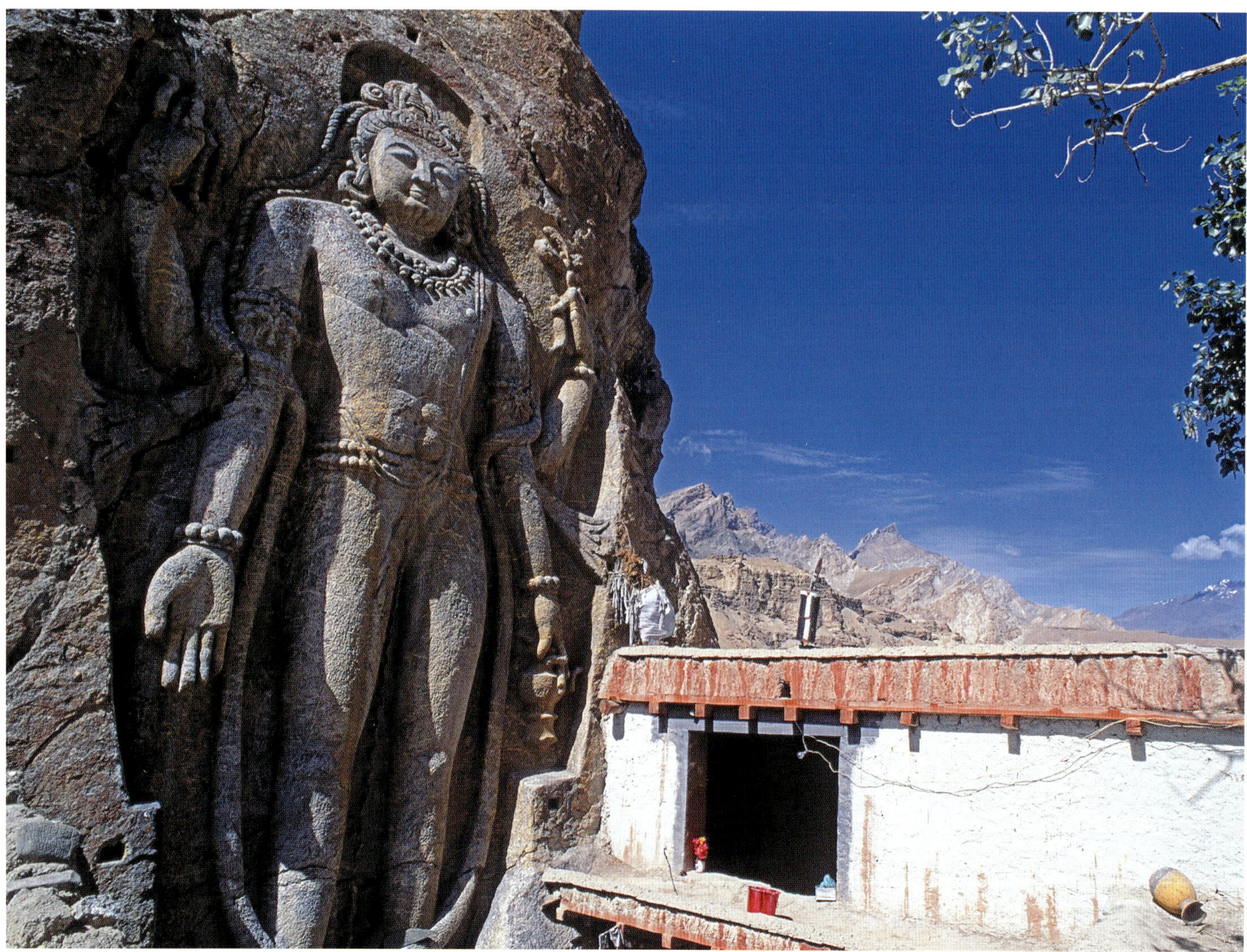

100. Figure of the Bodhisattva of compassion, Avalokitesvara, hewn out of the rock at Mulbekh. Ninth to tenth century CE. Ladakh, India. Photo 1998.

The most important sites in these three regions are:

Western Tibet

- **Ruthok** is a district in westernmost Tibet; there are petroglyph sites dating from the Bronze Age to the Buddhist period. At the site of **Renmudong** there are several Iron Age petroglyphs in the Animal Style. In total, about 70 sites have been recorded in western Tibet.[10]

Ladakh and Zanskar[11]

- **Murgi Tokpo**, in the Nubra Valley, northern Ladakh, has petroglyphs mainly from the Bronze Age.

- **Domkhar** and neighbouring **Khalatse** in western Ladakh have numerous petroglyphs in the Animal Style of the Saka Iron Age.

- **Zamthang**, also known locally as Char, is in Zanskar. Here, several Bronze Age petroglyphs have been over-pecked by Buddhist petroglyphs of chortens (stupas).

- **Gyalwa Ringna**, near Padum, Zanskar. On a huge boulder situated at an altitude of 3,700 m asl are carved the large images of the Five Tathagata Buddhas and on another boulder nearby the Five Bodhisattvas. The images on both boulders date to the Middle Ages.

- **Shey**, south of Leh, Ladakh's capital. On the road from Leh to the palace and monastery of Shey is a huge boulder with the engravings of the Five Tathagata Buddhas.

- **Tanktse (Drangtse)** is located in eastern Ladakh. Besides petroglyphs from the Bronze Age and in the Animal Style, there is a boulder with historically important inscriptions and Nestorian Christian crosses.

- **Kharul**, situated north of Kargil in western Ladakh, has a boulder with a long Tibetan inscription commemorating the achievements of a western Tibetan councillor in the service of a western Tibetan king of Purang, dating from the second to fourth quarter of the eleventh century CE.[12]

- **Alchi Bridge**, one of the largest petroglyph sites of Ladakh, is situated on the left bank of the Indus opposite Saspol on the way to Alchi, near the ancient bridge. As in some other sites, the petroglyphs were carved next to a dangerous crossing point over a torrential river, which is an indication that such places had a sacred character. Unfortunately, many rocks with petroglyphs from the Bronze Age to the Buddhist period have been ruthlessly destroyed or pushed into the Indus in the course of construction of the road to the village of Alchi.[13]

- Several smaller sites are located along or in the vicinity of both banks of the river Indus, namely, from west to east, at **Mulbekh**, **Khalatse** (which also has interesting inscriptions), **Nurla**, **Saspol** and between **Phyang** and **Taroo.**

- In Ladakh, huge Buddhist figures of the Bodhisattva Maitreya and Avalokitesvara have been carved in high relief into the rock at places including **Mulbekh** and **Khartse Khar** in western Ladakh; the former is 9 m high and the latter 7 m high. Further large high-relief Buddhist figures are at **Apati** and at **Tumail**, both north-east of Kargil.

- Besides petroglyphs and high-relief figures, there are also several carved, free-standing Buddhist stone steles in Ladakh, for example at **Changspa** and **Skara** near Leh, **Dras** west of Kargil in western Ladakah, south-east of **Shey**, at **Digar** in the Nubra Valley and at **Sani** in Zanskar.[14]

Excluded from consideration in this list are the so-called *mani* stones which are portable stone pebbles or plates inscribed with the six-syllable mantra of Bodhisattva Avalokitesvara *Om mani padme hum*, in Tibetan ༀ་མ་ཎི་པ་དྨེ་ཧཱུྃ. The mantra is also carved on immobile boulders and cliffs (fig. 105). It is considered auspicious to engrave or donate *mani* stones as votive offerings. They are often grouped along roads and rivers or on top of mountain passes to form mounds or walls up to several hundred metres long. The mantra is usually carved in high relief and each syllable is painted in a different symbolic colour. According to Buddhist beliefs, such piles and walls have to be circumvented or passed clockwise from the left-hand side, but according to the teachings of Bön, Tibet's pre-Buddhist religion, they should be passed anticlockwise from the right-hand side.[15]

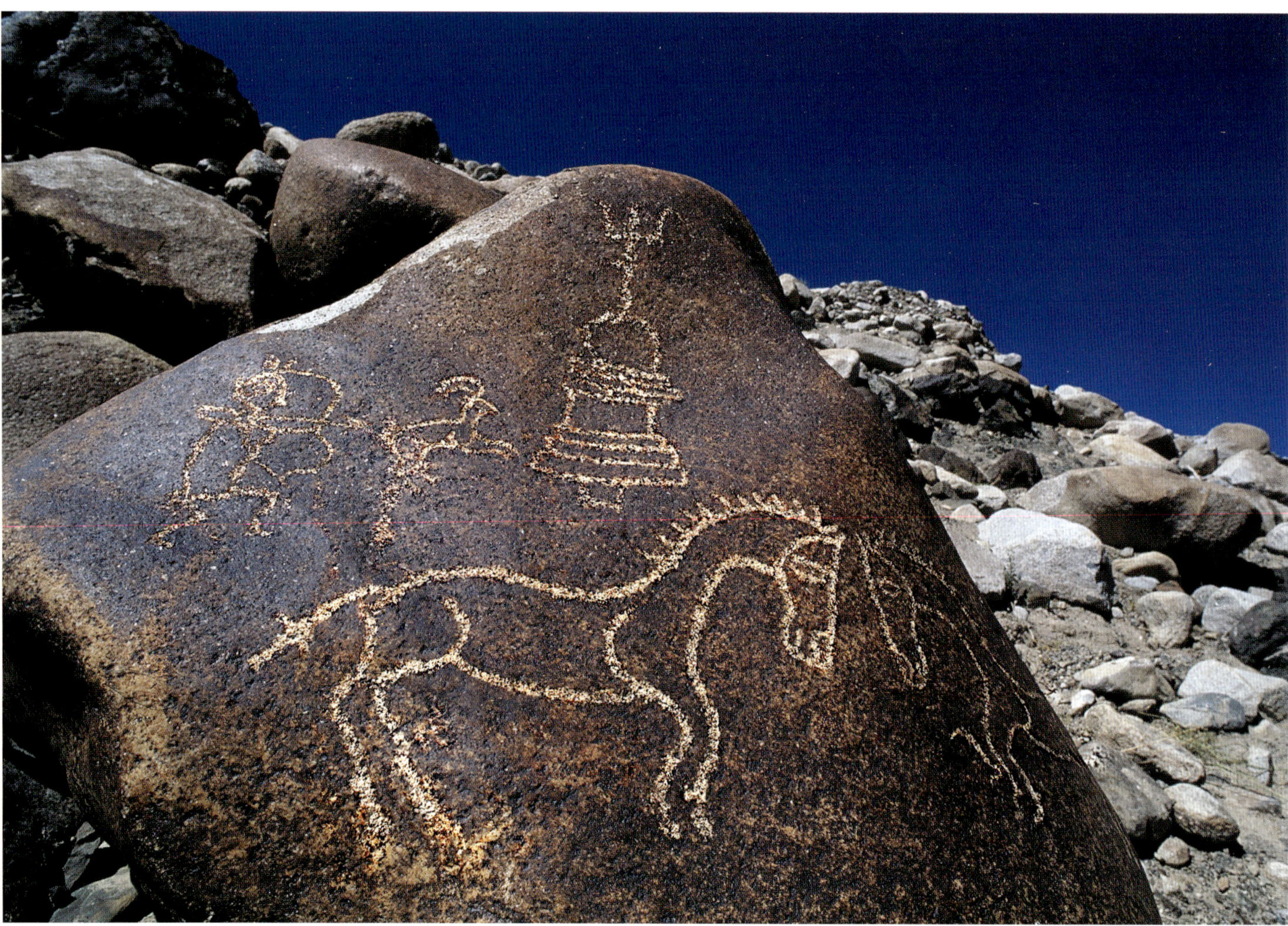

101. Boulder with a hunting scene to the left and two horses facing each other, on the left bank of the Indus near the Alchi Bridge, Ladakh, India. The two mirrored horses show influence from the Steppe Animal Style. Photo 1998.

Back in 1982, the German Tibetologist Gerd Koenig published an article entitled 'Scythians in Tibet?' Starting from an ancient amulet (*tokcha*) found in Ladakh and made of a copper alloy in the shape of a backward-looking bird of prey similar to Scythian Animal Style metal raptor fittings, Koenig hypothesized that this amulet, which probably originated in western Tibet, pointed to 'a temporary incorporation of western Tibet into the cultural space of the Central Asian steppes'.[16] He dated this small find, which was probably originally a fitting on a horse's harness, to the early Iron Age of Tibet. Later, in 1990, the French archaeologist Henri-Paul Francfort gave specificity to Koenig's hypothesis, based on published research of petroglyphs in northern Pakistan, Ladakh, Zanskar and western Tibet: 'It seems that the upper Indus Valley and its geographical extension into Tibet were crossed by peoples related to those of Central Asia in the second and first millennia BCE.'[17] Judging from the striking similarities between Bronze and Iron Age petroglyphs in Central Asia and those and the regions under discussion, Francfort concluded:

Tribes from the Andronovian and later the Sako-Siberian steppe populations visited Ladakh, Zanskar and western Tibet extensively from the Bronze Age at least until the fourth century BCE and were in contact with the empires of China in the east and Persia in the upper Indus.[18]

Indeed, as will be shown below, the comparison between the petroglyphs south of the Hindu Kush–Karakoram line of mountain ranges and those in Central Asia strongly suggests intense cultural contacts between these regions, most probably caused by migration. As noted by John V. Bellezza, genetic studies have indicated that the genetic heritage of the Tibetans, who are closely related to other Sino-Tibetan populations, includes an ancient genetic admixture from Central Asia which occurred through migration movements from the central Asian steppes into western Tibet.[19]

Some five major routes existed to reach the northern fringes of the Indian subcontinent from the north, with Xinjiang serving as a thoroughfare in each case. As suggested by petroglyphs located in the Kuruk Tagh Mountains[20] between the oases of Turfan and Korla, by archaeological finds discovered at Satma Mazar and Yuan Sha along the course of the former lower Keriya River,[21] and by petroglyphs located in the Kunlun Mountains south of the oasis of Qiemo,[22] there were two routes crossing the Kunlun Mountains into western Tibet; from there, routes continued north-westward to Ladakh and then to Zanskar or Kashmir. A third, important caravan route from Yarkand, at the southern edge of the Tarim Basin, crossed the 5,540-metre-high Karakoram Pass. From here, the route continued in three directions: one led over the 5,411-metre-high Saser Pass into the Nubra Valley, and then via the 5,359-metre-high Khardung Pass to Leh; a second made

a detour to the east via Tanktse, which is a rich petroglyph site, before reaching the River Indus at Karu and continuing to Leh; the third ran southward from the Karakoram Pass and the upper Nubra Valley, but avoided following the Nubra River downwards and led instead to the neighbouring Shyok Valley and then downstream to Leh. This was the route taken by the famous second mission of Sir Thomas Forsyth to Yarkand and Kashgar in 1873–74.[23] A fourth route led from Yarkand or Kashgar over the 4,709-metre-high Mintaka Pass and the 4,827-metre-high Kilik Pass into the Hunza Valley to Gilgit. Further south, at the confluence of the Astor River and the Indus, one route led southwards over the 4,100-metre-high Burzil Pass to Kashmir, whereas a second bifurcated eastward

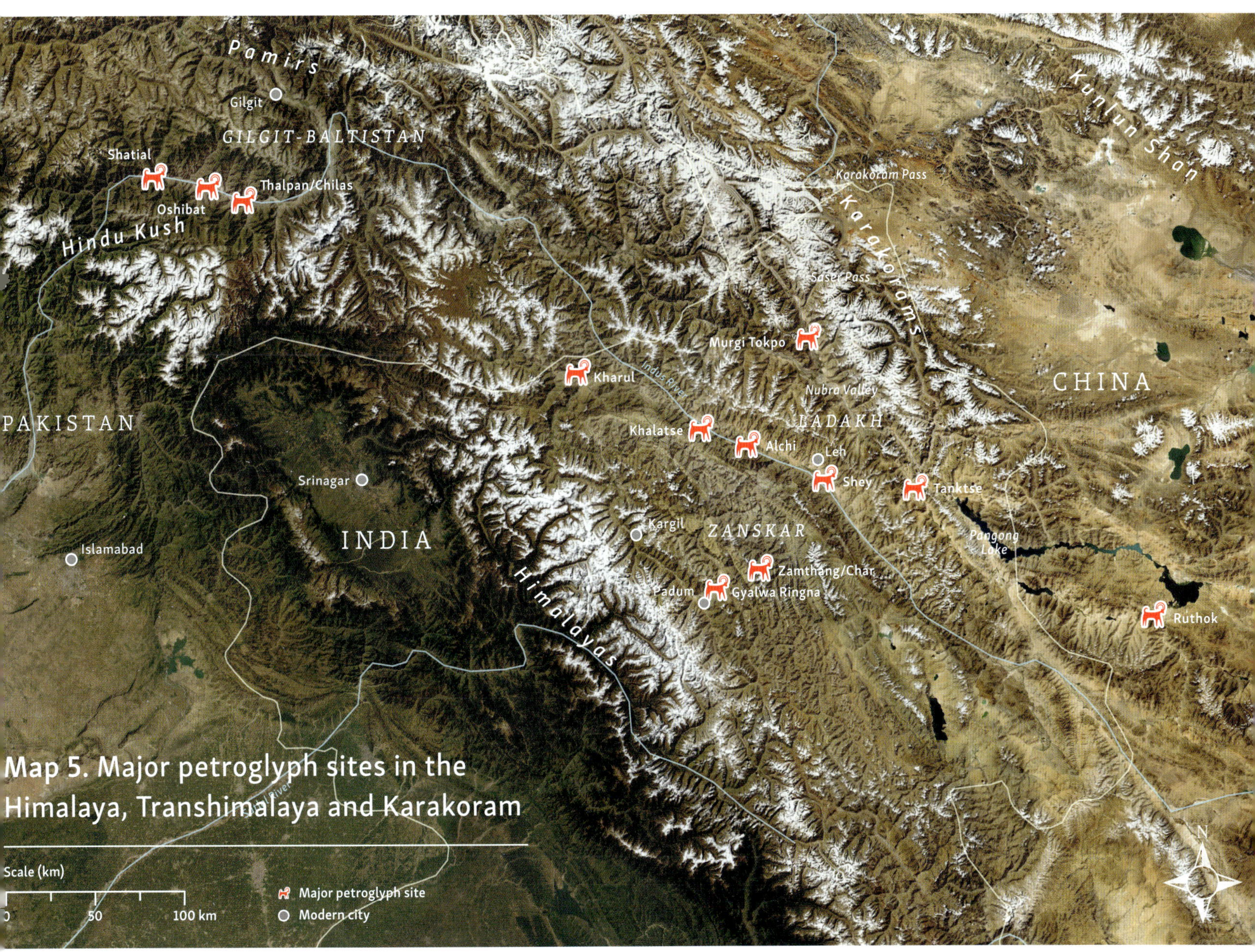

Map 5. Major petroglyph sites in the Himalaya, Transhimalaya and Karakoram

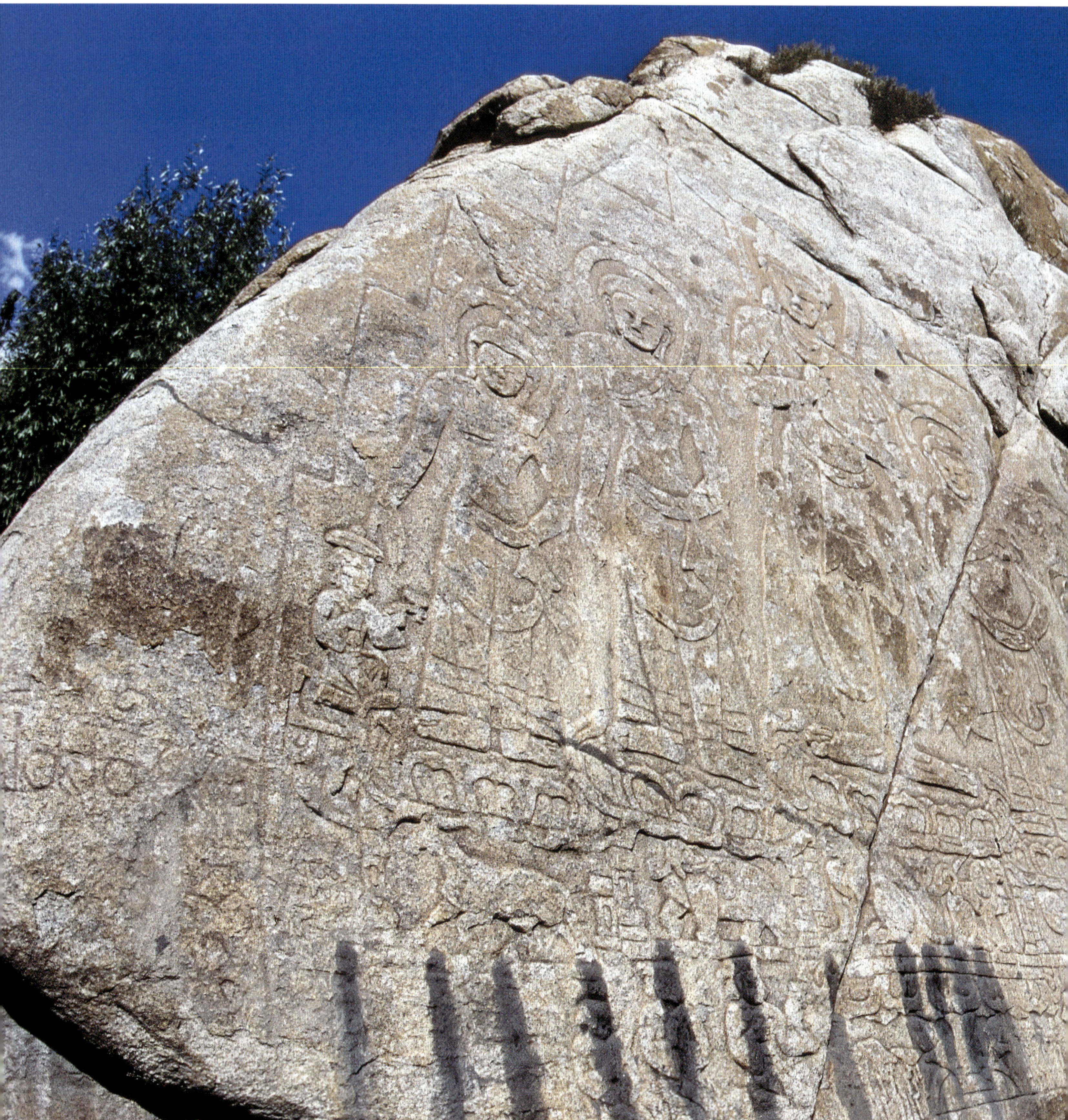

102. The Five Tathagata Buddhas carved into a boulder close to the palace and monastery of Shey. *ca.* tenth century CE. Ladakh, India. Photo 1998.

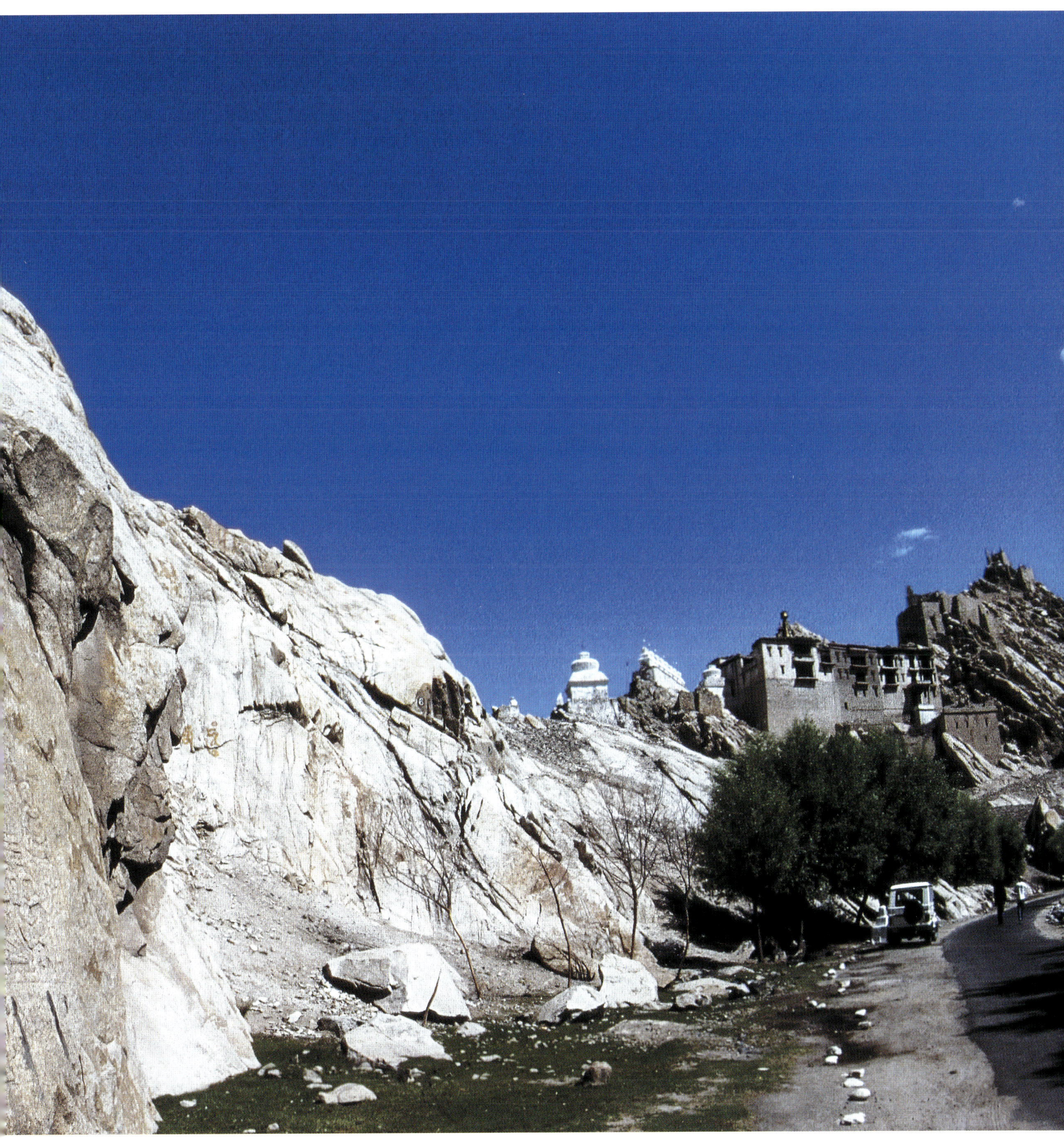

following the Indus, passing the rich petroglyph sites of the Chilas region, and then leading southwards through the infamously dangerous Indus Gorges – called 'hanging passages' by the Chinese pilgrim-monk Faxian (d. *ca.* 418 or 423 CE)[24] – to today's Khyber Pakhtunkhwa province of Pakistan. The fifth route, finally, led over the Pamirs to the region of Lake Zorkul and from there either via the 4,630-metre-high Khora Burt Pass into the upper Gilgit Valley or via the 3,798-metre-high Broghil Pass to Chitral.

Although Ladakh and western Tibet formed transit corridors for people from Central Asia, they remained relatively isolated and only adopted technological innovations such as metallurgy after a time lag. This is reflected in the chronological classification established by Bellezza and Bruneau:[25]

- **Neolithic** period (to *ca.* 1500 BCE)

- **Bronze Age** (*ca.* 1500–900 BCE, possibly later in western Tibet).

- **Iron Age** (*ca.* 900 BCE–100 BCE, possibly later in western Tibet).

During this period, an Indo-Aryan people called Mon came from the Gilgit region, northern Pakistan, to Ladakh.[26]

- **Early historic** period in Ladakh (*ca.* 100 BCE–*ca.* 650 CE). An inscription in Kharosthi carved in a boulder near the **Khalatse** bridge across the Indus names the Kushan ruler 'Uvima Kavthisa', that is Vidma Kadphises (r. *ca.* 102–127 CE), showing that in the first and second centuries CE Ladakh belonged to the Kushan Empire.[27] In the fourth or fifth century CE, the Indo-Aryan Dards, who also came from northern Pakistan, subjugated the Mon.[28] About two centuries later, Ladakh came under the influence of the poorly known western Tibetan Kingdom of Zhangzhung, which, for its part, passed in the later 640s under the control of King Songtsen Gampo (r. *ca.* 627 or 632–650 CE) from the central Tibetan dynasty of Purgyal.[29]

- **Protohistoric** period in western Tibet (*ca.* 100 BCE–*ca.* 650 CE). Western Tibet was during this period the centre of the elusive Kingdom of Zhangzhung.[30]

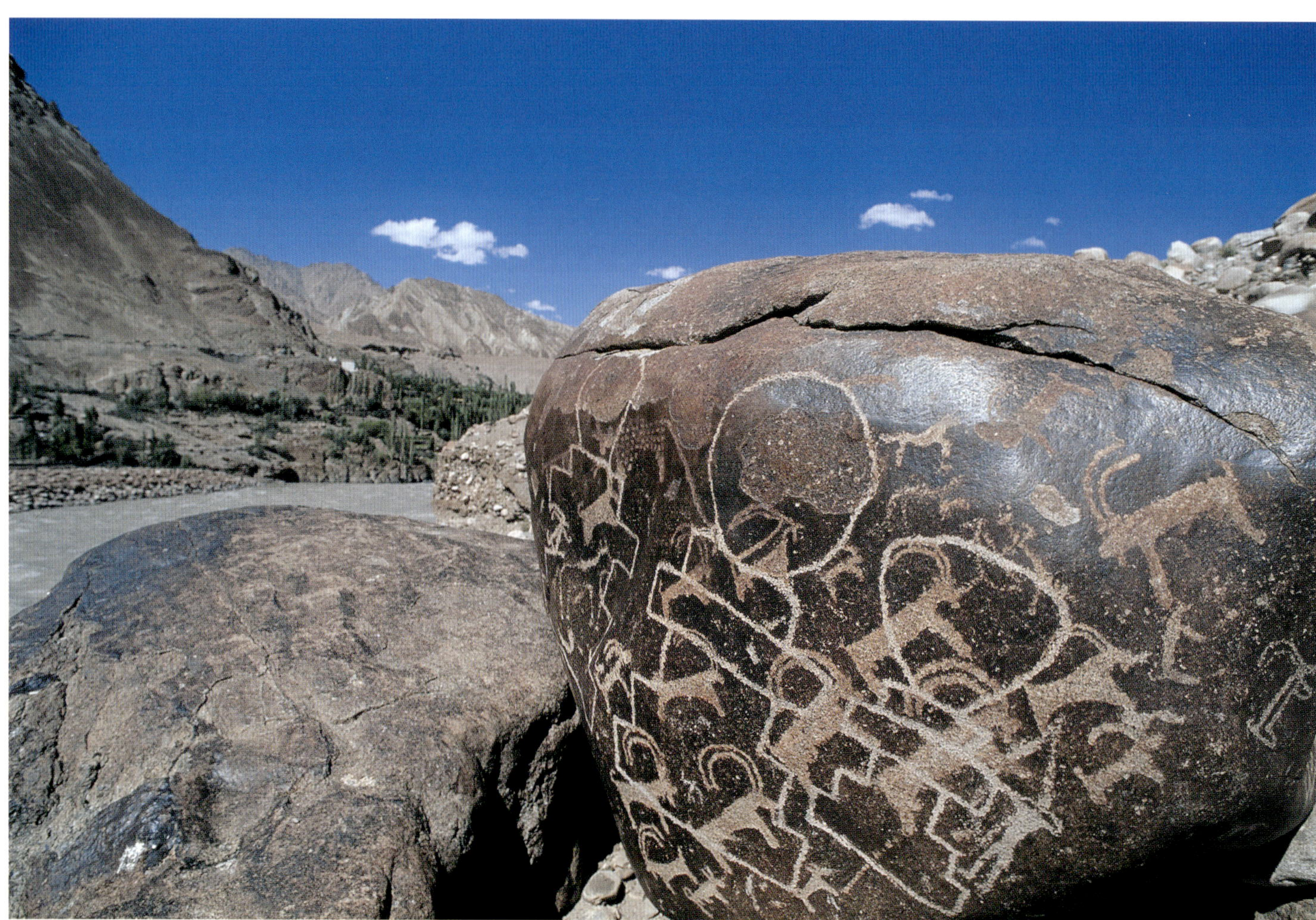

103. Petroglyph palimpsest of Bronze Age ibexes superimposed by Buddhist stupas. Left bank of the Indus near the Alchi Bridge, Ladakh, India. Photo 1998.

- **Imperial** period (*ca.* 650–*ca.* 850 CE) and **post-Imperial** period (*ca.* 850–1000 CE). Following the murder of King Langdarma of the Purgyal dynasty in 842 CE, the Tibetan Empire fell apart and sank into civil war. Langdarma's great-grandson Kyide Nyimagon (r. *ca.* 900–930 CE) fled to western Tibet and around 912 CE founded the Kingdom of Guge to which Ladakh and Zanskar also belonged. At Kyide Nyimagon's death, the kingdom was divided among his three sons into Guge-Purang (western Tibet proper), Maryul (Ladakh) and Zanskar-Spiti.[31] During this period Ladakh became more deeply Tibetized.

- **Second diffusion of Buddhism** and period of the **Buddhist schools** (*ca.* 1000–1642 CE). Following an intermittent and partial Buddhist proselytization during the Imperial period, the second diffusion of Buddhism began in western Tibet and Ladakh at the instigation of King Khor De of Guge-Purang (r. late tenth century), better known under his later monastic name Lhachen Yeshe Ö. He commissioned the Buddhist teachers Atisha (d. 1054) and Rinchen Zangpo (d. 1055) to spread Buddhism through his realm. It was in this period that the engraving of Buddhist inscriptions on cliffs and boulders began, which has lasted till the present day. In Ladakh, the new dynasty of Namgyal seized power in 1470, holding it until 1834. As for Tibet, in 1642 the leader of the Khoshut-Oirat, Güshi Khan, installed the Fifth Dalai Lama as political ruler of Tibet, thus founding the theocracy of the Dalai Lama which lasted until 1951 when the Chinese People's Liberation Army (PLA) occupied Lhasa.[32]

In **Murgi Tokpo** in the northern Ladakhi Nubra Valley and, albeit to a lesser degree, in the western Tibetan district of **Ruthok** can be found various specific petroglyph motifs dating to the Bronze Age which are very similar to contemporaneous images from Central Asia.[33] These include, for example, archers on foot armed with a mace or, more likely, with a ball flail; duels between archers; animals with bi-triangular bodies; and humans with triangular-shaped torsos as at Saimaluu Tash in Kyrgyzstan.[34] Common to both Murgi Tokpo and Central Asia, furthermore, are petroglyphs of giants, solar symbols, solar anthropomorphs, 'dumbbell' objects, bulls or yaks whose tail ends have the shape of a ball, the flight of an arrow shown as a straight line reaching from the bow to the prey, and anthropomorphs wearing a mushroom-shaped headdress.[35] The last figure is also found at Zamthang in Zanskar.[36] Some of these images, such as giants, mushroom-headed humans and dumbbell objects are not found in Ruthok, which is,

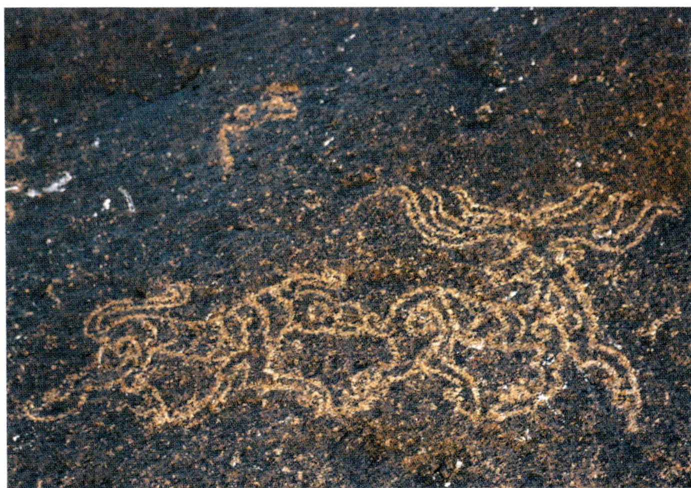

104. A feline engraved in the dynamic Animal Style hunts a stag at Tanktse. *ca.* 600–400 BCE. Pangong Region, Ladakh, India. Photo 1998.

according to Bellezza and Bruneau, an indication that western Tibet was more isolated and enjoyed less contact with the Central Asian Andronovians than did Ladakh.[37]

Petroglyphs of light, spoked chariots, a less specific motif, occur in Ladakh only at Trishul, in the Valley of the Indus close to the monastery of Hemis, but more than twenty times in western Tibet.[38] Finally, the images of masks which are widespread in Central Asia, Tuva and southern Siberia, are also found in Ruthok (western Tibet), in the Nubra Valley (Ladakh), in Zamthang (Zanskar) and in the region of Chilas (northern Pakistan). They are interpreted either as real masks or as representations of painted or tattooed faces. Some masks have tiny feet and hold a bow with an arrow ready to shoot; these masks represent hunters hiding behind a large painted shield.[39] Such images are mostly associated with the Bronze Age Okunev culture, but also to a later phase of the preceding Afanasievo culture.[40] All these findings strongly suggest that the Nubra Valley formed, via the Karakoram and Saser passes further north, an important transit route for people belonging to the Okunev, Andronovo and later the Karasuk cultures. In view of the scarcity of archaeological excavations in western Tibet and Ladakh, petroglyphs represent, besides archaeogenetics, the only source of information for understanding such Bronze Age migrations.

That rock pecking continued during the Iron Age at Murgi Tokpo, although on a smaller scale, is exemplified by the unique scene of two armed men engaged in a mortal duel where either opponent hits the head of his adversary with a battle pick.[41] Very similar petroglyphs exist at Sagyr (Kazakhstan) and Tsagaan Salaa (Mongolia).[42] Whereas the site of Murgi Tokpo has the

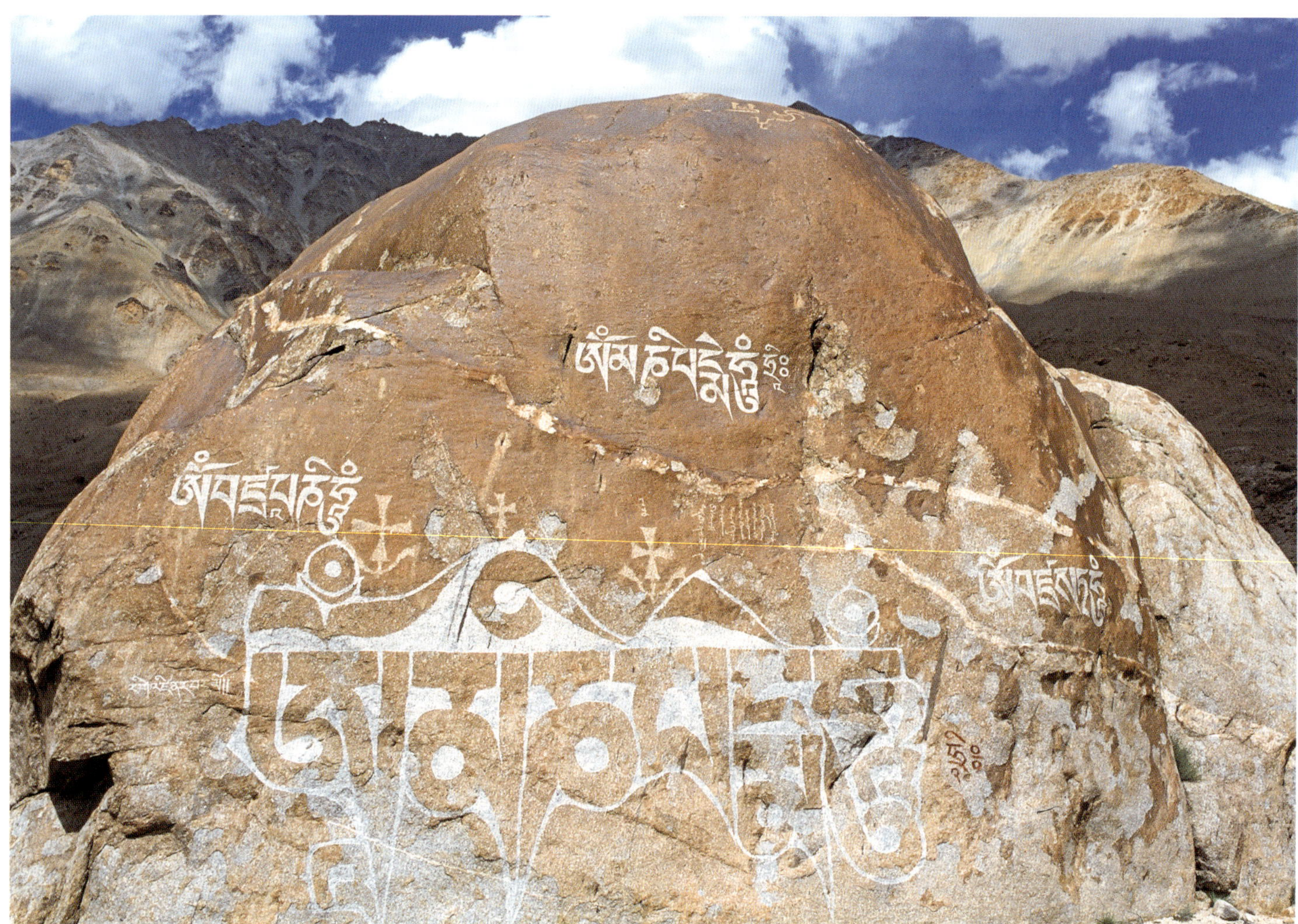

105. The top of a large boulder at Tanktse is covered with Bronze and Iron Age images while its southern side is engraved with inscriptions in Tocharian, Sogdian, Chinese, Arabic and Tibetan as well as Christian crosses. A Sogdian inscription records that a Sogdian merchant and a Nestorian Christian monk travelled in the year 825/6 CE to the king of Tibet. Pangong Region, Ladakh, India. Photo 1998.

richest collection of Bronze Age petroglyphs in Ladakh, the sites of **Domkhar** and **Khalatse**, **Alchi** and **Tanktse** (all Ladakh) as well as **Zamthang** (Zanskar) are replete with images from the Iron Age, which are also well represented in **Renmudong** and other places in Ruthok[43] as well as in the region of Chilas (northern Pakistan). Among the typical Central Asian, Tuvan and Altaian scenes from the Saka Iron Age we find in this region first the image of a feline predator attacking a herbivore, then petroglyphs of animals standing on their tiptoes or with their legs tucked under their bodies, and images of herbivores looking backwards[44] toward a predator attacking them from behind.[45] Motifs of animals such as predators, deer, ibexes and yaks shown in strict profile with only two legs and with an S-shaped decoration engraved inside their bodies also belong to the repertoire of Central Asian Saka petroglyphs; the same applies to animals depicted with four legs and volute designs on their shoulders and thighs.[46] The sources of these

obviously Scythian influences on the Iron Age rock art of western Tibet, Ladakh, Zanskar and Chilas are multiple. Saka pastoralists or their ancestors may have come from the steppes and travelled via the Pamirs or the Karakoram. Other groups of early Saka lived at the fringes of or inside the Tarim Basin, as suggested by the evidence of archaeological excavations. Wooden vessels engraved with animals shown walking on tiptoe and decorated with volute designs, which were excavated at the graveyards of Zaghunluk (*ca.* 800 BCE) situated in the oasis of Cherchen (Qiemo), of Jumbulakum (Yuan Shah, sixth century BCE) and of Satma Mazar (fourth–third century BCE), clearly indicate a Saka cultural environment (fig. 38). These two latter sites were located in the riparian zones of the former Keriya River which 2,500 years ago still carried water; the environment of the Keriya was then a grass steppe instead of today's bare sand desert.[47] These early Saka or proto-Saka communities were, so to speak, bridgeheads for the future Saka Kingdom of Khotan. In the course of the second century BCE, the Indo-Iranian Saka living in the Chuy and Ili valleys in today's Kyrgyzstan and Kazakhstan were displaced by the Indo-European Yuezhi and moved into Greek Bactria, the Hindu Kush, western Karakoram and ultimately into northern India, as well as into the oases of the Tarim Basin where they founded or occupied the emerging Kingdom of Khotan.[48] The Khotan kingdom and the north Indian Kushan Empire were in close trade contact, and one of the links was through Ladakh as suggested by the Kharosthi inscription at Khalatse mentioned above. The Tarim Basin and north-eastern Xinjiang clearly represent the links between the world of the Central Asian steppes and the regions south of Karakoram and the Hindu Kush.

Ladakh in the first millennium was not an isolated backwater, but an important transit region for international trade and travel. The largest carved boulder of **Tanktse** (Drangtse) in eastern Ladakh bears witness to this. Standing in an environment of Bronze and Iron Age petroglyphs situated west of Lake Pangong,[49] this free-standing boulder and several smaller rocks carry three large and eight smaller crosses of the Maltese type which are typical of the so-called 'Nestorian' Church of the East.[50] Besides these there is a bird – possibly a dove – and inscriptions in Tocharian, Sogdian, Chinese, Arabic and Tibetan. A longer Sogdian inscription reads, 'In the year 210 [of the Arabs, i.e. 825/6 CE] we sent Caitra of Samarkand, together with the monk Nosfarn, as ambassadors to

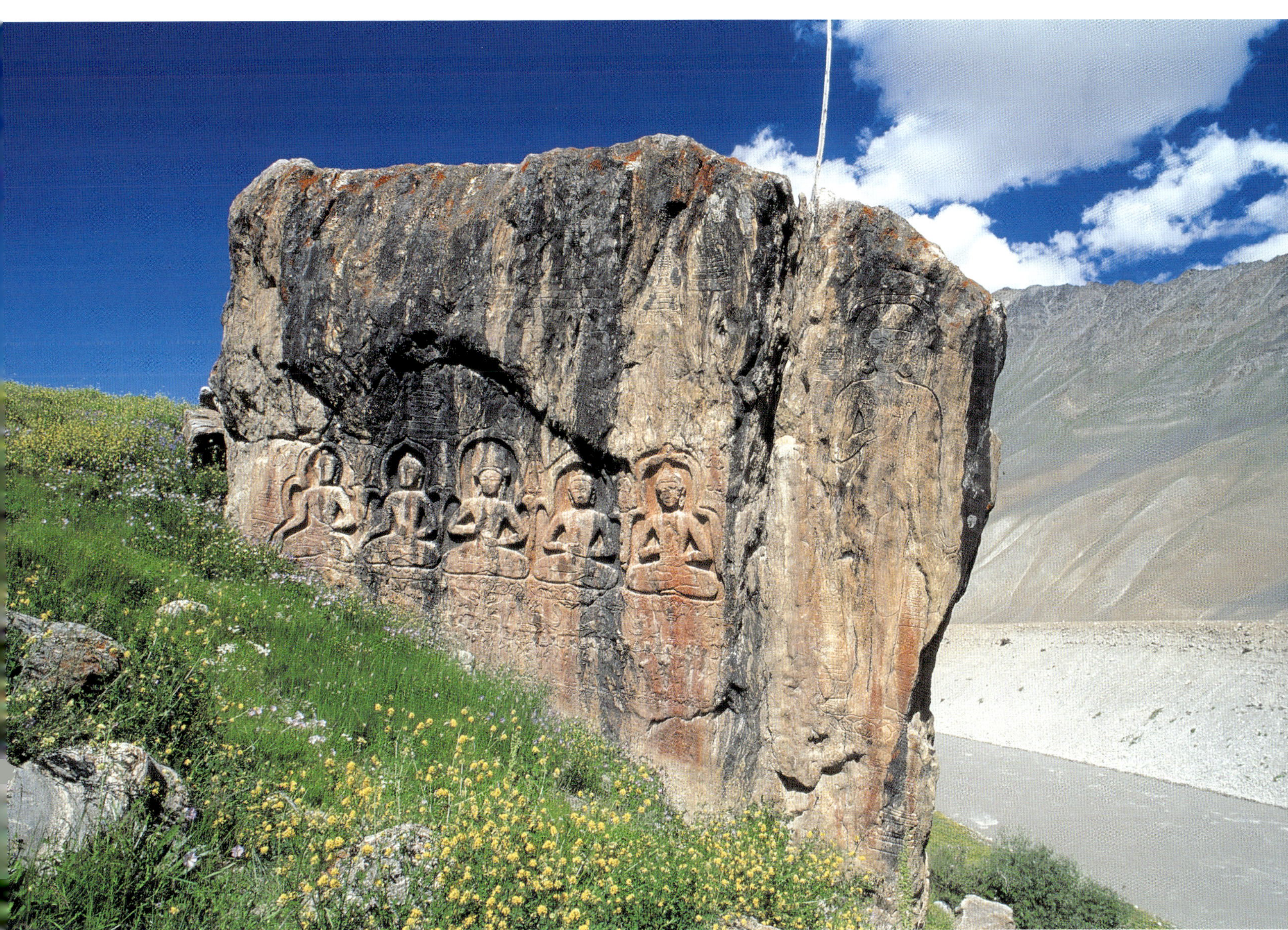

106. Images of the Five Tathagata Buddhas and of the standing Boddhisattva Maitreya are engraved at an altitude of *ca.* 3,750 m asl on a boulder named Gyalwa Ringna near Padum. Ninth to tenth century CE. Zanskar, India. Photo 1998.

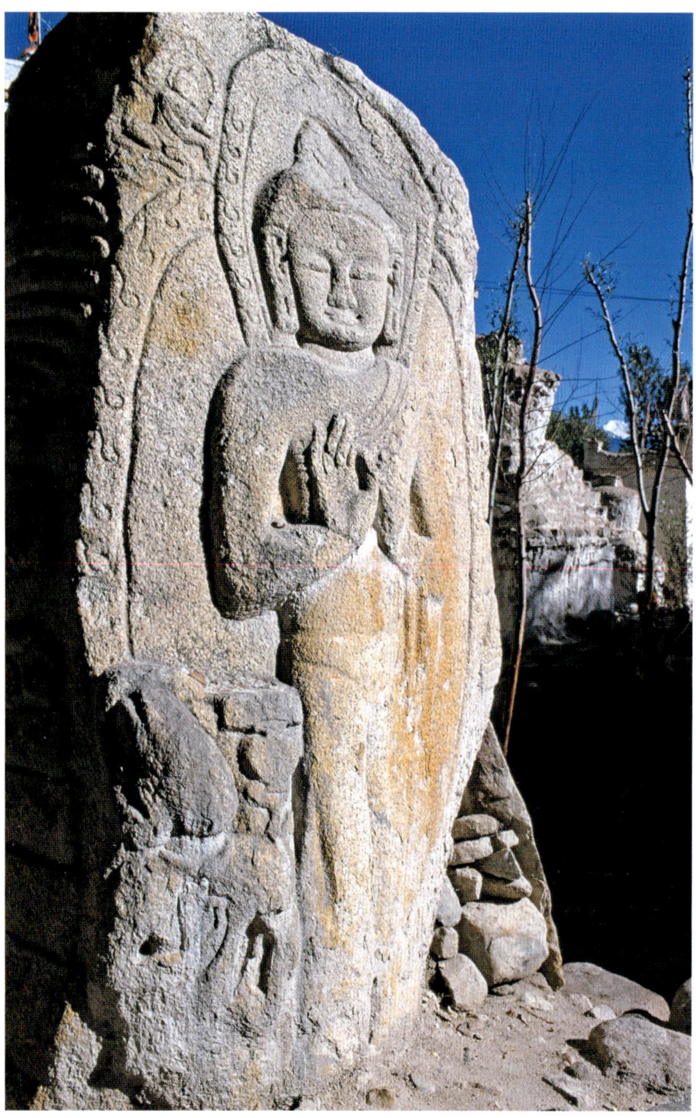

107. Free-standing stone stele featuring the Buddha with attendants, Changspa near Leh, Ladakh, India. Photo 1998.

the Tibetan king.' Another short Sogdian inscription, placed above a cross, may mean Yisaw, that is Jesus. Finally, there is a Tibetan inscription dating from 774 or 834. If one assumes that the two Sogdian inscriptions and the three large crosses are connected, we can conclude that a (probably Christian) Sogdian trader accompanied a Nestorian monk in 825/6 to the king of Tibet.[51] This boulder was already important in the pre-Christian period, since the upper side, facing the sky, is engraved with many Bronze and Iron Age motifs, such as hunting scenes, yaks, deer, spirals and swastikas. These two Sogdian inscriptions indicate that Tanktse lay on one of the branches of the Silk Road linking Sogdia (the eastern half of today's Uzbekistan) and Bactria (northern Afghanistan and southern Uzbekistan) with Khotan and Central Tibet. At that time, Sogdian merchants speaking an eastern Iranian language controlled long-distance trade and maintained trading settlements in many large cities, presumably including Lhasa. Although the majority of Sogdians were Zoroastrians, there were also significant minorities of Sogdian Christians, Manichaeans and Buddhists. The inscription at Tanktse is particularly valuable because it is dated and provides information about the cultural contacts of that time. Later, in the period of the Second Diffusion of Buddhism, the boulder was symbolically 'converted' to Buddhism by the addition of images of Buddhist mantras and chortens. Nevertheless, the pre-Buddhist petroglyphs remained mostly intact, probably as a sign of respect towards previous beliefs.

Whereas the main thrust of Buddhist proselytization came from the east – as of the eleventh century from Tibet – evidence of an earlier partial presence of Buddhism can be found in Ladakh and Zanskar. These are, on the one hand, large petroglyphs carved into massive boulders and featuring groups of Buddhist deities, and, on the other hand, huge figures of the Bodhisattvas Maitreya and Avalokitesvara which were carved in high relief on cliffs and boulders. Since Buddhism had hardly taken root in Tibet before the Second Diffusion, it could not have been introduced into Ladakh from the east prior to the eleventh century. This early propagation could only come from the west, namely from Kashmir, where Buddhism was already well established in the early second century CE. Stylistic studies of early Buddhist stone monuments in Ladakh and stone as well as bronze figures from Kashmir confirm the hypothesis of a preliminary diffusion of Buddhism from Kashmir. An outstanding example of almost life-size petroglyphs is to be found at **Gyalwa Ringna**, a large boulder situated at an altitude of *ca.* 3,750 metres above sea level on a bank of the Lungnak River near Padum, the capital of Zanskar (fig. 106). On the boulder are engraved images of the Five Tathagata Buddhas in a seated position; they represent Ratnasambhava, Akshobhya, Vairocana, Amitabha and Amoghasiddhi. To the right of the five Buddhas, nearest to the river, a more than life-size standing Bodhisattva Maitreya is carved. These petroglyphs may be attributed to the ninth to tenth centuries CE. On another boulder also located near Padum, the Five Bodhisattvas Manjusri, Vajrapani, Avalokitesvara (Padmapani), Maitreya and Ksitigarbha are engraved in a standing position.[52] The Five Tathagata Buddhas were also carved into a huge boulder at **Shey**, situated 11 kilometres south-east of Leh under the eponymous palace (fig. 102); they probably date from the tenth century.[53] Another site with large pre-Tibetan Buddhist petroglyphs is to be found at **Byama Khumbu** near the village of Sanku, located 30 kilometres south of Kargil. It represents Bodhisattva Avalokitesvara flanked by two female deities or attendants.[54]

Several mighty Buddhist figures carved out of the rock in high relief also date from the pre-Tibetan period. Such monumental figures hewn from rocks were of course not unique to Ladakh, but were one of the characteristics of Buddhist art, as they are to be found everywhere where Buddhism flourished. The largest Ladakhi Buddhist high-relief is the nine-metre-high figure of Avalokitesvara, the Bodhisattva of Compassion, at **Mulbekh** in western Ladakh. As observed by Phuntsog Dorjay, the rosary held by the figure in its upper right hand is an indication that Avalokitesvara is featured, and not the future Buddha, Bodhisattva Maitreya, as is locally believed.[55] This impressive figure had already been noted by the explorer William Moorcroft in 1820.[56] Almost as big is the seven-metre-high carved figure of Maitreya at **Khartse Khar** whose garment and three-pointed crown or diadem are reminiscent of Kashmiri works of art. It is situated in the Suru Valley near the road linking Kargil with Padum, Zanskar.[57] Both figures at Mulbekh and Khartse Khar may be dated to the ninth to tenth centuries. Other large high-relief Buddhist figures stand at **Apati** and at **Tumail**, both north-east of Kargil.[58]

Finally, the carved, free-standing stone steles representing Buddhist deities have to be mentioned, for example those at **Changspa** (fig. 107) and **Skara** near Leh, at **Dras** west of Kargil in western Ladakh, those to the south-east of **Shey**, at **Digar** in the Nubra Valley and at **Sani** in Zanskar.[59] Since the Second Diffusion, countless Buddhist mantras and images or chortens were engraved on rocks and boulders, often superimposed on already existing figurative petroglyphs. Such palimpsests expressed an act of resacralization of the landscape, that is an exorcism of the symbols of previous beliefs. Several inscriptions show that petroglyphs of stupas as well as three-dimensional stupas and mani walls were made as votive offerings. The donors wanted to earn spiritual merit for their deceased parents and for themselves, or to express gratitude for the birth of a son. Other inscriptions were of a secular kind, for example regulating the distribution of water for irrigating the fields.[60]

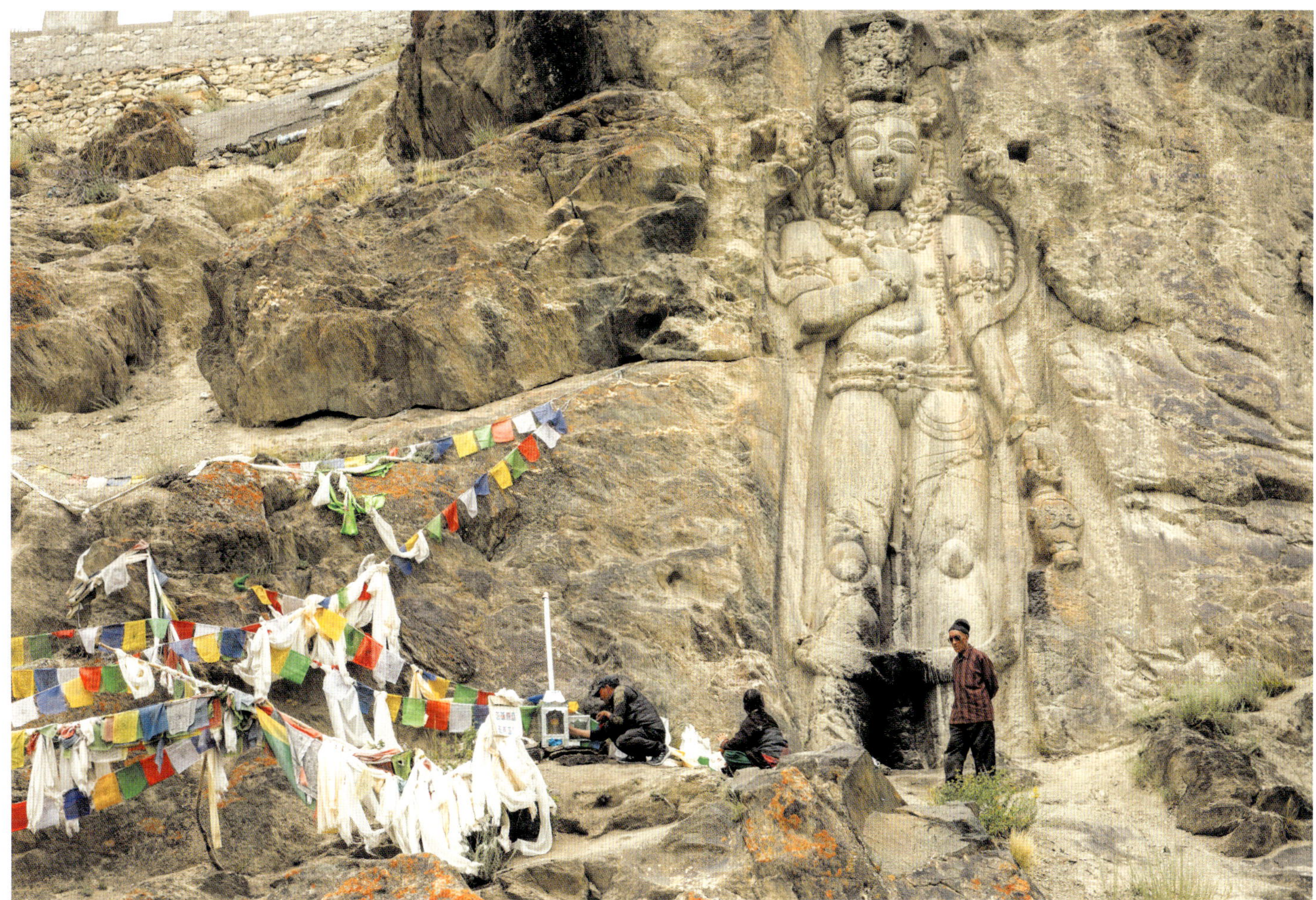

108. The 7-m-high stone figure of Maitreya, the future Buddha, at Khartse Khar. Ninth to tenth century CE. Ladakh, India. Photo 2021.

2. Gilgit-Baltistan

The gorges of the Upper Indus extend over a distance of 60 kilometres to the west, and 40 kilometres to the east of the small city of Chilas, and are full of petroglyphs dating from the Neolithic to the coming of Islam in the fourteenth century. In total, more than 50,000 petroglyphs, of which more than 5,000 are inscriptions, have been documented. A significant proportion of the petroglyphs date from the Buddhist period, from its introduction in the region in the early first century CE to its blossoming in the fifth to eighth centuries. Later petroglyphs suggest a post-Buddhist solar cult. This region, together with Arabia and the Sahara, is one of the richest in the world in terms of inscriptions, which are found in Kharosthi, Brahmi, Proto-Sarada,[61] Sogdian, Bactrian, Middle Persian, Parthian, Chinese, Tibetan and even one each in Hebrew and Syriac.[62] In contrast to Christianity and Islam, in Buddhist Gilgit-Baltistan as well as in Ladakh and Zanskar, creating petroglyphs was an accepted way of expressing one's affiliation to a complex religion. Although Kargil in western Ladakh and Chilas are only 210 kilometres apart as the crow flies and relatively accessible via the Burzil Pass and Astor, the thematic foci in Gilgit-Baltistan and Ladakh-Zanskar were in some ways different; these two areas were hardly a cultural unit.

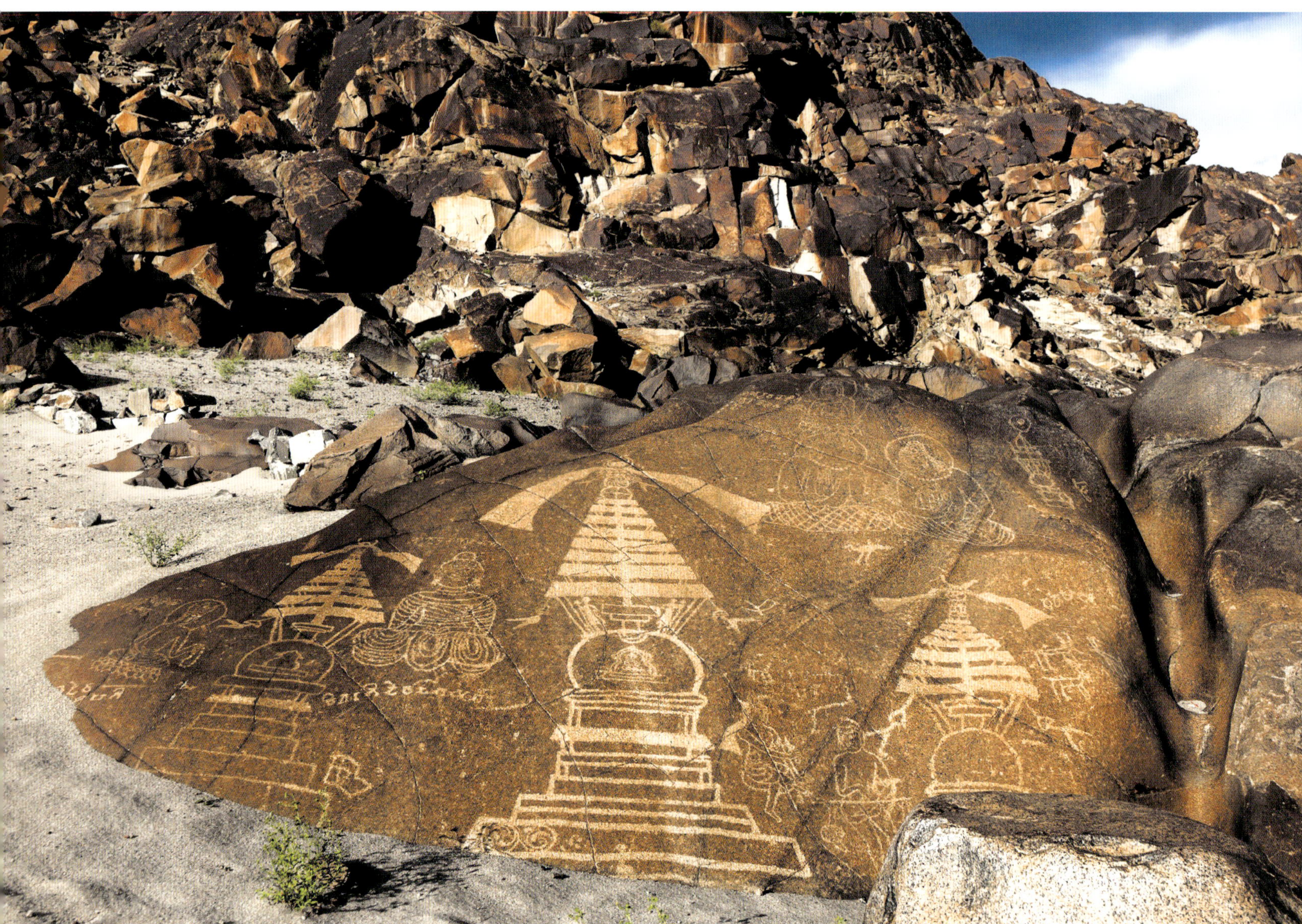

109. Stupas and sitting Buddhas in meditation, second to third quarter of the first millennium CE. Thalpan, autonomous region of Gilgit-Baltistan, northern Pakistan. Photo 2010.

The most important sites, listed from west to east, are:

- **Shatial** numbers *ca.* 1,800 petroglyphs, which are divided into 1,100 inscriptions and 700 figurative petroglyphs. The Sogdian inscriptions account for 565 items, the majority, followed by 411 in Brahmi, 15 in Kharosthi, nine in Bactrian, eight in Chinese, seven in Proto-Sarada, two each in Middle Persian and Parthian and one in Syriac. The remaining ones can no longer be identified. Each type of script gives clues about dating: Sogdian inscriptions date to the Sasanian period (224–651 CE), and Bactrian, which used the Greek script, was utilized in the Kushan Empire and its successor states until the seventh century. Kharosthi was used from the third century BCE to the third century CE, Brahmi from the third to the eighth century and Proto-Sarada from the seventh century. At Shatial, the figurative petroglyphs feature, besides 138 stupas, a rich variety of motifs from Kushan deities, fire altars, Buddhas and a *Jataka* story[63] to portraits of Hunnic rulers with artificially induced turricephaly (fig. 111), along with many small anthropomorphs and ibexes.

- **Oshibat** has more than 1,000 petroglyphs, of which 298 are inscriptions. Among the latter, the 230 Brahmi inscriptions make up the vast majority, followed by 25 Sogdian and 9 Kharosthi inscriptions. The petroglyphs are mainly pre-Buddhist, of giants, screw-horned goats and small anthropomorphs, and later, stupas.

- **Hodar.** In contrast to Shatial, the *ca.* 200 inscriptions are a relatively small minority compared to the 1,700 figurative petroglyphs, of which 400 are anthropomorphs. Particular to Hodar are the 127 discs which look like solar symbols and 18 free-standing axes. The solar discs and the axes suggest a post-Buddhist solar cult. Also noteworthy are numerous horsemen, (possibly) Nestorian crosses and heraldic *tamgas* in the shape of stylized lions.

- **Chilas** lies on the southern shore of the River Indus, opposite the site of Thalpan. It counts *ca.* 550 petroglyphs, of which 150 are inscriptions, mainly Brahmi, followed by some in Proto-Sarada. Several of the petroglyphs are distinguished by the high quality of their execution, for example of Buddhas, *Jatakas*, Bodhisattvas, worshippers and stupas.

- **Thalpan** and several other smaller sites along the northern shore of the Indus together form the region's largest complex with thousands of mainly figurative petroglyphs. As on the other side of the Indus, in Thalpan there are some very carefully executed petroglyphs. These include Buddhist motifs such as the Buddhas Shakyamuni, Maitreya and Manjusri, the Bodhisattvas Vajrapani and Avalokitesvara, ascetics, finely dressed worshippers and elaborate stupas; one of the worshippers holds in one hand a portable incense burner, in the other a lotus.[64] In addition, there are striking non-Buddhist figures such as men dressed in Median or Achaemenid garments, saddled horses, a horse represented in the Achaemenid *knielauf*, that is with the left front leg bent, and carnivores in the Animal Style (fig. 110). Also of interest are petroglyphs of giants,[65] armed horsemen, armed men on foot holding axes, swords or bows, battle scenes, hands, feet, screw-horned goats, an elephant, birds of prey, *tamgas*, numerous solar discs and axes.

- **Shing Nala** is a smaller site with petroglyphs mainly of stupas and Buddhas from an earlier period, around the fourth to fifth century CE.

- **Alam Bridge** is located *ca.* 60 kilometres north of Shing Nala on the road to Gilgit. Its petroglyphs consist mainly of figures, including various animals and stupas as well as inscriptions in Kharosthi and Brahmi which again highlight the cultural influence from the Indian subcontinent at that time.

- **Hunza Valley.** In the Hunza Valley between Gilgit and Altit, numerous boulders and rocks also carry petroglyphs similar to those around Chilas, such as Buddhas, stupas, anthropomorphs holding a shield, ibexes, horses, inscriptions and *tamgas* in the shape of a Maltese cross within a second, outer cross.[66]

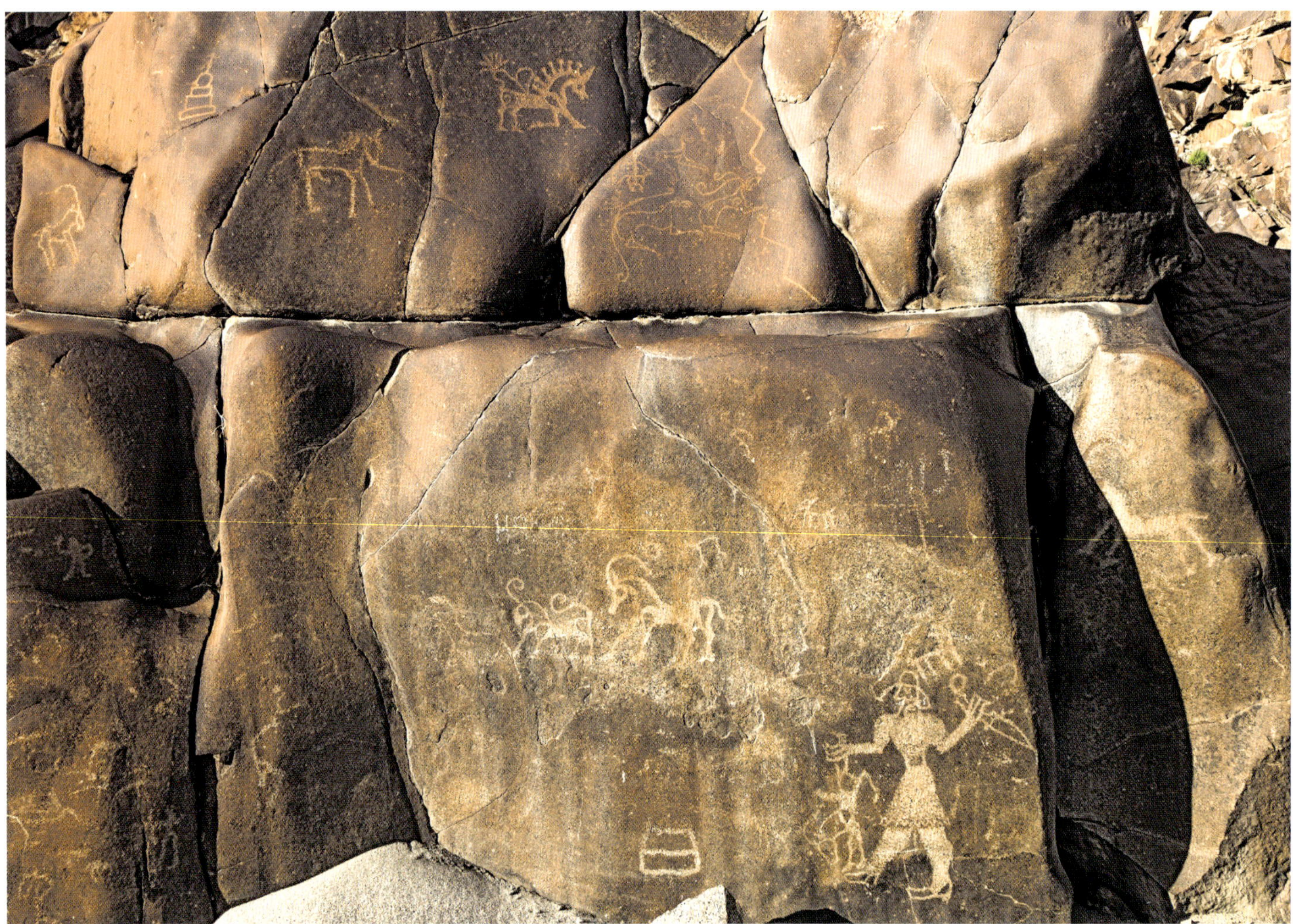

110. Above, a horse in the so-called *knielauf* (knee-walk) with its left front leg bent, just below a predator rendered in the Saka Animal Style. At the bottom right is a man in Median or Achaemenid dress, holding a dagger in one hand and a goat in the other, which he is presumably about to sacrifice. Sixth to second century BCE. Thalpan, Gilgit-Baltistan, northern Pakistan. Photo 2010.

The simultaneous engraving of figural petroglyphs and inscriptions observed in Gilgit-Baltistan shows that the rise of literacy in a society did not necessarily lead to an end of petroglyph making: both were used as complementary media. Unfortunately, about 5,900 boulders and rocks with *ca.* 37,000 petroglyphs will be submerged by the mid 2030s, due to the construction by a Chinese company of the 272-metre-high Diamer-Bhasha Dam which means that three-quarters of this unique cultural heritage will be lost for ever.[67] Moreover, due to the construction of a new road on the north bank of the Indus, boulders covered with petroglyphs have been dynamited. Additional destruction of rock art must be expected in the course of the building of facilities linked to the power plant.[68] Furthermore, in the last few decades, other petroglyphs have already been wantonly destroyed, blasted away or, in the case of Buddhist images, whitewashed with paint.[69] As of 2022, construction works make the access to the site of Shing Nala very difficult.

As in Central Asia, with the onset of the Holocene the mountainous region of Gilgit-Baltistan enjoyed a relatively mild and moist climate. These conditions allowed rich vegetation to grow and thus an abundant diversity of wildlife to thrive, which in turn attracted hunting communities. They have left traces in the form of simple prehistoric petroglyphs featuring ibexes, blue sheep and screw-horned goats as well as occasional hunting scenes.[70] These petroglyphs have not yet been reliably dated. As in Ladakh, in the Bronze Age towards the end of the third millennium BCE, petroglyphs of giants in a frontal position and, occasionally, of masks and of a chariot appear. In the Iron Age, Baltistan came into increased contact with expanding neighbouring peoples; first with the Iranian Achaemenid Empire (550–330 BCE) which extended into the regions of Gandhara and Sind. Obvious testimonials of an Achaemenid cultural presence are the petroglyphs showing men wearing Median or Achaemenid garments – one of them holds a knife and is in the process of sacrificing a goat which he holds by a hind leg (fig. 110)[71] – and of horses or mythological animals shown in the typical Achaemenid *knielauf* with a front leg bent (fig. 110).[72] Later, the Parthians (247 BCE–224 CE) extended their influence to today's Afghanistan and came into contact with the Upper Indus region. On some petroglyphs, men seem to wear Parthian garments. A few decades later, in the second century BCE, groups of Saka entered from the north into today's Afghanistan and Gilgit-Baltistan. From this period come the petroglyphs of deer, ibexes and carnivores executed in the Animal Style.

In the first to second century CE the region of the Upper Indus came into the political and cultural realm of the Kushan Empire (30–*ca*. 350 CE), which had been founded by the Yuezhi horsemen who came from the north-east, from Xinjiang and Gansu.[73] To visually express their deities, the early Kushans adopted figures from the Hellenistic and Iranian pantheons as well as aspects of the Bactrian fire cult. Such adoptions are noticeable in rock art; for example, in the petroglyphs of the Iranian wind god Oado,[74] the moon god Mao[75] or the sun god Miiro[76] who are also featured on Kushan coins. In addition, worshippers standing in front of a fire altar or fire altars are represented in petroglyphs and on Kushan coins as well as in later Sogdian murals from Panjikent (sixth-seventh centuries CE).[77] As the Kushan started to decline, the Kabul and eastern Upper Indus valleys came under the influence

of the Iranian Sasanian Empire, then the Hunnic Kidarites and, in the fifth century CE, the Hunnic Alkhan. Their legacy is visible in the petroglyphs of male portraits with pronounced turricephaly, that is high, artificially deformed skulls.[78] These portraits look like the bust found on silver dinars of the Alkhan king Khingila (r. *ca*. 430/40–490) (fig. 111)[79]. The strong Hunnic influence in Gilgit-Baltistan is further exemplified by several inscriptions containing the ethnonym 'Hun', which was used as a personal name.[80]

Whereas in Ladakh during the first eight centuries CE Buddhism remained marginal, under the Kushan it spread to Afghanistan in the first century BCE, and to the Upper Indus of Gilgit-Baltistan a century later. The earliest witnesses to Buddhism in rock art are petroglyphs of stupas, pilgrims revering a stupa, Buddhas and inscriptions in Kharosthi. Sir Aurel Stein was right when he suggested in 1942 that 'many of the short inscriptions attached to representations of stupas are votive, to record the names of the persons who in lieu of erecting stupas had to content themselves with offering such rock-pictures as modest proofs of their devotion'.[81] Indeed, many of the hundreds of engraved stupas at Shatila, Chilas Bridge, Thalpan, Hodar and Shing Nala are inscribed with a dedication, and dozens of them state 'This is the religious donation of …'.[82] Stylistic comparisons between some engravings of stupas and portable stupas made from stone or metal suggest that the earliest stupa petroglyphs date to the early first century CE or even the late first century BCE.[83] In general, numerous petroglyphs of stupas, Buddhas and Bodhisattvas show clear similarities with analogous portable statues made from metals or stone; obviously the carvers of these elaborate petroglyphs were accomplished artisans who were aware of the trends in Buddhist figurative art.[84]

The heyday of Buddhism in this region was in the fifth to eighth centuries CE, although it was a time of fierce competition between three smaller local powers and the great powers, China and Tibet. The local powers were the kingdoms of Lesser Bolor (in Tibetan *Bruzha*), which comprised the Gilgit and Yasin valleys, Greater Bolor (in Tibetan *Balti*), that is Baltistan, and the land of the Daradas situated south-west of Chilas.[85] The latter controlled the important trade hub of Chilas where routes from Sogdia, Xinjiang, Gandhara, Swat, Kashmir and Ladakh joined. From the late sixth century to the 750s, the Buddhist dynasty of the Palola-(Patola-) Shahis ruled parts of both Bolors, probably from Skardu in Baltistan.[86] The expansionist empires of China and Tibet, for their part, were engaged from 704 to 842 CE in a bitter struggle over the Pamirs, Hindu Kush and Karakoram for control of the trade routes to the west and south.[87]

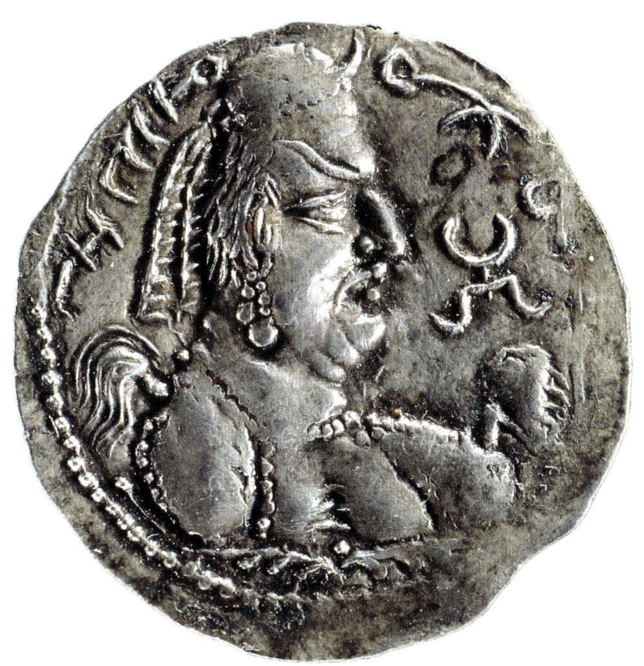

111. Silver dinar of the Hunnic king Khingila (r. *ca*. 430/40–490) from the Alkhan dynasty, which ruled over Gandhara and the Kabul region. The Trustees of the British Museum, London. Similar portraits are found at the Shatial petroglyph site.

The starting point for this long conflict was China's reconquest of the Four Garrisons[88] in 692 CE, that is of the Tarim Basin, which seriously threatened Tibet's trade communications with the Caliphate and northern India. As a result, Tibet needed to secure alternative routes through the Pamirs, Karakoram and Hindu Kush. China, on the other hand, wanted to capitalize on its victory by denying Tibet such an alternative. After Tibet had reconsolidated its control over Ladakh by 704 CE, it captured Greater Bolor, that is Baltistan, around 719/722, whereupon it attacked Lesser Bolor and forced its King Mojinmang to flee the Gilgit Valley.[89] Mojinmang, however, turned to the Chinese military governor of Beiting in Xinjiang, who put a 4,000-strong army at his disposal. This army first captured Sarikol from the Tibetans before crossing the Wakhan and driving them out of Yasin and Gilgit. So it was that Greater Bolor fell within the Tibetan sphere of influence, and Lesser Bolor within the Chinese.[90] Then, between 730 and 733, the Tibetans succeeded in taking the Wakhan, so that they not only threatened Lesser Bolor from the north-west as well as from the

east, but were in a position to attack the Four Garrisons from the Wakhan.[91] To relieve Tibetan pressure in the Pamirs, China successfully launched an unexpected attack 2,000 kilometres further east, in Eastern Tibet, in 737,[92] which did not however prevent Tibetan forces in the Pamirs from conquering Lesser Bolor between 745 and 747. Now the whole area extending from western Tibet, across Baltistan, Gilgit and Yasin to the Wakhan and the Oxus was in Tibetan hands. China immediately launched a counter-offensive and in 747 General Gao Xianzhi proceeded with 10,000 men from Kucha to Kashgar and Tashkurgan, whereupon he captured the Tibetan fortress of Sarhad situated in the Wakhan on the River Panj.[93] Gao Xianzhi then crossed the Broghil Pass and the difficult, 4,650-metre-high Darkot Pass and invaded Lesser Bolor, whose king, a Tibetan vassal, capitulated without a fight. With this lightning campaign, which caught the Tibetans unprepared, General Gao had driven a wedge between the Tibetans and the Arabs, with the Wakhan, Yasin and Gilgit now coming again under Chinese control. In 749–50 Gao took advantage of the new situation to advance once

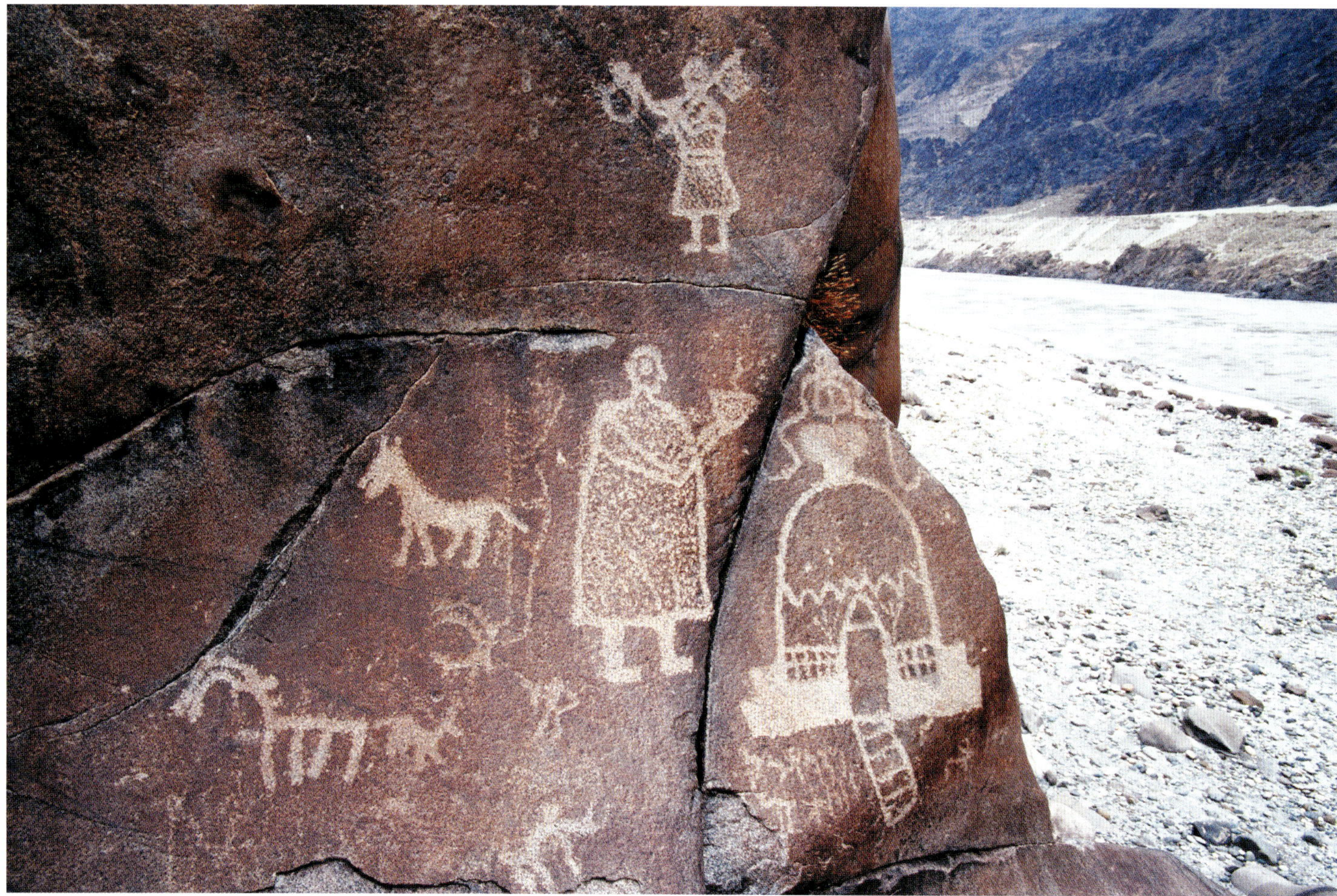

112. A Buddhist believer offers a libation to a stupa; above, a man seems to hold a bag or flag over his left shoulder and a large torc or wreath. To the left of the stairs leading to the stupa there is an inscription in Kharosthi. Second quarter of the first millennium CE. Chilas II, Gilgit-Baltistan, northern Pakistan.

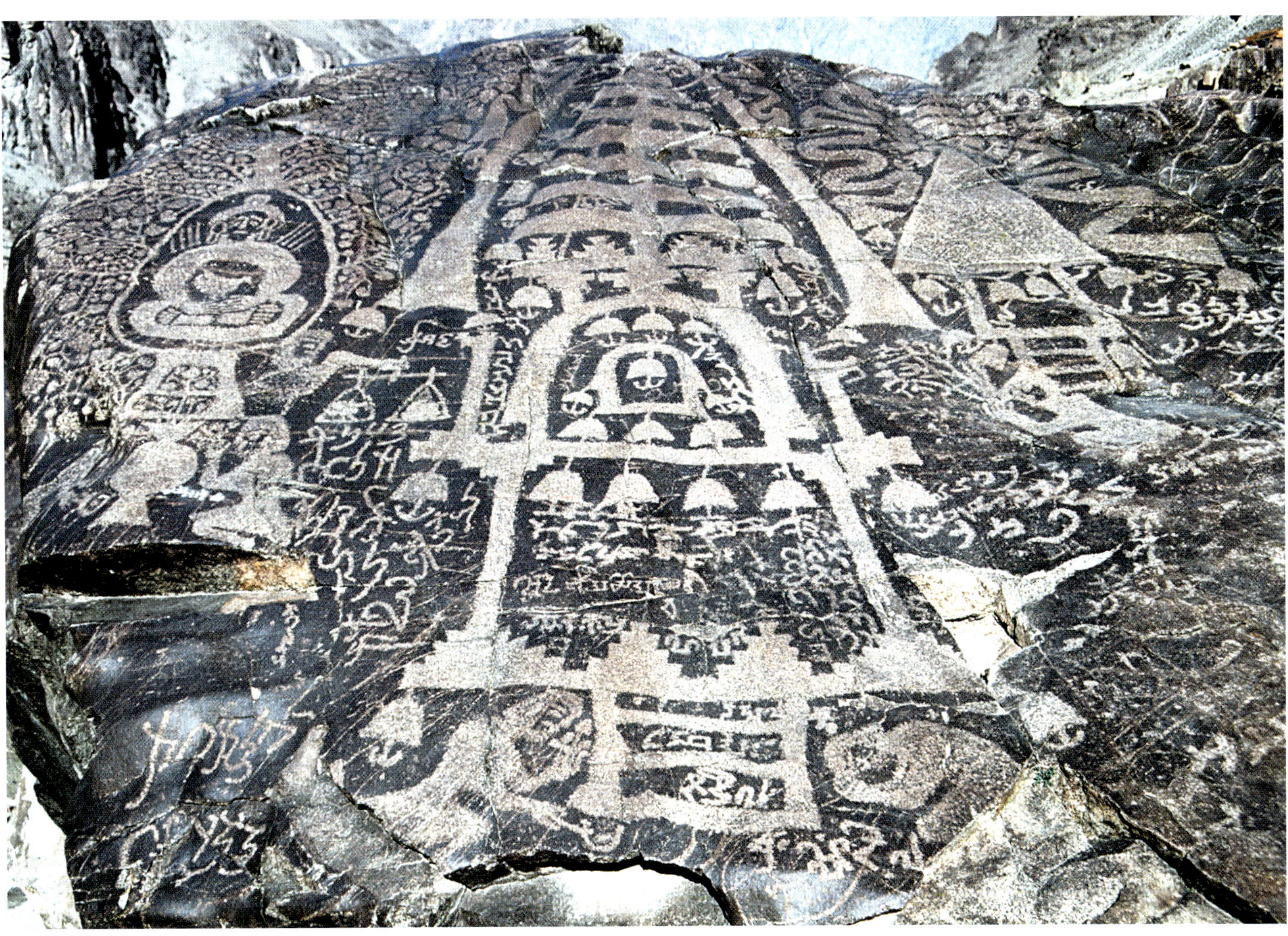

113. Petroglyphs and inscriptions on rock 34 at Shatial near the left bank of the Upper Indus. In the middle and on the right, two unique pagoda-shaped stupas are engraved as well as venerating devotees, and on the left sits a Buddha with flaming shoulders, holding a bird in his lap. The scene illustrates the *Sibi-Jataka*, which tells how the gods Indra and Agni put the generosity of the pious King Sibi, an earlier incarnation of Buddha Shakyamuni, to the test. At first, they transformed into a hawk and a dove, and then the hawk chased the dove which fled in terror and sought protection in the lap of the king. When the hawk demanded that he hand over the dove, Sibi refused and as compensation offered the equivalent in weight from his own flesh. The falcon accepted but though the king cut several large slices of flesh from his body and threw them on to the scales, they never equalled the weight of the dove. Finally, king Sibi put his whole body on the scales, prepared to die. But even then, the dove was heavier – at which point Indra and Agni revealed their true identities and praised the king for his boundless beneficence. Thanks to the inscriptions in Kharosthi, Brahmi and Sogdian, most of the petroglyphs can be dated to the third and fourth centuries CE. Shatial, Gilgit-Baltistan, northern Pakistan. Photo Felsbild-Archiv, Heidelberg Academy of Sciences and Humanities.

more into the Pamirs, where he again defeated a Tibetan army to reach Chitral.[94] Although China's forward strategy suffered a setback in 751, when General Gao Xianzhi was crushingly defeated by the Arabs at the Battle of Talas, the initiative in Central Asia remained in the hands of the Chinese. In 753, General Feng Chang Qing invaded Greater Bolor, driving the Tibetans from their last major outpost in the Pamirs. However, in 755–57 the rebellion of An Lushan, a Sogdian general in Chinese service, provided Tibet with the opportunity to re-establish its control over the Wakhan from 758 to 815/16, and occasionally also over Yasin and Gilgit. An Arab army drove the Tibetans out of Wakhan around 815 or 816, but the latter retained their influence in the Gilgit Valley until the collapse of the Tibetan Empire after 842.[95] In spite of these conflictual times, Buddhism and Buddhist rock art blossomed in Gilgit-Baltistan, in part due to the support of the local petty rulers. Outstanding examples of Buddhist art of that period are the high-relief figure of the Buddha at **Kargah** near Gilgit[96] and the large scene carved in the six-metre-high **Manthal** Buddha Rock near Skardu in Baltistan (fig. 114). Here the meditating Buddha Shakyamuni sits inside a mandala of smaller Buddhas and the scene is flanked by the standing Bodhisattvas Padmapani (Avalokiteshvara) and Maitreya. However, as will be discussed below, in the second half of this period Buddhism was confronted by a hostile religious movement which was probably connected to a solar cult.

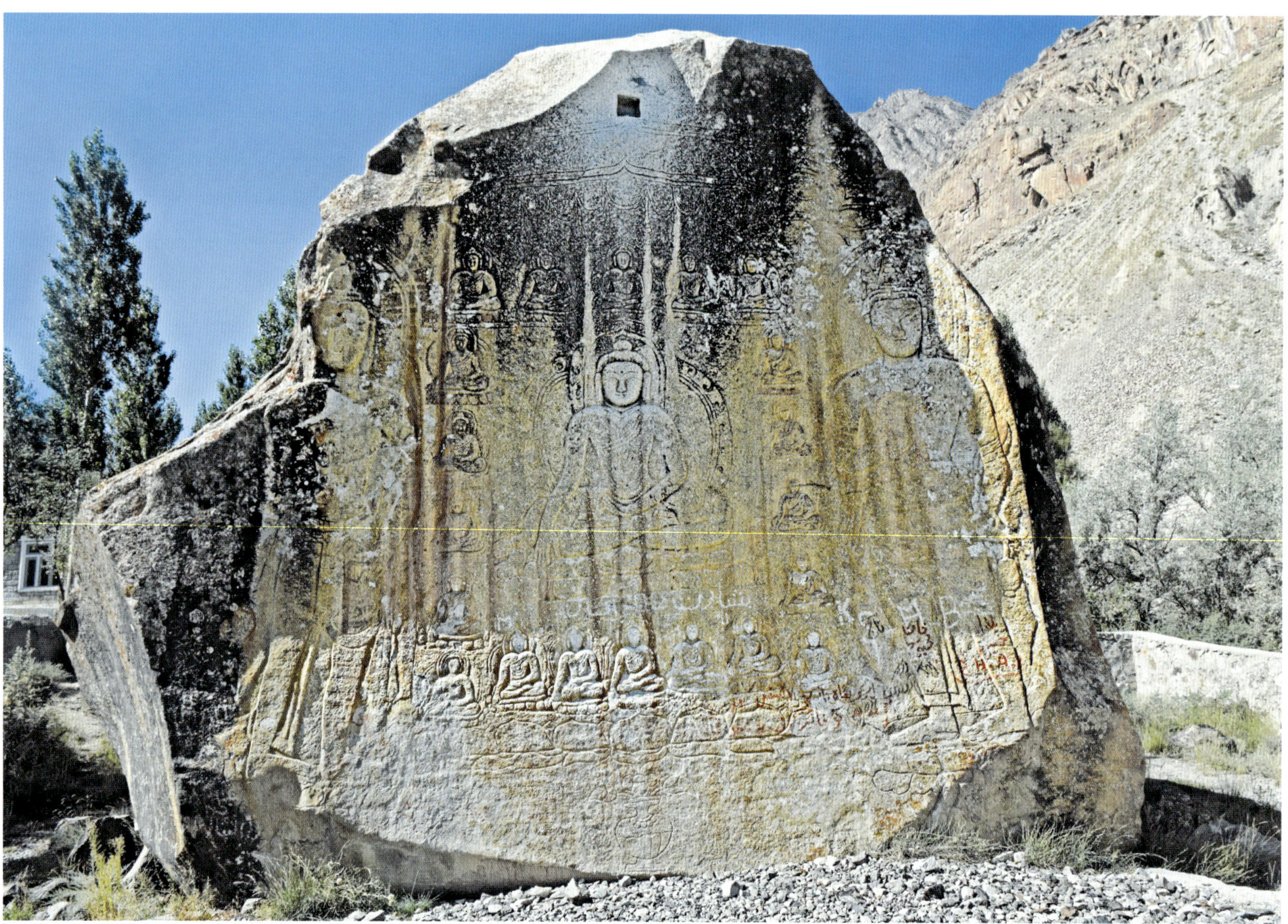

114. The meditating Buddha Shakyamuni is surrounded by twenty smaller Buddhas and flanked by the Bodhisattvas Maitreya to his right and Padmapani, who holds a lotus flower, to his left. This relief reveals Tibetan influence and dates from the eighth century CE. Manthal rock near Skardu, Gilgit-Baltistan, northern Pakistan. Photo 2015 by Sepahi Kamzam.

In this period of Buddhist blossoming, rock art consisted not only of single images such as Buddhas or stupas, but of complex scenes. These are either episodes from Buddha Shakyamuni's life or from the lives of his previous incarnations, told in the *Jatakas*. Three petroglyph scenes of *Jatakas* are located at the Chilas Bridge and neighbouring Thalpan. They are the *Vyaghri-* or 'Tigress' *Jataka*,[97] the *Rsipancaka-Jataka* or 'Jataka of the Greatest Misery',[98] and the *Sibi-Jataka* or 'Jataka of the Flesh Offering'; this last is also represented at Shatial on boulder 34, in a petroglyph scene from the fourth century.[99] The first *Jataka* narrates how Prince Sattva, a previous incarnation of Shakyamuni, sacrifices himself to feed a hungry tigress. The carved scene shows the Buddha who threw himself off a cliff into the depths and is now offering his lifeless body to the tigress and her four cubs to be devoured. Directly above, a tree has been carved into the rock with a woman growing out of its trunk instead of a branch.[100] She is probably a tree deity or a

nymph. In the second *Jataka*, a wealthy Brahman who became an ascetic holds a discussion with animals concerning the 'greatest misery', namely the physical body. This depiction of the *Rsipancaka-Jataka* seems to be unique of its kind (fig. 115).[101]

In the third *Jataka*, King Sibi cuts chunks of meat out of his body to save a dove from a hungry hawk. Noteworthy in this scene is the petroglyph of the sitting Bodhisattva Sibi holding the saved dove on his lap, because from each of his shoulders four flames are rising (fig. 113). The motif of the flaming shoulders is an allusion to the Great Miracle of Sravasti, also called 'the miracle of fire and water', when Shakyamuni caused flames to shoot from his shoulders and water from his feet. This motif was not only popular with the Kushan emperors whose representations on golden coins showed them with flaming shoulders, but also in Buddhist Gandhara[102] from where it spread to the Tarim Basin and mainland China. In fact, the oldest gilt-bronze figure manufactured in China, towards the end of the second century CE, is a sitting Shakyamuni with flaming shoulders.[103] Also remarkable among the scenes from Shakyamuni's life is his temptation by the beautiful daughters of the king of demons, Mara – in the petroglyph scene at Thalpan, a meditating Shakyamuni is flanked by two lasciviously dancing, bare-breasted women.[104] Other scenes at Thalpan illustrated Shakyamuni's first sermon to five disciples and two deer in the deer park of Sarnath,[105] or Shakyamuni with his protector, Bodhisattva Vajrapani.[106] A slightly later petroglyphic scene at Hodar West shows two Buddhas sitting on a pedestal flanking a stupa; they are Shakyamuni and the past Buddha Prabhutaratna.[107] This motif was also popular in the shape of gilt bronzes and rock reliefs in the Tarim Basin, Gansu and China proper.

As in Ladakh, important petroglyph sites in Gilgit-Baltistan were situated close to river crossings, for example at Chilas–Thalpan or at Shatial. The latter seems to have been an international meeting place. For one thing, the more than 400 Brahmi inscriptions were carved by Buddhists and are religious in content. Moreover, across the Indus and a few kilometres to the north, there probably stood an important Buddhist shrine or temple. Two Chinese Buddhist pilgrims, the above-mentioned Faxian[108] and Xuanzang (600–664),[109] who both travelled to Buddhist India, mentioned in their accounts a highly venerated statue of

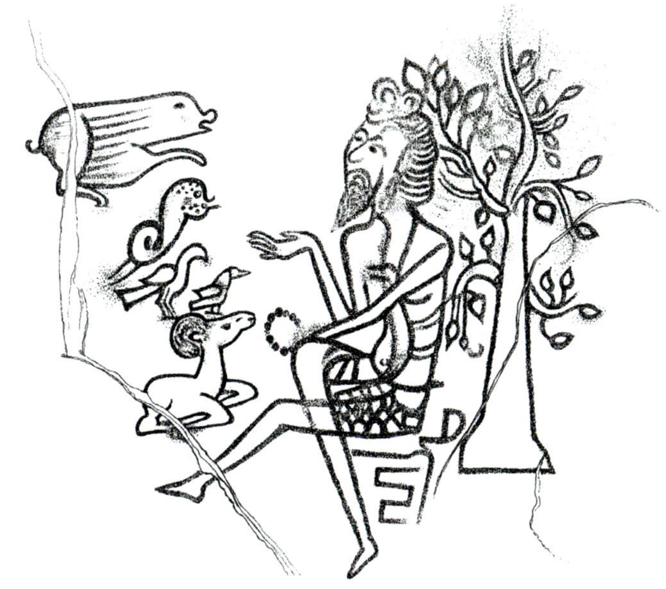

115. Ink drawing of a petroglyph scene illustrating the Buddhist *Rsipancaka-Jataka* according to which a wealthy Brahman, who had turned ascetic and in fact was a previous incarnation of Buddha Shakyamuni, was asked by a pigeon, a crow, a snake and a gazelle for instruction. The four animals were of different opinions about the greatest evil in the world. The dove thought that love was the most dangerous evil, the crow hunger, the snake anger and the gazelle believed it was the everlasting fear of death. But the ascetic replied that they were all wrong, for the greatest calamity was to be born, that is to have a physical body. Second to third quarter of the first millennium CE, Thalpan, Gilgit-Baltistan, northern Pakistan. After Hauptmann, Harald (ed.), *Materialien zur Archäologie der Nordgebiete Pakistans*, vol. 6 (Mainz: Philipp von Zabern, 2003), pl. 88.

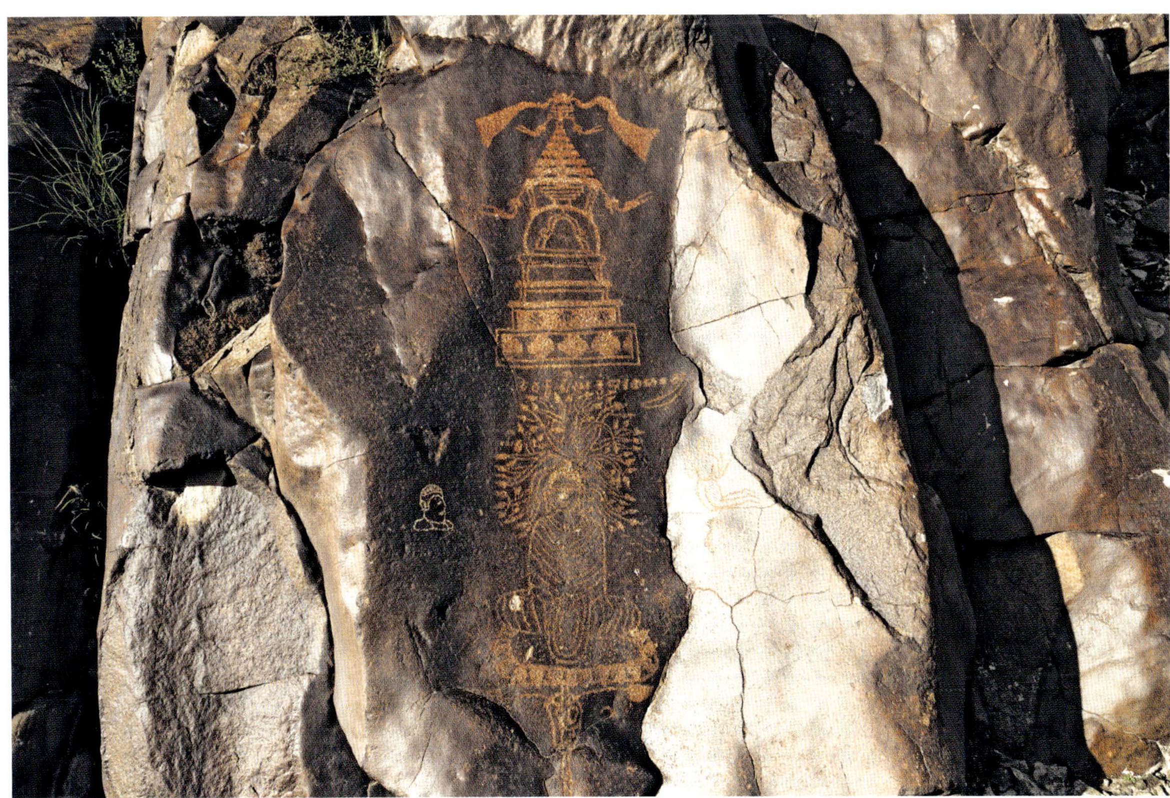

116. Buddha Shakyamuni meditating under the Bodhi Tree, a fig tree (*Ficus religiosa*) where he attained enlightenment. Above features a stupa, and at the right a kneeling devotee. The small portraits to the left and right of the Buddha are recent additions. Third quarter of the first millennium CE. Thalpan, Gilgit-Baltistan, northern Pakistan. Photo 2010.

Bodhisattva Maitreya made from gilded sandalwood at a place called 'To-leih' ('Ta-li-lo'). In 1913, Sir Aurel Stein confirmed the hypothesis of Major General Sir Alexander Cunningham (1814–1893), whereby To-leih (Ta-li-lo) was a transcription of 'Darel' which was derived from Darada. The Darel Valley and the place called Darel are situated across from Shatial.[110] And, as in Ladakh, stupas, Buddhas or Bodhisattvas were carved here by Buddhist believers mostly to acquire merit for themselves or their relatives; some petroglyphs were an expression of gratitude. On the other hand, at Shatial the Buddhist Brahmi inscriptions are outnum-bered by the 565 Sogdian inscriptions which were not carved by locals but by Sogdian traders, and were of secular content. The Sogdians, whose realm lay mostly in present-day Uzbekistan and western Tajikistan, did not form a unified state, but rather lived in independent city-states. Nevertheless, they controlled to a very great extent the international trade between India and Sogdia, India and Iran, and later the Arab Caliphate, as well as between China and the Caliphate, and China and India.[111] The concentra-tion of Sogdian inscriptions at Shatial strongly suggests that Shatial had two functions: it was an important Sogdian trading hub and, together with To-leih, a Buddhist pilgrimage centre.[112] The Sogdians

trading at Shatial most probably came not only from Sogdia, but also from the Tarim Basin, Kashmir and Gandhara.

Concerning the beliefs of the Sogdians, since there was no unified Sogdian state, there was no state religion. Whereas the majority of Sogdians followed a polytheistic variant of Zoroastrianism which included some 23 to 24 divinities, there were also minorities of Sogdian Christians, Manichaeans and Buddhists. The petroglyphs in the Shatial–Chilas–Thalpan region are thus testimonials of a once-intensive trade and cultural contact between India, Iran, Sogdia, China and Tibet. However, it is noteworthy that in view of the many Sogdian inscriptions at Shatial there are hardly any figurative petroglyphs related to Sogdian Zoroastrianism, apart from some fire altars.[113] Since the Sogdians did amply represent their deities in temple murals and in private houses, as well as on portable painted wooden boards, one may assume that within this Buddhist environment the Sogdians were allowed to carve only their names, but not their anthropomorphic deities. It is also possible that the Sogdian traders, who were otherwise hardly acquainted with rock art, did not care to represent their deities on rocks, and that by pecking inscriptions they were only following the practice of Buddhist pilgrims and traders. Since they

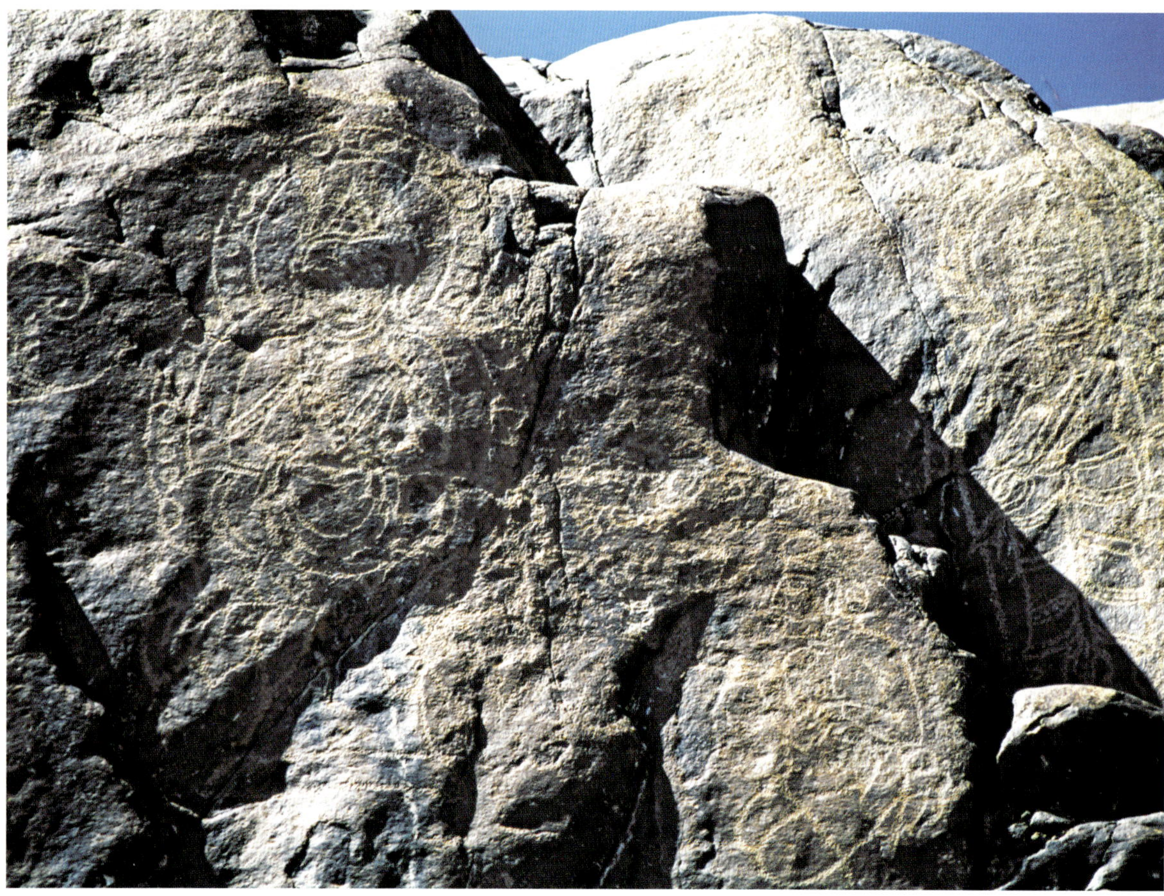

117. Petroglyphs of Buddha Vipassi who preceded Buddha Shakyamuni, and Bodhisattva Maitreya (right). According to a Brahmi inscription, the kneeling figure in the lower centre is the donor Sinhota.[3] Both Vipassi and Maitreya wear a three-pointed crown; the faces of all three figures have been recently vandalized. Second to third quarter of the first millennium CE. Chilas Bridge, Gilgit-Baltistan, northern Pakistan. Photo 2017.

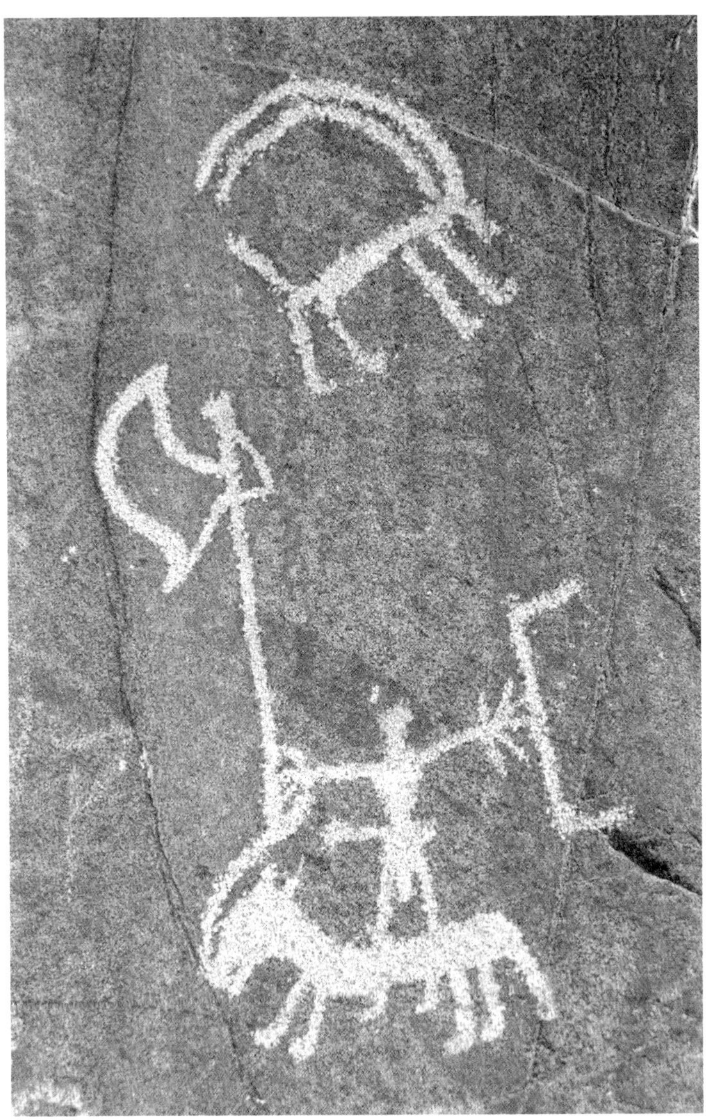

118. A warrior, girded with a short sword, holds a huge ceremonial axe and an unknown object, possibly a schematized bow. Chilas II, Gilgit-Baltistan, northern Pakistan.

were tolerant in religious matters, it could do no harm to ask for the protection of a local Buddhist deity. This latter interpretation is supported by the Sogdian inscription no. 36:38 at Shatial:

[I], Nanai-Vandak, the [son of] Nariasaf, have come [here] on the tenth [day/year] and have requested the grace of the spirit of the holy place of Kart [Shatial?] to reach Kharvandan [Tashkurgan] very quickly and to see with joy my brother in good [health].[114]

Evidently a Sogdian, who was on his way to Tashkurgan in today's Xinjiang, invoked the protection of Buddha or a Bodhisattva for him and his brother.

In the ninth and tenth centuries, a significantly different type of petroglyph emerged, mainly at Hodar and at Chilas, which were sometimes carved over existing Buddhist petroglyphs. That they are more recent is confirmed by their lesser degree of repatination. These petroglyphs are rather rough representations of mounted warriors or on foot, who tend to look like stick figures; some of them hold huge battle axes (fig. 118). Often, battle axes alone are carved, alone or in groups. Some of the horsemen wear armour and their mounts too are armoured. Occasionally the horsemen carry a crested flag, as the ancient Turkic horsemen did. These images are often associated with representations of solar discs (fig. 119) which, in certain cases, seem to represent shields, or warriors holding a huge round shield. These new types of petroglyph suggest the arrival of different people with a different ideology or the emergence of a different culture among local people who opposed the traditional Buddhist dominance. The hostility towards Buddhism is not only suggested by the over-pecking of stupas, as at Thalpan,[115] but also at Hodar by a battle scene between armed men protecting a stupa and attackers armed with bows, axes and swords and commanded by a larger figure.[116] There are several hypotheses concerning the nature and origin of this people. The *Hudud al-Alam* (*The Regions of the World*), a Persian geography from the tenth century, gives an interesting indication whereby the ruler of Bolor was no longer a Buddhist but an adept of a solar cult: 'Bolor is a vast country with a king who declares that he is the Son of the Sun. And he does not rise from his sleep until the Sun has risen, saying that a son must not rise before his father.'[117] This means that in Bolor a martial solar cult, probably hostile to Buddhism, was prevailing, at least among its rulers and parts of society. The sun disc and battle axe were symbols of this new power and ideology. Although Karl Jettmar believed that this solar cult was imported from Multan in Punjab, where there stood a famous sun temple, or that it had been influenced by Manichaeism,[118] the glorification of mounted warriors and the crested flags point rather to a people of horsemen. Furthermore, warriors from Punjab or other parts of India mainly fought on foot. At present, the most likely guess is that a group of Turkic or Iranian horsemen entered Bolor where they either seized power or enabled a section of society which disapproved of Buddhism to assert itself. Nevertheless, even if Buddhism declined, it did not disappear and experienced a modest renaissance in the tenth to eleventh centuries.

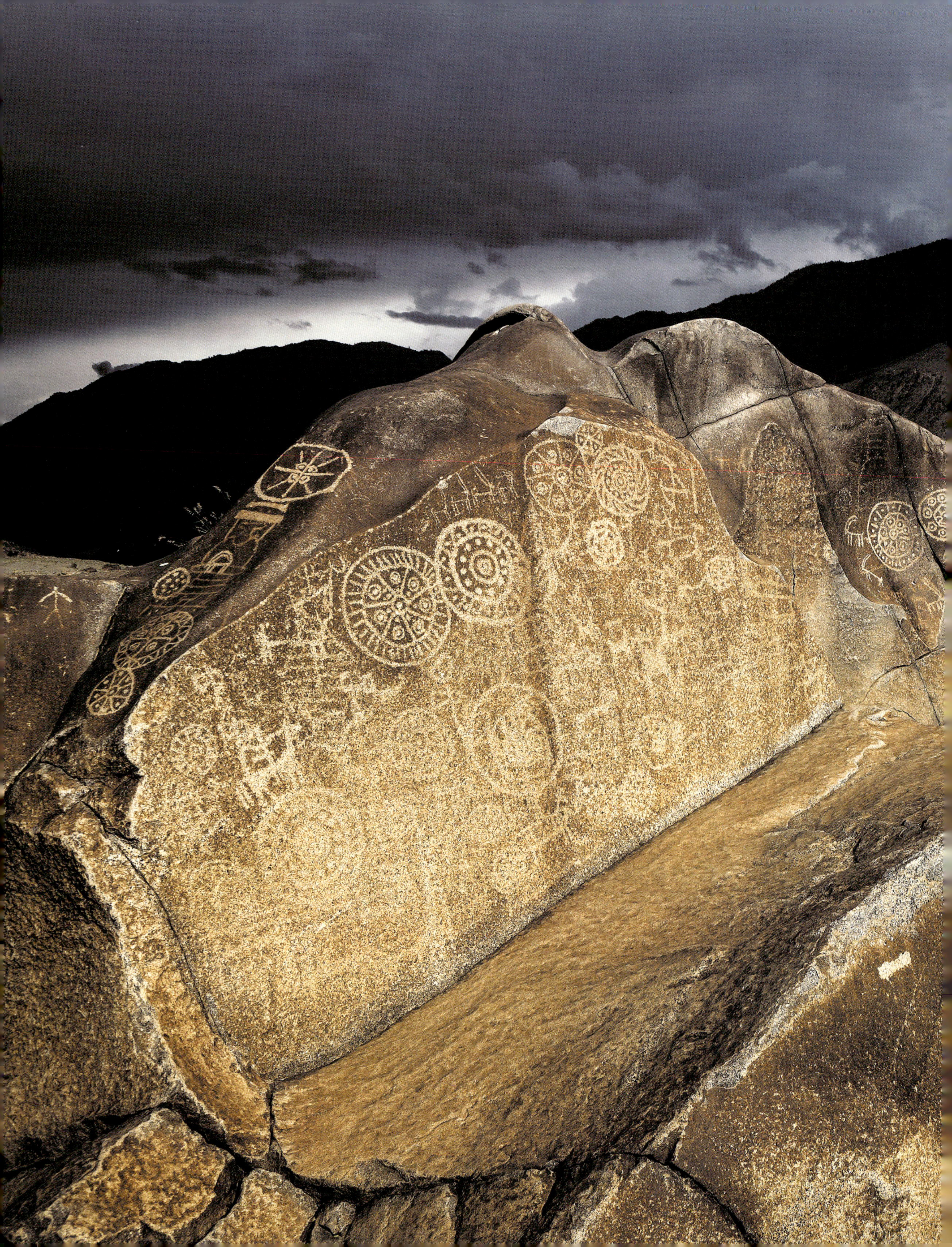

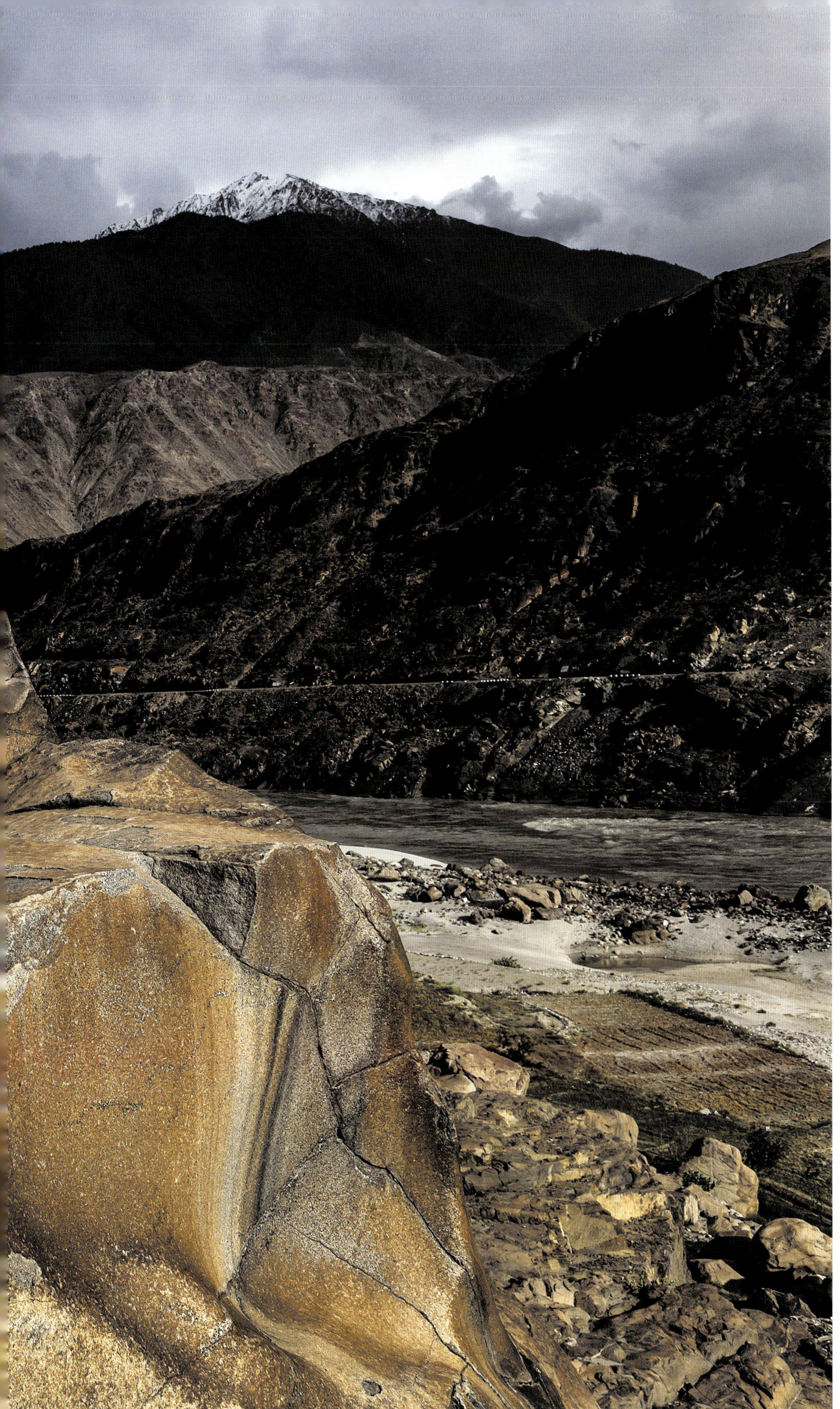

119. Solar discs, goats and axes dating from the ninth to tenth century CE, superimposed on older petroglyphs of Buddhist stupas. Thalpan, Gilgit-Baltistan, northern Pakistan. Photo 2010.

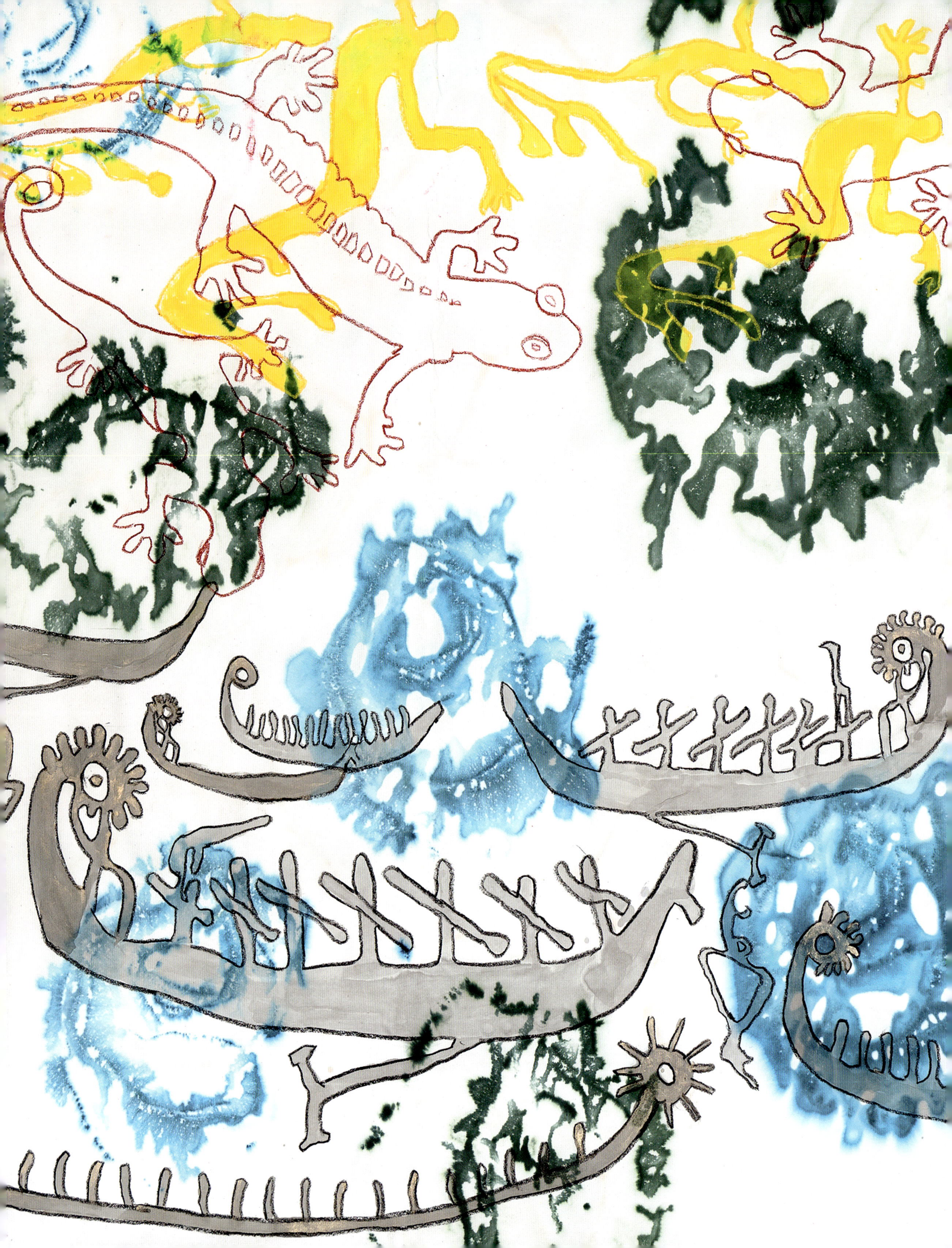

V. Caucasus

In the Caucasus, petroglyphs are concentrated in Dagestan, Azerbaijan and Armenia. In Dagestan there are several smaller sites scattered over the whole country,[1] but the major complexes are in the South Caucasus, in Azerbaijan and Armenia. Whereas the largest site of Azerbaijan is close to the Caspian Sea, the richest sites of Armenia are in the high mountains. At the former, the petroglyphs were pecked into sandstone, while in the latter they were engraved into volcanic rock that has been polished by the movements of glaciers.

The most important sites are:

Azerbaijan

- **Gobustan** is a complex of five different sites *ca.* 60 km south of the Azerbaijani capital Baku. The petroglyphs date from the late Upper Palaeolithic to the medieval period, and their history is linked to the oscillations of the Caspian Sea.

- **Absheron Peninsula**. Here the petroglyphs mostly date from the Bronze Age when the so-called Kurgan people, that is tribes of horsemen, came from the north. In order to safeguard these petroglyphs, and also the stone figures and carved plaques associated with the Kurgans, from destruction, several specimens have been moved to the Qala open-air museum five kilometres north-east of Baku, and to the Shirvanshah Palace Museum in Baku.

- **Gamigaya** is located in the south-east of Nakhchivan; the site consists of petroglyphs from the Bronze and Iron Age featuring wild animals and hunting scenes, two-axle carts pulled by oxen, and geometric signs such as concentric circles and triangles which resemble the decorations on ceramics from the second millennium BCE.[2]

- **Kalbajar** lies in western Azerbaijan.[3] Its petroglyphs are located in volcanic highland at *ca.* 3,000 m asl. They date mainly from the Bronze Age and feature hunting scenes, dances, carts pulled by oxen, ibexes, wolfs and leopards.[4]

120. ← Therese Weber, *Punctuation in Hard Rock I.* Symbols of mobility, living creatures and topographies condense into a landscape. On the bow of the boats is a sun symbol analogous to the petroglyphs in Gobustan on the Caspian Sea, Azerbaijan. Representations of amphibians, a discovery on a boulder in the wild topography of Ughtasar, Armenia. 84 × 68 cm. Chinese ink painting and chalk drawing on Zerkall laid paper, 2024.

Armenia

- **Ughtasar** is a complex in the south-eastern province of Syunik about 150 km south-east of Yerevan. It consists of three high-altitude sites situated between 2,950 and 3,270 m asl. A major part of the petroglyphs date from the Bronze and Iron Ages.

- **Gegham Mountains**. At the foot of Mount Astghaberd in the Gegham Mountains in central Armenia there are petroglyphs from the Bronze Age spread over more than 66 sites that include some unusual motifs.[5]

- **Aragats Volcano**. The petroglyphs in the Kasagh Valley and those between Aghavnatun and Voskehat within the Aragats region are situated in western Armenia. They feature hunting and ploughing with harnessed oxen, ibexes and herds of goats.[6]

1. Azerbaijan

The landscape of the littoral zone along the Caspian Sea has been strongly impacted and shaped by the eustatic oscillations of the sea, that is the changes of its water levels compared to the average global ocean level. The Caspian, which is almost tideless, became an inland body of water about 5.5 million years ago. It was thus separated from the Black Sea and from the smaller, shallow Sea of Azov.[7] Yet there were later, relatively short periods during three large marine transgressions[8] in which these seas were connected. At the time of the Cimmerian regression, 4 mya, the Caspian Sea had shrunk to its southern, deeper third, and the northern, shallow two-thirds had dried up. But during the subsequent Akchagylian transgression which occurred about 3.2–3.0 mya and was due to tectonic processes, the Caspian Sea, which today is 1,160 kilometres long on its north–south axis, expanded to the north to a total length of more than 2,200 kilometres, reaching roughly as far as the present-day city of Kazan on the Volga. The sea also expanded

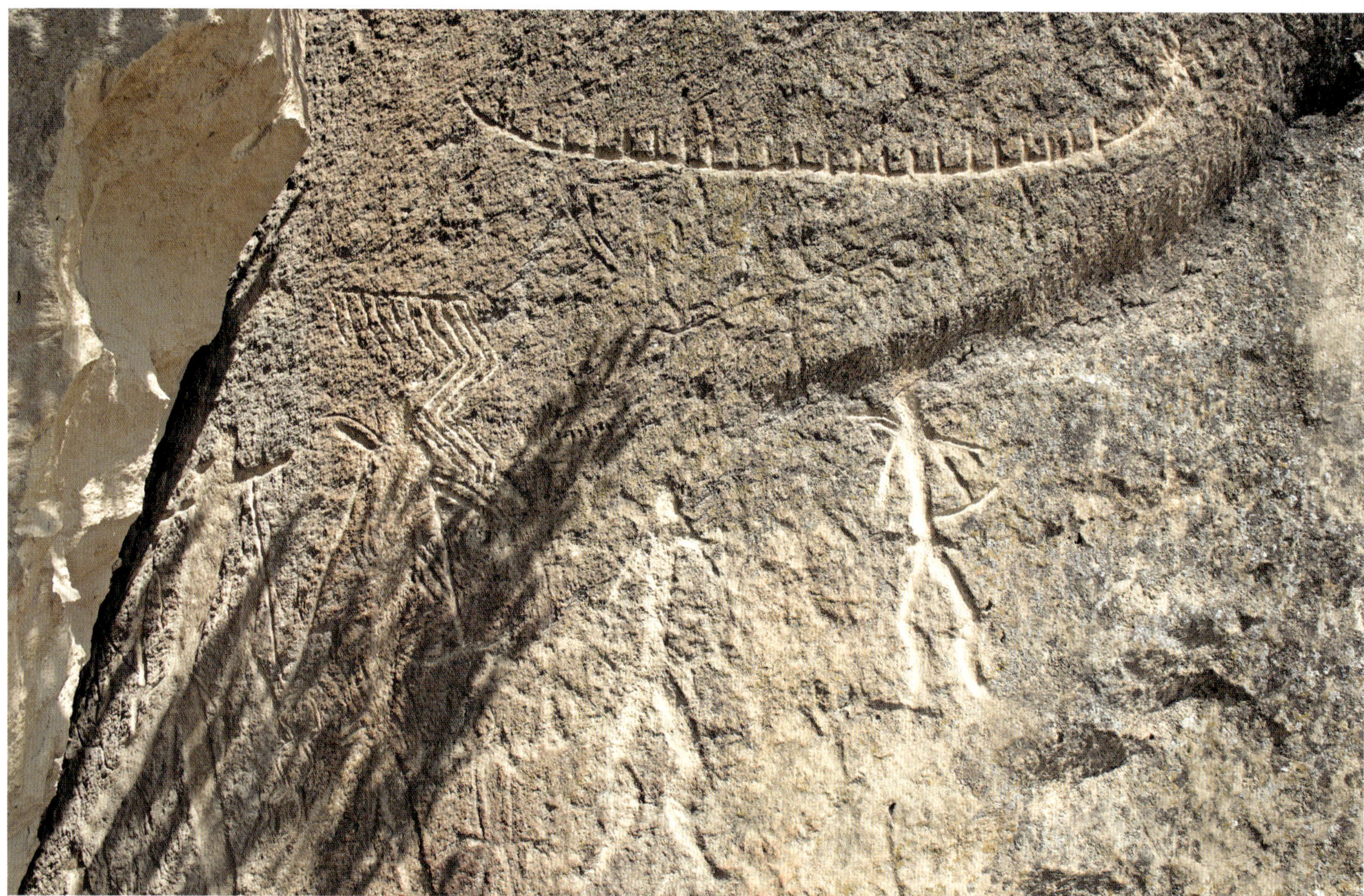

121. At the top of the image is a 150-cm-long boat with 21 passengers. On the left, two large and one small human figure are superimposed on zigzag motifs that probably depict water; the two larger figures are carrying bows on their back (possibly added later). These petroglyphs date from the Mesolithic (*ca.* 8000–7000 BCE), but the two brighter figures in the centre are later, probably from the Neolithic. Upper terrace, Boyukdash, Gobustan, Azerbaijan. Photo 2016.

eastwards as far as the Aral Sea and was connected by the Manych Depression to the Black Sea and the Sea of Azov, which, in turn, were joined to the Mediterranean.[9] The next major transgression, the Absheronian, is variously dated between 2.0 mya (van Baak) and 1.1 mya (Boomer). The surface area of the four interconnected bodies of water was almost as extensive as it had been during the Akchagylian transgression.[10] The third transgression, the Early Khazarian (0.3 mya), was less extensive and failed to reach the Aral basin.[11] There are various causes for the oscillations of the sea. The long-term factors are tectonic processes and large-scale climate change. The medium and short-term factors are regional climate oscillations, earthquakes, solar activity and sunshine intensity, which influence the degree of evaporation, and, very importantly, precipitation in the Volga catchment area, since the Volga accounts for 80 to 85 per cent of the sea's freshwater intake.[12]

Of relevance for the petroglyphs at Gobustan are the Caspian's later oscillations: after the Early Khvalynian transgression (32–25/24 ka BP) which led to a significant rise of the Caspian water level, came the Yenotavian regression (24–17 ka BP) with a dramatic sinking of the water level to 51 metres below ocean sea level. During the subsequent Late Khvalynian transgression (16–9/8 ka BP) levels rose again to, according to different studies, between 12 metres below sea level and 50 (or even 130) metres above; but with the Mangyshlak regression shoreland was once more drained as water levels sank to 21.5 (or 41) metres below sea level. The Caspian Sea remains notorious today for its rapid swings in water level. Over the last 50 years, the world's oceans have fluctuated by an average of 1.8 +/- 0.3 mm per year, while the Caspian Sea in the 1980s fluctuated on a number of occasions by 38 centimetres per year, almost 200 times more than the average. At present, the Caspian Sea's water level is *ca.* 26.9 metres below the mean sea level of the world's oceans.[13]

Table 2: Major sea-level fluctuations of the Caspian Sea in the Late Pleistocene and Holocene[14]

Oceanic period	Time period	Sea level compared to global level
Late Khazarian transgression	114–75 ka BP	−20 to −10 m
Atel regression	75–35/32 ka BP	−120 to −140 m
Early Khvalynian transgression	32–25/24 ka BP	−5 m to 0 m (Mamedov) +48 to +50 m as a short-term peak (Yanina)
Yenotavian regression	24–17 ka BP	−51 m or lower
Late Khvalynian transgression	16 ka–9/8000 BP	−12 m (Mamedov); 0 m (Yanina); +50 m highstand (Kakroodi) or even +130 m (Chepalyga)
Mangyshlak[15] regression	8000–4000 BP	−41 m or even −113 m extreme regression (Kakroodi) −21.5 m (Mamedov)
Neocaspian Period: eight cycles of 450 to 500 years each	4000 BP–present Present time	−20 m to −32 m −26.9 m

The petroglyphs of **Gobustan**, whose name means 'land of dry riverbeds', represent unique works of art from the Late Palaeolithic to the Middle Ages. In total, the three main petroglyph complexes of Gobustan – **Boyukdash**, **Kichikdash** and **Jinghirdagh** – and the two minor ones – **Shikhgaya** and **Shongar** – contain more than 6,000 petroglyphs. The three major sites are situated at a height of *ca.* 100–200 metres above sea level; Boyukdash and Kichikdash are one and a half to two kilometres away from the Caspian coast, Jinghirdagh around ten kilometres. The petroglyphs were not carved on rocks, but on massive stone blocks that slid down from the mountains as a result of nearby volcanic eruptions and earthquakes. Some of these boulders happened to form pseudo-caves used by prehistoric hunters. The fact that some of the rocks fell only in recent millennia is shown by those boulders on which aurochs were engraved in the Upper Palaeolithic or early Neolithic but are now upside down, whereas animals like ibexes, which were superimposed during the Bronze Age on the older petroglyphs

of aurochs, stand the right way up. The geology of the boulders consists of a thick layer of sedimentary limestone which includes many species of shells and other marine fossils stemming from previous marine transgressions. These various submersions shaped the littoral zone into datable strata. On some rocks located in the south-east of the Gobustan petroglyph complex at Kichikdash there is a band around 20 to 30 centimetres wide with small encrusted shells separating the upper, pre-Bronze Age petroglyphs from the lower, Bronze and Iron Age petroglyphs. In the words of Dario Sigari, 'it is possible to use the Caspian eustatic movements as a valid chronological indicator for rock art chronology.'[16] In spite of the changes in the landscape due to the maritime fluctuations, the area of Gobustan remained populated or at least frequented over a period of *ca.* 14,000 or 15,000 years by people who adapted to marine transgressions and regressions by following the shoreline. Consequently, the petroglyphs of a particular terrace can be assigned to a specific time period.

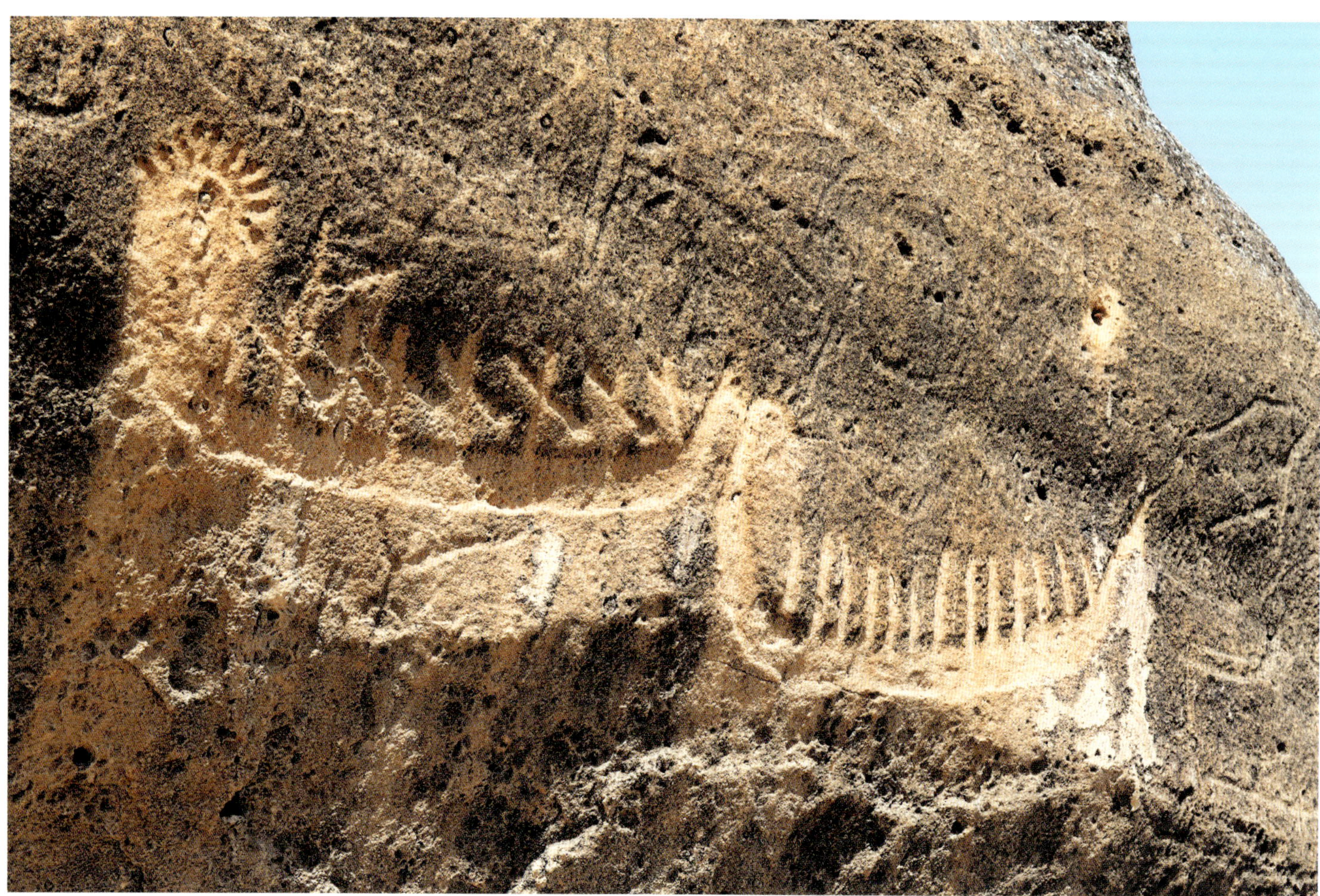

122. Two boats with solar symbols at the prow. Transition from the Mesolithic to the Neolithic (*ca.* 7000–6000 BCE). Lower terrace, Boyukdash, Gobustan, Azerbaijan. Photo 2016.

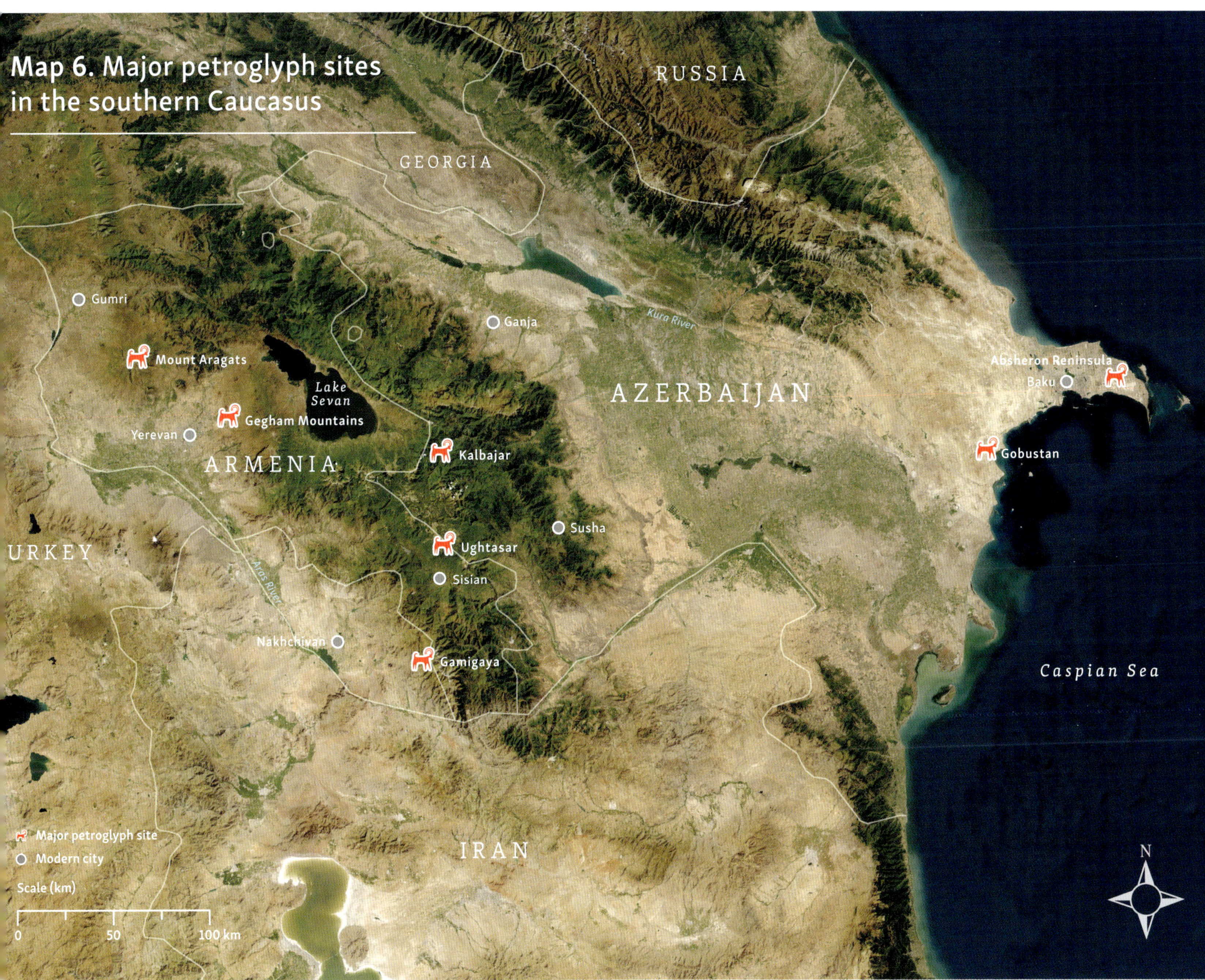
Map 6. Major petroglyph sites in the southern Caucasus
RUSSIA
GEORGIA
Gumri
Ganja
Kura River
Mount Aragats
AZERBAIJAN
Absheron Reninsula
Lake Sevan
Baku
Gegham Mountains
Yerevan
Kalbajar
ARMENIA
Gobustan
URKEY
Susha
Ughtasar
Aras River
Sisian
Caspian Sea
Nakhchivan
Gamigaya
Major petroglyph site
Modern city
Scale (km)
IRAN
N
0
50
100 km

The history of Gobustan's petroglyphs is classified into five periods:[17]

- **I. Late Upper Palaeolithic–Early Holocene** (15th–10th millennium BP). The petroglyphs of this period were created during the Late Khvalynian transgression (16–9/8 ka BP) when the sea level rose sharply, which is why they are located on the upper strata of Boyukdash and Kichikdash, many of them in rock shelters and pseudo-caves. Archaeological investigation of the surrounding layers of earth and debris revealed that people at that time lived from fishing and hunting. Neither traces of agricultural activity nor advanced stone tools were found. From the first half of this period come images of aurochs or aurochs heads as well as of women with pronounced breasts, hips and buttocks but without a head, or with only amorphous heads rendered in profile. Some images feature pregnant women.

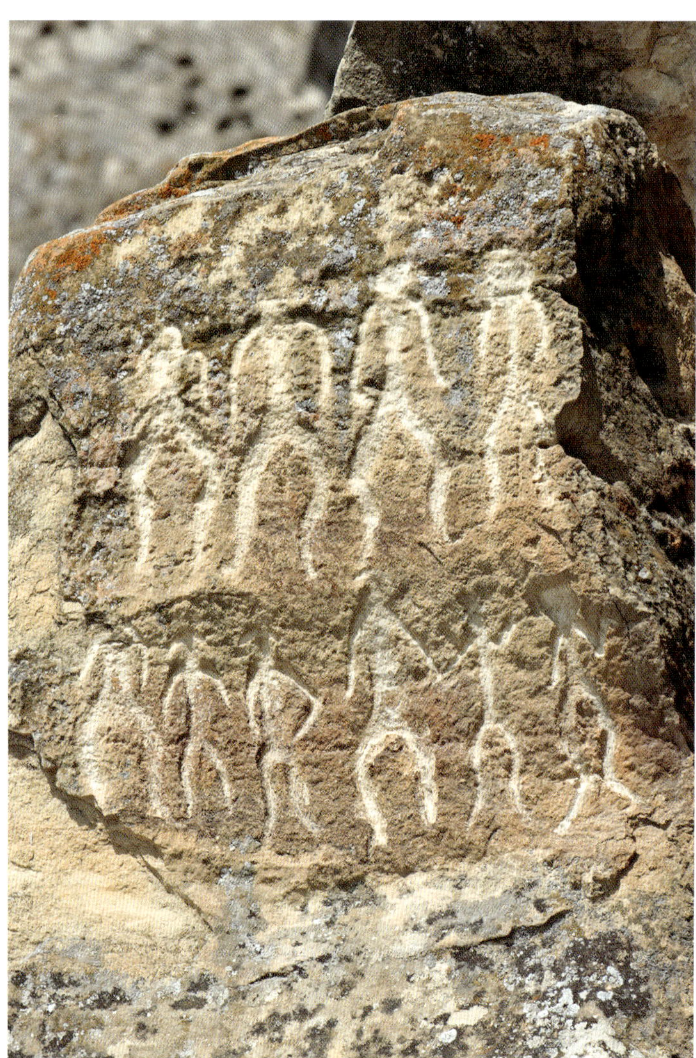

123. A group of ten dancing humans from the Neolithic (*ca.* 5000–4000 BCE). Upper terrace, Boyukdash, Gobustan, Azerbaijan. Photo 2016.

These highly stylized images often form groups. They display clear similarities to contemporaneous petroglyphs of curvaceous women from Jubbah in Saudi Arabia, to Palaeolithic figurines from Western Europe, and to the silhouette-like representation of headless women in the cave carvings of Gönnersdorf, Germany, dating from the final Magdalenian.[18] These similarities may suggest that the concept of such female images was common to several pre-Neolithic cultures. In the middle phase of this first period, images of schematic, larger-than-life-size males appeared; and in the last two millennia of this period, three additional motifs emerged. First, petroglyphs of men holding bows and arrows; sometimes bows and arrows were added to older male images (fig. 121). This new element most probably coincided with the introduction of the bow and arrow in hunting; hunters had previously used spears.[19] Next, in the Mesolithic, petroglyphs appeared featuring humans with tattoos or body painting; and finally, images of rowing boats. More than 60 representations of boats have been found; many of them carry a sun symbol at their bow which may suggest that the people of those times believed that a boat carried the sun during its journey through the sky. Alternatively, the figure at the ships' prow may represent the star with the help of which early seafarers oriented themselves when navigating on the Caspian Sea (fig. 122). The largest ship pecking is 150 centimetres long and there are about twenty people on board, represented as stick figures. The boats were probably made from reeds bundled together.[20] These boat peckings date from the later phase of the Late Khvalynian transgression when the Caspian Sea lay much closer to the petroglyphs than it does today.

- **II. Neolithic–Chalcolithic** (seventh–fourth millennium BCE). Into this period fall the hunting scenes of aurochs and wild asses as well as dancing scenes (fig. 123). In the second half of this period images of ibexes, boars, deer and domesticated oxen appear, and the animals are rendered in more stylized shapes.

- **III. Bronze Age** (fourth–second millennium BCE). During this period the petroglyphs tend to become smaller and more realistic, and the fauna depicted reflect the economic changes to food production. There are no more aurochs, and only a few domesticated oxen and wild equines; ibexes and deer now predominate. Striking are the images of the East Caucasian tur (*Capra cylindricornis*) with its large body and huge horns (fig. 124). The middle Bronze Age witnessed a population exchange when the local, south-east Caucasian

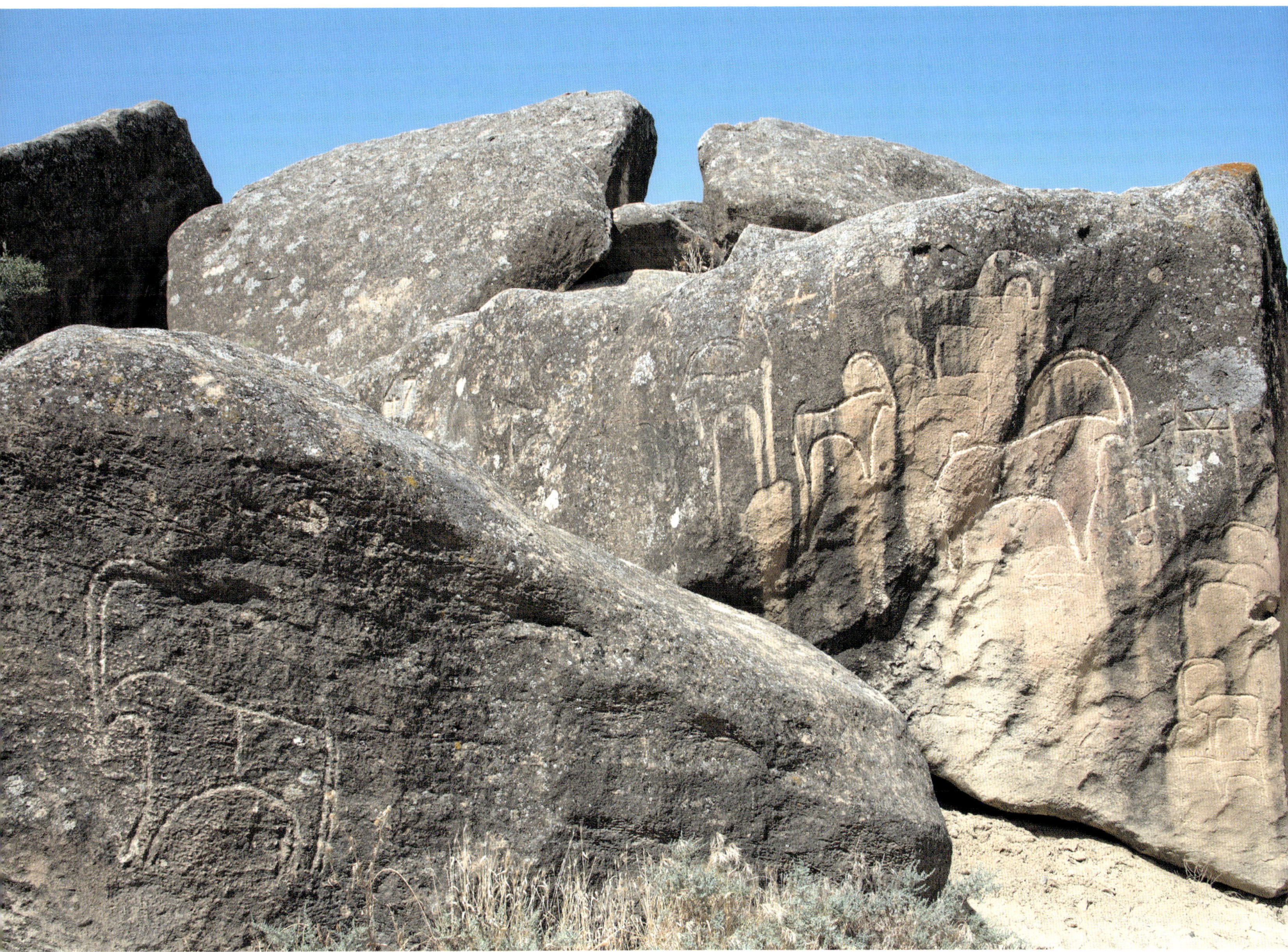

124. Petroglyphs of East Caucasian tur (*Capra cylindricornis*) at Jingirdagh. Bronze Age (*ca.* 3000–2500 BCE). Gobustan, Azerbaijan. Photo 2016.

sedentary farmers began to migrate southward into eastern Anatolia and the Iranian highlands due to a climatic aridification from *ca.* 2400 BCE, and at the same time semi-mobile cattle breeders from the North Caucasus started to move southward into today's Azerbaijan in search of new pastures.[21] The most visible cultural markers of these immigrants are the kurgans, the funeral tumuli usually surrounded by stone circles. Such kurgans are widespread in Azerbaijan, and are found at Gobustan and on the Absheron Peninsula; occasionally an anthropomorphic stone stele or slabs carved with a standing or seated anthropomorphic figure formed part of the outer stone circle.[22] In the later

Bronze Age petroglyphs, images of carts and chariots, bears, lions and wolves appeared.

- **IV. Iron Age** (late second–first millennium BCE). In the early Iron Age, petroglyphs of horsemen hunting deer began to emerge. Also from the Iron Age are scenes of two ibexes confronting each other and standing on their hind legs, as well as images of anthropomorphs without arms.

- **V. Albanian[23] antiquity to the Middle Ages** (late first century BCE–fifteenth century CE). The most striking petroglyph from ancient Albania is an important historical document.

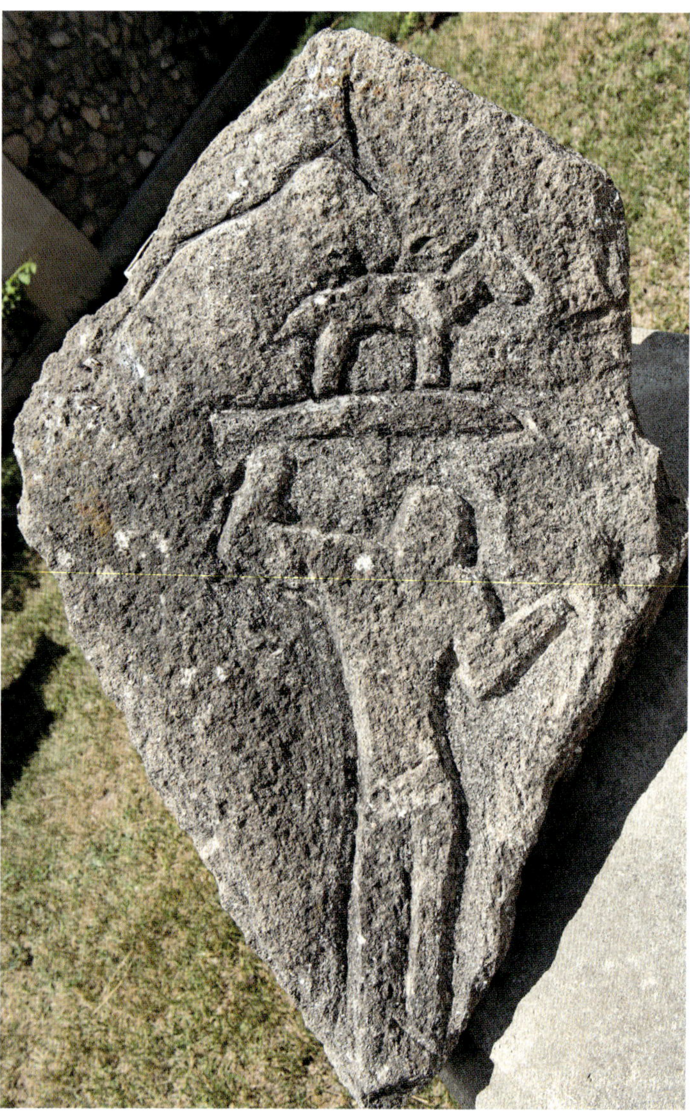

125. A hunter holds a bow in his left hand and with his right he lifts a plate with a horse on it. Early second millennium BCE. Relief from Agdash Duzu, central Azerbaijan, now in the open-air archaeological museum, Gala State Historical and Ethnographic Reserve, Absheron, Azerbaijan. Photo 2016.

It is the inscription made by a Roman centurion of the Legio XII Fulminata, which was stationed there under Emperor Domitian (r. 81–96). Following a military initiative into Iberia (today's Georgia)[24] launched by Emperor Vespasian in 75 CE, Domitian extended the Roman zone of influence to the Caspian Sea. At Emperor Trajan's death in 117 CE, his successor Hadrian (r. 117–138) pulled the Roman out-post back behind the Surami Mountain Range which divides western and central Georgia.[25] Other petroglyphs from antiquity and the Middle Ages feature horsemen armed with spears, hunting scenes, a camel caravan, *tamgas* and Arabic inscriptions.

2. Armenia

The petroglyph complex of **Ughtasar** lies 20 kilometres north of the small city of Sisian. It consists of three sites. Two of them, **Naseli** and **Sepasar,** are located on the outer slopes of the eponymous volcanoes at an altitude of 2,950 and 2,980 metres above sea level respectively. The third site borders the small **Lake Ughtasar** located inside the caldera of the volcano Tskhuk at an altitude of 3,270 metres above sea level. The geology of the whole area is volcanic. The volcanic rock was ground smooth during the last Ice Age after which manganese–iron varnish formed on the basalt blocks. The rock varnish is either dark blue when there is a high manganese content, or reddish brown showing a high iron content. When the glaciers retreated in the course of the Holocene, pastures expanded on the mountain slopes, which were used in summer by semi-mobile pastoralists as far as Lake Ughtasar. In terms of motifs, petroglyphs of animals form the majority, followed by those of humans and a few objects. Besides hunts of ibexes and deer, there are few scenes involving action. Noticeable exceptions are dancing humans, two men fighting with swords, and a man armed with a bow and a shield surrounded by five felines. About two-thirds of all images are simplified representations of ibexes; after this come humans (*ca.* 15 per cent) and felids which account for a relatively high 7 per cent of all images (fig. 126). The latter portray snow leopards or cheetahs chasing and attacking deer; smaller felines may represent Pallas's cats (also known as manul). It remains unknown whether this high proportion of felines points to a symbolic or cultic meaning or whether it simply reflects a high density of those carnivores during the Bronze Age.

Several humans have huge hands with outstretched fingers, as at Mount Astghaberd in central Armenia. Then there are images of bears, horses, snakes and wavy lines, possibly representing rivers or mountain paths, as well as swastikas and cup marks. As at Saimaluu Tash in Kyrgyzstan, there are also petroglyphs of carts pulled by oxen and a ploughing scene with two harnessed oxen.[26] Close to the lake there is a flat stone with a curious spatial arrange-ment: on the larger left half are images from daily life such as a hunter shooting an arrow at an ibex, other ibexes, another human holding an object, and two small bovines. On the smaller half of the stone at the right is a long wavy line, separated from the scene on the left by a straight rake whose 18 to 20 prongs point left (fig. 127). Whether this undulating line represents a river or three mountains is impossible to assess; in any case it seems that the rake represents an insurmountable obstacle between the two halves. Surprisingly, close to the tiny lake there are also two petroglyphs featuring a small boat although the nearest significant body of water, Lake Sevan, is 70 kilometres away.[27] The petroglyphs at Ughtasar date from the Bronze and Iron Ages.

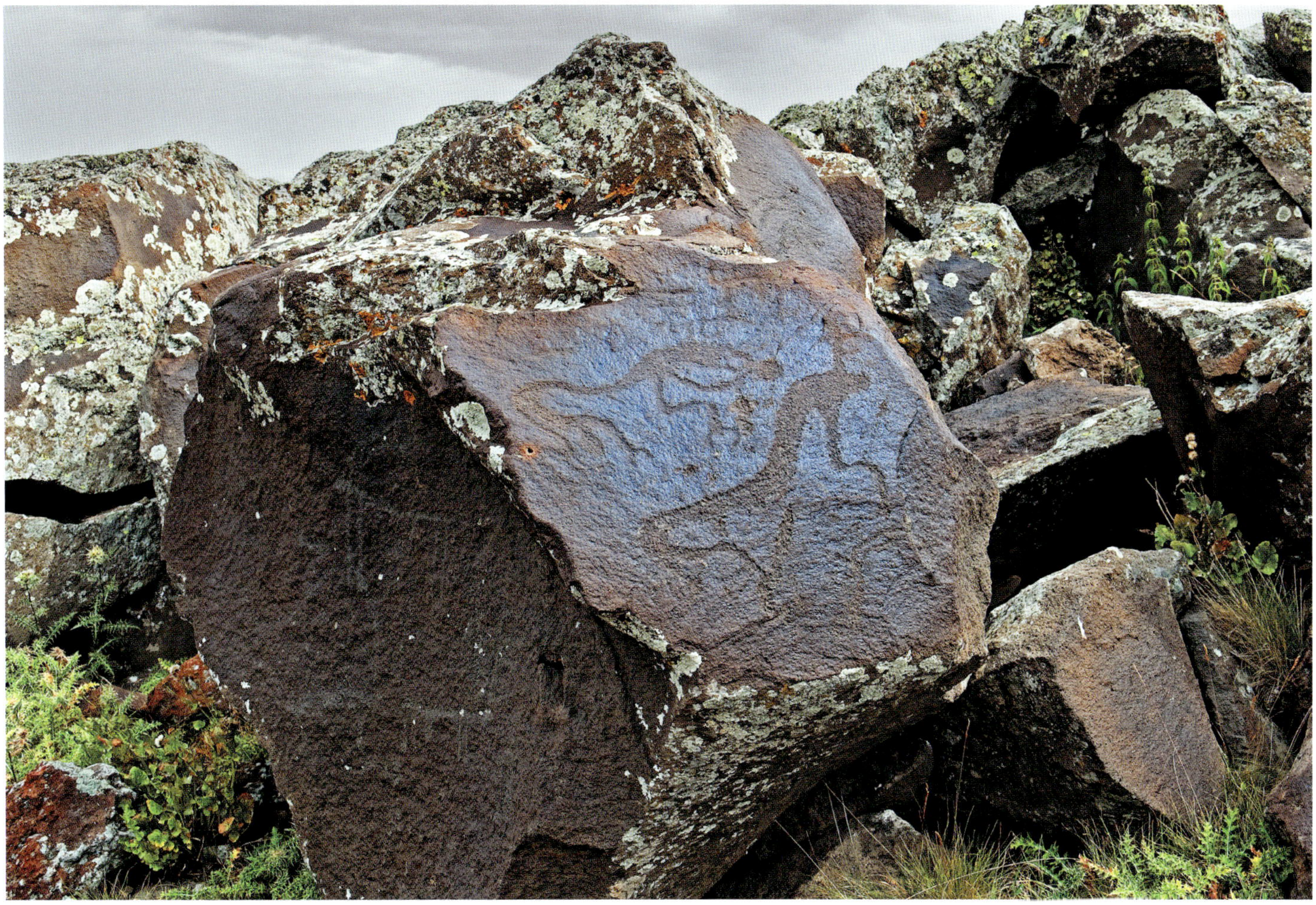

In the **Gegham Mountain** Range most of the petroglyphs are located on the slopes of **Mount Astghaberd**; they date from the Bronze and Iron Ages. Besides widespread motifs such as ibexes, deer, oxen, leopards, bears, foxes, stick figures, hunting scenes, carts, humans with huge hands and outstretched fingers, there are more unusual images. These include suns with undulating rays, the moon, constellations of stars, possibly a celestial map, spirals, a kind of chessboard, swastikas, coniferous trees, birds and numerous snakes. The latter most probably represent *vishaps*, mythological animals in Armenian folklore in the shape of a dragon or a snake. The *vishaps* were venerated since they caused thunder and rain, and feared because they could obscure the sun. Other remarkable scenes feature two men fighting each other with their fists, hunters shooting arrows at a leopard, a man holding a large deer on a leash, and the sacrifice of an ox with a battle axe or hammer – a scene similar to the sacrifice scene at Tamgaly, Kazakhstan.[28]

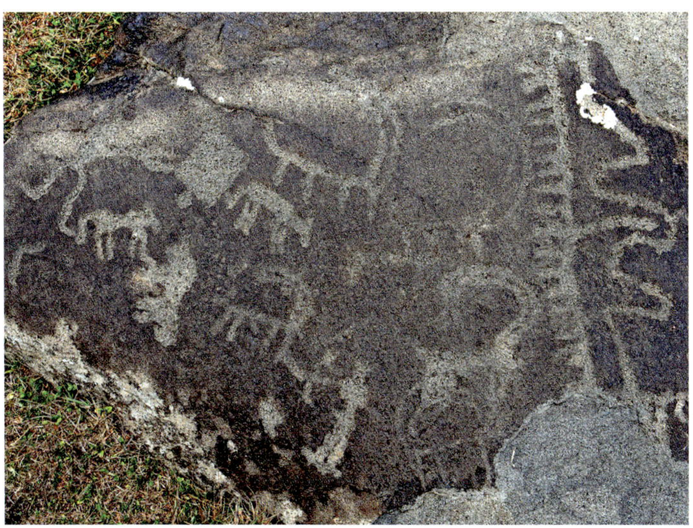

126. ↑ Petroglyphs of two slender animals, possibly carnivores, although the lower one seems to wear antlers. Bronze Age, Ughtasar mountains, Armenia. Photo 2015.

127. Petroglyphs showing at the bottom a hunter taking aim with a bow at a near ibex or a predator standing further away; then a human holding a rectangular object, ibexes and, at the right, a kind of rake and a wavy line. Seen from the left side, the latter two figures may signify a border below a mountain range. Bronze Age, Ughtasar mountains, Armenia. Photo 2015.

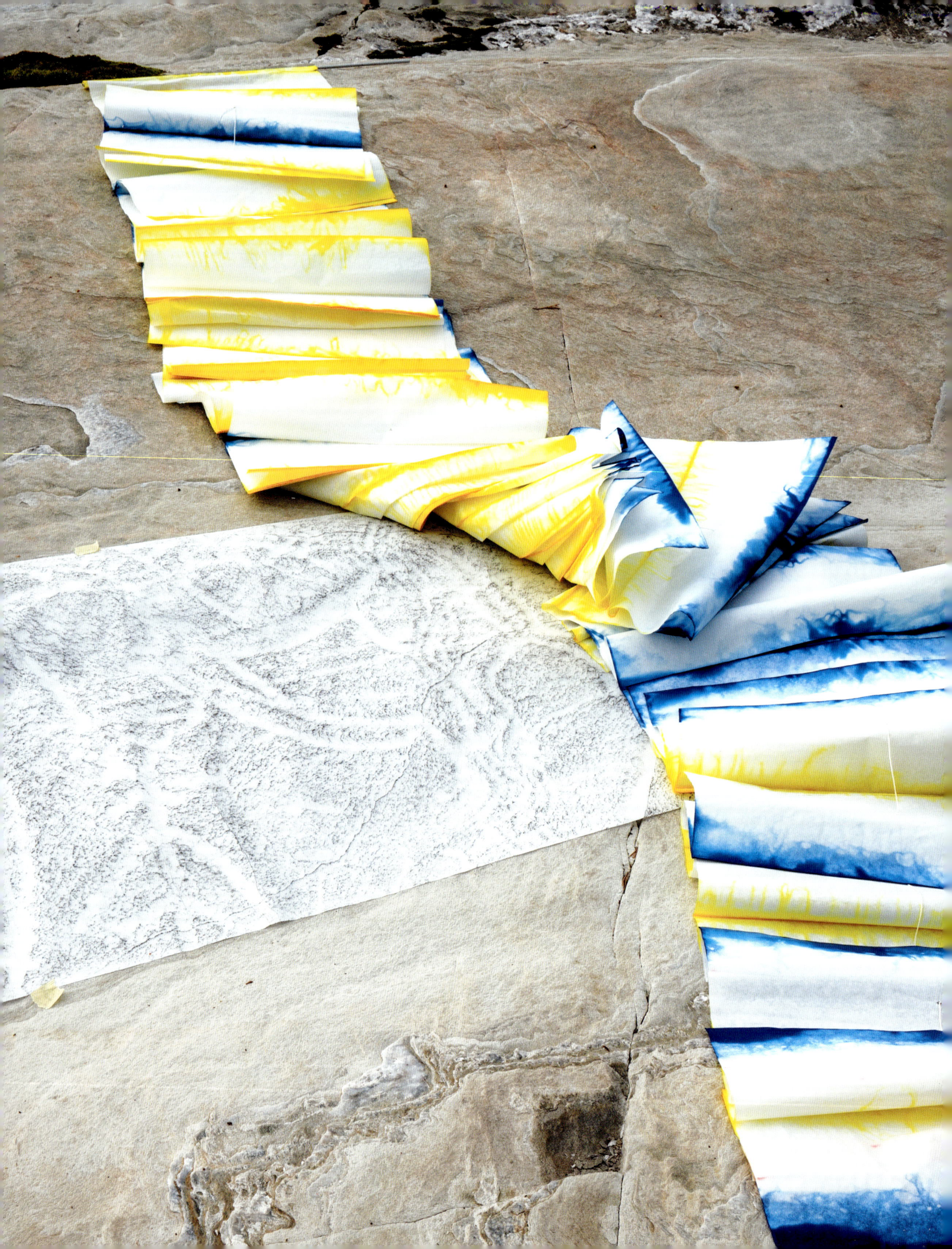

VI. Europe

The art of petroglyphs in Europe dating from the later Mesolithic to the late Iron Age or early Roman period can be divided into two large groups: Nordic and Alpine. The Nordic group comprises Fennoscandia – which includes Sweden, Norway and Finland,[1] along with the Murmansk oblast and Republic of Karelia in Russia. The Alpine group mainly consists of the huge southern Alpine sites of Val Camonica (Italy) and Mont Bégo (France), some tiny sites in Alpine Switzerland and Austria, and a few smaller sites in Iberia (Spain and Portugal). While independent centres of petroglyphs emerged in both regions, with their own characteristics and styles reflecting their respective climatic conditions and fauna, surprising similarities in content are also noticeable, triggered by trade contacts across Europe and even with the Near East during the Bronze Age. Given the relatively rare occurrence of copper and especially tin, the spread of bronze required a brisk trade in these raw materials within Europe and the Mediterranean, which brought with it a trade in equally rare goods such as Baltic amber. But since iron ore is much more widespread than bronze and tin, the European trade in raw materials shrank rapidly in the earlier Iron Age, and with it the corresponding cultural contacts.

128. ← Therese Weber, *Forms of the Present, Narratives of the Past.* Past and present are linked by the interaction of frottage and the spread-out leporello/accordion book. The fascination of working in the context of the ancestors and in the same landscape as them creates a dynamic balance between action and knowledge transfer. Frottage on Mulberry paper (total 115 × 488 cm) and installation at the petroglyphs in Amtmannsnes, Alta, Norway. Accordion book: coloured paper band of mulberry fibre (total of folded paper band: 46 × 5000 cm), 2022.

1. Northern Europe: Fennoscandia

Although the petroglyph area of Fennoscandia stretches along a north–south axis from 70° to 55° latitude over a distance of 1,600 kilometres, it forms a single entity in terms of timescale and content. The similarities that occur across the region in terms of motifs, and in part also of meanings, are due to a common climatic and geological history that resulted in comparable animal populations, as well, initially, as human economies and ways of life. As each sub-region, however, has a different focus in terms of its predominant motifs, Fennoscandia is best understood as a network of petroglyph complexes. Common to petroglyphs across Fennoscandia are their references – both in terms of location and of content – to seas, lakes or rivers, especially at cataracts such as Vyg in Russian Karelia or Nämforsen in Sweden. The petroglyphs were mostly created in the vicinity of water and the predominant motifs are, in Karelia, belugas and waterfowl, and in Alta (Norway) and southern Fennoscandia, boats and ships. In this context, 'boats' are smaller vehicles designed for inland and coastal waterways, while 'ships' refers to larger, seaworthy craft. Also characteristic of Fennoscandian petroglyphs is the fact that, compared to those from other regions, they feature a disproportionate number of complex scenes, even including narratives of events that occurred only at specific times of the year, for example the hunting of belugas in summer or autumn or the corralling of reindeer in autumn.[2] As a result, Fennoscandian petroglyphs should not be understood one-dimensionally as an expression of magical thinking or of myth, but also as a depiction of real events; most probably both aspects, the real and the imaginary, were being referred to at the same time. As an example, in a high mountainous environment in Central Asia where light battle chariots were of no real use, such petroglyphs could have had only a figurative significance. But in the coastal and riverine areas of Fennoscandia, boats were the preferred means of transport, which is why such petroglyphs will also have had a concrete meaning. The rendering of real-life activities was intertwined with mythological beliefs. Finally, common to all northern petroglyphs from the Mesolithic and early Neolithic is the fact that they illustrate exclusively outdoor situations and activities, most probably related only to men; humans marked as female and indoor scenes are absent. Clearly female figures appear for the first time at Amtmannsnes II, Alta, dating from *ca.* 3000–2000 BCE.

There were however two factors that subdivided Fennoscandia into northern and southern halves. One was the last of several stages of the Weichselian Fennoscandian Ice Sheet which reached its final maximum around 19.0 to 18.5 ka BP and covered most of Fennoscandia's interior, thus separating the northern and eastern parts of the region from the narrow coastal and southern parts. Most of Fennoscandia's flora disappeared and the fauna migrated south. The Ice Sheet rapidly shrank as of 15 ka BP and disappeared at the onset of the Holocene around 12 ka BP.[3] An additional obstacle was the brackish Yoldia Sea, which connected the North and Baltic Seas.[4] Due to the isostatic uplift[5] of Scandinavia, this connection was closed off between 10.7 and 10.0 ka BP and the saline Yoldia Sea turned into the freshwater Ancylus Lake (which ultimately became the – once more salty – Baltic Sea). These barriers impeded the migration of populations. The second, more determining factor was the climate during the Neolithic, Bronze and Iron Ages north of the 64th degree. When agriculture began to spread in southern Scandinavia in the Late Neolithic (2400–1800 BCE), it expanded along the Norwegian coast as far as the Trondheim Fjord (63° 30' north) thanks to the favourable influence of the Gulf Stream, but in Sweden only as far as an area north of Uppsala, *ca.* 60° north. Beyond these limits, forestry, hunting, trapping and fishing were more productive than agriculture, which in most of the region was in any case impossible, except close to the coast as at Alta where barley could be grown. These limits fluctuated slightly over time, but they meant that there was a sharp economic, social and cultural line dividing Scandinavia.[6] People north of this divide remained mainly hunter-gatherers, while to the south a gradual shift took place towards sedentary pastoralism and farming, albeit hunting and fishing remained significant and maritime trade played an important economic and social role. This socioeconomic divide is reflected in the petroglyphs. While petroglyphs of boats and of animal hunts on land are ubiquitous, there are no whaling or bear-hunting scenes in the south, or any ploughing scenes, chariots, carts or domestic animals in the northern petroglyphs. Nevertheless north and south remained in trading contact, mainly for furs and hides.

1.1. Northern Fennoscandia

The pulse of climatic changes also determined the movements of the human population and of fauna. During the relatively mild late Pleistocene Bølling–Allerød interstadial (14.7–12.9 ka BP), the tundra, and in tandem with it reindeer, moved northwards; reindeer hunters living in present northern Germany followed this 'walking larder' into southern Scandinavia.[7] However, this warmer climatic trend was soon interrupted by a renewed climatic deterioration during the Older Dryas (13.9–13.15 ka BP) which was followed by the sharp cooling of the Younger Dryas (12.9–11.7 ka BP) and a return to glacial conditions.[8] Prey and hunters returned south. With the end of the Younger Dryas, reindeer and hunters rapidly repopulated southern Scandinavia, which led to the emergence of the **Fosna–Hensbacka culture** (*ca.* 11.5 or slightly before 10.5 ka BP) which shows affinities with the final Palaeolithic Ahrensburger culture of the north-western European plain.[9] Since the Fennoscandia Ice Sheet rapidly vanished as climate became warmer, the migrations of fauna and humans quickly continued northwards, initially along the ice-free Norwegian coast. By this stage these northbound settlers already had boats.[10] The maritime **Komsa culture** (after 11.5 or around 11.2–10 ka cal. BP), which is considered to be an extension of the Fosna–Hensbacka culture, emerged around the 70th latitude.[11] It was probably from these migrating pioneers and their descendants that the earliest known petroglyphs in Fennoscandia originate, north of the Arctic Circle[12] in the region of **Ofoten** at 68° 28' north. They are dated to *ca.* 9000–7000 cal. BCE.[13] The often life-size and naturalistic, though quite weathered, petroglyphs feature hunted wildlife including elk, reindeer, bears and swans, a whale more than seven metres long, possibly a porpoise, and, according to the Norwegian rock art archaeologist Jan Magne Gjerde, a 4.3-metre-long boat. The latter most probably represents a lightweight Arctic skin boat made from a wooden rib frame and seal hide, similar to the *umiak* used by the Inuit and Yupik peoples. It is estimated that the early settlers of the northern Norwegian coastline, which was dotted with small, settled islands, were dependent on boats propelled by paddles in order to survive in this maritime environment.[14] Nitrogen and carbon isotope analyses have pointed to an 'extremely maritime diet' for these early fisher-hunter-gatherers.[15] After *ca.* 5000 BCE,

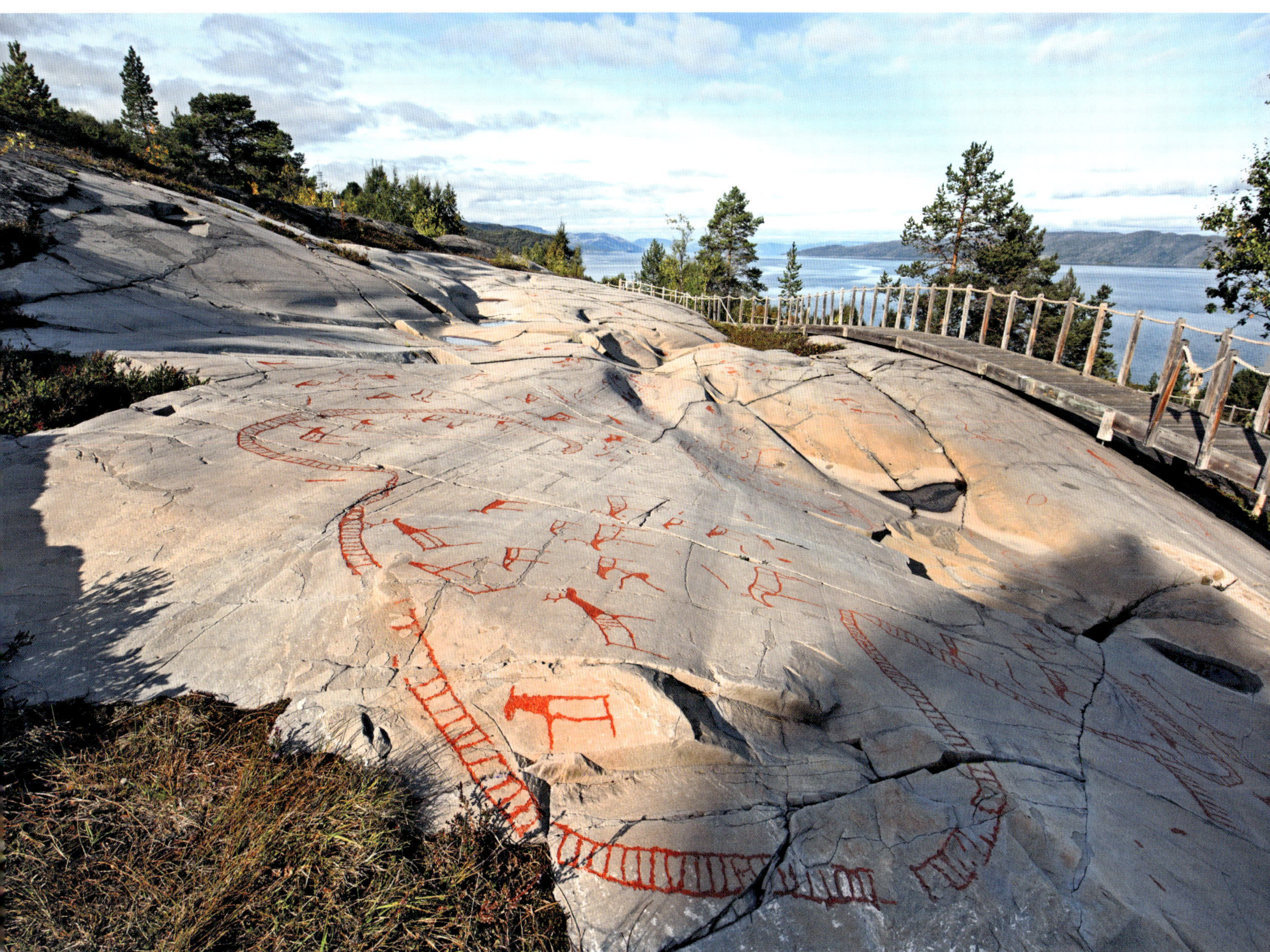

129. Petroglyphs, recently enhanced by paint, of reindeer and elk kept within an enclosure. *ca.* 4200–3000 BCE. Hjemmeluft, panels 6–7, Alta, northern Norway. Photo 2022.

the repertoire of petroglyph motifs became wider, including other animals, humans and man-made objects such as boats.

Petroglyphs are in general notoriously difficult to date, but in the coastal areas of Fennoscandia a quite reliable dating method is made possible by analysing and reconstructing the shoreline over time. The fundamental assumption is that in a maritime environment and culture, ancient petroglyphs were made close to the shoreline. This is the more plausible as there remains only a three- to four-metre-wide littoral band of rock next to the water, which in Fennoscandia, thanks to the tidal spray, is free of vegetation. Beyond this band, lichen, moss and shrubs quickly cover the rock

surface. Furthermore, it is only such littoral strips of rock that remain free of snow, making them visible during the long winters. Finally, in the late Mesolithic and Neolithic the inland regions were thickly forested and hard to cross, which is why waterways were preferred for transport; people travelled along the shores. The respective level of the shoreline is a result of two physical mechanisms, namely eustasy, the global oscillations of sea levels, and isostasy, the geological balance between the lithosphere – the solid outer layer of the earth – and the underlying mantle. During the last peak of the Weichselian glacial period, most of northern Europe and Fennoscandia was covered by an ice sheet two to three

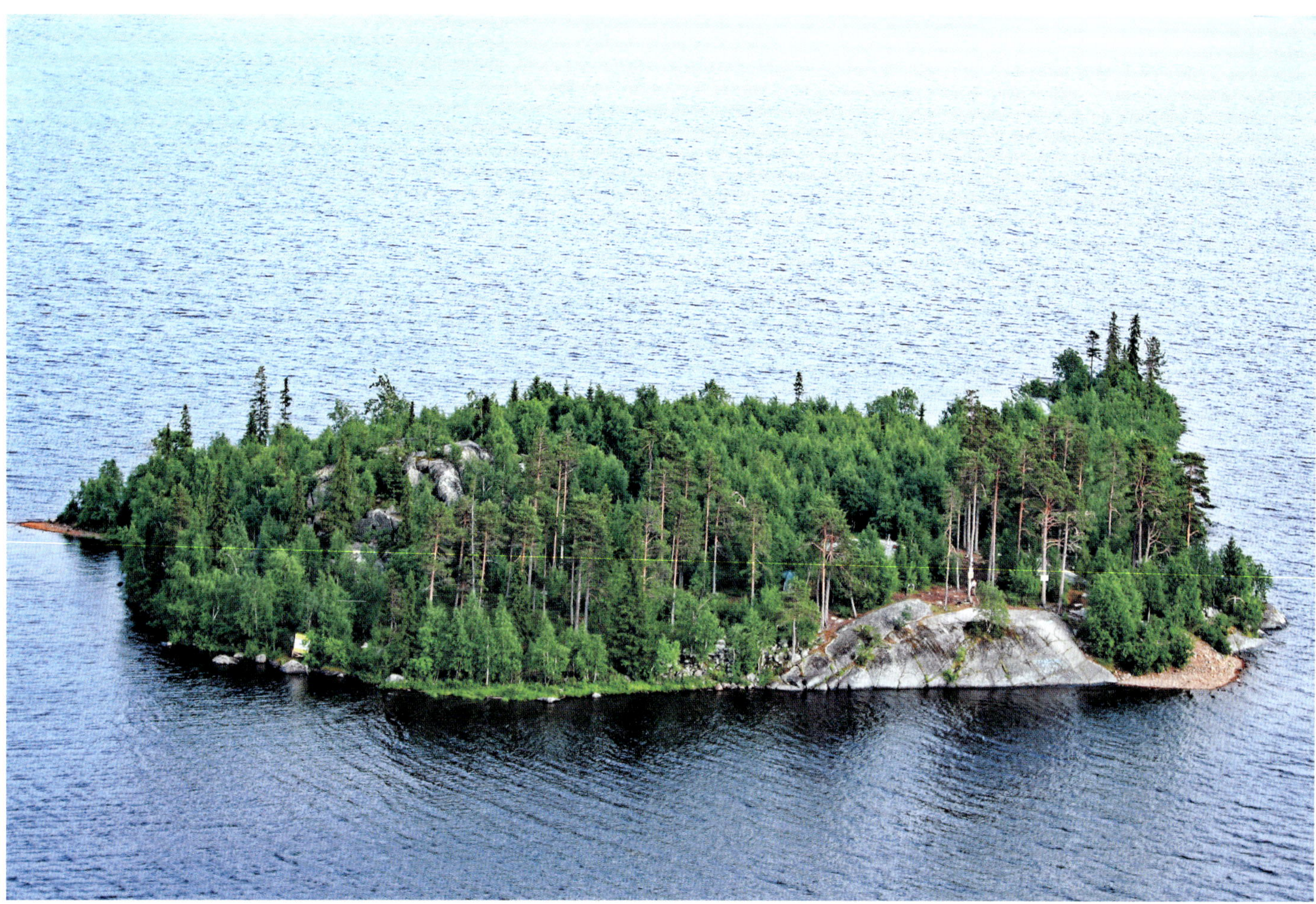

130. The island of Kamenny in Lake Kanozero is rich in petroglyphs dating from the fourth to the second millennium BCE. Karelia, Russian Federation. Photo 2022 by Vadim Likhachev, Russian Federation.

kilometres thick, carrying stones beneath it that would grind the faces of the underlying rocks, thus creating ideal 'canvasses' for future petroglyphs. The enormous weight of the ice masses provoked an isostatic depression as the lithosphere dipped into the astheno-sphere, the relatively soft upper mantle of the earth lying beneath. At the same time, a sizable share of the globe's water was captured in the ice shields, meaning a reduction of sea levels of up to 120 metres and an alteration in the outline of continents: for example, in those days Doggerland connected Britain to continental Europe.[16]

The rapid rise in temperatures at the beginning of the Holocene activated two mechanisms: at first, the melting ice caused a maritime transgression, that is a rise of global sea levels and a corresponding inundation of coastal land. Doggerland was submerged around 6500–6200 BCE and Britain became separated from continental Europe. However, in Fennoscandia the melting of the ice triggered a spectacular isostatic uplift. Freed from the immense weight of ice, the lithosphere, which had previously been pressed down, rebounded as the ice loads diminished. In

Fennoscandian coastal areas and especially in inner fjord regions where the ice sheet had been especially thick, local isostatic uplifts outpaced the global eustatic rise in sea level.[17] Even today, some areas in the Gulf of Bothnia, which was 'the epicentre of the isostatic rebound',[18] are rising by nine millimetres per annum.[19] Whereas people living in Doggerland had to migrate landward, those in Fennoscandia pursuing a maritime economy had to gradually move downward to sea level in order to access their retreating fishing grounds.[20] As they moved seaward, they found previously submerged, well-polished rocks ideal for rock pecking. And as the land rebound continued, the bands of rock which had previously marked the shoreline, on which petroglyphs had been chiselled, would rapidly be overgrown by vegetation, and new petroglyphs would be created closer to the shore, in other words at a lower level. What we perceive today as landscape along Fennoscandian coastal regions was at the time of the creation of the petroglyphs 'seascapes'.[21] As a rule of thumb, the higher on a cliff petroglyphs are located within a coastal area, the older they are, and vice versa; and petroglyphs which were made at the shoreline during the Neolithic or Bronze Age are today far away from the sea. For example, in Bohuslän, south-western Sweden, the oldest petroglyph sites are located 10 to 15 kilometres away from the sea at a height of 20 to 10 metres above sea level.[22] By means of algorithms adapted to local conditions, the age of petroglyphs can be assessed based on their present situation above the level of the sea.[23] Of course, one has to bear in mind that shoreline data from maritime regressions provide *post quem* dates and, conversely, data from marine transgressions give *ante quem* dates.

The shoreline data from the Arctic north suggest the following Mesolithic (9500–4500 BCE) dates for its oldest petroglyph sites: **Jo Sarsakluben** (9250–9185 cal. BCE), **Nes** (9250–9185 and 8730–8630 cal. BCE), **Valle** (9150–8840 cal. BCE), **Leiknes** (8300–8280, 7050–6830 cal. BCE).[24] Due to the land uplift, the Mesolithic petroglyphs at Valle are today situated 73 metres, and at Leiknes up to 50 metres above sea level, but when they were originally made they were close to the shoreline. Given the size of these petroglyphs and their location on cliffs close to the waterline, they were meant to be seen from boats and possibly also served as landmarks. These ancient petroglyphs were mainly created by grinding and rubbing the rock surfaces with a hard stone, thus producing lines about 20 millimetres wide. Towards the end of the Mesolithic and in subsequent periods petroglyphs were made with chisel and stone hammer.[25]

Still in the Mesolithic, petroglyphs appeared in the area of the former Komsa culture, first at **Slettnes** (*ca.* 5500 or 5300 BCE), and soon after at **Alta**, around 5300–5200 cal. BCE.[26] From now on, petroglyphs were quite often arranged in scenes, showing for example whaling or reindeer hunting. The period between *ca.* 5300 and 4500 or 4200 BCE witnessed the emergence of all the major petroglyph sites of northern Fennoscandia, which is rightly described by Jan Magne Gjerde as the period of 'rock art explosion'.[27] These far northern Nordic petroglyphs are also counted under the heading of the **Northern tradition** made by hunter-gatherers, as opposed to the later **Southern tradition** made by pastoralists and farmers who were also involved in the international maritime trade which blossomed south of the Trondheim Fjord. Contrary to what was previously believed, the carriers of the Southern tradition were definitely not purely agriculturalists, but are best described as maritime trading and agro-pastoralist farmers. While petroglyphs of boats are ubiquitous in the major early sites of the Northern tradition, each of these sites has a predominant animal motif, reflecting the most important respective prey. These are at **Vyg** (Karelia) the beluga whale and reindeer, at **Kanozero**

(Murmansk oblast) the bear and reindeer, at **Lake Onega** (Karelia) the swan, at **Alta** (Norway) the reindeer and elk, and at **Nämforsen** (Sweden) the elk. Rock art was made at those sites for thousands of years, except where it was interrupted by a natural event such as a maritime transgression. Most probably, these rich petroglyph sites were located close to places where large animals gathered and were hunted in specific seasons, for example the summer/autumn beluga hunt and the winter/spring elk hunt at Vyg, the late summer/autumn hunts of reindeer at Alta and of elk at Nämforsen, and the autumn swan (or goose) hunts at Lake Onega. Such hunts, targeting dozens or hundreds of migrating animals, had to be communal activities and the sites probably also functioned as gathering places for hunting-related social rituals and events which in turn strengthened intra-societal cohesion.[28] From this viewpoint, the choice of important rock art sites was also determined by the seasonal migration patterns of prey. The high importance of hunting in the societies of the Northern tradition is underscored by the high proportion of clearly identifiable hunting scenes in petroglyphs, namely 56 per cent at Vyg, 49 per cent at Kanozero and 19 per cent at Alta.[29] The hunting of sea mammals like belugas was often organized at cataracts located near the sea, as at Vyg, or in narrow fjords where the prey could be trapped. Land mammals such as reindeer, elk and red deer were ambushed for preference at the crossing points of rivers, either from boats or from the shores using bows and spears.[30]

Archaeological and genetic analyses indicate that there was a dual- or even triple-route migration into northern Fennoscandia, as it was colonized not only from the south-west, but also from the south-east and east. Immigrations also occurred into the Karelian isthmus between Vyborg and Lake Ladoga after 8800 cal. BCE, and from there continued further north. Finally, archaeological finds from Sujala, northern Finland, dated to 8300–8200 cal. BCE, point to an immigration from the east and south-east.[31] The analysis of the lithic tools found at Sujala (69° 43' north) indicate that their makers were so-called 'Post-Swiderian' hunter-gatherers. They came in the course of the ninth millennium BCE from the north-western Russian plain, centred in the region of today's Moscow, along the upper courses of the rivers Volga and Oka, and from the eastern Baltic.[32] A few centuries earlier, people from the east had colonized sites closer to the seas such as Stahrenjunni (66° 40') at the north-eastern end of the Kandalaksha Gulf in the White Sea, Løkvika (70° 47') on the Barents Sea, and Slettnes (70°) at the meeting of the Norwegian and Barents Seas, within the realm of the Komsa culture.[33] Genetic data have confirmed archaeological conclusions whereby northern Fennoscandia was populated in the first instance by 'western hunter-gatherers', soon followed by immigrating 'eastern hunter-gatherers'.[34] Three millennia later, in the second half of the sixth millennium BCE, eastern hunter-gatherers brought knowledge of ceramic manufacture from the east to northern Fennoscandia marking the beginning of the 'Forest Neolithic'.[35] From here it soon spread south.[36] Three millennia later again, a second Neolithization occurred in Scandinavia with the arrival of agriculture.[37] That the northern Mesolithic people enjoyed a high level of mobility is emphasized by the findings in northern Fennoscandia of sledge runners and paddles dating from the ninth millennium BCE; skis have also been found from the Boreal or even a pre-Boreal period (later ninth–eighth millennium BCE), albeit further east, in central and north-eastern Russia. By the fourth millennium BCE at the latest, skis were widely used in Karelia as can be seen at the petroglyphs of Zalavruga, Vyg, where no fewer than 30 skiers have been identified.[38] The fact that initially there was no technological transfer between the western and eastern lithic industries of northern Fennoscandia suggests that at first both groups coexisted with only limited cultural exchange. At the turn of the ninth to the eighth millennium BCE, the two lithic traditions became blended.[39]

1.1.1. Murmansk oblast and Russian Karelia

During the Last Glacial Maximum Russian Karelia and the Kola Peninsula, which forms the eastern, larger part of today's Murmansk oblast, were, like Scandinavia, covered by an ice sheet two kilometres thick. In the Holocene, temperatures rose and the Kola Peninsula and eastern Karelia around Lake Onega became ice-free during the earlier eighth millennium BCE, and western Karelia about half a millennium later.[40] Earlier, around 8000 BCE, the water level of the glacial lake inside the White Sea Basin fell by 50 to 60 metres within 200 years when the Gorlo Strait opened up, connecting the White Sea with the Barents Sea and the world's oceans. Karelia and the Kola Peninsula were populated towards the end of the ninth millennium BCE, enjoying a climatic optimum from *ca.* 5500 BCE to 2800 BCE.[41] In this region there are three major petroglyph complexes:

- **Kanozero** is a lake located in the south-west of the Kola Peninsula within Murmansk oblast. The lake is crossed by the River Umba which discharges into the White Sea. Three of its tiny islands and a site on the mainland have petroglyphs from the Neolithic and Bronze Age.

- **Vyg** lies in eastern Karelia. Zalavruga, the centre of the complex, is located 5 km west of the town of Belomorsk which is situated on the western shore of the White Sea. The petroglyphs date from the later Mesolithic and the Chalcolithic (Copper Age), from *ca.* 5300 until 2000 BCE.

- **Lake Onega** lies south of the White Sea and north-east of Lake Ladoga, 325 km south of Vyg. The petroglyph complex includes four major and a few minor sites, all of them close of the lake's eastern shore since in this area there was minimal isostatic uplift.

Lake Kanozero, whose name means Wild Reindeer Lake (*kan* in the Sami language signifies 'wild reindeer', and *ozero* is Russian for 'lake'), is principally fed by the River Umba which then flows 28 kilometres further south into the White Sea.[42] During the Holocene, Lake Kanozero was never part of the White Sea, but during the Neolithic, the river system of the upper Umba joined with the system of the Voronya via lakes Umbozero and Lovozero. Since the Voronya River flows into the Barents Sea, there existed during the Neolithic a 'Stone Age water highway' linking the White Sea to the Barents Sea 285 kilometres further north.[43] Archaeological remains of several Neolithic settlements and a few small petroglyph sites found along this continuous waterway underscore its importance.[44] The petroglyphs were only discovered in 1997; they were found on the three small islands Kamenny, Elovy and Gorely and on the mainland at Odinnokaya, numbering in total 1,800 petroglyphs distributed over 23 panels.[45] Most of the petroglyphs are on Kamenny Island, and they are at their highest concentration in the large panel **Kamenny 7** which counts more than 430 images (fig. 131).[46] Virtually all its petroglyphs are hammered out over the whole surface of the image. From comparison of the most ancient petroglyphs at Kamenny with similar ones at Vyg, a date around 3700 BCE has been advanced for the oldest figures, representing whaling scenes. The production of petroglyphs at Kanozero continued throughout the third millennium and ended in the second half of the second millennium BCE.[47]

In terms of subjects, 22 per cent are boats, 21 per cent tracks of animals or humans, 16 per cent humans, 14 per cent land animals and 10 per cent ichthyomorphs including whales.[48] As in Vyg, the high proportion of complex scenes with several actors is highly unusual. Most of them are intricate hunting scenes, dominated by the 33 different beluga whale hunts, from boats and using spears and harpoons. Other hunting scenes involve bears, elk, reindeer and beavers.[49] At Kamenny 7, a bear-hunting scene in winter,

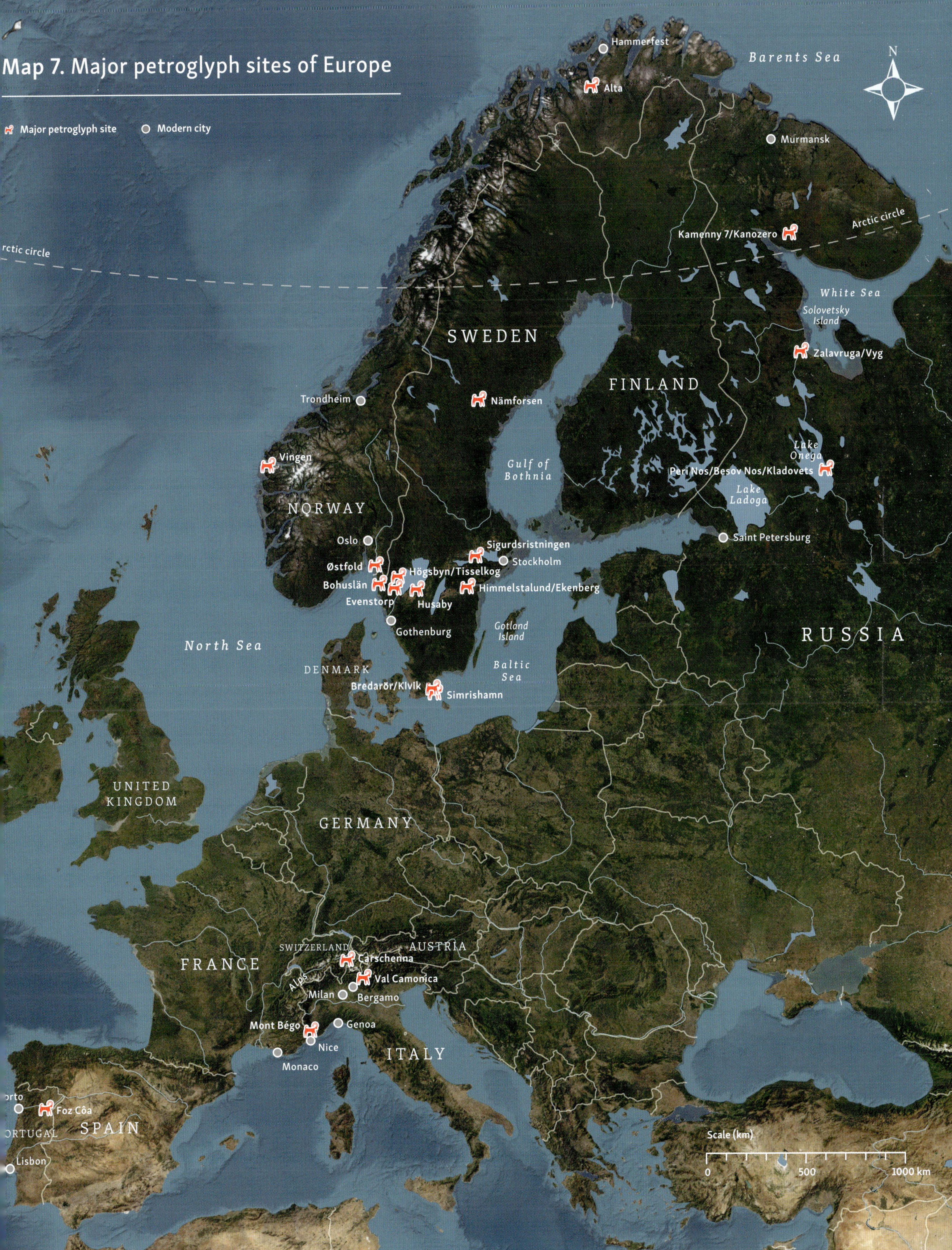

Map 7. Major petroglyph sites of Europe
Major petroglyph site
Modern city
Barents Sea
N
Hammerfest
Alta
Murmansk
Arctic circle
Arctic circle
Kamenny 7/Kanozero
White Sea
Solovetsky Island
SWEDEN
FINLAND
Zalavruga/Vyg
Trondheim
Nämforsen
Lake Onega
Vingen
Gulf of Bothnia
Peri Nos/Besov Nos/Kladovets
NORWAY
Lake Ladoga
Oslo
Sigurdsristningen
Østfold
Högsbyn/Tisselkog
Stockholm
Saint Petersburg
Bohuslän
Himmelstalund/Ekenberg
Evenstorp
Husaby
RUSSIA
Gothenburg
Gotland Island
North Sea
Baltic Sea
DENMARK
Bredarör/Kivik
Simrishamn
UNITED KINGDOM
GERMANY
SWITZERLAND
AUSTRIA
Carschenna
FRANCE
Val Camonica
Alps
Milan
Bergamo
Mont Bégo
Genoa
Nice
ITALY
Monaco
Porto
Foz Côa
SPAIN
PORTUGAL
Lisbon
Scale (km)
0
500
1000 km

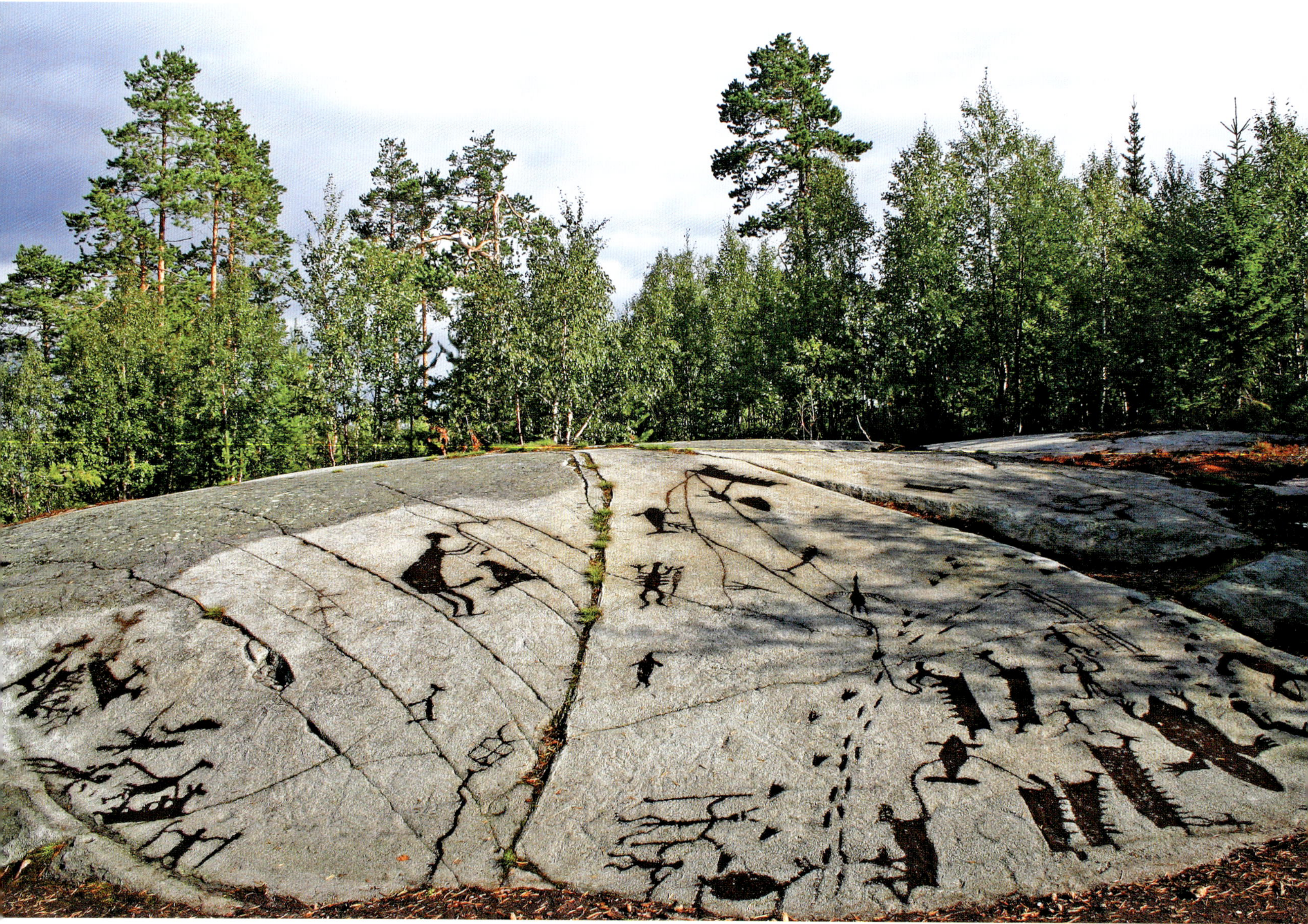

131. In the centre a beluga hunt involving six ships, from two of which the beluga has been hit by harpoons. To the right of the larger ship features a large beaver or a salamander, and, further right, a hunter stabs a bear with his javelin. The bear hunt begins to the left of the beluga hunt: at first, the footprints of the hunter who wears skis and the paw prints of the bear run in parallel upwards. When the prints turn 90° to the right, long strokes replace the hunter's footprints since he is skiing downhill. Since the skiing hunter is faster downhill than the bear, he manages to overtake and kill his prey. In the photo, only a small proportion of the petroglyphs have been enhanced by paint, and there are several more hunting scenes. Since 2015, the panel has been covered by a plexiglass dome. Panel 7 at Kamenny Island, Lake Kanozero, Karelia, Russian Federation. Photo 2005 by Vadim Likhachev, Russian Federation.

where the prey is tracked by hunters on skis, has been superimposed on an older scene featuring a beluga hunt involving at least two, and probably six boats with bow figureheads shaped like elk heads. Bears were hunted in autumn and winter as is indicated by the hunters on skis and the tracks of prey and pursuers in the snow. In one scene from Kamenny 7, it seems that in the context of a complex bear hunt, an elk has been killed which will then serve to lure a bear into a trap.[50] In another scene at Kamenny 3, it has been suggested that human footsteps emerge from the lake to climb a hill.[51] Since reindeer and elk were also hunted from boats

while they crossed rivers, it is possible that in this scene a hunter is pursuing a prey that managed to escape from the water to land. Since an elk or reindeer was much slower in water than on land, hunters liked to drive the animals into water and to attack them from boats.

The predominance of beluga hunts with harpoons and spears and the shapes and decorations of the vessels involved, as well as the depiction of winter hunts with skis, all show great similarities between the petroglyphs of Kanozero and those of Zalavruga at Vyg, 285 kilometres to the south. Clearly the climatic and faunal conditions at Kanozero and Vyg were comparable and so were the human economic responses to them. The identical representation at Kanozero (panels Kamenny 7 and Elovy 3), Vyg and, to a lesser degree, at Alta, of boats with a high stem post in the shape of an elk or reindeer head, with a keel protruding forward and with a stern post curved backwards, suggests the hypothesis that these petroglyphs rendered real boats such as were used for whaling and hunting in rivers.[52] The carved micro-landscape of the boulder known as Kamenny 7 was understood as a rendering of the real land- and seascape during the Neolithic. Finally, there are a small number of petroglyphs with a somewhat peculiar appearance. First, five petroglyphs of two crosses engraved one inside the other (Elovy 1, 2, 3; Kamenny 1, 7);[53] this image is also found at Kåfjord, Alta, and is dated to the third millennium BCE.[54] Its meaning is unknown; maybe it was the mark of a social group. Also, the petroglyphs of wheels or solar motifs found at Elovy 3 look strange in the maritime environment of Kanozero; they may suggest a

cultural contact with southern Sweden in a later phase, during the second millennium BCE.

The petroglyph complex of **Vyg** is situated in the mouth of the eponymous river which discharges into the White Sea at 64° 30' north. It mainly consists of four sites, namely Novaya (New) Zalavruga with 1,176 petroglyph images, Staraya (Old) Zalavruga[55] with 216, Besovy Sledki (530) and Yerpin Pudas with 157. The sites and their petroglyphs are witness to an eventful geological history.[56] Like most of Karelia, Vyg was covered before the onset of the Holocene by a thick ice sheet which then slowly melted away. The earliest petroglyphs were made at **Yerpin Pudas** *ca.* 5300–4300/4200 BCE, and are poorly preserved; their altitude today is 23.7–21.5 metres above sea level.[57] Then followed the figures at **Besovy Sledki** from *ca.* 4350–3100 BCE, at 21.6–20.4 metres above sea level. When the dam for the Vyg hydroelectric power stations was constructed in the late 1950s and 1960s, a protective pavilion was built over the larger, northern part

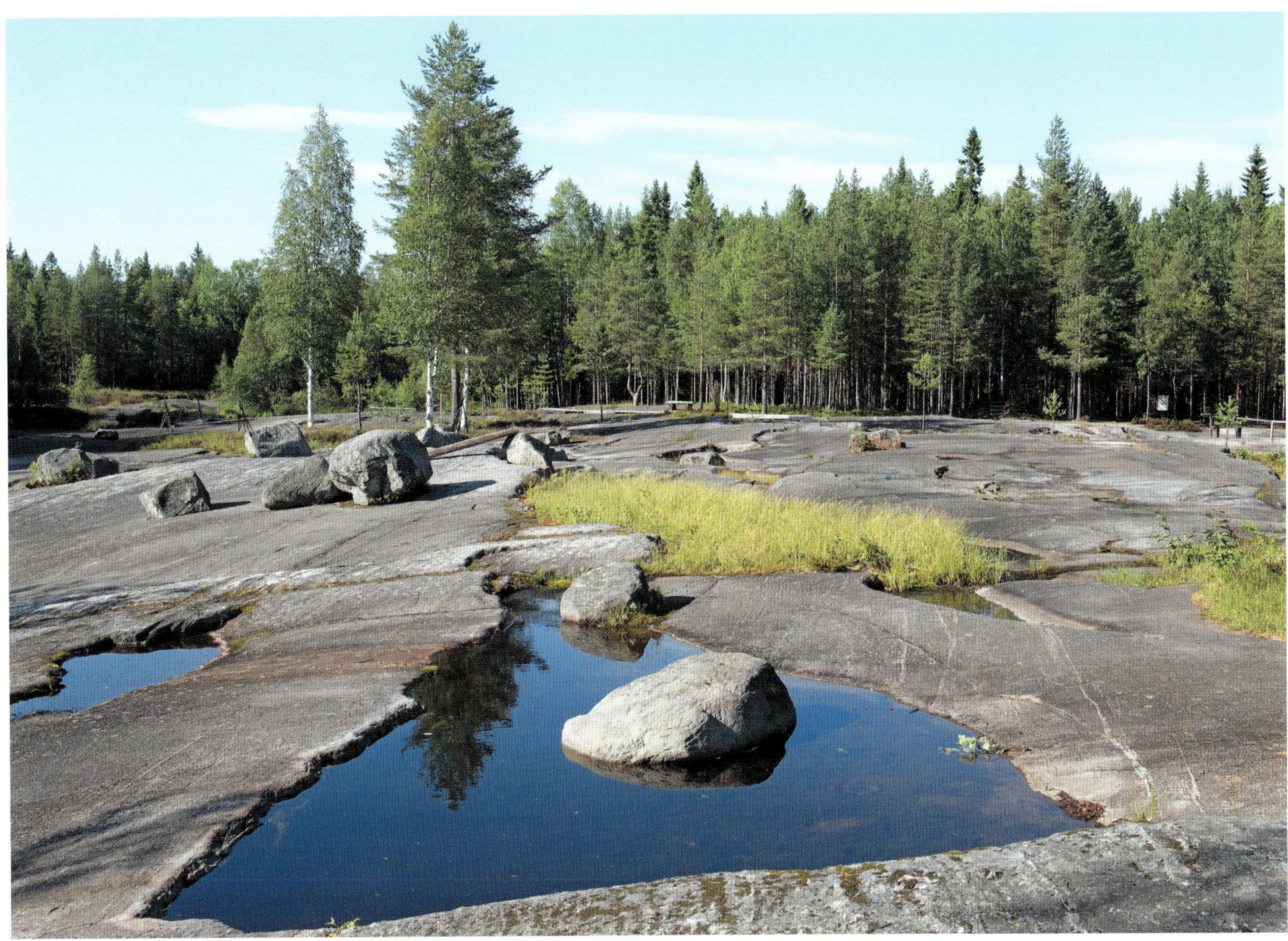

132. The petroglyph site of Novaya Zalavruga looking northward. Karelia, Russian Federation. Photo 2019.

133. Ink drawing of the large panel IV at Novaya Zalavruga which consists of several complex scenes. From left to right: three hunters on skis track and kill three elk; the tracks of the skiers and the elk run for a while in parallel. In the centre and lower right there are not only a couple of beluga hunts and one or two bear hunts, but also a mortal fight between humans. Archers are shooting at each other and one of them is hit from behind by two arrows. At the upper right, a crew of twelve fishermen has just harpooned a beluga. Just below, a hunter kills a bear, in whose back sticks an arrow, with a javelin. Fourth to third millennium BCE. Karelia, Russian Federation. After Sawwatejew, Juri, *Karelische Felsbilder* (Leipzig: VEB E.A. Seemann Verlag, 1984), pp. 164f.

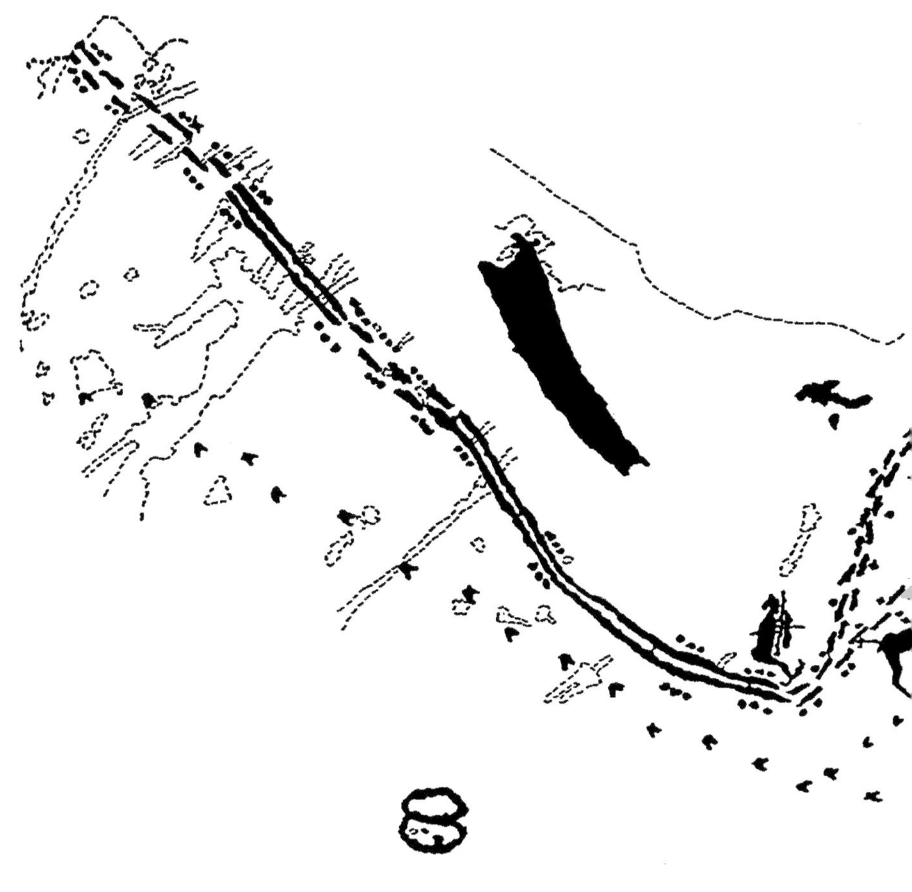

of Besovy Sledki. However, it later collapsed and buried the petroglyphs under its debris; for years they were inaccessible but in 2021 the pavilion was renovated.[58] Judging from drawings, images of coveted prey such as reindeer and elk (63 petroglyphs) and beluga whales (36) predominated, followed by half a dozen bears and walruses, and flocks of waterfowl. Especially striking is the petroglyph of an anthropomorph shown in profile with a humped back, a huge phallus and an enormous right foot. The figure's meaning remains unknown. Unfortunately, the petroglyphs of Besovy Sledki South are lost, since they have been covered over by the construction of a road.[59]

In the early fourth millennium, the level of the White Sea was about 18–19 metres higher than today and the granite rocks of

Zalavruga (today 20.8–13.7 metres above sea level) would have been partially protruding out of the water. As the marine regression continued, further polished rock surfaces emerged. Petroglyphs were created at **Novaya Zalavruga** from *ca.* 3700 to 2500 BCE, and at **Staraya Zalavruga** from *ca.* 3400 to 2100 BCE. A rapid and brief marine transgression then set in which inundated Zalavruga and deposited a layer of sand up to one metre thick over the rock art. Soon after, the White Sea regressed again and humans reliant on fishing occupied the re-emerging island, as is demonstrated by a layer of Chalcolithic findings including ceramics and the remains of settlements.[60] As a result, the petroglyphs were covered first by sand and alluvial sediments and then by Chalcolithic settlements.[61] Later, when the settlements were abandoned in the early

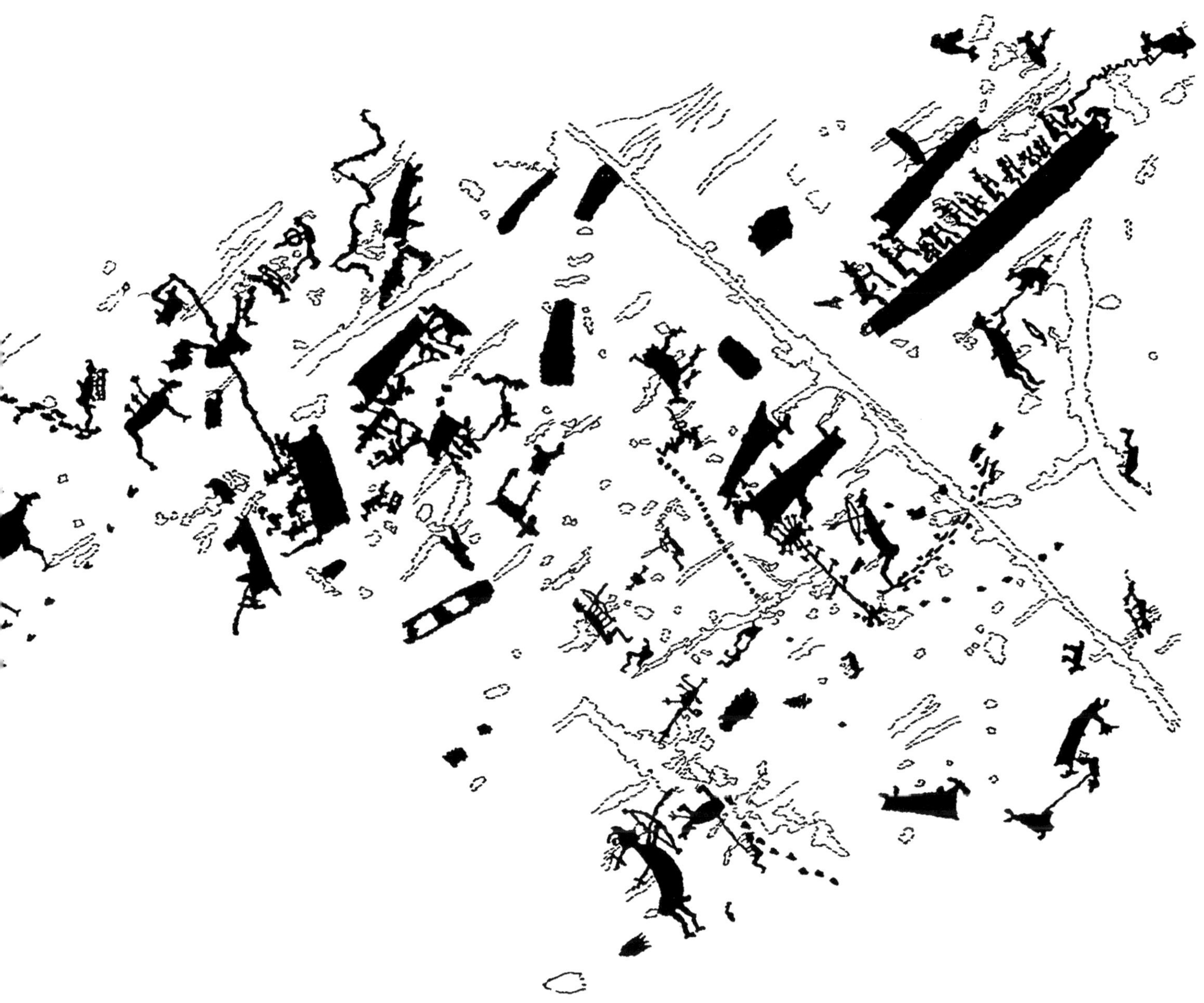

second millennium BCE, the river partially flushed the sand away from the petroglyphs, and the area gradually became swampy. In the twentieth century, the petroglyphs reappeared. In 1926, local people led the ethnologist A.M. Linevsky to the site of Besovy Sledki, where he was followed in the 1930s by V.I. Ravdonikas. The construction of the hydroelectric plant and its dam dramatically altered the landscape as water levels dropped and the petroglyphs reappeared. Occasional floodings by the power plant further flushed the sand layers away. Due to the construction of another power station, about a third of the Vyg petroglyphs have been submerged since 2017.

As at Kanozero, complex hunting scenes predominate at Zalavruga, namely beluga whale hunts and elk hunts. Today the petroglyphs of Vyg are six kilometres away from the White Sea, but more than five millennia ago the region formed a large river estuary with several streams among which stood the island of Zalavruga. Since such estuaries are often rich in fish, it would have attracted belugas for feeding. During summer and early autumn, belugas would also enter the warmer, shallow estuaries for mating and calving. Cataracts blocked the River Vyg upstream so that the estuary became a natural beluga trap where organized groups of hunters could ambush them from downstream. The importance of these seasonal, communal hunts is illustrated by the more than 60 beluga-hunting scenes.[62] In many scenes, for example at the sites Novaya Zalavruga VIII, XIII and XX, several boats pin down a whale using spears and harpoons. At Novaya Zalavruga IV, a large

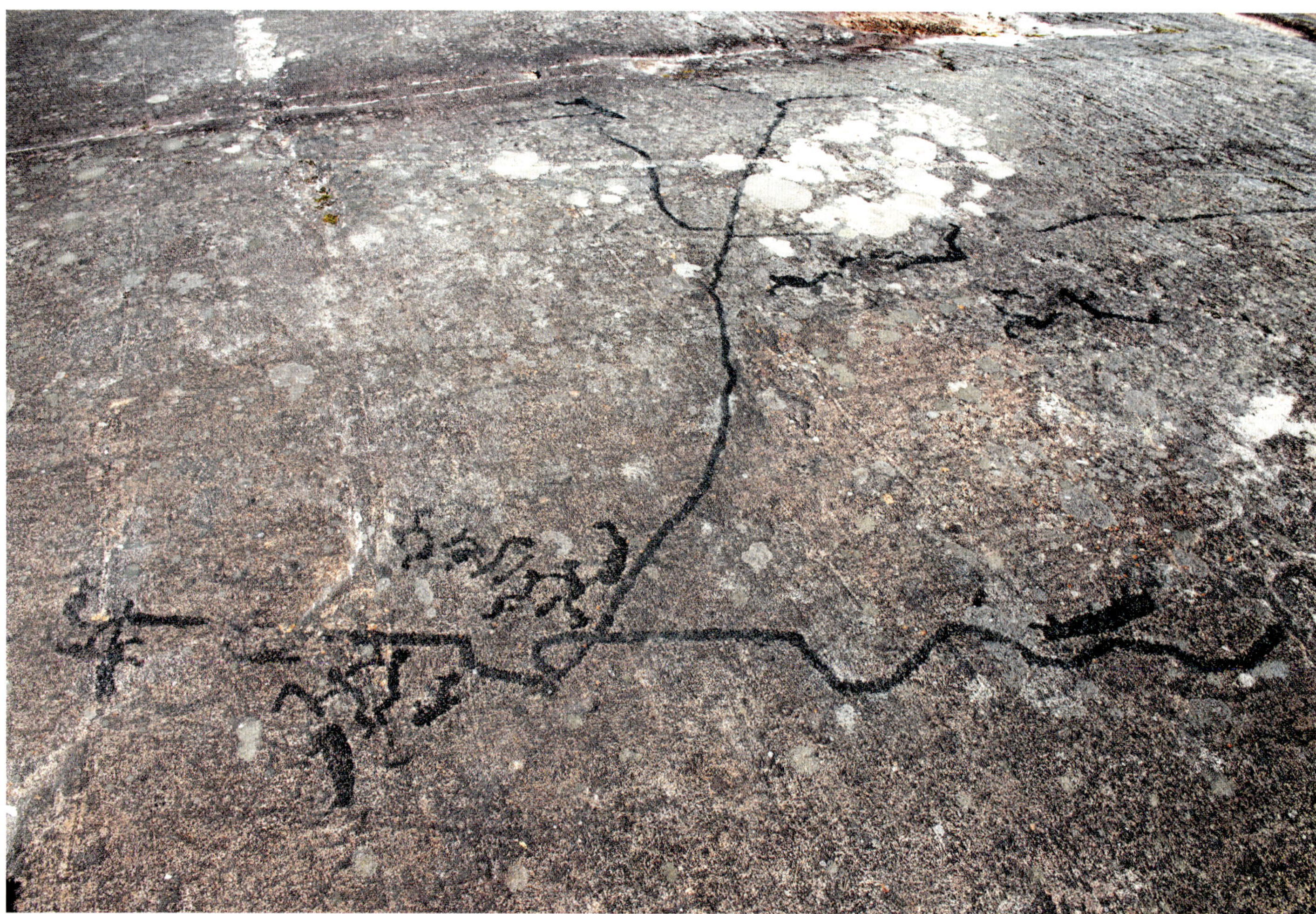

134. A sea map and a beluga hunt. Fourth to third millennium BCE. Detail from site XV at Novaya Zalavruga, Karelia, Russian Federation. Photo 2019.

boat manned by twelve people chases a beluga which has just been harpooned, as the line is still loose (fig. 133). Below, a bear is killed. At Zalavruga, no fewer than 328 boats carrying 732 people have been identified, which underscores the importance of fishing and hunting from boats.[63] The beluga hunters not only had to know the seasonal patterns of their prey – whales, like reindeer and elk, are migrating animals – but also the routes taken by the whales. This is suggested by site XV which represents a map of the winding river with half a dozen boats blocking one end and groups of hunters lurking in three different places. A striking detail shows a couple of hunters carrying elk-shaped poles, a scene which looks similar to ones at Alta (figs 148, 150).[64] Jan Magne Gjerde hypothesizes that the absence of beluga images at this site indicates that belugas no longer entered the estuary due to a change of landscape – either a continued land uplift or a change in the course of the river. As a consequence, the hunters focussed increasingly on hunting elk.[65] Indeed, in the more recent petroglyphs at Staraya Zalavruga, belugas are absent and elk hunts predominate. As sites VI and

XII illustrate, other aquatic creatures were also hunted, such as waterfowl and salmon.

Besides whaling, elk hunting was also of paramount importance for these hunter-gatherers. Judging from the numerous elk hunts at both Novaya and Staraya Zalavruga, these usually took place in winter or early spring since the pursuing hunters often wear skis.[66] Most spectacular is the site Novaya Zalavruga IV where three hunters on skis pursue and kill three elk. The illustration starts at the upper left of the rock face with tracks of humans, alternatively walking and running on skis, who follow the elk's tracks. At a sharp turn, the three elk separate. One is hit by an arrow shot by a hunter. A second hunter soon manages to catch up with another elk whose tracks are seen in the snow; hunters on skis were faster than the heavy animals whose hooves sink into the hard snow. The second hunter kills the largest elk with his spear. Finally, the third hunter kills the last elk with three arrows shot in its back. Boulder IV is also highly interesting for other reasons. There are not only several whaling scenes – among them the one mentioned above with the large boat, elk and bear hunts – but also scenes of conflict between humans. Two archers seem to shoot at each other, and another, large archer is shooting an arrow while he is hit by arrows in his back and the back of his head.[67] Additional scenes of violence between humans are found at Staraya Zalavruga. There, a man is hit by an arrow in his back and another is pierced by at least five arrows.[68] Then, six men who hold spears in one hand flee on skis from an invisible enemy; four of them have been hit in the back by arrows while the last one topples backwards, and a seventh lies dead in the snow.[69] One may speculate that such violent scenes illustrated real conflicts, possibly conflicts over hunting grounds. Finally, at panel XIV, three hunters bag a bear. Two hunters shoot arrows at the animal which has already been hit by four arrows, and the third hunter finishes it off with a spear (fig. 135).

In the west of Staraya Zalavruga a large palimpsest documents the transition from Neolithic–early Chalcolithic whaling to late Chalcolithic elk hunting. The bottom layer shows seven large boats, over which small figures such as skiers wearing rucksacks were later carved. In a third stage, three huge elk were superimposed on the earlier images, as well as two long rows of male and female elk meeting at a 90° angle; one row numbers fourteen animals, the other six (fig. 137).[70] Whether the two rows of elk represent a battue, where the animals are driven into a river to be ambushed, remains a matter for conjecture. To conclude, the petroglyphs at Zalavruga appear close to nature and realistic. As in the much later Animal Style of the Iron Age Scythians and Saka, the carvers achieved this closeness to nature by emphasizing the main characteristics of the animals or humans involved. The images were the result of accurate observation and conscious reflection. While there is hardly any doubt that these scenes illustrated real hunting events, they probably also had an additional purpose, namely to magically summon up further luck for hunting. The site can be understood as a microcosm, a miniature replication of the landscape at that time.

As in prehistoric times, waterways have remained important in northern Fennoscandia. For more than 90 years, **Lake Onega** has been linked to the White Sea by the 227-kilometre-long White Sea–Baltic Canal, which rises 133 metres across 19 locks. The 'Stairs

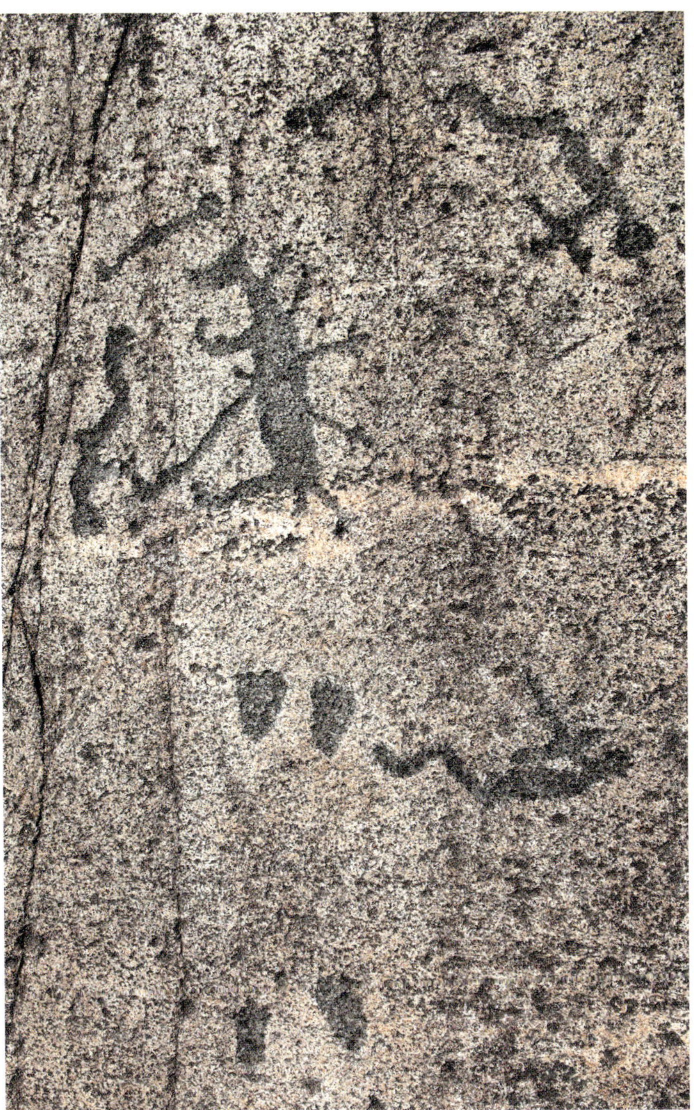

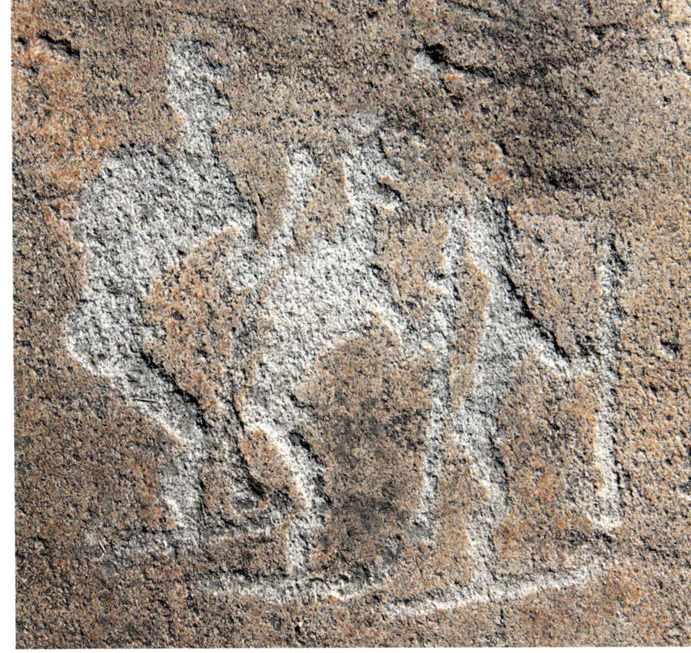

135. ↗ Two archers shoot at a wounded bear which is hit by three arrows; a third hunter kills the bear with a spear. The prints of the bear's paws are engraved in the lower part of the scene. Fourth to third millennium BCE. Novaya Zalavruga XIV, Karelia, Russian Federation. Photo 2019.

136. → Three hunters on skis. Fourth to third millennium BCE. Staraya Zalavruga XV, Karelia, Russian Federation. Photo 20HP.

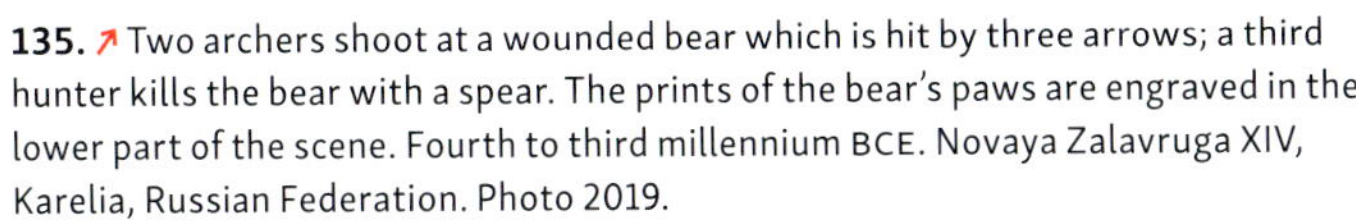

of Povenets', only twelve kilometres long, rises 67 metres in seven locks. The canal is part of the 1,248-kilometre-long waterway from Arkhangelsk on the White Sea to St Petersburg via Lake Ladoga. The canal is both famous and infamous since it was built between October 1931 and August 1933 by around 125,000 forced labour prisoners and gulag inmates, of whom between 12,000 and 20,000 died during the work.[71] After the completion of the canal, 12,500 prisoners were released and 59,500 received a reduced sentence. Such pardons remained unique and were never repeated. For all this, the canal has only limited commercial significance, as it is unusable by larger ships due to its narrow width, 15 metres, and draught of a mere 3.5 metres. Moreover, it is not ice-free in winter.

With a surface of 9,700 square kilometres, Lake Onega is Europe's second-largest lake. On the reddish granite boulders at its eastern shore roughly 1,300 petroglyphs were engraved between the mouths of the Rivers Vodla and Chornaya, a distance of sixteen kilometres as the crow flies. From north to south, the major sites are **Cape Swan** (in Russian **Lebediny Nos**), **Peri Nos**, **Besov Nos** and **Kladovets**. Like at Kanozero, isostatic uplifts were significantly less pronounced at Lake Onega than at Vyg or Alta, and marine transgressions also remained relatively modest. However, as the authors experienced in summer 2019, the strength and direction of wind as well as air pressure can produce fluctuations in the lake level on the eastern coast of +/-90 to +/-100 centimetres, which means that the difference between low and high levels is almost 2 metres.[72] Since in average weather conditions the petroglyphs lie very close to the waterline, they can be rapidly submerged in a storm. The region between the Rivers Vodla and Chornaya has been populated since the Mesolithic, as has been shown by archaeological excavations. A transgression of three to four metres at the beginning of the fifth millennium BCE brought this cultural period to an end; yet after three to five centuries a gradual regression set in and this coastal region was resettled, as indicated by archaeological finds dating from the Neolithic Pit-Comb Ware culture. Most probably, the petroglyphs of Lake Onega were created by these Neolithic Pit-Comb Ware communities. These settlements and the

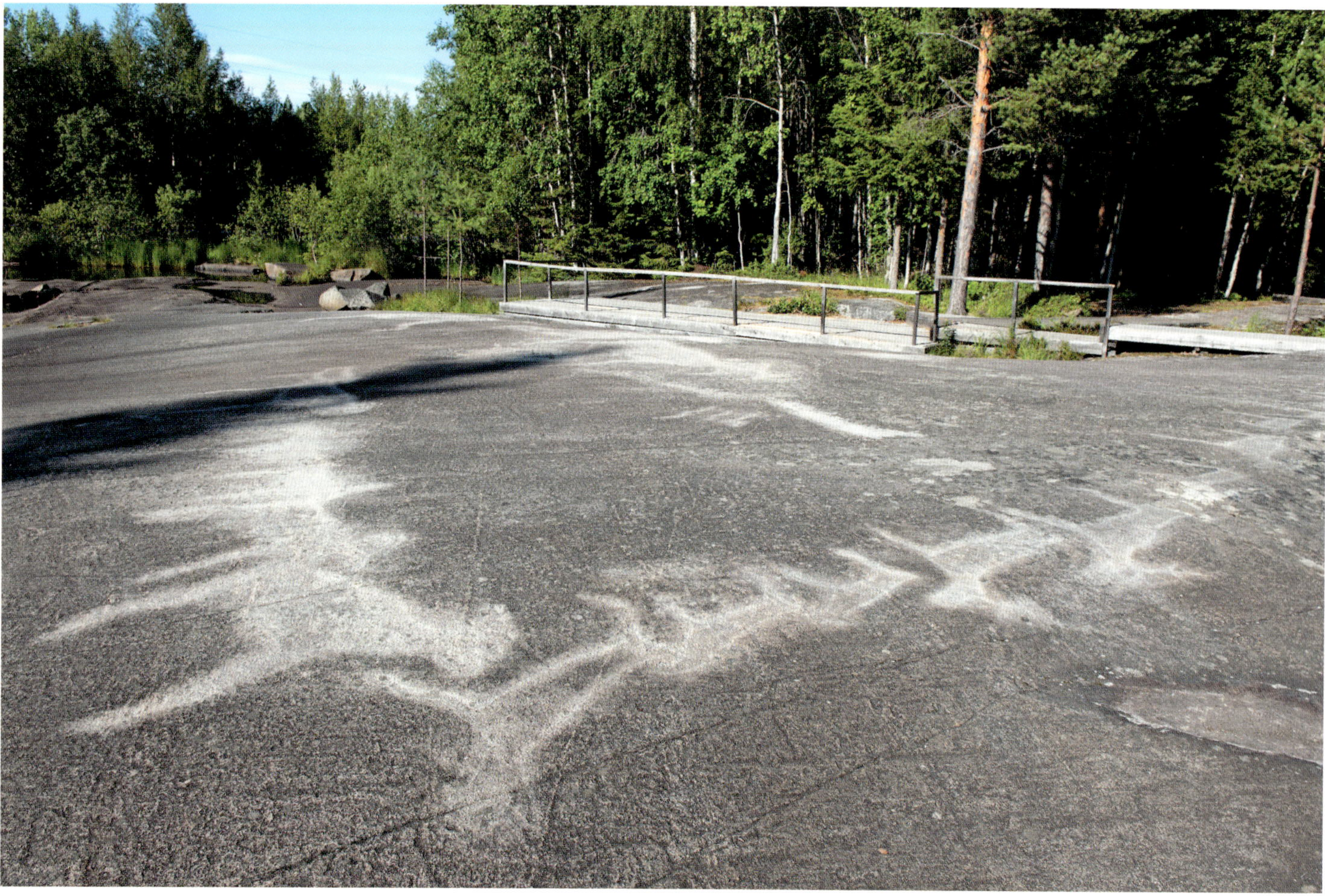

137. Petroglyphs from the late third millennium BCE of two rows of elk meeting at a 90° angle were superimposed on older images of boats dating from the fourth millennium BCE. Staraya Zalavruga, Karelia, Russian Federation. Photo 2019.

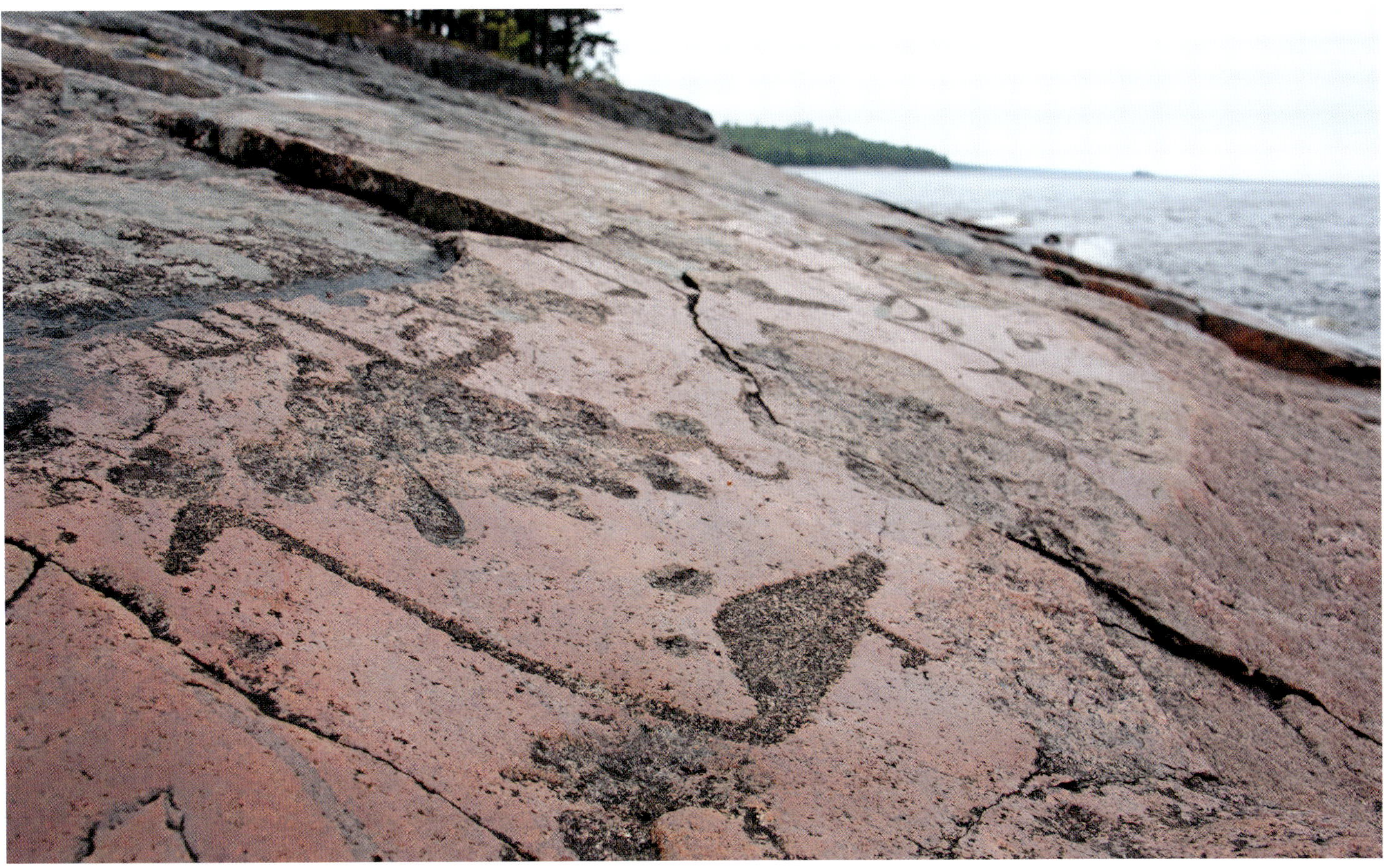

138. Long-necked swans at the site of Kladovets on the eastern shore of Lake Onega. When a strong wind blows from the lake, the petroglyphs are submerged. Neolithic period, *ca.* fourth millennium BCE. Karelia, Russian Federation. Photo 2019.

creation of petroglyphs came to an end around 2900 BCE in the Late Neolithic with the Early Subboreal transgression which lasted until *ca.* 2500 BCE. It is improbable that the sparse population of the ensuing Chalcolithic resumed the pecking of rock art.[73] That no petroglyphs were made in post-Neolithic periods is also indicated by the absence of petroglyphs representing livestock, agriculture or metallic weapons.

Like at Kanozero, Vyg and Alta, it appears that at Lake Onega the pecking of petroglyphs took place at the shoreline not only for practical reasons such as the absence of vegetation and snow, but also for mythological reasons. Starting from the widespread concept of a tripartite universe consisting of an upper, a middle and a nether world, the shore represented not only the 'contact zone' of these three cosmological realms – sky, earth and aquatic netherworld – but also of these realms with the world of nature. As explained by Knut Helskog, 'the rock carvings signify liminal places where communication between the human and the spirit worlds of the cosmos was made.'[74] This interpretation is further supported by the fact that 16 per cent of identifiable petroglyphs represent astral bodies, solar, lunar and stellar motifs, which rank

second only to the dominant motif of waterfowl which account for a staggering 50 per cent of identified images (44 per cent of the total).[75] Other motifs, albeit in much smaller numbers, are boats and cervids. Among the waterfowl, swans represent the large majority; they depict migratory Whooper Swans (fig. 138). Whether the swans were hunted remains unclear, as hunting scenes are virtually absent at Lake Onega, apart from a couple depicting whaling, even though there were never belugas in freshwater Lake Onega.[76] The virtual absence of hunting scenes and the highly unusual motifs suggest that the petroglyphs at Lake Onega had additional symbolic meanings.

The swans, which were often rendered with disproportionate necks, up to four metres long, were probably not featured as game, but rather have a symbolic or mythological meaning. As Whooper Swans are migratory birds, their annual arrival from southern regions marked the return of spring, warmth and life. Conversely, their departure announced winter, cold and death. People in Arctic and sub-Arctic regions were especially aware of the importance of seasonality due to the terrifying period of brutal cold and total or semi-darkness in winter. The annual return of migratory birds

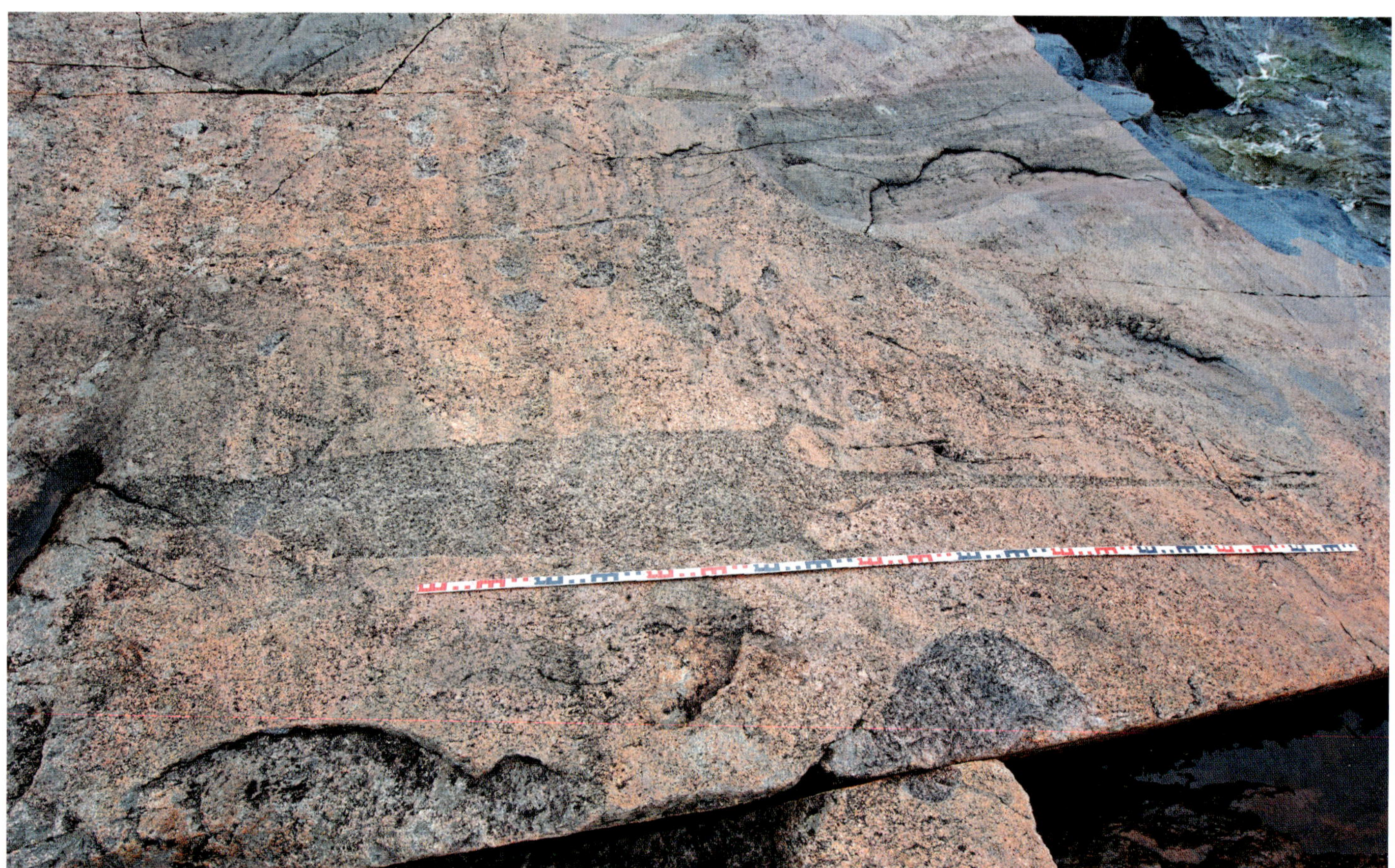

139. Petroglyph of a lizard, salamander or Eurasian otter 261 cm long; behind, a long-necked swan. Neolithic period, *ca.* fourth millennium BCE. Besov Nos at Lake Onega, Karelia, Russian Federation. Photo 2019.

– swans, geese or ducks – must have been a long-desired and joyful event, which was celebrated in rock art. Another characteristic of swans and other waterfowl is their capability to live in all three worlds, sky, earth and water. Taking an 'informed approach', the Finnish archaeologist and anthropologist Antti Lahelma has analysed ancient Finnish-Karelian folklore, which probably had its roots in prehistorical Finno-Ugric mythology.[77] And indeed, in this lore 'waterbirds play an important role as messengers between the world of humans and that of spirits or gods since they are able to journey from one to the other'.[78] Lahelma, and subsequently Jean-Loïc Le Quellec, have related petroglyphs of these strange, almost supranatural swans at Lake Onega to the 'diving-bird myth'.[79] According to this creation myth, which is widely disseminated among speakers of the Finno-Ugric family of languages throughout northern Eurasia, a water-bird, often a duck, is ordered by the creator god to dive into the primordial ocean and bring back some silt from which the earth is created.[80] A different, yet related interpretation was advanced by the Soviet ethnologist Konstantin Laushkin in the 1960s concerning a distinct arrangement of five petroglyphs on the small island of Bolshoi Guri in Lake

Onega. Within a grey, oval rock formation in the shape of an egg there are five petroglyphs featuring a swan standing close to an egg-shaped figure, a solar symbol and two elk. Laushkin connected this composition with the myth of the primordial egg which was also widespread in northern Eurasia and Siberia. In this myth, a supranatural bird flies from a mountain to the earth (or the primordial ocean) to lay an egg from which the world will emerge.[81] Whereas the primordial egg interpretation seems somewhat far-fetched, that of the diving-bird myth looks plausible.[82] That the petroglyphs of swans at Lake Onega had any connection to the Late Bronze Age solar cult that spread in southern Scandinavia is highly unlikely.

Another intriguing scene at Besov Nos represents a skier wearing the mask of a wolf or bear and pursuing an elk.[83] He holds in his hands two objects which represent either a crescent moon and a sun or, less likely, a large trap. Above his head there is a second crescent, behind him a second solar symbol and a swan (fig. 140).[84] Then there are two isolated, unusual motifs which share obvious similarities with petroglyphs in faraway Bohuslän, southern Sweden, 1,400 kilometres to the south-west. One represents men with huge, even giant-like calves,[85] which are also found at Backa in Brastad, Lövåsen, Torsbo, Vitlycke and elsewhere in Bohuslän. The other striking motif at Cape Swan features a maypole dance, as also seen at Gerum in Bohuslän. Maypole dances are still performed in Nordic regions at the summer solstice. In the maypole petroglyph at Cape Swan, the torsos of the two men dancing at the right of the scene form the body of a swan, which creates a strange hybrid palimpsest.[86] Direct cultural contacts between Karelia and Bohuslän must be excluded since the latter petroglyph dates from the Bronze Age, about 1,000 years later than those from Lake Onega; the inspiration for both scenes must go back to a common Nordic mythological heritage.

Finally, the most spectacular arrangement of petroglyphs lies at the south-western tip of the Besov Nos promontory, very close to the waterline. It shows, from west to east, four swans, a schematized tree 87 centimetres tall, a lizard, salamander or Eurasian otter 261 centimetres long, a swan with a neck 102 centimetres long, a sturgeon 95 centimetres long, an anthropomorph 248 centimetres long with a quasi-rectangular head, and a fish 262 centimetres long, probably a wels catfish. All the animals, the tree and the anthropomorph are aligned exactly parallel to each other and form a group.[87]

It seems that these prominently arranged figures enjoyed some kind of veneration from their makers, although their relation to each other remains unknown. The huge lizard or salamander may possibly be compared to the petroglyph of a crocodile-like monster at Shishkino in Siberia which symbolizes a version of the myth narrating the abduction of the sun. In that case, the lizard would symbolize the forces of darkness and death. The main figure is the eerie-looking anthropomorph who is divided into two practically symmetric halves by a longitudinal crevice in the rock. The location was deliberately chosen by the artist, because the fissure already existed before the petroglyph was made. The knees are bent and the feet turned outwards; the arms are turned upwards with the fingers spread. Much later, a large Orthodox cross was engraved above the left arm of the anthropomorph and above the cross an oval shape, perhaps suggesting a halo. Local people in the nineteenth and early twentieth centuries interpreted this mysterious figure as a demon, which also gave the name of the cape *Besov Nos*, in Russian 'Devil's Cape'.[88] Whereas the 'demon' was made in the Neolithic, the Orthodox cross was superimposed much later, most probably in the sixteenth century by Orthodox monks from the nearby Muromsky or Shalsky monastery. The intention

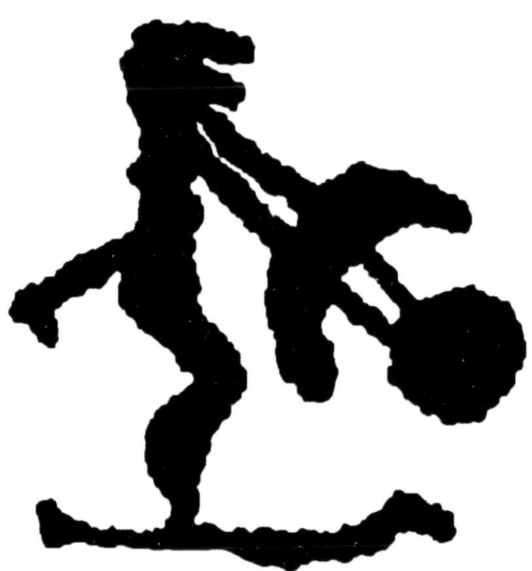

140. Petroglyph of an anthropomorph on skis wearing a bear or wolf mask and girded with a short sword or dagger. He holds in his hands two objects, either the symbols of sun and moon or a trap; Neolithic period, *ca.* fourth millennium BCE. Besov Nos at Lake Onega, Karelia, Russian Federation. After Poikalainen, Väino and Ernits, Enn, *Rock Carvings of Lake Onega*, vol. 3: *The Besov Nos Region: Besov Nos, Kladovets, Gazhi and Guri Localities* (Tartu: Estonian Society of Prehistoric Art, 2021), p. 41.

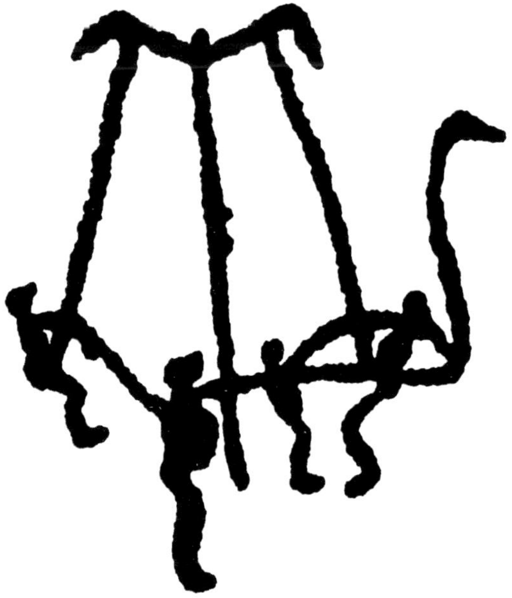

141. A maypole dance from the Neolithic period at Cape Svan, Lake Onega, Karelia, Russian Federation. Maypole dances are still held today in Nordic communities to celebrate the summer solstice. The bodies and arms of the two dancers on the right form the body of a long-necked swan. After Poikalainen, Väino and Ernits, Enn, *Rock Carvings of Lake Onega*, vol. 1: *The Vodla Region* (Tartu: Estonian Society of Prehistoric Art, 1998), p. 157.

was surely to desacralize and neutralize the uncanny figure, since in 1534 an archbishop of Novgorod had ordered the eradication of any remaining pagan customs in Karelia and Ingria.[89] Since another cross was superimposed on a swan near the catfish and a third one, albeit unfinished, on the lizard,[90] we may conclude that these petroglyphs were still venerated in the sixteenth century.

1.1.2. Alta, Norway

Alta lies at 69° 57' north, 380 kilometres north of the Arctic Circle, which means that the sun remains below the horizon from 21 November until 21 January. Thanks to the mitigating effect of the Gulf Stream, the Alta Fjord has a sub-arctic climate without permafrost. As in other parts of northern Fennoscandia, the ice sheet started to melt at the beginning of the Holocene and the Alta region was populated around 9000 BCE.[91] However, the process of isostatic uplift and of marine regression came to a brief halt during the Tapes transgression when the rise in sea level matched and even outpaced the terrestrial uplift. This began *ca.* 7000 BCE and peaked around 5000 BCE, or a couple of centuries earlier. Since some of the petroglyphs at Slettnes on Sørøya Island, about 70 kilometres north of Alta, are water-worn, covered by molluscs and were previously hidden under a layer of marine sediment, it is probable that they antedate the Tapes transgression and can be dated to *ca.* 5500 or 5300 BCE. Whether the very oldest petroglyphs at Kåfjord at Alta also predate the peak of the Tapes transgression is debated and questionable.[92] The petroglyphs at Alta are spread across a height of from 26.5 to 8.5 metres above the present sea level, the majority being between 26.5 and 17 metres asl. Today, the average variation between high and low tides is about 1.8 metres.[93] Based on shoreline data, it is judged that rock pecking was produced at Alta over a period of five millennia from *ca.* 5200 to 200 cal. BCE, the majority between *ca.* 5200 and 3000 BCE.[94] Following the work of Gjerde, the following periodization of Alta rock art is proposed:[95]

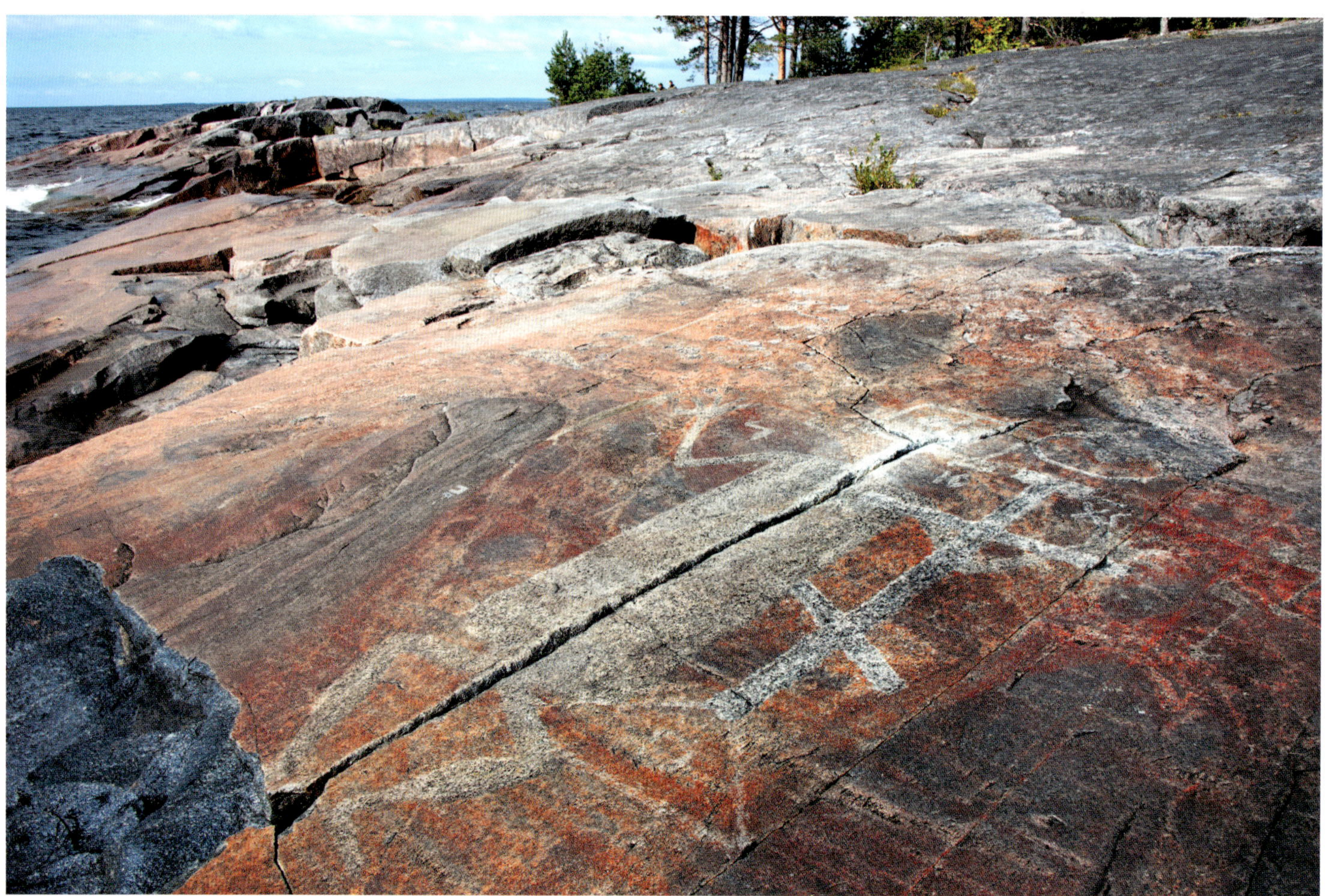

142. Image of an anthropomorph 248 cm long, divided by a natural rock fissure into two halves. Neolithic period *ca.* fourth millennium BCE. An Orthodox cross standing on a pedestal was added in the later sixteenth century. Besov Nos at Lake Onega, Karelia, Russian Federation. Photo 2019.

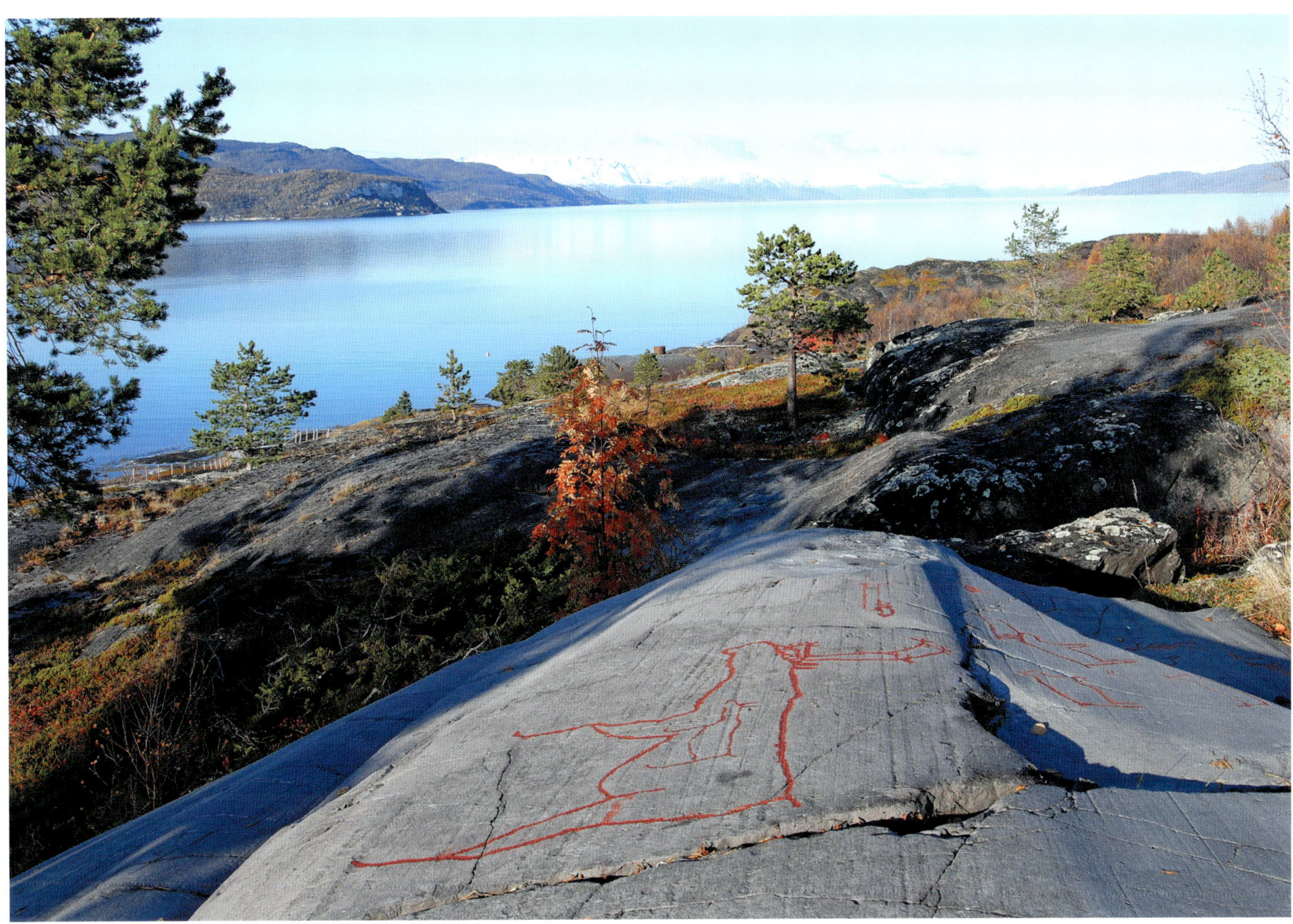

143. Repainted petroglyph of a pregnant elk at Ole Pedersen 11 A; in the background is the Altafjord. Alta, northern Norway. Photo 2010: Karin Tansem / World Heritage Rock Art Centre – Alta Museum.

Period	m asl	Time span (cal.)	Temperatures compared to present	Specific elements
I	26–22	5200–4200 BCE	+3/−2 °C	Elk, reindeer, waterbirds, elk with striped bodies.
II	21[96]–17	4200–3000 BCE	+1.7/−1 °C	Great diversity and complex scenes such as organized hunts. Elk, reindeer, bears, halibut, whales, waterbirds, necklaces, boats with elk-shaped prows, hunters, fishermen, men holding elk-headed poles.
III	17–14	3000–2000 BCE	+0.8/−0.3 °C	Outside Amtmannsnes: similar motifs as in Period II, but fewer scenes and a sharp decline in quantity. New site at Amtmannsnes with large schematic humans, partly females; deer, elk and fish; no boats. Probably a new population.
IV	12.5–11	1700–1200 BCE	Close to present	Small, simple humans, reindeer and again boats. Boats begin to have a rectangular hull, similar to those in Bohuslän, no longer with elk figureheads at the prow.[97]
V	10–8.5	1100–200 BCE (or 100 CE)[98]	Close to present	Long ships with large crews, some holding their paddles upright; elk with long legs. Humans rendered as simple line figures. A sword fight heralds a new epoch of conflicts.[99]

Whereas in southern and central Scandinavia a dividing line is assumed between an egalitarian society of hunter-gatherers and a socially stratified society of settled agro-pastoralists beginning around 1700 BCE, this division does not apply to the northernmost regions where a culture of fishers, hunters and gatherers, who slowly also adopted pastoralism, existed till the first centuries CE.[100] There, people started to become settled in coastal areas while people living inland remained hunter-gatherers, with a greater or lesser degree of mobility.

The most important sites at Alta are:

- **Kåfjord** is a large (700 square metres) single panel of mudrock with *ca.* 1,500 figures situated 26–18 m asl. The upper 70% of the steep slope dates from Period I, the lower part from Period II.[101]

- **Hjemmeluft** is located 3 km south-east of Kåfjord on the opposite side of the bay. It is the largest site of Alta, with *ca.* 2,700 petroglyphs spread over 100 panels; 25 panels are marked with signage and open to the public.

- **Amtmannsnes** lies 7 km north-east of Hjemmeluft. The emergence of new motifs in a unique style suggests that these petroglyphs were made by a new group of people.

- The smaller sites of **Ole Pedersen, Apana Gård, Bergheim** and **Apanes** are the northern extensions of Hjemmeluft.[102] As at Hjemmeluft, there are petroglyphs from the second, fourth and fifth periods.

- **Storsteinen** lies midway between Hjemmeluft and Amtmannsnes; it is a single sloping rock about 3 m high and it has a surface area of almost 50 sq m. The petroglyphs are an unusually dense palimpsest dating from all five periods. Since the rock lies at an altitude of 22–21 m asl, from Period III onwards countless other rocks emerged from the retreating sea, yet petroglyphs continued to be made on the Storsteinen rock and the other boulders were ignored. The place must have been favoured for rituals linked to petroglyphs.

- **Transfarelv** is, of the eight places with known rock paintings, the best preserved. Today, it is located 12 km north-east of Hjemmeluft in a thick forest at an altitude of 20 m asl. This distance from the present shoreline suggests a date around 4000 BCE, but the Transfarelv paintings are traditionally dated around 1500 BCE; in fact, they could indeed be older.[103] The images feature a human with arms ending in a circle, reindeer and geometrical figures; for the painting, iron oxides mixed with fat, blood or another binder were used.

A peculiarity of the sites of Kåfjord and Hjemmeluft is their reddish surface. As analysed by Karin Tansem and Per Storemyr, the coastal rocks at Hjemmeluft consist of hard, originally grey sandstone with a strong mineral lamination comprising mainly magnetite, but also zircon, rutile, tourmaline and haematite, from which a reddish film emerged on the surface. It is believed that the carved rocks were red at the time the petroglyphs were made; but as a consequence of continued uplift, the older petroglyphs became overgrown by vegetation causing acidification, which gradually removed the reddish film and returned the surface to a grey appearance. At Kåfjord however, the bedrock is naturally reddish as it is 'strongly laminated volcanoclastic or tuffaceous mudstone', which has a high content of magnetite.[104] When the petroglyphs were discovered in the 1970s,[105] they were covered with moss, turf, lichen and tiny shrubs. In fact, the best method of searching for petroglyphs was to examine coastal rocks overgrown with such vegetation, rather than forested locations, since trees have deep roots. In order to keep the petroglyphs visible for the public, they are regularly cleared of vegetation and cleaned. Previously, the ever-regenerating vegetation was removed in early summer and the panels covered before winter to prevent frost wedging. At the single, large panel of Kåfjord, thin plastic sheets were initially used which were found to be vulnerable to precipitation in storms. A second attempt, using a combination of PVC plastic and fibreglass mats as a permanent protection, also failed since this tight cover lacked air circulation and risked becoming a greenhouse for all kind of fungi and bacteria.[106] Since then, the petroglyphs of Kåfjord and Hjemmeluft have been regularly chemically treated with a 70 per cent ethanol concentration to prevent any biological growth.[107] As in Sweden, some of the petroglyphs in Alta and also in southern Norway have been painted red or white to improve their otherwise poor visibility. This practice is controversial. On one hand, it makes rock art accessible to the wider public and is said to protect it from weathering. On the other hand, it compromises the authenticity of the petroglyphs and may turn out to be harmful to the rock in the long term.[108] Whether the petroglyphs were originally painted is doubtful.

The dominating motifs at Alta in all periods are reindeer and elk, although petroglyphs of reindeer and elk hunts disappeared around 500 BCE, which indicates a shift in economic priority among petroglyph makers from hunting and trapping to maritime trade. Boats are another key motif from Period II, but they are absent in Period III when the focus of rock art making shifted to Amtmannsnes. Humans are present in all periods but the first, and they markedly predominate at Amtmannsnes in Period III. Birds such as geese or great auks were represented in Periods II and III, fish in Periods II to V and bears mainly in Period II and to a small extent in Period IV. The predominance of reindeer and, to a lesser degree, of elk in petroglyphs is understandable since these two cervids were the most important source of meat and of animal raw material. In a few petroglyphs their rib cages and inner organs are illustrated (fig. 146). Reindeer, which are recognizable by their shorter legs, appear in rock art either alone or in hunting scenes. On panels 6–9 at Hjemmeluft, complex hunting scenes are featured involving one to two dozen reindeer and several hunters armed

with bows and spears. The hunts are clearly well-planned cooperative activities. In one kind of hunt, a man armed with a spear drives a flock towards other hunters armed with bows, or into a fenced enclosure where they are trapped and slaughtered.

To be distinguished from these hunts are scenes where numerous reindeer stand inside a fenced corral; they have probably been captured to prevent them from undertaking their seasonal winter migration. Another type of hunt is shown on panel 8: at the right of the scene, a hunter shoots from a boat at a fleeing herd of ten reindeer, but they are caught on the shore by a second archer. Such communal hunts were seasonal as they took place either in spring or autumn when the herds were migrating (fig. 147).[109] As illustrated by petroglyphs at Bergheim, in the snowy season hunters wore skis or double-pointed and hardwood-framed snow

---

145. → In the centre of panels 6 and 7 at Hjemmeluft the petroglyphs illustrate reindeer and elk kept inside enclosures. At the right, hunters attack three bears with bows and lance. 4200–3000 BCE. Alta, northern Norway. Photo 2022.

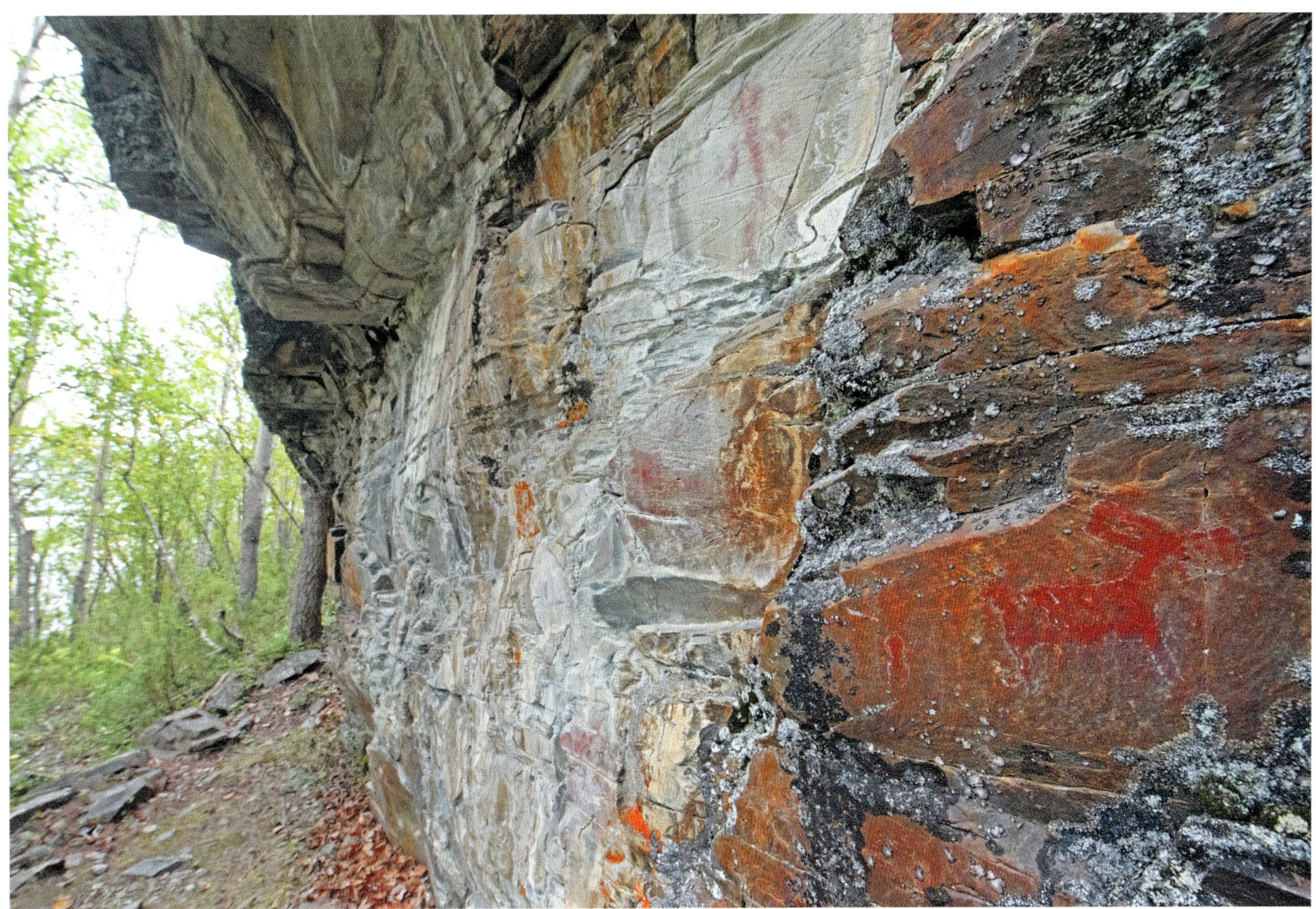

144. Rock painting of a reindeer at the right and of a human above; fourth to second millennium BCE. Transfarelv, Alta, northern Norway. Photo 2022.

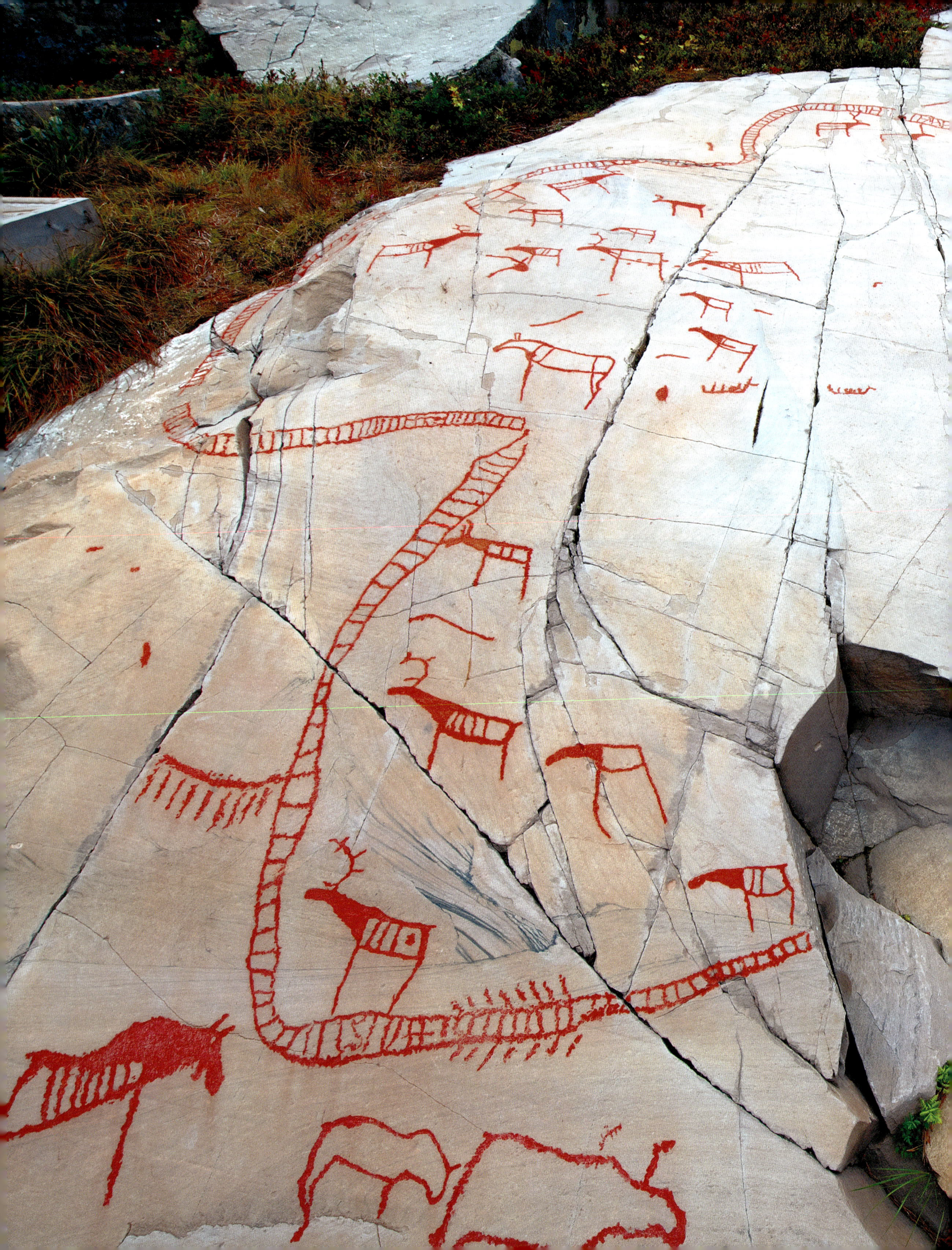

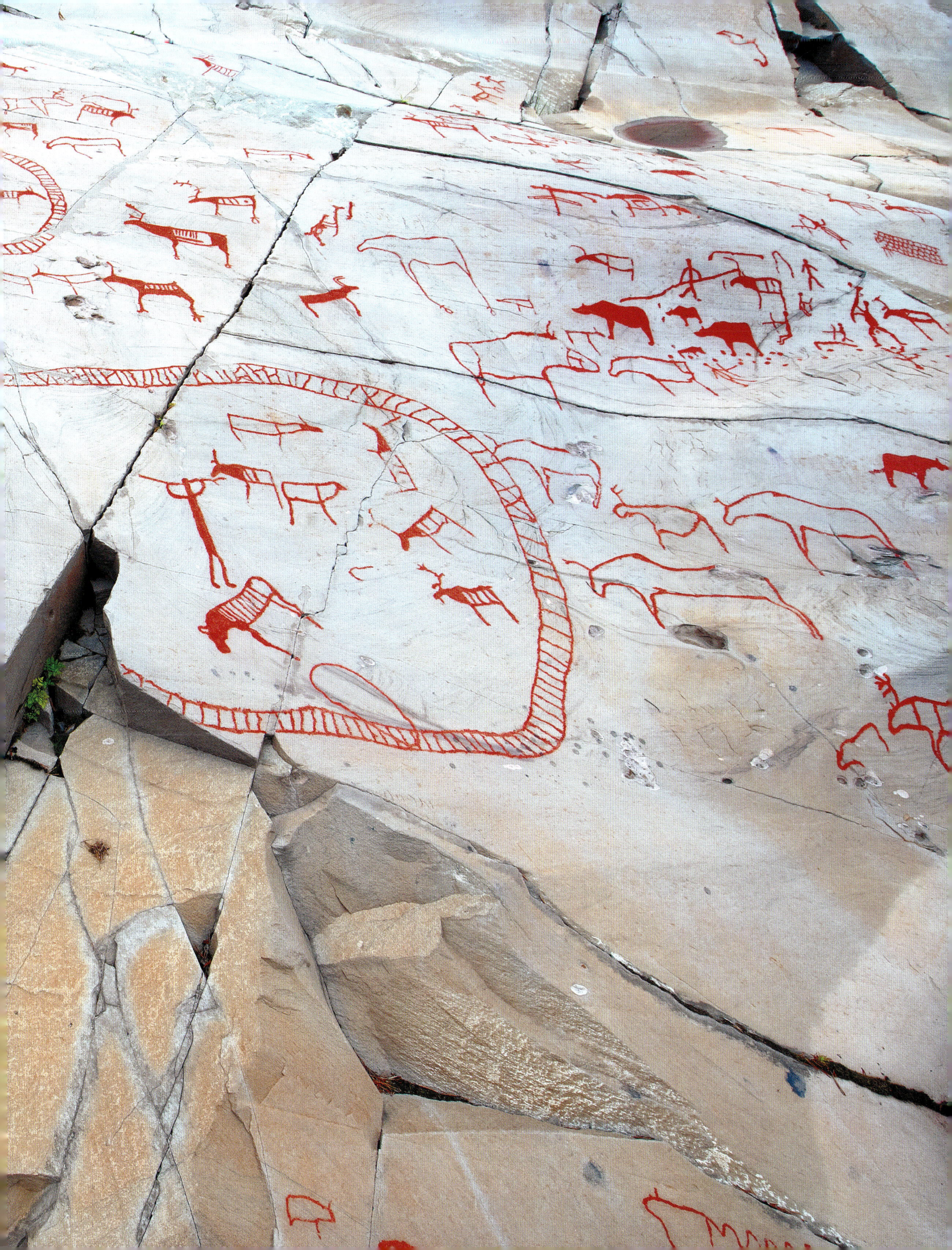

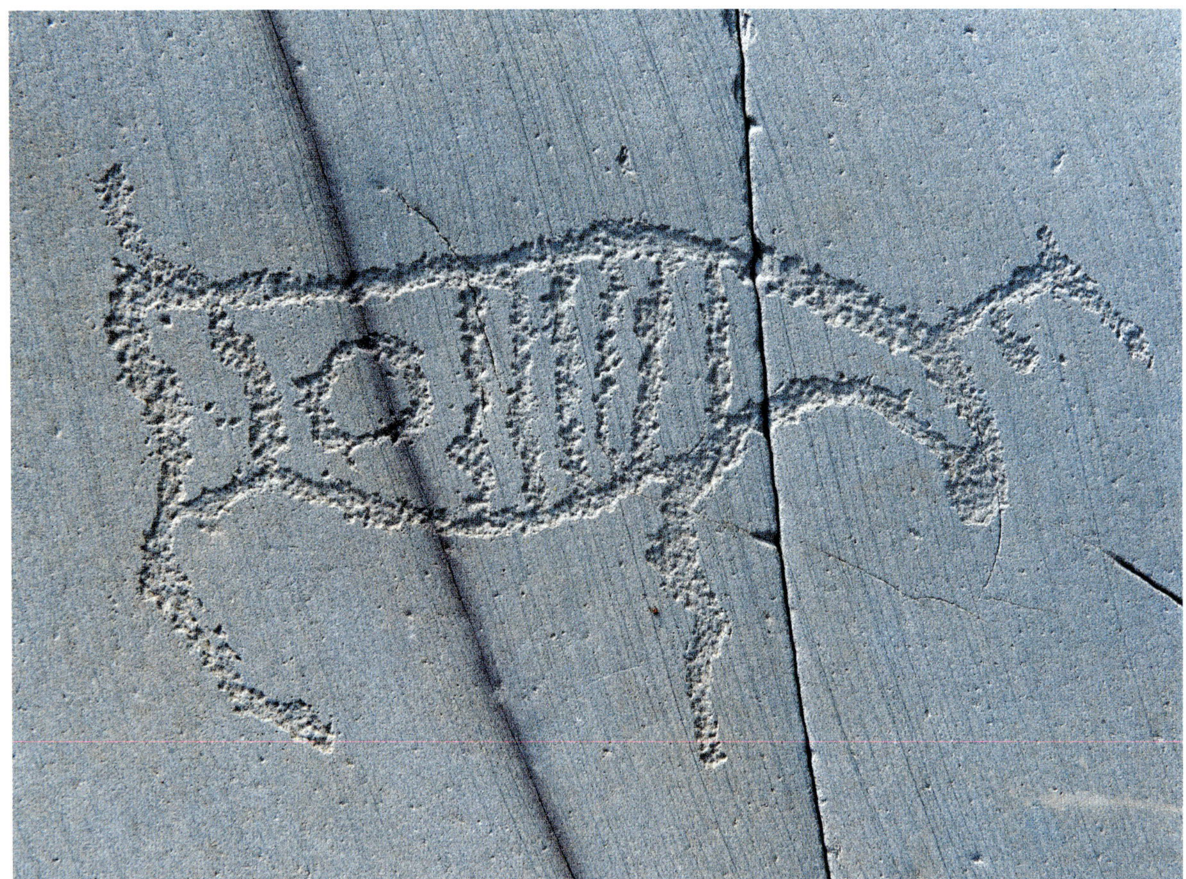

146. Petroglyph of an elk. The internal lines and the circle may represent the ribs and stomach of the animal. Fifth millennium BCE. Hjemmeluft, panel 9 A, Alta, northern Norway. Photo 2022.

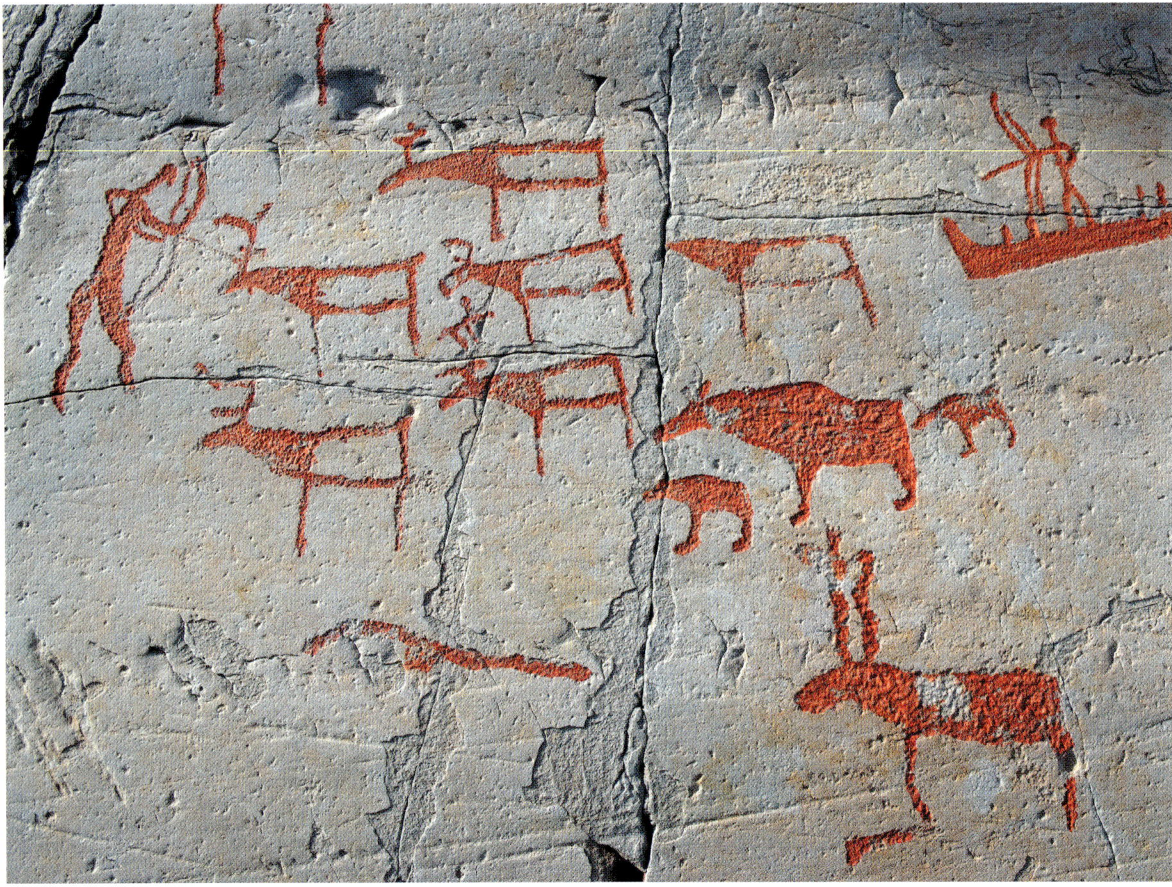

147. Illustration of a reindeer hunt both from the water and on land. The archer standing in the boat drives the prey from the river to the shore where a second hunter is waiting in ambush. 4200–3000 BCE. Hjemmeluft, panel 9, Alta, northern Norway. Photo 2022.

148. A man hits a young reindeer on the snout with an elk-headed staff; the object engraved below the reindeer could be a trap. 4200–3000 BCE. Hjemmeluft, panel 9, Alta, northern Norway. Photo 2022.

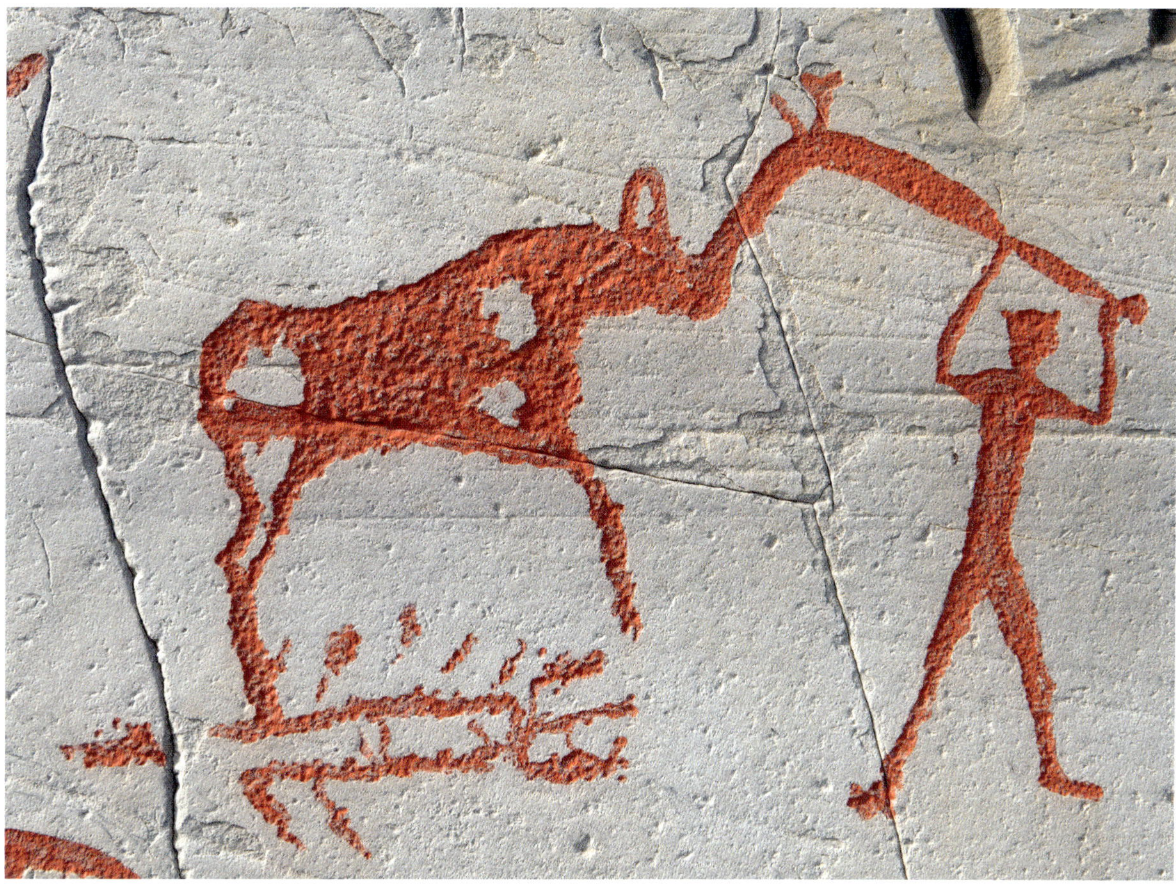

149. An archer and a fisher holding nets stand in a boat with an elk-shaped prow. 4200–3000 BCE. Hjemmeluft, panel 9, Alta, northern Norway. Photo 2022.

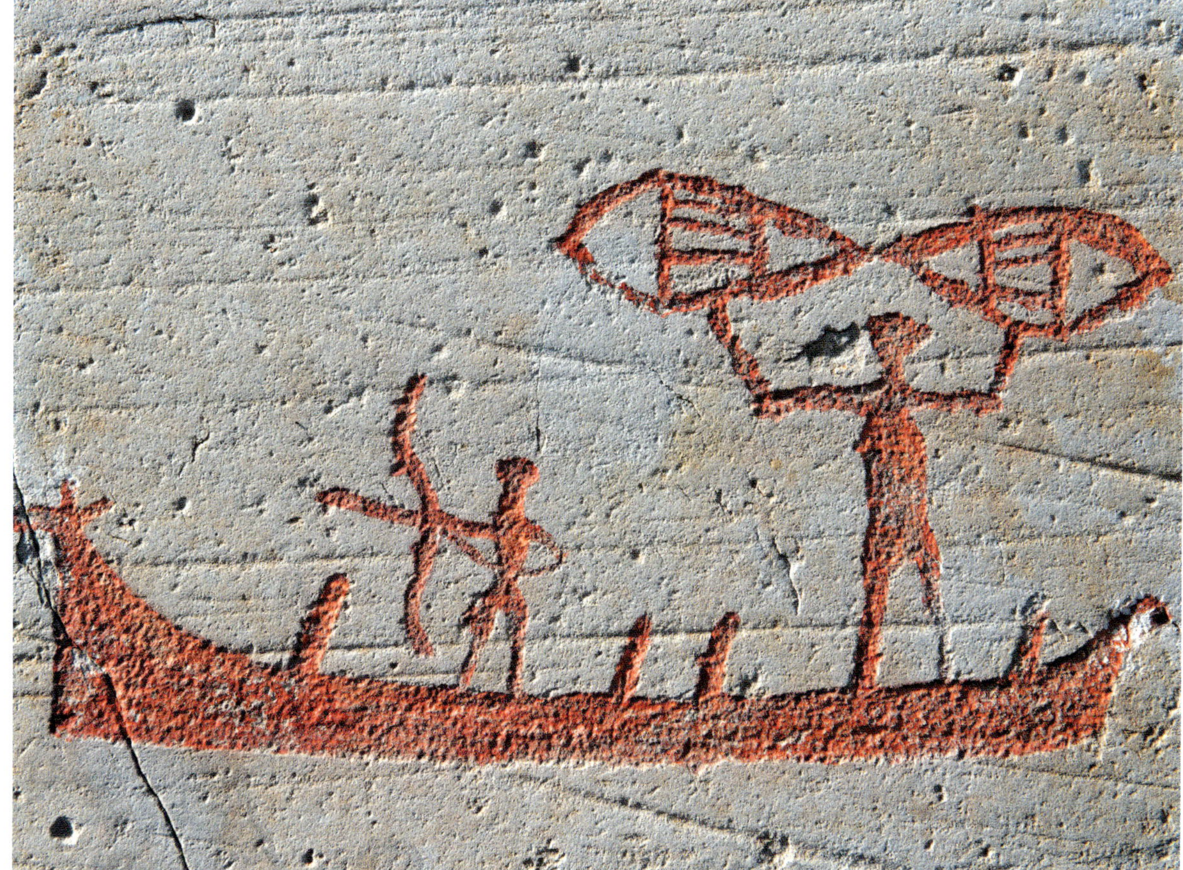

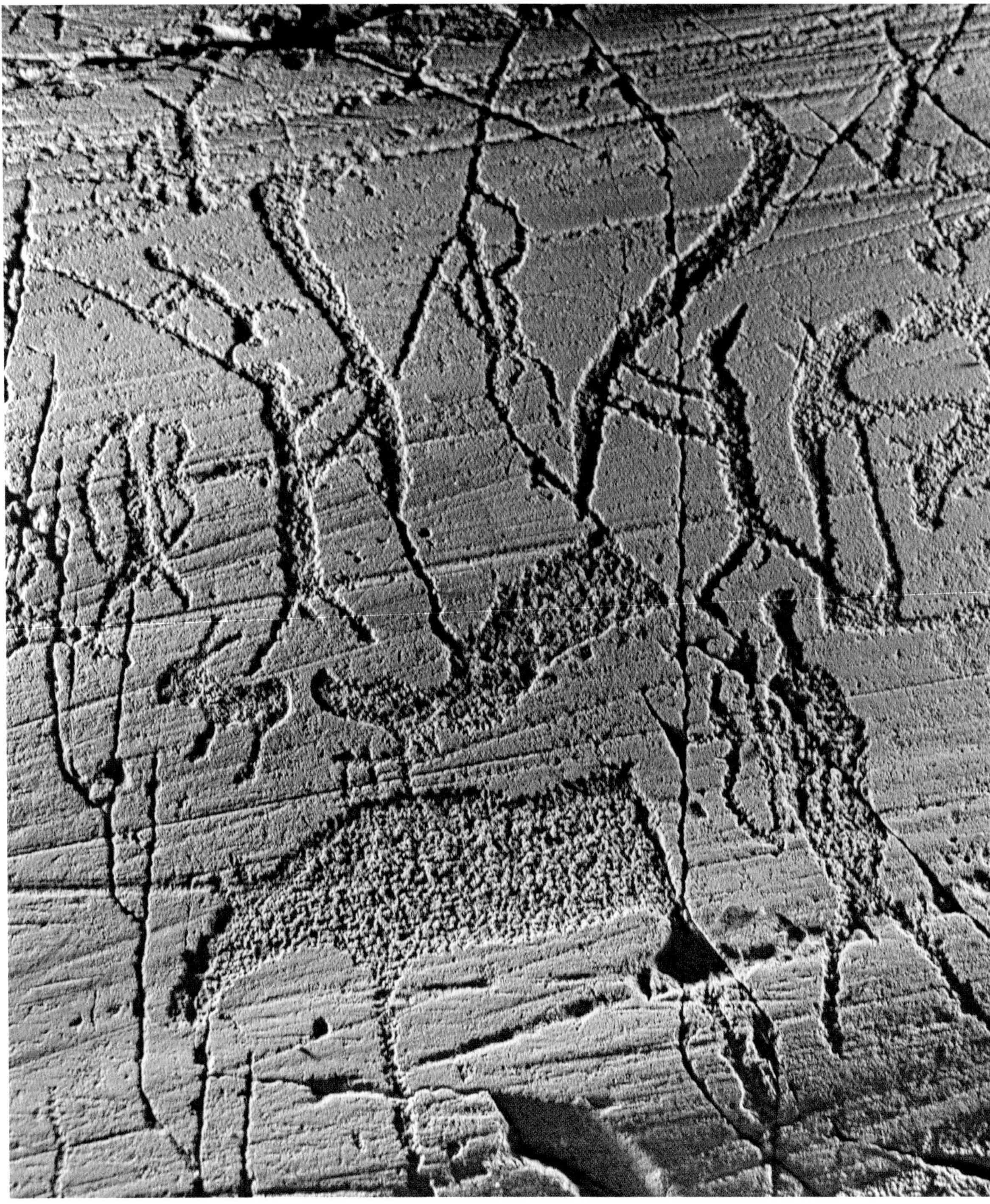

150. Two men face each other while holding elk-headed poles; one of them wears a pointed cap. The one standing on the left seems to be threatened from the front by a lancer and from behind by an archer. Below is a hare, and an archer shoots at a reindeer from behind. 4200–3000 BCE. Hjemmeluft panel 19, Alta, northern Norway. Night photo 2022.

shoes made from rawhide latticework (fig. 154). The importance of reindeer is further highlighted by scenes where one or more men hold poles whose upper ends are shaped like a reindeer (or elk) head. In such a scene on panel 19 of Hjemmeluft (also called Ole Pedersen 9) two men holding elk-headed poles face each other (fig. 150). It remains unclear if this scene represents a ritual or a violent confrontation, for between the two pole-holders stands a man who threatens the left pole-holder with a spear; at the same time, an archer shoots an arrow at the threatened pole-holder from behind. It is possible that this scene addresses two topics, hunting rituals and fights over hunting grounds.[110] In similar scenes, a human touches the head of a reindeer with such a staff (fig. 148). According to Knut Helskog, these poles were used in hunting rituals to ensure the continued presence of game. The spirit of the reindeer or the ancestral animal was supposedly asked for permission to kill animals of his kind. The reindeer spirit's wrath had to be avoided at all costs, or it could change the animal's migration routes.[111] Considering the hunting rituals of the Sami and other Nordic peoples recorded in the past, we may safely assume that the various scenes featuring hunting scenes had at least a twofold purpose, a concrete one and a magic one: they first illustrated and celebrated real hunting activities and, second, were intended to magically ensure successful hunts in the future. Finally, some compositions carried additional mythological or symbolic connotations which remain hard to detect.[112] Petroglyphs featuring poles with an elk head are also found at Alta, Vingen, Nämforsen, Zalavruga and Kanozero.

The significance of these two cervids was not confined to hunting, since dozens of such staves or figures, mainly of elk, but also reindeer and deer heads, have been found in burials and peatbogs in northern Fennoscandia. The oldest are *ca.* 8,000 years old.[113] In total, almost 50 such elk and reindeer heads have been discovered; they were made from wood, bone, antlers and soapstone.[114] The symbolic importance of the elk, which is an excellent swimmer and also survives easily in bogs, is further underscored in northern Fennoscandia by the fact that the bows of boats made from hides, and possibly also of log-boats, often ended in the shape of an elk's head, which symbolically bestowed the endurance of the elk on the craft (fig. 149).[115] The elk was associated with speed not only in water, but also on land, for skis with elk carvings on their surface dating from the Mesolithic were found at Vis in the Vychegda Basin, in the Russian Komi Republic.[116] It seems that there were mythological topics in common between northern Fennoscandia and peoples further east towards the Urals. Since the elk was well adapted to both dry ground and aquatic environments, it may have represented a metaphor for mediation between earth and water, the realm of

humans and the netherworld. This excellent adaptation of the elk to both land and water is also expressed in the elk-shaped ship's bows. Such boat figureheads do not have antlers; they represent either female elk or male elk in the wintertime. These northern petroglyphs of elk-headed boats predate similar petroglyphs in southern Scandinavia by more than two millennia, and with the difference that in southern and central Scandinavia the prows of boats and seagoing ships were mostly horse-headed. In spite of this chronological gap, an inspiration from the north seems plausible. Probably the elk-headed northern boats were known to the seafarers in the south, and the people in southern Scandinavia simply started to peck petroglyphs considerably later than in the north.

The scene mentioned above, on panel 19 at Hjemmeluft, might also establish a link to the Siberian myth of the cosmic hunt and the giant elk Kheglen. According to one version, the giant elk steals the sun at nightfall, but loses it to a hare which returns it to its proper place in the sky.[117] In panel 19, there is a hare (an animal very rarely depicted in Nordic petroglyphs) between the shooting archer and his target, the left-hand holder of an elk-headed pole. Another scene on panel 19 at Hjemmeluft remains enigmatic. Four people aligned at the cardinal points hold a diamond-shaped object; one of the people's

---

151. ↙ Detail of the bear hunt from panel 7 at Hjemmeluft. Three hunters with drawn bows attack a female bear and her cub while another hunter is in the process of sticking a long lance into the back of another female bear. The prints of the bears' paws indicate that the animals have just left their den. At the right a man raises an elk-headed pole over the head of a reindeer. 4200–3000 BCE. Alta, northern Norway. Photo 2022.

152. ↘ A female bear is leaving her den with her cub. Fourth millennium BCE. Hjemmeluft, panel 9 A, Alta, northern Norway. Photo 2022.

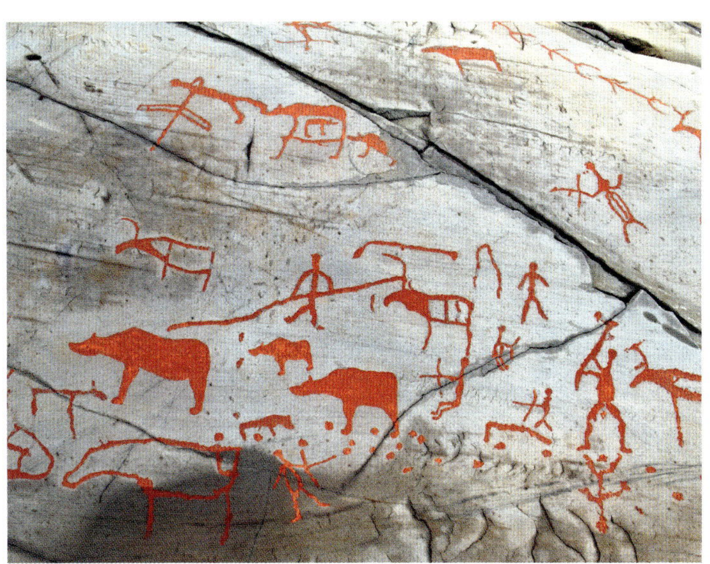

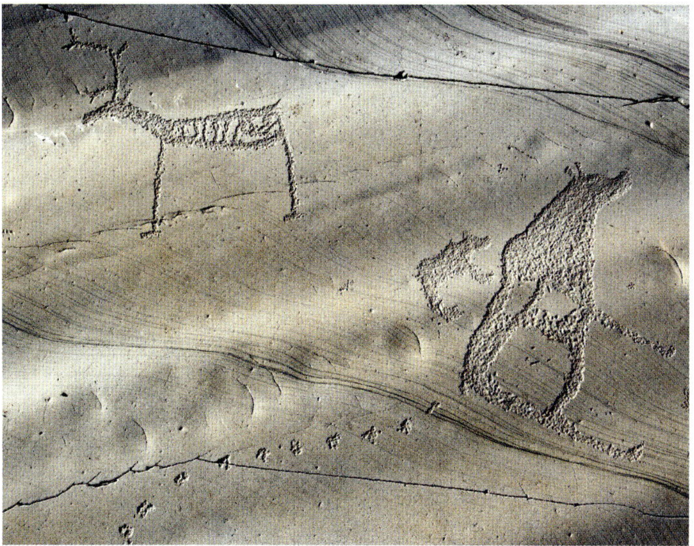

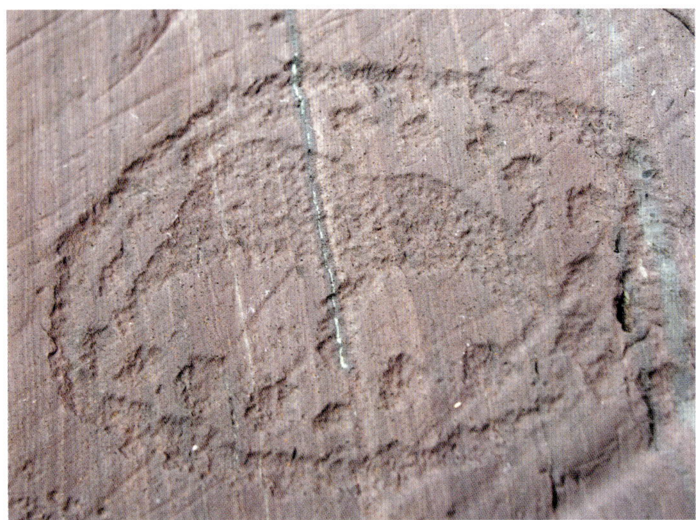

153. A bear has walked in circles inside its den and is preparing to leave it at the beginning of spring. 4200–3000 BCE. Kåfjord, Alta, northern Norway. Photo 2022.

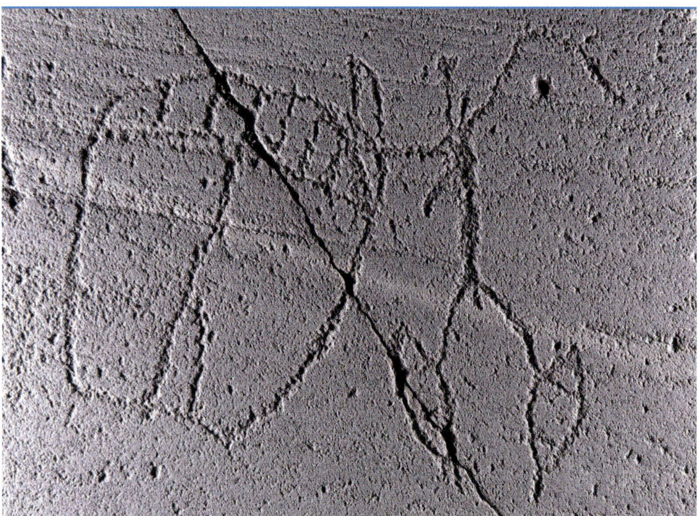

154. Footprints and an archer wearing snow shoes at Bergheim. 3800–3000 BCE. Alta, northern Norway. Night photo 2022.

legs end in the body of an elk. Possibly the central object represents the sun and the composition encapsulates a solar ritual.

Although fishing and hunting sea mammals were of high importance in the diet and economy of coastal northern Fennoscandia, there are relatively few petroglyphs at Alta representing aquatic animals, such as halibut, salmon, seals and possibly a shark. Probably, the numerous petroglyphs of boats implied fishing and marine fauna. By contrast, the bear is much more prominent in Alta's petroglyphs. In some scenes, such as Hjemmeluft panel 6, two archers and a hunter armed with a long spear attack two adult bears and their two cubs, which have just left their den. Above the hunting scene is a pregnant bear with a cub (figs 145, 151). The den is represented by two concentric circles and the distance covered by the four bears is indicated by their pawprints. The two concentric circles recall the custom of medieval Sami hunters who would draw a circle around a bear's winter lair before the bear was driven out and killed.[118] Other complex scenes illustrate the important role of bears in people's minds and in their rock art. At Kåfjord, several petroglyphs show bears hibernating inside their dens or in the process of leaving them in spring (fig. 153). In the upper parts of Hjemmeluft, located south-east of panels 6–9 at an altitude of 25–22 metres above sea level, dozens of bears are pecked in the polished sandstone (fig. 152). There are hunting scenes, a depiction of one huge bear almost a metre long, and several compositions where female bears and their cubs leave their dens, which are mostly located in the cracks and fissures of the sandstone. In another scene, bear tracks lead from the den to a cavity in the rock where water remains after rain, thus suggesting the bear's movement from its den to a pool. These and other scenes show how fissures, cracks, indents and holes in the rocks' surfaces were integrated into the petroglyph scenes as design features. Bears obviously referred to seasonality, as they retreated to their dens in late autumn, thus announcing the impending winter, and later they would leave their dens when spring was approaching. The retreat of bears into their dens heralded cold and darkness, their reappearance warmth and the renewal of life. Possibly bears also symbolized a mediation between our terrestrial world and the underworld. In any case, bears enjoyed much respect in Arctic regions and successful bear hunts had to be followed by rituals. The hunters apologized for the killing or put the blame for the slaughter on others, and the bones of the killed bear had to be buried in the correct anatomical order.[119] On the same boulder east of panels 6–9, there are also several images of men holding long, elk-headed staves, of axes ending in an elk head, and of two pregnant elk.

A kind of revolution occurred in Alta's petroglyphs in the third millennium BCE, for the centre of rock art shifted north-eastward to **Amtmannsnes** and new motifs emerged, expressed in a totally different style. At that time, Amtmannsnes was still an island. While petroglyphs in the wider Alta region mainly depicted people as relatively small, gender-neutral figures hunting, fishing, boating or performing rituals, the new petroglyphs show large humans, up to 210 centimetres long, standing inactively or lying down, with schematic faces and grid designs on their bodies; some have abnormally long rib cages with thirteen ribs on each side. A few humans have stick-like bodies, others almost rectangular or oval-shaped ones, suggesting big bellies. Some figures are identified as males by their penis, others are most probably females; two females are clearly identified by their vulva. These somewhat skeletal-looking anthropomorphs hardly look like humans, rather like the wire-framed figures sometimes seen sprayed on walls today. A few reindeer have stripes on their coat.[120] The radical departure from the previous style and motifs suggests that these petroglyphs were made by immigrants from the east. At Amtmannsnes, the making of petroglyphs stopped around 2000 BCE, and the focus of petroglyph making shifted back to the previous sites. For what reasons the previous repertoire of images (with the exception of birds) was also revitalized remains unclear.

As of *ca.* 1600 BCE, the production of petroglyphs declined at all sites and towards the end of the millennium, a new type of boat began to appear; about six centuries later, hunting scenes disappeared. These developments suggest a change in economic activity and new cultural contacts. The new type of boat has a rectangular-shaped hull, with an elongated gunwale. Sometimes, vertical strokes protruding from the hull suggest crew members; one petroglyph at Apana Gård shows a ship crew of 32. These boats and ships are distinctly different from those featured in Period II; they could well represent plank-built boats such as are featured in Bronze Age petroglyphs of Bohuslän, southern Sweden, almost 1,400 kilometres south of Alta. These apparent similarities between the late boat and ship petroglyphs of Alta and those from Bohuslän indicate intensive maritime contact between both regions, which did not however reach the Kola Peninsula or Karelia where such boats are absent from petroglyphs.[121] Interestingly, at the time when petroglyph production declined in Alta, it virtually exploded in Bohuslän. To conclude, as in other places in Fennoscandia, the rock art at Alta illustrates a world of outdoor activities mainly associated with males, such as hunting, fishing and conducting rituals. With the exception of the schematic representations of women at Amtmannsnes II, the world of indoor domestic activities associated with females, such as the rearing of children, householding and domestic craft is absent.

The pecking of petroglyphs ended at Alta after 200 BCE for uncertain reasons. Possibly the making of petroglyphs had become

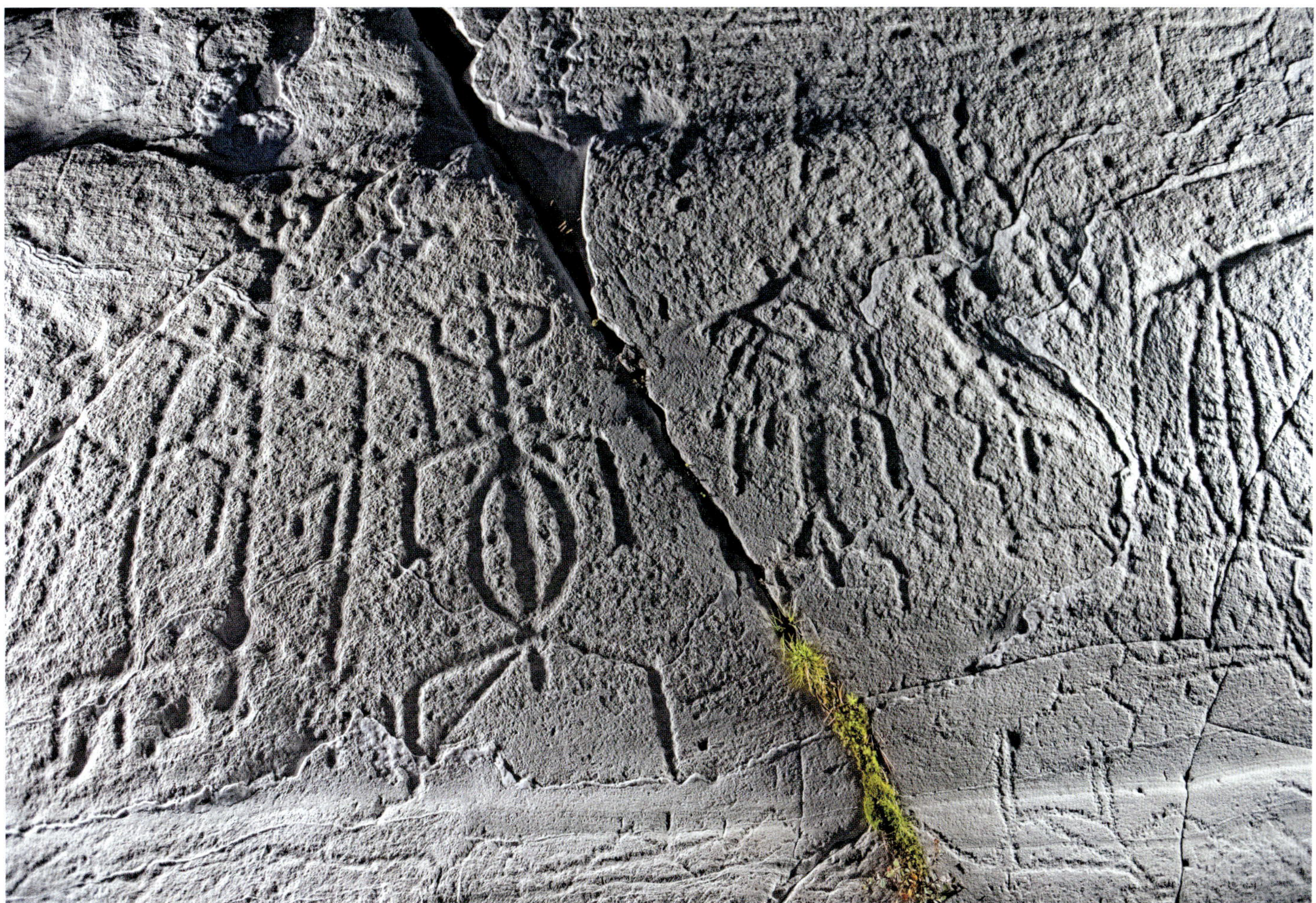

155. Male and female humans at Amtmannsnes. Third millennium BCE. Alta, northern Norway. Night photo 2022.

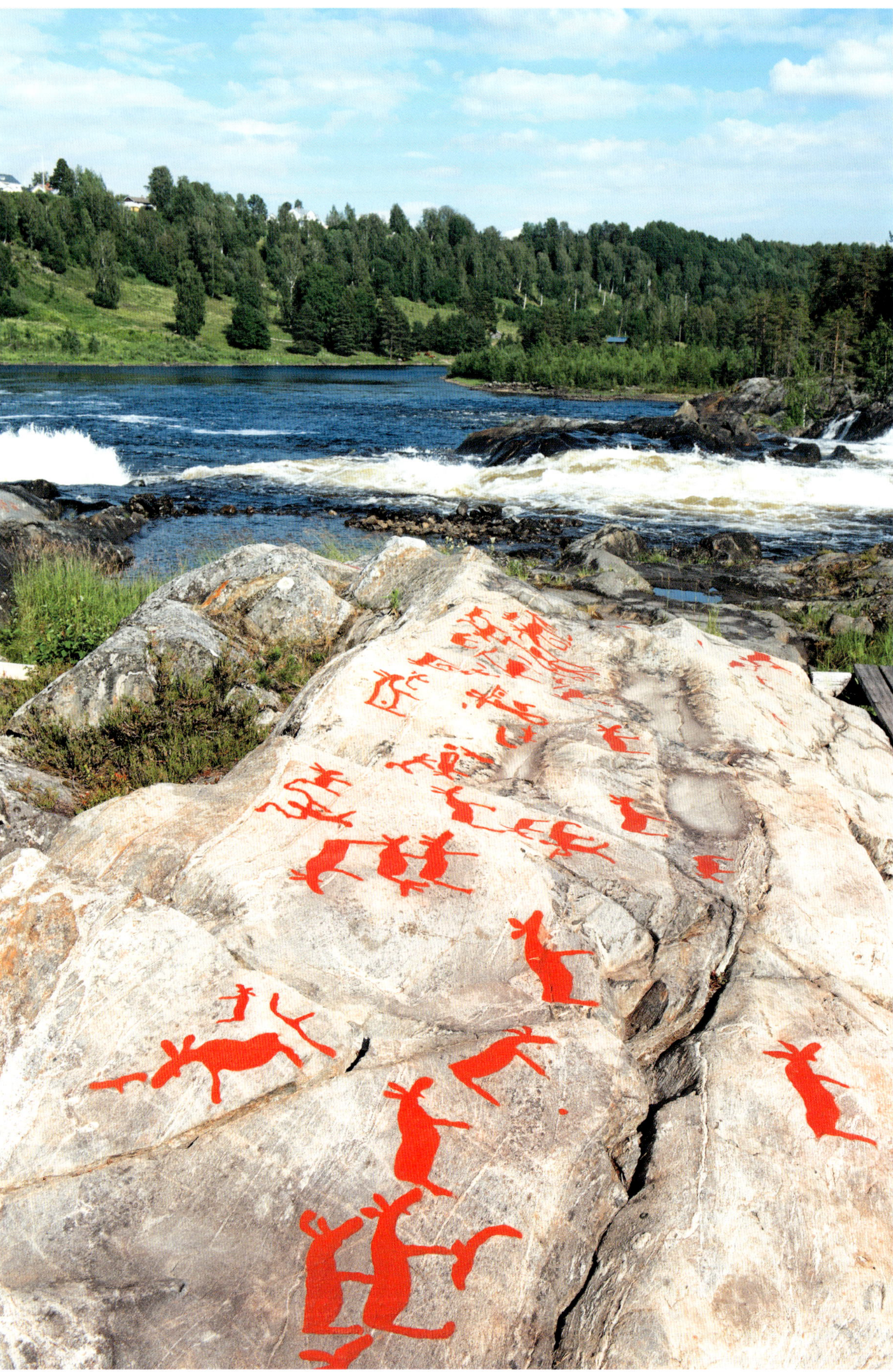

156. Recently overpainted petroglyphs of elk at Nämforsen and, in the background, part of the rapids of Ångermanälven. Late Neolithic to early Bronze Age, central Sweden, Photo 2021.

irrelevant or Alta was no longer a meeting point linked to seasonal hunting activities; or perhaps the values expressed in petroglyphs were now expressed orally in epics. Nevertheless, the mythological contents attached to the petroglyphs remained relevant and were transmitted by other means. This is suggested by the few Sami shaman drums which survived confiscation and destruction by Christian missionaries in the eighteenth century. On these drums there are painted images of bears, reindeer, deer, geese, skiers, archers, boats and so on, which look very similar to petroglyphs.[122] Whereas it is highly unlikely that shaman drums existed at the times of petroglyph making and even impossible that the medieval shamans ever saw the petroglyphs, which by then were heavily overgrown with vegetation, it is conceivable that the mythological contents implied in the petroglyphs were preserved and transmitted to later generations by being recorded on perishable materials such as bark or leather which have long since disappeared.

1.1.3. Nämforsen, central Sweden

Nämforsen lies at 63° 26′ north in the south of northern Fennoscandia. Although situated at the same latitude as Trondheim, Nämforsen never benefitted from the mitigating factor of the Gulf Stream and was therefore unsuitable for agriculture. The petroglyphs, which were first recorded in 1705, are located in the rapids of the Ångermanälven river on the three small islands of Laxön, Notön and Bradön as well as on the left shore of the river. Due to the construction of a hydroelectric power plant just upstream of the petroglyphs, the cataracts have lost some of their vigour. Nevertheless, the islands of Notön and Bradön can only be reached in later summer when the plant greatly reduces or ceases operations. During the late Mesolithic and the Neolithic, however, the region looked very different from today. The petroglyphs, which today are situated at an altitude of 87 to 73 metres above sea level at a distance of almost 100 kilometres from the Gulf of Bothnia, date from *ca.* 5000 to 1800 BCE; a few carried on being made until 1000 BCE.[123] During the first period, lasting until *ca.* 4000 BCE, the site was located in the mouth of the fjord into the sea and the easternmost island, Notön, stood not in the estuary but in the sea itself. These petroglyphs, on the highest panels, are mostly surface-pecked images of elk.

At Nämforsen, the isostatic uplift was swift and the sea retreated eastward. The fjord became a river and the rapids were formed. Nevertheless, the Neolithic people continued to make petroglyphs in this dangerous cataract environment. The site was considered auspicious for rock art, most probably because there was a river crossing nearby for elk during their seasonal migrations. In the second period of rock art making, only the contours of images were pecked, and they were no longer scooped out. Although the

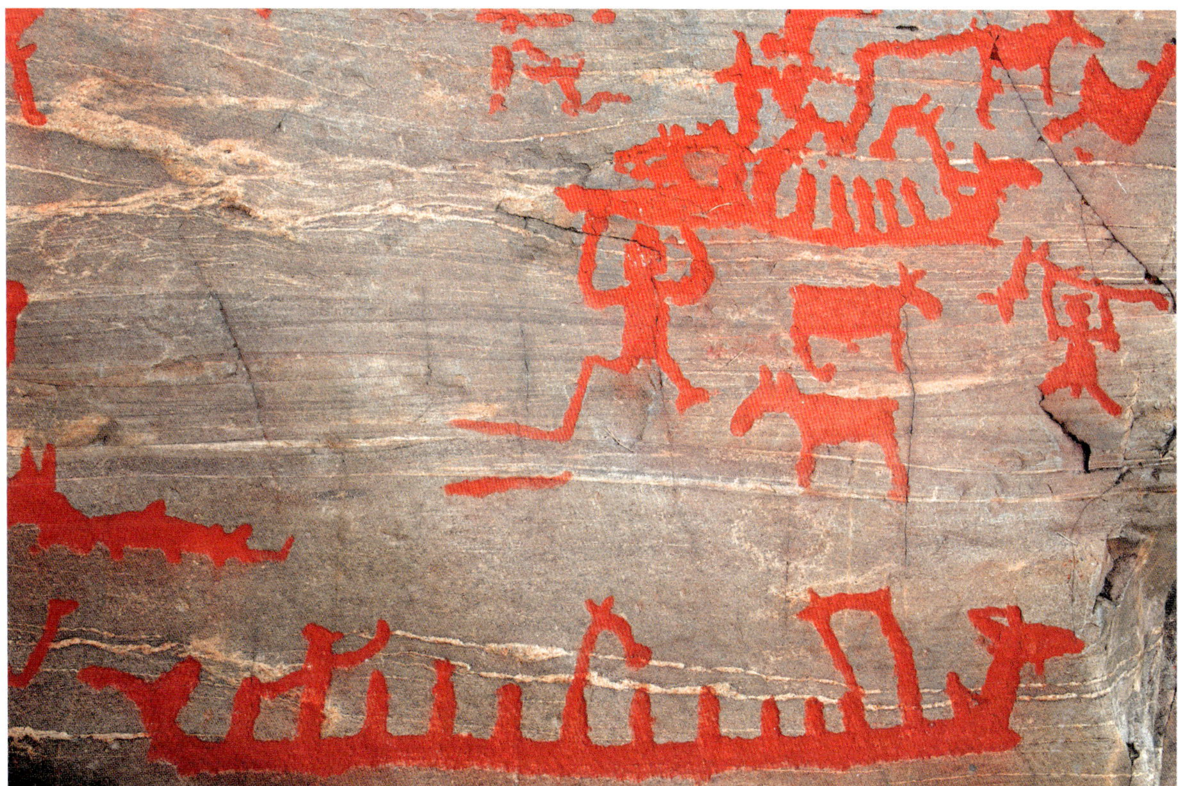

157. In the centre, a man seems to carry a boat and to the right another man lifts an elk-headed pole. At the bottom a boat with an elk-headed prow and *ca.* twelve passengers. Early Bronze Age, Nämforsen, central Sweden, Photo 2021.

sea continued to retreat – by 2000 BCE it was already 35 kilometres from Nämforsen – the Ångermanälven river remained navigable and served as an important connector to the Gulf of Bothnia and from there to the North Sea.[124] The pictures of some larger ships with a dozen or even 50 crew members indicate an intensive use of the waterway.[125] In order to navigate further upstream than Nämforsen, the lightweight hide boats were emptied and carried around the obstacle on foot, as it is illustrated in some petroglyphs (fig. 157). Similar petroglyph images exist at Novaya Zalavruga (Vyg), Alta and Massleberg (Bohuslän). However, in a different context, such petroglyphs may also illustrate a ritual where small boat models were carried in a procession.

Due to the abundance of salmon in the Ångermanälven and of elk and reindeer in the forests on either side, its valley has been well populated since the late Mesolithic. Not only have traces of about 1,000 Mesolithic and Neolithic settlements and numerous hunting pits been identified there, but also fifteen sites with rock paintings.[126] Although salmon was the most important supplier of animal nutrition for the Neolithic and early Bronze Age hunter-fishers at Nämforsen, elk is predominant in the rock art, with 54 per cent of the total images, followed by boats (31 per cent) and humans (9 per cent); salmon account for a mere 1 per cent.[127] Without doubt, the rapids were an ideal trap to catch salmon swimming upstream. Yet the importance of the large cervids is also highlighted, as in Alta, by the numerous petroglyphs of boats with elk-headed prows, and of elk-headed staves. The dominance of wildlife in petroglyphs and the absence of domestic stock or of agriculture clearly position the rock art of Nämforsen within the Northern tradition.

The economy of the Neolithic people around Nämforsen did not solely consist of fishing, hunting and gathering, but also of trade. In one settlement there was a production centre of red ochre which lasted from 4200 to 2400 BCE. Red ochre was not only used for rock paintings, but was a key element in late Mesolithic and Neolithic burial customs across vast areas of north-western Eurasia where it was used to sprinkle the dead. Most probably the Nämforsen people were exporting their ochre. Another indicator for supra-regional trade lasting far into the Bronze Age are petroglyphs illustrating objects which were known further south, such as a horned helmet and pick-shaped and hooked axes, similar to rock peckings found at Vingen (Norway), Järrestad (Skåne, Sweden), Bohuslän and carvings on megalithic burials in Brittany (France).[128] In one scene at Nämforsen, a human holds in each hand an axe with an extra-long shaft ending in a loop; over one of the axe heads a male elk has been superimposed (fig. 159). Interestingly,

at Nämforsen, two early Bronze Age petroglyphs illustrate a duel involving spears and swords, similar to scenes in Bohuslän.[129] Most probably, trade contacts existed in the Bronze Age between Nämforsen and Bohuslän, which was 600 kilometres away by land and 1,500 kilometres by boat.

1.2. Southern Fennoscandia

Like northern Fennoscandia, the region's southern parts remained covered by a thick ice sheet up to the onset of the Holocene; during the late Palaeolithic and early Mesolithic the western and eastern coastal areas experienced more or less pronounced marine transgressions due to a rise in sea level. However, during the Boreal Period (8700–7300 BCE), the isostatic uplift began to outpace the eustatic sea rise which led to gradual marine regressions in both the western and eastern coastal areas.[130] In contrast to the north where petroglyph making started around 5200 BCE, in the south it did not start until three millennia later, at the transition from the Neolithic to the early Bronze Age around 1750 BCE. As in the north, rock art came to an end *ca.* 200 BCE.

1.2.1. Bohuslän and Østfold

Today, the Bohuslän region is located in the south-west of Sweden, north of Gothenburg, but before the Peace of Roskilde of 1658, it belonged to Norway and formed a cultural unit with today's Østfold in south-eastern Norway.[131] This area of mainly granite boulders which represents the largest petroglyph complex in Europe – or even the world – with more than 1,500 sites, is politically divided with the far larger part in Bohuslän (Sweden) and a much smaller part in Østfold (Norway). As at Alta, during the Bronze Age (*ca.* 1750–500 BCE) the landscape looked very different from the present since it was then a 'seascape' and 'about 30 percent of today's arable land was covered by the sea'. As explained by Johan Ling, 'a majority of the rock art sites were located close to the shore and … contemporary settlements were on higher ground, about 500–1000 m away from the sea',[132] the major exception to this rule being the petroglyph site of Fossum which never lay at the seashore. In the Bronze Age, most of the sites lay on shores of the sea or fjords or on tiny islands. Within this environment of seascapes and swampy as well as forested landscape, boats were the best means of transport and travel. From this point of view alone it is not surprising that boats are the second most prevalent motif after cup marks, outnumbering humans, animals, footprints, wheels/sun symbols and weapons.[133] Cup marks are tiny concave depressions pecked into the rocks. The meaning of single cup marks is virtually impossible to decipher, since the simpler a form is, the

158. A hybrid creature, possibly a mermaid. Bronze Age, Nämforsen, central Sweden, Photo 2021.

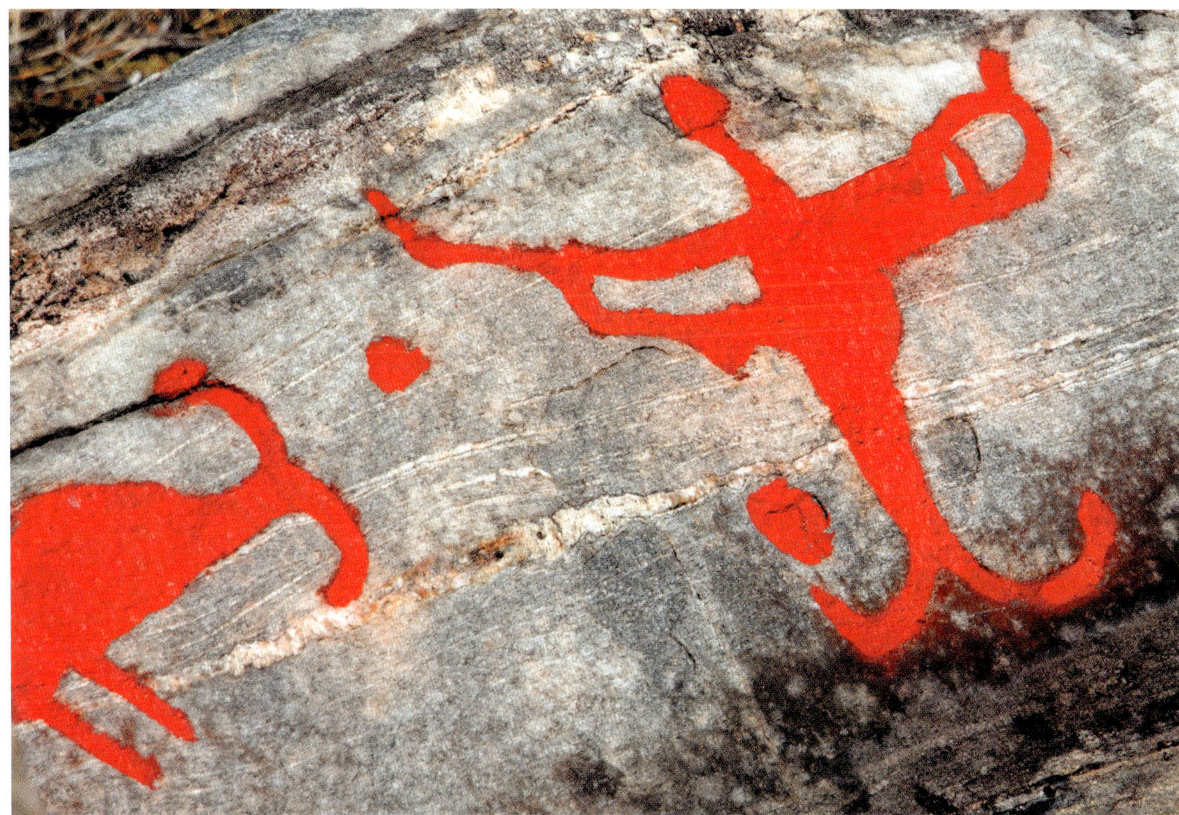

159. A man holds a large pole and an elk which is being pushed by a woman from behind. Bronze Age, Nämforsen, central Sweden, Photo 2021.

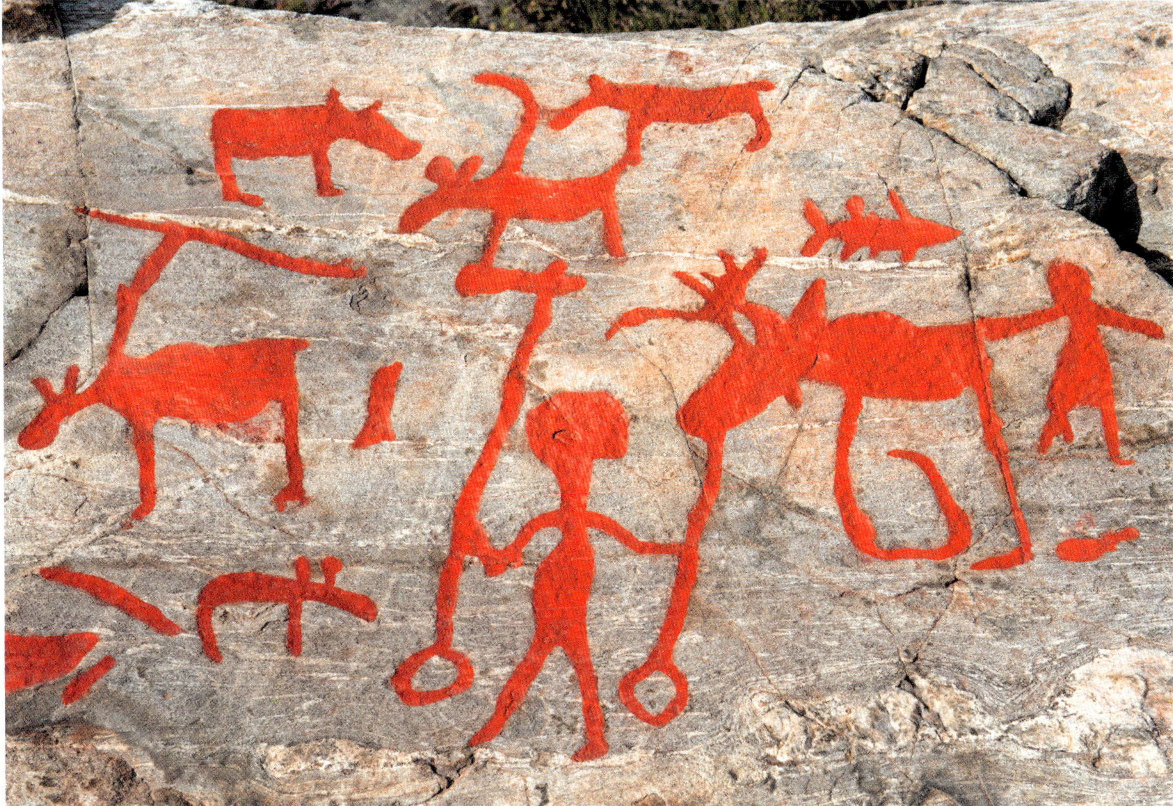

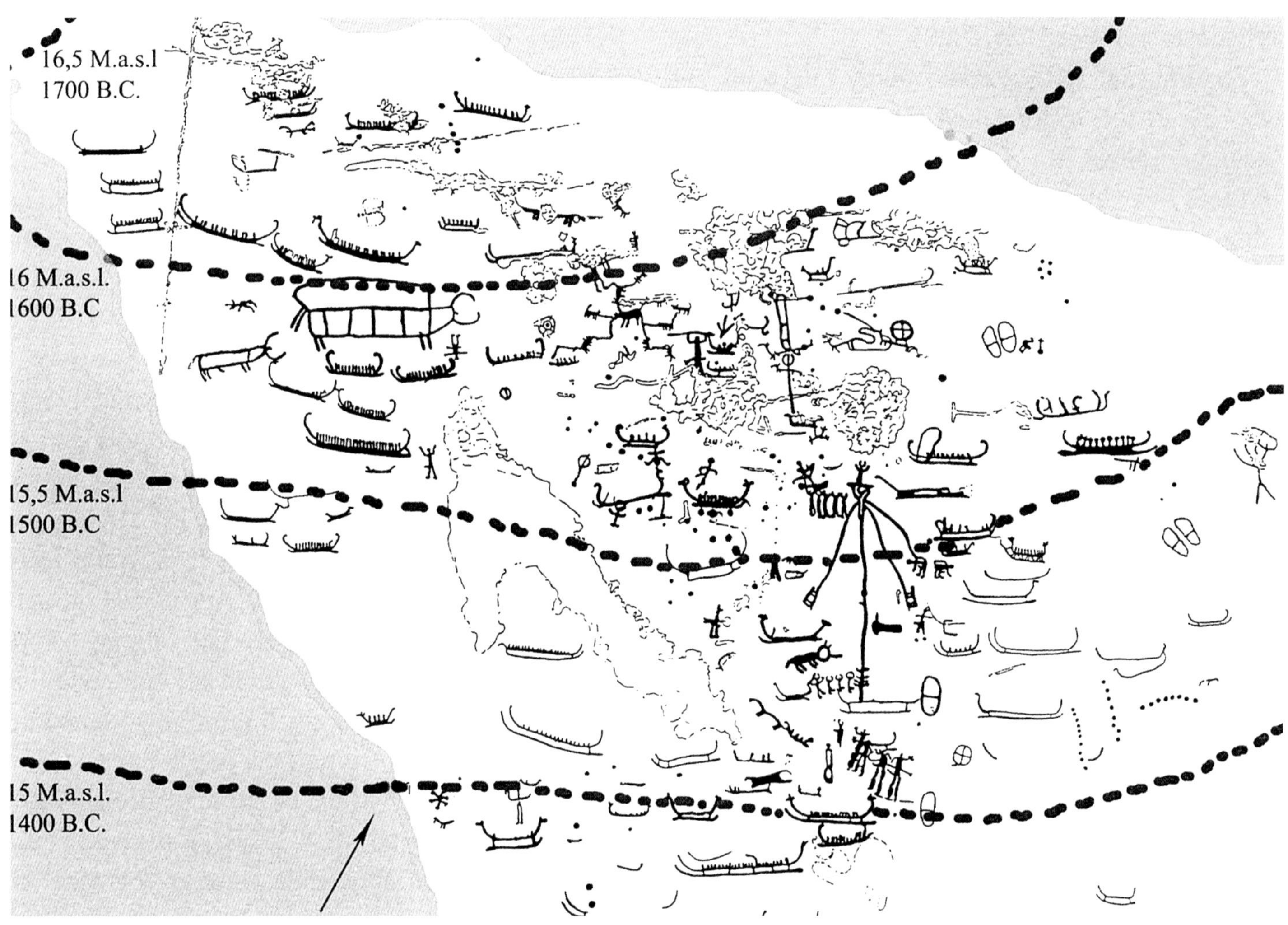

160. Drawing of the site of Gerum in Bohuslän. In the centre of the panel a small man stands on a narrow platform with his arms raised on top of a pole. Three ropes fall from the platform to half the height of the pole; on two of the ropes stands an animal, a cow or a dog, and on the third rope a man is tied to the rope by his stomach. At the foot of the tree are four small (dancing) people, and to the left of the platform five people lift their arms. The scene illustrates a maypole dance. The dotted lines indicate the date and relative altitude when sections of the boulder emerged from the water. For example, the maypole scene was engraved earliest, by *ca.* 1440/30 BCE. Courtesy Johan Ling, *Elevated Rock Art: Towards a Maritime Understanding of Rock Art in Northern Bohuslän, Sweden* (Oxford: Oxbow, 2014), p. 91.

greater the number of possible interpretations. Their meaning can only be guessed when they occur in groups or in combination with other images.[134] Cup marks were not only pecked into rocks, but in the Middle Ages also into church walls where they formed part of burial ceremonies as well as fertility rituals. It seems that the powdered rock produced by the hammering was believed to have healing properties.[135] Also, as at Alta, the marine regression forced the fishing people of prehistoric Bohuslän to follow the receding sea and move their mooring places accordingly, while the band

of rock at the shore where petroglyphs were carved also shifted seaward. At the beginning of the Bronze Age the shoreline lay *ca.* 19–20 metres, and at its end *ca.* 10–11 metres above the present sea level.[136] In Østfold the shorelines were probably a couple of metres higher.[137] In both regions, petroglyph dating according to the shoreline has to take into consideration the fact that some of the coastal areas have been cultivated for the last few centuries which has led to an accumulation of agricultural sediment of up to a metre.[138]

Documentation of and research into petroglyphs began in Europe in 1627 when Peder Alfsön sent a watercolour image of a petroglyph panel at Backa, in Brastad parish in Bohuslän, to the Norwegian antiquarian Ole Worm, who collected information on ancient monuments and legends. The panel featured ships, humans with prominent calves, animals and the famous so-called 'cobbler', a 150-centimetre-tall image of an ithyphallic male holding a battle axe in his raised right hand (fig. 161); the image, however, was not published until 1784. Eight years later, the officer C.G.G.

Hilfeling made an ink drawing of a similar figure, the 'Spear God' of Litsleby (fig. 188). A renewed interest in petroglyphs arose in the early nineteenth century when the state antiquarian J.G. Liljegren commissioned C.G. Brunius to make exact copies of the petroglyphs of Bohuslän that were then known. The impulse behind this was a letter from Jean-François Champollion, decipherer of the Egyptian hieroglyphs. He wanted to evaluate whether the petroglyphs of southern Scandinavia might represent a forerunner of a hieroglyphic script. Brunius carefully documented more than 100 panels using a grid to measure sizes and distances. Half a century later in 1874, Lauritz Baltzer began the ambitious project of recording all the petroglyphs of Bohuslän, the results of which were published between 1881 and 1908.[139]

Whereas previous interpretations had attributed the petroglyphs to local stone cutters (Alfsön) or to the Vikings (Sven Lagerbring), in 1838 Brunius dated them to the Neolithic. He observed that most of petroglyphs were located near former harbours and ancient shorelines. By analysing the distance from the sea and the corresponding height above sea level, he was the first to use shoreline data to determine the age of petroglyphs.[140] Forty years later, Oscar Montelius convincingly argued for a Bronze Age date for the petroglyphs and in 1917 he published his pioneering classification of the petroglyphs into six Bronze Age periods. Among other things, he based his classification on comparisons between specific ship images in petroglyphs and those engraved on bronze razors found in tombs. At the end of the twentieth century, Flemming Kaul refined and vastly extended the base for such a classification by analysing 420 bronze objects bearing boat and ship images from Denmark dating from the Bronze Age periods IV-VI, that is 1100-500 BCE, the only earlier exception being the Rørby sword dating from Montelius Period I, *ca.* 1600 BCE.[141] The six periods of the Scandinavian Bronze Age were defined by Montelius as follows: **I** (1750/1700–1500 BCE), **II** (1500–1300 BCE), **III** (1300–1100 BCE), **IV** (1100–920 BCE), **V** (920–720 BCE), **VI** (720–550/500 BCE).[142]

Regarding the interpretation of petroglyphs, once their alleged association with the Vikings had been discredited, in the second half of the nineteenth and the early twentieth centuries a debate raged as to whether they illustrated religious rituals (A.L. Croll), religious symbols (Jens J.A. Worsaae), a solar cult (Joseph Helander), a death cult (C.A. Holmboe) or were an expression of hunting magic (J.G. Frazer).[143] The Swedish archaeologist Oscar Almgren (1869-1945) was the first to make a synthesis of various interpretations. Starting from the conviction that many petroglyph scenes rendered cultic rituals, he used comparative cultural analysis as a tool to interpret rock art. For example, he highlighted the similarities between the Scandinavian petroglyphs featuring boats carrying solar symbols and the Egyptian paintings and carvings illustrating the night journeys of the sun god Re on his barque through the netherworld.[144] Almgren put this and other interpretations of various scenes in the context of a comprehensive fertility cult which he claimed had been brought by agricultural-ists migrating from the south. For Almgren, the supposed death cult and hunting magic were aspects of an all-embracing fertility cult. Almgren believed that the petroglyphs had been created by farmers close to their fields and settlements to invoke the protection of the gods and foster fertility.[145] Almgren's interpretative approach,

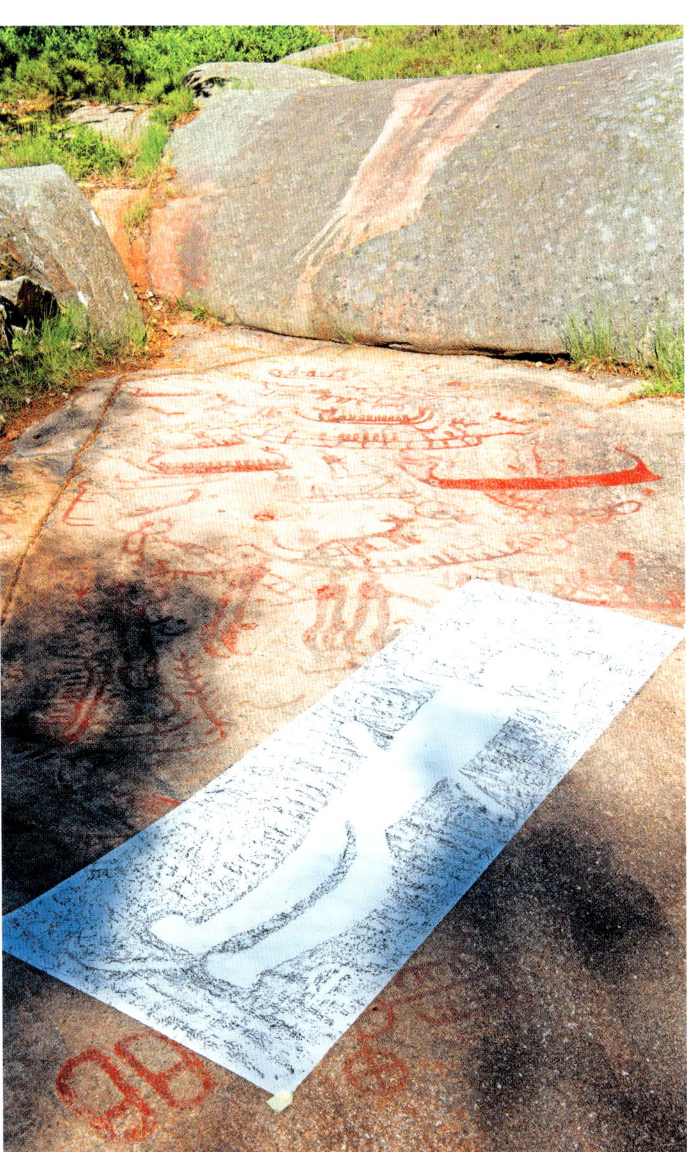

161. Rubbing on paper (206 × 69 cm) made in situ of the so-called 'cobbler' at Backa Brastad, in fact the petroglyph of a late Bronze Age warrior. Bohuslän, south-western Sweden. Photo 2021.

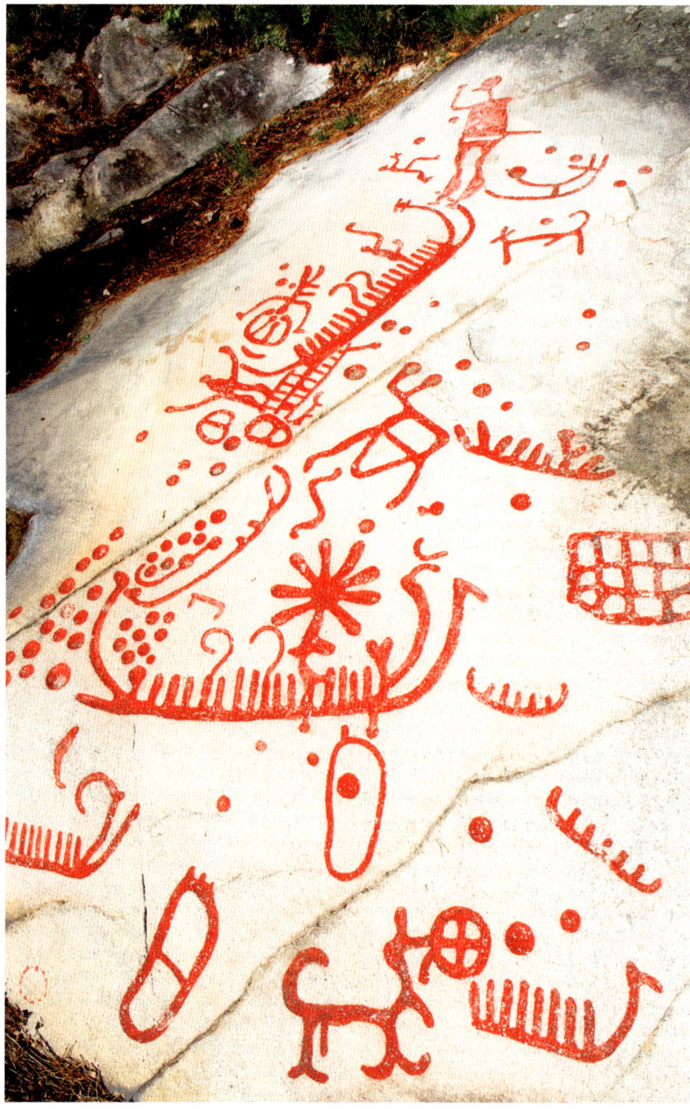

162. In the centre, a small deer standing in a boat carries a radiating sun, and below a hybrid animal consisting of a horse with the tail of a dog lifts a solar disc onto a ship with its snout. Bronze Age, Massleberg, Bohuslän, south-western Sweden. Photo 2021.

which put petroglyphs into the context of ancient worldviews, and the application of comparative cultural analysis have remained relevant up to the present, all the more so as it became apparent that the Bronze Age people of Bohuslän were in contact with cultures of Western and Central Europe and the Mediterranean, thanks to a lively trade in raw materials such as metals and amber.

However, Almgren overestimated the land-based agrarian factor and underestimated the maritime orientation of the Bronze Age economy, since he saw the boats and ships in the petroglyphs only in cosmological terms and not as factual depictions from a maritime society. The petroglyphs speak clearly for themselves, given that the 27 ard ploughs and the few domestic animals rendered in Bohuslän and Østfold are vastly outnumbered by no

fewer than 11,240 images of boats and ships.[146] The economy along the coast was neither purely agro-pastoral nor purely maritime; agriculture, pastoralism and, to a lesser degree, hunting played an important role, but the economy also relied on fishing and maritime trade. Moreover, as will be explained, the makers of petroglyphs were most probably more closely associated with the elite which controlled trade than with the peasant stratum. Some later interpretations of Bohuslän's petroglyphs have taken a semiotic approach, claiming that they express not a kind of magic communication of humans with deities, but a communication between humans.[147] Finally, following the end of the Cold War and the prevalence of a utopian belief in a conflict-free future that led to a refusal to accept war as a historical norm, the role of warfare and conflictual migration was downplayed not only in historiography and archaeology, but also in the interpretation of petroglyphs. The interpretation of battle scenes and weapons as illustrations of real events and killing tools was considered taboo, and they were understood as ritual mock fights and dummy weapons for parade purposes. In a nutshell, contemporary welfare society tried to ignore the phenomenon of warfare. When applied to all conflict scenes in petroglyphs, this approach is too rigid.

In southern Scandinavia, the agrarian Neolithization took place after the introduction of ceramics at the turn of the sixth to fifth millennium BCE. Whereas the dissemination of ceramics occurred when the local people acquired the knowledge of pottery from the north through trade contacts, agriculture spread as a consequence of migration from the south. It was around 6000 to 5000 BCE that several sizable groups of early farmers coming from the Near East arrived in what are now Hungary, Spain and Germany, which led to a substantial flow of Near Eastern genetic heritage into the gene pool of European Mesolithic hunter-gatherers and thus to a population replacement.[148] At first, the southern Scandinavian late Mesolithic hunter-gatherers adopted a few Neolithic tools, but not farming.[149] Within a few centuries after 4000 BCE, agriculturists migrated from Germany to southern Scandinavia where agriculture and the material elements of the north-central European **Funnel Beaker culture** (4300–2800 BCE) rapidly spread.[150] 'Farming practices were brought to northern Europe by a group of people that were genetically distinct from resident hunter-gatherers.'[151] Later, a second wave of Neolithization occurred in the second half of the third millennium BCE when farming was introduced northward along the Norwegian Atlantic coast as far as about 100 kilometres south of the Arctic Circle.[152] The introduction of agrarian technology was a major addition to the traditional strategies of hunting and gathering for food provision.

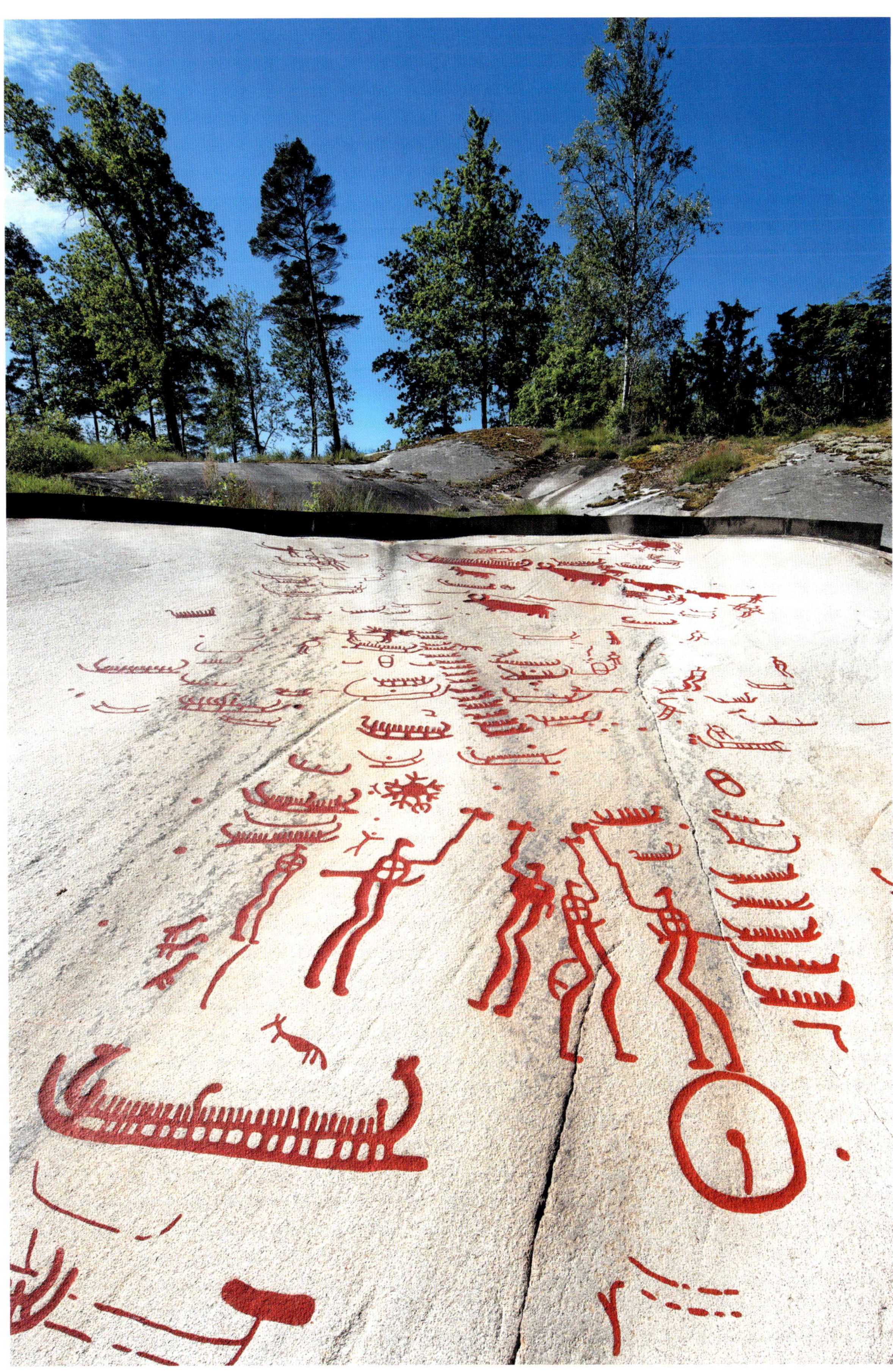

163. The largest petroglyph area at Aspeberget. From bottom to top: a ship with two helmsmen and thirty crew members, four warriors brandishing axes, ships stacked on top of each other, a ploughing and a herding scene and a solar disc. Bronze Age, Bohuslän, south-western Sweden. Photo 2021.

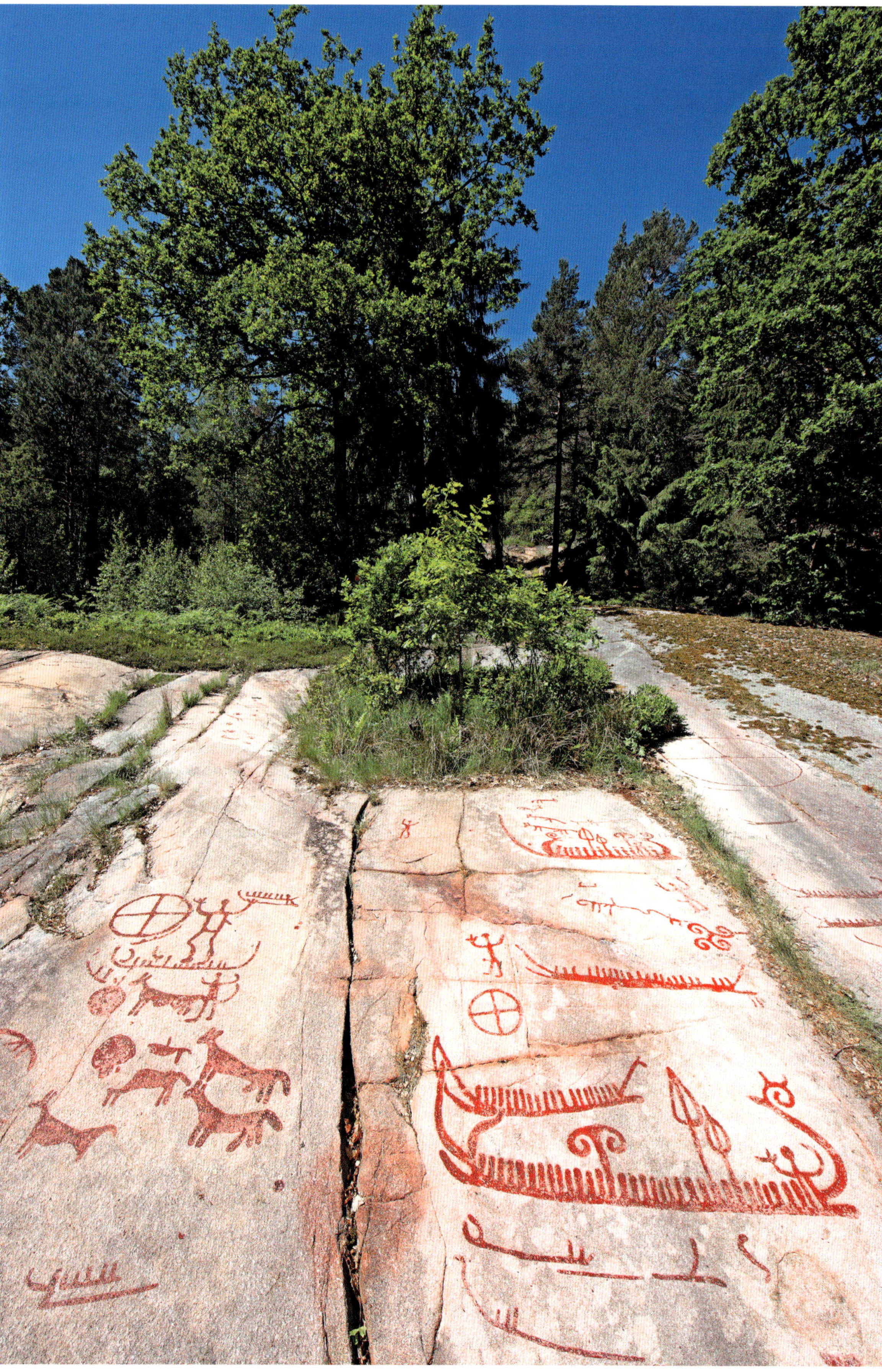

164. In the right half of the main panel of *Åbyhällen* are two ships with large crews and huge ceremonial axes and lances; in the left half a man standing on a boat lifts a small boat, probably a model. Bohuslän, south-western Sweden. Photo 2021.

This significant increase in available and storable foodstuffs not only provided surpluses, but allowed for an increased division of labour and long-distance trading which in turn generated new cultural contacts and stimuli.

As already mentioned, a second, massive wave of immigration from the east, from the Pontic–Caspian Steppes, impacted Europe in the course of the third millennium BCE. This second population replacement added to the existing gene pool of ancient Western and Central European hunter-gatherers and Near Eastern farmers a third element, namely that of the carriers of the Yamnaya steppe culture which also included gene heritage from the Caucasus.[153] From this genetic and cultural influx resulted the widespread **Corded Ware culture** which extended from mid Scandinavia in the north as far as the Alps in the south and from today's Netherlands in the west to the Volga in the east. The Corded Ware culture, which is named after a pottery decoration, is known in southern Scandinavia and southern Finland as **Battle Axe culture** (*ca.* 2800–2300 BCE).

This name refers to a funerary gender distinction whereby battle axes were only placed in male burials and amber necklaces only in female ones.[154] The Yamnaya immigrants not only brought their metallurgical skills, their worldview and mythological heritage to Europe, but also their Proto-Indo-European languages, as they did in their eastward migration to Central Asia. The Neolithic farmers of Western and Central Europe would not previously have spoken Indo-European languages.[155] Another far-reaching consequence of the introduction of farming into southern Scandinavia was the clearing of forests to create agricultural land and pastures in order to sustain a growing population. The construction of houses and ships as well as the demands of metallurgy put additional pressure on forests.

The concentration of petroglyph sites in Bohuslän and Østfold is incredibly dense, and several sites consist of hundreds of single images which is why only the most important ones are listed below, in order from south to north:[156]

Bohuslän

- **Backa,** near **Brastad**, consists of three sites a few hundred metres apart. Famous are the aforementioned 'cobbler' who represents an idealized late Bronze Age warrior wielding an axe (fig. 161), ships with horse-headed prows and chariots carrying solar symbols.

- **Lökeberg** lies today in a forest clearing and has numerous petroglyphs of boats and ships. The largest ship measures 138 cm and carries a crew of 31 or 62 rowers and two steersmen.[157] There are also several footprints and, very unusually, a coniferous tree 91 cm high.

- **Åbyhällen** has more than a dozen petroglyphs featuring large ships up to 230 cm long. On several ships huge ceremonial axes and spears are set vertically, indicating that these are warships (fig. 164). Also striking are the petroglyphs illustrating a scene of bestiality between a male anthropomorph and a mare, and a procession of five adorants.

- **Kallsängen** is one single small boulder featuring the unusual figures of five winged male hybrids with birds' heads (or masks). One of them is double-headed, another sodomizes a mare. Another scene features a pack of hunting wolves.

- **Torsbo** is a large site consisting of several granite boulders featuring numerous ships, of which the longest measures 4.5 metres and carries the unlikely number of 70 or even 140 rowers. There are petroglyphs of, unusually, a *Taxus baccata* (common yew), acrobats and armed men with pronounced calves.

- **Södra Ödsmål**. Here there are two rare scenes of fishing from boats. The disproportion between the economic importance of fishing in the Bronze Age and the scarcity of fishing scenes in petroglyphs indicates that fishing was either a low-prestige activity or it was symbolically included in the countless ship images.

- **Sötetorp** consists of two huge boulders. Striking are the scenes of an acrobat making a somersault over a ship steered by two helmsmen wearing horned helmets (fig. 184) and of a large fishing net held by two ships.

- **Lövåsen** also features at least two acrobatic scenes involving ships. Notable is the petroglyph of a ship where a tall helmsman with marked calves and wearing a horned helmet commands a crew of seven paddlers who lift their paddles (or spears) (fig. 171).

- **Gerum**. Famous scenes here are a maypole dance as at Cape Swan at Lake Onega, and a hunting scene where two hunters and seven dogs encircle a deer.

- **Kalleby** (Tanum 248)[158] is a small site with a spectacular scene in which three men wearing horned helmets (or masks) blow lurs, that is bronze horns, which were up to two metres long; above them stand two warriors with large calves (figs 165, 166). Lurs were sounded during rituals and have been found in pairs in bogs.

- **Trättelanda**. Here there is a unique petroglyph of a so-called goblin. His very long arms are stretched out above his body which has the shape of a honeycombed net (fig. 173).

- **Litsleby** (Tanum 75) is a large boulder with the famous, 235-cm-tall 'Spear God' who holds a spear 195 cm long (fig. 188). In fact, he represents a late Bronze Age hero-warrior. Noteworthy are also two ships 190 cm long with solar symbols at bow and stern.

- **Tegneby** (Tanum 72) lies on a small hill in a forest. The small panel from the early Iron Age illustrates a unique battle between two groups of horsemen armed with spears and rectangular shields (fig. 189). Whereas shields were

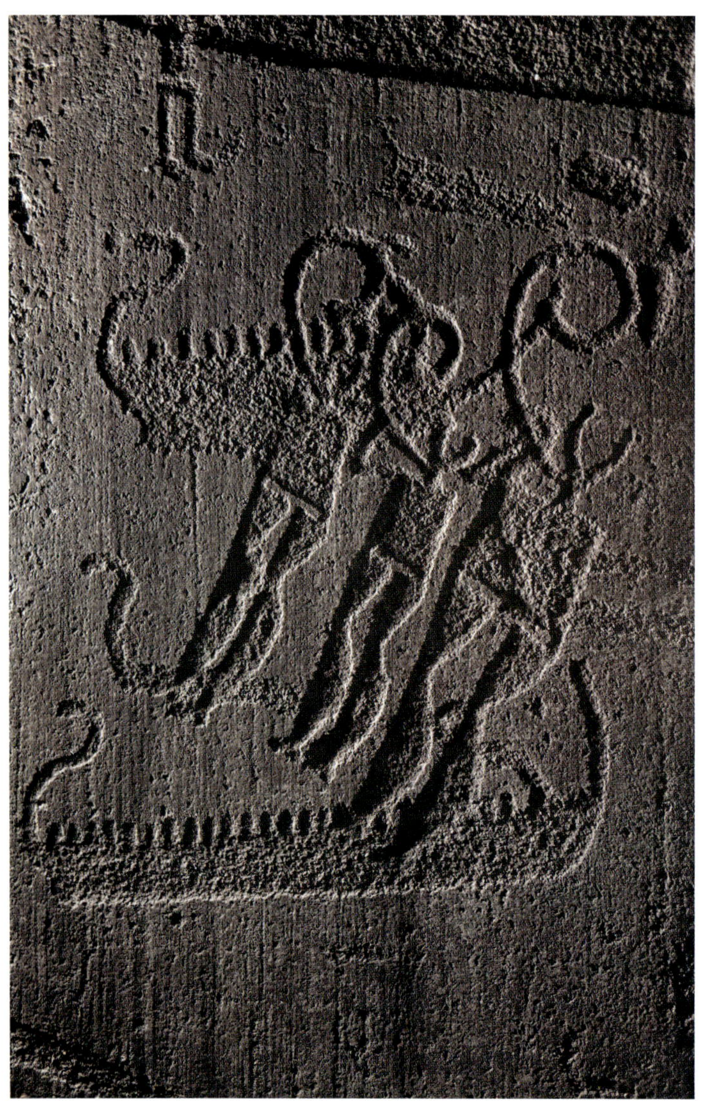

165. The petroglyphs of three men with powerful calves who are blowing the lur are superimposed on three ships. Bronze Age, Kalleby, Bohuslän, south-western Sweden. Night photo 2021.

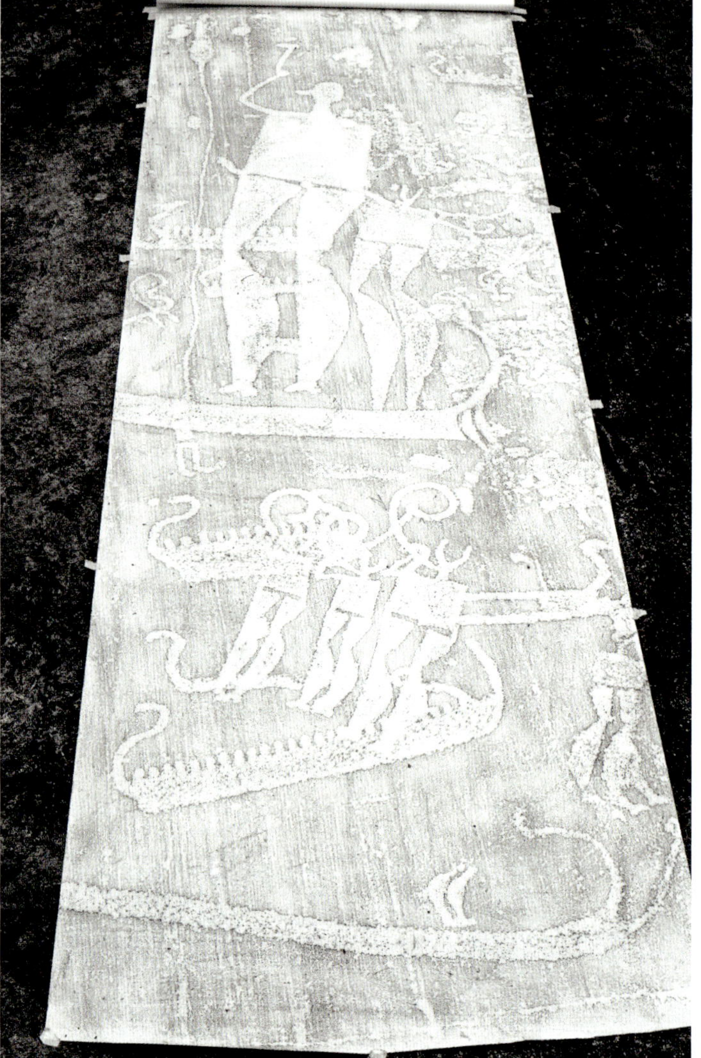

166. Rubbing (180 × 92 cm) made *in situ* from the main panel at Kalleby. Above, two men with powerful calves stand above a ship; the taller holds a lance. Below, three men blowing lurs are superimposed on three ships. Bohuslän, south-western Sweden. Photo 2021.

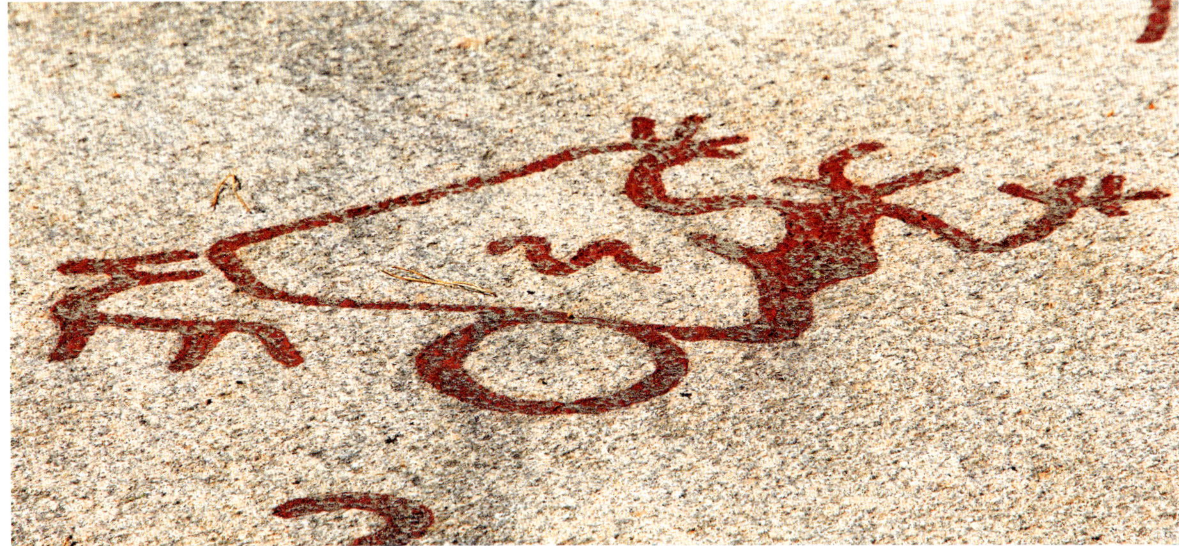

167. A man wearing a horned bird mask drives a single-axle chariot pulled by a horse. Bronze Age, Vitlycke, Bohuslän, south-western Sweden. Photo 2021.

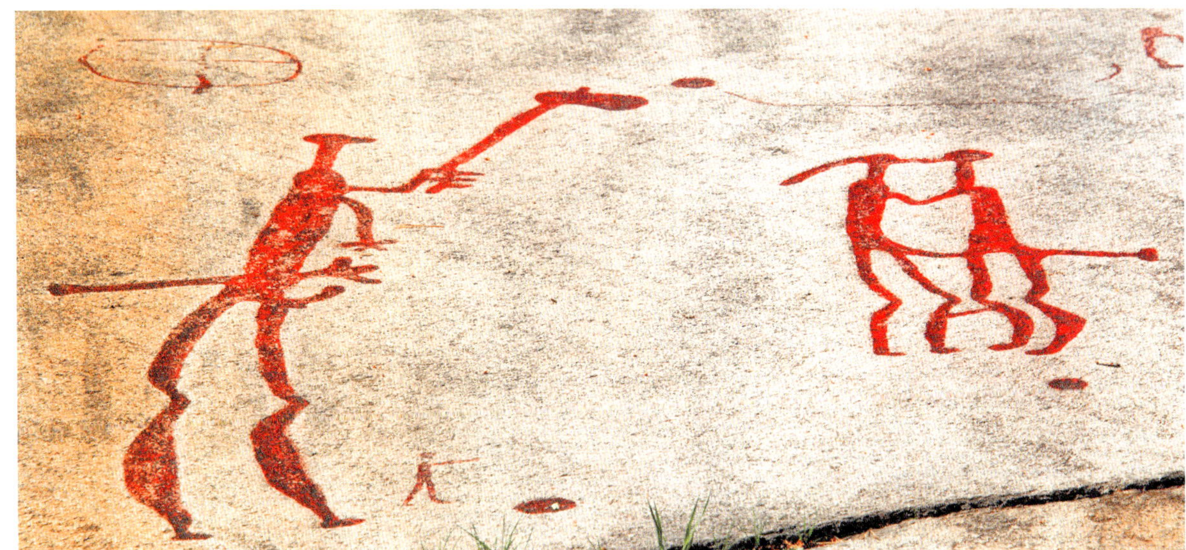

168. In this small scene, an erotic couple is either threatened or protected by a warrior with huge calves who brandishes an axe and is girded with a sword. Bronze Age, Vitlycke, Bohuslän, south-western Sweden. Photo 2021.

rectangular in the early Iron Age and relatively small for horsemen, they were circular in the Bronze Age and of large size, as seen at the southern site of Aspeberget T 18 and Finntorp. In other renderings, the small shield forms part of the warrior's body, as at the main site of Aspeberget.

- **Aspeberget** is the largest complex in Bohuslän and consists of five sites (fig. 163). There are countless boats and ships, solar symbols, a ploughing scene, domestic bulls, men brandishing battle axes, duels, two-axled chariots, and a group of eleven dancing (?) men.

- **Greby**. On two ships an adorant with raised arms is standing, which seems to illustrate a special ritual.

- **Finntorp**. Striking are a duel between a shield-bearer wielding a lance and a man brandishing an axe, a net or map, and a ploughing scene with an ard.

- **Vitlycke** consists of a highly interesting, huge granite boulder and some smaller panels hidden in the forest. Today, the site is 5 km from the sea, but in the Bronze Age it was only 65 m (figs 167, 168). The main scenes are confrontations between armed men, ships, possibly a naval battle, an embracing couple, a whale, a lur player, a man wearing a horned bird mask who drives a single-axle chariot pulled by a horse and who may represent a precursor of Týr, god of the sky and thunder. Another singular scene shows a woman mourning a man lying on the ground. Four-wheeled vehicles

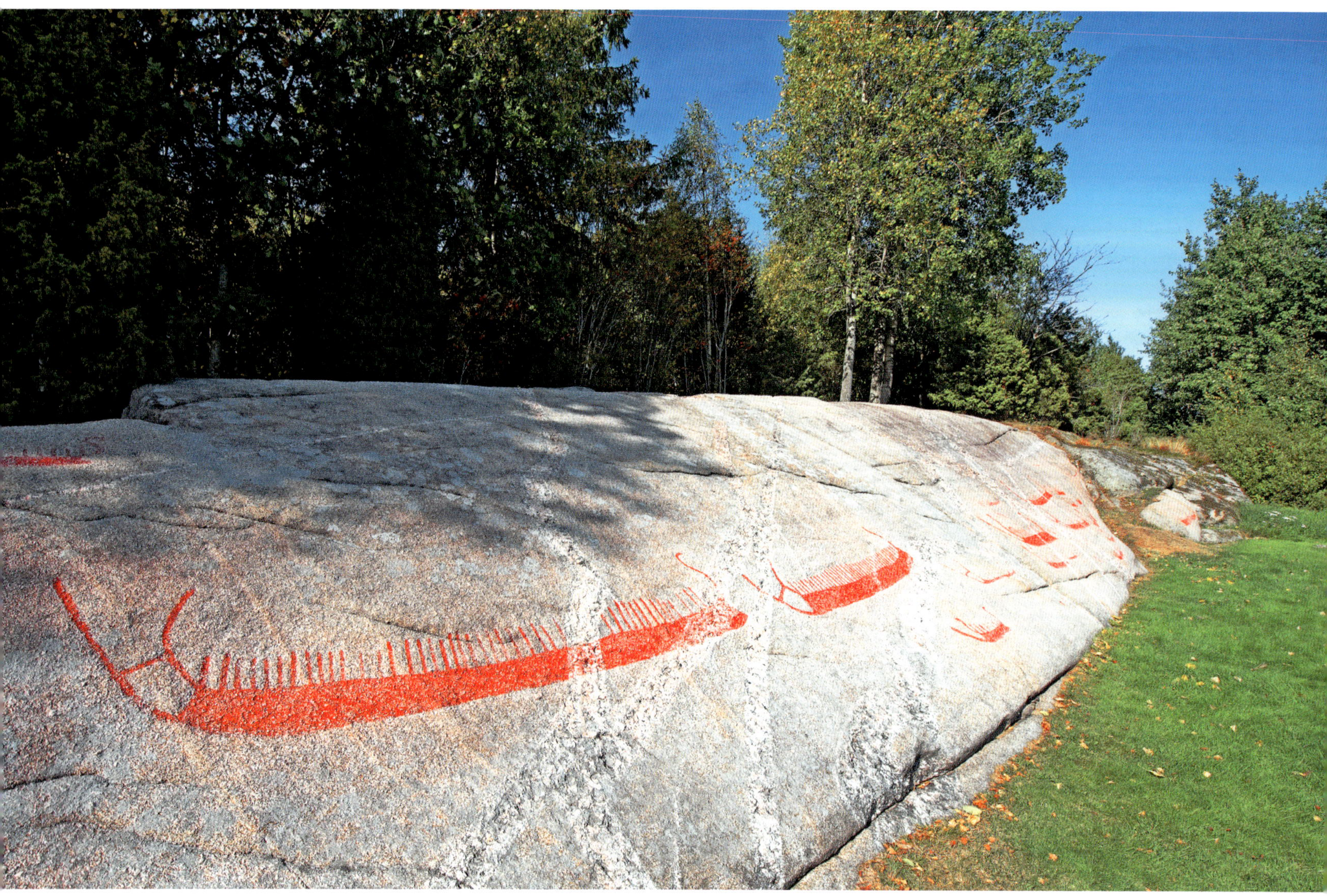

169. The huge boulder of Horness in Østfold has 22 petroglyphs of ships; the largest one is 3 m long. Southern Norway. Photo 2022.

were certainly used during the Bronze Age while single-axle chariots were probably used in parades.

- **Fossum** and **Balken**. Fossum lies five kilometres north-east of Vitlycke and was never at the seashore. On the huge principal granite boulder there are several conflict scenes, lur blowers, duels between two men armed with battle axes and standing on ships, a hunting scene, a sun surrounded by birds (?) and a boat carrying storage vessels (figs 179, 180). At nearby Balken is the famous petroglyph of a horse pulling the sun (fig. 181).

- **Massleberg** and **Jörlov** are 27 km north of Fossum. At Massleberg, a scene shows two men standing on a ship who

are engaged in a duel with spears over the possession of a woman (fig. 185). There are also dogs attacking a stag, a man holding on his raised arms a ship (or the model of a ship) with 40 crew members (fig. 176), and a ship carrying a small deer above whose head features a sun (fig. 162). About one km away lies Jörlov where ships, hybrid animals and a sledge are pecked into two boulders.

- **Torp Hogdal**. This single boulder stands in a private garden. Here, among other images, two seafarers stand on the deck of a ship and, armed with spears and flails, fight off the attacks of three men.

Østfold

- **Horness** lies 28 kilometres north of Massleberg. At least 22 ships are pecked into a long granite boulder; the largest is 3 metres long and carries 47 or possibly 94 seamen (fig. 169).

- **Solberg** is 500 metres east of Horness. There are petroglyphs of ships, three double-axle wagons, armed men, horses, birds and numerous cup marks.

- **Begby** consists of a large complex and a smaller site; all are located in a forest of conifers and larches. At the top of one high boulder there is a pothole. When it fills with rain, water flows down towards the ships engraved further down and they appear to be floating in water (fig. 177). As in other petroglyph sites, this micro-landscape replicated the surrounding macro-landscape. On all the boulders ships predominate; there are also several single-axle chariots, one of which is transported on a boat, and armed men; another man seems to wear ice skates.

- **Bjørnstadskipet.** The longest ship of Fennoscandia is pecked here. It measures 4.6 metres and carries 50 seamen commanded by the captain standing at the bow and the helmsman at the stern.[159] While no such ship has yet been excavated in Sweden nor Norway, a similar ship was discovered in Denmark at Hjortspring dating from *ca.* 400/300 BCE which carried about 24 seamen. This vessel, a canoe 21 metres long, was made from sawn wooden planks and follows the typical Bronze Age tradition of boat building as is seen on the Rørby sword.[160]

- **Kalnes.** On this boulder are depicted at least 21 ships; on nine of them the paddlers lift their paddles (fig. 175). Over or close to three of the ships there is a solar symbol, suggesting a close relationship between ship and sun.

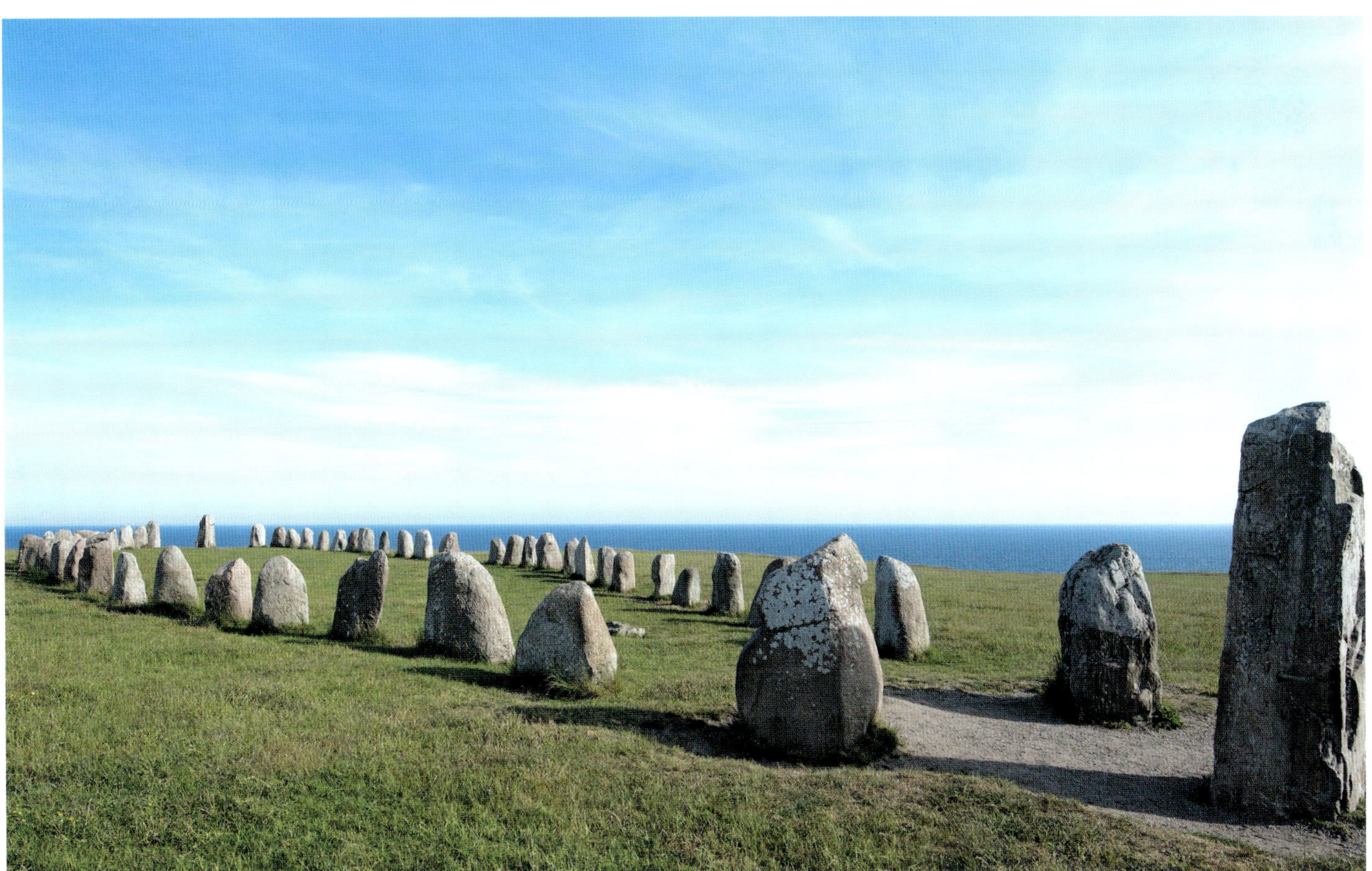

170. Megalithic monument 67 m long in the shape of a ship at Ales Stenar; in the background the Baltic Sea. The monument was erected in connection with a cremation and also had astronomic functions, since the stones are positioned in such a way that, viewed from the longitudinal axis, the sun sets exactly behind the front bow menhir at the summer solstice and rises behind the stern menhir at the winter solstice. While Ales Stenar was erected around 600 CE, like the majority of such ship-shaped monuments, the earliest examples date from the later Bronze Age. Skåne, southern Sweden. Photo 2021.

Bohuslän and Østfold are not only very rich in petroglyphs, there are also dozens of cairns and kurgans (tumulus tombs), tombs marked by menhirs, stone labyrinths and ship settings. The latter are graves or cremation burials which were surrounded by slabs or stones in the shape of boats or ships.[161] Their size varies in southern Scandinavia from a couple of metres to 67 metres for the Ales Stenar ship setting at Kåseberga in Skåne in southern Sweden (fig. 170). All these monuments date from the Bronze Age to the Middle Ages.

The specific evolution of Bronze Age and early Iron Age petroglyphs in Bohuslän and Østfold is closely linked to the region's economic development which brought about a flourishing of trade and contacts with non-Scandinavian cultures. Whereas the Bronze Age began in the Mediterranean region around or shortly before 3000 BCE and in the temperate zones of Europe around 2300 BCE, in southern Sweden it began only around 1750 BCE. Bronze objects had first been introduced to southern Scandinavia by the mobile carriers of the **Bell Beaker culture** (*ca.* 2800–1800 BCE).[162] Initially, bronze had been made from copper and arsenic or lead, but as of 2000 BCE tin bronze spread rapidly through Central and Western Europe, and soon after to southern Scandinavia. However, since it lacked tin and had only little copper which was not mined, southern Scandinavia had to import either finished bronze objects, bronze ingots or the requisite metals. Analysis of its chemical composition, and lead isotope analysis of southern Scandinavian bronze objects has been able to pinpoint the provenance of the raw materials sourced over a period of 1,200 years from various distant places.

- In the **first period** (to 1600 cal. BCE), Scandinavia sourced its copper mainly from northern Tyrol in the Austrian Alps; a secondary source of copper as well as of alloyed ingots and finished products was the British Isles. The import of finished goods is reflected in the petroglyphs of Simrishamn in Skåne, which represent 'two Anglo-Irish inspired flange axes' dated 2000–1700 BCE and axes of the Arreton type known from Stonehenge, 1750–1500 cal. BCE.[163] Contacts also existed with the Carpathian Mountains where high-quality bronze weapons and tools were produced.[164]

- The **second period** (1600–1300 cal. BCE) witnessed a change of suppliers, for most of the copper now came from Cyprus and Greece, and northern and southern Iberia, with only

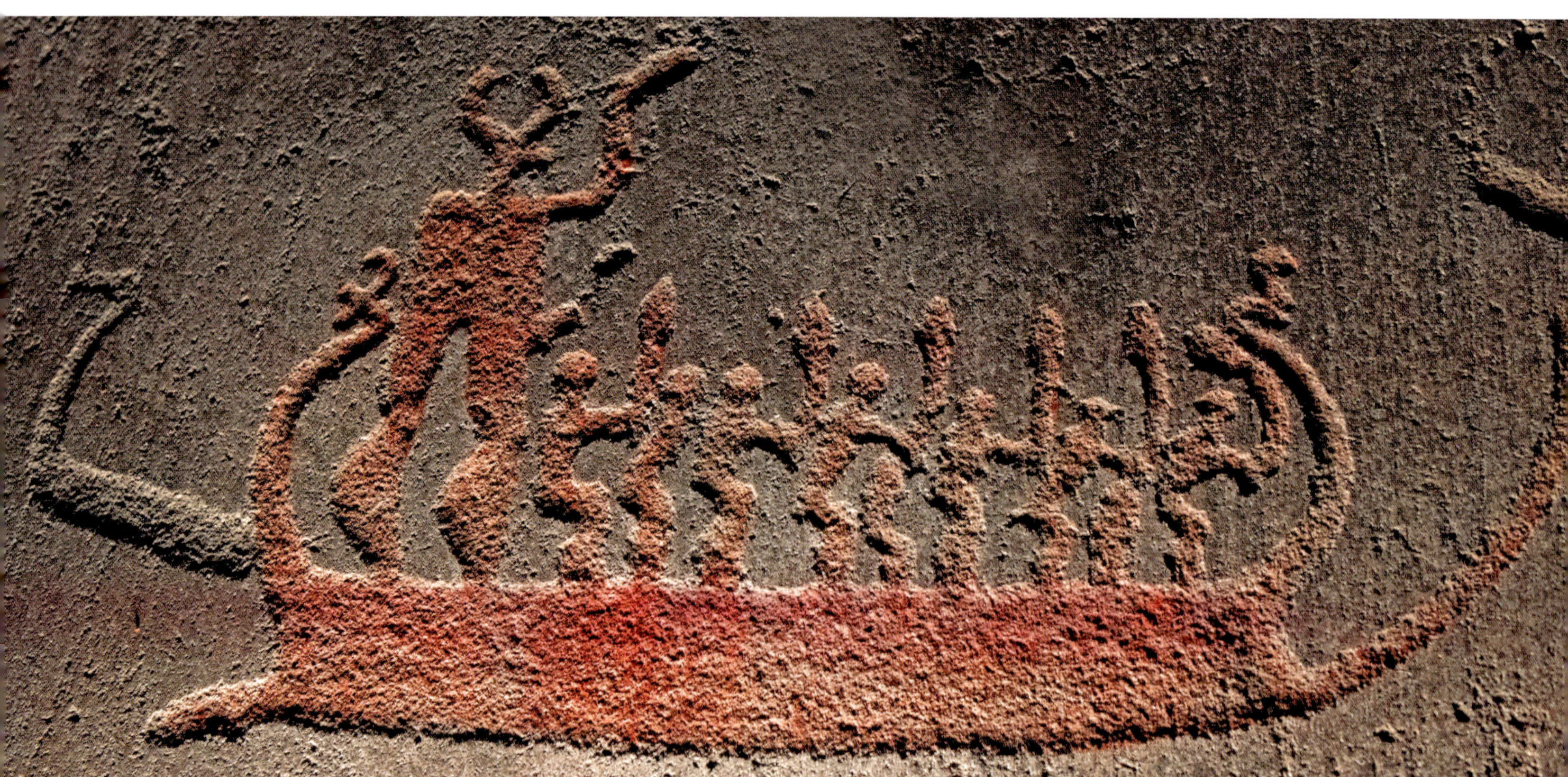

171. A helmsman with strong calves and wearing a horned helmet directs a crew of seven, or possibly nine seamen who lift their paddles. Bronze Age, Lövåsen, Bohuslän, south-western Sweden. Night photo 2021.

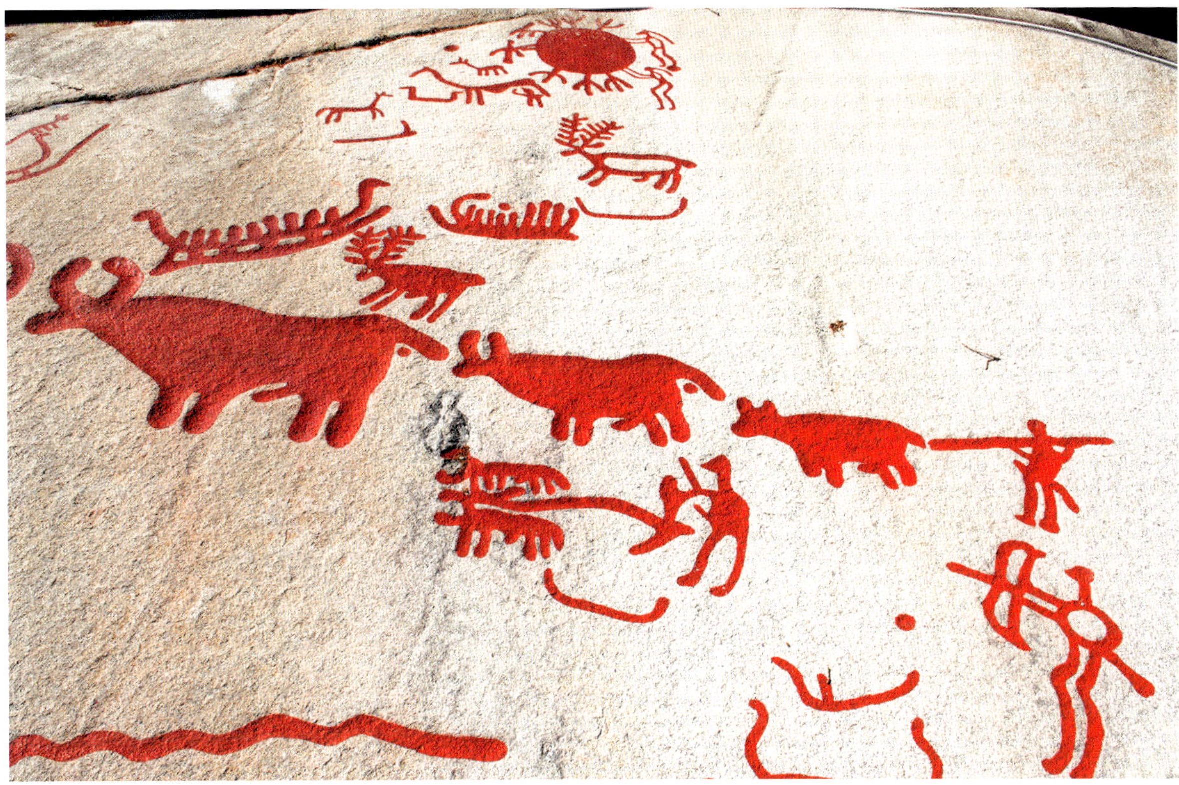

172. At the top, two humans with long hair, most likely women, touch the sun in an adorant position while eight birds surround it. Below, a herding and a ploughing scene illustrate the agrarian and pastoral aspects of the local Bronze Age economy. Detail from the main panel at Aspeberget. Bronze Age, Bohuslän, south-western Sweden. Photo 2021.

small proportions from Wales, the Alps and Sardinia.[165] The main export of Scandinavia was Baltic amber (a fossilized resin of conifers), as is suggested by the numerous finds of amber jewellery in the Aegean and the Near East, notably in Greece, Syria, Iraq and Egypt where Baltic amber beads were part of the breast ornament of the Pharaoh Tutankhamun (r. *ca*. 1333–1324 BCE).[166] Other Scandinavian export items, such as hides, furs and probably women, were perishable and left no archaeological traces. On the other hand, southern Scandinavia also acquired glass beads from Egypt and the Near East.[167] The maritime route followed the Iberian coast to reach the Atlantic and then led northward to the British Islands and Scandinavia. A second route led to southern France from where it headed overland to the River Garonne and then continued to the Atlantic. These new cultural contacts were again reflected in petroglyphs, first in the images at Torsbo and Norrköping (eastern Sweden) of ships loaded with 'oxhide ingots'[168] which look identical to contemporary ingots weighing 20–30 kilogrammes from Crete dating to the Late Minoan Period I (1700–1470 BCE). The cultural influence from the Mediterranean appears in other new rock art motifs such as acrobats, horse-drawn battle chariots, long swords, and scenes expressing a solar mythology such as the sun travelling at night on its barque. Glass beads from Egypt and

Mesopotamia found in south Scandinavian tombs are further indications of these far-reaching contacts.[169]

- In the **third period** (1300–550/500 cal. BCE), for the first 200 years Sardinia and Iberia were equally involved in copper exports to the north, while the Cypriot supply stopped, probably as a consequence of the activities of the Sea People which disrupted maritime trade.[170] Then, from 1100 to 900 BCE, this export business in copper and also tin was dominated by Iberia, followed by the Tyrolian Alps. Towards the end of this period, the Alpine regions became once more the prime supplier of copper and ingots, followed by Iberia and Sardinia. One of the most spectacular visual signs of the contacts between the western Mediterranean and southern Scandinavia are the representations of warriors or leaders wearing horned helmets, seen both in Scandinavian petroglyphs and metal figurines and in Nuragic (Sardinian) stone statuettes (fig. 183).[171]

Rarer than copper was tin, and specifically its main ore cassiterite, whose main deposits were located in Cornwall (England), Brittany (France), Galicia (Spain) and Erzgebirge and Fichtelgebirge (Germany). The gold found in southern Scandinavia came from Ireland.[172] It was the presence of the raw materials required for the production of quality bronze, copper and tin, in

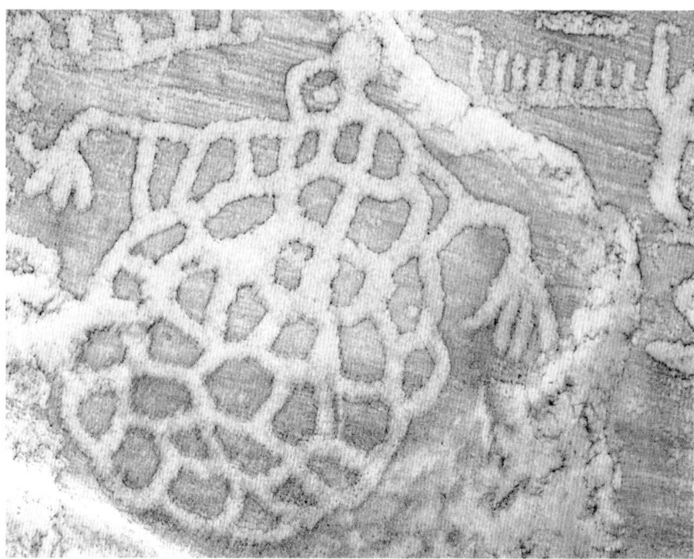

173. Cutout of a rubbing (196 × 97 cm) of the so-called goblin of Trättelanda in Bohuslän. The mysterious creature has a tiny head and its arms are stretched over its body which looks like a net. Bronze Age, south-western Sweden. Rubbing 2021.

southern England and Brittany[173] that turned the former island of Thanet at the easternmost tip of Kent into an important Bronze Age trading hub. Here both key trading goods, small bronze ingots and amber, have been excavated. The island was perfectly located for access to England and Brittany, and midway along the route from Iberia to Scandinavia. Analysis of strontium and oxygen isotope signatures in late Bronze Age human bones from Thanet has revealed, besides local people from Kent, individuals originating from southern Sweden and Norway as well as from the western Mediterranean. It became apparent that the late Bronze Age population of Thanet 'was dominated by migrants, some of whom had moved between two locations only to be buried in a third'.[174] Another trading hub for the coveted tin was the Island of Ictis. The Greek historian Diodorus Siculus (1st century BCE) wrote in his *Library of Histories*:

Then they [the people of Belerium, that is today's Cornwall] work the tin into pieces the size of knuckle-bones and convey it to an island which lies off Britain and is called Ictis; for at the time of ebb-tide the space between this island and the mainland becomes dry and they can take the tin in large quantities over to the island on their wagons ... On the island of Ictis the merchants purchase the tin of the natives and carry it from there across the Strait to Galatia or Gaul.[175]

The exact location of Ictis is unknown, the most plausible candidates being the tidal island Saint Michael's Mount in Cornwall and the Mount Batten peninsula in the Plymouth Sound.[176] These

findings strongly suggest that maritime trade was carried out via long-distance voyages across the open sea, rather than following the coast in short stages and with changes of crew. Probably, the Scandinavian seafarers travelled as far as Thanet and Ictis where they met traders from Iberia who in turn were in intensive contact with Mediterranean merchants. A second metal trade hub existed in the Carpathian Mountains, as some of the Cypriot copper was exported northward via Greece to the Carpathians and from there to Germany and Scandinavia.[177] Thus, during the European Bronze Age different cultures thousands of kilometres apart were directly or indirectly interconnected by the trade in metals and amber. Changes in petroglyphs went roughly in tandem with specific cultural developments in the metal-supplying regions. Yet it would certainly be an exaggeration to hypothesize a pan-European culture based on metal trade.

The food surplus generated by agriculture allowed not only for the division of labour, in other words the emergence of traders, but also the accumulation of wealth which could be invested in mercantile operations. Trading in metals required capital which had to be invested and remained tied up for months or even years. Since the risks involved in such long-distance trade, such as shipwreck, piracy or robbery, were great, margins and profits had to be high as well. This build-up of wealth led to economic and social inequalities as well as the emergence of a hierarchically stratified society which replaced the previous, rather egalitarian social organization made up of self-sufficient households.[178] And because both the new wealth and the trading journeys needed protection from theft and robbery, traders had to either arm themselves or engage the services of warriors. That life was not peaceful in the Northern European Bronze Age is best exemplified by the archaeological findings at the battleground of Tollense, northern Germany. In that battle, which took place around 1250 BCE, at least 150 to 500 combatants were killed. Since numerous casualties showed scars of older, healed wounds, it is clear that these men were war veterans. Results from recent research which analysed the different types of weapons used in this battle – mainly arrowheads – indicate that in the battle a local party fought against an incoming force of non-local, southern Central European origin. Since the majority of arrowheads which had perforated bones were locally made, it is probable that the local defenders prevailed over the attackers coming from a southern region.[179] Extrapolating from petroglyphs featuring armed helmsmen and duels taking place on ships as well as images glorifying armed men, one can conclude that there existed in southern Scandinavia an armed elite which controlled the surplus wealth as well as the trade in amber and metal.[180] It also regulated the local manufacture and sale of the coveted bronze products, including the distribution of metal weapons. It was most probably this elite class which was associated with the making of petroglyphs, rather than farmers or people involved in domestic work. It is no coincidence that images of ships appeared in southern Scandinavian petroglyphs at the same time as the import of bronze began.[181] The position and power of this mercantile social stratum depended on the control of bronze for whose acquisition seaworthy ships were essential. The sea, for its part, was both a means of transport and a larder. Nevertheless, agriculture and pastoralism kept their economic importance, something that is implied by the (relatively few) petroglyphs featuring ploughing scenes and bulls, as at Aspeberget and Finntorp. A unique composition on the smaller, southern panel of Aspeberget named Tanum 25 combines the motifs of ship and bull in one image, since the small bull's head has the shape of a ship.[182] In other petroglyphs, the antlers of a reindeer look like a boat. Rare petroglyphs like this, of a reindeer with boat-like antlers, invert the more widespread image of a boat with a prow in the shape of a reindeer's or elk's head.

With the spread of iron, whose ore is much more commonly found throughout Eurasia, the demand for copper and tin for the manufacture of weapons and tools declined rapidly; bronze remained in demand only for the manufacture of jewellery. The new metal was all the more attractive as the output from the Alpine copper mines had been declining since the ninth century BCE and the quality of bronze alloys worsened throughout northern Europe due to the use of tin with too high a lead content.[183] As iron prevailed, international trade between Scandinavia and the British Isles, Iberia and the Mediterranean came to a standstill. Soon after, the making of petroglyphs also slowed down and then stopped, possibly because the former trading elite lost the source of its business since iron ore, which has been called a 'democratic metal',[184] was locally available in most regions.

The immense number of petroglyphs in Bohuslän and Østfold depicting boats and ships leaves no doubt that the social class involved was maritime-orientated. All these boats and ships were either paddling or rowing vessels; the difference between the two

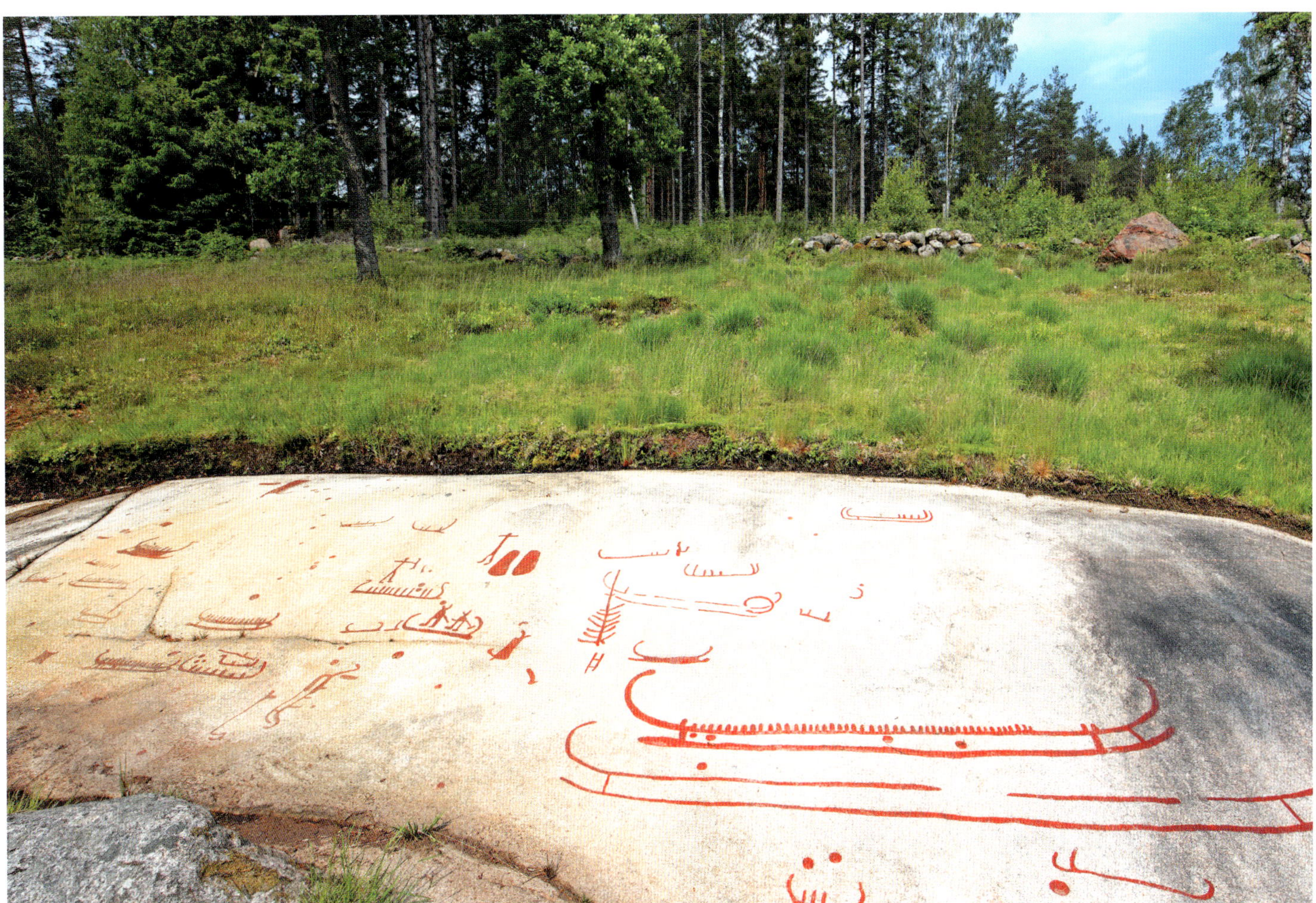

174. Partially unfinished petroglyphs of long ships, footprints and an evergreen tree. Stone 156 at Torsbo, Bohuslän, south-western Sweden. Photo 2021.

being that paddles are freely held by the seamen while oars are attached to the gunwale by a pivot. Rowers always sit in pairs, while paddlers using a single-blade paddle may sit or kneel in pairs and those using double-blade paddles sit or kneel one behind the other. Small boats were made from hide, larger ships from sewn wood planks, like the famous 21-metre-long Hjortspring ship. The Roman historian Tacitus left an interesting description of the north Germanic tribe of the Suiones who lived in southern Scandinavia:

The design of the ships is different from ours, in that the prow being at both ends makes it always ready to touch land with the front. It is not worked with sails, nor do they have an orderly row of oars on either side; the oars are free, as on some river ships, and can be swapped to one side or the other as required.[185]

Many ships rendered in the petroglyphs do indeed have prows at each end and on the larger ships there is a helmsman at each end which allowed for swift changes of direction at sea and for landing or departing from shore without having to turn. Like the Hjortspring ship, these Bronze Age ships had a steering oar at both ends and could navigate in both directions, which was a significant advantage in a fight.[186] With one exception at Järrestad, Skåne, ships are depicted in petroglyphs without sails.[187]

The majority of petroglyphs of ships are meant to illustrate real vessels – fishing boats, merchant vessels or war ships – while others had a symbolic meaning. The ship represented power and wealth, and possibly also knowledge of the world at large. In other, more significant petroglyphs, two warriors stand on a ship deck duelling each other, men lift up a ship in their hands, or ships carry a solar disc. Like other petroglyphs, the ship was

175. Rubbing (252 × 69 cm) of three rowing boats with seamen lifting their oars; in the centre a solar symbol. Bronze Age, Kalnes, Østfold, southern Norway. Rubbing 2022.

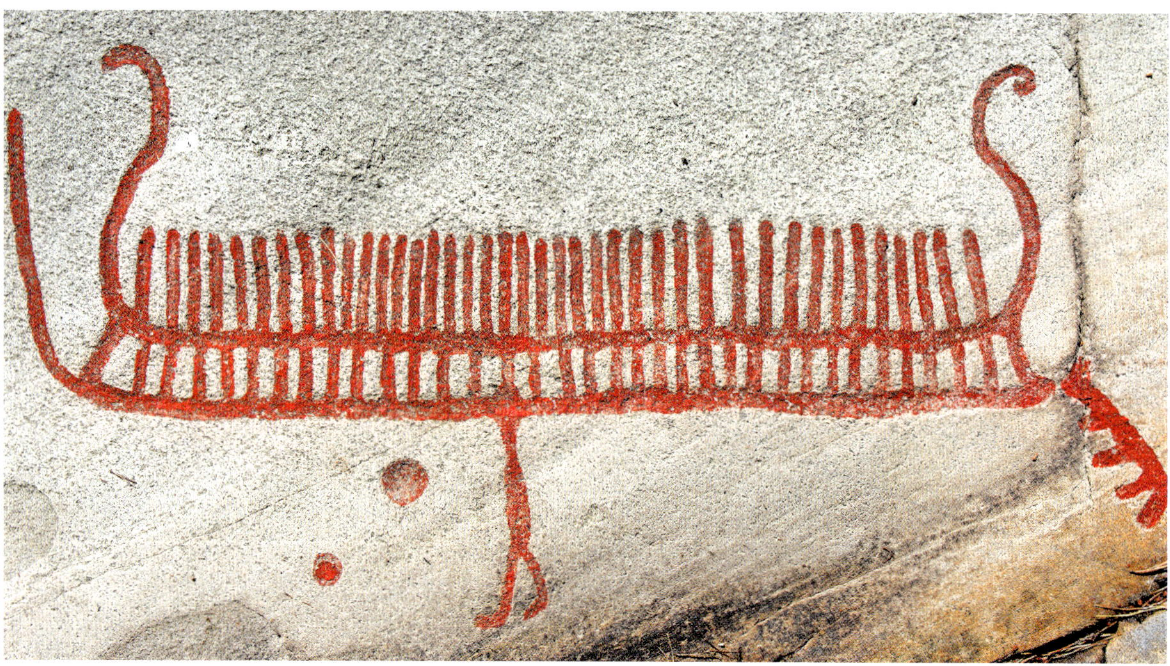

176. The petroglyph scene at Massleberg of a human carrying a ship with a crew of 40 seamen probably illustrates a tradition in which people carried model ships during an unknown ritual. A similar scene exists at Ekenberg, near Norrköping. Bohuslän, south-western Sweden. Photo 2021.

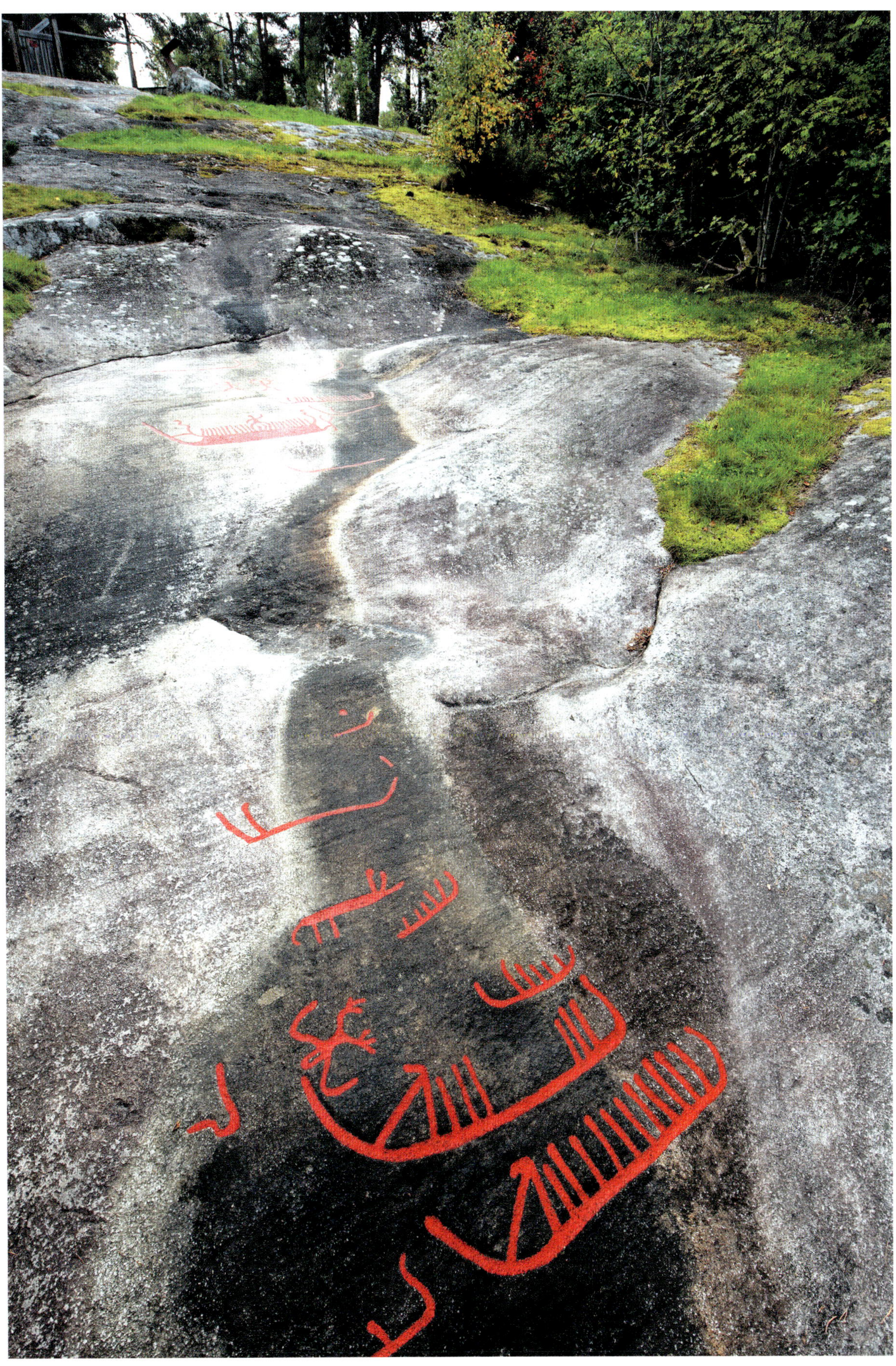

177. Petroglyphs representing ships. When the pothole at the top of the boulder is filled with rainwater, it flows down downhill and the engraved ships seem to float in water. Begby, Østfold, southern Norway. Photo 2022.

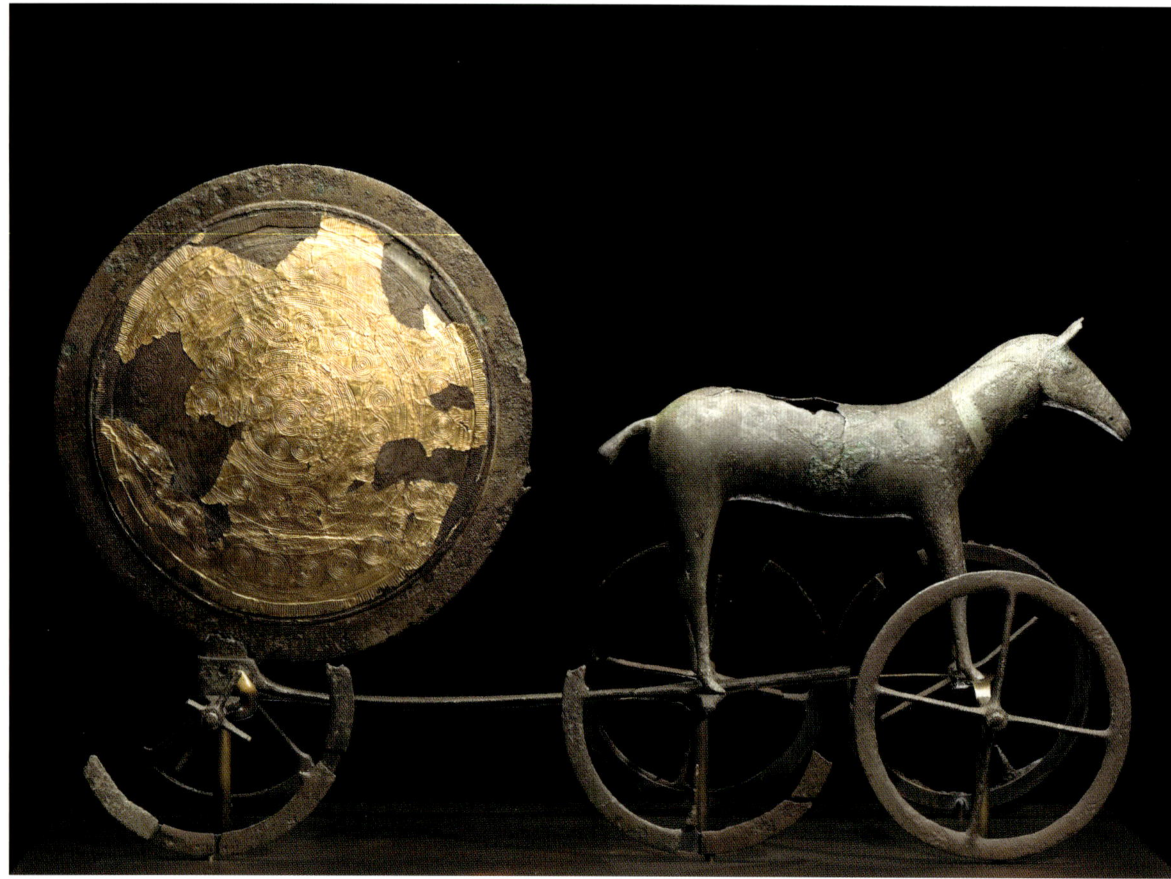

178. The Trundholm sun chariot, dated to *ca.* 1350 BCE. The composition represents the sun-horse pulling the shining sun through the firmament, since, seen from the northern hemisphere, the sun rises at the left, that is east, and disappears at the right, the west. Originally a band connected the neck of the horse with the solar disc. The six-wheeled, two-part carriage, 56 cm long, is not part of the mythical concept, but simply served to move the composition during a ritual or procession. Photo: CC BY-SA, Roberto Fortuna & Kira Ursem, The National Museum of Denmark, Copenhagen.

polysemantic, that is it communicated several meanings. The paramount importance of the ship within the worldview of Bronze Age southern Scandinavia is highlighted by the fact that ships were represented in very different ways, often in the context of burials. High-ranking individuals were buried in small wooden boats, or stone ship settings were erected over burials. Small models of ships made from clay or gold were given as grave goods. In the instance of a burial at Nors, Denmark, almost a hundred tiny boats made from shining gold sheet were placed into the grave. Finally, boats and ships were engraved on bronze razors which were burial gifts for males.

The possibilities for dating petroglyphs are unique in southern Scandinavia in that three different tools are available for establishing a chronology. These are the height above the shoreline, stylistic developments in the illustration of ships, and the evidence of bronze objects found in burials, mainly razor blades engraved with ships. It soon became apparent to specialists researching petroglyphs that the form of the ships, above all the design of their stems and the shape of their keel extensions, varied depending on the height above sea level, which made it possible to establish a chronology. The ship images at the highest altitudes,

that is the oldest petroglyphs from Montelius Period I, have high-raised stems which are clearly turned inward while the keel extensions are either horizontal or only slightly turned upwards. A petroglyph from Simris in Skåne and the ship engraved on the blade of the Rørby sword are perfect examples for this early type of ship.[188] In Periods II and III, at a slightly lower altitude, keel extensions tend to become longer and slightly higher, and in Period III horse-headed stems start to appear. In Period IV, the keel extension gains further in height and the horse- or waterfowl-headed prows become more stylized, but some ships still have inward-turning stems. Finally, in the late Bronze Age Periods V and VI, the keel extensions become very high, sometimes virtually vertical, and the horse- or waterfowl-headed prows become S-shaped or curled. Some ships now appear symmetrical. Most probably, the depictions of ships in rock art followed the development of real ships. Concerning the rendering of the crews, a major change occurred in Period IV: in the first three periods they are shown as simple lines, but thereafter also as full-bodied paddlers, armed warriors and helmsmen or lur players. Large ceremonial axes and spears are also depicted standing upright on deck, and acrobats perform somersaults over ships.

The third parameter for dating ship petroglyphs is a comparison with the ship depictions engraved on late Bronze Age (Periods IV–VI) razor blades, hundreds of which have been discovered in Danish graves and sacrificial sites and dated accordingly. Analysing more than 400 such blades, the Danish historian Flemming Kaul found that the development of ship typology on the razor blades was very similar to that on petroglyphs and that the respective dates correlated with each other.[189] Although petroglyphs of ships are found almost exclusively in the Scandinavian Peninsula and not in Denmark, where there is a lack of adequate rocks, and conversely razor blades engraved with ship motifs have only been discovered in Denmark, there is little doubt that they originate from the same cultural realm and have the same ideological significance. A formal clue is given by the petroglyphs from Torsbo, which appear to depict half-finished ships but in fact show open razors. In Litsleby there is even a unique depiction of a ship that looks like a half-opened razor. Conversely, several bronze razors have ship-like shapes and their handles look like a ship stem.[190]

As far as the interpretation of ship motifs is concerned, Kaul took an interesting, albeit slightly reductionist approach. His starting point is the famous Trundholm sun chariot which was discovered in 1902 in a Danish peat bog. It consists of a circular disc made from two cast bronze plates joined together by an outer bronze ring, and of a cast figure of a horse. Both disc and horse

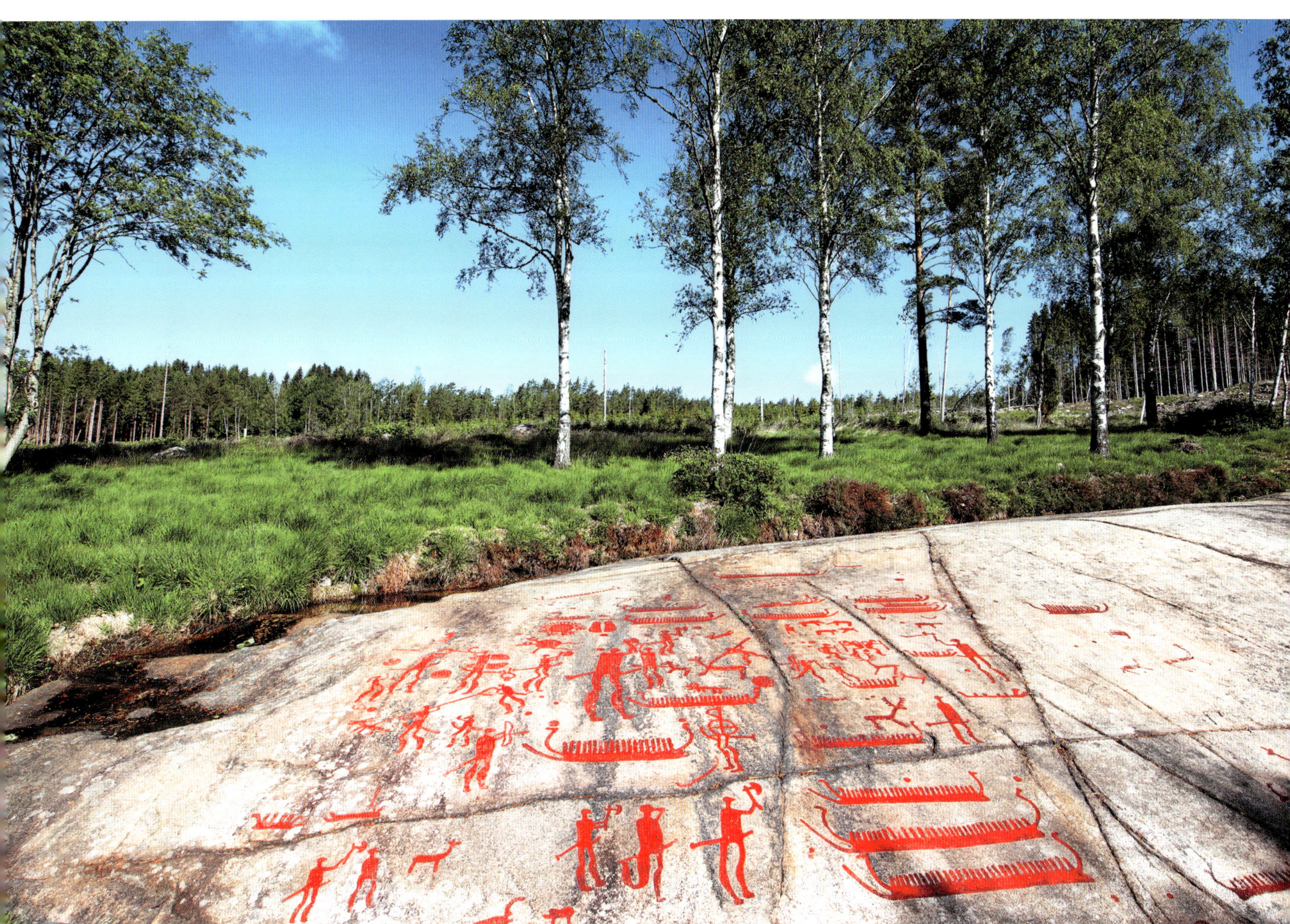

179. Part of the large panel at Fossum. The petroglyphs show ships with crews numbering up to 32 seamen, men blowing lurs or brandishing axes, duels, hunts, footprints and a solar disc. Bohuslän, south-western Sweden. Photo 2021.

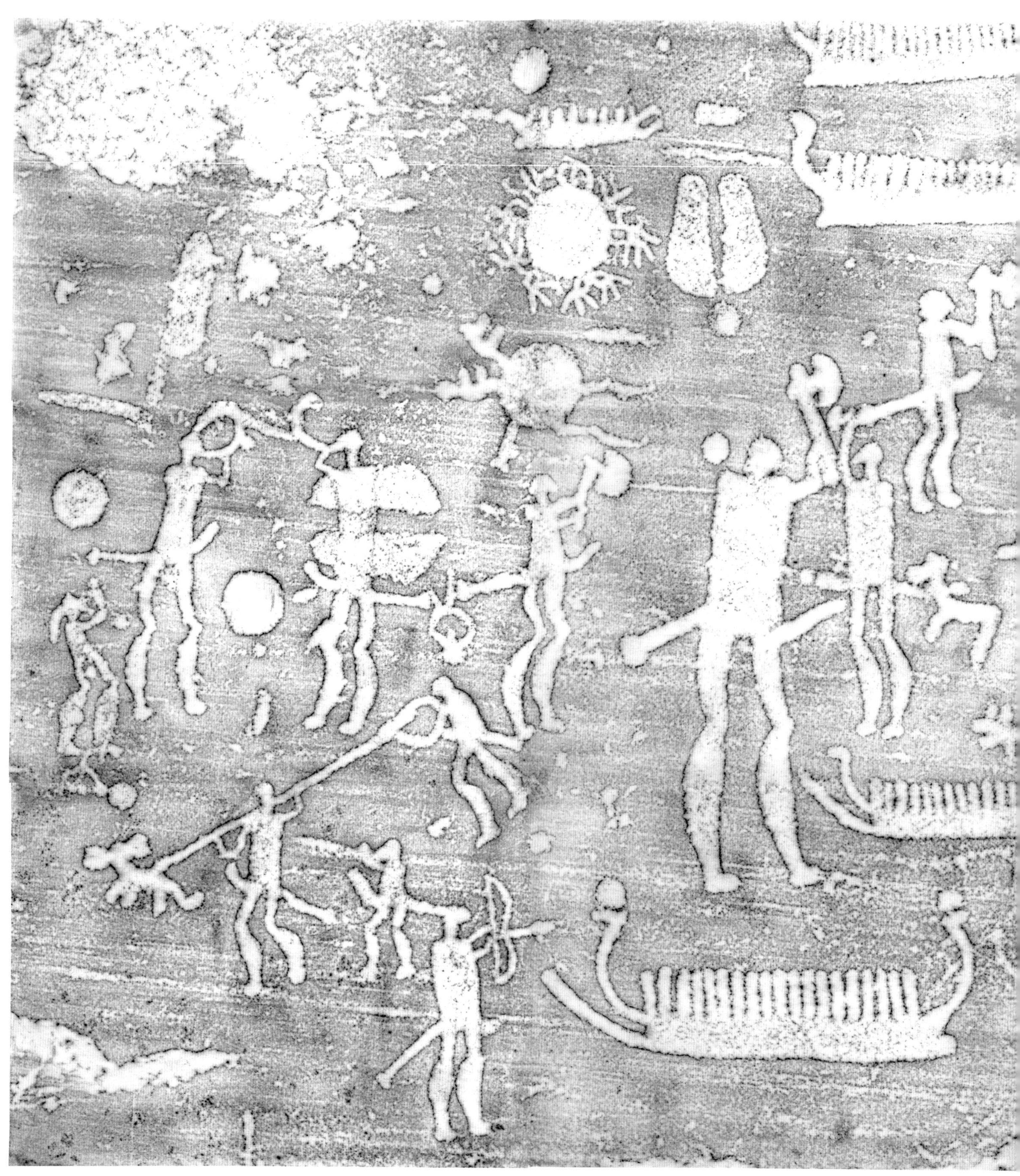

are mounted on a six-wheeled wagon with four-spoked wheels. Possibly, the four spokes symbolize the four cardinal directions or the four seasons. Only one side of the disc is covered with gold foil, whose outer edge is decorated with fine lines probably symbolizing rays; the other side remained dark. The object, 54 centimetres long, is dated to *ca.* 1350 BCE, that is to Montelius Period II; it was probably designed to be pulled during ceremonies (fig. 178).[191] This spectacular composition strongly suggests the interpretation that it symbolizes the movements of the sun: when the horse faces right, the chariot and the sun move from east to west and the gilded disc symbolizes the brilliant day-sun pulled by a horse across the sky. But when the horse faces left, it returns from west to east and the dark night-sun symbolizes darkness. Traces of reins linking the horse with the solar disc show that the sun itself is driving the horse. This interpretation joins up with Almgren's belief that the petroglyphs featuring ships were connected to a solar cult.[192] Among the petroglyphs, the counterpart of the Trundholm sun chariot is the striking Sun-Horse of Balken (Tanum 262) where a rope connects the sun disc to a horse which moves to the right, thus visualizing the daily movement of the sun across the sky (fig. 181). There are other petroglyphs featuring sun horses in Bohuslän, namely at Kalleby, Lilla Arendal, Varløs, Backa near Brastad and possibly Gerum.[193]

The sun-horse at Lilla Arendal reveals an intriguing detail as the sun is surrounded by four small figures consisting of four short lines.[194] These do not represent the sun's rays, but are possibly stylized humans in an adorant position, or, more likely, flying birds. There are two similar representations of an isolated sun at Fossum, where ten birds circle the sun, and at Aspeberget, where eight flying birds seem to have just reached the sun while two humans with long hair, probably women, touch the sun in an adorant position with outstretched arms (fig. 172).[195] These three scenes are hard to decipher. Possibly the birds are migratory, which may allude to the fact that the sun disappears and reappears on a daily and annual basis. The role of the two presumed women in the Aspeberget scene remains mysterious. However, there is a possible link to a specific female burial gift from the early to middle Bronze Age, namely a circular bronze plate with engraved

spirals circling around a central point. Such a disc was also found in the famous burial of the Egtved girl dated to 1370 BCE; it was probably a mark of high social status.[196] When worn on her front in sunshine, it must have reflected the sunlight, thus symbolically associating the woman with the sun. But the exact mythological or ritual background remains unknown.

Naturally, engravings on a smooth razor blade can express finer details than petroglyphs hammered onto an uneven rock. Analysing such details allowed Kaul to further refine the Scandinavian myth of the sun travelling through the sky. However, some aspects of this reconstruction cannot be properly traced in the petroglyphs. Kaul identified twelve scenes or situations, which narrate the daily cycle of the sun's journey in which the ship and a number of animals serve as vessel and helpers. At sunrise, a fish transfers the sun from the night-ship to the morning vessel and accompanies the travelling sun until it is snatched by a bird of prey. At the same time, two sun horses approach the ship and at noon a sun-horse pulls the sun across the sky with a rope, exactly like the sun-horse petroglyph at Balken (fig. 181). In this specific scene, the congruence between images on razor blades and on rocks is perfect.[197] In the afternoon, the sun- horse (or two sun horses) land on the afternoon ship like at Massleberg (fig. 162). At sunset, a snake takes over the sun, hides it in its curled body and dives into the water where two ships are ready to take the invisible sun on board and to carry it through the dangerous night. The cycle is completed when the fish joins the night-ship(s) in order to transfer the sun once more to the morning boat.[198] It is striking that in Homer's *Iliad*, too, the sun crosses at day the sky in a chariot while it returns at night by boat through Okeanos to its starting position in the east.[199] This cosmological myth was especially powerful for people of the North where the sun disappears or wanes not only daily, but annually for months in winter. The historian Kristian Kristiansen suggests an alternative interpretation of the ship, horse and sun symbols in Scandinavian petroglyphs. However, his association with the myth of the sun maiden, daughter of the sky god, and her heavenly twin brothers who, disguised as a horse and a ship, have to rescue her from the claws of nocturnal monsters, lacks corresponding visualization in petroglyphs.[200]

The concept of the sun being pulled across the sky by a horse was widespread in antiquity and appeared first in the Indo-Aryan *Rig Veda* hymns which had their roots in an older Indo-Iranian tradition. In the 130th hymn of the first book, the supreme god Indra is addressed: 'Let thy bay horses bring thee hither like the sun, as every day they bring the sun.'[201] It is plausible that the concept of the horse-drawn sun reached Scandinavia during the

180. ← Rubbing on paper (400 × 280 cm) of a part of the Fossum panel. In the top row are a solar symbol, a pair of footprints and ships. In the middle section two men can be seen blowing lurs and to their left a smaller woman; then a duel between a giant wielding an axe and a smaller man holding a sword, the killing of a deer, a man hitting the head of an archer from behind with an axe, and a stag. In the lower section are a hunting scene, an archer, a ship, a warrior whose body is covered by a round shield, another ship and a stag. Bohuslän, south-western Sweden. Rubbing 2021.

181. The Sun-Horse at Balken near Fossum pulls the sun with a rope through the sky by day. Similar images exist at Lilla Arendal, Bohuslän, and on late Bronze Age razor blades from Denmark. Bohuslän, south-western Sweden. Night photo 2021.

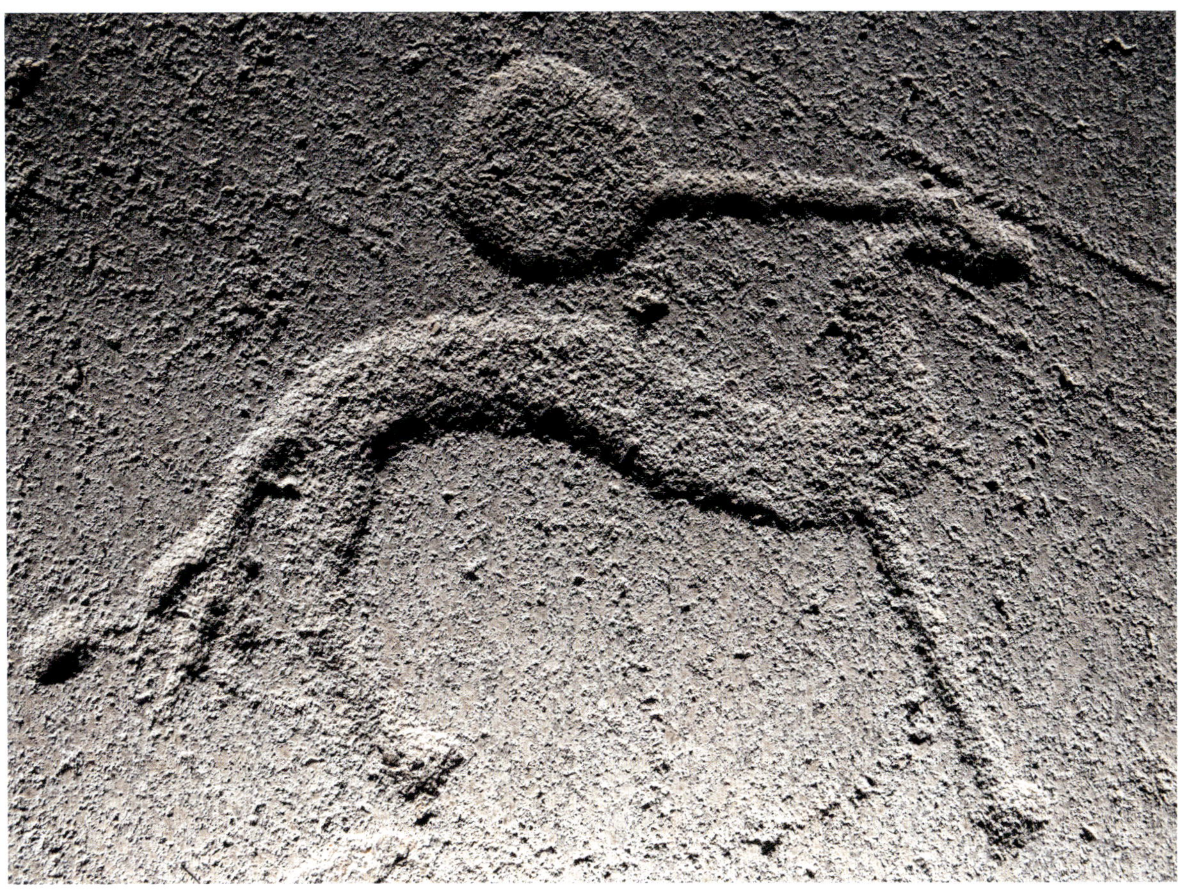

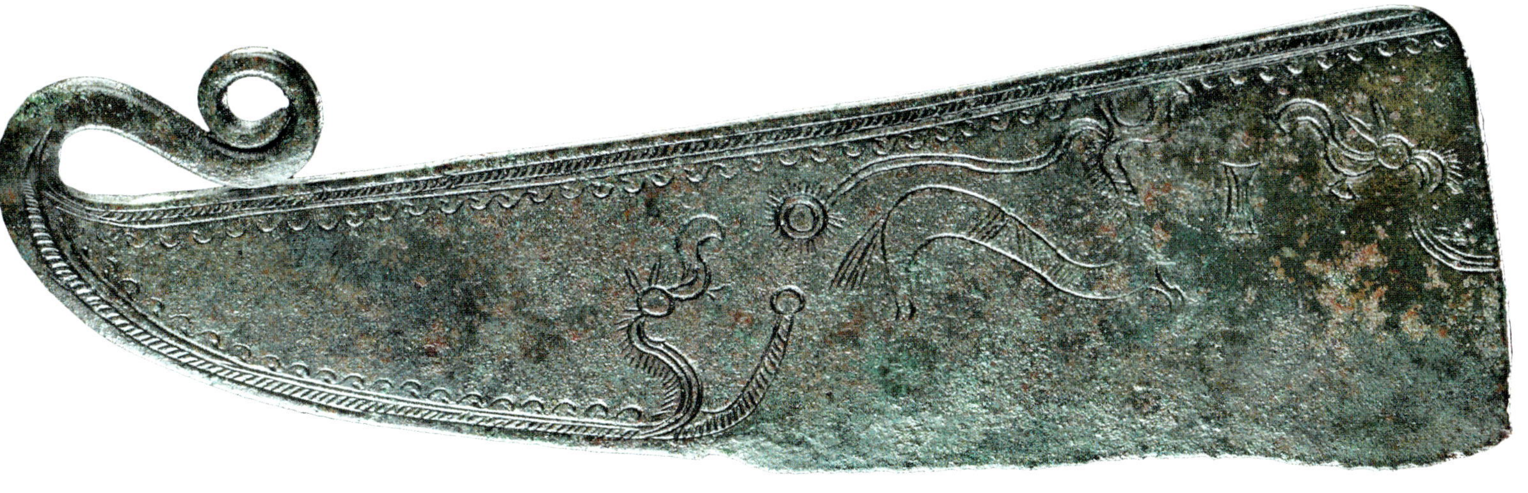

182. On a razor blade made from bronze a sun horse pulls the sun away from a ship whose prow is decorated with a solar symbol, and a bird leads the sun-horse westward towards the approaching evening. Razor blades and weapons were often given as burial goods and were important markers of adult male identity. Late Bronze Age, Denmark. Photo: CC BY-SA, John Lee, The National Museum of Denmark, Copenhagen.

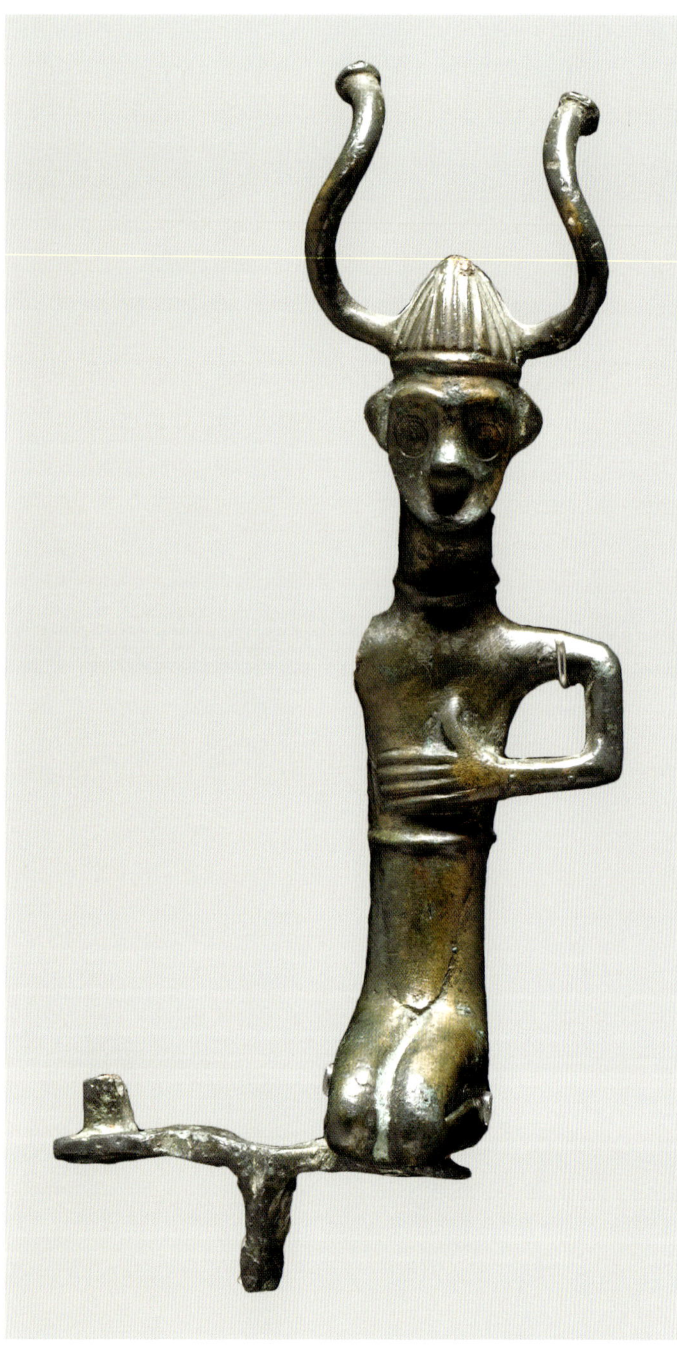

183. Bronze figurine of a kneeling warrior wearing a horned helmet. This figurine and another of an acrobat, as well as four or five now lost figurines, were most probably fixed to a miniature ship. Late Bronze Age hoard from Grevensvængen, Denmark. Photo: CC BY-SA, Roberto Fortuna & Kira Ursem, National Museum of Denmark, Copenhagen.

migration of the Indo-European Yamnaya people to Northern Europe. This idea remained part of the Scandinavian mythological heritage for millennia, for it is reported in the epic *Gylfaginning* from the thirteenth century CE that 'Odin took Night [the daughter of a giant], and Day, her son [by a war god], and gave to them two horses and two chariots, and sent them up into the heavens, to

ride round about the earth every two half-days.'[202] While the oldest petroglyph illustrations of this myth feature the sun being pulled by a horse, variants soon appeared, such as the sun placed on a chariot (at Backa and Disåsen, in Brastad) or carried on a ship (Lökeberg and many other sites). The most famous rendering of a solar deity driving a heavenly chariot is of course the Greek sun god Helios steering across the sky with his four-horse team. The interchangeability of horse and ship as vehicles of the sun is further signified in southern Scandinavia by the countless petroglyphs of ships with horse-headed stems. A scene at Ekenberg near Norrköping in central Sweden expresses the close relation between ship and horse, for here a boat (or less likely a sledge) is towed by two horses walking towards a solar symbol (fig. 198). In other petroglyphs, a solar symbol forms the top of a ship's stem or the ship is held by humans, as at Aspeberget, Massleberg and Ekenberg (fig. 176). Both Almgren and, later, Kaul insisted that such petroglyphs did not represent the myths themselves but the corresponding rituals.[203] Since these rituals were re-enactments of the myths and tightly connected to them, this differentiation may seem at first sight somewhat redundant, unless one believes that the petroglyphs were substitutes for rituals. This latter interpretation is supported by the numerous depictions of a person holding a ship with one or both hands. Either the petroglyph illustrates the offering of a votive gift in the context of a ritual or the making of the petroglyph was the votive gift itself.[204]

The concept of the sun travelling on a ship appears not only on numerous razor blades from Denmark, but also on the famous Nebra sky disc found in Central Germany and dating from the early Bronze Age. The disc is the oldest known representation of the sky and was altered four times during its use, which probably lasted from *ca.* 1800 until 1600 BCE. The ship, made of gold sheet, which carries the sun and moon, was added to the disc around 1700 BCE.[205] The sun was, especially in the North, a most powerful symbol, for its daily return from nocturnal darkness and its annual resurgence after a hostile winter heralded renewed brightness and life. Therefore, the burial gift of a razor with an engraved scene illustrating the sun travelling on its ship must have been understood as a kind of amulet promising a further life. From this perspective, the ship represents not only the vehicle of the sun, but also of the dead. The latter symbolism is also expressed in boat burials and in the ship settings.[206] Just as the ship brings the crew safely through the chaos of the sea and transports the sun through the dangerous night, it should lead the deceased to new, hopeful shores. In this context, the hundred miniature golden ships from the Nors burial in Denmark symbolized the hope that they would carry the dead through the netherworld to a renewed life. That the concept of a ship carrying the sun through the sky is not limited to the realm of Northern Europe is apparent when one considers the illustrations of the Egyptian sun god Re travelling on his barque.

Acrobats performing a somersault over a ship, as featured at Lövåsen, Torsbo or Sötetorp, is another motif with a reference to the eastern Mediterranean cultural realm and with a parallel in Bronze Age metalwork (fig. 184). Instead of jumping over a bull, as in the Minoan murals and figurines dated 1600–1450 BCE which illustrate the famous ritual of bull-leaping, in Scandinavian petroglyphs humans jump over a ship. There was a very similar depiction in the Grevensvængen hoard found in Denmark in the eighteenth century. Out of the six or seven bronze figurines, dating from the late Bronze Age, only two have survived, but the others were recorded in a drawing from 1779. They represented two

kneeling warriors wearing horned helmets and holding ceremonial axes, one or two standing women wearing a long shirt, and three female acrobats wearing only a cord skirt (fig. 183).[207] All the figures had a peg allowing them to be fixed onto a base. Since the two remaining figurines, a female acrobat and warrior with horned helmet and axe, look exactly like corresponding figures in rock art, one can safely assume that all the figurines were originally fixed on a miniature ship. Most probably the petroglyphs and the figurines represent the actual performance of ritual acts.

Whereas petroglyphs illustrating somersaults are relatively scarce, there are at least 175 images of warriors wearing horned helmets.[208] They are mostly engaged in activities related to travel, conflict or rituals, such as commanding a ship, driving a light chariot, fighting a duel or blowing a lur. That such helmets were actually worn, whether in rituals or maybe in combat, is indicated

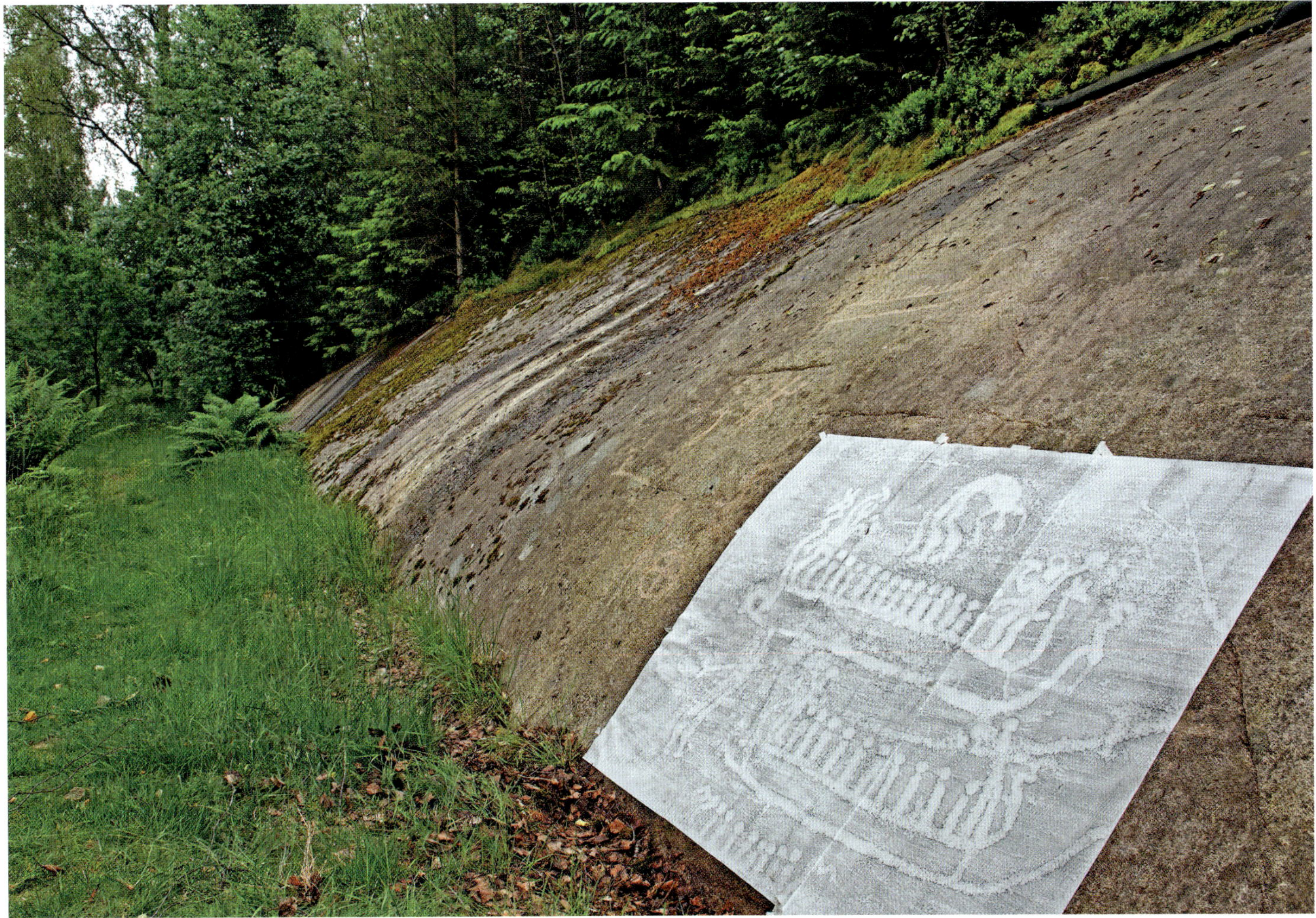

184. Rubbing (138 × 112 cm) made *in situ* of a petroglyph scene showing three boats stacked upon each other. An acrobat performs a somersault above the upper ship which is commanded by two helmsmen wearing horned helmets and standing at the prow and stern respectively. A very similar scene was illustrated by finds at Grevensvængen, Denmark which consisted of three somersaulting female acrobats, two kneeling warriors wearing a horned helmet, and one or two standing women. Sötetorp, Bohuslän, south-western Sweden. Photo 2021.

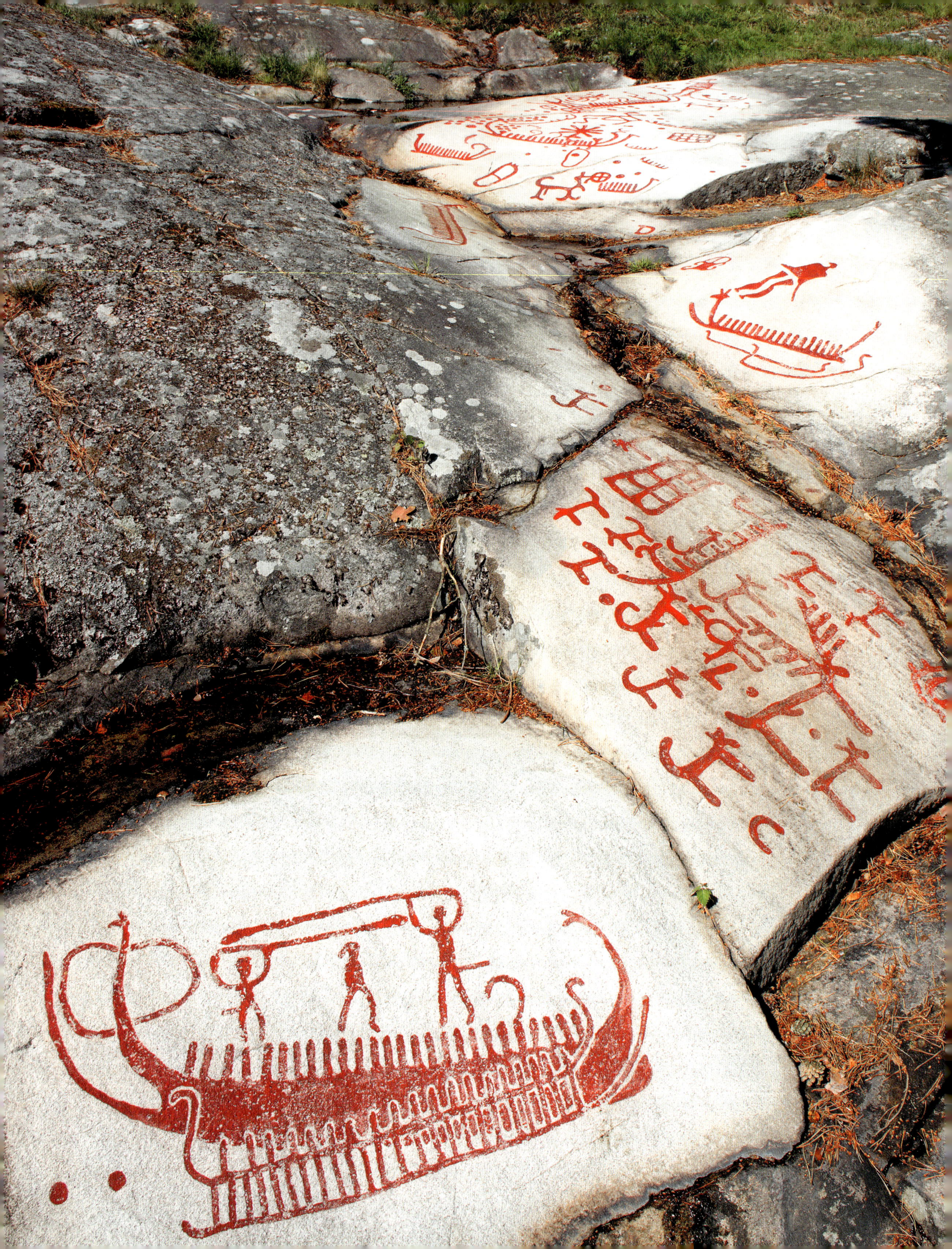

185. ← On the lower panel at Massleberg, two men duel each other with lances, and between them stands a woman. The image is of rich mythological content. It may either show the Valkyrie Hild trying to stop the fight between her lover Hedin and her father Hogni.[4] Or, if the two warriors stand for two armies, the scene may illustrate the eternal battle in Valhalla where a Valkyrie brings the slain warriors back to life in the evening so that they can feast during the night and resume the battle next morning. This never-ending battle serves to train Odin's army for the final battle of Ragnarök, the twilight of the gods. This continuous battle is also illustrated on the Stora Hammars stone stele no. I which dates from the seventh century CE, the beginning of the Viking age. This suggests that the roots of this Nordic myth lay in the Bronze Age. Bohuslän, south-western Sweden. Photo 2021.

186. → The Stora Hammars stele no. I from the seventh century CE standing in the Gotland Island, Sweden. The carvings show, at the top, death in battle and the hanging of a man; a rope is wound around his neck and attached to the top of a tree which is tied down by a second rope. When this second rope is cut, the tree will immediately spring back and strangle the condemned man. Below is the scene illustrating either the fight between the followers of Hild's father Hogni and of her lover Hedin, or the perpetual battle in Valhalla. Further down, death in battle is again visualized and at the bottom a Viking warship. Photo Berig.

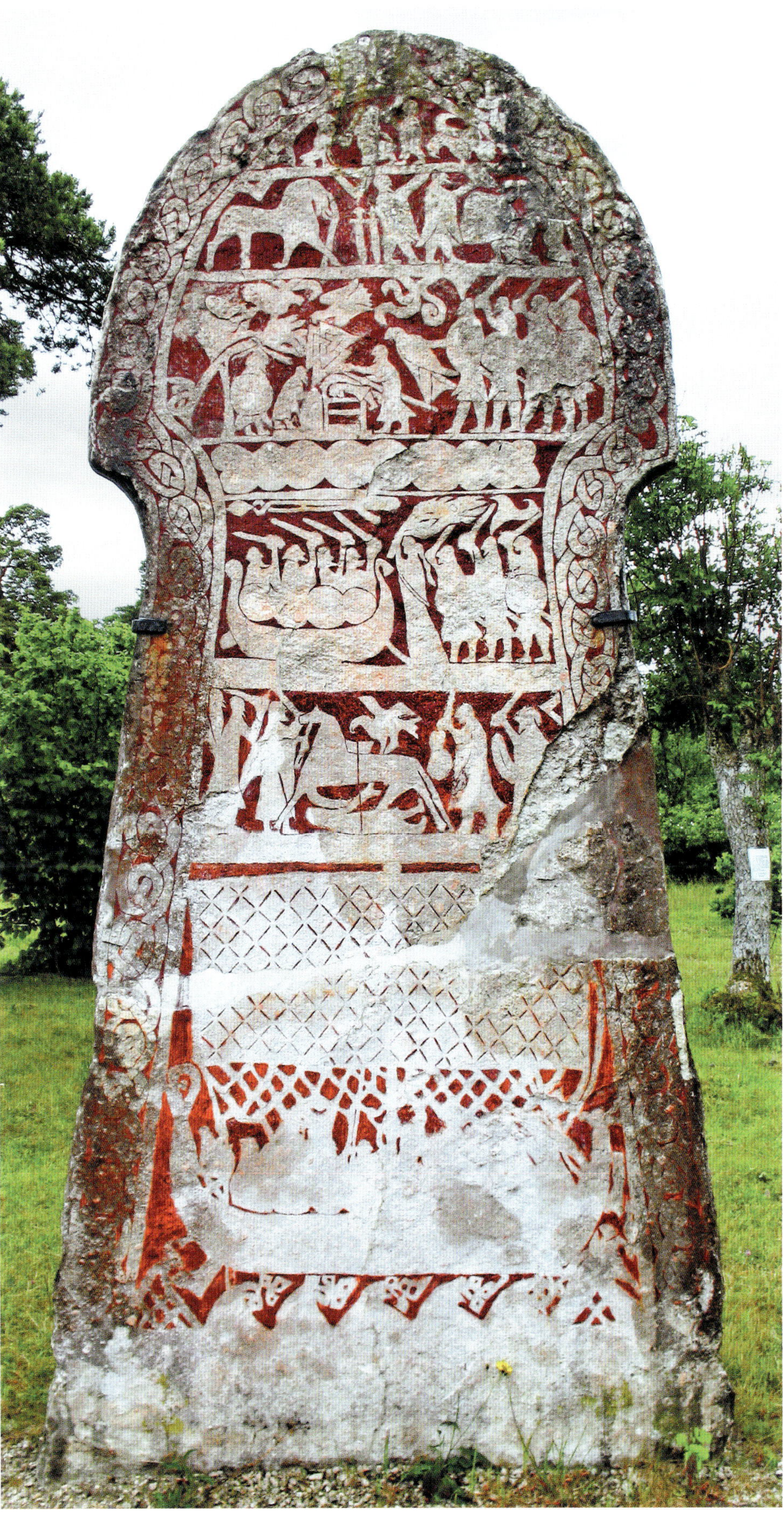

by the two bronze helmets from Viksø, Denmark, whose horns look very similar to those of the Grevensvængen male figurine (fig. 183). Since their fronts are decorated with two bulging eyes, the helmets can also be viewed as masks. These Scandinavian representations of warriors with horned helmets share strong similarities with contemporary metal figurines from Sardinia and stone steles from Iberia, two regions that were key suppliers of copper for Scandinavia.[209] Most probably, the horned helmet emphasized the strength and bellicosity of its wearer, and its simultaneous appearance in Sardinia, Iberia and Scandinavia fits the impression of a strong interconnection between trading Bronze Age cultures. That the bull was an important symbol of power for Mediterranean Bronze Age people is evident at the huge petroglyph site of Vallée des Merveilles in the South of France where by far the largest number (80 per cent) of figurative petroglyphs represent bull's heads, followed by daggers and halberds (figs 216, 217).[210]

To conclude this section on Bohuslän and Østfold, the amount of violence illustrated is striking, for of the more than 1,800

petroglyphs in Sweden showing people with an offensive weapon, the vast majority are in Bohuslän.[211] There are many scenes on land and on ships where warriors fight duels with battle axes or, at Fossum, a giant wielding an axe is attacked by a warrior fighting with a sword (fig. 187). Some of the duels fought with axes, as illustrated at Aspeberget and Fossum, were probably part of a ritual, for the protagonists seem to wear bird-like masks with round heads and beak-shaped noses. On the other hand, in a few scenes, the act of killing is also shown, for example at Fossum where a warrior hits an archer from behind with his axe, at Tanum 319 where a warrior armed with a sword pierces a man from behind with a spear, or at Brastad 617 where a man spears another man armed with a club.[212] Judging from petroglyphs and burial finds, in the early and middle Bronze Age the spear, including the two-handed spear, and the battle axe were the preferred weapons.[213] But the sword had not long to wait to be added to the armoury, for 40 per cent of humans in Bohuslän petroglyphs carry a sword, usually worn at the waist inside a scabbard. The sword was the first weapon that

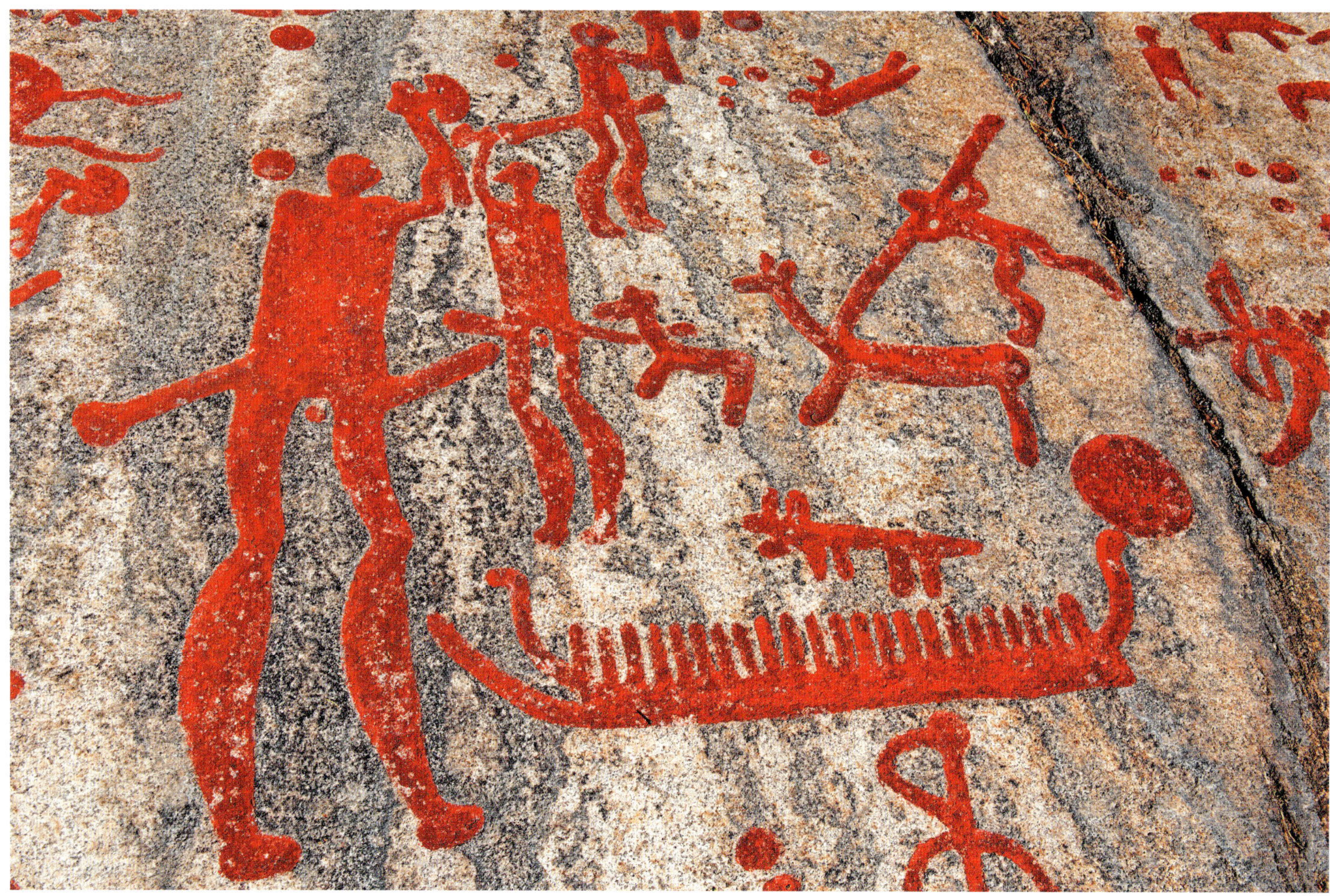

187. A detail from the Fossum panel illustrating a fight between a large warrior armed with an axe and a smaller adversary fighting with a sword. In the image, the modern repainting is misleading, as the smaller figure holds a sword, not an axe. Photo 2021.

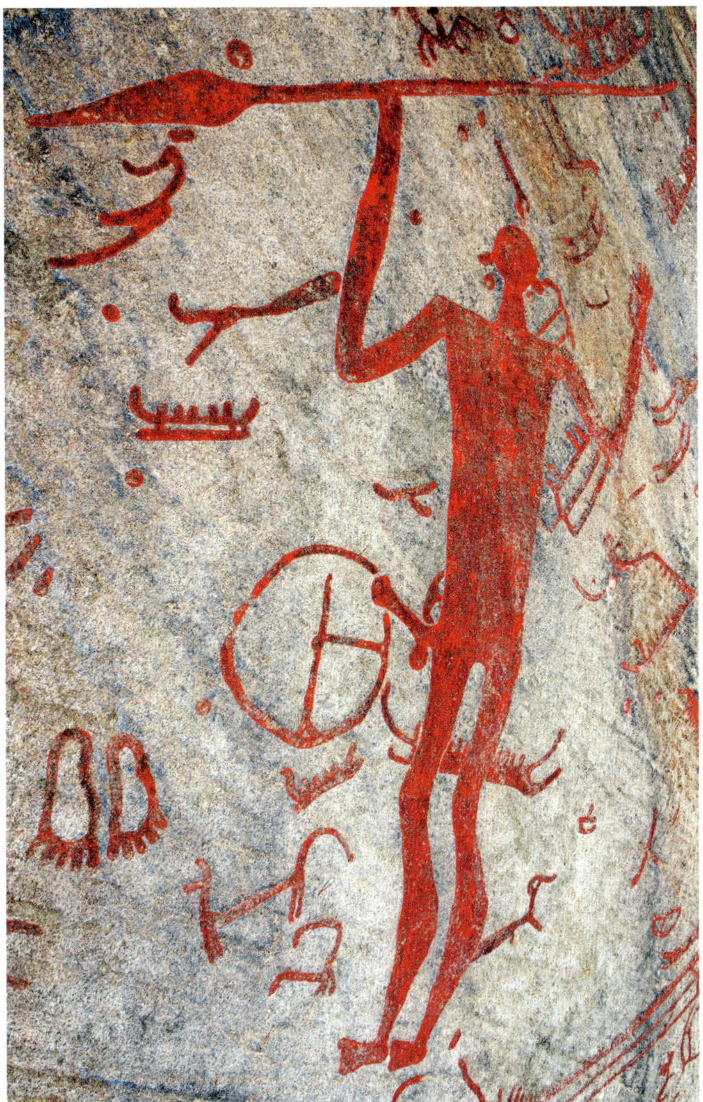

188. Petroglyph of an ithyphallic hero-warrior from the late Bronze Age; the warrior measures 235 cm, his spear 195 cm. Litsleby, Bohuslän, south-western Sweden. Photo 2021.

sword began to spread among warriors, that is in the thirteenth century BCE, the influence of the Central European Urnfield culture (*ca.* 1300–750 BCE) led to a change in burial customs, namely from inhumation to cremation. The ashes were placed in an urn and buried in small stone cists; soon full-size swords were no longer placed as grave goods, but only miniature ones.[217]

Little doubt remains that in the course of the Bronze Age, a kind of militarization of societies took place and that warrior aristocracies, uncontrolled by any central power, emerged in southern Scandinavia, as in most societies in Europe. This societal trend went hand in hand with a warrior elite ideology, where the idealized warrior mutated into a hero. The phallic giants at Backa and Litsleby from Montelius Period V exemplify this gradual idealization of the warrior. Later, in the course of the Iron Age and concurrent with the emergence of an orally transmitted Norse mythology, the warlike ideals of the late Bronze Age evolved into personifications of supranatural weapon-bearers, that is weapon-wielding gods. Paramount among these warlike Nordic gods are Odin, the god of battle and death whose key attribute is a spear, and Týr, god of the sky, thunder and lightning, whose attribute is the axe. It is Týr who temporarily binds the monstrous wolf Fenrir who will break loose and kill Odin at Ragnarök, the twilight of gods and destruction of the created world. Over time, Týr was absorbed by Thor whose weapon is a hammer.[218] However, it must be emphasized that Bronze Age people most probably had neither a pantheon nor personifications of supranatural powers, that is human-like gods. Their rituals are best understood as a kind of magic whose aim was achieve an objective or change an unsatisfactory situation without the involvement of supranatural or transcendent powers.[219] At the same time, rituals reinforced the social cohesion of communities.

1.2.2. Central and south-eastern Sweden

Although the petroglyphs of central and south-eastern Sweden share many similarities with those in Bohuslän, there are some significant differences. As mentioned earlier, the epicentre of the isostatic rebound lay in the Gulf of Bothnia with local uplifts of up to 286 metres. This means that the rebounds were more pronounced in Uppland, in central-eastern Sweden, than in Bohuslän. In south-western Uppland they were 25 metres above sea level for a date around 1700 BCE, 23 metres for 1500 BCE, 21 metres for 1300 BCE, 18 metres for 1100 BCE, 17 metres for 900 BCE and 15 metres for 700 BCE.[220]

was specifically developed to kill humans and it soon became the hallmark of warriors. Whereas several axes discovered in Danish and southern Swedish tombs were indeed purely ceremonial, since they were made from fired clay and had only a thin bronze coat,[214] 71 per cent of the bronze swords with organic hilts excavated in Danish tombs and bogs had been resharpened, which is a clear indication that they had been used in combat.[215] Whether weapons, primarily the axe, were venerated as such, remains unclear. Concerning the representation of the sword, it is striking that in Bohuslän only a few swords were individually pecked, whereas at Ekenberg and Himmelstalund, sites near Norrköping in central Sweden, there are no fewer than 23 individual petroglyphs of swords rendered at virtually life size (figs 195, 196).[216] At about the same time as the

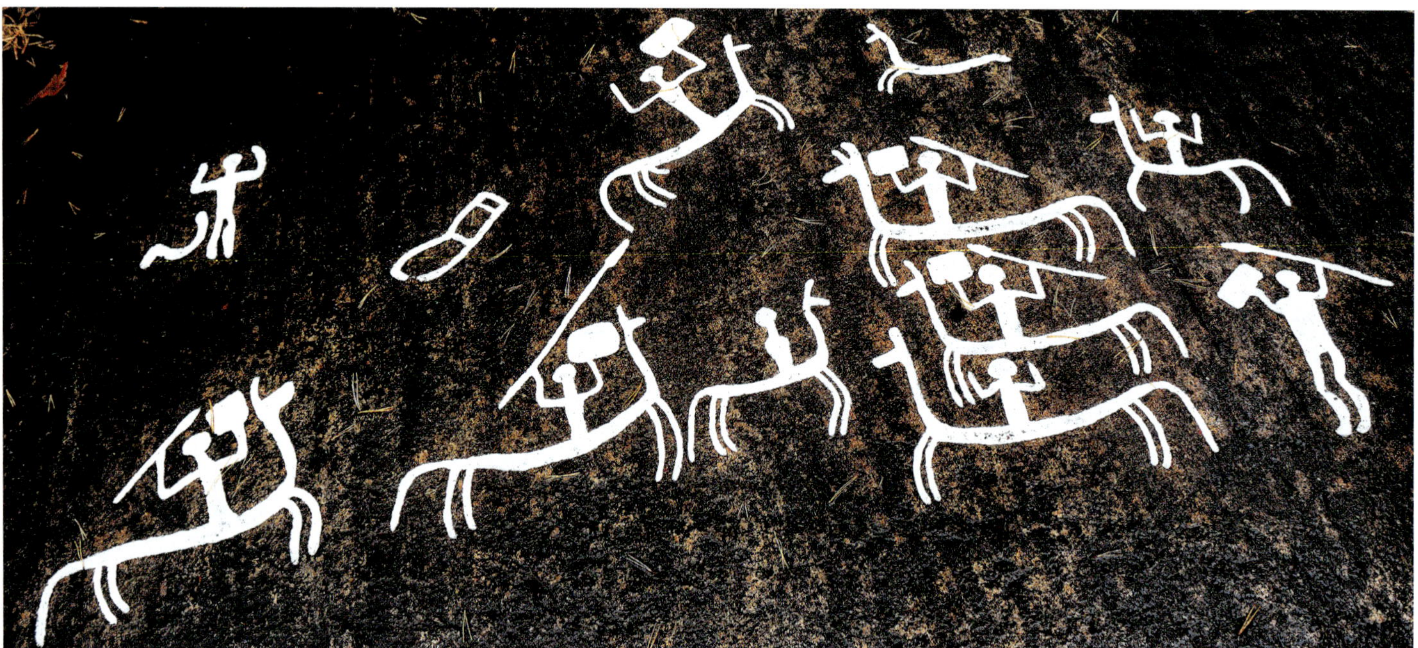

189. Battle scene between horsemen and one foot soldier from the early Iron Age. Tegneby, Bohuslän, south-western Sweden. Photo 2021.

The major sites are, listed from east to west and north to south:

- **Högsbyn** lies in the nature reserve of Tisselskog by the shore of the small Lake Råvarpen. As in Bohuslän, there are two scenes of acrobats performing a somersault over a ship; a lur player stands on one of the ships. There are also numerous footprints, ships and wheels.

- **Evenstorp.** Here two groups of stick-humans with tiny heads, around 30 in total, walk in two rows. There are also four figures of concentric circles, ships and snakes.

- **Husaby** features several interesting scenes involving ships. On one ship, some members of the crew stand on deck while others are head-down under the ship's keel. Another ship carries a solar disc of different design at either stem; possibly they represent the sun by day and night. Behind two other ships a large fishing net is spread.

- **Sigurdsristningen** at Sundbyholm lies west of Stockholm close to Lake Mälaren. The complex scene from around 1030 CE illustrates an episode from the saga of Sigurd, the slayer of the dragon Fafnir.

- **Himmelstalund, Ekenberg, Leonardsberg** and **Fiskeby** near Norrköping are four sites which in the Bronze Age lay on a promontory separating a deep fjord of the Baltic Sea from Lake Glan in the west, which was larger then than it is today.

Near Himmelstalund there was probably a harbour which connected the Baltic Sea with inland waterways and routes. Some petroglyph motifs are unique to these sites.

- **Hästhallen** near Möckleryd today lies in a forest in south-eastern Sweden. On a single boulder of *ca.* 200 sq m there are 85 petroglyphs of ships, eighteen imprints of feet, a dozen animals which are hard to define, and two horses which gave the site its name. Quite a few ship images seem to have been reworked over the course of time; some of them have marks like small compartments and are strangely bent which gives them the look of ringed earthworms.

- **Bredarör** at Kivik, south-eastern Sweden, is not an outdoor petroglyph site, but a Bronze Age kurgan whose burial chamber consisted of ten stone slabs. The eight slabs on the long sides have highly interesting petroglyphs facing inwards, dating from the late sixteenth or fifteenth century BCE. Another kurgan with interior slabs decorated with petroglyphs stands at **Sagaholm** south of Jönköping.

- **Simrishamn** and **Järrestad** are 17 km south of Kivik. Simrishamn is famous for its multitude of pecked axes and huge ceremonial halberds, Järrestad for the petroglyph of a dancing warrior 80 cm tall and the possibly unique representation of a sailing ship.

Several petroglyphs at **Simrishamn** and neighbouring **Järrestad** in Skåne (the south-eastern tip of Sweden) are among the oldest in southern Scandinavia. Compared to the Gulf of Bothnia, in Skåne the isostatic uplift was minimal, no more than about two metres.[221] The main site at Simrishamn is called **Yxornas häll** which means 'Rock of axes'; it lies only twenty metres from the sea. The name is indeed appropriate, for on this flat quartzite rock there are 50 images of axes, some of them ceremonial, as well as 45 ships. Some of the axes have counterparts in bronze axes discovered in hoards such as the Fjälkinge hoard, while others look similar to Bronze Age Anglo-Irish axes or Carpathian shaft-hole axes, which suggests a date around 1700/1500 BCE for the oldest such petroglyphs as well as trading contacts with the British Isles and the Carpathian Mountains.[222] A few men hold oversized ceremonial axes, and in one instance the axe and its extra-long shaft are one and a half times the height of the man; these axe-holders raise their ceremonial axes like flags (fig. 190).[223] Such huge ceremonial axes with thin blades have been excavated, proving that they

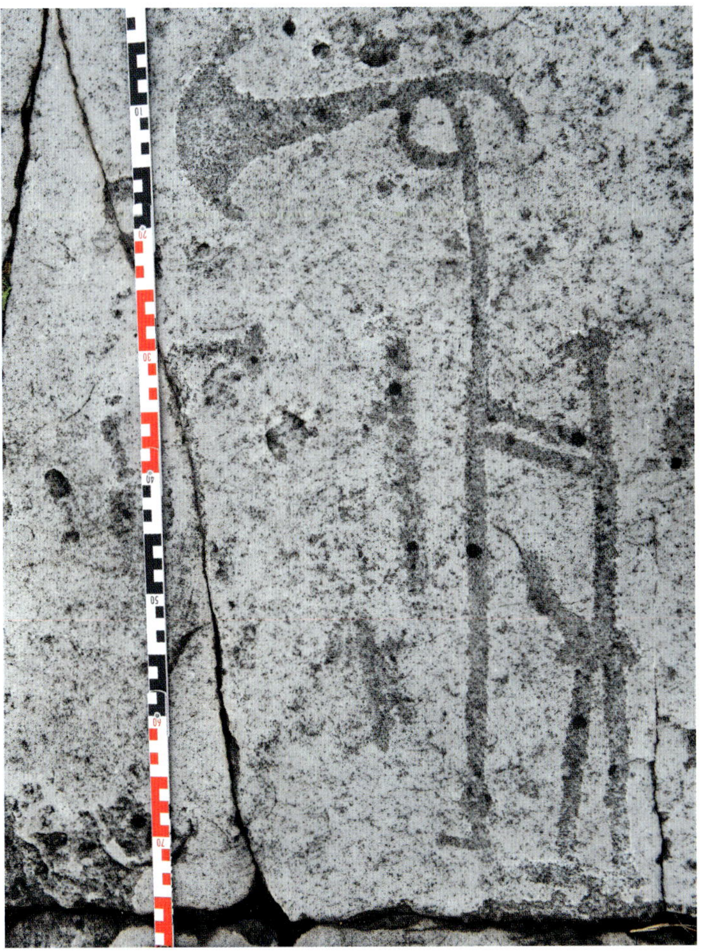

190. An ithyphallic man holds a huge ceremonial halberd. Bronze Age, Yxornass häll, Simrishamn, Skåne, southern Sweden. Photo 2021.

really existed.[224] Two similar axes were carved on slab I of the Bredarör tomb at Kivik.[225] Other motifs are the solar wheel, humans and two wagons. The petroglyphs at the neighbouring site of **Stenkilsristningen** are extremely weathered, and can only be discerned at night using lateral grazing light.

Five kilometres west of Simrishamn is **Järrestad** where, on a quartzite boulder with a surface of *ca*. 500 square metres, there are more than 1,200 images. More than half of them are cup marks, followed by about 90 footprints. Most of these footmarks replicate real feet fully carved out with toes and probably date from Montelius Periods I–II. Interestingly, as observed by Peter Skoglund, the axis marked out by the footprints corresponds to the turning points of the year. 'Northeast and northwest mark the direction of the midsummer sunrise and sunset respectively while southeast and southwest indicate the same events at midwinter.'[226] Obviously the early Bronze Age people paid attention to the solstices, when days reached their longest and shortest duration. In the later Bronze Age, other footprints were rendered in outline.[227] Then there are images of groups of two or three palstaves (a type of axe) associated with footprints, spirals, snakes and five horsemen who do not sit but stand on their horses; possibly they are acrobats. Singular too are the petroglyphs of a ship with a crew of around eighteen sailors which seems to have a large sail looking like a Mongol yurt, and of a dancing warrior 80 centimetres tall. Since he wears a sword-scabbard with a winged chape, of a type that is also known from Bohuslän, this petroglyph dates from the transition from Montelius V to VI, that is around 700 BCE.[228] Next to the petroglyphs there are three kurgans. At both sites, Yxornas häll and Järrestad, petroglyph pecking continued until 200 BCE.

The kurgan of **Bredarör** near **Kivik** lies only 300 metres from the sea. With its unusual size, 75 metres in diameter and approximately 3.5 metres high, the cairn has been known for centuries. It caught the interest of scholars in 1748 when two farmers who were quarrying its stones came upon a rectangular grave chamber which consisted of ten stone slabs, four along each side and one at each end, all 110 to 120 centimetres in height. The two men looted the cist by night, but rumours quickly spread about their finds and they were arrested. It remains unknown what kind of objects they had taken, and they were acquitted in 1749. Although famous scholars such as the renowned naturalist Carl von Linné (Linnaeus) visited the site soon after its rediscovery, it was only in 1756 that the petroglyphs were discovered by the antiquarian Nils Wessman on the long inner sides of the cist; the petroglyphs were to be seen by the dead, not by mourners or visitors.[229] Luckily, Wessman hired the artist Gustaf Feldt to make faithful drawings of the rock art on eight of the ten slabs, as the archaeological site continued to be neglected. Stones continued to be stolen and three slabs disappeared, of which two were found again, but one slab remains lost. The only official archaeological excavations were conducted in 1931, but the report was never published, and only the find of a few fragmented Bronze Age objects was reported. The tumulus was rebuilt in 1932–33 and the slabs were rearranged in its centre. About 300 metres east of the kurgan, the large graveyard of Ängakåsen dating from the Bronze and Iron Ages was discovered, which included a large ship setting. Five kilometres further northwest, at Ravlunda, seven Roman coins from the second century CE were also found.[230] In the absence of sufficient facts, the hypotheses arose that a tribal leader from the Bronze Age or a widely travelled trader from the Imperial Roman period was buried at Bredarör.

A breakthrough in research came in 2006 when the bones which had been excavated in 1931 were analysed. It then became clear that this was not the site of a single burial for one leader, but that at least five or six individuals had been buried here over a period of 600 years. Four or five of them were juveniles, 13 to 17 years old, the last was an adult about 25 to 35 years old. Furthermore, the burials occurred in three stages, the first around 1450–1200 BCE, the second between 1200 and 1000 BCE, and the third, of the adult, between 900 and 700 BCE. As the petroglyphs are dated to around 1400 or even 1550–1400 BCE based on stylistic criteria,[231] and since the few discovered grave goods are from Montelius Periods II and III, the burial chamber and grave goods cannot have been intended for the buried adult. The first to be buried were one or two juveniles. The archaeological investigations resumed in the immediate neighbourhood of the kurgan in the 2010s. They revealed that there had been a settlement since the Mesolithic and that the first cairn was built for burial purposes around 2000 BCE. Around 1400 or even as early as 1550 BCE, the cairn was rebuilt and expanded, and the cist was erected with the ten stone slabs. At least eight of them are of quartzite, while slab V is of gneiss and completely weathered. When comparing the dates for the earliest burial with those of the excavated objects (Montelius Period II–III) and those suggested by the majority of researchers for the petroglyphs, the conclusion is that the engraved cist was constructed for one or two juveniles. However, if the earlier dating of the petroglyphs is accepted, then another scenario emerges: the decorated slabs were made for an earlier burial, the bones from which are missing.

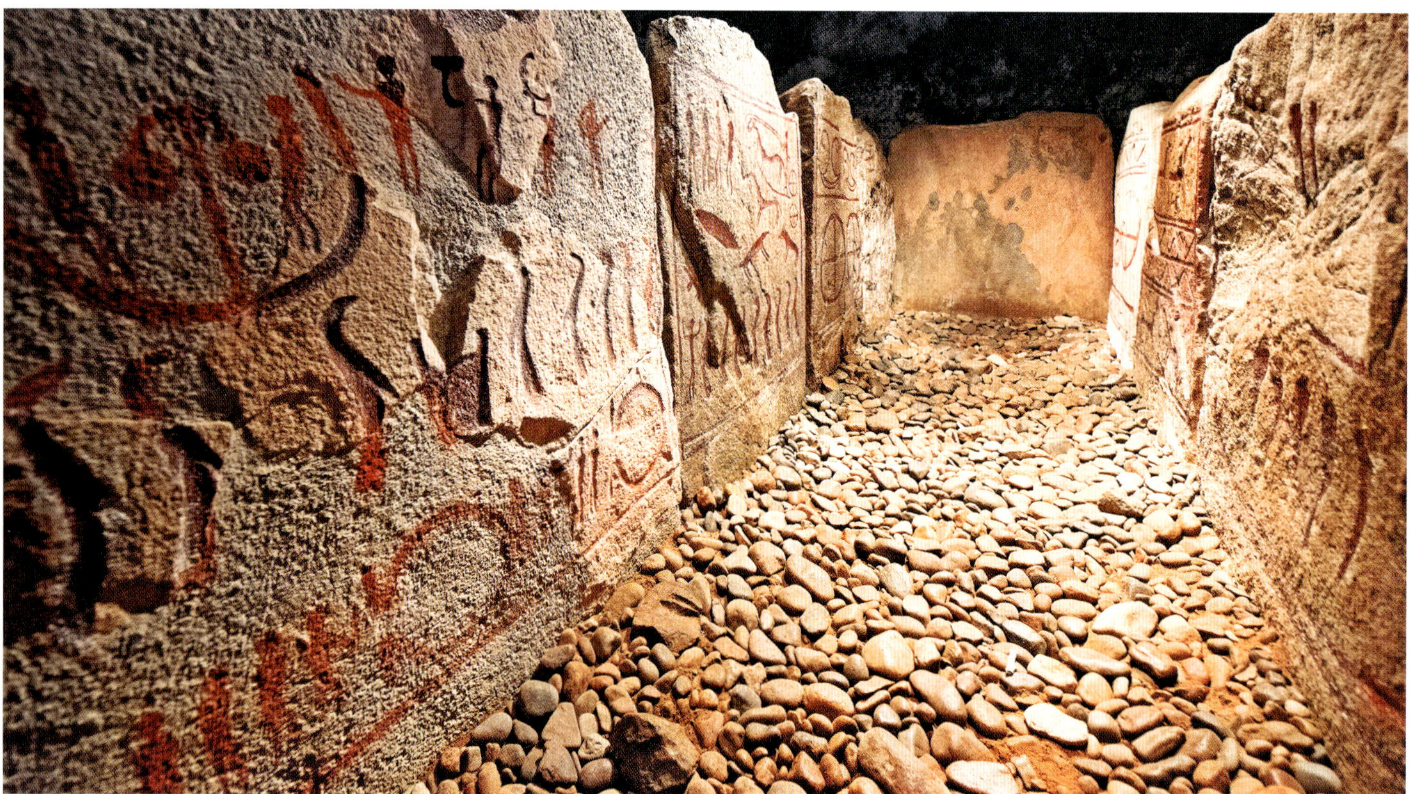

191. The burial chamber in the Bredarör barrow at Kivik consists of ten stone slabs and measures 360 × 110 cm. Of at least five or six burials, the first occurred around 1400 BCE, the last around 700 BCE. The petroglyphs on the inner sides of the cist probably date to the time of the first burial; at the left are slabs VII and VIII. Southern Sweden. Photo 2021.

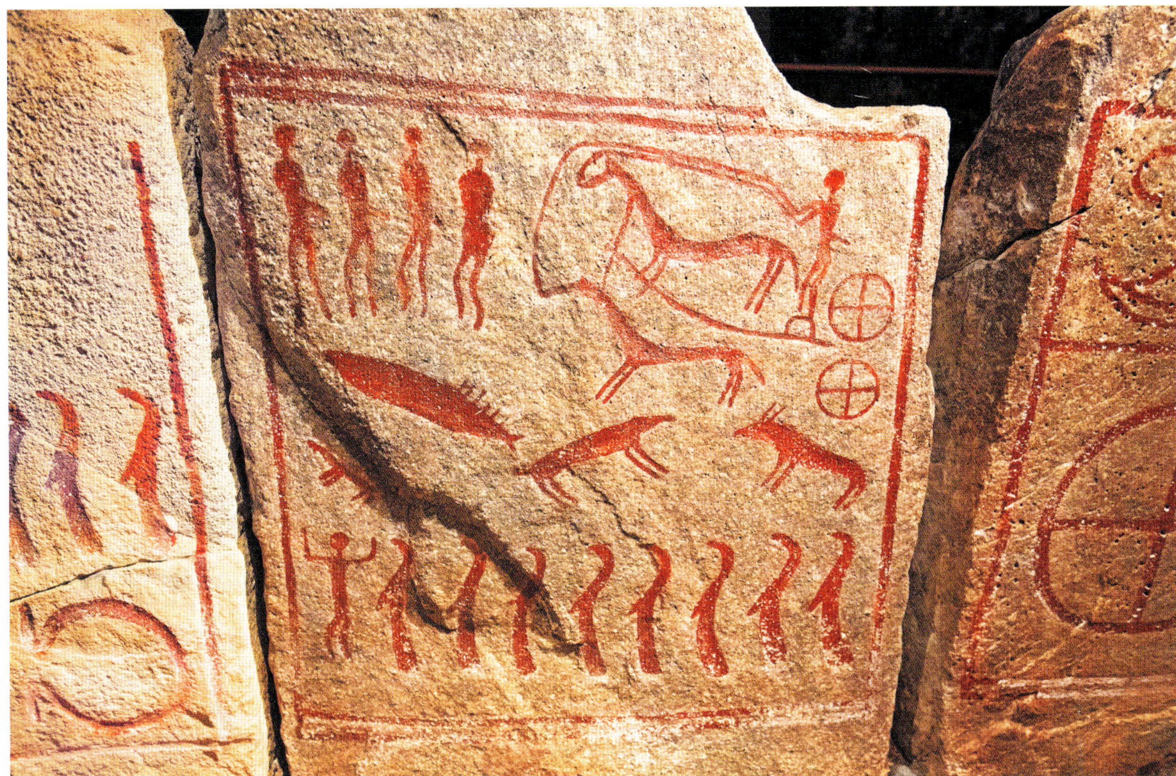

192. Slab VII in the Bredarör barrow. At the top, a light battle chariot resembling an early Mycenaean chariot is driven towards four men. In the middle row are a wels catfish or whale, then three quadrupeds. At the bottom, eight women wearing bird masks and long robes advance in procession towards an adorant with raised arms. Kivik, southern Sweden. Photo 2021.

The eight engraved slabs were most probably made at the same time and form a coherent group. The assumed order of the slabs follows the drawings made by Feldt, and by the antiquarian Carl Gustav Gottfried Hilfeling in 1775.[232]

- **Slab I**, which has now disappeared, featured two shafted axes, two spearheads standing on either side of a long, cone-shaped object, and below, a boat with stems bent inwards and a keel slightly bent upwards. The two shafted axes are similar to those at Simrishamn, and the boat is also of the Montelius Period II type.

- **Slab II** is quite weathered. At the bottom features a similar boat to slab I; five axes are fixed upright on the boat's deck. Then there are three horses, one small player of a lur and two figures shaped like a hat which have no counterparts in Scandinavian petroglyphs or in any excavated objects.

- **Slab III** depicts four horses, two on either side of a horizontal diamond-shaped band. The horse was introduced to southern Scandinavia at the beginning of the Bronze Age. Bones from a horse were found inside the cist. Whether these horse engravings are associated with the mythical sun-horse known from Bohuslän remains unknown.

- **Slab IV** is damaged. Two four-spoked wheels are placed between two zigzag lines. Both wheels strongly resemble so-called 'sun-wheel' petroglyphs from Bohuslän. Since slabs III and IV stood next to each other, an implied combination of horses and suns seems plausible.

- **Slab V** is of gneiss and extremely weathered. Only the beginning of two zigzag lines can be made out.

- **Slab VI** features two ceremonial axes and, underneath, two four-spoked wheels as on slab IV.

The last two slabs are much richer and illustrate complex scenes.

- **Slab VII** numbers twenty images arranged in three rows (fig. 192). On top, a charioteer armed with a short sword drives a light chariot with four-spoked wheels drawn by two horses towards four standing men, three of which wear a short sword. The chariot and driver of slab VII look very similar to images of early Mycenaean chariots. A similar, although more schematic petroglyph was found twenty kilometres south of Kivik in the **Villfara** stone monument.[233] The chariots from Kivik and Villfara are quite unique in the southern Swedish context

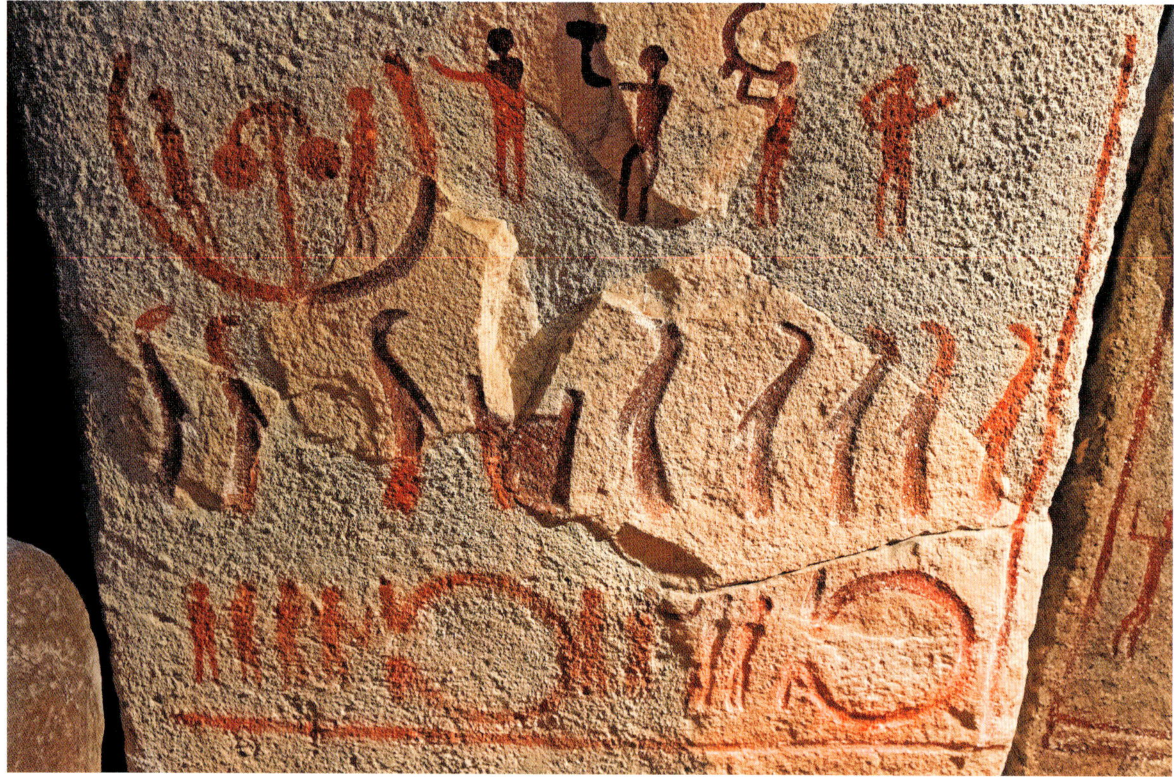

193. Slab VIII in the Bredarör barrow. In the top row, two men play the lur and two others a double gong. Below, a group of nine women wearing bird masks and long robes stand on both sides of a stone cist or an altar, and at the bottom two groups of men stand near two omega-like figures, possibly representing giant torcs. The scenes on slabs VII and VIII illustrate burial rituals and ceremonies. Kivik, southern Sweden. Photo 2021.

because they are depicted three-dimensionally, in contrast to most petroglyphs of chariots which are usually rendered two-dimensionally. The only exceptions are the petroglyphs at Hemsta in Boglösa parish, Uppland, and at Ekenberg near Norrköping.[234] In the middle row of slab VII two quadrupeds, possibly a horse and a wolf, face each other. Then there are another quadruped and a large aquatic animal, a wels catfish or a whale. The lower row depicts a procession of eight humans (probably women) in long robes and bird masks. They have S-shaped bodies and are moving towards an adorant standing on the left with raised arms. The top and bottom rows seem to illustrate a procession, probably in conjunction with a funeral. The middle row would in that case feature the sacrificial animals.

- **Slab VIII**, which was broken, was reassembled in 1915; it includes at least 28 figures, again arranged in three rows (fig. 193). Under an unidentifiable figure at the top stand six men, of whom two blow lurs, and another two men stand within a semicircle and hit a double gong. The fifth male possibly holds a rattle. The eight (probably originally nine) women wearing bird masks from slab VII stand now on both sides of a figure which could well represent the stone cist or an altar. At the bottom, a group of four and a second group of four or five men stand in front of two figures like a capital omega (Ω), which

could represent large torcs (neck rings), worn during special ceremonies.[235] The presumed females with S-shaped figures on panels VII and VIII, which obviously belong together, and the driving charioteer rendered three-dimensionally are foreign to the pictorial language of southern Swedish petroglyphs and indicate an external influence. The hypothesis of Kristian Kristiansen and Thomas B. Larsson whereby the scenes on slabs VII and VIII display influence from the early Mycenaean world is worth consideration since Mycenaean burials included processions, mourning, the playing of music and chariot races, as was later also described by Homer. Furthermore, as noted by Peter Gelling and Hilda Ellis Davidson, the S-shaped bodies of the females bear similarities to Minoan renderings of the human body.[236] The petroglyphs illustrating acrobats jumping backwards over a ship from Bohuslän already indicated Aegean influence in Bronze Age southern Sweden. All these elements suggest cultural contacts between the eastern Mediterranean and southern Sweden in the wake of the metal and amber trade. Probably, a harbour located on the east coast of Skåne was the entry point of such contacts.

Besides Bredarör and Villfara, there are a few more burials which included stones with petroglyphs. Among them are the burials at Järrestad, at Klinta on the Swedish island of Öland, in

194. Two hunters with dogs attack a wild boar with lances; one of the dogs has been killed and lies on its back. Early Bronze Age, Himmelstalund, Norrköping, central Sweden. Photo 2021.

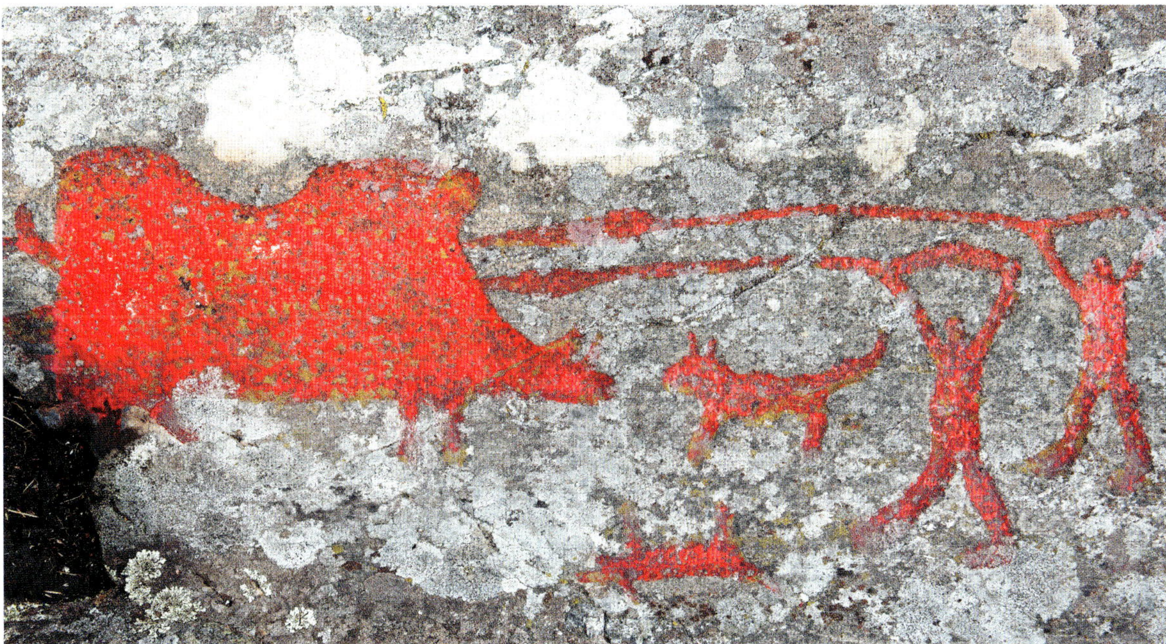

195. The main panel at Ekenberg, Norrköping, central Sweden with petroglyphs of ships, boats, swords and axes. In the centre on the left, two horses pull a ship (see the corresponding detail fig. 198). Photo 2021.

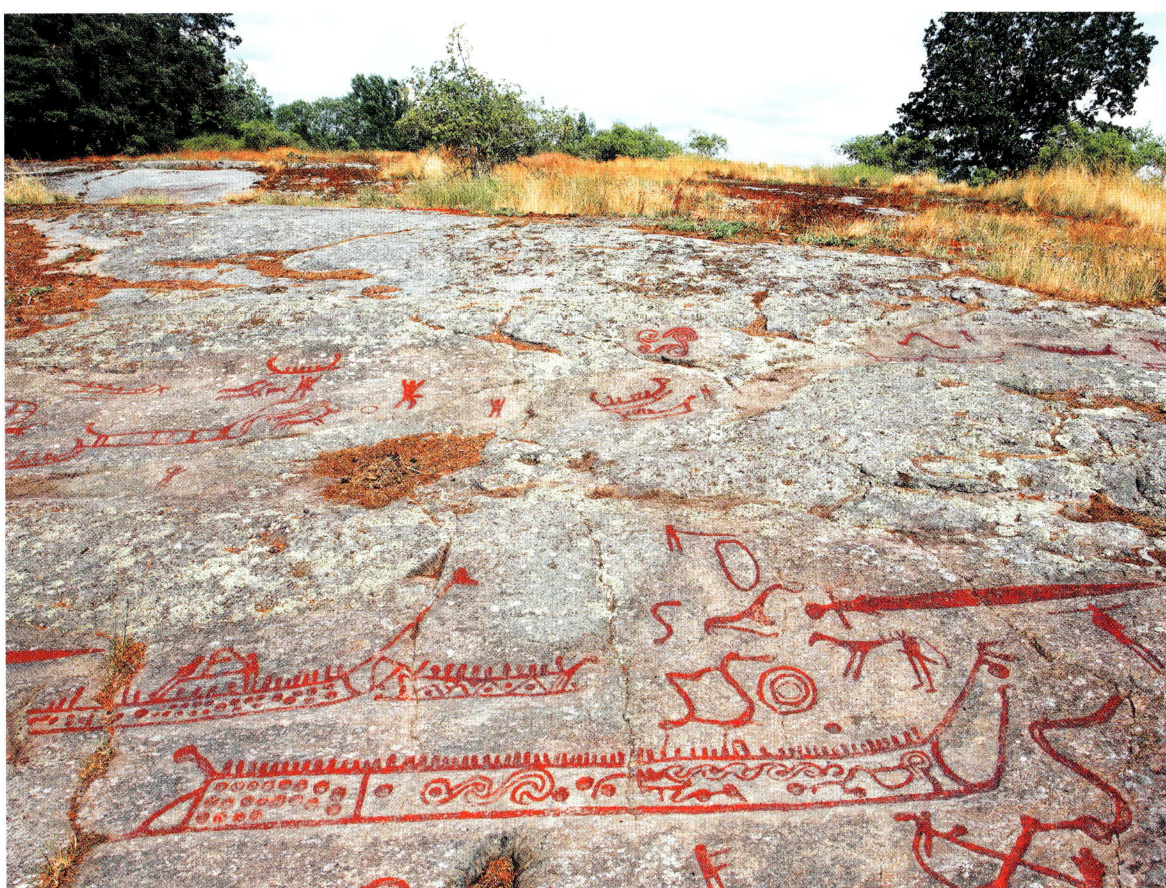

Birkerøgel in Zealand, Denmark, and at Sagaholm near Jönköping, central southern Sweden. Inside the **Sagaholm** barrow, which had a diameter of 22 metres, stood a kerbstone circle consisting of around 100 sandstone slabs of which 45 were excavated. Of these, eighteen were engraved with petroglyphs of mainly horses, then ships, humans, hunting scenes and a scene of zoophilia. Fifteen slabs were found *in situ*, three more were stray finds. Unlike the cist at Bredarör, the slabs at Sagaholm were facing away from the buried person towards potential outside viewers, yet it seems that the chamber and the slabs were covered with gravel and earth immediately after the burial ceremony. Judging from the remaining kerbstones it is unclear how the petroglyph motifs were related to the burial and the corresponding ceremonies. Whether the fact that all the horses but one are oriented to the right allows for an interpretation associating them with the sun-horse of Trundholm, which faces to the right during the day, remains uncertain. The burial has been dated to Montelius Periods II–III, that is 1500–1100 BCE, a little later than Bredarör.[237] The fact that petroglyphs were created to be placed inside tombs hidden from the world of the living exemplifies the fact that they were laden with a high level of symbolism.

In the west and south-west of **Norrköping** are the petroglyph sites of **Himmelstalund, Ekenberg, Leonardsberg and Fiskeby**, of which the first two are the most impressive. At Norrköping, the isostatic uplift was less pronounced than at Bohuslän; it is estimated that during the early Bronze Age Himmelstalund stood about 15 metres above present sea level, and about 10 metres above sea level during the late Bronze Age.[238] By measuring heights above sea level and comparing petroglyphs of weapons and tools like swords and axes with dated metal equivalents, the petroglyphs can predominantly be dated to the early Bronze Age (1700–1100 BCE), with a smaller part dating from the later Bronze Age.[239] In terms of motifs, out of the *ca.* 1,660 images at Himmelstalund, 630 are ships, 260 animals and 60 humans interacting with animals, often in a hunt using spears. Then there are fully carved-out axes and swords at life size. At the smaller site of Ekenberg, out of 400 images about 115 are ships, followed by about 70 humans and 50 animals.

It is striking to what extent the petroglyphs at Norrköping exude a spirit of martial ideals, along with competitiveness and hunting skill against dangerous animals such as boars. Unique to Himmelstalund and Ekenberg are the above-mentioned 23 fully carved full-hilt swords dating from Montelius Period II (figs 195, 196).[240] Unlike the hunting scenes at other sites of southern Scandinavia where relatively harmless quadrupeds are hunted and wild boar are absent, at Himmelstalund the hunt of wild boar dominates (fig. 194). Due to the speed, robustness and aggressiveness of wild boar, such hunts are dangerous, especially with Bronze Age equipment, and require the cooperation of at least two men and the assistance of dogs. In the corresponding petroglyph scenes, hunters act in pairs and attack the wild boar with spears, and possibly also javelins, and they are assisted by dogs. As in other societies with combative ideologies, the fight of man against wild animals was part of the social life of the elite. Successfully hunting boar or lions

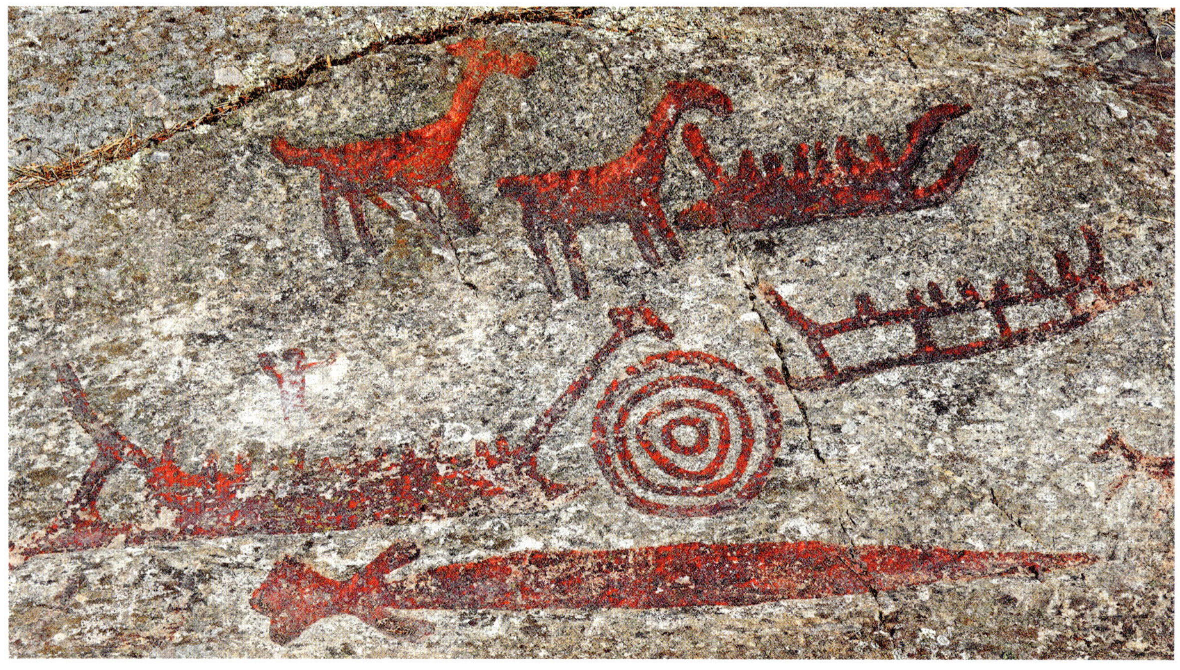

196. A typical Bronze Age sword, four concentric circles, a boat whose prow has the shape of a long-necked elk, two smaller ships and two horses. Ekenberg, Norrköping, central Sweden. Photo 2021.

197. In the lower part of the panel, two men lift a huge rectangular object with ribbed patterns. This could indicate the preparation for a boar hunt when nets are placed near a boar's lair to trap the animal. Bronze Age, Himmelstalund, Norrköping, central Sweden. Photo 2021.

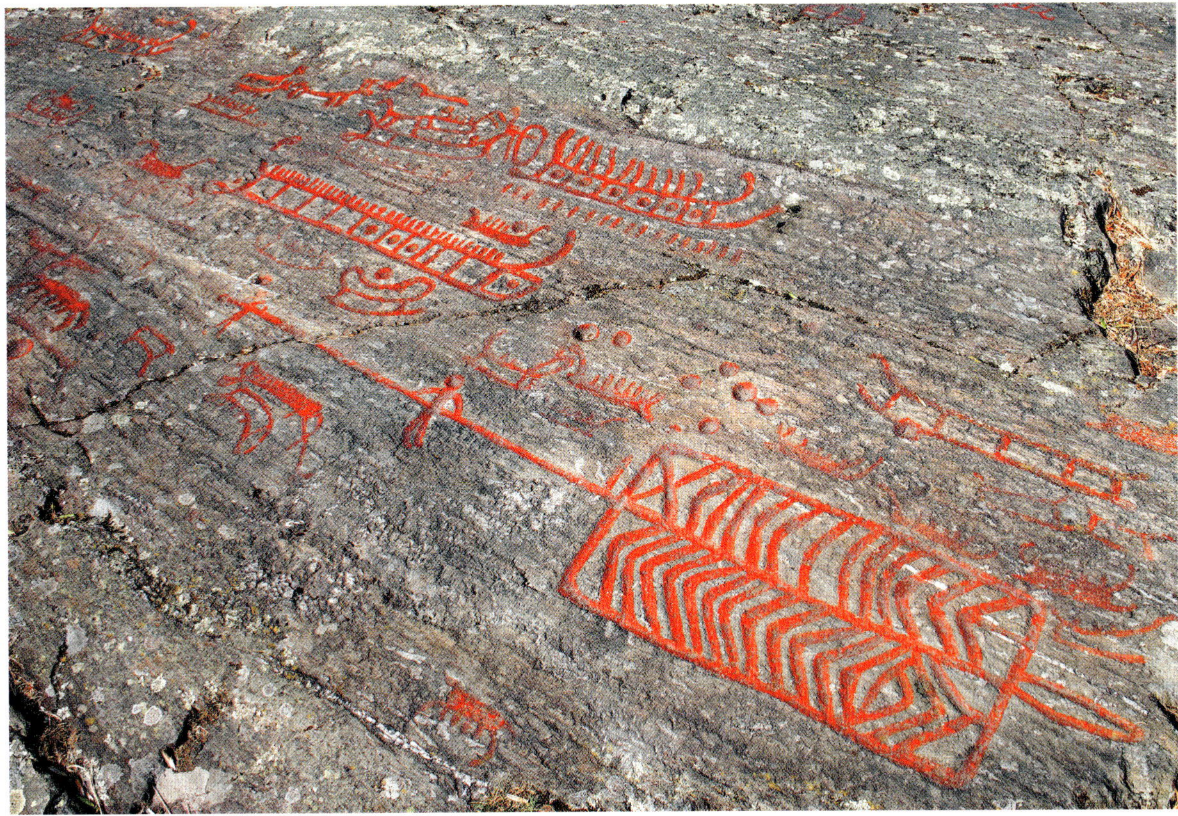

198. In the lower part of the image two horses pull a ship towards a solar disc (not in the photo), and above a man seems to lift a model boat. Bronze Age, Ekenberg, Norrköping, central Sweden. Photo 2021.

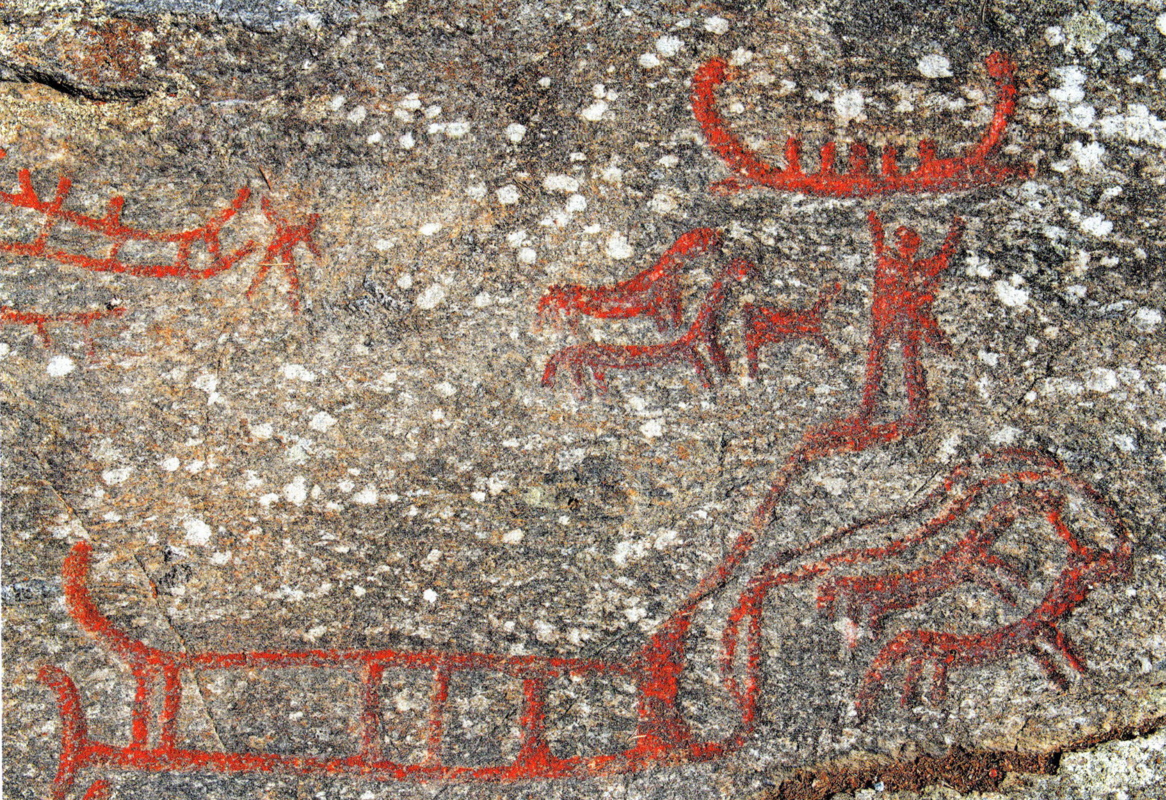

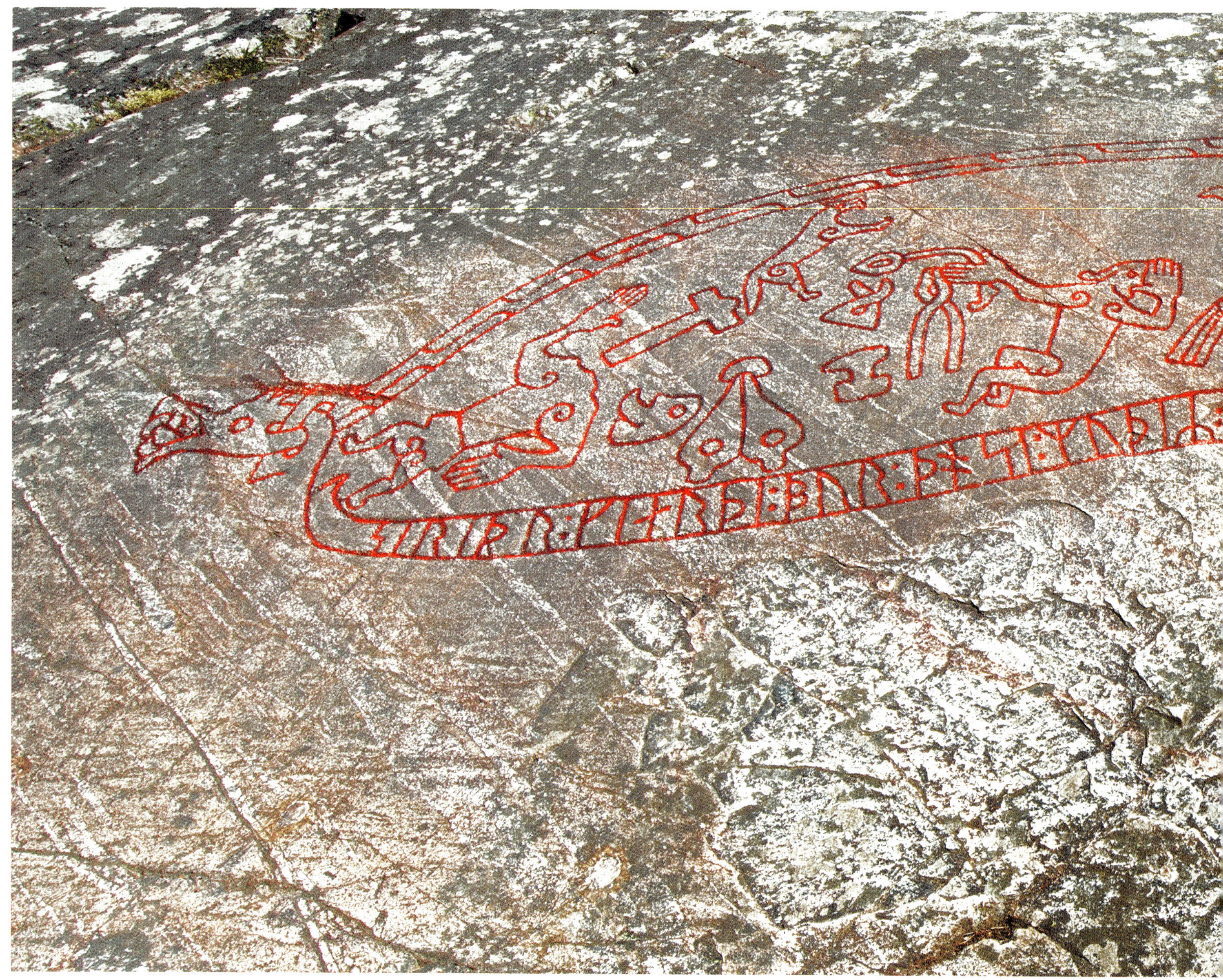

199. The medieval panel of Sigurdristningen near Lake Mälaren, 460 cm long, dates from the Viking period around *ca.* 1030 CE. In the panel, Sigurd pierces the dragon Fafnir with his sword Gram. In the centre, Sigurd's horse is tied to a tree on whose crown is a bird while the hero sits on the ground and roasts Fafnir's heart for his foster father the blacksmith Regin who wants to eat it. But Sigurd burns his thumb and cools it in his mouth. When the dragon's blood touches his tongue, he begins to understand the language of the bird on the tree above him. The bird warns Sigurd that Regin wants to kill him so that he can have the hoard of gold for himself. Sigurd then kills Regin, whose headless corpse and disembodied head are visualized on the left of the scene. Central Sweden. Photo 2021.

was not only considered proof that one lived up to the values of the relevant social class, it also sharpened skills needed in combat. In one scene at Himmelstalund, where a single man holds a spear turned downward towards the earth, it is unclear whether the man is preparing himself for a boar hunt or whether he is guarding a herd of more than twenty pigs and piglets; a few lie on their backs and have probably been slaughtered. The various visualizations of the act of killing are also particular to Norrköping. Finally, martial arts are also celebrated at Fiskeby where petroglyphs illustrate several duels fought with spears and a combat between at least nine warriors.

Other striking petroglyphs at Himmelstalund are a ship 2.4 metres long with a crew of 73, bear paw prints, paired lurs, a double-axle wagon, ship hulls decorated with spirals, circles and conifers, and a runic inscription inscribed next to a sledge or unfinished ship. Assuming that the inscription is authentic, it dates to the late Iron Age or early medieval period. It has been deciphered as 'Brajdo' which is a female name meaning 'the broad one', or as

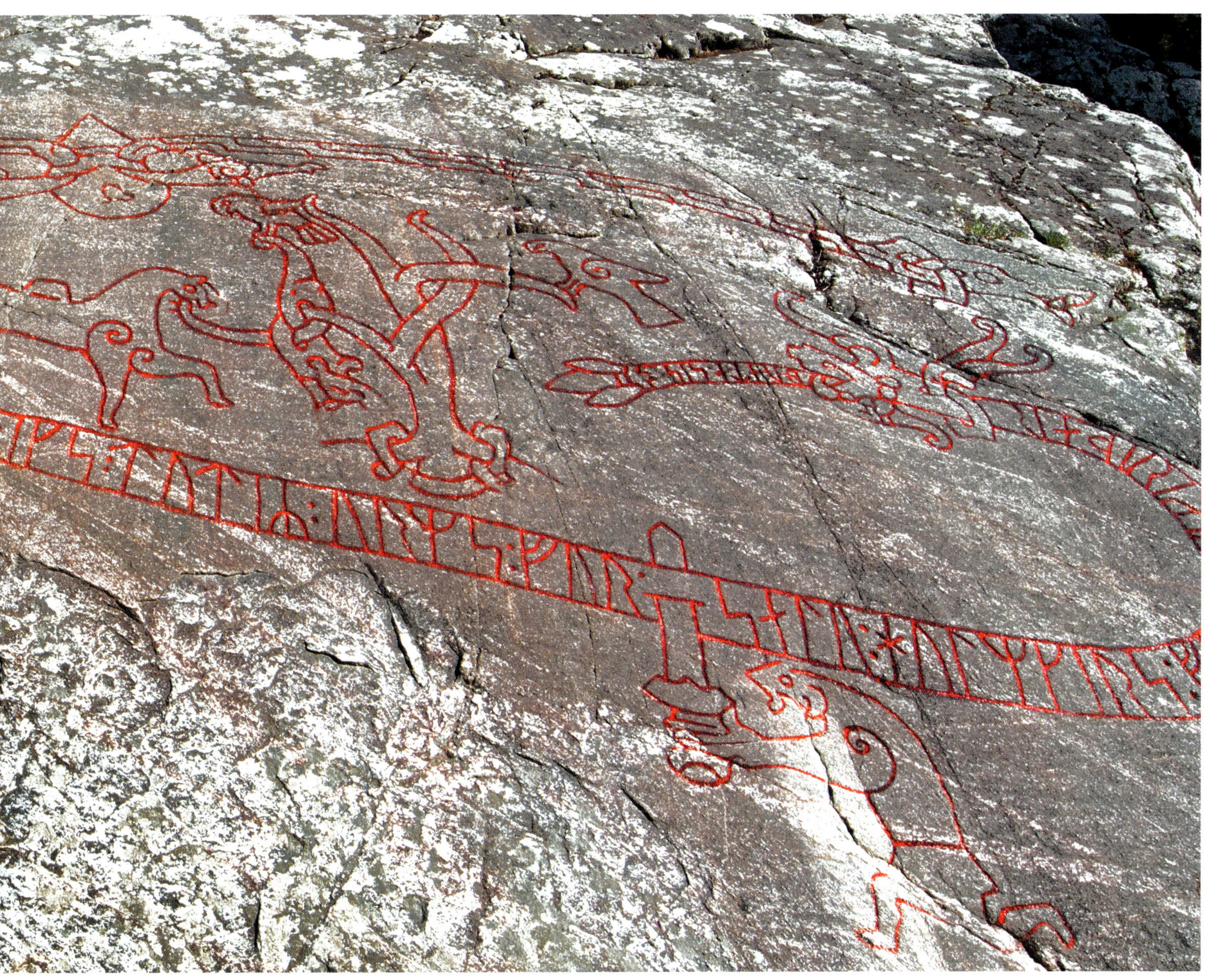

'buajdo', 'I did'.[241] Then there are two men holding a huge rectangular structure with a ribbed pattern on a horizontally held pole (fig. 197). This scene could well illustrate the beginning of a boar hunt when hunters would set up nets in the bushes in front of a boar's lair, in which it would become entangled. At Ekenberg, there are several particular scenes which are hardly found elsewhere, for example a scene where two horses pull a ship (or, less likely, a sledge) towards a solar symbol, and above them an armed man seems to lift the model of a boat (fig. 198). The first scene is most probably an illustration of the 'sun-horse' myth, and the second visualizes a votive offering. Then there is a group of seventeen men armed with swords standing beside a tall leader. Above this group are a ship and several concentric circles, and below, a ship is shown upside down, as if capsized.

Finally, there is the striking image of an armed man holding a large sun symbol, consisting of concentric circles and an inner double spiral, above his head. These scenes probably illustrate rituals.

The medieval rock art at **Sigurdristningen** goes back to the initiative of the Viking woman Sigrid who sponsored this rock image and a bridge over the River Ramsundsån which flows just below the rock, in honour of her deceased husband Holmger. Today, a road runs along the former riverbed, but at that time, Lake Mälaren was five metres higher than it is today. The bridge served the living and symbolically also the dead husband of the female donor as a passage to the afterlife, as is recorded in runic script within the body of the dragon Fafnir which frames the whole scene. In the past, such runic inscriptions were painted in bright colours; it is now in red.[242]

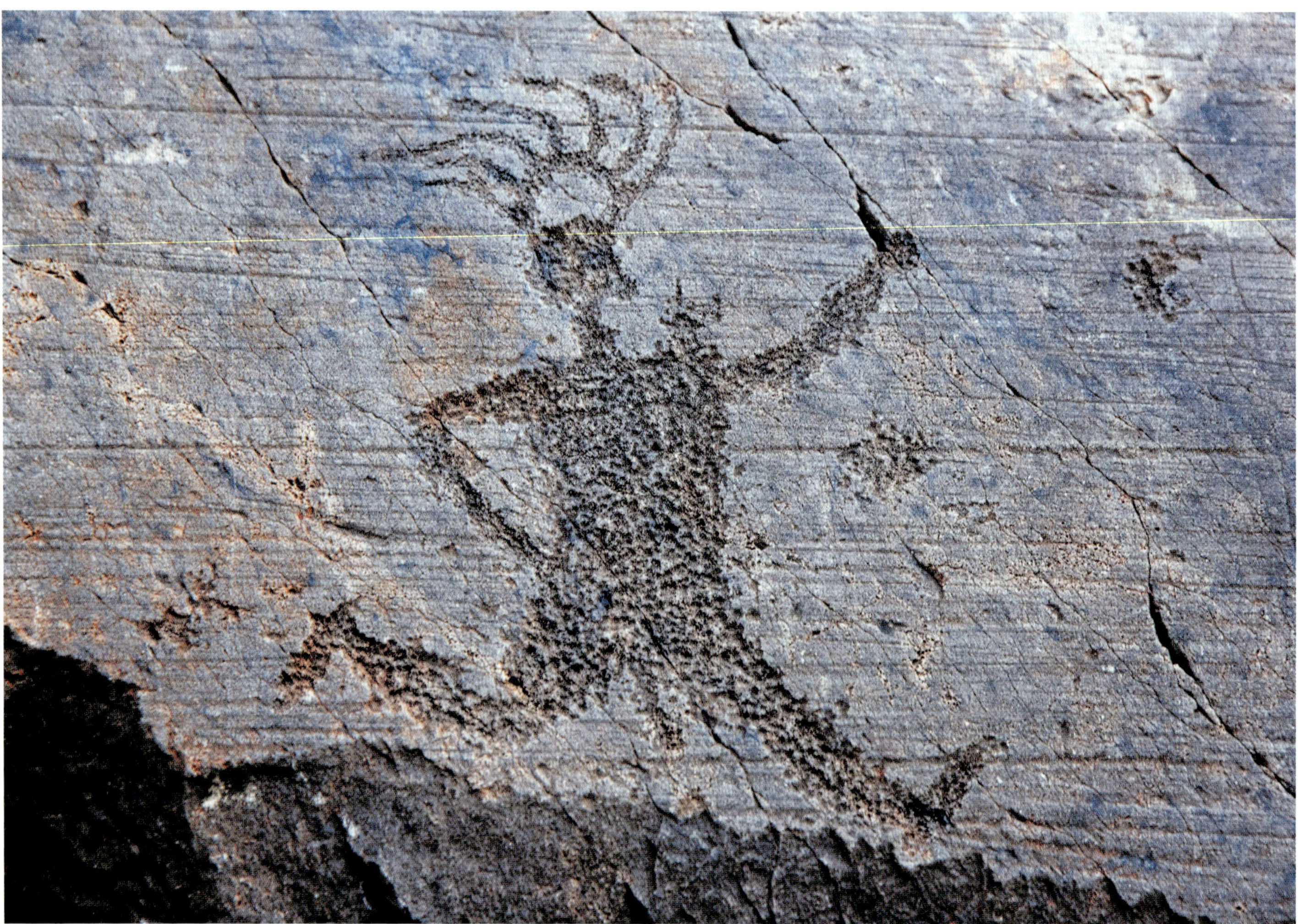

200. A running man wearing a feathered headdress on boulder 35 at Naquane. Such a dynamic image is unusual. Iron Age, Capo di Ponte, Val Camonica, northern Italy. Photo 2019.

The rock art is 4.6 metres long and 1.9 metres high; it dates from around 1030 CE and illustrates an episode from the saga of Sigurd, the slayer of the dragon Fafnir. (Sigurd is called Siegfried in the *Song of the Nibelungs*.) According to the saga, the god Loki once killed the fisherman Otter, who was fishing in the guise of an otter. His enraged father Hreidmar demanded that Loki fill the skin of his slain son with gold. Loki extorted the gold and a magic gold ring from the dwarf Andvari, who cursed the treasure which from now on would bring death to its possessor. As Hreidmar refused to share the gold with his two other sons, Fafnir and Regin, Fafnir murdered his father and took on the form of a dragon, and hid the gold in a cave. Regin then incited his foster son Sigurd the Volsung to kill Fafnir and forged the special sword Gram for him. In the rock art, Sigurd pierces the dragon Fafnir with his sword Gram. Then, in the centre left of the picture, Sigurd rests, his horse tied to a tree on whose crown a bird is sitting. Sigurd sits on the ground and roasts Fafnir's heart for Regin who wants to eat it. But Sigurd

burns his thumb and cools it in his mouth. As soon as the dragon's blood touches his tongue, he immediately understands the language of the birds and the bird on the tree above him. The bird warns him that his foster father Regin wants to kill him so that he can have the gold for himself. Sigurd listens to the bird's warning and kills the blacksmith Regin, whose headless corpse and disembodied head can be seen on the left of the scene.[243] It is implied that the curse of the dwarf Andvari will now pass to Sigurd since he will appropriate the treasure.

Related to this rock art are the more than 400 illustrated stone steles from the Migration and Viking periods, most of which stand in Gotland, Sweden. Usually painted, they illustrate not only episodes from Nordic mythology such as the entry of a dead warrior riding Odin's eight-legged magic horse into Valhalla, but also much older motifs from the Bronze Age such as ships carrying solar symbols and single combats.[244] However, it would go beyond the scope of this book to discuss this interesting subject in detail.

2. Alpine Central Europe

The two main sites of Alpine petroglyphs are situated in Val Camonica (Italy)[245] and Mont Bégo (France); both of them lie within the southern flanks of the Alps. A secondary site is the large rock called *Rupe Magna* at Grosio in Valtellina, Italian Lombardy, which is 84 metres long and 35 metres wide, where hundreds of rather simple petroglyphs similar to those in Val Camonica are engraved.[246] In the Swiss and Austrian Alps there are a few much smaller sites, for example Carschenna (Switzerland). The central European Alpine petroglyphs mostly date from the Bronze and Iron Ages and show significant visual differences from the petroglyphs in southern Fennoscandia. Although the intellectual and societal developments of this region were similar to southern Scandinavia, the thematic visualization was quite different. In both regions the development can be observed of a rather egalitarian, pre-Bronze Age society into a hierarchical society with a corresponding glorification of the warrior and his weapons. However, due to environmental conditions, only a few boats or sea creatures can be found in the southern Alps, whereas scenes related to agriculture and settlements are common. Among the few petroglyphs featuring a boat, two of them located on rock 50 at Naquane in Val Camonica have an inscription in the North Etruscan, or more specifically Camunian, script engraved on the hull. Since the inscriptions are names, these petroglyphs may possibly illustrate the journey of a dead person to the netherworld by boat.[247] Unique to Val Camonica are the seven petroglyphs which feature what are without any doubt wooden vertical looms. Weaving is traditionally associated with domestic activities performed by women which are in general only rarely thematized in European petroglyphs. Hunts, depictions of duels and weapons are common to both southern Fennoscandia and the Alpine regions; schematized heads of bulls are unique to Mont Bégo.

2.1. Val Camonica

The huge petroglyph complex of Val Camonica National Park which has been a UNESCO World Heritage site since 1979 lies in the north Italian province of Brescia. The petroglyphs are spread over a distance of 25 kilometres within a valley more than 100 kilometres long. More than 140,000 petroglyphs[248] are distributed over some three dozen sites; the most important ones are:

- **Naquane**, Capo di Ponte municipality, is, together with Seradina-Bedolina, the largest and most interesting site. It lies on the eastern side of the valley through which the river Oglio flows. Naquane contains 104 rocks with petroglyphs dating from the Neolithic to the Iron Age.

- **Seradina-Bedolina**, Capo di Ponte municipality, is on the west side of the valley, only 1 km away from Naquane as the crow flies. Its petroglyphs date from the Bronze and Iron Ages.

- **Massi di Cemmo** lies 200 m south of Seradina-Bedolina. Here two huge rocks covered with petroglyphs were, in the Chalcolithic period, part of a large megalithic sanctuary which was rearranged in the late Bronze Age and turned into a large ceremonial site. The sanctuary was in use until the first three centuries CE, under Roman rule, and was dismantled in the fourth or fifth century CE with the spread of Christianity. Next to the two rocks, at least 30 additional engraved monoliths were excavated, many of them in fragments, and brought to the local museum. Also from the Chalcolithic are the two engraved menhirs from **Bagnolo**, 10 km south of Capo di Ponte.

- The **Museum of Prehistory** stands in the centre of the village of Capo di Ponte, and contains, among other things, about 50 engraved stone steles or fragments dating from the Chalcolithic which in the Alpine region covers the late fourth and the whole third millennium BCE. The stone monoliths come from Massi di Cemmo and other places in the valley.

- **Asinino-Anvòia** and **Luine** near Darfo Boario Terme are smaller and lie a few kilometres south-west of Naquane. At Asinino-Anvòia the alignment of menhirs has been reconstructed based on archaeological excavations; at Luine are found the oldest petroglyphs, which date from the final Upper Palaeolithic or the Mesolithic. At **Corni Fresci** north-east of Boario Terme a composition of nine halberds from the Chalcolithic period is engraved on a large boulder.

- **Sellero** and **Sonico** are a few kilometres north of Naquane.

- **Foppe di Nadro, Cimbergo** and **Paspardo** are 1–2 km east and south-east of Naquane. Noteworthy are the petroglyphs of houses built on stilts, weapons and duel scenes, all from the Iron Age.

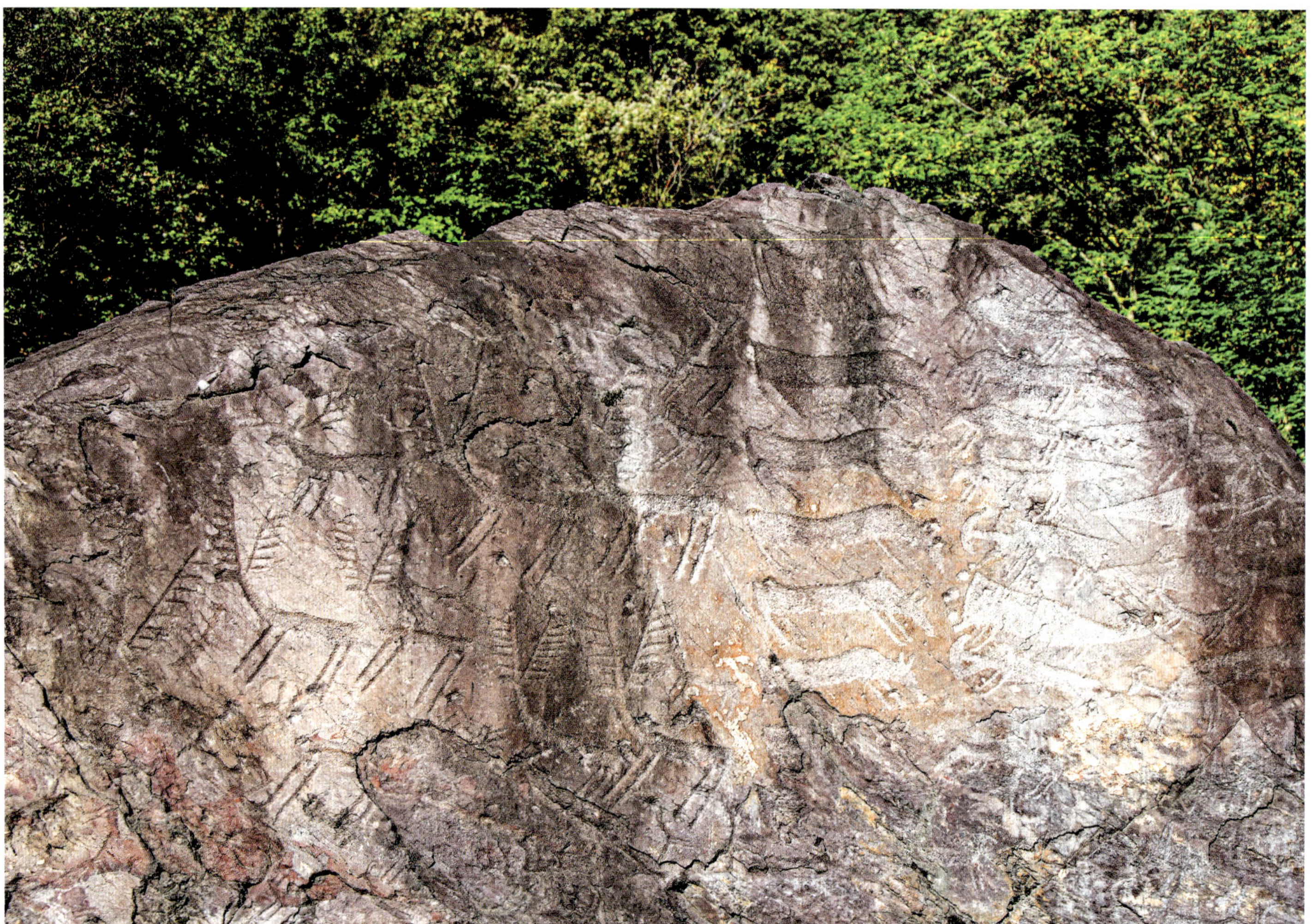

201. The upper part of one of the two main rocks *in situ* at Massi di Cemmo, Capo di Ponte municipality. On the right, images of so-called Remedello daggers are superimposed on petroglyphs of stags. Such engraved daggers were probably substitutes for the offering of real daggers. Chalcolithic period, fourth to third millennium BCE. Val Camonica, northern Italy. Photo 2019.

The rock of Val Camonica used for pecking petroglyphs is Permian sandstone which was formed in the Permian Period 299–252 million years ago. These rocks were later exposed several times to glaciation. The advancing and retreating glaciers shaped and smoothed them creating polished and striated surfaces. When in the Mesolithic the last glaciers withdrew, hunter-gatherers ventured into the valley in the tenth to ninth millennium BCE; they made the earliest petroglyphs, mainly of schematized large prey, spears and abstract signs. During the Neolithic, farmers and pastoralists settled in the valley, displacing the hunter-gatherers. They introduced new technologies such as agriculture, cattle breeding, ceramics, the loom, and possibly also the bow and arrow. In the course of the third millennium BCE metallurgy spread, and soon afterwards the wheel. In the second millennium BCE, Val Camonica was one of several transit routes leading from northern Italy over the Alps to Central Europe. At the beginning of the Iron Age, around 900 BCE, the horse was introduced. All these stages can be followed in the petroglyphs of specific weapons, agricultural tools, looms, metal processing, houses and plans of settlements.

Also in the earlier Iron Age, the local people of the valley, whom the Romans called Camuni or Camunni, brought rock art to its highest flowering.[249] According to the Greek geographer Strabo (64/63 BCE–23 CE), the Camuni belonged to the Rhaetian people[250] whose language was related to Etruscan; for their script, the Camuni adapted the North Etruscan alphabet to their needs and created the Camunian alphabet. The importance of rock art for the Camuni is highlighted by the fact that of the 280 recorded Camunian inscriptions – which are mainly divine and human names – 60 per cent were found on rocks and stone menhirs. When the Celtic Gauls invaded Italy and conquered Rome in 390 or 387 BCE, the Camuni were in contact with those Gauls who had settled in the plain of the Po Valley. The famous petroglyph of the Celtic god Cernunnos, protector of animals and god of nature and fertility, refers to this Celtic cultural influence (fig. 210). In the years 16–15 BCE, the Roman generals Drusus, Tiberius and Publius Silius Nerva brought Val Camonica and neighbouring parts of the Alps under Roman rule.[251] With the Roman conquest, the pecking of petroglyphs virtually came to an end and was limited to a few Latin inscriptions and later to some Christian symbols such as crosses and keys. In the fourth or fifth centuries, the ancient pre-Christian sanctuaries were dismantled.

The petroglyphs of Val Camonica were first officially mentioned in 1909 by the alpinist Walther Laeng; his first publication followed in 1914. But it was only in 1929 that research in Val Camonica really began, conducted by Giovanni Marro and Raffaello Battaglia. In the second half of the 1930s, the petroglyphs were misused for political purposes when the Germans Franz Altheim and Erika Trautmann conducted research in the valley. The first two expeditions in 1935 and 1936 were organized by the Institut für Kulturmorphologie, founded and directed by

the pioneer of rock art research Leo Frobenius (1873–1938), who was free of ideological bias. But, as a result of Trautmann's close connections with high-ranking Nazi officials, the next expeditions up to 1940 were conducted under the financial and ideological auspices of Heinrich Himmler's pseudo-scientific SS organization Ahnenerbe (Ancestral Heritage) and with the support of Hermann Göring. Altheim and Trautmann identified alleged similarities between southern Scandinavian petroglyphs and those at Val Camonica and claimed, in line with Nazi ideology, that both were rooted in the common heritage of the so-called prehistoric 'Aryan race'. The Val Camonica petroglyphs were declared to be the product of a migration of Aryans form Northern Europe, the home of the superior Aryan race, southward to the Alps. Following the appropriation by Altheim and Trautmann of the Val Camonica petroglyphs as the product of the superior Nordic-German Aryan race, the Italian Marro did not hesitate to claim the authorship of Val Camonica rock art for a similarly

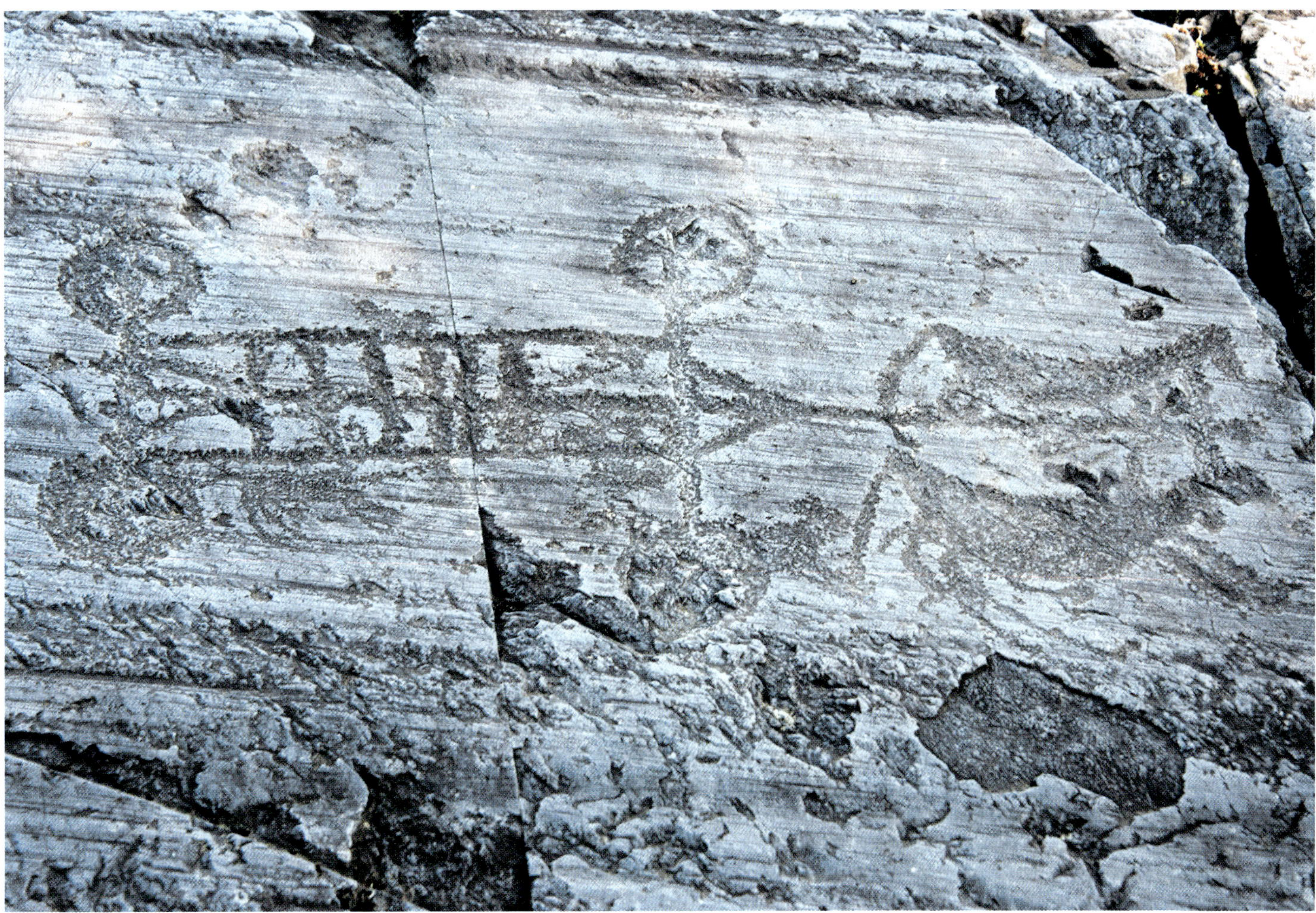

202. A two-axle wagon pulled by two horses. Later Bronze Age, Boulder 23 at Naquane, Capo di Ponte, Val Camonica, northern Italy. Photo 2019.

superior 'Italic race'. Scientific research started in 1956 when the archaeologist Emmanuel Anati (b. 1930) arrived in Val Camonica in order to compare its petroglyphs with those at Mont Bégo in the French Alpes-Maritimes. Although he had originally planned to stay only a few days, he immediately grasped the potential of the site and dedicated the rest of his life to the research of Val Camonica.[252] In 1964, he founded the Centro Camuno dei Studi Preistorici (Camunian Centre of Prehistoric Studies), and in 1979, Val Camonica became the first Italian monument to be listed as a World Heritage site.[253]

Mainly based on stylistic criteria, a chronology of the Val Camonica rock art has been established in six periods, whose cornerstone figures are supported by archaeological data.[254]

I. Final Upper Palaeolithic to Mesolithic (Proto-Camunian) period, eleventh (?) to sixth millennium BCE. This tiny group of a dozen larger petroglyphs represent mainly elk and deer rendered in outline and being hit by spears; there are also two images of fish.[255] As temperatures continued to rise in the early Holocene, elk left the Alpine region and no longer appear

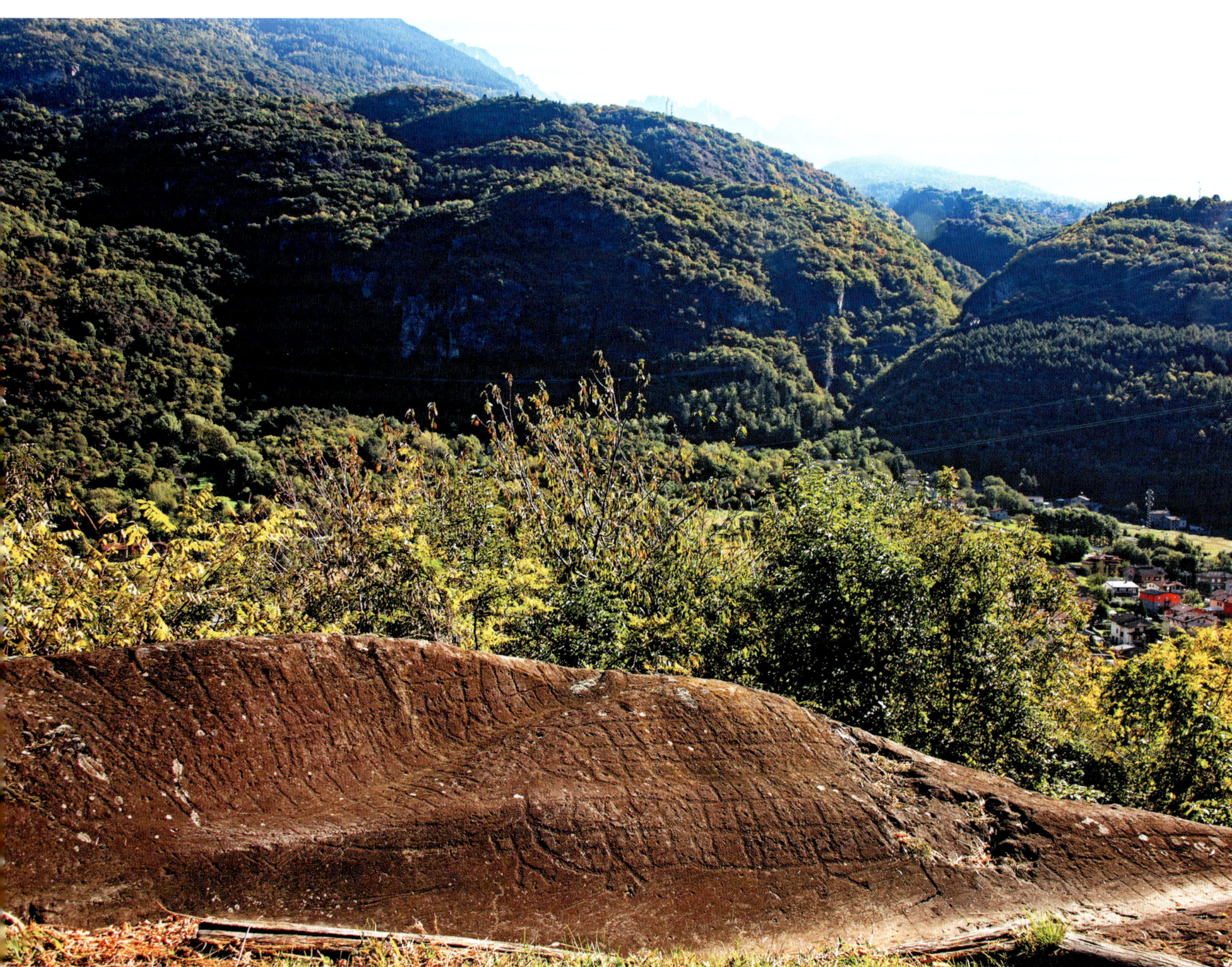

203. A kind of schematic map of the local settlements with a few superimposed humans. Boulder 57 at Seradina I, image taken looking east. Early Iron Age, Capo di Ponte, Val Camonica, northern Italy. Photo 2019.

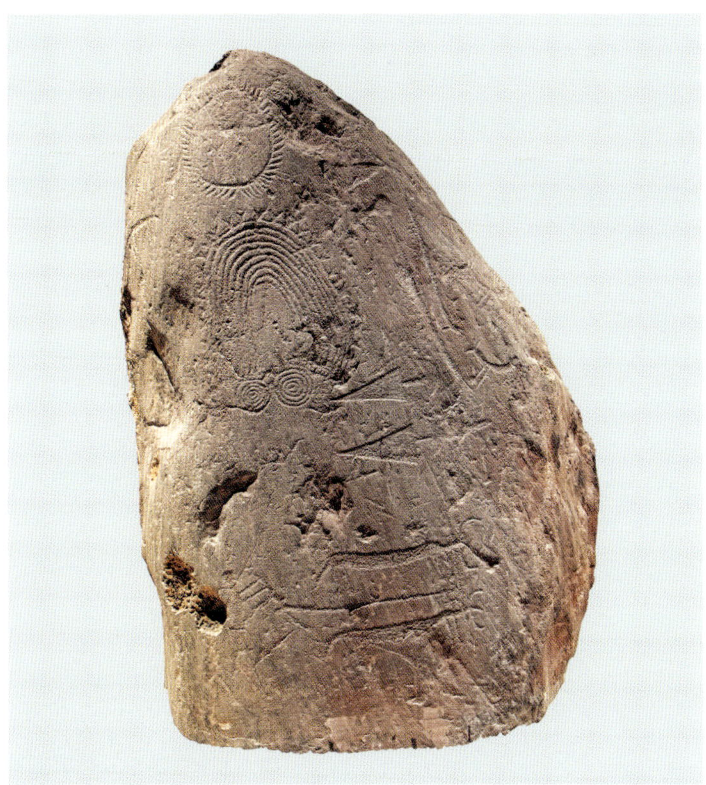

204. Menhir 2 from Bagnolo. From top to bottom are engraved: a solar symbol or a necklace; a U-shaped necklace with two pendants consisting of circular circles; to its right two palstaves; and below two Remedello-type daggers and a ploughing scene. It seems that both male and female attributes or markers appear on this stone block: the sequence of the engraving is uncertain. National Museum of Prehistory, Val Camonica, northern Italy. Photo 2019.

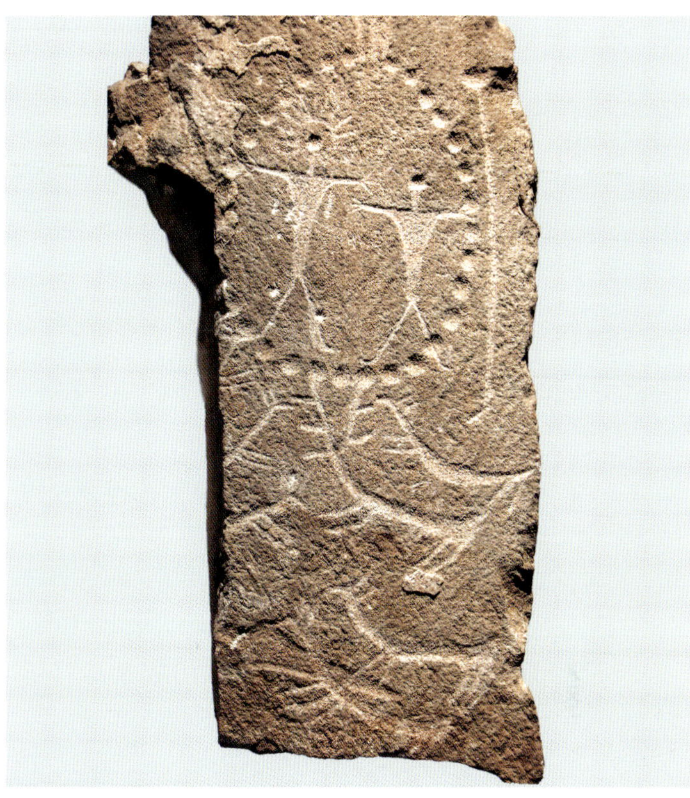

205. Menhir 4 from Massi di Cemmo. At the top, two humans stand inside a circle of pearls, the head of the larger one is surrounded by rays; beneath are stags and does. Chalcolithic period. National Museum of Prehistory, Val Camonica, northern Italy. Photo 2019.

in petroglyphs. These early petroglyphs, made by hunter-gatherers, show some similarities with petroglyphs in northern Norwegian Nordland, and with the carvings on schist plaques from the Franco-Cantabrian Azilian culture.[256]

II. Late Neolithic to Early Chalcolithic period, late fifth to early third millennium BCE. There was possibly a hiatus in the production of petroglyphs between the first and the second period. In Period II, petroglyphs were mainly non-figurative and consisted of cup marks of different sizes, spirals and rectangles.[257]

III. Chalcolithic period, *ca.* 2800–2200 BCE. In this period, figurative rock art returned, this time not on rocks embedded in the ground, but on free-standing stone steles as well as on isolated blocks from landslides, such as Cemmo 1 and Cemmo 2 (fig. 201). The steles were most probably anthropomorphic as is suggested by the occasional schematic representations of shoulders. In this aspect the figurative steles differ from menhirs which lack iconographic anthropomorphic markers. The

only vaguely human character of the Val Camonica steles and those from Valtellina (northern Italy) sets them apart from other Alpine groups such as those of the Val d'Aosta (Italy) and Sion (southern Switzerland) which are more clearly shaped as anthropomorphs (fig. 213). However, the engraved figures display some similarities in both groups. In the first phase at Val Camonica, petroglyphs of the so-called 'Remedello' dagger predominate, which is characterized by a triangular blade and a half-moon-shaped pommel (figs 201, 204). Such daggers, made from arsenic copper, were excavated in the grave-yard of Remedello di Sotto, in Brescia province, northern Italy, and are dated to 2900–2500 BCE.[258] They feature also on the Chalcolithic steles of the Remedello culture of Aosta and Sion. On the Val Camonica steles, the daggers appear together with other weapons such as axes and halberds, and with animals, mainly deer, ibexes, wolfs, foxes and wild dogs. There are also renderings of wagons and several ploughing scenes using bulls which show that the Chalcolithic petroglyph makers were agriculturalists who had acquired the technologies of copper metallurgy and of wheeled vehicles (fig. 204).[259] It is probable

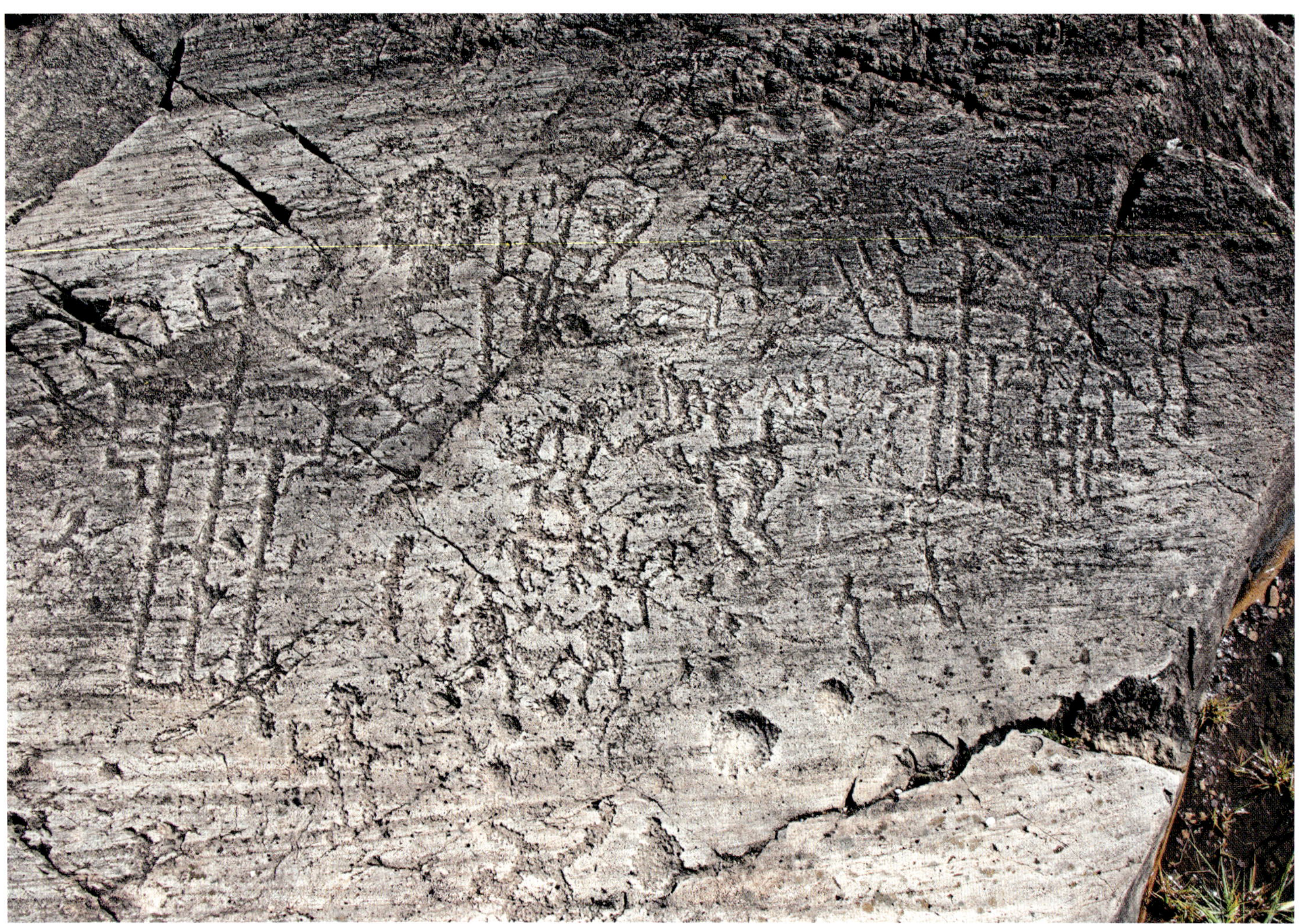

206. Two duels in the courtyard between two houses or barns. Detail from boulder 18 at Seradina II. Iron Age, Capo di Ponte, Val Camonica, northern Italy. Photo 2019.

that farmers had moved from the Po Valley plain northwards into Val Camonica in the later fourth millennium BCE. Whether the acquisition of those technologies and of certain elements of their worldview such as the veneration of weapons and the solar disc represent 'Indo-European' influences, as suggested by Anati, is debatable. Concerning the supposed subdivision of the universe into the three spheres of sky, earth and nether-world, which Anati reads into the Chalcolithic stone steles, one has to bear in mind that (in the words of Lawrence Barfield and Christopher Chippindale) 'the Chalcolithic in northern Italy appears to fall a little earlier than the Indo-European incur-sions into south-central Europe'.[260] Anati's hypothesis that 'the Indo-European ideology was born or had an important devel-opment in the Alpine area', is definitely untenable as it contra-dicts all the linguistic evidence.[261]

These Chalcolithic steles were, like many from Sion and Aosta, gendered. Masculine steles are characterized by daggers, axes, halberds, a solar disc, wild animals, ploughing and a horizontal belt.[262] Occasionally, rectangles with a chequerboard pattern and fringes also decorate the masculine steles, which may possibly represent a cloak.[263] Female steles are marked by pendants consisting of concentric circles and large U-shaped necklaces, which correspond to excavated copper jewellery (fig. 204). Smaller U-shaped figures may represent diadems. At Val Camonica and Valtallina, the U-shaped motif is often associated with the so-called 'sun with three rays'.[264] Additional female markers are concentric circles, earrings and the schematic indication of eyebrows and nose as well as breasts. Female steles lack weapons and animals. These markers of sex engraved on steles are matched by the grave goods excavated in burials dating from the same cultural time frame. In the second, transitory phase, anthropomorphs begin to appear on steles and animals are rendered in a more naturalistic way, whereas in the third phase anthropomorphs dancing in a row or in circles dominate, together with slim-bladed daggers of the Ciempozuelos type and halberds of the Villafranca type, which were widespread in the Bell Beaker culture. On some steles, such as Masso di Cemmo 3, the dancing humans are superimposed on images of daggers, halberds and deer. On another stele, the deer are superimposed over the daggers.[265] The fact that these steles were re-engraved and reconfigured centuries after they had first been erected shows that they remained *per se* relevant objects of veneration although their initial meaning had become obsolete. The enduring veneration of these ancient steles is underscored by the nearby availability of countless similar, unused stones, since it would have been easier to engrave these unused stones than to recut the old ones.[266]

On one singular stele, two people stand in the upper half within a circle of pearls, with the head of the larger, probably male figure, surrounded by a halo of rays; this latter aspect may suggest an anthropomorphizing of the earlier solar symbol (fig. 205). In the lower part of the stele, the images of two schematic stags were superimposed on an earlier petroglyph of a dagger. As explained by Alberto Marretta, the Chalcolithic period at Val Camonica is divided into two periods, the first associated with Remedello daggers (*ca.* 2900–2500 BCE) and the second with the Bell Beaker culture, lasting until 2200 BCE. This corresponds with the division into an earlier 'symbolic' period using 'iconic signs' such as the dagger and the solar disc, followed by an anthropomorphic phase. This sequence went in parallel with the gradual switch from a worldview focussing on ancestor worship to one where selected members of the community are idealized.[267] However, whereas at Sion we find steles which were associated with burials and which are understood as the representations of ancestors of the founders of clans, this link is missing at Cemmo and other sites with steles in Val Camonica.[268] Whether the steles of Val Camonica represented ancestors or deities remains unknown. What is certain is that such places, with their alignments of steles and menhirs, served as markers in the open landscape and as a sanctuary for rituals. Concerning the numerous representations of daggers and halberds, it is possible that they were offered in place of the non-existent grave goods; and even at Sion and Aosta, only small numbers of weapons were bequeathed to the buried persons as grave goods.

IV. Bronze Age period, 2200–900 BCE. During the Bronze Age, the representation of weapons continued, hardly ever any longer on free-standing steles but now on the rocks and boulders which are part of the landscape. In contrast to the weapons on the Chalcolithic steles which were rendered in a regular and orderly manner they now appear in heterogenous groups and without any recognizable spatial arrangement. Most of these weapons have their counterparts in metal weapons excavated from burials. As in Fennoscandia, one can hypothesize that the pecking of such petroglyphs was a kind of substitute for real offerings. Whereas weapons were a male symbol, the so-called *paletta*, a kind of shovel, was a female marker, since such objects were found in female burials from the Later Bronze Age. The *paletta* was used for managing fire during cooking and for gathering ashes. Also during the Bronze Age, females remained visible in petroglyphs, sometimes prominently, as at rock 32 at Naquane from the late Bronze Age where seven humans, most probably females, stand or

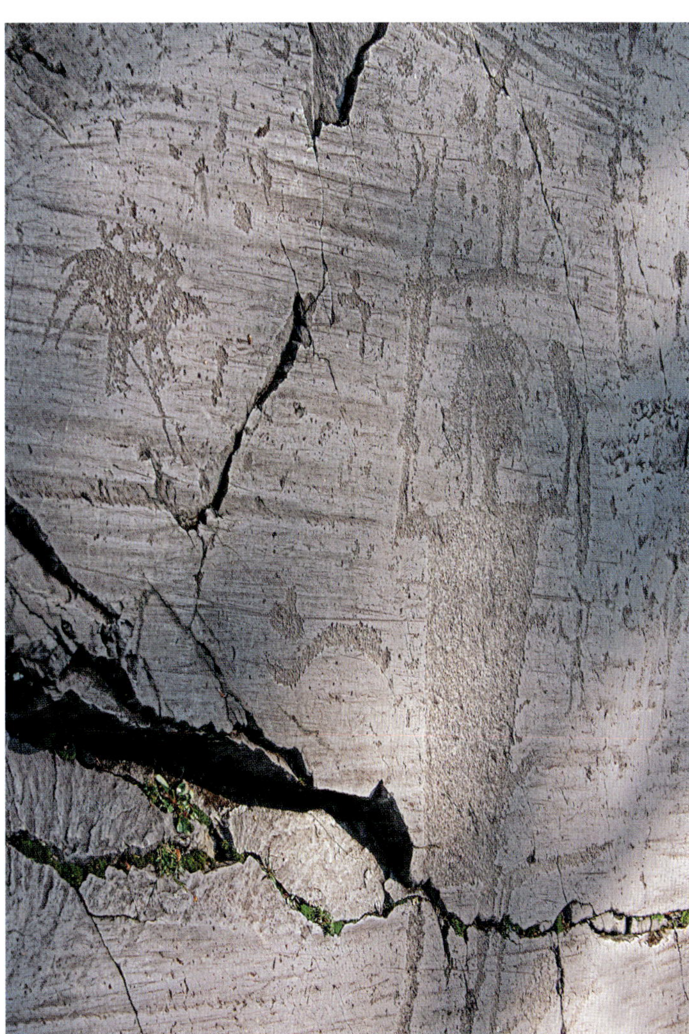

207. Petroglyph of a tall warrior wearing an Etruscan helmet and armed with a sword or short spear and a shield. Iron Age, rock 50 at Naquane, Capo di Ponte, Val Camonica, northern Italy. Photo 2019.

dance with arms raised, above a woman and a second human of undefined sex lying on the ground; to the right stands another human, probably male. The two lying humans are pecked inside a natural small channel, and when it rains, water flows through the channel. The scene has been interpreted as an initiation, a birthing or, more likely, a mourning scene.[269] In the Iron Age, women disappear from petroglyphs except in sexual scenes. Also from the Bronze Age date the petroglyphs of vertical looms. The threads stretched on the loom were kept under tension by small pierced stones or clay objects which were attached at the threads' lower end. They are illustrated in the petroglyphs by rows of tiny hanging discs. This illustration of domestic scenes is a major difference compared to the petroglyphs of southern Fennoscandia.

V. Iron Age period, 900–15 BCE. About 80 per cent of Val Camonica's petroglyphs date from the Iron Age when the Camuni emerged as an ethnic group. The rock art reflects an apparent militarization of society with the emergence of a martial elite, since images of warriors and scenes expressing martial values now occupy a prominent place. Whereas in

the previous two periods weapons appeared alone in rock art, they are now held by humans engaged in action (figs 206, 207). Petroglyphs of warriors on foot wearing helmets, holding shields and wielding swords and spears are often shown with their weapons raised in a pose of self-glorification and exaltation, but also in actual combat, either between warriors on foot or between horsemen and fighters on foot, as on rock 21 of Seradina II. In addition, there are many images of duellists and mounted warriors.[270] All these motifs signal a new ideology centred on martial values. Hunting scenes by single hunters or groups of horsemen armed with spears (rock 12, Seradina I) and the illustration of the act of killing the prey (rock 1, Naquane) underline this set of competitive values. The duellists are often only lightly armed with a sword or a short spear and a small shield; sometimes they fight flanked by their seconds who hold spear and shield (fig. 208). Since in such scenes the assistants are taller than the duellists, the latter are probably adolescents undergoing trials of courage and martial skills in order to be admitted into the group of warriors; occasionally, such trials ended with a fatal outcome.[271] The petroglyphs of four-wheeled wagons pulled by horses show for their part striking similarities

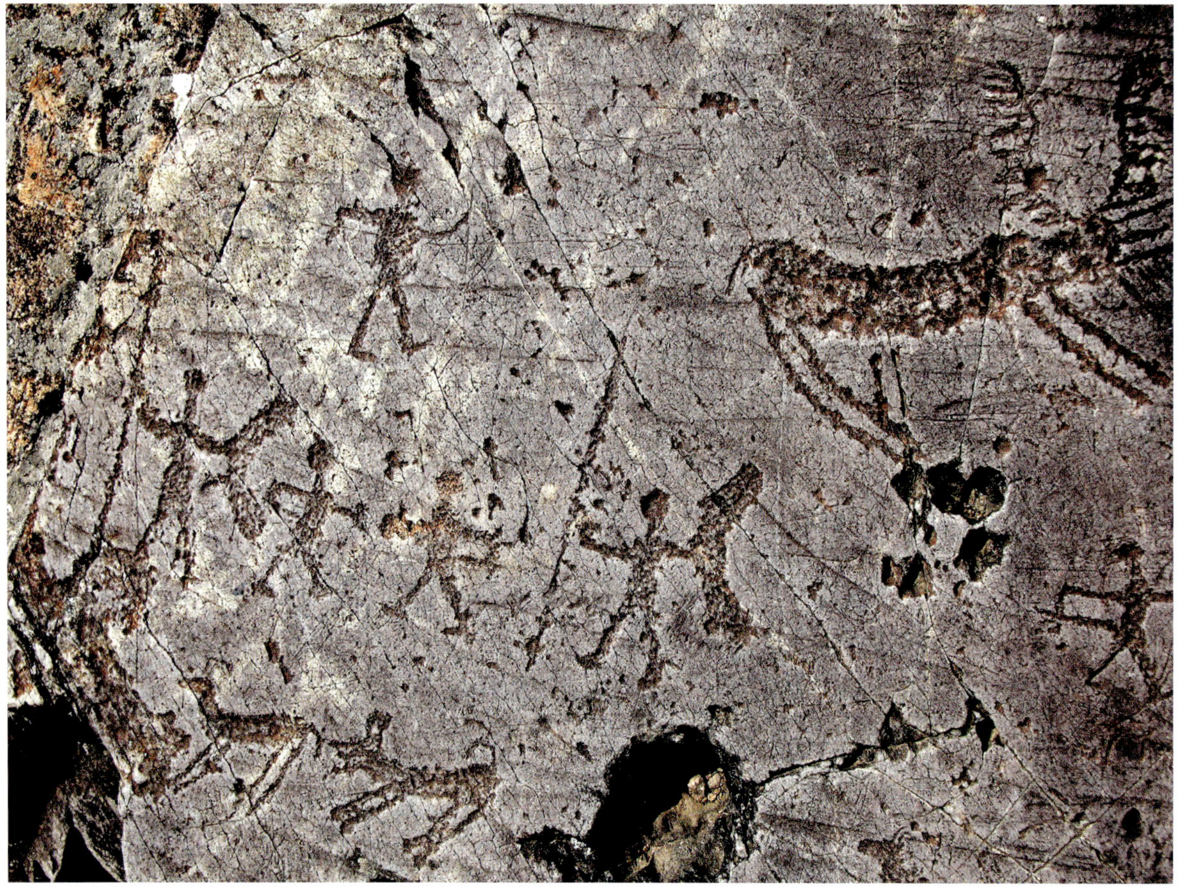

208. Two lightly armed, adolescent duellists fight under the observation of their referees or assistants. Iron Age, rock 12 at Seradina II, Capo di Ponte, Val Camonica, northern Italy. Photo 2007.

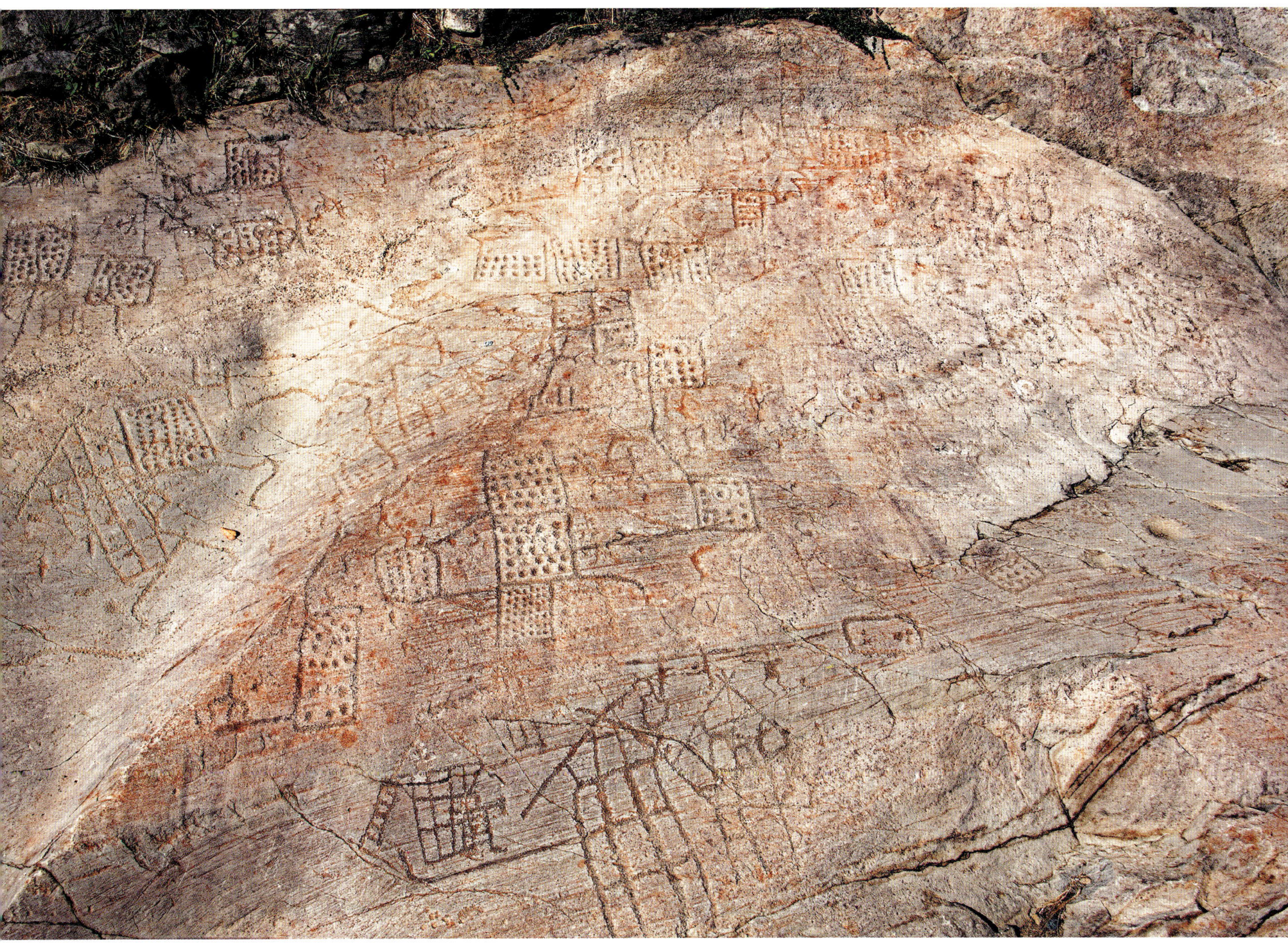

209. The so-called 'Bedolina Map' on rock 1 at Bedolina measures 350 × 250 cm and probably visualizes a village that could be seen from the location. Early to middle Iron Age, Capo di Ponte, Val Camonica, northern Italy. Photo 2019.

with the image of a wagon on the recliner of Hochdorf, a Celtic burial from the sixth century BCE belonging to the early Iron Age Hallstatt culture (800–450 BCE) (fig. 202). Such wagons were used in Celtic Central Europe to transport deceased members of the upper class to the funeral place where they would be buried together with other grave goods and, occasionally, also with the sacrificed horses.[272]

Other images deal with agriculture and settled life. To these belong ploughing scenes, in one of which a sex scene is rendered immediately behind the plougher, most probably as a further symbol of fertility. In another agricultural scene, a man leads two donkeys pulling a harrow, on which a second man

stands to weigh it down (both scenes on rock 12, Seradina I). Also clearly associated with settled life are the various topographical compositions, mainly at Seradina and Naquane.[273] Most spectacular is the 'Bedolina Map' engraved on rock 1 at Bedolina, a sandstone rock nine metres long and four metres wide located high above the valley (fig. 209). Here, the 109 figures replicate the landscape seen from this rock and show cultivated fields, meadows, demarcation walls, paths and a village which corresponds to the Bronze and Iron Age village of Dos dell'Arca. The map of the village alone measures 3.5 by 2.5 metres. The village is illustrated with multistorey houses (perhaps including barns and food stores) with gabled roofs and standing on some kind of stilts; in some houses a ladder leads to the top floor from outside. These buildings were made from wood. According to Dietrich Evers, the houses were not constructed on stilts driven into the ground, but on wooden pillars which stood in a box frame tightly filled with heavy rubble.[274] Paths connect the houses and cultivated gardens with each other, and between them there are humans and various animals. The map includes a so-called 'Camunian Rose' which is formed of a winding, closed line curving around nine cup marks; it either forms a kind of cross or a swastika. Whether it is a solar symbol remains unknown. The Bedolina Map is one of the oldest existing maps in the world and dates to the Middle Iron Age, that is the middle of the first millennium BCE.[275] The topographical compositions at Seradina I, rock 57 and II, rocks 18, 21, among others, are also spectacular. In the first

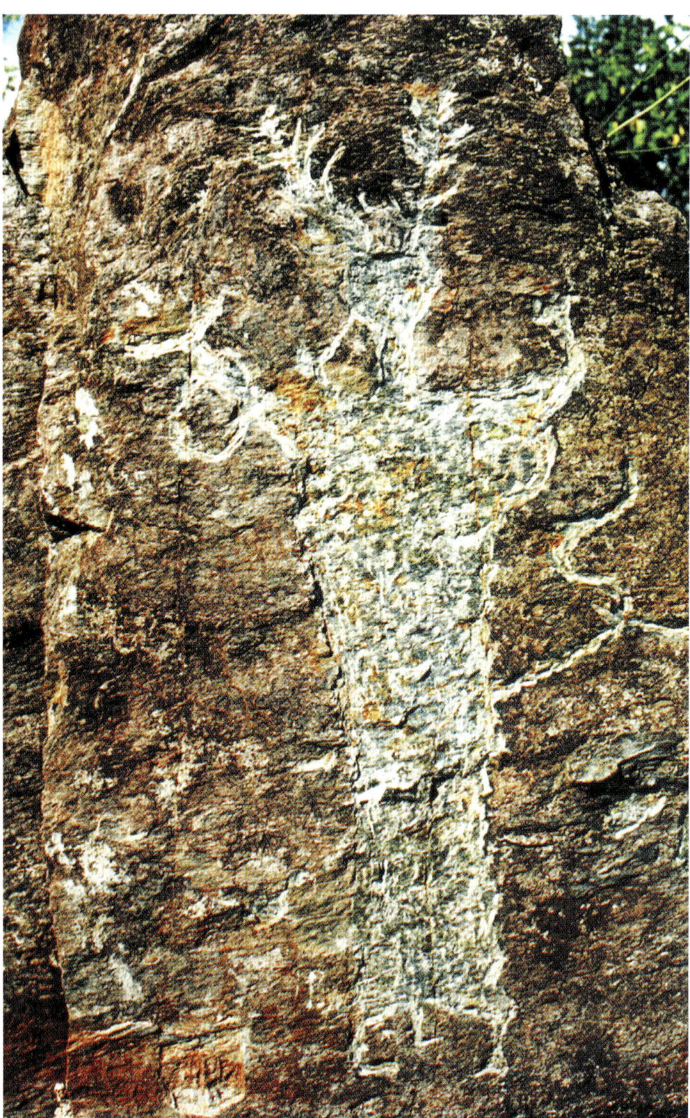

two of these compositions, duels are fought near or between the houses, and both feature a Camunian inscription (fig. 206). Opposite Seradina, at Naquane rock 35, are engraved nine structures with gabled roofs. Goats are shown inside the three largest constructions, which may indicate that they represent barns. At Naquane 35 there is also a unique petroglyph of a running man wearing a hat adorned with feathers; petroglyphs expressing such dynamic movement are rare (fig. 200).

Some of the motifs serve as chronological markers giving *post quem* dates. Horse riding began in the valley in the ninth or eighth centuries BCE, the Camunian script based on the North Etruscan alphabet was developed around the fifth century BCE, and Latin inscriptions first appear only at the end of the first century BCE following the Roman occupation. The Etruscan influence is also visible in the life-sized image of a standing warrior armed with a spear and a shield wearing an Etruscan helmet with a comb-like crest (fig. 207). This image is on Naquane, rock 50; another one is at Cimbergo, rock 62. After the Gauls had invaded Italy in 390 or 387 BCE and settled in the Po Valley, cultural exchanges with the Etruscans were interrupted and Celtic influences prevailed, which is clearly apparent in the life-size petroglyph featuring Cernunnos, the Celtic god of nature and fertility, at Naquane, rock 70 (fig. 210).[276] Cernunnos, whose name means 'the horned god', wears antlers and holds in his left hand a cornucopia and in his right a torc (a large and stiff metal ring), while a snake appears behind his hips. In fact, this Camunian petroglyph is believed to be the oldest depiction of Cernunnos.[277] Another famous image of the antlered god Cernunnos can be found on the large silver **Gundestrup Cauldron** which was discovered in a Danish bog (fig. 211). This unique piece has a diameter of 69 centimetres, stands 42 centimetres high and weighs 9 kilogrammes. The silver used came apparently from two sources, one from northern France and the other from the Taunus Mountains in western Germany; the alloyed tin, for its part, came from Cornwall. The cauldron is decorated on the inside with five concave plates and on the outside with eight convex plates, of which one is missing.

210. The life-size petroglyph of an anthropomorph with antlers who holds in his left hand a cornucopia and in his right a torc. It represents the Celtic god of nature and fertility Cernunnos; a snake appears behind the god. Iron Age, rock 70 at Naquane, Capo di Ponte, Val Camonica, northern Italy. The photo was made before overly aggressive cleaning removed the contrast between the petroglyph and the surrounding patina. Scientific image quotation: Widmer, Jean-Pierre, *Ces fascinantes gravures de l'art rupestre du Val Camonica* (Weinstadt: Bernhard-Albert Greiner, 2013), fig. 118.

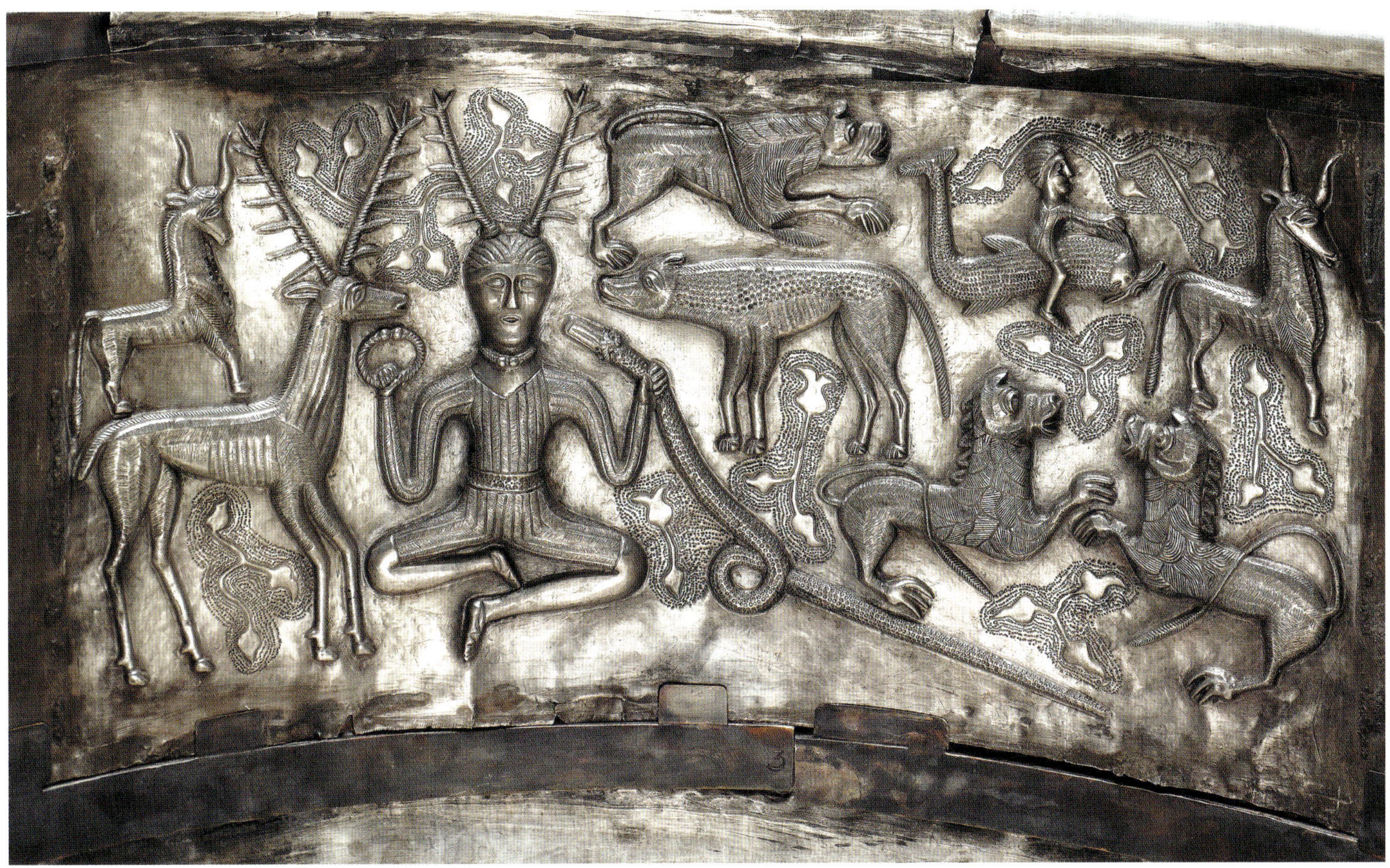

211. The Celtic god Cernunnos with his typical antlers; in his hands he holds a snake with a ram's head and a torc. He is flanked by two bulls or antelopes, a stag with similar antlers to Cernunnos, three lions, a wolf and a man riding a dolphin. Inside plate of the Gundestrup Cauldron, probably fourth to third century BCE. Photo: CC BY-SA, Roberto Fortuna & Kira Ursem, The National Museum of Denmark, Copenhagen.

Cernunnos is represented on an inside plate. There the god is seated holding in one hand a snake with a ram's head, and with the other a torc. To his right stands a stag with the same kind of antlers as the god. Cernunnos is further surrounded by two bulls or antelopes, a wolf, three lions and a man riding a dolphin. In this plate, Cernunnos is represented as the Lord of Animals, a widespread concept within the Eurasian realm. The slightly gilded silver plates, made using the *repoussé* technique (hammering from the reverse side), reveal a Celtic world of ideas executed in a Thracian style. The commissioner of the cauldron was most probably a Celt, but the artist a Thracian.[278] The cauldron has been traditionally dated between 150 and 1 BCE, but two accelerator datings of beeswax from the reverse of the plates gave older datings as far back as the fourth or third centuries BCE which would place the cauldron into the same age bracket as the corresponding petroglyph at Naquane.

VI. Roman and Christian period, 15 BCE–Middle Ages. With the integration of Val Camonica into the Roman Empire, the making of figurative rock art came to an end, probably due to an assimilation of Roman culture and because the social class which had commissioned the pecking of petroglyphs lost its power and relevance. The only petroglyphs made in this period represent, first, Latin inscriptions, then, as of the fourth or fifth century, Christian symbols such as crosses and keys. Rocks with dozens or even hundreds of crosses are to be found at Sonico, Aprica and Cimbergo. The petroglyphs at Val Camonica are unique inasmuch as they document at least seven millennia of history, beginning with Mesolithic hunter-gatherers, followed by Neolithic and Bronze Age farmers among whom, with the coming of the Iron Age, a warrior elite later emerged. Following this, the petroglyphs visualize cultural contacts with Etruscans and Celtic Gauls, and finally, continuing up to the Middle Ages, document first the valley's assimilation into the Roman realm and then the spread of Christianity.

The anthropomorphic stone steles in the south-western Alps

Many of the petroglyph motifs found in Val Camonica during the Chalcolithic period are also found on stone steles of the same age in the south-western Alps and neighbouring regions, namely at Le Petit Chasseur and Don Bosco in Sion in the Swiss Valais; in Aosta, Trentino, Tuscany and Liguria, all in Italy; in south-eastern France; in Sardinia and Corsica. This simultaneous occurrence of engraved motifs on natural rocks and steles during the European terminal Neolithic, Copper and early Bronze Age is comparable to the occurrence of identical figures on rocks and deer stones in Mongolia during the late Bronze Age. The phenomenon of engraved anthropomorphic steles stretched far beyond the Alps, since from 4000 BCE onward steles of up to 395 centimetres in height appeared in several regions reaching from the Pontic Steppe north of the Black Sea and Crimea in today's Ukraine[279] as far as Brittany and the Iberian Atlantic coast. In the region of Sion in the southern Swiss canton of the Valais alone, more than 30 such steles have been excavated,[280] with another 80 steles in the region of Lunigiana in Liguria, 50 steles or stele fragments in Val Camonica, 46 in Aosta, 18 in Trentino, a dozen in Valtellina, and in south-eastern France more than 250 steles or fragments.[281] Several types of stones were used, such as quartzite, micaceous marble, grey marble, gneiss, limestone, trachyte and sandstone. The geographical distribution of these engraved anthropomorphic steles seems random at first glance, but a closer look reveals that their centres of concentration were located near sea coasts, in the catchment areas of major navigable rivers such as the Rhone, the Dnieper and the Dniester, or in selected valleys leading to important mountain passes such as, in the Alps, the Great Saint Bernard, Simplon and Lötschberg. All these places played an important role in the trans-European trade by sea and land in ores, metals and salt.[282] In this context it is surprising that no such steles have so far been found in the British Isles even though they were part of this trading network and possessed a highly developed megalithic culture.[283] Within this huge supra-regional cultural complex, the steles from the Alpine region such as at Sion, Val Camonica, Riva del Garda, Teglio and Aosta share several iconographic similarities which suggests a more or less homogenous cultural realm. These similarities implied a lively cultural exchange within this 280-kilometre-wide region.

Most of the central and south European steles are obviously anthropomorphic with carved shoulders, faces, arms and hands as well as attributes such as belts, weapons, jewellery and clothing. About half of these steles feature facial details such as eyes, nose and mouth whereas those of Sion and Aosta have neither eyes nor mouth; instead, their faces are rendered like a nasal helmet. Numerous steles are also gendered, with breasts, various types of necklaces and other jewellery as well as long tunics decorated with geometric patterns characterizing females, while males are identified by weapons such as daggers, halberds, battle axes, bows and arrows, by a small bag attached to the belt as well as by tools including ploughs, small axes and occasionally a wagon. Interestingly, the attribute of a double-spiralled pendant is found on steles of both sexes belonging to the intermediary period between archaic and developed steles. This gender identification by means of jewellery and weapon attributes can also be found in the tombs of the respective cultures. A smaller number of steles are non-gendered. The majority of all these steles are dated to the terminal Neolithic and the Copper Age, from the later fourth to the third millennium BCE, the engraved Remedello daggers being one of the chronological markers.[284] The steles of Lunigiana represent an exception as they continued to be erected well into the Bronze Age. Even in the Iron Age several Chalcolithic steles from Lunigiana were 'updated', that is reworked, by adding arms, legs or new objects. In addition, steles from Sion and Aosta were supplemented during the third millennium BCE with additional attributes or even modified so that they became three-dimensional palimpsests. Moreover a few steles from Aosta, Val Camonica and Valtellina underwent a change of sex by the superimposition of gendered attributes on older marks signifying the opposite sex: for example, weapons were engraved over

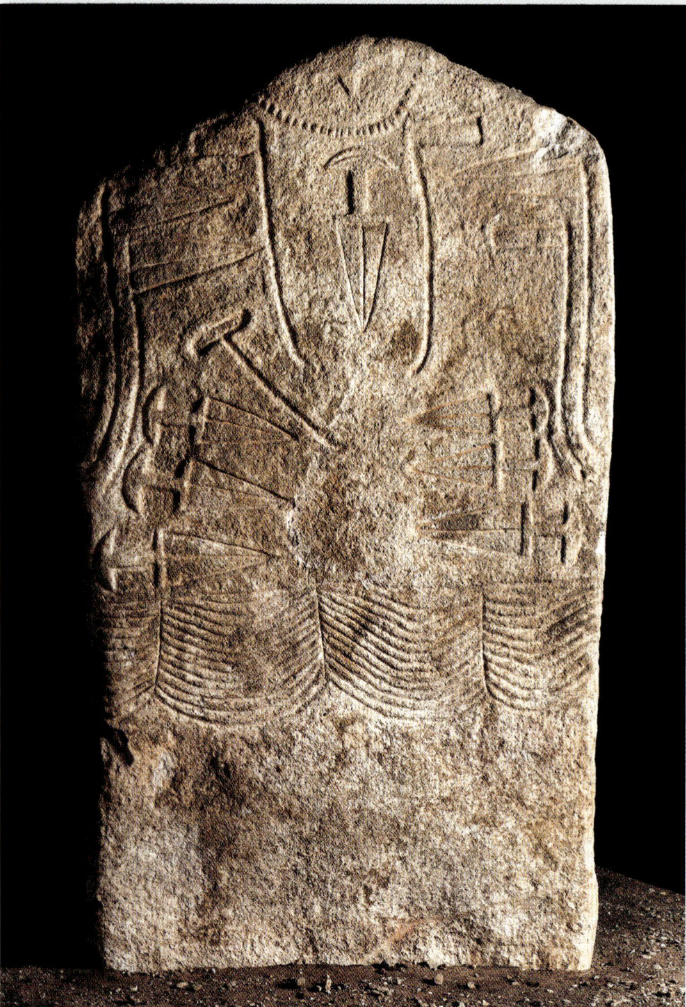

212. The stone stele Arco 1 from Trentino–Alto Adige (South Tyrol), *ca.* 3000–2500 BCE. The stele wears a necklace, and the engraved axes, halberds and daggers marks it as male. At this date, weapons were not buried as grave goods at the death of their owner but handed to his successor. Archivio Museo Alto Garda, Italy. Photo Gardaphoto.

jewellery, and vice versa. In a singular case, stele no. 20 from Sion was first marked on one side as male by a bow and arrow and later on the other side as female by a large necklace, a broad belt and a tunic, both decorated with rhombic patterns.[285] In another singular instance, the 'male' stele no. 1 from Sion originally had a schematized face at its top, which was later replaced by a shining sun with distinctive rays, reminiscent of steles from the Central Asian Okunev culture.[286]

These hundreds of steles signal a change in culture within societies. The Chalcolithic epoch witnessed societal changes triggered by earlier technical innovations whose economic impact became increasingly decisive, namely developments in agriculture and pastoralism, wheeled transport, metallurgy in general and weaponry in particular. The ability to store goods and competition for raw materials led to a stratification within society and the rise of elites. Anthropomorphic steles were often erected in lines or circles close to sacrificial platforms where rituals were performed and votive gifts were offered. They most probably represented high-ranking men and women (or their ancestors) who were members of the emerging elite. Their high status was also indicated by the fact that the objects engraved on them, such as metallic weapons, jewellery or ploughs, highlighted those technologies which had created the conditions for the elites to emerge.

The well-preserved sacred districts of Aosta and Sion were discovered by chance during construction work in the 1960s; in the case of Aosta the development can be reconstructed over a period of two and a half millennia.[287] Deep furrows preserved in the ground show that a ritual surface area of at least 5,000 square metres was first marked out with a ploughshare around 4200 BCE, that is in the late Neolithic.[288] These furrows represent the oldest evidence of ploughing using animal traction in central and south-western Europe.[289] For millennia, ploughing rituals were linked to fertility and were later also part of the foundation rituals of Roman cities and colonies. The discovery that human teeth had been 'sown' in the furrows after ploughing was highly unusual. This ritual bears striking similarities to the Greek myths of Iason (Jason) and Kadmos, who threw dragon's teeth into freshly ploughed furrows from which armed men immediately grew and fought each other. It is possible that the fertility ritual of sowing human teeth was also known in the Greek environment. Soon thereafter, towards the end of the fifth or at the beginning of the fourth millennium BCE a cluster of *ca.* fifteen pits were dug inside the perimeter which were filled with offerings of cereals, seeds and millstones for grinding. About eight centuries later, a long row of *ca.* twenty wooden posts was erected; they probably had an astronomical as well as a religious function.[290] Then, at the beginning of the third millennium BCE, the wooden posts were supplemented by rows of tall menhirs with few traces of working, and by perforated polygonal slabs. Soon after, anthropomorphic steles were erected, which stood either in straight lines or at right angles. The replacement of the probably unworked, rather anonymous wooden posts by anthropomorphic steles reflected the emergence of stratified societies and the veneration of leading personalities or ancestors.

As in Sion, so also in Aosta three types of anthropomorphic steles can be distinguished: first came the archaic ones featuring arms and hands, belts and daggers of the Remedello type as well as clothing with simple geometric patterns. They were followed by a few intermediary

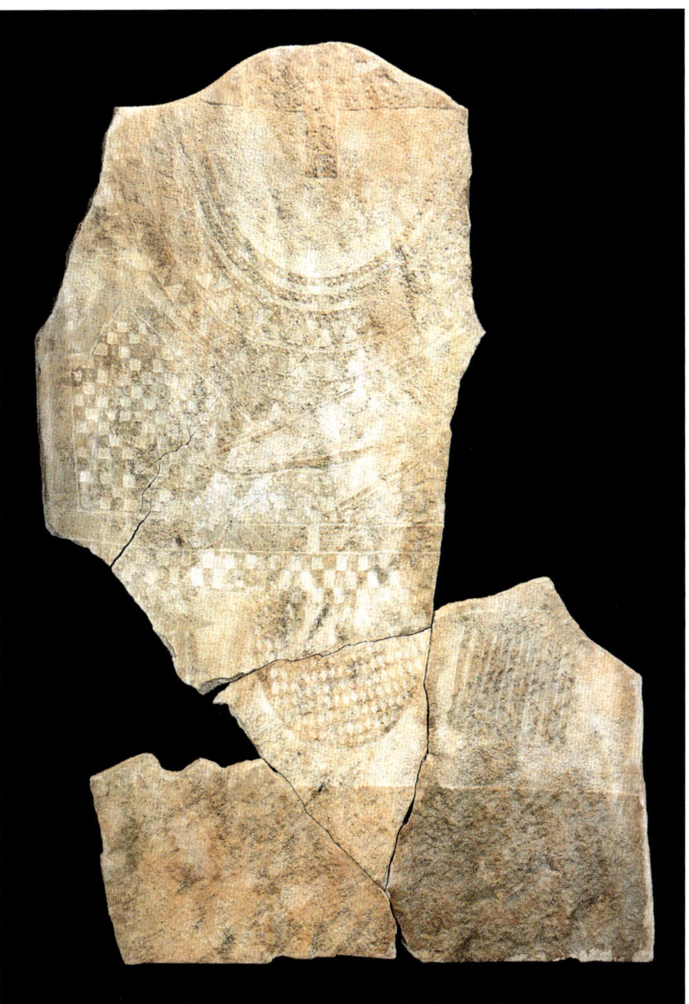

213. The anthropomorphic stone stele 30 from Saint-Martin-de-Corléans in the Aosta Valley, Italy, *ca.* 2750–2400 BCE; height 250 cm, width 174 cm. The stele was reconstituted from four fragments, and the shoulders and one arm are missing. The face has a distinctive T-shaped pattern. The figure wears a hat, four collars and a garment or breastplate decorated with a chequered pattern. The chest features an axe on the left and a banded bow and two arrows on the right which identifies the stele as male. Two daggers and a semicircular purse hang from the belt. The stele displays striking similarities with steles 8 and 25 at Sion which indicates that the arrangements of Aosta and Sion belonged to the same cultural realm. Parco Archeologico e Museo, Aosta, Italy. Photo D. Cesare. On concession of the Autonomous Region of Valle d'Aosta, Italy.

specimens on which the featured persons wear a large double spiral pendant. Similar pendants feature on steles at Val Camonica and have also been found in Chalcolithic tombs in today's Austria and Slovakia.[291] In the third, developed style the engravings of weapons such as battle axes, bows and arrows, jewellery and patterned garments became more sophisticated and detailed. At Aosta and Sion, steles were gendered solely by attributes, not by sexual markers. All of these steles were about 150 to 275 centimetres high, 40 to 120 centimetres wide and 6 to 19 centimetres (occasionally even up to 33 centimetres) thick.

A drastic repurposing of steles took place in Sion after 2500 BCE, shortly before the onset of the Bell Beaker culture, and in Aosta around its beginning, *ca.* 2350 BCE; in both places the steles were reused for the construction of megalithic dolmens.[292] These dolmens were above-ground funeral constructions which were visible and accessible through a hole carved within one of the vertical slabs. This hole was usually closed by another stone slab or plug which was temporarily removed when further human remains, that is bones or ashes, were to be deposited into the dolmen. For the reuse of the steles in dolmens and also in large, covered stone cists, the steles had to be trimmed accordingly; often, the protruding head was cut away.[293] It seems that at Sion steles were not only reused to construct a dolmen or a large cist, but that they were initially also placed directly in front of dolmens. Around 2300–2250 BCE, the Bell Beaker people emptied the largest dolmens for their own usage and later built smaller, simpler ones, also reusing steles in the process.

These dolmens then served as communal graves for families; at Aosta, the largest dolmen contained the remains of at least 39 individuals, most of them male, and grave goods such as ceramic artefacts and metal objects. At both sites, a few steles were also reused as altar slabs; in the case of stele no. 12 at Aosta, more than a hundred cup marks were hewn into its surface after it had been turned into an altar slab. The function and meaning of these cup marks remain unknown.

The dolmens of Sion and Aosta strongly resemble in function and shape the more or less contemporaneous dolmens located in the western Caucasus in the coastal area along the north-eastern Black Sea, that is a zone stretching from Anapa in the north southwards to Abkhazia.[294] Another characteristic of the Aosta and Sion dolmens is also found in the north of the Caucasus, namely in the culture of Maikop. At the huge kurgan of Nalchik (3092–2943 cal. BCE,) today's capital of the Kabardino-Balkarian Republic, the sunken burial chamber consisted of 24 orthostates which had originally been free-standing steles; nine of them were engraved with geometric patterns, and at least six had an anthropomorphic shape.[295] These graveyards ceased to be used around 1600 BCE. A unique reuse of a Chalcolithic stele was discovered in 1992 during the restoration of a church in Vinschgau, in South Tyrol (Alto Adige), when the Gothic altarpiece turned out to be a former 'male' stele with engraved weapons, dogs and stags.[296]

2.2. Alpine Switzerland and France

Although almost half of Switzerland's territory lies in the Alps, is has only a few small petroglyph sites,[297] the most important one being that at **Carschenna** in the Grisons in south-eastern Switzerland. The site is situated on a hill at the edge of a sheer cliff several hundred metres deep; it is close to an ancient mule track which led to the passes of Splügen and San Bernardino and avoided the dangerous gorge of Viamala whose name means 'bad road'. The *ca.* 300 images are spread over 12 boulders which lie at the very edge of the precipice; they were found by chance in 1965 during the construction of a high-voltage power line. The petroglyphs consist mainly of concentric circles with a cup mark in the centre. There are also solar symbols, lattices and schematized horses or mules carrying loads, a horseman and some undefined quadrupeds. Very close to the petroglyphs, traces of a Bronze Age settlement were excavated. Since the schematic equids were carved over the concentric circles, the latter must be older, dating probably to the middle Bronze Age around 1500 BCE, while the equids are from the Iron Age. The site's name contains the word *carschen* which in the Rhaeto-Romance language means 'rising moon' which may suggest, together with its location close to a mountain path, that this complex had a cultic function and was a kind of wayside shrine.[298] Similar images of equids and concentric circles are found in Val Camonica, at **Senslas** near Tinizong in Grisons, and at **Val Cenischia** in the western Alps of Piedmont.

Another interesting small petroglyph site lying on a steep mule track is **Sasso delle Croci**, whose name means 'Rock of the Crosses'. On this rock in the southern Swiss canton of Ticino 224 equal-armed crosses and twenty cup marks are engraved.[299] The rock looks very similar to the two rocks covered with crosses at Sonico, Val Camonica, and can be dated to the earlier Middle Ages. In the case of Sasso delle Croci, the stone lies alongside the path like the small chapels further down the way. Travellers probably stopped here to ask for a safe journey. It is also likely that here, as in Val Camonica, crosses were engraved in order to Christianize a pagan landscape, in a similar way that in the Himalayas petroglyphs of Buddhas and stupas were pecked on boulders already containing older, pre-Buddhist figures. There are further places with numerous pecked crosses, namely in Switzerland at **Rivera** in Ticino and **Salvan** in Valais, in Italy at **Valchiusella**, Piedmont, and in France at **Macôt-la-Plagne** in the Savoie.[300]

Mont Bégo lies in southern France, 80 kilometres north of Nice and the Mediterranean coast. The region came to France only in 1947 by plebiscite, having previously belonged to Italy. Although it is one of the southernmost regions of the Alps, its petroglyphs, which lie at an altitude between 2,300 and 2,500 metres above sea level, are covered by snow for eight months of the year. At the peak of the last glaciation around 18 ka BCE, the ice sheet was probably up to two kilometres thick. A general deglaciation began *ca.* 13 ka BCE and around 8000 BCE the Vallée des Merveilles (Valley

214. Petroglyph of concentric circles at Carschenna. Middle Bronze Age, Grisons, Switzerland. Photo 2023.

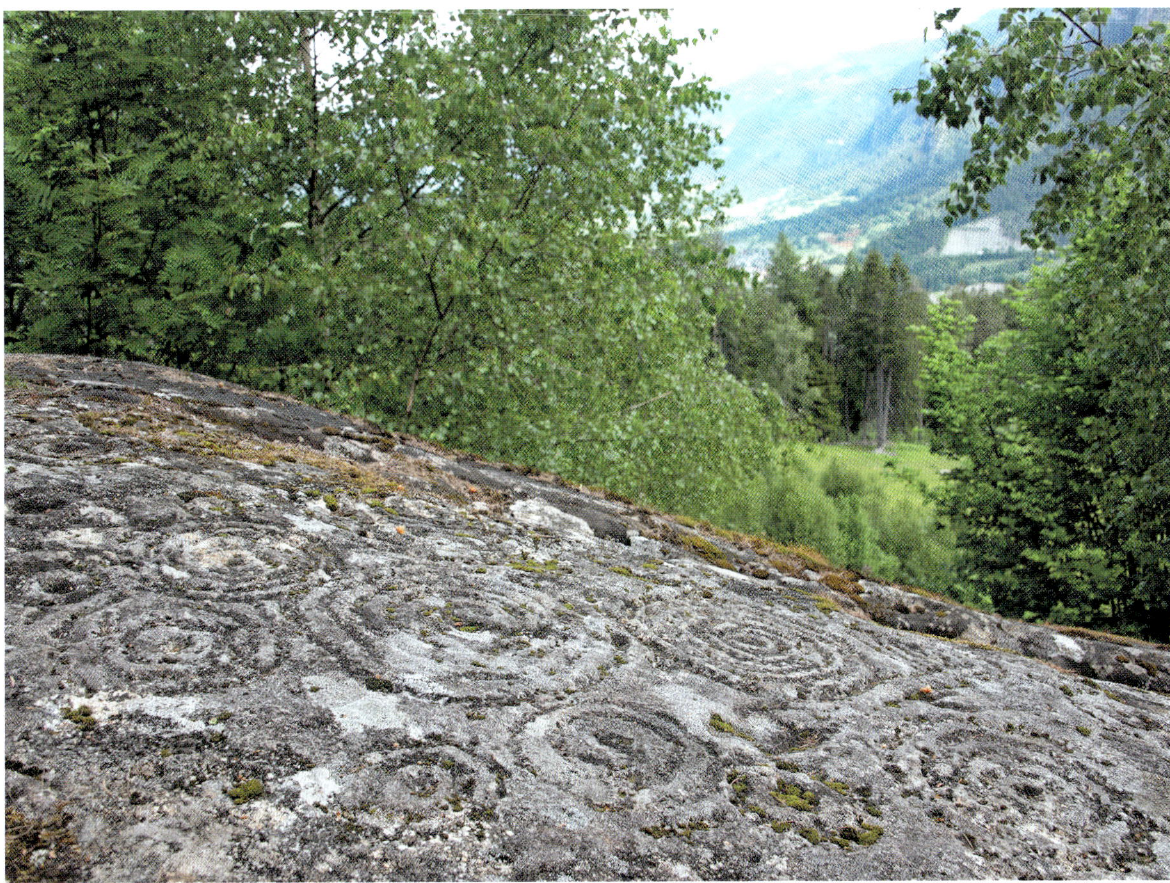

215. In total, 224 equal-armed crosses are engraved in the Sasso delle Croci dating from the earlier Middle Ages. Ticino, southern Switzerland. Photo 2023.

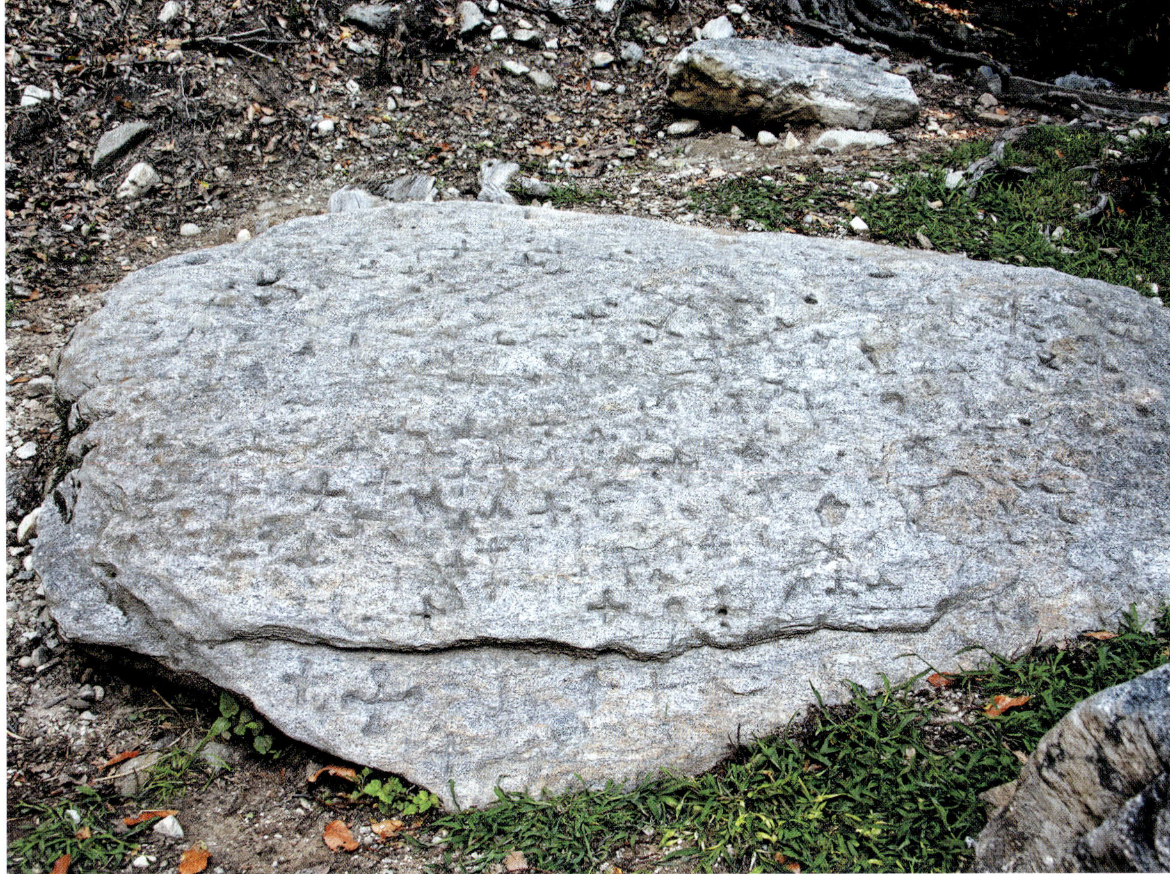

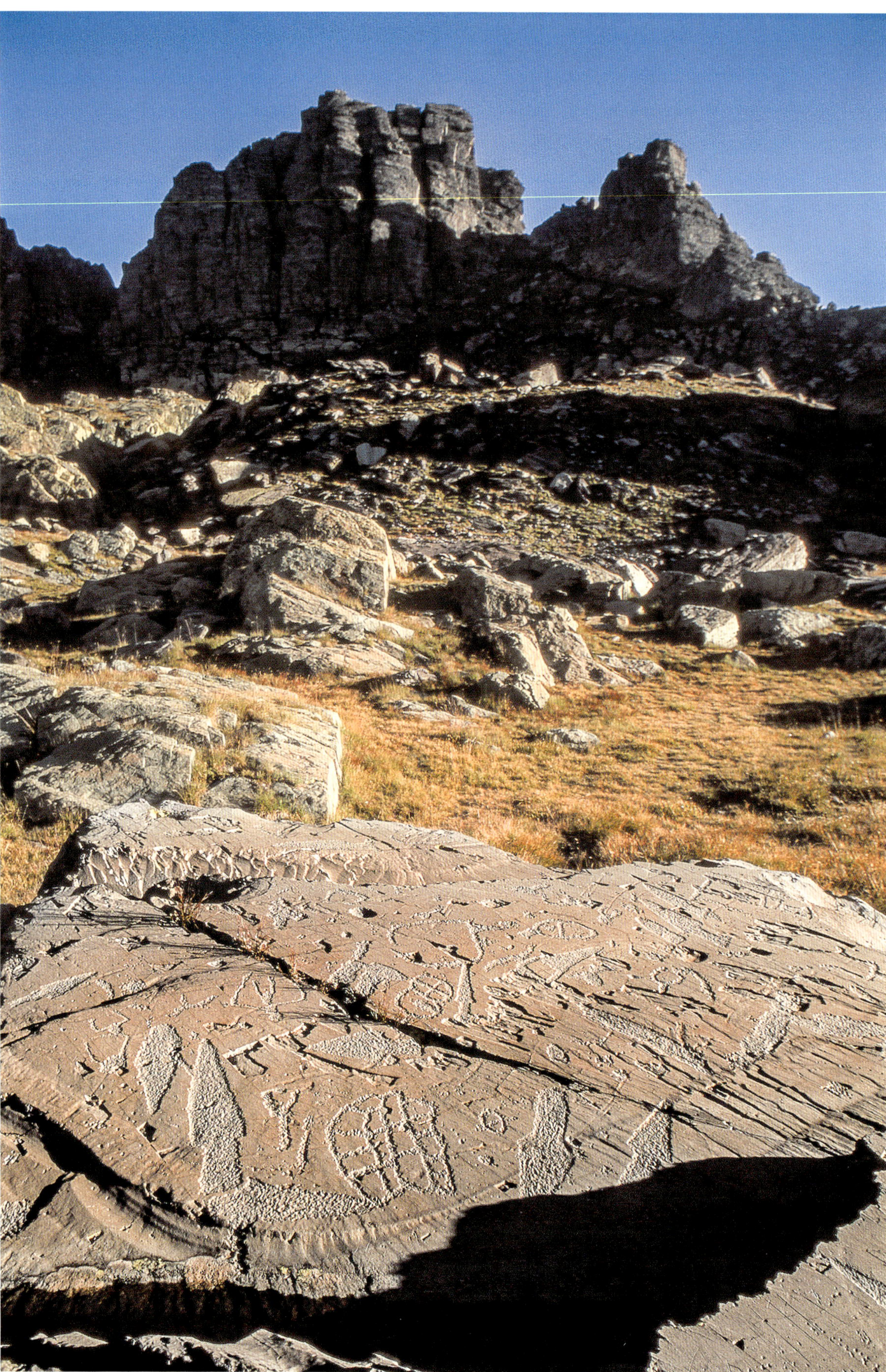

216. A multitude of engraved daggers and schematized heads of bulls in frontal view. Early Bronze Age, Vallée des Merveilles, Mont Bégo, southern France. Photo by Emmanuel Breteau.

of Wonders), where most of the petroglyphs are located, became ice-free. The retreating glaciers left a well-polished landscape whose surface consists of greenish slate (65 per cent) and grey sandstone (35 per cent). As mentioned in chapter II, the petroglyphs were first described in 1460 as a 'hellish place'. In the following centuries Mont Bégo was visited several times by scholars, but it was only in 1878 that the French prehistorian Émile Rivière dated the petroglyphs to the Bronze Age. In 1885, the London-born botanist and former clergyman Clarence Bicknell came to the sites and was so fascinated by the petroglyphs that in 1897 he settled in their neighbourhood and stayed there until his death in 1918. Since 1967, the palaeoanthropologist Henry de Lumley and his team have researched the petroglyphs.[301]

In total, there are about 36,000 petroglyphs at Mont Bégo spread over seven areas, of which the Vallées des Merveilles and Fontanalba are the largest. Setting aside the non-figurative petroglyphs, 80 per cent of the images represent schematized bulls, either as heads in a frontal position or in pairs yoked to an ard (a simple plough without a mouldboard) and seen from above. Then follow weapons and tools (7 per cent), geometric patterns (3 per cent) and anthropomorphs (1 per cent) (figs 216, 217).[302] The petroglyphs of highly schematized bulls pulling an ard, with or without a human driver, as well as images of single ards and harrows, indicate that the petroglyph makers were familiar with agriculture although agricultural activities took place almost 2,000 metres lower than Mont Bégo, similar to Saimaluu Tash in Kyrgyzstan. Petroglyphs featuring rectangles divided into small squares probably represent cultivated fields and animal enclosures which confirm the importance of farming. As often with petroglyphs, weapons at Mont Bégo are valuable indicators for dating purposes. Since there are no images of daggers of the Remedello type and since the kind of halberds featured belong to the local Polada culture (*ca.* 1800–1400 BCE in Piedmont) which succeeded the Remedello culture, the upper date for the Mont Bégo petroglyphs may be set at 1800 BCE. On the other hand, the lack of petroglyphs showing swords suggests a terminal date for figurative images around 1500 BCE, which gives a relatively brief 300 years' period within the earlier Bronze Age.[303] Since the bull's heads are closely associated with the weapons, the former can be dated to the same period. This short period of figurative petroglyph production explains the apparent lack of stylistic development. The simple linear figures, however, are much later and were made well into the Middle Ages.[304] One of the earliest linear petroglyphs is a weird Latin inscription reading: HOC QVI SCRIPSIT PATRI MII FILIVM PIIDICAVIT (i.e. *Hoc qui scripsit patris mei filium pedicavit*) which means 'the one who wrote this defiled the

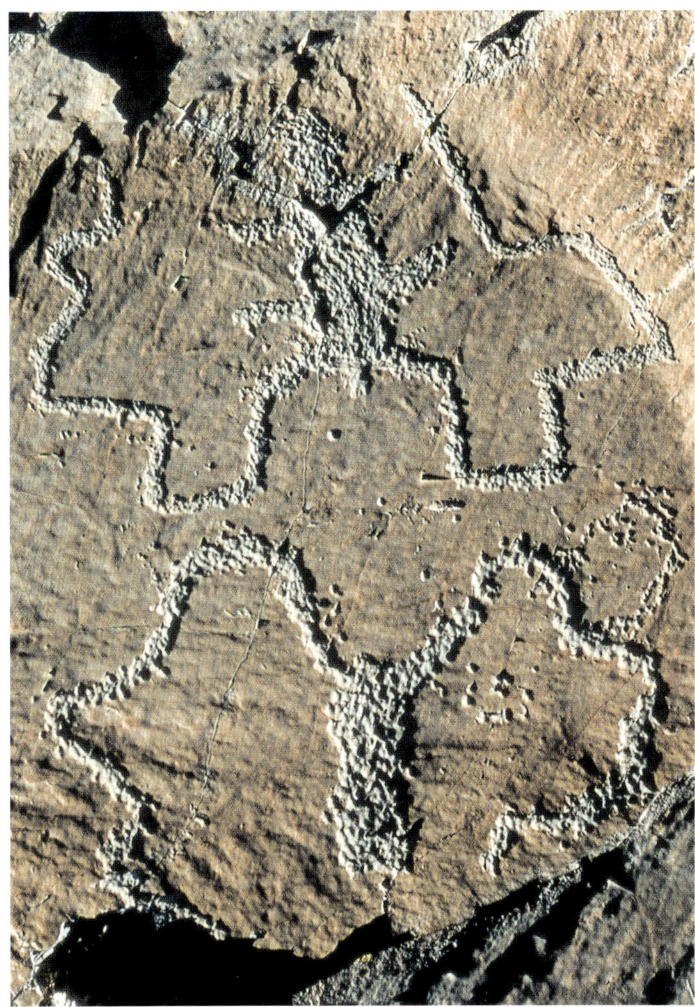

217. Two bull heads with huge horns. Early Bronze Age, Vallée des Merveilles, Mont Bégo, southern France. Photo by Emmanuel Breteau.

son of my father'.[305] Later graffiti-like images include sailing ships, bayonets and epigrams from Italian mountain soldiers. In contrast to Val Camonica, at Mont Bégo there are hardly any scenes, with the exception of males holding halberds with rather slim, triangular blades and very long handles.[306] Such disproportioned halberds could only be used in ceremonies or rituals. That the bull, which is virtually omnipresent at Mont Bégo, represented strength, power and fertility in the Bronze Age is undoubted, but its association with this specific mountain that is famous for its violent thunderstorms remains unknown; maybe the mountain and the bull were subject to a common veneration.

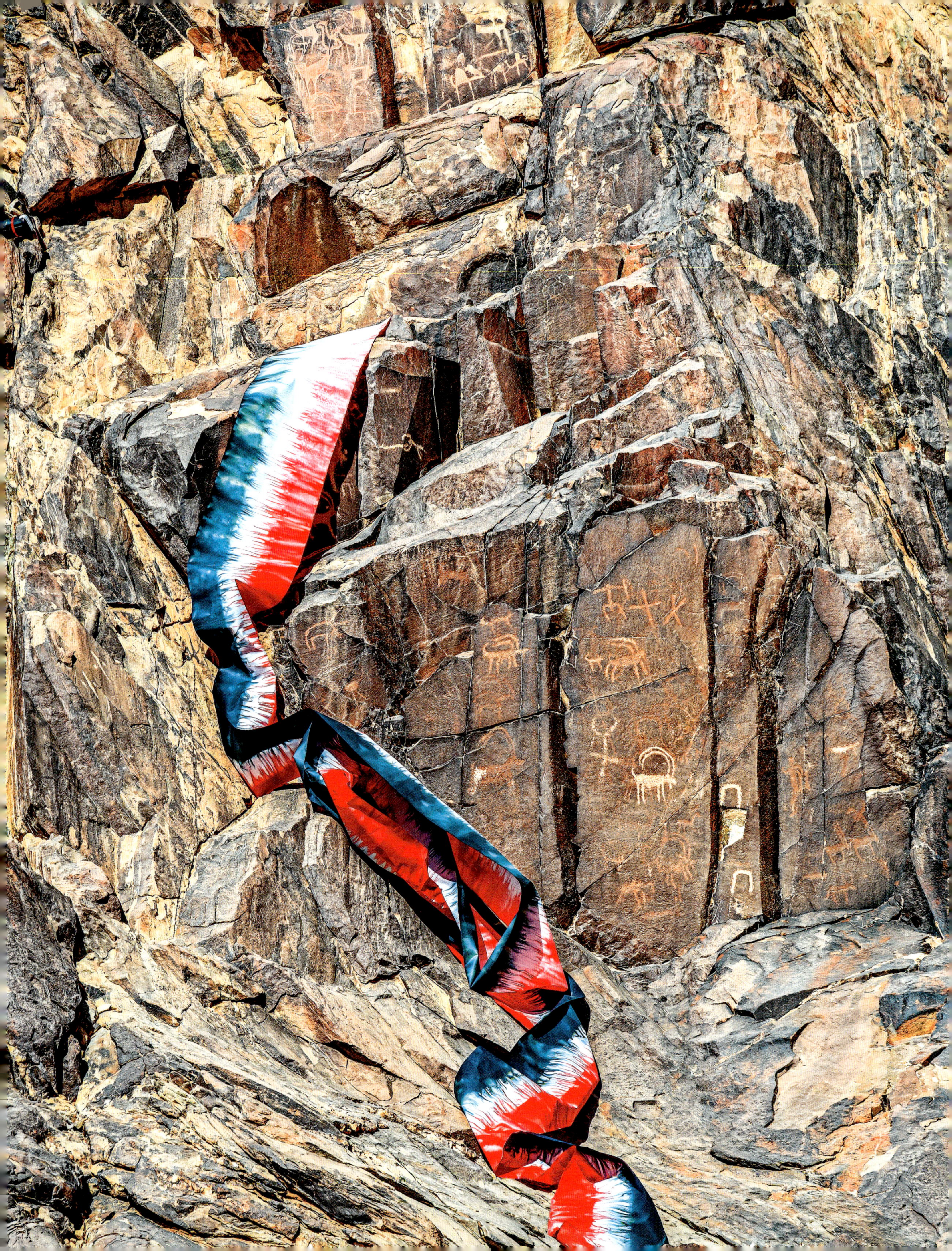

VII. Arabia

In political terms the Arabian Peninsula includes, from north-west to south-east, Jordan, southern Iraq, Kuwait, Saudi Arabia, Bahrain, Qatar, the United Arab Emirates, Yemen and Oman. This chapter focuses on the countries with the richest petroglyph heritage, foremost among them Saudi Arabia, followed by Jordan, Oman and the United Arab Emirates.[1] The largest petroglyph complex of Jordan lies in its south, in Wadi Rum. These petroglyphs reveal similarities to those in north-western Saudi Arabia, for Wadi Rum is only 25 kilometres north of the Saudi–Jordan border and 85 kilometres north of the petroglyphs in the region of Jabal al-Laws in Saudi Arabia.[2] The petroglyphs of Oman, on the other hand, are stylistically quite different from those in Saudi Arabia, for there was, until a couple of centuries ago, little contact between these two regions which are separated from each other by the fearsome Rub' al-Khali desert. In prehistoric times, from the sixth to the fourth millennium BCE, fishermen and pastoralists of eastern Arabia maintained maritime contacts with Mesopotamia, as is suggested by the numerous finds of Mesopotamian Ubaid pottery along the eastern Arabian littoral.[3] Later, around the middle of the third millennium BCE, eastern and central Arabia had indirect trading relations with Oman, since they sourced copper from Dilmun, which comprised the region between today's Kuwait and Qatar, including the island of Bahrain. Dilmun, in turn, imported the ore from Magan in northern Oman. Magan was a key exporter of copper, and the harbours along the Gulf, above all Dilmun, served as entrepôts for long-distance trade. Oman, in turn, traded not only with Dilmun and Mesopotamia, but also with Iran and South Asia; several stamp seals and much ceramic ware from the Indus Valley have been found along the Omani littoral as well as in Bahrain.[4] In fact, based on its geographical position and maritime orientation, Oman was a facilitator for trade and cultural exchange between Mesopotamia and the Indus Valley civilization then called Meluhha.[5] North and central Arabians, for their part, maintained contacts in prehistoric times with the Levant, and later also with Egypt. However, in spite of these contacts outside the Arabian Peninsula, exchanges and migrations within Arabia remained rather marginal until the domestication of the dromedary for transport purposes in the tenth century BCE.[6] This isolation of the various regions from each other is reflected in the emergence of regional petroglyph styles.

---

218. ← Therese Weber, *Early Codes of Mankind in Equilibrium with the Present.* On the steep rock face near Jada'a, Saudi Arabia, the petroglyphs inspired Weber to unfurl a sign of the present. The ephemeral paper band coexists with the petroglyphs, some of which are only preserved in fragments. These petroglyphs have been exposed to the elements for thousands of years. Performative action by Therese Weber, near Jada'a, Saudi Arabia. Coloured paper band of mulberry fibre (total paper band: 45 × 2500 cm), 2022.

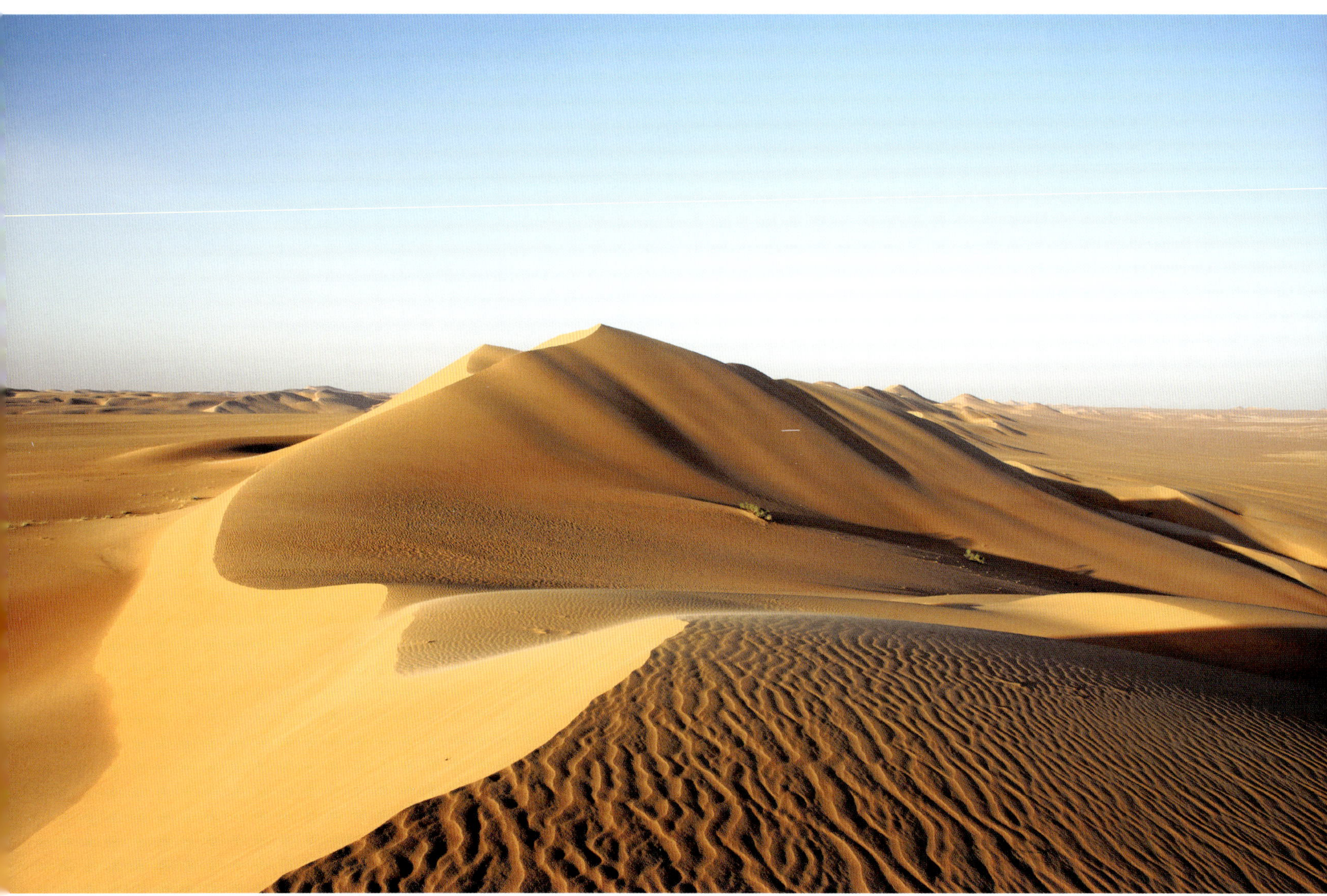

219. Sand dunes in the evening light in the Rub' al-Khali south-east of Qaryat al-Faw, Saudi Arabia. Photo 2022.

1. Saudi Arabia

The desert societies of the Arabian interior are often considered timeless and unchanging. However, an analysis of rock art up to *ca.* 9,000 years old reveals a history of flexible adaptations in economy and social organization to dramatic climatic and environmental changes. Some economic innovations were adopted from the Levant or Assyria; others developed within Arabia itself. The interior of Saudi Arabia is a land of sweeping deserts and unforgiving climate. In the south lies the Rub' al-Khali – the Empty Quarter – which, with an area of *ca.* 650,000 square kilometres, is the largest pure sand desert in the world, while the north holds the Great Nafud Desert, which extends to some 104,000 square kilometres. Rain in these deserts is minimal, with less than 100 millilitres

a year, against an evaporation potential of approximately 45 times that.[7] However, as with the Sahara or the Taklamakan Deserts, earlier climatic conditions in Arabia were not as hostile to life as those prevailing today. An examination of former lake sediments indicates that the Arabian Peninsula experienced several climate fluctuations. During the Chibanian and Upper Pleistocene periods, for example, there were lakes in existence in the Nafud at various points around 410 thousand years ago (kya), 320 kya, 200 kya,125 kya, and 100 kya.[8] Since the earliest remains of hominins outside Africa, which are *ca.* 1.78 million years old, were found at Dmanisi in Georgia,[9] the question arose by what route these early migrants had reached the Caucasus. It was long believed that the only possible route led through the Levantine Corridor. While finds of Oldowan lithic tools in al-Jawf (northern Saudi

Arabia) and the Hima–Kaukab region (southern Saudi Arabia) are questionable,[10] the identification of Acheulean lithic devices is certain in the Saudi Arabian Nafud Desert[11] and at Dawadmi in central Arabia as well as along the Red Sea littoral. They show that humans populated certain regions of Arabia *ca.* 800,000 years ago; should the identification of Oldowan tools be confirmed, a date around 1.3 million years BP could be considered.[12] *Homo sapiens*, for his part, migrated to the region of the Nafud Desert around 95,000 to 86,000 years ago on a longer-term basis; these were not just brief incursions during winter rain periods.[13] The recent discovery, by the shore of a long-disappeared palaeolake in the western Nafud Desert, of human and animal footprints which have been dated using the Optically Stimulated Luminescence method indicate that *Homo sapiens* was living there 112,000 to 121,000 years ago. One can assume that this palaeolake formed in the penultimate interglacial period (MIS 5e).[14]

The presence of humans, most probably *H. sapiens*, in a comparable time period can also be traced in the Rub' al-Khali desert. It was St John Philby who in 1932 first found and reported freshwater shells and man-made Neolithic artefacts inside the Rub' al-Khali. He correctly deduced that in prehistoric times humans would have hunted the animals which came to drink at now-vanished rivers and lakes. Philby's assessment that by *ca.* 5000 BCE climatic conditions in the desert began to worsen, making life unsustainable, was also quite accurate.[15] Scientifically dated human artefacts have been found in south-western Saudi Arabia, in Najran province. During the wet pluvial periods of MIS 5e (124–119 ka BP, peak at 123 ka BP), MIS 5c (peak at 96 ka BP) and MIS 5a (peak at 82 ka BP) the Mundafan al-Buhayrah palaeolake in the south-western Rub' al-Khali had a surface up to 300 square kilometres. It was fed by a drainage system originating in the Asir Mountains, to which the Wadi Najran also belonged.[16] In those periods, Lake Mundafan was surrounded by savanna grasslands. Stratified lithic artefacts which were found in the Mundafan area have been dated to 100–80 ka BP and thus testify to the presence of *Homo sapiens* at the time.[17]

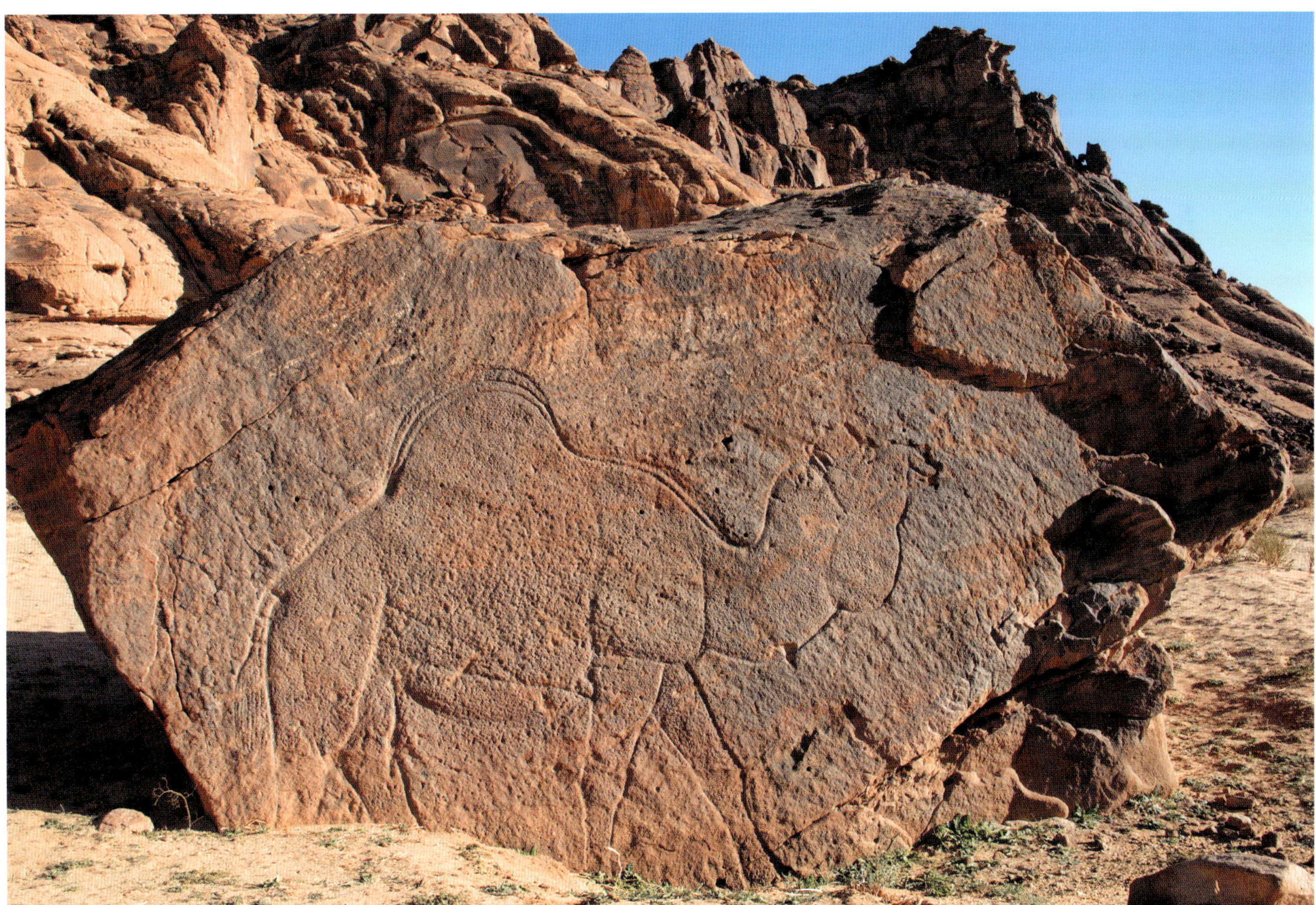

220. An almost life-size Bronze Age wild camel. Neolithic period, Southern al-Misma, Great Nafud Desert, northern Saudi Arabia. Photo 2020.

But it seems that about 40,000 years later people left Arabia again, for only scarce attestations of human presence have been found so far for the last three decades of the Upper Palaeolithic, that is for the period *ca.* 42– 12 ka BP, in spite of the fact that the climate during this period was not continuously hyperarid.[18] The likelihood is that the Upper Palaeolithic people of Arabia left the interior of the peninsula when hyperaridity set in and moved into the region of the present Persian Gulf. During the last glacial period, the sea level of the Gulf fell by *ca.* 120 metres and its shallow basin turned into a huge oasis. In those days, the common estuary of the rivers Euphrates and Tigris lay at today's Strait of Hormuz.[19] In the words of Jeffrey Rose,

At that time, the interior savannas of Arabia desiccated while tens of thousands of square kilometres of fertile land in the Gulf basin were exposed. It is possible these shifting environmental dynamics forced hunter-gatherers to increasingly rely on coastal resources rather than big- and medium-game hunting in the interior.[20]

With the onset of the Holocene, sea levels rose rapidly and the Persian Gulf was quickly replenished, forcing people to leave, returning either to Arabia or southern Mesopotamia and Iran.[21] This process in the Persian Gulf of colonization of areas released by the retreating sea during a global cold period, followed by renewed flooding due to global warming, is comparable to the course of events in Doggerland: a dry, extremely cold period drives people from the arid interior to a coastal region that has become free of water, whereupon a subsequent climate warming causes sea levels to rise and forces people to return from the flooded coastal regions to a now wetter interior with richer vegetation and fauna. In the early Holocene people also returned to Lake Mundafan in the south-western Rub' al-Khali which by then had a reduced surface of *ca.* 50 square kilometres. By comparison, in the Sahara the more or less contemporaneous Lake Mega Chad had a surface of *ca.* 360,000 square kilometres, which highlights that environmental conditions in the two deserts were not comparable. The discovery near Lake Mundafan of Neolithic arrowheads, knives and scrapers dated to

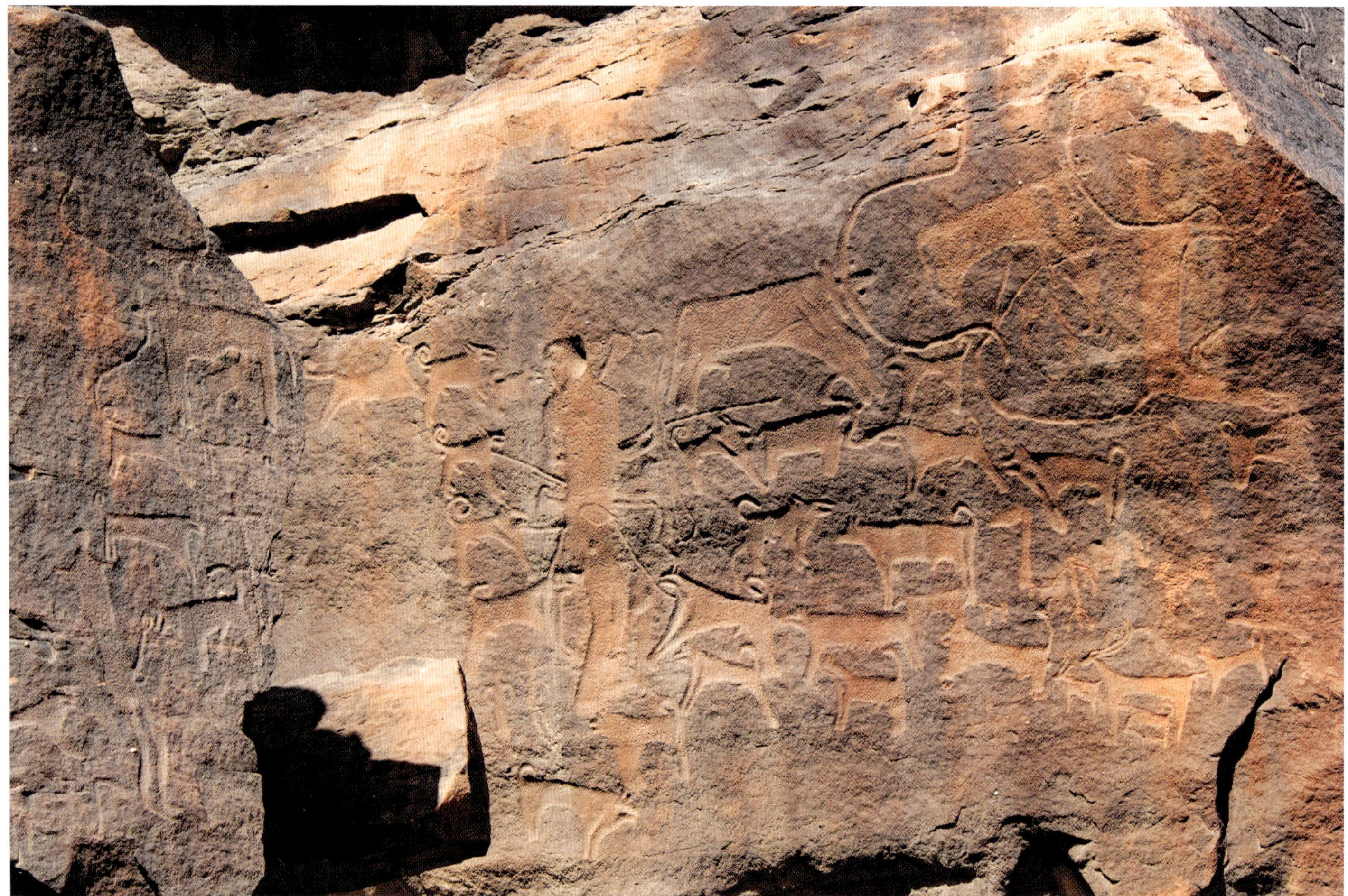

221. On the left, an ithyphallic pastoralist with bovines and dogs; on the right, a hunter with his pack of hounds and two buffaloes; on the far right, a leopard. Neolithic and the transitional period to the early Bronze Age, Jabal Raat, Shuwaymis, central Saudi Arabia. Photo 2020.

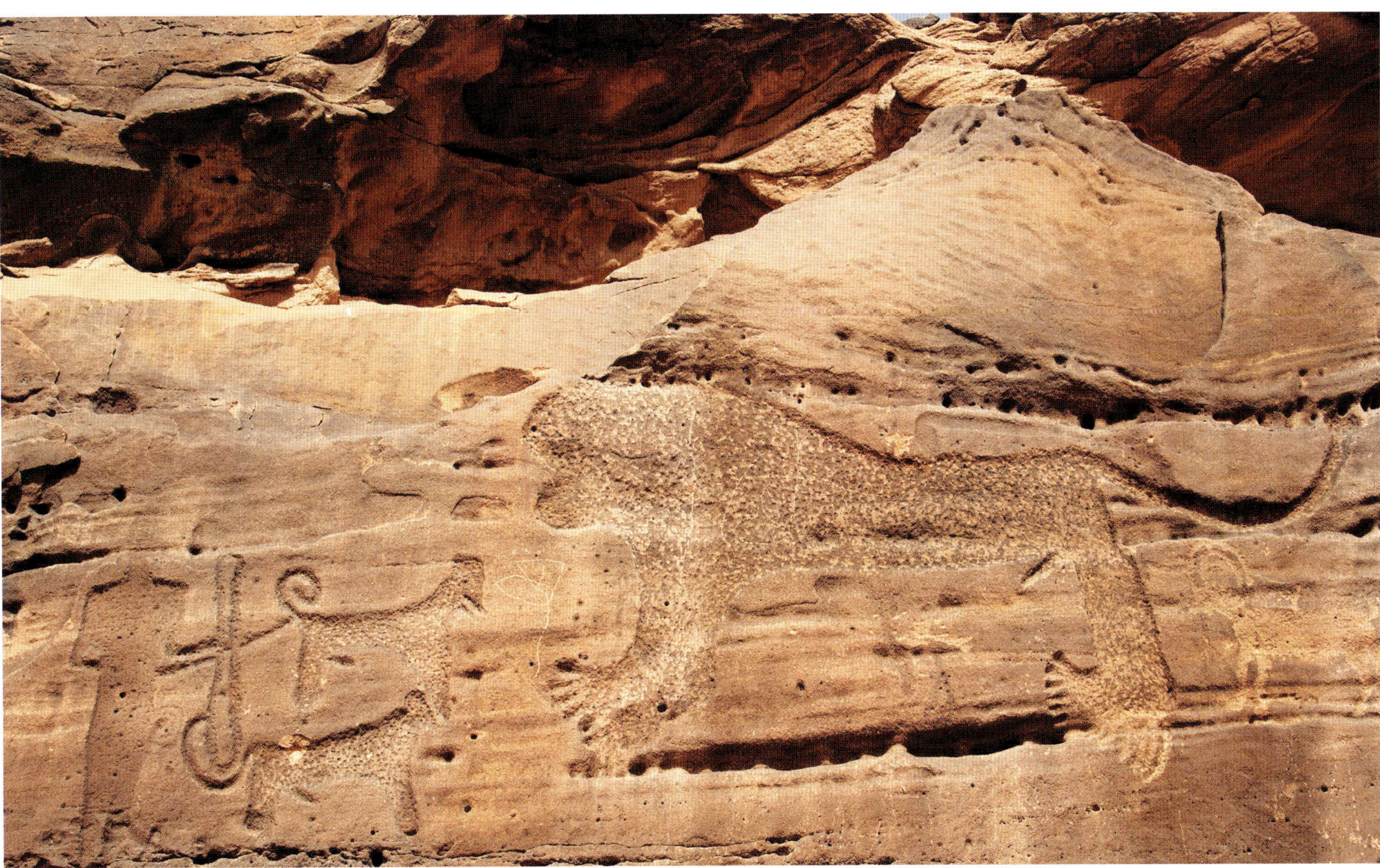

222. A hunter, armed with a bow, and his two dogs confront a lion. Late Neolithic period, Jabal al-Manjor, Shuwaymis, central Saudi Arabia. Photo 2020.

the seventh and sixth millennia BCE, and the absence of sedentary remains, indicate that hunts took place on a short-term basis near the lake where animals came to drink.[22] Unlike the early Neolithic hunters in the region of the Nafud Desert, those in Najran do not seem to have made any petroglyphs.

While it is difficult to imagine those lost worlds today, traces of more recent shifts can be found in the country's remarkable rock art, which illustrates the intricate relationship between human life and the climate. The Great Nafud is surrounded by a belt of spectacular sandstone mountains and outcrops to the south and west; a similar landscape stretches north-westwards up to Wadi Rum in present-day Jordan. In the centre of the kingdom, south-west of its capital, Riyadh, the landscape is dotted with various mountain ranges and smaller deserts interspersed with oases. Whereas the Rub' al-Khali desert predominantly consists of huge sand dunes, the eastern foothills of the neighbouring Asir Mountains extend as far as the desert's south-western edge. All of these various sand and limestone mountain ranges, which are in parts heavily weathered, provided vast 'canvases' for creating rock art, including inscriptions. Many of the human social and economic adaptations

to changes in fauna and flora are mirrored in the petroglyphs. In fact, the deserts of Saudi Arabia are exceptionally abundant in rock art. More than 1,500 rock art and inscription sites are registered, and they form an important part of Saudi Arabia's rich cultural heritage.[23] A distinctive feature of Saudi Arabian rock art from the first millennium BCE onward is its close association with inscriptions, written in at least seventeen different scripts of which the majority were local developments. While most of these inscriptions are brief epigraphs, a few of them are highly important official records that shed light on Arabia's pre-Islamic history. Timewise, the petroglyphs stretch from the earlier pre-Neolithic to the first centuries of the Islamic period, and sporadically even up to the present. In contrast to the Sahara, the overwhelming majority of rock art in Saudi Arabia comprises petroglyphs; and only a few larger pictograph (rock painting) sites exist, such as at Mahraga al-Agil in the Jabal al-Lawz, northern Tabuk province, or al-Hamdha in the Asir province.

1.1. History of research

One of the first European travellers to take note of Arabian petroglyphs and inscriptions was the Englishman James Wellsted who reached Oman in 1835–36 and researched the ancient inscriptions.[24] Within Saudi Arabia, the Finnish Orientalist and explorer Georg August Wallin was the first to notice petroglyphs when he visited Jubbah in 1845.[25] He was followed by James Hamilton who described a panel with petroglyphs and inscriptions along the Ri' al-Zallalah pass on the road from Ta'if to Mecca.[26] After Hamilton, Charles Montagu Doughty, who spent two years (1876–78) in Arabia, visited the same panel and published a not very accurate illustration of it.[27] In terms of petroglyphs and inscriptions, Doughty explored, among other things, the sites of Talaat al-Salaby in the Jabal Abu Mughair, Tayma, Jubbah and Mada'in Saleh.[28] Following on his heels, in 1879, were Lady Anne Blunt and her husband, Wilfrid Scawen Blunt, who reached the oases of Ha'il and Jubbah, situated on the southern edge of the Great Nafud.[29] Scientific investigation of rock inscriptions began with the Alsatian epigrapher Charles Huber who embarked on his first journey to Arabia (1880–81) from the north through the Wadi al-Jawf, crossed the Great Nafud Desert and reached the petroglyphs of Jubbah. Next, he studied ancient inscriptions in the region of Ha'il, explored the inscriptions in the Jabal al-Misma, and visited the ancient sites of Tayma, al-Ula and the Nabataean site of Hegra (Mada'in Saleh).[30] On his second journey of 1883–84, Huber travelled with the German epigrapher Julius Euting. Both were fascinated by the reports of Doughty's travels, especially his discoveries at Hegra.[31] They first journeyed together to Jubbah and Ha'il. Here, and in the mountainous southern edge of the Nafud Desert, they explored several sites with inscriptions and petroglyphs, and also hammered their own names into the rocks. Next, they reached Tayma where it was Euting, and not Doughty or Huber,[32] who was the first to see and identify the famous Tayma Stele which probably dates to the sixth century BCE when the Neo-Babylonian King Nabonid (r. 556–539 BCE) stayed there.[33] The Aramaic text on the stele states that the priest Salm-Shezeb, son of Pet-Osiri, introduced in Tayma the new god *slm* (Salm, Sulmus), who is represented in petroglyphs as a bull's head in frontal view[34] and on stone altars as a bull wearing a solar disc between his horns.[35] Leaving the stele in Tayma intending to retrieve it on their return journey, they continued to Khaybar, al-Ula, and Mada'in Saleh in order to document further ancient inscriptions. In the meantime, Huber had intrigued against Euting with Emir Ibn Rashid, ruler of Ha'il, and the emir allegedly forbade Euting his planned return to Ha'il, meaning that Euting was unable to recover the stele to which he was contractually entitled.[36] Euting retreated to al-Wajh after

having successfully defended himself against robbers and killed three assailants. Huber, for his part, continued alone towards Ha'il, in the course of which journey he was murdered by his own guides.[37] As it turned out, Huber's intrigue against Euting had unwittingly saved the latter's life. Thanks to the manoeuvres of Jacques-Félix de Lostalot, the French vice-consul in Jeddah, the Tayma Stele was secured for the Louvre in Paris.[38] Huber (posthumously) and Euting published hundreds of pre-Islamic inscriptions; but while Huber was only incidentally interested in petroglyphs, Euting paid full attention to them.[39]

In 1907, 1909 and 1910, the Dominicans Antonin Jaussen and Raphaël Savignac systematically studied pre-Islamic rock inscriptions at Mada'in Saleh, Tayma and Tabuk as well as Byzantine and Umayyad inscriptions in Jordan. Their photographic record of monuments and inscriptions is still a work of reference today.[40] Forty years later, they were followed by the Belgians Gonzague Ryckmans, his nephew Jacques, and Philippe Lippens in 1951–52.[41] The Ryckmans–Lippens expedition was guided by Harry St John Bridger Philby, who in the 1930s took advantage of his position as adviser to King Abd al-Aziz ibn Saud to explore the deserts of central and southern Arabia. Based on 232 photographs taken at one single site by the Ryckmans–Lippens expedition, Emmanuel Anati attempted to date and classify the petroglyphs according to styles and ethnic authorship.[42] Anati never visited Arabia and his interpretations are now dated.[43] In 1976, the Comprehensive Archaeological Survey of Saudi Arabia began, and from the 1980s, Majeed Khan conducted extensive fieldwork. Then followed the Palaeodeserts Project of the Max Planck Institute and research by the Royal Commission for AlUla. Recently, the French archaeologist and epigraphist Christian Robin and his team have made interesting epigraphic discoveries in central and southern Saudi Arabia, while Guillaume Charloux and Maria Guagnin discovered the spectacular life-sized carvings of camels in the al-Jawf region and the southern Nafud Desert.[44] Finally, Robert Bednarik and Majeed Khan conducted optical micro-erosion analysis on selected petroglyphs and inscriptions[45] while the team led by Meinrat Andreae of the Max Planck Institute researched the rate of desert varnish regrowth on petroglyphs.[46]

With the exception of precisely dated inscriptions, dating rock art is notoriously difficult – but in Saudi Arabia, as elsewhere, some important motifs are known to appear only in specific time periods, so they can offer a rough indication in terms of *ante quem* and *post quem* dates. Such temporal indicators are the extinction of certain animal species resulting from changing climatic conditions, and the beginning of the domestication of other animals. Other

Map 8. Major petroglyph sites of Arabia

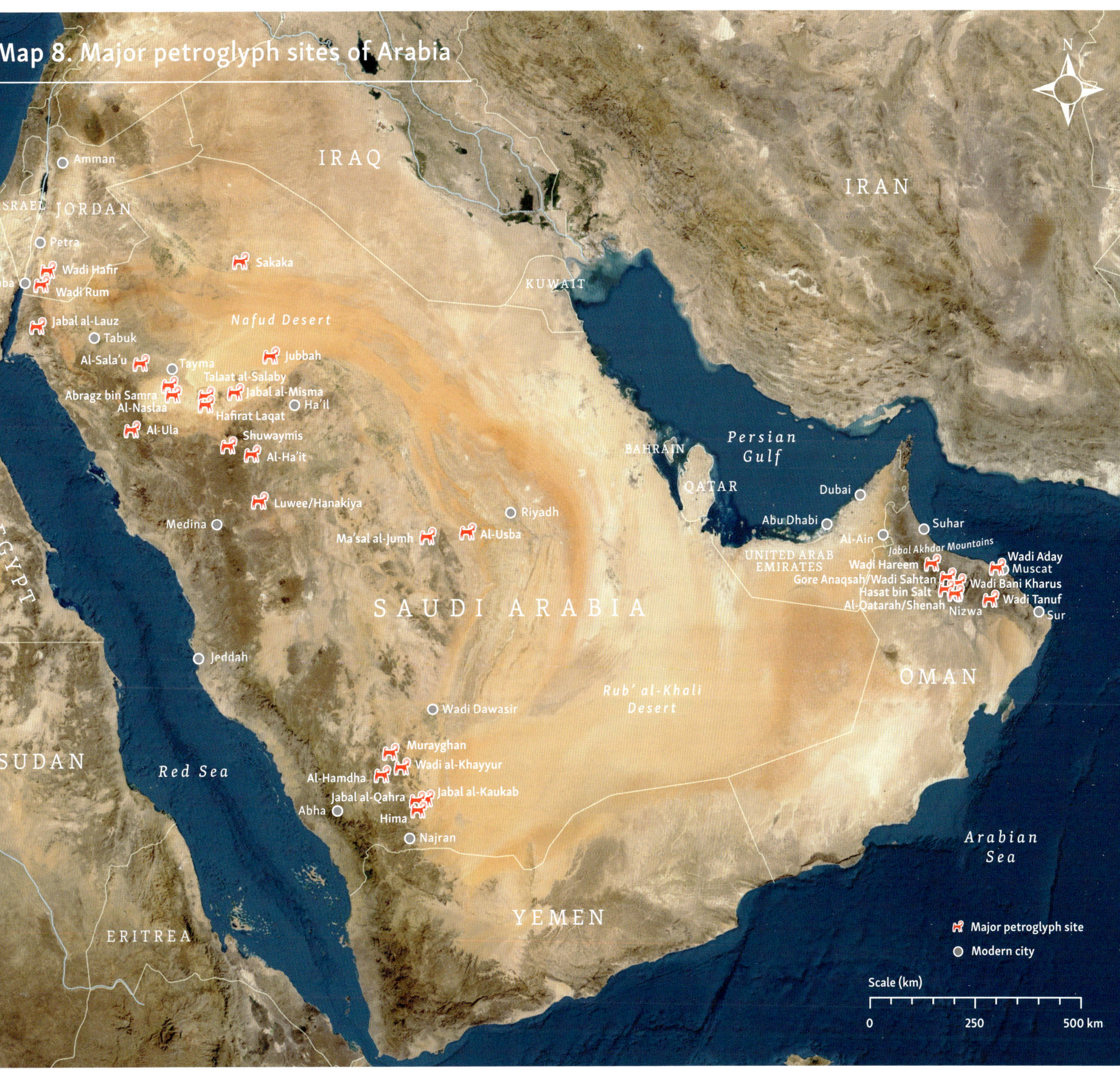

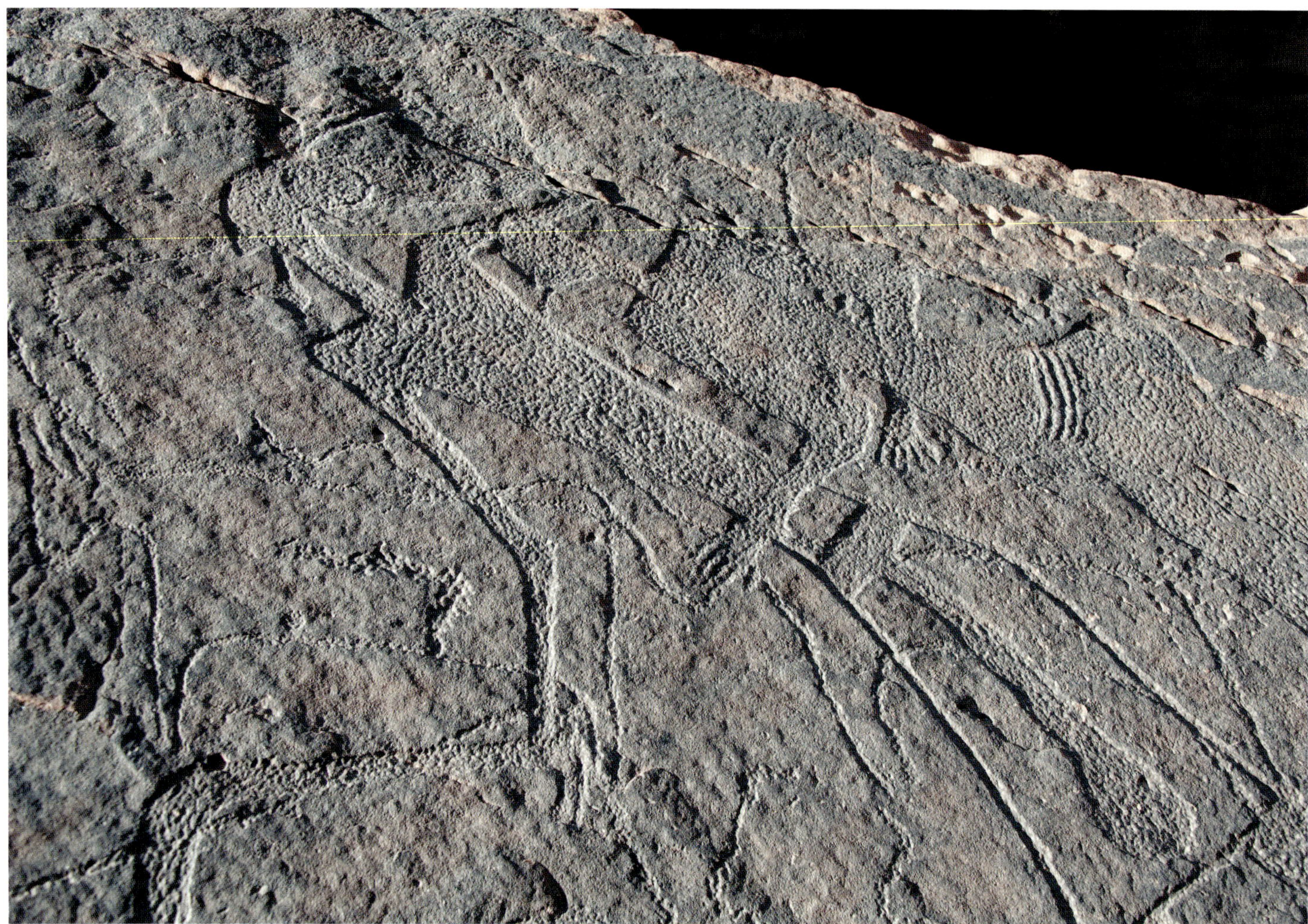

223. A Neolithic warrior in Jubbah style holding a boomerang; behind him stands a woman. Neolithic period, Talaat al-Salaby, Jabal Abu Mughair, Great Nafud Desert, northern Saudi Arabia. Photo 2020.

time-related markers are weapons, vehicles such as carts and light chariots, inscriptions and, occasionally, religious symbols. The use and reuse of some rock faces as a 'canvas' for petroglyphs has created superimposed banks of imagery dating to different periods. These palimpsests make it possible to sketch a relative chronology, which may then be compared with the direct dating achievable through archaeology. In terms of direct dating methods, the measurements of natural manganese (Mn) and iron (Fe) deposited as rock varnish on engraved petroglyphs compared to the adjacent natural varnish has made it possible to provide quantitative age estimates for a defined group of petroglyphs, so long as such rock art has been dated independently by other means such as a dated inscription. However, as Dorothea Macholdt has noted, 'Mn revarnishing measurements are not generally appropriate for deriving an "age" for an individual petroglyph.'[47]

1.2. Climate, fauna and rock art

As the hyperarid Terminal Pleistocene ended and the Holocene began around 10 ka BCE or slightly later, climate changed and Arabia experienced a relatively moist period, mainly driven by the north-westerly extension of the Indian Ocean monsoon.[48] This climatic shift first made its mark on the south-eastern portion of the Arabian Peninsula but, after a lag of *ca.* 1,700 years, the Nafud Desert also began receiving summer monsoons, albeit to a lesser extent. Lakes formed, which were replenished in the winter months by rainfall delivered by westerly cyclones from the Mediterranean, and parts of what had been desert landscape became steppe or, at favourable locations, savanna.[49] Big carnivores, such as lions and

224. → The lower part of this unique outcrop has petroglyphs of countless ibexes, a lion, a large bird, a single-axle chariot and archers shooting at each other. Bronze Age, southern al-Misma, Great Nafud Desert, northern Saudi Arabia. Photo 2020.

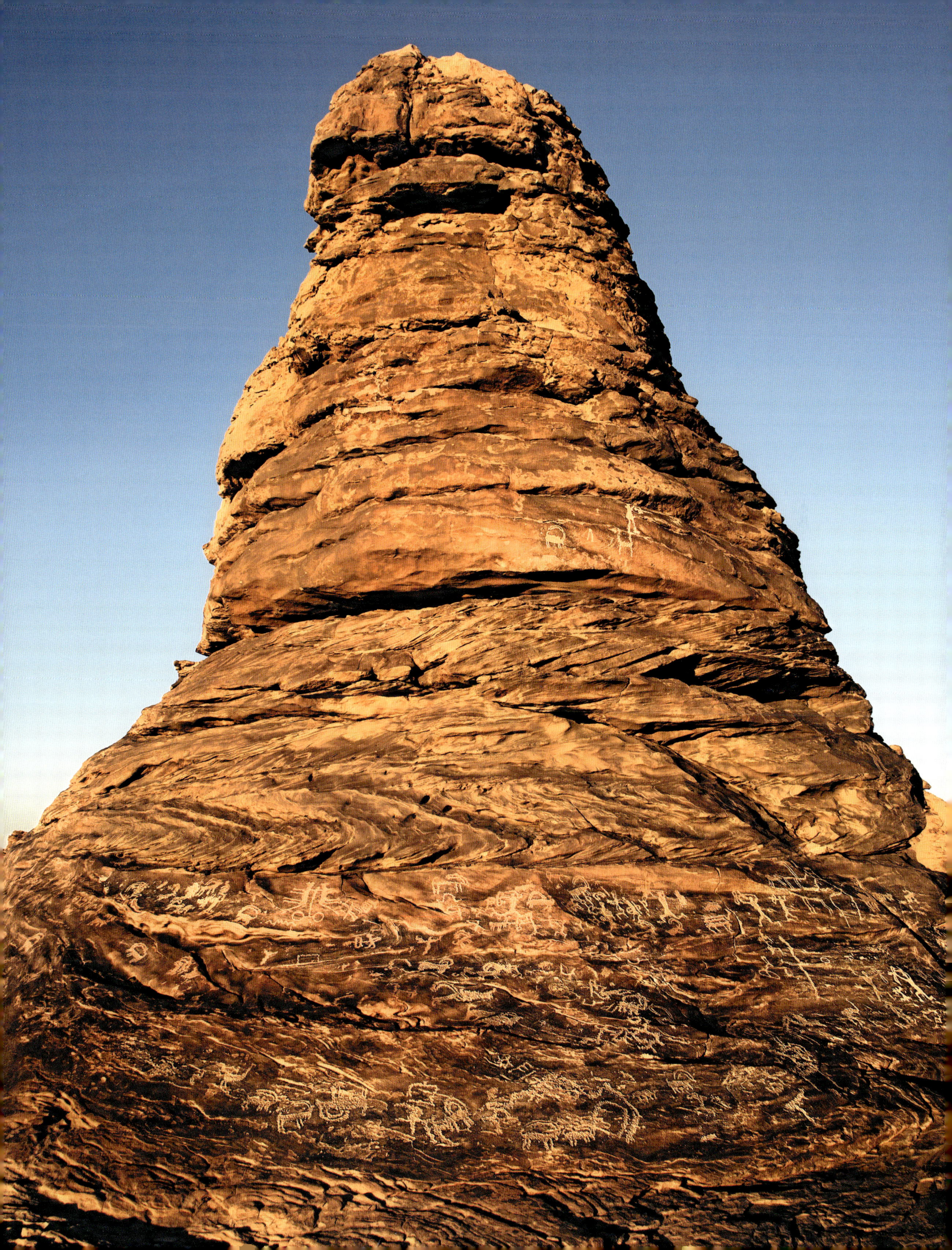

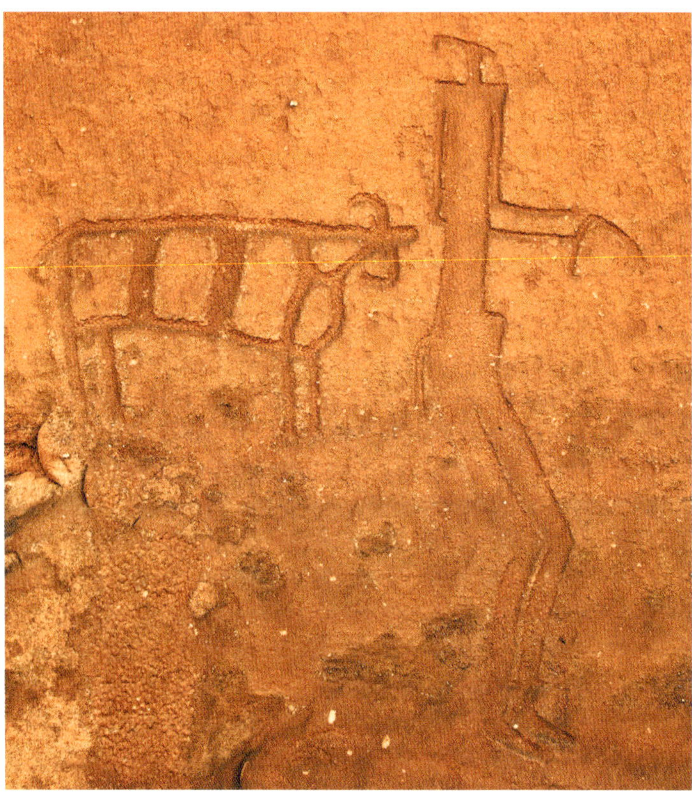

225. A tall man engraved in the Jubbah style holding what is probably a non-returning boomerang, and a bovine. Neolithic period, Jabal Umm Sanman, Jubbah, Great Nafud Desert, northern Saudi Arabia. Photo 2020.

leopards, and large herbivores like aurochs, long-horned buffalo, wild dromedaries and kudus thrived. At the onset of this wetter period, a hunter-gatherer economy dominated. Since lakes attracted carnivores and herbivores alike, these hunters also sought their prey there. Indeed, petroglyphs are quite often located in the immediate vicinity of palaeolakes or natural water sources.[50] Following what are probably the earliest pre-Neolithic, that is pre-pastoralist, petroglyphs at Jubbah featuring curvaceous women with round heads and large breasts from the eighth millennium BCE,[51] early rock art illustrated hunting scenes, sometimes involving packs of dogs (fig. 221), as well as confrontations between humans and lions (fig. 222) which may date from the seventh millennium BCE.[52] It is noticeable that petroglyphs often occur in concentrated form at water points, while other rock surfaces remained unworked. Where such water points were located along thoroughfares, one may find dated inscriptions from the Iron Age made by passing armies from the period of the Neo-Babylonians to the Christian and Jewish rulers of Himyar (Yemen), such as at the sites of al-Ha'it (ancient Padakku, alternatively ancient Yadihu),[53] Ma'sal, Murayghan, or around Bir Hima (see below).

The introduction of domestic cattle, sheep and goats from the Levant into Arabia around 6200 BCE[54] spurred a transition

to **Neolithic pastoralism**. This shift was not triggered by a mass migration from the Levant, but by the local herders of Arabia adapting to a subsistence based on livestock.[55] This major economic change is clearly mirrored in the rock art. Scenes featuring herding and domesticated animals became common and were often positioned to overlay older hunting images. Striking similarities between the petroglyphs in the southern Nafud in the so-called 'Jubbah style' (fig. 225) and slightly later images at Shuwaymis and Luwee, also called al-Hanakiya, which are respectively 200 and 350 kilometres south of Jubbah, at Musayqirah and Mughayra west of Riyadh, and at Wadi Rum in Jordan, 700 kilometres north-eastwards, suggest that the Nafud Neolithic pastoralists expanded both southwards and northwards.[56] Occasional examples of bovines in the Jubbah style exist *ca*. 400 kilometres south of Luwee at al-Ta'if and 500 kilometres south of Musayqirah at Khamasin (in Wadi Dawasir) which may suggest a further southward spread of this Neolithic style,[57] but it never reached the south of Saudi Arabia. Whereas the transition from hunting to herding is clearly visible in the Jubbah–Ha'il and Shuwaymis–Luwee regions, it is not apparent in the province of Najran in the south-west of the country, where the making of petroglyphs started later than in the north. In the Jubbah style, humans are featured with elongated and rather slim bodies, 40–190 centimetres high, and with tiny heads that seem to wear a head cover; together, the head and cover look like a hammer (fig. 226). The figures are often shown in motion with slightly bent knees; they have very slim arms and in one hand they often hold either a bow or an object that probably represents a boomerang or a throwing stick used in hunting. The bovines, for their part, are rendered in profile, their legs joined together in pairs with the same outline and the ears shown as fine lines on each side of the head. The very long and thin horns, however, are shown as seen from above making the shape either of a lyre or of pincers. The whole surface of these early images was often deeply pecked into the stone (fig. 225), while later petroglyphs were mostly created by removing the dark brown rock surface to expose the brighter, underlying stone so as to form just the outlines of the figures.[58]

In the south-western Nafud Desert, in Jabal al-Misma, the authors' 2020 expedition discovered one Neolithic petroglyph of an almost life-sized wild dromedary (fig. 220).[59] Nearby, two huge slabs had been used as a shelter and were adorned with stylistically very similar carvings of three wild dromedaries and the carving of an oryx. Under these four animals the outline of an earlier animal can be conjectured. In 2022, four rock panels featuring nine large, naturalistic wild dromedaries were discovered in the Sahout region at the southern edge of the Nafud Desert, close to another, already published, large, naturalistic dromedary petroglyph.[60] Some of them were superimposed over petroglyphs of small ibexes and were in turn superimposed by humans in the Jubbah style, domestic sheep, and a hunt of an equid with the assistance of dogs, the latter images belonging to the Neolithic. These ten naturalistically engraved camel petroglyphs look stylistically not only almost identical, but they are also very similar to the above-mentioned camel petroglyphs from Jabal al-Misma. There was clearly a norm for how wild dromedaries, most probably male ones, were to be featured in petroglyphs; possibly some of those images were made by the same artist. Excavations conducted in close proximity to these panels yielded lithic material, bones and a hearth with radiocarbon-dated charcoal remains which indicate repeated occupation of the site from the Terminal Pleistocene to the Middle Holocene,[61] that is from the twelfth to the seventh millennium BCE.[62] The fact that Neolithic images have been superimposed on the naturalistic dromedary petroglyphs suggests that the latter *may* be pre-Neolithic. Almost as old as the dromedary petroglyphs from Sahout are the seventeen life-sized high and low reliefs, dated to between 5200 and 5600 BCE, which were discovered in 2016 in Saudi Arabia's northern region of al-Jawf.[63]

Recent research conducted east of al-Ula has demonstrated that towards the sixth millennium BCE the Neolithic pastoralists were already building monumental stone structures which served ritual purposes. These structures, called *mustasils*,[64] consist of two parallel platforms built from sandstone or basalt which stand between 20 and 600 metres apart and are connected by two rows of stones positioned at right angles. More than 1,600 such *mustasils* have been identified in north-western Arabia with an especially dense distribution in the Khaybar–al-Ula region; the northern-most such structure was found at Dumat al-Jandal in the Saudi Arabian al-Jawf province, the southern most in Dhofar in Oman. The excavation of such a *mustasil* near al-Ula brought to light a large amount of faunal remains, of which 94 per cent belonged to cattle or wild bulls. Radiocarbon analysis dated these remains ranging from 5200 to 4850 cal. BCE.[65] These finds have been interpreted as implying that a large number of people ritually came together at such *mustasils* and offered animal sacrifices.

Towards the beginning of the fourth millennium BCE, drier conditions set in once more and the Jubbah style disappeared.[66] Limited winter rainfall and the retreat of the Indian Ocean monsoon led the sparse grassland to disappear as the steppes

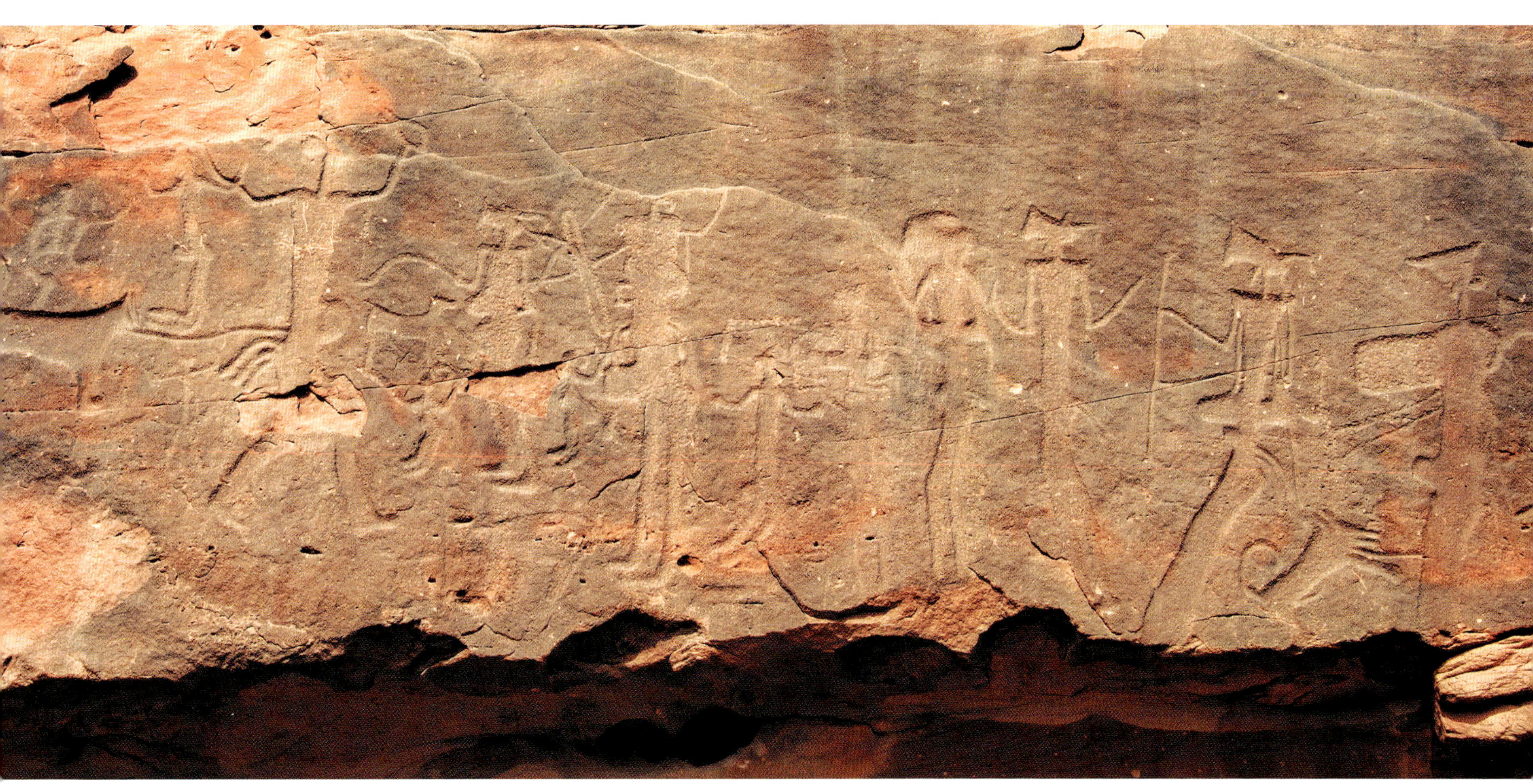

226. An eight metres wide panel with in total ten pastoralists in Jubbah style; one holds a bow. Neolithic period, Luwee, also called al-Hanakiya, al-Medina Province, central Saudi Arabia. Photo 2020.

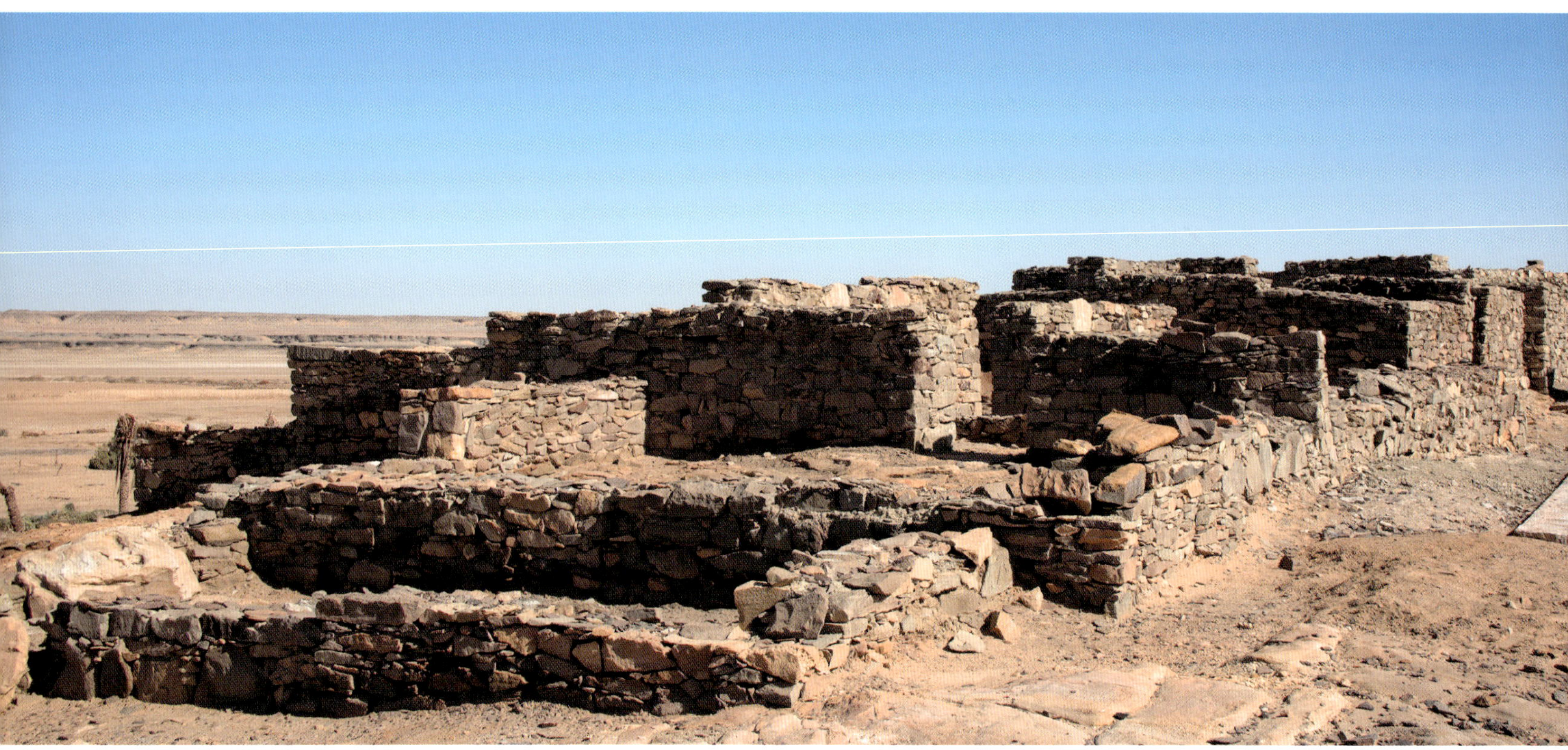

227. The al-Hamra Temple in Tayma at the southern edge of the Great Nafud Desert. The temple dates to the sixth century BCE, the period of the Neo-Babylonian king Nabonid. The first protective walls of the oasis were built in the third millennium BCE. Northern Saudi Arabia. Photo 2020.

gradually regressed to desert.[67] As a consequence, the savanna fauna was replaced by desert-adapted animals, first in the north, later also in the south of Saudi Arabia.[68] Humans responded not only by retreating to coastal areas,[69] but also by adopting two economic strategies. First, settlements harnessing artificial irrigation fed by wells flourished at the desert edges or in fertile oases such as Tayma at the south-western edge of the Nafud Desert.[70] In those days, and indeed until the 1960s, the phreatic level was relatively close to the earth's surface in certain regions of northern and north-central Saudi Arabia, and wells provided the needed water; at the wells, leather containers filled with water were pulled up by oxen, and later by camels.[71] Second, pastoralism diminished and hunting regained its importance.[72] The prey animals were wild camels, gazelles and goats. On a societal level, it is probable that the increased competition for the access to pastures and water fostered social cohesion among local populations which led to the emergence of tribal structures.[73] The renewed importance of hunting is also suggested by the increase in so-called 'desert kites', which are in fact huge traps. These are arrangements of stone walls in the shape of a kite, as they consist of two convergent walls hundreds of metres or even several kilometres long ending in an enclosure. Game animals would be driven into these 'kites' to be caught in the enclosure

which was surrounded by numerous pits up to four metres deep.[74] Quite often, individual neighbouring kites were linked together by walls and thus formed chains of kites from which it was nearly impossible for animals to escape.[75] Obviously the construction of these kites, their maintenance and their use required significant manpower and concerted efforts in planning. Such prehistoric mega-traps were mainly constructed in northern Saudi Arabia, eastern Jordan and Syria, but also in Armenia, north-western Uzbekistan and in the Ustyurt Plateau of Kazakhstan. The oldest examples in Jordan and northern Saudi Arabia have been dated to the seventh to sixth millennia BCE.[76] Interestingly, at two places where desert kites are located in Saudi Arabia and Jordan, large petroglyphs have been found illustrating such desert kites to scale. Since the layout of these huge stone structures, which were built on flat plains, can only be grasped from the air, one may assume that the rocks must have been engraved by the kites' builders or users.[77] In any case, these two complex petroglyphs testify to an advanced mental capacity for spatial perception and the ability to reproduce it to scale. Furthermore, in the Black Desert in eastern Jordan, dozens of somewhat smaller petroglyphs seem to illustrate kites as well.[78]

Also in the course of the Bronze Age, those large oases whose economies were based on agriculture and irrigation such as

Tayma and, a little later, Dadan[79] (today's al-Ula), developed into proto-urban settlements. Some of them invested in architectural defensive systems against environmental dangers and hostile human threats. For example, the oasis of Tayma with its palm groves was surrounded by a 128-kilometre-long, moderately high mudbrick wall which protected it from advancing sand and possibly also from seasonal flash floods in the wadis; its construction began in the third millennium BCE.[80] Tayma also possessed a second, inner defensive wall twelve kilometres in length which was higher and built from stone.[81] Such a wall also fulfilled a military function, namely protecting the inhabited and key agricultural areas from nomadic incursions and organized hostile armies. Soon after Tayma, Qurayyah too began to build protective walls. The construction and maintenance of such large protective and defensive architecture required a central power able to deploy sufficient labour forces. By the end of the second millennium BCE, the urbanization process at Tayma had developed further, for its inner defensive wall was now up to ten metres high.[82] Later, during the middle Iron Age, long walls protecting quasi-urban oases emerged at Dumat al-Jandal in the Jawf, and further south at Khaybar (ancient Hibra), Medina (Yatribu/Yathrib), al-Ha'it (Padakku), and al-Huwayyit (Yadi'u). All these oases as well as Tayma (Tema) belonged to the realm of King Nabonid.[83] The domestication and use of the dromedary for transport purposes triggered a revolution in long-distance transport and greatly stimulated trade. Tayma, Dadan and other central Arabian cities developed from agricultural proto-urban settlements to merchant cities, which brought them into contact and conflict with neighbouring empires of Egypt, Neo-Assyria and Neo-Babylonia, a development which is also recorded in petroglyphs and inscriptions.

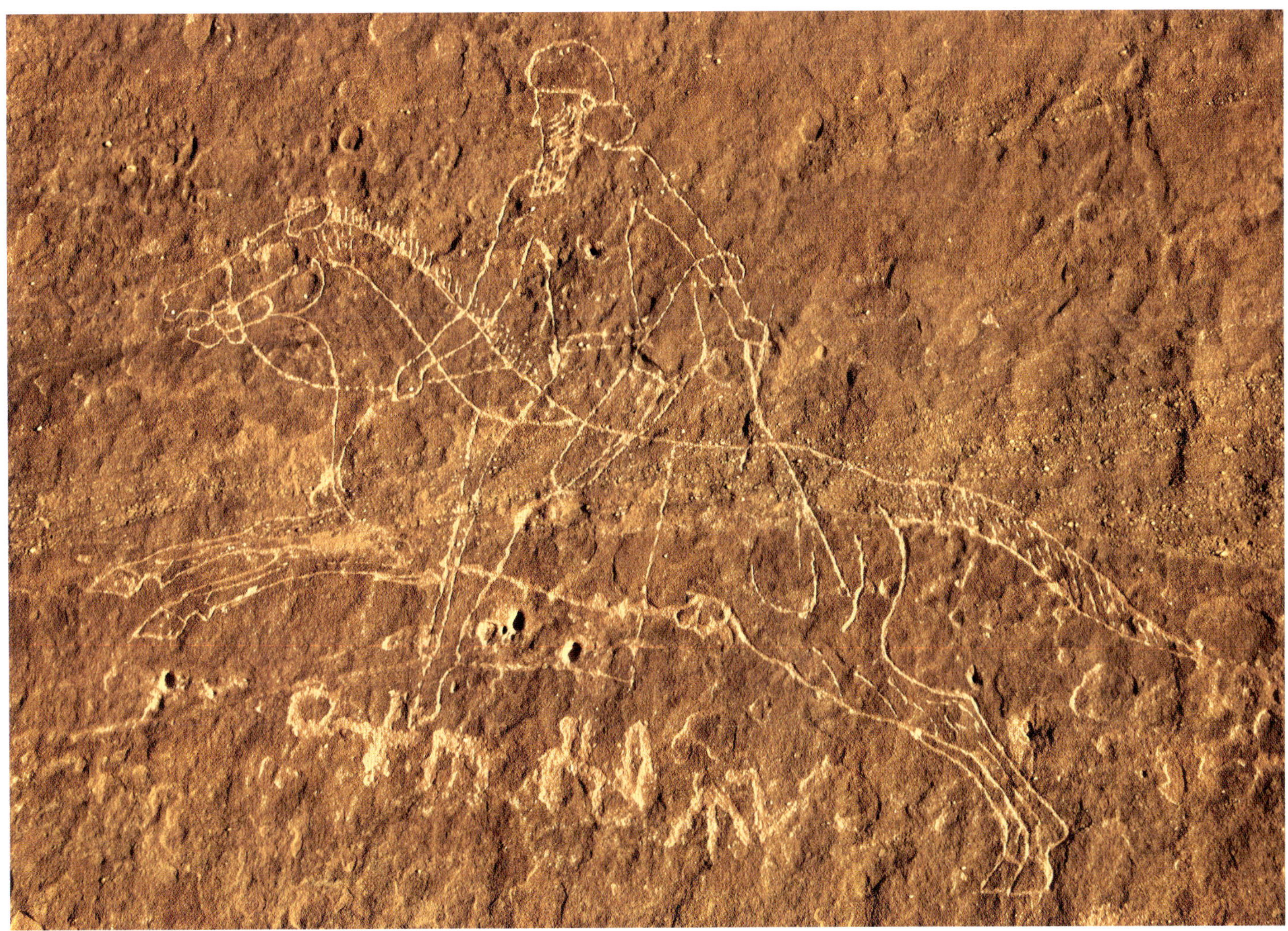

228. Petroglyph of a galloping horseman in the Neo-Assyrian and Neo-Babylonian style. He wears a beard and carries a quiver. A nearby inscription mentions border guards of [*nbnd*] *mlk bbl*, that is '[Nabonid], King of Babylon'. The petroglyph most probably dates from between 553/2 and 543/2 BCE. Whether the petroglyph is meant to show the king or one of his horsemen is unknown. Al-Khshaybowat, Great Nafud Desert, northern Saudi Arabia. Photo 2020.

As the region became drier, cattle disappeared from rock art and hunting scenes became dominant once more. Overhunting of wild dromedaries probably spurred their domestication around 1000 BCE, initially to ensure supplies of meat and milk.[84] Approximately one century later, dromedaries also began to be used for transport, substantially increasing the mobility of pastoralists and merchants – but also of raiders.[85] The late Bronze Age and early Iron Age witnessed the emergence of simple carts with four-spoked wheels pulled by equids, which are featured in rock art in plan view (e.g. at Jubbah or Abragz bin Samra south of Tayma; fig. 229) and, towards the middle of the first millennium BCE, of light chariots with eight- or ten-spoked wheels rendered in profile similar to Neo-Assyrian, Neo-Babylonian and Egyptian images; such chariots are found on petroglyphs at al-Sinya near al-Ula, Hafrat Berd in the southern Nafud or al-'Ayrayn south of Tabuk (fig. 236).[86] Since nomads and caravans depended on access to water, the question of who controlled the wells prompted an increase in violent confrontation.[87] Horses were domesticated slightly later than dromedaries but their use became common only around 400 BCE;[88] in southern Arabia the spread of the horse was slower and its use for riding became prevalent in the first century CE.[89] This encouraged a militarization of nomadic society which is reflected in rock art, with mounted lancers and swordsmen, fighters on foot, and battle scenes becoming dominant (fig. 264).

Today, the Arabian Peninsula, and Saudi Arabia within it, is divided into three distinct climatic zones: the north is impacted by the Mediterranean climatic pattern with dry summers and rainy winters, the large central zone has mild winters and hot, dry summers with occasional intermittent showers, while the eastern Indian Ocean coastal regions have a climatic regime characterized by high humidity, very hot summers and precipitation in winter.

As this brief overview shows, the relation between climate, economy and rock art can be divided into six periods:

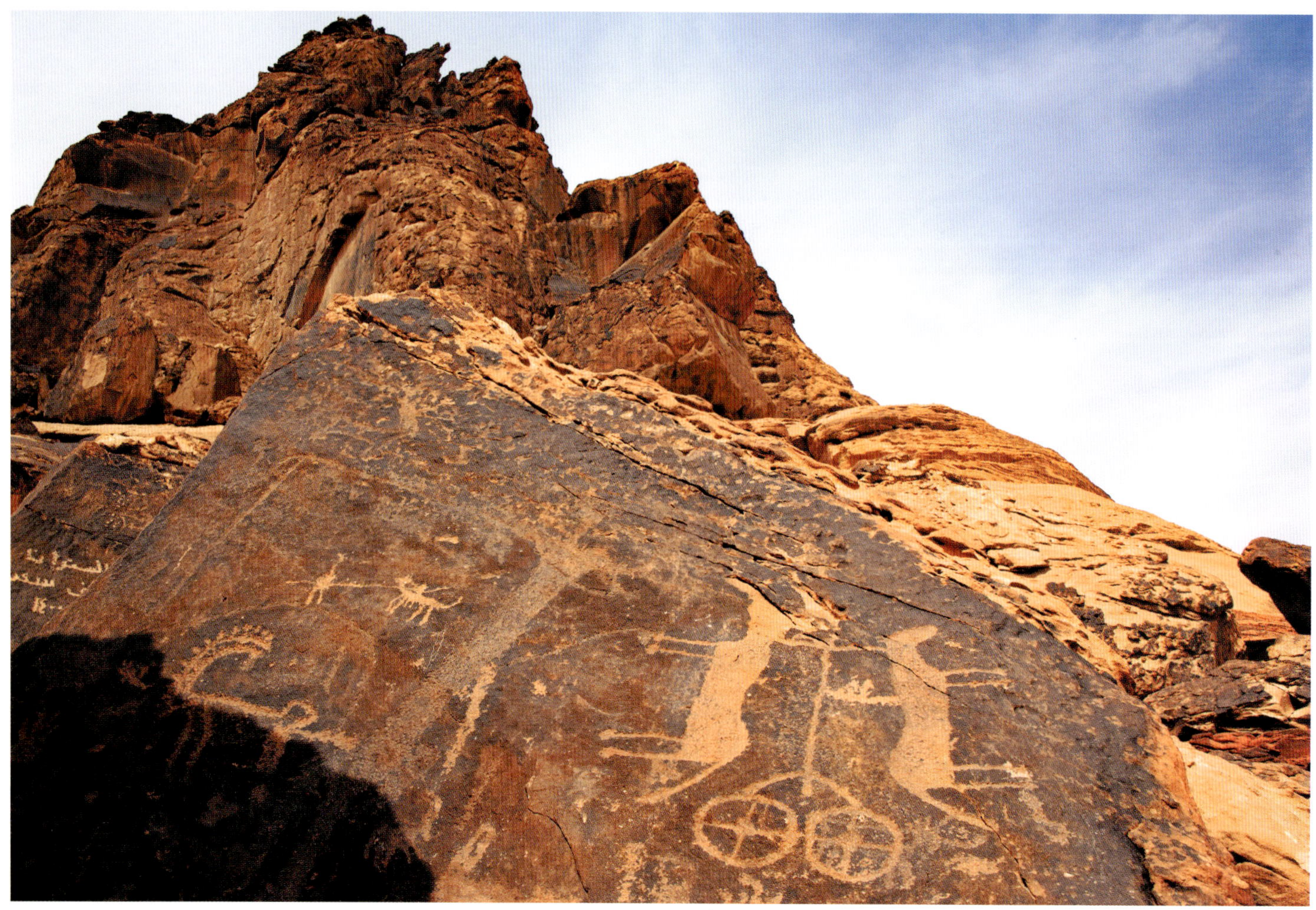

229. Petroglyph of a light chariot at the Jabal Umm Sinman. Bronze Age, Jubbah, Great Nafud Desert, northern Saudi Arabia. Photo 2020.

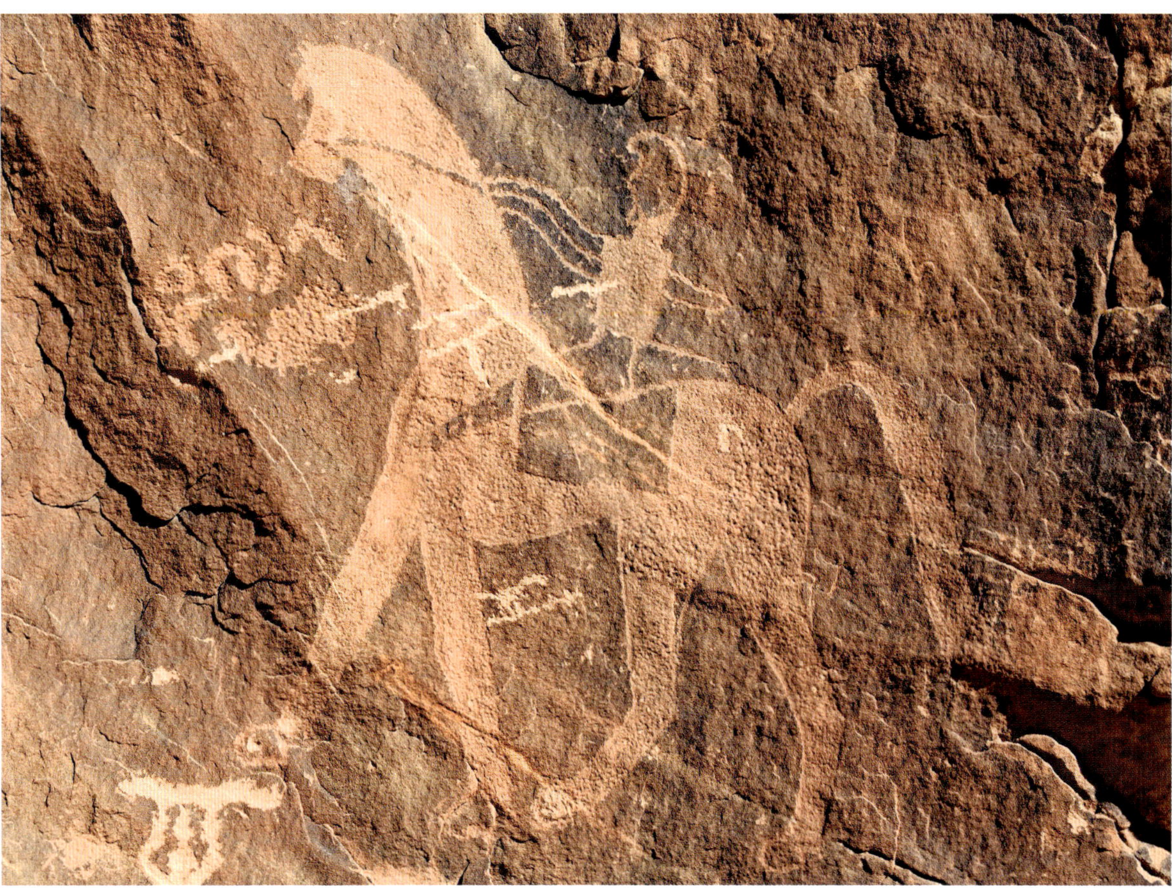

230. A horseman sitting on a blanket and wearing a Phrygian cap, a quiver and a sword. Iron Age, southern al-Misma, Great Nafud Desert, northern Saudi Arabia. Photo 2020.

- First, during the wet, early Holocene, a hunter-gatherer economy is reflected in petroglyphs featuring, at Jubbah, curvaceous women followed by hunting scenes.

- Second, in the era of Neolithic pastoralism (beginning in the later seventh millennium BCE) which still enjoyed a relatively humid climate, images of pastoralists and domesticated cattle, sheep and goats predominate.

- Third, in the late Neolithic and Bronze Age, a return of arid conditions led to the development of settlements relying on irrigated agriculture and to a resurgence of hunting.

- Fourth, in the Iron Age (*ca.* 1200–300 BCE), the domestication of the dromedary and horse brought a new level of mobility. Rock art now featured dromedaries, horses and riders (fig. 230), as well as numerous brief inscriptions; the latter were carved not only by literate travellers, but also by local pastoralists. Countless engraved figures were 'signed' with brief epigrams. Whereas royal proclamations were written in the South Arabian Sabaic script, the epigrams occur in a multitude of North Arabian scripts such as the various Thamudic scripts, Taymanitic, Dadanitic, Hismaic and Safaitic. In addition, there are inscriptions in Egyptian hieroglyphs, Imperial Aramaic, Nabataean, Greek, palaeo-Arabic and Arabic scripts. Hunting scenes tend to diminish in number, and dromedaries become common in rock art, sometimes in a schematic style with exceedingly long necks (fig. 234).

- Fifth, in the pre-Islamic period ending in 622 CE, continued aridification led to an increase in conflict. This development is mirrored in battle scenes and duels involving mounted lancers and archers as well as infantry. Especially in Najran, battle scenes continued to be carved in the early Islamic period.[90]

- The sixth, contemporary phase includes Arabic inscriptions and, from the nineteenth century onwards, also hunters and warriors armed with guns, and finally cars and trucks.

Of course, this classification is only a rough indicator and takes little notice of transitional periods. Furthermore, the economic importance of a species of animal was not always mirrored accordingly in rock art. For example, sheep appear only infrequently in rock art, mainly in the region of Hima.

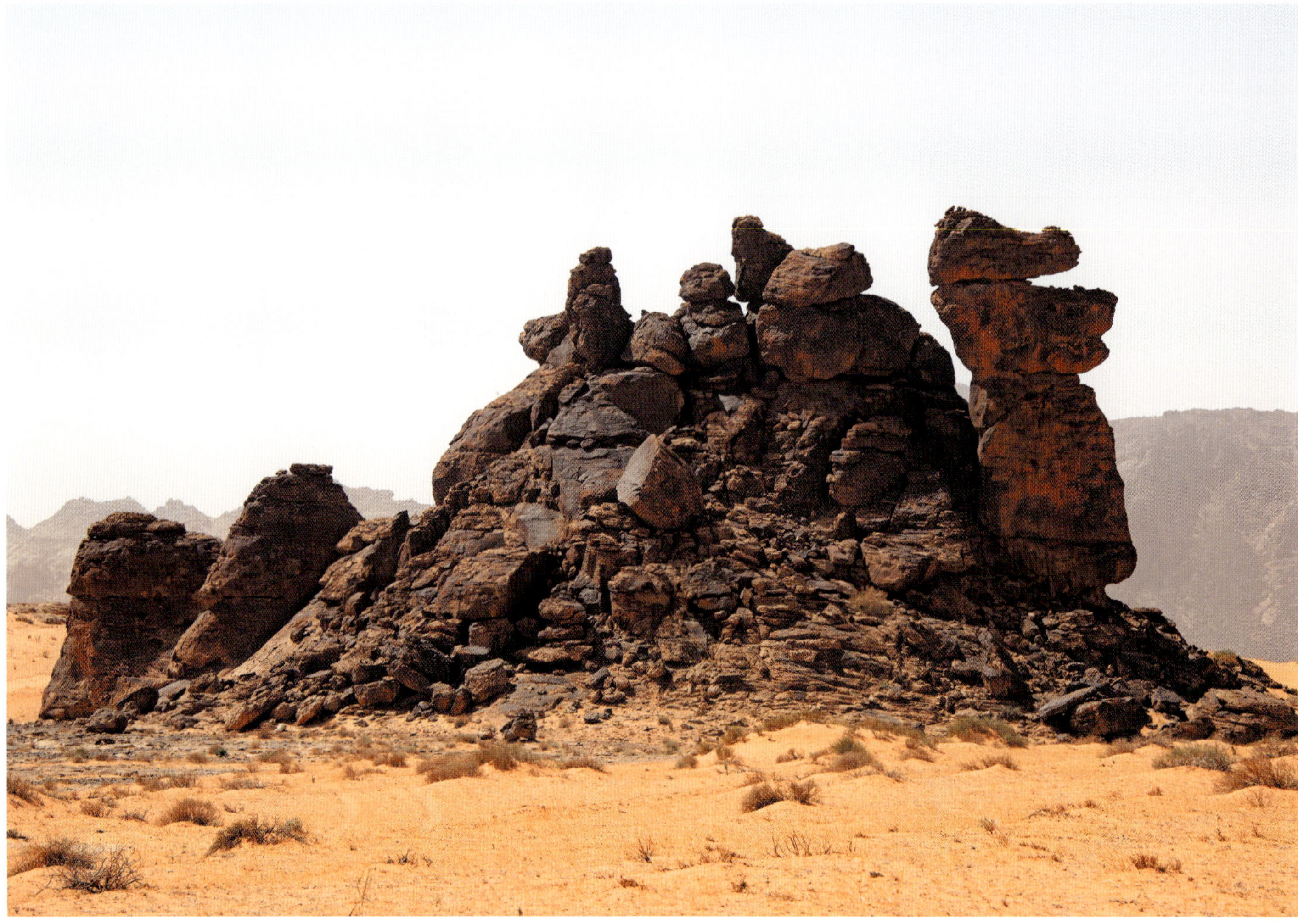

231. Stone formation in the shape of a crouching two-humped camel at Riya Azlek in the Jabal 'Arnan, Great Nafud Desert. Julius Euting drew this unique outcrop in his diary.[5] Northern Saudi Arabia. Photo 2020.

1.3. Rock art sites by region

In view of the multitude of rock art sites within Saudi Arabia, the choice of sites described is of necessity highly selective.

1.3.1. Northern Saudi Arabia

The main sites in northern Saudi Arabia, that is north of 25° latitude, are, from north to south and east to west:

The '**Camel Site**', located near the village of Sakaka in the northern province al-Jawf, was discovered in 2016. This unique site consists of 22 life-sized wild animals carved in a naturalistic way in high and low relief into beige-orange sandstone boulders. They represent seventeen dromedaries and five equids, most probably wild asses. These monumental reliefs have been dated to the Neolithic between 5600 and 5200 BCE. The only carvings comparable to those at the Camel Site are the two Nabataean life-sized high reliefs of camel caravans walking towards each other in the Siq at Petra, but they date from the first century BCE.

Since in those days al-Jawf belonged to the political-economic realm of the Nabataeans, it is conceivable that the Petra high reliefs were inspired by those at Sakaka.[91] Although any influence its excluded, the Sakaka reliefs also recall the famous two bison modelled from clay in the 16,000-year-old Tuc d'Audoubert Cave in Ariège, southern France (fig. 2). Tuc d'Audoubert was probably a sanctuary, as the Camel Site may have been as well.

Wadi Damm, Jabal al-Lauz and Jabal Hisma. In the region north of Tabuk, there are many locations with petroglyphs and early Arabic inscriptions in the Kufic calligraphic style engraved in the red sandstone typical of this region, for example at **Shahibuwat**, **Safinah**, **Wadi Damm** and a cave in the **Bajda–Neom** Desert. On a south-eastern foot of the 2,580-metre-high **Jabal al-Lauz** lies the little-known site of **al-'Agil al Mahruq**, which means 'the burnt calf'. In the shelter formed by a huge boulder, there are paintings of a dark red bull, a bright red bull 80 centimetres long with large horns in the shape of a lyre, a long animal (possibly a large cat), two small goats, and a human 33 centimetres tall painted in a strong red colour. In another tiny shelter, there are three or four gazelles painted in black. In the **Wadi Beidah**, Jabal Hisma, there are numerous inscriptions in the Dadanitic script (formerly called Lihyanite). Finally, at **Ruwafah**, there are not only many petroglyphs of horsemen armed with lances confronting each other, dating from the middle of the first millennium CE, but also inscriptions in Greek and a bilingual inscription in Greek and Nabataean. The latter declares that members of the central and north Arabian Thamud tribe serving in the Roman cavalry dedicated the nearby temple to the emperors Marcus Aurelius and Lucius Verus between 167 and 169 CE.[92] In those days, north-west Saudi Arabia belonged to the Roman zone of influence since the Roman Emperor Trajan had conquered and annexed Petra in 106 CE and transformed its realm into the Roman province of Arabia Petraea.

In **Wadi Asafir**, located about 20 kilometres south-west of Tabuk, there is a highly interesting petroglyph scene which suggests that light chariots were not only used for purposes of prestige and ceremony, but also in battle. It shows a chariot with eight-spoke wheels, as are familiar in the Neo-Assyrian period, pulled by a horse and driven by a charioteer standing in the box. Behind him stands an archer who shoots an arrow back at an enemy archer who has dismounted from his camel to shoot more accurately and one of whose arrows narrowly misses the head of the bowman in the chariot.[93]

Al-Sala'u. In 2010, the first pharaonic inscription within Saudi Arabia was discovered at al-Sala'u, 80 kilometres west of Tayma (fig. 232). The inscription is carefully made and includes a cartouche of Pharaoh Ramses III (r. 1192–1160 BCE). Such cartouches have an official character and were made in the course of military or commercial expeditions. Since no military campaign of Ramses III against Arabia is recorded, it was most probably made in the context of an official expedition to acquire raw materials, above all copper and gold. While there are no copper or gold deposits in the region of Tayma, they are plentiful further south-west. Three similar inscriptions have been found in the Sinai and Negev Deserts along ancient trade routes, which must have continued to the trading city of Tayma.[94] Clearly there existed trade connections between Tayma and Pharaonic Egypt. In the nearby **Wadi Zayadani** there are two rare Taymanitic inscriptions and a petroglyph of the bull-faced god Salm mentioned in the Tayma Stele.[95]

Jubbah is a major rock art complex 100 kilometres north-west of Ha'il, which consists of the four sites **Jabal Umm Sinman**, a UNESCO World Heritage site, **Jabal Oraf**, **Ghawtah** and **Jabal**

Qatar. Like other petroglyph sites in the Nafud Desert, Jubbah was close to a palaeolake which existed in the Late Pleistocene and during the Holocene Wet Phase up to *ca.* 3500 BCE, making the place attractive to wild animals and humans with their herds. At Jabal Umm Sinman, the Mesolithic petroglyphs of large-buttocked and big-breasted women are especially outstanding, as are the early Neolithic pastoralists in the Jubbah style (fig. 225); the latter sometimes hold a throwing stick in their hands to hunt rabbits and other small animals.[96] Other late Neolithic images feature a male 2.6 metres tall wearing a kind of crown with an attendant, a pastoralist 2.3 metres tall with a bull, and buffaloes with huge horns. Then there are hunting scenes of lions, ostriches and later a light chariot pulled by two horses (fig. 229), camel riders and lancers. Ostriches are virtually the only birds depicted in petroglyphs, with the exception of a few vultures in Najran

232. Cartouche of Pharaoh Ramses III (r. 1192–1160 BCE). Al-Sala'u, Tabuk province, northern Saudi Arabia. Photo 2020.

province. Also striking are the many Thamudic inscriptions, some of which are curses, such as 'O Rab' [God], cut off the head of Fual,' or 'O Rab, abandon Shafr' (whose name means 'the blade').

Ha'il and **Janin Cave.** To the east of the city of Ha'il there are several petroglyph sites, among them the **Janin Cave** and the nearby mountains. In the cave, which is around 100 metres deep, there are dozens of petroglyphs featuring hand prints and a few footprints, possibly from the Bronze Age (fig. 316); then later images of camels, leopards and many pre-Islamic Thamudic inscriptions. About two kilometres further east inside a steep canyon are found petroglyphs of aurochs with long horns, ibexes, wild asses and stick-like dancing humans.

Tayma to al-Ula. In this area, spread over a distance of 110 kilometres between the cities of Tayma and al-Ula in the south-western Nafud Desert, there are numerous petroglyph sites. At the site of **Abragz bin Samra**, 25 kilometres south-west of Tayma, the petroglyphs are not pecked as usual into a vertical rock face, but into the dark-brown patina of flat limestone boulders lying on the ground (fig. 233). Thanks to this specific location, the petroglyphs remained covered by sand for centuries and, despite their high age, show only slight patination. Particularly noteworthy are at least four petroglyphs featuring two seated humans drinking with straws from the same jug. The identical image was found on seals from the Dilmun culture, which flourished in Bahrain and the

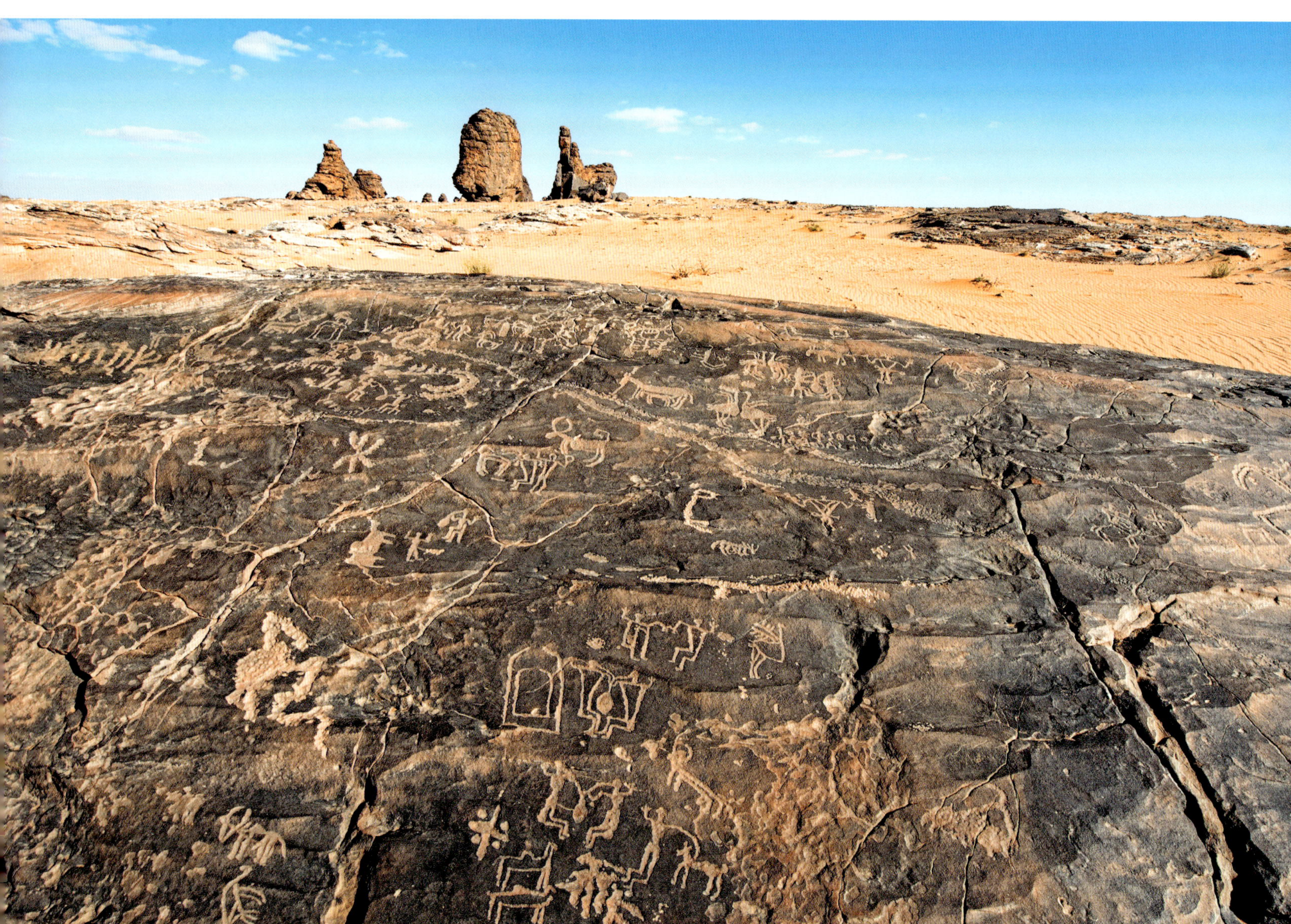

233. In the centre front, two pairs of seated humans drink from the same gourd and two other pairs are engraved behind. At the back right are petroglyphs of two pairs of mirrored ostriches and two armed men with triangular-shaped torsos. Bronze and Iron Age, Abragz bin Samra, Great Nafud Desert, northern Saudi Arabia. Photo 2020.

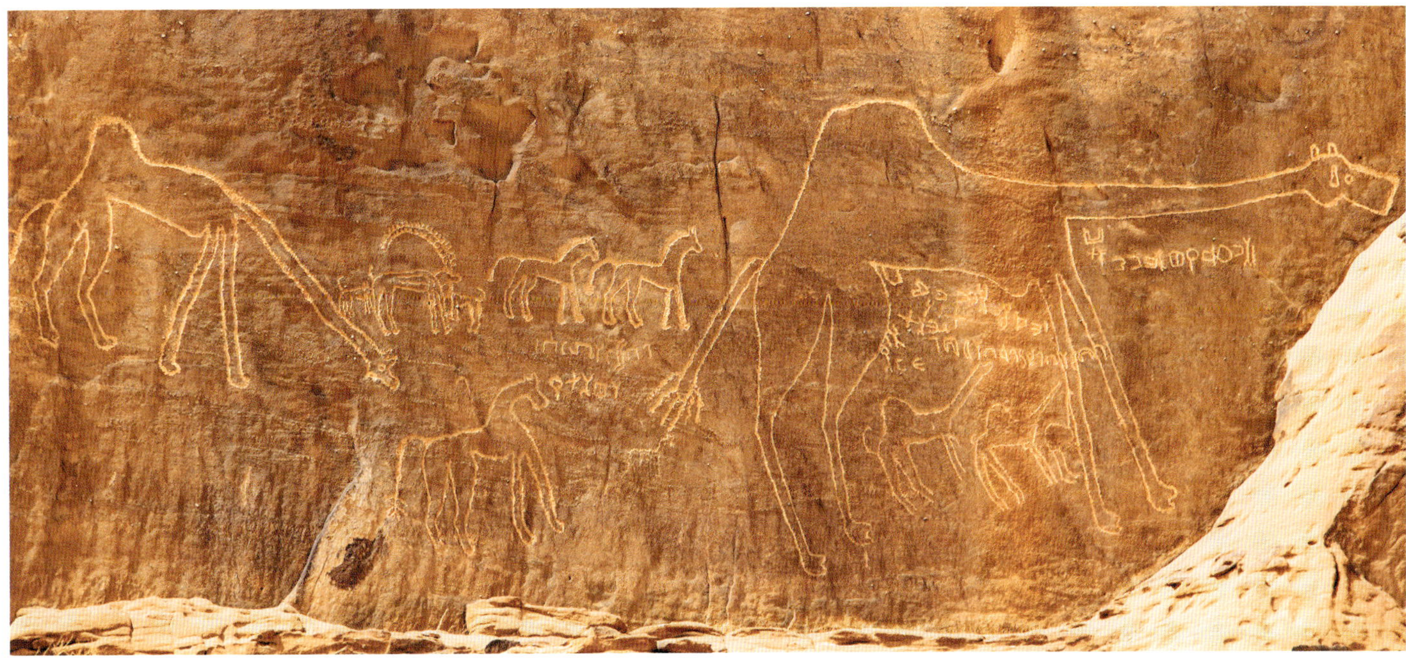

234. Images of camels and horses at Uqulq, also called al-Dogosh. Iron Age, Great Nafud Desert, northern Saudi Arabia. Photo 2020.

opposite east Saudi Arabian coast in the late 3rd and early 2nd millennium BCE. Striking are also petroglyphs of mirrored ostriches, of men with triangular-shaped torsi, a lizard, a cart, and later Taymanitic inscriptions.[96a]

About 37 kilometres south-west of Tayma at a place called **al-Khshaybowat** is found a finely engraved petroglyph of a galloping horseman, which shares strong similarities with Neo-Assyrian and Neo-Babylonian bas-reliefs from Nineveh (fig. 228). Next to the horseman, an equally finely engraved inscription 172 centimetres long in Taymanitic script (formerly named Thamudic A), mentions border guards of *mlk bbl*, that is a 'king of Babylon'. Since two inscriptions discovered in the Tayma region mention *nbnd mlk bbl*, that is 'Nabonid, king of Babylon',[97] and since the Neo-Babylonian ruler **Nabonid** (r. 556–539 BCE) spent about ten years of his reign in Tayma, the petroglyph of the horseman either represents Nabonid himself or, more probably, one of his guards. Both petroglyph and inscription are an important witness to a period when northern Arabia belonged to the Neo-Babylonian Empire. Nabonid, whose name means 'Nabu [god of wisdom] be praised', was the last king of Babylon. He lived in Tayma from 553/2 to 543/2 BCE, either to consolidate the Neo-Babylonian rule over northern Arabia, or, more likely, because he had been forced into exile by the Babylonian clergy of the god Marduk since he favoured the cult of the moon god Sin.[98] Nabonid was not of royal Babylonian blood, but a usurper who had forcefully deposed Neriglissar's son Labashi-Marduk, who only ruled for a couple of months. In this, he

followed Neriglissar (r. 560–556 BCE) who had himself forcefully ejected Nebuchadnezzar's son Awel-Marduk.[99] Most probably, the driving force behind the coup was Nabonid's son Belshazzar, who acted as regent in Babylonia during the ten-year absence of his father in Arabia. He had probably hoped that his aged father (born *ca.* 615 BCE) would soon die, allowing him to inherit naturally; but since Nabonid remained alive and propagated the cult of the moon god, Belshazzar forced his father into exile, while being obliged to let him command the core of the army.[100] At any rate, Nabonid conquered the northern half of today's Saudi Arabia as far south as Medina. When Nabonid returned to Babylon, he demoted his son Belshazzar and stripped him of his functions, replaced key officials with new men who were devoted to him and imposed the worship of Sin as the paramount deity of the Babylonian pantheon.[101] But in 539 BCE, the Persian ruler Cyrus, whose empire almost encircled the Babylonian realm, attacked it and defeated Nabonid in battle; Cyrus took Babylon on 12 October 539 without a serious fight.[102] In the Akkadian cuneiform inscription on the so-called Cyrus Cylinder dated to the 530s BCE, Cyrus claimed that the Babylonian god Marduk himself had requested him to remove Nabonid and to restore Marduk's cult.[103]

Some 260 kilometres south-east of al-Khshaybowat, Nabonid is present in another petroglyph and a long inscription which were discovered at **al-Ha'it** in 2011 (fig. 235). The large rock stands in the ancient, abandoned city which was surrounded by walls made from basalt at the bottom and clay higher up; hundreds of dead palm trees

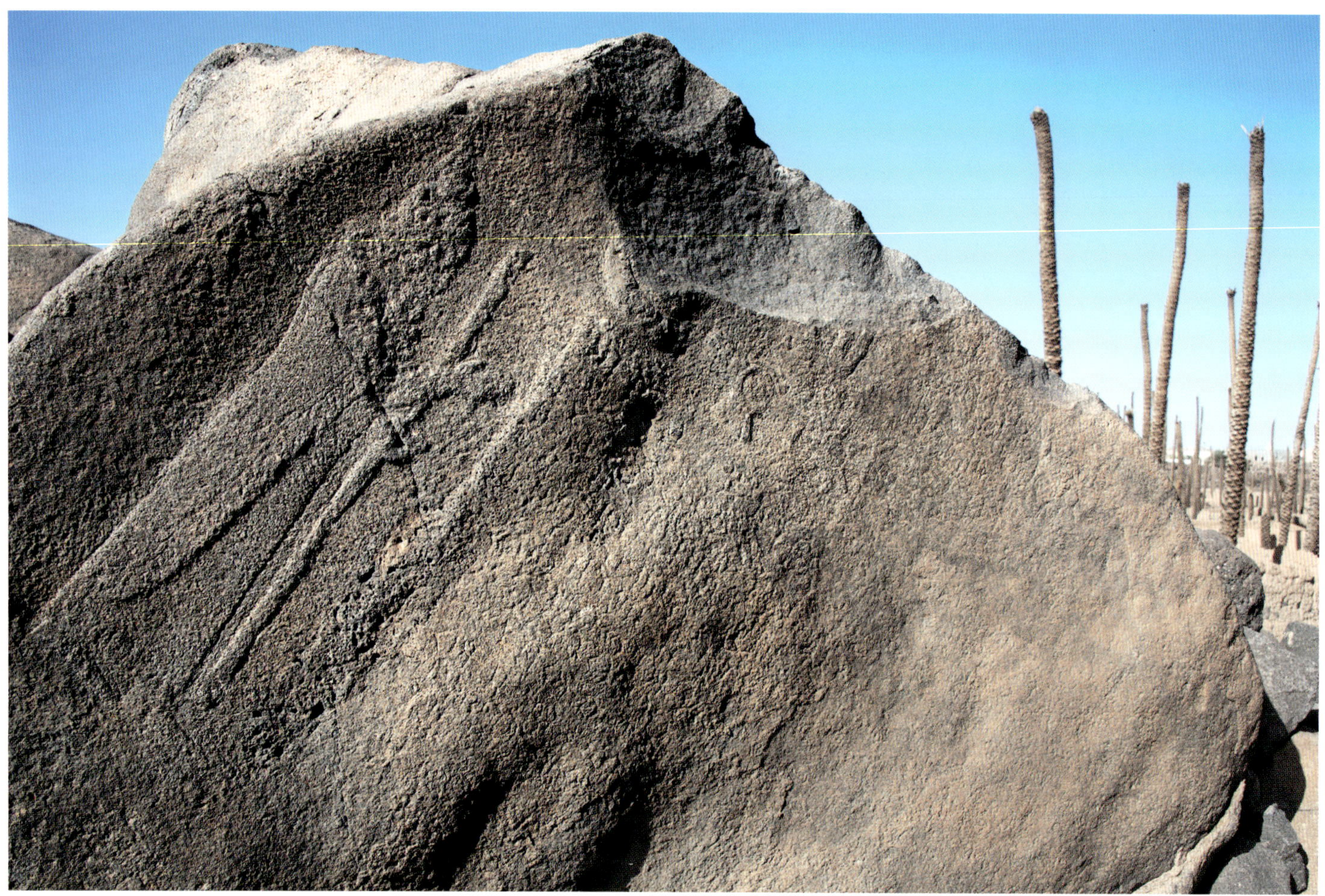

235. Petroglyphs on a basaltic rock of a standing bearded man holding a ceremonial staff, with four symbols and a 26-line cuneiform inscription which names the standing man: *Nabu-na'id sar Babil*, 'Nabonid, king of Babylon'. The symbols at the top are the crescent moon representing the moon god Sin, the sun representing Salm/Sulmus, and the morning star representing Ishtar, the goddess of love and war. Above the three astral symbols, a U-shaped sign may symbolize the local goddess of the morning star, al-'Uzza. The engraved rock stands in the ruins of al-Ha'it, the ancient Padakku, which had been conquered by Nabonid. The inscription dates from his reign in Arabia between 553/2 and 543/2 BCE. Central Saudi Arabia. Photo 2020.

stand around as reminders of the former fertility of the oasis. The whole petroglyph consists of a standing royal person 47 centimetres high, four symbols and a cuneiform inscription in 26 lines; it is in total 80 centimetres high and 108 centimetres wide. Lines ten and eleven name the ruler: *Nabu-na'id sar Babil*, 'Nabonid, king of Babylon'.[104] From other proclamations of Nabonid, among others the Harran Stele preserved in Şanlıurfa (Turkey), it is known that he used to inscribe rocks or erect steles at places he conquered. Within today's Saudi Arabia these were Tema (Tayma), Dadanu or Dadan (al-Ula), Padakku, mentioned in line 5 of the al-Ha'it inscription and also known as Fadak (al-Ha'it), Yadi'u (al-Huwayyit located 60 kilometres south of al-Ha'it), Hibra (Khaybar) and Yatribu (Yathrib, today's Medina).[105] Some 200 kilometres west of the Saudi border in Jordan, there is another proclamation and image of Nabonid at al-Sila.[106] On the inscription of al-Ha'it, to the right of Nabonid's head, are a half-moon, a winged and tailed sun and the radiant

morning star. The crescent moon represents the moon god Sin, Nabonid's favourite deity, the sun god Sulmus, and the morning star Ishtar, the goddess of love and war. Above the three astral symbols there is a further, U-shaped sign; it may symbolize the local goddess of the morning star, al-'Uzza.[107]

Three centuries before Nabonid, northern Saudi Arabia had already come into hostile contact with Mesopotamia, namely when the Neo-Assyrian king Shalmaneser III (r. 858–824 BCE) defeated a coalition of rulers from the Levant, among them 'Gindibu of the Arabs'. About a century later in 733 BCE, Tiglath-Pileser III (r. 744–723 BCE) proclaimed in an inscription that his army had defeated 'Shamsi, the queen of the Arabs' and forced the Arabs of Adummatu (today's al-Jawf) and Tayma to bring tribute of, among other things, female dromedaries.[108] These dromedaries were surely requested for breeding, to secure a stock of camels for military and trading purposes. In 691 BCE,

Sennacherib (r. 705–681 BCE) defeated another queen of the Arabs named Te'elhunu, and in 678 BCE, Esarhaddon (r. 681–669 BCE) installed yet another Arab princess called Tabu'a as queen of the Arabs of Adummatu. Following another revolt by the Arabs, around 650–649 BCE Assurbanipal (r. 669–631 BCE) installed a permanent garrison in Adummatu and forced both it and Tayma to submit tribute.[109] From these proclamations it becomes apparent that Neo-Assyria attached great importance to the control of northern Saudi Arabia and that a major confederation of Arab tribes was regularly ruled by women.

Between Tayma and al-Ula lie many other sites of interest, such as **Hafrat Berd** where a petroglyph shows a horse-drawn Assyrian battle chariot which transports three soldiers: a driver, a passenger and an archer (fig. 236). At **Jabal Habib** there is an impressive life-sized petroglyph of a horse, and at **al-Naslaa** a famous large boulder split vertically by a tiny (seven-centimetre) crack in the middle into two halves, each standing on a fragile pedestal; on the right half is the image of a man holding a spear and

leading a horse (fig. 237). At **al-Dogosh** (also called **Uqulq**), huge petroglyphs of dromedaries with long necks as well as of horses are located on a high ridge 20 metres above the ground (fig. 234). **Al-Wahaf**, for its part, consists of three complexes. On the main one, there are petroglyphs of leopards chasing ostriches, three large horses, a battle chariot, five antelopes and a hunter with a drawn bow and five menacing dogs who confronts a huge ibex. Finally, at **Jabal al-Sharqiya**, inside a complex formed by large boulders, are found petroglyphs of white and dark striped bovines. They look Chalcolithic, but since the peck marks appear rather fresh, they were either refreshed by re-engraving or are more recent copies.[110]

The fertile oasis of **Dadan**, today's **al-Ula**, was a famous trading city also mentioned in the Old Testament by Ezekiel (chapters 27 and 38) (fig. 240). Its surroundings are especially rich in ancient petroglyphs, with almost 2,000 rock inscriptions and monuments all lying within a breath-taking landscape. Based on the agricultural productivity of the oasis and its location along a trans-Arabian trade route, it evolved early into an Arabian kingdom. The first

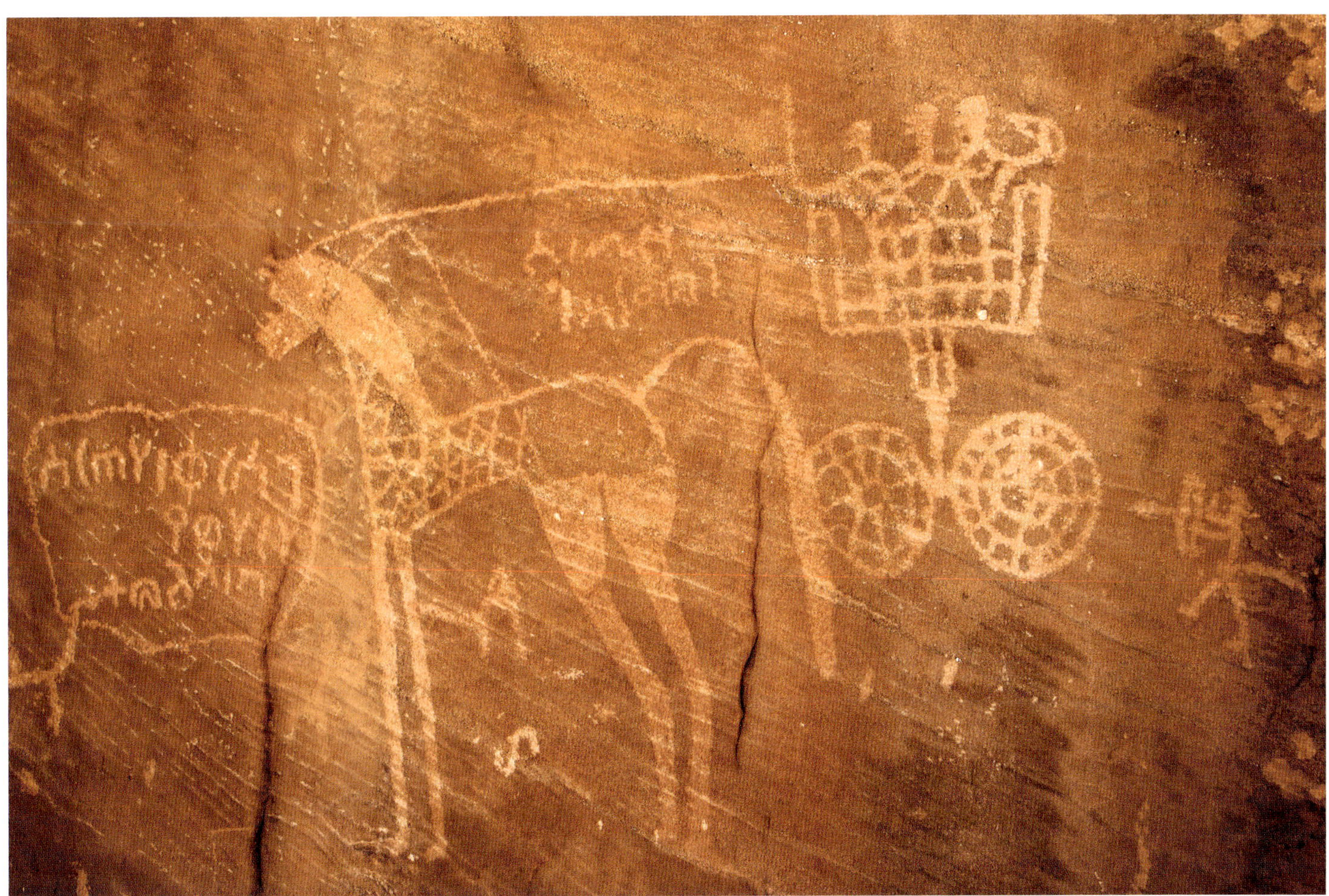

236. A rare petroglyph scene of a horse-drawn Assyrian chariot which carries three soldiers, a driver, a passenger and an archer. An archer on foot aims at the chariot from behind. Hafrat Berd, Great Nafud Desert, northern Saudi Arabia. Photo 2020.

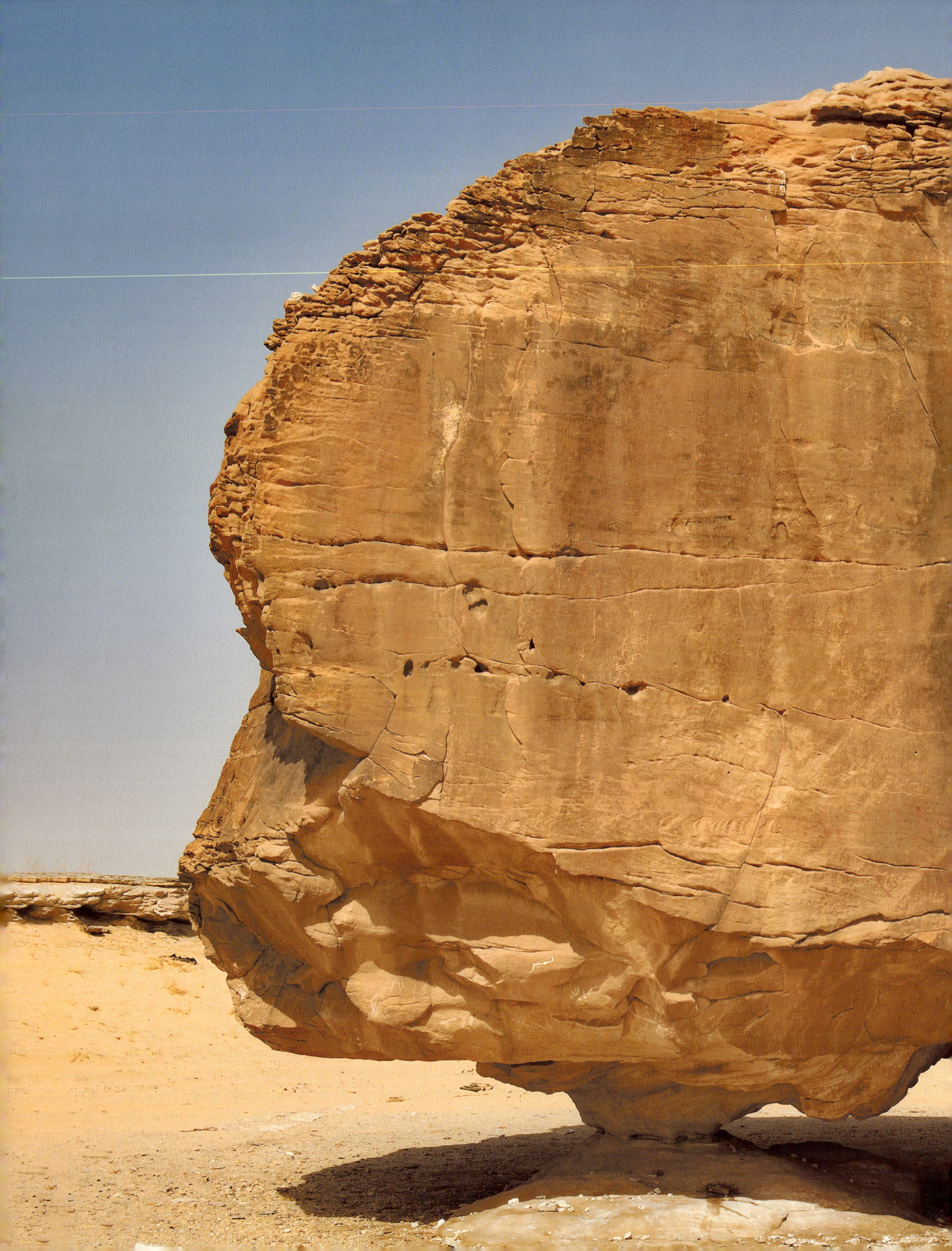

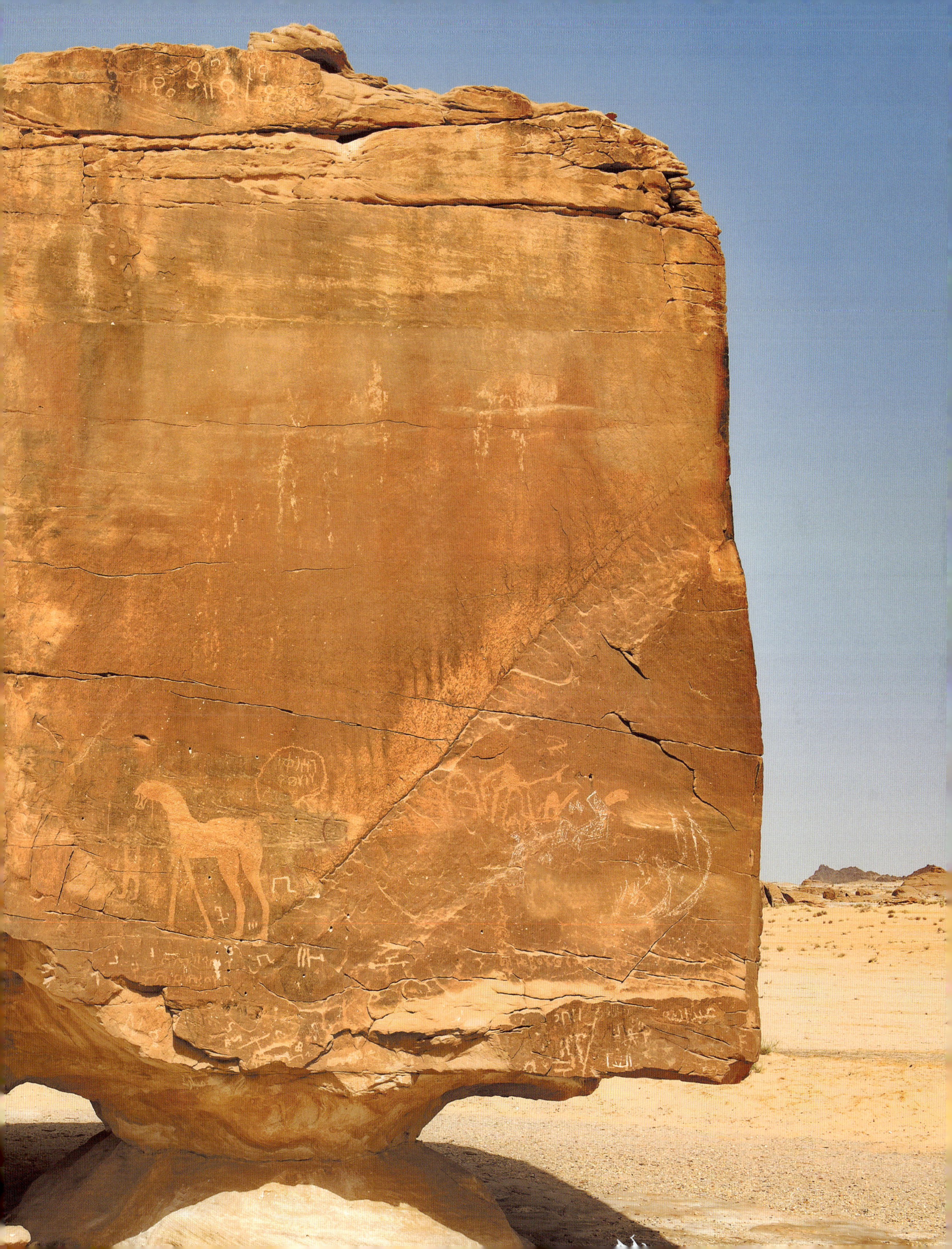

political entity was the Kingdom of Dadan (late ninth to early fifth century BCE), which was briefly conquered by Nabonid, like Tayma and other north and central Arabian cities. The Dadanite kingdom was followed by the Lihyanite dynasty which lasted until *ca.* 50 BCE when it was conquered by the Nabataeans. Under the Lihyanites, a south Arabian trading community from Ma'in flourished in the Dadan oasis, and a Hellenistic influence is also detectable.[111] The Nabataeans were originally trading pastoralists who had settled around today's Petra (Jordan) in the fourth to third centuries BCE; they dominated the land-bound trade in Arabian incense and myrrh. The Nabataeans moved the capital of their western Arabian vassal some twenty kilometres away from Dadan to Hijr (Hegra), today's Mada'in Saleh. A year after Rome had annexed Petra in 106 CE,

Hegra came under Roman hegemony, which lasted less than two centuries.[112]

Petroglyphs featuring slim humans, ibexes and lions are found not only on several boulders inside the city of **al-Ula**, but also in the **Wadi Ikmah** (also called Abu Ud) nine kilometres north of al-Ula. On a high cliff there are images of cattle from the later Iron Age on which are superimposed large vessels, rugs, schematic chariots, ibexes, duels of archers and about two dozen ostriches with strange rectangular bodies; all the latter petroglyphs date from the historic, that is Islamic period (fig. 239). A couple of kilometres to the west there are dozens of cattle petroglyphs. Three kilometres east of Wadi Ikmah, on the east side of **Jabal Ikmah**, there are dozens of well-kept Late Dadanitic, that is Lihyanitic, inscriptions in high or low relief. Here, as at a few other places, the rock faces were first smoothed to create even surfaces, allowing the inscriptions stand out as clearly as possible (fig. 238). Some are longer texts spread over a dozen or more lines; these were dedicated to the local deities and asked for specific favours. Others record the names and

---

237. ↵ The 'Split Rock' at al-Naslaa *ca.* 50 km south of the Tayma oasis, Great Nafud Desert, northern Saudi Arabia. The split, only 7 cm wide, and the absolutely flat faces of both rocks are natural. At the lower right a man leads a horse by a leash. Iron Age. Photo 2020.

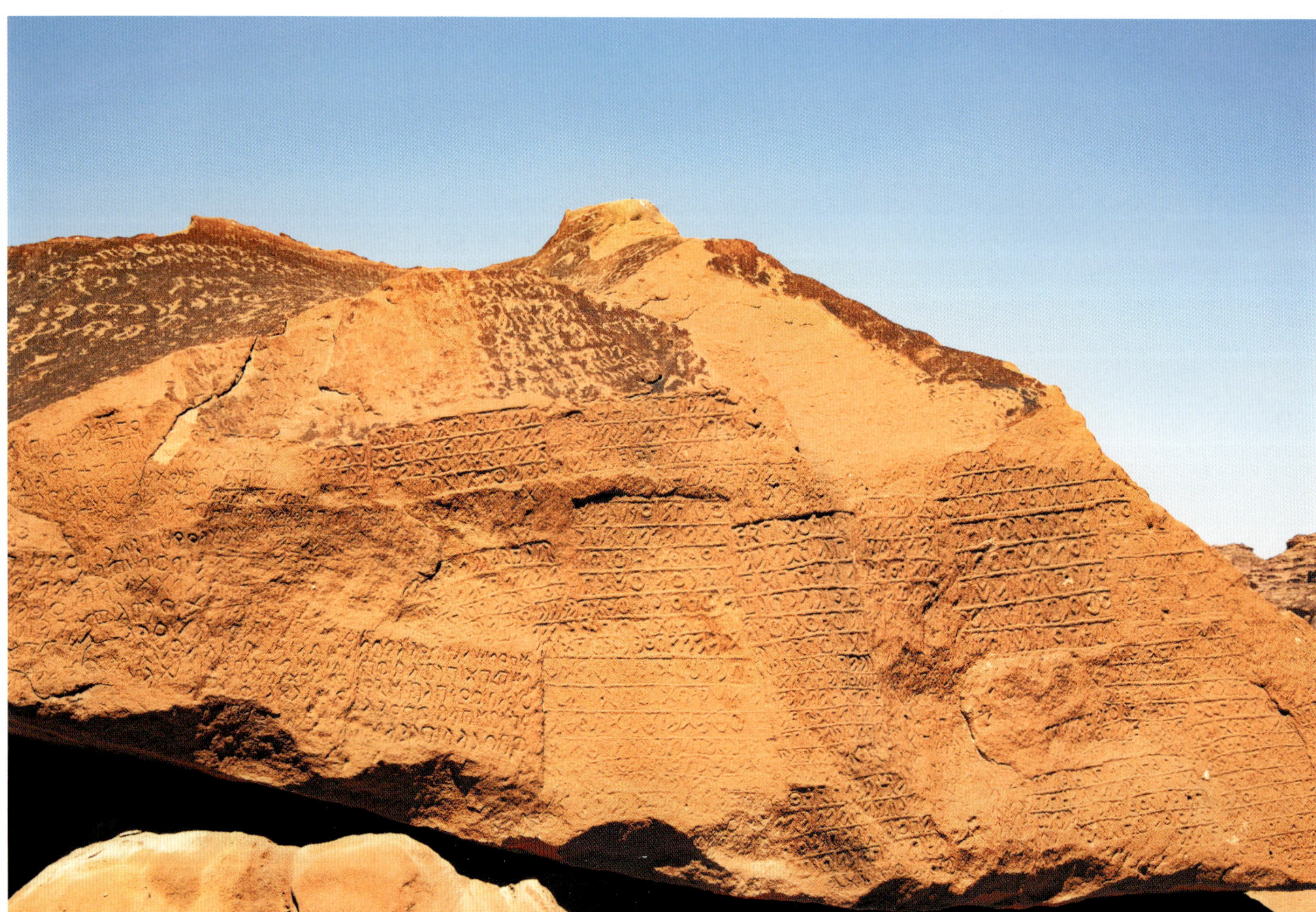

238. Late Dadanitic (formerly called Lihyanitic) inscriptions at Jabal Ikmah near al-Ula. Fifth to first century BCE. Western Saudi Arabia. Photo 2020.

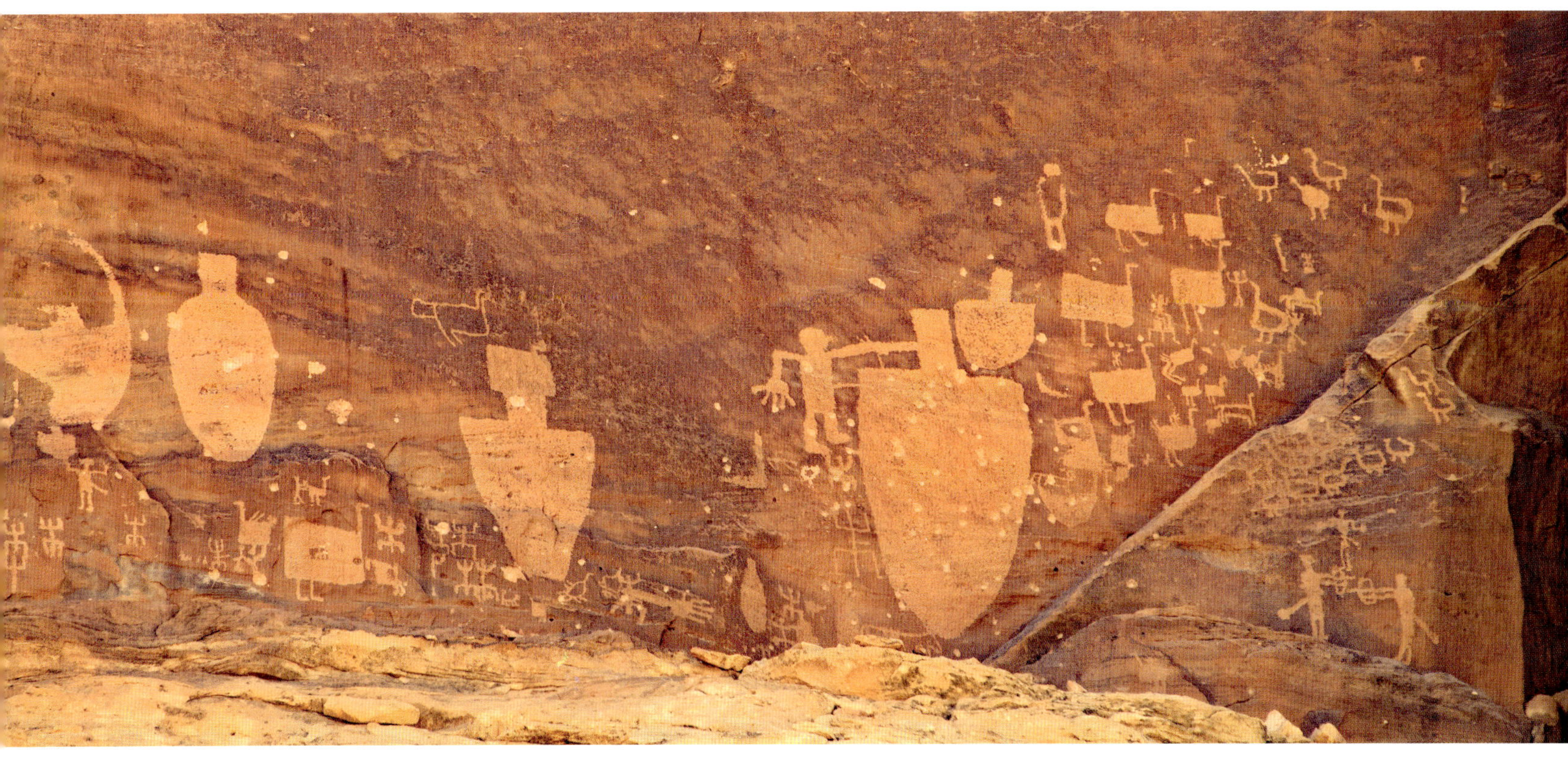

239. Images of large vessels, rugs and ostriches from the early Islamic period are superimposed on petroglyphs featuring cattle from the later Iron Age. The petroglyphs are engraved into an inaccessible cliff about twenty metres above the floor of the valley. Wadi Ikmah, also called Wadi Abu Ud near al-Ula, western Saudi Arabia. Photo 2020.

titles of rulers. The majority of the inscriptions are brief; a few of them are framed by a cartouche. In total, almost 300 inscriptions in Dadanitic, Thamudic, South Arabian Minaean, Aramaic and early Arabic scripts were engraved into the reddish-brown, soft sandstone. On an ancient trade route 25 kilometres further north lies the small pass of **Mabrak al-Naqah**, whose cliffs are inscribed with numerous inscriptions in Dadanitic, Thamudic, Nabataean, Greek, ancient South Arabian and Arabic. Unfortunately, these interesting inscriptions have been vandalized, mostly by spray-painting. The inscriptions had been studied in 1877 by Doughty and in 1907 by Jaussen and Savignac.[113] In Arabic Mabrak al-Naqah means 'Passage of the she-camel' which relates to the refusal of a pre-Islamic Thamudian tribe to follow the prophet Saleh's order to convert. According to the Quran, the pre-Islamic prophet Saleh requested of the people of Hegra that they abandon polytheism in favour of monotheism. They refused and killed Saleh's gift of the miraculous she-camel which gave as much milk every day as it drank water. Thereupon Saleh cursed the city and God sent an earthquake – a curse which was repeated by the Prophet Muhammad when he led a military expedition against Tabuk in the year 630 CE.[114] An earthquake which occurred in the first century CE at nearby Dadan gave rise to the legend of the prophet Saleh.[115]

A similar tradition was reported by Philby concerning Shabwa, the ancient capital of the Kingdom of Hadramawt in today's Yemen.[116]

Hegra's present name **Mada'in Saleh** relates to the prophet Saleh's curse, for its Arabic name means 'cities of Saleh'. This archaeological complex is not only famous for its Dadanitic, (Lihyanitic) and countless Nabataean inscriptions, but also for its Nabataean monuments, above all its monumental tombs cut up to a height of sixteen metres into sandstone boulders and outcroppings (fig. 241). There are 86 tombs with a rock-cut facade, and in total more than 131 tombs, dating from the first three quarters of the first century CE.[117] This compares to 600 façade tombs in Petra. No scaffolding was needed to cut the façades, since the stonemasons worked the rocks from top to bottom, moving down only when the upper storey was completed. About fifteen kilometres north-east of Mada'in Saleh, the **Wadi Ri' al-Maqtal**, the 'Gorge of the murder', extends within a spectacular landscape of towering outcrops; there is a rare petroglyph here of a light chariot seen in profile, as well as Thamudic and Nabataean inscriptions, a lioness and camels.

---

240. ↳ View from the Jabal al-Hamra over the oasis of al-Ula, western Saudi Arabia. Photo 2020.

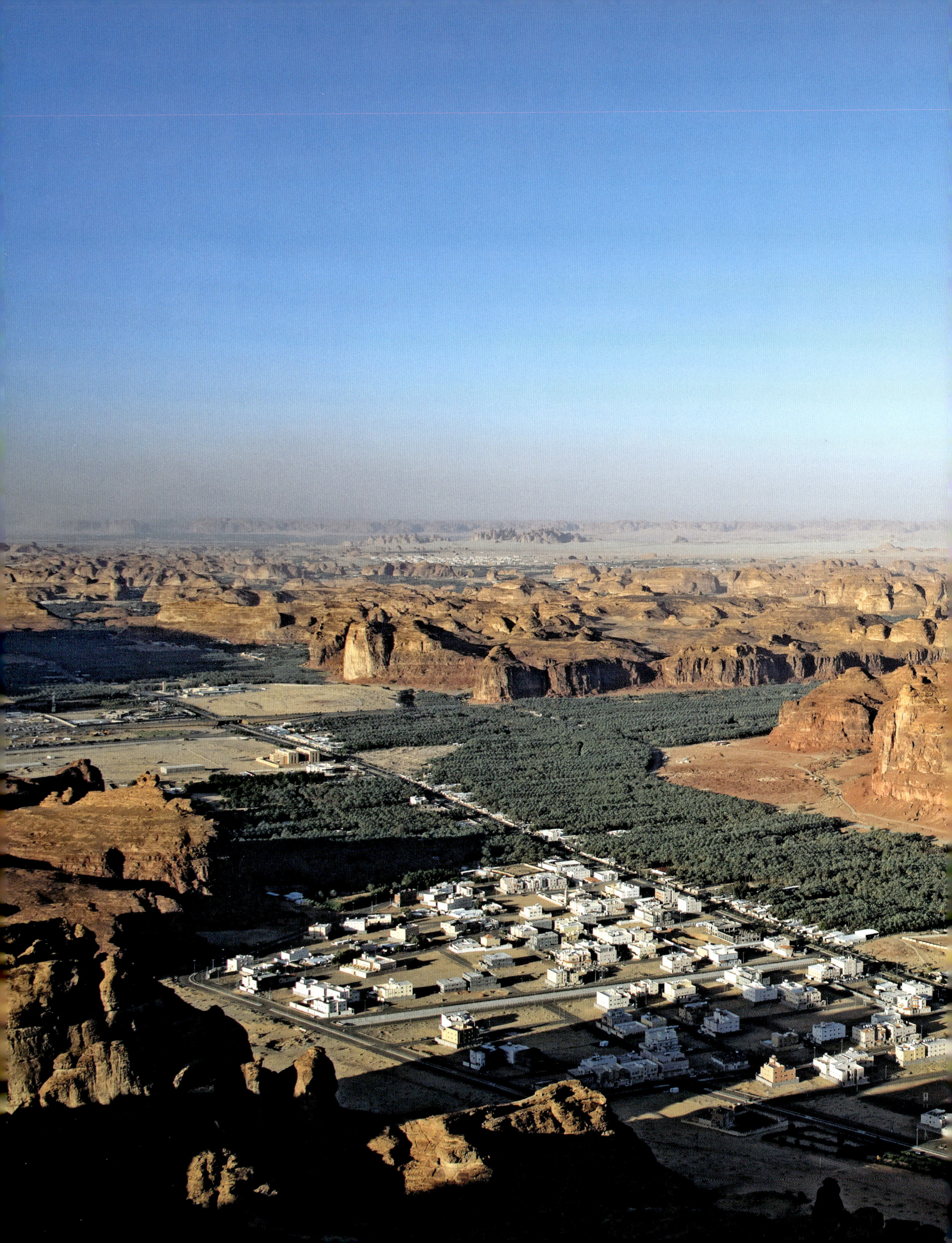

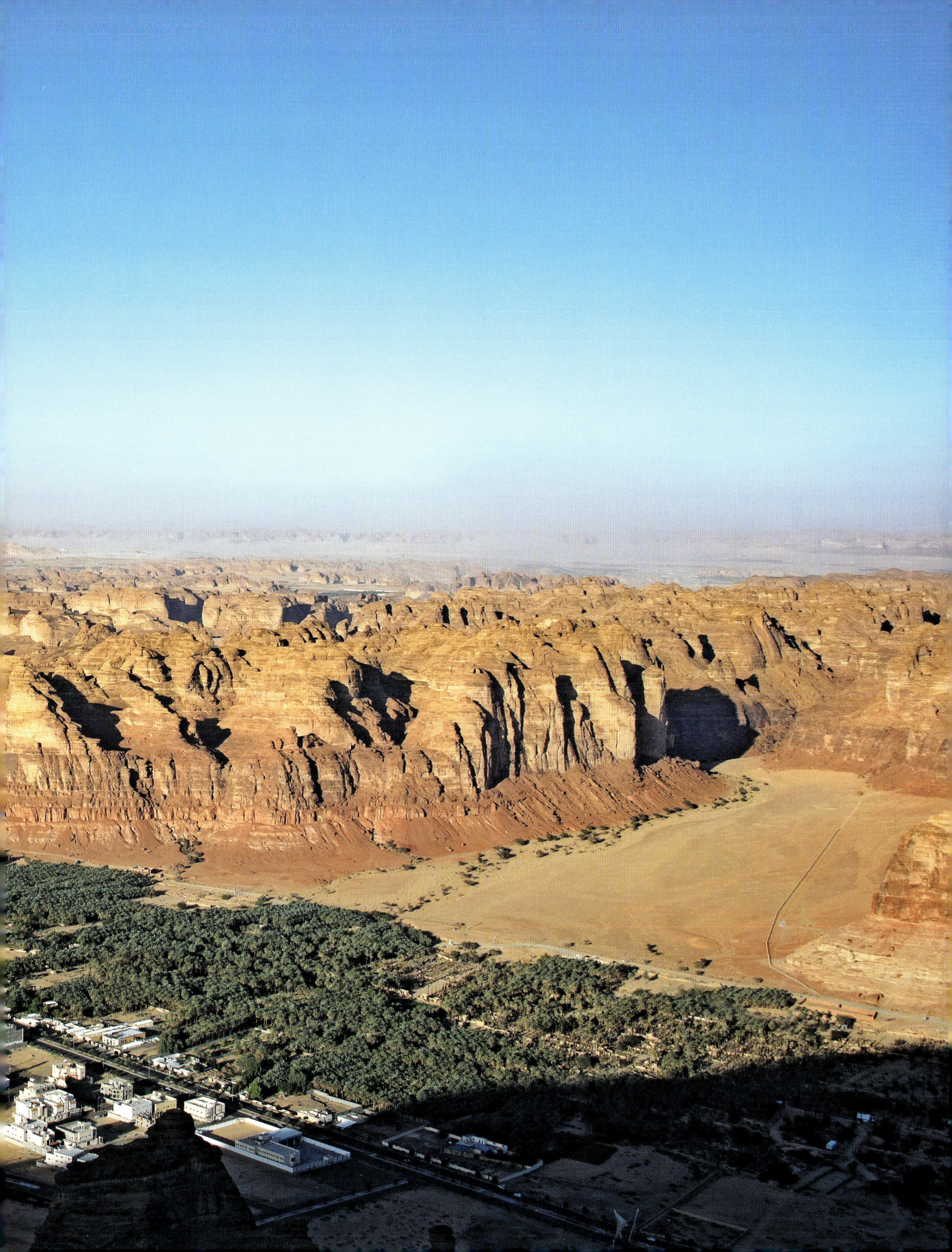

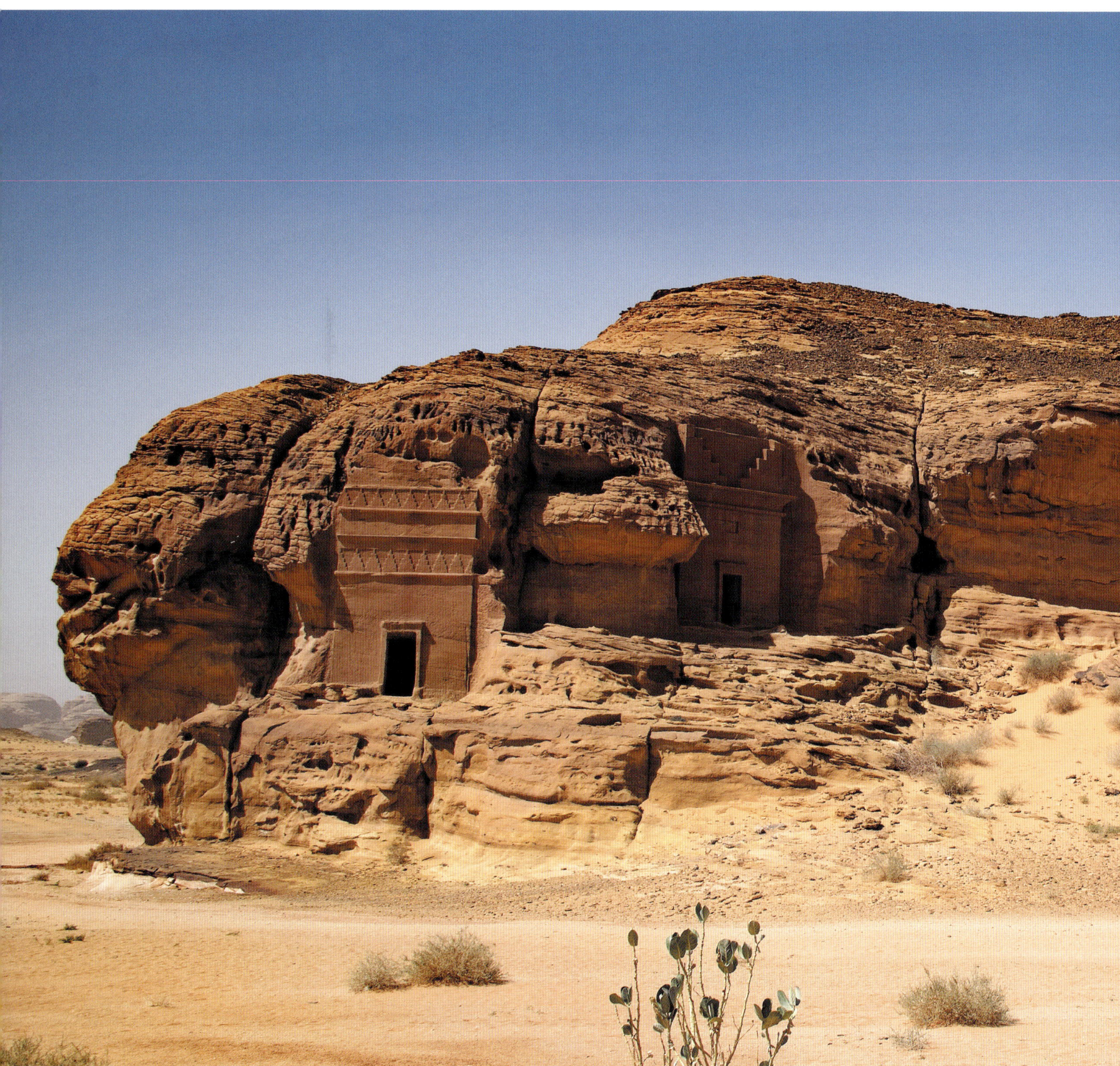

241. The Nabataean burial complex of Jabal Ahmar, the 'Red Mountain', at Mada'in Saleh, ancient Hegra. The complex includes at least 21 tombs; some of them contained dozens of burials. First to second century CE. Western Saudi Arabia. Photo 2020.

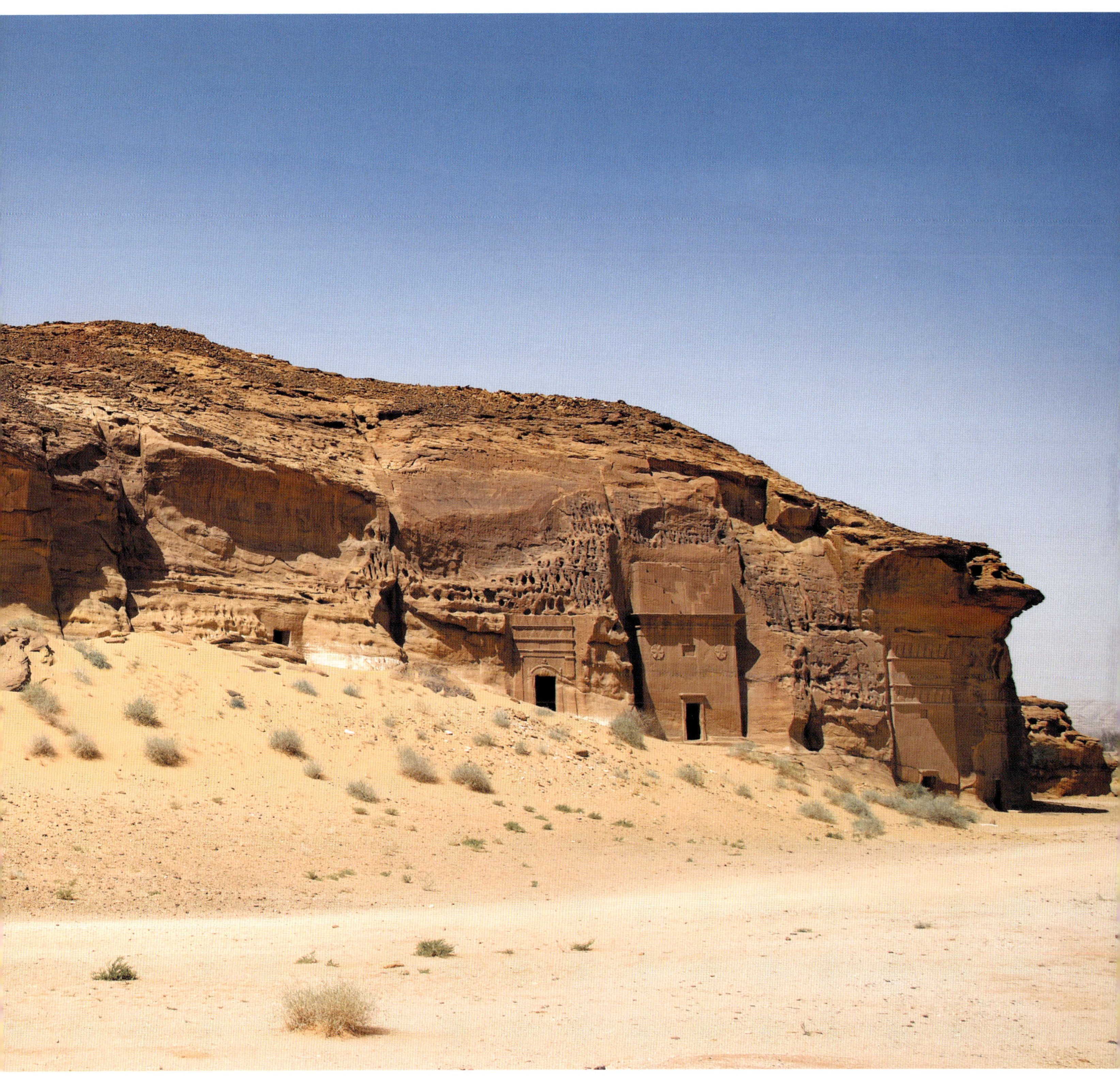

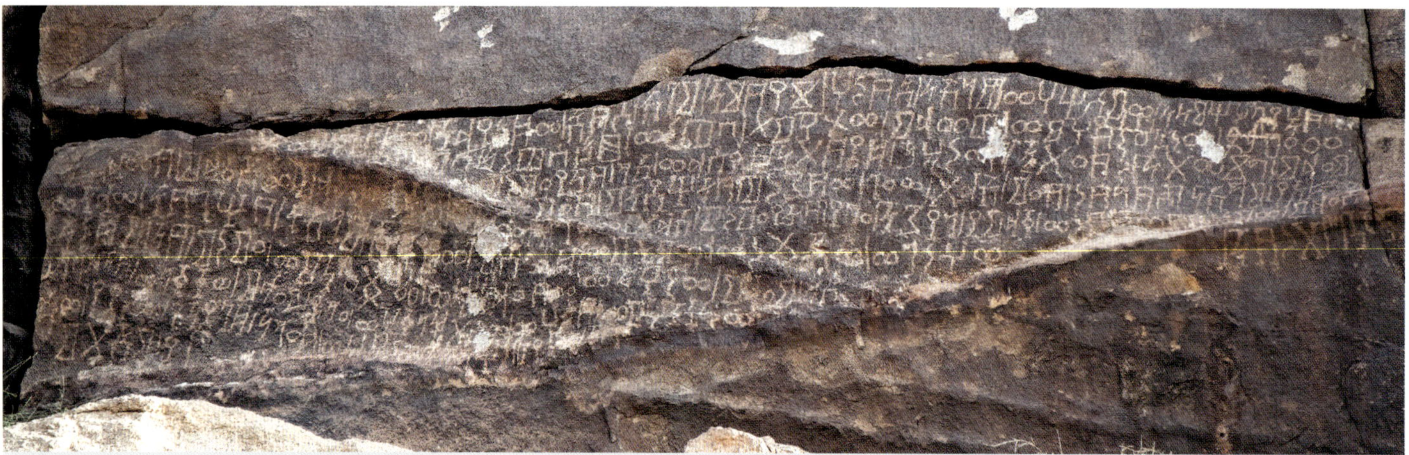

Ancient scripts of Arabia

From the early first millennium BCE, literacy spread in the western and central parts of Arabia as indigenous alphabets emerged and developed.[118] Within the Arabian scripts, two families have to be distinguished, the **South Arabian** script, also called the **Sabaic** or in modern Arabic the **Musnad** script, and the **North Arabian** alphabets. Since the most ancient versions of both families share similarities, they must have been developed from the same source, probably a non-Arabian script.[119] Whereas the South Arabian script hardly evolved and remained quite stable for its whole duration, the North Arabian scripts soon developed into different branches. The **South Arabian script** counted 29 monumental letters for its consonants; it was used in today's Yemen and southern Saudi Arabia for various languages such as Sabaic, Qatabanic, Minaean, Hadramitic, Himyaritic, as well as for Hasaitic in eastern Saudi Arabia. The only exception to the stability of the Musnad script is the adaptation to a cursive script called **Zabur** which was used in ordinary documents such as letters and lists; they were written on wooden sticks and the stalks of palm-leaves. Musnad and Zabur died out at the end of the sixth century CE.[120]

As noted by Jérôme Norris, the **North Arabian alphabets**, for their part, can be divided into '**urban scripts**' used in the large oases and '**desert scripts**' used by the nomadic tribes roaming the deserts.[121] Under the urban scripts are listed **Dumaitic** (used in al-Jawf and Dumat al-Jandal, northern Saudi Arabia), **Taymanitic** and **Dadanitic**, which counts 28 letters and whose later development was also called **Lihyanitic**. These scripts were written in any horizontal direction, mainly from right to left, but also from left to right and in boustrophedon, where the direction of writing alters line by line. These urban oasis scripts were replaced by the Nabataean Aramaic script in the course of the second century CE.[122]

Among the desert scripts figure the **Hismaic** script (formerly Thamudic E) used in southern Jordan and northern Saudi Arabia, **Safaitic** used in southern Syria and eastern Jordan, and a group of similar alphabets called **Thamudic B**, **C** and **D** which were used to write different languages spoken by nomadic desert dwellers. The name Thamudic relates to the ancient Thamud tribe from northern Saudi Arabia which is mentioned in the Quran. The oldest securely dated Thamudic inscription dates from *ca*. 550 BCE, the latest is from 267 CE; these Thamudic scripts probably died out in the fourth century CE.[123]

Another variant of Thamudic formerly called Thamudic F occurs in Najran, southern Saudi Arabia, and is called **Himaitic** which was in use until 630 CE.[124] Most of these alphabets, above all the desert scripts, were used to record personal names, prayers and invocations to gods or curses, memorial texts in the vicinity of burials, indications of property or authorship and other messages.[125] Desert inscriptions were made by itinerant merchants, but mainly by local nomads. Some of these inscriptions make clear that certain petroglyphs featuring camels or bulls were meant as ex-votos, that is substitutes for the offering of real animals (fig. 268).[126] Other alphabets such as Sabaic and Dadanitic also served to record business and governmental decisions or to write down royal proclamations and the record of military campaigns, for example at Ma'sal al-Jumh, Murayghan and Bir Hima (figs 242, 252, 262).

In addition to this multitude of autochthonous scripts, the corpus of rock inscriptions includes several non-Arabian scripts, namely ancient Aramaic, Imperial Aramaic, which was probably introduced into Saudi Arabia by Nabonid, Egyptian hieroglyphs, Nabataean, Greek and Latin. Concerning the **Arabic** alphabet, it seems that the Arabic language remained for a long time virtually unwritten even though there were indigenous Arabian scripts in existence. An exception was a brief inscription by a Syrian desert king writing his self-proclamation as 'king of all Arabs' in Arabic using the Late Nabataean script.[127] Until recently it was believed that the Arabic script emerged at the beginning of the sixth century CE in a Syrian environment as an adaptation of the Late Nabataean alphabet. The earliest Arabic inscriptions were dated 512, 528/9 and 568 CE; all were found in Syria within a Christian context. It was thought that the Arabic script had been developed to teach Christianity to desert-dwelling Arab tribes.[128] Yet the discovery in 2014 of the Christian necropolis of Hima in the southern Saudi province of Najran brought to light two mortuary inscriptions in an early form of Arabic dating from the years 470 and 513 CE (see below). These earliest known palaeo-Arabic inscriptions, however, recorded not an Arabic, but an Aramaic text.[129]

---

242. ↑ The inscription *Ry 506* at Murayghan in southern Saudi Arabia. It is written in the South Arabian Sabaean (Musnad) script and dates from the year 552 CE. The inscription records the successful fourth military expedition of the Christian King Abraha of Himyar and Najran against the central Arabian Ma'add tribe and crown prince Amr bin Mudhdhiran of al-Hira. Photo 2022.

90 kilometres south-east of Tayma stands the major petroglyph site of **Talaat al-Salaby** in the Jabal Abu Mughair. It was briefly visited by Charles Montagu Doughty in 1877 and Huber in 1884.[130] The site crowns a sandstone hill, where a spring waters some two dozen palm trees overlooking a panorama of sand punctuated by basalt outcrops. The petroglyphs at Talaat al-Salaby range from the Neolithic to late pre-Islamic times. They include several Neolithic hunters carved in the Jubbah style and wielding hunting throwing sticks and bows (fig. 223). This style of slim figure was succeeded (or complemented) by an opposite style: callipygian – that is, shapely buttocked – men and women possibly dating from the late Neolithic (fig. 243). There are also three birthing scenes, ithyphallic hunters shooting arrows, a wild ass, a long-horned buffalo, late Bronze Age leopards, ibexes, snakes and lizards, as well as Thamudic and Nabataean inscriptions. Unmentioned by Doughty and Huber, there is also a petroglyph, *ca.* 40 centimetres tall, of a menorah, the Jewish seven-armed candelabrum (fig. 244). The menorah is surrounded by Northern Thamudic epigrams, and the comparison of their respective varnishes suggests that the petroglyphs might date to the middle of the first millennium CE. The five brief Thamudic texts close to the menorah are probably not directly related to it as they record the presence of five different persons, such as 'I am Malik bin Aslam'.[131] Another inscription under the menorah is damaged and hard to decipher. Important Jewish communities once existed in central Arabia, with the largest established in the oases of Yathrib (today's Medina), Khaybar and Tayma. The Jewish community of Tayma existed from the first century CE until at least the later twelfth century, when the Jewish traveller Benjamin of Tudela visited Tayma in around 1170.[132]

Only twenty kilometres south of Talaat al-Salaby lies the huge site of **Hafirat Laqat**, which was briefly visited by Huber and Euting in 1884 (fig. 245).[133] It consists of a sandstone ridge approximately 160 metres long and up to six metres high, covered on its eastern side with hundreds of petroglyphs dating from the later Bronze Age to the pre-Islamic period. There, and along a second, shorter ridge, are found images of hand marks, a skeleton, countless life-sized camels, a large lion, a wolf, horses, dogs and/or hyenas, ostriches, palm trees, dancing humans and the solar deity *slm* (Salm/Sulmus), symbolized by a bull's head seen from the front. Later carvings show mounted lancers, swordsmen and archers, as well as at least two Nabataean inscriptions and many in Thamudic. A very rare image of a boat is striking within a desert environment. Its sickle-shaped hull looks similar to the petroglyph of a sickle boat in Wadi Asafir south-west of Tabuk;[134] both petroglyphs share similarities with Egyptian representations of such boats. Directly east of the ridges lies a

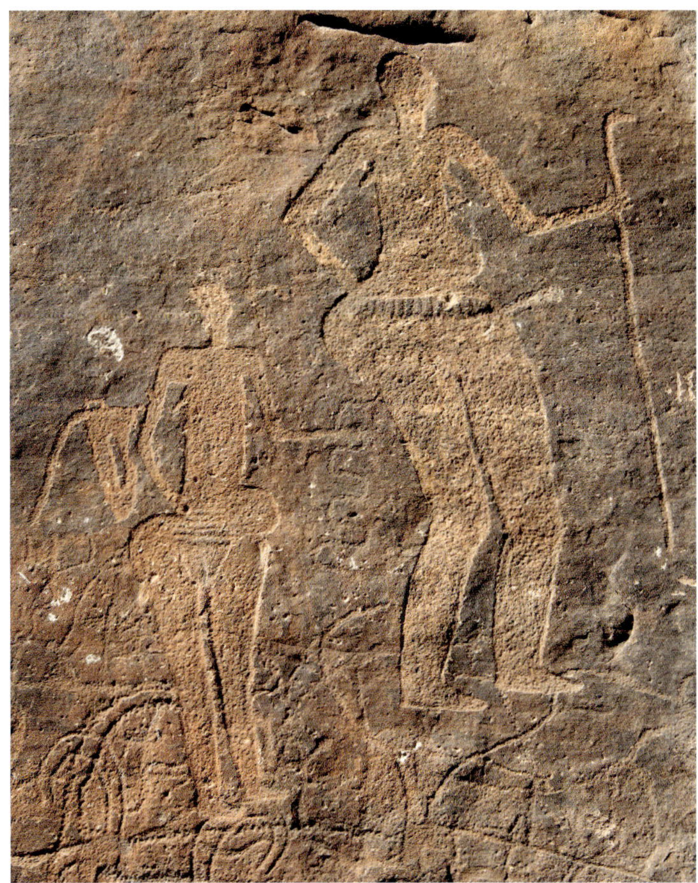

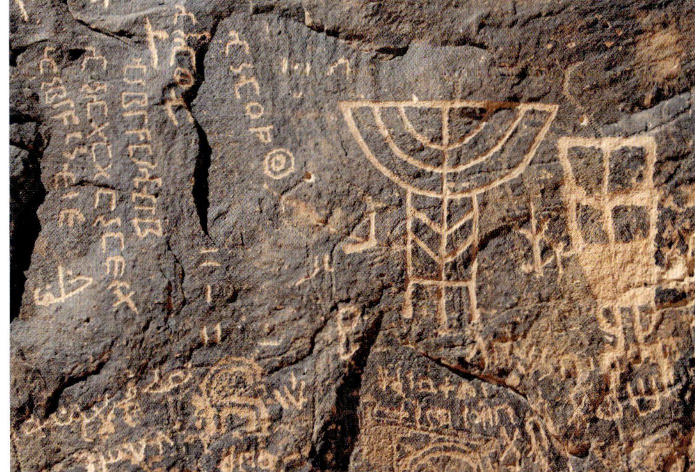

243. ↑ A male ithyphallic and a female herder, both callipygian, late Neolithic period. Talaat al-Salaby, Jabal Abu Mughair, Great Nafud Desert, northern Saudi Arabia. Photo 2020.

244. Menorah and Thamudic inscriptions at Talaat al-Salaby from the middle of the first millennium CE. The brief Thamudic inscriptions are unrelated to the menorah. Great Nafud Desert, northern Saudi Arabia. Photo 2020.

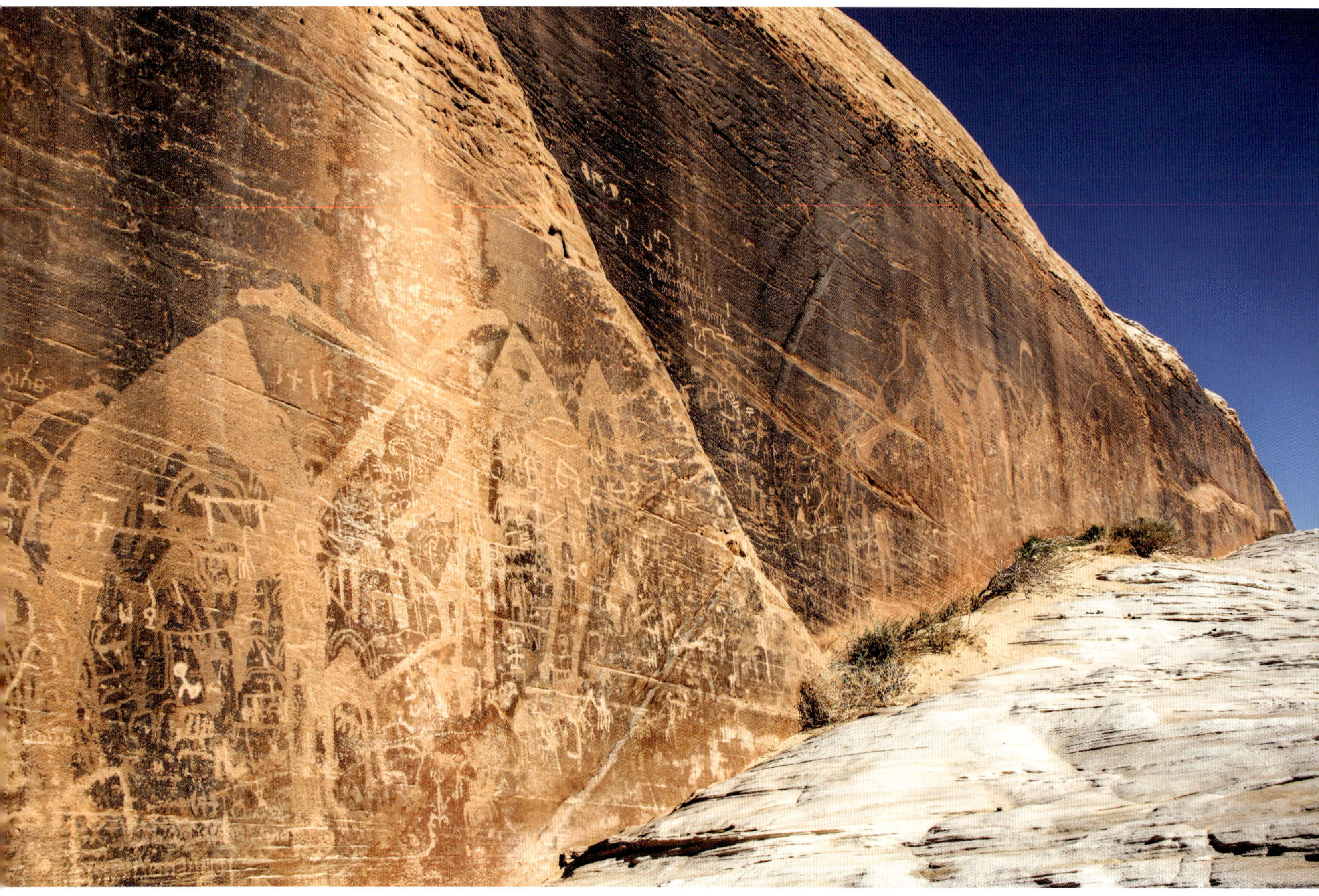

245. The southern half of the great ridge at Hafirat Laqat, Great Nafud Desert. The huge petroglyphs of schematized dromedaries from the later Iron Age were superimposed on late Bronze Age and Iron Age images of humans, ibexes, carnivores, ostriches, horsemen, a skeleton, palm trees and inscriptions in the Nabataean and Thamudic scripts. There is also a rare petroglyph of a boat and one of the sun god Sulmus/Salm. Saudi Arabia. Photo 2020.

depression possibly hinting at a former small lake which would have been a gathering place for nomadic pastoralists and their herds, and for wild animals.[135] The importance of water to its human visitors is underscored by the fact that at Hafirat Laqat 95 per cent of all the petroglyphs face this depression. By contrast, the far sides of the ridges are virtually devoid of imagery.

At Hafirat Laqat, on a boulder situated east of the presumed former tiny lake the present authors rediscovered two equilateral crosses drawn inside each other that had been mentioned by Euting (fig. 246).[136] The inner cross could be Christian, but the outer cross looks like a swastika as its four ends have the shape of ibex horns and heads, implying a rotating movement. The ibex was a popular object of veneration in south Arabia where it was one of the

attributes of the moon god Almaqah. But while Christian communities existed from the early fourth century CE in northern Arabia, for example the Banu Taghlib, this emblem could also represent a *wasm* (plural *wusum*), a tribal mark. Such swastika-like combinations of cross and ibexes are rare. The closest similar motifs are seals from Dilmun with four gazelle heads, the two theriomorph swastikas discovered in Zavkhan aimag in north-western Mongolia and at Mayemyr in eastern Kazakhstan,[137] as well as a Saka bronze ornament featuring four goat heads from the end of the first millennium BCE.[138] Yet the distance between those finds and Hafirat Laqat excludes such an influence. Only fifteen kilometres south-east of Hafirat Laqat stand the two spectacular **Arches of Mahajjah**, whose lower inner walls are decorated with images of life-sized camels (fig. 247). 90 kilometres further east lies the extensive site of **Dhubabiya** (or Dhubiya) where the petroglyphs of two large horsemen are striking; one of them holds a bow in one hand, the other one carries a quiver.

Two other extended petroglyph complexes lie in the mountains Jabal 'Arnan and Jabal al-Misma which are located in the Nafud Desert between Mahajjah and Jubbah. In **Jabal 'Arnan** there are staggering landscapes formed by towering outcrops which look from a distance like the back of a monstrous hedgehog. Other stone formations create arches or have the shape of a crouching dromedary (fig. 231). In this area there are many images of life-sized camels, smaller horses and camels carrying a *hawdah* (in Arabic *hawdaj*), a seat for one person fitted with a canopy and placed on the back of a camel or an elephant. Besides that, there are callipygian women and hunters, ostriches, dogs and ibexes as well as a multitude of small warriors brandishing spears; finally, an almost life-sized petroglyph of a lion with an accompanying inscription in Thamudic B which states 'the lion of Ma'al' (fig. 248).[139] In this way, the artist signed his work. As in the Sahara, most of the sites in Jabal 'Arnan and al-Misma are next to pools or seasonal water sources where animals and humans gather. In the northern part of **Jabal al-Misma**, which stretches over 60 kilometres in a north–south direction, there are petroglyphs of the bull-headed Tayma god *slm* (Salm/Sulmus), of horsemen holding spears, of four-wheeled carts, predators, camels and numerous Thamudic inscriptions. In the southern part of al-Misma can be found not only several dated carvings made by Euting and Huber in 1884 and modern images of planes, cars and trucks, but also a mysterious petroglyph showing nine concentric circles. Also impressive is the image of a horseman wearing a Phrygian cap, a quiver and a sword and riding on a blanket (fig. 230). Then there are images of duelling archers and of two-wheeled chariots. Finally, on an isolated boulder on the floor of a small wadi there is a spectacular Neolithic petroglyph showing an almost life-sized wild dromedary (fig. 220).[140] Nearby, two huge slabs have been used as a shelter and are adorned with stylistically very similar carvings of three wild dromedaries and a probably earlier carving of an oryx. Under these four animals the outline of an even earlier animal can be guessed at.

1.3.2. Central Saudi Arabia

In central Arabia, the most famous petroglyph sites are Shuwaymis, al-Ha'it (see above), Luwee, al-Usba and Ma'sal al-Jumh. The petroglyphs of **Shuwaymis** have been carved on Cambrian sandstone rocks emerging out of the Harrat Khaybar, a basaltic lava field 12,000 square kilometres in extent; the last lava stream

occurred around 2500 BCE, the last eruptions around 650 CE or even later.[141] The complex consists of two sites one kilometre apart, Jabal al-Manjor and Jabal Raat, which are located either side of the Wadi al-Mukhayet. During the wetter period of the earlier Holocene the wadi was probably filled with water. As mentioned above, at the end of the seventh millennium BCE, the hunter-gatherer economy was replaced by pastoralism, with the breeding of bovines, sheep and goats. The water and rich vegetation disappeared by *ca.* 3000 BCE at the latest and the region underwent a phase of aridization. After a presumed hiatus of almost 2,000 years, life and carving in the area began again around 1000 BCE, now with images of camels and horses.

The most interesting petroglyphs at **Jabal al-Manjor** are: three Neolithic hunters in the Jubbah style turned upside down and a row of small camels standing on their feet – clearly, the rock fell down after the completion of the Neolithic carvings and was later reused for the Iron Age camels, thus forming a genuine palimpsest. Next to this rock there are two Neolithic hunters and two bulls at a 90° angle to them; this rock too has fallen from a higher position. Also striking is the scene of a huge lion confronting a hunter armed with a bow and his two dogs (fig. 222). This image is one of the few

246. Double cross with four ibexes near Hafirat Laqat, Great Nafud Desert. The inner cross might be Christian or a tribal mark, but the outer one looks rather like a swastika whose branches, which are shaped like ibex horns, suggest a rotational movement. The whole figure could also represent a complex tribal mark. First millennium CE. Great Nafud Desert, northern Saudi Arabia. Photo 2020.

Neolithic representations of a lion. Besides many smaller images of camels, onagers and bovines, there is a spectacular, long panel with three large dromedaries with triangular humps and about twenty small camels; they all date from the Iron Age (fig. 249). As in Jubbah, some of the petroglyphs of **Jabal Raat** illustrate the transition from hunting to herding. On a huge boulder on top of the stony hill, there are two complex scenes: at the left stands a Neolithic ithyphallic pastoralist with bovines and dogs, while at the right, a hunter is surrounded by his pack of hounds, two gazelles and a tiny lion. To their right follow two buffaloes with enormous horns; their horns are superimposed on the image of a leopard (fig. 250). Nearby other hunters are rendered in the Jubbah style, one of them with two dogs. In the lower parts of the hill there are several large blocks which have fallen from their original position, as the petroglyphs of aurochs and slender figures of hunters are upside down. In

one instance, there are two large bovines turned upside down, onto which the curved horns of ibexes have been added oriented upwards, resulting in two strange hybrid animals. Finally, there are the images of a wild ass and of two carnivores, possibly leopards.

150 kilometres south of Shuwaymis is the complex of **Luwee**, also called **al-Hanakiya**, which consists of reddish sandstone; its petroglyphs mostly date from the Neolithic. In the southern section, there is a striking boulder with six bovines in the Jubbah style on which the animals are rendered in profile but their long, thin horns are shown from above. Near this boulder there is a spectacular panel eight metres long featuring at least ten slender humans in the Jubbah style with heads which look like a hammer; one or two of them hold a bow, which shows that these shepherds and pastoralists also practised hunting (fig. 226). Two individuals hold their arms and hands up while their legs remain straight; one human

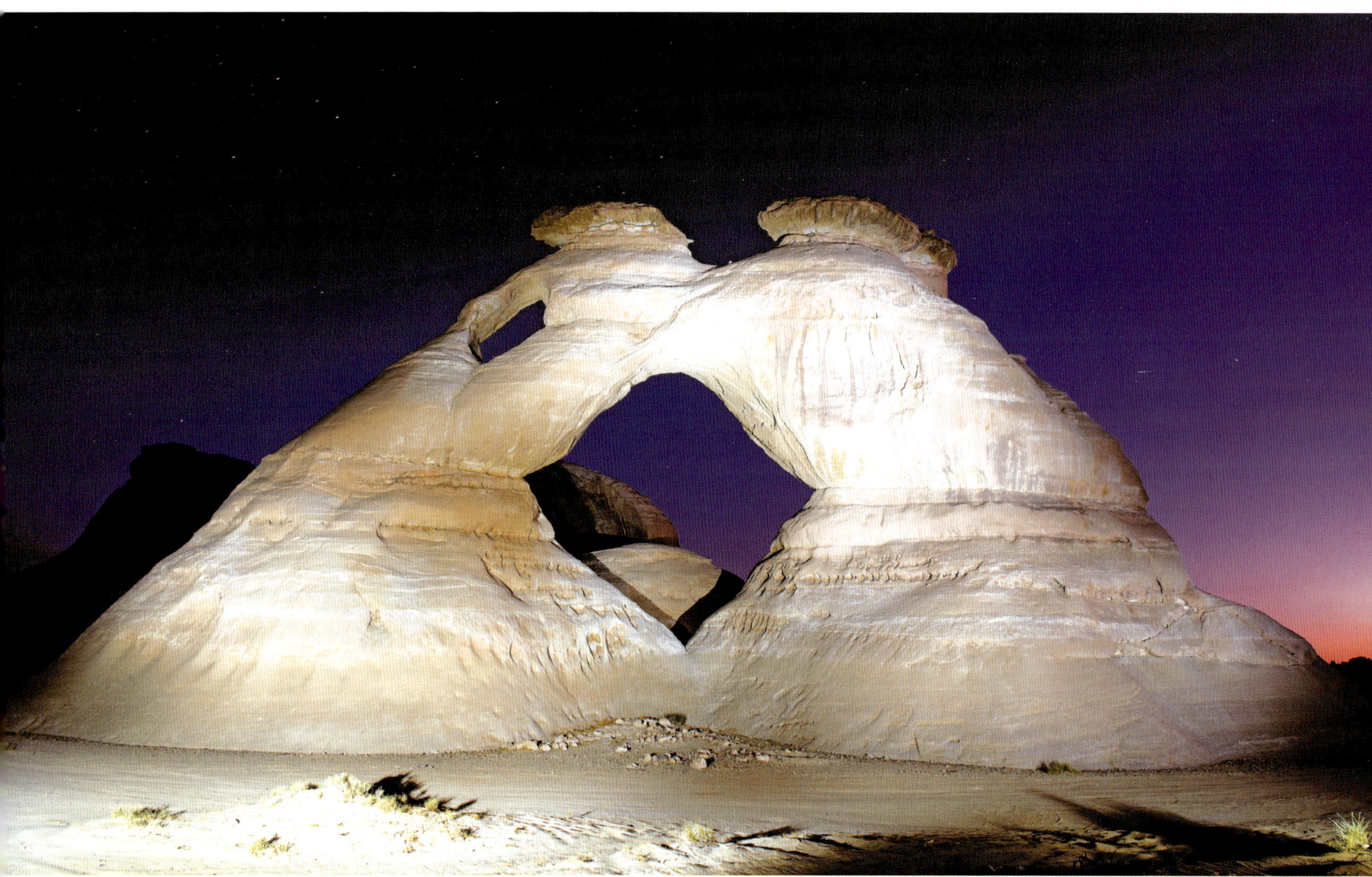

247. The forty-metre-high arch of Mahajjah, Great Nafud Desert. The middle mound features numerous Thamudic inscriptions; the third mound in the background has at least nineteen carvings of huge camels, the largest of which is 260 cm high. Northern Saudi Arabia. Night photo 2020.

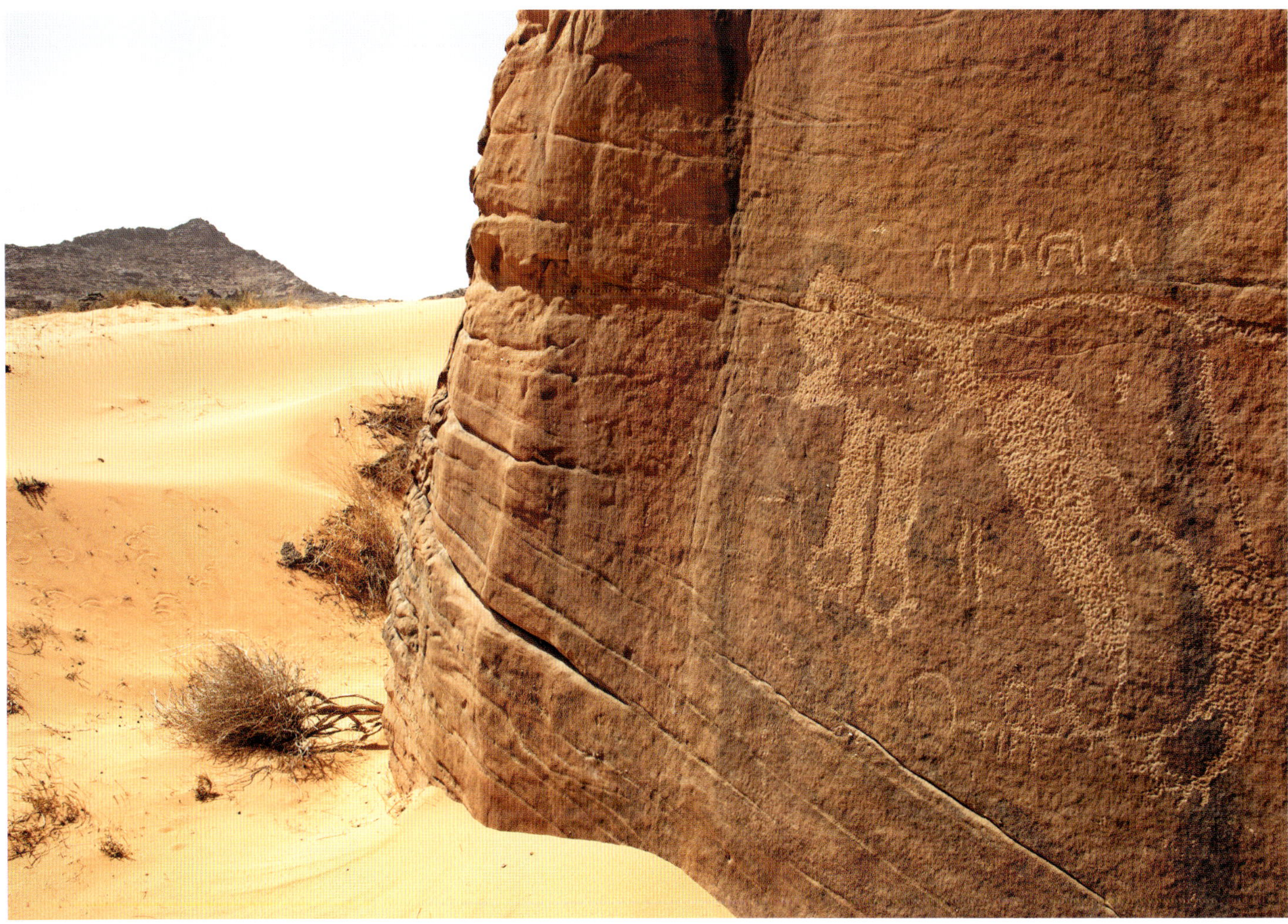

248. Petroglyph of a lion, 180 cm long. Iron Age, Riya Azlek in the Jabal 'Arnan, Great Nafud Desert, northern Saudi Arabia. Photo 2020.

seems to have both very large breasts and a penis. The humans are accompanied by bovines and dogs. In the eastern part of the complex, there are at least ten petroglyphs of large bovines in the Jubbah style, two lions and several pastoralists.

The site of **al-Usba**, near the village of **Musayqirah**, stands 110 kilometres west-south-west of Riyadh near an ancient caravan route; it is an isolated outcrop of sandstone with a dark brown varnish that is friable and fragile. The major concentration of petroglyphs is on the western side near the top of the hill which is around twelve metres high; on the eastern panel there are fewer images, dating from the late Neolithic and the Bronze Age.[142] The petroglyphs on the western side offer a cross section through most periods of rock art ranging from the later Neolithic to the late pre-Islamic and Islamic periods (fig. 251). In quantitative terms, camels (19 per cent), ibexes (17 per cent), *wusum* (13 per cent) and humans (12 per cent) predominate.[143] In chronological order, we find: bovines with large, curved horns rendered in

the Jubbah style, cattle, ibexes, gazelles, oryxes, wolves, hunting scenes with archers, two men dancing with raised arms, lions, a dancing skeleton, handprints, small armed ithyphallic men, a mother ostrich with her chicks, dromedaries – some of them carrying a *hawdah* – horses, a horseman swinging a sword and a palm tree. Although the date palm represented a vital factor in the life and economy of north Arabian oases for between five and seven millennia, it appeared only late and seldom in petroglyphs. Judging from the different degrees of patination on petroglyphs with identical motifs such as bovines and humans, it can be deduced that some of them have been refreshed, that is reworked. Finally, there are several *wusum* tribal marks. They were used not only to mark cattle, but also to signal the ownership of a site such as a well. In rock art, they also appear on the chests of armed men. About 150 kilometres south-west of Musayqirah are three other interesting sites. First, **Tayman** in the Ahara region, where it is surprising to find the petroglyphs of four broad-hipped dancing women, for such

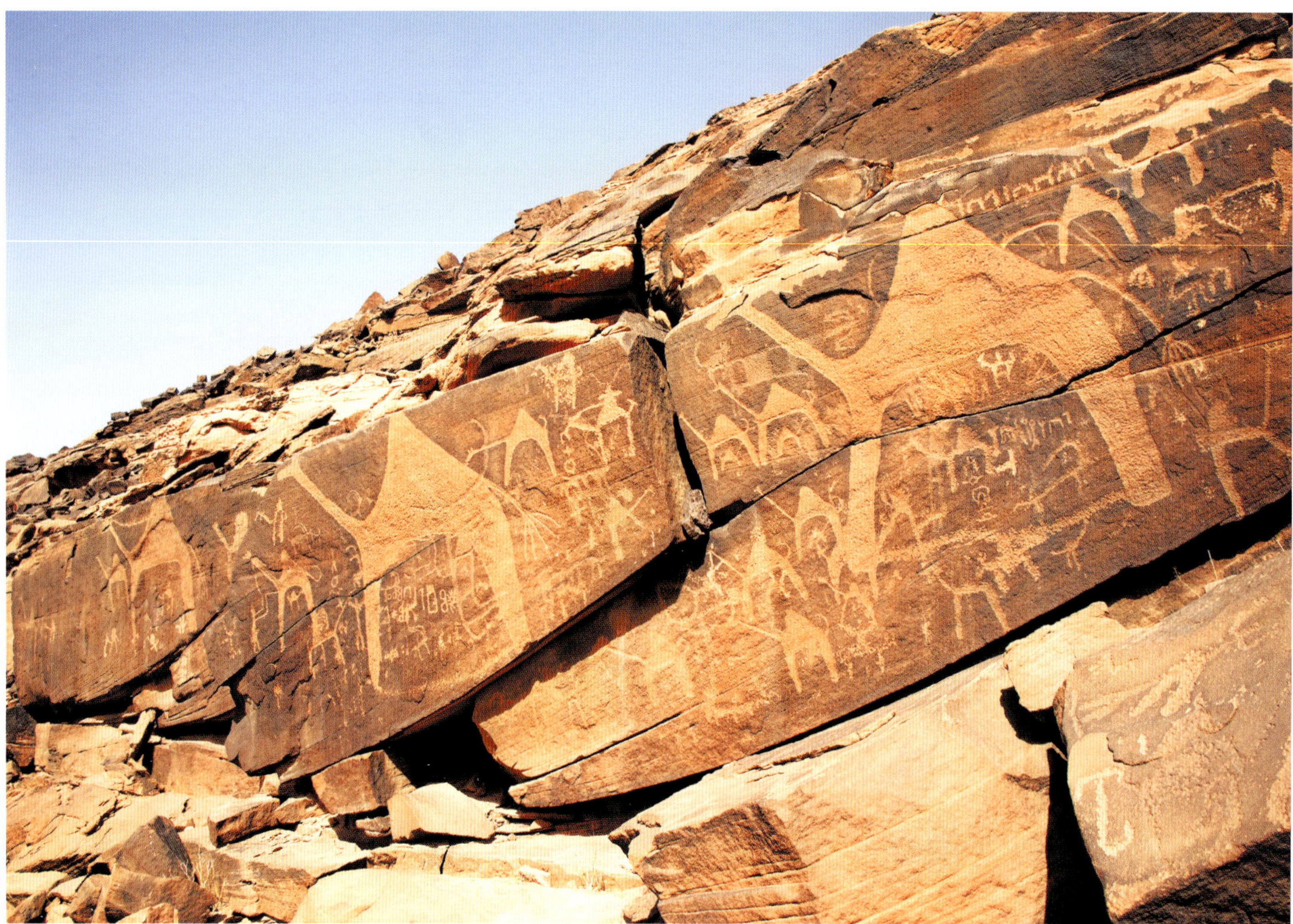

249. Palimpsest of late Iron Age dromedaries superimposed on Bronze Age cattle and early Iron Age inscriptions. Jabal al-Manjor, Shuwaymis, central Saudi Arabia, Photo 2020.

figures are otherwise only common in the al-Qahra–Kaukab–Hima region some 600 kilometres further south.

The second site is **Jada'a** which lies at the head of a wadi in the mountain of Jabal al-Ankir. The main panel, situated a few metres above a small pool, is 8.7 metres long and about two metres high. From left to right the main scenes are: ibexes from the Bronze Age on which Iron Age scenes have been superimposed, two further ibexes, then a battle between three horsemen and two fighters on foot, all of whom are armed with lances, while the foot soldier at the right is protected by a round shield. After this is the palm of a hand and an adorant raising his arms towards heaven. In pre-Muslim and Muslim Arabia the hand was a talisman protecting from malevolent *jinns* (spirits) and influences, and still remains so, for example in the symbol of the *hamsa* (Fatima's hand). Petroglyphs showing a hand or an arm including the hand may possibly also symbolize a request for blessing or a protection.[144] Further to the right a horseman holds a lance and next to him stands an armed man with raised arms

and long hair sticking out from his head like the crown of a palm tree. Finally, at **Zayidi al-Janubi** 60 kilometres further south-west, petroglyphs dating from the middle of the first millennium CE show numerous combat scenes between horsemen armed with lances and sabres which have been superimposed on older petroglyphs.

At **Ma'sal al-Jumh**, 210 kilometres south-west of the Saudi capital, there are three highly important Himyar Sabaic rock inscriptions from the fifth and sixth centuries CE. The site was first scientifically explored by the Philby-Ryckmans-Lippens expedition in 1951–52.[145] The first inscription, numbered *Ryckmans Ry 509*, was inscribed by the Himyar King Abikarib As'ad (r. *ca*. 390–420 CE), and his son, Hassan Yuha'min (r. 420–448) (fig. 252).[146] The neighbouring inscription, *Ry 510*, was commissioned by the Himyar ruler Ma'dikarib Ya'fur (r. 517/18–522 CE), who was murdered by his successor, the Jewish king Yusuf As'ar Yath'ar, aka Dhu Nuwas (r. *ca*. 522–527/30 CE).[147] This second inscription dates to spring 521 CE. In the later 510s, the Yemenite Kingdom of Himyar, whose rulers were traditionally inclined to Judaism, had become a vassal of the Christian Kingdom of Aksum. Previously, Himyar had oscillated between a pro-Byzantium policy which was friendly towards Christianity, and a hostile strategy favouring Judaism as a counterweight to the missionary efforts and political ambitions of Byzantium. Whereas around 354 CE Himyar had welcomed Bishop Theophilos the Ethiopian, an envoy of the Emperor Constantius II, and had allowed him to build three churches, about three and a half decades later the above-mentioned Abikarib As'ad converted to a Jewish-inspired monotheism, that is a non-Rabbinic form of Judaism.[148] The first culmination of hostility towards Byzantium and Christianity resulted in the massacres of Christians in Najran around 470 CE.[149] The later rise to power of Ma'dikarib Ya'fur was probably facilitated by Byzantium's ally Aksum, and this provoked the established Jewish elite to retaliate. The revolt of Dhu Nuwas against Ma'dikarib Ya'fur and the later massacre of the Christian nobles of the ancient city of Najran represented a reassertion of power by the former Judaeophile elite.[150] But, as recorded by the

Byzantine historian Procopius, the Negus of Aksum, Kaleb reacted forcefully and invaded Himyar, where he defeated Dhu Nuwas and installed the Christian Himyarite Sumuyafa Ashwa as new ruler. However, the Aksumite commander Abraha, a Christian, soon rebelled and sized power.[151] He subsequently successfully repulsed punitive expeditions sent by Negus Kaleb.[152]

Next to the inscription *Ry 510* is engraved a man wearing a loincloth and holding a lance, with an epigraph identifying him as Thamim dhu Hadeyat, secretary to the Himyar commander, Sharah'il Yaqbul dhu Yazan. The same Thamim is twice portrayed and named hundreds of kilometres further south in the Hima and Kaukab regions (see below).[153] Clearly, Thamim served both Himyar rulers, the Christian Ma'dikarib Ya'fur and the Jewish Dhu Nuwas. The Yemenite Kingdom of Himyar had come to dominate the various south Arabian kingdoms at the end of the third century CE. Since it controlled the production of incense in Hadramawt and Dhofar, it wanted to expand its control to the major trade routes leading to its clients in Mesopotamia and Rome; this implied the conquest of

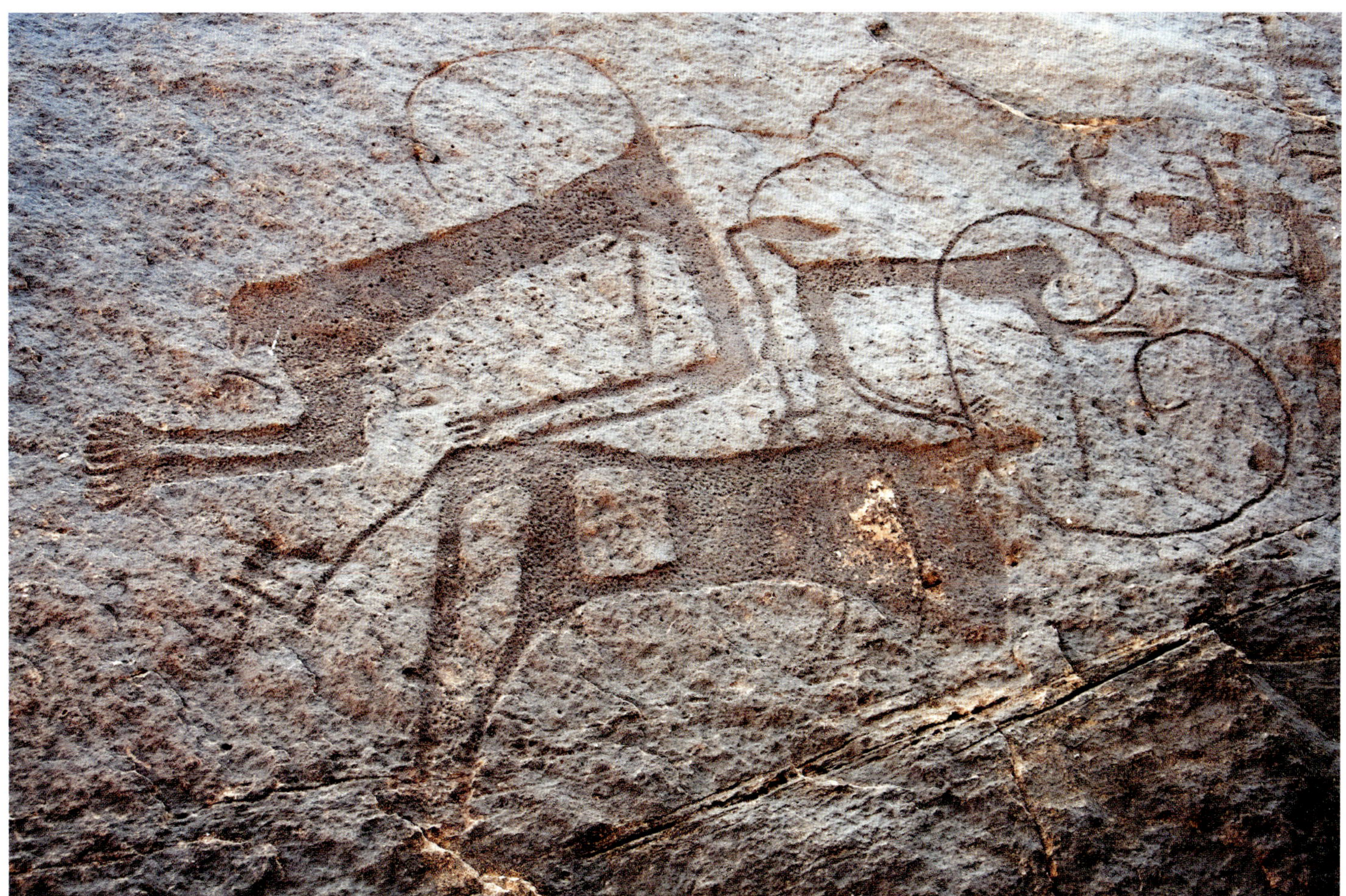

250. Petroglyphs of a buffalo with very long, thin, recurved horns and two leopards from the late Neolithic period or the early Bronze Age. The rendering of the attacking feline at the left is quite unique. Jabal Raat, Shuwaymis, central Saudi Arabia, Photo 2020.

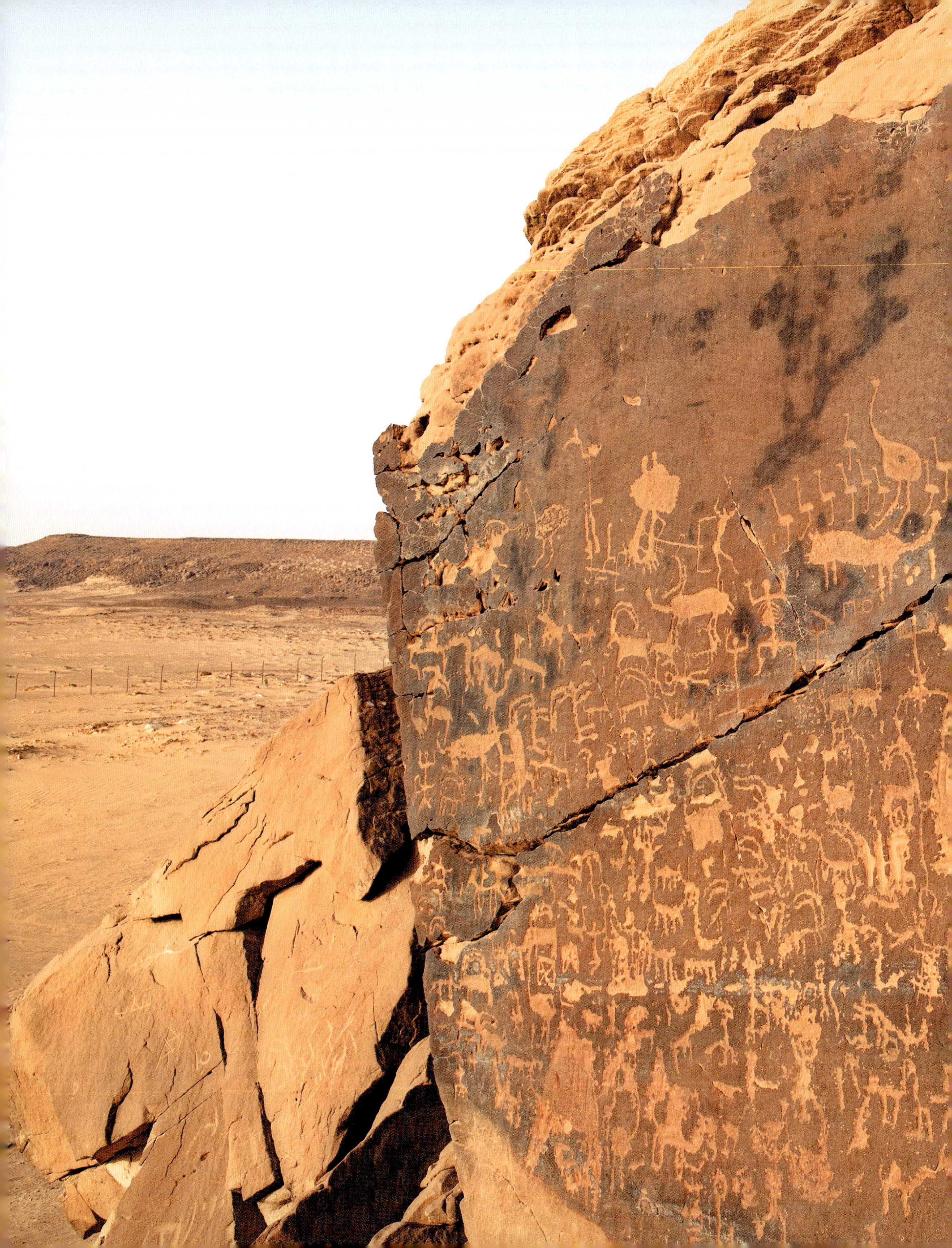

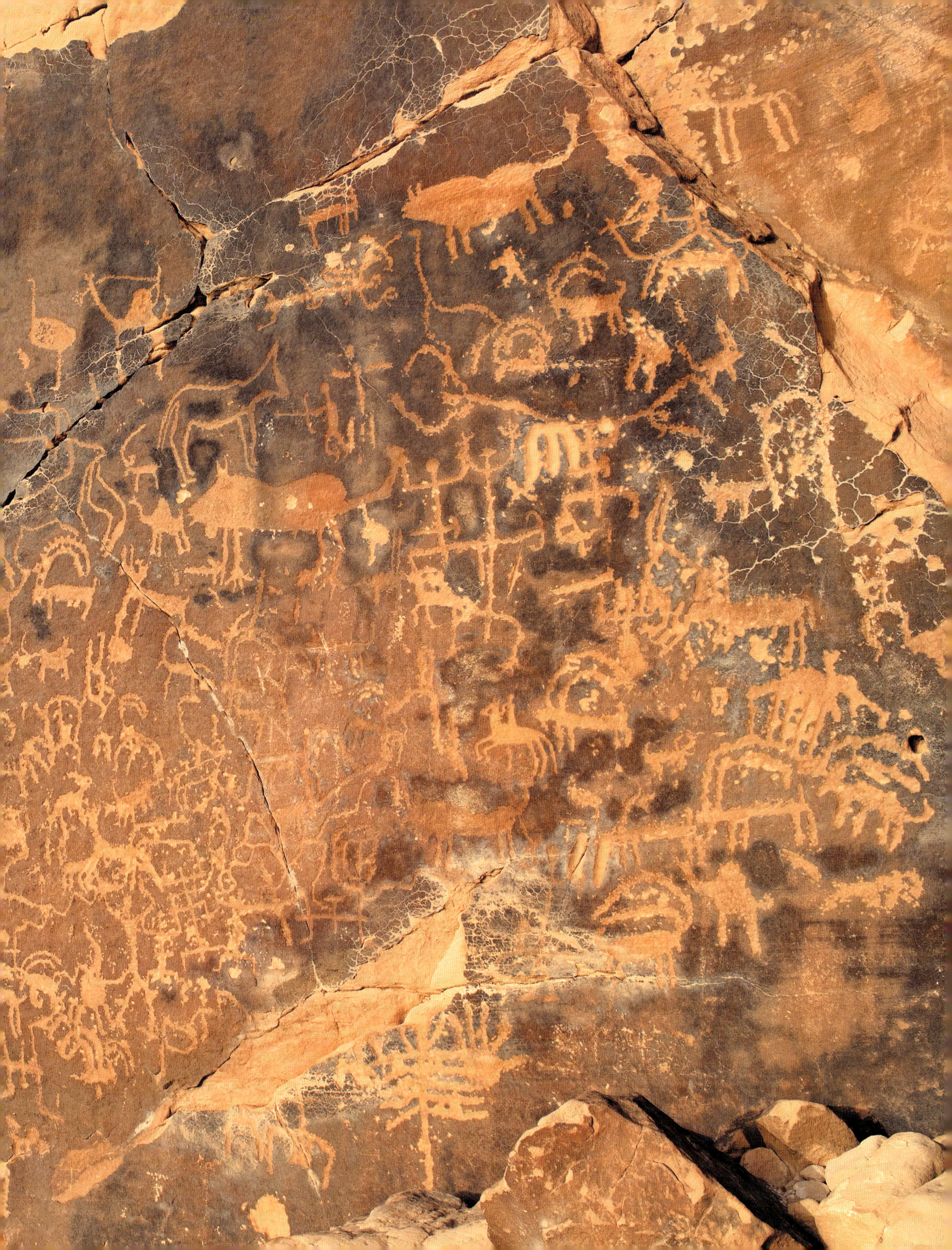

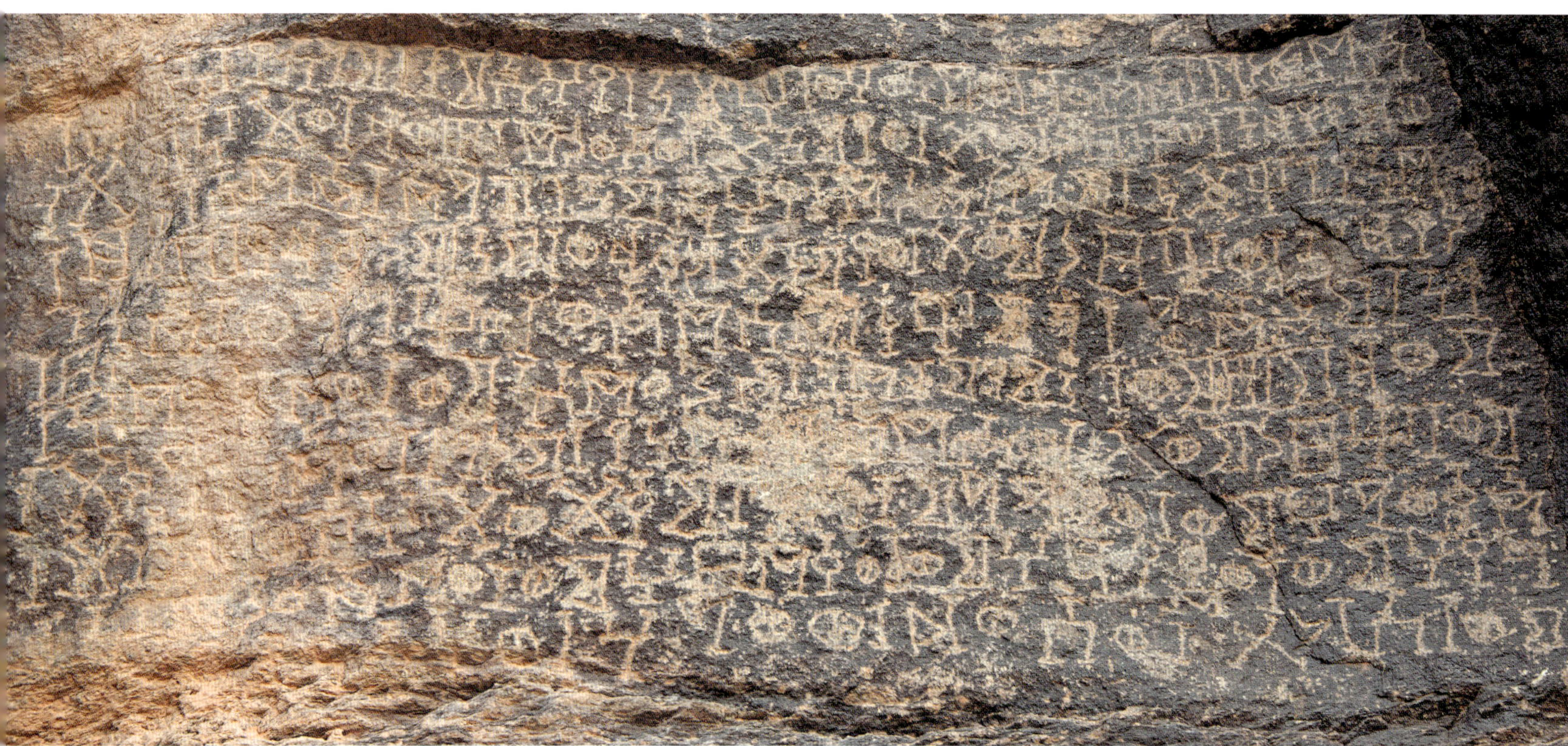

252. The inscription *Ry 509* at Ma'sal al-Jumh in the South Arabian Sabaean (Musnad) script was commissioned by the Himyar king Abikarib As'ad (r. *ca.* 390–420 CE), and his son, Hassan Yuha'min (r. 420–448). It records their military campaign against the central Arabian tribe of *M'dm* (Ma'add) which is also mentioned in the first and third inscriptions at Murayghan. Central Saudi Arabia. Photo 2022.

central and eastern Arabia. Both inscriptions celebrate the conquest of central Arabia by Himyar with the support of its vassal, the central Arabian Kingdom of Kinda, and a military expedition to southern Mesopotamia to subjugate Arab tribes beyond the lower Euphrates. The third inscription, discovered in 2008, stands on the same boulder 28 metres south of *Ry 510*, and is dated to 474–75 CE.[154] It describes a Himyar military expedition by King Shurihbi'il Yakkuf (a son of the above-mentioned Hassan Yuha'min) and his sons, Abishammar Nawf and Lahay'at Yanuf, into eastern Najd and beyond to conquer the capital of the Kingdom of Tanukh in the region of al-Hira, on the right bank of the lower Euphrates. The power of the Kingdom of Himyar can be further assessed by the fact that Ma'sal al-Jumh is 1,120 kilometres distant as the crow flies from the Himyarite capital at Zafar in today's Yemen. Further important rock inscriptions from the Himyar period exist further south, namely at Murayghan and Bir Hima (see below); they underline the importance of inscribed petroglyphs for the reconstruction of history.

---

251. ↵ The rich main petroglyph panel at the site of al-Usba near Musayqirah, central Saudi Arabia. The images range from late Neolithic bulls to dromedaries of the late pre-Islamic period. Photo 2020.

1.3.3. Southern Saudi Arabia

In the context of this survey southern Saudi Arabia refers to that part of the country lying south of 20° latitude. The exceptional role of Arabian rock inscriptions is underscored by the three Himyar inscriptions at the site of **Murayghan** in the province of Asir, 530 km south of Ma'sal al-Jumh. The first, labelled *Ry 506*, was discovered at the mouth of the wadi by the Philby–Ryckmans–Lippens expedition in 1951–52 (fig. 242).[155] It is dated to 552 CE and proclaims the victorious fourth military campaign of the Christian King Abraha of Himyar and Najran (r. after 527/31–after early 560s CE) against the central Arabian tribe of Ma'add and the crown prince Amr bin Mudhdhiran (r. as king 554–569) of al-Hira, son of King al-Mundhir III (r. 502–554).[156] Whereas the second inscription which also mentions King Abraha is rather short, the third consists of four lines and is 518 centimetres long; it is located 700 metres north-east of *Ry 506* and was discovered in 2009. It records one of the first three military expeditions of King Abraha to central Arabia between *ca.* 535 and 552 CE. The text begins with a Syriac cross 23.5 centimetres high and continues: *b-ḥyl Rḥmnn w-ms ḥ-hw mlkn 'brh*, 'by the power of Rahmanan and of his Messiah, King Abraha … wrote this inscription'.[157] These petroglyph inscriptions are very interesting. The designation of God as *Rahmanan*, 'the beneficent', was later used by Prophet Muhammad as the first name of Allah. Then, the second person of the Trinity is called neither Christ nor the Son (of God), but Messiah, which indicates that the Himyarite Christians probably denied the divinity of Jesus, as Muhammad would do eight decades later. Highly relevant also are the mentions of the subjugation of *M'dm* (Ma'add in central Arabia),[158] *Hgrm* (Hagar, today's al-Hufuf in eastern Saudi Arabia), *Ht* (Khatt in Ras al-Khaimah), *Tym* (Tayma), *Ytrb* (Yathrib, that is, Medina), and *Gzm* (north-western Arabia between Tabuk and Aqaba). This means that during the 530s–50s, virtually all of Arabia had to recognize the supremacy of the Christian King Abraha of Himyar.[159] As at other, larger rock art sites, wells and valleys with permanent or ephemeral water had become stops on caravan trails.

Sixty kilometres south-west of Murayghan stands the best-preserved site of rock paintings in Saudi Arabia, **al-Hamdha**.

It is a concave granite boulder *ca.* 80 metres long. Approximately eight metres above ground level, there is a panel some eighteen metres long with several red pictographs dating from the Neolithic to the Iron Age (fig. 253). They represent, among other things: a large aurochs or buffalo of the Jubbah type in bright red colour with huge horns seen from above, cows, a reddish camel painted over a geometric pattern consisting of five double hexagons arranged vertically, smaller camels, a man with enormous hands, a tiny, ten-centimetre-high foot soldier holding shield and sword, a tall adorant, and a Himaitic epigraph as well as *wusum* painted in black.

The eight-kilometre-long **Wadi al-Khayyur** is located 50 kilometres north-east of al-Hamdha, at whose head in March 2022 the authors discovered what are probably hitherto undocumented monumental petroglyphs. Within an area of one square kilometre, nine high-quality over-life-sized armed male figures are engraved

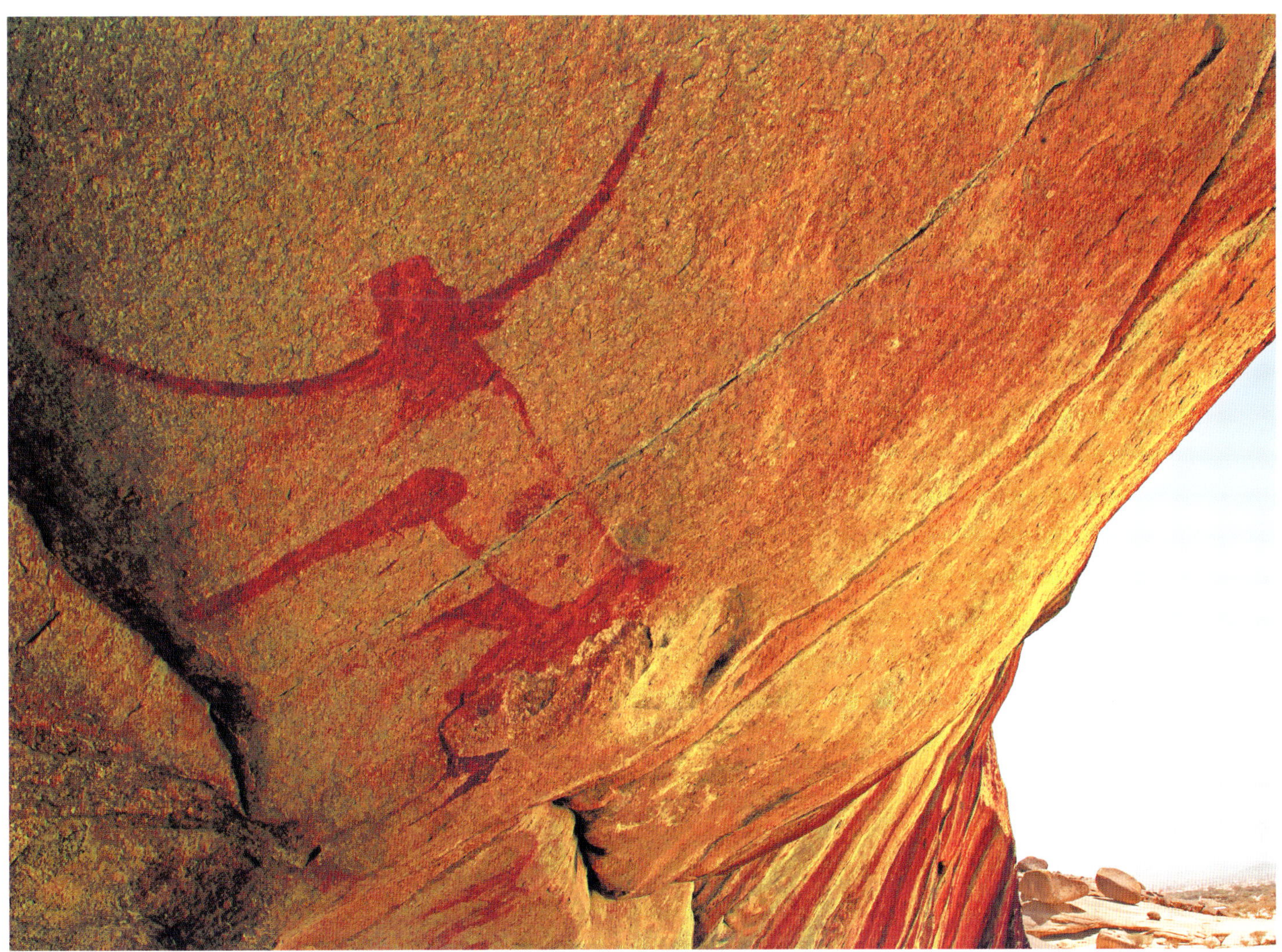

253. Rock painting of an aurochs or buffalo 110 cm long in the shelter of al-Hamdha. Early Bronze Age, Asir Province, southern Saudi Arabia. Image slightly enhanced with DStretch. Photo 2020.

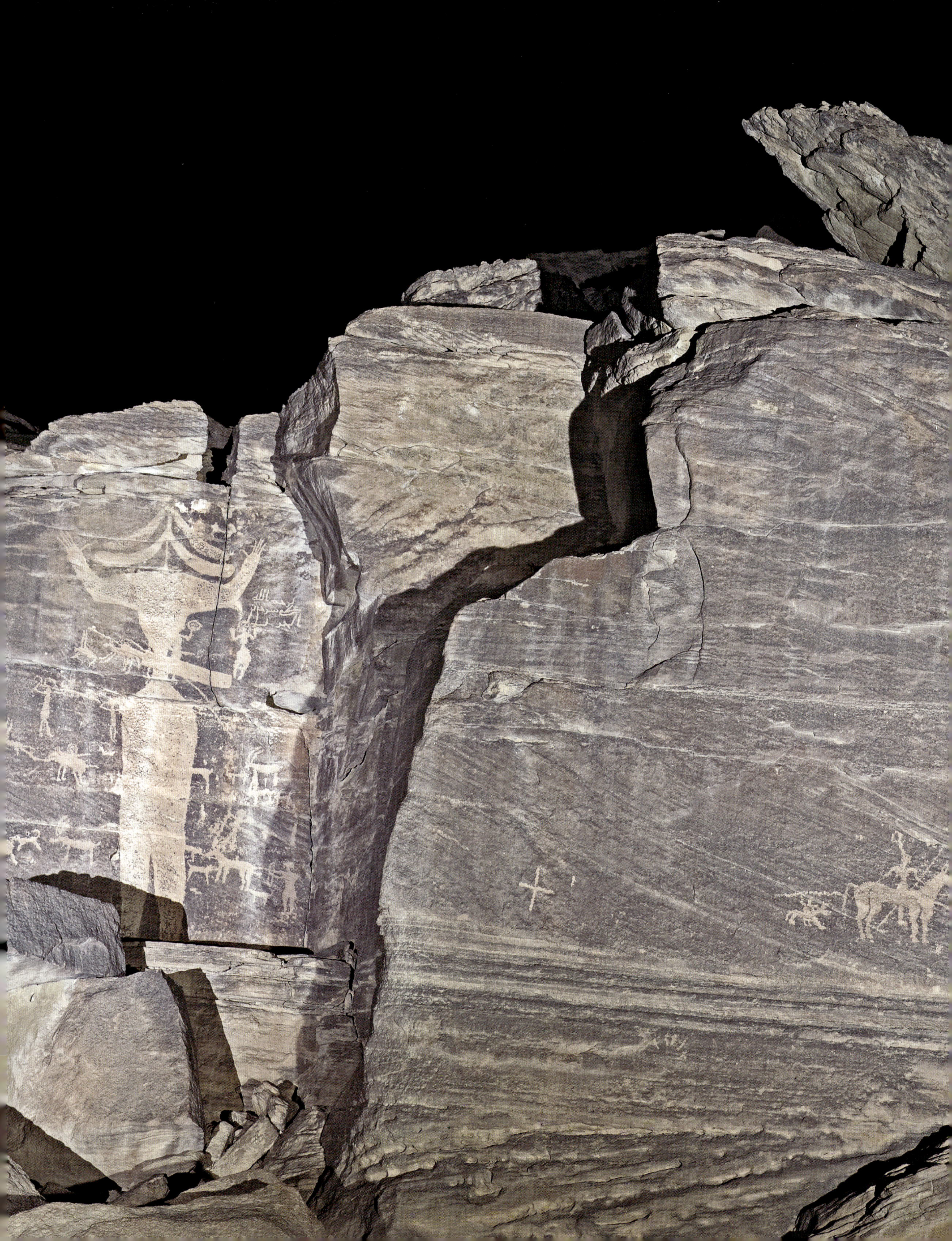

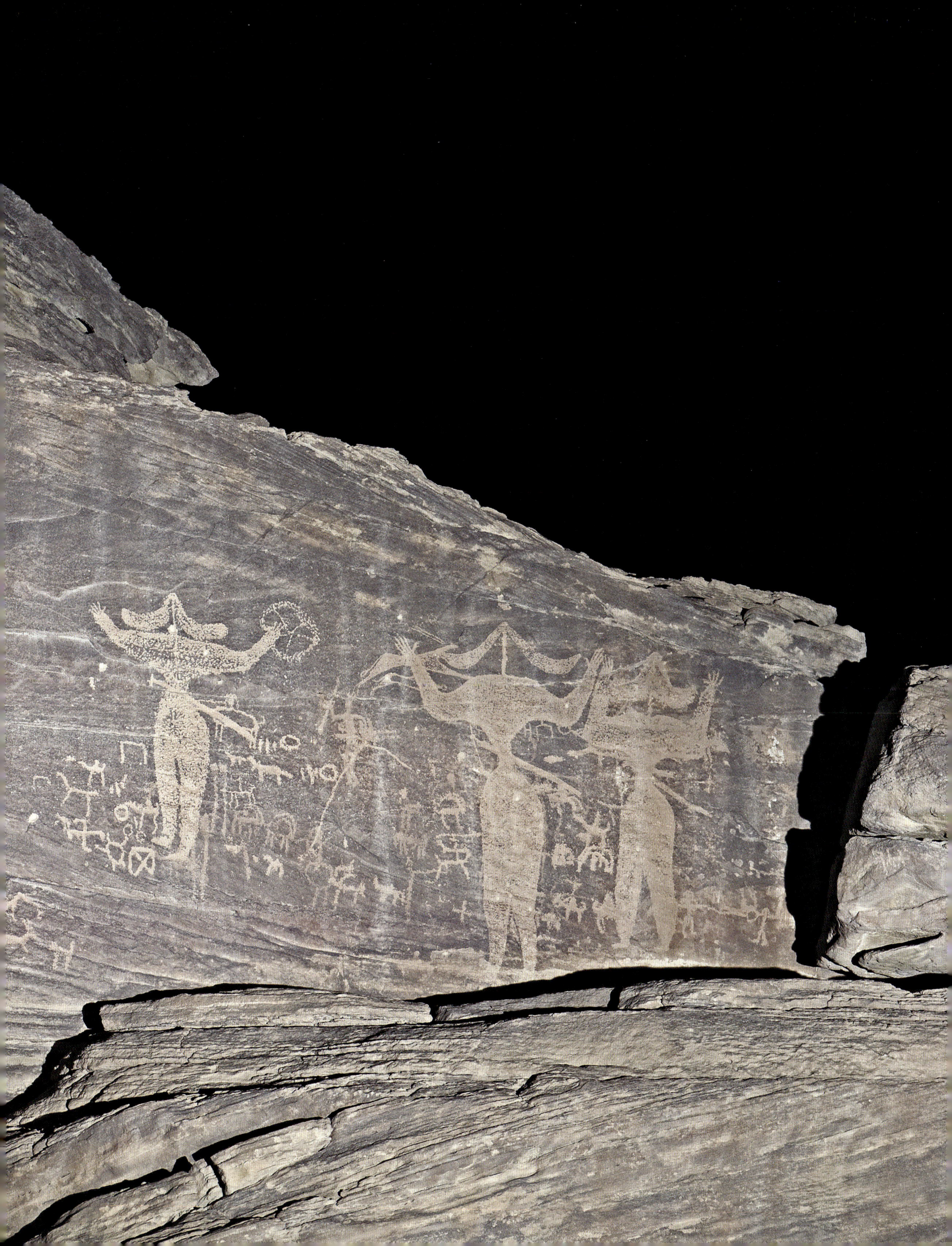

on three different boulders; the three largest are 3.2 metres tall, the smallest 2 metres (fig. 254). There are in addition five 1–1.4-metre-tall warriors from the same period. The giants were partly superimposed over petroglyphs of mounted lancers, felines, ostriches, hunting scenes, ibexes, swastikas and brief Thamudic inscriptions. Later Arabic inscriptions have been added. The men have ultra-slim waists and carry straight swords and curved daggers; one holds a shield, and all have a rod-shaped, ultra-slender head and long hair curving upwards. In some other, much smaller petroglyphs of horsemen, the riders are rendered in a similar style with slim waist and long hair curved upwards. On the second boulder there is a singular image of a person *ca.* 100 centimetres tall with arms raised. The outline is fully pecked and up to ten centimetres thick, but the inner part of the body is marked by a multitude of dots like cup-marks.

Based on the shape of the swords, the superimposed smaller figures and the Thamudic inscriptions, these monumental petroglyphs can be dated to the later pre-Islamic period, around 500–600 CE. Similar, but smaller, figures are known in Jabal al-Qahra and al-Kaukab in Najran province, the exception being at Tha'er where there are two unarmed females more than two metres tall.[160] At the end of the al-Khayyur wadi, where it leads into the desert, there are petroglyphs of similar, but much smaller warriors. About 27 kilometres south-east of al-Khayyur is **al-Kheir** where there are petroglyphs of at least ten standing warriors. Five of them hold lances, while the tallest of them has a double lance with two tips and a rectangular shield, and in his right hand he holds a curved club, a symbol of the moon god Almaqah.[161] An interesting inscription in Musnad reads *Amn Yatha*, whereby *Amn* designated the moon god of the ancient southern Arabian kingdom of Qataban which was conquered by Himyar,[162] and *Yatha* was a prefix to the names of some Qatabanian rulers. 33 kilometres east of al-Khayyur and close to the **Arch of Wajjid** are the petroglyphs of six warriors, five on foot and one mounted on a dromedary, and two women; on the chests

of three of the warriors a nail-shaped *wasm* is engraved; the tallest one holds two spears.

Najran province is exceptionally rich in petroglyphs, especially the neighbouring areas of **Jabal al-Qahra** and **Jabal al-Kaukab** as well as in the region of **Hima**. In contrast to north-western and central Saudi Arabia, this region on the south-western fringe of the Rub' al-Khali desert has no pre-Neolithic or Neolithic rock art and only a few petroglyphs from the Bronze Age. Most date from the Iron Age, the pre-Islamic and the Islamic periods.[163] The countless inscriptions were written in the following scripts, in decreasing numerical order: Sabaic, Himaitic, Arabic, Nabataean, Greek, Syriac and Hebrew.[164] In view of the extremely large number of sites, some of which have quite similar motifs, the most important sites will be listed first and, afterwards the most significant themes will be identified.

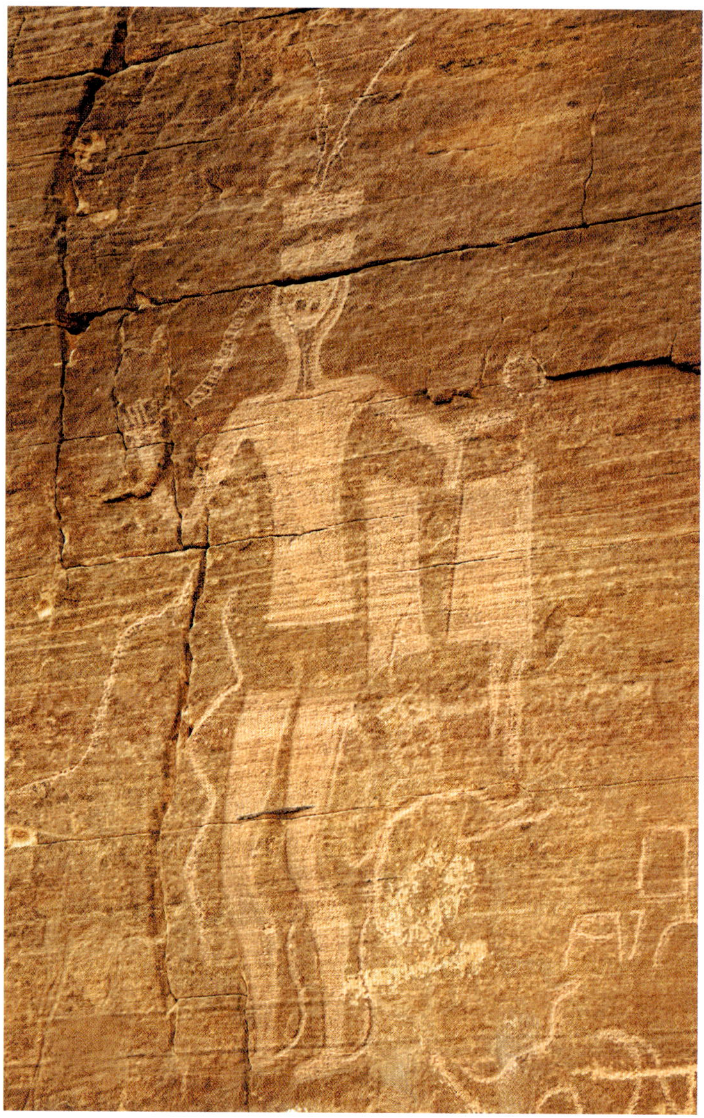

254. ↵ Four armed men, dating from the late pre-Islamic period, superimposed on Iron Age petroglyphs. The tallest figure is 320 cm high. Al-Khayyur site 6, Asir province, southern Saudi Arabia. Night photo 2022.

255. A tall male figure whose head is adorned with two feathers. Above his right hand is an object that looks like a slightly curved, narrow ladder, and in his left hand he holds what could be a rectangular shield. To the right there is a second rectangular object which is superimposed on the rear legs of an unidentified animal. The slightly curved object is an attribute of the southern Arabian moon god Almaqah. It is uncertain whether this figure represents Almaqah or one of his attendants. Iron Age, Aan al-Naam, Najran province, southern Saudi Arabia. Photo 2020.

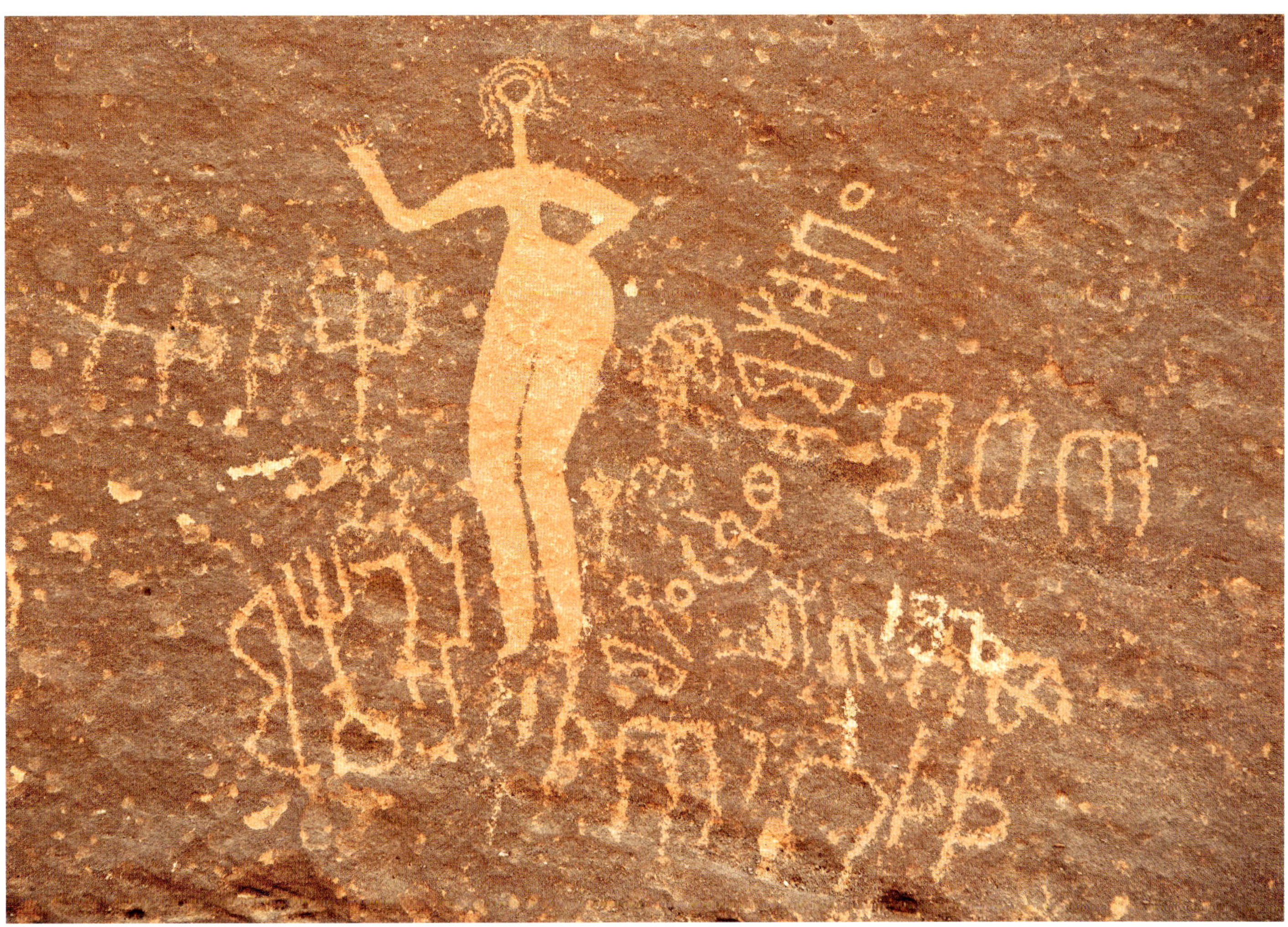

256. Petroglyph of a woman waving with an inviting gesture. One of the Himaitic inscriptions names the male owner of the location, another the goddess of purity and fertility Dhu Khalsa. Whether the engraved woman is related to the goddess is unknown. Tha'er, site 1, Najran province, southern Saudi Arabia. Photo 2022.

The centre of **Jabal al-Qahra** is about 70 kilometres south of the Arch of Wajjid. The main sites are from north to south:

- **Aan al-Naam** lies in the sandy plain 15 km north of Jabal al-Qahra. Striking images include a tall man, whose head is adorned with two feathers. Above his right hand there is an object that looks like a slightly curved, narrow ladder or a small club, and in his left hand he holds what could be a rectangular shield (fig. 255). This and the neighbouring shield were superimposed over the older petroglyph of a quadruped. Then there are several images of ostriches which became extinct in the desert only in the 1930s when they were exterminated by motorized hunting.[165] Typical of Aan-al Naam and the Najran area are women with raised hands and long plaited hair (see below) and men wearing long daggers with lunate pommels.

- **Fardat Sheyban** is 5 km south of Aan al-Naam and has striking combat scenes between mounted lancers; they date from the first millennium CE (fig. 264).

- **Umm Onaik** is 6 km south of Fardat Sheyban. Its main images are duels between horsemen fighting with flails, lances and sabres, tall women with long hair and ostriches.

- **Najd Sehi** and **Najd Musamma** form a large complex.[166] This flat sandy zone lies between Jabal al-Qahra and Jabal al-Kaukab. On an isolated large rock, the petroglyphs of eight tall women are especially noteworthy. They have long plaited hair and rise their arms towards the sky, and stand among two groups of horsemen battling with lances and sabres (fig. 261). In the same area, three warriors with long

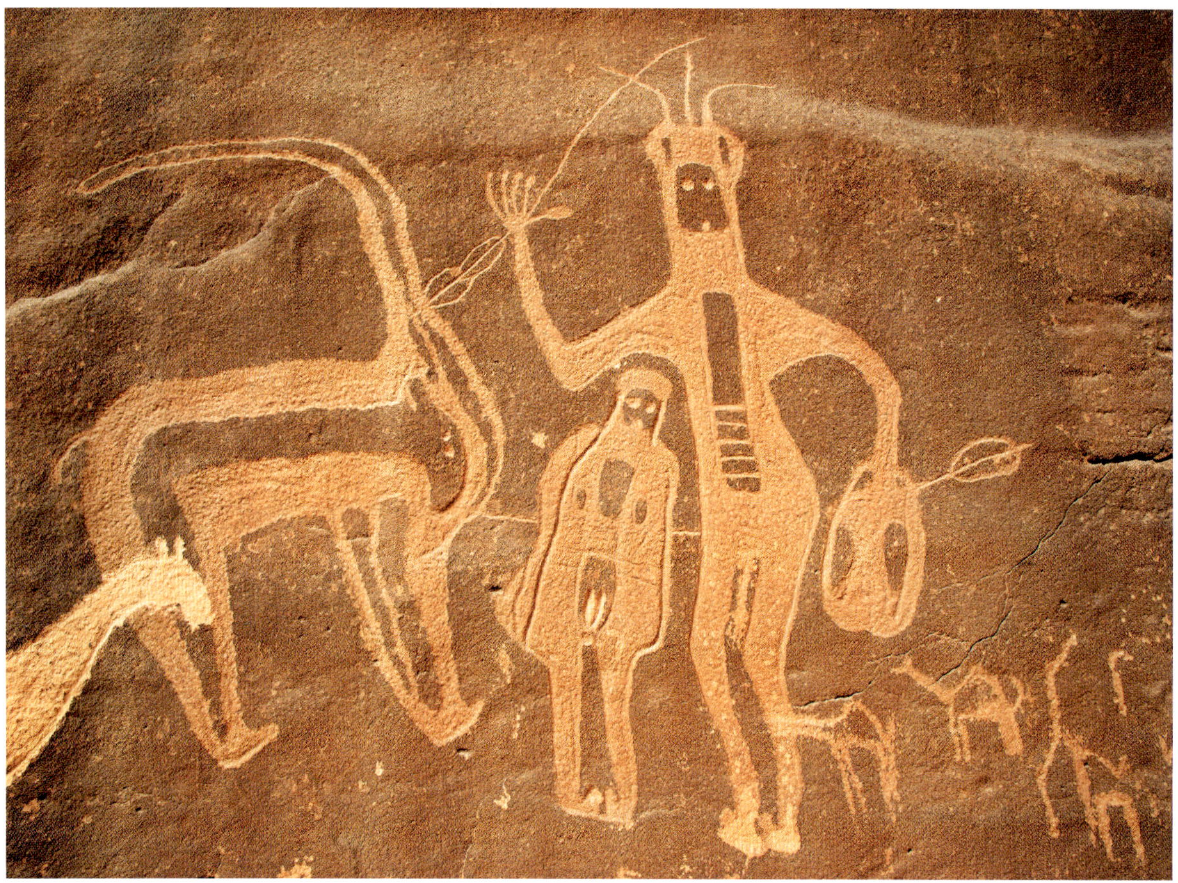

257. Images of a tall man who holds a shield pierced by an arrow in one hand and an arrow in the other; a woman; and a strange animal whose long neck is stretched back, and inside whose body there is a sheep. Pre-Islamic period; the sexual characteristics of the humans were added later. The dromedary at the lower left was added around the year 2000. Khayran, Najran province, southern Saudi Arabia. Photo 2022.

outward-curving hair hold in their left hand a bow and in their right two arrows; the tribal affiliation of one of them is indicated by a cross on his chest, another one by a *wasm* in the shape of a nail. A few hundred metres further on there is a single rock featuring an almost life-sized petroglyph of a cow and on another boulder three large, running ostriches; one of them is caught by a small hunter wearing a wolf mask.

- **Tha'er** is a large complex consisting of five sites. Unique here are the images of several women with relatively broad hips waving to the spectator in an inviting gesture (fig. 256). Next to them are Himaitic inscriptions naming the (male) owner of the place, for example 'this is the place of Abdu'l Hamid'; in one instance, another inscription placed close to the knee of the inviting woman names the goddess of fertility and purity Dhu Khalsa. However, the relationship between this goddess and the inviting women remains unclear. There are also several humans with either long or curly hair girded with swords and with a nail-shaped *wasm* on their chests, as well as women with raised arms and braided hair. In the narrower, upper part of the wadi there is a block with two women over two metres tall with ultra-slim waists and hair curving upwards, like the huge warriors at al-Khayyur, but without weapons.

- **Hareemah**, 5 km further south, is famous for its two large battle scenes involving lancers, swordsmen and fighters on foot. There are also petroglyphs featuring saddled camels, Arabian antelopes, ostriches and a vulture standing with spread wings.

- **Khayran** is located 6 km south-east of Hareemah in the region of Wadi Saad. Here the very well-executed images of two humans are striking; the taller, male one holds a spear and a shield pierced by an arrow (fig. 257). To the left of both persons stands a strange animal; it either has no face and very long horns or a long neck stretched backwards, and inside its body a sheep is engraved. The sexual characteristics of the humans were probably added later. Unfortunately, around the year 2000, the image of a plump dromedary has been added.

- **Daab al-Qurthi** is 3 km south-east of Khayran. Here there are petroglyphs of four ultra-slender women, about 1 m tall, with curly hair and wearing necklaces. One Himaitic inscription says 'The place of Karamat' (a female name), another 'the place of Thara'al' (a male name). A few hundred metres away are petroglyphs dating from the historic (Islamic) period which illustrate a battle scene between lancers. Then there are images of a large cheetah, of a lion, two stout boars, a camel wearing a blanket with a chevron pattern, a three-storey house, palm trees and a camel with a ladder leaning against it.

- **Wadi al-Naqha** lies 20 km south-east of Hareemah. On a huge boulder stands the petroglyph of a tall warrior adorned with a feather headdress. He wears chest armour and a lunate pommel-handled dagger in his belt. In his left hand he holds two spears and another in his right. His sandals each have a thorn at their back; he probably wears spurs, which suggests that he is a dismounted horseman or male deity (fig. 258). To his right a kneeling female musician plays a lyre or cithara, 80 cm high, and next to her stands a woman, 136 cm tall with rather short, braided hair. She wears two torcs, and to her left features a crescent moon which suggests that she, like the

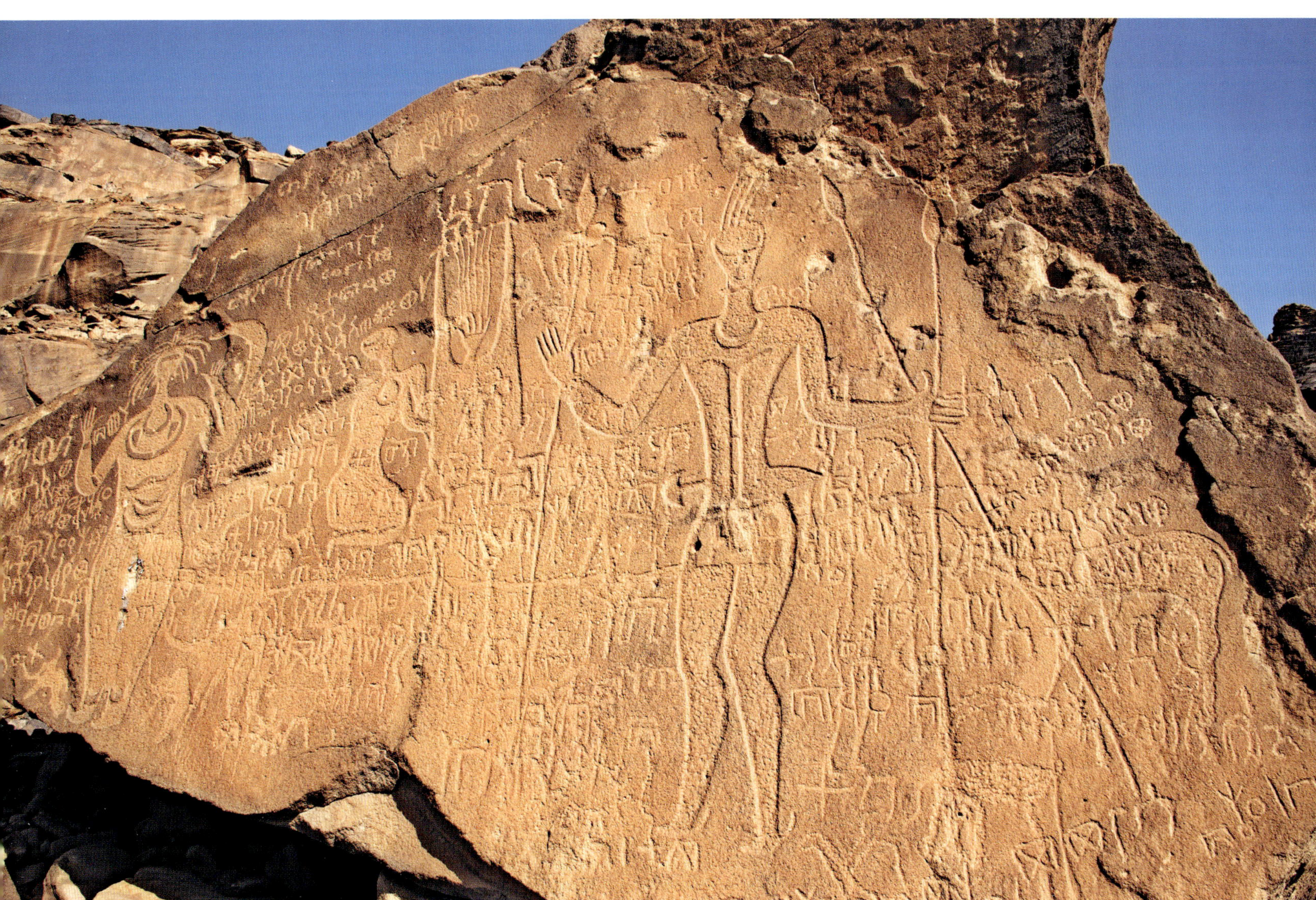

258. An isolated boulder in Wadi al-Naqha. From right to left: a bull; a warrior adorned with a feather headdress, holding two lances in his left hand and one in his right, wearing chest armour and a dagger, and spurs on his feet; a kneeling female musician who plays a lyre or cithara; and next to her another standing woman, with rather short, braided hair. She wears two torcs, and to her left is a crescent moon. Both she and the warrior are associated with the moon god Almaqah. Najran province, southern Saudi Arabia. Photo 2022.

warrior with the two spears, is associated with the moon god Almaqah.

Jabal al-Kaukab borders Jabal al-Qahra to the east; its main sites are:

- At the northern tip of the Jabal, about 10 km north of **Aan Halkan**, is a nameless site with two boulders 4 m in length. Noteworthy are a rare petroglyph of a fat-tailed sheep (fig. 260) – other petroglyphs of sheep are found at Fardat Sheyban, Umm al-Khorq and Thajar – and those of humans in an adorant position, a large donkey, dogs attacking an ibex, and straight daggers or short swords, and finally of an equilateral cross framed by a larger cross, probably a *wasm*. That this region was already inhabited in the Neolithic is clear in view of the numerous 'tombs with tails'. These consist of circular tumuli up to 1 m high made from flat

stones heaped on top of each other; their diameter varies from 2 to 5 m. Some tombs consist just of a tumulus, others have long tails of aligned stones 1 m wide, which may exceed 100 m in length.

- **Aan Halkan** is a complex containing several sites. In the central one, a small sanctuary dedicated to Dhu Samawi, the protector of the health of camel herds, was discovered in 2008.[167] Dhu Samawi was the paramount god of the Bani Amir tribe, and his pilgrimage site was at Yathill, today's Baraqish in north-western Yemen. The Aan Halkan sanctuary was unfortunately vandalized after its publication.[168] Nearby is the inscription *Ry 508*, one of the three monumental Sabaic inscriptions celebrating the military campaign of the Himyar king Dhu Nuwas against Zafar and Najran which is dated to 523 CE. The neighbouring inscriptions *Ry 513* and *Ry 514* mention Thamim dhu Hadeyat who is also recorded at Ma'sal

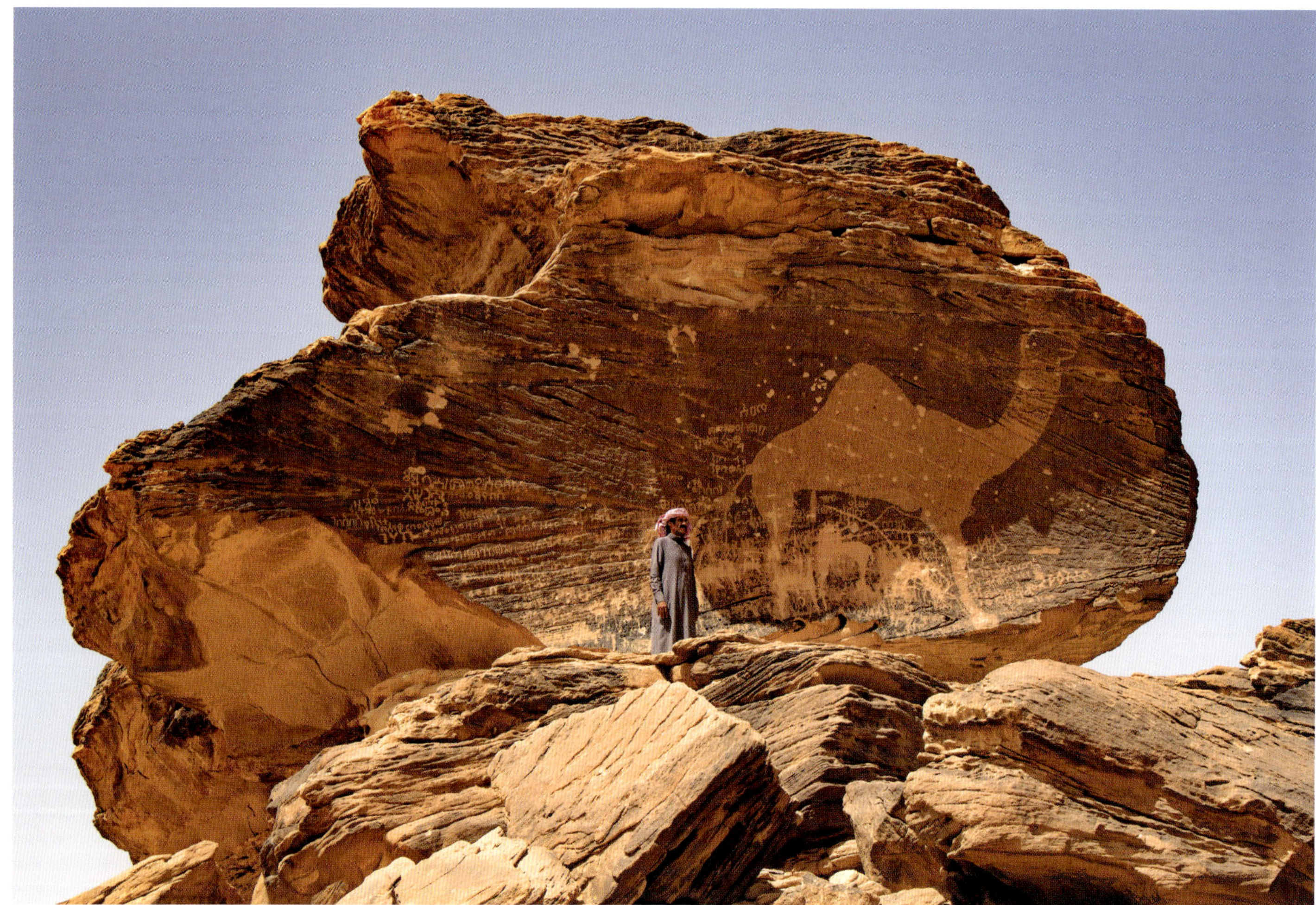

259. This huge dromedary at the site called al-Mawaqee is the largest single petroglyph in Najran province. Iron Age, southern Saudi Arabia. Photo 2020.

al-Jumh.[169] To the left of inscription *Ry 514* the image of Thamim is engraved; he is girded with a long sword and holds a lance in his right hand.[170] Petroglyphs elsewhere at Aan Halkan include riders on saddled camels, a couple of lions, arms and hands, at least five warriors holding two spears in one hand and in the other a kind of boomerang with two or three decorative horizontal lines or a tiny curved ladder which represents a symbol of the south Arabian moon god Almaqah.[171] Two of these warriors have spurs on their boots. On a neighbouring rock is the image of an Himyarite warrior named by an Thamudic inscription Thauba-El. Close by, there is a strange scene of a slender standing human over whose chest are superimposed the open wings of a raptor; to his left stands a horseman, who holds to his right a drawn bow and a hooked rod.

- **Habah** consists of a few scenes above the valley floor. In one are the petroglyphs of four armed men guarding three large dromedaries; the front dromedary looks back to the other two animals. In another scene, four men girded with daggers are dancing while holding bows and arrows or short spears.

- **Dhubabeen** is two kilometres south of Habah. Noteworthy are the images of three dromedaries, up to 210 cm long, two female humans with raised arms and a dozen Sabaic inscriptions.

- **Umm al-Khurq, site I.** Umm al-Khurq is a valley at the southern end of Jabal al-Kaukab. At site I there are unparalleled petroglyphs. Unique to here are the images of three women with legs spread out exhibiting their sexual organs or giving birth. On rocks a few metres up, two battles are shown. Above, four mounted lancers fight each other, and below, four warriors on foot wearing horned helmets and large daggers each hold in their raised arm a disc or ring; three of the four men are hit by a flying spear.

- **Umm al-Khurq, site II.** Here are found the petroglyphs of three fat-tailed sheep guarded by armed shepherds, bovines with geometric patterns inside their body, ostriches, small lions and a horseman armed with a lance. It is quite probable that these petroglyphs of cows and bulls with geometric patterns represent animals which were painted, a tradition which was also followed in the prehistoric Sahara. These cows and bulls definitely represent domestic cattle kept in oases, since wild bovines would have been unable to survive in such a dry environment as prevailed at the time the petroglyphs were created. Finally, there is an image 30 cm high of a man girded with a straight sword and holding a ring in his raised left hand; he has an ultra-slender head and long hair curving upwards, similar to the much larger images at al-Khayyur.

- **Gal al-Sidiri** is a concave boulder of red sandstone 40 m long, with petroglyphs of armed horsemen, bovines decorated with geometric patterns, two crosses and Himaitic inscriptions.

- **Thajar** lies 15 km east of Jabal al-Kaukab in the desert plain. On a single sandstone boulder, the petroglyphs show almost life-sized camels, horsemen wielding spears, a large fat-tailed sheep and ibexes as well as Sabaic and Himaitic inscriptions. Noteworthy are three men armed with bows and arrows of which two wear a bird mask; two other men hold the symbol of the moon god Almaqah.

- **Al-Mawaqee** is an isolated sandstone outcrop 20 km south-west of Thajar. On the rock at the hill summit is the petroglyph of a huge dromedary measuring 3.3 by 2.8 m (fig. 259). It is the largest petroglyph in Najran.

Hima lies south of both Jabals and counts the following sites:

- **Barqa al-Mahanet** is a long, concave sandstone boulder on top of a small hill. Here there are petroglyphs of life-sized cows decorated with stripes and geometric patterns probably dating from the Iron Age, Himaitic inscriptions and later, schematic horsemen swinging swords, as well as palm trees.

- **Nazim** is a widely spread-out complex. At the main, southern site, the images of seven large cows are overlaid over older petroglyphs of bovines and antelopes. In one corner, two men are duelling with swords and axes.

- **Thalatha Afial** ('three elephants') in the Jabal Dhibah consists of two rocks evoking a crucial, quasi-historical event in the pre-Islamic history of Arabia, namely the attack on Mecca by the Christian King Abraha of Himyar mentioned

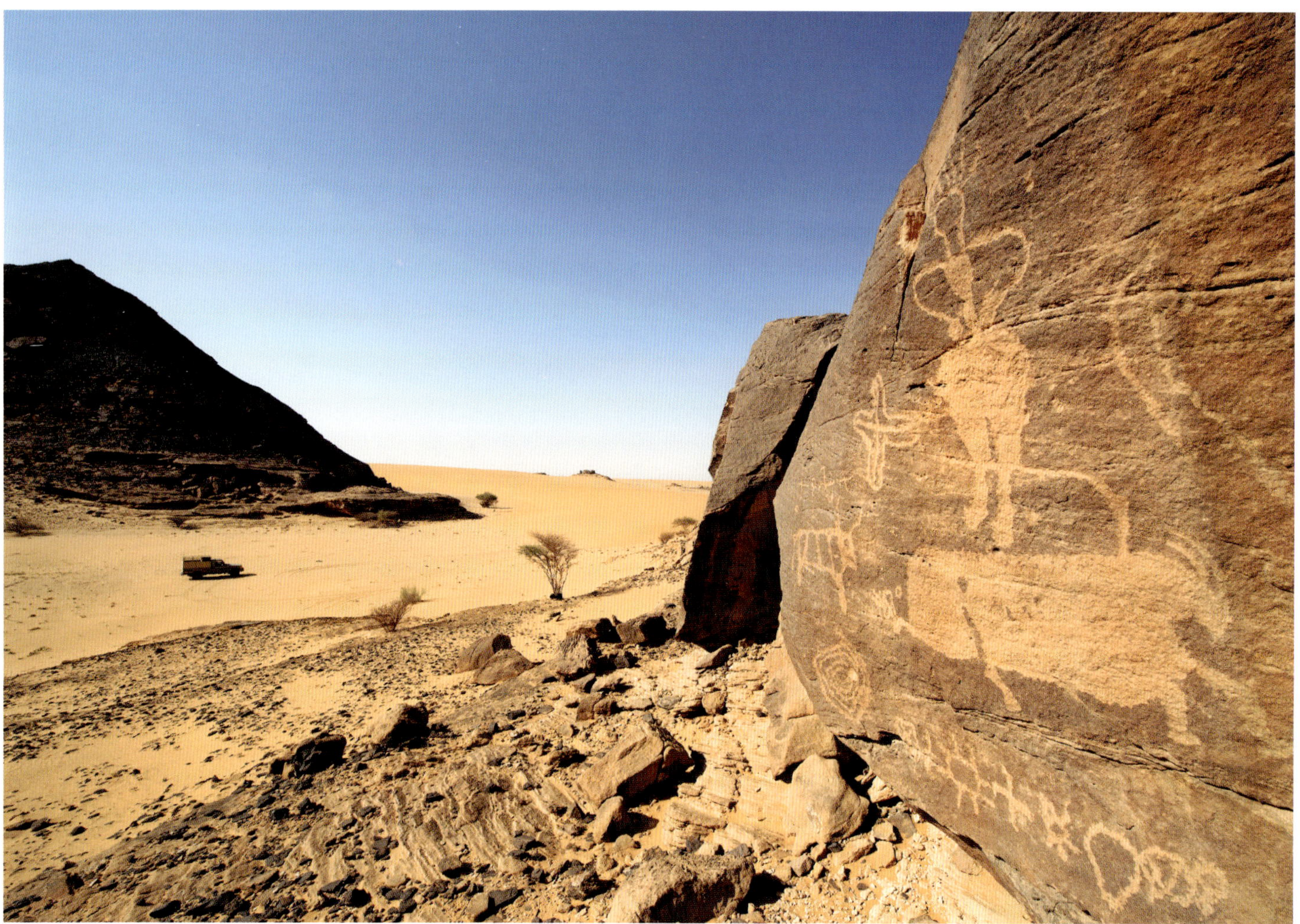

260. Petroglyphs of a woman, a fat-tailed sheep, a bull and a small cross framed by a larger one. This is probably a *wasm*. Nameless site in Jabal al-Kaukab, Najran province, southern Saudi Arabia. Photo 2022.

above. A zealous Christian, Abraha is said to have built a great church at Sana'a in today's Yemen. According to the Quran, Abraha launched a military expedition against Mecca in the year of Prophet Muhammad's birth, that is in 570 (or 572) CE, known as the Year of the Elephant.[172] Abraha allegedly planned to destroy the Kaaba in order to direct all pilgrims to his new cathedral in Sana'a instead of to Mecca which in pre-Islamic times was already an important pilgrimage destination. But Abraha's army, in front of which an elephant was marching, failed to reach Mecca; according to tradition, the elephant refused to continue his march and Abraha died in the same year.[173] Christian Robin believes that this was indeed a historical event which took place between 555 and 565 CE and that the outbreak of an epidemic in Abraha's army forced the king to cancel his campaign.[174] The three petroglyphs at Thalatha Afial of elephants mounted by their drivers are

unique in Saudi Arabia, for the elephant was unknown in Arabia and could only have been imported from Ethiopia, King Abraha's homeland. In addition, 2.6 km further north there is a large Musnad inscription which says *Abraha zabeyan malik*, that is 'Abraha, His Highness the King'.[175] Since Abraha had to pass through Najran on his expedition against Mecca it is very tempting to link the inscription and the three pecked mounted elephants with that event. 5 km to the west of this inscription an emblem of a star of David is pecked into a sandstone boulder otherwise covered with petroglyphs featuring ostriches as along with armed camel-riders and horsemen. Judging from the weak repatination, these petroglyphs can be dated to the middle of the first millennium CE.

- **Dabah** is a steep rock formation about 900 m south of Thalatha Afial. On the top there are many Musnad inscriptions and the image of a couple playing the flute. The name of the standing male musician is Bahsam the Hadramawti. The image of the seated female player has been damaged by bullet shots. This is not the only site where petroglyphs have been abused as shooting targets. On a nearby, smaller boulder there is an armoured lancer, a standing woman with plaited hair and a man with a triangular-shaped upper body who holds two sticks or arrows. A few hundred metres away is the site of **Aan Jamal**, a rocky outcrop covered with a multitude of Sabaic and Himaitic inscriptions. The site is fenced with a metal grid and the inscriptions are inaccessible.[176]

- **Bir Hima**, whose name means 'Well of Hima', is the place of four ancient and two more recent wells. Here stands one of the most famous historical petroglyph inscriptions not only in Arabia, but in the whole Middle East, comparable to the Achaemenid royal inscription of Behistun. It consists of a panel in four text sections written in the monumental Sabaic script. It reports on the early wars of the Jewish Himyarite king Yusuf As'ar Yath'ar, aka Dhu Nuwas, in the year 523 CE (fig. 262). It is no coincidence that this royal proclamation and the very similar one at nearby **Saydah** were hewn in the rocks of Bir Hima, for the main trade and military road leading northwards from the southern Arabian kingdoms in

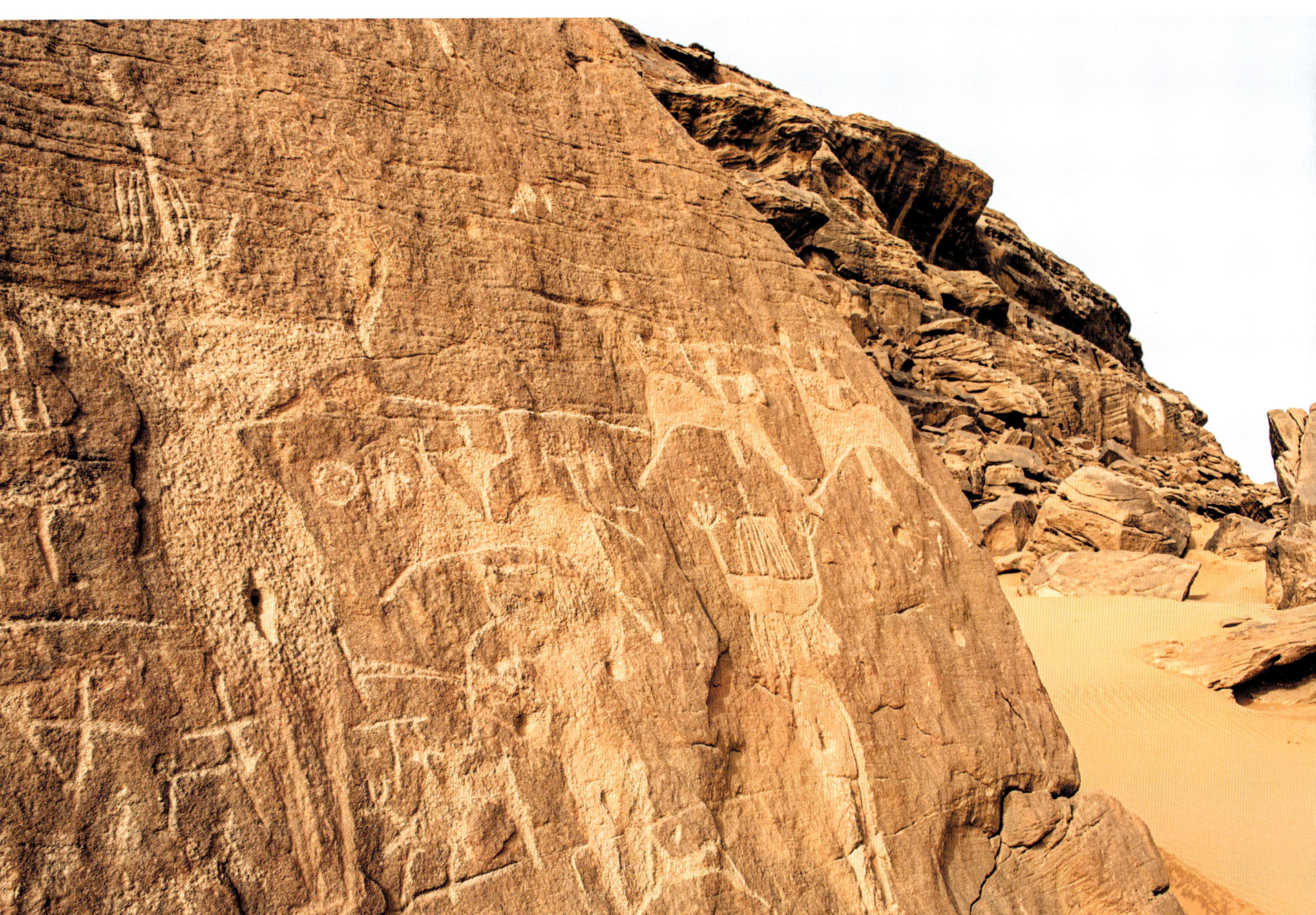

261. Tall women with long plaited hair and arms raised towards the sky stand among two groups of horsemen battling with lances and sabres. In total, eight such women are engraved on this boulder; they possibly represent military 'cheerleaders' exhorting their tribesmen to valiant battle. *ca.* middle first millennium CE. Najd Sehi, Najran province, southern Saudi Arabia. Photo 2022.

today's Yemen led first to the ancient city of Najran and then to the wells of Bir Hima 85 km further north. East of Najran, the desert precluded the passage of any large caravan, and to the west the paths led either through the Asir and Hijaz Mountains or into the murderous heat of the Tihama coastal plain. North of Najran and Bir Hima, the main route split, going either north-westwards in the direction of Yathrib (Medina), Dadan, Tabuk, Petra and the Mediterranean Sea or north-eastwards to Qaryat al-Faw and the port city of Gerrha on the western shore of the Persian Gulf.

The four inscribed panels are numbered from left to right as follows:

- *Ja 1032*: The inscription names *Naimat*, an officer of the Himyarite commander Sharah'il Yaqbul dhu Yazan; to the left of the brief inscription a camel is pecked.[177]

- *Ja 1031*: The inscription names *Hugayya Ayhar*, half-brother (by a slave-mother) of the chief commander Sharah'il Yaqbul, and quartermaster of the army. He is shown climbing a palm tree.[178]

- *Ja 1030*: The inscription names *Thamim dhu Hadeyat*, secretary of commander Sharah'il Yaqbul. Thamim wrote the proclamation; he is shown armed with a sword.[179]

- *Ja 1029* is a tribal monogram.[180]

- *Ja 1028* is the proclamation ordered by commander Sharah'il Yaqbul dhu Yazan. The text is 12 lines long and is engraved in a panel 4.05 m wide and 1.24 m high.[181] Monograms of the Himyarite ruler and of the tribes participating in the campaign are engraved to the top right of the main text.

The text records how Dhu Nuwas seized power and killed the Christian Ethiopian garrison stationed in the Himyarite capital Zafar in spite of initially offering them a safe withdrawal in

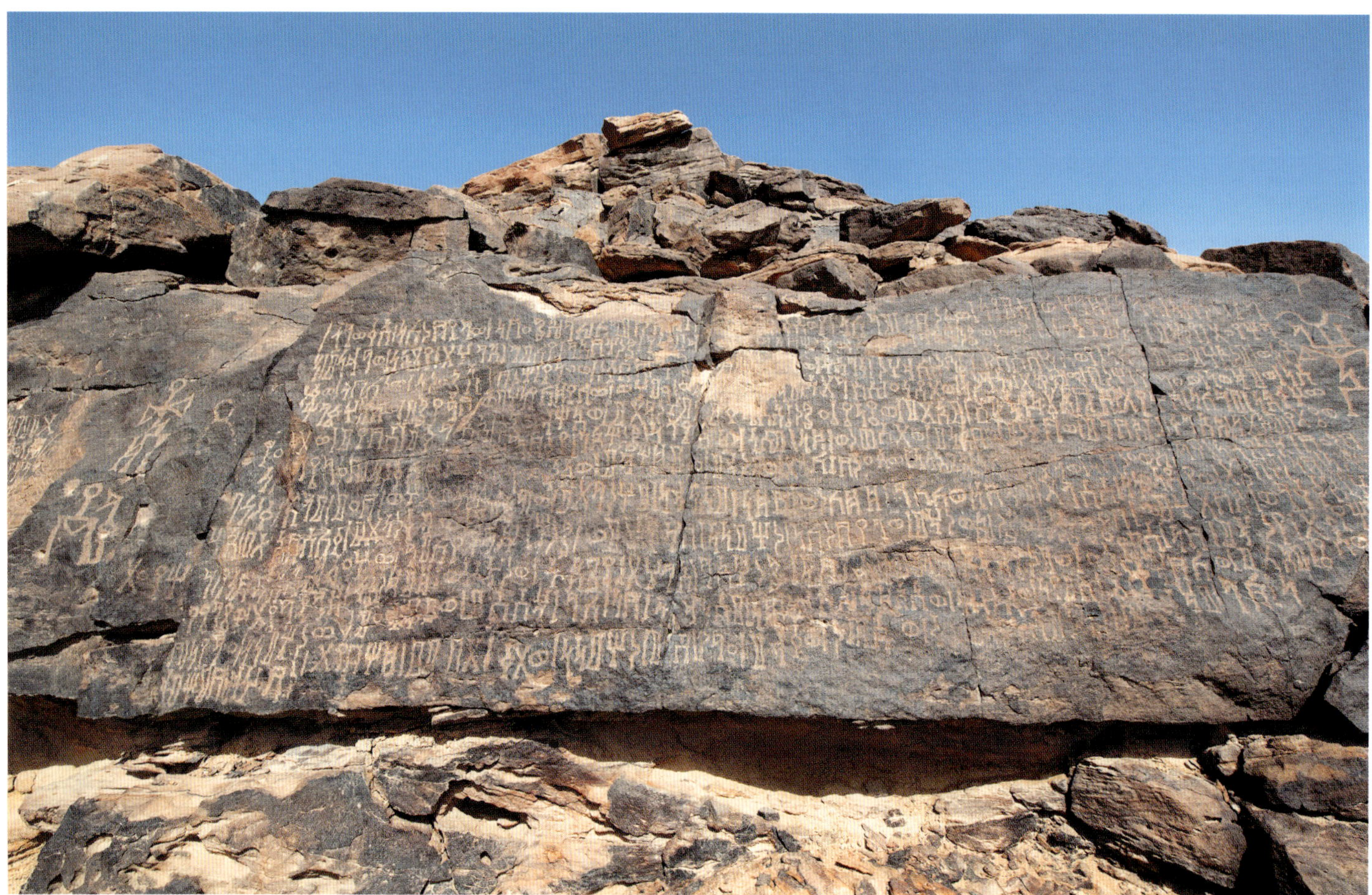

262. The inscription *Ja 1028* at Bir Hima, dated 523 CE, is part of a complex of four inscriptions and one tribal *wasm*. It proclaims that the Jewish king of Himyar, Dhu Nuwas, burnt down the Christian church in Zafar and massacred 12,000 pro-Aksumite people there, after which he directed his army against Najran. Najran province. Iron Age, southern Saudi Arabia. Photo 2020.

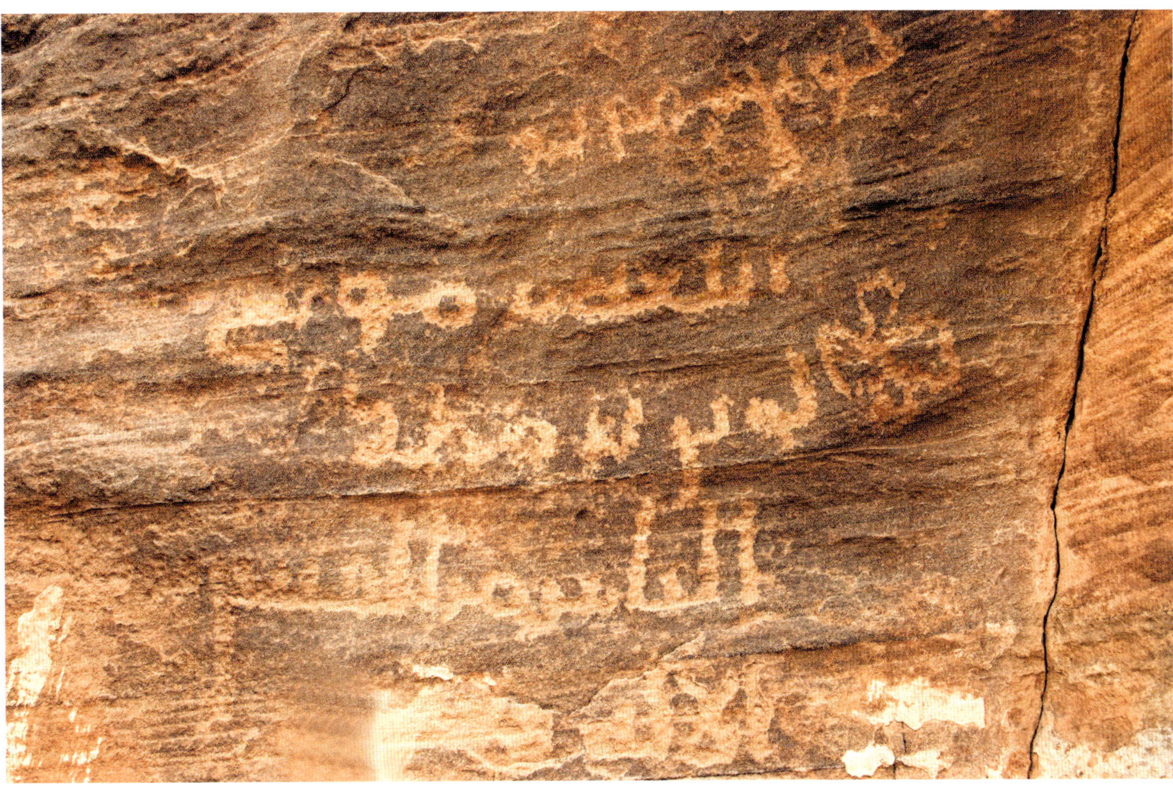

263. Palaeo-Arabic inscription *PalAr 8* at the Christian necropolis at Hima. To the right, a small Maltese cross; on the left, an inscription from the later fifth or early sixth century CE. It states: Thawban (son of) Marthad / Rabiʾa (son of) Musa (Moses) / Cross / Thawban (son of) Marthad / Eliah (son of) ʾImruʾ al-Qays (son of) Taym / (may be protected by) l-ʾIh [or rather al-ʾIlh]. Photo 2022.

return for capitulation.[182] Since he feared an Ethiopian counter-attack, he then ravaged the Tihama, the coastal region of the Red Sea opposite Ethiopia. In the Tihama, he put some 12,000 people, probably pro-Aksumite Christians, to death as stated in *Ja 1028*.[183] But the rich oasis of Najran, which had an important Christian minority, refused to recognize the new king and rebelled, whereupon Yusuf divided his forces: with the main army he continued the campaign in the Tihama while in summer 523 he sent another army against Najran whose first move was to cut communications between Najran and central Arabia. The two inscriptions *Ja 1028* at Bir Hima and *Ry 507* at nearby **Saydah** as well as *Ry 508* at Aan Halkan all date from summer 523. They reflect the victories and accomplishments over Zafar and Tihama thus far. It is clear that these three proclamations were engraved before the fall of the rebellious city of Najran later in the same year for there are no mentions of its conquest. Afterwards, in autumn 523, King Dhu Nuwas left the coastal region, as the early winter winds and storms would make an Ethiopian naval landing impossible, and reached Najran.[184] According to the sources, Dhu Nuwas repeated his treacherous offer to the besieged Christians of Najran by promising them pardon and freedom of religion if they submitted. When they capitulated in November 523,[185] Dhu Nuwas allegedly murdered the clergy and the nobility, burnt the church and massacred the Christians who refused to convert to Judaism.[186]

There is an allusion in the Quran to the massacre of Najran's Christians by Dhu Nuwas. The 85th surah, the *Surah al-Buruj*, narrates in verses 4–10 how the city's 'believers' (in pre-Islamic times the Christians) were burnt alive in a large ditch. A vast field of ruins called *al-Ukhdud*, whose name means 'wide trench', lies 10 km south of modern Najran. It was visited by Philby in 1936[187] and by the Philby-Ryckmans-Lippens expedition in 1951–52;[188] in both cases it was identified with the place where the Christian minority (or possibly even majority) of ancient Najran were massacred. But according to the archaeologist Jérémie Schiettecatte, no Christian monument has ever been identified inside the walled city, while pottery sherds with stamped cross-motifs have only been found *extra muros*.[189] The city's main rectangular structure no. 32, which is built of stone blocks, is rather related to Wadd, the Minaean god of the moon and love, since its outer walls include petroglyph-like engravings of snakes, the animal symbolizing Wadd, or of the apotropaic formula *Wadd Abb* written in Musnad script. This formula, which means 'Wadd, our father', was often inscribed on temples and amulets.[190] In southern Arabia, the moon god was worshipped in Maʾin under the name Wadd and in Saba as Almaqah. It seems that the Minaeans continued to worship Wadd even after the disappearance of their kingdom after 100 BCE. It remains uncertain whether this temple was dedicated to Wadd or Almaqah.

- **Hima necropolis** or **martyrion**. About 5 km south-east of Bir Hima, a Christian necropolis or memorial place was discovered in 2014. On two stone steles and on neighbouring rocks 16 brief inscriptions in either South Arabian Musnad (4 inscriptions) or palaeo-Arabic script (11 inscriptions) were identified; one inscription mixes the two scripts.[191] All inscriptions are provided with a Christian cross. The term **palaeo-Arabic** encompasses two groups: texts written in archaic Arabic script but whose language is Aramaic/Nabataean, which are called Nabataeo-Arabic, and texts written in archaic Arabic script and the Arabic language, which is known as pre-Islamic Arabic.[192] Three inscriptions are especially important, namely *PalAr 1, 2* and *8*:

- *PalAr 1* is a stone stele measuring 115 by 72 cm, which probably served as funeral stone.[193] The epitaph reads *Thawban Malik, in the month of Burak 364.* The date of *Burak 364* according to the Bosra era corresponds to February–March 470 CE which makes this palaeo-Arabic epigraph the oldest known inscription in Arabic letters.[194] The name *Thawban Malik* (i.e. *Thawban, son of Malik*) is engraved ten times on the various inscriptions of the necropolis which indicates that this person was highly venerated. The date of 470 falls in the period of the first persecution of Christians in the Najran region. From this one can extrapolate that Thawban Malik was a Christian martyr and the place was venerated as a martyrion. An Ethiopian source referring to the persecution of Christians in Najran in the year 470 also mentions the martyrion of a priest called Azqir; possibly Azqir and Thawban Malik were the same person. The fact that several names such as Isaac, Elijah and Moses mentioned in the sixteen epitaphs of this martyrion are clearly Christian names indicates that this place formed a Christian necropolis or memorial where, in addition, clerics were buried or remembered, for in ancient Christian southern Arabia only the clerics took unambiguously Christian names while the lay believers kept their traditional Arab names.[195]

- *PalAr 2* is also a stone stele measuring 1.85 by 1.3 m; its epitaph names *Ishaq, son of Amir.* The cross is framed by an aedicula, a tiny temple which probably indicates that Ishaq (Isaac) was a bishop.[196]

- *PalAr 8* is a rock inscription consisting of five lines and one Maltese cross; it says: *Thawban (son of) Marthad / Rabi'a (son of) Musa (Moses) / Cross / Thawban (son of) Marthad / Eliah (son of) 'Imru' al-Qays (son of) Taym / (may be protected by) l-'lh* [or rather *al-'Ilh*] (fig. 263). Important in this inscription, as well as in epitaph *PalAr10*, is the fact that they carry the word *l'lh*.[197] This proves that the Christians from Najran called their God '*al-Ilah*' – which corresponds to the Syriac term *Alaha*.[198] This term was not used by the Himyarite church based in Sana'a which named God *Rahmanan*, the 'beneficent'.[199]

To summarize the characteristics of petroglyphs in Najran, the high number of duel and battle scenes is striking. These deadly encounters mainly occurred between groups of light cavalry armed with long lances, flails, swords, sabres and, occasionally, bows. The lances often have discs fixed behind the iron point. These discs would stop the lances from passing too far through the body of a slain enemy or horse, which would prevent them from being retrieved. The horses are rendered in a gallop with legs stretched forwards and backwards, giving an arched shape. The riders are mostly mounted on horses, less often on camels. Typical examples of such battle scenes are at Fardat Sheyban (fig. 264), Umm Onaik, Najd Sehi, Barqa al-Mahanet, and especially spectacularly at Hareemah. As late as the early twentieth century, tribal armies would ride on camels on campaign or in raids and only mount their horses just before joining battle.[200] Dromedaries are much more enduring and resilient than horses which are swift and agile, but quickly tire out in action. In the petroglyphs, small dots surrounding the body and horse suggest scale armour, which was used in the Sasanian Iranian Empire (224–651 CE). Due to the hot climate, armour could only be worn for a brief period during battle. Occasionally, newer carvings featuring warriors armed with rifles are added. These numerous battle scenes indicate the warlike character of pre-Islamic society in which tribes and clans would raid and fight one another. It was the Prophet Muhammad who brought these permanent raids and tribal wars to an end and channelled the bellicose energies of the Arabs into a united war effort of conquest.

Another eye-catching motif within the petroglyphs of Najran are the more than 100[201] female figures with hands raised to the sky and long plaited or shoulder-length hair who stand in the middle of battle scenes or at their edges. All of these figures are shown without facial features such as eyes, nose, mouth or chin. Most of them have a narrow waist and wide hips, others have less pronounced hips and somewhat resemble the figures at al-Khayyur, but carry neither sword nor dagger. There appear to be no inscriptions providing information about their identity.[202] Spectacular examples are to be found at Aan al-Naam, Najd Sehi (fig. 261), Najd Musamma, Umm Onaik and Tha'er; these women are obviously connected to the battles. One interpretation identifies these lightly dressed or even naked women as the evening star Venus, whom the Arabs called Alilat according to Herodotus[203] – that is, the pre-Islamic goddess of love and war, al-Lat, one of the three daughters of Allah. Another interpretation equates this female figure with the stellar deity, *rdw* (Ruda) of Nabataean origin.[204] Both interpretations are unlikely since both goddesses were mainly popular in northern Arabia and Syria. As suggested by Michael Macdonald,[205] the solution may be found in the evidence of the British captain Gerard Leachman from 1910 and the German traveller Carl Schmidt, aka Carl Raswan, from 1928.[206] They reported that beautiful girls would ride with the warriors into battle, wear their long hair loose, and show their bare breasts while exhorting their tribesmen to courage and valour. In short, these girls acted like military cheerleaders.[207] Unfortunately, these petroglyphs of women with raised arms are not infrequently abused as shooting targets; in a few places such as Daab al-Qurthi, a contemporary petroglyph of a man aiming with his gun at such a female figure has been added. Next to these supposed 'cheerleaders', in Saudi Arabia's southern rock art one finds numerous other female figures such as birthing women or slender, standing females, whereas petroglyphs of females are less frequent in the north.

Another interesting figure specific to this southern region is an armed, tall warrior. He holds in his left hand one or two spears, occasionally also a rectangular shield, and in his right hand an object that looks like a slightly curved, narrow ladder or a small, slightly curved club with two short decorative horizontal lines; sometimes the curved club is not directly held by the warrior, but is placed close to his hand (fig. 255). This is the symbol of the south Arabian moon god, Almaqah.[208] The most important temples of Almaqah stood in the Sabaean cities of Marib and Sirwah in today's Yemen; both belonged to the Sabaean kingdom until the late third century CE. A further famous temple dedicated to Almaqah (or Wadd) stood in Najran. Whether these petroglyphs represent Almaqah himself[209] or warriors

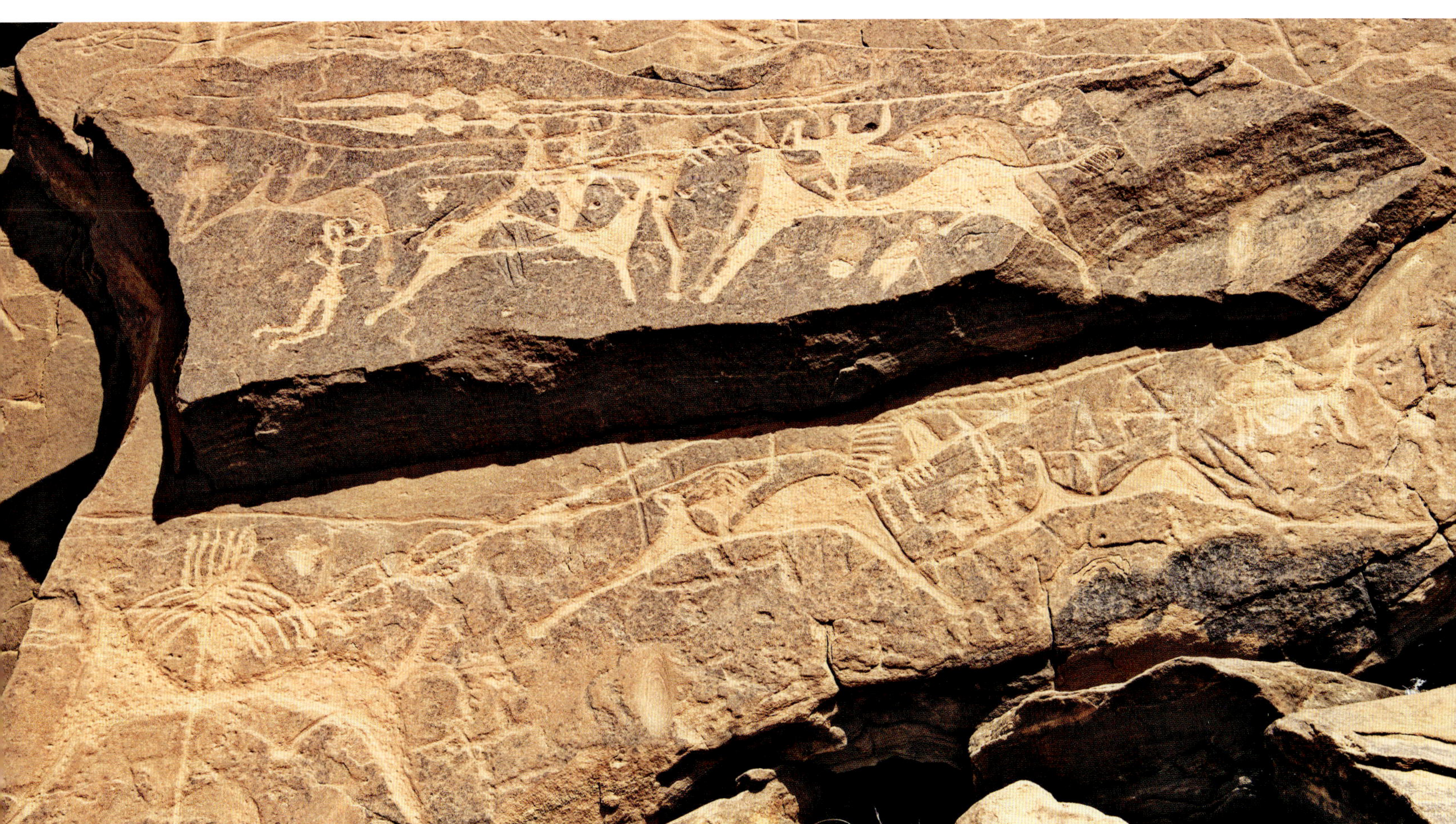

264. Combat scene between mounted lancers at Fardat Sheyban, *ca.* middle first millennium CE. The lances of the horsemen above have small discs fixed behind the iron point in order to stop the lances from passing too far through the body of a slain enemy or horse, which would make it difficult to retrieve them. Najran province, southern Saudi Arabia. Photo 2020.

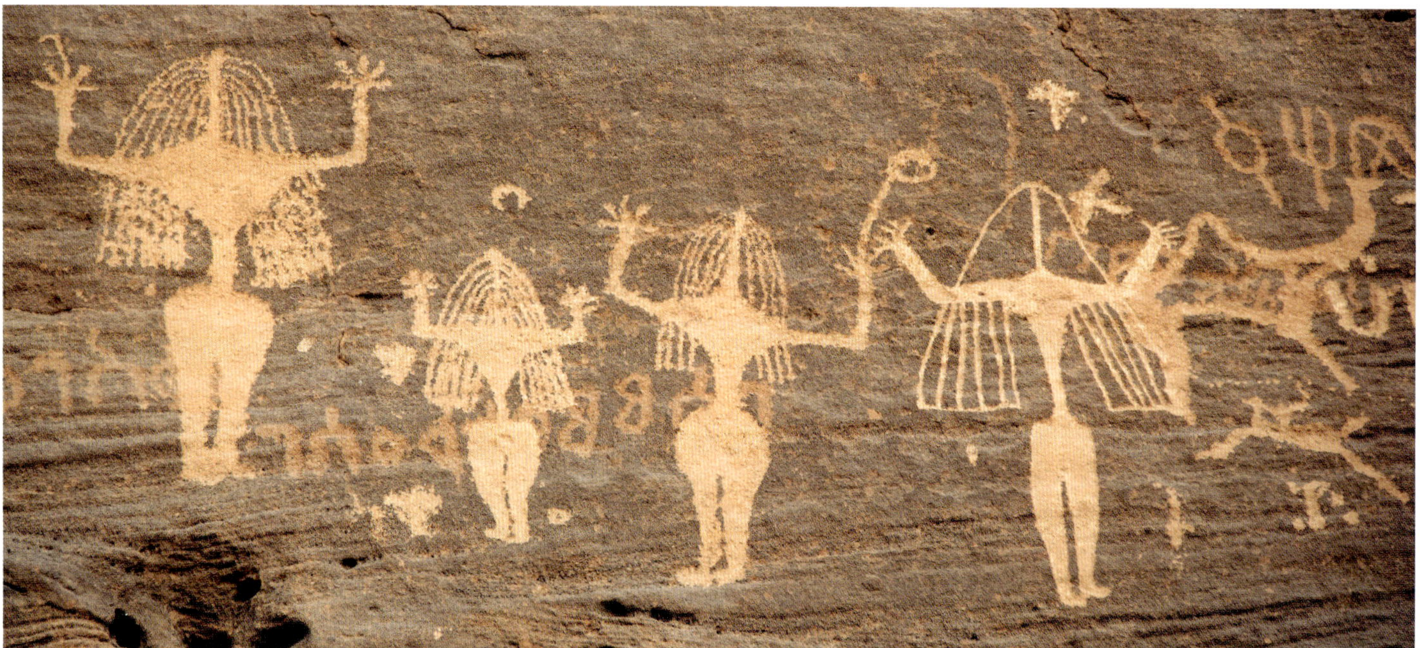

265. Four women with raised arms and long braided hair. *ca.* middle first millennium CE. Tha'er, site 4, Najran province, southern Saudi Arabia. Photo 2022.

in his service remains unknown; such figures are featured, among other places, at Aan al-Naam, al-Kheir and Thajar. A very similar attribute to the curved ladder looks like a large letter H with two straight horizontal cross-beams whose vertical bars are not curved, but straight; this is associated with Dhu Samawi, the protector of camels. Such petroglyphs are found at Qaryat al-Faw,[210] Aan Halkan East and al-Kheir. Like Almaqah and Wadd, Dhu Samawi was also a lunar deity.

Similar figures, but without the curved club, appear in petroglyphs at Wajjid and in the Wadi al-Naqha. At the latter site the warrior wears a feathered headdress, chest armour and a lunate pommel-handled dagger. He holds two spears in his left hand and one in his right, whereas the figure at Wajjid holds one spear in each hand; both warriors wear spurs (fig. 258). Probably these two petroglyphs at Wajjid and Wadi al-Naqha are also connected to Almaqah. The association of these singular petroglyphs with the southern Arabian god Almaqah is the more likely as according to Strabo, in the last decades of the first millennium BCE Najran belonged to the Kingdom of Saba which soon became a protectorate of Himyar.[211] After a subsequent period of independence, around 275 CE Saba was annexed by Himyar.[212]

Also conspicuous in Najran are the petroglyphs testifying to the former presence of Christianity. Relatively often inscriptions are encountered beginning with a cross at their right-hand side. As already mentioned, a cross was not only used as a Christian symbol; it could be a tribal mark or the Thamudic letter 'ta'. But in certain

contexts, this petroglyph signals Christianity. Examples are the two Maltese crosses at Gar al-Sidiri, since one of the inscribed names reads *sml* which most probably means 'Samuel'. The region of Hima and the trading city of Najran had a significant Christian community around the middle of the first millennium.[213] The Christians of Najran thrived until Caliph Umar (r. 634–644) ordered their eviction from southern Arabia and their transfer to Iraq.[214] The most obvious proof of a Christian presence is the above-mentioned necropolis or martyrion of Hima with its Christian inscriptions. Finally, a very surprising Christian symbol was discovered by the authors in Wadi al-Naqha, namely what looks like the petroglyph of a crucifix overlaid on the recurved horns of an ibex (fig. 266). The fifteen-centimetre-high crucified body and drooping head are easily recognizable; much later, another cross was carved over the bottom portion of the image.

What is striking when attempting to interpret the petroglyphs of Saudi Arabia is the apparent difficulty of connecting them to myths, for within the realm of the Arabian Peninsula little remains of the heritage of myths, or rather little is known about them. Whereas many local or regional deities are recorded thanks to inscriptions, there exists hardly any mythological lore characterizing these deities and their relationships with each other and with the human race. Either there never existed a mythology in Arabia comparable to the Indian Vedas or the Norse or Greek myths revolving around gods and goddesses, or, more likely, they were never written down. And when Islam prevailed, the myths were devalued as a relic of *Jahiliyya*, the Age of Ignorance, and fell into oblivion.[215]

2. Jordan

The Kingdom of Jordan shares a border with Saudi Arabia for 700 kilometres and its geology and climatic conditions are in its eastern half comparable to those in the Saudi kingdom. Jordan's eastern part can be roughly divided into three regions: in the north is the so-called 'panhandle' which borders Syria, Iraq and Saudi Arabia and was created in the early 1920s by the British mandatory power, to separate Syria from the expansionary Sultanate of Najd, the predecessor of the Kingdom of Saudi Arabia. This region includes the governorates of Mafraq and Zarqa and mainly comprises the Black Desert, a desertic volcanic landscape of basalt, similar to the Saudi Arabian *harrat*. To the south comes Ma'an governorate whose territory is mainly filled by mountainous desert landscapes. The south-west of Ma'an governorate borders Wadi Rum which is a desertic system of valleys cut into ferrous sandstone. Granite blocks occasionally protrude from the layer of sand. In all three regions, petroglyphs and inscriptions are found. Being close to Saudi Arabia, the climates of these regions are similar to those on the other side of the border, with the difference that the western disturbances originating in the Mediterranean region bring sudden and heavy winter rains which are more pronounced in Jordan than in Saudi Arabia.

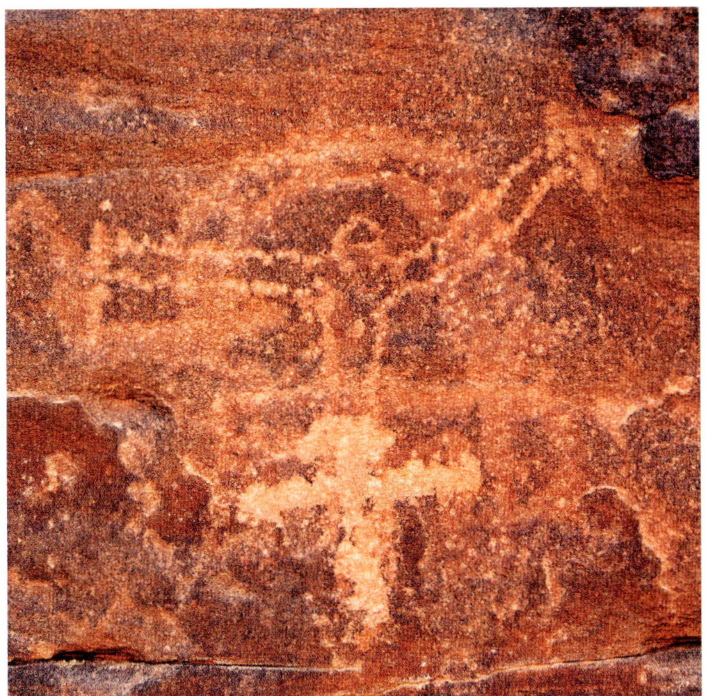

266. What is probably a crucifix superimposed on the horns of an ibex; the brighter cross is more recent. Wadi al-Naqha, Najran province, southern Saudi Arabia. Photo 2020.

2.1. The Black Desert

The Black Desert, also called *Harrat al-Sham*, stretches from south-eastern Syria through the western half of Jordan's 'panhandle' into north-western Saudi Arabia, over an area of about 40,000 square kilometres. In administrative terms, this hyper-arid desert of vast basalt fields covers the western half of Mafraq governorate and the northern half of that of Zarqa. In the north-western corner of Mafraq governorate, petroglyphs were made on black basalt rocks and on reddish, ferrous basalt stones which look similar to sandstone. In the Black Desert, it is not only the ancient monuments built from black basalt such as the medieval fortress of Azraq[216] or the Byzantine town of Umm al-Jimal that are famous, but also the 'desert kite' traps (see p. 258) and the petroglyphs that illustrate them. Whereas large and detailed petroglyphs of kites, made to scale, are very rare, there are dozens of smaller kite engravings. Whether they served as a kind of simple instruction on how to build kites or as a kind of charm to secure a lucky hunt remains unknown. The huge traps were built for catching large herd-dwelling desert and steppe animals such as gazelles, lesser kudu, Syrian wild asses and possibly also wild dromedaries. Interestingly, the openings of these desert traps, which were often linked together, were mostly oriented to the south-east, that is against of the wind which predominantly blew from the north-west.[217] This gave the pursuing hunters the advantage, since they were able to attack their prey from downwind and thus remain for a long while unnoticed. So far, desert kite traps have not been properly dated, with the estimates for the majority of them varying between 7000 and 3000 BCE.[218]

Particular to the Black Desert, in addition, are the more than 20,000 Safaitic inscriptions (fig. 267). The Safaitic alphabet comprised 28 letters and was used to write North Arabian dialects. It was widespread from the first century BCE to the fourth century CE in south-eastern Syria, eastern Jordan and north-western Saudi Arabia. By far the majority of the Safaitic inscriptions were personal messages such as names, genealogical records, prayers for successful raids or for rain, votive donations or captions to petroglyphs. For example, such a caption was engraved on a ferrous basalt stone whose petroglyphs show a woman playing a flute and a dancing man. The Safaitic inscription explains: 'By Aqraban, son of Kasit, son of Saad, the beautiful woman playing the reed pipe'.[219] Other petroglyph motifs include the Nubian ibex, the scimitar-horned oryx with long curving horns bent backwards, the Arabian oryx with long, rather vertical horns, addax antelopes with slightly twisted horns as well as greater and lesser kudu with strongly twisted horns. The petroglyphs also illustrate onagers,

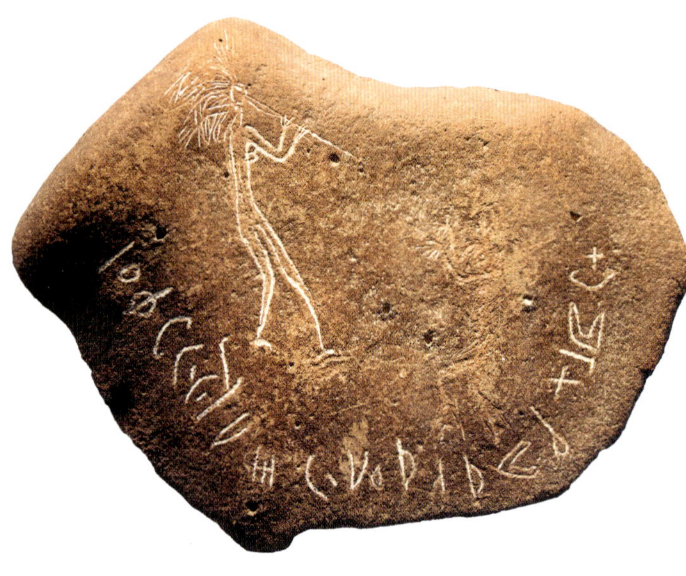

267. Petroglyphs on a ferrous basalt stone of a slim woman playing the flute for a dancing man. The Safaitic inscriptions explains: 'By Aqraban, son of Kasit, son of Saad, the beautiful woman playing the reed pipe'. Jordan National Museum, Amman.

mausoleum or funerary marker. The image of the pair of feet inside the *nefesh* suggests the symbolic presence of the deceased; it is a memorial not connected to any actual tomb. The two *nefeshes* also contain inscriptions which unfortunately are illegible. To imply the presence of a dead person by his footprints alone fits with the religious attitude of the Nabataeans who avoided representing their deities in an anthropomorphic way and restricted themselves to suggesting their presence in the shape of betyls, that is four-sided stones or pilasters.

About 50 kilometres north of Petra and ten kilometres south of Tafila lies the village of Qaryat al-Sila and the archaeological site of **al-Sila**. The latter consists of a rugged sandstone outcrop whose highest plateau towers some 200 metres above the surrounding valleys. The place was once part of the Kingdom of Udumu (Edom) and served as a stronghold of refuge. On the plateau there are ruins of fortifications, dwelling caves, houses, sanctuaries and cisterns. The site was first mentioned in 1907 by the Czech orientalist, explorer and spy Alois Musil, yet its petroglyph of a standing human figure and the inscription in the Neo-Babylonian Akkadian language and cuneiform writing were only rediscovered in 1994. The relief and inscription were engraved on the steep eastern face

horsemen, camels, ostriches and occasionally bovines, lions and *wusum*.[220] Finally, besides Safaitic inscriptions, there are also ones in Thamudic and Arabic.

2.2. Petra and al-Sila

In the west of Ma'an governorate lies the ancient capital of the Nabataeans, **Petra**, which was annexed to the Roman Empire by Emperor Trajan in the year 106 CE. While its monumental rock-cut mausolea are world-famous, its petroglyphs, at the top of its highest peak, Umm al-Biyara, are hardly known. Next to a Nabataean sanctuary with cultic niches, the petroglyphs represent small ibexes, horsemen armed with spears, hunting scenes, camels and prints of shoe soles.[221] The latter probably suggest the presence of the believers who visited the sanctuary. That the petroglyphs of shoe soles have a religious meaning within the Nabataean environment is also implied by the few large petroglyphs at the archaeological site of Beidha (Bayda) located a few kilometres north of Petra. These petroglyphs mainly represent several prints of shoe soles and feet with marked toes. Especially noteworthy are two pairs of feet placed within the lower part of an engraved tower-like structure ending in a pointed pyramid.[222] This tower-like structure represents, in a Nabataean context, a *nefesh*, that is a

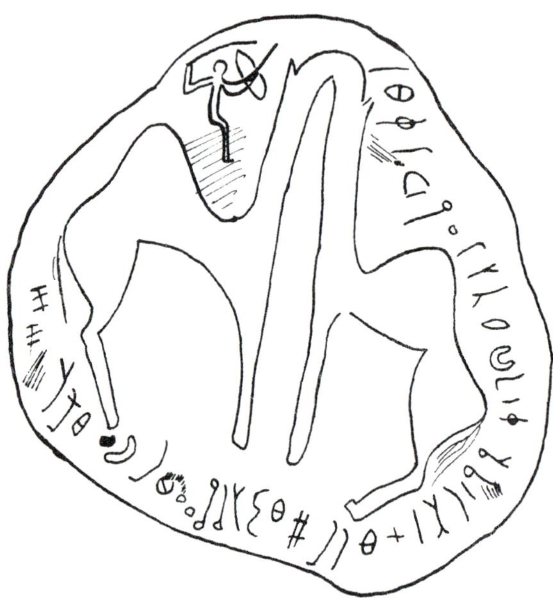

268. Ink drawing of two dromedaries which are connected at their heads. The Safaitic inscription says: 'By Wqr [Waqar], son of Ya'l, are the two male camels which have been dedicated to 'lt [al-Lat] and to Rdw [Rudaw]; so, O Yt̲' [Yayta], blind whosoever would efface this [writing].' Safaitic inscription copied by Maurice Dunand in Syrian Harrah in the 1920s–30s. Published in Ryckmans, Gonzague (ed.), *Corpus Inscriptionum Semiticarum. Pars V, Inscriptiones Saracenicas Continens*, vol. 1: *Inscriptiones Safaiticae* (Paris: Imprimerie nationale, 1950–51), pl. 70, siglum C 1658 (= Dunand 388).

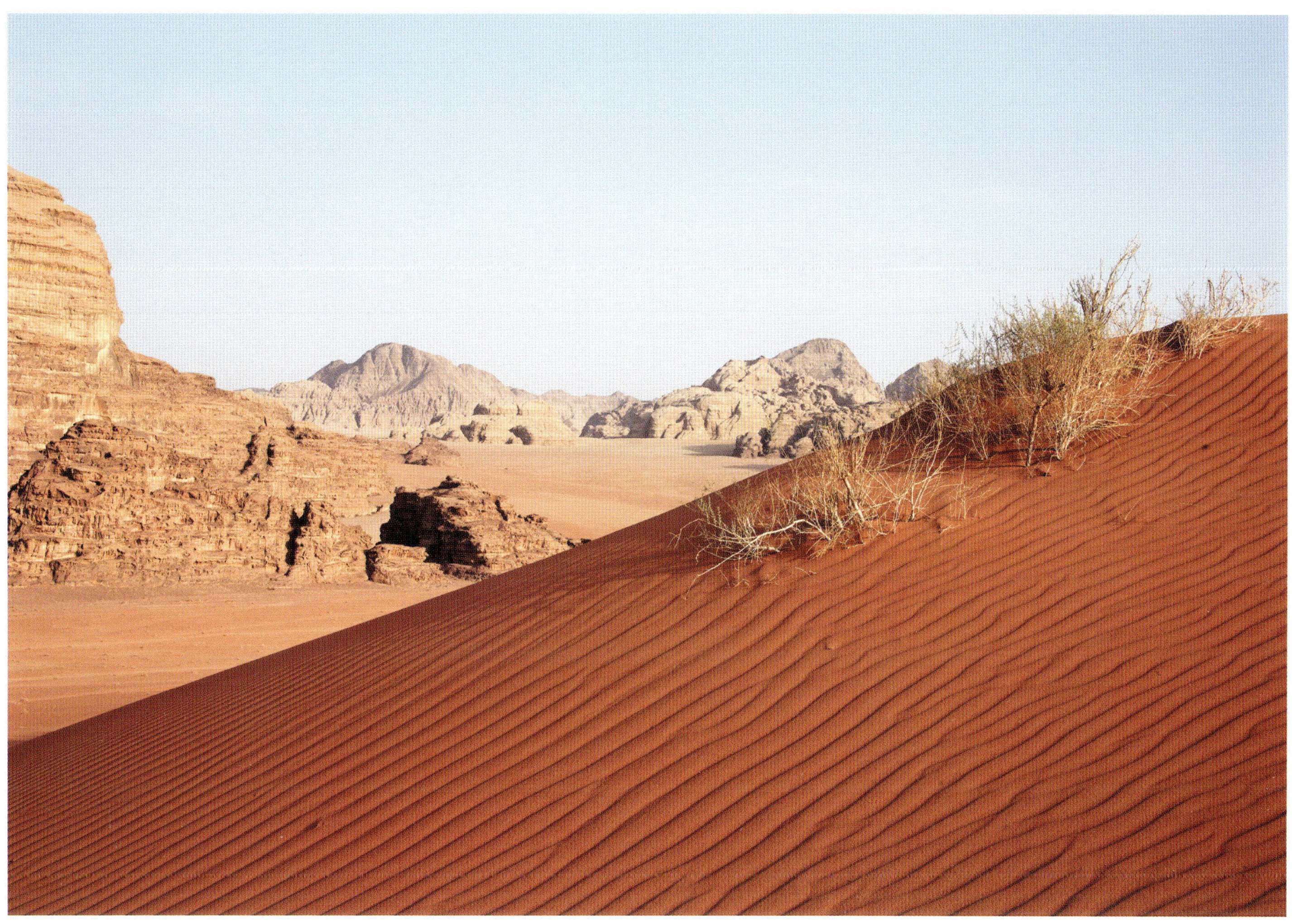

269. Sand dune near Jabal Nadur, Wadi Rum, Jordan. Photo 2022.

of the main promontory at an inaccessible place about 120 metres above the floor of the valley and 90 metres above a narrow terrace. It is probable that the makers of the inscription had to abseil from the top, about 20 metres above the rock art, or they had to build a scaffolding from the narrow terrace. The petroglyphic monument is 302 centimetres long and 224 centimetres high, and was probably originally painted in bright colours.[223] Unfortunately, the two inscriptions are so weathered that they are indecipherable except for a few lines.

The design of the petroglyphic scene is very similar to the Nabonid rock relief at al-Ha'it, Saudi Arabia. As it is confirmed in the inscription, which states 'I am Nabonid, king of Babylon',[224] the petroglyph of the standing man wearing a long robe and a conical headdress represents King Nabonid. By his head is a high relief of a crescent moon, the symbol of Nabonid's favoured moon god Sin. Then follow the solar disc symbolizing the sun god Samas (Salm) and the star indicating the goddess of the morning star Ishtar. So

far, the design of the al-Sila relief follows the one of al-Ha'it, but the solar symbol is slightly different. At al-Ha'it, the sun has two wings and a trapezoid tail which was a common representation in a Neo-Assyrian context. But at al-Sila, the sun symbol is not only winged and tailed, but it has a second trapezoidal figure on its top which looks like a second tail shown upside-down. This additional element seems to transform the solar symbol into a cross symbol, namely a so-called cross pattée, a Greek cross with four equal arms that flare at the ends. However, as observed by the Assyriologist Rocio Da Riva, there are no indications that the petroglyph of the traditional Assyrian winged and tailed sun symbol was transformed into a Christian symbol at a later date. Furthermore, the cross pattée had already appeared in conjunction with the solar disc in Neo-Assyrian stone monuments.[225] Based on an uncertain reading of a couple of words as 'fifth year', it is assumed that this time mark dates the inscription into the fifth year of Nabonid's reign, that is 551 BCE.[226]

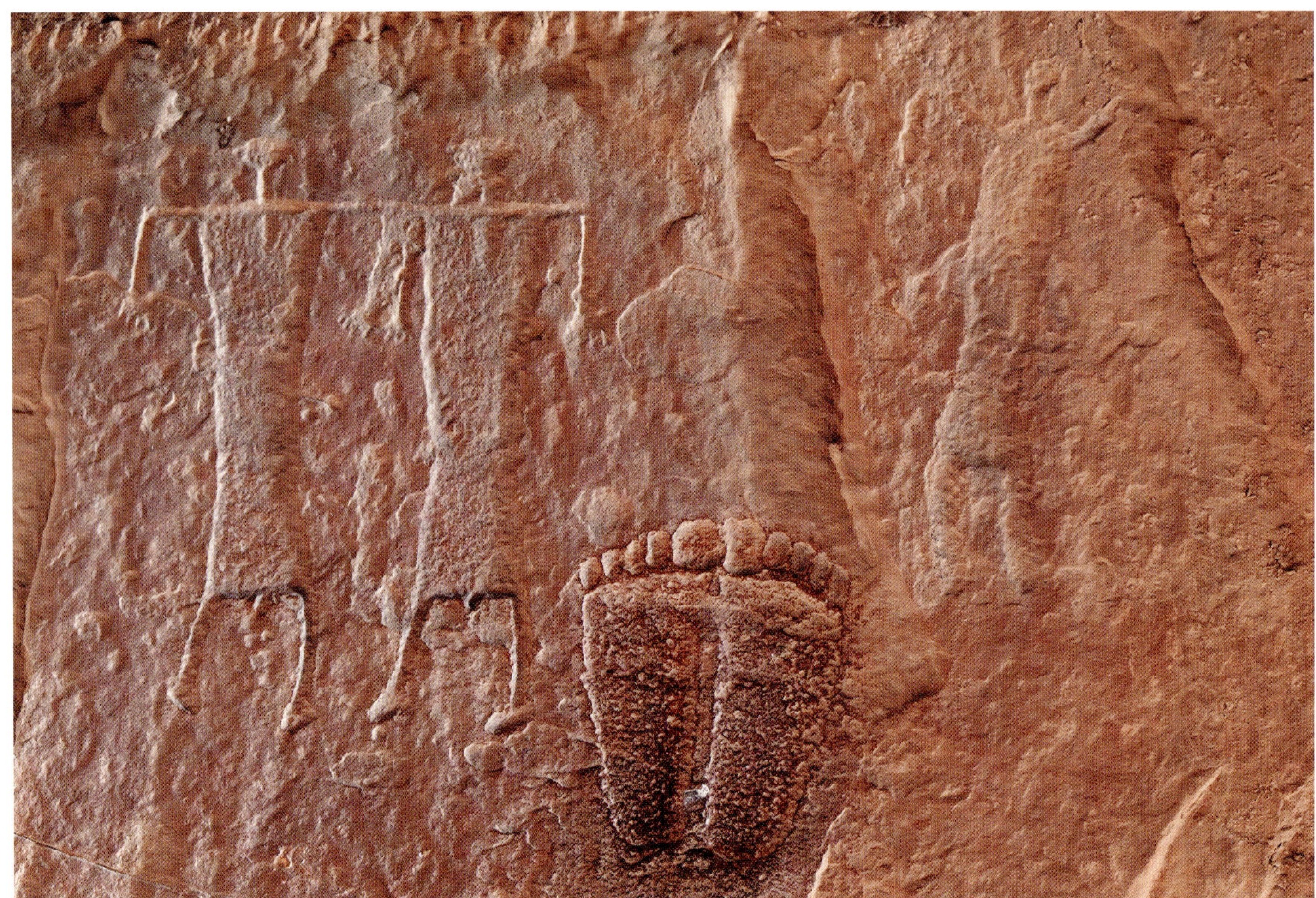

270. Three slender human figures and a pair of footprints, Kaz'ali Siq, Wadi Rum, Jordan. Photo 2022.

2.3. Wadi Rum

Like the fortress of Azraq, Wadi Rum is associated with T.E. Lawrence, for it was from this mountainous desert valley, which served him as an operational base, that he mounted the successful attack on Aqaba in July 1917.[227] The canyons and wadis of Wadi Rum, whose surface area extends over 730 square kilometres, began to be formed 20 million years ago when aeolian and fluvial erosion started to cut through the 700-metre-thick sandstone layer to create the spectacular shapes that are visible today. In addition, the landscape has often been subject to suddenly alteration by earthquakes. Here, as in other mountainous desert regions, geology and climate act as 'landscape sculptors'. Extrapolating the past developments into the future, one can assume that in around twenty million years only isolated sandstone pillars will remain, like at Gharameel in Saudi Arabia's Ha'il Province. Due to a high concentration of iron oxide in the sand particles, some of the dunes have a bright orange-red colour. In areas near Wadi Rum, archaeological excavations indicate human occupation since the Upper

Palaeolithic, about 19,000 years ago.[228] Thanks to the numerous water sources, nomadic settlements existed inside the valley from the Neolithic, about 7,000 years ago. Flints found in rock shelters indicate that people were occasionally visiting the area about two millennia earlier. Water sources were available, since the winter rainwater brought by the Mediterranean westerlies seeped through the porous sandstone and was held back by the underlying impermeable layer of granite. The accumulated water then either emerged in the valley as springs or formed subterranean pockets of water that were easy to tap. Petroglyphs of bovines hint at a wetter climate during the Neolithic and suggest, together with the remains of Neolithic settlements,[229] a partial sedentarism when cattle were able to survive. The finds of numerous sherds of Qurayyah Painted Ware indicate that during the thirteenth to eleventh centuries BCE the region of Wadi Rum most probably belonged to the realm of the Midianite confederation whose main settlement was Qurayyah, north of Tabuk.[230] The zone of influence of the northern Arabian Midianites extended as far as Wadi Araba, located 100 kilometres north of Wadi Rum, which possessed rich deposits of copper ore. Wadi Rum was right in the middle of the direct line of communication between Qurayyah and Wadi Araba, and its sources and wells made an ideal stopping place for trade caravans. The lack of evidence for Iron Age settlements, however, indicates a return to a mobile life and economy. As told by the al-Sila inscription 140 kilometres north of Wadi Rum, Nabonid occupied Edom, which probably also controlled Wadi Rum, around 551 BCE. About two centuries later, the Nabatu, that is the Nabataeans, expanded into Wadi Rum and incorporated it into their network of trade routes. But in the periods of Roman and Byzantine domination, Wadi Rum declined in importance as a caravan stop, since the majority of trade between the Empire and southern Arabia and India now went via the maritime route through the Red Sea.

Wadi Rum counts not only *ca.* 25,000 figurative and geometrical petroglyphs, but also about 20,000 inscriptions, mainly in Hismaic (Thamudic E), Safaitic, Nabataean and Arabic Kufic scripts, occasionally also in Minaean,[231] Greek and Latin. It also boasts a spectacular landscape with bizarre sandstone formations, red sand dunes and huge natural arches such as the easily accessible **Khor al-Ajram Arch**, the highly impressive fifteen-metre-high **Umm Fruth Arch** and the *ca.* 30-metre-high **Jabal Burdah Rock Bridge** in the south-east of Wadi Rum. Since petroglyphs and inscriptions are found at countless places, only the most important ones are listed here.

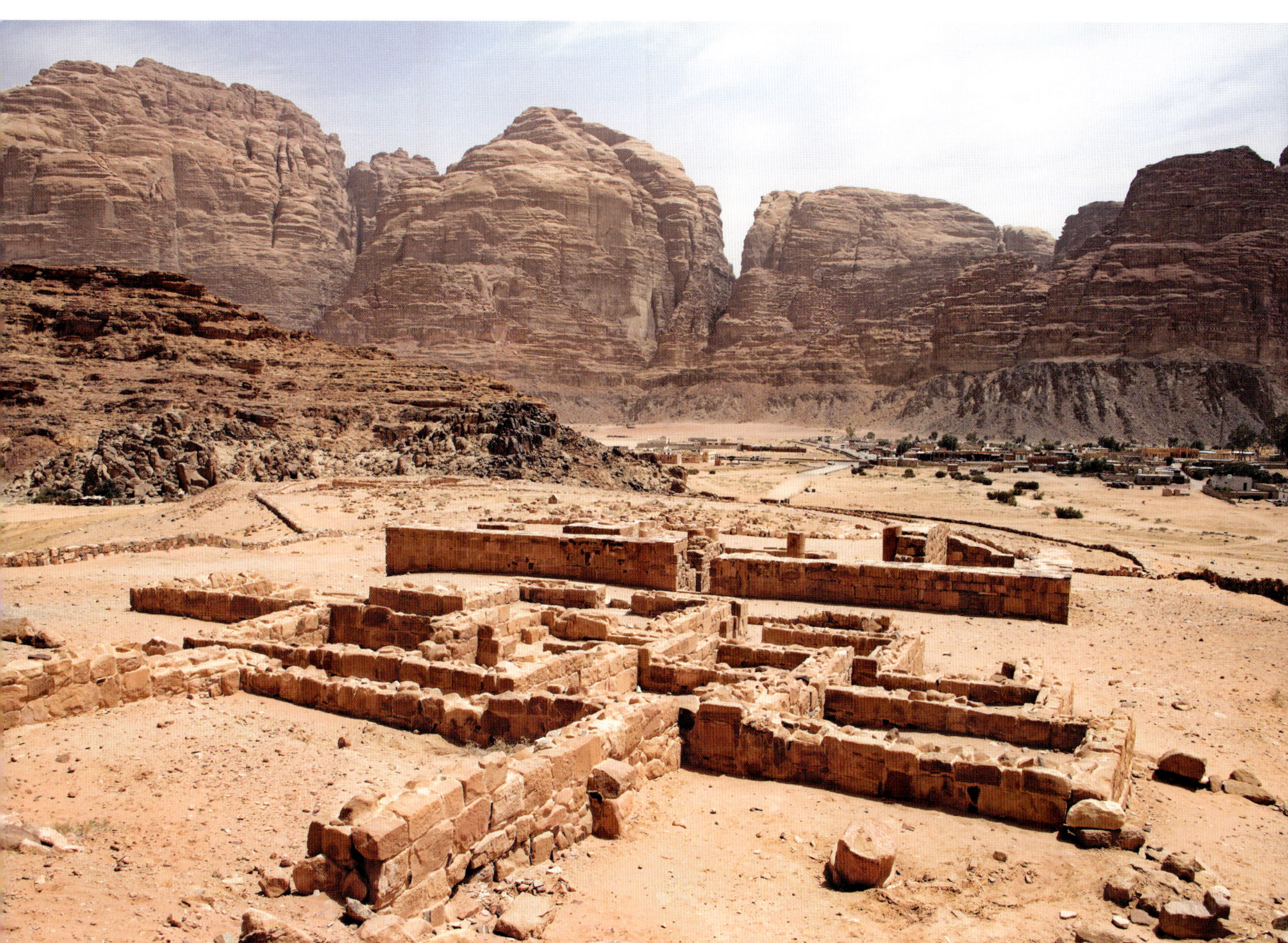

271. Ruins of the Nabataean temple in Wadi Rum which was completed in 100–101 CE. Jordan. Photo 2022.

- **Kaz'ali Siq.** The Gorge of Kaz'ali is a narrow abyss in the centre of the wadi with numerous inscriptions in Hismaic and the early Arabic Kufic script. As well as this there are petroglyphs of horses, lions, ibexes, bovines, ostriches, a swastika, horsemen and schematized quadrupeds each with two humans engraved inside their bodies. Very intriguing are the petroglyphs, executed in a singular style, of two fully chiselled-out figures of slim humans 42 cm tall next to a 25-cm-long pair of footprints (fig. 270). Two other slender humans stand nearby. These striking petroglyphs most likely had a commemorative function; they were either a memorial for deceased persons or votive offerings made by pilgrims.

- **'The Map'** lies 2 km north of Kaz'ali. The three rocks lying at the edge of a basalt ridge have no maps engraved, but one of them features a bovine which dates to the late Neolithic and earlier Bronze Age when the climatic conditions were more favourable to cattle raising. Other petroglyphs show a scared man harassed by a snake and a wolf, a small lion, a camel and Hismaic inscriptions.

- **Anfasieh, Al-Meleh** and **Udayb al-Rin** are sites lying relatively close to each other with inscriptions (most of them Hismaic), camels and camel-riders, lancers and humans with raised arms. At **Hadeibat al-Gawafel**, the 'Hill of caravans', two petroglyphs of ibexes with ultra-long recurved horns are striking. All these petroglyphs date from the late Iron Age and the first millennium CE.

- **Umm Sabatah** is 4 km south of Kaz'ali. Here, a larger panel features a duel between a foot soldier armed with a bow against a mounted lancer, hunters, two ostriches and a leopard attacking an ibex.

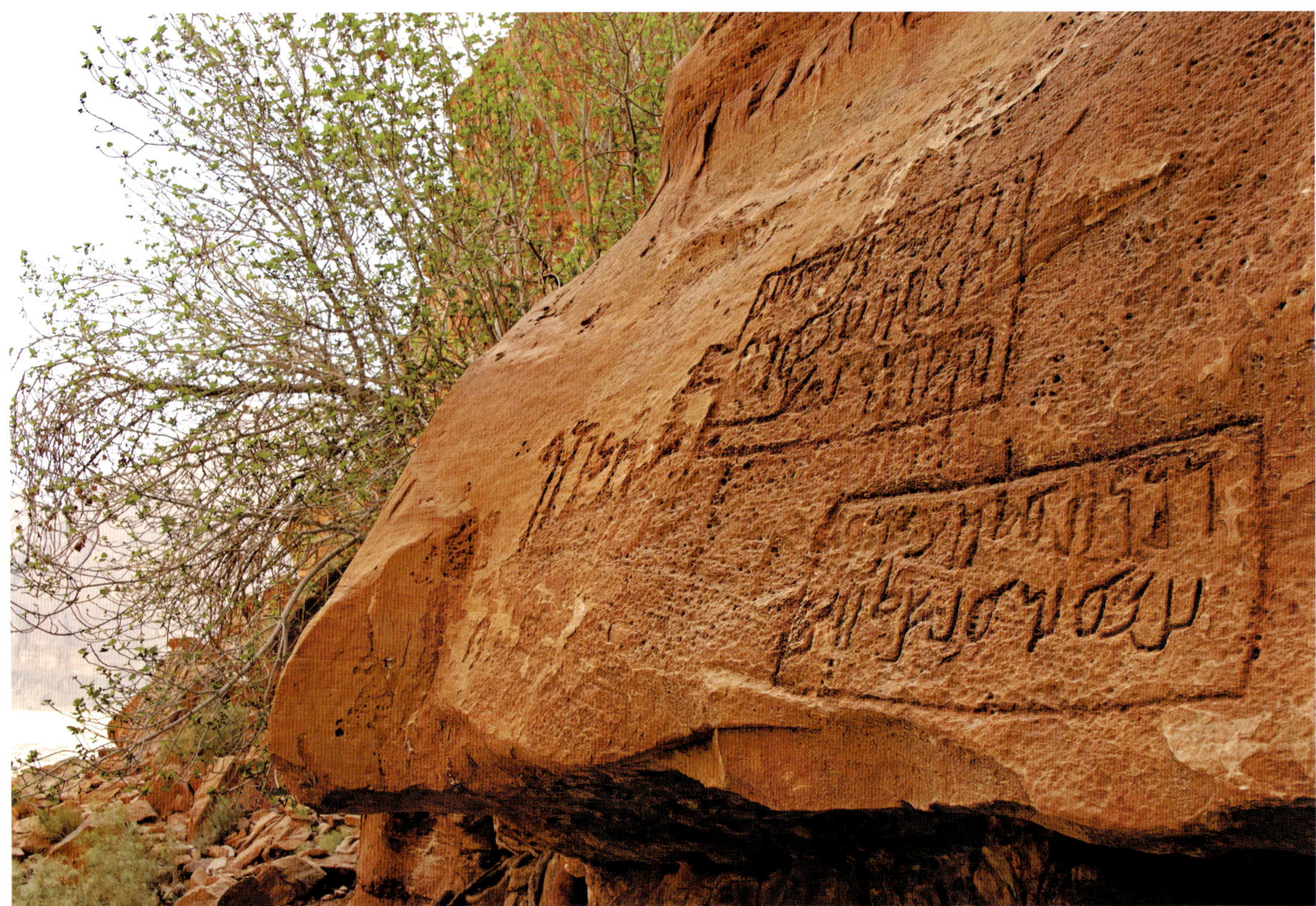

272. Nabataean inscriptions at the Nabataean rock sanctuary of Ayn Sallaleh, Wadi Rum, Jordan. Photo 2022.

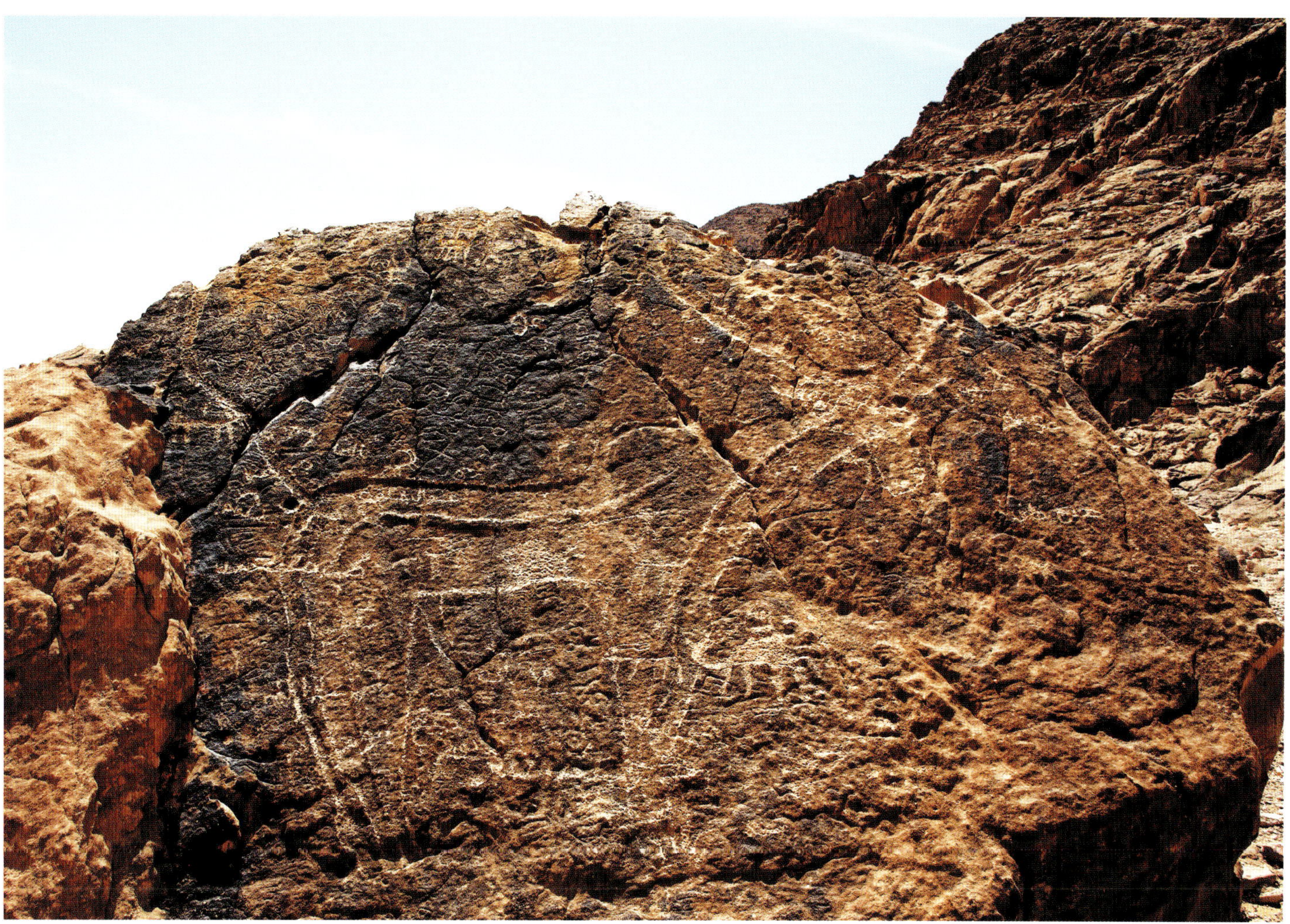

273. Petroglyph of a large bull with mighty horns which looks like an East African Sanga long-horned bull on an isolated boulder in Wadi Hafir north of Wadi Rum. Middle of first millennium CE. Jordan. Photo 2022.

- **Umm al-Dami** is further south, about 19 km south of Umm Sabatah. At this site the petroglyphs of foot- and handprints as well as of arms are noteworthy.

- **Al-Husn** is a solitary boulder in the plain east of the Jabal Burdah Rock Bridge. The strongly weathered petroglyphs show a dozen ibexes, four bulls with large horns in the shape of a lyre which date from the late Neolithic or the Bronze Age, and an oryx whose horns are double the length of its body. Whereas cattle have not been able to survive in Wadi Rum since the Iron Age, the oryx disappeared only in the 1930s due to the new fashion of hunting from cars.

- **Nabataean Temple**. Just to the west of the small village of Rum stand the ruins of a Nabataean temple (fig. 271). As we know from an inscription, the first sanctuary was pre-Nabataean and dedicated to the pre-Islamic goddess al-Lat, to whom another smaller sanctuary was dedicated within the valley at Umm al-Qesir. This dedication reads: 'In remembrance of Hayan, son of Abd Allahi, son of Ibn ʾAtmu, for al-Lat, the goddess [who resides] in Iram, for ever.'[232] Based on this evidence, and on another inscription in Nabataean script at the spring Ayn Sallaleh near the main temple, it has been assumed that Wadi Rum is identical with the *Land of Iram* mentioned in the Quran in the Surah al-Fajr (verses 6–14).[233] In this surah, the Quran warns those who refuse to recognize Allah as the only god by mentioning the divine punishment inflicted on Iram and its Thamud population. Assuming that the Quranic Iram designates Wadi Rum, it follows that its settlement was, by the time of the Prophet, an abandoned ruin. The second, Nabataean temple was probably built in two stages, for one inscription mentions King Aretas IV (r. 9 BCE–40 CE) and another states: 'This is the sanctuary commissioned by Ailamu, son of Amru, for Dushara [the main god of the Nabataeans], the god of our master Rabbel the king, in the year 31 of Rabbel, king of Nabataea'.[234] Since Rabbel II ruled from 70 to 106 CE, the dedication dates from 100–101 CE.

- **Ayn Sallaleh.** High above the Nabatean temple there are a couple of natural springs in the mountain which still give water in spite of the arid climate. The path to the sources is lined with boulders engraved with petroglyphs such as camels, horses, camel riders, geometric signs and Hismaic and Arabic inscriptions. The largest spring is Ayn Sallaleh, whose Nabataean inscriptions, close to a Nabataean rock sanctuary, were first mentioned by T.E. Lawrence (fig. 272).[235] In the cliff, four betyls are engraved, one of them featuring a crescent moon lying on a kind of altar, from whose concave side rises a short column. Three of the Nabataean inscriptions are framed by a rectangle with handles on both sides. Some of the inscriptions are official dedications to different deities, others are personal invocations. Among the deities invoked are those mainly venerated in northern and central Arabia such as the goddesses al-Lat, al-'Uzza and al-Kutba,[236] then Dushara, the principal god of the Nabataeans and the Syrian god Baalshamin. As mentioned above, one inscription names the place Iram and is dated to the reign of King Rabbel II.[237]

- **Wadi Hafir.** This 15-km-long wadi lies north-east of Wadi Rum and harbours countless petroglyphs dating mainly from the Iron Age and earlier as well as thousands of Hismaic inscriptions. About 34 km north-east of Kaz'ali, in the middle of the wadi, there is a unique petroglyph of a huge bull with mighty horns; the image is 3.1 m long and 2.4 m high. The bull was carved onto Hismaic inscriptions and got later superimposed by images of camels, an oryx, and Arabic inscriptions (fig. 273). The head and horns of the bull look similar to those of the large Sanga long-horned cattle originating in East Africa. In the whole of Wadi Rum and surrounding areas there is no other petroglyph of this size or style. Since the bull image dates from a late or post-Hismaic yet pre-Islamic period around 500 CE, the inspiration cannot come from Jubbah or Shuwaymis, where the large petroglyphs of bulls are four to six millennia older and, moreover, have a different appearance.

3. Oman

The Sultanate of Oman shares in the south a 275-kilometre-long border with Yemen, in the west a 650-kilometre-long frontier with Saudi Arabia and in the north-west 320 kilometres with the United Arab Emirates (UAE). Oman is isolated from the rest of Arabia on its western side by the Rub' al-Khali desert, and on its eastern flank it is exposed to the extensions of the Indian Ocean Monsoon. This means that during the early Holocene wet period, Oman was the first region of Arabia to receive higher rainfall, and conversely, when the ongoing climatic aridification began, Oman benefited the longest from the rainfall that was retreating to the east. A reconstruction of the palaeoclimate of northern and central Oman over the last 30,000 years shows a relatively close correlation with the climatic developments in the Rub' al-Khali in central Saudi Arabia. Following a relatively wet, pluvial period interspersed with brief dry intervals from *ca.* 30 ka to 19 ka BP, aridification set in which in Oman culminated in a hyper-arid period from 16.3 to 13 ka BP. In central Saudi Arabia, this hyper-arid period had already begun around 17 ka BP while Oman continued to benefit from the retreating monsoon rains for about 700 years. At that time, the Persian Gulf was virtually dry and its earlier potential for vaporization had become non-existent. From 13 ka BP, the early Holocene climatic improvement set in, triggering a renewed pluvial period that lasted till *ca.* 4500 BCE; at the same time, water quickly refilled the basin of the Persian Gulf.[238] A sub-pluvial transitional phase then began which gradually led, around 2000 BCE or shortly thereafter, to the present arid conditions.

The human history of Oman's later Pleistocene is not well known. In April 2023, an international team claimed to have found in the southern Omani governorate of Dhofar stone hand-axes at least 300,000 years old.[239] More broadly supported are the conclusions drawn from the surface finds of dozens of stone tools in Dhofar in 2010–11. These lithic artefacts belong to the so-called Late Nubian cultural complex, previously only known from Sudan and the Horn of Africa, which is roughly dated to 128–74 ka BP, that is to MIS 5. Applying the Optically Stimulated Luminescence method, the Dhofar finds have been dated to 106 ka BP.[240] Later expeditions identified similar artefacts manufactured in the Nubian Lavallois technology in other regions of Arabia, namely in the southern Rub' al-Khali, in northern Oman, in the Jawf basin in northern Saudi Arabia, and at al-Kharj in central Saudi Arabia; the latter finds from al-Kharj date from the later phase of MIS 5 around 90–70 ka BP.[241] These finds imply a population exchange between north-eastern Africa and Dhofar at a time when the Red Sea was rather shallow and easier to cross.[242] However, no skeletal remains have been found so far in conjunction with Late Nubian complex artefacts. Not only the assumption that these tool makers were anatomically modern humans, but the very concept of a Late Nubian complex itself remain debated.[243] With the onset of the Holocene, a classification of human prehistory into archaeological epochs becomes possible, which in turn can be brought approximately into correlation with the phases of petroglyph-making.[244] Within the Jabal al-Hajar, the 'Rocky Mountains', of northern Oman where most petroglyphs are located, rock art may be classified mainly on stylistic criteria into six phases:[245]

I. Maritime animals – Early Neolithic. Before the fifth millennium BCE no petroglyphs were made and people were concentrated along the coasts living mainly on marine and coastal resources, while in the sparsely populated mountainous areas, hunting and gathering was practised. From the fifth millennium BCE date heavily weathered petroglyphs representing maritime animals such as green turtles, fish and sea anemones. In this period, the husbandry of goats and sheep began in addition to be practised both in coastal and mountain regions. Agriculture was still absent. Most people were sedentary with graveyards close to settlements. Interestingly, the grave goods were not classified by gender since bracelets, necklaces, shells and turtle shells were deposited with the deceased irrespective of sex. The fact that more than half of the burials contained turtle shells suggests that a special significance was attributed to turtles; their importance was also reflected in their representation in petroglyphs. Already in the late fifth millennium BCE trade contacts existed between the littoral of

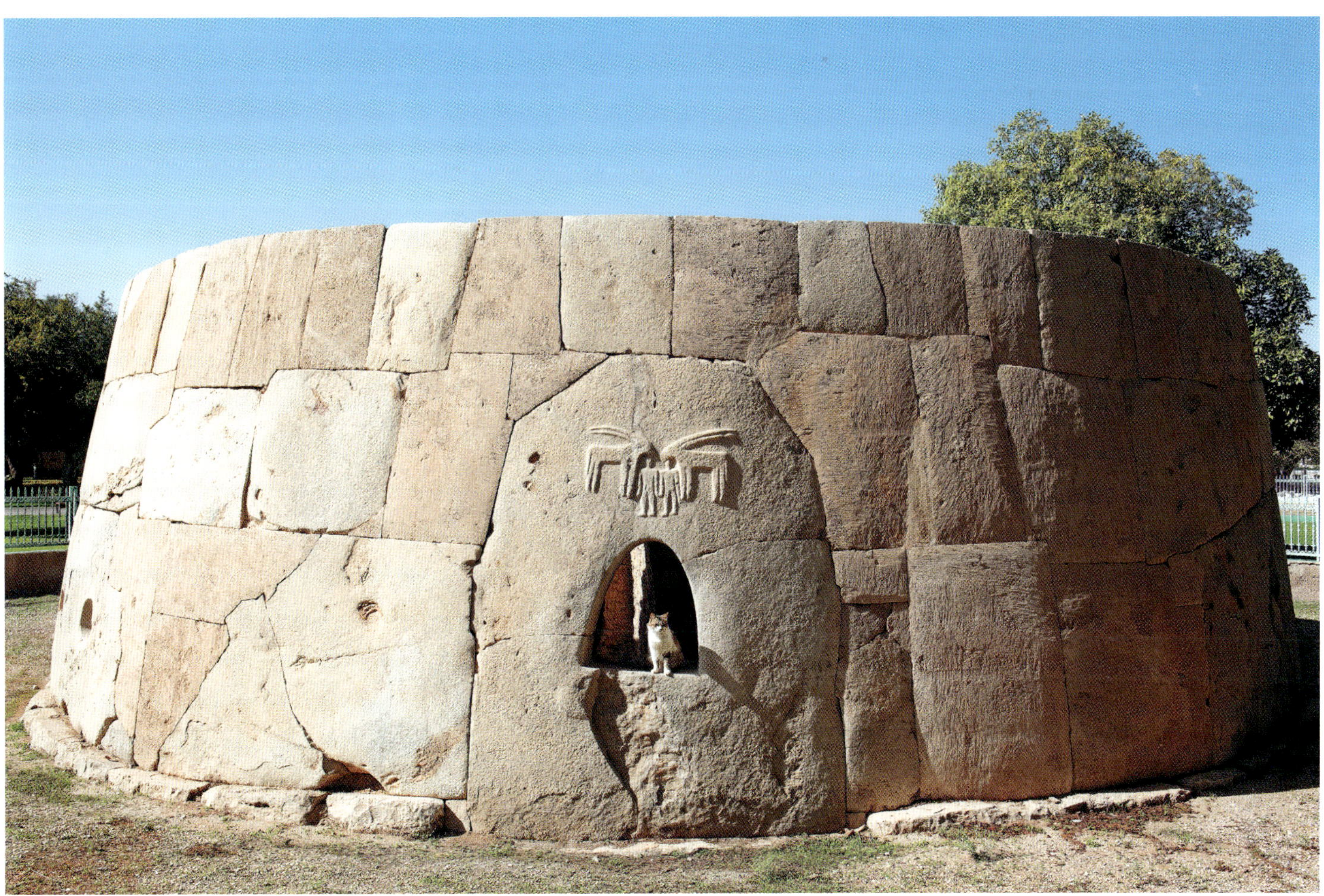

274. Funeral tower no. 1059 from the Umm al-Nar Period (2600–2000 BCE) in al-Ain, United Arab Emirates. Above the north-western entrance are bas-reliefs of two humans holding hands, flanked by two oryxes. The monument was reconstructed from the original limestone blocks following the 1965 excavations. Photo 2024.

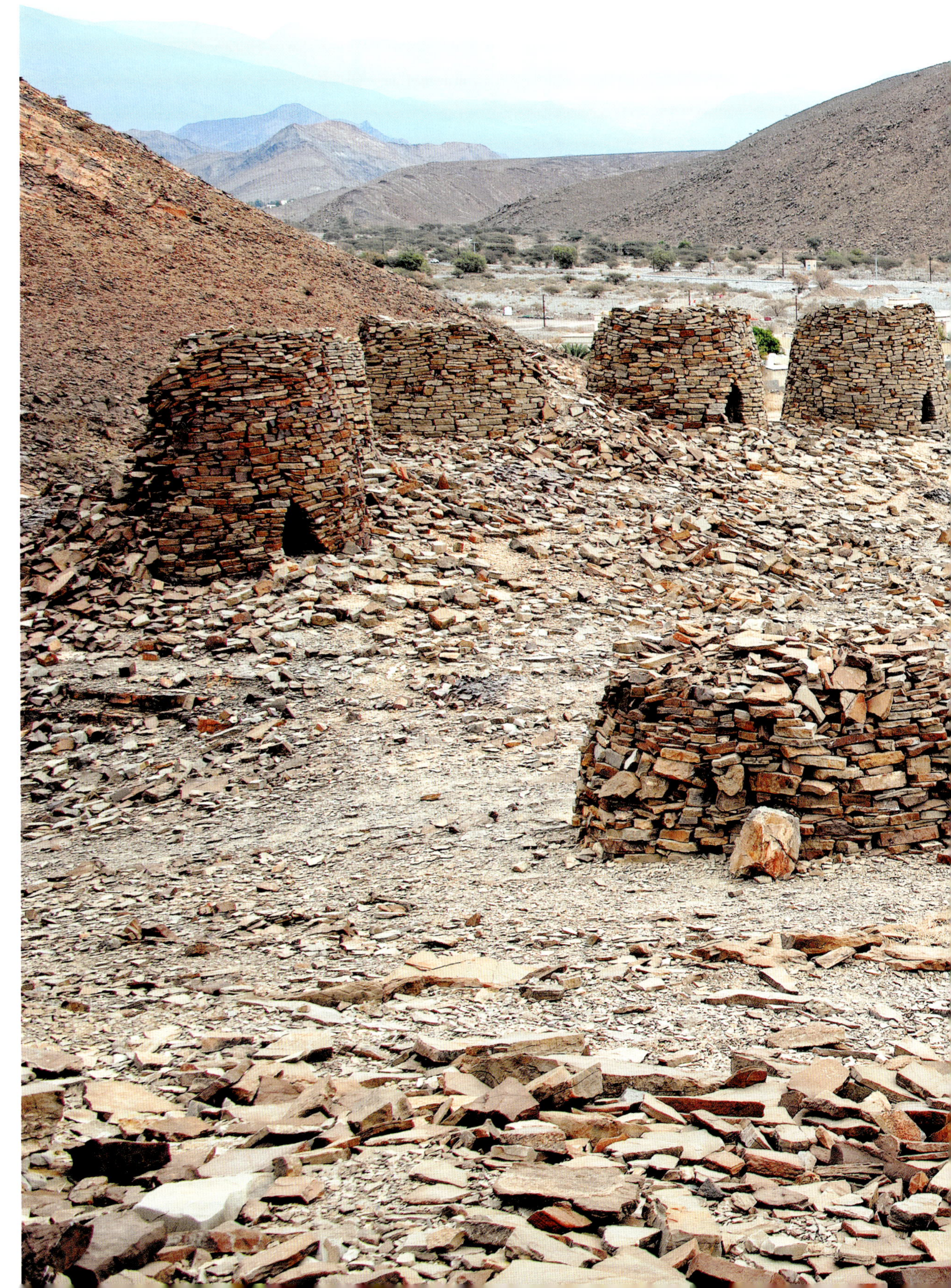

275. The 'beehive' funeral towers at al-Ain from the Hafit period (3100–2600 BCE). Oman. Photo 2024.

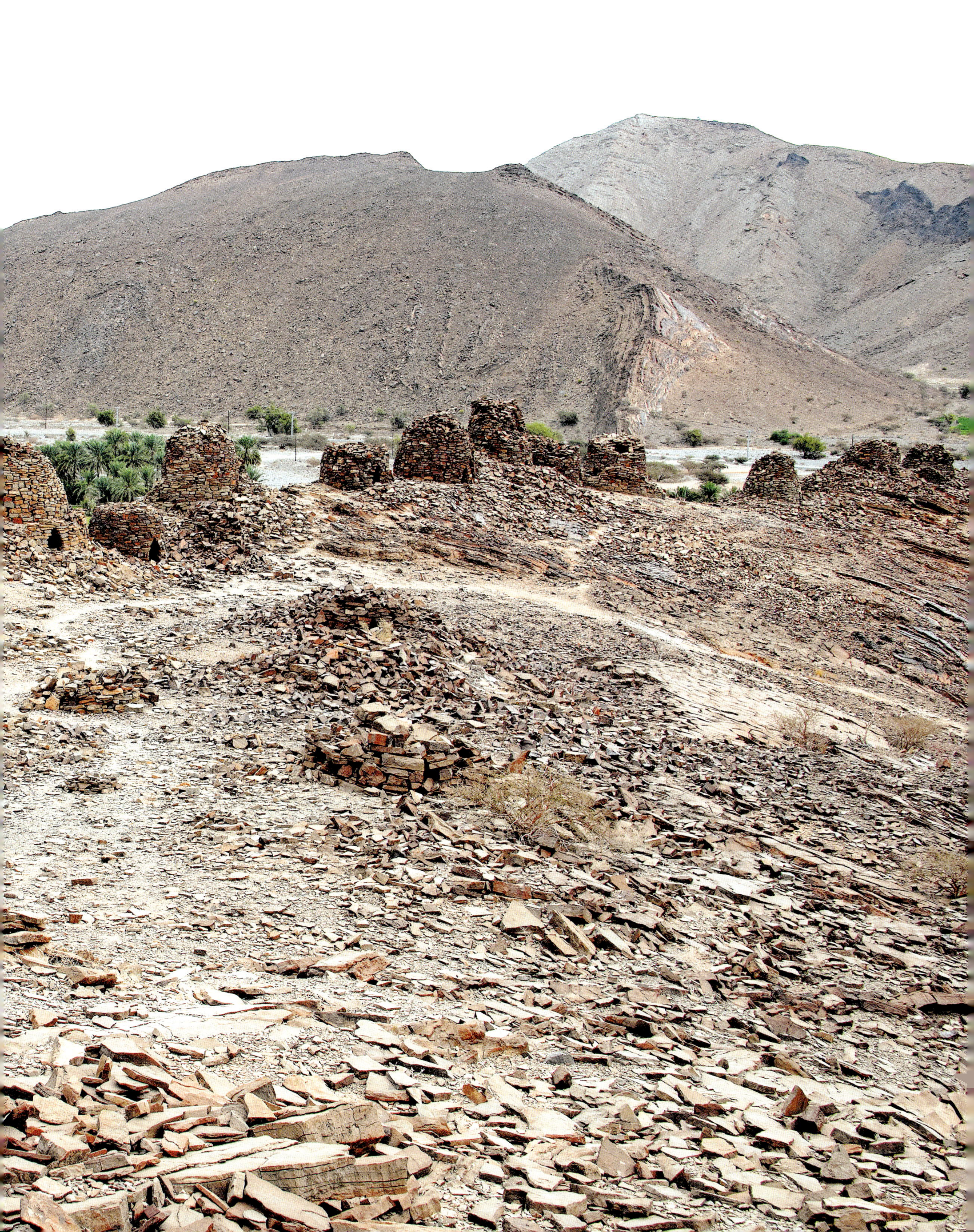

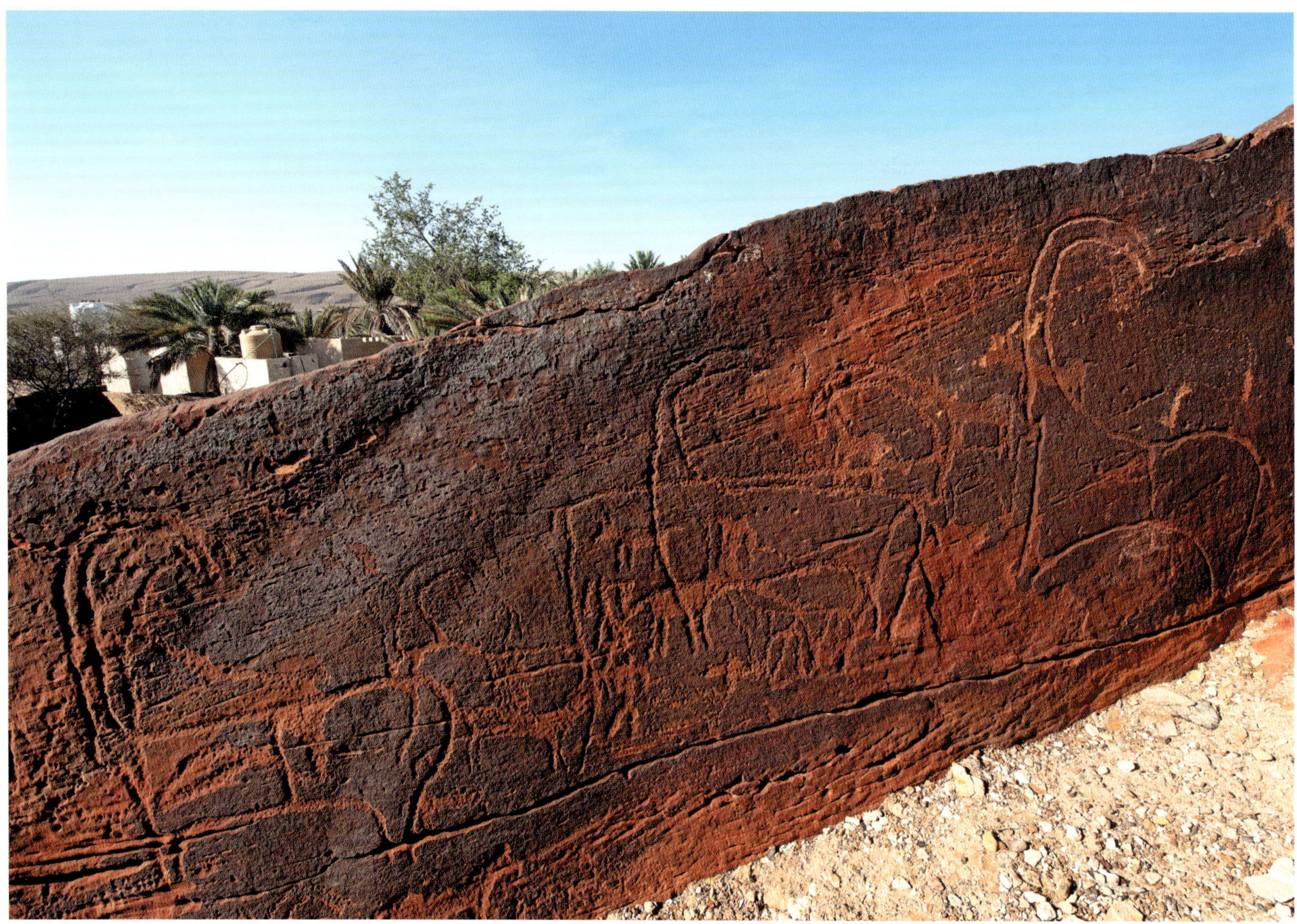

276. Petroglyphs of caprids, probably Nubian ibexes or Arabian tahrs, made in the 'three-strokes style' from the Late Neolithic were superimposed on older images of wild asses, ibexes and oryxes. Al-Qatarah 1, Shenah, central Oman. Photo 2024.

north-eastern Arabia, that is today's United Arab Emirates, and southern Mesopotamia, as can be deduced from pottery finds in the Mesopotamian Ubaid style.[246]

II. Land mammals – middle to late Neolithic. In the fourth millennium BCE, maritime animals are displaced in rock art by completely pecked petroglyphs of wild asses, oryxes and ibexes. In a second sub-phase, images of cattle and leopards also appear. In this second sub-phase, the petroglyphs are no longer fully pecked, but the outlines are engraved and sometimes filled with small dots. This period witnessed a climatic aridification which forced the people to reorganize their lifestyle, grouping families into structured clans and later tribes.

III. Stylized humans and daggers – Copper and Bronze Ages. The first half of this epoch stretching from *ca.* 3100 to 2600 BCE corresponds to the **Hafit Period** which is characterized by

monumental funeral towers in the shape of truncated cones, four to five metres high (fig. 275). These 'beehives' consisted of two or three concentric circular stone walls built around a central chamber. Such burial towers were collective tombs probably owned by groups of families or small clans and used over longer periods. The towers often stood on outcrops or even mountain ridges, and were visible from afar; they acted as symbols of power and territorial markers.[247] The distribution of such Bronze Age Hafit-style funeral towers was not limited to the northern half of Oman and the United Arab Emirates, but also spread to south-western Saudi Arabia, for example in the Wajjid Desert and north of Hima in Najran province. This spread, which implies a similar cultural horizon and close social contacts over a huge area, is striking, since the Holocene Wet Period had long since come to an end in the Bronze Age and the Rub' al-Khali desert now separated Najran and Dawasir from Oman and what is now the UAE. Other characteristics of the Hafit Period were the exploitation of copper ore in the Jabal al-Hajar and agriculture based on irrigation fed by wells. In this period, totally new rock art motifs appeared in the shape of stylized male and female humans with angular torsos, for example at Hasat bin Salt (fig. 279) or Gore Anaqsah (figs 280, 281) in Wadi Sahtan. The women were also rendered seated on a kind of throne, attended by a smaller servant; whom these petroglyphs represent is unknown.

The ensuing **Umm al-Nar Period** (2600–2000 BCE) witnessed an expansion of irrigation-based agriculture and the introduction of the first underground water channels, called *falaj* (plural *aflaj*). Later, in the second millennium BCE, such channels were developed into underground irrigation systems kilometres long.[248] In the Umm al-Nar Period the exploitation of copper in the shape of ingots or finished products intensified, and the majority was exported to Mesopotamia via Dilmun. So far, about 150 deposits of copper ore have been detected in Oman and the UAE.[249] The continued supply of copper ore from Oman was of such importance for Mesopotamia that its ruler did not hesitate to intervene militarily. For example, the Akkadian king Naram-Sin (r. 2254–2218 BCE) boasted on a statue of himself: 'Naram-Sin, the mighty king … He subjugated Magan and captured Manitan, the "lord" of Magan.' Whether northern Oman was really centralized under the rule of a king in those days is doubtful; maybe Manitan (or Mannium or Mannu Danu) was a temporal leader of a coalition or Naram-Sin wanted to magnify his victory by enhancing the position of the defeated enemy.[250]

Later, the Neo-Sumerian Empire (2112–2004 BCE) imported copper directly from Magan, which required control of the waterways.[251] Magan, for its part, was famous for its shipbuilding, and the second major export article of Oman to Mesopotamia was, after copper, wood for use in ship construction.[252] Other exported goods were dates, goats and diorite. In return, Magan imported from Mesopotamia cereals and textiles, and from the Indus Valley spices.[253] The finds of Harappan potsherds and of a few Harappan seals confirm direct maritime contacts with the Indus culture.[254] Oman in the third millennium BCE represented the southern corner of a Mesopotamia–Oman–Indus Valley trading triangle. During the Umm al-Nar Period, the funeral towers became even more monumental; their outer walls were now built from polished limestones of cyclopean size, up to 2.25 metres long and weighing up to 2.125 tons. They were no longer sited on mountain ridges, but on flat locations in the plain. The interior was always divided into two main chambers, each having its own entrance, and two or four additional compartments. The largest stands in the Hili Archaeological Park of al-Ain in the United Arab Emirates; its diameter is twelve metres and its height four metres (fig. 274). The dead bodies were first kept in one of the two central rooms,

and once the flesh had decayed, the bones were placed in one of the two lateral chambers. In total, the mortal remains of some 600 persons have been found, including grave goods such as clay objects, pottery, daggers, arrow heads, local and imported beads as well as silver and gold jewellery. The monument was excavated in 1965 and then reconstructed from the existing blocks. Above the north-western entrance are bas-reliefs of two humans holding hands, flanked by two oryxes. On the opposite side, the bas-reliefs feature two Arabian leopards devouring a deer and, above, an equestrian riding a donkey who is followed by a man on foot and two humans embracing.[255] On the north-eastern side there are two bas-reliefs of oryxes, of which only one is left intact as the other one has been redrawn. These bas-reliefs have no equivalent in local petroglyphs. The monumentality of these towers reflects a spirit of competition among wealthy dynasties. The towers served over longer periods for the burial of dozens and hundreds of persons. A second, similar tower stands nearby, others on Umm al-Nar Island north of Abu Dhabi.[256] The repertoire of petroglyph motifs now

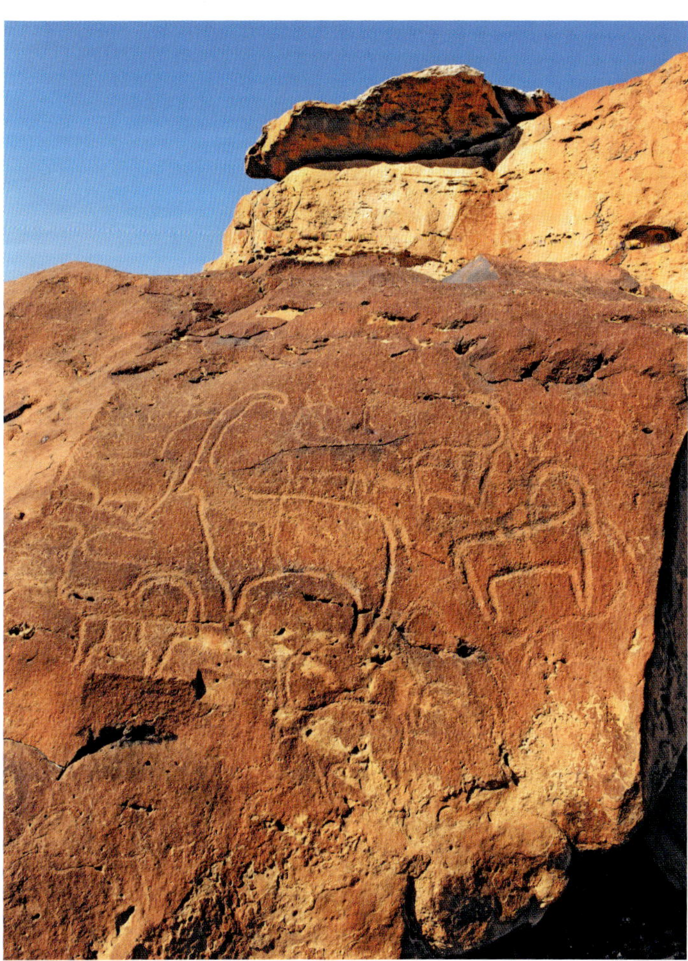

277. Petroglyphs of caprids made in the 'three-strokes style' at al-Qatarah 2, Shenah, central Oman. Photo 2024.

comprised not only schematic humans, but also wild cats, probably nocturnal caracals, and large T-shaped daggers. The latter heralded an incipient shift towards male and combative values. Whether the signs engraved on two stamp steals discovered at Ras al-Jinz near Sur in Oman, which were carved on a steatite bowl dating from *ca.* 2200 BCE, really represent 'a form of writing' as claimed by Serge Cleuziou and Maurizio Tosi is questionable.[257]

IV. Daggers and symbols – Late Bronze Age. Soon after 2000 BCE, trade exchanges with the Indus Valley and Mesopotamia declined and coarse pottery replaced the previously fine ware. In this period of continued aridification the **Wadi Suq** culture (2000–1600 BCE) emerged, which is marked by increased mobility and more modest burial architecture. However, male burials now often contained bronze weapons such as long swords, javelins and arrow heads. The dominant petroglyph motifs were now daggers and geometric forms such as solar symbols, spirals and zigzags, plus a few schematized humans. The radical change in grave goods and simultaneously in petroglyph motifs from jewellery and turtle shells in the Neolithic to weapons in the Later Bronze Age testifies to radical transformations in terms of the prevalent set of values and probably also of societal organization.

V. Warrior attributes – Iron Age and beyond. From *ca.* 1000 BCE, petroglyphs illustrate warriors fighting on foot and mounted, armed horsemen and camel riders as well as the traditional curved dagger called a *khanjar*, the symbol of masculine adulthood par excellence. In the Iron Age, the international export of copper from Oman resumed and previously abandoned copper mines were put back into operation,[258] but in the tenth century CE, the mining of copper suddenly stopped, probably due to a lack of available wood. In the first millennium CE, inscriptions in Musnad and classical Arabic are included, as well as images of ostriches, cattle and boats. From this period also date the rare paintings of horsemen from the Wadi Bani Kharus. In political terms, from the sixth century BCE until the rise of Islam the northern coastal areas of Oman came intermittently under Iranian influence or even control.

VI. Vehicles – Present period. As in neighbouring Saudi Arabia, the petroglyphs made in the last decades illustrate cars, trucks, planes and ships as well as rifles, musical stringed instruments and cup marks arranged like a game board.

The most important rock art sites of northern and central Oman, that is excluding those in Dhofar,[259] are located in the al-Hajar mountain range, which stretches over 700 kilometres from the easternmost tip of Oman as far as the Musandam Peninsula. They are, in chronological order:

- **Shenah**. Close to the village of Shenah in the al-Sharqiyah governorate is the district of al-Qatarah where at least twenty sites have been identified; in their surroundings stand several Hafit-type funeral towers (or their ruined remains).[260] At Shenah, the numerous superimpositions help to establish a chronological sequence. Deeply engraved and strongly revarnished images of wild asses, oryxes and ibexes belong to its oldest period, that is Period II from the middle to late Neolithic. They are overlapped by relatively large images, 30 to 60 cm wide, of caprines which may represent Nubian ibexes, Arabian tahrs and/or other kinds of goat-like caprines. Only the outlines of these animals were pecked, and they were made in the so-called 'three-strokes style' where the outline consists of three lines.[261] The 'three-strokes style' petroglyphs belong to the late Neolithic; outstanding examples of such palimpsests are to be found at Fossati's site al-Qatarah 1 (east of Shenah), al-Qatarah 2 (north-east of the village), and Insall's al-Qatarah 5 (north of Shenah at the falaj al-Zam) (figs 276, 277).[262] Some of these petroglyphs are upside down, so obviously the lintels and boulders fell from a higher position after the rock art had been engraved. From Phase III, the Copper and Bronze Age, date the T-shaped images which are often superimposed over 'three-strokes style' images; such a slab with at least a dozen T-shaped petroglyphs lies at the bottom of al-Qatarah 2. The upper bar of the T may be either straight, curved or shaped like a half-moon. This petroglyph type probably represents a dagger, sometimes possibly a pickaxe. In addition, between al-Qatarah 3 and 5 lies a limestone boulder measuring 3.6 by 2.2 m which is engraved with a dozen heavily schematized horsemen executed in the stick-figure style; they date from the first centuries CE. Other images at Shenah feature horses, camels, footprints and goats within enclosures.

278. The petroglyph site Hasat bin Salt in central Oman. In total, at least thirteen human figures have been either engraved in bas-relief or pecked into the metamorphosed limestone rock. They probably date from the period between the first century BCE and the sixth or seventh century CE. Photo 2024.

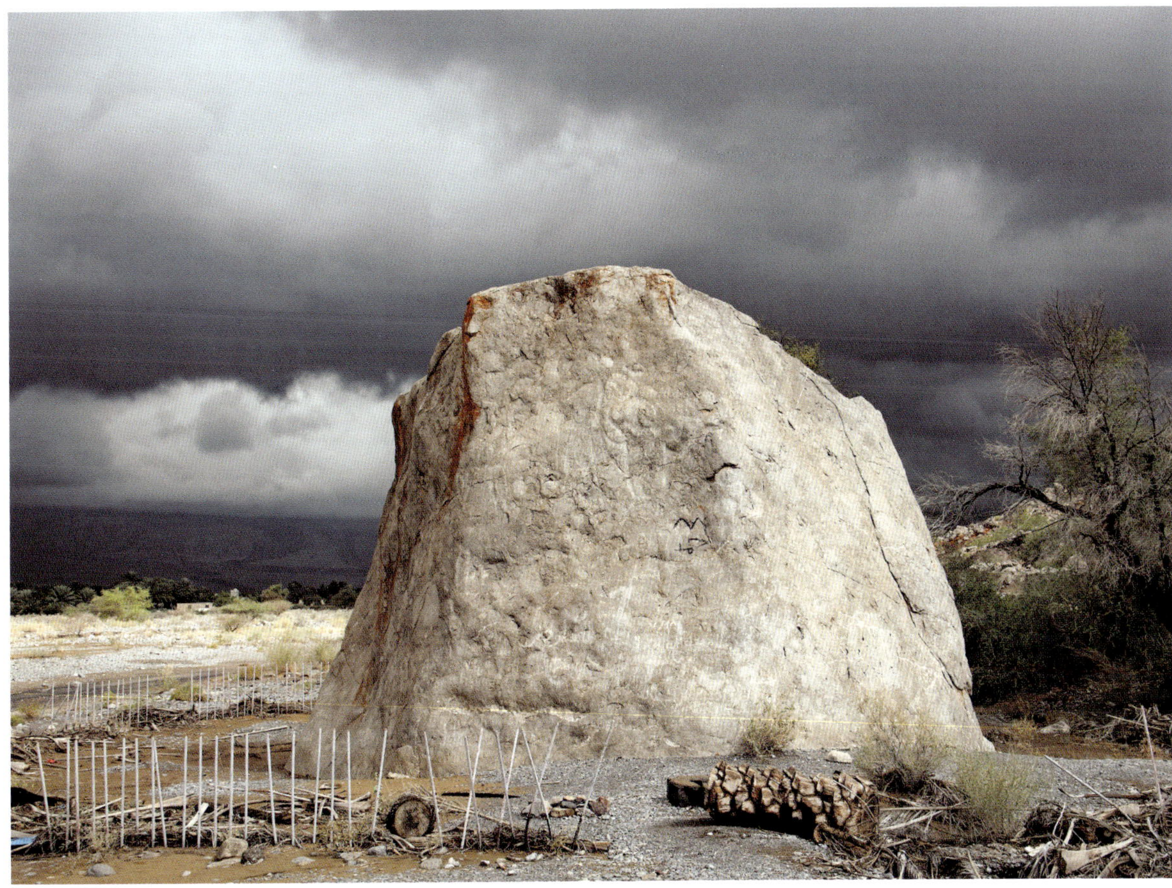

279. Detail from the southern face of the rock of Hasat bin Salt. From left to right: a standing man and below his bent right elbow a male youth whose image extends onto the western rock face. In the centre of the rock stands an adult woman with noticeable breasts and wearing a skirt, and to her left stands again a man who holds in his raised right hand a mace, thunderbolt or double-edged dagger with two blades. To his left stands a child. First century BCE to sixth or seventh century CE. Central Oman. Photo 2024.

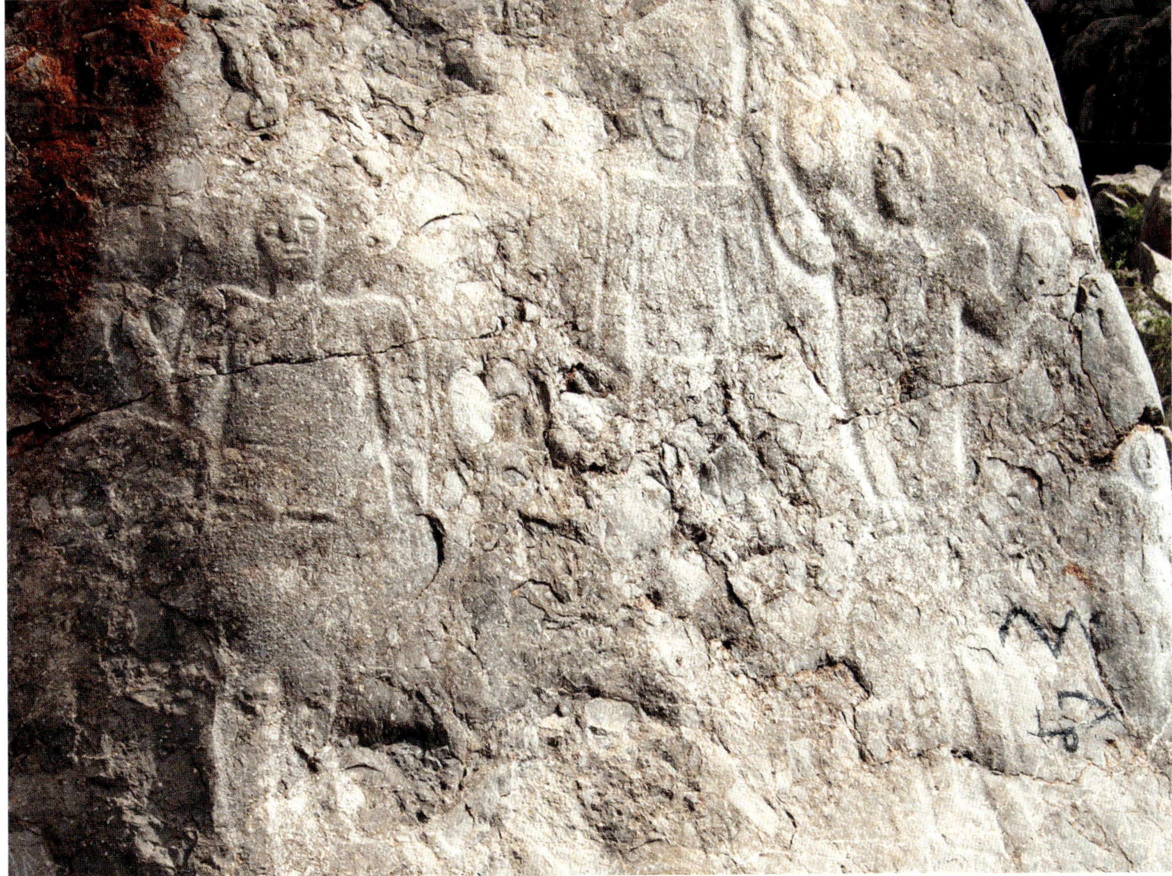

- **Hasat bin Salt** and **Bilad Sayt** lie in the central Omani governorate of al-Dakhiliyah on a southern slope of Jabal Akhdar, the 'Green Mountain'. **Hasat bin Salt** is a metamorphosed limestone monolith around 6 m high and 3.6 m wide standing a couple of kilometres south of the town of al-Hamra. On the southern, western and northern faces at least thirteen human figures have been either engraved in bas-relief or pecked (figs 278, 279). On the best-preserved, southern side there are five figures, from left to right, first a standing man 1.6 m tall; just below his bent right elbow stands a male youth 1.1 m tall whose image extends onto the western rock face. In the centre of the composition stands an adult woman *ca.* 1.8 m tall with noticeable breasts and wearing a skirt, and to her left stands a man 1.95 m tall who brandishes in his raised right hand a mace, thunderbolt or double-edged dagger with two blades. To his left stands a child 1 m tall. Cleuziou and Tosi dated these engraved figures to the second half of the third millennium BCE, but Paul Yule and Eric Olijdam consider that they date to the Parthian or Sasanian periods, *ca.* first century BCE to sixth or seventh century CE.[263] Since the two tall males seem to wear a kind of loose-fitting trouser as are known from Parthian and Sasanian rock reliefs, the present authors tend to agree to the later dating. However, the central female figure could have been made at an earlier time. Whom these figures represent remains unknown. The central position of the female is certainly striking and the tall male next to her is the only figure with an attribute. If one were to assume that this dominant figure holds a thunderbolt, he hypothetically could represent a thunder and rain deity similar to the Babylonian thunder god Hadad or Bel. As for the woman, who has a rectangular torso, figures bearing a slight similarity are found at Gore Anaqsah in Wadi Sahtan, in the northern Jabal Akhdar.

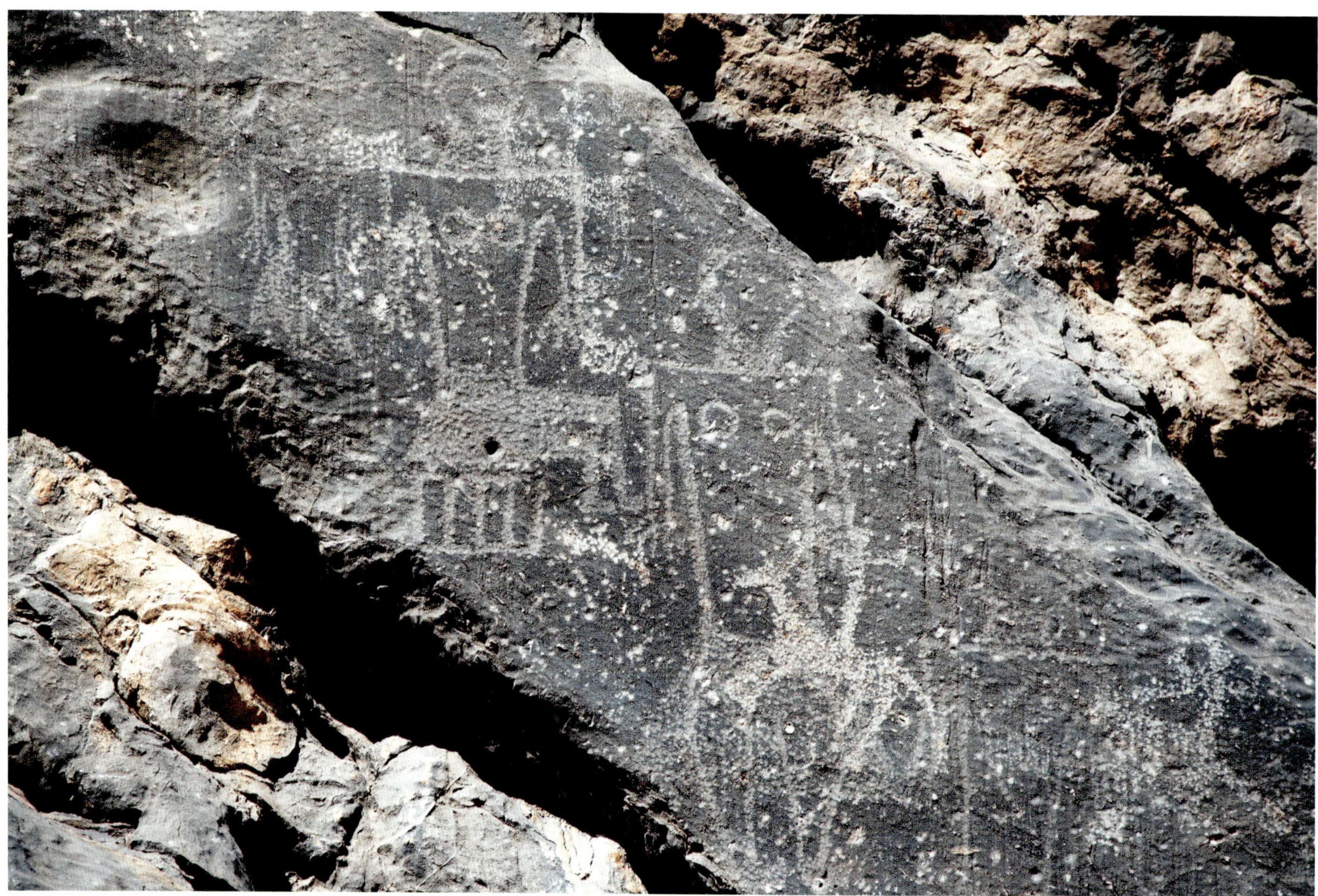

280. Two women sit on a chair or a throne, at the bottom only the torso of a third is visible; beside the upper woman stands a small person. These petroglyphs possibly date from the second millennium BCE; they were later superimposed with petroglyphs of horsemen. Gore Anaqsah, Wadi Sahtan, central Oman. Photo 2024.

A few hundred metres west of Hasat bin Salt is the site called **Bilad Sayt** where there are petroglyphs of a few bulls executed in the 'three-strokes style', of a leopard, goats, humans, horsemen and a solar symbol.[264]

- **Gore Anaqsah** lies in Wadi Sahtan, in the al-Batinah South governorate. Unique to this site is the group of four women, *ca.* 60 cm tall, seated on a throne or chair along with one tall standing woman. They wear skirts and their rectangular torsos are in a similar style to the central female at Hasat bin Salt. But in contrast to the latter, the females at Gore Anaqsah are purely pecked, not carved in bas-relief. Head, torso and arms are shown frontally, the legs from the side (fig. 280). There is another seated woman 2 m diagonally above. These petroglyphs are significantly revarnished and have been superimposed with at least five smaller horsemen. To the left of the seated women there are two felines with five sharp claws which seem to be attacking prey. They probably represent caracals, a lynx-like medium-sized wild cat. Above the upper caracal there is a solar symbol. About 60 m further south is the petroglyph of a standing woman *ca.* 120 cm tall flanked by two smaller humans. The torso of the woman has been over-engraved with two small warriors on foot duelling with short swords and holding round shields (fig. 281). Due to a lack of material with which to compare them, it is hardly possible to date these intriguing petroglyphs; the degree of revarnishing suggests a date around the later second millennium BCE. Other interesting petroglyphs include ostriches, standing warriors and horsemen with so-called bi-triangular or hourglass-shaped bodies, and several pre-Islamic inscriptions in an ancient South Arabian alphabet. Finally, there are also modern images of cars. A couple of kilometres further north there are two additional sites with medieval and recent petroglyphs.

- **Wadi Bani Kharus** lies, like Wadi Sahtan, in the northern Jabal Akhdar, in the al-Batinah South governorate. It consists of at least six sites located either in the main wadi or in side valleys. At the site near the restored fortress of Awabi numerous blocks of limestone are covered with encrusted, fossilized shells and other sea animals which were petrified during the Cretaceous (145–66 mya). Besides two heavily weathered petroglyphs of bulls, recent and finely executed petroglyphs predominate. They represent a lion, a panther, a giraffe, a rhinoceros, dogs and a cock as well as mounted

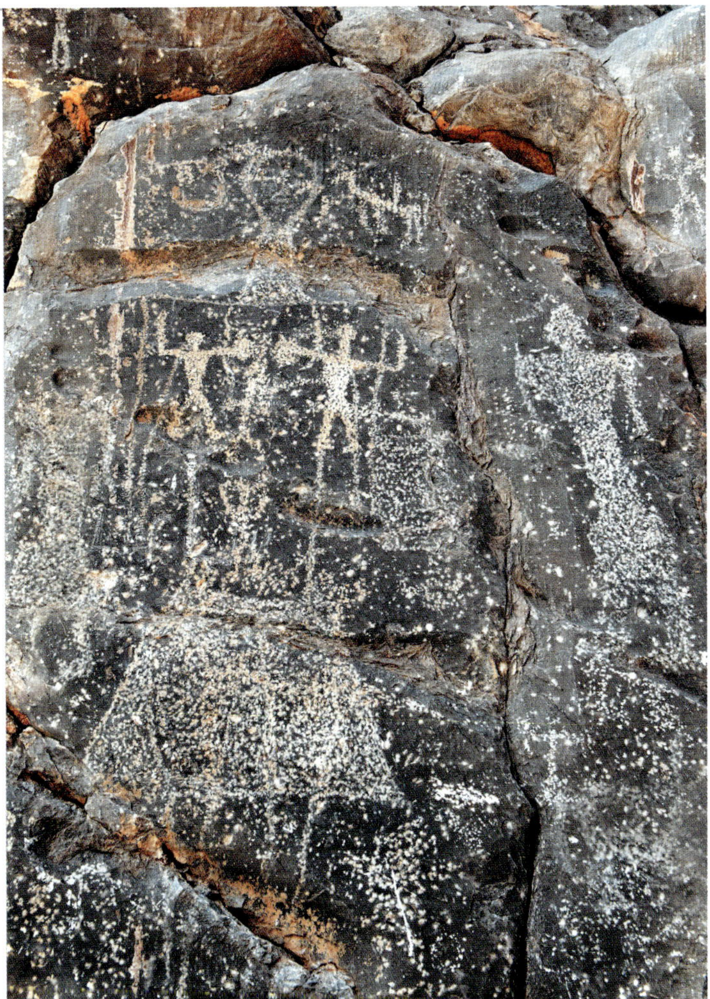

281. Two human figures flank a tall woman 120 cm high, who wears a skirt. Her torso has been superimposed with two small warriors on foot duelling with short swords and holding round shields. The older images possibly date from the second millennium BCE. Gore Anaqsah, Wadi Sahtan, central Oman. Photo 2024.

lancers, humans with jackal heads reminiscent of Anubis, the Egyptian god of funerary rites, and Oman's coat of arms consisting of a *khanjar* (curved dagger) overlying two crossed long knives. Also striking is the petroglyph of a sailing ship which has been engraved over the Late Neolithic image of an ibex (fig. 282). An Arabic inscription informs the reader that the petroglyph represents the *Jewel of Muscat*, which was a replica of a ninth-century Omani ship that was shipwrecked in Indonesia. The *Jewel of Muscat* successfully sailed in 2010 from Muscat to Singapore.[265] There are two other petroglyphs sites in the Wadi al-Hijir 10 km further south; at the wadi's entrance a group of mounted lancers and at the entry to a narrow gorge near the eponymous village there are three rock art complexes: a large boulder is covered with medieval petroglyphs of horsemen brandishing spears or swords,

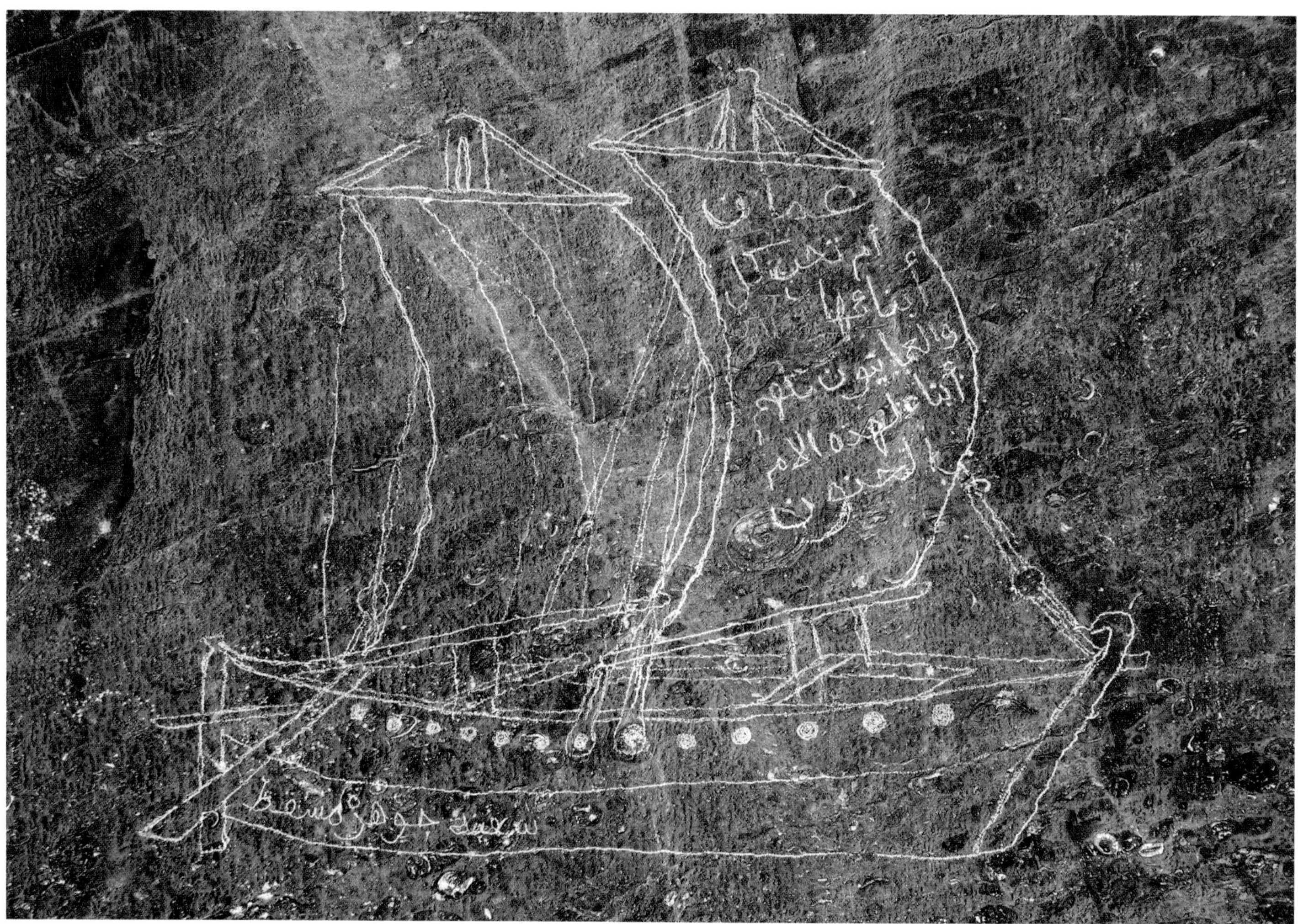

282. Contemporary petroglyph of the ship *Jewel of Muscat* which was made after July 2010 when this replica of a medieval dhow concluded its journey from Muscat to Singapore. Wadi Bani Kharus, site 1, northern Oman. Photo 2024.

foot soldiers and recent, carefully done images of lancers and khanjars. In a nearby natural shelter formed by huge boulders which fell down from the mountain one boulder is covered with the petroglyphs of horsemen and Arabic inscriptions. Finally, a narrow path leads from the shelter uphill to a pre-Islamic archaeological complex and passes a rock which is inscribed with numerous Arabic epigraphs. They mention the names and origins, even Mecca and Medina, 1,800 km away, of people who apparently made pilgrimages in medieval times to the pre-Islamic shrine along this exposed mountain path.

In the main wadi about 12 kilometres south of Awabi lie Istal and Mesfat al-Hatatlah, with several petroglyph sites. At al-Saloot near Istal there stand two tiny mosques of a rectangular floor plan, astonishingly, right in the middle of the wadi bed. On an adjacent boulder there are not only petroglyphs of ibexes, tahrs, equids and lancers but also Arabic inscriptions. One of them refers to the Quran and describes how the prophet Musa (Moses) debated with the wicked pharaoh who held the Israelites prisoner; another, dated AH 900 (1494/5 CE), records the complaints of a father about his quarrelling son. High above the two mosques on a high ridge of difficult access stand the remains of a third mosque which is reported to have served in early Islamic times as a retreat for Muslim hermits, similar to Christian monks of that time. Then, near Istal, there are a few unusual petroglyphs likely representing turtles seen from above.[266] Later petroglyphs feature a few caprines made in the 'three-strokes style', horsemen, a combat scene between a horseman and two warriors on foot, a human wearing ibex horns or a horned helmet, and men firing guns. An Arabic inscription dated AH 981 (1573/4 CE) commemorates a deceased tribal leader whose dated tombstone stands in the nearby cemetery.

- **Wadi Aday** is located 8 km south of the capital Muscat. On both sides of the wadi panels carry petroglyphs featuring rather schematized equids, ibexes, hunters, humans and quadrupeds framed by a kind of cartouche, T-shaped objects that are probably daggers, and modern graffiti in Arabic and Latin scripts. Some of the petroglyphs are pecked in a pronounced pointillé style.

- **Wadi Hareem** is in the al-Batinah North governorate *ca.* 80 km south of Sohar. Most petroglyphs are concentrated on two boulders situated on the left shore of the brook. Three sides of the upper boulder are engraved with more than 100 horsemen armed with spears and swords (fig. 283). About 90 per cent of the warriors are oriented to the east. From the bright desert varnish, the date of these petroglyphs can be estimated to the last few centuries. Since all the petroglyphs look alike, a single authorship may be assumed. The unusually high number of armed and galloping equestrians suggests an event like a battle or a tale. The lower boulder has petroglyphs, again of equestrians holding spears or swords, then camels and humans with big hands and outstretched fingers. A few warriors are on foot, either single or duelling; there are also Arabic inscriptions and a few camels. Further upstream dozens of boulders are also decorated with petroglyphs, although to a much lesser extent than the two main ones. They illustrate mainly horsemen, warriors on foot, a few large stick-humans and a sailing ship manned by two sailors.

- **Wadi Tanuf, Salut** and **Nizwa** are located in the Dakhiliyah governorate. The petroglyphs in **Wadi Tanuf** are north of the abandoned village of Old Tanuf which was destroyed in 1959 at the end of the Jabal Akhdar Civil War (1954–59) in which the major tribes of Jabal Akhdar, who were followers of Imam Ghalib ibn Ali, opposed Sultan Said bin Timur (r. 1932–1970). The petroglyphs along the shores of the river[267] feature ibexes, goats, bulls, camels, horsemen, standing males wearing daggers or short swords, T-shaped objects and the unusual image of a mounted warrior brandishing a battle axe.[268] South-west of Nizwa stands the Iron Age fortress of **Salut.** On the neighbouring Jabal Hammah petroglyphs were found rendering schematized, 'comb-shaped' horses and horsemen, humans and T-shaped objects. Significant for dating purposes is the fact that at nearby Qaryat Salut an engraved stone featuring a human with arms raised had been reused in the lower part of an early Iron Age wall which was no longer visible once the construction was complete. The corresponding *ante quem* date is the thirteenth century BCE.[269] Hermetically trapped under the weathered crust of another stone with a petroglyph featuring a man holding a huge T-shaped object resembling a pick-axe was organic material which has been dated to the ninth to eighth century BCE, that is the Iron Age.[270] Finally, an unusual location for rock art is a large plaster panel at an entrance to the fort of **Nizwa** which is covered with engravings from the early twentieth century featuring horsemen holding shields and spears, horses, camels and ships. In terms of style, these recent petroglyphs resemble those from the Middle Ages.

It is striking how different the petroglyphs in Oman look from those in Saudi Arabia, apart from the ubiquitous simple stick-humans and almost comb-shaped horses and horsemen; exchange between these two vast regions seems to have been minimal. With the exception of hunting and duel scenes, there are few scenes in Omani rock art in which the figures depicted clearly relate to each other. Also, only a very few figures have specific attributes that go beyond common weapons like spears, swords, daggers and shields. All these factors make it largely impossible to establish links between the petroglyphs and any myths or beliefs. Furthermore, there are no points of reference for interpreting the stylistically unique petroglyphs of Hasat bin Salt and Gore Anaqsah.

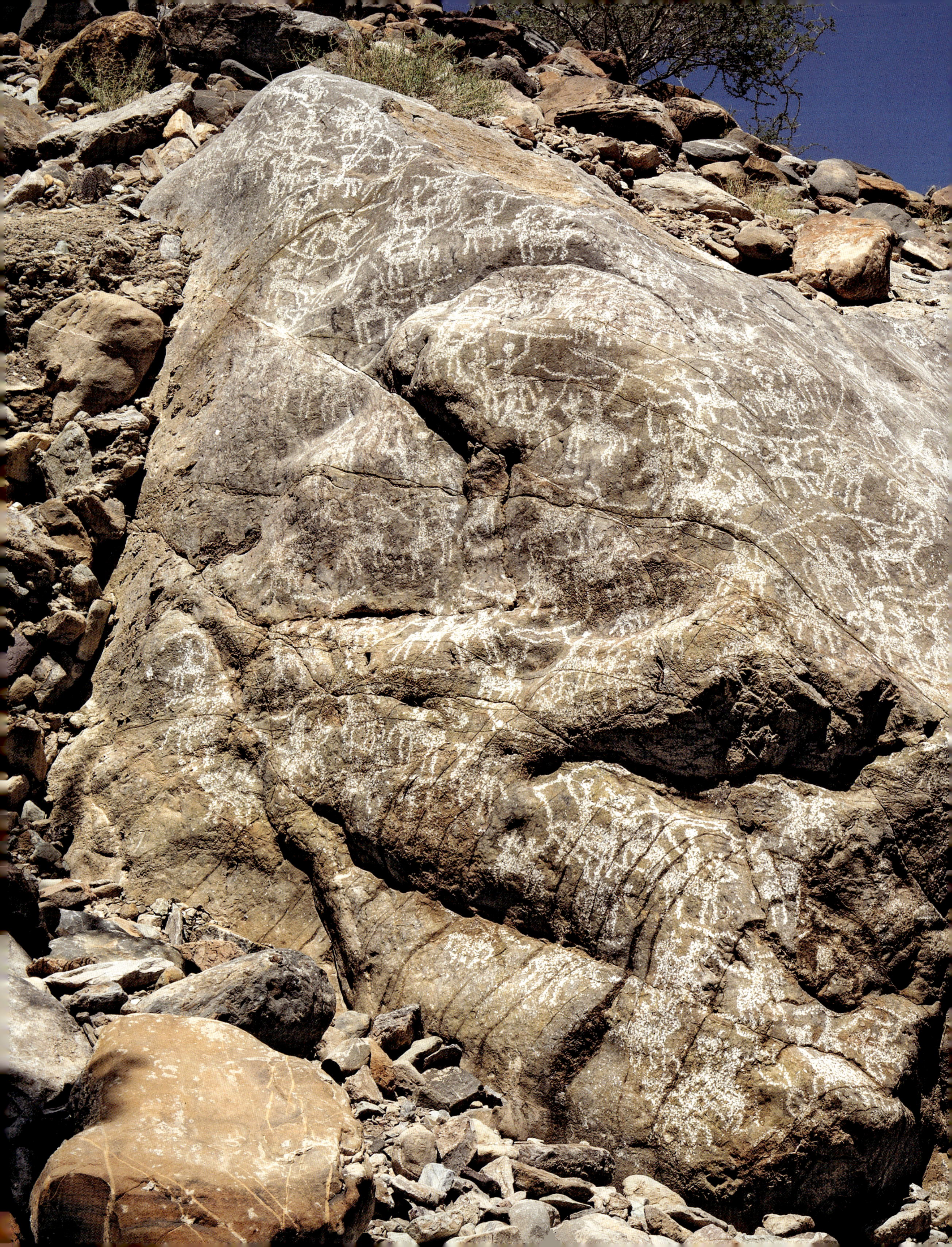

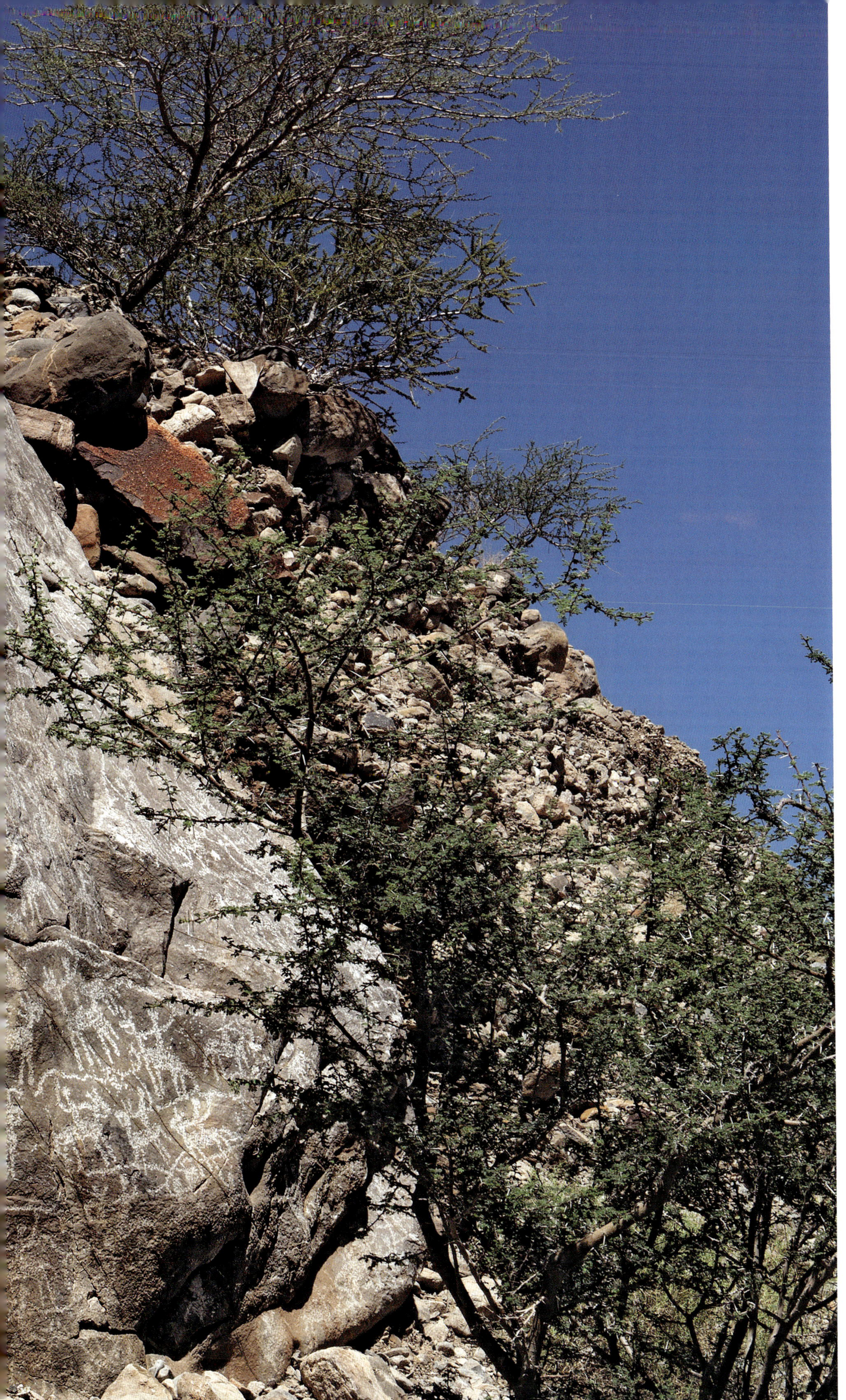

283. The upper boulder in Wadi Hareem is covered with more than 100 petroglyphs of horsemen armed with spears and swords. About 90 per cent of the warriors are oriented to the east. They were probably carved by the same person since all these petroglyphs look alike. 18th–19th century CE. Northern Oman. Photo 2024.

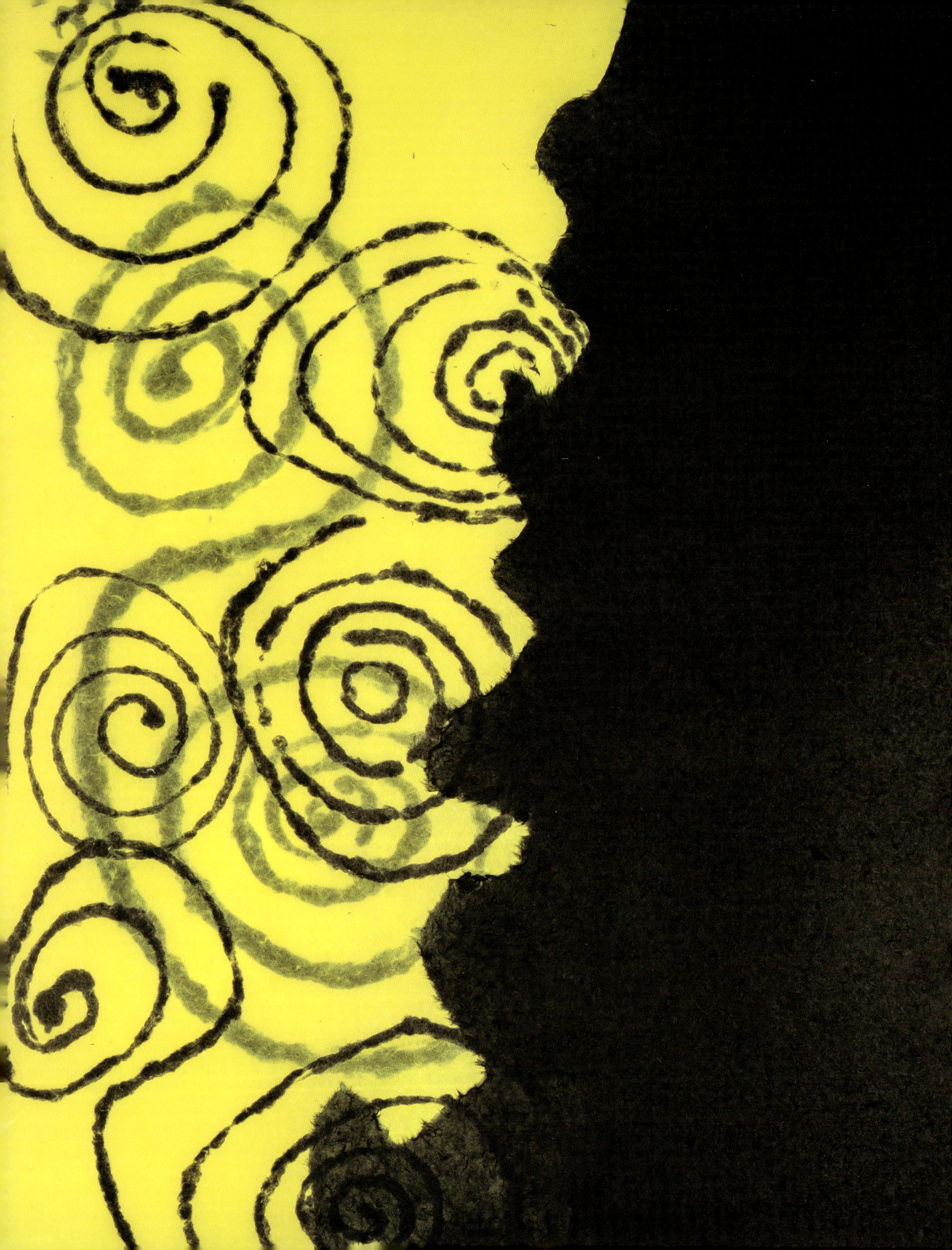

VIII. Central Sahara

1. Introduction

The Sahara is, with a surface of 9.2 million square kilometres, the largest non-polar, hot desert of the world. South of the Sahara lies the Sahel belt, also called the Sahelian Acacia Savanna, which is a transition zone, on average 450 kilometres wide, to the more humid Sudanian savannas. About 20 per cent of the Sahara is covered by sand, and 70 per cent by stone plateaus and mountains which could in principle be sites for rock art.[1] In contrast to Central Asia and Arabia, where petroglyphs predominate and rock paintings appear relatively rarely, in the Sahara the proportions are reversed. Pictographs are widely spread, but petroglyphs are mainly concentrated in three sandstone regions of the central Sahara:

- The **Wadi (Oued) Djerat** in the Tassili n'Ajjer in today's south-eastern Algeria is one of the most extraordinary petroglyph sites of the world, for in this deep narrow valley, *ca.* 70–150 m wide and in total more than 50 km long, a rich variety of petroglyphs as well as paintings are found spread over a walking distance of some 35 km.

- About 300 km to the east of Wadi Djerat in south-western Libya, the adjoining ranges of **Messak Settafet** (including the neighbouring valley of **Wadi al-Ajal** to the north) and **Messak Mellet** together form a crescent-shaped, table-like mountain range almost 500 km long. Unique to both Messak regions and Wadi Djerat are petroglyphs of therianthropes, that is animal–human hybrids, which are engraved in a particularly expressive and distinctive style (figs 286, 303, 304, 308). In addition, **Tadrart Acacus**, a mountain range which runs for some 250 km parallel to the lower part of Messak Settafet and Messak Mellet some 70 km to the west, has, besides numerous paintings, a number of petroglyphs.[2]

- The **Ahaggar Mountains** lie *ca.* 500 km south-west of Wadi Djerat in southern Algeria. The petroglyph sites are famous for their numerous Tifinagh inscriptions.[3]

284. ← Therese Weber, *Solar Tides, Tassili VI*. The inner outline of the curvy, dark area in the centre of the picture represents the geographical shape of the narrow Wadi Djerat, Tassili n'Ajjer, Algeria, and has the appearance of a silhouette. Recognizing topographical connections is part of the survival strategy in this inhospitable region. The painted spirals are a reference to the petroglyphs of prehistoric cultures, in which engravings of spirals played an important role. Full size: 200 × 100 cm. Detail: 160 × 100 cm. Washi, coloured and cast mulberry fibre; pulp painting on both sides, 2023.

At the edges of the Sahara there are other petroglyph complexes, which are beyond the scope of the present work. They are, from north to south and west to east:

- In **Morocco**, the main petroglyph concentrations are in the High Atlas Mountains, mainly at the four sites of **Oukaïmeden**, and in the country's south in the Sahara at **Aït Ouazik, Aït Ouabelli, Umm La Leg, Oued (Wadi) Mestakou, Tiggane, Akka** and **Imaoun**.

- In **Niger** the main concentrations of petroglyphs are in the Aïr Mountains, at **Anakom**, **Tagueit** and **Iwellene**, and at **Dabous**, on the western side of the Aïr Mountains in the Ténéré Desert, where there is, among other things, a famous, well-preserved petroglyph of a six-metre-tall giraffe (fig. 287).

- The highlights of the site of **Niola Doa** in the Ennedi region of eastern **Chad** are the large and in parts more than life-sized petroglyphs of humans with richly decorated bodies and steatopygic figures (fig. 285).[4] They are possibly females, but could also be young males who ritually overeat in order to acquire a steatopygic shape for a limited time.[5] The site lies on the southern edge of the Sahara.

- In the **Eastern Sahara**, in the area where Libya, Egypt and Sudan meet, the **Gilf Kebir** plateau and the **Jabal al-Uweinat** mountain range are rich in rock art, mainly paintings but also petroglyphs. In both regions, sandstone is the dominant rock.[6] Further south-east, beyond the Sahara, there is a rich rock art heritage in Ethiopia and the Horn of Africa, that is Somaliland and Djibouti.[7]

- The site of **Qurta** and its neighbouring locations lie on the east bank of the River Nile on the northern fringe of the Egyptian Kom Ombo oasis. Their figurative engraved images are the oldest scientifically dated petroglyphs in Africa. First discovered in 1962–63, then forgotten and rediscovered in 2005, the petroglyphs have been dated using the Optically Stimulated Luminescence method to the late Palaeolithic around 17–15.5 ka cal. BCE when the hyperaridity began to subside.[8] The rather large images were engraved in sandstone and mainly represent naturalistically drawn animals such as wild bovines, hippopotami, birds, gazelle and fish. In addition, there are about a dozen highly stylized humans with pronounced buttocks but no heads. Dirk Huyge,[9] one of the rediscoverers in 2005, highlighted similarities between the petroglyphs of stylized humans at Qurta with the so-called 'headless women' in figurines and engravings such as those from Gönnersdorf, Germany, from the European late Magdalenian (*ca.* 15.5–14.5 ka cal. BP) as well as with the petroglyphs of 'headless females' in Gobustan in Azerbaijan.[10] A few km north of Qurta, in the **Wadi Silwa Bahari**, there are petroglyphs of two types of boats: real boats used for transport and boats for ritual and religious purposes; the images date from the second and first millennium BCE.[11]

- In Egypt's Western Desert lies the **Dakhleh Oasis** where in its central and eastern areas petroglyph sites are to be found dating mainly from the Neolithic to the Fifth and Sixth Dynasties of the Old Kingdom. Within the high number of different featured animals, giraffes dominate; other important groups are female figures rendered with schematic heads and torsos but with pronounced lower bodies, and sandal prints.[12] 170 km to the east of Dakhleh Oasis, *ca.* 17 petroglyph sites have been identified in the **Kharga Oasis**.[13]

- In the region of the **Fourth Nile Cataract** in Sudan, 370 km north of Khartoum, there are hundreds of petroglyph sites. The sites are dominated by images of cattle, camels and hundreds of crosses and cross-shapes as well as of geometric figures probably representing churches or reliquaries. Most of the crosses date to the earlier Christian period from the third/fourth to the seventh centuries CE.[14]

285. → Life-sized petroglyphs of humans with painted bodies and steatopygic shapes from the Late Pastoral Period. Niola Doa, Ennedi, eastern Chad. Photo 2018 by Takayuki Hanafusa, Japan.

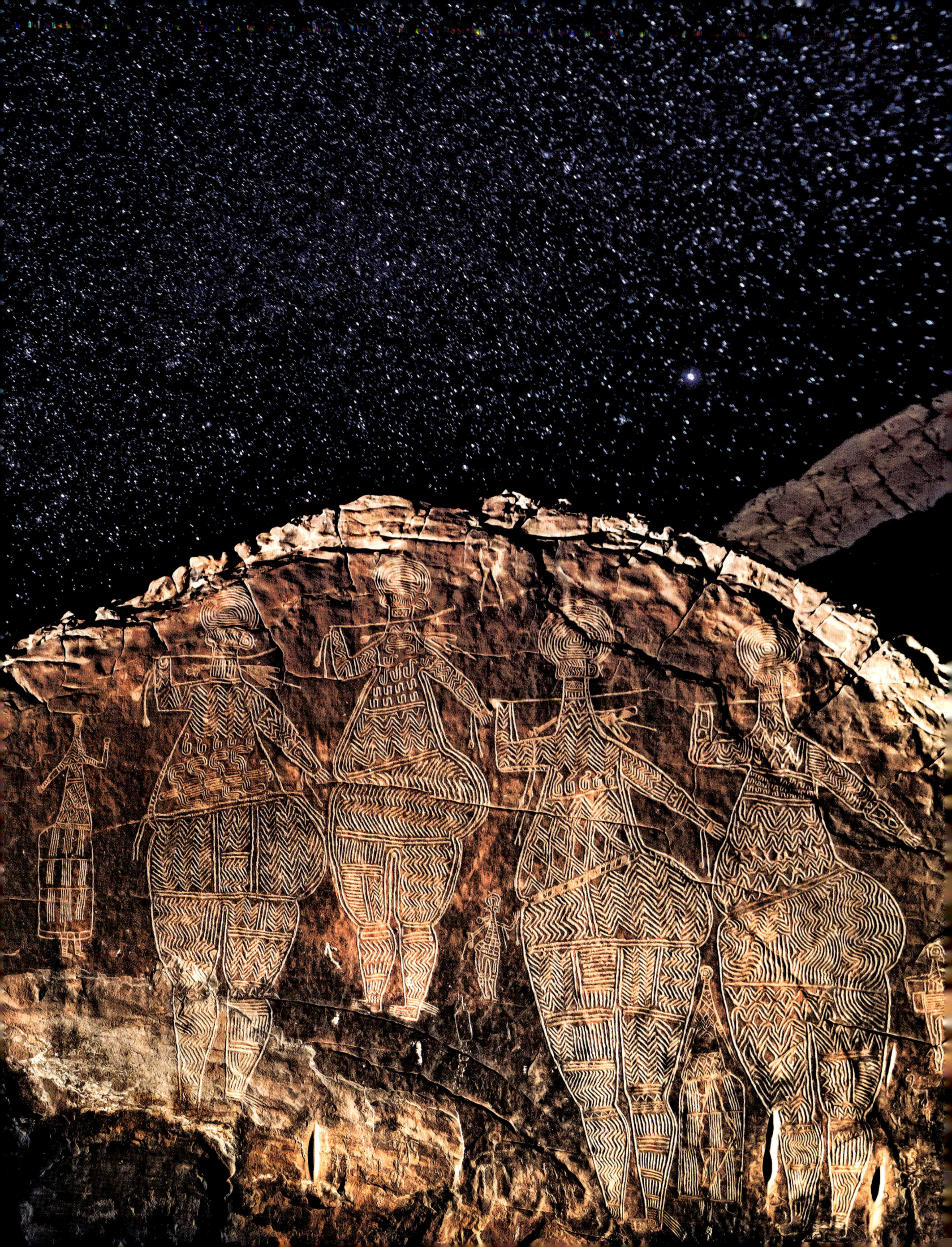

The first to discover and publish Saharan petroglyphs was the German explorer Heinrich Barth (1821–1865) who made a pioneering crossing of the desert from Tripoli to Timbuktu in 1850–55.[15] When he camped on 5 July 1850 in the Wadi Telissare (Tilizaghen) in the Libyan Messak, he discovered figures of animals and therianthropes engraved on the smooth rock faces. In one scene, a larger therianthrope has a human body and a horned bull or antelope head; he is armed with a shield and a drawn bow. He attacks a smaller therianthrope who carries what is either a bow without an arrow or a shield. Between the two therianthropes stands a bovine, probably the object of the dispute (fig. 286). Barth interpreted the larger therianthrope as the 'Apollo of the Garamantes', the mythic forefather of the Garamantes (mentioned by Herodotus) whose realm centred in the Fezzan, south-western Libya.[16] By associating the petroglyphs with the Garamantes, Barth acknowledged their antiquity. He was furthermore amazed to notice that the engraved animals, such as buffalo, cattle and ostriches, could have ever survived in the prevailing climate. Barth also wondered at the absence of camels in the petroglyphs although the dromedary was ideally adapted to desert environments. By reminding the reader that the camel had only been introduced in Egypt under the Ptolemaic Dynasty (in fact it was in the seventh century BCE), he implied that the petroglyphs dated from older, prehistoric times when the Sahara included grasslands.[17] Although Barth did not elaborate further on the connection between climate, fauna and rock art, he sensed that petroglyphs could open a door to an unknown past. Later European explorers who followed in the footsteps of Barth were also struck by the contrast between the arid Saharan landscape and petroglyphs of crocodiles, elephants, rhinoceroses and hippopotami which all required wet or at least humid environments.

Indeed, as in Saudi Arabia, the Sahara has seen an eventful tectonic and climatic history with its fauna thriving and disappearing to the rhythm of the climatic pulsation. The same observation applies to the human populations of these regions and their economies which adapted to varying climatic conditions. And,

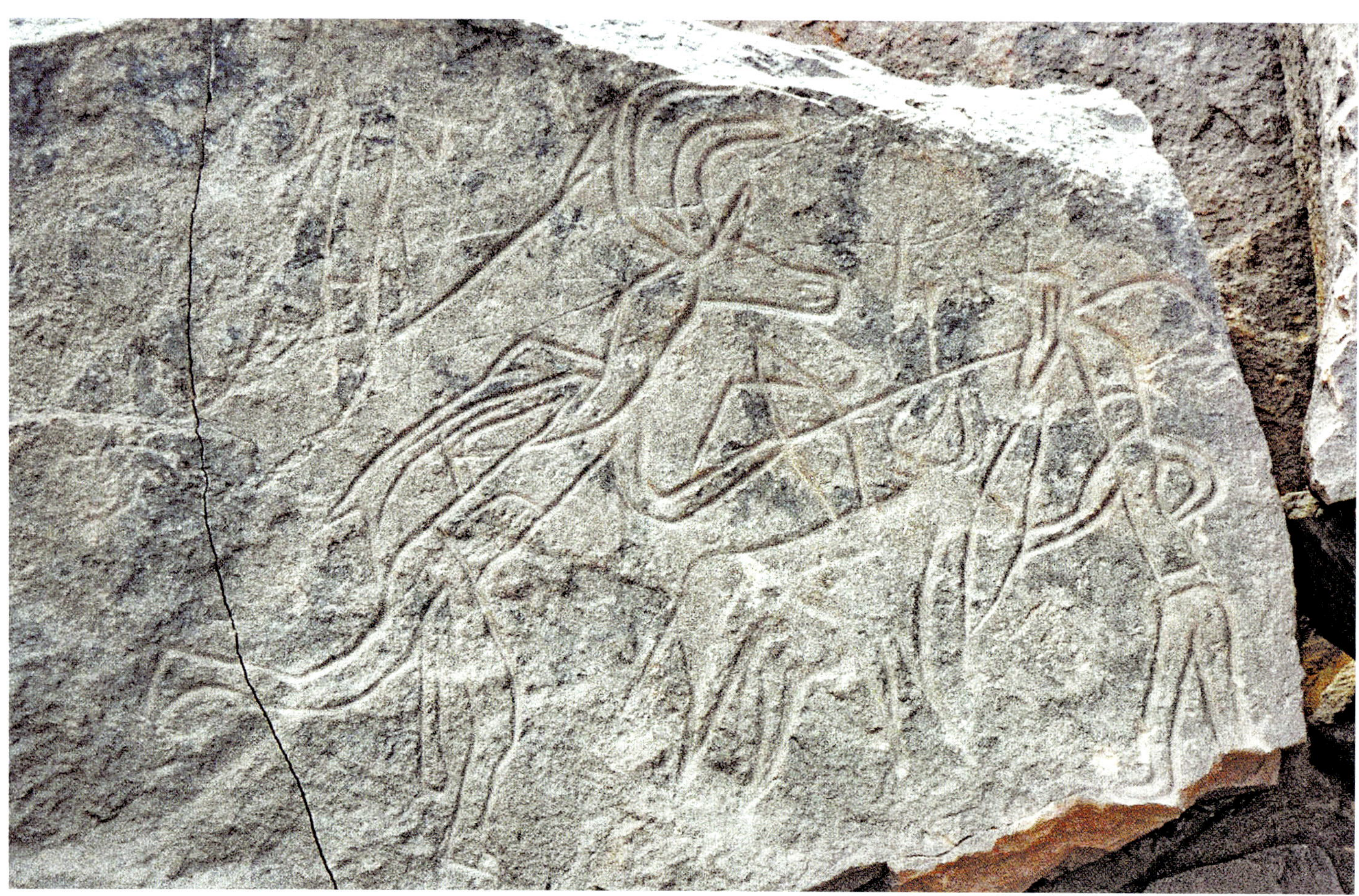

286. The famous petroglyph scene in Wadi Tilizaghen (Telissare) which was named 'Apollo of the Garamantes' by Heinrich Barth in 1850. The larger figure has a human body and a bull or antelope head; the scene seems to illustrate a conflict over a bovine. Early to Middle Pastoral Period, Messak, south-western Libya. Photo 1999 by Martin Emch.

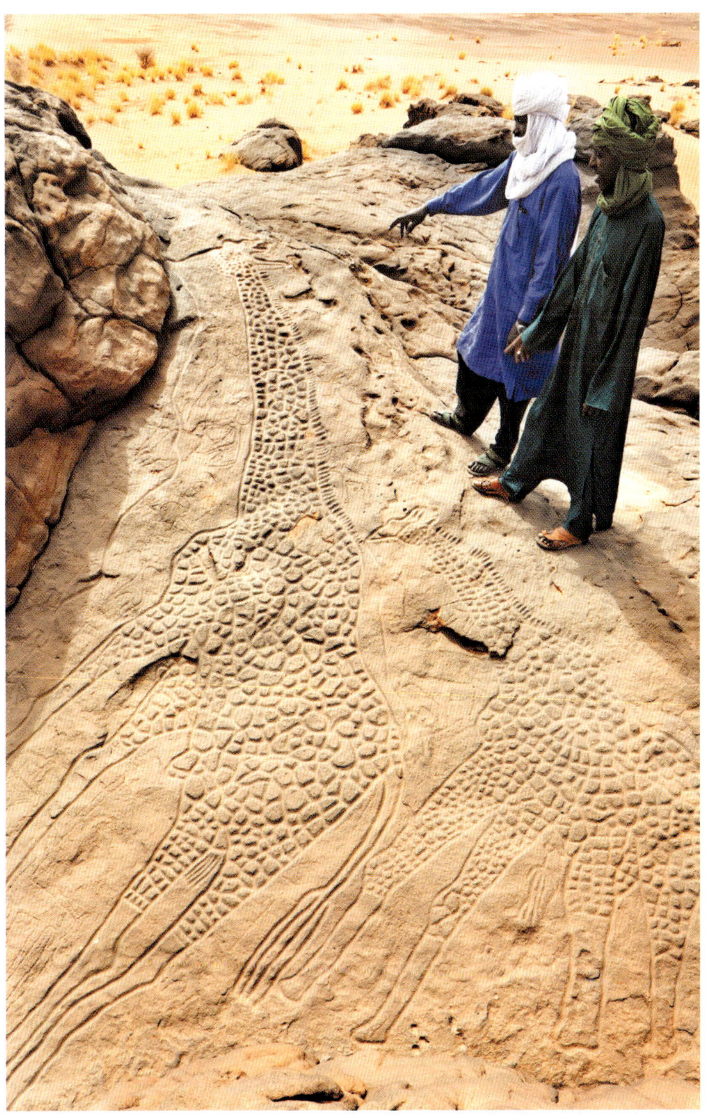

287. Petroglyphs up to six metres long of two giraffes at Dabous in the Aïr mountains. Early Pastoral Period, Ténéré Desert, Niger. Photo 2010.

as in Arabia and Central Asia, the changes in fauna and human activities were reflected in rock art. The multitude of inscriptions, both engraved and painted, in the Tifinagh script which are found in Wadi Djerat represents another parallel with Arabian rock art. The Tifinagh script was used to write Berber Tuareg languages; it is a successor to the ancient Libyco-Berber alphabet which emerged around the middle of the first millennium BCE, probably as a development of the Phoenician script with the addition of local symbols. However, the development from the Libyco-Berber script to Tifinagh was a gradual one, and contemporary Tifinagh is somewhat different from ancient Libyco-Berber.[18] Today's Tuaregs who are literate in Tifinagh can only recognize some of the ancient letters, and do not understand their meaning. But unlike the epigraphic rock art in Arabia, the engraved Tifinagh inscriptions in Wadi Djerat are exclusively brief and simple personal communications, and there are no official proclamations.

Based on Barth's publication and on unverified information from local Tubu (herders living in the Tibesti Mountains and southern Libya) who gave reports about very ancient wheel ruts and petroglyphs of carts pulled by zebus in the Fezzan and Messak regions, the French geographer Henri Duveyrier (1840–1892) developed the theory that there existed in the antiquity a road that crossed the Sahara from the Libyan coast via Garama, the capital of the central Saharan Garamantes in today's south-western Libya, to the Aïr in northern Niger. He even linked this supposed road to three Roman military expeditions across the Sahara led by Cornelius Balbus in 20–19 BCE, Septimius Flaccus around 77–81 CE and Julius Maternus *ca.* 82–85 CE. Although Duveyrier had never travelled to the Fezzan, the French explorer Henri Lhote (1903–1991) adopted this theory of a presumed Trans-Saharan road suitable for carts and chariots.[19] Later research conducted *in situ* failed to confirm these alleged wheel ruts and petroglyphs of cart-pulling zebus.[20] The German ethnologist and explorer of rock art Leo Frobenius (1873–1938), for his part, left an enduring heritage, for he recognized in the African petroglyphs and pictoglyphs the original expression of prehistoric autochthonous African cultures.[21] For Frobenius, researching and documenting the rock paintings was an essential part of his ambitious endeavour to systematically record the cultures of Africa before they were drowned out by European influences in the course of colonial administration.

2. Climate, fauna and petroglyphs

Today, the Sahara stretches from the Atlantic Ocean to the Red Sea and from *ca.* 17° north in the south to *ca.* 34° north at its northern edge, which corresponds to a north–south distance of 1,900 kilometres. But not only the climate of the Sahara, but also its geographical position was once very different from today. About 420 million years ago (mya), the cratons[22] forming today's Africa were joined together to form part of the supercontinent Gondwana which was fully located in the southern hemisphere. Although it is hard for us to imagine, what is today the Sahara was twice mostly covered by thick ice, around 450 and 300 mya.[23] Around 335 mya, Gondwana fused with the northern land masses of Laurasia and Siberia to form the even larger supercontinent of Pangaea which was now centred at the equator. But this new supercontinent was subject to internal pressures and tectonic movements northwards by the

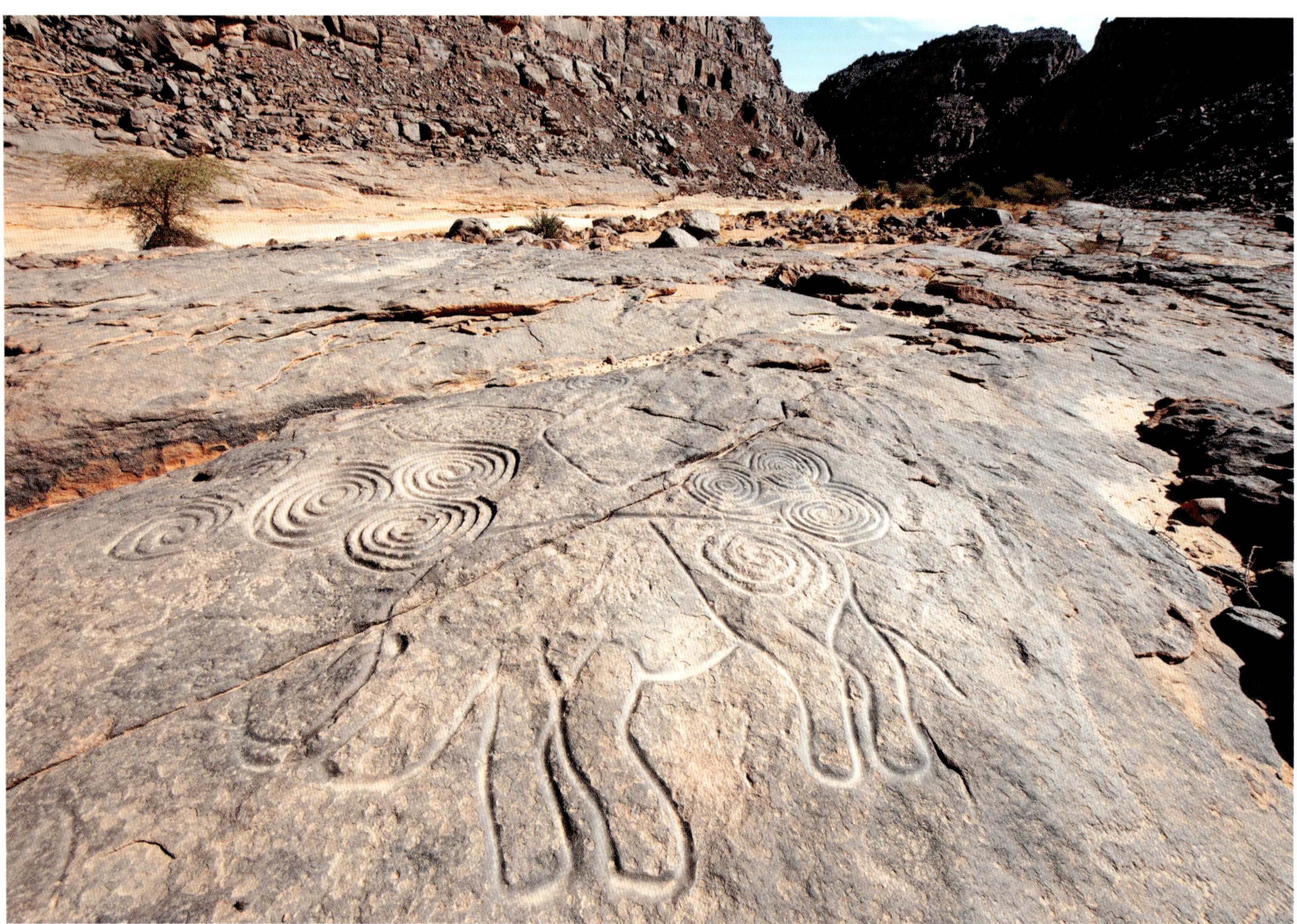

288. Deeply engraved petroglyphs of a rhinoceros, two triple spirals and additional single spirals. Middle Pastoral Period, site L 28, Wadi Djerat, Tassili n'Ajjer, south-eastern Algeria. Photo 2023.

former African cratons. This encroachment of the African plate on the Eurasian plate triggered the slow uplift of the Atlas Mountains and the Saharan Upland in northern Africa and of the Alps in Europe. These uplifting forces and volcanic activities that continued till the Miocene (23–5.3 mya) created the Saharan Upland and its high mountain ranges such as the Tibesti (up to 3,415 metres), Jabal Marra (3,088 metres) and Ahaggar (Hoggar, 2,998 metres). These mountain ranges were later highly important for the survival of plants and animals since they attracted clouds. They secured a minimum of water supply by obtaining significantly more rain than the surrounding arid plains; moreover, the seeping rainwater refilled the groundwater springs around which oases flourished. In the Holocene, these mountains and adjacent valley systems would function as refuges for flora and fauna during arid intervals.

About 200 mya Pangaea started to break up. By *ca.* 130 mya Africa had broken away from South America and the Atlantic Ocean began to form.[24] During the Cretaceous period (145–66 mya), when

dinosaurs thrived in today's Sahara,[25] Africa was still positioned south of its present location and the equator ran across the Sahara.[26] The continued northward drift of the African plate not only further contributed to the Alpine orogeny (mountain formation),[27] but also pushed the landscape that is today the Sahara northwards out of the humid equatorial zone into latitudes dominated by dry aeolian flows. As a consequence, the wet rainforest climatic regime that was previously dominant in the Sahara moved southwards and by the end of the Eocene (56–33.9 mya) the north of the Sahara began to desiccate. Even so, around 6 mya, the monsoon line was at times about 1,650 kilometres further north than it is today and the Sahara, defined as a hot and arid landscape with minimal rainfall, had practically disappeared. As of *ca.* 2.4 mya, the Sahara was more or less desertic, albeit cyclically interspersed with longer wetter periods.[28] Such warmer, wetter periods, in which grasslands expanded, existed between 340 and 200 ka, around 124 ka, 102 ka and 81 ka BP. Finds of Acheulean[29] and Levallois lithic tools on the northern borders of the Sahara as well in central regions such as Tassili n'Ajjer and Ahaggar indicate that early humans not only crossed the Sahara but also lived in it, taking advantage of its wildlife. However, a renewed cold and arid period from 71 ka to 57 ka BP forced these Middle Palaeolithic hunter-gatherers out of the Sahara. Apart from milder intervals around 39–36 and 28–25 ka BP the Sahara remained an arid, cold zone hostile to human life, whose harshness peaked in the Last Glacial Maximum around 21–19 ka BP. Except for the milder interludes, the Sahara remained for tens of thousands of years virtually empty of humans.[30]

The warmer Bølling–Allerød interstadial (14.7–12.9 ka BP) was, in spite of the subsequent renewed sharp and brief cooling of the Younger Dryas (12.9–11.7 ka BP), a real climatic game-changer. As the northern ice sheets melted at the onset of the Holocene and global sea levels rose, much humidity was released into the atmosphere and the climate of North Africa became moister. This development initiated the African Humid Period which lasted until about 3500 BCE.[31] During the climatic optimum of the Humid Period, the landscape of the Sahara included lakes, among them the Mega Fezzan and the Mega Chad. The latter's maximum surface was then *ca.* 360,000 square kilometres,[32] with forests growing around it. Outside the lacustrine and fluvial regions, the landscape was a mix of grass savanna, steppe and bushes. The expansion and shrinking of the Sahara was essentially a function of the reach and strength of the African monsoon. Whereas during the Last Glacial Maximum the Sahara Desert expanded southwards by 500 to 800,[33] or even 1,000[34] kilometres compared to its present dimensions, during the African Climatic Optimum around 8500–8000 BCE, its southern border regressed by a similar amount – *ca.* 500 to 800 kilometres[35] or even 800–1,000 kilometres[36] – to the north of the current border (map 9). The rapidly improving climatic conditions triggered the return of vegetation soon followed by herbivores and their predators and in turn by hunter-gatherers. The repopulation of the Sahara began soon after 11 ka BP from the south when sub-Saharan hunter-gatherers followed the monsoon rains and the consequent northward expansion of flora and fauna. Since a fairly lush vegetation and wildlife developed, the migrating hunter-gatherers found plentiful food resources and opted for a relatively sedentary kind of life.[37] Possibly at the same time or slightly later, hunter-gatherers left the valley of the Nile, which had become swampy and therefore unsuitable for human life, and migrated westward into the eastern Sahel region. From there, they subsequently migrated northward into the eastern Sahara.[38] Also in the same time bracket, hunter-gatherers moved from the southwest, from today's Mali, into the wooded and grassy savannas of

the Sahara. These migrants brought the knowledge of the manufacture of ceramics with them. The oldest ceramic sherds of Africa were found in Mali at 14° 38' north; they are dated to *ca.* 9400 BCE, at the time when the African monsoon began to reach 14° north. From here, the knowledge of ceramic production spread rapidly northwards and reached 20° north in northern Niger at the beginning of the ninth millennium BCE and southern Algeria and southern Libya around or shortly after 8000 BCE.[39] The spread of ceramics, which in the Sahara marked the beginning of the early Neolithic,[40] was of huge practical consequence, since it allowed people to conserve and to process plant-based foodstuffs such as wild cereals through cooking or fermenting.

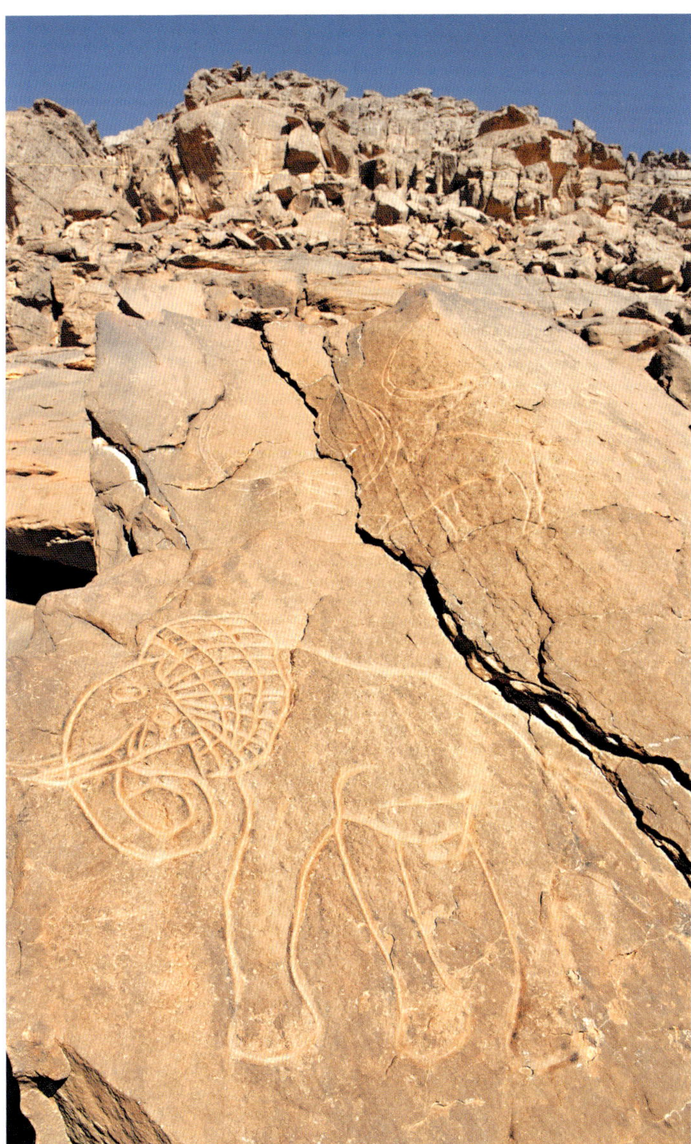

289. Petroglyphs of an elephant (below) and two wild buffaloes (above). Early to Middle Pastoral Periods, site L 52, Wadi Djerat, Tassili n'Ajjer, south-eastern Algeria. Photo 2023.

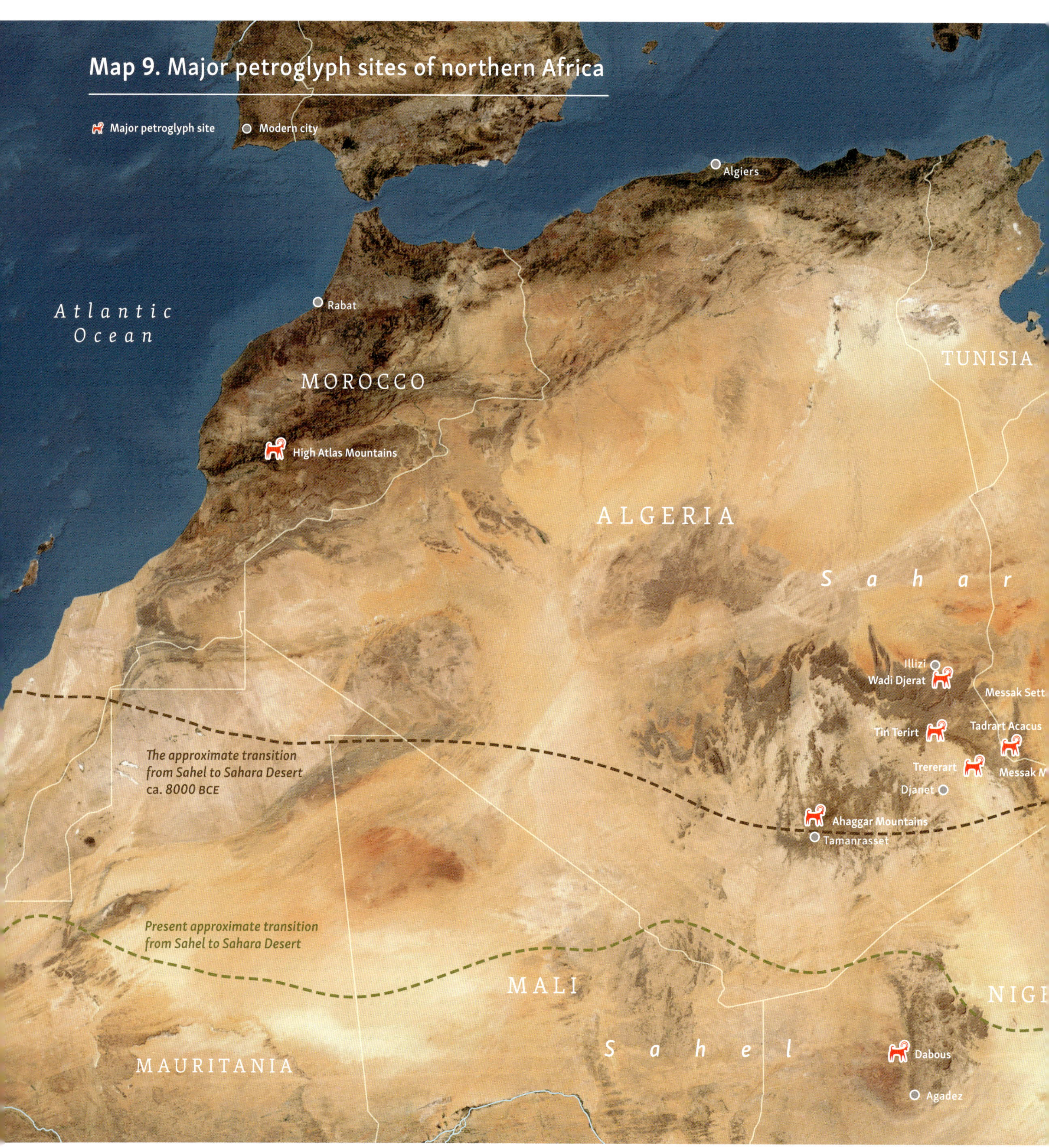
Map 9. Major petroglyph sites of northern Africa
Major petroglyph site
Modern city
Algiers
Atlantic Ocean
Rabat
MOROCCO
TUNISIA
High Atlas Mountains
ALGERIA
Sahar
Illizi
Wadi Djerat
Messak Sett
Tin Terirt
Tadrart Acacus
Trererart
Messak M
Djanet
The approximate transition from Sahel to Sahara Desert ca. 8000 BCE
Ahaggar Mountains
Tamanrasset
Present approximate transition from Sahel to Sahara Desert
MALI
NIG
Sahel
MAURITANIA
Dabous
Agadez

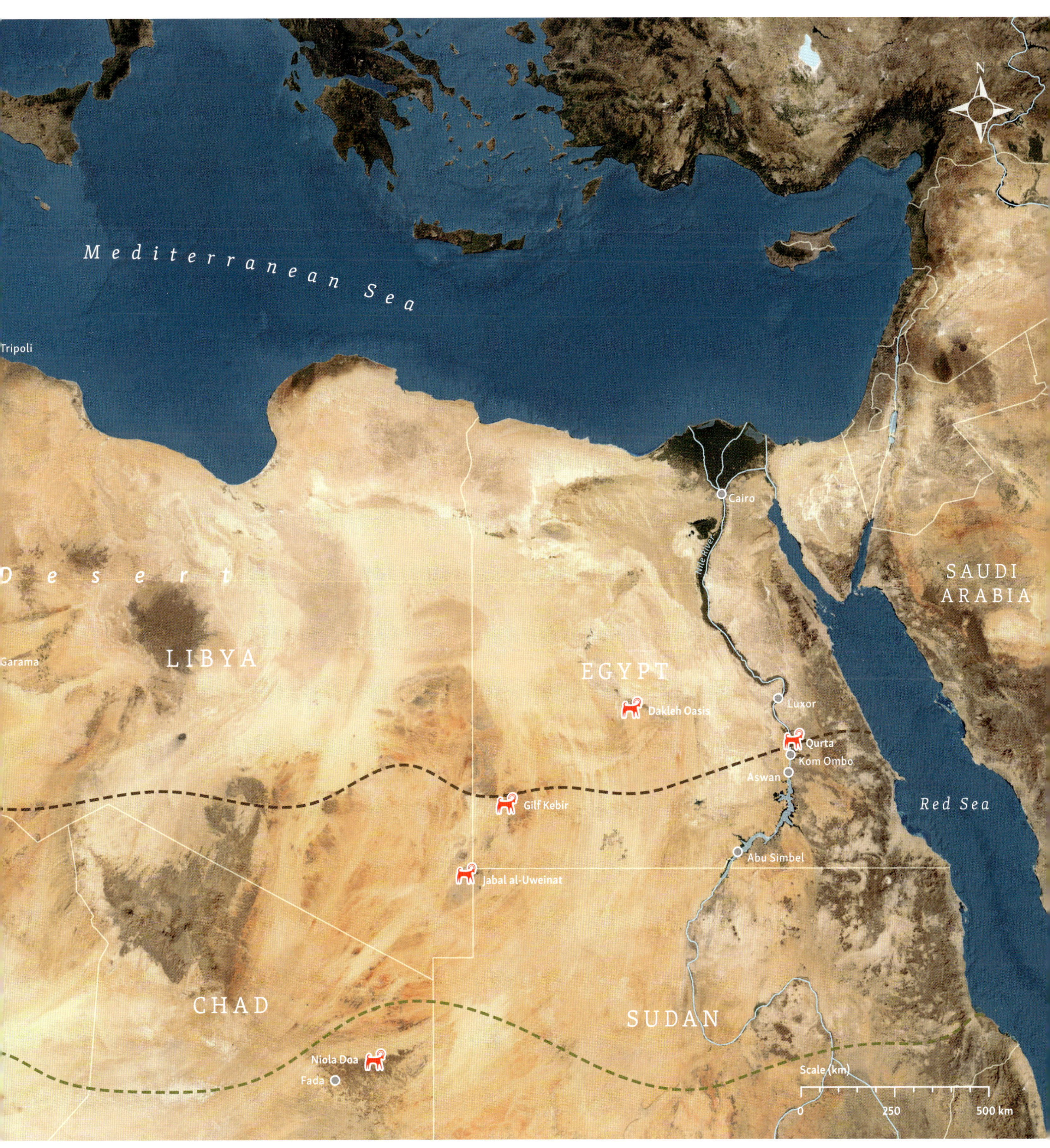
N
Mediterranean Sea
Tripoli
Desert
LIBYA
Garama
EGYPT
Cairo
Nile River
Dakleh Oasis
Luxor
Qurta
Kom Ombo
Aswan
Gilf Kebir
SAUDI
ARABIA
Red Sea
Abu Simbel
Jabal al-Uweinat
CHAD
SUDAN
Niola Doa
Fada
Scale (km)
0
250
500 km

At the onset of the Holocene, rainfall advanced into the Sahara not only from the south northwards, but also from the north southwards. Witness to a southward migration of Mediterranean–North African hunter-gatherers are the lithic tools found in the Central African Acacus region where a rich centre of petroglyph production would later emerge. This microlithic industry from the Early Acacus phase, which is dated to the ninth to eighth millennium BCE, reveals strong similarities with the lithic production of the late North African **Iberomaurusian culture**.[41] Genetic analyses have confirmed that Mediterranean people migrated during the Holocene Climatic Optimum into the central Sahara. Their distant descendants were the Garamantes who, in turn, are the forefathers of today's Tuaregs. The latters' significant, but younger sub-Saharan genetic heritage was most probably introduced through the Trans-Saharan slave trade which the Garamantes already practised in the sixth century BCE.[42] Whereas the Early Acacus period of pure hunter-gatherers was aceramic, a millennium later the Late Acacus hunter-gatherers had pottery and followed a less mobile lifestyle since they herded Barbary sheep, a native North African caprine, and collected and stored wild cereals.[43]

Occurring around 6200 BCE, the global **8.2-kiloyear event** was a significant climate cooling lasting for about 300 years. It happened during an underlying climatic cooling phase which had become noticeable in the Levant several centuries earlier, possibly since *ca.* 7300 BCE.[44] This cooling trend was reinforced when the north-east American Laurentide Ice Sheet finally melted away discharging icy water into the North Atlantic Ocean. This cooling triggered an acceleration of the ongoing reduction in humidity and precipitation which, in the fundamentally fragile ecosystem of the Sahara, led to a sharp shrinkage of lakes and a reduction in vegetation.[45] It is likely that this gradual increase in dryness and cold as of *ca.* 7300 BCE motivated farmers and pastoralists from the Levant to migrate south into the Nile Delta, bringing with them know-how in agriculture and livestock breeding. Whereas agriculture never really took root in the Sahara, domesticated sheep and goats soon spread from the Nile Delta westwards; first along the Mediterranean coast to the Maghreb and

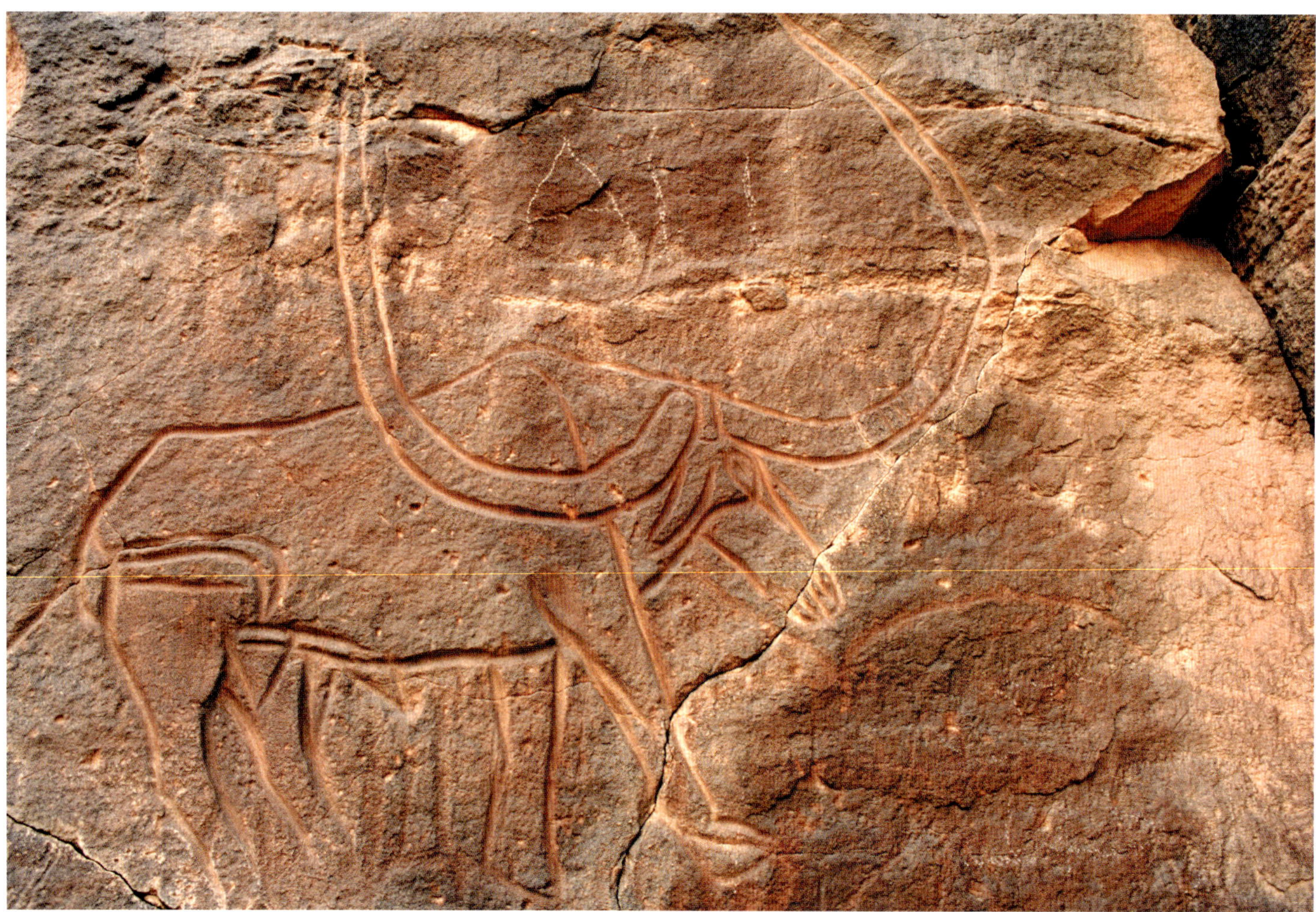

290. Wild African buffalo *Bubalus antiquus* (*Syncerus antiquus*) with spreading horns. Early to Middle Pastoral Period, Messak, south-western Libya.

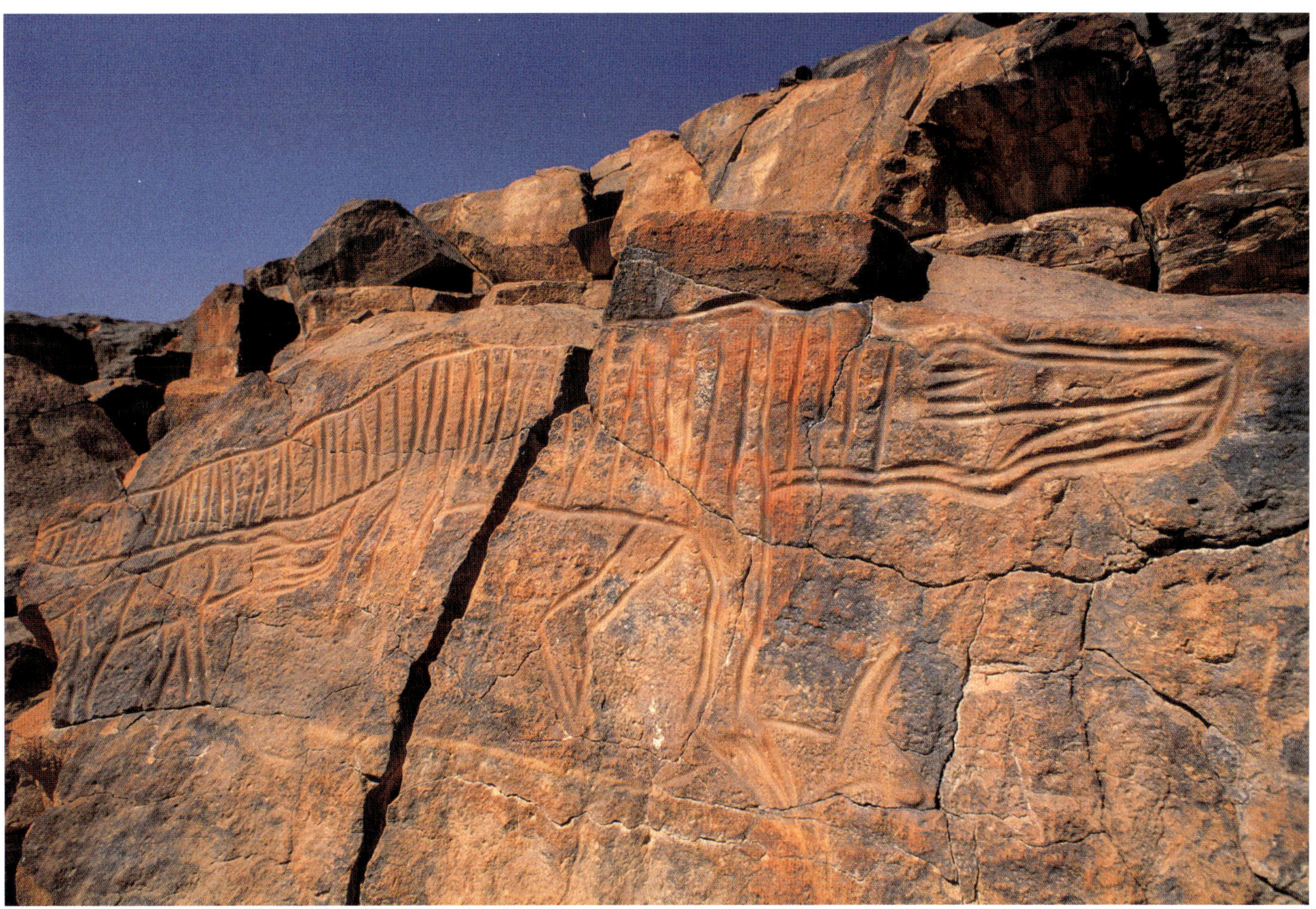

291. Petroglyphs of two crocodiles. Early to Middle Pastoral Period, Messak, south-western Libya.

the Nubian Desert, and then in a second stage to the Acacus region in the central Sahara by around 6300 BCE.[46] It seems that the spread of sheep and goats preceded that of cattle by one or two centuries.[47] It is conceivable that the earliest petroglyphs of bovines in the Tassili n'Ajjer and Messak date from this period.[48] While there is no doubt that sheep and goats were first domesticated in Anatolia and were introduced from Egypt to Northern Africa and the Sahara – the African Barbary sheep (*Ammotragus lervia*) is not closely related to domesticated caprines[49] – it has been debated whether the cow (*Bos taurus*) was also introduced into Africa from outside or whether it was domesticated locally, possibly in the eastern Sahara, that is the Western Desert of Egypt. The most recent genetic testing indicates that cattle were originally domesticated in Mesopotamia and spread from there to the Middle East and then to Africa. However, in Africa imported domesticated cows were hybridized with native wild aurochs.[50] The introduction of caprines and bovines into the Sahara changed its Neolithic economy from one of hunter-gatherers to pastoralism; nevertheless, both hunting and the gathering of

wild cereals continued to play a role. This represented a successful adaptation to fundamental environmental changes. As warmer and more humid conditions returned in the first quarter of the sixth millennium BCE, the Saharan lakes filled up again, albeit not to their previous levels, and vegetation recovered.

The fact that cattle were the most important resource for the central Saharan Neolithic pastoralists may be deduced from the fact that *ca.* 60 per cent of Saharan rock art depicts cattle or activities related to cattle,[51] and from the cattle burials in Messak. These monuments consisted of a platform which was surrounded by sandstone slabs that were often decorated with petroglyphs featuring bovines; a few of these petroglyphs illustrate the sacrifice of cattle.[52] The surrounding rocks were also engraved with the images of bulls or cows. Excavations of such monuments revealed the bones of bovines, mostly cows. These finds suggest that in the context of a cattle cult cows were ritually sacrificed, their meat eaten and their bones buried, whereupon engraved slabs were erected. These cattle burials have been radiocarbon dated to between 5200 cal. and

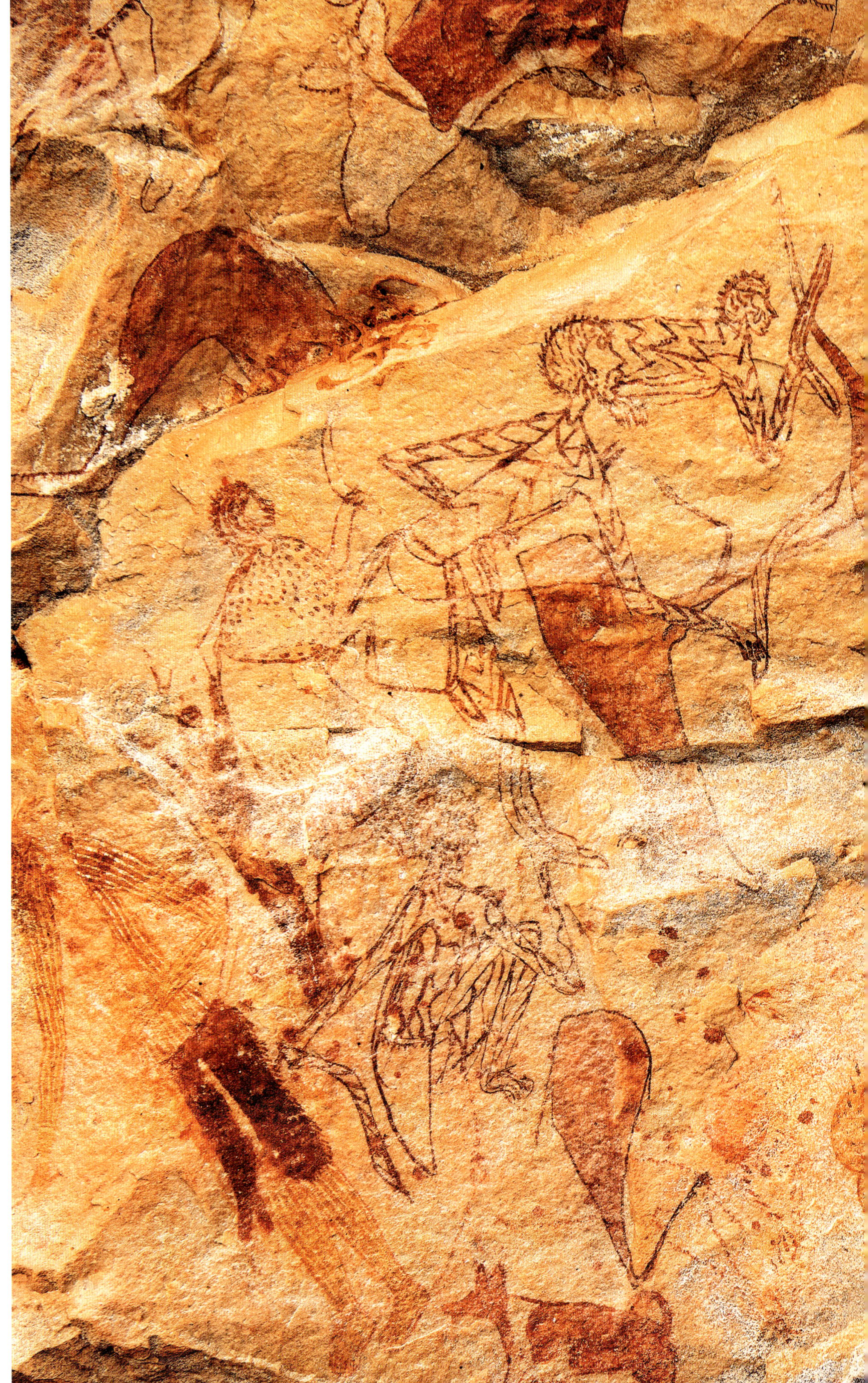

292. Painting in the naturalistic Saharan Iheren–Tahilahi style at the shelter of Tikadiouine. In the image, of the central and right sections: three men and one woman butcher an antelope with their knives. Below the lower man there is a dog, and to its left stands a human whose torso is painted with long stripes. Around the butchering scene crouch four rabbits, probably the prey from a recent hunt. To the right, three giraffes flee from two pairs of pursuing men armed with curved knives. The bodies of all four hunters as well as of two of the men doing the butchering have rich body painting or tattooing. One of the hunters catches the tail of one of the giraffes which tramples on a Barbary sheep lying on the ground. Late to Final Pastoral Period, Tassili n'Ajjer, south-eastern Algeria. Photo 2023.

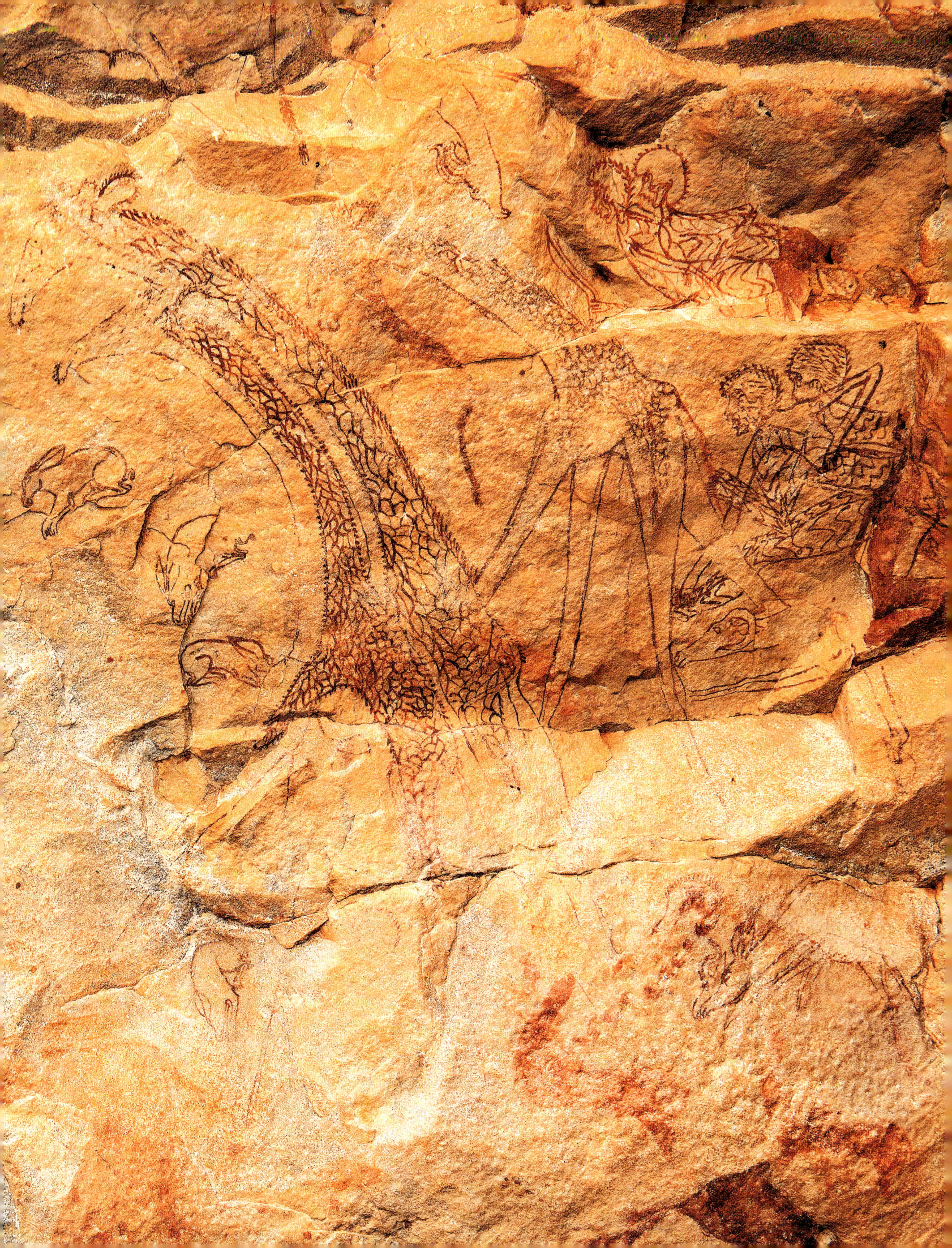

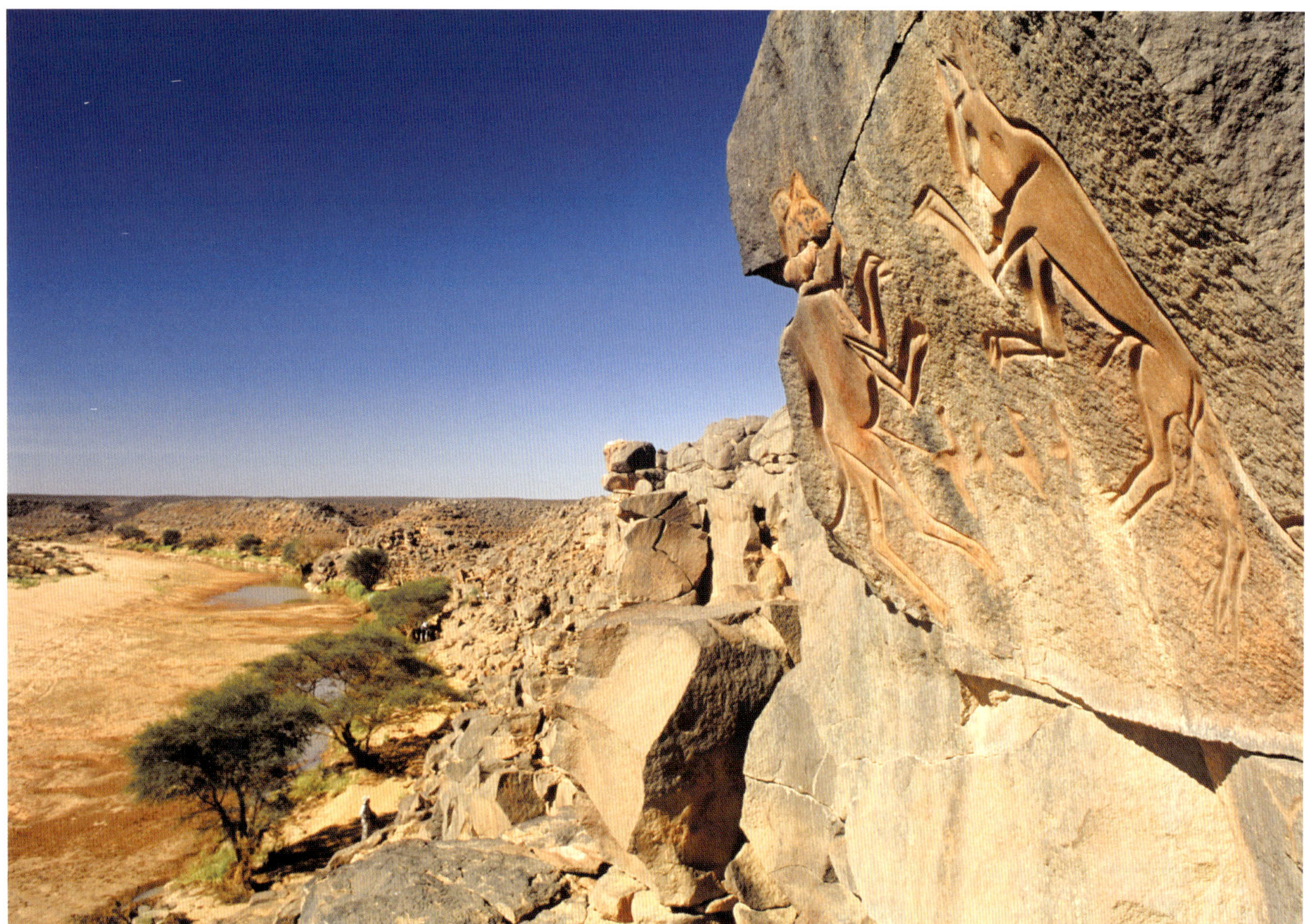

293. Deeply engraved and polished petroglyph panel of the so-called 'two fighting cats' in Wadi Mathendous. Pastoral Period, Messak Settafet, south-western Libya.

3800 cal. BCE, that is the Middle Pastoral Period.[53] Even earlier, in the sixth millennium BCE, circular stone arrangements were placed over the ritual burials of cattle in the eastern Sahara.[54] As surmised by Barry Cunliffe, it is likely that this Saharan cattle cult was transferred to the Nile Valley in the first half of the fourth millennium BCE when a renewed trend towards aridity that had already begun in the eastern Sahara at the end of the sixth millennium BCE forced the eastern Saharan pastoralists to relocate to the Fayum oasis and the Nile.[55] When the African monsoon precipitation began to recede southwards, aridification set in first in the eastern Sahara while the central and western Sahara still received rain from the Atlantic which continued to ensure viable conditions for pastoralists, especially in mountainous uplands like the Tassili n'Ajjer, Messak Settafet and Tadrart Acacus. In those regions, pastoralists adopted a strategy of vertical transhumance, moving with their herds to semi-permanent mountain camps when the seasonal conditions were wetter in the mountains than in the plains.[56] Yet

the reduction in precipitation and thus in the sizes of lakes and rivers led to a gradual disappearance of water-bound animals like crocodiles and an exodus of large herbivores such as hippopotami, elephants and rhinoceroses, and later also of giraffes.

However, when the monsoon further retreated and aridification increased at the beginning of the third millennium BCE, pastoralists began to migrate either south into the Sahel, north towards the Mediterranean coastal regions or east to the Nile. Judging from wall paintings in the Tassili n'Ajjer, where facial features can be recognized much more clearly than from petroglyphs, soon after 3000 BCE virtually the only people represented in the prevailing **Iheren–Tahilahi style** are of a Mediterranean, gracile type, and black African people are almost absent from these paintings (fig. 292). The latter had by that time probably migrated south together with their herds. It is possible that a renewed migration from the North African Mediterranean region into the Sahara stimulated the shift from a pastoral economy to a primarily agricultural economy in the central Saharan Fezzan.[57] In spite of a marginal improvement of climatic conditions during the second millennium BCE, major parts of the Sahara became inhospitable and uninhabited except by frugal semi-nomads practising small-stock husbandry, such as herding goats and sheep.[58] Only oases like those in the Tassili n'Ajjer or, especially, in the Fezzan, had enough resources to sustain substantial populations. Most probably, the aridification and retreat of vegetation was not solely caused by this global climate change, but was at a local and regional level also man-made, a result of overgrazing.[59] Around 1000 BCE, the climatic conditions of the Sahara were similar to those of today.

In the Fezzan, however, as observed by Nick Brooks et al., the aridification also triggered an inward migration which led to an increased population density, an adapted use of landscape and planned water management. These changes in turn resulted in a new social stratification and, in the case of the Garamantes, in the formation of a semi-agrarian, semi-urban civilization.[60] The process in the Fezzan was similar to the one in the Nile Valley two millennia earlier, since the climatic deterioration triggered an increase in population density which in turn fostered social stratification, the emergence of new technologies such as artificial irrigation, and the development of a unique civilisation. Since there were no natural water courses linking the wells and aquifers with the fertile plains, the Garamantes adopted and further developed the *qanat* water transportation system which the Persians had introduced in Egypt after its conquest in 525 BCE. The *qanats*, called *aflaj* in the Arabian Peninsula and *foggaras* in North Africa, are underground aqueducts which transport the water to the desired destination.[61] Since the aqueducts are underground, evaporation is minimal; as so often in history, in the Fezzan adversity turned out

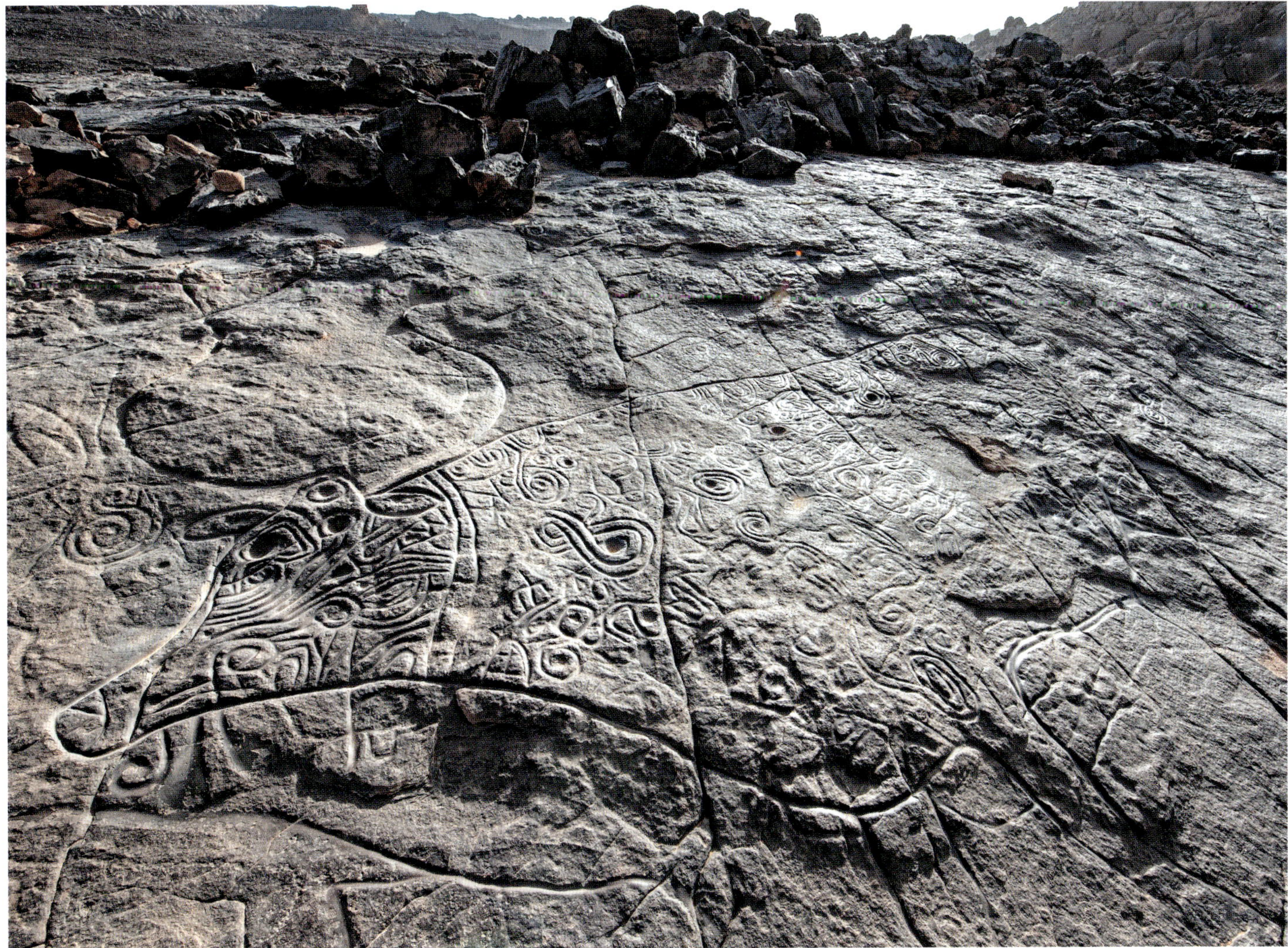

294. A buffalo 4.45 m long at Tin Teghert whose body is decorated with a multitude of signs and ornaments. Middle Pastoral Period, Tassili n'Ajjer, south-eastern Algeria. Photo 2023.

to be a driver for innovation. Some of these new technologies which appeared in the central Sahara came from outside, like the horse, the chariot and the camel. The two-wheeled battle chariot pulled by two horses was first introduced into Egypt in the course of the invasion of the lower Nile Valley by the Hyksos, of Levantine origin, around 1650 BCE.[62] From Egypt, horse and chariot gradually spread westward along the Mediterranean coast and into the Sahara, to the Fezzan and Tassili n'Ajjer (fig. 312).[63] The dromedary, in turn, reached the Sahara several centuries later. In Arabia, the dromedary has been domesticated for transport purposes since the tenth century BCE, but the date of its spread in Egypt and North Africa remains unknown. While it is probable that the dromedary was occasionally introduced into Lower Egypt in the wake of the trade contacts between Arabia and Egypt, it was used there for military purposes only after the Neo-Assyrian invasions of 671–663 BCE.[64] This means that the dromedary spread to the Sahara after the seventh century BCE, and it probably became widespread in the third century BCE.

In many locations of the Sahara, for example in Wadi Djerat, there are petroglyphs and paintings of light chariots, which could never have been used in such rocky and mountainous environments. This is not the only place with rock art illustrating chariots where deep sand made the use of such chariots impracticable. Most probably, in some areas of the Sahara, like in mountainous Central Asia, the chariot was an object of prestige or perhaps remembered in myths. However, there were regions where the rapid *biga*, *triga* and *quadriga* were certainly used. Herodotus, who reported that the Garamantes cultivated cereals and kept long-horned cattle, also wrote: 'The Garamantes hunt the Ethiopian troglodytes in four-horse chariots, for these troglodytes are exceedingly swift on foot.'[65] By 'Ethiopians' Herodotus did not mean the inhabitants of today's Ethiopia more than 3,000 kilometres away from the Fezzan, but sub-Saharan black people, since the Greek term *Aithiops* means 'burnt face'. As surmised by Jean-Loïc Le Quellec, Herodotus' 'Ethiopians' may here denominate the Tubu living south of the Garamantes who raided their neighbours to obtain slaves and were involved in slave-trading.[66] The occasional argument that the Garamantes hardly used any light chariots because there were only three such rock art depictions in their heartland[67] falls short of the mark, as the production of rock art in general declined in their heartland during the Garamantes' heyday but continued in neighbouring areas such as Messak, Tadrart, Tassili n'Ajjer and the Ennedi Plateau where hundreds of such images are found.

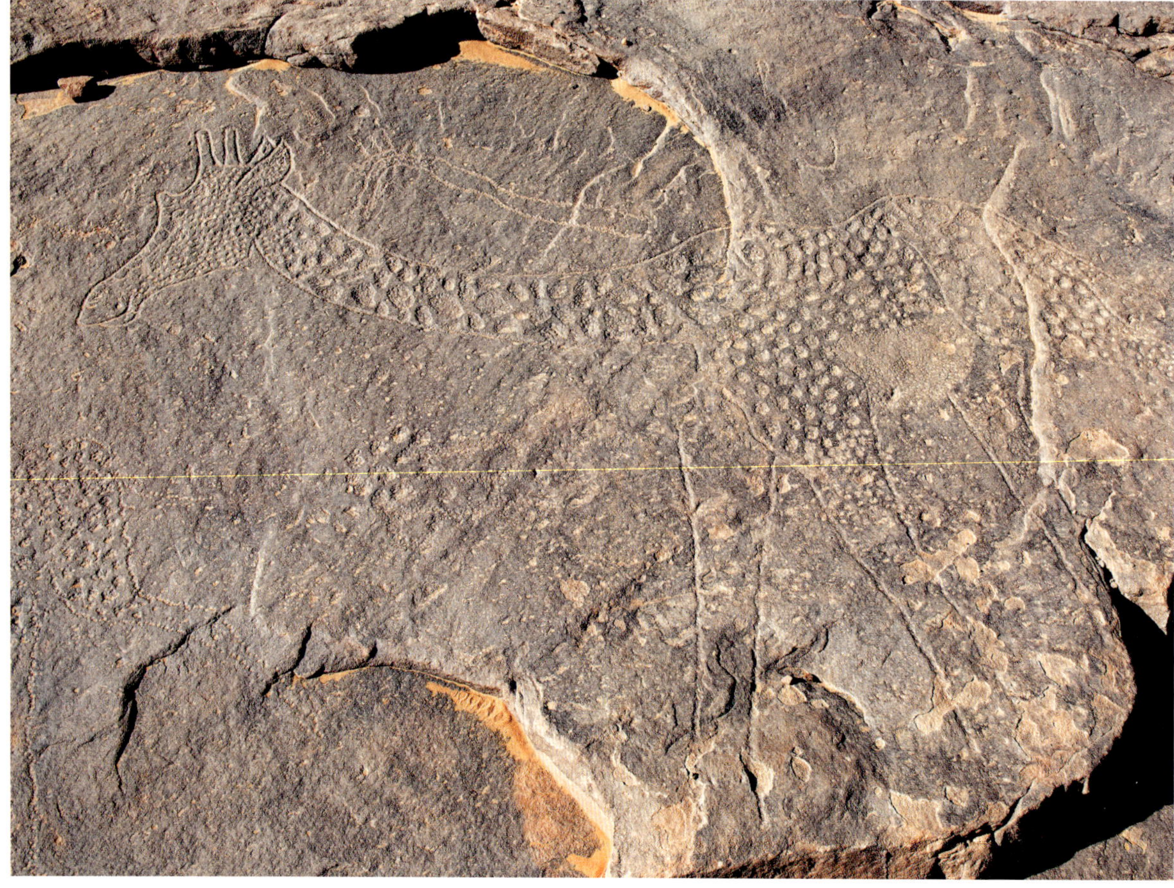

295. Petroglyph of a giraffe at site L 21, Wadi Djerat. Middle Pastoral Period, Tassili n'Ajjer, south-eastern Algeria. Photo 2023.

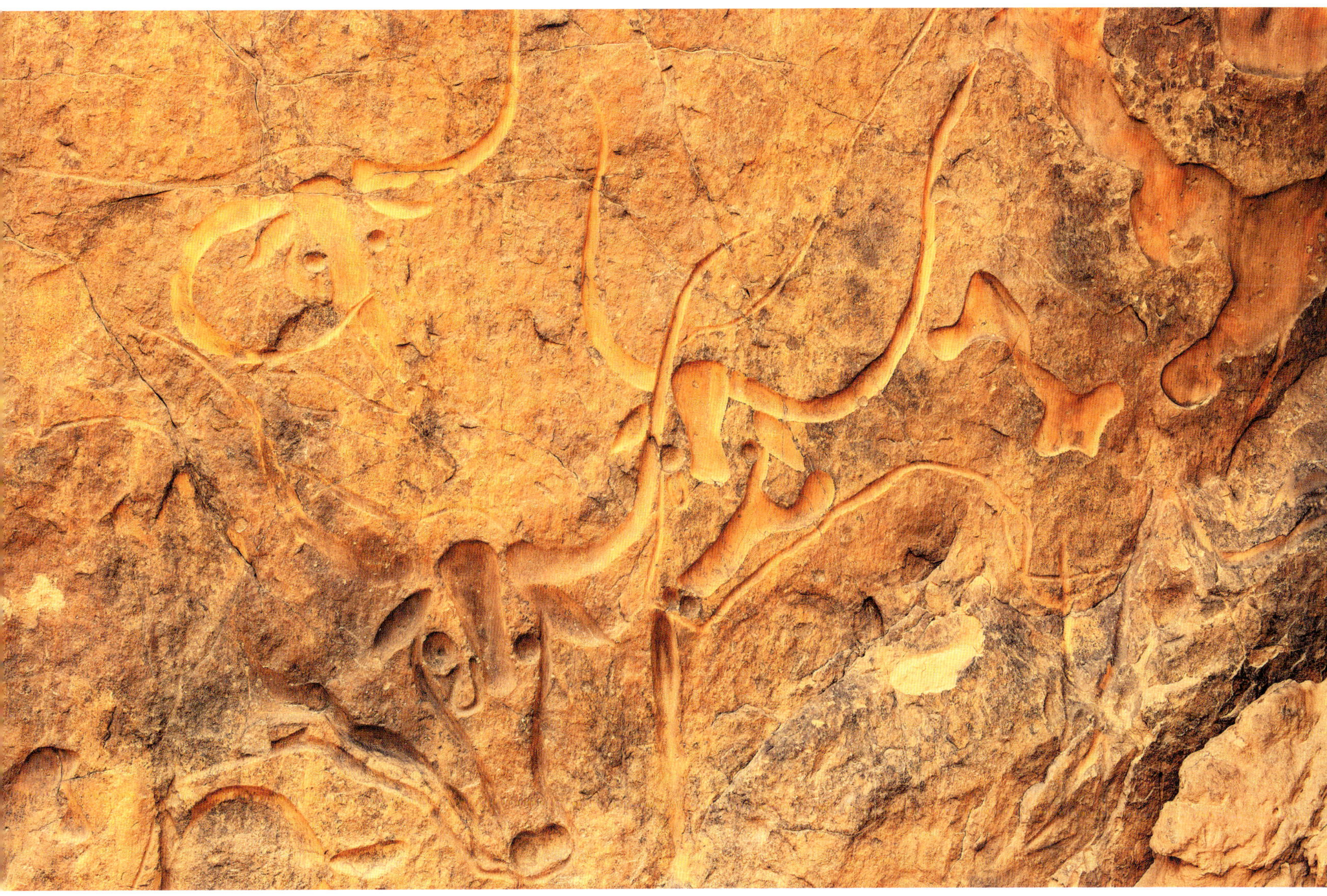

296. Panel of the so-called 'crying cows' at Tegharghart south of Djanet, from the Middle Pastoral Period. When it occasionally rains, the tiny depression at the base of the outcrop is filled with water, which creates the impression that the cows, from whose eyes a drop seems to trickle, bend their heads to drink. In folklore, cows are said to shed tears when they suffer from thirst. Middle Pastoral Period, Tassili n'Ajjer, south-eastern Algeria. Photo 2023.

3. The chronology of Saharan petroglyphs

When the first rock art was created in the Sahara, and especially the earliest petroglyphs, has been a controversial question for decades. The traditional chronology of petroglyphs goes back to the sequence outlined by Heinrich Barth. He described the oldest petroglyphs as those of extinct animals such as buffalo and ostriches, followed by domesticated cattle, then depictions of horses, later camels and finally rough Tifinagh inscriptions.[68] The Africa explorer Théodore Monod (1902–2000) deepened Barth's categorization into four phases which were adopted by Henri Lhote, Leo Frobenius and other authors.[69] They named the oldest period of petroglyph the **Bubalus Period** (*ca.* 8000–6000 BCE) in which large wild animals that are now extinct were rendered in a naturalistic yet expressive style, above all the wild African buffalo *Bubalus antiquus*, also called *Syncerus antiquus*, which is characterized by powerful, curved horns.[70] These petroglyphs were allegedly made by pre-pastoralist hunter-gatherers. In the next phase, the **Bovidian Period** (*ca.* 6000–1200 BCE), petroglyphs of domesticated cattle and scenes related to livestock husbandry predominated, which were created by pastoralists. The third period was called **Caballine** (*ca.* 1200–1 BCE) as images of more or less stylized horses became preponderant. It was followed by the **Camelline Period** (after *ca.* 1 CE) which reflected the widespread introduction of camels in the Sahara in the second half of the first

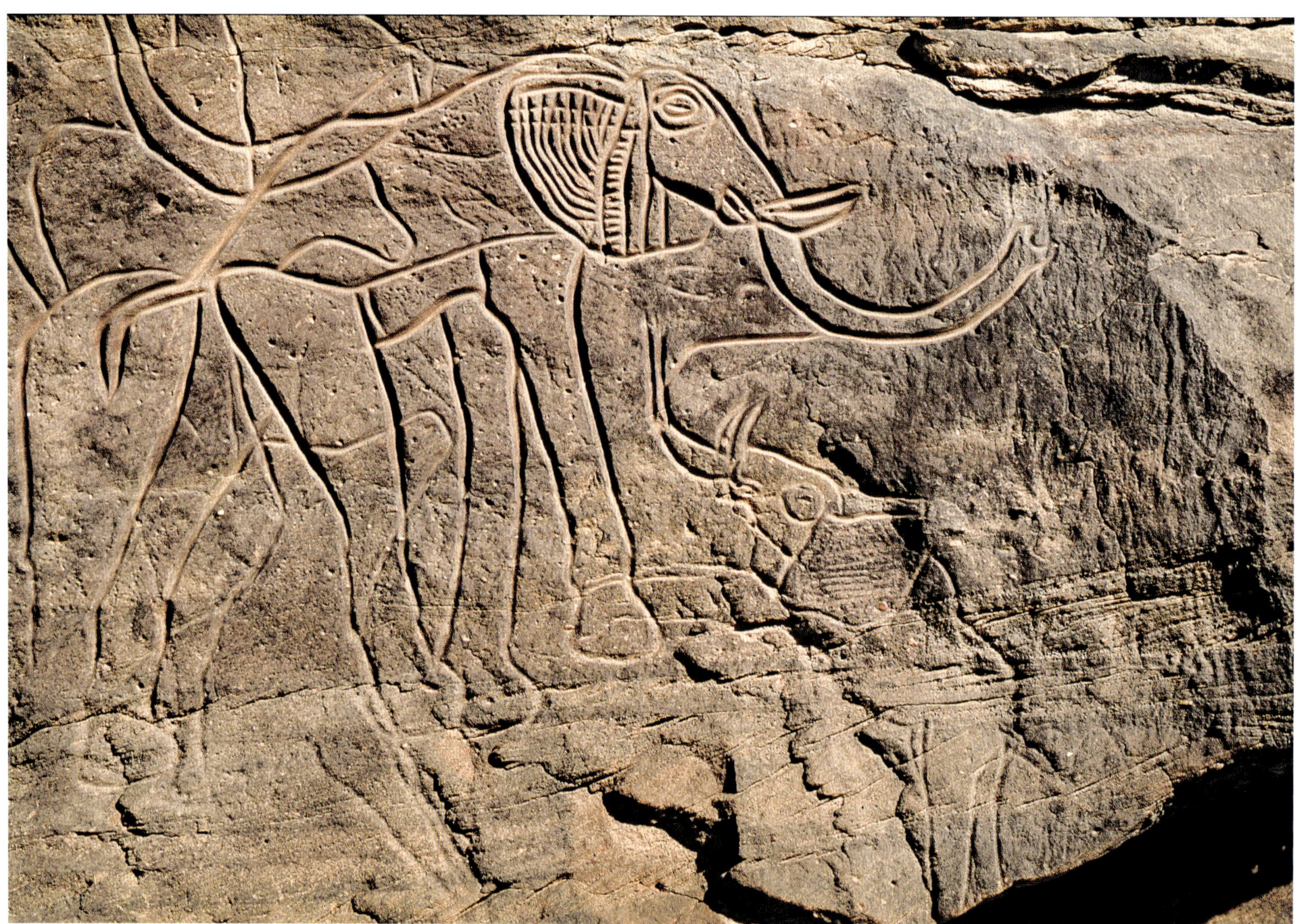

297. Polished engravings of two elephants. The larger elephant has been made over an older petroglyph of a quadruped and a young bovid has later been superimposed over his back. Pastoral Period, Messak, south-western Libya. Photo by Emmanuel Breteau.

millennium BCE.[71] However, as early as 1932 Monod, and Lhote in 1960, expressed doubts whether the Bubalus and Bovidian periods were two clearly distinct phases. Lhote admitted that petroglyphs of domesticated cattle already appeared in the Bubalus Period, while Monod questioned the validity of this distinction and considered that the two periods should be treated as one.[72] Nevertheless, Barth's categorization, which clearly distinguishes petroglyphs made by pre-pastoralist hunter-gatherers from those of pastoralists, forms the basis of the so-called 'long chronology' which is upheld by, among others, Karl-Heinz Striedter,[73] Rüdiger and Gabriele Lutz,[74] Anne-Michelle and Axel Van Albada[75] and David Coulson and Alec Campbell.[76]

However, as noted by Alfred Muzzolini and later Jean-Loïc Le Quellec, the so-called Bubalus Period is not an interval of time, but a style of petroglyphs applied by early pastoralists. Petroglyphs of domesticated oxen were already being engraved in the early period when bubalus images were made, for petroglyphs of bubali

and tropical big fauna can be found superimposed on images of cattle, and on other petroglyphs bovines looking like bubali are nevertheless rendered with ornamentation or carrying loads. For Muzzolini and Le Quellec, there was no culture of petroglyphs among pre-Neolithic hunters, in other words no Bovidian rock art was made before the introduction of domesticated cattle.[77] These convictions led to the 'short chronology' which amalgamates the supposedly separate Bubalus and Bovidian periods into a single category of petroglyphs created by pastoralists. However, among the proponents of a 'short chronology' there are noticeable differences concerning the absolute dating of the earliest central Saharan petroglyphs. Le Quellec declared categorically: 'Nowhere in the central Sahara are domestic cattle known to have existed before the fifth millennium [BCE] and the Bovidian paintings, which depict such livestock on a massive scale, can therefore be no older.'[78] Le Quellec applied the same limitation to petroglyphs. The first half of Le Quellec's statement seems too restrictive, for there are secure dates from the Tadrart Acacus for the introduction of domesticated cattle and ovicaprines by 6300 BCE.[79] Of course, as noted by Savino di Lernia, 'an early date for domestic cattle does not necessarily imply an early date for the rock art.'[80] Although the transition to a comprehensive exploitation of pastoralism, including dairy products, might have taken a couple of centuries, it is highly unlikely that the rock art rendering pastoral themes appeared more than a millennium after the switch to herding. For these reasons, while adopting a 'short chronology' that places images of bubali and cattle in the same period, several researchers, and the present authors, place the beginning of central Saharan petroglyph making around 6300 to 6000 BCE.[81]

But the question of dating the so-called 'Round Head' rock paintings, which are concentrated in the Tassili n'Ajjer, complicates the issue. The Round Heads represent an artistic style that is characterized by anthropomorphic figures with a distinctly round head and no or hardly any facial features such as mouth, eyes or nose; only a few have sexual markers. They are occasionally associated with Barbary sheep and antelopes which suggests that the makers of those paintings practised the corralling of sheep.[82] Most authors concur that the Round Heads belong to the oldest rock art in the central Sahara, and predate the appearance of Bovidian petroglyphs in the Central Sahara.[83] However, no definite date has been established yet since the Optically Stimulated Luminescence dating of sediments from two Round Head sites merely confirmed that the paintings had been done in the Holocene, but not earlier than 10,000 to 9,000 years ago.[84] Concerning the unanswered question of the appearance of petroglyphs in relation to the Round Heads, di Lernia surmised: 'Could the apparent overlap between an archaic style (recalling the Round Head) and the pastoral subject be considered the material representation of contacts and negotiations between foragers and herders?'[85] These foragers would have belonged, in Messak, to the Late Acacus Period (8200–6300 BCE) who practised corralling Barbary sheep.[86] Whether these hunter-foragers and pastoralists belonged to different populations remains unknown.

To conclude, the following categorization of Central Saharan petroglyphs is suggested;[87] it is based on ecological, stylistic, historical and chemical criteria.[88] It must be noted that it is often difficult to assess the date of the initial creation of some petroglyphs, especially those of big fauna like elephants or bubali, since their outlines were reworked and repolished in later periods.[89]

Period	Rock art	Climate	Repatination
Late Acacus Corralling 8200–6300 BCE	Round Heads? Barbary sheep? Archaic petroglyphs?	African Wet Period	n/a
Early Pastoral 6300–5200 BCE	Bubalus, cattle, big fauna including elephants, rhinoceroses, giraffes, lions, rarely crocodiles and fish, therianthropes, fabulous animals	African Wet Period	Black, manganese-rich varnish
Middle Pastoral 5200–3800 BCE	Giraffes, elephants, ostriches, large cattle, sheep, antelopes, pelicans or shoe-billed storks, fish, therianthropes, fabulous animals, naked women, sexual scenes, spirals Burial of cattle in cairns in Messak	Gradual aridification	Grey, less rich manganese varnish
Late Pastoral 3800–1600 BCE	Cattle herds and pastoral scenes, goats, antelopes, ostriches, hunting, sexual scenes, humans In paintings, people with Mediterranean physiognomy, daily life, Iheren–Tahilahi style. Human burials in cairns replace cattle burials in Messak	Increased aridification	Red, iron-rich patina
Final Pastoral 1600–1000 BCE	Cattle, sheep, goats, wild asses, people with Mediterranean physiognomy, battle and duel scenes	Desertic conditions	Red, less pronounced iron-rich patina
Garamantian and Islamic 1000 BCE–present	Horses, camels, chariots,[90] schematic small horse and camel riders, fighting scenes, bi-triangular style, stick-heads, goats, palm trees, Tifinagh inscriptions. Spread of the camel in the third century BCE, ethnographic petroglyphs	Desertic conditions	Weak to none

4. Wadi Djerat

Wadi Djerat in the Tassili n'Ajjer in south-eastern Algeria is, together with the Libyan sites of Messak, a unique place of rock art which lines the valley floor for a length of 35 kilometres.[91] The valley harbours not only countless petroglyphs but also several shelters with paintings; in fact, the wadi is one of the few places where petroglyphs and paintings are found side by side. Research on Wadi Djerat is closely associated with the French explorer of rock art Henri Lhote who was a pupil of the famous rock art expert Abbé Henri Breuil. Lhote at first wanted to become an army pilot, but an accident ended his career and he went to North Africa as part of a programme to fight locusts.[92] According to Lhote, the rock art of Wadi Djerat had already been brought to the attention of the French Africa explorer Fernand Foureau (1850–1914) during his Trans-Saharan expedition of 1892–93.[93] Forty years later, in 1933, Lieutenant Charles Brenans (1902–1955) of the French Camel Corps rediscovered the petroglyphs of Wadi Djerat by chance during a patrol tour. He then sent his drawings to Maurice Reygasse, curator of the Bardo Museum in Algiers. During the winter of 1934 Brenans guided to the site Reygasse and another scholar, Émile Félix Gautier, who studied the rock art and published several brief papers.In November of the same year, Henri Lhote accompanied the geographer Robert Perret and studied the rock art for two months. During the winter of 1935 Reygasse returned to Wadi Djerat, accompanied by the painter Maurice Rigal who made some copies of engravings and paintings.[94] After World War II and a long period of illness, in 1956–57, with the support of the Musée de L'Homme in Paris, Lhote led a small team to the Tassili n'Ajjer for sixteen months, including to Wadi Djerat.[95] Probably the most important team member was the Tuareg guide Machar Jebrine ag Mohammed (d. 1981) who had already guided Brenans and Lhote in 1933 and 1934; many discoveries were to his credit.

The main objective of the 1956–57 expedition was to make full-scale coloured copies of the rock paintings based on *in situ* tracings. Unfortunately, in order to reshape the contours of figures

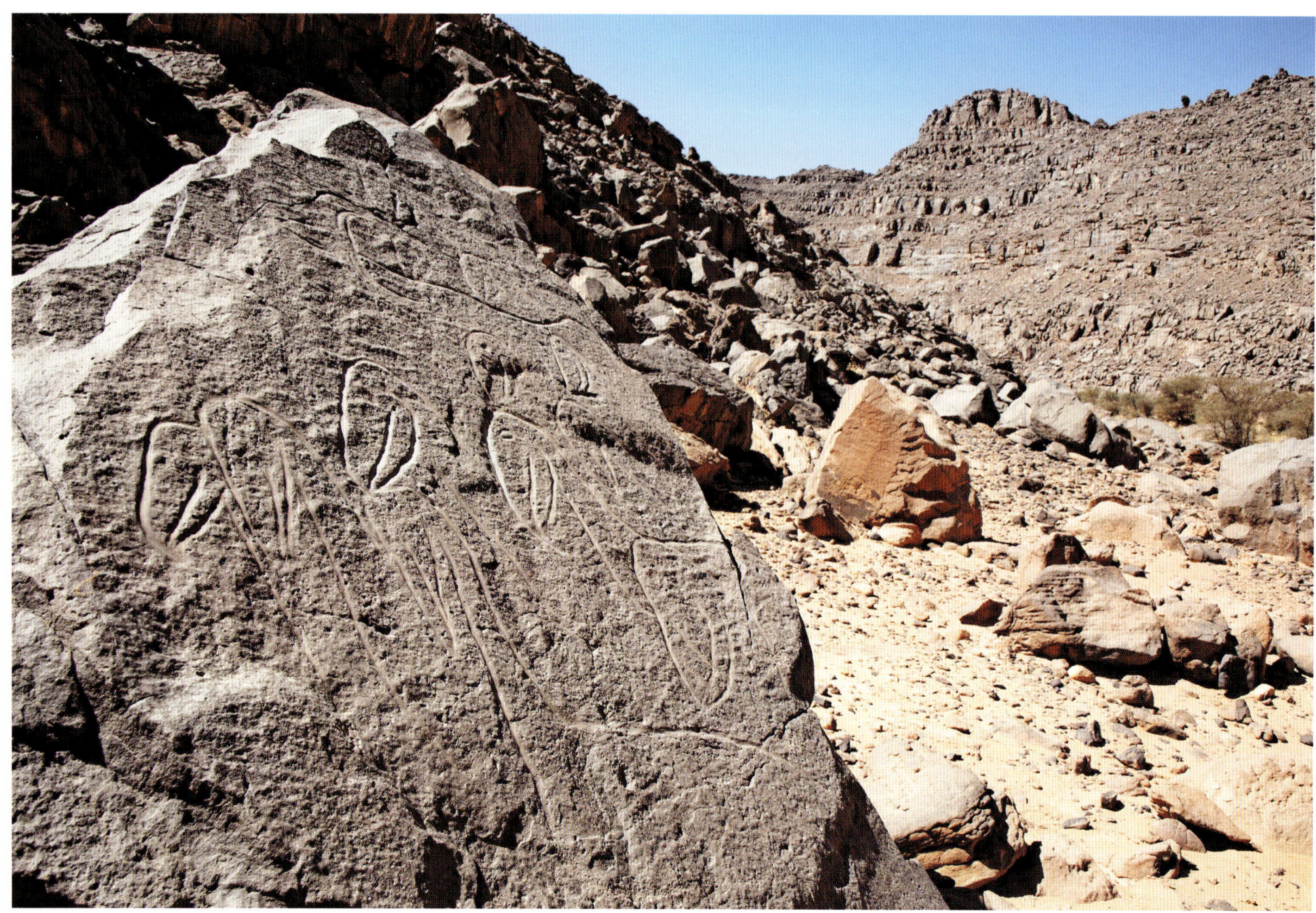

298. Seven shoe-billed storks or, less likely, pelicans. Middle Pastoral Period, site L 46, Wadi Djerat, Tassili n'Ajjer, Algeria. Photo 2023.

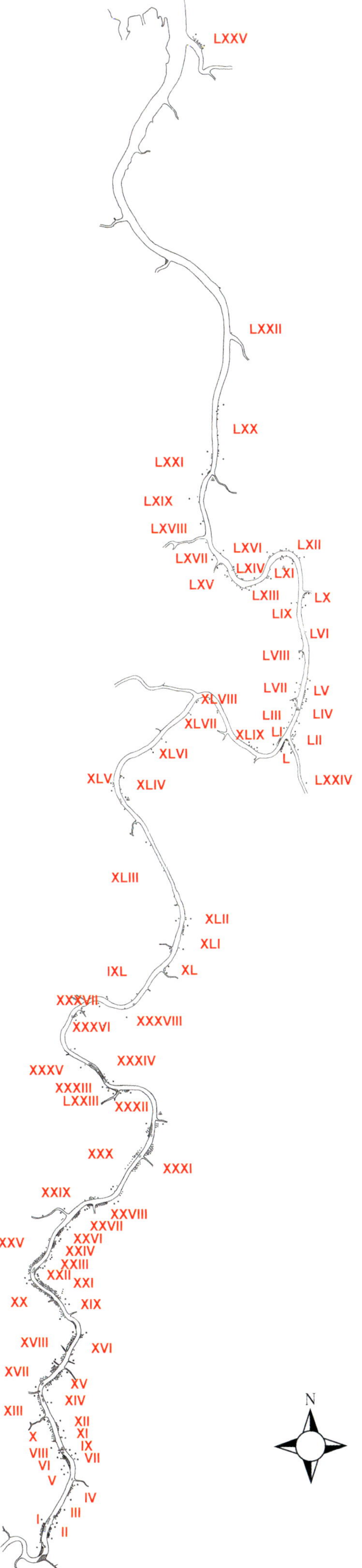

and to revive the colours, Lhote and his painters wetted the millennia-old rock paintings repeatedly and scrubbed them with sponge and brush to remove the dust, which caused irreversible damage. Due to this barbaric treatment and the ensuing chemical processes resulting from the applied moisture, many of the most beautiful paintings have disappeared.[96] Nevertheless, the paintings and photographs were then successfully exhibited in the Musée des Arts décoratifs in Paris. Thanks to the support of General de Gaulle, Lhote managed to return to the Tassili n'Ajjer in 1959, 1960 and 1962. During the first expedition, his team of French and Tuareg collaborators made an inventory of the petroglyphs in Wadi Djerat.[97] In his two-volume report, published in 1975, Lhote described 75 sites including 2,600 figures, although he noted that several panels had not been included in his inventory and that the total number of engravings would exceed 4,000.[98] On Lhote's map, site 1 lies in the south, in the oasis of Nafeg supérieur[99] from where a steep mountain path leads to the Fadnoun stone plateau where there are hundreds of neolithic burials in the shape of stone tumuli, circular stone arrangements and so-called keyhole-shaped monuments.[100] From Lhote's site 1, the rock art locations follow the flow of the seasonal river northwards as far as site L 75 which lies twenty kilometres south-east of the small city of Ilizi.[101] The petroglyphs were mostly engraved on flat or gently sloping rock panels, blocks that had fallen from the cliffs or, more rarely, on vertical surfaces.

The wadi has some peculiarities. It is narrow and the mostly dry riverbed fills a considerable part of it, which limits the available habitat. Furthermore, it is enclosed by high cliffs that are so steep that only Barbary sheep can climb them. Although there are numerous petroglyphs of tropical megafauna such as elephants, rhinoceroses, hippopotami and lions in the wadi, it is hard to imagine that these large herbivores could ever proliferate here, let alone find enough food. Water was less of a problem, since there existed, like today, several *gueltas*, that is ponds which last for months. Large animals could only have lived in the lower estuary of the river near site L 75, where lakes and swamps formed and pastures existed. Coexistence between humans and megafauna is even less conceivable in this confined space. Furthermore, the occasional torrential downpours would cause flash floods and also inundate the narrow terraces flanking the riverbed; at some narrow

---

299. Map of Wadi Djerat with the sites identified by Henri Lhote. Compiled and assembled from: Lhote, Henry, *Les gravures rupestres de l'Oued Djerat (Tassili-n-Ajjer)* (2 vols, Algiers: Centre de recherches anthropologiques, préhistoriques et ethnographiques, 1975).

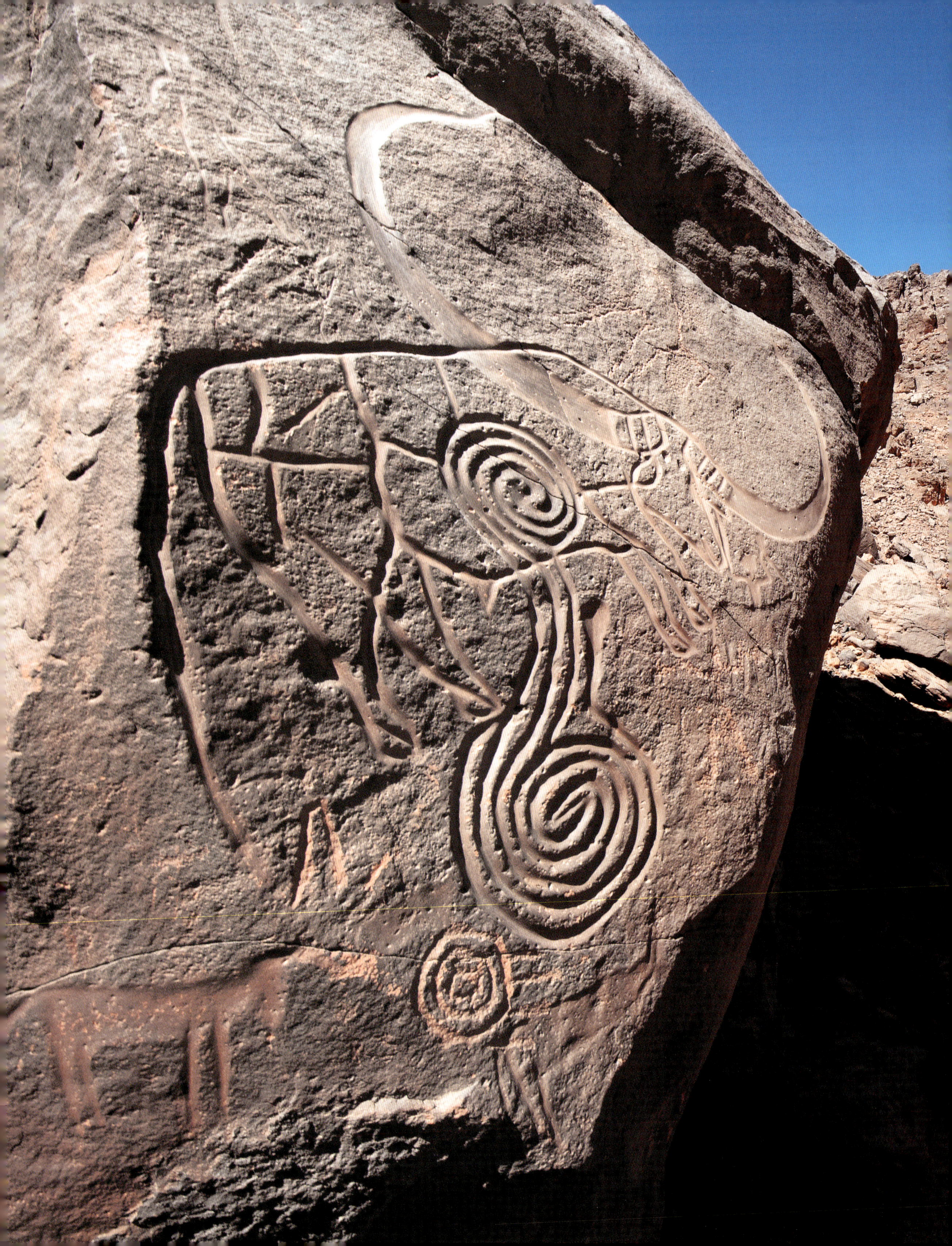

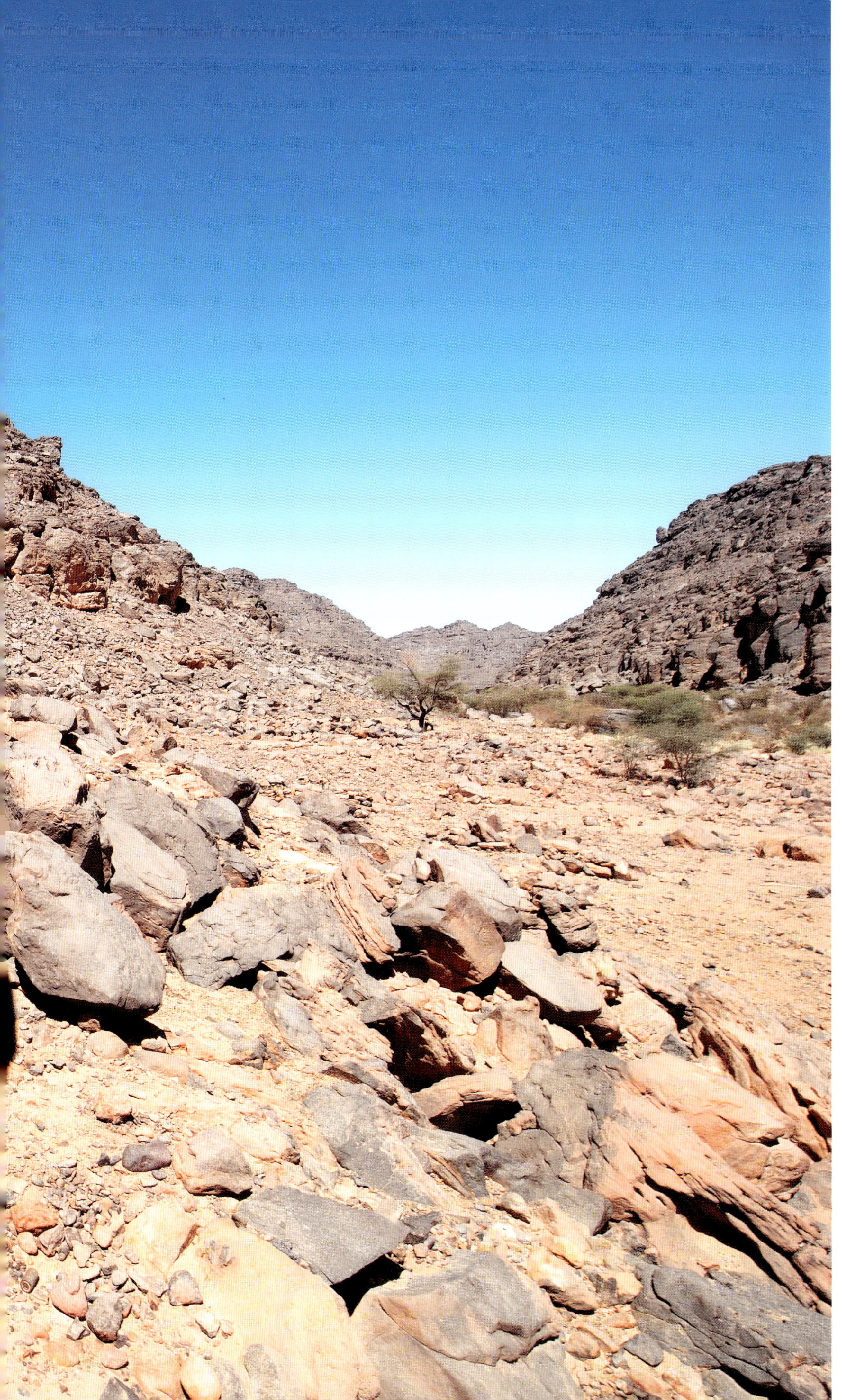

300. Polished petroglyph of a wild African buffalo *Bubalus antiquus* (*Syncerus antiquus*) which was superimposed with the figure of an eight-shaped double spiral. Early Pastoral Period, site L 58, Wadi Djerat, Tassili n'Ajjer, south-eastern Algeria. Photo 2023.

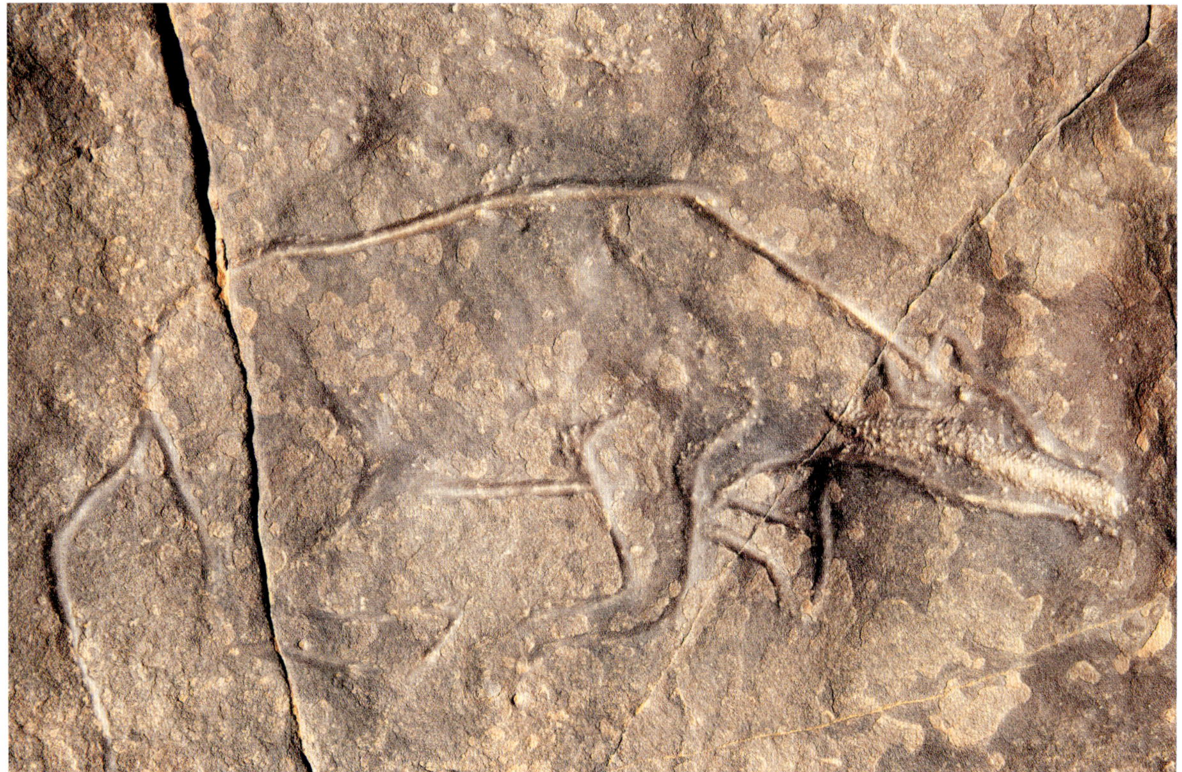

301. A hybrid animal consisting of the body of a hippopotamus and the front legs and snout of a crocodile. Early to Middle Pastoral Periods, site L 28, Wadi Djerat, Tassili n'Ajjer, south-eastern Algeria. Photo 2023.

places, the floods would have blocked the valley. The presence of animals was likely only occasional or seasonal, but this attracted hunters who set traps. Finally, the wadi could hardly have served as a transit route for it comes to a dead end of steep cliffs that can only be mastered by Barbary sheep, felines, humans and pack animals like camels and donkeys. The contrast between the abundance of rock art and the relative dearth of archaeological finds[102] confirms the assessment that thousands of years ago Wadi Djerat could not have served as an ordinary habitat for cattle breeders, but rather as a kind of sanctuary for pastoralists who also practised hunting. As hyperbolically formulated by Malika Hachid, 'Wadi Djerat, an open-air site, functioned like a cave art site in Europe, where all the known wild animals of the Palaeolithic period lived side by side, without ever having entered the cave.'[103]

At the beginning of petroglyph making in the Early Pastoral Period, images of *Bubalus antiquus* with enormous horns predominated in Wadi Djerat, for example at sites L 27, L 47 and L 58, whereas in Messak there are many renderings of aurochs (which also appears at L 26 in Wadi Djerat) with rather short, sturdy horns that curve forward or are shaped like pincers. Isolated cattle appeared in petroglyphs at the same time as wild buffalo. From the same epoch come petroglyphs of hippopotami, rhinoceroses, elephants, giraffes, lions, lycaons (African wild dogs), crocodiles[104] and fish,[105] which can be found inter alia at L 1, 2, 9, 10, 14, 15,

16, 17, 20, L 21, 25, 26, 27, 28, 30, 32, 39, 41, 44, 47, 50, 51, 52, 54, 58, 60, 61, 65, 71, 73, 74 and at **Tin Teghert**.[106] In most of these earlier petroglyphs the animals are depicted individually and, in a sense, glorified. The anatomy of the megafauna is rendered realistically, yet expressively; the artists obviously also practised hunting and had developed sharp observation skills. In these periods, humans are absent or visualized only in diminutive sizes, quite contrary to the more or less coeval Round Head paintings. Some of the animals featured are enormous; for example, there are ostriches 2.3 metres high at L 28, a buffalo 4.45 metres long at Tin Teghert, a 3.32-metre-high elephant at L 17 and an even taller one, 4.7 metres high at L 25, and a group of 12 giraffes at L 73 of which the tallest measures 8.5 metres. One may safely assume that the petroglyphs featuring large tropical fauna and the Round Heads were the expressions of different cultures and likely also of different peoples.

Although cattle and herbivores are disproportionately represented in the petroglyphs of Wadi Djerat, all the large animals living in the Tassili at that time were depicted, so that they provide a realistic picture of the large fauna of the time. The preference for wild buffaloes and other large herbivores may be explained by the fact that they were edible, diurnal and mostly lived in larger groups whereas carnivores, by contrast, are inedible, nocturnal and live in small groups. While edible – and thus economically highly important – animals were rendered in petroglyphs,

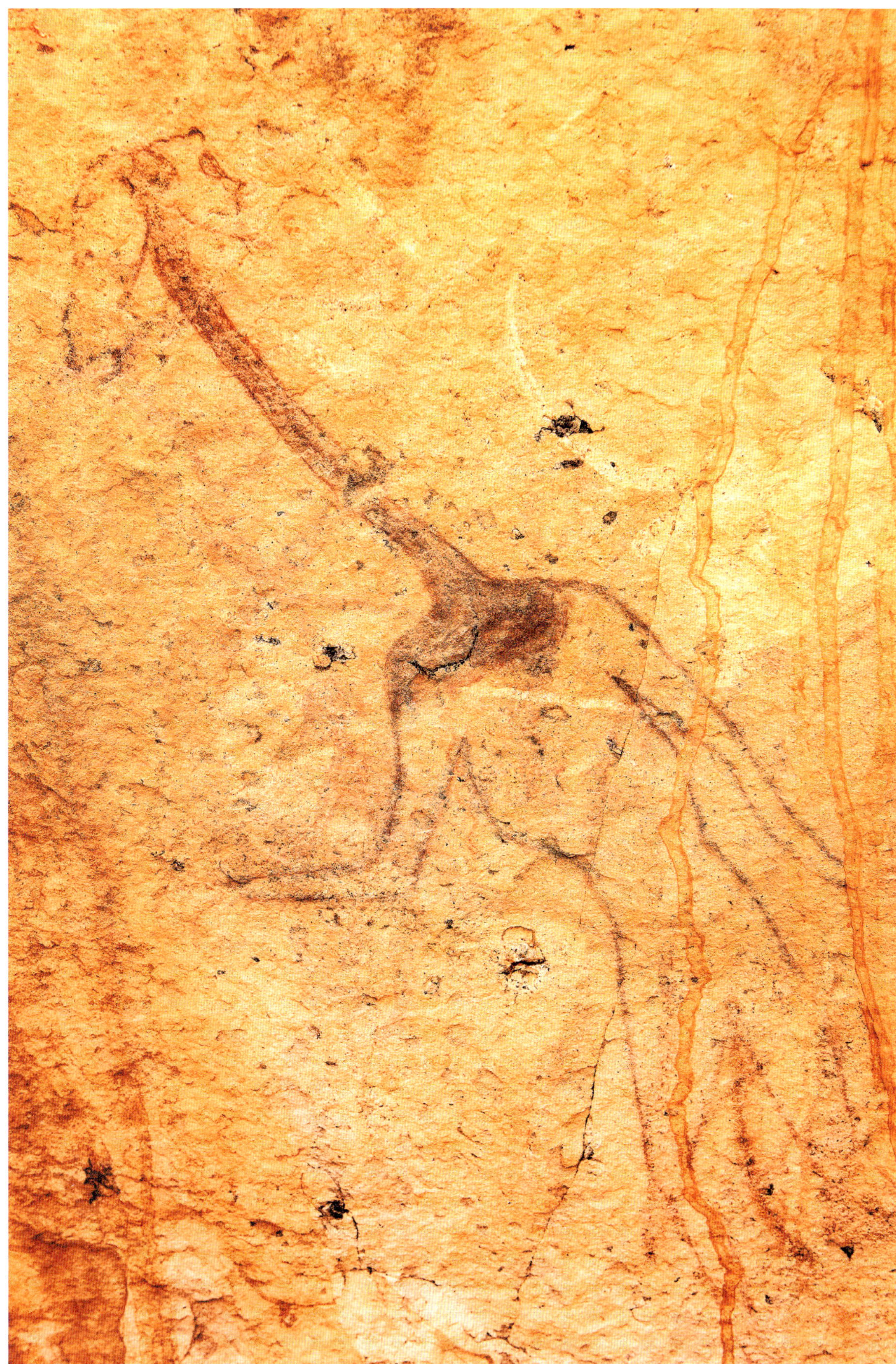

302. Cave painting of a therianthrope with a human body, the neck of a giraffe and Janus-like double-sided head; one side may represent the head of a giraffe, the other of a human or monkey. Late Pastoral Period, shelter of Adjoudjel, Tassili n'Ajjer, south-eastern Algeria. Photo 2023.

scenes that unambiguously depict hunting are absent in the early period. If there is human–animal interaction, it is limited to gently touching or merely capturing a wild animal. For example, in L 47 three masked and unarmed men or therianthropes try to capture a bubalus and in L 51 a trap consisting of rope slings attached to heavy stones has been placed near a rhinoceros. In Messak, petroglyphs show also how aurochs, wild donkeys or hippopotami were trapped using such slings in combination with a trapping pit.[107] Clearly recognizable hunting scenes appear later in the Late Pastoral Period, mainly in paintings. A potential exception to the absence of violence in early petroglyphs might exist at L 31 where a man is in the process of hitting a domesticated bull with a curved object, possibly an axe. The scene is reminiscent of the sacrificial cattle burials at Messak.

Before the paradigm shift from the dominance of animals to the dominance of humans during the Middle Period, the therianthropic hybrid appeared in Messak and Wadi Djerat as an intermediate step, so to speak.[108] They mostly consist of a human body and an animal head, usually of a canid such as a lycaon or a jackal, whose head is narrower and ears more pointed than those of the lycaon. Other therianthropes have the heads of buffaloes, elephants, hares, lions, cats, owls (possibly) and even crocodiles and ibises, yet while all these heads are without doubt those of animals, they display human facial features. An exceptional, and probably unpublished, therianthrope is represented in a painting of the shelter of **Adjoudjel** east of Tin Teghert. It consists of the body of a man, the long neck of a giraffe and a Janus-like double head of a giraffe and a human or monkey (fig. 302). With one exception in Messak, all therianthropes appear to be male.[109] Therianthropes must be distinguished from human mask wearers, as the latter can often be recognized as wearing an animal mask over their heads.[110] Such masks may represent an aurochs, a donkey, a canid, a gazelle or an owl (fig. 305). The therianthropes are often characterized by enormous strength since they effortlessly carry a killed buffalo on one shoulder or a rhinoceros under their arm. Like humans, some of the therianthropes are hunters, but whereas humans use bow and arrows, boomerangs and throwing knives, therianthropes prefer clubs and stone axes. In these contexts, the therianthropes and humans wearing animal masks are associated with the hunt and hunting rituals. The ancient practice of hunters disguising themselves with masks and animal skins was indeed widespread in Africa and the Eurasian continent. In his *Geographica*, Strabo mentions the African *Strutophagi* who hunted ostriches wearing ostrich skins.[111]

However, the meaning of therianthropes in rock art is more complex. There are ethnological indications that the concept of the animal–human hybrid belonged to a very ancient African heritage. For example, the Sao, the legendary ancestors of Chadian people, were said to be giants capable of carrying killed elephants on their backs.[112] And, according to the mythology of the South African San (Bushmen), therianthropes emerged from the first creation, and only in the second creation did distinctly separate humans and animals appear.[113] Considering this archaic mental heritage, the therianthropes of Wadi Djerat and Messak probably symbolized the residual animality of mankind, and in turn the hidden humanity of large animals. In view of the enormous strength with which the therianthropes were endowed, they most probably also represented the attempt to acquire by magic the strength and capabilities of the respective animals. Since several therianthropes are featured in a hunting context which also implies death, it is tempting to wonder whether Anubis, the Egyptian god of funerary rites, who is depicted as a man with the head of a jackal or a dog, was inspired by the lycaon- and jackal-headed therianthropes.[114] Or both representations, the canid-headed therianthropes of Saharan rock art and the Egyptian god Anubis, might share a common ancestral mythic heritage. However, although the Egyptian religion knew several deities who, among other features, also possessed a human body and animal head, they were not prehistoric therianthropes, since there are no indications that the therianthropes in rock art were venerated like deities. Furthermore, it is highly doubtful whether a petroglyph at Lhote 21 where a bull seems to carry a disc between its horns has any connection with the Egyptian deities represented by a bull (Apis) or a cow (Hathor) carrying a solar disc in their horns. In other images the horns are bent inwards to such an extent that they form a circle without necessarily having a solar connotation.[115] Yet the mythological concept of human–canid hybrids, called *cynocephali* in Greek and Latin, was widespread in the Mediterranean world in antiquity. Hesiod in the seventh century, Scylax of Caryanda in the sixth to fifth, Ctesias of Cnidus in the fifth and Megasthenes (according to Pliny) in the fourth to third centuries BCE mentioned *cynocephali* living in Northern Africa and India.[116] Later, bishop Augustine (354–430 CE), who was a North African Berber, mentioned *cynocephali* and believed that they were animals rather than humans. In the seventh or eighth century CE, a legend about Saint Christopher related that the saint was originally a man-eating *cynocephalus* and that he acquired human features by the grace of God.[117] The *cynocephali* represented a long-lasting myth for they are also present in *The Travels of Marco Polo* as the inhabitants of the Andaman Islands.[118]

Another aspect of therianthropes was sexuality which is expressed in numerous scenes where canid-, leporid- (rabbit)

303. Tracing on photo. A lycaon-headed therianthrope riding an elephant returns from the hunt with the body of a rhinoceros placed in front of him. Early to Middle Pastoral Period, Wadi Meseknan, Messak Settafet, south-western Libya. Photo and tracing 2005 by Jörg Mollet.

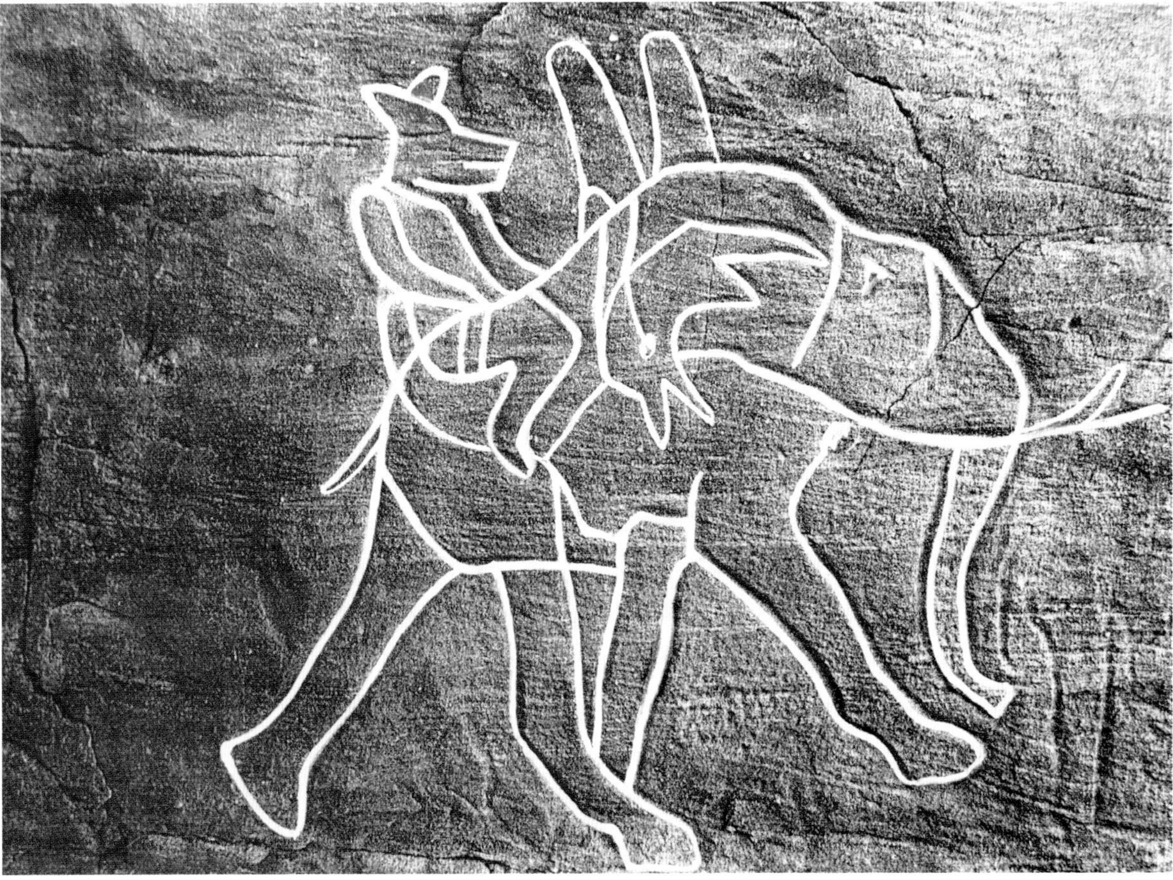

304. Tracing on photo. Two lycaon-headed therianthropes prepare a captured gazelle for a banquet. Early to Middle Pastoral Period, Wadi Anou al-Aurer, Messak Settafet, Libya. Photo and tracing 2005 by Jörg Mollet.

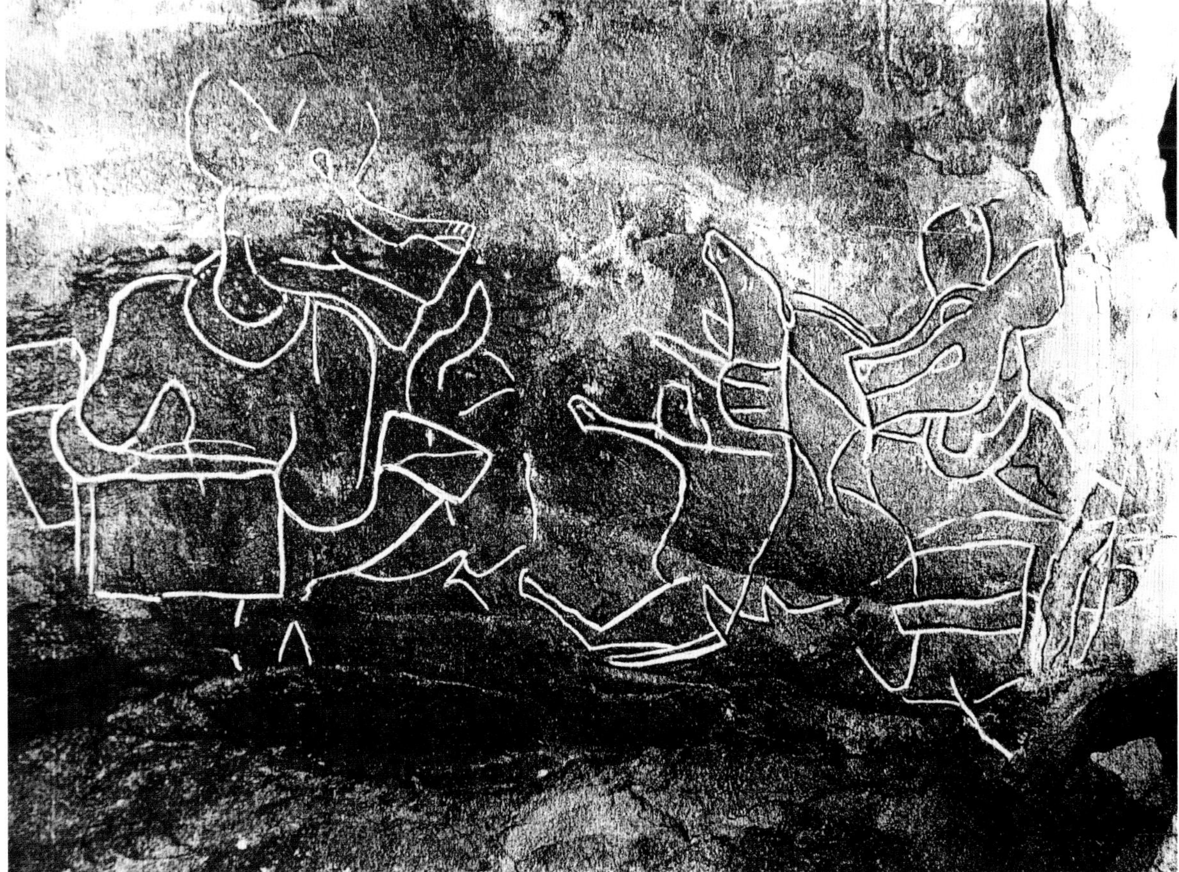

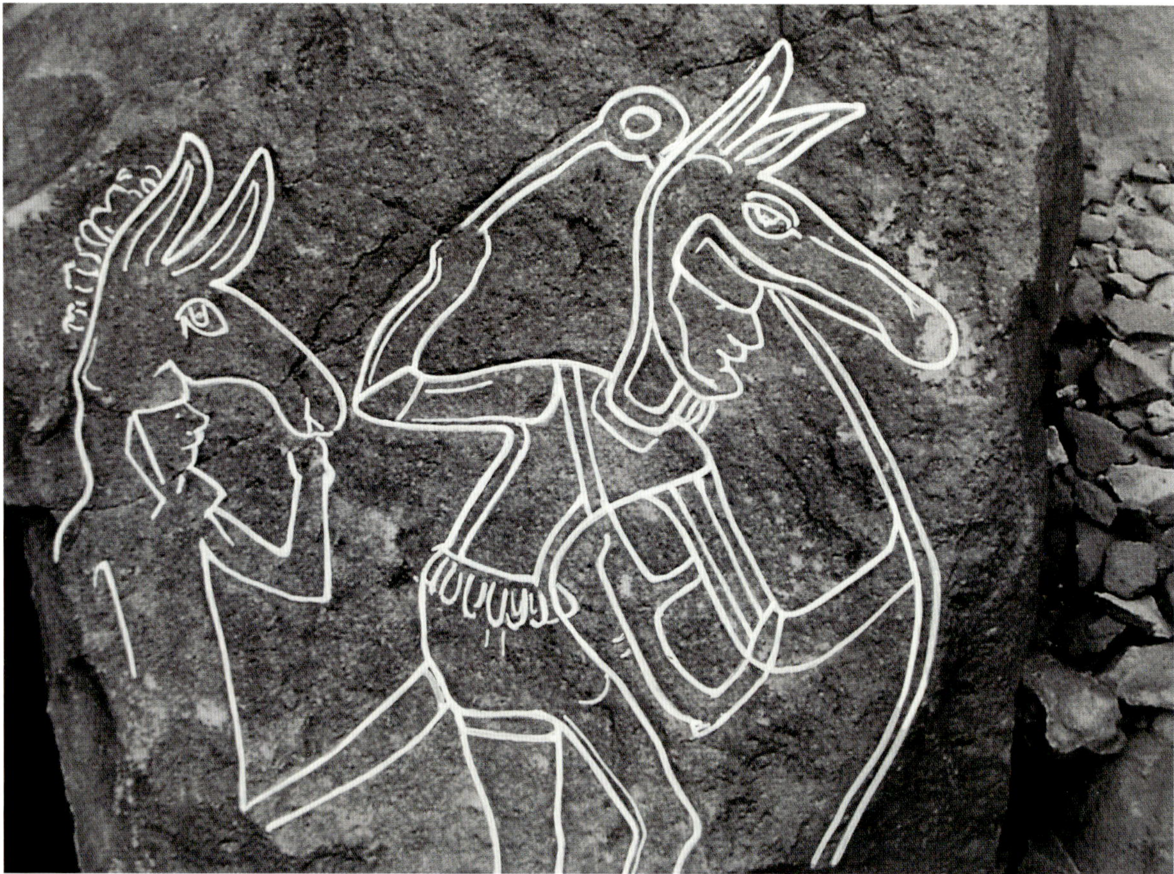

305. Tracing on photo. Two human hunters wearing donkey masks. Early to Middle Pastoral Period, Wadi Imrawen, Messak Settafet, south-western Libya. Photo and tracing 2005 by Jörg Mollet.

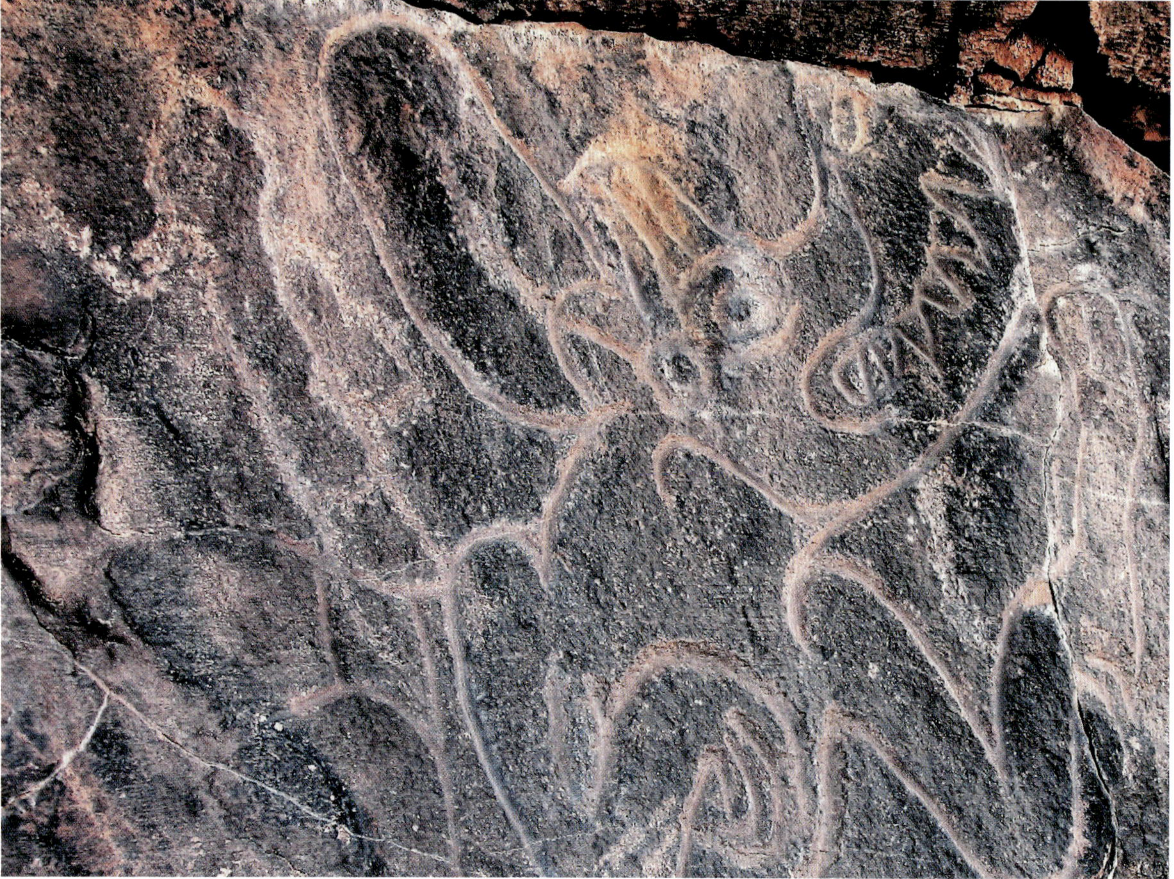

306. A Lycaon-headed therianthrope with sharp teeth. Early to Middle Pastoral Period, Wadi Taleshout, Messak Mellet, south-western Libya. Photo 2006 by Jörg Mollet.

and felid-headed therianthropes copulate with women.[119] These images recall the ancient myth of a Berber woman from the Fezzan mating with a dog.[120] In the later Early or in the Middle Pastoral Period sexuality gained greatly in importance, especially in Wadi Djerat. Not only are there scenes of copulation between man and woman, but also of sodomy with animals, that is bestiality, where men either copulate with rhinoceroses, elephants and buffaloes or approach these animals from behind with an erect phallus. In a couple of scenes, a tall woman wearing a long skirt and a hat is approached by ithyphallic men from behind and frontally. More frequent are images of naked, squatting women with spread legs and exposed sexual organs being penetrated or approached by a long phallus, and of ithyphallic males engaged in various activities like running and hunting (fig. 309).[121] In one unique scene, a small theriomorph with the head of rhinoceros rides a rhinoceros while ejaculating towards the beast's eye (fig. 308). In other, crudely executed and probably later petroglyphs, caricature-like, felid-headed therianthropes exhibit phalli that are as long as their own bodies. According to Malika Hachid, images of ithyphallic hunters allude to the widespread African taboo whereby a successful hunt should be preceded by a period of sexual abstinence.[122] Concerning

bestiality, the same author quotes ritual customs of the San and Maasai where young hunters had to copulate with an antelope or a donkey.[123] Judged from a broader perspective, it may be assumed that in the wake of a gradual climatic aridification taking place in these periods, themes of fertility and how to ensure fertility became of paramount importance. Another expression of fertility and creation of life might have been the more than 100 spirals[124] which were either superimposed on bubali, hippopotami and rhinoceroses or placed near their heads or above ithyphallic males (figs 300, 309); at Tin Teghert, the numerous spirals and the lemniscate[125] were engraved at the same time as the outlines of the huge domesticated buffalo. At other sites in Wadi Djerat, petroglyphs of spirals make up groups of their own.

When the aridification in the Central Sahara intensified, water-dependent animals like hippopotami and rhinoceroses disappeared, later followed by lions, elephants and giraffes, the latter enduring dry climates and savannas better than the former two. Small crocodiles, for their part, survived in *gueltas* of the Tassili until the twentieth century CE.[126] In the Later Pastoral Period, normal people take the centre stage in rock art and cattle take a back seat. Bovines are no longer represented as impressive

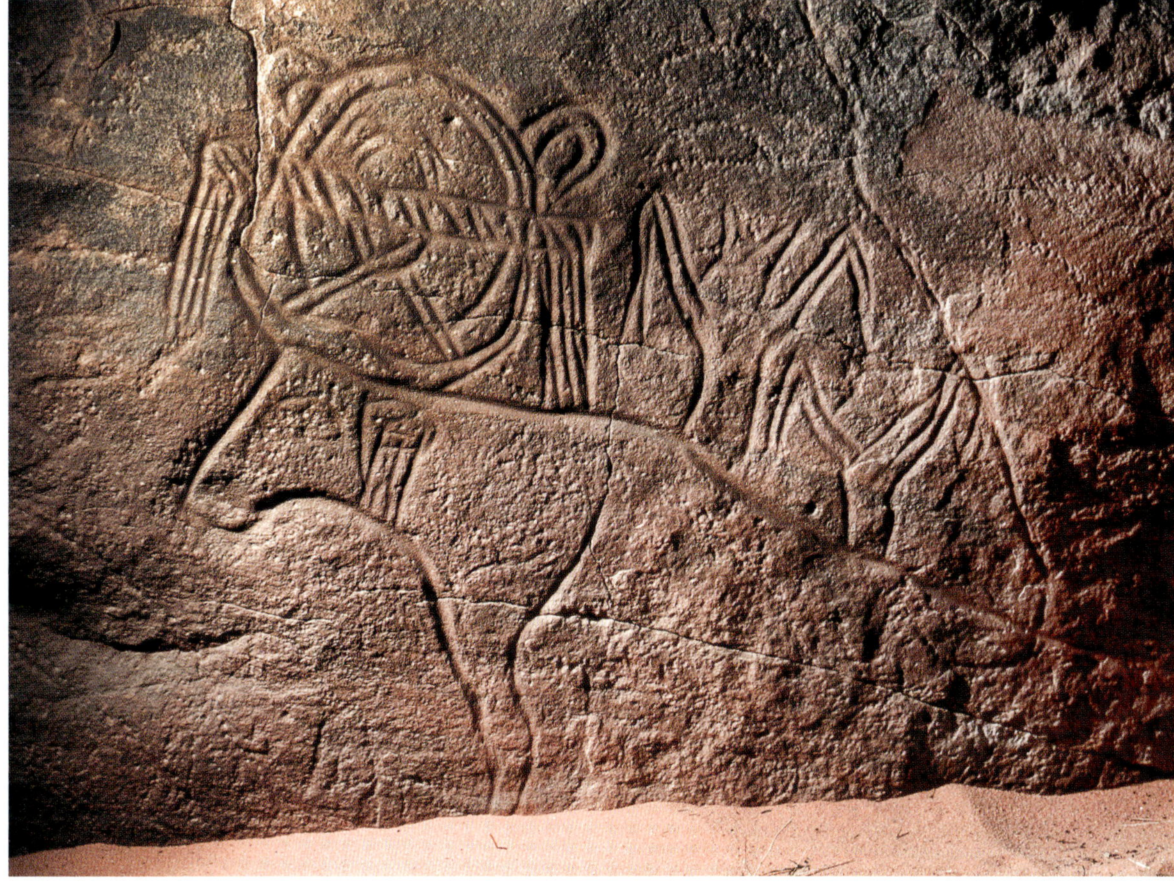

307. Deeply engraved petroglyph of a bull whose horns are extended to make a full circle, possibly suggesting a solar symbol. Behind its back stands a therianthrope with a feline head. Middle Pastoral Period, Messak, south-western Libya. Photo by Emmanuel Breteau.

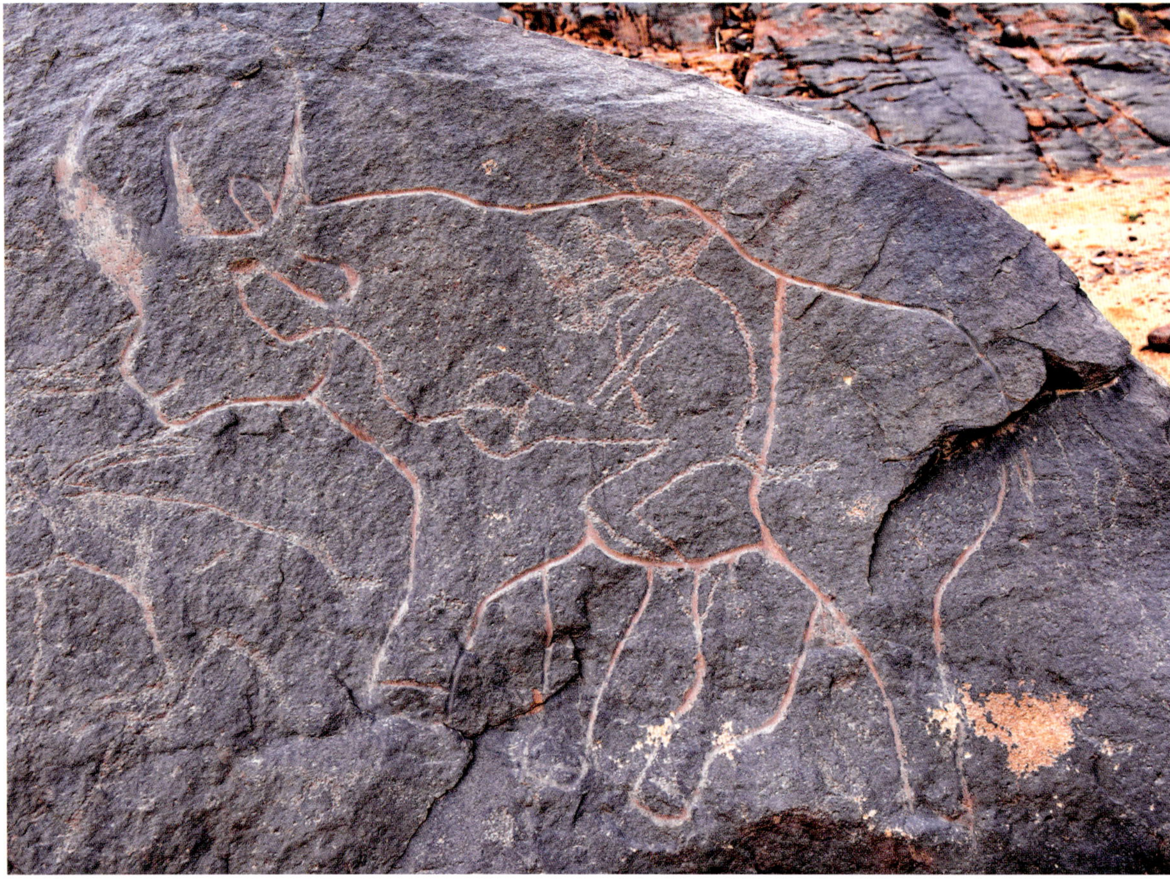

308. A theriomorph with the head of rhinoceros rides a rhinoceros while ejaculating towards the mount's eye. Middle Pastoral Period, site L 30, Wadi Djerat, Tassili n'Ajjer, south-eastern Algeria. Photo 2023.

individuals, but in herds which are led by proportionally larger humans who show themselves as the masters of cattle. In rock art, idealized beings or concepts are no longer visualized, but rather the everyday life of semi-settled pastoralists. At the same time, in Wadi Djerat rock paintings tend to become the preferred means of expression at the expense of petroglyphs.[127] In Wadi Djerat, the pigments for painting were made from minerals and not from organic material. Ochre (a mixture of ferric oxides) was used for yellow and red colours, manganese oxide for black, and white clay, and possibly gypsum, for white. Key topics of paintings are herding and milking cattle, goats and sheep, caravans with loaded oxen, hunts of Barbary sheep, wild buffaloes and giraffes with dogs, and domestic scenes.

Exemplary of the Late Pastoral Period are the paintings in the **Tikadiouine** shelter 50 kilometres north-west of Tin Teghert, which illustrates the daily life of herders who also practised hunting (fig. 292). These paintings are a pinnacle of the Saharan Iheren–Tahilahi painting style which is characterized by technical mastery in an elegant, naturalistic technique based on fine brushstrokes. The humans are of a tall and slim Mediterranean-Europid type with long noses and pale skin which is often decorated with body painting or tattoos. Women wear long dresses and over the shoulders often a shawl, men a short skirt and a stubby beard. The preferred weapons are throwing knives, javelins, and bow and arrows. On the ceiling of the ten-metre-wide Tikadiouine shelter the following scenes can be seen, from left to right: a relatively small giraffe and a group of three people who face an approaching herd of long-horned, red-and-white spotted cattle; the tallest of the three men holds a long knife in his right hand and possibly he will slaughter the goat standing beside him. Above to the right there follows a seated woman with her hair braided in a bun; in front of her stand a child and three calabashes, and an older man holding a throwing stick is approaching her. Below the three humans facing the herd stand two long-horned buffalo, and a man touches the back of the smaller buffalo from behind. In the centre of the scene three men and one woman are butchering an antelope with knives. Below the lower man there is a dog. To the left of the people doing the butchering stands a strange anthropomorph whose upper body is ornated with long stripes. Around the butchering scene four rabbits are crouching, which are probably the quarry from a recent hunt.[128] To the right, three giraffes flee from two pairs of pursuing men armed with curved knives. The bodies of all four hunters as well as of two of the men doing the butchering have rich body painting or tattooing. One of the hunters catches the tail of one of the giraffes which tramples on a Barbary sheep lying on the ground – probably another hunting bag. At the far right a goat watches the scene. This rich 'canvas' illustrates daily activities of pastoralists and hunters; whether it also symbolizes 'the ideal life trajectory of a male subject from childhood to elderhood' as postulated by Augustin Holl and Gao Chang remains speculative.[129]

That the Saharan pastoralists hunted giraffes with throwing knives is also illustrated in the painting at the shelter of **Adjoudjel** (fig. 311). In the main scene, there is a tight group of ten running giraffes which are preceded by three oryxes, four antelopes and five ostriches. An isolated giraffe at the lower right, however, is attacked by six or seven hunters armed with throwing knives, two from behind and four or five from the front. Two knives stick in the back of the giraffe's head, two others fly towards its upper neck

and the animal bleeds at two points on its lower jaw. The furthest-left giraffe of the fleeing group is also attacked by two hunters brandishing throwing knives, one of whom is an adolescent. Below the hunting scene four women with long knives butcher two large cows. Since late pastoralists did not use metal, such knives were probably made from very hard wood with inserted stone blades. However, it is doubtful whether such light weapons could bring down a giraffe; maybe the knives were first dipped in poison.

The accelerated aridification of the environment in the Late and Final Pastoral Periods not only led to a gradual shift from cattle to sheep and goat herding, but also to stiffer competition for pastures and access to water.[130] These changes are reflected in a few petroglyphs and numerous paintings featuring duels, battles and even death. An interesting petroglyph scene is engraved at L 50 in Wadi Djerat where two groups of armed men confront each other.

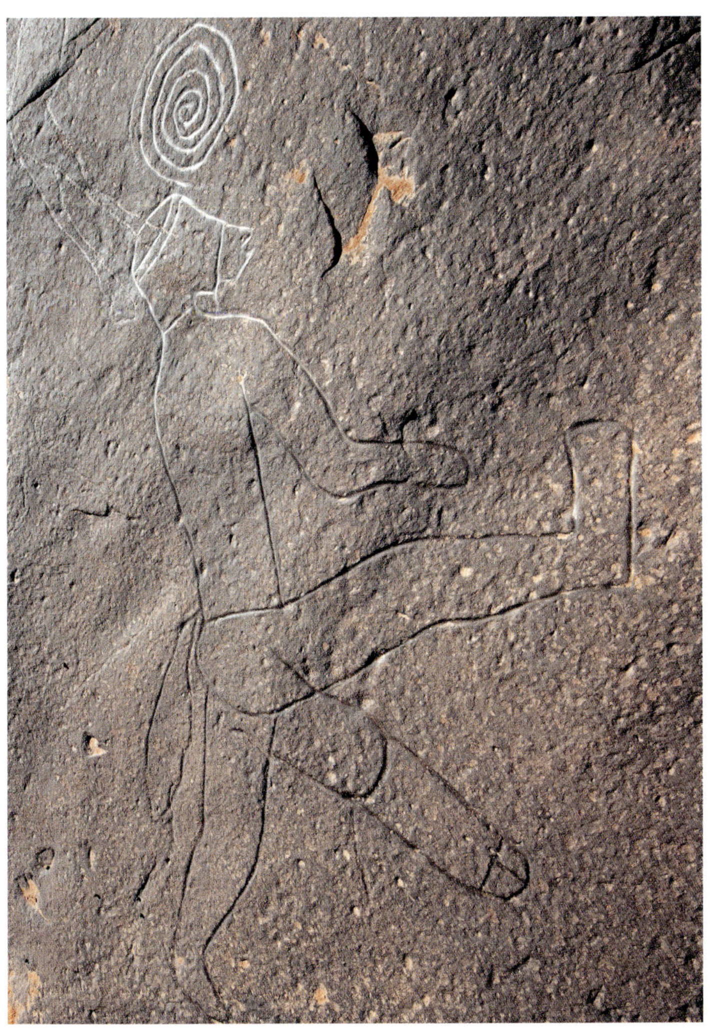

309. Male human or therianthrope with a dog-like face, an enormous phallus and a false tail. A spiral features above his head. Middle to Late Pastoral Period, site L 47, Wadi Djerat, Tassili n'Ajjer, south-eastern Algeria. Photo 2023.

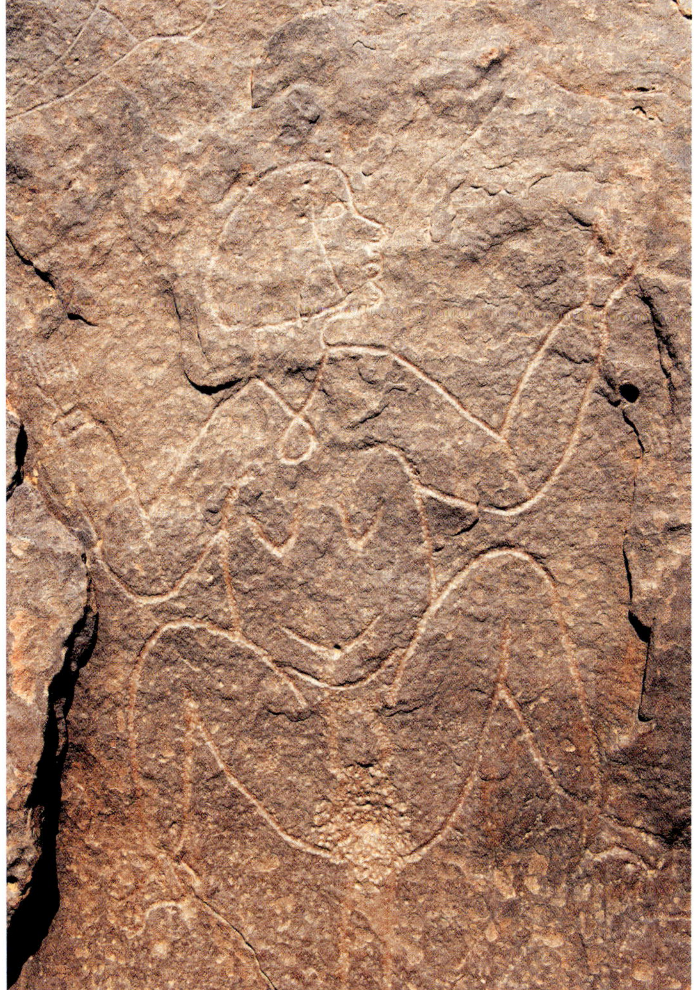

310. Naked woman exhibiting her sexual organs. Middle to Late Pastoral Period, site L 28, Wadi Djerat, Tassili n'Ajjer, Algeria. Photo 2023.

Those standing in the front row are all armed with bows, the others behind also with javelins and long-shafted axes.[131] The scene shows an obviously hostile encounter between two parties. The leader of the armed band at the left sits on an ox which indicates that this scene dates from the early Late Pastoralist Period. The left-hand group counts eleven fighters on foot plus their mounted leader, the right-hand one twelve fighters on foot. In another petroglyph scene at L 4, two warriors on foot, each wearing a headcover with three feathers, shoot arrows at each other. Nearby at L 2, two mounted lancers duel each other and, in the adjacent painting, two groups of four warriors each fight each other armed with javelins and shields. Still in Wadi Djerat, at L 17, besides two hunting scenes of Barbary sheep, there are two battle scenes showing men armed with lances, javelins, shields and occasionally a bow battling each other (fig. 313). One man lies on the ground and another kneels before his victorious adversary who directs a lance against his neck. In addition, a light battle chariot manned by a driver and a warrior holding three javelins[132] rushes from the right to join in the battle. These paintings fall into the Garamantian Period.[133] Mortal battle scenes were not limited to Wadi Djerat, for at **Sefar**, north of Djanet, there is a painted battle scene involving more than three dozen archers shooting at each other,[134] and at **Tin Ibrahim** a defeated man lies on the ground with a javelin stuck in his body.[135] Taken as a whole, these petroglyphs and paintings indicate how the prevailing values in these societies

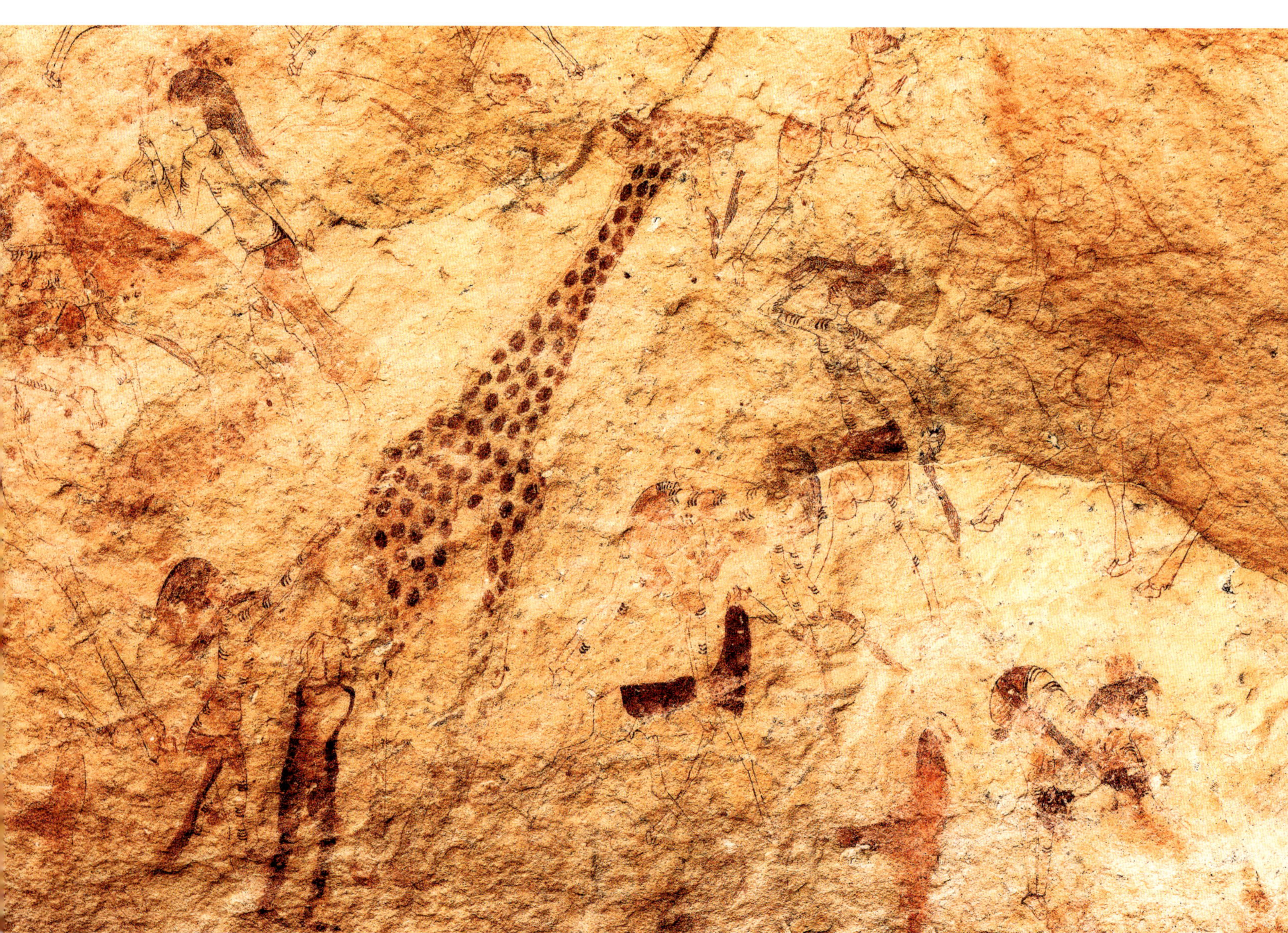

311. Six or seven hunters attack a giraffe with throwing knives. Detail from the painting panel at the shelter of Adjoudjel. Late Pastoral Period, Tassili n'Ajjer, south-eastern Algeria. Photo 2023.

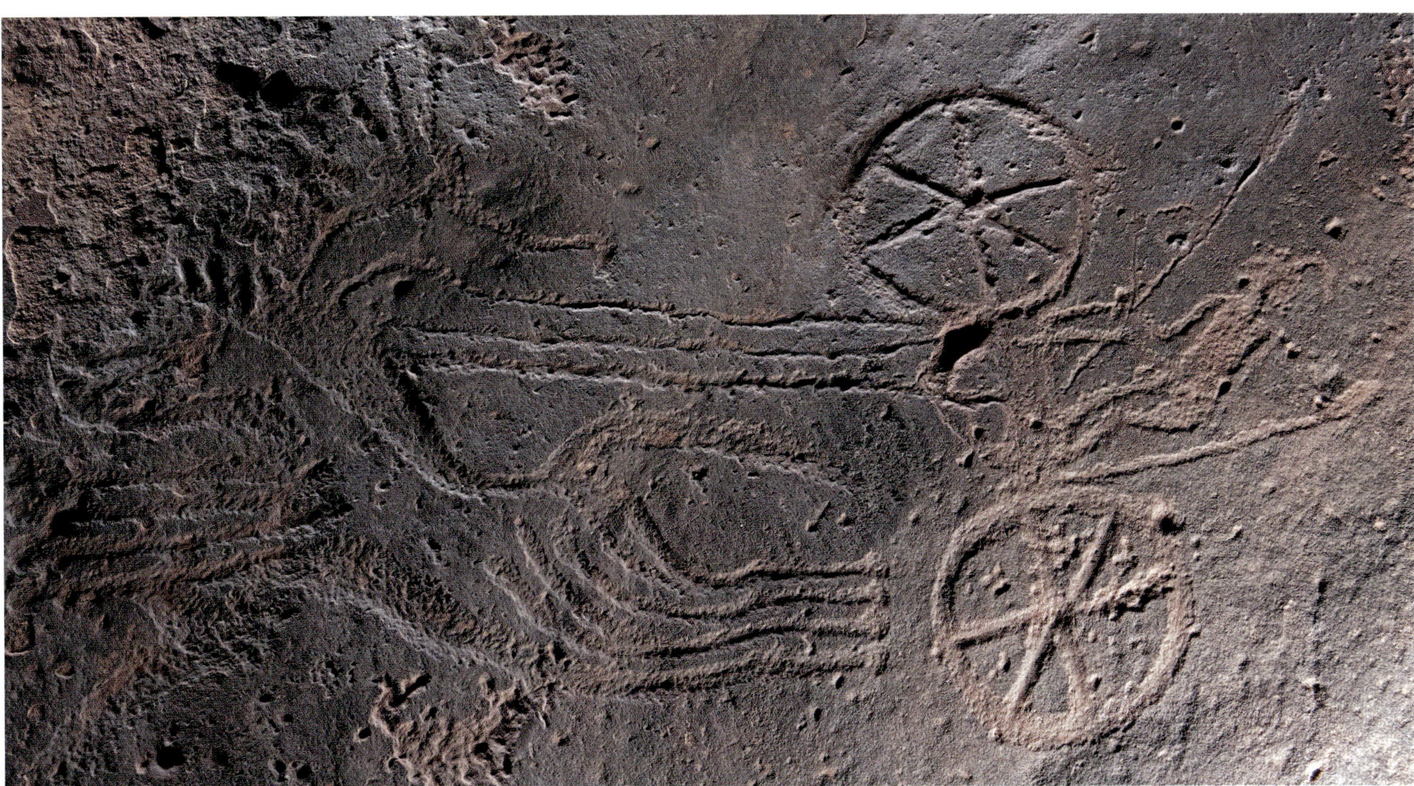

312. Petroglyph of a light battle chariot pulled by horses at a flying gallop viewed from the side; the driver holds two javelins. Garamantian Period, site L 21, Wadi Djerat, Tassili n'Ajjer, south-eastern Algeria. Night photo 2023.

changed over time from the veneration of tropical megafauna to the depiction of human–animal hybrids and sexuality as the epitome of fertility, followed by the evocation of the everyday life of hunting cattle breeders and finally of successful warriors.

As in other regions of the world with petroglyphs, numerous representations of chariots appeared in the Sahara too, albeit a little later. The horse spread into the central Sahara around 1000 BCE, the chariot followed around or after 700 BCE.[136] At present, more than 1,500 painted and engraved chariots are known in the Sahara, of which 60 per cent are located in the central Sahara and 40 per cent in the north-west, in Morocco and Mauritania.[137] A small minority of these chariot representations feature vehicles pulled by oxen, while another group illustrates unharnessed two-wheeled vehicles. The images of single-axle chariots pulled by two horses seen from above, in which the animals and the driver are 'folded out', are widespread within the universe of petroglyphs; sometimes chariot and driver are seen from above while the horses are seen from the side. Virtually unique in the world of rock art are some hundred central Saharan images of light single-axle chariots pulled by two or four horses galloping at full speed and rendered from the side in a proper perspective.[138] The overwhelming majority of these images are paintings.

In Wadi Djerat, there are at least six well-preserved petroglyphs of light chariots, three at L 21 and one each at L 20, L 31 and L 65 (fig. 312). One of them, at L 21, is a conventional representation seen from above with the horses and the driver folded out; the one at L 20 is a hybrid, for the chariot is seen from above and the driver is folded out, but the horses are shown standing in profile. The chariot at L 31 is not harnessed. The other three images depict the chariots, horses and driver from the side in a flying gallop, which is rare in petroglyphs. At L 21, one of the drivers wears a headdress decorated with a feather, and he holds two javelins which clearly identifies him as warrior.[139] Paintings of light chariots in a flying gallop are found, among others, at sites L 2, 5, 6 and 17, of which L 5 consists of three neighbouring shelters (fig. 313). In one of them there are, besides hunting and butchering scenes, at least six single-axle chariots pulled by one or two oxen, one chariot harnessed to two horses, one chariot with uncertain draught animals and an unharnessed chariot. In a neighbouring shelter, the paintings illustrate cattle herds, hunts, two therianthropes with giraffe-like heads, humans with stick-like heads, and at least four light chariots pulled by horses in a flying gallop. Whether the representations in rock art of light chariots pulled by galloping horses generally illustrate a myth or represent real

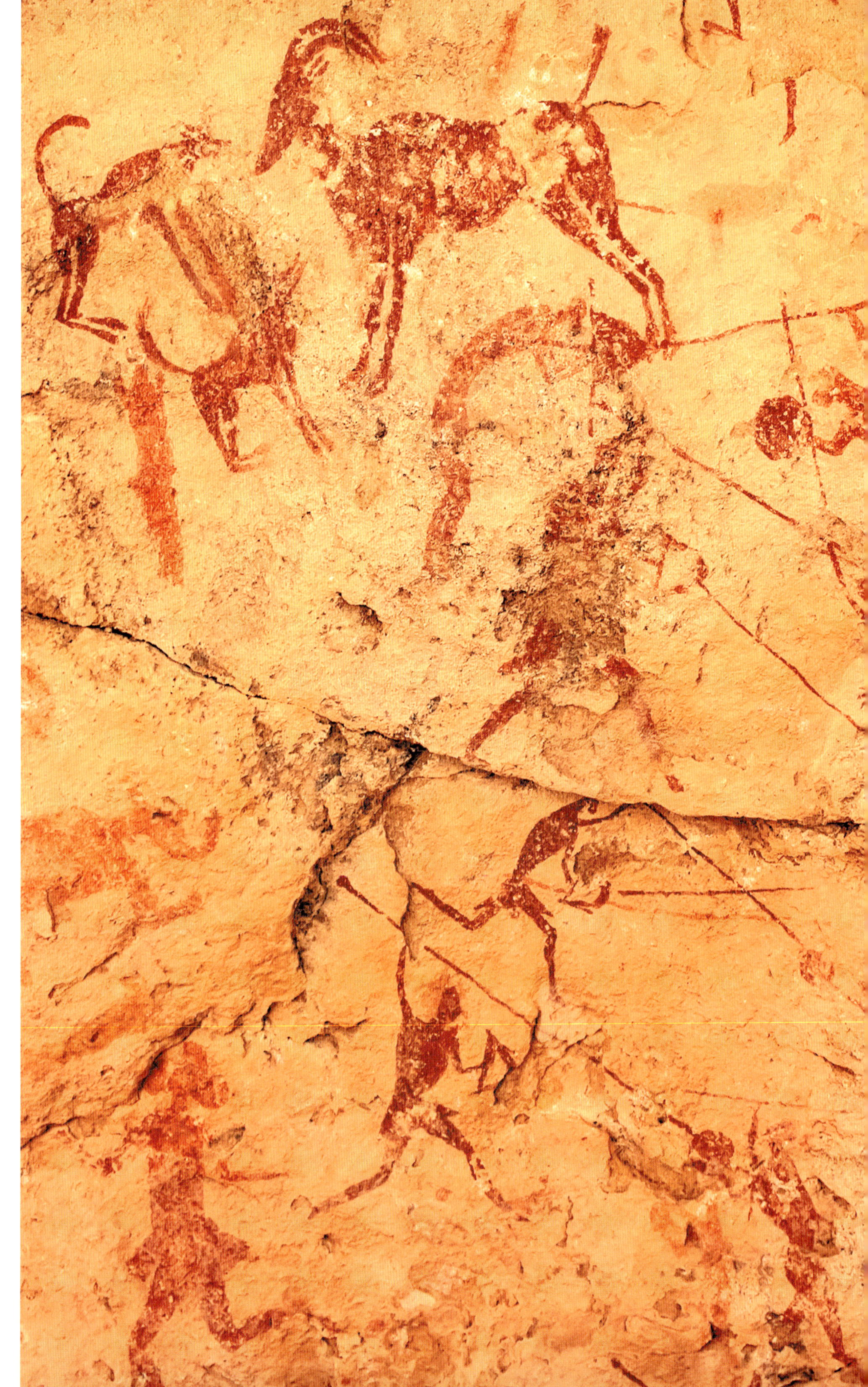

313. Central and right sections of the painting panel at shelter L 17 in Wadi Djerat. From left to right: a gazelle is hit by arrows and confronted by two dogs; a battle scene between lancers armed with small shields; and a battle chariot joins the battle at a flying gallop. Final Pastoral to Garamantian Period, Tassili n'Ajjer, south-eastern Algeria. Photo 2023.

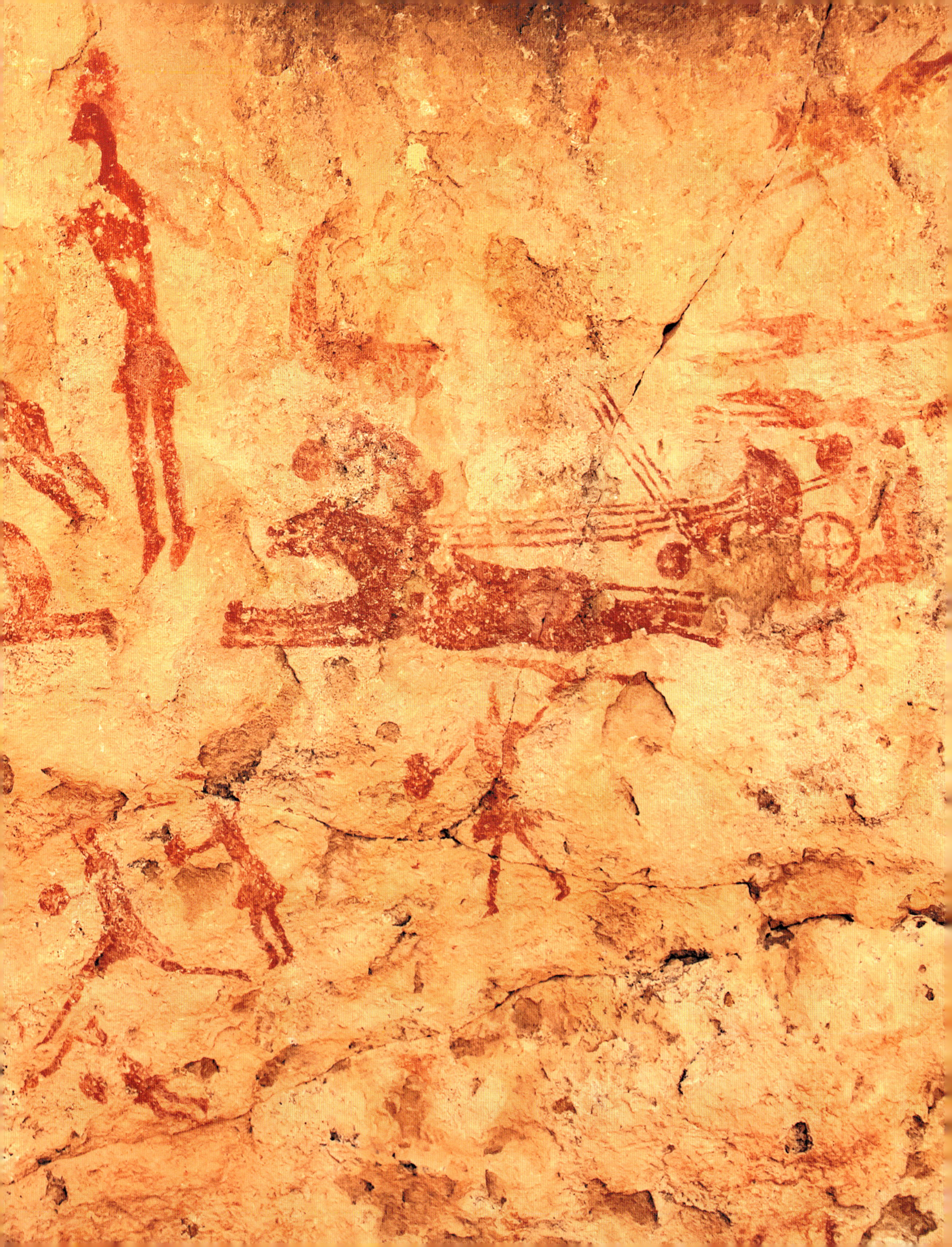

scenes, for example as *pars pro toto* of a hunt, a conflict, a sporting or ritual race remains difficult to determine.[140] Since chariots shown moving at high speed are often integrated in 'canvases' illustrating activities of daily life, such images had at least a partial reference to real events.[141]

Another individual feature of central Saharan rock art is the series of Libyco-Berber inscriptions, from which the Tifinagh inscriptions evolved. They are spread from the Mediterranean all the way to the Sahel zone, but only west of the Tibesti Mountains, the Ennedi Plateau and the Uweinat region; 80 per cent of them are located in Libya and Algeria.[142] There seems to be quite a significant overlap between site complexes with chariots and those with inscriptions; furthermore, as far as the date of the first appearance of inscriptions is concerned, they emerged around or shortly after the middle of the first millennium BCE, probably a couple of centuries after the first chariots.[143] Since both chariots and Libyco-Berber (and subsequently Tifinagh) inscriptions are concentrated in those parts of the central Sahara which would later become the land of the Berber Tuaregs, they may reflect the acquisition by these Berber populations first of the wheel and soon thereafter of writing.[144] In the third century BCE, the usage of the camel as a means of transport became widespread in the Sahara. The introduction, one after another, of irrigation systems, the horse, iron, the wheel, the camel and writing decisively transformed the pastoralist culture of the Fezzan into an urban one centred at Garama, the Garamantian capital. In this Garamantian Period the quantity of petroglyphs as well as the quality of their execution declined; motifs were restricted to schematized dromedaries, simple stick humans and animals and inscriptions. It is clear that petroglyphs had by now lost their relevance in the worldview of this society, as other means of expression prevailed, such as written texts, oral transmission and religious beliefs.

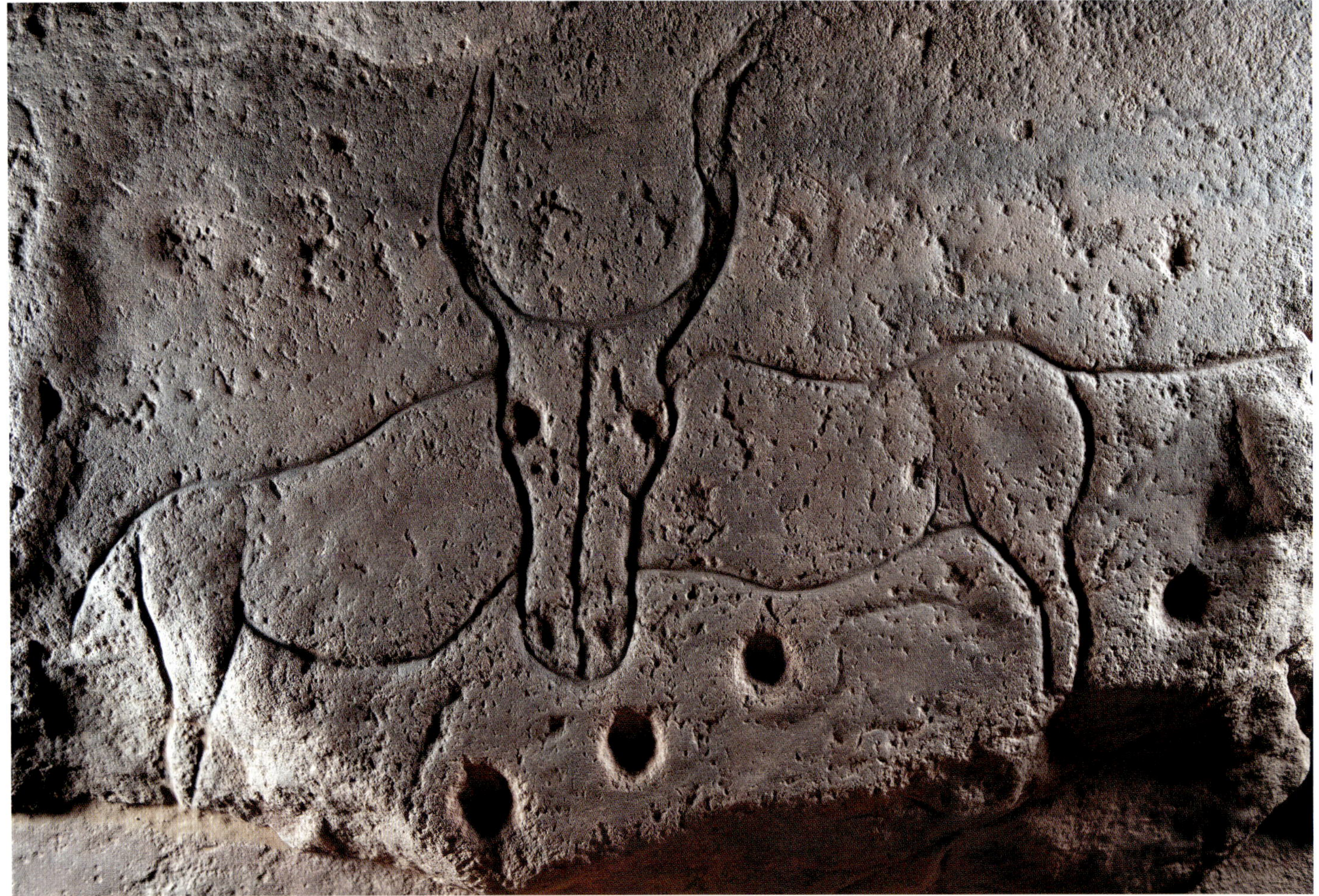

314. Two bulls seem to share the same head at site L 65, Wadi Djerat. Middle Pastoral Period, Tassili n'Ajjer, south-eastern Algeria. Night photo 2023.

3

The Influence of Rock Art on Contemporary Art

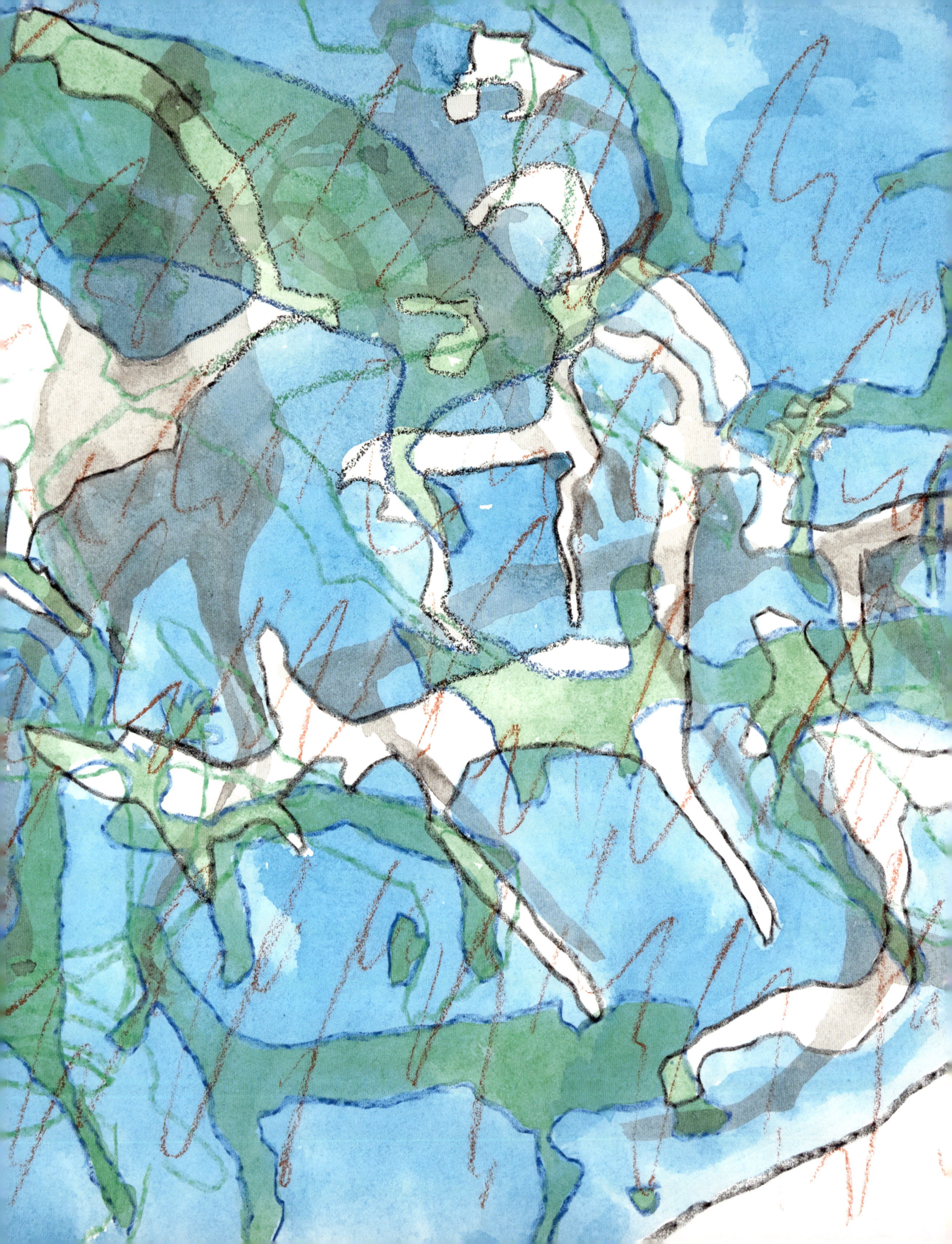

IX. Transferring the Past into the Future

By **Therese Weber**,
translated from the German by Diana Renker

1. Pioneers of narration

In rock art, we find information analogous to an encyclopaedia. Understanding petroglyphs means immersing oneself in landscapes, pictorial spaces, pictorial surfaces, pictorial objects and signs. Their narrative language focuses on motifs that refer to cultures, events and ways of life. Their complexity and forms of interpretation provide possibilities for developing new pictorial languages to this day.

1.1. The emergence of a dialogue with rock art

In the early twentieth century, painters began drawing inspiration from rock art for their own artistic processes. For some artists, it became the central impetus for their art. Leo Frobenius, a German ethnologist, became fascinated by African cultures at a young age. He founded his Africa Archive in 1898 when he was just 25 years old. Between 1904 and 1912, he led five ethnological expeditions to Africa, before turning his attention to African rock art during his sixth expedition to the Sahara and the Atlas Mountains. He subsequently conducted eight more expeditions, focusing on the discovery and documentation of African rock paintings and petroglyphs. During these expeditions, which continued until

1935, qualified artists on site copied rock paintings onto canvas and paper, preserving this prehistoric art and creating a valuable visual archive for the history of art.[1] Starting in 1934, Frobenius sent independent teams to research rock art outside Africa, starting with Val Camonica in Italy, then Scandinavia, southern France and northern Spain, and from 1937 Indonesia, Australia, Central and South America. His teams also returned to Africa several times, primarily to Libya and Ethiopia. These expeditions focused on the heritage of rock art and ethnography and occasionally incorporated archaeological excavations.[2] Frobenius' institute continued these research expeditions until 1974, long after his death in 1938. Through their fieldwork and publications, Frobenius and his team opened the door to the rock paintings first of Africa and later of other continents. Between 1927 and 1937 alone, Frobenius exhibited his copies of rock paintings twenty times across Europe, followed by exhibitions in New York and 29 other North American cities.[3] As the German ethnologist Karl-Heinz Kohl noted, these exhibitions had a profound impact on artists, even though Frobenius himself was critical of contemporary art. 'Conservative in his basic attitude and sceptical of modernism, Frobenius himself thus became a midwife to modern art.'[4]

Prehistoric pictorial representations date from a time when there were no written records, and neither cultural nor art history existed in written form. Therefore, the beginnings of recording art history do not coincide with the beginnings of art itself. It was only in the later twentieth century that a critical examination of rock art beyond mere interpretative approaches was undertaken, mainly by André Leroi-Gourhan (1911–1986). For him, writes the art historian

315. ← Therese Weber, *Palimpsest X*. Overlays of animals orienting themselves to the east and west, transparent surfaces intersecting, and disproportionately sized people appearing in the background are all embedded in green, symbolizing growth, and blue, evoking associations with the cosmos. Full size: 35 × 42 cm. Detail: 35 × 29 cm. China chalk and ink drawing on Zerkall laid paper, 2006.

Toni Hildebrandt, 'the origin of the images lies in the abstraction written into the line as a trace of the liberated hand, that is, in the interweaving of gesture and technique. From this abstraction, the complex mythograms and cosmographies of prehistoric "cave painting" evolved.'[5] Leroi-Gourhan, adhering to an evolutionary perspective on the development of art, formulated his own theory and divided the art of the Palaeolithic, both rock paintings and that of small figurative objects and sculptures, into four stylistic periods. According to his 'Genealogy of Prehistoric Artists', art began in the Aurignacian period (and to a lesser extent earlier in the Châtelperronian period) with simple carvings and ochre drawings on bone and stone depicting the outlines of animals, such as mammoths and horses. The second stage, during the Gravettian and early Solutrean periods, saw the emergence of larger, stylized paintings and engravings in shelters and at cave entrances. In the third period, encompassing the Solutrean and early Magdalenian periods, paintings featured finer lines and depicted movement. For Leroi-Gourhan, this third style, evident in the paintings of

Lascaux, represents the pinnacle of rock art. Most Palaeolithic artworks were created in the fourth period, the Middle and Late Magdalenian, where both paintings and sculptural objects were predominantly realistic.[6] This theory was later refuted by the discovery of highly sophisticated figurative art in the Swabian Jura and the masterly rock paintings of Chauvet, both of these sites dating to the Aurignacian.

The discovery of prehistoric art in Europe and Africa sparked an interest in the diverse ethnic groups and cultures that created these visual communications. The artists creating this rock art lived under vastly different conditions and economic and social structures from how we do today. Who were these early creators of visual records who felt the need to communicate through images alongside the development of language? They skilfully used simple forms to create abstract depictions of living beings, events and objects from the real world of their time. Were the creators predominantly men? Or were women, children and young people also involved in making these early artworks?

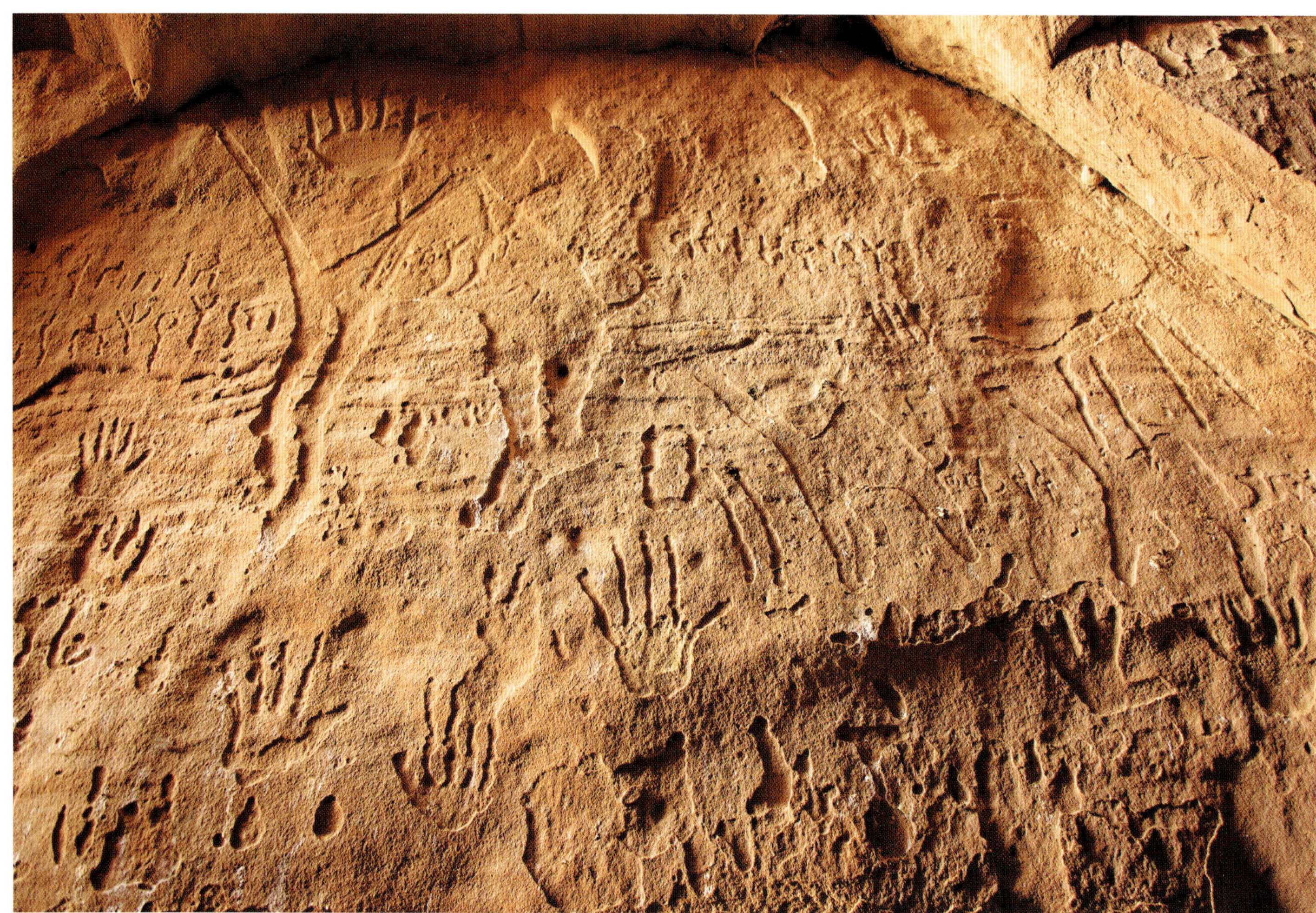

316. Hand marks and camels in the Janin Cave, Ha'il region, north-western Saudi Arabia. Photo 2020.

The debate on authorship and gender of the makers of rock art is so far unresolved.[7] The issue is further complicated by the fact that identifying authorship in rock art depictions is impossible. There are no signatures, so any information on authorship is largely hypothetical. The most reliable insights come from the depictions of hands. There is scant concrete information on the proportion of women involved in creating rock paintings, with most of our understanding based on statistical analyses. In 2013, for example, archaeologists studied hand depictions in rock paintings in eight caves in France and Spain. The hands had been placed on the rock as stencils and pigment was sprayed or blown on to the surrounding surface to create a negative image. Using an algorithm developed by the American archaeologist and anthropologist Dean Snow, it was found that 75 per cent of the hand shapes were likely those of females.[8] Similar studies have been conducted in southern Africa.[9] However, it is unclear whether these findings also apply to other cultures and regions. Of course, it cannot be excluded that the hands one sees as negatives belonged to the artists themselves. It is furthermore important to note that any conclusions about the gender of the artists drawn from handprints assumes that the bodies of men and women at that time differed significantly in size. As Kelley Hays-Gilpin pointed out, even today in southern Africa, hunters and gatherers have smaller bodies than farmers and herders of the same ethnic group.[10] Therefore, different hand sizes do not necessarily indicate different genders; they can also reflect different lifestyles. To gain more accurate information, handprints must also be compared with skeletal remains from the same era.

The content of Palaeolithic rock art – what is depicted, in other words – does not provide further clues as to the gender of the artists. The prevalence of powerful wild animals in the art suggests male authorship. It was the men who usually hunted dangerous animals, though women likely participated as beaters in collective hunts. However, the increasing prevalence of themes of rivalry, combat and victory in petroglyphs from the Bronze and Iron Ages in Europe, Central Asia, Arabia and the Sahara might at a first glance suggest a male dominance in rock art.[11] Even though there are indications that women also participated in battles in the era of the nomadic horse-riding peoples of Central Asia and north-eastern Europe (such as the Sarmatians), archaeological finds clearly prove that defence and warfare were male domains. Female skeletons from those eras very rarely show evidence of injuries caused by weapons and, aside from the Sarmatians, most male burials were accompanied by weapons and riding gear, whereas women were almost exclusively buried with jewellery and occasionally a knife or a small dagger. We can therefore assume that Bronze Age and

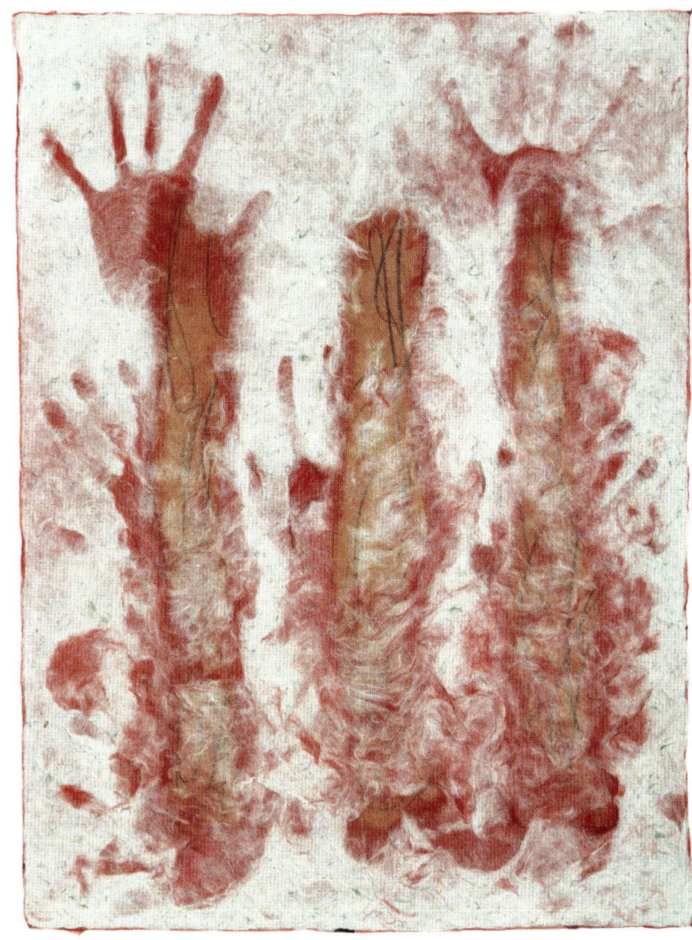

317. Therese Weber, *Hand into the Future II*, front side. 64 x 49 cm. Washi, coloured and cast mulberry fibre; pulp painting on both sides, 2023.

Iron Age petroglyphs more likely reflect the ideas of the male world and were also created by men. However, the authors of petroglyphs may have varied within each culture. In Val Camonica, for instance, there are countless duelling scenes but also petroglyphs of looms, which most likely belonged to the female realm of activities. In general, everyday scenes of a domestic nature and depictions of children are very rare in petroglyphs.

Another unresolved, and perhaps also unanswerable, question is that of the gender of simple stick figures. In rock paintings, gender is often indicated by clothing or long hair, less frequently by the depiction of sexual characteristics. In contrast, petroglyphs are naturally less detailed, and the depiction of gender varies depending on the region and culture. Some carvings indicate gender through the more or less explicit depiction of phalluses, vulvas or breasts. However, most are not gender-specific. This lack of differentiation can be interpreted in several ways. Because armed figures are often identified as men, gender-neutral figures might depict unarmed males. Alternatively, these figures could represent women, considering that in various European and Central Asian cultures, men were often defined by their weapons. It is also possible that in certain cultures, gender was of little relevance in the context of petroglyph art.

An analysis of Palaeolithic handprints also shows that the left hand was predominantly depicted, as seen in the cave paintings at Lascaux in France.[12] Consequently, most of the work was done with the right hand. In petroglyphs, however, the hand was not used as a stencil, so that both hands were free to be used for engraving. This is not only the case in Europe but also on the Arabian Peninsula. For example, in the spectacular Janin Cave, about 30 kilometres east of Ha'il on the eastern edge of the Great Nafud Desert in Saudi Arabia, engravings depict both right and left hands.[13] Some questions remain unanswered: were these images of hands made by individuals or by a team? Are the hands depicted in cave paintings those of the artists or those of others who were present? In the case of smaller hands, it is conceivable that adults reproduced the hands of children as part of a ritual (fig. 316).

Can these depictions be considered the beginnings of art? This question has been revisited repeatedly and is interpreted differently depending on artistic practices and the time period. The art historian Sir Ernst Gombrich (1909–2001) declared in 1950: 'There really is no such thing as art: there are only artists.'[14] Gombrich built bridges between art history and other fields of research by questioning basic concepts and developing new perspectives. The Saudi researcher Muhammad al-Mustaneer, who investigates Saudi Arabian petroglyphs, points out that a prehistoric visual work perceived as art today represented something quite different for its creators and their society. Referring to the petroglyphs in the province of Najran, he notes: 'For the people back then, these works were to leave behind traces of their perceptions, their views and their everyday lives. For me today, it is art.'[15]

The debate on the influence of prehistoric rock art on modern art was initiated by Alfred H. Barr, Jr (1902–1981), the founding director of the Museum of Modern Art (MoMA) in New York City. He asked how prehistoric rock art had influenced and was influencing the genesis of contemporary art in Paris and New York between 1930 and 1960. In 1937, he dedicated an exhibition at MoMA to rock art and its creators.[16] In the wake of this seminal exhibition, a trend in art appreciation emerged that aimed to challenge traditional ways of thinking and seeing. The aim was to obtain through a multi-perspective approach new insights beyond the discipline-specific views. John Kay Clegg (1935–2015) was the first scholar to teach rock art at an Australian university.[17] According to his approach, petroglyphs should be viewed from multiple perspectives. As he succinctly put it: 'different ways of looking will result in different ways of seeing'.[18] His background as both a practising artist and an archaeologist enabled him to develop a comprehensive approach from the perspectives of technology, aesthetics, history and science.

Let us return to the hand, both a versatile tool for many tasks and itself a subject of art. Hands are used to create petroglyphs as well as rock paintings; but they also serve as stencils and are among the oldest motifs in rock art. Today, various artists still use their hands as creative tools and forms of artistic expression, with some continuing to employ techniques from prehistoric times. For example, the Australian Indigenous artist Dale Harding creates images directly on museum walls using his hand as a stencil and spraying pigments around it to create a negative form. He also uses the same technique to create large-scale prints, including the ones shown at *documenta 14* in Kassel in 2017.[19] In her work '*Impression of my Left Hand*' from 1984, Meret Oppenheim (1913–1985) referred to a photograph made by Man Ray and coated the palm of her hand with paint and pressed it onto paper, thus creating a positive image of her hand. She signed the work with her poem 'La rosée sur la rose'.[20]

In my own artistic work, my hands play a crucial role in a complex and unique technique that I have developed. I place one hand in thin layers of coloured fibres made of the inner bark of the mulberry tree *Broussonetia papyrifera* which have been poured into a cast paper sieve frame. At the same time I use my other hand to control how the fibres flow and to add more layers. This process of creating paper art results in a multi-layered surface with my hand practically 'inscribed' in the paper. The shape of my hand remains visible and can be seen from both the front and the back due to the transparency of the subtly coloured fibrous material. The piece is both the support and the image with the paper pulp substrate an essential part of the composition. The two works titled *Hand into the Future* were created in Japan in 2023 (figs 1, 317).

1.2. Transfer methods: sketches, photos and frottages

Unlike rock paintings, petroglyphs typically exhibit distinct characteristics due to the specific techniques and tools (of stone and later metal) used in their creation. During the carving process, depictions were rendered in a linear or dotted manner. Sometimes, the entire image or a part of it was created by chipping or scraping away the surface. Lines vary in width and depth and were shaped by scoring, engraving or punching. They can also be made up of dots. The line's edges can be smooth or sharp-edged, chipped or polished. Scraped areas have different surface textures depending on the tools used. Petroglyphs are created through actions that are 'irrevocable' as they involve carving, engraving or punching into the stone or rock surface rather than applying paint or pigment.

Also, unlike rock paintings, petroglyphs are mostly not located in caves or protected by rocky outcrops but are in open terrain exposed to the elements. [21] They are exposed in the landscape and susceptible to the threat of impermanence. Their eventual disappearance is just a matter of time. Over thousands of years, climate-related influences such as rain, snow, water and ice can damage these historical 'drawings in stone', as can overgrowth by shrubs, lichen or moss. Human activities, such as the construction of roads and bridges or the building of dams, can also cause irreparable damage to rock art. More recently, inappropriate conservation methods, vandalism and, in the case of the petroglyphs in the Chilas region of northern Pakistan, religious fanaticism against pictorial representations of humans and animals have further endangered this valuable cultural heritage. Since not all of these threats can be eliminated, the documentation of petroglyphs

has become increasingly important. Various methods facilitate the documentation of rock art. Each method comes with its own advantages and disadvantages, highlighting the importance of applying the right method according to context and purpose and preserving the results in an archival format. It is crucial that these methods are non-invasive and do not leave behind any traces.

Sketching allows for interpretation and is often schematic. Drawing by hand can capture motifs in greater detail but does not qualify as a scientific record. Historically, emphasis was often placed on certain 'relevant' details while neglecting other 'disruptive' elements that might have been added at a later date. Some elements were simply omitted as they were considered offensive, such as the depictions of sexual content. An example is the watercolour painting by the Norwegian Peter Alfsön (see pp. 21, 190), who in 1627 depicted the great warrior in the petroglyph composition of Backa in Brastad without his erect phallus. Similar selective renderings can be found in Henri Lhote's reproductions of Saharan rock paintings, where he omitted certain figures or

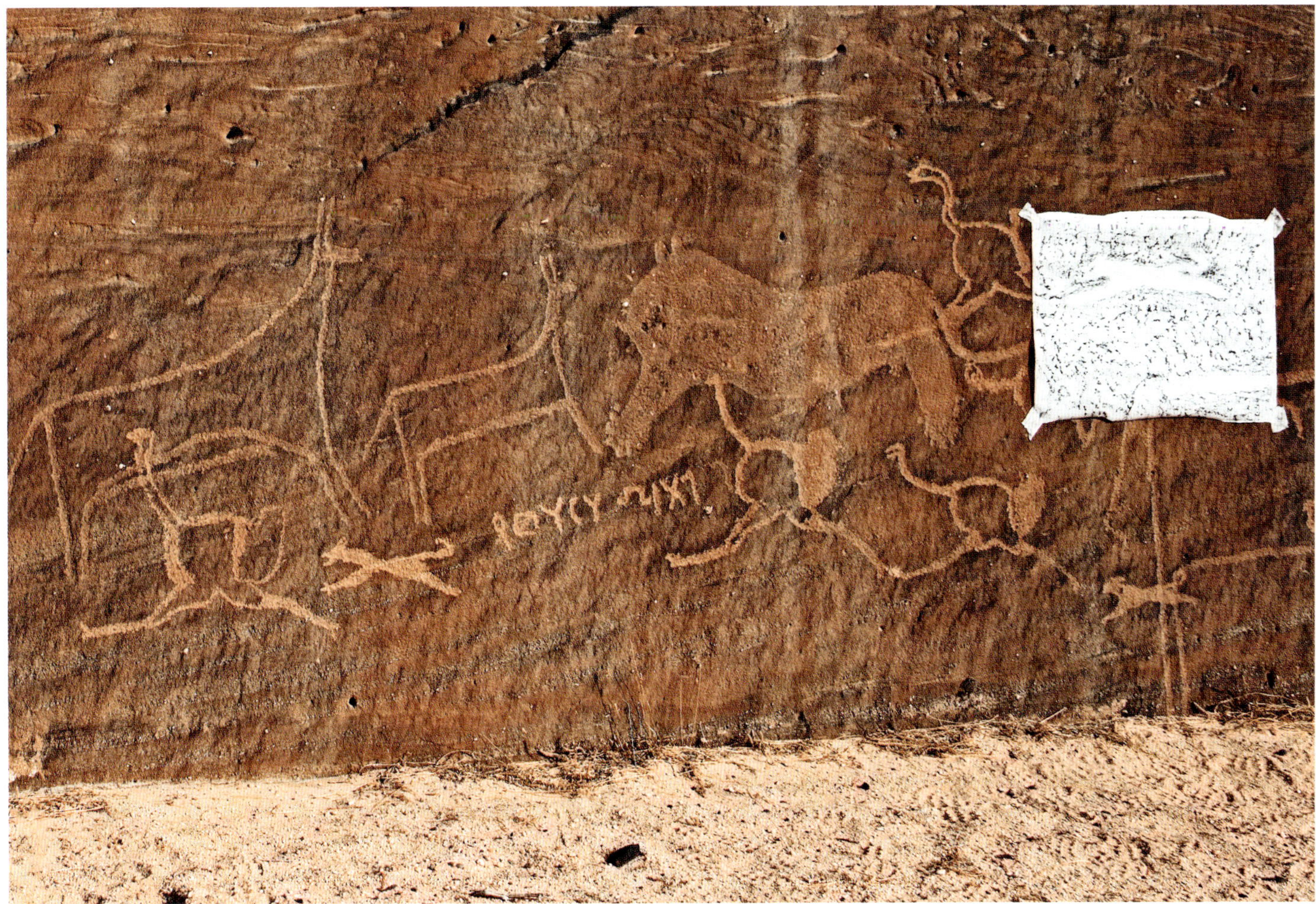

318. Frottage by Therese Weber of a jumping leopard *in situ* at the petroglyph site of al-Wahaf, Saudi Arabia. Frottage, graphite pencil on mulberry paper, 52 × 69 cm, 2020.

combined unrelated and distant figures to create a new scene. Carl Gustav Gottfried Hilfeling's ink drawings from 1792, a century after Alfsön, are more nuanced. Hilfeling was clearly a skilful draughtsman.[22] However, as far as precision is concerned, the drawings by the Swedish historian and archaeologist Carl Georg Brunius (1773–1869) were far more accurate. He used a grid system in his documentations to scale down sizes, ensuring reproductions were as true to scale as possible.[23]

Using photographic documentation as a tool for viewing is crucial for refining visual perception of the artistic process. Differences and subtle textures are often more discernible on a computer screen than when viewing the artwork at first hand. This clarity enhances our ability to trace individual figures and superimpositions, and this helps with research and dating. Photographs also provide a suitable starting point for tracing, whether manually, using tracing paper or transparent foil, or digitally. Digitizing images and employing processes like 3D scanning or the DStretch method[24] are effective methods for making details visible and highlighting what is barely noticeable *in situ*. This is because visual perception in the field can also be significantly influenced by varying light and weather conditions.

Transfer methods that can be used directly in the field include tracing on transparent foil and making rubbings (frottages). Tracing involves placing the foil over the petroglyph and accurately following the image at a 1:1 scale, reproducing the image as a linear outline. This method requires precision and care. Rubbings on paper document the format, content and texture of the surrounding rock at a 1:1 scale, capturing the tactile qualities and faithfully reproducing both the figurative representations and the natural texture of the rock. Rubbings can reveal structural details that are difficult, if not impossible, to capture in photographs. When done carefully, the frottage method does not damage the surface of the petroglyphs. Depending on their size, one or several sheets of paper are placed next to each other over the petroglyphs and the surface details are transferred to the paper by rubbing with graphite, carbon paper or chalk. These rubbings create records of historical artefacts that may eventually disappear due to erosion or human activity. The technique is based on an ancient Chinese method primarily used for copying texts on stone steles. The artist Max Ernst also recognized the potential of frottage for the visual arts, and although he did not work with petroglyphs, he applied and further developed this method from 1925 onwards.[25]

The transmission of rock art into contemporary art typically occurs through painting and drawing. We must distinguish between artists with a direct biographical connection to rock art and those who explore it through travel, research or literature. The first group, which includes artists like Dale Harding (Australia), Abdulmagid Abdulrahman (Libya), Lydia Ourahmane (Algeria), Ibrahim N. al-Fassam (Saudi Arabia), and Joane Cardinal-Schubert (Canada), are motivated by their personal, ethnic or geographical ties to rock art. The second group includes the notable artists featured by Alfred Barr in his MoMA New York exhibition and those showcased in the *Ten Americans: After Paul Klee* exhibition at the Zentrum Paul Klee in Bern (2017–18), as well as other contemporary artists.

1.3. Approaches to rock art

How we approach art and what we experience very much depends on who we are, and on our specific objectives. In the words of John Berger, 'The relation between what we see and what we know is never settled. […] The way we see things is affected by what we know or what we believe.'[26] The discourse on rock art involves different levels of understanding, depending on the researcher's approach. As is evident from the previous chapters in this book, anthropologists and archaeologists focus on the way of life of the makers of petroglyphs and aim to understand their economic environment, their worldview, objectives and aspirations. Art historians, on the other hand, use different strategies and methods to decode and categorize rock art. From the standpoint of their own discipline, they are able to identify additional contexts within the pictorial compositions. Their visual analytical approach gives rise to different questions relating to iconography, style and genres of art. For example, interrelationships and parallels between rock art and Cubism are noted in relation to works by Pablo Picasso (1881–1973), Paul Klee (1879–1940), or Joan Miró (1893–1983). Rock art is thus placed in a dialogue with modern art, forming a bridge from archaic visual elements to contemporary art and raising an awareness of the significance of prehistoric art.

Artists bring a different perspective again, that includes interdisciplinary and creative technical approaches. They try to identify the rules underlying representation and drawing methods, as well as the styles and types of figures featured. They see graphic qualities that emphasize how these motifs are depicted. They note how figures and proportions interact, and how surface is expressed and differentiated, how silhouette and contour are rendered, and how individual figures and groups are arranged. They also analyse how movement is implied to make specific activities visible. The depiction of animals walking or running was already conceived in prehistoric times through the multiplication of legs, similar to how images are staged in animated films. Activities and actions

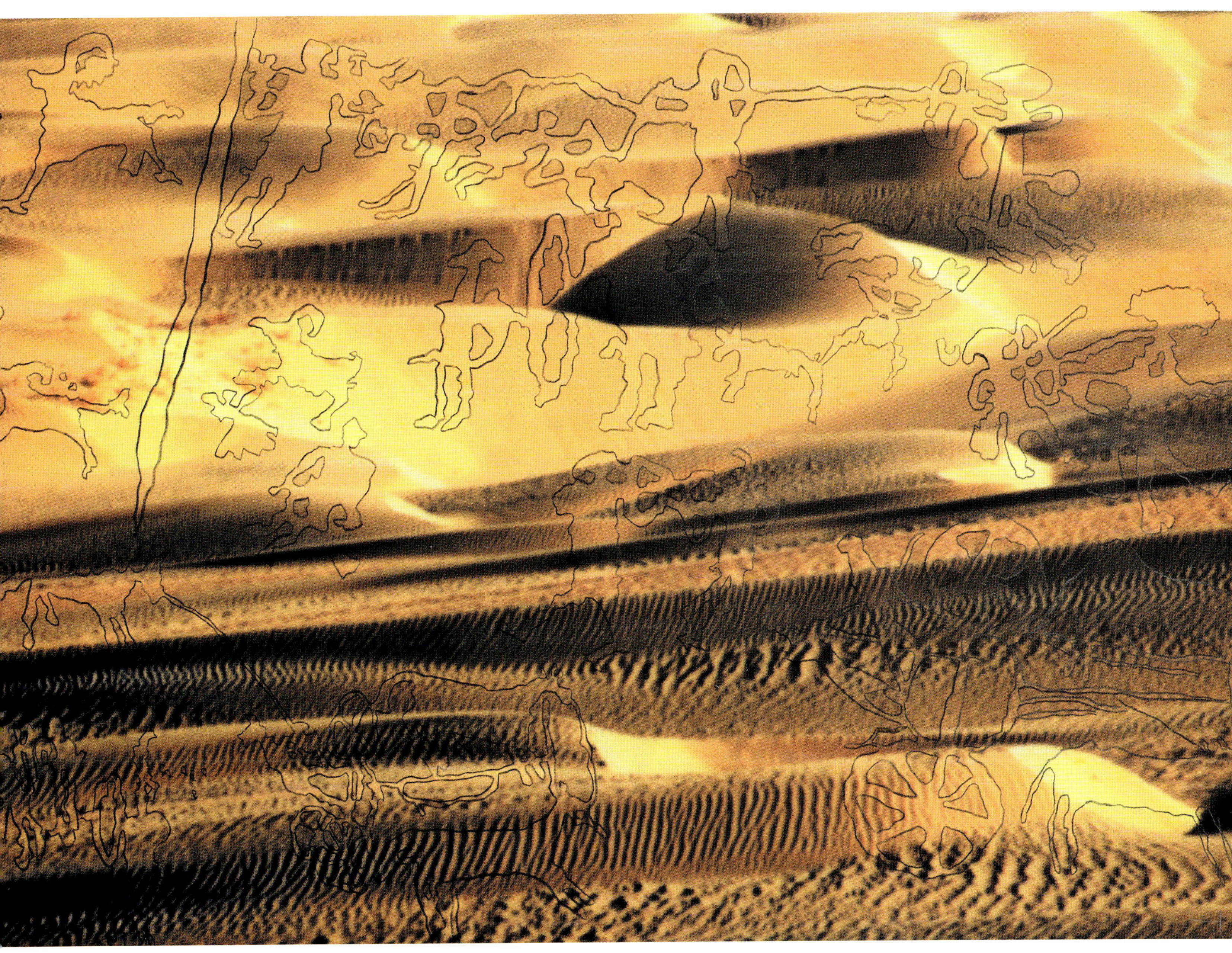

319. Therese Weber, *Metamorphoses IV*. 80 × 100 cm. Photograph (digital airbrush process), China ink, chalk drawing, on Zerkall laid paper, 2007.

are expressed by attributes that take on the function of a *pars pro toto* – a harpoon, for example, may signal whaling, or a sword a conflict situation. Deciphering these attributes helps us understand the intentions expressed in the rock art and the thought processes behind the illustrations. Perception, inspiration and intention are very individual and depend on the artist's knowledge. They use their own vocabulary to decipher and then communicate their own artistic messages.

The 'artists' of prehistoric times applied their images to rock formations, shelters and caves, depending on the topography. These rocks not only served as the support and background for the signs

and motifs, but through their colour, structure, consistency, shape and surface texture they even dominated the images imposed on them and became part of the composition. In most two-dimensional contemporary art, by contrast, the background is made, for example, of linen or cotton, paper, wood or metal, and mostly recedes, becoming purely a support material. Quite often, an artist's perspective on art changes after they have spent time engaging with prehistoric rock art. Their understanding of ancient art, as well as their own approach to art, is renegotiated and expanded.

There are various reasons why artists are fascinated by rock art. For Pierre Soulages (France, 1919–2022), for example, it was not

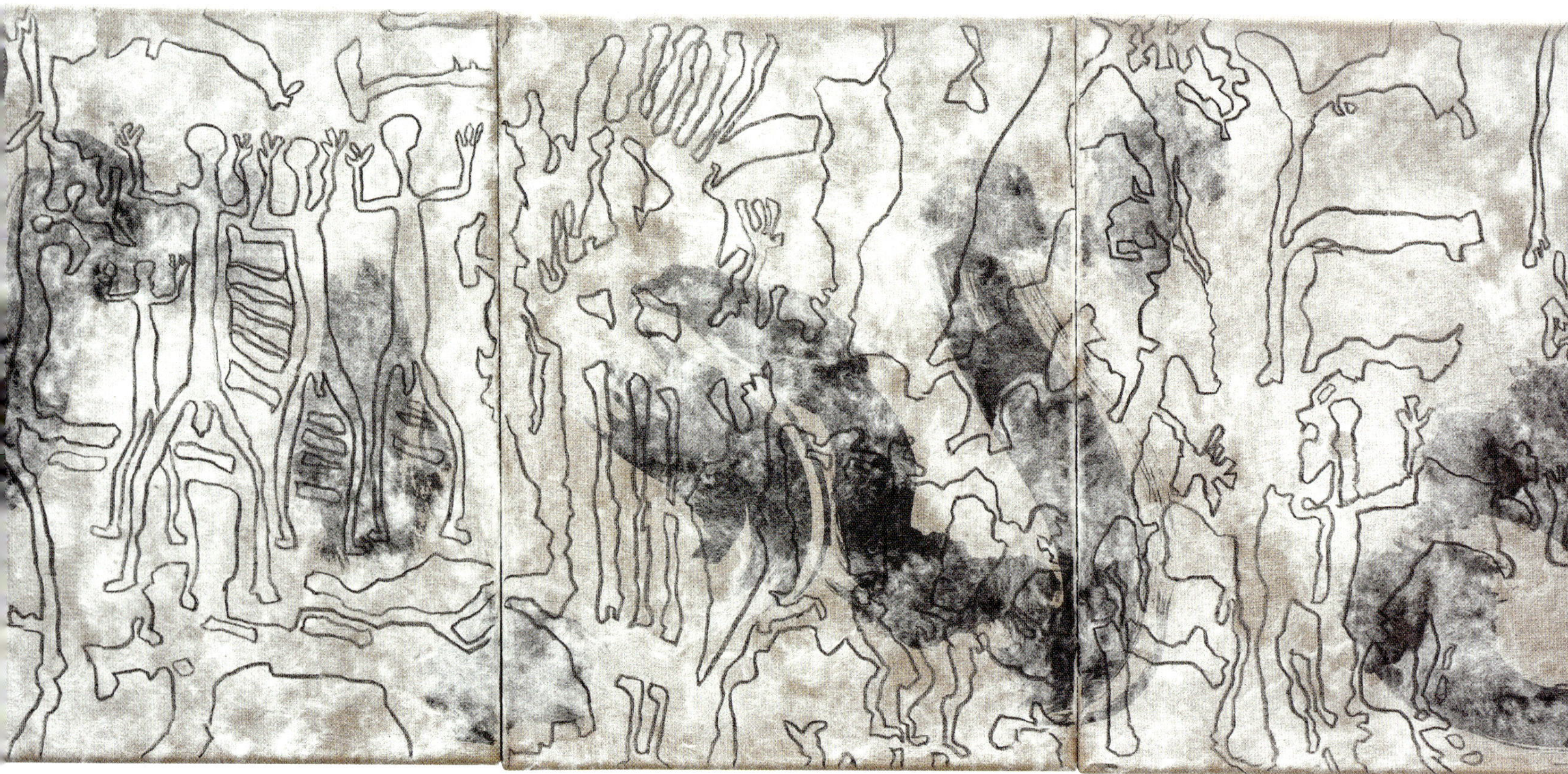

320. Therese Weber, *Signs of the Moment*. 50 × 120 cm. Calligraphy and mulberry fibre on linen fabric, chalk drawing, 2019.

the motif that inspired his work but soot, the material used for the first cave drawings. 'Art emerged from darkness,' Soulages stressed. 'It was painting with black soot. Its first colour was black.'[27] He was referring to the first, Palaeolithic people who began to paint. 'What interests me about these ancient paintings is what happened with the people who made them, in terms of materials – that is the best way to approach these things, far better than trying to figure out their meaning ... because it's well known that when you talk of meaning, you're only talking about yourself.'[28] Black remained the dominant 'colour' throughout his oeuvre.

Art critics and curators have also discovered the relevance of differentiating between the perception, meaning and composition of rock art. The American art historian Lucy R. Lippard,[29] for example, analysed a continuum of forms and symbols that artists have used for thousands of years, so as to document her own approach. What interested Lippard most about prehistory was the unknown – all that we do not know about these forms of expression. For her, focusing on these forms allowed her to immerse herself in a new, 'speculative' art history. She concentrated her attention on how things are and how they develop in specific situations. Since she had previously written mainly on

contemporary art, the inclusion of prehistoric art within her field of study required a departure from conventional ways of looking at art. The merging of two disparate realities, the prehistoric period and contemporary art, changes one's perception of contemporary culture. In these 'overlays', as she calls them, contemporary artists incorporate prehistoric images into their work. In her book *Overlay: Contemporary Art and the Art of Prehistory*, Lippard focuses on works by artists from different continents who have all looked at prehistoric culture. This includes the Cuban-American artist Ana Maria Mendieta (1948–1985), but most of the artists Lippard discusses are from the USA, such as Robert Smithson (1938–1973), Michael Heizer (b. 1944), and Richard Fleischner (b. 1944). By studying these 'overlays', she established new spaces that were to shape her thinking from then on. 'Art has trained me to do whatever I want to do. The ideas that I got from artists have formed the ways I look at the world.'[30]

2. Open-air archives: an artist's narrative

When I visit places, they become intricately connected to certain themes in my art and research projects. Some of these places bear traces of prehistoric times, which I encounter as silent witnesses in the form of 'open-air archives'. They are not only important manifestations that preserve the treasures of history, but they can also generate new stories and spark metamorphoses. The interplay between past and present events, each embodying different thought processes and methods, provides fertile ground for extraordinary imaginative and creative processes. Each of my pictures, installations and performances is closely connected to a specific area. For me, finding a suitable 'topography' in the global world means finding a place for my own development. Every landscape, every place reflects a story, a memory. Through my individually developed procedures and methods of artistic research and practice, I broaden my understanding of both history and traditions. This often begins with researching the culture and geography of an area. In doing so,

I make connections between intersecting themes so as to generate a new discourse. It is the unknown that draws me in and inspires new thinking. Without this curiosity and thirst for knowledge, there are no questions, and without questions, there are no answers. Literary research and participating in expeditions are essential for exploring transcultural perspectives and examining the visual language of prehistoric times. I focus specifically on petroglyphs, a form of communication that provides clues and information about the way of life in various cultures throughout different periods. These recording systems trace back to the origins of pictorial expression, predating by millennia the invention of paper,[31] and even of parchment and papyrus.[32]

Each of my projects has a focus, and travelling is essential to realize it. *In situ* encounters and observations are formative and help to further develop concepts and ideas. Inspiration and imagination require one to step out of traditional ways of thinking and seeing and allow for unexpected input. Being on the road advances the process, creating a dialogue with places, topographies and artefacts from earlier times, and enables encounters

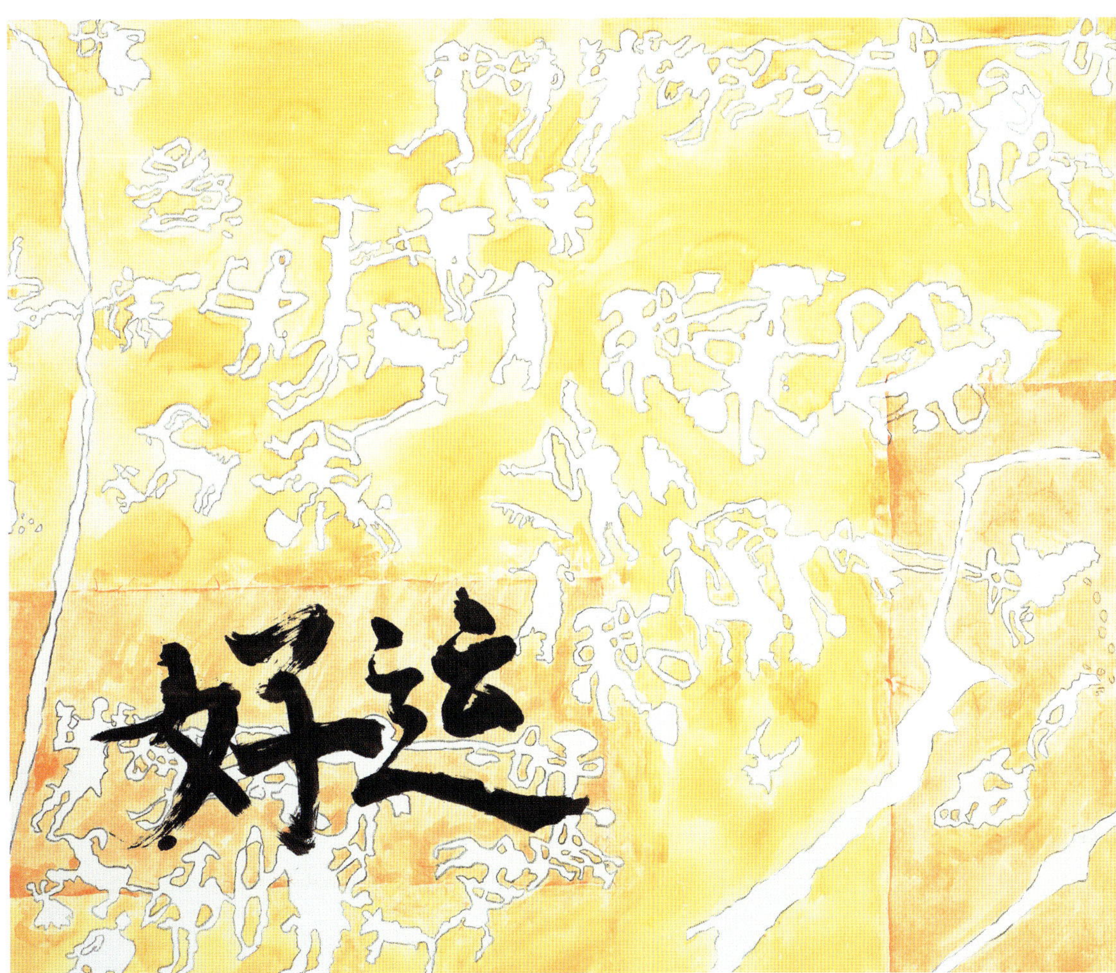

321. Therese Weber, *Synthesis II.* The Chinese calligraphic sign means 'luck'. 120 × 140 cm. China ink, chalk drawing on canvas, collage from mulberry paper, 2014.

with people and their worldviews. These elements interweave to form a multi-layered structure – spaces for thought and action in artistic practice. They become a part of my life, entering my mental archive as a store of personal insights. Reflecting on one's approach and perception and scrutinizing one's own narrative is also important. As an artist and researcher, I am fascinated by the interactions between different themes, methods and places. These form the foundation for linking and documenting exploration, analyses and records through photography and text. This work constantly evolves due to new pursuits in all my areas of interest. Consequently, my work is shaped by my life story and created in the context of a specific time and history.

For me, the work balances technological innovations and the preservation of tradition through the transfer of stone engravings using the technique of rubbing, incorporating them into my art. In this interactive field, unique experiences and new connections between place, space and time emerge. My art attempts to bundle together historical, social and climatic elements in order to visualize an interplay of different cultures and eras. This approach is linked to my desire to explore ideas that I might otherwise not have considered. My work is based on various systems and concepts that I am constantly questioning in order to look for new solutions. While there are certain rules and principles, each piece has its own objective: it focuses on a specific theme and follows a unique stylistic

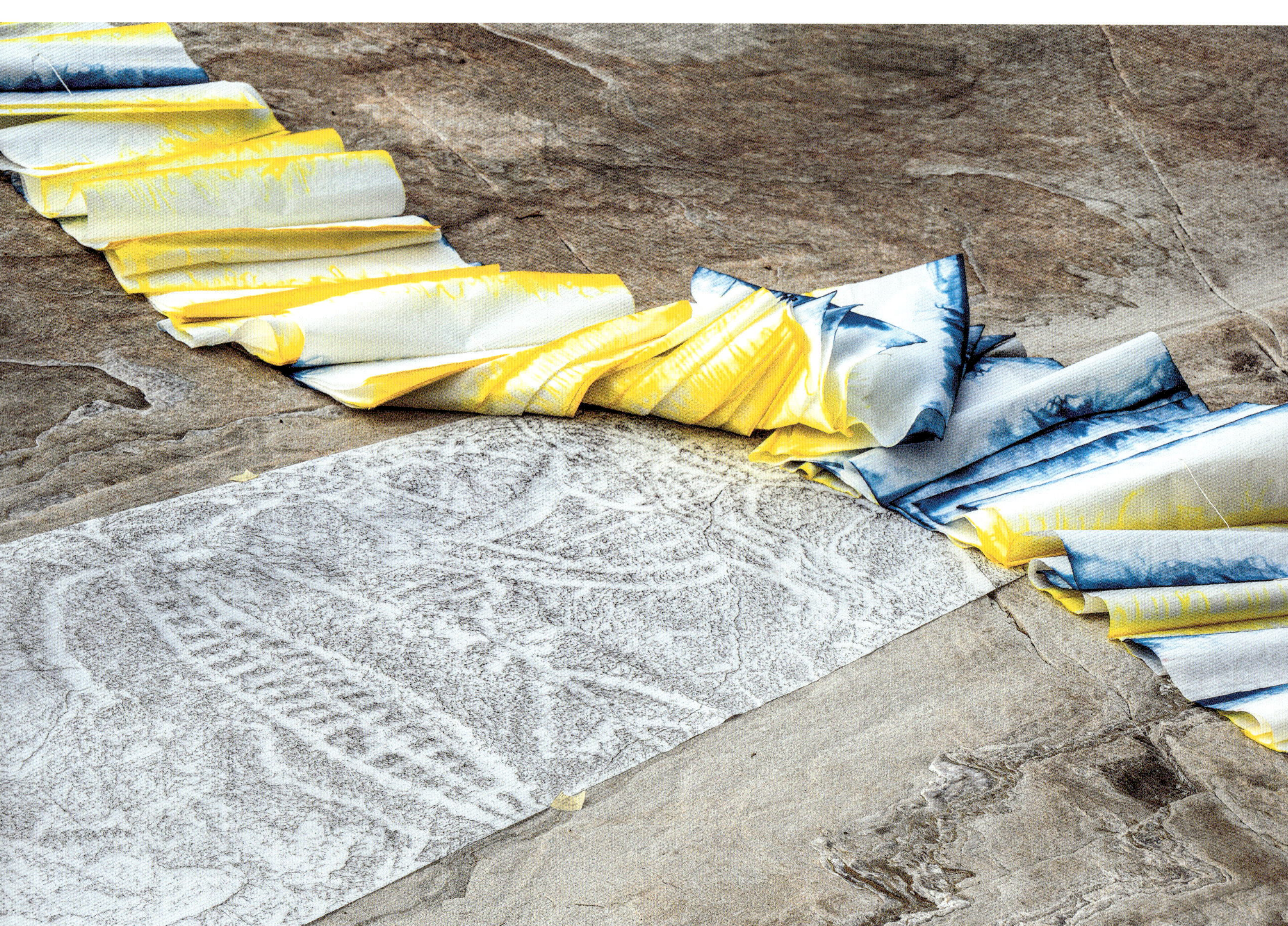

322. Therese Weber, *Forms of the Present, Narratives of the Past*. Frottage on Mulberry paper (total 115 × 488 cm) and installation at the petroglyphs in Amtmannsnes, Alta, Norway. Accordion book: coloured paper band of mulberry fibre (total of folded paper band: 46 × 5000 cm), 2022.

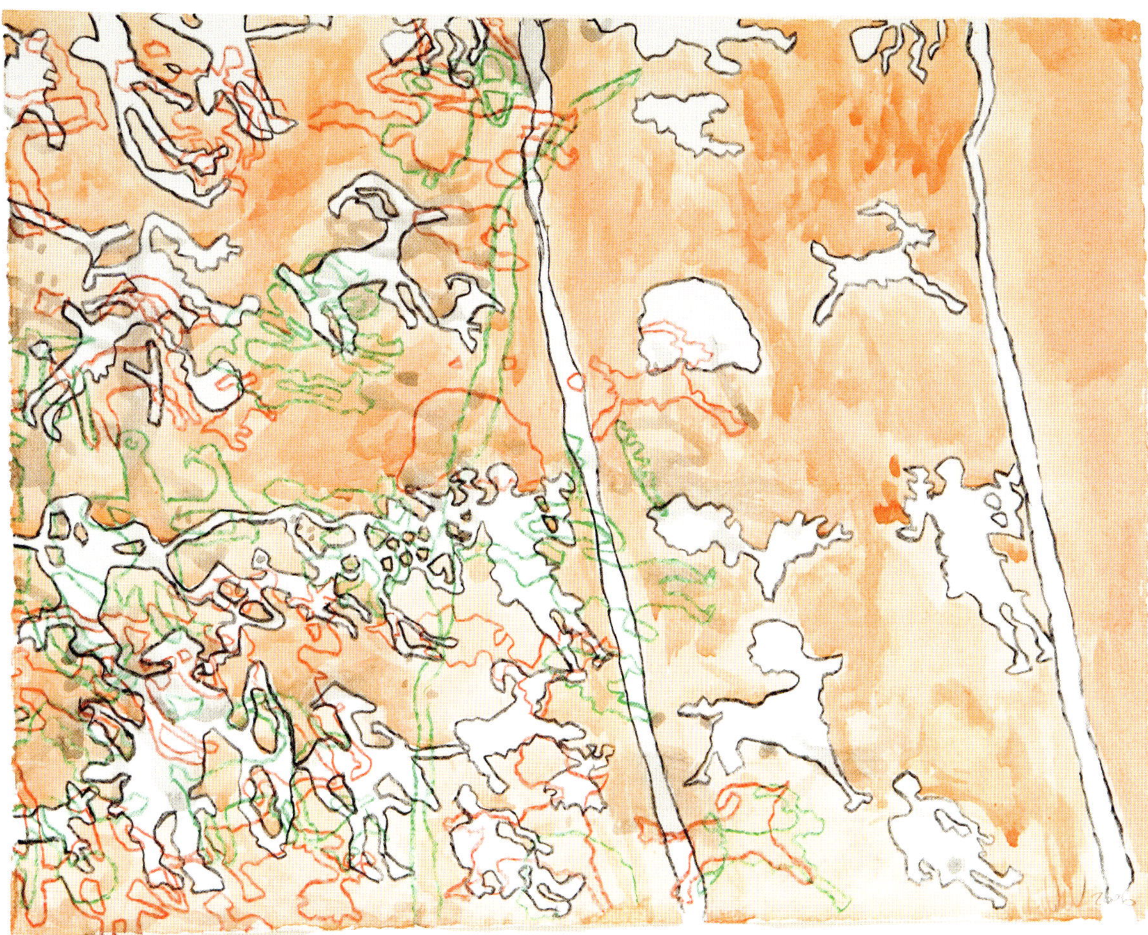

323. Therese Weber, *Palimpsest I*. 35 × 42 cm. China chalk and ink drawing on Zerkall laid paper, 2006.

direction. Starting from sketches, mapping processes, frottages and photographs, the concepts and ideas are transferred into my art in the form of pictures, installations, performances and texts. Several domains can overlap, such as photography and drawing in *Metamorphoses IV*, 2007 (fig. 319), or pulp paintings and drawing in *Signs of the Moment*, 2019 (fig. 320).

The artworks made from paper are unique in this context. I build them up layer by layer by scooping or pouring the paper fibre material, also known as pulp, onto a screen base. This creates a transparent, solid, smooth or structured surface, depending on the technique and raw material used. The fibres from plant-based raw materials such as the inner bark of mulberry, cotton or abaca[33] are first prepared in a complex process. After harvesting and removing the cellulose fibres, they are cleaned, boiled, beaten or defibrated using a Hollander or Naginata beater.[34] Depending on the intended outcome, they may then be dyed. Next the fibres are suspended in water and used like liquid dye as a medium for painting. I first started working with these little-known processes in 1985 in California and the following year in Japan. In paper art, which originated in the United States in the 1970s, 'paper' becomes autonomous and frees itself from its servile role as a carrier

material for images and writing. It becomes a language and means of artistic expression in its own right.

However, stone and rock are also fascinating. I first encountered stone as a carrier of knowledge in China in 1997, when a new world opened up for me at the Beilin (or Stele Forest) Museum in Xi'an, the former capital of the Tang Dynasty (618–907 CE). The museum houses more than 3,000 engraved stone steles, over a thousand of which are on display. These limestone slabs, some up to 2,000 years old, nearly three metres high, and weighing up to two tonnes, immortalize Confucian classics, Buddhist texts and selected poems, and also document significant events. During that pivotal encounter, I discovered the technique of rubbing, which was invented in China. This method, which predates block printing, also preserves the original written document, that is the text engraved on the stone slab. The knowledge-conveying tandem of stele and rubbing not only guaranteed the preservation of the original text but also its literal reproduction, unlike the error-prone work of medieval copyists in Europe.

A rubbing frequently becomes the starting point for further artistic engagement, especially if it depicts figurative petroglyphs. I first encountered these prehistoric figures and signs around the

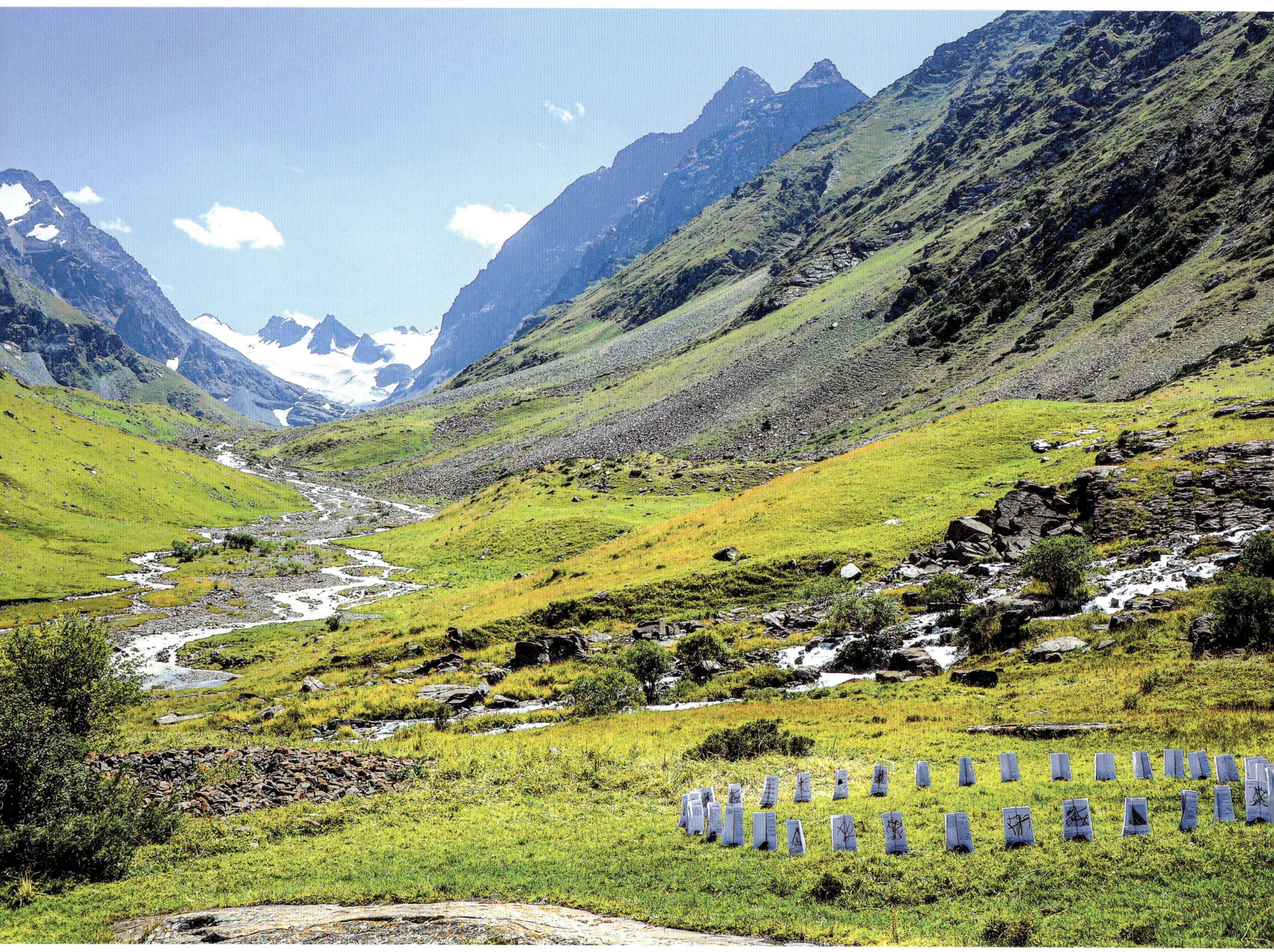

324. Therese Weber, *Identities of Different Periods.* Installation with 37 pieces, Zhaltyrak Tash, north-western Kyrgyzstan. Paper, microscope photographs, text, drawing, 2017.

turn of the millennium in Tibet, and later in Mongolia and Central Asia. These engraved petroglyphs are found in special places that were often associated with a place of worship or burial site. Discovering petroglyphs as a means of communication that makes comprehensible a world that is no longer visible was formative for me. My experience of these 'open-air archives' sparked a new direction in my creative intention and simultaneously opened a new field of research. From then on, figurative motifs entered my pictorial vocabulary, which had previously been characterized primarily by abstract forms. What emerged were multiple overlays of black-and-white and coloured petroglyph drawings

on handmade paper, some of which were derived from original rubbings on thin mulberry paper. Revitalized in this way, revered supernatural beings, status symbols, wars and battles immortalized in stone more than 5,000 years ago find their way into my works. The past merges with contemporary art.

A particularly complex work, *Synthesis II* (fig. 321) from 2014, depicts a large petroglyphic scene with two prominent Chinese characters superimposed on it. Indeed, the Mongolian land of nomadic cattle breeders and the Chinese territory, shaped by sedentary farmers, have been interacting culturally and economically for more than 3,000 years. In this work, the confidently inscribed Chinese characters meaning 'luck' remind us of the fact that from the late seventeenth century CE, the sedentary people of China, who had also developed writing, dominated the once-proud horse people of the steppe.

The Bronze Age petroglyphs from Amtmannsnes near Alta, Norway, almost 400 kilometres north of the Arctic Circle, inspired me to perform a dual artistic intervention. These petroglyphs, dating from the third of the five periods of local petroglyph art, that is *ca.* 3000–2000 BCE, reflect the social worldview of the time. They depict large, passively standing female figures with pronounced pelvises. Unique in all of Scandinavia, these petroglyphs were likely created as a result of a cultural exchange with immigrants from the east. In my multi-dimensional installation *Forms of the Present, Narratives of the Past*, 2022 (fig. 322), a 50-metre-long, blue-and-yellow-coloured book object in zigzag folds made of mulberry paper opens and expands across the frottage over the rock with its petroglyphs. The blue colour serves as a reminder that the hills of Amtmannsnes were still

underwater not long before the rock paintings were created around 4,500 years ago.

In my oeuvre, the world of paper and the world of petroglyphs enter a creative dialogue. Since participating in an archaeological research expedition to the Taklamakan Desert in Xinjiang, China, in the autumn of 2003, I have been combining paper traditions with petroglyph research and incorporating these explorations into my artistic practice. During this process, I create rubbings that depict the engraved figures at their original size. These valuable documents contribute to building an archive of prehistoric records. For me, they provide an impulse to translate these non-verbal messages from the rock carvings into my unique visual language, linking them with my concepts and objectives. This process creates a metamorphosis between my photographs from the Taklamakan Desert and figures of people and animals, as well as two-wheeled chariots drawn by horses or camels from the prehistoric world of petroglyphs. These overlays document how the currently hostile sand sea once, thousands of years ago, harboured flourishing oases. Two different time periods

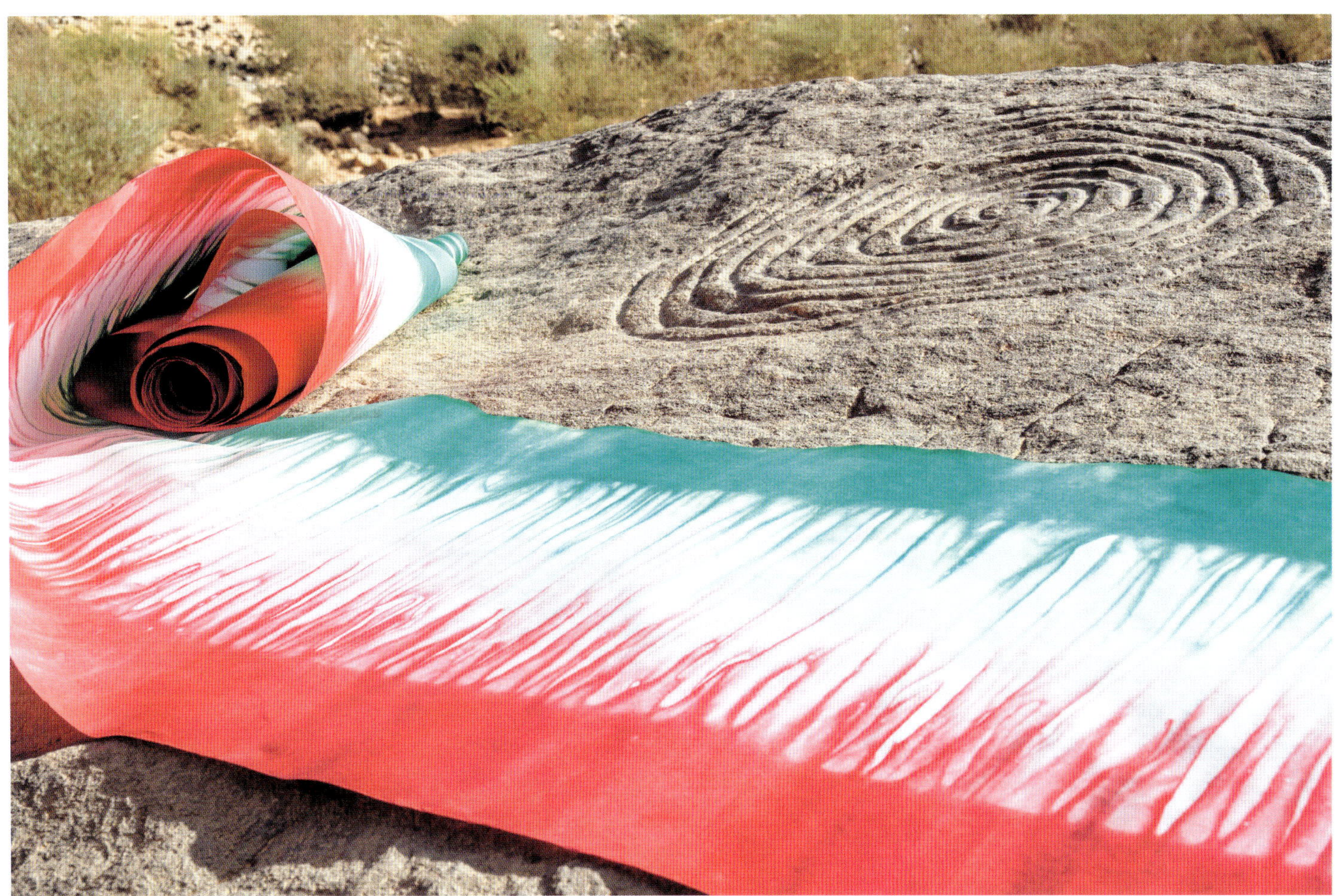

325. Therese Weber, *The Point in the Middle.* Installation near the petroglyph site Lhote 28 in Wadi Djerat, Sahara, Algeria. Dyed paper band of mulberry fibre, 45 × 2500 cm, 2023.

are combined, highlighting the mobility of these early peoples. In the work *Metamorphoses III*, 2018 (fig. 11), these two territories coexist like palimpsests. The inhospitable Taklamakan Desert is overlaid with animals, people and wagons reminiscent of prehistoric times, but given a new context that reminds us that many desert regions were once populated. The question of the visions and worldview of the people who once lived there and left behind these early records is left unanswered.

In the land art project *Identities of Different Periods*, 2017 (fig. 324), installed at the foot of the large petroglyph rock face in Zhaltyrak Tash, north-western Kyrgyzstan, at an altitude of 2,701 metres, different worlds and periods came together once again. My previously designed book object, featuring photographs of microscopic images of paper fibres and inscribed with quotations from the philosopher Bruno Latour (1947–2022), testifies to a relationship between natural phenomena and cultural conditions. Latour's experimental, multi-layered way of thinking and his powerful texts, such as his book *An Inquiry into Modes of Existence*,[35] convey challenging theses that allow me to develop further visions and methods. In this installation, I arranged the artist's book, divided into 37 book blocks, in a circle next to a kurgan, a circular burial mound from the early Iron Age, to initiate a discourse between three eras. The work, set in the peaceful landscape by the Kaman-Suu River, with a glacier in the background and a multitude of animal motifs on the smooth surface of the large rock face, invites the viewer to engage with these three different worlds from the past, the present and the future.

In the rocky Tassili n'Ajjer, an area of the central Sahara, another encounter took place. Here, a delicate roll of white paper meets the hard stone, contrasting with the rock engravings of a

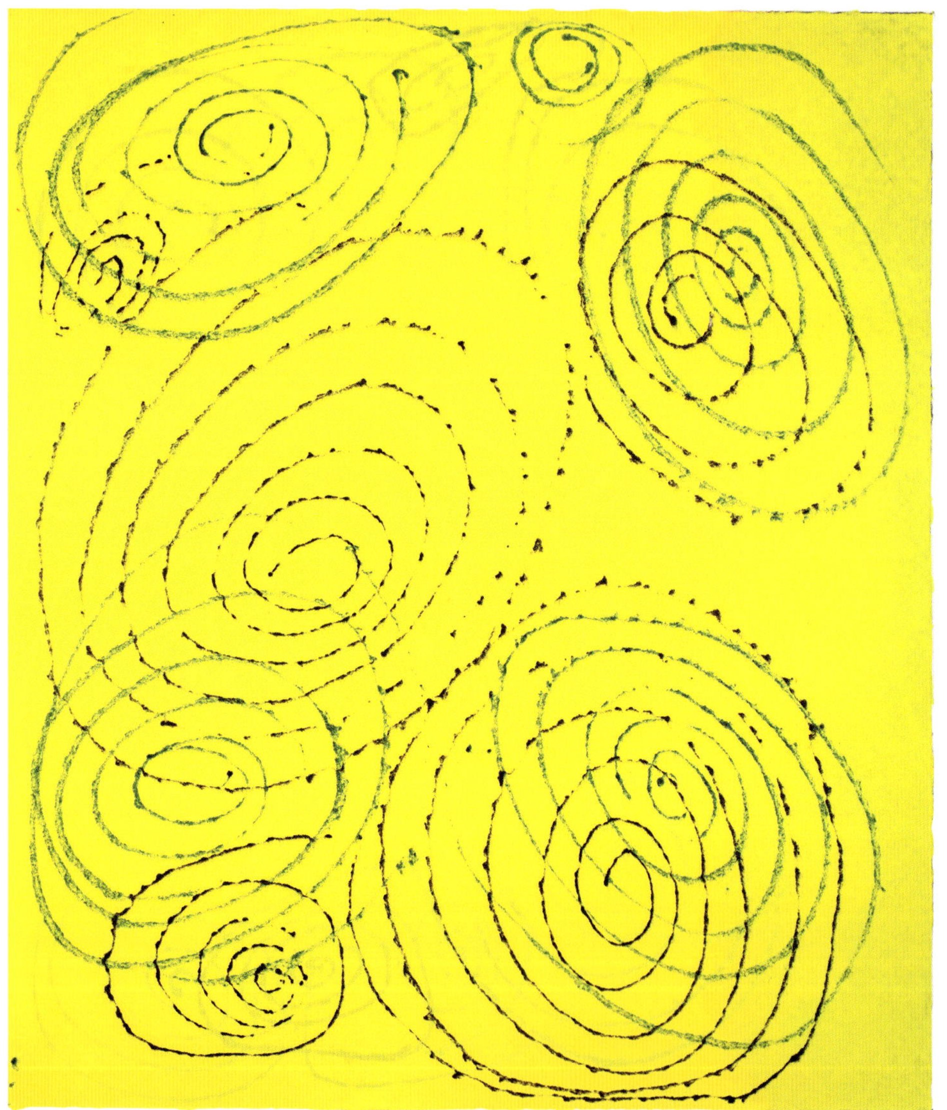

326. Therese Weber, *Solar Tides, Tassili V.* Several petroglyph sites in the narrow Wadi Djerat, Tassili n'Ajjer, Algeria, provided the stimulus for working with spiral shapes. 200 × 180 cm. Washi, coloured and cast mulberry fibre; Pulp painting on both sides, 2023.

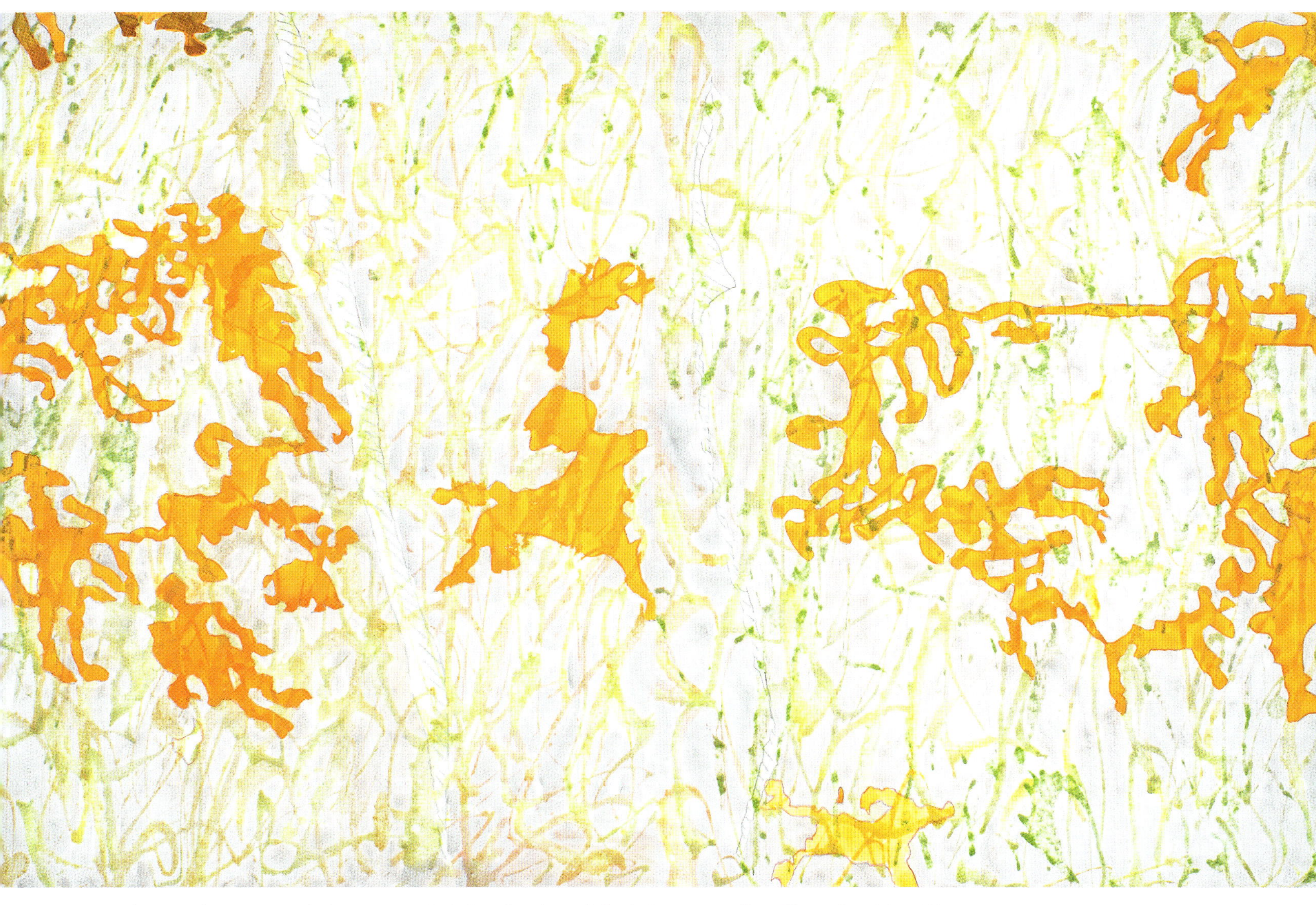

327. Therese Weber, *Disputes in the Bronze Age I*. 140 × 240 cm. Drawing and ink painting on cast mulberry fibre on linen fabric, 2022.

triple spiral and a small rhinoceros. Engraved in the sandstone, the spirals emerge from a circumferential line, which expands at the top into more spiral shapes that extend far beyond the petroglyph field. Similarly, the paper roll expanded into a three-dimensional object. In *Things Seen from the Edges and from the Centre I*, the spiral form mediated between the prehistoric and the contemporary. *The Point in the Middle* (fig. 325) and *Solar Tides, Tassili V*, both 2023 (fig. 326), originate from the same valley and were also developed around petroglyphs of spirals. The painting *Solar Tides, Tassili V* is double-sided and carries image information on both sides. The painted motifs lie between and on top of the layers of fibres. This creates different compositions of spiral shapes on both sides of the painting. For this technique, the pre-dyed mulberry fibres are applied in layers in a wet process and only solidify during the drying process to form the picture surface.

The multi-dimensional work *Disputes in the Bronze Age I*, 2022 (fig. 327) consists of delicate layers of mulberry tree fibres on canvas. Here, dark yellow petroglyph figures, painted with chalk and ink, appear against a light-flooded background. It seems as if they have left their place on the rocks and are coming alive in the space, fighting, chasing and dancing. In the atmospheric colours of the deserts – in hot deserts the colours of sand and sky dominate, in cold deserts those of ice and snow – the overlapping layers are reminiscent of the strong colours such as red and green that were once part of the palette of a living landscape. My work illustrates that today's 'empty' deserts used to be filled with life and that today's fertile landscapes, full of vibrant life, could one day become deserted. Be it living beings, cultures, mountains or even continents – at some point, everything that has grown will inevitably disintegrate and mutate into new life forms. Through these overlays, the desert space becomes a habitat

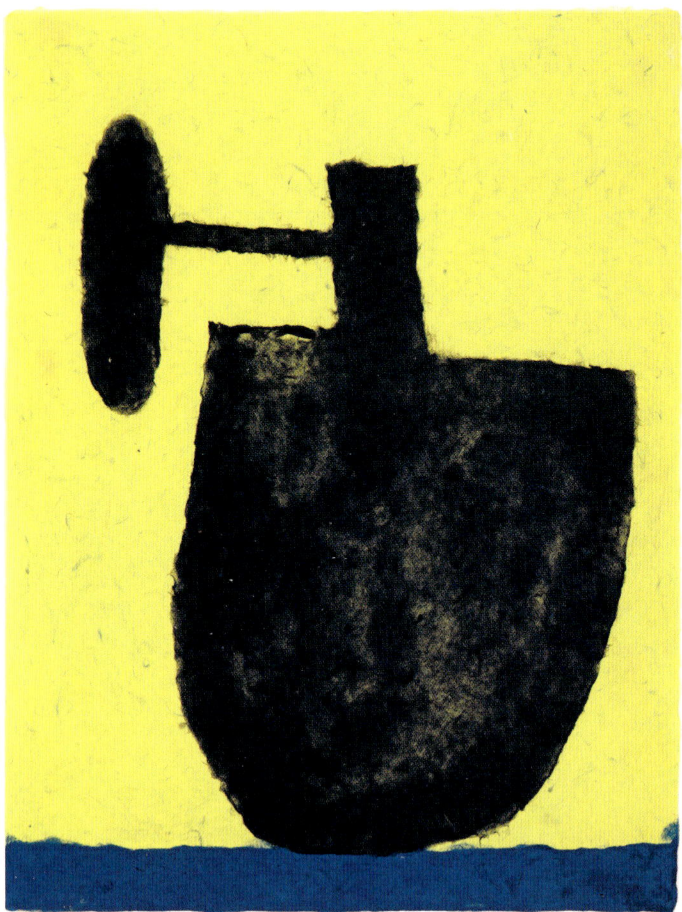

328. Therese Weber, *Inside the Vessel Precious Goods, North of Al-Ula I.* 64 × 49 cm. Washi, coloured and cast mulberry fibre, 2023.

again, and vice versa. The petroglyphs in the upper part of a gigantic rock face in Wadi Ikmah, north-east of al-Ula in Saudi Arabia, are unique indications of early life forms within what is today a desolate landscape (fig. 239). They depict bulbous vessels, slender amphorae and carpets from the ancient world, which formed the starting point for the image sequence *North of Al-Ula*, 2023. Although vessels are among mankind's oldest cultural artefacts, they are very rarely depicted in petroglyphs (fig. 328).

To animate in a fleeting moment what has been frozen in time was also my intention with the ephemeral installation *Revival of Space*, 2021 (fig. 329), at the Early Bronze Age petroglyphs near Nämforsen, Sweden. The meandering drape of the paper band coloured with ink reflects the waves of the Ångermanälven river rushing past and breathes new life into the 5,000 to 6,000-year-old petroglyphs. Each gust of wind changes the position of the band. Only a thin thread stops it from disappearing into the water and dissolving.

The performative action *Early Codes of Mankind in Equilibrium with the Present*, 2022 (fig. 218) on a steep rock face in Saudi Arabia required maximum concentration and a head for heights. The

fragile and ephemeral red-blue paper band coexists with the petroglyphs, which have been exposed to climatic conditions for thousands of years. Individual boulders have become detached from the rock face and are lying, mostly upside down, in the valley below. The original petroglyph compositions are no longer intact but exist only in fragments. It was a challenge for me to shape this 'puzzle' into a new story.

For such installations or actions, the conceptual work takes place in three stages. It begins in my studio, where I first sketch and develop the concept and design and colour the paper band. Here, the hand and mind play a central role. On the one hand, the design process demands technical and artistic expertise; on the other, the mind wanders into the yet-to-be-explored surroundings, either through reading or exploring with Google Earth. My aim is to assess the landscape as accurately as possible from a distance in order to then be able to develop the idea further *in situ*. On site, I explore the area, analyse topographies, and assess options for interventions in the context of the petroglyphs. In this process, I balance my artistic intention, the situational circumstances and the technical and material-specific challenges in order to achieve a specific goal – or to deviate from it if the terrain or climatic conditions do not allow it. At the same time, my mind returns to the studio at home, as ephemeral works must be photographed in a way that allows them to either have a continued existence as works in their own right or serve as a foundation for further development in the studio. Through photography, ephemeral actions and installations become crystallized into a fixed form. Following the action, everything in the landscape remains unchanged; only footprints in the sand remind us of it until they, too, are blown away by the wind.

An integral part of my perception and the way it is reflected in my work are the moments I spend in deserts, whose shapes are constantly changing. In the supposed 'emptiness' between heaven and earth, magnificent perspectives open up, leading to bare rock faces, narrow valleys and caves. I experienced this in Wadi Rum, Jordan, where there are several interesting petroglyph scenes in the lower part of a gigantic, seemingly polished rock face. One striking image shows a camel with its front legs tied and a striding man wielding a raised sword behind it. Some of the figures are outlined, while others are fully detailed using different techniques, presumably from different eras. Also distinctive are the perfect depictions of slender, clothed people – reminiscent of the Jubbah style in Saudi

329. → Therese Weber, *Revival of Space.* Installation at the petroglyphs on the island of Laxön, Nämforsen, central Sweden. Coloured paper band of mulberry fibre, 46 × 5000 cm, 2021.

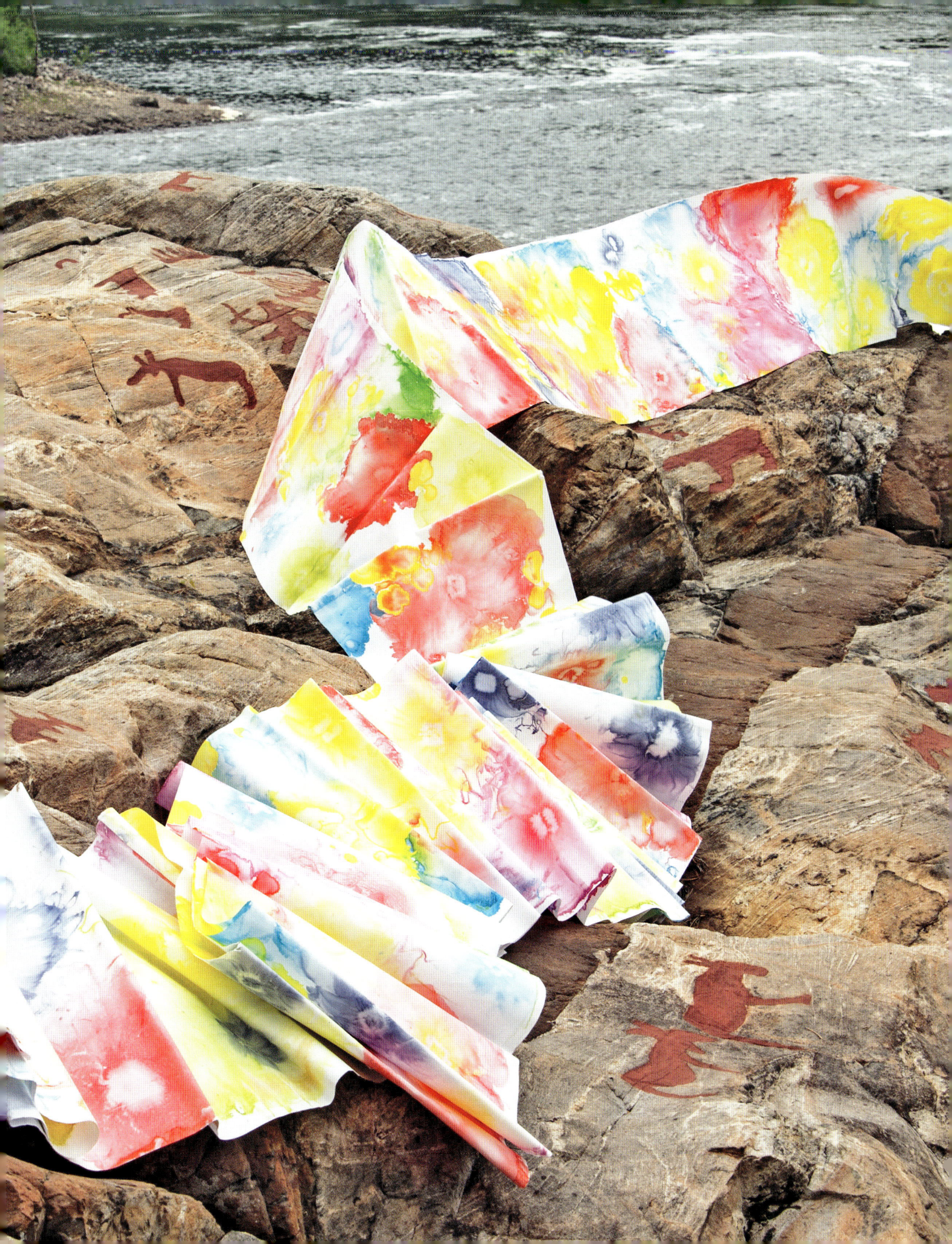

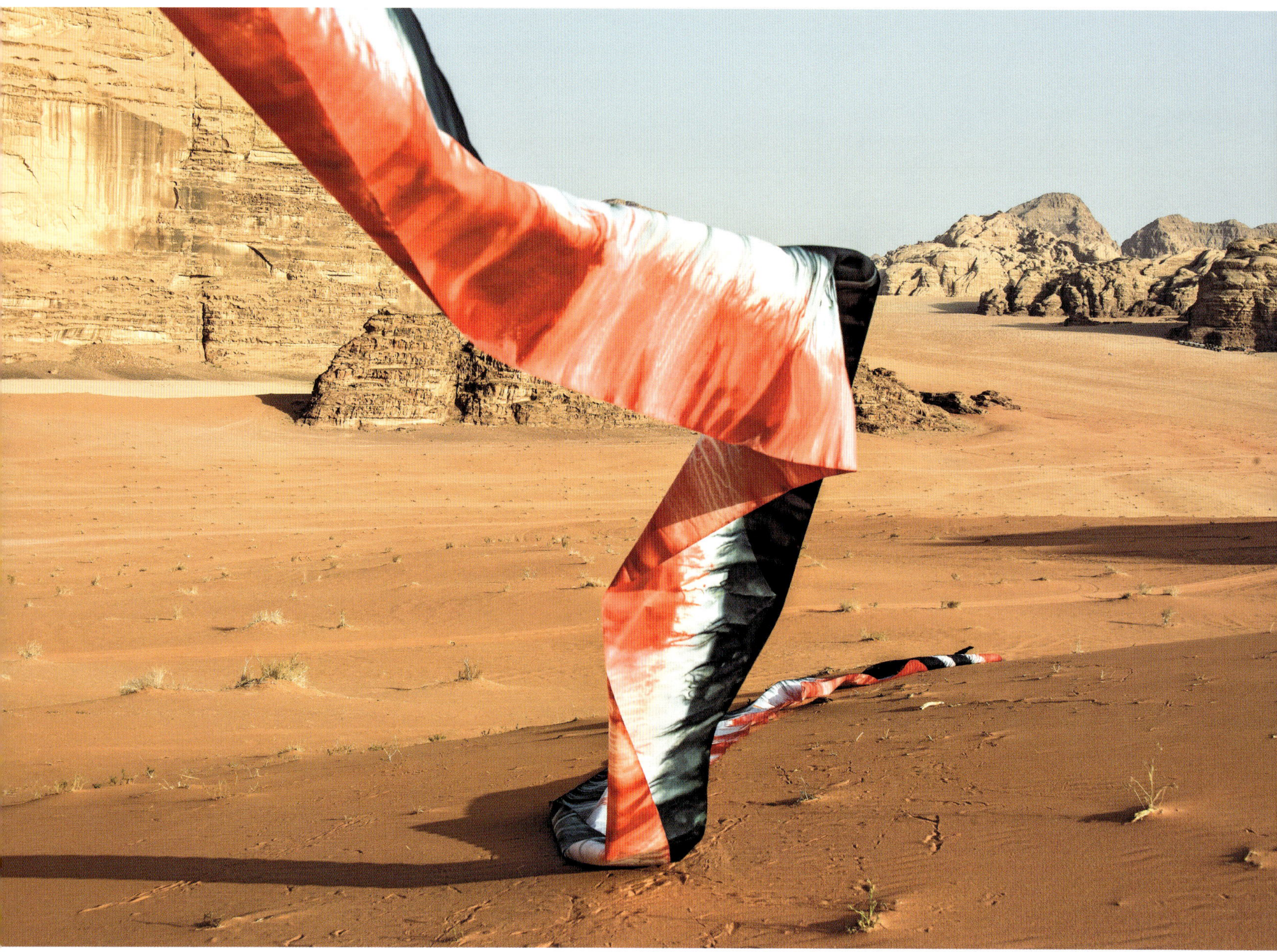

330. Therese Weber, *Units of Sediments and Materiality*. Performative action, Wadi Rum, Jordan. Dyed paper band of mulberry fibre, 45 × 2500 cm, 2022.

Arabia – as well as hands and pairs of feet found in the Kaz'ali Gorge (fig. 270). In the presence of the ancestral records that make up this open-air museum, the momentum emerged for the performative action entitled *Units of Sediments and Materiality*, 2022 (fig. 330).

Through transformative overlays, petroglyphs are transported into the present and regain their topicality. In the landscape installations, the vector of artistic intention is similar to that of palimpsests, but the method and temporality differ. The installations interweave documents from different eras with ephemeral elements shaped by the wind. In palimpsests, on the other hand, the message remains immovably fixed; the individual layers of superimposition can no longer be deconstructed. I define part of my work

as palimpsests – pieces of writing that have been overwritten multiple times, similar to archaeological processes where layers are uncovered in stages. Much like an archaeological cross section that reveals cultural layers from different epochs, these works illustrate overlapping, chronologically successive worlds on a single pictorial plane. This artistic repertoire thus conveys information and tells stories. The environment not visible in the work is also intended to be included through the viewer's imagination. Viewers are invited to activate their own ideas, perceptions and knowledge in order to develop their own personal perspective.

3. Contemporary artists and rock art

This chapter focuses on artists who either have a biographical and cultural connection to prehistoric rock art or who have explored the subject in depth. Certain key artists whose work closely relates to rock art have already been discussed elsewhere in various publications, and are consequently mentioned here only in the context of exhibitions. One who nevertheless deserves further consideration is Paul Klee.

3.1. Paul Klee and the departure from the norm

The connection between prehistoric rock art and the work of the Swiss artist Paul Klee (1879–1940) was first showcased in 1937 at MoMA, New York. This exhibition, which included works by Joan Miró, Hans Arp, André Masson and Wassily Kandinsky, among others, was held alongside the *Prehistoric Rock Pictures in Europe and Africa* show. Both exhibitions were initiated by Alfred H. Barr, Jr, then director of MoMA.[36] Barr had previously highlighted Klee's significance as a pioneering artist with a solo exhibition at MoMA in 1930.

Klee was a well-read artist who constantly asked questions and was deeply preoccupied with the subject of the origin of art. He saw this as a way to turn away from the academic canon and develop his own figures of thought. His analytical and critical view of objects, natural phenomena and the relationship between humans and animals drew him to prehistoric rock art. In 1928, together with his wife, Lily, he visited the series of menhirs in Carnac in Brittany, France, and the prehistoric museum there. They bought books and collected postcards of the large site in Locmariaquer with the dolmens of the 'Table des Marchands'. His subsequent work contains images that strongly resemble the abstract palaeolithic engravings found at these sites. One example of his processing of prehistoric artefacts is the painting *Temptation*, 1934, whose figures can be traced back to a book on rock art research in Brittany. These images on paper were drawn into the wet paste paint with an object or a finger, giving them a relief-like character. Books provided Klee with important impulses for his work.

It was in the book *Propyläen – Weltgeschichte*[37] that Klee found an ink drawing of the large petroglyph scene at Aspeberget 1 in Tanum, southern Sweden. Its dynamics fascinated him.[38] This large petroglyph composition reflects the worldview of a Bronze Age people who combined the settled life of farming with maritime trade (fig. 163). Klee also studied the work of Frobenius, who published his research in Africa in the *Cahiers d'Art* (1930)[39] – where Klee's art was also featured – as well as in the journal *Documents: doctrines, archéologie, beaux-arts, ethnographie*, founded in 1929.[40] Some of the elements showcased in

these publications were central to Klee's work. Klee continuously pursued his aim of developing a universal and timeless visual language by broadening his horizons. In the United States especially, Klee's work was increasingly juxtaposed with prehistoric art. Such a juxtaposition featured in the exhibition *The Sources of Modern Painting*, 1939. In the catalogue his painting *Im Bann des Gestirns* (Under the Spell of the Stars), from 1921, was placed beside a copy of a painting from the Mutoko Cave in South Africa which had been made by the Frobenius team, with the following comment: 'Klee's search for primitive expression took him further back than historical times. This linear, grotesque composition is reminiscent of the carvings of prehistoric people found on the walls of their cave sites.'[41]

In his search for new forms of expression that reflected the social and cultural upheavals of his time, Klee also drew inspiration from his own children's drawings. According to Fabienne Eggelhöfer, 'he noted in his diary: "I want to be like a newborn, knowing nothing of Europe, nothing at all … to be free of influences; almost at the origin." In his children's drawings, Klee discovered an expression that focused on reduction and the essential, which is what he tried to realise in his art.'[42] He saw this spontaneous, immediate creativity as one of the ways that his art aligned with rock art.

It is possible that Klee came across so-called 'X-ray pictures' while researching children's drawings.[43] In the painting *Muttertier* (Mother Animal), a kind of therianthrope,[44] he uses a technique of visualizing the inner life of a figure by showing the skeleton of the animal (fig. 331). The eyes are also fascinating; both are visible in the silhouette-like depiction. X-ray depictions can also be found in petroglyphs, for example at Gore Anaqsah in Wadi Sahtan in Oman, where in the depictions of clothed women their anatomy remains partially visible through the clothing.[45] The pictorial representation of 'transparent' layers makes it easier to understand how bodies and things function.

Klee also felt a connection with the diversity, structures and processes found in nature. He wanted to understand their laws and analogies, in order to create work in a similar way to nature. His animal or hybrid creatures, for example, are often radically simplified and consist of just a few strokes. Klee mastered a wide range of techniques and materials, including etching into a plaster surface, tracing and drawing into paste paint on canvas, collage, and spray techniques similar to those used in prehistoric times. In 1934, he created a series of watercolours using the spray technique with empty spools of thread from a weaving mill as stencils.[46] Weaving was part of his technical and creative vocabulary from his time at the Bauhaus, as were other mixed techniques. His deep interest in scientific knowledge and technical and creative processes remained with him throughout his life.

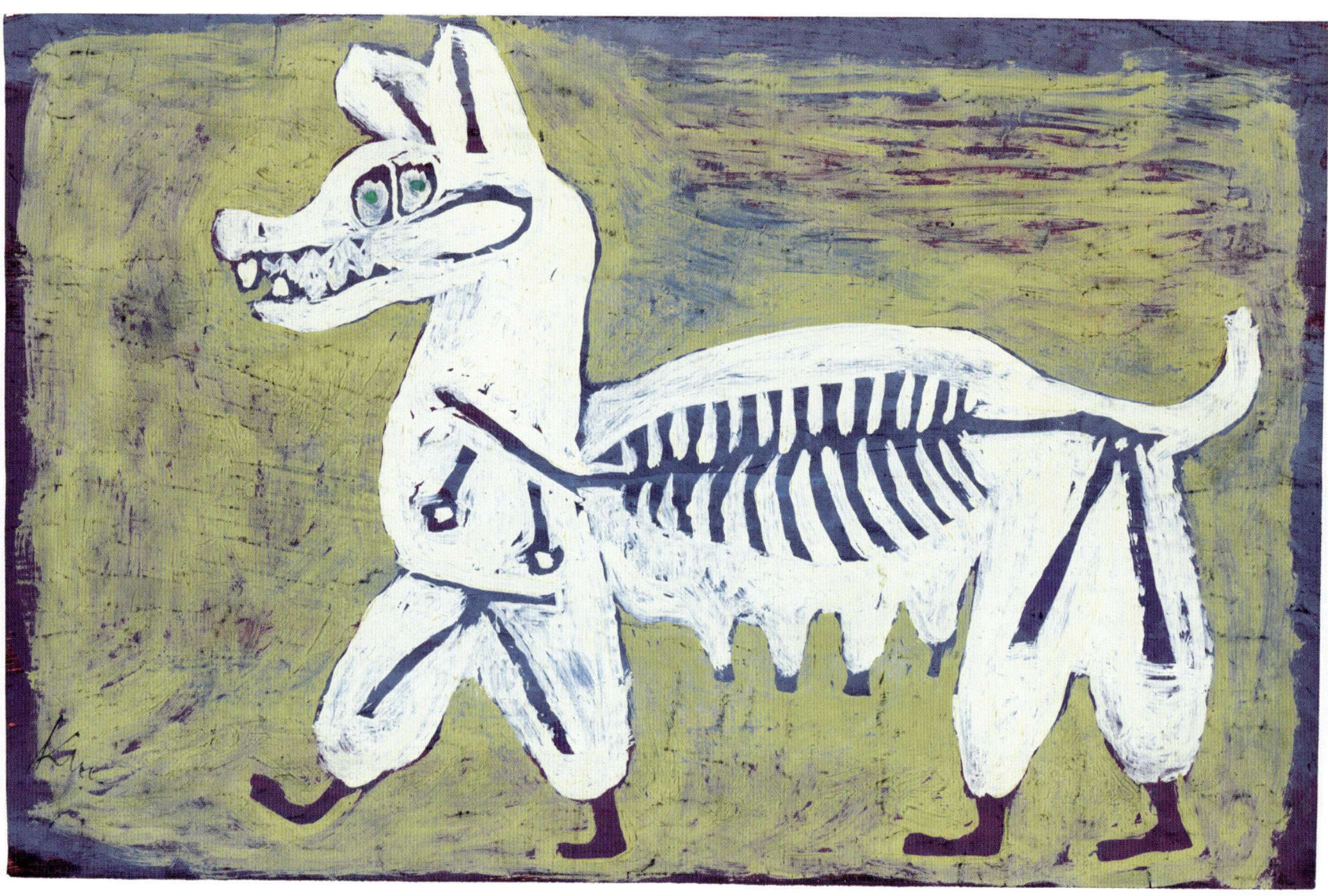

331. Paul Klee (1879–1940). *Mother Animal (Muttertier)*. 20.9 × 32.8 cm. Oil paint on primer on paper on cardboard, 1937. © Zentrum Paul Klee, Bern, picture archive.

3.2. Engagement with petroglyphs in Arabia and northern Africa

The common denominator of the artists thematized in this section is their conscious engagement with the prehistoric and thus pre-Islamic heritage of their long-distant ancestors while remaining connected and committed to their religion, Islam. In contrast to some artists of Central Asia and southern Siberia who are discussed in the next section, these Muslim artists are not searching for a replacement for a recently vanquished belief or ideology; they seek an enrichment of the prevalent Islamic worldview.

Ibrahim N. al-Fassam, Saudi Arabia

Ibrahim al-Fassam's large-scale paintings were already displayed on the walls of his school while he was still in middle school. At that time, he painted with gouache on plywood panels. Born in 1955 in Diriyah, the capital of the first Saudi emirate in the eighteenth century, he completed his training as an art teacher in 1973. However, he only taught for a short time before deciding to become

a designer at a state printing company. In 1986, al-Fassam created his first mural (measuring 14.64 by 2.44 metres) in Riyadh, the current capital of Saudi Arabia. This led to numerous awards and a commission at King Fahd International Airport in Dammam, the capital of Saudi Arabia's Eastern Province.

In terms of cultural politics, al-Fassam is dedicated to critically engaging with contemporary art as well as researching and preserving Saudi Arabia's unique cultural heritage. He is interested in the latest developments of various arts movements within the Kingdom, and his biography reflects his strong commitment to engaging with the current art scene on the Arabian Peninsula, including the broader issue of artistic freedom throughout the Arab world. At the same time, al-Fassam draws inspiration from folk traditions and is deeply interested in the anthropology of people and particularly the psychology of human interaction.

From 2001 onwards, the evolution of his visual language has centred on Arabic calligraphy, leading him to incorporate calligraphic elements into his works. In folk traditions and traditional calligraphy, he found a deeper meaning beyond the popular decorative elements. At the same time, al-Fassam saw something new in the diverse antiquities of the Arabian Peninsula, leading him to turn to archaeology, and especially rock art. He wants to share this experience with society, saying: 'I aim to show the beauty of rock engravings in my art, especially the spontaneity expressed in them, which invites the viewers to explore such artwork.'[47] Archaeology and its artefacts became a source of inspiration for him. In 2008, the art critic and artist Professor Muhammad al-Muneef stated on the *Al Jazeera* news channel: 'The artists overlooked it [the heritage of petroglyphs] despite its importance, but al-Fassam succeeds in employing archaeological drawings in his paintings.'[48]

From that point on, al-Fassam's visual vocabulary expanded as he integrated 'archaeological drawings', that is petroglyphs, into his work. His experience of drawing inspiration from archaeology and antiquities made him realize the vast scope of prehistoric culture. Drawings, figurines of animals and people and highly sophisticated signs and fonts became sources for his contemporary works. Unlike prehistoric artists, he doesn't use stone or metal tools on a stone surface; instead, he uses a brush on canvas and paper.

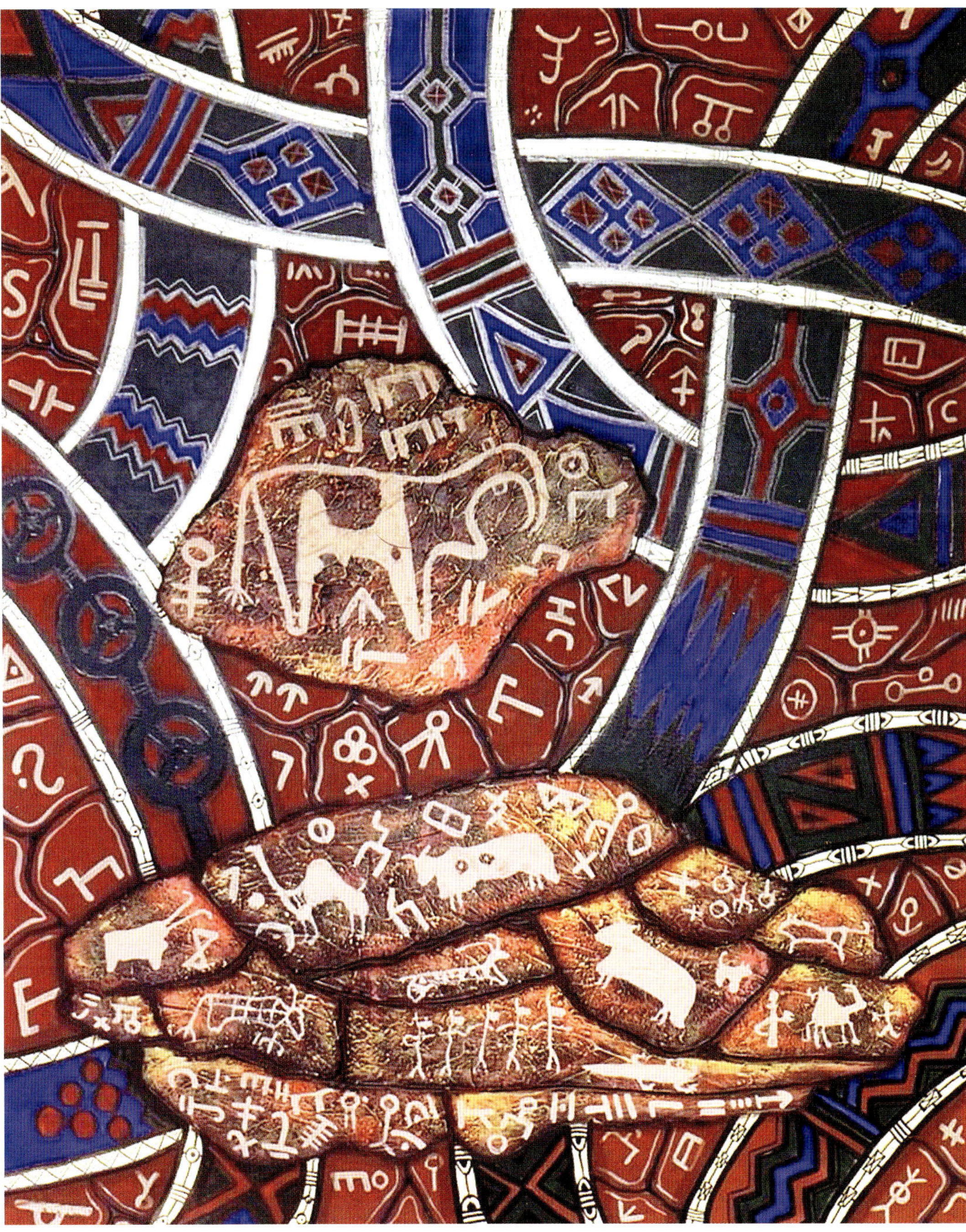

332. Ibrahim N. al-Fassam, *Antiquities of the Arabian Peninsula*. 120 × 100 cm. Acrylic paint on canvas, 2021. © By permission of Ibrahim N. al-Fassam, al-Riyadh, Saudi Arabia.

His motifs of animals and people unmistakably echo stone engravings that are still preserved today, particularly in Saudi Arabia. At a major exhibition in Riyadh in 2022, the artist showcased works inspired by archaeological elements from the Arabian Peninsula.[49] These works all include elements from rock art, such as animals, people, hieroglyphic-like signs and invented characters based on the long-extinct ancient South Arabian Sabaean script.

Al-Fassam's pieces don't have titles that describe the motifs, but simply give the format, medium and material of the picture surface. In one of his works, human figures appear that strongly resemble the petroglyphs of Jubbah and Luwee (also known as al-Hanakiya) from the Neolithic period.[50] These figures are characterized by their slender form. They are often depicted standing with slightly bent knees and with schematically drawn heads, sometimes in the shape of a hammer, and are adorned with traditional geometric patterns that occasionally resemble tattoos. Another work is dominated by a large bovine animal with a small head and a huge body, similar to the late Neolithic petroglyphs of Jabal al-Sharqiya. The body of the bovine has been painted over with seven smaller bovine animals and pseudo-Sabaean

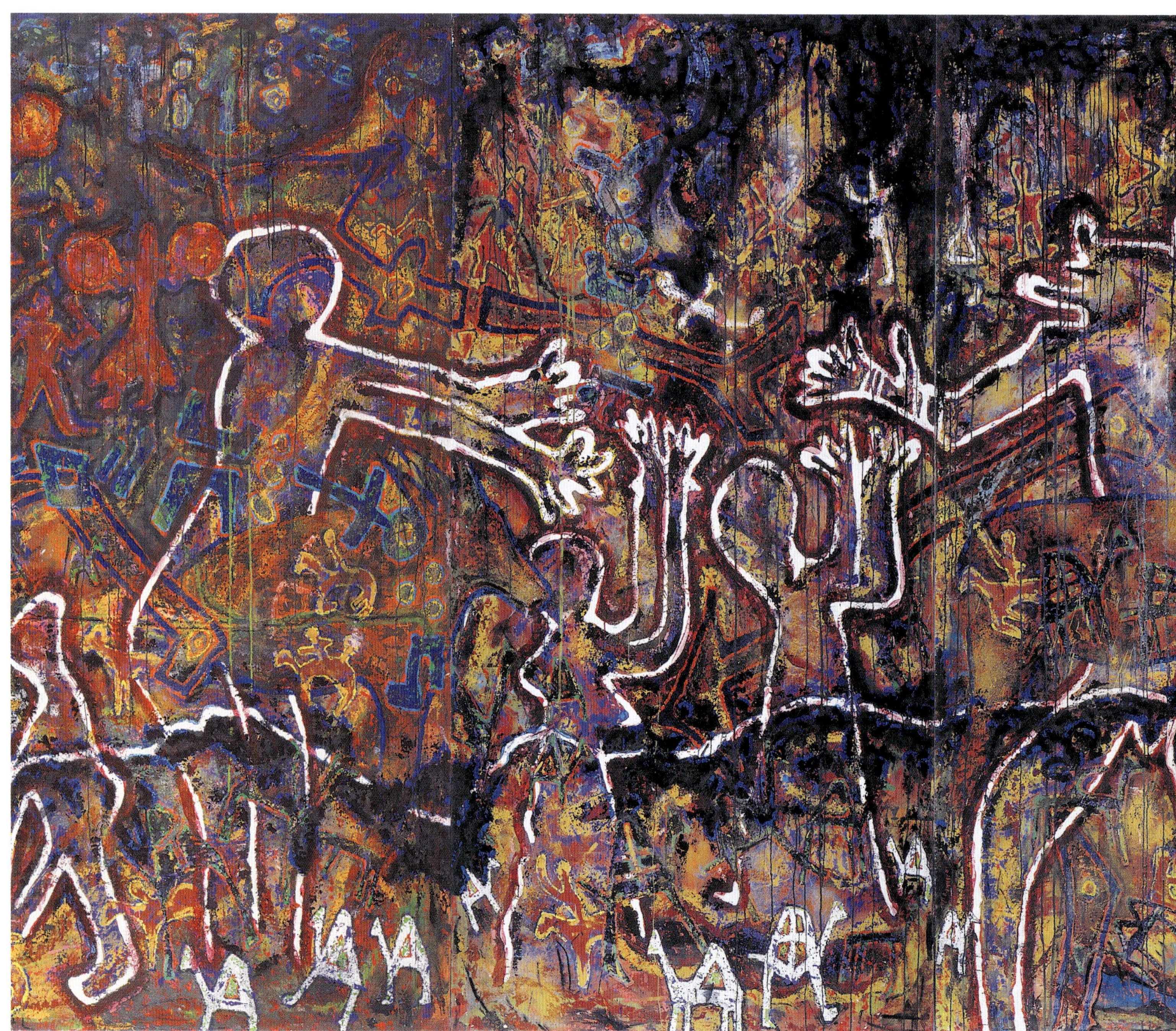

characters. The painting in another work resembles typical patterns on a Bedouin rug or a traditional ceremonial plate, with concentric bands adorned with floral motifs around the outer area. The circle in the centre features well-known petroglyph motifs like camels, people and characters, alongside a frontal depiction of a bull's head which, 3,000 years ago, symbolized the ancient Arabian solar deity *slm* (Sulmus). In yet another painting, dominant forms from traditional calligraphy stand out against a bluish background, and these forms are decorated with figures from the world of petroglyphs.

In other works, the artist combines rock art motifs with contemporary references through superimpositions. In one such piece, our attention is immediately drawn to blue and purple patterned bands with white frames which overlap in parts and run through the entire composition. These bands resemble motorway intersections seen from above, yet their elegance evokes calligraphy (fig. 332). Hieroglyphic signs fill the spaces between the bands. Painted over these layers are two shapes resembling desert rocks. These 'rocks' are adorned with familiar motifs from prehistoric petroglyphs, such as buffaloes, cattle, camels, the ultra-slim figures characteristic of the Jubbah style, and hieroglyphic signs that evoke traditional tribal marks of Bedouins. In other similar works, the bands suggest not roads but labyrinths viewed from above, or even an archaeological dig divided into geometric segments. Ibrahim al-Fassam's works are striking for their successful fusion of prehistoric heritage and modernity, with each element maintaining its distinct identity.

Abdulmagid Abdulrahman, Libya

The artist and architect Abdulmagid Abdulrahman (b. 1972) is culturally very close to the content of his paintings due to his birthplace in the Tripoli region of Libya, where he lived until 2004. He then moved to Germany to study art, where he also completed his doctorate. There, he wrote a paper on 'Rock art and cave paintings from Libya'. For him, petroglyphs and cave paintings are part of Libya's history and culture. As he states, his academic work and artistic expression cannot be separated: 'My works are intended to depict a period that belongs to the early history of art, to which all other artistic epochs are connected and oriented. I believe that the artistic development of ancient times does not receive enough attention and appreciation … it is my concern to sensitise people … to this important time and to engage with this significant period of art history.'[51] In the nineteenth century the German explorer Heinrich Barth, who had discovered a few petroglyphs in the Messak region in 1850, noted that these carvings were of high artistic quality, both in terms of the expression of the figures and their technical execution.

For Abdulrahman, ancient rock art is the model and inspiration for his large-format pictures, which can be up to twelve metres in length. In these works, he refers to the millennia-old art of the Sahara. In Abdulrahman's canvases, the figures appear to be

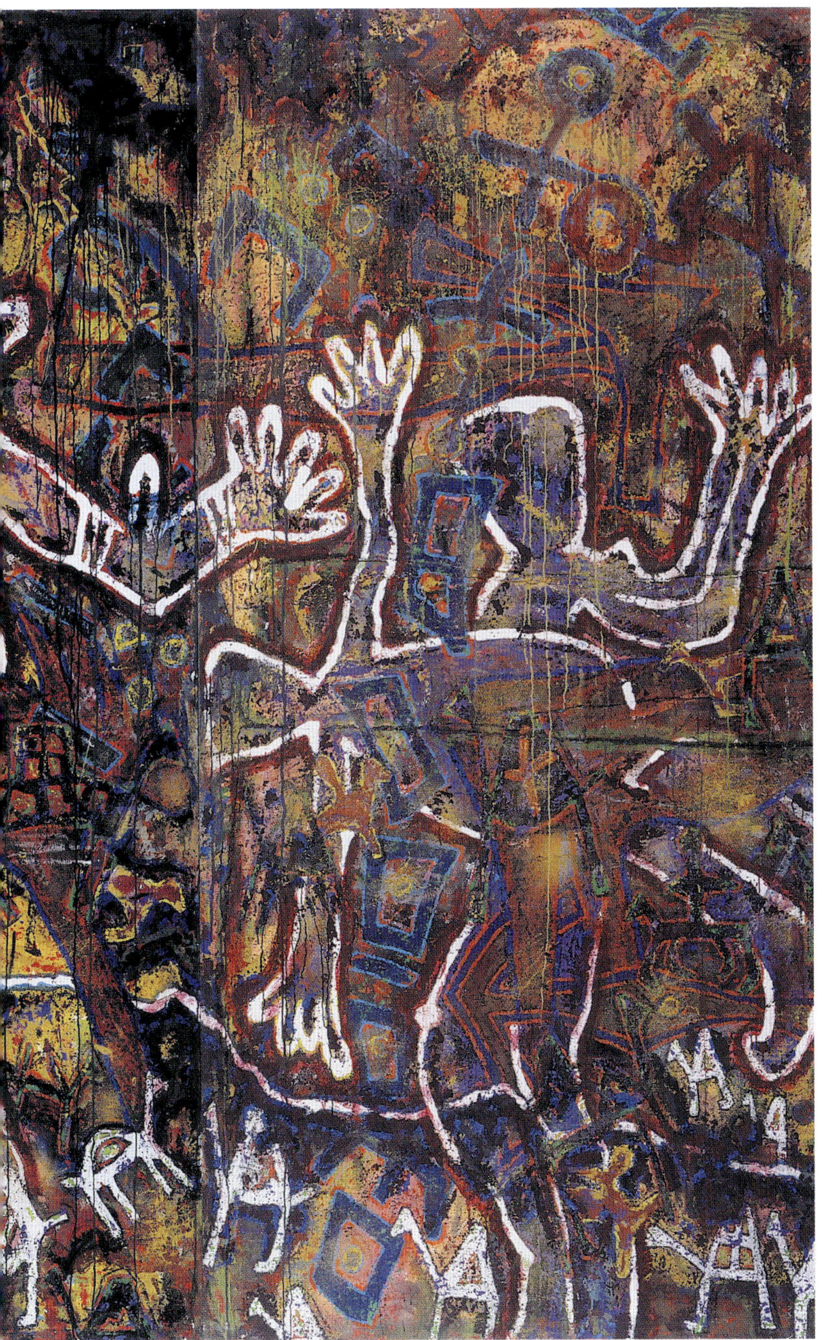

333. Abdulmagid Abdulrahman, *Masked People.* 310 × 600 cm. Acrylic paint and sand on canvas, 2007. © By permission of Jörg Mollet, Solothurn, Switzerland.

engaged in dialogue and gesturing. The figures in the foreground are emphasized with striking white contours. Earthy colours dominate the background – yellow, ochre, dark red, brown and black. Several layers of painting and drawing are superimposed in a palimpsest-like manner. Animal and human figures, geometric signs and symbolic motifs cover the canvas and occupy the background of the painting *Masked People*, measuring 3.1 by 6 metres (fig. 333). In the foreground, at the lower edge of the picture, tiny camels cavort, most of them striding to the left. At first glance, it seems as if the artist is not interested in proportional relationships, for the tiny animals are dominated by the gigantic creatures depicted with outstretched arms. The frontally depicted figure in the centre, with arms stretched out to both sides, is particularly eye-catching. Do the figures perhaps tell of a particular ritual? What links can be drawn between the painted anthropomorphs and the way in life of that time? In any case, the rock art in the shelter of Sefar, Tassili n'Ajjer, Algeria, was definitely an important source of inspiration for Abdulrahman's monumental pictorial composition. This rock painting, 30 metres square and more than 8,000 years old, is dominated by a 3.25-metre-high, frontally depicted male figure painted with translucent white pigments. Approaching from the left are female figures, also painted with white. They reverently raise their arms, and one of them is presumably pregnant. There is also a white antelope. On the right are a pregnant antelope, a woman lying in labour, and a theriomorph. This painting is evocative of the beginnings of Saharan rock art and is made in the style of the 'Round Heads', in which human figures have few or no facial features, as the faces are depicted purely in two dimensions. The sexual characteristics in the human figures in Sefar, however, are rather unusual for this style of painting.

This spectacular image recalls the shadowy figures by the American artist Keith Haring (1958–1990), often outlined in black spray paint, such as in the mural *Untitled (FDR NY) #5-22*, 1984.[52] His Subway Drawings (1980–85)[53] also share this visual language. Haring drew motifs exclusively with white chalk on blank, black billboards in New York's subway stations. From a young age, he was fascinated by figures in comics and spent much of his time drawing. Throughout his studies and creative work, he retained the style of the schematically depicted figures. Even though Abdulrahman and Haring carry on the legacy of very different cultures and histories, they are united by a visual language that is characterized by diverse attitudes and knows no boundaries. The works of both artists are documents of a specific period – an era with a multitude of styles and stylistic currents – yet their expressions are self-sufficient and deeply rooted in their biographical and geographical backgrounds. Both aspire to create art for all.

Jörg Mollet, Switzerland

Mollet (b. 1946) is an artist specializing in painting, drawing and photography. He works with lines and surfaces to question established visual habits. Based on his interest in the signs of Indigenous peoples, he undertook several expeditions to the Sahara Desert between 2005 and 2012 to explore rock art, together with the writer and cultural journalist Aurel Schmidt (1935–2024) and the sculptor Ernesto Oeschger (1931–2022).[54] At the same time, he focused on the expanse of the desert and the quality of light, which also defines space in the desert. He later incorporated both of those components into his pictures. Mollet also aimed to scientifically document, measure, and visualize figures and their details. Using photographs, he traced the individual figures and depicted them graphically against the rocky background (figs 303–305). The goal of better understanding the culture and art of the region and discovering connections to Western art was also a key feature of the Swiss-Libyan Art Project, which took place both *in situ* and later in local studios.

Mollet's research in the field, through photography and documentation, was followed by in-depth study and development in the studio, particularly for the Libya project. After his explorations, Mollet archives his photographs, and on the other hand, uses them to realize multi-layered crops and redrawings of the images. These transformations emphasize the characteristics and details of individual figures, making them more accessible to the viewer. The artist thus works with an extended form of drawing. His redrawings help to precisely visualize the graphic elements of a motif, such as lines, dots and shapes. They enhance the legibility, analysis and interpretation of petroglyphs. Mollet intuitively sensed that the rock paintings of the Sahara represent one of those cradles of civilization that could serve as a bridge to contemporary art. The stylized drawings possess a certain modernity that offer a unique conceptual perspective.[55]

One of his artistic transformations of petroglyphs is a collage-like combination of graphics and photography titled *Carneval des Animaux* (Carnival of the Animals).[56] The photograph features a circular, ritual stone setting overlaid with translucent Japanese Shoji paper. Drawings of animals based on motifs from various rock paintings in Libya were then added using a pigment printing process. Mollet also initiated an exchange with local Libyan artists who incorporated rock paintings into their work, describing their cultural heritage in the desert region as a culture of remembrance. Lectures and exhibitions of his photographs and redrawings also formed part of the project, enriching the collaboration.

Lydia Ourahmane, Algeria

Lydia Ourahmane (b. 1992) was born in Saïda, Algeria, and currently lives in Algeria and Barcelona. In 2024 she was awarded the Rosa Schapire Art Prize at the Kunsthalle Hamburg, Germany. Her artistic language and different conceptualizations are closely related to her biographical roots and history. In her film project *Tassili n'Ajjer*, 2022,[57] she conceived a film that is closely linked to the topography and rock formations of her homeland. The 45-minute film was first shown in 2022–23 at the Fondation Louis Vuitton in Paris; it was projected onto the walls and the dome-shaped ceiling to completely fill the room.

The Tassili n'Ajjer region of the Sahara is home to thousands of prehistoric petroglyphs and cave paintings that depict the transformation of life in the Sahara over thousands of years. In her film project, Ourahmane focuses on her own inner perception as she tries to explore the meaning of the cave art images. At the same time, she expands her observations and examines history and traditions, including elements of spirituality, migration and the history of colonialism. The film is divided into four parts, each accompanied by the sounds of a different musician, which gives it a rhythmic quality. The artist dispensed with words in the film, allowing the images to speak for themselves – because, she reasoned, what else can be said about images that have been communicating in their own way for thousands of years? She leaves it up to the viewer to ask questions and find answers. In the film, the camera moves at walking pace over extensive, impressive topographies from a bird's-eye view, while it repeatedly passes close to the rocks, revealing details of rock formations. This movement brings together images that have also been presented as large-format film stills in other exhibitions entitled *Tassili*, including at the SculptureCenter, New York, 2022.[58]

Ourahmane uses her conceptualizations to ask profound questions. She reflects on her personal experiences in encounters with rock art and how these engagements influence and shape her way of experiencing them. In the context of her wordless *Tassili* film, she formulates philosophical questions about life in an interview,[59] questions that complement her considerations in the film and highlight the issues that are important to her. These questions include: What are we looking for? Who benefits from this desert experience? What does the desert region trigger in me? What do I leave behind, apart from my footprints?

3.3. Prehistoric rock art as a path to Indigenous identity

Whereas the artists described in the previous section feel ideologically and emotionally at home in the environment in which they have grown up, the artists of the next group have become estranged from their ideological environment. In the case of Central Asians, the collapse of the Soviet Union and of its doctrines has left an ideological void and a lack of identity-forming cultural anchor points. Artists from Indigenous communities, for their part, seek their cultural roots beyond the frame of a heteronomous, colonial past which they increasingly question.

Behzod Nurillayevich Choriyev, Uzbekistan

Various factors contribute to one's decision to become an artist. For the Uzbek Behzod Choriyev (b. 1985), it was the cultural heritage in the immediate vicinity of his home village in the Navoiy district of central Uzbekistan. He explained: 'The village where I grew up is close to Sarmishsay, near the place where petroglyphs were carved in stone. I've been interested in the history of these petroglyphs since I was young, and this interest motivated me to become an artist.'[60] The 5,000-hectare Sarmishsay Nature Reserve is on the list for consideration as a UNESCO World Heritage Site. Of the more than 4,000 petroglyphs, the oldest date back to the fourth millennium BCE and span a period up to the eighteenth century CE.[61]

For Choriyev, who was born into a family of artists, the historical and cultural heritage of his region serves as the catalyst for his visual language. In his works, which are painted in a historical style, national traditions and universal human values, with their inherent spiritual component, are deeply intertwined. The artist's work is inspired by traditions and juxtaposes aspects of the past and present. Choriyev's own biography, life and work are woven together, combining his interest in history, tradition and contemporary issues. In his pictures, he adopts the visual language of the petroglyphs engraved on large rock faces in the Sarmishsay Valley. The valley is reminiscent of an open-air museum: individual groups of petroglyphs engraved on a relatively smooth surface are visible from a great distance far into the valley, while others are more difficult to see because they have been 'washed out' by the weather or are in hard-to-access terrain. Choriyev immerses himself in this atmosphere and later incorporates his impressions and drawings of individual figures into his pictorial compositions. The motifs remain almost unchanged but are presented in a completely different configuration featuring superimpositions and different formats (fig. 334). The materiality of the often smooth rocks shining in the sun is also mirrored in his pictures. The rather dark backgrounds show the

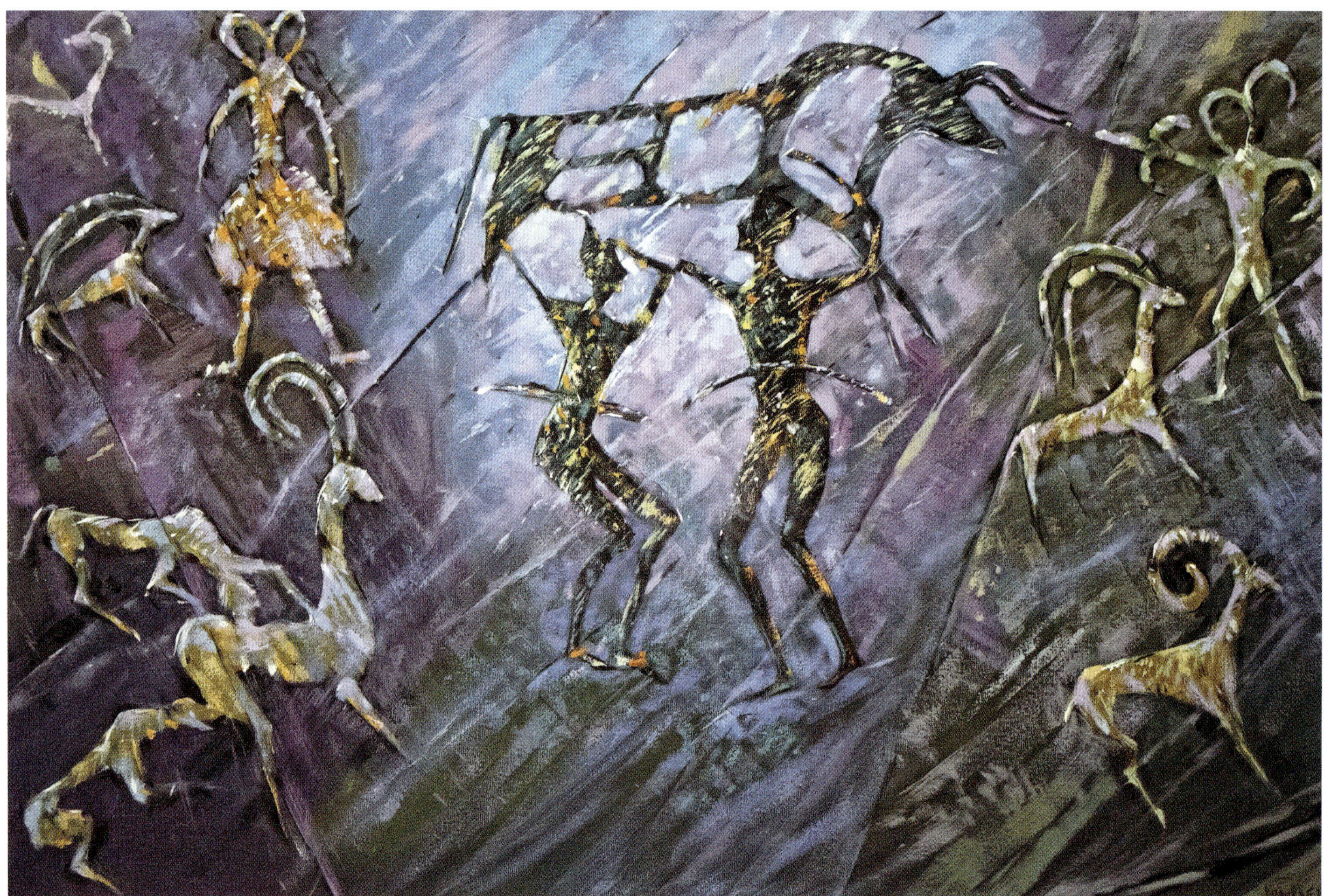

334. Behzod Nurillayevich Choriyev, *Petroglyphs of Sarmishsay*. 60 × 90 cm. Oil on canvas, 2021. © By permission of Behzod Nurillayevich Choriyev, Navoiy, Uzbekistan.

crevices and structures of the rocks into which human and animal figures have been inserted. Through the artist's use of colour, the signs on the somewhat shimmering background appear as if they have been chiselled into the surface.

Timur Akanaev, Kazakhstan

Different worlds unfold on the canvas of the Kazakh Timur Akanaev (b. 1982). In the background of his work *Nomads* from 2010, an expansive, barren landscape suggests heaven and earth. In the foreground, a gigantic animal – a camel or horse – is pulled through the landscape by a leaping, human-like creature. The creature's head consists of a circle with rays all around it and dots in between that could symbolize planets. In the middle of the circle, there is a solid area with a centre, comparable to a sun symbol. In the body of the animal another scene appears, set in relief against the background. There are various groups of animals depicted in small format as well as riders on horseback and three yurts. We also see the heads of a herd of camels or horses galloping

to the right. These multifaceted scenes are all packed into this thrilling painting. They illustrate the life of Kazakh nomads. It is a metaphorical depiction that transcends geographical and cultural boundaries and incorporates facets of prehistoric symbols. Akanaev thus shows a world in constant flux. The juxtaposition and meeting of people, animals and dwellings create a dynamic image that suggests vitality and new beginnings (fig. 335).

With the sun symbol, Akanaev points us towards the Kazakhs' nomadic past. The running figure with the sun-like head on the right-hand side of the picture is undoubtedly inspired by one of the most important scenes from the petroglyphs of Tamgaly, south Kazakhstan, described on pp. 75–77. This composition from the Middle or Late Bronze Age depicts seven anthropomorphic figures with sun-like heads. These figures presumably represent solar deities that played an important role in the mythology of Bronze Age Indo-Iranian cultures. Given that the rock near Tamgaly contains micaceous schist and conglomerates with mineralized copper, it is likely that the somewhat shimmering, copper-like colour that dominates in the painting *Nomads* is linked to the material consistency of the mountains.

Akanaev draws on his biographical background to define his artistic and cultural identity – it plays a central role in the composition of his pictures. His ethnic roots can be felt in the narratives through which he transports his cultural heritage, by way of the significance and complexity of rock art, into today's world. In many of his works, he documents nomadic life in a multifaceted way. Mobility, for example, is humorously portrayed in several pictures. In the painting *Caravanserai*, a camel carries an entire caravanserai – the mosque, minarets and yurts, as well as camels and objects – on its back. All this is depicted on the elongated body of the camel, which strides through a colourful landscape. [62]

As Andrzej Rozwadowski pointed out, old, nomadic ways of life and their attributes such as yurts, camels or horses, as well as sun symbols, are important themes in the modern movement of Tengrism. [63] Originally, the collective term 'Tengrism' referred to the religious worldviews of ancient Turco-Mongolian peoples such as the Xiongnu, Old Turks, Mongols, Kyrgyz and Kazakhs. What these beliefs have in common is the concept of the almighty heaven, called Tengri, which embodies the universal principle guiding the cosmos. Since the collapse of the Soviet Union, intellectual circles of Turco-Mongolian ethnic groups have sought to revitalize Tengrism

as a vehicle for establishing an authentic and pre-colonial identity, i.e., one that is neither Soviet, Christian nor Islamic. Prehistoric petroglyphs constitute an important link to the ancient nomadic life of Turco-Mongolian peoples.

Alexey Ulturgashev, Khakassia (Russian Federation)

The Khakassian Alexey Ulturgashev (1955–2020) was another artist who was deeply engaged with prehistoric rock art. Like the Kazakh Akanaev and other south Siberian artists, he was associated with the informal group of Siberian–Kazakh *Archaeoart*, whose goal it was to address the identity crisis that emerged when the Soviet Union collapsed by reappropriating cultural elements from prehistoric petroglyphs, engraved steles, shamanism and mythological heritage. The spectacular archaeological discoveries made since the 1950s in southern Siberia and eastern Central Asia had already prepared the ground for an increased interest in and a nascent return to reflection about these prehistoric cultures. In one of his works, a large stag with antlers extending over his whole back and painted in blue is obviously inspired by the typical late Bronze Age petroglyphs engraved on the deer stones of Mongolia. Under the stag which dominates the sky there are ibexes with long, strongly recurved horns, and at the bottom a long boat manned by a crew of about twenty is floating on a river. [64] In another painting,

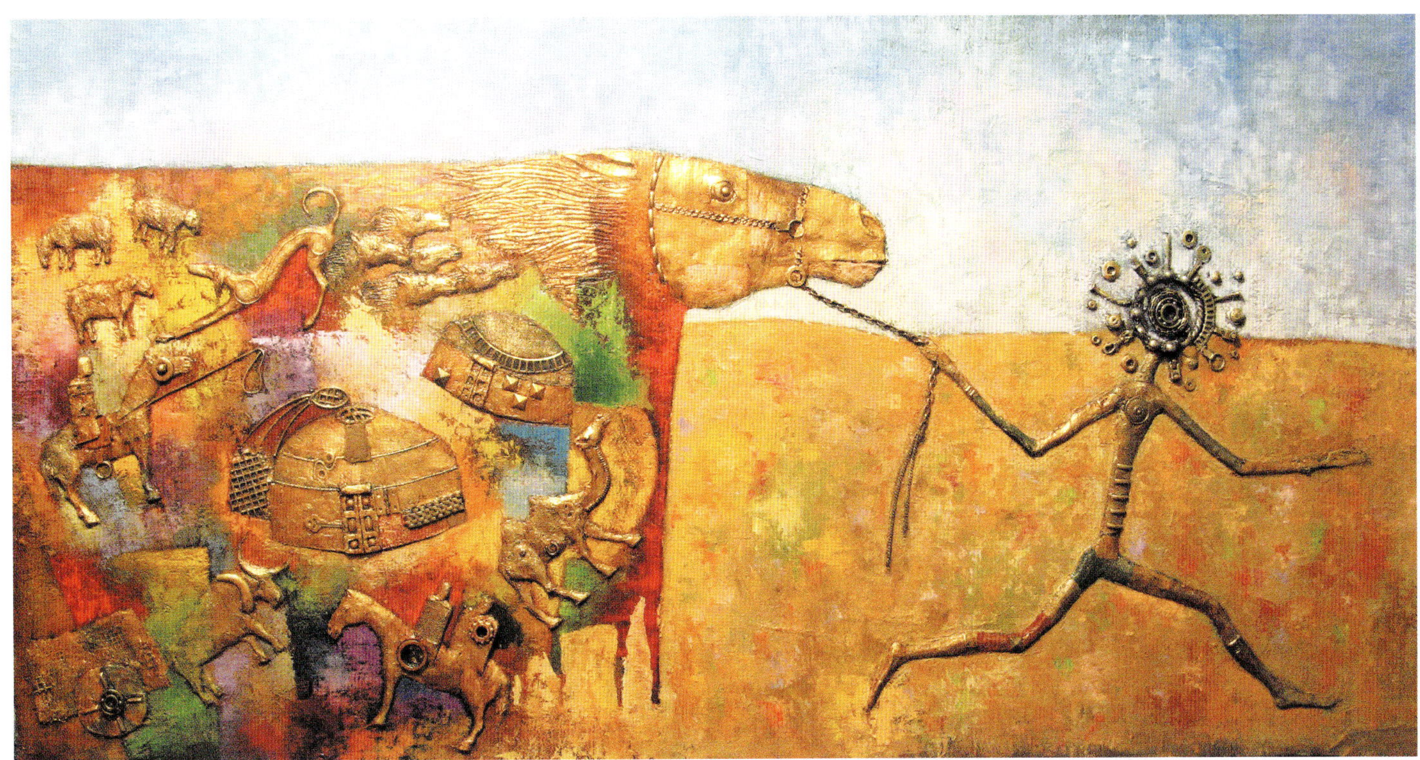

335. Timur Akanaev, *Nomads*. 160 × 80 cm. Mixed media, 2010. © By permission of Timur Akanaev, Almaty, Kazakhstan.

The Shaman's Kamlanie, from 2005, a shaman beats a drum in front a monumental stele inscribed with fantasy runic signs.[65] The shaman is inspired by a petroglyph and the monumental stele resembles steles from the Okunev culture (fig. 336). The south Siberian painters Aleksandr Domozhakov (1955–1998) and Georgy N. Sagalakov (b. 1955) also incorporated iconic motifs from the Okunev culture in their paintings, such as a solar head with radiant crown or the anthropomorphic face of a monumental stele.[66]

However, as noted by Rozwadowski, a reappropriation of Neolithic or Bronze Age cultural elements in the framework of a revival of an alleged ancient Turkic heritage may be problematic from a historical point of view, for the emergence of a Turkic ethnic family and Turkic languages can only be traced back to the last centuries BCE.[67] Furthermore, numerous petroglyphs and engraved steles from the Okunev and Andronovo cultures were likely created by people speaking an Indo-Iranian language, not a Turkic or Altaic one. From a historical perspective, it is therefore questionable to attribute those creations of rock art, whose meaning belonged to the Indo-Iranian mythological worldview, to a cultural Turkic heritage.

Joe Feddersen, USA

As a mediator of traditions and stories, materials and craft techniques play a central role in the work of the American artist Joe Feddersen (b. 1953), who is a member of the Indigenous Confederated Tribes of the Colville.[68] He interweaves themes and traditions relating to time and geography that can be categorized as separate parts of his work. They are rooted in the traditions of his homeland and at the same time reflect the present day. Feddersen explained: 'In this region where I live there are an abundance of pictograms [and petroglyphs]. These works record our histories and tell our narratives. I view them as our

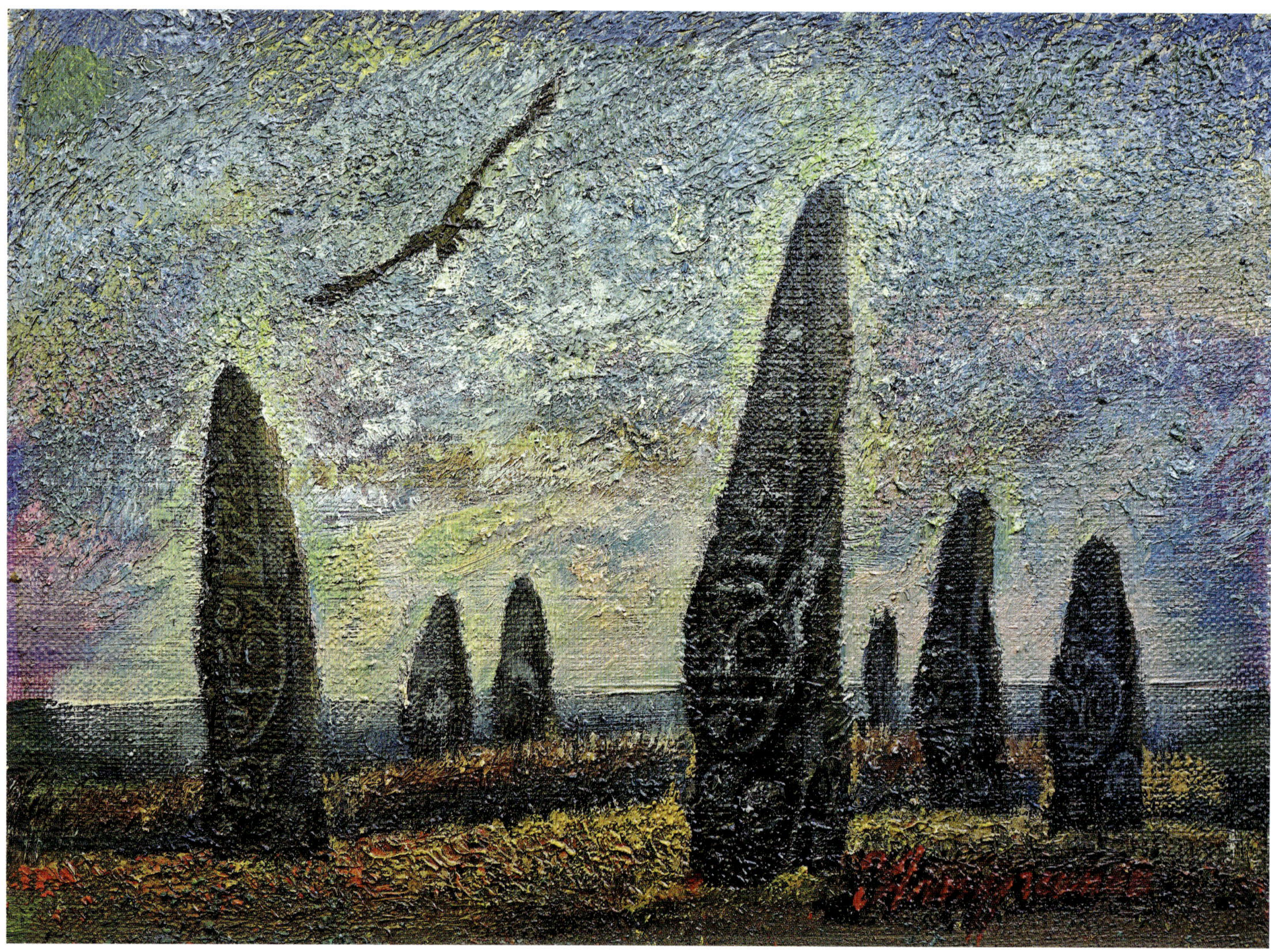

336. Also this painting is connected to the Okunev culture since it features prominently Okunev steles (see fig. 31). Alexey Ulturgashev, *The Call of Spirits*. 27 × 33 cm. Oil on canvas, 1992. © Minusinsk Regional Museum for Local Heritage named after N.M. Martyanov, Minusinsk, Russian Federation.

stories that tie us to place.'[69] For Feddersen, ancient rock art forms a cultural anchor point for his self-conception as an Indigenous person. The materials he works with play a role as carriers of information; they can be triggers for chains of associations and new processes. With his complex glass installations, for example, he suggests that the traditional should not be abandoned but that solutions can be found by testing materials to see how the old and the new can function together and enter into a dialogue.

Based on these considerations, he has dedicated himself to the task of integrating rock art and glyphs – graphic representations of symbolic characters – into his work as a connecting element and basic principle that gives each work a different character. These range from collages, ceramic objects and graphic prints to room-sized wall pieces made of molten glass, a material he has been working with for over twenty years and that was used as early as the third millennium BCE in the form of glass beads for jewellery. His work is dominated by references to rock art. The symbols Joe Feddersen uses always have a cultural and historical significance. He focuses on petroglyphs from Indigenous North American tribes. His large installation *Charmed (Bestiary)*, 2022/23, which has a strong tactile quality, consists of hundreds of suspended, transparent, figurative glass ornaments. These ornaments move ever so slightly and produce gentle sounds as they touch each other, as if part of a ritual that activates the space through sound. The objects of the glass 'petroglyph wall' refer to prehistoric rock art, but they also incorporate symbolism related to the world around us. These glass objects depict stylized creatures and motifs such as those found in rock art. They contain iconography in a traditional and contemporary context, a mixture of forms rooted in the Indigenous culture of the plateau: fish, horses and humanoid figures, some of which are shown hunting while others are likely warriors, shamans or deities. These symbols are interspersed with images of modern urban life, such as helicopters, cars or handguns. Past and present exist equally in the same space, overlapping and interconnected through the composition of these motifs. In addition, the shadows of the installation project a drawing onto the wall, transferring the continuous movement of the objects and, in their blurriness, conveying the sense of lightness and fragility of the material that is glass.

Joane Cardinal-Schubert, Canada

Another artist who transferred the art of Indigenous peoples into her visual language is Joane Cardinal-Schubert (1942–2009), who was also a writer and activist. She focused primarily on the significance of the petroglyphs and pictograms located along the Milk River in South Alberta, Canada. For her, these engravings and images serve as reminders that Indigenous peoples had developed their own culture long before the arrival of European settlers. By combining Native American patterns and scenes with contemporary motifs and painting styles, Cardinal-Schubert created visual statements that extended the past into the present. Her later work, in particular, is characterized by intense colours combined with indigenous iconography and texts.

In one of her works, the painting *Letters to Emily: Borrowed Power*, 1992, the contrast between light and dark conveys an almost cave-like atmosphere (fig. 337). The work is in two parts, each dominated by two stretched animal skins placed on the surface. A coat hanger is inserted at the upper edge of each skin, referencing modern civilization. She integrates other animals, wolves painted in silhouette, into these large-format skins, creating a link to the living environment of earlier civilizations. Below the wolves, she places either a text or another animal. To the right or left of the animals, we can make out paper money. Below the skins, Cardinal-Schubert places white and red imprints of her hands, always in the sequence left–right. At the very bottom of the left-hand picture, four horses are striding to the right, and in the right-hand picture, the title 'Borrowed Power' is written. Both are drawn in delicate white strokes.[70] The artist used techniques and motifs that combine aspects of rock art and contemporary art to create a palimpsest of past and present.

For Cardinal-Schubert, referencing the knowledge and spirituality of Indigenous peoples was of key importance and provided her with a way to express herself politically. Cardinal-Schubert was a role model. She inspired and motivated young Indigenous artists across the continent to challenge and reclaim their creative identity. She was instrumental in creating a favourable environment for contemporary Indigenous art in Canada.[71]

Dale Harding, Australia

Dale Harding (b. 1982) and his mother Kate Harding aim to connect the past and the present. In doing so, they also explore the relationship between mother and son and the culture that has shaped them both. As descendants of the Indigenous Bidjara, Ghungalu and Garingbal peoples, they have a direct connection to the artefacts of early cultures and are closely associated with the famous Carnarvon Gorge in Central Queensland, known for its high concentration of rock art. The gorge is also a site of spiritual significance to the Aboriginal people. In their work, Kate and Dale Harding show this culture from different perspectives and their individual viewpoints. Dale Harding uses a range of different techniques and materials, while Kate Harding is a textile artist who works mainly with quilts.[72] They exhibit together to showcase and juxtapose their work.[73]

Dale Harding's multi-layered work explores the links between modernity and Aboriginal culture. He also employs various techniques and materials traditionally used by the Aboriginal peoples, such as spray painting and stencilling. Harding is considered one of the most influential representatives of his generation and culture. His creative practice does not just represent the past in a present form but offers a new vision of the past, present and future, opening up new narratives and contexts. He achieves this through his pictorial and object language, expanding the visual and cultural heritage emerging from historical rock art traditions. His recent projects demonstrate an inclusive and pluralistic approach with the aim of sharing knowledge and recognizing the connections between Aboriginal and non-Aboriginal cultures. This includes viewing Indigenous art as an aesthetic phenomenon linked to the search for identity, belonging and reorientation. His exhibitions are complex and thought-provoking, allowing art-historical and practical approaches to provide new insights and interventions into the methods and discourse of rock art.

With his contemporary artistic direction, Harding offers a cultural continuum that is intended to stimulate dialogue among viewers. He achieves this through his art practice, which expands cultural heritage and visual languages, thereby emphasizing the tradition of rock art and its significance. This was his aim with his installation *Body of Objects* (2018), which consisted of eleven sculptural works that he developed using stencils based on forms found in the rock art in Carnarvon Gorge. These ochre-coloured, mouth-blown images depict various weapons and ceremonial objects relating to Harding's own ancestry. In response to these stencil images, Harding produced objects made of black silicone rubber, horseshoe nails and drawing pins that follow the same theme and presents them on white plinths in a contemporary curatorial context.

His deep engagement with rock art was also evident at *documenta 14* in Kassel (2017) with his project *Composite Wall Panel*. Monochrome, ultramarine blue screenprints of hands, boomerangs and human figures on a white background were applied to the wall in a large format.[74] His pictures take us back into history. They are in a state of flux, mirroring the process of the artist discovering stories on the walls of the Carnarvon Gorge and creating new images from these scenes, palimpsest-like, layer upon layer, in the style of the rock art works.[75]

Ana Mendieta, USA and Cuba

The artist Ana Mendieta (1948–1985) straddled her birthplace, Cuba, and the USA, where she spent most of her life. Throughout her life, she remained very close to the culture and Indigenous people of the Taíno in Cuba. This led to her interest in petroglyphs, which influenced her landscape-based work. Her relief sculptures are mainly focused on the body and reflect female figures or their attributes, for example in the caves of the Parque Escaleras de Jaruco outside Havana, where Mendieta honoured the goddesses of the Taíno creation story with a group of works titled *Guanaroca: First Woman* (1981), where she cut the contours of her own body into the earth. In other works, such as the Silueta Series (1973–80), she lay naked on the ground and dug herself into the earth, thereby moulding life-size figures into the ground.[76] During this period, she created over 200 *siluetas*, also known as 'earth-body work'. Mendieta said, 'I use the earth as a canvas and my soul as a tool.'[77]

In her often ephemeral *silueta* reliefs, Mendieta explored the connections between the female body and nature, as well as feminist and political topics. In addition, she incorporated themes such as memory, history, displacement and rebirth into her performances. Mendieta explored public spaces, such as nature, that are free from patriarchal barriers and which she also used for her political statements. She felt that such places, being outside the museum business, offered women in the 1970s an opportunity to showcase themselves and their work since they were in those days rarely represented in museums and galleries. Rituals were also a defining component of closeness to nature in prehistoric times, celebrating humans' dependency on natural elements, mythological powers and social events. For Mendieta, performance and ritual, incorporating the forces of nature, included the need for healing.

Robert Smithson, USA

Robert Smithson (1938–1973) developed an interest in the archetypal nature of things at a young age. His fascination with geology and geosciences provided him with the knowledge of mapping, which was essential for his projects. He was also interested in the origins and beginnings of things. Finding the right place for his land art installations was paramount to him, and his understanding of geology and how continents and oceans were formed gave him a special sensitivity for this. His photos of petroglyphs in Utah, USA, document his interest in rock art.[78]

Several of Smithson's land art works are constructed in the form of a spiral within the landscape, echoing images from prehistoric times. The extensive project *Spiral Jetty*, 1968–72, built into the Great Salt Lake in Utah from black stones, salt crystals and earth,

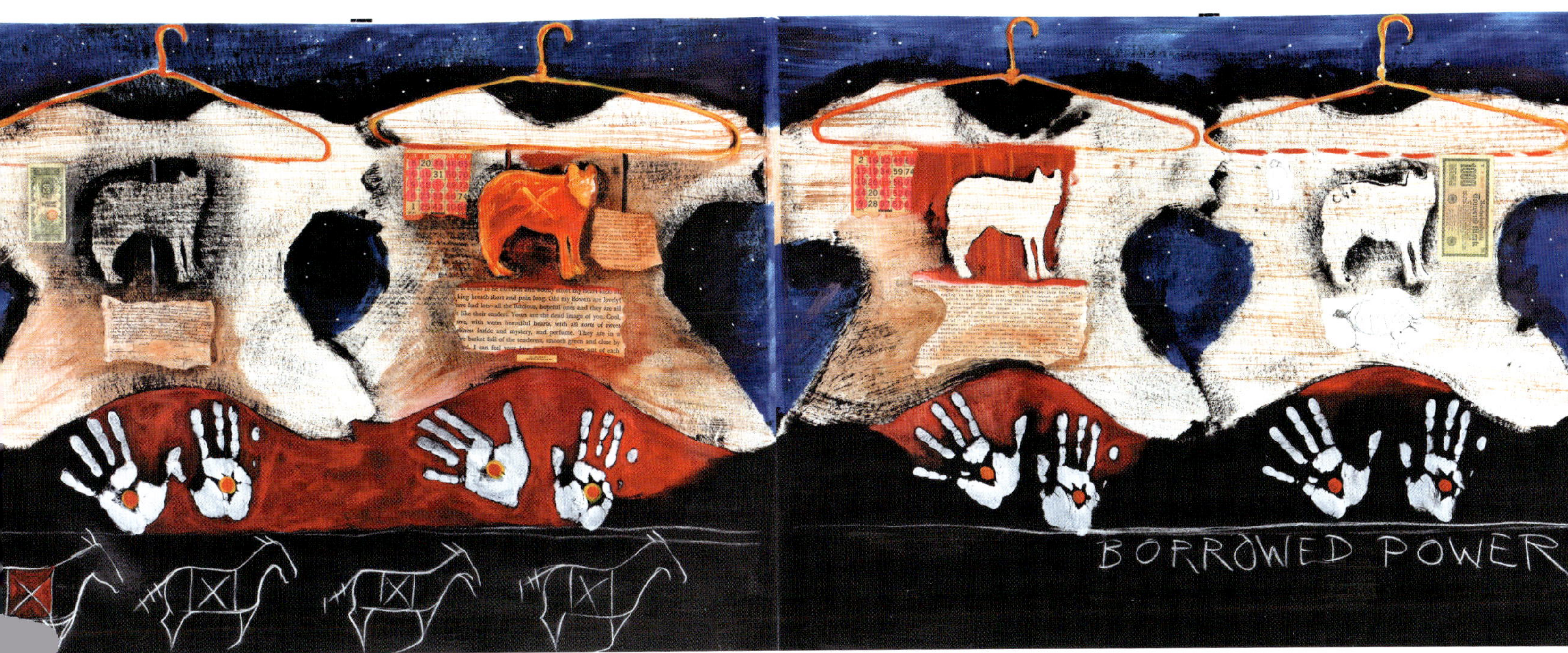

337. Joane Cardinal-Schubert, *Letters to Emily: Borrowed Power*. 91.4 × 243.8 cm. Collage and painting on rag paper, 1992. © Estate of Joane Cardinal-Schubert & The Alberta Foundation for the Arts, Edmonton, Canada.

is reminiscent of spiral forms found in the petroglyphs of various cultures, such as in Wadi Djerat, Algeria, or Val Camonica, Italy.

Smithson, who was self-taught, had a wide range of interests, including the influence of religion and language on art, and this is reflected primarily in his paintings, drawings, collages and writings. In his work, he aimed to bring together different time periods – the history and prehistory of a place, as well as the time it took to create and experience a work. By exploring the conceptual and physical limits of knowledge, Smithson raised fundamental questions about the position of people in the world. As a theorist and artist, he favoured landscapes that reminded him of prehistory. For him, both dimensions – place and history – were closely linked and also raised the question of time, with which he constantly grappled. 'The investigation of a specific site is a matter of extracting concepts out of existing sense-data through direct perceptions. [...] One does not impose, but rather expose the site ... The unknown areas of sites can best be explored by artists.'[79]

Lisa Schroeter-Bieler, Germany

In 1981, the physicist Lisa Schroeter-Bieler (1923–2018) travelled to Scandinavia for the first time to explore rock engravings. She discovered a remarkable concentration and variety of petroglyphs in the Bohuslän region, which inspired her to develop a new method of documentation. Equipped with index cards and copies from a petroglyph book, she initially planned to visit only five sites. However, she was so captivated by the petroglyphs that over the following years (1982–86), she travelled to Sweden twice each summer as a 'field researcher' and twice each winter as a 'library worm'.[80] She became increasingly interested in the sometimes encoded meaning of the depictions and tried to interpret them, even though they often puzzled her. She continued to question each message, attempting to get closer to understanding the meaning. In her descriptions, she placed the information conveyed in this visual language into a figurative, historical and mythological context.

Schroeter-Bieler's analysis of a famous, enigmatic scene is an example of her deep engagement with the petroglyphs of Bohuslän in south-western Sweden:

The picture with the 'world axis' at Lilla Gerum is so large that it takes two sheets of paper [of 88 × 126 centimetres] to capture it (fig. 160). What we see is not one of the common 'maypoles' ready to be climbed, but something more extraordinary. A tree trunk, unevenly grown and with a small spherical reinforcement in the middle, towers in the centre of the picture. It sits on a rectangular kind of box, which looks like the central section of a ship hull. Three 'ropes' extend from the cup-shaped top of the pole, with two of them showing a creature with four extremities and a round head clinging to the rope. We must think of them as human beings, [...] We see a man holding on to the rope with only one arm while the next phase, his fall or jump, is depicted simultaneously. [...] The person is at a crossroads. Is the hammer-shaped device also being used against him? Is it a weapon of death or a weapon of blessing? Light emanating from this ambiguous event falls on the four waiting people at the bottom left with their arms raised in the shape of a circle and the five above them in a reversed position. [...] Could those 'hanging' up here be the dead, sacrificed in a game of death? Did the cosmos, the sun or the moon demand sacrifices so that the course of the stars could continue with new momentum?[81]

However, Schroeter-Bieler was also an analyst and developed methods for categorizing the rock paintings into groups such as genus, family, order, class or tribe, as well as for assigning to time periods and to geographical categories, as detailed in her book.[82]

Schroeter-Bieler approached the process of visually documenting petroglyphs with an element of creativity. She used a double frottage technique and then also drew over the images. For the first step, she used a cotton swab to apply a rarely used graphic medium, a water-soluble Syrian asphalt in the form of a blackish-brown powder, with which she rubbed down the entire paper. The petroglyphs became visible while retaining a certain transparency. In the second step, Schroeter-Bieler outlined the petroglyphs with a black wax crayon.[83] She would decide which signs to outline and to what degree they should be emphasized. In some instances, she first made a rubbing and then moved the position of the paper slightly before, in a second step, tracing the outlines with the wax crayon. Usually, the petroglyphs are recorded on lightly grained, sized paper measuring 88 by 126 centimetres with a weight of 170 gsm. These sheets are sometimes also cut into smaller formats. Such firm and opaque paper is not commonly used for frottages. Since Schroeter-Bieler could no longer identify the petroglyphs visually because of the thickness of the paper, she had to locate them by touch. By tracing the grooves in the rock with her fingertips, she was able to exactly determine the contours of the figures.

Schroeter-Bieler's works attracted much interest at the 1985 exhibition *Felsbilder in den Alpen* (Rock Art in the Alps) in the Museum für Ur- und Frühgeschichte, Freiburg im Breisgau, Germany. The German artist Hans Benesch (b. 1946)[84] continued the dialogue with the petroglyphs of Scandinavia by selecting certain pages from Schroeter-Bieler's book *Skandinavien* as the starting point for his overpainting, a technique he has pursued since 1993. The pictorial background he uses as his starting point is already rich in history, featuring two aesthetic components: the figures of the Scandinavian rock engravings, dating back to the Bronze Age, and Schroeter-Bieler's frottages on paper that evoke the textured surface of the rock and petroglyphs. On a third level, Benesch's overpainting adds his personal touch and a contemporary element.

3.4. The allure of prehistoric art and mythology

For several artists, the combination of working in both natural settings and urban environments while engaging with rock art created a dynamic tension that unlocked new creative possibilities. For Joseph Beuys in particular, who worked across all artistic genres and adhered to his idea of an expanded concept of art, his connection to mythology and rituals provided a gateway to the art of his ancestors.

Joseph Beuys, Germany

The artist and political activist Joseph Beuys (1921–1986) was interested in prehistoric rock art. He was particularly drawn to animal representations which reveal the living environment of the era and, according to Beuys, evoke magic and enchantment. For him, animals also served as a benchmark for the human–animal relationship, symbolizing constantly evolving meanings and characterizations.[85] He was not only interested in animals from a biological and anatomical point of view but also saw them as important partners to humans and felt a kinship with them. In rock art, he reflected on fundamental anthropological constants to describe living environments that resonated with him. Prehistoric motifs inspired his creative approach and artistic processes, using a variety of methods and procedures.

Besides his installations and performances, Beuys's work is characterized by engravings in slate, wood reliefs and prints, as well as creations made with stencils and outline drawings or watercolours on various backgrounds. Everyday materials served as pictorial surfaces, along with certain favourite types of paper. In a drawing from 1982, for example, he used the floor as a background (fig. 338). Materials such as grease or felt also served as creative elements in his work. Beuys also integrated objects such as telephones, hoses, ladles and felt coats into his conceptualizations. His spectacular performances included, for example, *I Like America and America Likes Me*, 1974, an event featuring a live coyote. Animals played a fundamental role also in his paintings, where he gave them an expressiveness comparable to that found in rock art. In such works, the animals are painted in watercolour with his so-called 'Braunkreuz' paint, a red-brown hue that he likely created from commercially available anti-corrosion paint. In addition to red, he saw red-brown as a primordial colour, which he also associated with blood. It is a colour that he believed speaks to our mythical consciousness. Beuys's interest in archaic traditions was not purely formal but absolute – setting him apart from Picasso, for example, who was mainly interested in the formal aspects of prehistoric art and less with their implied meaning.[86] His preference for side views or frontal silhouettes, which he depicts as schematized figures, is evident in his many drawings. They show an affinity with rock art, particularly prehistoric etchings, reliefs and outline drawings. In an interview in 1984, he said 'Perhaps I am a reincarnated cave artist.'[87] In his work, drawing, thinking, acting and communicating merged and overlapped, similar to palimpsests in many petroglyphs.

Cave paintings and stone engravings from various cultures inspired Beuys's work. Above all, he was fascinated by their overall structure. He was interested both in how ancient traditions were embedded in cultural memory and in the spiritual aspects of evolution and revolution. The cultural anthropologist Aleida Assmann, describing the concept of 'cultural memory' in relation to several artists, stated: 'It seems as if memory, which no longer has a cultural form or social function, has found refuge in art.'[88] Beuys was also closely aligned with Rudolf Steiner's anthroposophical cosmology and believed that human cognition does not reveal reality but creates it. He was a mystic, visionary and provocateur. His greatest concern was that art should change the world and was convinced of the transformative power of art.

A.R. Penck, Germany

A.R. Penck (born Ralf Winkler, 1939–2017), explored many aspects of art, history, mythology and politics. Though his simplified forms align him with modern graffiti art, his distinctive pictorial language, combining figurative and abstract elements, places him well ahead of renowned artists like Keith Haring and Jean-Michel Basquiat.

In his work, A.R. Penck focused on ideas about the earth, humans and their soul. In the epilogue to his book *Mein Denken* (My Thinking), he wrote:

What kind of planet is the earth? ... What processes take place inside a human being? ... Does the soul have a core? ... These are all questions that move me and that I try to answer in my drawings. Anyone who sees my drawings will quickly realize that there are about five different types of images. But you can easily come up with more, depending on how you differentiate. The first is the abstract symbolic type, the second is the figurative type, the third is the purely automatic type, the fourth is a kind of illusion, and the fifth is the destructive type.[89]

By introducing these types, Penck wanted to shed light on the complexity of his signs and images, which are populated with archetypal figures. A similar typology could also be applied to petroglyphs, whose authorship lies in many hands and various thinking strategies.

Penck's enigmatic stories and mysterious rituals also reflect his life as an outsider, both in East Germany, where he repeatedly had to struggle with opposition, and as an emigré in the West.

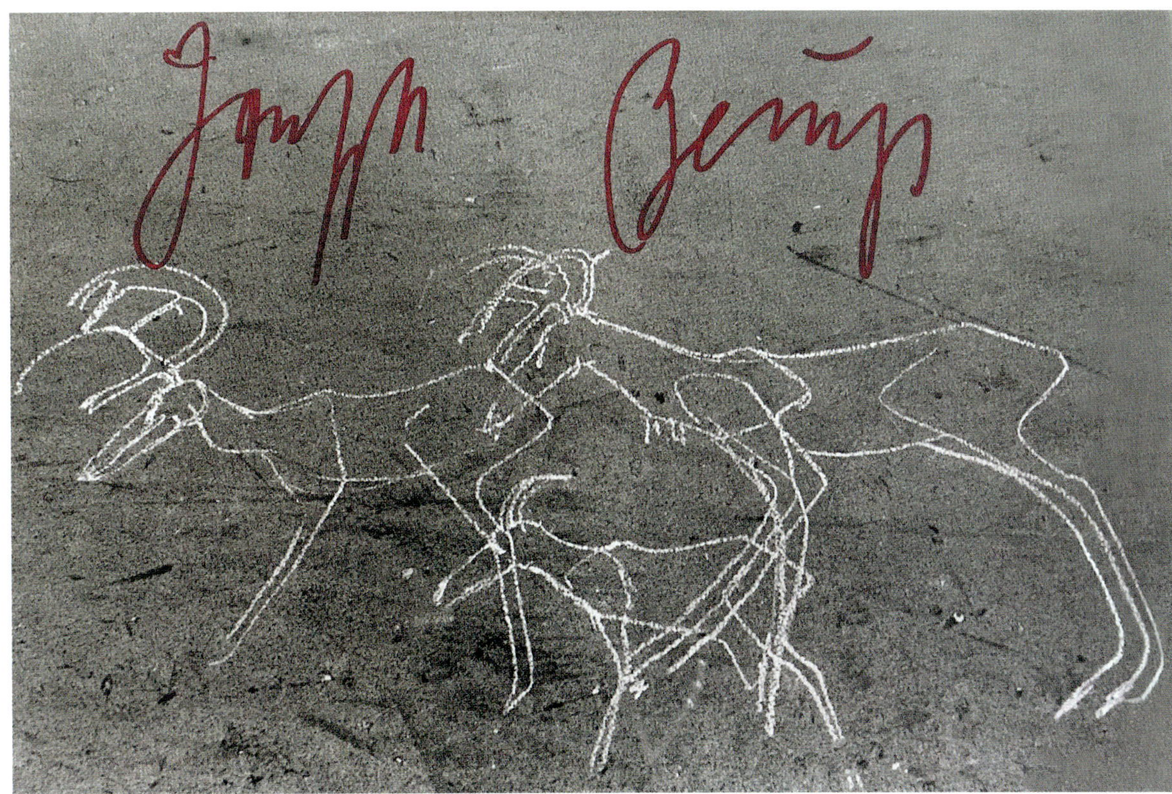

338. Joseph Beuys, *Floor Drawing (Fussbodenzeichnung), Herzogstrasse 79, 6.6.1982.* 30 × 40 cm. Lithograph, 1982. © 2024, ProLitteris, Zurich, Switzerland and Rainer Rappmann, Achberg, Germany.

Reflecting on his struggles with these adversities, he wrote: 'The attitude of "hands up" is not only an attitude of surrender but also one of freedom.'[90] This posture is also found in petroglyphs, and there are various hypotheses as to its meaning. On the one hand, it can be seen as a position of reverence; on the other, as an attitude of confrontation. These interpretations from different cultures align with Penck's way of thinking.

Penck questioned conventional ideas in art and developed his own visual vocabulary. He applied this unique pictorial language to a wide range of materials and media, capturing the zeitgeist of the time and simultaneously transcending cultural boundaries, as was seen at his major retrospective in 2008 at the Schirn Kunsthalle in Frankfurt am Main, Germany; the exhibition included many of his sketchbooks and artist's books.[91] From an early stage, Penck forged his own path beyond traditional art. In 1961, for example, he started to create his so-called 'world pictures', which he described as modern history paintings. These include his typical style of 'stick men' shown from the front or the side. The term 'man' is significant here, as the majority of these figures includes a phallus, just as in prehistoric petroglyphs. There is a clear emphasis on the male gender in petroglyphs across most cultures, while depictions of people with female attributes are rather rare.

The artist favoured a wide range of materials and could be very spontaneous in his choices. The present author was able to observe his impulsive and loose approach during the installation of the Biennale PaperArt in the Leopold-Hoesch-Museum in Düren, Germany (1994). As Penck worked to realize his vision of the installation *Neue Logik 17 / 5 / 94*, he moulded a four-metre-tall male figure using crumpled newspaper arranged as a series of lines in the form of a relief mounted on the museum wall. It looked like a gigantic representation on a

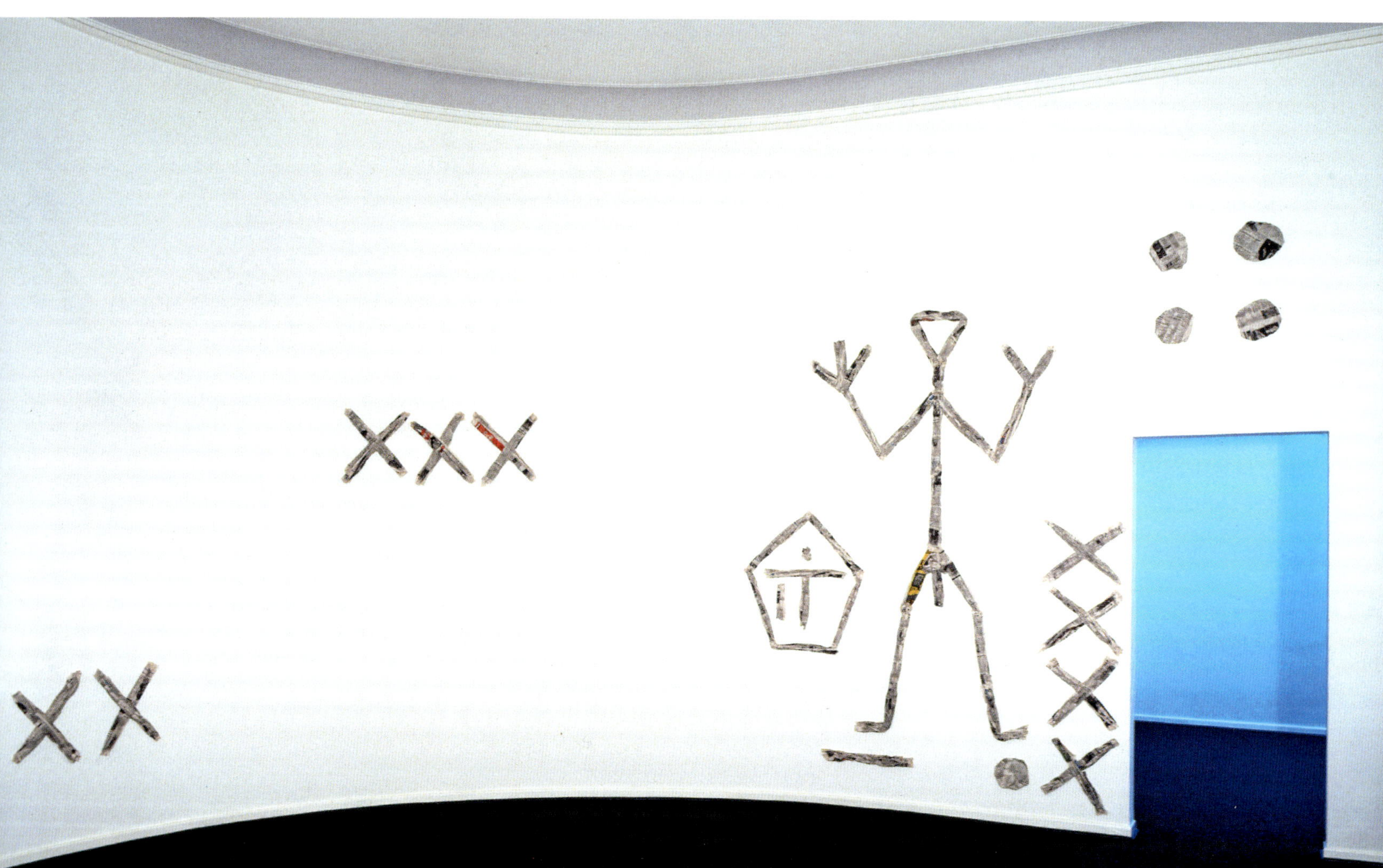

339. A.R. Penck, *New Logic 17 / 5 / 94*. Installation made with crumpled newspaper at the *PaperArt*, Leopold Hoesch Museum Düren, Germany, 1994. Approx. 680 × 680 cm. © By permission of Anne Gold, Aachen, Germany.

smooth rock face in a bare, open landscape (fig. 339). In contrast to this work made of consumables, other works feature his signs engraved in precious, hard marble just as in prehistoric times, albeit with the help of modern tools. An excellent example is the five-part marble sculpture *Himmlische Stürze* (a title implying 'objects crashing from heaven', 1995–96) in Wuppertal.[92] It features engravings of double spirals, serpentine or zigzag shapes (found in prehistoric signs in many cultures), as well as cross-like shapes and other motifs such as characters and mathematical formulae.

A.R. Penck is often referred to as 'the cave painter of postmodernism'. However, in his complex pictorial compositions and sculptures, the artist combined the individual, the social and the political to create timeless events and truths. He developed his very own pictorial logic and methodology and continued to scrutinize it, leading him to change and reinvent motifs and themes over the course of his career.

Peter Piller, Germany

In his research into Stone Age art, Peter Piller (b. 1968) focuses primarily on rock art from France, Spain and Portugal. But his research also takes him to libraries, where he searches for photos and images that illustrate rock art. His art projects also include his own photographs and drawings, which are often inspired by his travels. As early as 1994, he began a serial documentation of these works under the theme *Peripheriewanderungen* (Peripheral Hikes). It was also during this period that he started the Peter Piller Archive, in which he organized, categorized and compiled thousands of images from various sources into series; some of these are published in the books *Archiv Peter Piller, Spekulationen* (Speculations).[93] For some years now, his work has focused on the connection between Stone Age art and its presence in his daily life. This research, which includes many photographs taken from publications on prehistoric art, photographs from his travels and images from scientific publications across various disciplines, is documented in the three volumes of *Spekulationen*.

He says of his interest in rock art: 'My interest in prehistoric art began when I discovered the relationship between cave paintings and my own drawings. Then I … looked at the art on site in many caves and one door after another opened for me.'[94] In the process, he discovered that his perception of the everyday world and his own photographs had an affinity with rock art. In this interplay between prehistoric and contemporary images, he primarily examines visual relationships, which are more important to him than references to content. Piller's interest in prehistoric rock art is mainly focused on rock engravings with, as he says, non-figurative or indeterminate

lines, such as those found in the Pech Merle Cave in south-western France.[95] The present author agrees with the art historian Rémi Labrusse in seeing hints of mammoth representations and female figures in them. Labrusse categorizes these engravings as figurative representations with the designation 'Tracés digitaux figuratifs'.[96] Piller reproduces photographs of these symbolic representations as archival pigment prints[97] in a 44 by 64-centimetre format and juxtaposes them with his so-called 'site drawings' done in a smaller, A4 format. These were created during his stays in the original caves or their exact replicas,[98] or later in his studio. These drawings also do not depict any clear figures. They offer subjective traces of imagination and memory that graphically recreate particular features and situations in the caves, similar to cartographic documentation. The photographs and drawings have been shown in juxtaposition in various exhibitions in recent years.[99]

3.5. Rock art and modern technologies

Some artists combine their biographical background with an interest in prehistoric rock art and then also use modern technologies to formulate their perceptions and visions.

Zhou Brothers, China/USA

The brothers Shan Zuo Zhou (b. 1952) and Da Huang Zhou (b. 1957), who live in Chicago since 1986, always develop their works together. They grew up in China's province of Guangxi where they became interested in the cave paintings of the Fa Shan caves. The motifs of the rock art left a formative impression and influenced their later works. Amorphous figures – silhouetted people with legs apart and arms outstretched, floating in some scenes, perhaps dancing – are central to their paintings, some of which are very large. Similar depictions can be found in petroglyphs on all continents. Between the figures, the brothers place pictographic signs such as circles, crosses, meandering shapes, the sun, the moon or totem symbols, as well as characters. In addition, they incorporate traditional calligraphic characters as traces of their culture into their canvases or works on paper. Their aim is to enrich present phenomena with elements of the past.

Robin Rhode, South Africa/Germany

Robin Rhode (b. 1976), originally from South Africa, studied rock art in his home country, mainly in the Cederberg Mountains where thousands of rock art images are found. He presents his subtle, personal interpretation and visual ideas in museums and public spaces in the form of street art and performances. His artistic interventions are captured as photographs and then exhibited together with his drawings in a new context. He creates a link between rock art and photography, street art and graffiti as well as comic drawings. In an interview in the art magazine *Monopol* in 2023, he said: 'I painted a lot on walls myself and did extensive research on ancient rock art from southern Africa. It was an attempt to reconnect with my roots. I wanted to explore the aesthetic and creative continuity that underpins my art. The petroglyphs are a source code of humanity and act as our story of human origin.'[100] Rhode is particularly fascinated by therianthropy, the ability of individuals to metamorphose into animals or hybrids, where the body possesses both animal and human characteristics. In his work *Celestial Body*, 2022, this is illustrated by the depiction of a female figure with horns posing in front of a wall with an eight-pointed star and its shadow. Such hybrid creatures can also be found in petroglyphs from other cultures and reference rituals and myths.[101]

Analia Saban, Argentinia/USA

In recent years, artists have explored new, innovative ways of appropriating rock art. Such explorations have become a focal point in the digital age, driven by advances in computer technology. In a rock drawing measuring approximately eight by ten metres, the Argentinian artist Analia Saban, Argentinia/USA (b. 1980) references prehistoric rock art and cave paintings. As part of the biannual outdoor exhibition of land art called Art Safiental in Switzerland, she created in 2018 the work *Circuit Board for Rock Painting* that brings together nature and technology by combining fast-changing technology with the permanence of rock. This linear figuration in the form of oversized computer circuit boards was first digitally projected onto the rock and then traced with chalk paint. The work, applied to an exposed rock face, is subject to transience and will erode over time.[102]

3.6. Street art as a global discourse

Finally, the transfer of prehistoric art into modern times can also be expressed as street art, since it exists to a large extent on all continents.

In our urban environments, man-made walls and surfaces have replaced rock faces as a platform for art. These walls carry a piece of the past into the present. Some of the art is applied in secret, as is the case with the English street artist Banksy.[103] His unauthorized satirical and often irreverent stencil graffiti can be found all over the world in public spaces – such as the scene *Reindeer Stretched in front of a Bench* on a brick wall in Birmingham, England[104] – but at the same time they are also exhibited in museums. Just as in prehistoric times, these murals are a reflection of their respective society. They visualize thoughts, actions, events, memories and visions.

Another, one could say, 'official' form of street art was created in 2022 in the northern Saudi Arabian city of Ha'il (fig. 340). This Saudi street art is created by a team of female artists painting large murals depicting prehistoric petroglyphs and Thamudic characters in numerous public squares and at intersections, the airport road and the regional airport. The painted motifs are based on the famous Jubbah petroglyphs located not far from Ha'il (fig. 229), as well as the Thamudic letters that were used by the nomadic Bedouin throughout northern and central Arabia more than two thousand years ago, mostly in the form of petroglyphs at desert wells and trail junctions. A Ha'il government spokesperson, Saud al-Ali said: 'These murals are anything but silent, they are expressive. They have inspired young people to study the ancient languages.'[105]

4. Bringing the past into the present: Exhibitions featuring rock art and contemporary art

Prehistoric Rock Pictures in Europe and Africa, MoMA New York, 1937

Prehistoric rock art became a subject of public interest in 1937, with the presentation of copies of rock art simultaneously with modern art at MoMA, New York. The combination of representations from prehistoric times with works by contemporary artists was extraordinary. It shed light on social structures from different continents and across a broad time period. In the groundbreaking exhibition *Prehistoric Rock Pictures in Europe and Africa*, 150 images of prehistoric, mostly painted copies of rock art from the collection of the German ethnologist Leo Frobenius were placed in the unusual context of a modern art museum.[106] The modern art and the rock art were exhibited in separate sections, making it difficult to draw direct connections between the prehistoric and modern images. Nevertheless, this first pioneering pictorial dialogue between past and present was a major step in art history, a discipline that previously had hardly mentioned or considered prehistoric art.

40,000 Years of Modern Art, London, 1948

The exhibition *40,000 Years of Modern Art: A Comparison of Primitive and Modern Art*[107] at the Institute of Contemporary Art in 1948 was initiated and curated by Herbert Edward Read and Roland Penrose,

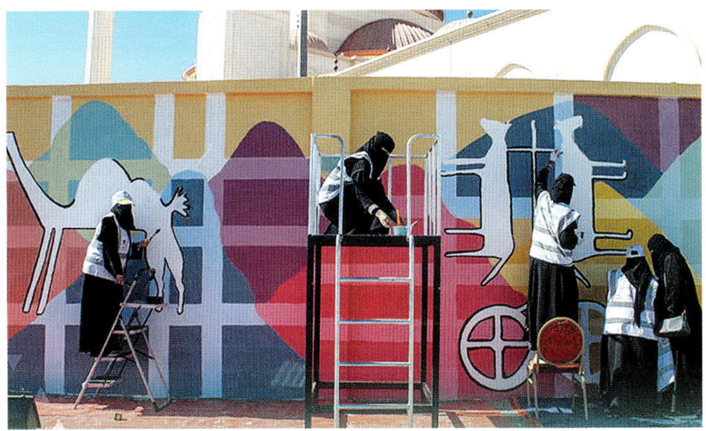

340. Painters decorating a public wall with motifs taken from Bronze and Iron Age petroglyphs, Ha'il, Saudi Arabia. Source: *Arab News*, 1 August 2022, 'Saudi heritage: Silent Thamud inscriptions speak of Hail's ancient cultural legacy'. © *Arab News*, al-Riyadh, Saudi Arabia.

the founders of the Institute of Contemporary Art and advocates of British Modernism. The exhibition concept connected pictures from both eras, conveying a spatial and temporal continuity to the visitors. One of the representatives of modern art was Joan Miró, whose painting *Hommage à Nusch Eluard*, 1937, was positioned directly next to a rock painting from Western Australia and a photograph of Indigenous people. (Miró only visited the famous Palaeolithic rock painting of Altamira twenty years later, in 1957.) The curator Penrose himself saw art as a vital necessity that was not limited by any concrete or historical boundaries. In an interview, he declared that 'art is eternal', indeed, that it is 'an instinct without which the human species cannot survive'.[108] The comparison and juxtaposition of works of so-called 'primitive' and 'modern' art triggered heated discussions.

40,000 ans d'art moderne, Paris, 1953

In 1953, another thematic exhibition was staged under the title *40,000 ans d'art moderne. La naissance de l'art dans les grands centres préhistoriques*' (40,000 Years of Modern Art: The Birth of Art in the Great Prehistoric Centres).[109] It was conceived as a collaboration between three Parisian museums: the Maison des Beaux-Arts, the Musée d'Art Moderne, and the Palais de Tokyo. 'The extraordinary collaboration between these three museums defined the approach to the exhibition and was evident in the title. A strange reversal had taken place, whereby modern art was used to legitimize prehistoric art, which had not yet unanimously been recognized as authentic art'.[110] The concept and the exhibits led to a number of controversies, partly because some of the allegedly prehistoric artefacts turned out to be archaeological forgeries. The exhibition was shown at the Musée d'Art Moderne as well as at the Palais de Tokyo.

Ten Americans after Paul Klee, Bern and Washington DC, 2017–18

With the exhibition *Ten Americans after Paul Klee* at the Zentrum Paul Klee in Bern[111] and the Phillips Collection in Washington DC (2017–18),[112] Klee was honoured for his pioneering role in the development of mid twentieth-century American art. In *Ten Americans*, key American abstract expressionist and colour field painters were presented in dialogue with works by Klee for the first time, highlighting the cultural exchange between Europe and the United States. These representatives, who had never met Paul Klee personally, included Adolph Gottlieb, Bradley Walker Tomlin, Mark Tobey, Norman Lewis, Robert Motherwell, William Baziotes, Theodoros Stamos, Jackson Pollock, Gene Davis and Kenneth Noland. The exhibition focused on how and to what extent the artists' visual thinking was inspired by ethnographic works, in particular the simplification and schematization of archaic symbols and signs. Analogies with rock art could be observed in the works of all participating artists. Another goal was to present modern art from a new, global perspective.[113]

Préhistoire, une énigme moderne, Centre Pompidou, Paris, 2019

After a long period in which it was overlooked, the link between the art of prehistoric times and modernity has recently been revisited by various museums, for example in the exhibition *Préhistoire, une énigme moderne* (Prehistory, a Modern Enigma) at the Centre Pompidou in Paris (2019). It covered a broad range of encounters between the creative visual language of the past and present.[114] The exhibition was structured around specific themes that methodically and didactically guided visitors through a series of rooms, from displays of rock art copies and prehistoric artefacts through to exponents of modern art. Topics included the start of the Lower Palaeolithic era, the first use of tools made out of carved stone, the appearance of the first *Homo sapiens*, the invention of carved stone hand axes, and the first writing system in Mesopotamia. These topics covered aspects such as traditions, rituals and design concepts in the form of paintings, drawings, sculptures and objects. References to prehistoric art could also be found in the rooms featuring contemporary artists – the intention was to form a bridge back to the art of prehistoric times. Representatives of the modern epoch included Joan Miró, Jean Dubuffet, Gyula Halász (Brassaï), Paul Klee, Jean Arp, Jacques Lipchitz, Jean Fautrier, Alberto Giacometti, Pablo Picasso, Ernst Ludwig Kirchner, Tacita Dean, Mario Merz, Robert Smithson, Carl André and Richard Long. Their works contain both obvious and hidden reflections on prehistory that connect the past with the present.

Art of Prehistoric Times: Rock Paintings from the Frobenius Expeditions, Museum Rietberg, Zurich, 2021

The exhibition *Art of Prehistoric Times: Rock Art from the Frobenius Expeditions* at the Museum Rietberg in Zurich (2021), on the other hand, focused on the pioneering work of Leo Frobenius and his teams.[115] Following the discovery of Palaeolithic cave paintings towards the end of the nineteenth century, the Frobenius copies of palaeolithic rock art further highlighted the need to question and revise the established notions about the beginnings of art. Large-format copies such as the *Large Elephants, Other Animals and People, Painted in Many Layers* (Zimbabwe, 1929), measuring 283 by 678.5 centimetres, revive a lost world. Most of Frobenius' copies were created by women painters who had completed a fine arts degree. They made copies of the rock art on site.[116] While most of the copies were drawn and painted on paper, they were later mounted on canvas for conservation reasons. These copies and photographs offer highly valuable insights into prehistoric cultures, and some of them are the only records we have from certain regions and eras since the original paintings have faded or even vanished.[117] Moreover, the coloured copies, executed with great skill, are works of art in their own right.

Urknall der Kunst. Moderne trifft Vorzeit, Darmstadt, 2023

In the exhibition *Urknall der Kunst. Moderne trifft Vorzeit* (Art's Big Bang: Modernity meets prehistory), in Darmstadt, 2023, the results from the expeditions by Frobenius and his team formed the basis for a discourse about early rock art and art created between 1868 and 1987. The featured artists all engaged with foreign cultures and prehistoric artefacts in their own way. The work of the Spaniard Joan Miró includes handprints and archaic forms inspired by his visit to Altamira in 1957. The German painter and graphic designer Willi Baumeister (1889–1955) visited Altamira in 1950, and his archaic scenes *Urzeitgestalten* (Primeval Figures), 1945, and *Ur-Nirgal* (Primeval Nirgal) from 1955 mirror figures from rock paintings in abstracted depictions. Pablo Picasso (1881–1973), for his part, is said to have allegedly visited the cave of Lascaux in 1941. He was interested in naturalism, timeless abstraction and the gradual reduction of the formal language, which he applied in works such as the eleven-part lithograph series *Le Taureau* (The Bull) in 1945–46.[118]

The presence of rock art in contemporary art also means connecting past and present. Such an inclusion builds bridges to preserve ways of transmitting knowledge and to keep the 'codes' of our ancestors alive, thus transferring a past reality into the future.

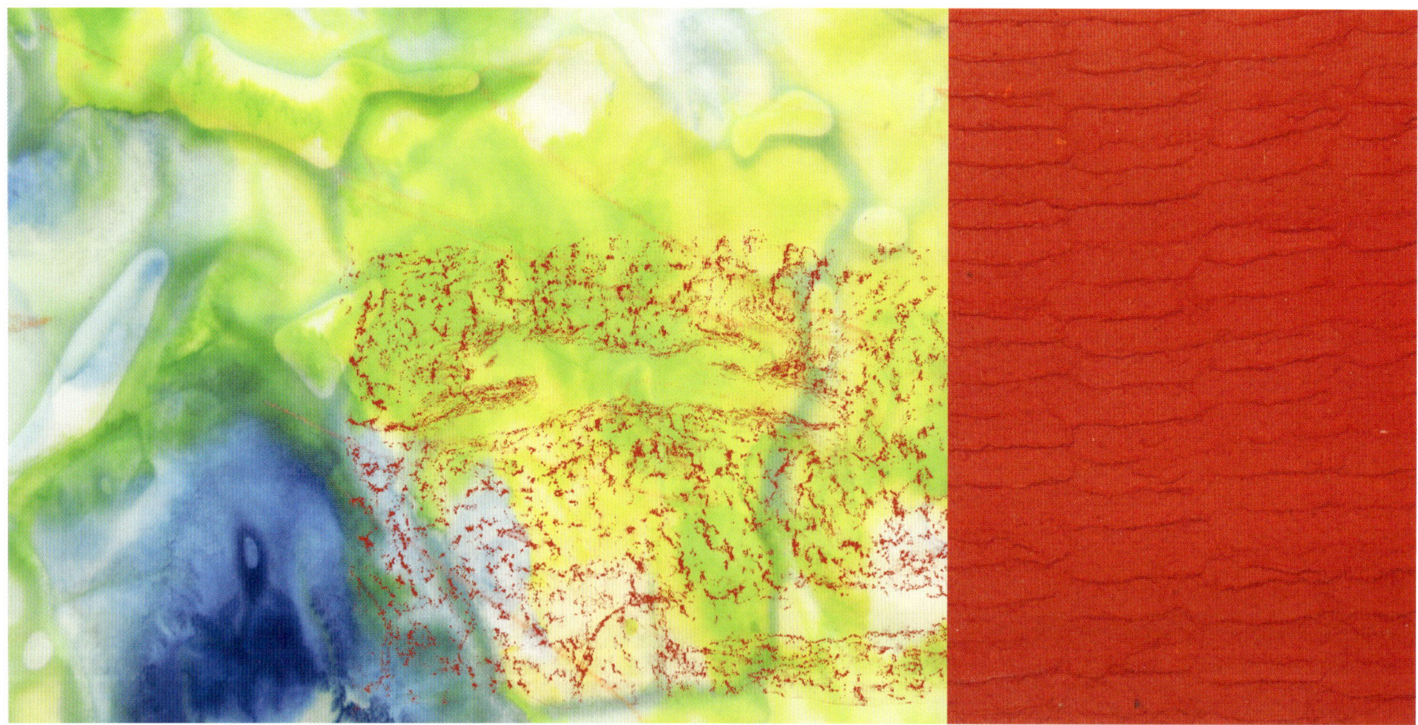

341. Therese Weber, *What is the leopard doing in the room?* 39 × 89 cm. Left: Frottage, graphite pencil on mulberry paper, digitally collaged on watercolour paper, print on handmade paper. Right: Scooped and cast pulp, hand-textured, detail: 39 × 79 cm, 2021.

Appendices

Notes

Part 1. Definitions and Methods

I. Defining Rock Art and Contextualizing Petroglyphs

1 In literature, petroglyphs are often described as 'rock carvings' or just 'carvings', although in reality most engravings are in fact pecked, and sometimes subsequently polished. Therefore 'peckings' is more correct, and 'petroglyphs' or, to a lesser degree, 'engravings' are more neutral terms since they do not specify a method of creation.

2 White, Randall, *Prehistoric Art: The Symbolic Journey of Humankind* (New York: Henry N. Abrams, 2003), pp. 158, 161. Casoli, Antonella, 'Research on the organic binders in archaeological wall paintings', in: *Applied Sciences*, vol. 11, no. 19, art. no. 9179 (Basel: MDPI, 2021).

3 Wall paintings were also exposed to various dangers inside caves. These include the formation of soot from torches, physical contact from humans and animals, increased humidity from human respiration, water ingress and, last but not least, bats. This is because the water vapour released by the bats' breathing condenses on the cave walls, also incorporating CO_2. This trickle of acidic water dissolves the limestone on the walls, leading to the formation of tiny blisters. In addition, the nitric acid in their urine and the strong acids released by the fermentation of guano piles also attack the walls, smoothing their surfaces as effectively as sandpaper. During the cold periods when the cave paintings were made, bats had left what is now France, but they returned at the beginning of the Holocene, which is why Palaeolithic cave paintings have only survived where the entrances were buried by rockfalls, such as in Lascaux, Chauvet and Cussac, or flooded by rising sea levels, as at Cosquer. In other caves, paintings only remained in galleries far from the entrance. Bruxelles, Laurent et al., 'Biocorrosion et art pariétal: une exclusion mutuelle à l'origine de vides archéologiques: Méthodologie, premiers résultats et nouvelles perspectives de recherche', in: *Hiatus, lacunes et absences: identifier et interpréter les vides archéologiques. Actes du 29e Congrès préhistorique de France, 31 mai–4 juin 2021* (Paris: Société préhistorique française, 2024), pp. 87–89, 99f.

4 The time reference BP stands for Before Present whereby 'Present' is defined as 1 January 1950, the set beginning of the radiocarbon dating practice. This time scale is mainly used in archaeology and geology: ka stands for kiloyear, that is 1000 years.

5 Upper Palaeolithic is an archaeological term, Pleistocene and Holocene are geological epochs. The Last Glacial Period is dated 115000–11700 cal. BP, the present Holocene began in 11700 cal. BP. For the abbreviation 'cal.' see note 10 below.

6 Aubarbier, Jean-Luc and Binet, Michel, *Sites préhistoriques en Périgord* (Rennes: Ouest-France, 1984). David, Bruno, *Cave Art* (London: Thames & Hudson, 2017), pp. 23–26, 179–182, 193.

7 Bovagne, Marilyne et al., 'Bellegarde. Un voyage à travers les âges', in: *Archéologia*, no. 627 (Dijon: Faton, 2024), pp. 48f.

8 The engravings and paintings at Cova Dones are over 24,000 years old since the species of cave bear which scratched its claws into the art works had become extinct by that time. Symonds, Matthew, 'Cova Dones: A surprising palaeolithic cave-art site', in: *Current World Archaeology*, vol. 123 (London: Current Publishing, 2024), pp. 16–21.

9 The graffiti-like engravings in the Addaura Cave date from the late Magdalenian and the Mesolithic.

10 Conventional radiocarbon measurements or accelerator mass spectrometry (AMS) provide raw data with an inherent deviation. Since the production of ^{14}C isotopes and thus the ^{14}C content of the atmosphere have fluctuated greatly over time, these raw data do not correspond exactly to calendar years and must be calibrated accordingly. From a date of more than 25,000 years BP, non-calibrated data provide age determinations that are too recent, whereby age underestimations can be up to five millennia. The lower limit for radiocarbon measurements is approx. 60,000 years BP. Calibrated dates are given as 'cal. BP' or 'cal. BCE'. Sauvet, Georges, 'In search of lost time. Dating methods for prehistoric art: The example of Aurignacian sites', in: *Palethnologie: Archéologie et Sciences humaines*, vol. 7 (Toulouse: CNRS / UMR 5608, 2015), pp. 2–4. Steelman, Karen L. and Rowe, Marvin W., 'Radiocarbon dating of rock paintings: Incorporating pictographs into the archaeological record', in: McDonald, Jo and Veth, Peter A. (eds), *Companion to Rock Art* (Chichester: Blackwell, 2012), pp. 567–572. A widely used algorithm to calibrate radiocarbon data is OxCal 4.4: https://c14.arch.ox.ac.uk/oxcal.html (accessed 5 Feb. 2024).

11 Bégouën, Robert at al., 'Parietal art and archaeological context: Activities of the Magdalenians in the cave of Tuc d'Audoubert, France', in: McDonald and Veth, *Companion to Rock Art* (2012), pp. 365, 377–379.

12 David, *Cave Art* (2017), pp. 174f.

13 Aubarbier and Binet, *Sites préhistoriques en Périgord* (1984), pp. 7, 9, 14, 18, 27.

14 In Pompeii alone more than 5,000 graffiti have been identified. Lohmann, Polly, 'Antike und historische Graffiti als Forschungsgegenstand', in: *Antike Welt*, vol. 21, no. 2 (Darmstadt: WBG, 2021), p. 11.

15 Typical examples of such vandalism are the personal names carved repeatedly by ignorant tourists on the walls of highly important historical monuments such as the Colosseum in Rome. https://www.arabnews.com/node/2329241/offbeat (accessed 3 Feb. 2024). Some of the oldest graffiti connected to rock art were made between 1641 and 1660 in the cave of Niaux, French Pyrenees: Bahn, Paul G., *Prehistoric Rock Art, Polemics and Progress* (Cambridge: Cambridge University Press, 2010), p. 6.

16 Other types of carved steles which have no connections to petroglyphs, like those at Göbekli Tepe, southern Turkey, will not be discussed.

17 This focus excludes both the above-mentioned cave petroglyphs and large-scale stone engravings such as Newgrange (Ireland) or Gavrinis (France).

18 In particular the cave paintings from Western Europe, and some of the cave engravings, have been thoroughly researched and are widely published, which would make yet another general publication on parietal art redundant.

19 Among the few cave paintings in Eastern Europe are those located in the Magura Cave in Bulgaria; they mainly date from the Neolithic period and the Bronze Age.

20 Plato, *The Republic*, trans. Benjamin Jowett (1888), book X: http://classics.mit.edu/Plato/republic.11.x.html.

21 Pliny the Elder [C. Plinius Secundus], *The Natural History*, trans. John Bostock and H.T. Riley (1857), book XXXV, ch. 5: www.gutenberg.org/cache/epub/62704/pg62704-images.html#BOOK_XXXV_CHAP_5.

22 Pliny, *Natural History*, book XXXV, ch. 36.

23 Since the distinction between fine and applied arts emerged only in the seventeenth to eighteenth centuries, such a distinction is irrelevant regarding rock art.

24 Kant, Immanuel, *Kritik der Urteilskraft*, part I, sections 1, § 2, 6, 9 (1790).

25 Hegel, Georg Wilhelm Friedrich, *Introductory Lectures*

on *Aesthetics*, trans. Bernard Bosanquet ([1886] London: Penguin, 2004), § XLIX, LV, LXVf, LXIX, pp. 35, 40, 50f, 56f.

26 Translation from the French by the author. Paillet, Patrick and Robert, Éric (eds), *Arts et préhistoire* (Paris: Museum national d'histoire naturelle, 2022), pp. 10, 12. Le Quellec, however, considers these two statements of Picasso apocryphal. Le Quellec, Jean-Loïc, *La caverne originelle. Art, mythes et premières humanités* (Paris: La Découverte, 2022), p. 351.

27 Translated from the German by the author. Krüger, Werner and Pehnt, Wolfgang, *Documenta – Documente. Künstler im Gespräch* (Cologne: Artemedia, 1984), pp. 43f.

28 Quoted from: Bradley, Richard, *Image and Audience: Rethinking Prehistoric Art* (Oxford: Oxford University Press, 2009), p. 26.

29 Ouzman, Sven, 'Towards a mindscape of landscape: Rock-art as expression of world-understanding', in: Chippindale, Christopher and Taçon, Paul S.C. (eds), *The Archaeology of Rock Art* (Cambridge: Cambridge University Press, 1998), pp. 32f.

30 Breuil, Henri, 'L'évolution de l'art pariétal dans les cavernes et abris ornés de France', in: *Compte rendu de la onzième session, Congrès préhistorique de France, Périgueux, 1934* (Paris: Société Préhistorique française, 1935), pp. 102–118.

31 Museo de Altamira, https://www.cultura.gob.es/mnaltamira/en/cueva-altamira/cronologia.html (accessed 3 Feb. 2024).

32 Kohl, Karl-Heinz et al., *Kunst der Vorzeit. Felsbilder der Frobenius-Expeditionen* (Munich: Prestel, 2021), pp. 14, 54f.

33 Conrad, Nicholas J. and Kind, Claus-Joachim, *Als der Mensch die Kunst erfand. Eiszeithöhlen der Schwäbischen Alb* (Darmstadt: Teiss/WBG, 2017), p. 11. Concerning whether modern *H. Sapiens* and Neanderthals met and interbred in Western Europe, the questionable Châtelperronian industry, the possible copying by Neanderthals of objects made by *H. sapiens*, and why *H. neanderthalensis* died out *ca.* 40000 BP, see: Baumer, Christoph, *History of the Caucasus*, vol. 1: *At the Crossroads of Empires* (London: I.B.Tauris/Bloomsbury, 2021), pp. 27–30, 357 n54. Also: Cummings, Vicki et al., *The Oxford Handbook of the Archaeology and Anthropology of Hunter-Gatherers* (Oxford: Oxford University Press, 2014), pp. 203–208, 282. David, Cave Art (2017), pp. 102–117. O'Hara, Kieran D., *Cave Art and Climate Change* (Bloomington: Archway, 2014), pp. 11f. Slimak, Ludovic et al., 'Modern human incursion into Neanderthal territories 54,000 years ago at Mandrin, France', in: *Science Advances*, vol. 8, no. 6 (Washington DC: AAAS, 2022); id., 'The three waves: Rethinking the structure of the first Upper Paleolithic in Western Europe', in: *PLOS ONE*, vol. 18, no. 5, art. no. 0277444 (San Francisco: PLOS, 2023). White, *Prehistoric Art* (2003), pp. 67f.

34 Lewis-Williams, David L., 'Art for the living', in: Cummings, *The Oxford Handbook of the Archaeology and Anthropology of Hunter-Gatherers* (2014), p. 626.

35 A sign has a communicative property and points to something other than itself.

36 The Upper Palaeolithic associated with *Homo sapiens* is divided, for Western and Central Europe, into several cultural periods named after an archaeological site. The dates of the periods vary by region and also depending how transitional periods are categorized.

For Western and Central Europe the periods are: **Aurignacian** (*ca.* 43000–32/31000 cal. BP), **Gravettian** (*ca.* 32/31000–26000 cal. BP), **Solutrean** (26,000–20,000 cal. BP) and **Magdalenian** (20,000–14,000 cal. BP); the **Azilian** (14,300–11500 cal. BP) falls into the transitional period from the late Upper Palaeolithic to the Mesolithic. In Southern and Eastern Europe, the Epigravettian followed the Gravettian and is dated similarly to the Solutrean. Conrad and Kind, *Als der Mensch die Kunst erfand* (2017), p. 45. O'Hara, *Cave Art and Climate Change* (2014), pp. 10, 15–19.

37 Rifkin, Riaan F. et al., 'Characterising pigments on 30,000-year-old portable art from Apollo 11 Cave, Karas Region, southern Namibia', in: *Journal of Archaeological Science: Reports*, vol. 5 (Amsterdam: Elsevier, 2016), pp. 336f, 339.

38 White, *Prehistoric Art* (2003), pp. 168–172. Ofer, Bar-Josef, 'The Natufian Culture in the Levant, threshold to the origins of agriculture', in: *Evolutionary Anthropology*, vol. 6, no. 5 (Hoboken: Wiley, 1998), pp. 162–169.

39 Finch, Damien et al., 'Ages for Australia's oldest rock paintings', in: *Nature Human Behaviour*, vol. 5 (London: Macmillan, 2021), pp. 310, 317.

40 Sadier, Benjamin et al., 'Further constraints on the Chauvet cave artwork elaboration', in: *Proceedings of the National Academy of Sciences*, vol. 109, no. 21 (Washington: PNAS, 2012), pp. 8002–8006.

41 The paintings in the Cosquer Cave were discovered in 1991, six years after the discovery of the cave itself whose entry lies today at 37 m below sea-level. They date from the Gravettian and the Solutrean periods. Since the level of the Mediterranean Sea was at that time *ca.* 130 m lower than today, its entry was then *ca.* 90 m asl and 10 km away from the shoreline. Lima, Pedro and Psaïla, Philippe, *La grotte Cosquer révélée. Les secrets du sanctuaire préhistorique englouti* (Montélimar: Synops, 2021), pp. 11, 26, 56, 64, 88f.

42 Quiles, Anita et al., 'A high-precision chronological model for the decorated Upper Paleolithic cave of Chauvet-Pont d'Arc, Ardèche, France', in: *Proceedings of the National Academy of Sciences*, vol. 113, no. 17 (Washington: PNAS, 2016), pp. 4670–4675. See also: David, Cave Art (2017), pp. 148–158.

43 Since the task of hunting fell probably primarily to men, with women presumably taking part in driving hunts, it is supposed that the cave paintings and petroglyphs were primarily made by men. So far, few robust clues are available by which to determine the distribution of roles between men and women in hunting and gathering; the same applies to rock art.

44 Charcoal finds suggest that in some caves the track from the entrance to the location of paintings, tens or hundreds of metres inside, was marked by small devices for holding wood which could be lit, or by stone lamps fuelled with animal fat (tallow) which did not smoke.

45 The Aurignacian was also revolutionary compared to the Mousterian industry associated with the Neanderthals in terms of hunting weapons, manufacturing of clothes, technologies for working primary materials like stone, bone and antlers, social organization and long-distance contacts. Additional innovations took place in the Gravettian and Solutrean with the inventions of fired ceramic figurines, spear-throwers, possibly the longbow and eyed bone needles. Parzinger, Hermann, *Die Kinder des Prometheus.*

Eine Geschichte der Menschheit vor der Erfindung der Schrift (Darmstadt: WBG, 2015), pp. 69–71. White, *Prehistoric Art* (2003), pp. 94, 135, 147.

46 Engravings on, or figurines made from, bone, ivory, reindeer antlers or limestone dating from the late Aurignacian to the Magdalenian soon spread across Western Europe and Southern Russia. It is noteworthy that significantly more animal species were featured in portable figurines or in engravings on utility articles than in paintings. The paintings were probably related to magic, rituals and myths and were therefore more codified than the small figurines and engravings which were personal amulets or decorations.

47 This term is derived from the Greek *theríon* meaning 'wild animal' and *ánthropos* 'human'. In rock art therianthropes usually have a human body and an animal head, in a few cases an animal body and a human head. Sometimes they are difficult to distinguish from humans wearing masks.

48 Wehrberger, Kurt (ed.), *Die Rückkehr des Löwenmenschen. Geschichte, Mythos Magie* (Ostfildern: Jan Thorbecke, 2013), p. 48.

49 Conrad and Kind, *Als der Mensch die Kunst erfand* (2017), pp. 94–102, 116, 125–129, 149f. Wehrberger, *Die Rückkehr des Löwenmenschen* (2013), pp. 98f.

50 d'Errico, Francesco et al., 'A 36,200 year-old engraving from Grotte des Gorges, Amange, Jura, France', in: *Scientific reports*, vol. 13, art. no. 12895 (London: Nature Portfolio, August 2023), pp. 1f, 8.

51 Aubert, Maxime et al., 'Pleistocene cave art from Sulawesi, Indonesia', in: *Nature*, vol. 514 (London: Macmillan, 2014), pp. 223–227.

52 Aubert, Maxime et al., 'Earliest hunting scene in prehistoric art', in: *Nature*, vol. 576 (London: Macmillan, 2019), pp. 1, 2, 4.

53 Brumm, Adam et al., 'Oldest cave art found in Sulawesi', in: *Science Advances*, vol. 7, no. 3 (Washington DC: AAAS, 2022), pp. 1–2, 6, 9.

54 A common denominator of all these wall paintings and carved animal figures from the Upper Palaeolithic is of a geographical nature, as they are found in karst landscapes with many caves and shelters that were used by prehistoric people. These karst landscapes have remained unchanged to this day and have preserved the artworks.

55 Pike, Alistair W.G. et al., 'U-series dating of paleolithic art in 11 caves in Spain', in: *Science*, vol. 336, no. 6087 (Washington DC: AAAS, 2011), pp. 1409–1414.

56 Hoffmann, D.L. et al., 'U-Th dating of carbonate crusts reveals Neandertal origin of Iberian cave art', in: *Science*, vol. 359, no. 6378 (Washington DC: AAAS, 2018), pp. 1–4.

57 See chapter 2, p. 20.

58 White, Randall et al., 'Still no archaeological evidence that Neanderthals created Iberian cave art', in: *Journal of Human Evolution*, vol. 144, art. no. 102640 (Amsterdam: Elsevier, July 2020).

59 The Mousterian is a prehistoric lithic industry belonging to the Middle Palaeolithic. In Europe, it is characteristic of Neanderthals but Mousterian tools were also produced at the same time by *H. sapiens* in North Africa and the Middle East. In Europe it lasted roughly from 160000 to 40000 BP.

60 The hypothesis put forward by Slimak whereby *Homo sapiens* crossed the River Rhône as early as 54,000 years ago and advanced at least as far as the cave of Mandrin in south-eastern France, remains highly disputed.

Slimak, 'Modern human incursion into Neanderthal territories' (2022); id., 'The three waves' (2023).

61 Marquet, Jean-Claude et al., 'The earliest unambiguous Neanderthal engravings on cave walls: La Roche-Cotard, Loire Valley, France', in: *PLOS ONE*, vol. 18, no. 6 (San Francisco: PLOS, 2023), pp. 1–28.

62 Hublin, Jean-Jacques et al., 'New fossils from Jebel Irhoud, Morocco and the pan-African origin of Homo sapiens', in: *Nature*, vol. 546 (London: Macmillan, 2017), pp. 289–292.

63 Neubauer, Simon et al., 'The evolution of modern human brain shape', in: *Science Advances*, vol. 4, no. 1 (Washington DC: AAAS, 2018).

64 Garvey, Raven and Bettinger, Robert L., 'Adaptive and ecological approaches to the study of hunter-gatherers', in: Cummings et al., *The Oxford Handbook of the Archaeology and Anthropology of Hunter-Gatherers* (2014), p. 82.

65 The bison is one of the few Ice Age animals that managed to adapt to warmer temperatures.

66 The mammoth was unable to adapt to the higher temperature and to a new vegetation which was toxic for Ice Age herbivores. O'Hara, *Cave Art and Climate Change* (2014), p. 40.

67 Haak, Wolfgang, Krause, Johannes et al., 'Palaeogenomics of Upper Palaeolithic to Neolithic European hunter-gatherers', *Nature*, vol. 615 (London: Macmillan, 2023), pp. 117, 124.

68 Aubry, Thierry and Balbin-Behrmann, Rodrigo de, 'Le plein air, un espace d'expression', in: *Art paléolithique. Dossiers d'Archéologie*, no. 417 (Dijon: Faton, 2023), pp. 56–59. Paillet and Robert, *Arts et préhistoire* (2022), pp. 235, 258.

69 Naudinot, Nicholas et al., 'Divergence in the evolution of Paleolithic symbolic and technological systems: The shining bull and engraved tablets of Rocher de l'Impératrice', *PLOS ONE*, vol. 12, no. 3 (San Francisco: PLOS, 2017), pp. 1, 20f.

70 This homogeneity is greater in paintings than in portable works; in paintings, herbivore mammals predominate.

71 Haak, Krause et al., 'Palaeogenomics', (2023), p. 124.

72 Maier, Andreas, 'Population and settlement dynamics from the Gravettian to the Magdalenian', in: *Mitteilungen der Gesellschaft für Urgeschichte*, vol. 26 (Tübingen: MGFU, 2017), pp. 87–89. Schmidt, Isabell and Zimmermann, Andreas, 'Population dynamics and socio-spatial organization of the Aurignacian: Scalable quantitative demographic data for western and central Europe', in: *PLOS ONE*, vol. 14, no. 2 (San Francisco: PLOS, 2019), pp. 1, 5–8.

II. Petroglyphs as a Mirror of Climate Changes, Economic Transformations and Beliefs

1 In contrast to myths, fables deal with anthropomorphized animals, and sagas narrate fantastic events which are linked to real events or persons.

2 Lévi-Strauss, Claude, *La pensée sauvage* (Paris: Plon, 1962), p. 24.

3 The flora was only rarely reflected in petroglyphs.

4 O'Hara, *Cave Art and Climate Change* (2014), p. 105.

5 Isostasy is the geological state of balance between the lithosphere, that is the masses of the Earth's crust, and the underlying mantle.

6 Cummings, Vicki, 'Hunter-gatherers in the post-glacial world', in: ead., *The Oxford Handbook of the Archaeology and Anthropology of Hunter-Gatherers* (2014), pp. 439f. Warren, Graeme, 'Transformations? The Mesolithic of North-West Europe', in: ibid., pp. 539f. In Kimberley, Australia, sea levels rose in the early Holocene by 125 m and the shoreline advanced inland by 159 to 200 km, in places even 300 km. Finch, 'Ages for Australia's oldest rock paintings' (2021), p. 317. The end phase of the Last Glacial Maximum had also allowed for the migration from north-eastern Siberia to North America via Beringia in a period when the sea level was about 125 m lower than present. Parzinger, *Die Kinder des Prometheus* (2015), p. 97.

7 See pp. 159, 188ff.

8 Buis, Alan, 'The atmosphere: Getting a handle on carbon dioxide, part 2' (Pasadena: NASA's Jet Propulsion Laboratory, California Institute of Technology, 2019), no pagination.

9 Baumer, Christoph, *The History of Central Asia*, vol. 1: *The Age of the Steppe Warriors* (London: I.B.Tauris, 2012), pp. 17f.

10 Cunliffe, Barry, *Facing the Sea of Sand: The Sahara and the Peoples of Northern Africa* (Oxford: Oxford University Press, 2023), pp. 6f.

11 One of the most famous examples in modern times is the eruption of the Mount Tambora volcano on the island of Sumbawa, Indonesia, from April to July of 1815, after which, in 1816, the world suffered the 'year without summer' with correspondingly widespread crop failures.

12 Lee, Jane J. and Wang, Andrew, 'Tonga eruption blasted unprecedented amount of water into stratosphere' (Pasadena: Jet Propulsion Laboratory, California Institute of Technology, 2 August 2022). Sellito, Pasquale et al., 'The unexpected radiative impact of the Hunga Tonga eruption of 15th January 2022', in: *Communications Earth and Environment*, vol. 3, no. 1, art. no. 288 (London: Macmillan, 2022).

13 Concerning these various factors, see: Chiotis, Eustathios, 'Reconstructing the environment as a scenery of human history and civilization', in: id., *Climate Changes in the Holocene: Impacts and Human Adaptation* (Boca Raton FL: CRS Press, 2019), pp. 5–11, 31. Crucifix, Michel, 'Pleistocene glaciations', in: ibid., pp. 78f. Kardulias, P. Nick, 'Migration of *Homo sapiens* out of Africa', in: ibid., p. 151. Wagner, Sebastian and Zorita, Eduardo, 'High resolution climate reconstruction of the last 2,000 years', in: ibid., pp. 124–129.

14 Interpreting measurements from charcoal requires especial caution since the wood from which the charcoal was produced may have died centuries or millennia before it was burnt. Furthermore, the charcoal may have been produced a long time before it was used in cave painting.

15 O'Hara, *Cave Art and Climate Change* (2014), p. 70.

16 Findeklee, Antje (ed.), *Frühe Kunst. Was Höhlenmalereien und Felszeichnungen verraten. Spektrum Kompakt*, 19 Oct. 2021 (Heidelberg: Spektrum der Wissenschaft), p. 63. Pike, Alistair W.G., 'Uranium–thorium dating of cave art', in: David, Bruno and McNiven, Ian (eds), *The Oxford Handbook of the Archaeology and Anthropology of Rock Art* (Oxford: Oxford University Press, 2018), pp. 953–957. Sauvet, 'In search of lost time' (2015), p. 6.

17 The speed of varnish regrowth decelerates over time.

18 Macholdt, Dorothea S. et al., 'Growth of desert varnish on petroglyphs from Jubbah and Shuwaymis, Ha'il region, Saudi Arabia, in: *The Holocene*, vol. 28, no. 9 (Thousand Oaks CA: SAGE Publications, 2018), pp. 1495–1497, 1503. 'Rock varnish on petroglyphs from the Hima region, southwestern Saudi Arabia: Chemical composition, growth rates, and tentative ages', in: *The Holocene*, vol. 29, no. 8 (Thousand Oaks CA: SAGE Publications 2019), pp. 1379–1389, 1391. Whitley, David S. (ed.), 'In suspect terrain: Dating rock engravings', in: McDonald and Veth, *Companion to Rock Art* (2012), pp. 607f.

19 The speed and degree of rock varnish regrowth is mainly a function of: time; surface texture such as porosity and smoothness; mineral density of the rock; initial Mn or Fe content; degree of acidity; amount of mineral dust flow; air pollution; temperature; exposure to water and wind. Andreae, Meinrat O. et al., 'Archaeometric studies on the petroglyphs and rock varnish at Khilwa and Sakaka, northern Saudi Arabia', in: *Arabian Archaeology and Epigraphy*, vol. 31 (Hoboken: Wiley, 2020), pp. 219–244. Dorn, Ronald et al., 'Rock varnish', in: Nash, D.J. and McLaren, S.J. (eds), *Geochemical Sediments and Landscapes* (Malden: Blackwell, 2007), pp. 246–297. Macholdt, 'Rock varnish on petroglyphs from the Hima region' (2019), p. 1391.

20 For a critical assessment of varnish measurement see: Harry, Karen G., 'Cation-ratio dating of varnished artifacts: Testing the assumptions', in: *American Antiquity*, vol. 60, no. 1 (Cambridge: Cambridge University Press, 1995), pp. 118–130.

21 McCarthy, M.C, 'Lichenometry', in: *Earth Systems and Environmental Sciences: Encyclopedia of Quaternary Science* (2nd ed., Amsterdam: Elsevier, 2013), pp. 565–572.

22 Roberts, Richard G., 'Optical dating of rock art', in: David and McNiven, *The Oxford Handbook of the Archaeology and Anthropology of Rock Art* (2018), pp. 945–948.

23 The drawings were only published in 1784. Bertilsson, Ulf, 'From folk oddities and remarkable relics to scientific substratum', in: Skoglund, Peter, Ling, Johan and Bertilsson, Ulf (eds), *Picturing the Bronze Age* (Oxford: Oxbow, 2015), p. 6.

24 Bahn, Paul G., *The Cambridge Illustrated History of Prehistoric Art* (Cambridge: Cambridge University Press, 1998), pp. 1–3. Taçon, Paul S.C., 'The rock art of South and East Asia', in: David and McNiven, *The Oxford Handbook of the Archaeology and Anthropology of Rock Art* (2018), p. 178.

25 Chen Zao Fu, *China. Prähistorische Felsbilder* (Zürich: U. Bär Verlag, 1989), pp. 35f.

26 'C'estait lieu infernal avecques figures de diables et mille démones partout taillez en rochiers': De Lumley, Henry, *Le mont Bego. Vallées des Merveilles et de Fontanalba* (Paris: Éditions du patrimoine, 2003), p. 23.

27 Le Quellec, Jean-Loïc, *La caverne originale* (2022), pp. 35f, 684.

28 Bahn, *The Cambridge Illustrated History of Prehistoric Art* (1998), p. 8.

29 Bahn, *The Cambridge Illustrated History of Prehistoric Art* (1998), pp. 16–18.

30 Strahlenberg, Philipp Johann von, *Das Nord- und Östliche Theil von Europa und Asia, in so weit solches das gantze Russische Reich mit Siberien und der großen Tartarey in sich begreiffet* (Stockholm: published by the author, 1730), pp. 338f, tables V, XI–XII.

31 The burial chamber was opened in 1748.

32 Goldhahn, Joakim, *Bredarör på Kivik, en arkeologisk odysse = Bredarör on Kivik: An Archaeological Odysse* (Simrishamn: Artes Liberales AB, 2013), pp. 62–79.

33 Bertilsson, 'From folk oddities and remarkable relics to scientific substratum' (2015), p. 7. The pioneering research into petroglyphs of each region will be briefly touched upon at the beginning of its respective chapter.

34 Bahn, *The Cambridge Illustrated History of Prehistoric Art* (1998), pp. 24–29.

35 Bahn, *The Cambridge Illustrated History of Prehistoric Art* (1998), p. 20.

36 Dorn, Ronald et al., 'Revisiting Alexander von Humboldt's initiation of rock coating research', in: *The Journal of Geology*, vol. 120, no. 1 (Chicago: Chicago University Press, 2012), pp. 1–14.

37 Paillet and Robert, *Arts et préhistoire* (2022) pp. 134, 152.

38 The leading denier of Altamira's palaeolithic dating, Émile Cartailhac, did not even bother to visit Altamira. Breuil, Henri, *Quatre cents siècles d'art pariétal. Les cavernes ornées de l'âge du renne* (Montignac: Centre d'études et de documentations préhistoriques, 1952), p. 15.

39 Bradley, *Image and Audience* (2009), p. 5.

40 Jürgens, Ekkehard, 'Pictures – What for? Seven hypotheses on the origin of art', in: Sachs-Hombach, Klaus and Schirra, Jörg (eds), *Origins of Pictures: Anthropological Discourses in Image Science* (Cologne: Herbert von Halem, 2013), p. 523.

41 Le Quellec, *La caverne originelle* (2022), pp. 36f, 42f, 56.

42 Breuil, *Quatre cents siècles d'art pariétal* (1952), p. 23. Jürgens, 'Pictures – What for?' (2013), pp. 526f.

43 Frobenius, Leo, *Das unbekannte Afrika: Aufhellung der Schicksale eines Erdteils* (Munich: Beck, 1923), p. 34f. Frobenius, Leo and Fox, Douglas C., *Prehistoric Rock Pictures in Europe and Africa* (New York: The Museum of Modern Art, 1937), 22f. A similar ritual has been reported for the Evenki living in the Amur Basin. Rozwadowski, Andrzej, 'Rock art of Northern, Central and Western Asia', in: David and McNiven, *The Oxford Handbook of the Archaeology and Anthropology of Rock Art* (2018), p. 163.

44 Jürgens, 'Pictures – What for?' (2013), pp. 527f.

45 Le Quellec, Jean-Loïc, *La caverne originelle* (2022), pp. 394f, 401, 406f, 415.

46 Totem is an ethnological term for a symbol or group insignia that represents a mythical, kinship-based connection between a person or group and a particular natural phenomenon, mostly animals, and less often plants, mountains, rivers or springs. In a totemist approach, the animals are interpreted as mere proxies of tribal communities.

47 The term animism refers to the belief that both living beings and inanimate objects have a soul.

48 Bahn, *Prehistoric Rock Art* (2010), p. 82.

49 Eliade, Mircea, *Shamanism: Archaic Techniques of Ecstasy* (Princeton: Princeton University Press, 1964).

50 'Hunter-gatherer religion and ritual', in: Cummings et al., *The Oxford Handbook of the Archaeology and Anthropology of Hunter-Gatherers* (2014), pp. 1224, 1235.

51 For example Devlet, Ekaterina and Marianna, 'Siberian shamanistic rock art', in: Rozwadowski, Andrzej and Kośko, Maria M. (eds), *Spirits and Stones: Shamanism and Rock Art in Central Asia and Siberia* (Poznán: Instytut Wschodni UAM, 2002), pp. 120–136. 'Rock art studies in Northern Russia and the Far East, 2000–2004', in: Bahn, Paul G. et al., *Rock Art Studies: News of the World*, vol. 3 (Oxford: Oxbow, 2008), pp. 123f.

52 Rozwadowski, 'Rock art of Northern, Central and Western Asia' (2018), pp. 164f. See also: 'Shamanism in indigenous context: Understanding Siberian rock art', in: McDonald and Veth, *Companion to Rock Art* (2012), pp. 458–465. For likely late Iron Age petroglyphs of shamans in Khakassia and the Russian Altai see: Devlet, Ekaterina and Marianna, *Myths in Stone: World of Rock Art in Russia* (Moscow: Aletheia, 2005), pp. 346f. Kšica, Miroslav and Ksicová, Olga, *Felsbilder zwischen Schwarzem Meer und Beringstrasse* (Brno: *PREH-ART-EXPO*, 1994), p. 152.

53 Molodin, Vjačeslav, Cheremisin, D.V. et al., 'Chronology of rock art of the Russian and Mongolian Altai: From the Paleolithic to the late Middle Ages', in: *Archaeology, Ethnology and Anthropology of Eurasia*, vol. 51, no. 4 (Novosibirsk: Russian Academy of Sciences, 2023), p. 75.

54 'Les grottes [pariétales] étaient des passages qui conduisaient à l'étage inférieur du cosmos chamanique. … Les chamanes visitent le monde inférieur au cours de leurs hallucinations. Pendant le Paléolithique supérieur, ils s'y rendaient non seulement pendant leurs visions mais aussi littéralement'. Clottes, Jean and Lewis-Williams, David, *Les Chamanes de la préhistoire. Transe et magie dans les grottes ornées* (Paris: Le Seuil, 1996), p. 99.

55 Francfort, Henri-Paul, 'Art, archaeology and the prehistories of shamanism in Central Asia', in: Francfort, Henri Paul, Hamayon, Roberte N. and Bahn, Paul G. (eds), *The Concept of Shamanism: Uses and Abuses* (Budapest: Akadémiai Kiadó, 2001), p. 260. See also: Rozwadowski, Andrzej, 'Sun gods or shamans? Interpreting the "solar-headed" petroglyphs of Central Asia', in: Price, Neil (ed.), *Archaeology of Shamanism* (Abingdon: Routledge, 2001), pp. 65f. 'Did shamans always play the drum? Tracking down prehistoric shamanism in Central Asia', in: *Documenta Praehistorica*, vol. 39 (Ljubljana: University of Ljubljana Press, 2012), pp. 278f.

56 Lewis-Williams, David, 'Monolithism and polysemy: Scylla and Charybdis in rock art research', in: Helskog, Knut (ed.), *Theoretical Perspectives in Rock Art Research* (Oslo: Institute for Comparative Research in Human Culture, 2001), pp. 30, 37.

57 Leroi-Gourhan, André, *Les religions de la préhistoire (Paléolithique)* (Paris: Presse Universitaire de France PUF, 1964). *Préhistoire de l'art occidental* (Paris: Mazenod, 1971), pp. 80–112.

58 Martel, Álvaro Rodrigo, 'Semiotics and meaning of Rock Art', in: Smith, Claire (ed.), *Encyclopedia of Global Archaeology* (New York: Springer, 2014), p. 3.

59 Lewis-Williams, J. David, *Believing and Seeing: Symbolic Meanings in Southern San Rock Paintings* (London: Academic Press, 1981). *The Rock Art of Southern Africa* (Cambridge: Cambridge University Press, 1983).

60 Lewis-Williams, David, 'Art for the living', in: Cummings et al., *The Oxford Handbook of the Archaeology and Anthropology of Hunter-Gatherers* (2014), p. 637.

61 Solomon, Anne, 'Rock arts, shamans, and grand theories', in: David and McNiven, *The Oxford Handbook of the Archaeology and Anthropology of Rock Art* (2018), pp. 566f.

62 Bahn, *Prehistoric Rock Art* (2010), pp. 72, 78, 86–104. Solomon, Anne, 'Rock arts, shamans, and grand theories' (2018), pp. 565–572.

63 Taçon, Paul S.C. and Chippindale, Christopher, 'An archaeology of rock art through informed methods and formal methods', in: Chippindale, Christopher and Taçon, Paul S.C. (eds), *The Archaeology of Rock Art* (Cambridge: Cambridge University Press, 1998), p. 6. See also: Chippindale, Christopher, 'Theory and meaning of prehistoric European rock art: "Informed methods", "formal methods" and questions of uniformitarianism', in: Helskog, *Theoretical Perspectives in Rock Art Research* (2001), p. 69.

64 Translation by the author from the English edition. Lévi-Strauss, Claude, *Structural Anthropology*, tr. Claire Jacobson and Brooke Grundfest Schoepf (New York: Anchor Books, 1967), p. 267.

65 Groups of potentially similar myths have been investigated utilizing phylogenetic software which is used for building evolutionary branching diagrams. This makes it possible to assess the relations between the various mythical versions and, eventually, to identify the primordial myth. d'Huy, Julien, 'The evolution of myths', in: *Scientific American*, vol. 315, no. 6 (New York: Springer Nature, 2016), pp. 64–69.

66 There are no global myths present in all cultures emerging from a mysterious 'collective unconsciousness' as was postulated by C.G. Jung. For example, in a European context the notion of 'Mother Earth' is widespread, yet in other cultures the earth has a male connotation, for example in Egypt it is personified by the male god Geb.

67 Anthony, David W., *The Horse, the Wheel and Language: How Bronze Age Riders from the Eurasian Steppes Shaped the Modern World* (Princeton: Princeton University Press, 2007), p. 454.

68 Frye, Richard N., *The Heritage of Central Asia: From Antiquity to the Turkish Expansion* (Princeton: Markus Wiener Publishers, 1996), pp. 68f.

69 Rozwadowski, Andrzej, 'From semiotics to phenomenology: Central Asian petroglyphs and the Indo-Iranian mythology', in: Helskog, *Theoretical Perspectives in Rock Art Research* (2001), p. 156.

70 Francfort, Henri-Paul, 'De l'art des steppes au sud du Taklamakan', in: *Bulletin of the Asia Institute*, vol. 12 (Bloomfield Hills MI: Asia Institute, 1998), pp. 45–58. 'Central Asian petroglyphs: Between Indo-Iranian and shamanistic interpretations', in: Chippindale and Taçon, *The Archaeology of Rock Art* (1998), pp. 302–318. Francfort, Henri-Paul et al., 'Pétroglyphes archaïques du Ladakh et du Zanskar', in: *Arts Asiatiques*, vol. 45 (Paris: Musée national d'art asiatique Guimet, 1990), pp. 5–27.

Part 2. Rock Art by Region

III. Central Asia

1 The Arctic Circle runs along latitude 66° 34' north.

2 Derev'anko, Anatoliy P. et al. (eds), *The Palaeolithic of Siberia: New Discoveries and Interpretations* (Novosibirsk: Institute of Archaeology and Ethnography, 1998), pp. 8, 126–129, 241–246, 329.

3 The extent of the share of anthropogenic factors relative to climatic ones contributing to the extinction of the glacial megafauna is disputed.

4   Rasmussen, S.O. et al., 'A new Greenland ice core chronology for the last glacial termination', in: *Journal for Geophysical Research: Atmospheres*, vol. 111, no. D6 (Washington DC: AGU, 2006), p. 12.

5   Since climate and pollen data may vary from region to region and the dating methods are not uniform, the dates given for climate periods can vary as well.

6   Sher, Jakov and Francfort, Henri-Paul (eds), *Répertoire des Pétroglyphes d'Asie centrale* (Paris: De Boccard, 1994–2006; individual fascicles are listed in the bibliography). See also: Devlet, Ekaterina and Marianna, *Myths in Stone: World of Rock Art in Russia* (Moscow: Aletheia, 2005).

7   Sher and Francfort, *Répertoire des Pétroglyphes d'Asie centrale*, fasc. 2 (1995), p. 13.

8   de Barros Damgaard, Peter et al., '137 ancient human genomes from across Eurasian steppe', in: *Nature*, vol. 557 (London: Macmillan, 2018), pp. 371–374.

9   Mallory J.P., *In Search of the Indo-Europeans: Language, Archaeology and Myth* (London: Thames & Hudson, 1989), pp. 143–185. For the rejected hypothesis which locates the homeland of PIE in Anatolia see: Renfrew, Colin, *Archaeology and Language: The Puzzle of Indo-European Origins* (London: Jonathan Cape, 1987).

10   For the expansion of the Indo-Europeans see: Baumer, *The History of Central Asia*, vol. 1 (2012), pp. 96f, 124, 136f. See also: Anthony, *The Horse, the Wheel and Language* (2007). Alexev, V., 'The physical specificities of Paleolithic hominids in Siberia', in: Derev'anko et al., *The Palaeolithic of Siberia* (1998), pp. 334f.

11   Haak, Wolfgang et al, 'Massive migration from the steppe was a source for Indo-European languages in Europe', in: *Nature*, vol. 522 (London: Macmillan, 2015), pp. 207–211. Wang, Chuan-Chao et al., 'Ancient human genome-wide data from a 3000-year interval in the Caucasus corresponds with eco-geographic regions', in: *Nature Communications*, vol. 10, art. no. 590 (London: Macmillan, 2019), pp. 1, 6–9.

12   Goldberg, Amy et al, 'Ancient X chromosomes reveal contrasting sex bias in Neolithic and Bronze Age Eurasian migrations', in: *Proceedings of the National Academy of Sciences*, vol. 114, no. 10 (Washington DC: National Academy of Sciences, 2017), p. 2657.

13   de Barros Damgaard, Peter et al., 'The first horse herders and the impact of early bronze age steppe expansions into Asia', in: *Science*, vol. 360, no. 6396 (Washington: AAAS, 2018), p. 2f. Heyd, Volker, 'The Mobility and Migration Revolution in the 3rd Millennium BC Europe', in: Fernández-Götz, Manuel et al. (eds), *Rethinking Migrations in Late Prehistoric Eurasia* (London: The British Academy, 2023), p. 43.

14   Haak, 'Massive migration from the steppe' (2015), p. 5.

15   Heyd, 'The Mobility and Migration Revolution in the 3rd Millennium BC Europe' (2023), p. 48.

16   Heyd, 'The Mobility and Migration Revolution in the 3rd Millennium BC Europe' (2023), p. 48.

17   The Okunev culture adopted and independently developed the culture inherited from Afanasievo.

18   For an overview of different types of carts and chariots in rock art and Eurasian antiquity in general see: Novozhenov, Victor A., *Communications and the Earliest Wheeled Transport of Eurasia*, ed. E.E. Kuzmina (Moscow: TAUS Publishing, 2012).

19   Nuristani is the third subgroup of Indo-Iranian. Mallory J.P., Adams D.Q. (eds), *Encyclopedia of Indo-European Culture* (London: Fitzroy Dearborn, 1997), pp. 290–311.

20   Grenet, Frantz, 'An archaeologist's approach to Avestan geography', in: Curtis, Vesta Sarkhosh and Stewart, Sarah (eds), *The Idea of Iran*, vol. 1: *Birth of the Persian Empire* (London: I.B.Tauris, 2005), pp. 35f.

21   Jones, Eppie R. et al., 'Upper Palaeolithic genomes reveal deep roots of modern Eurasians', in: *Nature Communications*, vol. 6, art. no. 8912 (London: Macmillan, 2015), p. 5.

22   Nowgorodowa, Eleonora, *Alte Kunst der Mongolei* (Leipzig: VEB E.A. Seemann, 1979), p. 39. Okladnikov, Aleksej Pawlowitsch, *Der Hirsch mit dem goldenen Geweih. Vorgeschichtliche Felsbilder Sibiriens* (Wiesbaden: F.A. Brockhaus), 1972, p. 162f. The paintings of the abri of Zaraut-Kamar (Uzbekistan), once dated to the Upper Palaeolithic or Mesolithic, are of a much more recent date and are presumably just a few centuries old. The same holds for the ostensibly Upper Palaeolithic paintings of Shishkino and Tal'ma in Siberia. Bednarik, Robert, 'Pleistocene rock art in Central Europe?' in: *International Newsletter on Rock Art*, no. 45 (2006), p. 29. Rozwadowski, Andrzej and Lymer, Kenneth, 'Rock art in Central Asia: History, recent developments and new directions', in: Bahn et al., *Rock Art Studies: News of the World*, vol. 4 (2012), pp. 151f.

23   Okladnikov, *Der Hirsch mit dem goldenen Geweih* (1972), p. 162; *E. namadicus* is now known as *Palaeoloxodon namadicus*.

24   The dating of the paintings of Khoid Tsenkeriin has been debated. Esin, Yury N. et al., 'Images of camels on a mammoth tusk from West Siberia', in: *Archaeological Research in Asia*, vol. 2 (Amsterdam: Elsevier, 2020), p. 9.

25   Nowgorodwa, *Alte Kunst der Mongolei* (1979), pp. 45–7, 55. The two-humped Bactrian camel (*Camelus bactrianus*) and the one-humped dromedary (*C. dromedarius*) are the descendants of two different subspecies of the wild camel (*C. ferus*). Its original habitat was in Mongolia, north-western China and eastern Kazakhstan. Potts, Daniel T., 'Bactrian camels and Bactrian dromedary hybrids', in: *The Silk Road*, vol. 3, no. 1 (Berkeley: The Silkroad House, 2005), p. 49.

26   Esin, 'Images of camels on a mammoth tusk from West Siberia' (2020), pp. 1, 3.

27   Okladnikov, *Der Hirsch mit dem goldenen Geweih* (1972), p. 163.

28   Ščelinskij, Vjačeslav E., et al., *Höhlenmalerei im Ural. Kapova und Ignatievka. Die altsteinzeitlichen Bilderhöhlen im südlichen Ural* (Sigmaringen: Jan Thorbecke, 1999), p. 34.

29   Paillet and Robert, *Arts et préhistoire* (2022), p. 276. Pakhunov, Alexander et al., 'The camel in the cave: Ice Age art in the Ural Mountains', in: *Current World Archaeology*, vol. 87 (London: Current Publishing, 2018), p. 10. Paillet and Robert, *Arts et préhistoire* (2022), p. 276. Rozwadowski, 'Rock art of Northern, Central and Western Asia' (2018), p. 152. Ščelinskij, *Höhlenmalerei im Ural* (1999), pp. 17–85.

30   Pakhunov, 'The camel in the cave' (2018), p. 11.

31   Paillet and Robert, *Arts et préhistoire* (2022), p. 276.

32   Ščelinskij, *Höhlenmalerei im Ural* (1999), pp. 94–132. Sher, Jakov and Garyaeva, Olga, 'The rock art of Northern Eurasia', in: Bahn, Paul G. et al., *Rock Art Studies. News of the World*, vol. I (Oxford: Oxbow, 1996), p. 107.

33   Ščelinskij and Sirokov, *Höhlenmalerei im Ural* (1999), pp. 136f.

34   Sher and Francfort, *Répertoire des Pétroglyphes d'Asie centrale*, fasc. 1 (1994), fasc. 2 (1995).

35   Nowgorodowa, *Alte Kunst der Mongolei* (1980), pp. 50–54.

36   Jacobson-Tepfer, Esther, 'Late Pleistocene and Early Holocene rock art from the Mongolian Altai: The material and its cultural implication', in: *Arts*, vol. 2, no. 3 (Basel: MDPI, 2013), p. 176.

37   In the present author's opinion, the animal in question is indeed a rhinoceros. Tseveendorj, D., Kubarev, V.D. and Jacobson, E., *Арал Толгойн хадны зураг = Петроглифы Арал Толгой (Монголия) = Petroglyphs of Aral Tolgoi (Mongolia)* (Ulaan Baatar: Mongolian Academy of Sciences, 2005), pp. 121, 123. Jacobson-Tepfer, Esther, 'The rock art of Mongolia', in: *The Silk Road*, vol. 4, no. 1 (Berkeley: The Silkroad House, 2006), p. 10. Moreover, the dating of the nearby petroglyphs at Kalgutinsky Rudnik on the Russian Ukok Plateau to the Final Pleistocene based on stylistic criteria remains questionable. Molodin, Vyacheslav and Cheremisin, D.V., 'The "Kalgutinsky" style in the rock art of Central Asia', in: *Archaeology, Ethnology and Anthropology of Eurasia*, vol. 47 (Novosibirsk: Archaeological Institute and Academy of Sciences, 2019), pp. 12–26.

38   South of Mongolia, in the Inner Mongolia Autonomous Region of the PRC, there are several additional petroglyph sites which are outside of the scope of this publication. See: Chen Zao Fu, *China. Prähistorische Felsbilder* (Zürich: U. Bär Verlag, 1989). *The Rock Arts of China* (Hangzhou: Zhejiang Photographic Art Press, 1989).

39   Klinge, Michael and Sauer, Daniela, 'Spatial pattern of Late Glacial and Holocene climatic and environmental development in Western Mongolia: A critical review and synthesis', in: *Quarternary Science Reviews*, vol. 210 (Amsterdam: Elsevier, 2019), p. 27.

40   Mongolia's horses prior to domestication were the tarpan (*Equus ferus ferus*) and the takhi (*E. ferus przewalskii*). Today's domesticated horse is not descended from the so-called Botai horse which was first bred around 3000 BCE as a food source and which was related to the takhi, but from the tarpan. Today's Przewalski horse is a descendant from the Botai horse which returned to the wild. De Barros Damgaard et al. 'The first horse herders' (2018), pp. 2, 6, 10. Novozhenov, Victor A., *Rock Art Chronicles of Golden Steppe*, vol. 1: *Model of Communication in Antiquity and Early Middle Ages* (Almaty: UNESCO Centre for the Rapprochement of Cultures, 2020), p. 278.

41   Deforestation occurred as a consequence of expanding pastures and the cutting of firewood for heating and metallurgy, while overgrazing due to rapidly increasing herd sizes accelerated the climate-driven trend to desertification, especially in the Gobi. Klinge and Sauer, 'Spatial pattern of Late Glacial and Holocene climatic and environmental development' (2019), pp. 27, 45f.

42   This table is adapted from: Baumer, *The History of Central Asia*, vol. 1 (2012), p. 46, which was inspired by Jacobson-Tepfer, Esther and Meacham, James E., *Archaeology and Landscape in the Mongolian Altai: An Atlas* (Redlands: ESRI Press, 2010), pp. 20f. Additional sources are: Jacobson-Tepfer, 'Late Pleistocene and Early Holocene rock art from the Mongolian Altai' (2013), pp. 151–181. *The Anatomy of Deep Time: Rock Art and Landscape in the Altai Mountains of Mongolia*

(Cambridge: Cambridge University Press, 2020), pp. 15–23. Klinge and Sauer, 'Spatial pattern of Late Glacial and Holocene climatic and environmental development' (2019), pp. 26f, 41, 45–47. Kurochkin, Evgeny N. et al., 'The timing of ostrich existence in Central Asia: AMS 14C age of eggshells from Mongolia and southern Siberia (a pilot study)', in: *Nuclear Instruments and Methods in Physics Research Section B: Beam Interactions with Materials and Atoms*, vol. 268, nos. 7–8 (Amsterdam: Elsevier, 2010), pp. 1091–1093. Morgan, Christopher et al., 'Paleolakes, archaeology, and Late Quarternary palaeoenvironments in northwestern Mongolia, in: *Quarternary Research*, 2022 (Cambridge: Cambridge University Press, 2022), pp. 1–15. Wright, Joshua and Janz, Lisa, 'The Younger Dryas in arid Northeast Asia', in: Eren, Metin I. (ed.), *Hunter-Gatherer Behavior: Human Response during the Younger Dryas* (New York: Routledge, 2012), pp. 231–247. A table highlighting the evolution of motifs and styles in Mongol petroglyphs from the Upper Palaeolithic to the Late Middle Ages is given by Molodin, Cheremisin et al., 'Chronology of rock art of the Russian and Mongolian Altai' (2023), pp. 68f.

43 Novozhenov, *Rock Art Chronicles of Golden Steppe*, vol. 1 (2020), p. 260.

44 For a detailed overview of the petroglyphs of Tsagaan Salaa in the form of ink drawings and photographs see: Sher and Francfort, *Répertoire des Pétroglyphes d'Asie centrale*, fasc. 6 (2001).

45 This Palaeolithic dating has also (not very convincingly) been challenged. Molodin and Cheremisin, 'The "Kalgutsinsky" style' (2019), p. 22.

46 The absence of representation of certain species does not of course mean they did not exist or played no economic role. For example, domestic pigs, poultry and insects are virtually excluded from Central Asian petroglyphs; birds are only rarely shown.

47 Jacobson-Tepfer, Esther, *The Life of Two Valleys in the Bronze Age: Rock Art in the Altai Mountains of Mongolia* (Eugene: Luminare Press, 2019), p. 166.

48 The present author observed this hunting tactic in central Mongolia in 2001.

49 Erdenebaatar D., 'Burial materials related to the history of the Bronze Age in the territory of Mongolia', in: Linduff, Katheryn M. (ed.), *Metallurgy in Ancient Eastern Eurasia from the Urals to the Yellow River* (Lampeter: Edwin Mellen, 2004), p. 197.

50 Shvets, Irina, *Studien zur Felsbildkunst Kasachstans* (Darmstadt: Philipp von Zabern, 2012), p. 188. There are petroglyphs where people on foot carry ball flails or throw stones. Jacobson-Tepfer, Esther, *Monumental Archaeology in the Mongolian Altai: Intention, Memory, Myth* (Leiden: Brill, 2023), p. 179, fig. 7.20.

51 Kšica and Kšicová, *Felsbilder zwischen Schwarzem Meer und Beringstrasse* (1994), pp. 175–179, 269.

52 Kšica and Kšicová, *Felsbilder zwischen Schwarzem Meer und Beringstrasse* (1994), pp. 201, 203.

53 Sher and Francfort, *Répertoire des Pétroglyphes d'Asie centrale*, fasc. 6, vol. 1 (2001), fig. 382. See also: Devlet, *Myths in Stone* (2005), p. 131.

54 Jacobson, Esther, *The Deer Goddess of Ancient Siberia: A Study in the Ecology of Belief* (Leiden: Brill, 1993), p. 195.

55 Ernits, Enn, 'On the cosmic hunt in Northern Eurasian rock art', in: *Folklore*, vol. 44 (Tartu: Folkloristenserver Haldjas, 2010), pp. 69–72. Hunters used skis to pursue deer or elk in winter since a skier would not sink, while deep snow would hamper the prey's flight. The

oldest excavated skis from *ca.* the seventh to sixth millennium BCE were found in the Ural region, Russia. Jacobson-Tepfer, E. and Novozhenov, V.A., *Rock Art Chronicles of Golden Steppe*, vol. 2: *From Karatau to Altai* (Almaty: UNESCO Centre for the Rapprochement of Cultures, 2020), pp. 146f.

56 Kšica and Kšicová, *Felsbilder zwischen Schwarzem Meer und Beringstrasse* (1994), p. 267. Devlet, *Myths in Stone* (2005), pp. 119f.

57 Kšica and Kšicová, *Felsbilder zwischen Schwarzem Meer und Beringstrasse* (1994), pp. 244f. A similar petroglyph exists at Tomskaya Pisanitsa on the right bank of the River Tom' west of Khakassia. Devlet, *Myths in Stone* (2005), p. 119.

58 Less probably, the myth could also be connected to solar or lunar eclipses.

59 Devlet, *Myths in Stone* (2005), p. 236.

60 Okladnikow, *Der Hirsch mit dem goldenen Geweih* (1972), pp. 47f.

61 Leont'ev, Nikolaj V. and Kapel'ko, Vladimir F., *Steinstelen der Okunev-Kultur* (Mainz: Philipp von Zabern, 2002), p. 48.

62 Leont'ev and Kapel'ko, *Steinstelen der Okunev-Kultur* (2002) p. 49, fig. 19.

63 Translation from the German by the author. Okladnikow, *Der Hirsch mit dem goldenen Geweih* (1972), p. 46.

64 Devlet, *Myths in Stone* (2005), p. 164. Mykhailova, Nataliia, '"Celestial Deer": The flight from the Stone Age to the Middle Ages', in: Anati, Emmanuel (ed.), *The Function of Art* (Capo di Ponte: Atelier, 2021), p. 99.

65 Okladnikow, *Der Hirsch mit dem goldenen Geweih* (1972), p. 100.

66 Davidson, H.R. Ellis, *Scandinavian Mythology* (Feltham: Newnes Books, 1984), pp. 51–54, 120.

67 Nash Briggs, Daphne, 'Reading the images on Iron-Age coins: 3. Some cosmic wolves' (n.d.).

68 A similar myth is known among the Iroquois (Haudenosaunee). d'Huy, Julien, 'The evolution of myths', in: *Scientific American*, vol. 315, no. 6 (New York: Springer Nature, 2016), p. 64. According to d'Huy, this myth is also found among the North African Berbers. 'A cosmic hunt in the Berber sky: A phylogenetic reconstruction of a Palaeolithic mythology', in: *Les Cahiers de l'AARS*, no. 16 (St-Benoist-sur-Mer: AARS, 2013), p. 101. See also: Berezkin, Yuri, 'The cosmic hunt: Variants of a Siberian–North American myth', in: *Folklore* (Tartu: Folklore Electronic Journal, 2005), pp. 79–100.

69 Kardulias, P. Nick, 'Migration of *Homo Sapiens* out of Africa', in: Chiotis, Eustathios (ed.), *Climate Changes in the Holocene* (Boca Raton FL: CRS Press, 2019), p. 151. Sala, Renato, 'Interaction of climate, environment and humans in North and Central Asia during the Late Glacial and Holocene', ibid. (2019), p. 347. Ernits questions the representation of the cosmic hunt in rock art anywhere in Eurasia and northern Fennoscandia. Ernits, 'On the cosmic hunt' (2010), pp. 61–73.

70 For an overview of these steles see: Leont'ev and Kapel'ko, *Steinstelen der Okunev-Kultur* (2002), plates 1–120.

71 Leont'ev and Kapel'ko, *Steinstelen der Okunev-Kultur* (2002), figs 3, 32, 169, 174, 277.

72 For a photo see: Baumer, *The History of Central Asia*, vol. 1 (2012), p. 138.

73 Devlet, *Myths in stone* (2005), pp. 30, 185, 255, 286–288.

74 Kšica and Kšicová, *Felsbilder zwischen Schwarzem Meer und Beringstrasse* (1994), pp. 305–307.

75 Altuntas, Leman, 'Orta Asya'da ilk defa bir Boğa Jeoglifi Keşfedildi = A bull geoglyph discovered for the first time in Central Asia', in: *Arkeonews* (29 September 2021).

76 Kovalev, Alexey A. and Munkhbayar, Ch., 'Петроглифы на чемурчекских ритуальных оградах в высокогорье Монгольского Алтая (3 тыс до н.э.): репертуар образов = Petroglyphs of the Chemurchek ritual fences in the highlands of the Mongolian Altai (3rd millennium BC): Repertoire of images', in: Batbold, N., *Төв Азийн эртний нүүдэлчдийн хадны зураг = Petroglyphs of Ancient Nomads from Central Asia* (Ulaan Baatar: Nuhus, 2022), pp. 84–101. Kovalev, Alexey A. and Solodovnikov, K N. et al., 'Палеоантропологическое изучение черепа погребенного в захоронении на чемурчекском святилище Хулагаш (Баян-Ульгийский аймак Монголии) = 'Paleoanthropological study of a skull from a burial at the Chemurchek sanctuary Hulagash (Bayan-Ulgii aimag, Mongolia)', in: *Вестник археологии, антропологии и этнографии = Bulletin of Archaeology, Anthropology and Ethnography*, 48.1 (Novosibirsk: Institute of Archaeology and Ethnography, 2020), pp. 92f.

77 See below, pp. 66f.

78 See below, p. 166.

79 Kovalev, Alexey A. (ed.), *Древнейшие европейцы в сердце Азии: чемурчекский культурный феномен, vol. 2: Результаты исследований в центральной части Монгольского Алтая и в истоках Кобдо; памятники Синьцзяна и окраинных земель = Earliest Europeans in the Heart of Asia: The Chemurchek Cultural Phenomenon, vol. 2: Excavations in the Central Mongolian Altai and in the Headwaters of the Khovd River; Sites and Finds in Xinjiang and in Outlying Regions* (St Petersburg: MISR, 2015), pp. 155–214. Kovalev and Munkhbayar, 'Петроглифы на чемурчекских ритуальных оградах в высокогорье Монгольского Алтая' (2022), pp. 84–101.

80 Baumer, *The History of Central Asia*, vol. 1 (2012), pp. 175–186.

81 Petroglyphs of carts pulled by oxen or horses appeared earlier during the Okunev culture. Nowgorodowa, *Alte Kunst der Mongolei* (1980), pp. 98f.

82 Camels pulling wagons are not found in Tsagaan Salaa but are seen in Kazakhstan, for instance in Arpa-Uzen.

83 Sher and Francfort, *Répertoire des Pétroglyphes d'Asie centrale*, fasc. 6, vol. 1 (2001), figs 983, 986, vol. 2, pl. 327, 328.

84 Jacobson-Tepfer, Esther, *The Hunter, the Stag, and the Mother of Animals: Image, Monument, and Landscape in Ancient North Asia* (Oxford: Oxford University Press, 2015), pp. 211–218. *The Life of Two Valleys* (2019), p. 245.

85 Kortum, Richard, 'Sacred imagery and ritual landscape: New discoveries at the Biluut petroglyph complex in the Mongolian Altai', in: Lami, Martina Revello and Fernandez, Mónica Palmero (eds), *Time and Mind*, vol. 7, no. 4 (Abingdon: Routledge, 2014), pp. 364–367. *Ceremony in Stone: The Biluut Petroglyph Complex, Prehistoric Rock Art in the Mongolian Altai* (Ulaan Baatar: Nepko, 2018), p. 193. Judging from a painted copy, it seems that in the Zheminay district of the Chinese Altai there exists a similar petroglyph of galloping horses pulling a chariot. Novozhenov, *Communications and the Earliest Wheeled Transport* (2012), p. 68.

86 Samashev, Zainolla, *The History of Kazakhstan Fine Art: Ancient Time and Middle Ages* (Astana: Margulan Institute of Archaeology et al., 2013), fig. 106.

87 Hermann, Luc, 'The rock art site of Akterek in Kazakhstan (Almaty Oblast)', in: *International Newsletter on Rock Art*, no. 76 (Foix: 2016), fig. 10.

88 A similar petroglyph scene existed at Oglakhty until its destruction in 1966. Sher and Francfort, *Répertoire des Pétroglyphes d'Asie centrale*, fasc. 1 (1994), p. xxviii. Jacobson-Tepfer, 'The rock art of Mongolia' (2006), fig. 8.

89 Another, albeit unclear, image of a Lord of Animals exists at Saimaluu Tash, Kyrgyzstan. The farthest west image of a Lord of Animals is a limestone lintel featuring a double-headed male figure taming two horses from *ca.* 300–100 BCE from Cuevas del Almanzora, Spain. https://mac.colleccions.cat/objecte/mac-bcn-019892/ (accessed 24 Nov. 2024).

90 Homer, *Iliad*, XXI.470.

91 Sources: personal archive of the author and a lecture given by the archaeologist Laurent Gorgerat in November 2022 in Basel, Switzerland. See also: Sher and Francfort, *Répertoire des Pétroglyphes d'Asie centrale*, fasc. 1 (1994), p. xxviii–xxxi.

92 The same Bronze and Iron Age development towards the representation of combat scenes in petroglyphs occurred throughout Central Asia.

93 Jacobson-Tepfer, Esther, 'Rock Art research in Mongolia, 2005–2009', in: Bahn, et al., *Rock Art Studies: News of the World*, vol. 4 (2012), p. 175, fig. 11.22. For additional duel and battle scenes see: Sher and Francfort, *Répertoire des Pétroglyphes d'Asie centrale*, fasc. 6, vol. 1 (2001), figs 124–129, 832, 1193, 1262.

94 The Greek epics have survived, the Nordic and Alpine ones have been lost or are only fragmentarily preserved in later sagas.

95 Aruz, Joan et al. (eds), *The Golden Deer of Eurasia: Perspectives on the Steppe Nomads of the Ancient World* (New York: The Metropolitan Museum of Art, 2000), p. 193.

96 Not all khirigsuurs were actual burials: many of them were cenotaphs where commemorative rituals were performed. Takahama, Shu et al., 'Preliminary report of the archaeological investigations in Ulaan Uushig I (Uushigiin Övör) in Mongolia, in: 金沢大学考古学紀要 = *Kanazawa University Archeology Bulletin*, vol. 28 (Kanazawa: The University of Kanazawa, 2006), pp. 67, 76. Williams, James, 'The Tahilt region: A preliminary archaeological survey of the Tahilt surroundings to contextualize the Tahilt cemeteries', in: *The Silk Road*, vol. 5, no. 2 (Berkeley: The Silkroad House, 2005), p. 43.

97 Fitzhugh, William, 'Stone shamans and flying deer of northern Mongolia: Deer goddess of Siberia or chimera of the steppe?', in: *Arctic Anthropology*, vol. 46, nos 1–2 (Madison: University of Wisconsin, 2009), p. 77. 'The Mongolian deer stone–khirigsuur complex: Dating and organization of a late Bronze Age menagerie', in: Bemmann, Jan et al., *Current Archaeological Research in Mongolia* (Bonn: R.F.W.-Universität, 2009, p. 183.

98 Leont'ev and Kapel'ko, *Steinstelen der Okunev-Kultur* (2002). Rogozhinsky, Alexey and Novozhenov, Viktor, Культурные ландшафты с петроглифами центральной Азии в вопросах и ответах: *Central Asia Cultural and Rock Art Landscapes: Frequently Asked Questions* (Samarkand: International Institute for Central Asian Studies, 2018), p. 80.

99 See below, p. 66. The Chemurchek culture is dated to 2600–1800 BCE. Kovalev, Alexey A., 'The Chemurchek (Qie'muerqieke) cultural phenomenon as a result of Western European migration to Dzungaria and the Mongolian Altai', in: Baumer, Christoph, Novák, Mirko and Rutishauser, Susanne (eds), *Cultures in Contact* (Wiesbaden: Harrassowitz, 2022), pp. 534, 547.

100 Kubarev, Gleb V., *Alttürkische Gräber des Altaj* (Bonn: Habelt, 2017), pp. 238f, figs 228–30.

101 Translation from the German by the author. Radloff, Wilhelm, *Aus Sibirien* (2 vols, Leipzig: Weigel Nachfolger, 1893), vol. 2, p. 92.

102 Essin, Yury N., 'Les peintures dans l'art pariétal de la culture Okuniev', in: *Bulletin Musée d'Anthropologie préhistorique de Monaco*, vol. 54 (Monaco: MAP, 2014), pp. 167–177. 'Paint on deer stones of Mongolia', in: *Archaeology, Ethnology and Anthropology of Eurasia*, vol. 45 (Novosibirsk: Russian Academy of Sciences, 2017), pp. 80, 85.

103 Nowgorodowa, *Alte Kunst der Mongolei* (1980), pp. 131–169. See also: Fitzhugh, 'Stone shamans and flying deer' (2009), p. 78.

104 One stele can be found in the museum of the nearby village of Mörön. When the fallen deer stones were put back up, most were incorrectly oriented to the south instead of the east. For drawings of the carvings on the fifteen deer stones see: Takahama et al., 'Preliminary report' (2006), pp. 95–102.

105 The numbering follows Novgorodova, who was one of the first to explore the area. Nowgorodowa, *Alte Kunst der Mongolei* (1980), pp. 133–149. In her reconstruction Novgorodova presents three rows of steles, although there were presumably just two. Takahama et al., 'Preliminary report' (2006), p. 84.

106 Takahama et al., 'Preliminary Report' (2006), pp. 76, 79. Two other deer stones with human faces stand at the lower Tsagaan Gol. For an image see: Jacobson-Tepfer, *Monumental Archaeology in the Mongolian Altai* (2023), p. 175, fig. 7.17.

107 The deer stones at Jargalantyn Am have been re-erected since the authors' visit in 2001, destroying the Iron Age slab graves. Reckel, Johannes and Schatz, Merle, *Fliegende Hirsche und Sonnengötter. Prähistorische Gesellschaften in Felsbildern Zentralasiens* (Oppenheim am Rhein: Nünnerich-Asmus, 2022), figs 62, 63.

108 Lepetz S. et al., 'Customs, rites, and sacrifices relating to a mortuary complex in Late Bronze Age Mongolia (Tsatsyn Ereg, Arkhangai)', in: Lepetz S. et al., *Occupations et espaces sacrés dans l'Altaï mongol: les sites archéologiques de Burgast et Ikh Khatuu (1100 a.C.–1100 p.C.)* (Drémil-Lafage: Editions Mergoil, 2022), pp. 151–177. 'Cheval et pensée symbolique', in: *Archéologia*, no. 632 (Dijon: Faton, 2024), pp. 36f.

109 Magail, Jérôme et al., 'Bronze Age and Iron Age decorated megaliths and funerary complexes in Mongolia and Southern Siberia', in: Laporte, Luc and Large, Jean-Marie (eds), *Megaliths of the World*, vol. 2 (Oxford: Archaeopress, 2022), p. 749.

110 Menghin, Wilfried et al. (eds), *Im Zeichen des goldenen Greifen. Königsgräber der Skythen* (Munich: Prestel, 2007), p. 129, fig. 14. Rudenko, Sergei, *Frozen Tombs of Siberia: The Pazyryk Burials of Iron-Age Horsemen* (London: Dent & Sons, 1970), plates 119–124. Samashev, Zainolla et al., 'Le kourgane de Berel dans l'Altaï kazakhstanais', in: *Arts asiatiques*, vol. 55 (Paris: Musée national des Arts asiatiques-Guimet, 2000), pp. 13, 18.

111 Menghin et al., *Im Zeichen des goldenen Greifen*, p. 153. Molodin, Vjačeslav I. et al. 'Das skythenzeitliche Kriegergrab aus Olin-Kurin-Gol. Neue Entdeckungen in der Permafrostzone des mongolischen Altaj', in: *Eurasia Antiqua*, vol. 14 (2008) (Deutsches Archäologisches Institut, Berlin; Mainz: Philipp von Zabern, 2009), p. 258.

112 Menghin et al., *Im Zeichen des goldenen Greifen*, p. 134.

113 Molodin, Cheremisin et al., 'Chronology of Rock Art of the Russian and Mongolian Altai' (2023), pp. 68 (fig. 2.34), 73.

114 Véronique Schiltz hypothesizes a connection between this burial and an Indo-Iranian functionary in the service of the Mitanni state. Schiltz, *Die Skythen und andere Steppenvölker* (Munich: C.H. Beck, 1994), p. 269.

115 The term Andronovians is used as an ethnonym in the sense of 'carriers of Andronovian culture'.

116 In addition, there are the so-called *balbal*, mostly unworked stones, approx. 30 to 80 cm high, which were placed in straight lines next to graves or sacrificial platforms and which were supposed to symbolize the enemies killed by the buried person.

117 Both the Scythians and Saka belonged mainly to Europid peoples, but neither were homogenous. They were rather a cultural community of mostly Europid horsemen who spoke Iranian languages and dialects. Of these Iron Age horsemen, those living west of the Urals are referred to as Scythians, and those in the east as Saka.

118 The Scytho-Siberian Animal Style was also influenced by the figurative art of the Chinese Warring States period (475–221 BCE).

119 Baumer, *The History of Central Asia*, vol. 1 (2012), pp. 175–195, 224–253.

120 Baumer, Christoph, *Die Südliche Seidenstrasse. Inseln im Sandmeer. Versunkene Kulturen der Wüste Taklamakan* (Mainz: Philipp von Zabern, 2002), pp. 22f. Keller, Dominik and Schorta, Regula, *Fabulous Creatures from the Desert Sands: Central Asian Woolen Textiles from the Second Century BC to the Second Century AD* (Riggisberg: Abegg-Stiftung, 2001), pp. 23–45.

121 Baumer, *The History of Central Asia*, vol. 1 (2012), p. 255. Keller and Schorta, *Fabulous Creatures from the Desert Sands* (2001), pp. 39f.

122 Keller and Schorta, *Fabulous Creatures from the Desert Sands* (2001), pp. 15, 150.

123 Baumer, *The History of Central Asia*, vol. 1 (2012), p. 181. Devlet, *Myths in Stone* (2005), pp. 101–4. Rozwadowski, Andrzej, *Symbols through Time: Interpreting the Rock Art of Central Asia* (Poznań: Adam Mickiewicz University, 2004), pp. 89f.

124 Baumer, Christoph, *The History of Central Asia*, vol. 2: *The Age of the Silk Roads* (London: I.B.Tauris, 2014), p. 32.

125 Göktürk means 'Blue', that is 'Celestial', Turks.

126 Nowgorodowa, *Alte Kunst der Mongolei* (1980), p. 215.

127 Devlet, *Myths in Stone* (2005), p. 53. Kubarev, *Alttürkische Gräber des Altaj* (2017), pp. 144, fig. 146; 158, fig. 162. Jacobson-Tepfer and Novozhenov, *Rock Art Chronicles of Golden Steppe*, vol. 2 (2020), pp. 301–333.

128 Rudenko, Sergey I. and Glukhov, Alexey N., 'Kudyrge burial ground in Altai', in: *Materials on Ethnography*, vol. 3, no. 2 (Leningrad: State Publisher of Russian Museums, 1927), pp. 37–52.

129 Kenk, Roman, *Früh- und hochmittelalterliche Gräber von Kudyrge im Altai* (Munich: C.H. Beck, 1982), pp. 18, 45, fig. 10.

130 Konstantinov, Nikita et al., 'Battle and hunting scenes in Turkic rock art of the early Middle Ages in Altai', in: *Rock Art Research*, vol. 33, no. 1 (Darwin: International Federation of Rock Art Organizations, 2016), pp. 8–18. Kšica and Kšicová, *Felsbilder zwischen Schwarzem Meer und Beringstrasse* (1994), p. 153.

131 Tatiev, E.E., et al., 'Semiotic analysis of petroglyph "Ancient Turks and the Mother Goddess Umay/ Umai"', in: *Rupkatha Journal on Interdisciplinary Studies in Humanities*, vol. 13, no. 3 (Murshidabad: 2021), pp. 1–16.

132 Kovalev, 'The Chemurchek (Qie'muerqieke) cultural phenomenon' (2022), pp. 535, 547.

133 Kšica and Kšicová, *Felsbilder zwischen Schwarzem Meer und Beringstrasse* (1994), pp. 222–224.

134 Aubekerov, R.J., Sala R. and Nigmatova, S.A., 'Late Holocene paleoclimate and paleogeography in the Tien Shan–Balkhash region', in: *PAGES News*, vol. 11, nos 2–3 (Bern: University of Bern, 2003), p. 25. Shvets, *Studien zur Felsbildkunst Kasachstans* (2012), pp. 7f.

135 Manco, Jean, *Ancestral Journeys: The Peopling of Europe from the First Venturers to the Vikings* (London: Thames and Hudson, 2021), p. 139.

136 With minor changes, we follow the periodization of Sala and Deom. Sala, Renato and Deom, Jean-Marc, *Petroglyphs of South Kazakhstan* (Almaty: Laboratory of Geoarchaeology, 2005), pp. 54–57.

137 Clottes, Jean (ed.), *Rock Art in Central Asia: A Thematic Study* (Paris: ICOMOS, 2011), pp. 9–42. Sala and Deom, *Petroglyphs of South Kazakhstan* (2005), pp. 75–126.

138 The Chalcolithic, also called Copper Age, is the transitional period between the Neolithic and the Bronze Age.

139 Baipakov, Karl and Maryashev, Alexey N., *Петроглифы Баян-Журека / Petroglyphs of Bayan Zhurek* (Almaty: Credos, 2008).

140 Baipakov, Karl, Maryashev, Alexey N. et al., *Петроглифы в горах Ешкиольмес / The Eshkiolmes Rock's Petroglyphs* (Almaty: OST-XXI Vek, 2005), pp. 79, 83f.

141 Lymer, Kenneth, 'The petroglyphs of Terekty Aulie in central Kazakhstan', in: Anati, Emmanuel (ed.), *Expression*, no. 8 (Capo di Ponte: Atelier, 2015), p. 96f.

142 Baipakov, Karl and Maryashev, Alexey N., *Петроглифы Малого Каратау и западной оконечности Киргизского Алатау = Petroglyphs of the Lesser Karatau and the Western End of the Kyrgyz Alatau* (Almaty: Archaeological Expertise, 2013), p. 20.

143 Rogozhinsky, Alexey E, 'Shatyrtas: Discovery of rock paintings', in: Jacobson-Tepfer and Novozhenov, *Rock Art Chronicles of Golden Steppe*, vol. 2 (2020), pp. 110–129. 'Rock art in western Central Asia (2015–2019)', in: Bahn et al., *Rock Art Studies: News of the World*, vol. 6 (2021), pp. 120f.

144 Samashev, Zainolla, *Petroglyphs of the East Kazakhstan as a Historical Sources* (Almaty: Rakurs, 1993), pp. 62–65. *Петроглифы Казахстана = Petroglyphs of Kazakhstan* (Almaty: Öner, 2006), pp. 28–30. 'Petroglyphs of Kazakhstan', in: Tashbayeva K. et al., *Petroglyphs of Central Asia* (Bishkek: International Institute for Central Asian Studies, 2001), pp. 153–158.

145 A drawing by O.N. Gumirova of this scene published by Abay Saduakasuly et al. shows a circle above the horns of the bull which the authors interpret as the sun, suggesting the myth in which hunters chase the bull which carries the abducted sun on its horns. However, in the image (fig. 50) of a rubbing taken *in situ* and a photograph of the scene no circle about the

bull's horns is visible. Saduakasuly A., Zheleznyakov, B.A. and Hermann, L., *Құлжабасы сілемінің жартас өнері / Наскальное искусство хребта Кулжабасы = The Rock Art of the Kulzhabasy Range* (Almaty: Zhambyl, 2017), p. 115.

146 Rogozhinsky, Alexey E., *Petroglyphs within the Archaeological Landscape of Tamgaly* (Almaty: Margulan Institute of Archaeology, 2011), pp. 32–57.

147 Rogozhinsky, *Petroglyphs within the Archaeological Landscape of Tamgaly* (2011), pp. 170–178.

148 Baipakov, Karl, Maryashev, Alexey and Potapov, S.A., *Петроглифы Тамгалы / Petroglyphs of Tamgaly* (Almaty: Margulan Archaeological Institute, 2006), p. 69. See also: Shvets, *Studien zur Felsbildkunst Kasachstans* (2012), p. 117.

149 Rogozhinsky, *Petroglyphs within the Archaeological Landscape of Tamgaly* (2011), pp. 185, 187, 209.

150 Samashev, *Petroglyphs of the East Kazakhstan* (1993), p. 67, fig. 153.

151 Mar'yashev, A.N., *Petroglyphs of South Kazakhstan and Semirechye* (Almaty: Margulan Institute of Archaeology, 1994), photo 6. Novozhenov, *Rock Art Chronicles of Golden Steppe*, vol. 1 (2020), fig. 183 top.

152 Hermann, Luc, 'Rock art of Tamgaly, Kazakhstan', in: *Adoranten* (Tanumshede: Scandinavian Society for Prehistoric Art, 2011), p. 35.

153 Mar'yashev, *Petroglyphs of South Kazakhstan and Semirechye* (1994), p. 20. *Rig Veda*, book 1, hymn 130.10.

154 Baipakov, Karl and Maryashev, Alexey N., *Петроглифы Ак-Кайнара / Petroglyphs of Ak-Kainar* (Almaty: Credos, 2009), p. 36.

155 Francfort, Henri-Paul, 'Les pétroglyphes de Tamgaly', in: *Bulletin of the Asia Institute*, vol. 9 (1995) (Bloomfield Hills, MI: The Asia Institute, 1997), pp. 168, 185–190. Hermann, Luc, 'Les cultes du soleil et du taureau dans l'art rupestre de l'âge du Bronze en Asie centrale (Kazakhstan et Kirghizstan)', in: *Praehistoria*, vol. 1–2 (11–12), (Miskolc: University of Miskolc, 2019–2020), pp. 310–315.

156 Baipakov and Maryashev, *Петроглифы Ак-Кайнара / Petroglyphs of Ak-Kainar* (2009), pp. 40f. Verbal explanations to the author by Alexey Rogozhinsky on 5 August, 2018 *in situ*.

157 Francfort, 'Les pétroglyphes de Tamgaly' (1997), pp. 186, 188, 193f.

158 Shvets, *Studien zur Felsbildkunst Kasachstans* (2012), pp. 41f.

159 For an image see: Francfort, 'Les pétroglyphes de Tamgaly' (1997), p. 190, fig. 6.

160 Herodotus, *The Histories*, tr. Aubrey de Sélincourt (London: Penguin, 2003), I.216, p. 94.

161 *Rig Veda*, book 1, hymn 14.1. Anthony, *The Horse, the Wheel and Language* (2007), pp. 370–375, 405–411. Rozwadowski, *Symbols through Time* (2004), pp. 38–42.

162 For a drawing of the whole scene, see: Rogozhinsky, *Petroglyphs within the Archaeological Landscape of Tamgaly* (2011), p. 185.

163 Rogozhinsky, *Petroglyphs within the Archaeological Landscape of Tamgaly* (2011), p. 78,

164 At Ak-Kainar 30 sun-headed figures have been recorded. Hermann, Luc and Zheleznyakov, B., 'Tamga petroglyphs from Akkainar (Almaty Region) in Kazakhstan', in: *Қазақстан археологиясы = Archaeology of Kazakhstan*, no. 22 (Almaty: Margulan Institute of Archaeology, 2023), p. 142.

165 Today, 26 sun-headed deities are known in Tamgaly. Hermann, 'Rock Art of Tamgaly, Kazakhstan' (2011), p. 35. For the subject of bull and sun-headed figures see also: Hermann, 'Les cultes du soleil et du taureau dans l'art rupestre de l'âge du Bronze en Asie centrale' (2019–2020), pp. 303–327.

166 Baipakov and Maryashev, *Петроглифы в горах Ешкиольмес / The Eshkiolmes Rock's Petroglyphs* (2005), p. 118.

167 Francfort, 'Central Asian petroglyphs' (1998), p. 309.

168 Kubarev, Vladimir D., *Древние росписи Каракола = Old Paintings of Karakol* (Novosibirsk: Nauka Publishing House, 1988), pp. 28–31, 39–42, 50, 60, 69f, 168–172. Rozwadowski, *Symbols through Time*, p. 69.

169 Essin, 'Les peintures dans l'art pariétal de la culture Okuniev' (2014), figs 6, 13, 14.

170 Such vehicles are discussed below in the section on Saimaluu Tash, Kyrgyzstan, pp. 94ff.

171 Baumer, *The History of Central Asia*, vol. 1 (2012), pp. 98, 117.

172 *Rig Veda*, book 4, hymn 13.2; book 7, hymns 61.1, 63.5, 65.1,7,12. Shvets, *Studien zur Felsbildkunst Kasachstans* (2012), p. 115.

173 *Khorda-Avesta*, VII, XXVI.17–35; *Avesta. Die heiligen Schriften der Parsen*, trans. Friedrich Spiegel (1863; Reprint: Paris: Adamant, 2006), vol. III. pp. 9, 89–102.

174 Hermann, 'Rock art of Tamgaly, Kazakhstan' (2011), p. 35, fig. 21.

175 Hermann, 'Rock art of Tamgaly, Kazakhstan' (2011), p. 35.

176 Novgorodva, *Alte Kunst der Mongolei* (1980), pp. 152, 169.

177 Shvets, *Studien zur Felsbildkunst Kasachstans* (2012), p. 169, plate 91. Without suggesting any connection, it is striking that a very similar ibex-headed swastika was found in the Nafud Desert, Saudi Arabia. See below pp. 278f, fig. 246.

178 Rozwadowski, *Symbols through Time* (2004), pp. 60–63, 74. Samashev, *Petroglyphs of the East Kazakhstan* (1993), fig. 172.

179 Mar'yashev, *Petroglyphs of South Kazakhstan and Semirechye* (1994), fig. 121.

180 Baipakov and Maryashev, *Петроглифы Малого Каратау / Petroglyphs of the Lesser Karatau* (2013), p. 37, photo 16.

181 For drawings see: Shvets, *Studien zur Felsbildkunst Kasachstans* (2012), plate 33 top.

182 Baipakov, Maryashev, *Петроглифы в горах Ешкиольмес / The Eshkiolmes Rock's Petroglyphs* (2005), fig. 12.

183 Samashev, *Петроглифы Казахстана = Petroglyphs of Kazakhstan* (2006), pp. 94–99.

184 Shvets, *Studien zur Felsbildkunst Kasachstans* (2012), plates 115, 116.

185 Baipakov and Maryashev et al., *The Eshkiolmes Rock's Petroglyphs* (2005), figs 12, 13, 23, 134. Samashev, *Petroglyphs of the East Kazakhstan* (1993), fig. 87. Shvets, *Studien zur Felsbildkunst Kasachstans* (2012), plates 101, 104.

186 Baipakov and Mariashev, *Петроглифы в горах Ешкиольмес / The Eshkiolmes Rock's Petroglyphs* (2005), figs 23, 232. Samashev, *Petroglyphs of the East Kazakhstan* (1993), figs 25, 26, 174. Shvets, *Studien zur Felsbildkunst Kasachstans* (2012), plate 105.

187 Samashev, *Petroglyphs of the East Kazakhstan* (1993), pp. 16, 48, 50, fig. 26. A similar scene of homicide exists at Tsagaan Salaa, Mongolia. Sher and Francfort,

Répertoire des Pétroglyphes d'Asie centrale, fasc. 6, vol. 1 (2001), fig. 642.

188 Baumer, *The History of Central Asia*, vol. 2 (2014), p. 174.

189 I thank Alexey Rogozhinsky for having shown me this interesting site and for having shared his knowledge about it.

190 Belenizki, A.M., *Mittelasien. Kunst der Sogden* (Leipzig: VEB E.A. Seemann, 1980), plates 30, 38; p. 82 top.

191 Baumer, *The History of Central Asia*, vol. 2 (2014), figs 186f, 195.

192 Shvets, *Studien zur Felsbildkunst Kasachstans* (2012), pp. 37f.

193 Samashev, Zainolla et al., *Treasures from the Ustyurt Plateau* (Almaty: Aktau State University, 2007), pp. 192–200. Rogozhinsky, Alexey E. 'Medieval Petroglyph Tamgas of Southern Kazakhstan and Semirechie', in: Voyakin and Iskanderova, *Tamgas of Pre-Islamic Central Asia* (q.v. 2019), p. 249. Yatsenko, Sergey and Rogozhinsky A.E., 'Introduction', in: ibid; pp. 19f.

194 Yatsenko, Sergey, 'Signs of the Early Nomads on the Ustyurt Plateau', in: Voyakin and Iskanderova, *Tamgas of Pre-Islamic Central Asia* (q.v. 2019), p. 65. 'General and Special Use of Tamgas by the Ancient People of Central Asia', in: ibid; p. 399.

195 Baumer, *The History of Central Asia*, vol. 1 (2012), p. 261. Yatsenko, Sergey, 'Marks of the Ancient and medieval Iranian-speaking peoples of Iran, Eastern Europe, Transoxiana and South Siberia', in: Pim, Joám Evans et al. (eds) *Traditional Marking Systems: A Preliminary Survey* (London & Dover: Dunkling Books, 2010), pp. 139–41.

196 Yatsenko, Sergey and Ilyasov, Jangar, 'Tamgas/Nishan and socio-political history', in: Voyakin and Iskanderova, *Tamgas of Pre-Islamic Central Asia* (2019), pp. 299–306.

197 Yatsenko, Sergey, 'Signs of the Early Nomads on the Ustyurt Plateau', in: Voyakin and Iskanderova, *Tamgas of Pre-Islamic Central Asia* (q.v. 2019), p. 67. 'General and Special Use of Tamgas by the Ancient People of Central Asia', in: Voyakin and Iskanderova, *Tamgas of Pre-Islamic Central Asia* (q.v. 2019), p. 400. See also: Samashev, 'Petroglyphs of Kazakhstan' (2001), p. 212.

198 Yatsenko and Ilyasov, 'Tamgas/Nishan and socio-political history' (2019), p. 314. See also: Yatsenko, Sergey and Rogozhinsky A.E., 'Introduction', in: Voyakin and Iskanderova, *Tamgas of Pre-Islamic Central Asia* (q.v. 2019), pp. 27–30.

199 Sala and Deom, *Petroglyphs of South Kazakhstan* (2005), p. 109f.

200 Jacobson-Tepfer and Novozhenov, *Rock Art Chronicles of Golden Steppe*, vol. 2 (2020), p. 210.

201 Samashev, *Петроглифы Казахстана = Petroglyphs of Kazakhstan* (2006), pp. 150–161.

202 Belli, Oktay, *Kırgızistan'da Taş Balbal ve İnsan Biçimli Heykeller / Stone Balbals and Statues in Human Form in Kirghizistan* (Istanbul: Arkeoloji ve Sanat Yayınları, 2003), p. 108.

203 The Wusun (second century BCE–fifth century CE) were semi-mobile pastoralists who probably spoke an East Iranian language. They migrated from their homeland of Gansu to Semirech'e in the second century BCE. Baumer, *The History of Central Asia*, vol. 2 (2014), pp. 37f.

204 The Paraloid B-72 application was done in 2002 on the recommendation of the German professor Bodo Anke. Brajer, Isabelle et al., 'The removal of aged acrylic coatings from wall paintings using microemulsions': *ICOM-CC 17th Triennial Conference 2014 Preprints* ([Paris]: The International Council of Museums, 2014). Kęsik, Jacek et al., 'Documenting archaeological petroglyph sites with the use of 3D terrestrial laser scanners: A case study of petroglyphs in Kyrgyzstan', in: Milosz, Marek and Kęsik, Jacek (eds), *Applied Sciences*, vol. 12, no. 20, special Issue: *3D Information Technologies for Tangible and Intangible Cultural Heritage* (Basel: MDPI, 2022), art. no. 10521.

205 One of these two impressive deer was heavily vandalized between 2004 and 2017.

206 The author led a team of nine to the site in early August 2017, staying there a week. For transport, a Mi-8 helicopter was rented from the army.

207 Rogozhinsky, Alexey E., 'Petroglyph sites of Kazakhstan and Western Central Asia as part of the archaeological landscape: New challenges', in: *Archaeology, Ethnology and Anthropology of Eurasia*, vol. 36 (Amsterdam: Elsevier, 2008), p. 86.

208 The estimate given by Tashbayeva of 11,500 engraved stones seems too high. Tashbayeva, K., 'Petroglyphs of Kyrgyzstan', in: Tashbayeva K. et al., *Petroglyphs of Central Asia* (Bishkek: International Institute for Central Asian Studies, 2001), pp. 16, 21f. The estimate of *ca.* 5,000 stones advanced here is rooted in an extrapolation taken from the GIS-based map made of the main moraine at Saimaluu Tash I. Hermann, for his part, mentions about 3,000 rocks. Hermann, Luc, 'La sexualité dans l'art rupestre d'Asie entrale', in: *Notae Praehistoricae* 35 (Liège: Studia praehistorica belgica, 2015), p. 59.

209 Martynov, A.J., Mariachev, A.N. and Abetekov, A.K., *Gravures rupestres de Saimaly-Tach*, ed. Karl Baipakov (Almaty: Ministère de l'instruction publique, 1992), pp. 13f. After Bernshtam came the mathematician N.I. Podolsky in 1963, in 1966–68 the historian Yu.N. Golendukhin and in 1968–73 G.A. Pomaskina, 1977–8 again Golendukhin and Y.A. Sher; later E.A. Novgorodova, A.N. Maryashev, A.J. Martynov, K. Tashbayeva and A.E. Rogozhinsky. Martynov et al., *Gravures rupestres* (1992), pp. 6–13. Sher, Yakov, 'Interpretation of scenes on some petroglyphs of Saymaly Tash', in: Lukonin, V.G. (ed.), *Культура Востока: Древность и раннее средневековье = Culture of the East: Antiquity and Early Middle Ages* (Leningrad: Aurora, 1978), pp. 163–166. Tashbayeva, 'Petroglyphs of Kyrgyzstan' (2001), pp. 11–16. More recently, Luc Hermann researched the site from 2012 to 2017. For Hermann's publications, see the Bibliography.

210 On other rocks there are also scenes of bestiality between a man and a horse, foal or goat.

211 Rogozhinsky, 'Petroglyph sites of Kazakhstan and Western Central Asia' (2008), p. 88.

212 It remains difficult to decide if the petroglyphs of two humans facing each other with their arms held high are dancing, fighting or in veneration.

213 Sher, 'Interpretation of scenes on some petroglyphs of Saymaly Tash' (1978), pp. 168–170. Shvets, *Studien zur Felsbildkunst Kasachstans* (2012), pp. 24, 196.

214 Two different animals can indeed be yoked into a single harness. Semenenko Aleksandr, 'бычье-эквидные упряжки двухколёсных повозок в древности и современности = Two-wheeled ox-drawn carriages in antiquity and modern times' (Voronezh: 2021).

215 Martynov et al., *Gravures rupestres* (1992), p. 42.

216 Sher, 'Interpretation of scenes on some petroglyphs of Saymaly Tash' (1978), pp. 165–170.

217 *Rig Veda*, book 2, hymn 13.2. Baumer, *The History of Central Asia*, vol. 1 (2012), p. 94.

218 *Rig Veda*, book 1, hymn 116.18; book 1, hymn 34.19. Sher, 'Interpretation of scenes on some petroglyphs of Saymaly Tash' (1978), pp. 165–170.

219 https://www.clevelandart.org/art/2001.2. Semenenko, 'Two-wheeled ox-drawn carriages' (2021).

220 Herodotus, *The Histories*, VII.40 (2003), pp. 431f.

221 *Rig Veda*, for example, 1.50.1, 1.164.2, 5.63.7.

222 Martynov et al., *Gravures rupestres* (1992), p. 26.

223 Lhuillier, Johanna, 'Intercultural interactions of the Sine Sepulchro cultural community (Handmade Painted Ware cultures) of the Early Iron Age with the neighbouring cultures of Asia and the Near East', in: Baumer, Novák and Rutishauser, *Cultures in Contact* (2022), pp. 140–142.

224 Masson, V.M. and Ploskich, V.M., *По следам памятников истории и культуры Киргизстана = On the Track of Memorials to the History and Culture of Kyrgyzstan* (Frunze: Ilim, 1982), pp. 22f. Shvets, *Studien zur Felsbildkunst Kasachstans* (2012), pp. 25, 137.

225 As the author noticed in 2017 from dated graffiti, the site had been visited several times before the alleged rediscovery by Gaponenko in 1956, namely in 1939, 1946, 20 July 1947, 24 August 1949 and 24 August 1950.

226 Tashbayeva et al., *Petroglyphs of Central Asia* (2002), pp. 53–60. Tashbaeva K. and Francfort, H.-P. 'Studies of the Zhaltyrak-Tash petroglyphs', in: *Bulletin of IICAS*, vol. 1 (Samarkand: International Institute for Central Asian Studies, 2005), pp. 14f.

227 Jacobson-Tepfer and Novozhenov, *Rock Art Chronicles of Golden Steppe*, vol. 2 (2020), p. 68, figs 23–24; p. 236, fig. 24. Molodin, Cheremisin et al., 'Chronology of Rock Art of the Russian and Mongolian Altai' (2023), p. 72, fig. 5.

228 A figure at Saimaluu Tash possibly also represents a centaur. Tashbayeva, *Petroglyphs of Central Asia* (2002), p. 201, fig. 87.

229 The plates of Orlat date from the late fourth century CE and were manufactured in a Sogdian cultural environment. Baumer, *The History of Central Asia*, vol. 2 (2014), p. 96, fig. 74. Tashbayeva et al., *Petroglyphs of Central Asia* (2002), pp. 199f.

230 Aichner, B. et al, 'High-resolution leaf wax carbon and hydrogen isotopic record of the late Holocene paleoclimate in arid Central Asia', in: *Climate of the Past*, vol. 11, no. 4 (Göttingen: Copernicus Publications, 2015), pp. 619, 626–628.

231 Bobomulloev, Bobomullo, 'Rock art in Tajikistan', in: Clottes, *Rock Art in Central Asia* (2011), pp. 73–92. Ranov, Vadim, 'Petroglyphs of Tajikistan', in: Tashbayeva et al., *Petroglyphs of Central Asia* (2001), pp. 122–150.

232 It is possible that the front part of the roof of the shelter has broken off since the paintings were made.

233 Bobomulloev, 'Rock art in Tajikistan' (2011), pp. 75f. Ranov, Vadim, 'L'exploration archéologique du Pamir', in: *Bulletin de l'École française de d'Extrême Orient*, vol. 73 (Paris: EFEO, 1984), pp. 76f, 88, 94. 'Petroglyphs of Tajikistan' (2001), pp. 128–131.

234 Zotkina, Lydia, Bobomulloev, Bobomullo et al., 'Новые данные о наскальном искусстве Восточного Памира / New data on the rock paintings of Eastern Pamir', in: *Вестник НГУ. Серия: История, филология / Vestnik NSU Series History and Philology*, vol. 21, no. 3 (Novosibirsk: 2022), p. 65.

235 Naiza-Tash was reported in 1995 or earlier, but was researched only in 2016. Ranov, 'Petroglyphs of Tajikistan' (2001), p. 129. Zotkina, Lydia and Sayfulloev, Nuritdin, 'Изображения Навеса Куртеке (Восточный Памир) = Imagery of the Kurteke Rock-Shelter (Eastern Pamir)', in: *Теория и практика археологических исследований = Theory and Practice of Archaeological Research*, vol. 34, no. 4 (Novosibirsk: Institute of Archaeology and Ethnography, 2022), pp. 148, 156f.

236 Zotkina and Bobomulloev, 'New data on the rock paintings of Eastern Pamir' (2022), pp. 68f.

237 Masov, Rahim et al. (eds), *National Museum of Antiquities of Tajikistan* (Dushanbe: Donish Institute, 2005), pp. 221, 223. Ranov, Vadim and Veber, Cecile, *Guide to the Principal Archaeological Sites of the Eastern Pamirs (Tajikistan)*, (Khorog: ACTED, n.d.), pp. 11–13.

238 Ranov and Veber, *Guide to the Principal Archaeological Sites of the Eastern Pamirs* (n.d.), pp. 13f. See also: Bubnova, M. A., *Археологическая карта Горно-Бадахшанской АвтономнойОбласти: Восточной Памир = Archaeological Map of Gorno-Badakhshan Autonomous Oblast: Eastern Pamir* (Dushanbe: Donish Institute, 2015), pp. 37, 40–42.

239 Bubnova, *Archaeological Map of Gorno-Badakhshan Autonomous Oblast* (2015), pp. 56f. Ranov, Vadim, 'Petroglyphs of Tajikistan' (2001), pp. 132–138.

240 The spiritual leader of the Pamiri Ismailis has the title of Aga Khan.

241 Baumer, *The History of Central Asia*, vol. 1 (2012), p. 206. Bonmann, Svenja et al., 'A partial decipherment of the unknown Kushan script', in: *Transactions of the Philological Society*, vol. 121, no. 2 (London: The Philological Society, 2023), pp. 293f, 299–302. Fussman, Gérard, 'Dašt-e Nāwor', in: *Encyclopaedia Iranica*, vol. 7, fasc. 1 (1994). Powell, Eric A., 'Breaking the Code of the Kushan Kings', in: *Archaeology*, March/April 2024 (Boston: Archaeological Institute of America), pp. 50–55.

242 Bonmann, 'A partial decipherment of the unknown Kushan script' (2023), pp. 298, 317f.

243 For the Yuezhi and the Kushan Empire see: Baumer, *The History of Central Asia*, vol. 2 (2014), pp. 46–54.

244 Bonmann, 'A partial decipherment of the unknown Kushan script' (2023), p. 325.

245 Bonmann, 'A partial decipherment of the unknown Kushan script' (2023), p. 325. The name 'Eteo-Tocharian' seems to the present author unfortunate, seeing as it risks getting confused with the older, non-Iranian Tocharian languages, Kuchean and Agnean.

246 Kashchey, O.A. and Nedashkovsky, L.F., 'Хронология наскальных изображений Каракиясая II = Chronology of the Karakiyasay II rock art', in: *Вестник археологии, антропологии и этнографии = Bulletin of Archaeology, Anthropology and Ethnography*, 2023, no. 2 (61) (Tyumen: Tyumen Scientific Centre of Siberian Branch of the Russian Academy of Sciences: 2023), pp. 69–79.

247 For reproductions of Roginskaya's watercolours, see: https://meros.uz/object/zaraut-kamar-darasi; https://megalithica.ru/petroglifyi-zaraut-kamar.html.

248 Khujanazarov, M., 'Rock sites in Uzbekistan', in: Clottes, *Rock Art in Central Asia* (2011), pp. 109–111. In an earlier publication, Khujanazarov had not mentioned any critical points concerning the Zaraut-Kamar paintings. 'Petroglyphs of Uzbekistan', in:

Tashbayeva et al., *Petroglyphs of Central Asia* (2001), pp. 91–93.

249 Jasiewicz, Zbigniew and Rozwadowski, Andrzej, 'Rock paintings – Wall paintings: New light on art tradition in Central Asia', in: *Rock Art Research*, vol. 18, no. 1 (Darwin: International Federation of Rock Art Organizations, 2001), pp. 3–14.

250 mya: million years ago.

251 Reutova, M.A., *Petroglyphs in Sarmishsay: The Methodological Recommendations for Conservation* (Samarkand: International Institute for Central Asian Studies, 2009), p. 4.

252 As at other rock art sites, there are also modern scribbles and inscriptions of names.

253 Baumer, *The History of Central Asia*, vol. 1 (2012), pp. 50–52, 117.

254 Kuz'mina, Elena, *The Origins of the Indo-Iranians*, ed. J.P. Mallory (Leiden: Brill, 2007), p. 182.

255 Kuz'mina, *The Origins of the Indo-Iranians* (2007), p. 182.

256 Khujanazarov, M., 'Petroglyphs of Uzbekistan' (2001), pp. 110–118.

IV. Himalaya, Transhimalaya and Karakoram

1. Francke published more than a dozen articles on inscriptions and petroglyphs of Ladakh between 1902 and 1925. Bruneau, Laurianne, 'The rock art of Ladakh: A historiographic and thematic study', in: Kumar, Ajit (ed.), *Rock Art: Recent Researches and New Perspectives* (Delhi: New Bharatiya Book Corp., 2015), pp. 79f, 91. Devers, Quentin et al., 'A review of rock art discoveries in Ladakh over the last fourteen decades', in: Bellezza, John V. (ed.), *Flight of the Khyung*, September 2017.

2 Francke, A.H., 'Historische Dokumente von Khalatse in West-Tibet (Ladakh)', in: *Zeitschrift der Deutschen Morgenländischen Gesellschaft*, vol. 61 (1907), pp. 583–614 (repr. Ulm: Fabri, 2012), pp. 1–40.

3 Francke, A.H., *Antiquities of Indian Tibet* (1914; New Delhi: Asian Educational Services, 1992), vol. 1, pp. 58–60, 94; vol. 2, pp. 99, 107.

4 Hedin, Sven, *Scientific Results of a Journey in Central Asia, 1899–1902*, vol. 3: *North and East Tibet* (Stockholm: Lithographic Institute of the General Staff of the Swedish Army, 1905), pp. 189–192, figs 154–156.

5 Ujfalvy de Mezőkövesd, Károly Jenő (Karl Eugen), *Aus dem westlichen Himalaya: Erlebnisse und Forschungen* (Leipzig: Brockhaus, 1884; facsimile edition, 2011), p. 248, figs XVIII, XIX.

6 Mohammad, Ghulam, 'Festivals and folklore of Gilgit', in: *Memoirs of the Asiatic Society of Bengal*, vol. 1, no. 7 (Calcutta: Asiatic Society of Bengal, 1905), pp. 93–127.

7 Stein, Marc Aurel, *Innermost Asia*, vol. 1 (Oxford: Clarendon, 1928), p. 14.

8 Stein, Marc Aurel, 'Archaeological notes from the Hindukush region', in: *The Journal of the Royal Asiatic Society of Great Britain and Ireland*, vol. 1 (London: The Royal Asiatic Society, 1944), pp. 5f, 16f.

9 Hauptmann, Harald (ed.), *Materialien zur Archäologie der Nordgebiete Pakistans*, 11 vols (Mainz: Philipp von Zabern, 1994–2013).

10 Bruneau, Laurianne and Bellezza, John Vincent, 'The rock art of Upper Tibet and Ladakh', in: *Revue d'Études Tibétaines*, no. 28 (Paris: UMR 8155 (CRCAO) of CNR, 2013), p. 10. South of Tibet there are also smaller petroglyph sites in Nepal, for example in Mustang.

Pohle, Perdita, 'Felsbilder in Zentralasien. Quellen zur Kultur- und Landschaftsgeschichte', in: *Geographische Rundschau* (Braunschweig: Westermann, 1997), pp. 287–292.

11 For the rock art of Ladakh and Zanskar there is an excellent interactive map: https://ladakharchaeology.com/categories/petro-picto/.

12 Martin, Nils, 'A solemn praise to a West-Tibetan councillor at Kharul, Purik', in: *Zentralasiatische Studien*, vol. 46 (Bonn: ZAS, 2018), pp. 189–232.

13 As early as 1909, A.H. Francke deplored the wanton destruction by road workers of stone inscriptions and petroglyphs along the river Indus. Francke, *Antiquities of Indian Tibet*, vol. 1 (1992), p. 94.

14 Morup, Tashi, 'Pre-Tibetan Buddhist rock art of Ladakh' (2017). Thangspa, Tashi Ldawa, 'Petroglyphs of Ladakh' (2021).

15 Concerning Bön, see: Baumer, Christoph, *Tibet's Ancient Religion, Bön* (Bangkok: Orchid Press, 2002).

16 Translation from the German by the author. Koenig, Gerd G, 'Skythen in Tibet?', in: Müller, Claudius C. and Raunig, Walter (eds), *Der Weg zum Dach der Welt* (Innsbruck: Pinguin-Verlag, 1982), pp. 318, 320.

17 Translation from the French by the author. Francfort, Henri-Paul et al., 'Pétroglyphes archaïques du Ladakh et du Zanskar', in: *Arts Asiatiques*, vol. 45 (Paris: Musée national d'art asiatique Guimet, 1990), p. 5.

18 Translation from the French by the author. Francfort et al., 'Pétroglyphes archaïques du Ladakh et du Zanskar' (1990), p. 5.

19 Bellezza, John Vincent, 'The origins of the Tibetan people', in: *Flight of the Khyung* (May 2013).

20 Chen Zhao Fu, *China. Prähistorische Felsbilder* (Zürich: U. Bär, 1989), figs 60–63, p. 97.

21 Baumer, *The History of Central Asia*, vol. 1 (2012), pp. 216–223.

22 Chen Zhao Fu, *China* (1989), figs 48–51, 57–59, 98.

23 Baumer, Christoph, *The History of Central Asia*, vol. 4: *The Age of Decline and Revival* (London: I.B.Tauris, 2018), pp. 145f.

24 Deeg, Max, *Das Gaoseng-Faxian-Zhuan als religionsgeschichtliche Quelle* (Wiesbaden: Harrassowitz, 2005), pp. 117f, 188f, 518f.

25 Bruneau and Bellezza, 'The Rock Art of Upper Tibet and Ladakh' (2013), pp. 8f.

26 Weihreter, Hans, *Ladakh. Vergessene Feste. Botschaften im Fels* (Graz: ADEVA, 2010), p. 12.

27 Petech, Luciano, *The Kingdom of Ladakh, c. 950–1842 A.D.* (Rome: ISMEO, 1977), pp. 6f.

28 Weihreter, *Ladakh* (2010), p. 17. The ethnonyms 'Mon' and 'Dard' are both exonyms.

29 Baumer, *Tibet's Ancient Religion, Bön* (2002), pp. 106, 112.

30 Since there is a dearth of reliable texts concerning Zhanzhung, Bellezza and Bruneau name this period 'protohistoric' instead of 'early historic'. 'The Rock Art of Upper Tibet and Ladakh', p. 9.

31 Baumer, Christoph and Weber, Therese, *Eastern Tibet: Bridging Tibet and China* (Bangkok: Orchid Press, 2005), pp. 66f. It seems that around 1100 CE Maryul began to control Guge. Handa, Omacanda, *Buddhist Western Himalaya*, part 1: *A Politico-Religious History* (New Delhi: Indus Publishing, 2001), p. 130.

32 Baumer, *Tibet's Ancient Religion, Bön* (2002), p. 126. *The History of Central Asia*, vol. 4 (2018), pp. 72f. Shakabpa, Tsepon W.D., *Tibet: A Political History* (New York: Potala Publications, 1984), pp. 56–60.

33 In the areas under discussion, of course, are also found the ubiquitous images of ibexes.

34 Bruneau, Laurianne et al., 'Rock art research in Murgi Tokpo, Nubra Valley in Ladakh', in: *Purakala*, vols. 20–21 (Agra: Rock Art Society of India, 2010–11), pp. 93f. 'Étude thématique et stylistique des pétroglyphes du Ladakh (Jammu et Cachemire, Inde)', in: *Eurasia Antiqua. Zeitschrift für Archäologie Eurasiens*, vol. 18 (Bonn: Rudolf Habelt, 2012), pp. 73, 77–81. 'L'art rupestre du Ladakh (Jammu et Cachemire, Inde): ses liens avec l'Asie centrale', in: *Cahiers d'Asie centrale*, vols 21–2 (Paris: De Boccard, 2013), pp. 490f. Bruneau and Bellezza, 'The rock art of Upper Tibet and Ladakh' (2013), p. 45. Francfort et al., 'Pétroglyphes archaïques du Ladakh et du Zanskar' (1990), p. 6.

35 Bruneau, 'Rock Art Research in Murgi Tokpo'. (2010–11), p. 93. 'Étude thématique et stylistique des pétroglyphes du Ladakh' (2012), pp. 74–77, 80–83.

36 Vernier, Martin, 'Zamthang, epicentre of Zanskar's rock heritage', in: *Revue d'Études Tibétaines*, vol. 35 (Paris: UMR 8155 (CRCAO) of CNR, 2016), p. 88.

37 Bruneau and Bellezza, 'The rock art of Upper Tibet and Ladakh' (2013), p. 45.

38 Bruneau, 'Étude thématique et stylistique des pétroglyphes du Ladakh' (2012), p. 83. 'L'art rupestre du Ladakh' (2013), p. 493. Bruneau and Bellezza, 'The rock art of Upper Tibet and Ladakh' (2013), pp. 32–40.

39 Distantly related to these various masks and maskoids are four small anthropomorphic figures at Renmudong, with bird's heads or wearing masks of birds, a motif occasionally also encountered in Central Asia. Chayet, Anne, *Art et archéologie du Tibet* (Paris: Picard, 1994), pp. 66, 68.

40 Bruneau, 'Rock art research in Murgi Tokpo'. (2010–11), pp. 94f. 'Étude thématique et stylistique des pétroglyphes du Ladakh' (2012), p. 72–74. 'L'art rupestre du Ladakh' (2013), p. 492. Bruneau and Bellezza, 'The rock art of Upper Tibet and Ladakh' (2013), pp. 40–45.

41 Bruneau, 'L'art rupestre du Ladakh' (2013), p. 493.

42 See above, p. 79.

43 Bruneau and Bellezza rightly warn against using the stylistic characteristics of the Animal Style in Tibet as a reliable indication of dating to the Iron Age because such images sometimes acquired a heraldic function, meaning that they were kept unchanged as the emblem of clan, similar to Turkic *tamgas*, long after the end of the Iron Age. Bruneau and Bellezza, 'The rock art of Upper Tibet and Ladakh' (2013), p. 51 n177.

44 This specific motif of a deer or other ungulate with its head turned backwards has been traced back by Francfort to the jade plaques from the Chinese Western Zhou dynasty (*ca.* 1045–771 BCE), specifically those from the Rujiazhuang tomb no. 1 in Shaanxi dated before 841 BCE. However, Francfort leaves the question open as to whether this element of Animal Style reached Ladak and western Tibet directly from China or whether it originated in a Central Asian steppe environment. Francfort et al., 'Pétroglyphes archaïques du Ladakh et du Zanskar' (1990), pp. 11, 23f.

45 Bruneau, Laurianne and Vernier, Martin, 'Animal style of the steppes in Ladakh: A presentation of newly discovered petroglyphs', in: Olivieri, Luca Maria (ed.), *Pictures in Transformation: Rock Art Research between Central Asia and the Subcontinent* (Oxford: BAR, 2010), pp. 28–35, figs 3–6, 8–13, 15. Bruneau, 'L'art rupestre du Ladakh' (2013), p. 494f. Bruneau and Bellezza,

'The Rock Art of Upper Tibet and Ladakh' (2013), pp. 45–52. Francfort et al., 'Pétroglyphes archaïques du Ladakh et du Zanskar' (1990), pp. 11f, 19f, 23f. Vernier, 'Zamthang, epicentre of Zanskar's rock heritage' (2016), p. 92. According to Bruneau and Bellezza, a famous scene at Renmudong featuring three felines attacking three deer is not ancient since it lacks repatination. Bruneau and Bellezza, 'The rock art of Upper Tibet and Ladakh' (2013), p. 49 n166.

46 Bruneau and Bellezza, 'The rock art of Upper Tibet and Ladakh' (2013), pp. 47–50. Francfort et al., 'Pétroglyphes archaïques du Ladakh et du Zanskar' (1990), pp. 13–16. Vernier, 'Zamthang, epicentre of Zanskar's rock heritage' (2016), pp. 90f.

47 Baumer, *The History of Central Asia*, vol. 1 (2012), pp. 216–223.

48 Baumer, *The History of Central Asia*, vol. 1 (2012), pp. 290–296; vol. 2 (2014), pp. 138–142.

49 Tanktse is 150 km north-west of Ruthok. About 40% of the length of Lake Pangong lies within Ladakh, India, half within Tibet, China, and 10% is disputed between India and China.

50 The term 'Nestorian' has traditionally been applied to denominate the Assyrian Church of the East, which blossomed east of the Roman Empire from the fourth century and stretched from Mesopotamia to China and South India. On this church see: Baumer, Christoph, *The Church of the East: An Illustrated History of Assyrian Christianity* (London: I.B.Tauris, 2016).

51 Dauvillier, Jean, 'Les provinces chaldéennes "de l'Extérieur" au Moyen-Age', in: *Mélanges offerts au R.P. Ferdinand Cavallera* (Toulouse: Bibliothèque de l'Institut Catholique, 1948). pp. 293f. Gilman, Ian and Klimkeit, Hans-Joachim, *Christians in Asia before 1500* (Chicago: University of Michigan Press, 1999), pp. 223f, 337. Uray, Géza, 'Tibet's connections with Nestorianism and Manicheism in the 8th–10th centuries', in: Steinkellner, Ernst and Tauscher, Helmut (eds), *Contributions on Tibetan Language, History and Culture*, vol. 1 (Vienna: University of Vienna, 1983), pp. 404–407. However, a Manichaean interpretation cannot be entirely ruled out. Hunter, Erica, 'The Church of the East in Central Asia', in: Coakley J.F. and Parry K. (eds), *The Church of the East: Life and Thought. The Bulletin of the John Rylands Library*, vol. 78, no. 3 (Manchester: The John Rylands Library, 1996), pp. 135f. A Buddhist context is also not impossible. Sims-Williams, Nicholas, 'The Sogdian inscription in Ladakh', in: Jettmar, Karl (ed.), *Antiquities of Northern Pakistan: Reports and Studies*, vol. 2 (Mainz: Philipp von Zabern, 1993), pp. 151–163. But the Nestorian crosses carved next to the inscription are a strong argument that it is indeed Nestorian.

52 These five figures could also represent the Five Tathagata Buddhas.

53 Dorjay, Phuntsog, 'Penetration of Buddhist ideology in Ladakh: A study through rock sculptures', in: Olivieri, *Pictures in Transformation* (2010), p. 49. Snellgrove, David L. and Skorupski, Tadeusz, *The Cultural Heritage of Ladakh*, vol. 1 (New Delhi: Vikas Publishing, 1977), p. 11, fig. 5.

54 Dorjay, 'Penetration of Buddhist ideology in Ladakh' (2010), p. 45. Snellgrove and Skorupski, *The Cultural Heritage of Ladakh*, vol. 2 (1980), p. 4, fig. 2.

55 Dorjay, 'Penetration of Buddhist ideology in Ladakh' (2010), p. 46.

56 Moorcroft, William and Trebeck, George, *Travels in*

the Himalayan Provinces of Hindustan and the Panjab; in Ladakh and Kashmir; in Peshawar, Kabul, Kunduz, and Bokhara, from 1819 to 1825 (London: John Murray, 1841), vol. 2, p. 18.

57 Dorjay, 'Penetration of Buddhist ideology in Ladakh' (2010), p. 46, fig. 4. Snellgrove and Skorupski, *The Cultural Heritage of Ladakh*, vol. 2 (1980), p. 10, fig. 7.

58 Morup, 'Pre-Tibetan Buddhist rock art of Ladakh' (2017).

59 Dorjay, 'Penetration of Buddhist ideology in Ladakh' (2010), pp. 47–50, figs 6, 8–11; pp. 52–57, fig. 22. Morup, Tashi, 'Pre-Tibetan Buddhist rock art of Ladakh' (2017); Thangspa, 'Petroglyphs of Ladakh' (2021). Snellgrove and Skorupski, *The Cultural Heritage of Ladakh*, vol. 1 (1977), p. 112, fig. 108; vol. 2 (1980), p. 10, fig. 8; p. 26, fig. 19.

60 Francke, A.H., 'Historische Dokumente von Khalatse in West-Tibet (Ladakh)' (2012), pp. 7, 20, 26, 29–31.

61 The Kharosthi script, also named Gandhari, was used from the third century BCE until the third century CE to write Indo-Iranian languages in the north-west of the Indian subcontinent, Afghanistan and today's Xinjiang. It was then superseded by the Brahmi script, which was gradually replaced by the Proto-Sarada script in the seventh century CE. Hauptmann, *Materialien zur Archäologie der Nordgebiete Pakistans* (hereafter *MANP*), vol. 2: *Die Felsbildstation Shatial* (1997), pp. 5f.

62 Hauptmann, Harald, 'Felsbildkunst am Oberen Indus', in: Luczanits, Christian (ed.), *Gandhara – Das buddhistische Erbe Pakistans. Legenden, Klöster und Paradiese* (Mainz: Philipp von Zabern, 2009), p. 357. 'Felsbilder und Inschriften am Karakorum-Highway', https://www. hadw-bw.de/forschung/forschungsstelle/ felsbilder-und-inschriften-am-karakorum-highway.

63 *Jatakas* are moral tales from Buddha Shakyamuni's previous incarnations.

64 Hauptmann, *MANP*, vol. 10 (2011), p. 80, pl. 1, 39.

65 Jettmar, Karl, *Zwischen Gandhāra und den Seidenstrassen. Felsbilder am Karakorum Highway* (Mainz: Philipp von Zabern, 1985), fig. 44.

66 Bräker, Annette and Geerken, Horst H., *The Karakoram Highway and the Hunza Valley, 1998* (Norderstedt: Bukit Cinta, 2017), p. 45, 47, 224f.

67 https://www.thenews.com.pk/latest/658242-fwo- and-power-china-joint-venture-awarded-contract-of- diamer-bhasha-dam (accessed 26 Nov. 2024).

68 Aerde, Marike van, 'Routes beyond Gandhara: Buddhist rock carvings in the context of the early Silk Roads', in: Liang, Emlyn Yang et al. (eds), *Socio-Environmental Dynamics along the Historical Silk Road* (Cham: Springer Nature Switzerland, 2019), p. 459. Yusuf, Suhail, 'Threatened rock carvings of Pakistan', in: *Dawn*, 18 May 2011 (Karachi: Dawn, 2011).

69 Aerde, Marike van and Khan, Abdul Rani, 'Carvings and community: Inclusive heritage solutions for protecting ancient Karakorum petroglyphs under threat', in: *Journal of Archaeohistorical Studies*, vol. 2, no. 2 (Hochstadt: ASAS, 2021). See also: https:// www.archaeologistsconnected.org/research-projects (accessed 26 Nov. 2024).

70 Hauptmann, 'Felsbildkunst am Oberen Indus' (2009), p. 353.

71 Hauptmann, *MANP*, vol. 6, pl. 52f, 86.

72 Hauptmann, *MANP*, vol. 6, pl. 62, 64.

73 Baumer, *The History of Central Asia*, vol. 2 (2014), pp. 46–58.

74 Hauptmann, *MANP*, vol. 2, p. 10, pl. 2.

75 Hauptmann, *MANP*, vol. 2, p. 14, pl. 4.

76 Hauptmann, *MANP*, vol. 2, p. 14, pl. 4.

77 Hauptmann, *MANP*, vol. 2, pp. 11f, 34, 69, pl. 138, IIb.

78 Hauptmann, *MANP*, vol. 2, pp. 17, 269, 341, pl. 6,

79 Baumer, *The History of Central Asia*, vol. 2 (2014), p. 99.

80 Jettmar, *Zwischen Gandhāra und den Seidenstrassen* (1985), pp. 22f.

81 Stein, 'Archaeological Notes from the Hindukush Region' (1944), p. 22.

82 Hauptmann, *MANP*, vol. 2, pp. 41f; 8, p. 5.

83 Aerde, 'Routes beyond Gandhara' (2019), p. 465.

84 Mohns, Alexander D.L., 'Buddha on the rocks: Analyzing the anthropomorphic Buddhist rock carvings on the Silk Roads along the Upper Indus', bachelor thesis (Leiden: University of Leiden, 2018), pp. 22, 23–38.

85 Hauptmann, 'Felsbildkunst am Oberen Indus' (2009), pp. 354.

86 Schroeder, Ulrich von, *Buddhist Sculptures in Tibet* (Hong Kong: Visual Dharma, 2001), vol. 1, p. 62. However, as observed by Oskar von Hinüber, 'it is not possible to precisely outline the area of Palola or Balur based on the available sources'. *Die Palola Sāhis, ihre Steininschriften, Inschriften auf Bronzen, Handschriftenkolophone und Schutzzauber. Materialien zur Geschichte von Gilgit und Chilas* (Mainz: Philipp von Zaben, 2004), p. 7.

87 Baumer, *The History of Central Asia*, vol. 2 (2014), pp. 281–295.

88 The Four Garrisons were four Chinese military garrisons in the Tarim Basin, namely: Kucha, Khotan, Kashgar and Karashahr.

89 Philip Denwood, 'The Tibetans in the Western Himalayas and Karakoram, seventh–eleventh centuries: Rock art and inscriptions', in *Journal of Inner Asian Art and Archaeology*, vol. 2 (Turnhout: Brepols, 2007), p. 49; 'The Tibetans in the West, Part I' (2008), p. 14.

90 Denwood, 'The Tibetans in the West, Part II' (2009), pp. 152ff.

91 Denwood, 'The Tibetans in the West, Part II' (2009), p. 154.

92 Beckwith, Christopher I., *The Tibetan Empire in Central Asia: A History of the Struggle for Great Power among Tibetans, Turks, Arabs, and Chinese during the Early Middle Ages* (Princeton: Princeton University Press, 1987), p. 115.

93 Stein, Marc Aurel, 'A Chinese expedition across the Pamirs and Hindukush, A.D. 747', in *The Geographical Journal*, vol. 59, no. 2 (London: RGS, February 1922), pp. 122–125.

94 Denwood, 'The Tibetans in the Western Himalayas and Karakoram' (2007), p. 50; Stein, 'A Chinese expedition' (1922), p. 130.

95 Beckwith, *The Tibetan Empire in Central Asia* (1987), pp. 108–116, 123–142. 144–146, 157, 163, 168–712.

96 Hauptmann, 'Felsbildkunst am Oberen Indus' (2009), p. 356, fig. 7.

97 Hauptmann, *MANP*, vol. 6, p. 30, pl. 43.

98 Hauptmann, *MANP*, vol. 6, pl. 88.

99 Hauptmann, *MANP*, vol. 2, pp. 13f, 93, pl. 4, V a, b. Hauptmann, 'Felsbildkunst am Oberen Indus' (2009), pp. 355. Mohns, 'Buddha on the rocks' (2018), pp. 43–49.

100 Hauptmann, *MANP*, vol. 6, p. 45f, pl. 7. Mohns, 'Buddha on the rocks' (2018), pp. 40f.

101 Mohns, 'Buddha on the rocks' (2018), pp. 47f.

102 See for example the standing Buddha statue made from schist and dated to the third century CE from the monastery of Paitava near Bagram, in today's Afghanistan, Musée Guimet, Paris: https://www.guimet.fr/fr/nos-collections/afghanistan-pakistan/le-bouddha-au-grand-miracle (accessed 26 Nov. 2024).

103 Baumer, *The History of Central Asia*, vol. 2 (2014), pp. 48, 50.

104 Hauptmann, *MANP*, vol. 7, pl. 94.

105 Hauptmann, *MANP*, vol. 7, pl. 90.

106 Hauptmann, *MANP*, vol. 7, pl. 4.

107 Hauptmann, 'Felsbildkunst am Oberen Indus' (2009), pp. 353, fig. 2, 355.

108 Deeg, *Das Gaoseng-Faxian-Zhuan als religionsgeschichtliche Quelle* (2005), pp. 112, 188, 517f. Faxian, *A Record of Buddhistic Kingdoms: Being an Account by the Chinese Monk Fâ-Hsien of his Travels in India and Ceylon (ad 319–414) in Search of the Buddhist Books of Discipline*, tr. James Legge (Oxford: Clarendon Press, 1886; repr., n.d.) pp. 24f.

109 Xuanzang, *Si-yu-ki: Buddhist Records of the Western World*, trans. Samuel Beal (1906, repr. New Delhi: Manoharlal, 2004), p. 134.

110 Stein, *Innermost Asia*, vol. 1 (1928), pp. 20f. See also: Hauptmann, *MANP*, vol. 2, pp. 83–87, 104f.

111 Baumer, *The History of Central Asia*, vol. 2 (2014), pp. 221–231.

112 Hauptmann, *MANP*, vol. 2, pp. 62, 68f, 76, 81, 105f.

113 The identification at Shatial of a figure with a head surrounded by spikes as a 'sun god in Sogdian style' is hardly convincing. Hauptmann, *MANP*, vol. 2, pp. 69, 150, pl. 4.

114 Hauptmann, *MANP*, vol. 2, pp. 92f, 207f, pl. 86.

115 Jettmar, *Zwischen Gandhāra und den Seidenstrassen* (1985), fig. 50.

116 Jettmar, Karl, 'Symbolic systems in collision: Rock art in the Upper Indus valley', in: Allchin, Raymond et al. (eds), *Gandharan Art in Context. East-West Exchanges at the Crossroads of Asia* (New Delhi: Regency Publications, 1997), pp. 61f, fig. 62. Hauptmann, *MANP*, vol. 3, pp. 129–131, pl. 7, 19–24, 61f, 68–74, 114.

117 *Hudūd al-ʿĀlam: The Regions of the World, a Persian Geography 372 A.H./982 A.D.*, trans. V. Minorsky, ed. C.E. Bosworth (repr. Cambridge: Cambridge University Press, 1982), p. 121.

118 Allchin, *Gandharan Art in Context* (1997), pp. 62f. Jettmar, *Zwischen Gandhāra und den Seidenstrassen* (1985), p. 29. Hauptmann, *MANP*, vol. 3, pp. 131f.

V. Caucasus

1 For the rock art of Dagestan see: Kšica and Kšicová, *Felsbilder zwischen Schwarzem Meer und Beringstrasse* (1994), pp. 39–57.

2 Babayev, Rafael (ed.), *The Encyclopaedia of Nakhchivan Monuments* (Nakhchivan: National Academy of Sciences, 2009), pp. 127–131.

3 Kalbajar district was occupied by Armenian troops from 1993 to 2020.

4 Farajova, Malahat et al., *Cultural Heritage of Azerbaijan: Petroglyphs* (Baku: Heydar Aliyev Foundation, 2014), pp. 82–85.

5 Kšica and Kšicová, *Felsbilder zwischen Schwarzem Meer und Beringstrasse* (1994), p. 69.

6 Khechoyan, Anna, 'The rock art of the Mt. Aragats system', in: *Rock Art in the Frame of the Cultural Heritage of Humankind: Papers of the XXII Valcamonica Symposium 2007* (Capo di Ponte: CCSP, 2007), pp. 247–252.

7 Van Baak, Christiaan G.C. et al., 'A magnetostratigraphic time frame for Plio-Pleistocene transgressions in the South Caspian Basin, Azerbaijan', *Global and Planetary Change*, vol. 103 (Amsterdam: Elsevier, 2013), p. 119.

8 The term 'marine transgression' refers to an advance of the coastline inland as a result of an increase in sea level or a tectonic subsidence of the landmass; 'regression' designates the opposite movement.

9 Van Baak, 'A magnetostratigraphic time frame' (2013), pp. 119, 130; Boomer, Ian et al., 'The palaeolimnology of the Aral Sea: A review', *Quaternary Science Reviews*, vol. 19 (Amsterdam: Elsevier, 2000), pp. 1161f.

10 Van Baak, 'A magnetostratigraphic time frame' (2013), pp. 130, 133; Boomer, 'Palaeolimnology of the Aral Sea' (2000), pp. 1261, 1276.

11 Boomer, 'Palaeolimnology of the Aral Sea' (2000), p. 1262. Today, the Caspian Sea is only connected to the Azov and Black Seas via the 101-km-long Volga–Don Canal, completed in 1952.

12 Van Baak, 'A magnetostratigraphic time frame' (2013), pp. 129f.

13 Kakroodi, A.A. et al., 'Late Pleistocene and Holocene sea-level change and coastal paleoenvironment evolution along the Caspian shore', *Marine Geology*, vol. 361 (Amsterdam: Elsevier, 2015), p. 111.

14 Kakroodi et al., 'Late Pleistocene and Holocene sea-level change' (2015), p. 113, 123; Mamedov, A.V., 'The Late Pleistocene–Holocene history of the Caspian Sea', *Quaternary International*, vols 41–2 (Amsterdam: Elsevier, 1997), pp. 161–165; Yanina, Tamara A., 'Correlation of the Late Pleistocene paleogeographical events of the Caspian Sea and Russian Plain', *Quaternary International*, vol. 271 (Amsterdam: Elsevier, 2012), pp. 122–126.

15 Yanko-Hombach, Valentina et al., 'Controversy over the great flood hypotheses in the Black Sea in light of geological, paleontological and archaeological evidence', *Quaternary International*, vols. 167–68 (Amsterdam: Elsevier, 2007), p. 95.

16 Sigari, Dario, 'Gobustan Rock Art Cultural Landscape (Azerbaijan)', in: Smith, Claire (ed.), *Encyclopedia of Global Archaeology* (New York: Springer Nature, 2019), p. 2.

17 We follow a modified version of Anati's chronology. Anati, Emmanuel, *The Rock Art of Azerbaijan* (Capo di Ponte: Atelier, 2015), pp. 20–23.

18 Bosinski, Gerhard, d'Errico, Francesco and Schiller, Petra, *Die gravierten Frauendarstellungen von Gönnersdorf* (Stuttgart: Franz-Steiner Verlag, 2001).

19 Anati, *The Rock Art of Azerbaijan* (2015), pp. 64f.

20 Manco, *Ancestral Journeys* (2021), p. 62.

21 Baumer, *History of the Caucasus*, vol. 1 (2021), p. 46.

22 Anati, The Rock Art of Azerbaijan (2015), pp. 121–132.

23 The term 'Albanian' refers to the quasi-state of Caucasian Albania which occupied the most part of what is roughly the west of today's Azerbaijan. See: Baumer, *History of the Caucasus*, vol. 1 (2021), pp. 156–166, 205–208, 222–229.

24 The exonym Iberia in Greco-Roman geography was the term for the Georgian kingdom of Kartli, that is the nucleus of today's Georgia.

25 Baumer, *History of the Caucasus*, vol. 1 (2021), pp. 151f.

26 Knoll, Franziska, 'Petroglyphs in the Syunik Highlands

(Armenia): mapping (pre-)historic traces', in: *Adoranten* (2016), pp. 73–83. 'Die Felsbilder im Hochland von Syunik', in: *Archäologie in Armenien*, vol. 2 (Halle: Landesamt für Denkmalpflege und Archäologie Sachsen-Anhalt, 2013), pp. 209–234. Meller, Harald, Knoll, Franziska and Dresely, Veit, 'Die Felsbilder von Ughtasar, Provinz Sjunik', in: *Archäologie in Armenien* (Halle: Landesamt für Denkmalpflege und Archäologie Sachsen-Anhalt, 2011), pp. 131–142. Kšica and Ksicová, *Felsbilder zwischen Schwarzem Meer und Beringstrasse* (1994), pp. 69–78.

27 Hermann, Luc, 'Ship engravings in Armenia?', in: *Adoranten* (2011), pp. 93f.

28 For the petroglyphs of Gegham see: Martirosyan, Н.А., Գեղամա լեռների ժայռապատկերները = *Petroglyphs of the Gegham Mountains* (Yerevan: Haykakan SSR G. A. Hratarakchutyun, 1981).

VI. Europe

1 Rock art in Finland consists mainly of rock paintings which will not be addressed in this work. Since Finland has favourable rocks for petroglyph pecking, it remains unclear why there are apparently hardly any petroglyphs in that country.

2 Within this huge prehistoric cultural environment, whose petroglyphs are characterized by their complex arrangements and narrative character, the possibility must be considered that isolated petroglyphs could also represent *pars pro toto*, i.e. that a single image suggests a known story or myth.

3 Boulton, G.S. et al., 'Evidence of European ice sheet fluctuation during the last glacial cycle', in: *Developments in Quaternary Sciences*, vol. 2, part 1 (Amsterdam: Elsevier, 2004), pp. 441–460. Manninen, Mikael A., et al., 'First encounters in the north: Cultural diversity and gene flow in early Mesolithic Scandinavia', in: *Antiquity*, vol. 95, no. 380 (Cambridge: Cambridge University Press, 2021), p. 312. See also: https://www.sciencedirect.com/topics/earth-and-planetary-sciences/scandinavian-ice-sheet (accessed 28 March 2024).

4 Price, T. Douglas, *Ancient Scandinavia. An Archaeological History from the First Humans to the Vikings* (Oxford: Oxford University Press, 2015), pp. 32, 46, 87.

5 Concerning the isostatic uplift, see above, chapter 2, pp. 17f, 20, 159f.

6 Price, *Ancient Scandinavia* (2015), pp. 4, 20, 105. Sognnes, Kalle, 'Symbols in a changing world: rock-art and the transition from hunting to farming in mid Norway', in: Chippindale, Christopher and Taçon, Paul S.C. (eds), *The Archaeology of Rock Art* (Cambridge: Cambridge University Press, 1998), p. 156. Widgren, M. and Pedersen, E.A., 'Agriculture in Sweden: 800 BC–AD 1000', in: Myrdal, Janken and Morell, Mats (eds), *The Agrarian History of Sweden: From 4000 BC to AD 2000* (Lund: Nordic Academic Press, 2000), p. 47.

7 Riede, Felix, 'The resettlement of Northern Europe', in: Cummings et al., *The Oxford Handbook of the Archaeology and Anthropology of Hunter-Gatherers* (2014), pp. 561f. But see also: Wickham-Jones, C.R., 'Coastal adaptations', ibid., pp. 699f.

8 For a graph illustrating the sharp decline in temperature during the Younger Dryas, see: Nielsen, Poul Otto, *National Museum of Denmark: Danish Prehistory* (Copenhagen: The National Museum, 2016), p. 8.

9 Manninen et al., 'First encounters in the north' (2021), p. 313. Riede, 'The resettlement of Northern Europe' (2014), pp. 562–567. Wickham-Jones, 'Coastal adaptations' (2014), p. 700.

10 Gjerde, Jan Magne, 'A boat journey in rock art "from the Bronze Age to the Stone Age – from the Stone Age to the Bronze Age" in northernmost Europe', in: Skoglund, Peter, Ling, Johan and Bertilsson, Ulf (eds), *North Meets South: Theoretical Aspects on the Northern and Southern Rock Art Traditions in Scandinavia* (Oxford: Oxbow, 2017), p. 126.

11 Price, *Ancient Scandinavia* (2015), p. 52. Riede, 'The resettlement of Northern Europe' (2014), p. 567.

12 The Arctic Circle lies at 66° 33′ 55″ north.

13 Goldhahn, Joakim and Fuglestvedt, Ingrid, 'Engendering North European rock art: Bodies and cosmologies in Stone and Bronze Age imagery', in: McDonald and Veth, *Companion to Rock Art* (2012), p. 239. See also: Gjerde, Jan Magne, 'Rock art and landscapes: Studies of Stone Age rock art from northern Fennoscandia', doctoral thesis (Tromsø: University of Tromsø, 2010), p. 90.

14 Gjerde, Jan Magne, 'The earliest boat depiction in northern Europe: Newly discovered early Mesolithic rock art at Valle, northern Norway,' in: *Oxford Journal of Archaeology*, vol. 40, no. 2 (Hoboken: Wiley, 2021), pp. 146f.

15 Günther, Torsten et al, 'Population genomics of Mesolithic Scandinavia: Investigating early postglacial migration routes and high-latitude adaptation', in: *PLOS Biology*, vol. 16, no. 1 (San Francisco: PLOS, 2018).

16 Bengtsson, Boel, *Sailing Rock Art Boats: A Reassessment of Seafaring Abilities in Bronze Age Scandinavia and the Introduction of the Sail in the North* (Oxford: BAR, 2017), p. 10. Ling, Johan, *Elevated Rock Art: Towards a Maritime Understanding of Rock Art in Northern Bohuslän, Sweden* (Oxford: Oxbow, 2014), p. 47. Price, *Ancient Scandinavia* (2015), p. 15f.

17 The isostatic uplift was much less pronounced inland.

18 Nimura, Courtney, *Prehistoric Rock Art in Scandinavia: Agency and Environmental Change* (Oxford: Oxbow, 2016), p. 23.

19 Bengtsson, *Sailing Rock Art Boats* (2017), p. 10. Lødøen, Trond and Mandt, Gro, *The Rock Art of Norway* (Oxford: Windgather Press, 2010), p. 295.

20 Price, *Ancient Scandinavia* (2015), p. 66.

21 Ling, Johan, 'Elevated rock art: Maritime images and situations', in: Fredell, Åsa et al., *Representations and Communications: Creating an Archaeological Matrix of Late Prehistoric Rock Art* (Oxford: Oxbow, 2010), p. 31.

22 At Umeå in the Bay of Bothnia, where the ice sheet was thickest, the pre-isostatic uplift shoreline lay an incredible 286 metres above present sea level. Helskog, Knut, *Communicating with the World of Beings: The World Heritage Rock Art Sites in Alta, Arctic Norway* (Oxford: Oxbow, 2014), p. 30.

23 Lødøen and Mandt, The *Rock Art of Norway* (2010), pp. 53, 71, 295.

24 Gjerde, 'Rock art and landscapes' (2010), pp. 189–212. 'The earliest boat depiction in northern Europe' (2021), pp. 136f, 144, 148f.

25 Gjerde, Jan Magne, 'An overview of Stone Age rock art in northernmost Europe – what, where and when?', in: 해가 지지 않는 땅. 백해의 암각화 = *Land where the Sun Never Sets: Rock Art of the White Sea* (Ulsan: Ulsan Petroglyph Museum, 2019), pp. 208f.

26 Gjerde, 'Rock art and landscapes' (2010), pp. 246, 250–252, 259, 271, 285.

27 Gjerde, 'Rock art and landscapes' (2010), p. 394.

28 Gjerde, 'Rock art and landscapes' (2010), pp. 423–425. 'Snowscapes of rock art: Seasons and seasonality of Stone Age rock art in Northernmost Europe', in: Gjerde, Jan Magne and Arntzen, Mari Strifeldt, *Perspectives on Differences in Rock Art* (Sheffield: Equinox, 2021), p. 108.

29 Gjerde, 'Snowscapes of rock art' (2021), pp. 193–195.

30 Nielsen, *National Museum of Denmark* (2016), pp. 13, 18.

31 Damm, Charlotte and Forsberg, Lars, 'Forager–farmer contacts in Northern Fennoscandia', in: Cummings et al., *The Oxford Handbook of the Archaeology and Anthropology of Hunter-Gatherers* (2014), p. 839. Manninen et al. give earlier dates for the eastern migrations into northern Norway and northern Finland, namely 'pre-9,000 BCE' and '9,000–8,400 BCE' respectively. Manninen et al., 'First encounters in the north' (2021), p. 324.

32 Rankama, Tuija and Kankaanpää, Jarmo, 'Eastern arrivals in post-glacial Lapland: the Sujala site 10,000 cal. BP', in: *Antiquity*, vol. 82 (Cambridge: Cambridge University Press, 2008), pp. 885–888, 892, 895f. Sørensen, Mikkel et al., 'The first eastern migrations of people and knowledge into Scandinavia: Evidence from studies in Mesolithic technology, 9th–8th millennium BC', in: *Norwegian Archaeological Review*, vol. 46, no. 1 (Abingdon: Routledge, 2013), pp. 24, 44.

33 Manninen et al., 'First encounters in the north' (2021), p. 316.

34 Günther et al., 'Population genomics of Mesolithic Scandinavia' (2018), pp. 1f, 5–7.

35 Parzinger, *Die Kinder des Prometheus* (2015), pp. 401f, 406.

36 Price, *Ancient Scandinavia* (2015), pp. 64, 86. In Siberia and northern Fennoscandia the Neolithic is not defined by the introduction of food production, but by ceramic and new lithic technologies. Sala, Renato, 'Interaction of climate, environment and humans in North and Central Asia during the Late Glacial and Holocene', in: Chiotis, *Climate Changes in the Holocene* (2019), p. 344. Sawwatejew, Juri, *Karelische Felsbilder* (Leipzig: VEB E.A. Seemann Verlag, 1984), p. 22.

37 Kaul, Flemming and Rønne, Preben, 'Bronzes, farms and rock art: The agrarian expansion of North Norway', in: *Adoranten* (2013), p. 26.

38 Helskog, Knut, 'Snowshoes and skis in North European rock art', in: Dodd, James and Meijer, Ellen, *Giving the Past a Future* (Oxford: Archaeopress, 2018), pp. 240, 242. Sørensen et al., 'The first eastern migrations of people and knowledge into Scandinavia' (2013), p. 42.

39 Manninen et al., 'First encounters in the north' (2021), pp. 323f.

40 Boyes, Benjamin M., et al., 'The last Fennoscandian Ice Sheet glaciation on the Kola Peninsula and Russian Lapland (Part 2): Ice sheet margin positions, evolution, and dynamics', in: *Quaternary Science Reviews*, vol. 300 (Hoboken: Elsevier, 2023), pp. 12–19. Putkinen, Niko, 'Late Weichselian deglaciation chronology and palaeoenvironments in northern Karelia, NW Russia', doctoral thesis, Geological Survey of Finland (Espoo: University of Oulu, 2011), pp. 1, 16, 18. Sawwatejew, *Karelische Felsbilder* (1984), p. 10. Stroeven, Arjen P. et al., 'Deglaciation of Fennoscandia', in: *Quaternary Science Reviews*, vol. 14 (Hoboken: Elsevier, 2016), pp. 113f.

41 Putkinen, 'Late Weichselian deglaciation chronology and palaeoenvironments in northern Karelia' (2011), pp. 1, 18. Sawwatejew dates this event about two millennia later. Sawwatejew, *Karelische Felsbilder* (1984), p. 12.

42 Likhachev, Vadim, 'Kanozero petroglyphs: History of discovery and investigation', in: *Adoranten* (2018), pp. 48f.

43 Gjerde, 'Rock art and landscapes' (2010), p. 336.

44 Gjerde, 'Rock art and landscapes' (2010), pp. 333–339.

45 Kolpakov, Eugen M. and Shumkin, Vladimir Ya., *Rock Carvings of Kanozero* (St Petersburg: Russian Academy of Sciences, 2012), pp. 14–26. Likhachev, Vadim, 'New motives and compositions of the Kanozero petroglyphs', in: *Adoranten* (2021), p. 72.

46 In 2014–15, a lockable dome ten metres high made from plexiglass was placed over the site Kamenny 7. While it protects the petroglyphs from careless tourists and rain, temperatures rise sharply in summer and the high humidity inside the dome is suboptimal for the rock art.

47 Gjerde, 'Rock art and landscapes' (2010), pp. 332f, 346. Kolpakov and Shumkin, *Rock Carvings of Kanozero* (2012), p. 350. Petroglyphs continued to be made occasionally till *ca.* 1800 CE.

48 For a comprehensive overview of the petroglyphs at Kanozero including drawings of all scenes and images see: Kolpakov and Shumkin, *Rock Carvings of Kanozero* (2012).

49 Gjerde, 'Rock art and landscapes' (2010), p. 324. Kolpakov and Shumkin, *Rock Carvings of Kanozero* (2012), pp. 290, 331. Likhachev, 'New motives and compositions of the Kanozero petroglyphs' (2021), p. 76.

50 Likhachev, Vadim, 'Bow elk hunt: Composition of the Kanozero petroglyph complex', in: *Adoranten* (2017), p. 81.

51 Gjerde, 'Rock art and landscapes' (2010), pp. 342, 345.

52 Kolpakov and Shumkin, *Rock Carvings of Kanozero* (2012), pp. 344, 347.

53 Kolpakov and Shumkin, *Rock Carvings of Kanozero* (2012), pp. 75, 93, 105, 129, 199, 233, 312.

54 Gjerde, 'Rock art and landscapes' (2010), p. 333, fig. 231.

55 The denominations 'Old' and 'New' Zalavruga are misleading, for the petroglyphs at New Zalavruga are older than those at Old Zalavruga. These denominations go back to the archaeologist Vladislav Ravdonikas who first discovered Old Zalavruga in the 1930s; Sawwatejew later found New Zalavruga. In fact, both sites make up a contiguous area of *ca.* 5,000 sq. m. The numbering of panels follows the order of discovery, not their estimated age.

56 For the dating of the petroglyphs at Vyg, see: Gjerde, 'Rock art and landscapes' (2010), pp. 291–300. Janik, Liliana, 'The development and periodisation of White Sea rock carvings', in: *Acta Archaeologica*, vol. 81, no. 1 (Leiden: Brill, 2010), pp. 89–94. Lobanova, N.V., 'New data on the chronology of Lake Onega and the White Sea area petroglyphs', in: Gjerde and Arntzen, *Perspectives on Differences in Rock Art* (2021), pp. 207–213. Sawwatejew, *Karelische Felsbilder* (1984), pp. 41, 138–202.

57 The altitudes above present sea level are taken from: Lobanova, 'New data on the chronology of Lake Onega and the White Sea area petroglyphs' (2021), pp. 209f, and Janik, 'The development and periodisation of White Sea rock carvings' (2010), p. 86.

58 www.worldheritagesite.org/list/Petroglyphs+of+the+Lake+Onega+and+the+White+Sea (accessed 30 Nov. 2024). When the authors visited Besovy Sledki in 2019, they were unable to view the originals.

59 Gjerde, 'Rock art and landscapes' (2010), p. 309.

60 Sawwatejew, *Karelische Felsbilder* (1984), pp. 139, 171–181, 201.

61 Lobanova gives the following chronological classification for Karelia: Mesolithic 6500–4900 BCE, Neolithic 4600–2900 BCE, Chalcolithic 2800–1700 BCE, Bronze Age 1600–500 BCE. Lobanova, 'New data on the chronology of Lake Onega and the White Sea area petroglyphs' (2021), p. 211. The 300-year gap between the end of the Mesolithic and the beginning of the Neolithic is not explained by Lubanova. The present author is inclined to prolong the Mesolithic until 4600 BCE.

62 Gjerde, Jan Magne, 'Stone-Age rock art and beluga landscapes at River Vyg, North-Western Russia', in: *Fennoscandia Archaeologica*, vol. 30 (Helsinki: Helsinki University, 2013), pp. 40f.

63 Sawwatejew, *Karelische Felsbilder* (1984), p. 167.

64 Gjerde, 'Rock art and landscapes' (2010), p. 320, figs 217f.

65 Gjerde, 'Stone-Age rock art and beluga landscapes at River Vyg' (2013), p. 50.

66 It is sometimes difficult to distinguish elk from reindeer. As a rule, male and female reindeer carry antlers; the males shed their antlers in winter, females in spring. Female elk have no antlers, males shed their antlers around December. Elk may be identified by their broad nose and wide, overhanging upper lip, a small beard and long legs.

67 Sawwatejew, *Karelische Felsbilder* (1984), pp. 165f.

68 Sawwatejew, *Karelische Felsbilder* (1984), pp. 141, 145.

69 Helskog, 'Snowshoes and skis in North European rock art' (2018), pp. 243f.

70 Janik, 'The development and periodisation of White Sea rock carvings' (2010), p. 87, fig. 5.

71 Information concerning the casualties from the Solovetsky Museum, Karelia, and: https://allthatsinteresting.com/white-sea-baltic-canal (accessed 30 March 2024).

72 Kostianoy, Andrey G., 'Interannual variability of water level in two largest lakes of Europe', in: *Remote Sensing*, vol. 14, no. 3, art. no. 659 (Basel: MDPI, 2022).

73 Lobanova, 'New data on the chronology of Lake Onega and the White Sea area petroglyphs' (2021), p. 212. Poikalainen, Väino and Ernits, Enn, *Rock Carvings of Lake Onega*, vol. 1: *The Vodla Region* (Tartu: Estonian Society of Prehistoric Art, 1998), pp. 15–17, 37–39. Sawwatejew, *Karelische Felsbilder* (1984), pp. 113, 120.

74 Helskog, Knut, 'The shore connection: Cognitive landscape and communications with rock carvings in northernmost Europe', in: *Norwegian Archaeological Review*, vol. 32, no. 2 (Abingdon: Routledge, 1999), p. 73.

75 Poikalainen, Väino, 'Some statistics about rock carvings at Lake Onega', in: *Folklore*, vol. 11 (Tartu: Institute of the Estonian Language, 1999). See also: Kynällä, Joutsenen, *Rock Art from Lake Onega 4000–2000 bc: Swansongs* (Tartu: Estonian Society of Prehistoric Art, 1990), p. 6.

76 Gjerde, 'Rock art and landscapes' (2010), pp. 415f.

77 The ancestors of the Finnish-Karelian people who passed down their mythological lore were most likely Finno-Ugric hunter-gatherers.

78 Lahelma, Antti, 'Strange swans and odd ducks: Interpreting the ambiguous waterfowl imagery of Lake Onega', in: Cochrane, Andrew and Meirion Jones, Andrew (eds), *Visualising the Neolithic* (Oxford: Oxbow, 2012), pp. 21f, 29.

79 Lahelma, 'Strange swans and odd ducks' (2012), pp. 26f. Le Quellec, Jean-Loïc, *Avant nous le Déluge ! L'humanité et ses mythes* (Paris: Éditions du Détour, 2021), pp. 153f. Devlet also mentions this myth of a cosmogonic dive, but without relating it to Lake Onega. Devlet, *Myths in Stone* (2005), p. 234.

80 Lahelma, 'Strange swans and odd ducks' (2012), p. 26. Le Quellec, Jean-Loïc and Sergent, Bernard, *Dictionnaire critique de mythologie* (Paris: CNRS Éditions, 2017), p. 1050. Le Quellec, Jean-Loïc, *La caverne originelle. Art, mythes et premières humanités* (2022), pp. 606, 710.

81 From: Poikalainen and Ernits, *Rock Carvings of Lake Onega*, vol. 3: *The Besov Nos Region: Besov Nos, Kladovets, Gazhi and Guri Localities* (Tartu: Estonian Society of Prehistoric Art, 2021), pp. 293, 313–324. See also: Lahelma, 'Strange swans and odd ducks' (2012), pp. 26f. Le Quellec and Sergent, *Dictionnaire critique de mythologie* (2017), p. 10.

82 Also noteworthy is the observation made by Vincent Vieira that on a couple of palimpsests a swan has been superimposed on an elk in such a way that the elk's front leg formed the swan's neck or that 'an elk's head was used as a base for the bodies of two swans'. Vieira, Vincent, 'A context analysis of Neolithic *Cygnus* petroglyphs at Lake Onega', in: *Cambridge Archaeological Journal*, vol. 20, no. 2 (Cambridge: McDonald Institute for Archaeological Research, 2010), p. 257, fig. 2. However, as noted by Lahelma, in Finno-Karelian mythology there is hardly any substantive link between elk and swan. Lahelma, 'Strange swans and odd ducks' (2012), p. 29. On another palimpsest at Cape Swan, the body of a swan forms the upper bodies of two men dancing at a maypole. Kynällä, *Rock Art from Lake Onega* (1990), fig. 5. Poikalainen and Ernits, *Rock Carvings of Lake Onega*, vol. 3 (2021), pp. 156f.

83 It is possible that the masked anthropomorph does not stand on skis, but on a snake.

84 Poikalainen and Ernits, *Rock Carvings of Lake Onega*, vol. 3 (2021), pp. 40f; also pp. 237, 248. Sawwatejew, *Karelische Felsbilder* (1984), pp. 63f, 96f.

85 Poikalainen and Ernits, *Rock Carvings of Lake Onega*, vol. 2: *The Besov Nos Region: Karetski and Peri Localities* (Tartu: Estonian Society of Prehistoric Art, 2019), pp. 487, 504; vol. 3 (2021), pp. 202, 228f,

86 Kynällä, Rock Art from Lake Onega (1990), fig. 5. Poikalainen and Ernits, *Rock Carvings of Lake Onega*, vol. 1 (2021), pp. 156f.

87 Poikalainen and Ernits, *Rock Carvings of Lake Onega*, vol. 3 (2021), pp. 130–177.

88 Lahelma, 'Strange swans and odd ducks' (2012), p. 19.

89 Poikalainen and Ernits, *Rock Carvings of Lake Onega*, vol. 3 (2021), pp. 77, 152f.

90 Poikalainen and Ernits, *Rock Carvings of Lake Onega*, vol. 3 (2021), pp. 131, 159, 181.

91 Helskog, *Communicating with the World of Beings*. (2014), pp. 17, 30.

92 Gjerde, 'Rock art and landscapes' (2010), pp. 246, 250, 259; 'Marine mammals in the rock art of Alta, Norway, northernmost Europe', in: *Whale on the Rock*, vol. 2 (Ulsan, S. Korea: Petroglyph Museum, 2018),

p. 197. Helskog, 'Changing settlements, shores and boats through 5,000 years: Dating and connecting petroglyphs to the general archaeological record – a case from northernmost Norway', in: Gjerde and Arntzen, *Perspectives on Differences in Rock Art* (2021), pp. 49, 52, 71. Tansem, Karin and Storemyr, Per, 'Red-coated rocks at the seashore: The aesthetics and geology of prehistoric rock art in Alta, Arctic Norway', in: *Geoarchaeology*, vol. 36 (Hoboken: Wiley, 2021), p. 319.

93 Gjerde, 'Rock art and landscapes' (2010), p. 252. Tansem and Storemyr, 'Red-coated rocks at the seashore' (2021), pp. 319f.

94 Gjerde, 'Rock art and landscapes' (2010), p. 252. In northern Norway, the following archaeological classifications are applied: Mesolithic: 9000–4500 BCE; Neolithic: 4500–1800 BCE; Bronze Age: 1800–500 BCE; Iron Age: 500 BCE–800 CE.

95 Gjerde, 'Rock art and landscapes' (2010), pp. 252, 254, 285. For an illustrated table with six periods see: Helskog, *Communication with the World of Beings* (2014), p. 29; also: Helskog, 'Changing settlements, shores and boats' (2021), pp. 50f.

96 The one-metre gap between 22 and 21 m asl may indicate a short interruption in the making of petroglyphs between Periods I and II.

97 Helskog, *Communication with the World of Beings* (2014), pp. 192f.

98 Helskog dates the end of rock art making at 100 CE; *Communication with the World of Beings* (2014), p. 29.

99 Helskog, *Communication with the World of Beings* (2014), pp. 183f, fig. 203.

100 Helskog, *Communication with the World of Beings* (2014), p. 17.

101 Since the mud-rock at Kåfjord is highly fragile, it is closed to the public and not signposted. Permission for an accompanied visit may be obtained at the Hjemmeluft Museum. The authors were able to visit all sites of Alta in September 2022 in company of museum curator Ingvild Telle.

102 Some of these places, for example Ole Pedersen, are subsumed under Hjemmeluft in documentation available at the museum.

103 Helskog, *Communication with the World of Beings* (2014), pp. 211, 221.

104 Tansem and Storemyr, 'Red-coated rocks at the seashore' (2021), pp. 315–316, 322–324, 330.

105 The first petroglyphs of Alta were discovered by chance in 1938 during road construction works.

106 Hykkerud, Martin, 'The management of the Kåfjord Rock Art Site', in: Gjerde and Arntzen, *Perspectives on Differences in Rock Art* (Sheffield: Equinox, 2021), pp. 132–138.

107 Tansem and Storemyr, 'Red-coated rocks at the seashore' (2021), pp. 326, 330.

108 As the authors observed in Bohuslän at sites where the petroglyphs were not repainted for a longer period, the older paint seems to penetrate permanently into the rock.

109 Helskog, *Communication with the World of Beings* (2014), p. 62.

110 The humans involved in this scene are identified as male by their penis.

111 Helskog, *Communication with the World of Beings* (2014), p. 100. These staffs and a couple of alleged drums are also associated with shamanism although it remains unknown whether shamanism was practised in northern Fennoscandia 5,000 to 6,000 years ago. Herva, Vesa-Pekka and Lahelma, Antti, *Northern Archaeology and Cosmology: A Relational View* (Abingdon: Routledge, 2020), pp. 78–80. Gjerde, 'Rock art and landscapes' (2010), pp. 125f. Rozwadowski, Andrzej, 'Shamanism in indigenous context: Understanding Siberian rock art', in: McDonald and Veth, *Companion to Rock Art* (2012), pp. 458–460.

112 Whether animals that often appear in petroglyphs represented tribal totems, as is sometimes postulated, is doubtful. For while there are numerous scenes of elk and reindeer hunts in northern Fennoscandia and these cervids were indeed hunted in real life, the killing of totem animals is usually taboo or, at least, regulated by strict ritual prescriptions.

113 https://www.donsmaps.com/norge.html (accessed 30 March 2024). Gjerde, 'Rock art and landscapes' (2010), p. 123. Helskog, *Communication with the World of Beings* (2014), p. 63.

114 Kashina, Ekaterina and Zhulnikov, Alexandr, 'Rods with elk's heads: Symbol in ritual context', in: *Estonian Journal of Archaeology*, vol. 15, no. 1 (Tallin: Estonian Academic Publishers, 2011), pp. 2f (= 19f).

115 Elk-headed boats are also found at Nämforsen, Vyg, Kanozero and Lake Onega.

116 https://www.donsmaps.com/toolsmore.html (accessed 30 March 2024). Gjerde, 'Rock art and Landscapes' (2010), p. 142.

117 Eliade, Mircea (editor in chief), *The Encyclopedia of Religion*, vol. 1 (New York: Simon & Schuster Macmillan, 1993), p. 398.

118 Sveen, Arvid, *Felsbilder. Jiepmaluokta Hjemmeluft, Alta* (Tromsø: Sveen, 1996), p. 47.

119 Eliade, *The Encyclopedia of Religion*, vol. 1 (1993), p. 397. Le Quellec, Jean-Loïc, *La caverne originelle* (2022), pp. 542–47.

120 For a sketch of the large panel Amtmannsnes II: Helskog, *Communication with the World of Beings* (2014), pp. 156f, fig. 163.

121 Bertilsson, Ulf, 'Boundless rock art: Symbols, contexts and times in prehistoric imagery of Fennoscandia', in: Stebergløkken, Heidrun et al. (eds), *Ritual Landscape and Borders within Rock Art Research* (Oxford: Archaeopress, 2015), p. 84. Helskog, *Communication with the World of Beings* (2014), pp. 192f. Helskog, 'Changing settlements, shores and boats' (2021), pp. 68f.

122 Helskog, *Communication with the World of Beings* (2014), p. 225, fig. 252. Sveen, *Felsbilder* (1996), p. 17.

123 Gjerde, 'Rock art and landscapes' (2010), pp. 354–357. For a later dating of the beginning of rock pecking at Nämforsen see: Sjöstrand, Ylva, 'Memory and destruction: Pictorial practices surrounding red ochre paintings in late Neolithic northern Sweden', in: Stebergløkken et al., *Ritual Landscape and Borders within Rock Art Research* (2015), pp. 171f.

124 Gjerde, 'Rock art and landscapes' (2010), pp. 103, 347–381. 'A Stone Age rock art map at Nämforsen, Northern Sweden', in: *Adoranten* (2015), pp. 75f.

125 Bertilsson, Ulf, 'New 3D documentation reveals carved Stone Age and Bronze Age axes at Nämforsen, in Ångermanland, Sweden', in: *Adoranten* (2018), p. 79, fig. 19. 'Warriors and weapons: Engraved motifs in the Early Bronze Age rock art in Sweden', in: Bettencourt, Ana M.S. et al. (eds), *Weapons and Tools in Rock Art: A World Perspective* (Oxford: Oxbow, 2021), pp. 71–80.

126 Gjerde, Rock art and landscapes' (2010), pp. 361, 363. 'A Stone Age rock art map at Nämforsen' (2015), p. 84. In the paintings, images of elk predominate by far. Ramquist, Per, 'Rock-art and settlement: Issues of spatial order in the prehistoric rock-art of Fenno-Scandia', in: Nash, George and Chippindale, Christopher (eds) *European Landscapes of Rock Art* (Abingdon: Routledge, 2012), pp. 148–151.

127 Gjerde, 'A Stone Age rock art map at Nämforsen' (2015), p. 75. Linge, Trond Eilev, 'Seasons and landscape in North European hunter-gatherer rock art: The case of salmon at Honnhammar, central Norway', in: Gjerde and Arntzen, *Perspectives on Differences in Rock Art* (2021), p. 156.

128 A couple of these picks may represent boomerangs. Bertilsson, 'New 3D documentation reveals carved Stone Age and Bronze Age axes at Nämforsen' (2018), pp. 75–82, 88. '3D-models of Neolithic and Bronze Age axe images at Nämforsen, Sweden, reveals long-distance contacts and new implications for chronology and cultural context', in: *Adoranten* (2021), pp. 113–120.

129 Bertilson, 'Warriors and weapons' (2021), pp. 68, 78.

130 Nielsen, *National Museum of Denmark* (2016), p. 19.

131 Hygen, Anne-Sophie and Bengtsson, Lasse, *Felsbilder im Grenzgebiet. Bohuslän und Östfold* (Sävedalen: Warne Förlag, 2000), p. 19.

132 Ling, *Elevated rock art* (2014), p. 5.

133 Nimura, *Prehistoric Rock Art in Scandinavia* (2016), p. 91.

134 It remains debatable whether cup marks are rock art at all. Isolated cup marks or groups of cup marks without any apparent order definitely do not qualify as 'art', being rather cultural signs or markers.

135 Evers, Dietrich, *The Magic of the Image* (Warmsroth: Pulsar-Verlag, 1994), p. 43.

136 Ling, *Elevated rock art* (2014), pp. 33, 111, 245. See also Ling, Johan, 'Elevated rock art: Maritime images and situations' (2010), pp. 35–37. Another study gives for Bohuslän a decline from 17 to 9–10 m asl over the same period. Ibid. p. 247.

137 Coles, John, *Shadows of a Northern Past: Rock Carvings of Bohuslän and Østfold* (Oxford: Oxbow, 2005), p. 101.

138 Ling, 'Elevated rock art: Maritime images and situations' (2010), pp. 34f.

139 Bertilsson, Ulf, 'From folk oddities and remarkable relics to scientific substratum: 135 years of changing perceptions on the rock art carvings in Tanum, northern Bohuslän, Sweden', in: Skoglund, Ling and Bertilsson, *Picturing the Bronze Age* (2015), pp. 6–14.

140 Kaul, Flemming, *Ships on Bronzes: A Study in Bronze Age Religion and Iconography*, vol. 1 (Copenhagen: The National Museum, 1998), pp. 58–64. Vogt, David, 'Continuity and discontinuity in South Scandinavian Bronze Age rock art research', in: Helskog, *Theoretical Perspectives in Rock Art Research* (2001), p. 101.

141 Bertilsson, 'From folk oddities and remarkable relics to scientific substratum' (2015), pp. 9–11. Kaul, *Ships on Bronzes* (1998), vol. 1, pp. 66, 114; vol. 2, p. 7. Nimura, *Prehistoric Rock Art in Scandinavia* (2016), p. 87.

142 Bertilsson, Ulf, 'The Spear: Digital documentation sheds new light on Early Bronze Age spear carvings from Sweden – An analysis with some comparative examples from Valcamonica, Italy', in: *Adoranten* (2017), p. 64.

143 Vogt, 'Continuity and discontinuity in South Scandinavian Bronze Age rock art research' (2001), pp. 101–104.

144 Almgren, Oscar, *Nördliche Felszeichnungen als religiöse Urkunden* (Moritz Diesterweg, Frankfurt a.M., 1934), pp. XIV, 37–39, 69, 190f, 298f. The German work is the revised translation of *Hällristningar och kultbruk* (1926–7).

145 Almgren, *Nördliche Felszeichnungen als religiöse Urkunden* (1934), pp. 145, 289, 311.

146 In the whole of Scandinavia, there are 32 ard ploughs as against 19,322 boats. Nimura, *Prehistoric Rock Art in Scandinavia* (2016), p. 91.

147 Vogt, 'Continuity and discontinuity in South Scandinavian Bronze Age rock art research' (2001), p. 106.

148 Allentoft, Morten E. et al., 'Population genomics of post-glacial western Eurasia', in: *Nature*, vol. 625 (London: Macmillan, 2024), pp. 301, 303–307. Haak, Wolfgang et al., 'Massive migration from the steppe was a source for Indo-European languages in Europe', *Nature*, vol. 522 (London: Macmillan, 2015), pp. 1, 4 (= 207, 210). Skoglund, Pontus et al., 'Origins and genetic legacy of Neolithic farmers and hunter-gatherers in Europe', in: *Science*, vol. 336 (Washington DC: AAAS, 2012), p. 466.

149 Price, *Ancient Scandinavia* (2015), pp. 157f. See also: Bramanti, B. et al, 'Genetic discontinuity between local hunter-gatherers and Central Europe's first farmers', in: *Science*, vol. 326 (Washington DC: AAAS, 2009), p. 137.

150 Price, *Ancient Scandinavia* (2015), p. 158. Skoglund, 'Origins and genetic legacy of Neolithic farmers and hunter-gatherers in Europe' (2012), p. 469.

151 Skoglund, 'Origins and genetic legacy of Neolithic farmers and hunter-gatherers in Europe' (2012), p. 469.

152 Kaul and Rønne, 'Bronzes, farms and rock art' (2013), p. 25.

153 Allentoft, Morten E. et al., 'Population genomics of Bronze Age Eurasia', in: *Nature*, vol. 522 (London: Macmillan, 2015), pp. 167–169. 'Population genomics of post-glacial western Eurasia' (2024), pp. 301, 308f.

154 Price, *Ancient Scandinavia* (2015), pp. 162f.

155 Allentoft et al., 'Population genomics of Bronze Age Eurasia' (2015), pp. 170f. Haak, 'Massive migration from the steppe was a source for Indo-European languages in Europe' (2015), pp. 1, 4f. Ling, John and Koch, John, 'A sea beyond Europe to the north and west', in: Dodd and Meijer, *Giving the Past a Future* (2018), pp. 97, 99.

156 The two best guides to the petroglyphs of Bohuslän are by John Coles: *Images of the Past: A Guide to the Rock Carvings and Other Ancient Monuments of Northern Bohuslän* (Vitlycke: Hällristningsmuseet Vitlycke, 1990), and *Shadows of a Northern Past: Rock Carvings of Bohuslän and Østfold* (Oxford: Oxbow, 2005). At the most visited places such as Torsbo, Aspeberget, Litsleby, Vitlycke, Fossum, Massleberg, Begby and Solberg, most of the petroglyphs have been painted in red or white to enhance visibility. The petroglyphs at other sites are often hard to see unless one uses a torch at night; occasionally sites are overgrown by moss.

157 Crew members are either represented full bodied in profile or as mere strokes. In the latter case, if they are paddlers, there are as many paddlers on board as strokes. If they are rowers who often sit in pairs, the ship may carry double the number of rowers as there are visible strokes. Bradley, Richard et al, 'Imaginary vessels in the Late Bronze Age of Gotland and South Scandinavia', in: *Current Swedish Archaeology*, vol. 18 (Uddevalla: Svenska Arkeologiska Samfundet, 2010), pp. 87, 90. Ling, *Elevated Rock Art* (2014), p. 189.

158 The sites within the parish of Tanum are sometimes referenced by that name followed by a number.

159 There are still larger petroglyphs worldwide than the 4.6-m-long ship at Bjørnstadskipet: for example the 8.5-m-long giraffe at site L 73 in Wadi Djerat, the 6-m-long giraffe at Dabous, Niger, and the gigantic snake petroglyphs recently discovered (in 2015–2019) in the middle and upper Orinoco River of Venezuela and Colombia. The longest snake petroglyph measures more than 40 metres and dates from the pre-Columbian period (11th–15th century CE). Riris, Philip et al., 'Monumental snake engravings of the Orinoco River', in: *Antiquity*, vol. 98 (Cambridge: Cambridge University Press, 2024), pp. 724–729.

160 The Hjortspring ship and Rørby sword are on display in the National Museum of Denmark in Copenhagen.

161 About 2,000 ship settings have been recorded in southern Scandinavia; a few dozen are from the Bronze Age, the vast majority from the Vendel Period and the Viking Age.

162 Kristiansen, Kristian and Larsson, Thomas B., *The Rise of Bronze Age Society: Travels, Transmissions and Transformations* (Cambridge: Cambridge University Press, 2005), pp. 112–116. Melheim, Lene and Ling, Johan, 'Taking the stranger on board: The two maritime legacies of bronze age rock art', in: Skoglund, Ling and Bertilsson, *North Meets South* (2017), pp. 77f.

163 Ling, Johan and Uhnér, Claes, 'Rock art and metal trade', in: *Adoranten* (2021), pp. 24–26.

164 Kristiansen and Larsson, *The Rise of Bronze Age Society* (2005), pp. 123–125.

165 Ling and Koch, 'A sea beyond Europe to the north and west' (2018), p. 98. Ling and Uhnér, 'Rock art and metal trade' (2021), pp. 24, 26.

166 Graichen, Gisela and Hesse, Alexander, *Die Bernsteinstrasse* (Reinbeck: Rowohlt, 2012), pp. 94, 153f.

167 Varberg, Jeanette and Kaul, Flemming and Gratuze, Bernard, 'Bronze Age glass and amber: Evidence of Bronze Age long distance exchange', in: *Adoranten* (2019), pp. 5f, 15, 18, 23.

168 Oxhide ingots were mostly made from copper, but also of tin or other metals.

169 Ling and Uhnér, 'Rock art and metal trade' (2021), pp. 26–31.

170 Jensen, Jørgen and Kruse, Petra (eds), *Gods and Heroes of the Bronze Age: Europe at the Time of Ulysses* (London: Thames and Hudson, 1999), p. 48.

171 Ling and Uhnér, 'Rock art and metal trade' (2021), pp. 32–35. Vandkilde, Helle, 'Breakthrough of the Nordic Bronze Age: Transcultural warriorhood and a Carpathian crossroad in the sixteenth century BC', in: *European Journal of Archaeology*, vol. 17, no. 4 (Cambridge: Cambridge University Press, 2014), pp. 135, 139, 141.

172 Jensen and Kruse, *Gods and Heroes of the Bronze Age* (1999), p. 40.

173 In Brittany there was only copper ore and no tin.

174 McKinley, Jacqueline I. et al., 'Dead-Sea connections: A Bronze Age and Iron Age ritual scene on the Isle of Thanet', in: Koch, John T. and Cunliffe, Barry, *Celtic from the West*, vol. 2: *Rethinking the Bronze Age and the Arrival of Indo-European in Atlantic Europe* (Oxford: Oxbow, 2013), pp. 167f, 178f.

175 Diodorus Siculus, *Library of Histories*, V, 22.1 (Harvard: Loeb Classical, 1933-1967), p. 157.

176 Lobell, Jarret A., 'Which island is it anyway? Unidentified island, English Channel', in: *Archaeology*, vol. 77, nr. 3 (Long Island City: Archaeological Institute of America, 2024), p. 34.

177 Kristiansen and Larsson, *The Rise of Bronze Age Society* (2005), p. 200.

178 Price, *Ancient Scandinavia* (2015), pp. 112, 123, 158.

179 Garrow, Duncan and Wilkin, Neil, *The World of Stonehenge* (London: British Museum Press, 2022), pp. 227–230. Kristiansen, Kristian, 'Warfare and the political economy: Europe 1500–1100 BC', in: Horn, Christian and Kristiansen, Kristian (eds), *Warfare in Bronze Age Society* (Cambridge: Cambridge University Press, 2018), pp. 30, 40. Inselmann, Leif et al., 'Warriors from the south? Arrowheads from the Tollense Valley and Central Europe', in: *Antiquity*, vol. 98, no. 401 (Cambridge: Cambridge University Press, 2021), pp. 1252–1270. Price, *Ancient Scandinavia* (2015), p. 204

180 Although there are many scenes of duels, only a few petroglyphs show the act of killing and death. Exceptions are Brastad 617, Fossum (Tanum 255) and Tanum 319.1. Ling, Johan and Toreld, Andreas, 'Maritime warfare in Scandinavian rock art', in: Horn and Kristiansen, *Warfare in Bronze Age Society* (2018), pp. 68, 72.

181 In northern Scandinavia and Karelia, ships of course appear in petroglyphs at a much earlier date.

182 Ling, Johan and Rowlands, Michael, 'The "Stranger King" (bull) and rock art', in: Skoglund, Ling and Bertilsson, *Picturing the Bronze Age* (2015), pp. 90, 94, fig. 8.5.

183 Jensen and Kruse, *Gods and Heroes of the Bronze Age* (1999), pp. 50f.

184 Nielsen, *National Museum of Denmark* (2016), p. 137.

185 Translation by the author from the Latin. Tacitus, C. Cornelius, *Die Germania* [*De Origine et Situ Germanorum*, tr. Adolf Bacmeister (1868)], chapter 44.

186 Nielsen, *National Museum of Denmark* (2016), p. 141.

187 It is believed that sails were introduced in Scandinavia around the sixth, seventh or even eighth century CE. It is from this period that the first ship engravings on stone steles from Gotland are dated. Nylén, Erik and Lamm, Jan Peder, *Stones, Ships and Symbols: The Picture Stones of Gotland from the Viking Age and Before* (Stockholm: Gidlunds Bokförlag, 1988), pp. 22, 42. For a different opinion see: Bengtsson, *Sailing Rock Art Boats* (2017). It remains striking that the Nordic people did not use sails although they must have encountered them in their contacts with British and Iberian sailors at the isle of Thanet, and later with the Romans.

188 Milstreu, Gerhard, 'Updating rock art: Re-cut rock art images (with a special emphasis on ship carvings)', in: *Adoranten* (2017), p. 39.

189 Kaul, *Ships on Bronzes* (1998), vol. 1, pp. 88, 113f. Ling, 'Elevated rock art' (2010), pp. 44–47. *Elevated Rock Art* (2014), pp. 99–105.

190 Kaul, *Ships on Bronzes* (1998), vol. 1, pp. 98–104, 136f. Meller, Harald (ed.), *Der geschmiedete Himmel. Die weite Welt im Herzen Europas vor 3600 Jahren* (Stuttgart: Theiss, 2004), pp. 60f.

191 Nielsen, *National Museum of Denmark* (2016), p. 111. Another, smaller sun-horse chariot dated to Montelius Period II was possibly found in 1895 at Tågeborg, Denmark. Goldhahn, Joakim, *Sagaholm: North*

European Bronze Age Rock Art and Burial Ritual (Oxford: Oxbow, 2016), p, 78. Whether the first of the two miniature clay chariots from Dupljaja, Serbia, where an anthropomorph standing on a three-wheeled chariot is pulled by three birds, also represents a sun chariot as claimed by Kaul, remains unknown, but it is quite plausible. Kaul's hypothesis is supported by the second miniature chariot, which he does not mention. Although the draught animals are missing here, the bird-faced figure standing in the chariot is decorated with engraved swastika symbols, an ancient sun symbol widespread in Eurasia. Kaul, *Ships on Bronzes* (1998), vol. 1, p. 254. Powell, Eric A., 'Europe's lost Bronze Age civilization', in: *Archaeology*, November/December 2024 (Boston: Archaeological Institute of America), pp. 34–37.

192 Almgren, *Nördliche Felszeichnungen als religiöse Urkunden* (1934), pp. 38f, 190.

193 Almgren, *Nördliche Felszeichnungen als religiöse Urkunden* (1934), pp. 99f. Kaul, Flemming, 'The Chariot of the Sun and other sun horses of the Nordic Bronze Age – including some interesting anatomical details', in: Dodd and Meijer, *Giving the Past a Future* (2018), pp. 62f.

194 Kaul, 'The Chariot of the Sun and other sun horses of the Nordic Bronze Age' (2018), p. 62, fig. 9.

195 A similar-looking woman stands near two lur players at Fossum, but her role is unknown.

196 Nielsen, *National Museum of Denmark* (2016), pp. 97–99, 104f.

197 The close relationship between sun and horse is also expressed in the two gold bowls from Boeslunde, Denmark, which are decorated with engraved sun motifs and have handles shaped like a horse's head. Nielsen, *National Museum of Denmark* (2016), pp. 122f, see also p. 114.

198 Garrow and Wilkin, *The World of Stonehenge* (2022), pp. 139f. Kaul, *Ships on Bronzes* (1998), vol. 1, pp. 195–203, 258–265.

199 Homer, *The Iliad*, VII.421f; VIII.485; XVIII.239f.

200 Kristiansen, Kristian, 'Rock art and religion: The sun journey in Indo-European mythology and Bronze Age rock art', in: Fredell et al., *Representations and Communications* (2010), pp. 93–115. Kristiansen and Larsson, *The Rise of Bronze Age Society* (2005), pp. 294–303. Lahelma, Antti, 'The circumpolar context of the "sun ship" motif in South Scandinavian rock art', in: Skoglund, Ling and Bertilsson, *North Meets South* (2017), pp. 146–148.

201 *Rig Veda*, book I, hymn 130.

202 Snorri Sturluson, *The Prose Edda*, trans. Arthur Gilchrist Brodeur (1916).

203 Almgren, *Nördliche Felszeichnungen als religiöse Urkunden* (1934), pp. XIV, 69. Kaul, *Ships on Bronzes* (1998), vol. 1, pp. 11, 25, 49.

204 Hygen and Bengtsson suggested that the image of a man lifting a boat could also represent the Nordic god Donar, that is Thor. Hygen and Bengtsson, *Felsbilder im Grenzgebiet* (2000), pp. 95f.

205 Meller, *Der geschmiedete Himmel* (2004), pp. 28f. However, it cannot be ruled out that the disc above the ship does not represent the sun, but the full moon.

206 Bradley, *Image and Audience* (2009), pp. 143–146.

207 Nielsen, *National Museum of Denmark* (2016), pp. 115f. Price, *Ancient Scandinavia* (2015), p. 218.

208 Bertilsson, 'Warriors and weapons' (2021), p. 73.

209 Vandkilde, 'Breakthrough of the Nordic Bronze Age' (2014), pp. 130f, 135–145.

210 Lumley, Henry de, *Le mont Bego. Vallées des Merveilles et de Fontanalba* (Paris: Éditions du patrimoine, 2003), p. 43.

211 Bertilsson, 'Warriors and weapons' (2021), p. 71.

212 Almgren's interpretation of a scene at Tuvene (Tanum 302) as a warrior standing next to a decapitated corpse has not been confirmed. I thank Gerhard Milstreu for this information. The man lying on the ground looks dead, but he is not decapitated. Almgren, *Nördliche Felszeichnungen als religiöse Urkunden* (1934), p. 123.

213 In fact, many Bronze Age axes were multi-functional; they could be used for wood cutting and combat.

214 Gelling, Peter and Davidson, Hilda Ellis, *The Chariot of the Sun and other Rites and Symbols of the Northern Bronze Age* (London: J.M. Dent & Sons, 1969), pp. 30f. Hygen and Bengtsson, *Felsbilder im Grenzgebiet* (2000), pp. 88, 183.

215 Bunnefeld, Jan-Heinrich, 'The chief and his sword? Some thoughts on the swordbearer's rank in the Early Nordic Bronze Age', in: Horn and Kristiansen, *Warfare in Bronze Age Society* (2018), p. 201.

216 Bertilson, 'Warriors and weapons' (2021), p. 77.

217 Bertilson, 'Warriors and weapons' (2021), pp. 69f. Nielsen, *National Museum of Denmark* (2016), p. 104.

218 Davidson, *Scandinavian Mythology* (1984), pp. 21, 31, 35, 51, 57, 59, 120.

219 Ling and Toreld, 'Maritime warfare in Scandinavian rock art' (2018), p. 64.

220 Ling, Johan, *Rock Art and Seascapes in Uppland* (Oxford: Oxbow, 2013), p. 21.

221 Nimura, *Prehistoric Rock Art in Scandinavia* (2016), p. 101.

222 Skoglund, Peter, *Rock Art Through Time: Scanian Rock Carvings in the Bronze Age and Earliest Iron Age* (Oxford: Oxbow, 2016), pp. 24–27, 66–74.

223 Four more such images of men carrying huge ceremonial axes are found at Dungen, a few km south of Simrishamn. Svensson, Ann-Louise, *A Guide to the Rock Carvings of South-East Scania* (Simrishamn: Simrishamne kommun, 2013), p. 15.

224 Svensson, *A Guide to the Rock Carvings of South-East Scania* (2013), p. 10.

225 Moberg, Carl-Axel, *The Kivik Grave* (Stockholm: Central Board of National Antiquities, 1992), p. 5.

226 Skoglund, *Rock Art through Time* (2016), p. 78, quoting Bradley, *Image and Audience* (2009), pp. 195–196.

227 Nimura, *Prehistoric Rock Art in Scandinavia* (2016), p. 101

228 Skoglund, *Rock Art Through Time* (2016), pp. 35f, 42, 111. Unfortunately, this highly significant petroglyph was severely damaged in 2009 during a botched silicon impression. Svensson, *A Guide to the Rock Carvings of South-East Scania* (2013), pp. 32f.

229 It is possible the petroglyphs were already noted as early as 1752. Goldhahn, Joakim, 'To let mute stones speak: On the becoming of archaeology', in: Dodd and Meijer, *Giving the Past a Future* (2018), p. 44.

230 Goldhahn, Joakim, 'Bredarör on Kivik: A monumental cairn and the history of its interpretation', in: *Antiquity*, vol. 83 (Cambridge: Cambridge University Press, 2009), pp. 363–6. *Bredarör på Kivik, en arkeologisk odysse = Bredarör on Kivik: An Archaeological Odyssey* (Simrishamn: Artes Liberales AB, 2013), pp. 7–92. 'To let mute stones speak' (2018), pp. 37–53. Ferngård Svensson Ann-Louise, *Das Grab von Kivik. Bredarör, das Königsgrab* (Kivik: Asmiroca Kulturarvsupplevelser, 2017), pp. 1–7, 12.

231 Most scholars agree on a date around 1400 BCE for the petroglyphs; Bertilsson et al. propose 1550–1400 BCE and Kristiansen and Larsson the later sixteenth century BCE. Bertilsson, Ulf et al., 'The Kivik tomb: Bredarör enters into the digital arena — documented with OLS, SfM and RTI', in: Bergerbrant, Sophie and Wessman, Anna (eds), *New Perspectives on the Bronze Age* (Oxford: Archaeopress, 2017), pp. 303f. Goldhahn, 'Bredarör on Kivik' (2009), pp. 368f. Kristiansen and Larsson, *The Rise of Bronze Age Society* (2005), pp. 189, 193. Ferngård Svensson, *Das Grab von Kivik* (2017), p. 10.

232 Goldhahn, 'To let mute stones speak' (2018), pp. 48–50. The petroglyphs have been painted red to ensure their visibility. It is doubtful whether they were also painted in the Bronze Age.

233 This is the only stone bearing petroglyphs in the Villfara monument; it may possibly have come from elsewhere. The burial is dated to Montelius Period II. Johannsen, Jens Winther, 'The Villfara Monument: Rock carvings, death, cosmology and rituals in early Bronze Age Scania', in: *Lund Archaeological Review*, vol. 19 (Lund: Lund University, 2013), pp. 19, 23, 27f.

234 For an image see: https://www.megalithic.co.uk/article.php?sid=30022 (accessed 31 March 2024).

235 A connection with the Greek letter itself is excluded as it appeared in the Greek alphabet only in the seventh century BCE.

236 Gelling and Davidson, *The Chariot of the Sun* (1969), pp. 99–101. Kristiansen and Larsson, *The Rise of Bronze Age Society* (2005), p. 191.

237 Goldhahn, *Sagaholm* (2016), pp. 12–29, 51f, 68, 76, 79, 91.

238 Nielsson, Per, 'A Life Aquatic? Looking at the relationships between settlements, rock art and sea levels in the Himmelstalund region of eastern Sweden', in: Fredell et al., *Representations and Communications* (2010), p. 7.

239 Ranta, Michael et al., 'Hunting stories in Scandinavian rock art: Aspects of 'tellability' in the North versus the South', in: *Oxford Journal of Archaeology*, vol. 39, no. 3 (Hoboken: Wiley, 2020), p. 10.

240 Bertilsson, 'Warriors and weapons' (2021), p. 77. Ling, Johan, *Rock Art and Seascapes in Uppland* (2013), p. 58.

241 Nielsson, Per, 'The Beauty is in the Act of the Beholder: South Scandinavian Rock Art from a Uses of the Past-Perspective', in: Back Danielsson, Ing-Marie, Fahlander, Fredrik and Sjöstrand, Ylva (eds), *Encountering Imagery: Materialities, Perceptions, Relations* (Stockholm: Stockholm University, 2012), pp. 87f.

242 Price, *Ancient Scandinavia* (2015), p. 367.

243 Information taken from interpretation boards at the site. See also: Davidson, *Scandinavian Mythology* (1984), p. 101.

244 Nylén and Lamm, *Stones, Ships and Symbols* (1988), pp. 9–11, 13–14, 22, 70, 177.

245 For Palaeolithic rock art in Italy see: Sigari, Dario, *Palaeolithic rock art of the Italian Peninsula* (Capo die Ponte: Centro Camuno die Studi Preistorici, 2022).

246 Pace, Davide, *Petroglifi dei colli di Grosio* (Grosio: Istituto archeologico valtellinese and Pro Loco Grosio, 1977).

247 Galbiati, Alberto, *Naquane: National Park of Rock Engravings* (Capo di Ponte: Libreria del parco, n.d.), p. 36.

248 The UNESCO application was based on more than 140,000 registered petroglyphs. More recent estimations claim 300,000 images. Fossati, Angelo E., 'The rock art tradition of Valcamonica–Valtellina, Northern Italy: A World Heritage view', in: Nash,

George et al. (eds), *Landscape Enquiries: The Proceedings of the Clifton Antiquarian Club*, vol. 8 (Bristol: Clifton Antiquarian Club, 2007), p. 139.

249 Anati, Emmanuel, *The Rock Art of Valcamonica* (Capo di Ponte: Atelier, 2015), p. 49.

250 Strabo, *Geographica IV*, 6.8, tr. A. Korbiger (Wiesbaden: Marix, 2007), p. 280.

251 Anati, *The Rock Art of Valcamonica* (2015), pp. 20f. Fossati, 'The rock art tradition of Valcamonica–Valtellina' (2007), pp. 152f. The Camuni are mentioned on the Tropaeum Alpium in La Turbie inland of Monte Carlo. The stone monument was built in 6 BCE to commemorate the subjugation of the 45 Alpine tribes by emperor Augustus. https://www.trophee-auguste.fr/en/ (accessed 30 November 2024).

252 Anati remains active at the time of writing, May 2024.

253 Marretta, Alberto, 'Digging the past: One hundred years of research on Valcamonica rock art', in: *Adoranten* (2008), pp. 36–58. Marretta, Alberto and Cittadini, Tiziana (eds), *Valcamonica Rock Art Parks* (Capo di Ponte: Centro Camuno die Studi Preistorici, 2011), pp. 8–12.

254 The chronology outlined mainly follows that advanced by Fossati in: 'The rock art tradition of Valcamonica–Valtellina' (2007), pp. 139–153.

255 For drawings see: Anati, *The Rock Art of Valcamonica* (2015), pp. 162–164. Sigari, Palaeolithic rock art of the Italian Peninsula (2022), pp. 90–113.

256 Anati, *The Rock Art of Valcamonica* (2015), pp. 85–88. Lødøen and Mandt, *The Rock Art of Norway* (2010), pp. 70–82.

257 It is doubtful whether the schematic stick-humans with lifted arms on rock 50 of Naquane really date to the Neolithic as claimed by Anati. *The Rock Art of Valcamonica* (2015), p. 169. Galbiati, *Naquane*, pp. 31f.

258 Fossati, 'The rock art tradition of Valcamonica–Valtellina' (2007), p. 143.

259 Fossati, 'The rock art tradition of Valcamonica–Valtellina' (2007), pp. 142–144. Marretta, Alberto, 'When it all begun: The Copper Age roots of Valcamonica rock art', in: *Adoranten* (2012), p. 55.

260 Barfield, Lawrence and Chippindale, Christopher, 'Meaning in the later prehistoric rock-engravings of Mont Bégo, Alpes-Maritimes, France,' in: *Proceedings of the Prehistoric Society*, vol. 63 (London: The Prehistoric Society, 1997), p. 105.

261 Anati, *The Rock Art of Valcamonica* (2015), pp. 135–137, 139.

262 In the necropolis of Remedello Sotto, all male burials were given weapons (daggers, axes and arrowheads) as grave goods. Casini, Stefania and De Marinis, Raffaele C., 'Des pierres et des dieux. L'art rupestre de la Valteline et du Valcamonica', in: *Le Globe*, vol. 149 (Geneva: University of Geneva, 2009), p. 70. Defrasne and Fedele believe that the discs engraved on the top of the steles do not represent the sun but necklaces. Defrasne, Claudia and Fedele, Francesco, 'Contextualiser l'imagerie préhistorique: Les figures circulaires et la figure "a bandoliera" des monolithes chalcolithiques centre-alpins', in: *Bulletin de la Société préhistorique française*, vol. 112, no. 3 (Paris: Société Préhistorique Française, 2015), pp. 543, 557f.

263 Casini, Stefania, 'The Valtellina and Valcamonica statue-menhirs: Their characters, chronology and contexts', in: Hansen, S. and Molodin, V.I. (eds), *The Bronze Age Art. Proceedings of International Symposium, April 15–19, 2013, Stralsund, Germany* (Novosibirsk:

National Research University and Berlin: German Archaeological Institute, 2015), pp. 101, fig. 10, 103 fig. 12. Casini and De Marinis, 'Des pierres et des dieux' (2009), pp. 70, fig. 5, 78, fig. 13.

264 Schweizerisches Landesmuseum, *Menschen in Stein gemeisselt* (Basel: Christoph Merian Verlag, 2021), p. 57.

265 Frachetti, Michael and Chippindale, Christopher, 'Alpine imagery, Alpine space, Alpine time; and prehistoric human experience', in: Nash and Chippindale, *European Landscapes of Rock Art* (2012), pp. 123–126, figs 6.3, 6.4.

266 Frachetti and Chippindale, 'Alpine imagery' (2012), pp. 123, 137.

267 Marretta, 'When it all begun' (2012), p. 56. Schweizerisches Landesmuseum, *Menschen in Stein gemeisselt* (2021), pp. 55–59. At menhir 11 from Massi di Cemmo, three rows of standing humans were superimposed on Remedello-type daggers. However, at Cemmo 1 (fig. 201) the daggers seem to have been engraved over the deer.

268 A possible exception was identified at Anvoia near Ossimo, twenty kilometres south of Cemmo. Some burnt bones from more than one human were found near the steles, but no burials. Marretta, 'When it all begun' (2012), pp. 56–59. Schweizerisches Landesmuseum, *Menschen in Stein gemeisselt* (2021), pp. 24, 59.

269 Galbiati, *Naquane*, pp. 24f. Nash, George H., 'Art and environment: How can rock art inform on past environments?', in: David and McNiven, *The Oxford Handbook of the Archaeology and Anthropology of Rock Art* (2018), p. 427.

270 On Seraldina I, rock 12, alone there are 60 duel scenes. Marretta, Alberto, 'Enlightening a rock art masterpiece: New research on Seraldina I Rock 12 (Valcamonica)', in: *Adoranten* (2016), p. 122.

271 Fossati, 'The rock art tradition of Valcamonica–Valtellina' (2007), p. 151, fig 20.

272 Marretta, Alberto, 'Age of the heroes: A brief overview of Valcamonica rock-art during the Iron Age (I millennium BC)', in: *Adoranten* (2013), p. 79.

273 Other maps of villages or fields are to be found at Paspardo and Giadeghe rock 39.

274 Evers, Dietrich, *Berge und Boote* (Langenweissbach: Beier & Beran, 2002), pp. 30, 122.

275 Priuli, Ausilio, *Valcamonica: Valley of Prehistory* (Capo di Ponte: Priuli Edizione, n.d.), p. 36.

276 The photo was taken before an excessive cleaning of the petroglyph was undertaken which removed shades and contrasts.

277 Fossati, 'The rock art tradition of Valcamonica–Valtellina' (2000), p. 152.

278 Kaul, Flemming, 'The Gundestrup Cauldron: Thracian art, Celtic motifs', in: *Études Celtiques*, vol. 37 (Paris: CNRS Éditions, 2011), pp. 80, 85f, 95, 101, 104. Nielsen, *National Museum of Denmark* (2016), p. 148. Nielsen, Svend, 'The Gundestrup Cauldron: New scientific and technical investigations', in: *Acta Archaeologica*, vol. 76 (Hoboken: Wiley, 2005), pp. 4f, 35, 38, 53f, 57. Salo, Unto, *The Gundestrup Cauldron: Cultural-Historical and Social-Historical Perspectives* (Washington DC: Institute for the Study of Man, 2018), pp. 69–76.

279 For the famous stela of Kernosovka in Ukraine see: Baumer, *The History of Central Asia*, vol. 1 (2012), p. 79.

280 In Sion, 31 steles were found in 1961 at the place called Petit Chasseur and two more in 2018 at Don

Bosco. https://www.vs.ch/de/web/communication/detail?groupId=529400&articleId=4214984 (accessed 31 July 2024). In Aosta, the steles were found in 1969.

281 Jensen and Kruse, *Gods and Heroes of the Bronze Age* (1999), pp. 145–52. Schweizerisches Landesmuseum, *Menschen in Stein gemeisselt* (2021), pp. 22, 29, 34. https://statuestele.org/stele-statues/the-stele-statues-of-lunigiana-2/?lang=en, https://www.lovevda.it/en/database/8/archeology/aosta/megalithic-area-of-saint-martin-de-corleans-archaeological-museum-and-park/751 (both accessed 31 March 2024). There are no steles at Mont Bégo.

282 See above, pp. 200ff.

283 Southern Scandinavia became part of the trading network of metals only when the tradition of erecting engraved steles had virtually disappeared in Europe.

284 Jensen and Kruse, *Gods and Heroes of the Bronze Age* (1999), p. 145. Schweizerisches Landesmuseum, *Menschen in Stein gemeisselt* (2021), p. 7.

285 Corboud, Pierre and Curdy, Philippe (eds), *Stèles préhistoriques. La nécropole néolithique du Petit-Chasseur à Sion / Prähistorische Stelen. Die neolithische Nekropole Petit-Chasseur in Sitten* (Sion: Musées cantonaux de Valais, 2009), pp. 62–67. Gallay, Alain, *Autour du Petit-Chasseur. L'archéologie aux sources du Rhône 1941–2011* (Paris: Errance, 2011), pp. 22f. Schweizerisches Landesmuseum, *Menschen in Stein gemeisselt* (2021), pp. 37, 38, fig. 5, 91, 100.

286 Corboud and Curdy (eds), *Stèles préhistoriques* (2009), pp. 56–59.

287 The chronology and dating of the different periods within the sacral space of Aosta is debated. The present author follows the chronology upheld by Poggiani Keller et al. and the information boards of the museum which is based on radiocarbon measurements. Poggiani Keller, Raffaela et al., *The Megalithic Area Saint-Martin-de-Corléans Archaeological Park and Museum* (Aosta: Assessorato Instruzione e Cultura, 2016), pp. 12–33. A different chronology is proposed by Franco Mezzena who disregards the ^{14}C data as apparently incompatible with the stratigraphic findings. Mazzena, Franco, 'Les stèles anthropomorphes en Europe' and 'Les stèles anthropomorphes de l'aire mégalithique d'Aoste', both in: Cavazzini, Emma (ed.), *Dei di pietra. La grande statuaria antropomorfa nell' Europa del III millennio a.C. / Dieux de pierre. La grande statuaire anthropomorphe en Europe au IIIe millénaire avant J.C.* (Milan: Skira, 1998), pp. 15–127.

288 The total archaeological site of Aosta measures *ca.* 18,000 sq m.

289 Poggiani Keller, *The Megalithic Area Saint-Martin-de-Corléans* (2016), pp. 12–16.

290 Poggiani Keller, *The Megalithic Area Saint-Martin-de-Corléans* (2016), pp. 17–20.

291 Corboud and Curdy, *Stèles préhistoriques* (2009), pp. 28–31.

292 It seems that at Sion steles continued to be engraved when the construction of dolmens began whereas at Aosta there was a time gap between the last manufacture of steles and the beginning of their reuse in dolmens. Jensen and Kruse, *Gods and Heroes of the Bronze Age* (1999), pp. 151f. Schweizerisches Landesmuseum, *Menschen in Stein gemeisselt* (2021), pp. 31–33. By contrast, the anthropomorphic steles of Val Camonica and Valtellina were not reused for burial purposes.

293 In Sion, thirteen dolmens and large stone cists were found, at Aosta seven dolmens and cists.

294 Baumer, Christoph, *History of the Caucasus*, vol. 1 (2021), pp. 68–70.

295 Baumer, *History of the Caucasus*, vol. 1 (2021), pp. 67f.

296 Schweizerisches Landesmuseum, *Menschen in Stein gemeisselt* (2021), pp. 108f.

297 One of the reasons for there being relatively few petroglyph sites in the Swiss Alps may be that granite and gneiss predominate, which are hard to work on.

298 https://www.surselva-hausbuch.ch/contentLD/HBS/KulturC1Carschenna.pdf, http://www.rupestre.net/alps/carsch.html (both accessed 31 March 2024).

299 http://www.ipernity.com/doc/2247442/45894384 (accessed 31 March 2024).

300 Schwegler, Urs, 'Felsbilder der Alpen', in: Beier, Hans-Jürgen and Hinze, Hans-Peter (eds), *Botschaften in Stein – Dokumentiert, interpretiert und experimentiert* (Langenweissbach: Beier & Beran, 2015), pp. 108, 118, 124–126.

301 Lumley, *Le mont Bego* (2003), pp. 9–30.

302 Non-figurative images are cup marks and lines. Lumley, *Le mont Bego* (2003), p. 43. See also: Barfield and Chippindale, 'Meaning in the later prehistoric rock-engravings of Mont Bégo' (1997), pp. 110, 120, fig. 12.

303 Lumley, *Le mont Bego* (2003), pp. 91, 110–113. Other authors such as Nicoletta Bianchi date the featured daggers to the Chalcolithic period, specifically to 2900–2100 BCE. 'Mount Bego prehistoric rock carvings', in: *Adoranten* (2010), pp. 72, 75.

304 Lumley, *Le mont Bego* (2003), pp. 116, 119.

305 Lumley, *Le mont Bego* (2003), p. 115. 'Patri mii' might also be a personal name which would change the meaning to 'the son of Patrimius/Patrimeus'.

306 Barfield and Chippindale, 'Meaning in the later prehistoric rock-engravings of Mont Bégo' (1997), pp. 120, fig. 12, 123, fig 14. Lumley, Henry de and Clergue, Lucien, *Fascinant Mont Bego* (Aix-en-Provence: Edisud, 2002), pp. 104, 110.

VII. Arabia

1 Due to the ongoing civil war and the impossibility of travelling freely, the petroglyphs of Yemen are omitted in the present work. For the relatively modest corpus of petroglyphs in the United Arab Emirates, see: Al-Tikriti, Walid Yasin, *Rock Art in the Abu Dhabi Emirate* (Al-Ain: Abu Dhabi Cultural Heritage, 2011). Ziolkowski, Michele C., 'A study of the petroglyphs from Wadi al-Hayl, Fujairah, United Arab Emirates', in: *Arabian Archaeology and Epigraphy*, vol. 9 (Oxford: Wiley, 1998), pp. 13–89. 'Rock on art: Petroglyph sites in the United Arab Emirates', in: *Arabian Archaeology and Epigraphy*, vol. 18 (Oxford: Wiley, 2007), pp. 208–238.

2 The Arabic noun *jabal* means 'mountain'.

3 Magee, Peter, *The Archaeology of Prehistoric Arabia* (Cambridge: Cambridge University Press, 2014), pp. 68f.

4 Magee, *The Archaeology of Prehistoric Arabia* (2014), pp. 87, 99, 111–114, 156.

5 Méry, Sophie, 'The first oases in Eastern Arabia: Society and craft technology, in the 3rd millennium BC at Hili, United Arab Emirates', in: *Revue d'Éthnoécologie*, vol. 4 (Paris: Open Edition, 2013), p. 11.

6 Magee, *The Archaeology of Prehistoric Arabia* (2014), pp. 214, 260.

7 Sanlaville, Paul, 'Geographic introduction to the Arabian Peninsula', in: Al-Ghabban, Ali Ibrahim et al. (eds), *Roads of Arabia: Archaeology and History of the Kingdom of Saudi Arabia* (Paris: Musée du Louvre, 2010), p. 64. See also: Breeze, Paul S., 'Prehistory and palaeoenvironments of the western Nefud Desert, Saudi Arabia, in: *Archaeological Research in Asia*, vol. 10 (Amsterdam: Elsevier, 2017), p. 1.

8 Rosenberg, Thomas M., et al., 'Middle and Late Pleistocene humid periods recorded in palaeolake deposits of the Nafud desert, Saudi Arabia', in: *Quaternary Science Reviews*, vol. 70 (Amsterdam: Elsevier, 2013), pp. 109–23, esp. pp. 109, 118.

9 Baumer, *History of the Caucasus*, vol. 1 (2021), p. 19.

10 Andreae, Meinrat O. et al., 'Archaeometric studies on the petroglyphs and rock varnish at Khilwa and Sakaka, northern Saudi Arabia', in: *Arabian Archaeology and Epigraphy*, vol. 31 (Hoboken: Wiley, 2020). p. 222. Inizan, Marie-Louise, 'The prehistoric populations', in: al-Ghabban et al., *Roads of Arabia* (2010), pp. 143–147. Whalen, Norman M. and Fritz, Glen A. 'The Oldowan in Arabia,' in: *Adumatu*, no. 9 (Riyadh: Al-Sudayri Foundation, 2004), pp. 7–18.

11 Groucutt, Huw et al., 'Multiple hominin dispersals into Southwest Asia over the past 400,000 years', in: *Nature*, vol. 597 (London: Macmillan, 2021), pp. 376–380.

12 Petraglia, Michael D. et al., 'Acheulean landscapes and large cutting tools assemblages in the Arabian Peninsula,' in: Petraglia, Michael D., and Rose, Jeffrey I. (eds.), *The Evolution of Human Populations in Arabia: Palaeoenvironments, Prehistory and Genetics* (Dordrecht: Springer, 2009), pp. 103–08, 115. Rose, Jeffrey I. and Petraglia, Michael D., 'Tracking the origin and evolution of human populations in Arabia', ibid., pp. 5f, 8f. Shipton, Ceri et al., 'Large Flake Acheulean in the Nefud Desert of northern Arabia', in: *Paleoanthropology* (Paleoanthropology Society, 2014), pp. 446–462. 'Acheulean technology and landscape use at Dawadmi, central Arabia', in: *PLOS ONE*, vol. 13, no. 7 (San Francisco: PLOS, 2018).

13 Groucutt, Huw S. et al., 'Homo sapiens in Arabia by 85,000 years ago', in: *Nature, Ecology and Evolution*, vol. 2 (London: Springer Nature, 2018), pp. 800–809. Magee, *The Archaeology of Prehistoric Arabia* (2014), p. 47.

14 Stewart, Mathew, 'A taphonomic and zooarchaeological study of Pleistocene fossil assemblages from the western Nefud Desert', Saudi Arabia, doctoral thesis (Sydney: University of New South Wales, 2019), pp. 296, 315f, 345–347. MIS (Marine isotope stages) is a timescale used in archaeology which links data to periods of palaeoclimatology.

15 Philby, H. St J. B., *The Empty Quarter, Being a Description of the Great South Desert of Arabia known as Rub' al Khali* (London: Constable, 1933), pp. 138–140.

16 Crassard, Rémy et al., 'Middle Palaeolithic and Neolithic occupations around Mundafan palaeolake, Saudi Arabia: Implications for climate change and human dispersals', in: *PLOS ONE*, vol. 8, no. 7, e69665 (San Francisco: PLOS, 2013), pp. 4–6, 19. Groucutt, Huw S. et al, 'Human occupation of the Arabian Empty Quarter during MIS 5: Evidence from Mundafan Al-Buhayrah, Saudi Arabia', in: *Quaternary Science Reviews*, vol. 119 (Amsterdam: Elsevier, 2015), pp. 116f, 131.

17 Crassard et al., 'Middle Palaeolithic and Neolithic occupations around Mundafan palaeolake' (2013), p. 19. Groucutt et al., 'Human occupation of the Arabian Empty Quarter during MIS 5' (2015), pp. 116f, 132f.

18 Inizan, 'The prehistoric populations' (2010), p. 147. Maher, Lisa A., 'The Late Pleistocene of Arabia in relation to the Levant', in: Petraglia, and Rose, *The Evolution of Human Populations in Arabia* (2009), pp. 188f, 197–200.

19 Sanlaville, 'Geographic introduction to the Arabian Peninsula' (2010), p. 68.

20 Rose, Jeffrey I., 'New light on human prehistory in the Arabo-Persian Gulf oasis', in: *Current Anthropology* vol. 51, no. 6 (Chicago: Chicago Press Journals, 2010), p. 867.

21 It is possible that the widespread myth of a prehistoric flood has its distant roots in the refilling of the Persian Gulf. Rose, Jeffrey, I., 'New light on human prehistory in the Arabo-Persian Gulf oasis' (2010), p. 868. *An Introduction to Human Prehistory in Arabia* (Cham: Springer Nature, 2022), pp. 248f, 288f.

22 Crassard et al., 'Middle Palaeolithic and Neolithic occupations around Mundafan palaeolake' (2013), pp. 15–20.

23 Khan, Majeed, 'Rock Art of Saudi Arabia', in: *Arts*, vol. 2, no. 4 (Basel: MDPI, 2013), p. 448.

24 Hunziker-Rodewald, Régine, 'La redécouverte de l'art rupestre,' in: *L'art rupestre en Arabie. Dossiers d'Archéologie*, no. 407 (Dijon: Éditions Faton, 2021), p. 23.

25 Wallin, Georg August, *Skrifter*, vol. 4: *Färderna till Mekka och Jerusalem 1845–1847*, ed. Kaj Öhrnberg and Patricia Berg (Helsinki: Svenska littratursällskapet i Finland; Stockholm: Atlantis, 2013).

26 Hamilton, James, *Sinai, the Hedjaz and Sudan: Wanderings around the Birth-Place of the Prophet and across the Aethiopian Desert, from Sawakin to Chartoum* (London: Richard Bentley, 1857), p. 168.

27 Doughty, Charles M., *Travels in Arabia Deserta* (London: Jonathan Cape, 1936), vol. 2, pp. 562f.

28 Doughty, *Travels in Arabia Deserta* (1936), vol. 1, pp. 160–229, 328–335, 349f, 619; vol. 2, pp. 58f.

29 Blunt, Lady Anne, *A Pilgrimage to Nejd* (2 vols, London: John Murray, 1881),

30 Huber, Charles, *Journal d'un voyage en Arabie (1883–1884)* (Paris: Société asiatique et Société de géographie, 1891).

31 While Huber knew the region between Hail and al-Ula from his own experience, Euting contributed the bulk of the finances. The Francophone Alsatian Huber, however, who hated everything German since France had been forced to cede Alsace and Lorraine to Germany in 1871, completely ignored Euting in his posthumously published memoirs and intrigued against his travel companion. Facey, William, *Charles Huber: France's Greatest Arabian Explorer. With a Translation of Huber's First Journey in Central Arabia, 1880–1881* (Cowes: Arabian Publishing, 2022), pp. 3, 38–40, 44, 48f.

32 As outlined by William Facey, there is no doubt that Euting was the first to have seen the Tayma Stele; Doughty and Huber had previously seen other inscriptions at Tayma. Facey, *Charles Huber* (2022), pp. 64–7, 70.

33 Euting, Julius, *Tagebuch einer Reise durch Inner-Arabien* (Leyden: E.J. Brill, 1896), part 2, pp. 157–159. On Nabonid, see below, pp. 265f..

34 Euting, *Tagebuch einer Reise durch Inner-Arabien* (1896), part 2, p. 159. Facey, *Charles Huber* (2022), pp. 64–67, 70, 77 n252. Maraqten, Mohammed, 'The Aramaic pantheon of Tyamā', in: *Arabian archaeology and epigraphy*, vol. 7 (Oxford: Wiley, 1996), pp. 18–22.

35 Noujaim, Souraya and Daucé, Noëmi (eds), *Routes d'Arabie. Trésors archéologiques de l'Arabie Saoudite* (Beirut: Kaph Books, 2018), p. 41.

36 Huber's claim that the emir had forbidden Euting's return to Ha'il was most probably a lie, for the emir himself had earlier warned Euting about Huber's machinations. Facey, *Charles Huber* (2022), pp. 48–51.

37 Lozachmeur, H. and Briquel-Chatonnet F., 'Charles Huber und Julius Euting in Arabien nach französischen, auch heute nicht veröffentlichten Dokumenten', in: *Anabases*, vol. 12 (Toulouse: De Boccard, 2010), pp. 195–200. See also: Facey, *Charles Huber* (2022), pp. 61f, 76.

38 Facey, *Charles Huber* (2022), pp. 56f, 74–82.

39 Euting, *Tagebuch einer Reise durch Inner-Arabien* (1896).

40 Jaussen, Antonin and Savignac, Raphaël, *Mission archéologique en Arabie, 1907, 1909–10* (6 vols, Paris: Ernst Leroux/Roth-Hotz Reprise, 1909–1922).

41 Lippens, Philippe, *Expédition en Arabie centrale* (Paris: Adrien Maisonneuve, 1956).

42 Anati, Emmanuel, *Rock Art in Central Arabia* (4 vols, Louvain: Institut Orientaliste, 1968–74).

43 Bednarik, Robert G. and Khan, Majeed, 'Scientific studies of Saudi Arabian rock art', in: *Rock Art Research*, vol. 22, no. 1 (Darwin: International Federation of Rock Art Organizations, 2005), pp. 49–81. Khan, Majeed, *Prehistoric Rock Art of Northern Saudi Arabia* (Riyadh: Ministry of Education, 1993), pp. 30–49.

44 Guagnin, Maria et al., 'Life-sized Neolithic camel sculptures in Arabia: A scientific assessment of the craftmanship and age of the Camel Site relief', in: *Journal of Archaeological Science: Reports*, vol. 42, art. no. 103165 (Amsterdam: Elsevier, 2021). 'Before the Holocene humid period: Life-sized camel engravings and early occupations on the southern edge of the Nefud desert', in: *Archaeological Research in Asia*, vol. 36, art. no. 100483 (Amsterdam: Elsevier, 2023).

45 Bednarik and Khan, 'Scientific studies' (2005). Bednarik, 'Scientific investigations into Saudi Arabian rock art: A review', in: *Mediterranean Archaeology and Archaeometry*, vol. 17, no. 4 (Athens: University of the Aegean, 2017), pp. 50–51.

46 Andreae et al., 'Archaeometric studies on the petroglyphs and rock varnish at Khilwa and Sakaka' (2020), pp. 219–244. Macholdt, Dorothea S. et al., 'Growth of desert varnish on petroglyphs from Jubbah and Shuwaymis, Ha'il region, Saudi Arabia', in: *The Holocene*, vol. 28, no. 9 (Thousand Oaks CA: SAGE Publications, 2018), pp. 1495–1511. 'Rock varnish on petroglyphs from the Hima region, southwestern Saudi Arabia: Chemical composition, growth rates, and tentative ages', in: *The Holocene*, vol. 29, no. 8 (Thousand Oaks CA: SAGE Publications, 2019), pp. 1377–1395.

47 Macholdt et al., 'Rock varnish on petroglyphs from the Hima region' (2019), pp. 1381, 1389. See also: Macholdt et al., 'Growth of desert varnish' (2018).

48 Guagnin, Maria et al., 'An illustrated prehistory of the Jubbah oasis: Reconstructing Holocene occupation patterns in north-western Saudi Arabia from rock art and inscriptions', in: *Arabian Archaeology and Epigraphy*, vol. 28 (Oxford: Wiley, 2017), pp. 138f. Parker et al. set the beginning of the monsoon rainfalls about a millennium later than Guagnin. Parker, Adrian et al., 'The early to mid-Holocene moist period in Arabia: Some recent evidence from lacustrine sequences in eastern and south-western Arabia', in: *Proceedings of the Seminar for Arabian Studies*, vol. 36 (Oxford: Archaeopress, 2006), pp. 243–255. 'A record of Holocene climate change from lake geochemical analyses in southeastern Arabia', in: *Quaternary Research*, vol. 60 (Amsterdam: Elsevier, 2006), pp. 465–476. 'Pleistocene climate change in Arabia: Developing a framework for hominin dispersal over the last 350 ka', in: Petraglia and Rose, *The Evolution of Human Populations in Arabia* (2009), pp. 39–49. According to Hilbert, a shallow lake formed as early as around 12 ka BP west of Jubbah. Hilbert, Yamandú et al., 'Epipalaeolothic occupation and palaeoenvironments of the southern Nefud Desert, Saudi Arabia, during the Terminal Pleistocene and Early Holocene', in: *Journal of Archaeological Science*, vol. 50 (Amsterdam: Elsevier, 2014), pp. 460–474. Neugebauer however, sets the beginning of the Holocene wet phase around 8800–7900 BP. Neugebauer, Ina et al., 'The unexpectedly short Holocene Humid Period in Northern Arabia', in: *Communications Earth and Environment*, vol. 3, art. no. 47 (London: Macmillan, 2022), pp. 1, 2, 6. For the climatic changes in the region of Hima, south-western Saudi Arabia, see: Macholdt et al., 'Rock varnish on petroglyphs from the Hima region (2019), pp. 1379, 1384, 1386, 1390.

49 Parker et al., 'A record of Holocene climate change', pp. 465–467, 472–474.

50 Macholdt et al., 'Growth of desert varnish' (2018), p. 1496.

51 Guagnin et al., 'An illustrated prehistory of the Jubbah oasis' (2017), pp. 138–152, esp. pp. 142, 143, 150.

52 Guagnin et al., 'An illustrated prehistory of the Jubbah oasis' (2017), pp. 149–150. 'Pre-Neolithic evidence for dog-assisted hunting strategies in Arabia', in: *Journal of Anthropological Archaeology*, vol. 49 (Amsterdam: Elsevier, 2018), pp. 225–236.

53 Arbach, Mounir and Prioletta, Alessia, 'Les inscriptions royales rupestres de la péninsule arabique', in: *L'art rupestre en Arabie. Dossiers d'Archéologie*, no. 407 (Dijon: Faton, 2021), p. 60. Hausleiter, Arnulf and Schaudig, Hanspeter, 'Rock relief and cuneiform inscription of King Nabonidus at al-Ḥā'iṭ (Province of Ḥā'il, Saudi Arabia), Ancient Padakku', in: *Zeitschrift für Orient-Archäologie*, vol. 9 (Tübingen: Ernst Wasmuth, 2016), pp. 232–235.

54 Guagnin et al., 'The Holocene humid period in the Nefud Desert: Hunters and herders in the Jebel Oraf palaeolake basin, Saudi Arabia', in: *Journal of Arid Environments*, 178, art. no. 104146 (Amsterdam: Elsevier, 2020), pp. 1, 2, 15. Magee, *The Archaeology of Prehistoric Arabia* (2014), pp. 49–50, 85.

55 Macholdt et al., 'Growth of desert varnish' (2018), pp. 1496, 1501.

56 Whether the southward migration of pastoralists from Jubbah to Shuwaymis and Luwee was triggered by the beginning of aridification in the north is uncertain. Khan, *Prehistoric Rock Art* (1993), p. 107.

57 Nayeem, Muhammed Abdul, *The Rock Art of Arabia* (Hyderabad: Hyderabad Publishers, 2000), pp. 219–222, 228, figs 322f, 328.

58 On older, pre-Neolithic finely carved petroglyphs the varnish has grown back to 100% which makes them difficult to distinguish from the natural environment. Macholdt et al., 'Growth of desert varnish' (2018), pp. 1501–1503.

59 For the dating see: Charloux, Guillaume et al., 'A rock art tradition of life-sized, naturalistic engravings of camels in Northern Arabia,' in: *Antiquity*, vol. 96, no. 389 (Cambridge: Cambridge University Press, 2022), pp. 1301–1309.

60 Guagnin et al., 'Before the Holocene humid period' (2023).

61 A petroglyph of an Iron Age horseman was added later. Guagnin, et al., 'Before the Holocene humid period' (2023), p. 4.

62 Guagnin et al., 'Before the Holocene humid period' (2023), pp. 8–15.

63 Guagnin, 'Life-sized Neolithic camel' (2021), pp. 1, 17.

64 *Mustasil* means 'rectangle' in Arabic.

65 Kennedy, Melissa et al., 'Cult, herding, and "pilgrimage" in the Late Neolithic of north-west Arabia: Excavations at a mustatil east of AlUla', in: *PLOS ONE*, vol. 18, no. 3 (San Francisco: PLOS, 2023), pp. 1–3, 17–19, 24, 30, 35, 38.

66 Guagnin et al., 'An illustrated prehistory' (2017), p. 140. 'Rock art provides new evidence on the biogeography of kudu (*Tragelaphus imberbis*) …', in: *Journal of Biogeography*, vol. 45, no. 4 (Hoboken: Wiley, 2018), pp. 727–749, esp. p. 729. Magee, *The Archaeology of Prehistoric Arabia* (2014), pp. 43–44, 74.

67 Parker et al., 'Pleistocene climate change' (2009), p. 46.

68 Macholdt et al., 'Growth of desert varnish' (2018), p. 1496. Robin, Christian, 'La faune de l'Arabie heureuse: Les textes et les images rupestres de Himà', in: Jouanna, Jacques et al. (eds), *Vie et climat d'Hésiode à Montesquieu* (Paris: De Boccard, 2018), pp. 344f.

69 Guagnin et al., 'An illustrated prehistory of the Jubbah oasis' (2017), p. 139.

70 Magee, *The Archaeology of Prehistoric Arabia* (2014), pp. 145, 217–219, 256.

71 The rapidly increasing use of powerful motor pumps since the 1960s has caused a sharp drop in the groundwater level.

72 Magee, *The Archaeology of Prehistoric Arabia* (2014), p. 200.

73 Magee, *The Archaeology of Prehistoric Arabia* (2014), pp. 62, 66, 85.

74 There are thousands of 'desert kites' in Saudi Arabia, Jordan and northern Africa. Magee, *The Archaeology of Prehistoric Arabia* (2014), pp. 147–150.

75 Hill, Austin Chad et al., 'Inscribed landscapes in the Black Desert: Petroglyphs and kites at Wisad Pools, Jordan', in: *Arabian Archaeology and Epigraphy*, vol. 30 (Oxford: Wiley, 2020), p. 249.

76 Crassard, Rémy et al., 'Les cerfs-volants du désert dévoilent peu à peu leurs mystères', in : *Archéologia*, no. 628 (Dijon: Faton, 2024), p. 41. See also: https://www.globalkites.fr/articles (accessed 2 May 2024).

77 Crassard, Rémy et al., 'The oldest plan to scale humanmade mega-structures', in: *PLOS ONE*, vol. 18, no. 5, art. no. 0277927 (San Francisco: PLOS, 2023).

78 Hill et al., 'Inscribed landscapes in the Black Desert' (2020), pp. 250f. Rollefson, Gary O. et al., 'Images of the environment: Rock art and the exploitation of the Jordanian Badiah', in: *Journal of Epigraphy and Rock Drawings*, no. 2 (Amman: Department of Antiquities of Jordan, 2008), figs 42–44.

79 Dadan, however, was an 'open' oasis without an enclosing wall, and having only fortified sectors; the same applies to Qaryat al-Faw. Charloux, Guillaume et al., 'The "walled oases" phenomenon: A study of the ramparts in Dūmat al-Jandal and other pre-Islamic sites in north-western Arabia', in: *Arabian Archaeology and Epigraphy*, vol. 32, no. 1 (Oxford: Wiley, 2021), p. 27.

80 Hausleitner, Arnulf, 'The Oasis of Tayma', in: al-Ghabban, Ali Ibrahim et al, *Roads of Arabia. Archaeology and History of the Kingdom of Saudi Arabia* (Paris: Musée du Louvre, 2010), pp. 226–228.

81 Hausleitner, Arnulf, 'The Oasis of Tayma' (2010), pp. 226f. Charloux et al. give 16 km for the Tayma wall. Charloux, Guillaume et al., 'The "walled oases" phenomenon' (2021), p. 15.

82 Magee, *The Archaeology of Prehistoric Arabia* (2014), pp. 144f.

83 Charloux, Guillaume et al., 'The "walled oases" phenomenon' (2021), p. 28. 'The ramparts of Khaybar: Multiproxy investigation for reconstructing a Bronze Age walled oasis in Northwest Arabia', in: *Journal of Archaeological Science: Reports*, vol. 53, art. no. 104355 (Amsterdam: Elsevier, 2024). See also: *The Ancient Walled Oases of Northern Arabia*. World Heritage Site Nomination Document (Riyadh: Permanent Delegation of Saudi Arabia to UNESCO, 2022), pp. 1–12.

84 Magee, *The Archaeology of Prehistoric Arabia* (2014), pp. 206, 213.

85 Magee, *The Archaeology of Prehistoric Arabia* (2014), pp. 226, 259. According to Peter Magee, people from northern Arabia close to Syria were aware of the domestication and transport potential of the Bactrian camel from the late third millennium BCE, but did not use this knowledge to domesticate the wild dromedaries of Arabia. Ibid. pp. 207, 213.

86 Macdonald, M.C.A., 'Wheels in a land of camels: another look at the chariot in Arabia', in: *Arabian archaeology and epigraphy*, vol. 20 (Oxford: Wiley, 2009), pp. 156–184.

87 Magee, *The Archaeology of Prehistoric Arabia* (2014), pp. 62, 66.

88 Macholdt et al., 'Rock varnish' (2019), p. 1388.

89 Robin, Christian and Antonini de Maigret, Sabina, 'Le cheval dans l'Arabie méridionale antique', in: *Arabian Humanities*, vol. 8 (Paris: Centre français de recherche de la péninsule Arabique, 2017), pp. 4–7.

90 Robin, 'La faune de l'Arabie heureuse' (2018), pp. 319–384, esp. p. 338.

91 Charloux, Guillaume et al., 'Les dromadaires gravés en grandes dimensions. Un art rupestre monumental méconnu', in: *L'art rupestre en Arabie. Dossiers d'Archéologie*, no. 407 (2021), pp. 33, 35. 'A rock art tradition of life-sized, naturalistic engravings of camels in Northern Arabia' (2022), pp. 1301–1309. Guagnin et al., 'Life-sized Neolithic camel sculptures in Arabia' (2021), pp. 1f, 7.

92 Macdonald, M.C.A., 'The development of Arabic as a written language', in: *Supplement to the Proceedings of the Seminar for Arabian Studies*, vol. 40 (Oxford: Archaeopress, 2010), pp. 5–28. Philby, H. St J. B., 'The lost ruins of Quraiya', in: *Geographical Journal*, vol. 117, no. 4 (London: Royal Geographical Society, 1952), pp. 450, 458.

93 Macdonald, M.C.A., 'Wheels in a land of camels' (2009), pp. 162–181. Nayeem, *The Rock Art of Arabia* (2000), pp. 70, 74, figs 52f.

94 Sperveslage, Gunnar and Eichmann, Ricardo, 'Egyptian cultural impact on north-west Arabia in the second and first millennia BC', in: *Proceedings of the Seminar for Arabian Studies*, vol. 42 (Oxford: Archaeopress, 2012), pp. 371–384.

95 The more or less anthropomorphic steles from Tayma dating to the first millennium BCE will not be discussed here since, unlike the deer stones from Mongolia, they do not include petroglyphs.

96 There are also petroglyphs of Neolithic pastoralists at nearby Jabal Oraf 2. Guagnin, Maria et al., 'The Neolithic site of Jebel Oraf 2, northern Saudi Arabia: First report of a directly dated site with faunal remains', in: *Archaeological research in Asia*, vol. 9 (Amsterdam: Elsevier, 2017), pp. 63–67.

96a Bibby, Geoffrey, *Looking for Dilmun* (London: Stacey International, 1996), p. 272.

97 Kootstra, Fokelien, 'The language of the Taymanitic inscriptions and its classification', in: *Arabian Epigraphic Notes*, vol. 2 (Leiden: Leiden Center for the Study of Ancient Arabia, 2016), p. 68. See also: Jacobs, Bruno and Macdonald, Michael C. A., 'Felszeichnung eines Reiters aus der Umgebung von Taymā', in: *Zeitschrift für Orient-Archäologie*, vol. 2 (Berlin: Walter de Gruyter, 2009), pp. 364–376.

98 Dougherty, Raymond Philip, *Nabonidus and Belshazzar: A Study of the Closing Events of the Neo-Babylonian Empire* (1928; repr. Eugene OR: Wipf & Stock, 2008), pp. 2, 49, 60–63, 68, 86–88, 90, 97f. Al-Ghabban et al., *Roads of Arabia* (2010), pp. 74–77, 124, 220f, 233, 252, 263. Nehmé, Laïla and Alsuhaibani, Abdulrahman (eds), *Al Ula. Merveille d'Arabie* (Paris: Gallimard, 2019), p. 61.

99 Beaulieu, Paul-Alain, *The Reign of Nabonidus, King of Babylon 556–539 BC* (New Haven: Yale University Press, 1989), pp. 79, 81, 84, 97.

100 Beaulieu, *The Reign of Nabonidus* (1989), pp. 77, 98, 184f.

101 Beaulieu, *The Reign of Nabonidus* (1989), pp. 31, 43–45, 54–60, 63–65, 150ff, 165, 203.

102 Beaulieu, *The Reign of Nabonidus* (1989), pp. 225, 230.

103 Adkins, Lesley, *Empires of the Plain: Henry Rawlinson and the Lost Languages of Babylon* (London: Harper Perennial, 2004), p. 369.

104 Hausleiter and Schaudig, 'Rock relief and cuneiform inscription of King Nabonidus at al-Ḥāʾiṭ' (2016), p. 234.

105 Hausleiter and Schaudig, 'Rock relief and cuneiform inscription of King Nabonidus at al-Ḥāʾiṭ' (2016), p. 226.

106 Riva, Rocío Da, 'The Nabonidus Inscription in Sela (Jordan): Epigraphic study and historical meaning', in: *Zeitschrift für Assyriologie*, vol. 100, no. 2 (Berlin: De Gruyter, 2020), pp. 176–195.

107 Hausleiter and Schaudig, 'Rock relief and cuneiform inscription of King Nabonidus at al-Ḥāʾiṭ' (2016), pp. 232–235.

108 Magee, *The Archaeology of Prehistoric Arabia* (2014), pp. 268–270. Potts, Daniel.T., 'The story of the origins', in: Al-Ghabban, et al., *Roads of Arabia* (2010), p. 74.

109 Potts, Daniel.T., 'The story of the origins' (2010), pp. 75–77.

110 I thank Dr Maria Guagnin for her assessment of the age of these petroglyphs.

111 Nehmé and Alsuhaibani, *AlUla* (2019), pp. 60–65.

112 Nehmé, Laïla, *Archéologie au pays des Nabatéens d'Arabie* (Paris: Hémisphères, 2019).

113 Doughty, *Travels*, vol. 1 (1936), pp. 123, 407f. Jaussen and Savignac, *Mission archéologique en Arabie*, vol. 1 (1909), pp. 103–106.

114 *Quran*, Surah 7, 73–79; Surah 54, 23–31.

115 Nehmé, *Archéologie au pays des Nabatéens d'Arabie* (2019), pp. 16, 19.

116 Philby, H. St J. B., *Sheba's Daughters: Being a Record of Travel in Southern Arabia* (London: Methuen, 1939), pp. 301f.

117 In addition, about 2,000 non-monumental tombs have been identified.

118 The hypothesis proposed by Majeed Khan, according to which the petroglyphs of schematized stick people represented a pictographic precursor to the Thamudic alphabets, lacks any scientific basis. Khan, Majeed, *Prehistoric Rock Art of Northern Saudi Arabia* (1993), pp. 177–190.

119 Robin, Christian Julien, 'Languages and scripts', in: Al-Ghabban et al., *Roads of Arabia* (2010), pp. 126–129.

120 Macdonald, 'The development of Arabic as a written language' (2010), pp. 7f, 18.

121 Norris, Jérôme, 'Les inscriptions préislamiques associées à l'art rupestre de l'Arabie du Nord-Ouest', in: *L'art rupestre en Arabie. Dossiers d'Archéologie*, no. 407 (2021), pp. 57f.

122 Macdonald, 'The development of Arabic as a written language' (2010), pp. 18f.

123 Macdonald, 'The development of Arabic as a written language' (2010), p. 16.

124 Macholdt et al., 'Rock varnish on petroglyphs from the Hima region' (2019), p. 1384. Norris, 'Les inscriptions préislamiques associées' (2021), pp. 57f. Robin, 'Languages and scripts' (2010), pp. 129f.

125 For a table of these various ancient Arabian scripts see: Robin, Christian Julien et al., *A Stopover in the Steppe: The Rock Carvings of ʿĀn Jamal near Ḥimā (Region of Najrān, Saudi Arabia)* (Paris: Académie des Inscriptions et Belles Lettres, 2022), pp. 126f.

126 Charloux, Guillaume et al., 'Les dromadaires gravés en grandes dimensions' (2021), p. 50. Norris, 'Les inscriptions préislamiques associées à l'art rupestre' (2021), p. 59.

127 Robin, Christian Julien, 'Antiquity', in: Al-Ghabban et al., *Roads of Arabia* (2010), p. 85.

128 Robin, 'Antiquity' (2010), p. 86. 'Languages and scripts' (2010), p. 130.

129 Robin, Christian Julien, 'Inscriptions antiques de la région de Najran (Arabie séoudite méridionale)' in: *Comptes rendus des séances de l'Académie des Inscriptions et Belles-Lettres, CRAI*, no. 3 (Paris: 2014), pp. 1039f, 1088f, 1093, 1116. 'Les gravures d'une nécropole Chrétienne à Himà', in: *L'art rupestre en Arabie. Dossiers d'Archéologie*, no. 407 (2021), pp. 69f.

130 Doughty, *Travels* (1936), vol. 1, pp. 349f. Huber, *Journal* (1891), pp. 497–506.

131 Interpretation by Muhammad Abu Ahmad, Buraydah.

132 Adler, Marcus Nathan, *The Itinerary of Benjamin of Tudela* (New York: 1907).

133 Huber, *Journal* (1891), pp. 85f.

134 Aksoy, Ömer Can, 'A sickle boat petroglyph in Wadi Asafir: Possible evidence of Pre-Dynastic Egyptian influence on Northwest Arabia', in: *Antiquity*, vol. 94 (Cambridge: Cambridge University Press, 2020), p. 1.

135 A well still in operation today suggests that the phreatic level is quite close to the surface.

136 Euting, *Tagebuch* (1896), part 2, p. 143.

137 See above, p. 78. Bibby, *Looking for Dilmun* (1996), p. 255.

138 Mattet, Laurence (ed.), *Arts de l'Antiquité de l'Europe au Sud-Est asiatique* (Paris: Hazan, 2008), p. 203.

139 I thank Jérôme Norris and Christian Robin for deciphering this Thamudic B inscription.

140 For the dating see: Charloux, Guillaume et al., 'A rock art tradition of life-sized, naturalistic engravings of camels in Northern Arabia' (2022), pp. 1301–1309.

141 Olsen, Sandra L. and Bryant, Richard T., *Stories in the Rock: Exploring Saudi Arabian Rock Art* (Pittsburgh: Carnegie Museum of Natural History, 2013), p. 48.

142 On the flat top of the outcrop tourists recently engraved in Chinese texts.

143 Andreae, Meinrat O. et al.,'Iconographic and archaeometric studies on the rock art at Musayqira, Al-Quwaiyah governorate, central Saudi Arabia', in: *Arabian Archaeology and Epigraphy*, vol. 32, suppl. 1 (Hoboken: Wiley, 2020), p. 159.

144 A rock with seven images of an arm and hand from the southern Asir province and dating from the Bronze Age is on display in the National Museum in Riyadh. Grohmann, Adolf, *Göttersymbole und Symboltiere auf südarabischen Denkmälern* (Vienna: Alfred Hölder, 1915, repr. London: Forgotten Books, 2017), pp. 45f.

145 Lippens, *Expédition en Arabie centrale* (1956), pp. 192–195. Philby had already briefly visited the site in 1950 after Amir Abdullah, a brother of King Abd al-Aziz ibn Saud, had told him about its existence two years earlier.

146 For *Ry 509* and *Ry 510* see: *Digital Archive for the Study of Pre-Islamic Inscriptions DASI*; http://dasi.cnr. it/ (accessed 5 April 2024). The core of the Himyar empire was called *Dhu Raydan*. See also: Robin, Christian Julien, 'Le royaume Hujride dit "Royaume de Kinda", entre Himyar et Byzance', in: *Comptes rendus des séances de l'Académie des Inscriptions et Belles-Lettres (CRAI)*, no. 2 (Paris: Institut de France, 1996), pp. 675–687.

147 Robin, 'Le royaume Hujride dit "Royaume de Kinda"', (1996), p. 686f, 701f.

148 Al-Jallad, Ahmad and Sidky, Hythem, 'A Paleo-Arabic inscription on a route north of Tā'if', in: *Arabian Archaeology and Epigraphy*, vol. 33 (Oxford: Wiley, 2022), p. 210 n40.

149 Robin, 'Le royaume Hujride dit "Royaume de Kinda"', (1996), p. 699f.

150 Robin, Christian and Tayran, Salim, 'Soixante-dix ans avant l'Islam: l'Arabie toute entière dominée par un roi chrétien', in: *Comptes rendus des séances de l'Académie des Inscriptions et Belles-Lettres (CRAI)*, no. 1 (Paris: Institut de France, 2012), pp. 529, 547.

151 Procopius, *History of the Wars*, book I, XX, 3–8, trans. H.B. Dewing (1924; Cambridge MA and London: Harvard University Press, 2006), pp. 191–193.

152 Christian Robin, 'Abraha et la reconquête de l'Arabie déserte: un réexamen de l'inscription Ryckmans 506 = Murayghan 1', in: *Jerusalem Studies in Arabic and Islam*, vol. 39 (Jerusalem: Hebrew University, 2012), pp. 47–51. Robin and Tayran, 'Soixante-dix ans avant l'Islam' (2012), pp. 533f. 'Les expéditions militaires du roi Abraha dans l'Arabie désertique dans les années 548–565 de l'ère chrétienne', in: *Comptes rendus des séances de l'Académie des Inscriptions et Belles-Lettres (CRAI)*, no. 3 (Paris: Institut de France, 2018), pp. 1339–1346.

153 Arbach, Mounir, Christian, Robin et al., 'Projet Himà', in: *Centre Français de Recherche de la Péninsule Arabique* (Paris: 2015, 2018), n.p.

154 Arbach, Robin et al., 'Projet Hima' (2015, 2018).

155 Lippens, *Expédition en Arabie centrale* (1956), pp. 76, 78.

156 The first three campaigns of King Abraha against Central Arabia were possibly in 549, 550 and 551. Robin, 'Abraha et la reconquête de l'Arabie déserte' (2012), p. 48.

157 http://dasi.cnr.it/index.php?id=dasi_prj_epi&prjId=1&navId=798948552&recId=2447 (accessed 5 April 2024). Robin, 'Abraha et la reconquête de l'Arabie déserte' (2012), p. 12. Robin and Tayran, 'Soixante-dix ans avant l'Islam' (2012), pp. 539f.

158 That the Ma'add confederation of Central Arabia was a Himyarite vassal is confirmed by Procopius. *History of the Wars*, book I, XIX, 14 (1924–2006), p. 181.

159 Robin and Tayran, 'Soixante-dix ans avant l'Islam' (2012), pp. 525–553.

160 Khan, *Prehistoric rock art* (1993), pl. 11. Strachan, Laura and al-Mustaneer, Muhammad, 'Alia: The many manifestations of southern Saudi-Arabia's alleged goddess' (preprint received 10 March 2024 based on the lecture given at the Conference of the GCC Society for History and Archaeology on 9 February 2023 in Najran, Saudi Arabia.), p. 13, fig. 1.8.

161 See below under Aan Halkan, pp. 294f.

162 Ryckmans, Gonzague, *Les religions arabes préislamiques* (Louvain: Publications universitaires, 1951), p. 43.

163 Macholdt et al., 'Rock varnish' (2019), pp. 1384, 1390.

164 Robin et al., *A Stopover in the Steppe* (2022), p. 62.

165 Desert gazelles were also exterminated in the 1930 or 40s when hunting from cars became fashionable.

166 A *najd* is a sandy upland between mountains.

167 Robin, Christian Julien, 'Un sanctuaire rupestre au dieu dhu-Samawi à an-Halkan', in: Isabelle Sachet et al. (eds), *Dieux et déesses d'Arabie: images et représentations* (Paris: De Bocard, 2012), pp. 119–128.

168 The threat of such vandalism is the reason why the present authors do not give GPS data for the sites.

169 Robin, Christian Julien, 'Joseph, dernier roi des Himyar (de 522 à 525, ou une des années suivantes)', in: *Jerusalem Studies in Arabic and Islam*, vol. 34 (Jerusalem: Hebrew University, 2008), pp. 82–87. See also below under Bir Hima.

170 https://dasi.cnr.it/index.php?id=79&prjId=1&corId=27&colId=0&navId=594141674&recId=2453; https://dasi.cnr.it/index.php?id=dasi_prj_epi&prjId=1&corId=0&colId=0&navId=545361818&recId=2454 (accessed 3 Dec. 2024).

171 Grohmann, *Göttersymbole* (1915–2017), pp. 6–18.

172 Surah 105, *al-Fil* ('The Elephant'), https://quran.com/105 (accessed 5 April 2024).

173 Robin, Christian Julien, 'L'Arabie à la veille de l'islam. La campagne d'Abraha contre La Mecque, ou la guerre des pèlerinages', in: de La Genière, Juliette et al. (eds), *Les sanctuaires et leur rayonnement dans le monde méditerranéen de l'antiquité à l'époque moderne* (Paris: Institut de France, 2010), pp. 213–224. 'Abraha et la reconquête de l'Arabie déserte' (2012), pp. 50f. Robin and Tayran, 'Soixante-dix ans avant l'Islam' (2012), p. 535.

174 Robin, 'L'Arabie à la veille de l'Islam' (2010), pp. 231, 234, 241.

175 Arbach and Prioletta, 'Les inscriptions royales rupestres de la péninsule arabique' (2021), p. 61.

176 For the inscriptions and petroglyphs of An Jamal see: Robin et al., *A Stopover in the Steppe* (2022).

177 http://dasi.cnr.it/index.php?id=79&prjId=1&corId=27&colId=0&navId=274621895&recId=2420 (accessed 5 April 2024).

178 http://dasi.cnr.it/index.php?id=79&prjId=1&corId=27&colId=0&navId=274621895&recId=2419.

179 http://dasi.cnr.it/index.php?id=79&prjId=1&corId=27&colId=0&navId=274621895&recId=2418.

180 http://dasi.cnr.it/index.php?id=80&prjId=1&corId=27&colId=0&navId=274621895&recId=2417.

181 http://dasi.cnr.it/index.php?id=79&prjId=1&corId=27&colId=0&navId=274621895&recId=2416.

182 Robin, 'Joseph, dernier roi de Ḥimyar' (2008), pp. 16, 51f.

183 Robin, 'Joseph, dernier roi de Ḥimyar' (2008), pp. 17f.

184 Robin, 'Joseph, dernier roi de Ḥimyar' (2008), pp. 18f, 48–54.

185 Robin, 'Le royaume Hujride dit "Royaume de Kinda"' (1996), p. 691.

186 Robin, 'Joseph, dernier roi de Ḥimyar' (2008), pp. 54f, 60–64, 80.

187 Philby, *Sheba's Daughters* (1939), p. 16.

188 Lippens, *Expédition en Arabie centrale* (1956), pp. 108–112. Ryckmans, Jacques, 'Al-Ukhdud. The Philby–Rickmans–Lippens Expedition of 1951', in: *Proceedings of the Seminar for Arabian Studies*, vol. 11 (1980) (Oxford: Archaeopress, 1981), pp. 55–63.

189 Schiettecatte, Jérémie, 'L'antique Najrān: Confrontation des données archéologiques et des sources écrites', in: Beaucamp, Joëlle et al., *Juifs et Chrétiens en Arabie aux Vème et VIème siècles* (Paris: Association des amis du Centre d'histoire et civilisation de Byzance, 2010), pp. 32f.

190 Ryckmans, *Les religions arabes préislamiques* (1951), p. 43.

191 Robin, Christian Julien, 'Les gravures d'une nécropole Chrétienne à Himà', in: *L'art rupestre en Arabie. Dossiers d'Archéologie*, no. 407 (2021), pp. 68–71. Robin, Christian et al., 'Inscriptions antiques de la région de Najran (Arabie séoudite méridionale): nouveaux jalons pour l'histoire de l'écriture, de la langue et du calendrier arabe,' in: *Comptes rendus de l'académie des inscriptions (CRAI)*, no. 3 (Paris: Institut de France, 2014), pp. 1033–1128, esp. 1039.

192 Robin et al., 'Inscriptions antiques' (2014), p. 1039.

193 The steles *PalAr 1* and *2* have been removed by the authorities and are to be displayed in the Regional Museum of Najran.

194 Robin, 'Les gravures d'une nécropole Chrétienne à Hima', pp. 69f. 'Inscriptions antiques de la région de Najran' (2014), pp. 1087–92. For an overview of the palaeo-Arabic inscriptions known so far, see: Al-Jallad and Sidky, 'A paleo-Arabic inscription on a route north of Tā'if' (2022), p. 212, Table 12, 214f.

195 Robin, 'Les gravures d'une nécropole Chrétienne à Hima', pp. 70f.

196 Robin, 'Les gravures d'une nécropole Chrétienne à Hima', pp. 69f. 'Inscriptions antiques de la région de Najran' (2014), p. 1093.

197 Robin, 'Inscriptions antiques de la région de Najran' (2014), pp. 1099f.

198 Ryckmans, *Les religions arabes préislamiques* (1951), pp. 20, 22f, 47.

199 Robin, 'Les gravures d'une nécropole Chrétienne à Hima', pp. 70f. 'Inscriptions antiques de la région de Najran' (2014), pp. 1100f. Ryckmans, *Les religions arabes préislamiques* (1951), pp. 23, 47f.

200 Raswan, Carl R., *Black Tents of Arabia* (Boston: Little, Brown, and Co., 1935), p. 29.

201 Strachan and al-Mustaneer, 'Alia' (2023), p. 10, 16.

202 Strachan and al-Mustaneer, 'Alia' (2023), p. 13, fig. 1.8

203 Herodotus, *Histories*, I.131. Khan, *Prehistoric Rock Art* (1993), p. 38.

204 Ryckmans, *Les religions arabes préislamiques* (Louvain: 1951), p. 18, 22.

205 Macdonald, Michael, 'Goddesses, dancing girls or cheerleaders?', in: Sachet et al., *Dieux et déesses d'Arabie* (2012), pp. 261–297.

206 Bray, N., *A Paladin of Arabia: The Biography of Brevet Lieut.-Colonel G.E. Leachmann* (London: The Unicorn Press, 1936), p. 152. Raswan, *Black Tents of Arabia* (1935), p. 78.

207 This interpretation has been questioned by Macholdt et al., 'Rock varnish' (2019), p. 1388.

208 Grohmann, *Göttersymbole* (1915–2017), pp. 6–18. Ryckmans, *Les religions arabes préislamiques* (Louvain: 1951), p. 39.

209 Pre-Islamic Arabs usually refrained from representing their deities as anthropomorphic figures or in paintings. Instead, they venerated sacred stones called *betyls*. The term betyl comes from *Beit El (Al)* which means 'house of god'. Robin, Christian Julien, 'Images divines', in: Sachet et al., *Dieux et déesses d'Arabie* (2012), pp. 101f. The Black Stone placed in the eastern corner of the Kaaba was originally a pre-Islamic betyl.

210 Charloux, Guillaume et al., 'The protohistoric and antique landscape of Qaryat al-Faw', in: *Proceedings of the Seminar for Arabian Studies*, vol. 52 (Oxford: Archaeopress, 2023), p. 65, fig 5.

211 Strabo, *Geographica*, XVI. 4, 24 (2007), p. 1097.

212 Robin, 'Le royaume Hujride dit "Royaume de Kinda"' (1996), p. 666.

213 Robin, Christian Julien, 'Nagrān vers l'époque du massacre: notes sur l'histoire politique, économique et institutionnelle et sur l'introduction du christianisme', in: Beaucamp et al., *Juifs et chrétiens en Arabie aux Vème et VIème siècles* (2010), pp. 39–107. Schiettecatte, 'L'antique Najrân' (2010), pp. 11–38.

214 Schiettecatte, 'L'antique Najrân' (2010), p. 35.

215 An exception was the Arab historian Hisham ibn al-Kalbi (d. AH 206/822 CE) who collected orally transmitted and written information about pre-Islamic Arab deities. Hisham ibn al-Kalbi, *The Book of Idols*; translated by Nabith Amin Faris (Princeton: Princeton University Press, 1952).

216 In the winter of 1917–18, the fortress of Azraq served T.E. Lawrence as a base for his guerilla and sabotage operations. Lawrence, T.E., *Seven Pillars of Wisdom: A Triumph* (London: Jonathan Cape, 1943), pp. 294–297, 396f, 423f, 443f, 574–659.

217 Rollefson et al., 'Images of the environment' (2008), p. 48.

218 Hill et al., 'Inscribed landscapes in the Black Desert' (2020), p. 249.

219 Translation from a board in the Jordan Museum, Amman.

220 Rollefson et al., 'Images of the environment' (2008), pp. 18–41.

221 Bignasca, Andrea, 'Vergessene nabatäische Felsbilder auf dem Umm al-Biyara', in: Schmid, Stephan G., *Petra* (Basel: Schwabe, 2012), pp. 263–265.

222 Nehmé, Laïla, 'Nouvelles gravures rupestres à Petra: techniques, religion, épigraphie', in: *Studies in the History and Archaeology of Jordan*, vol. 5 (Amman: Department of Antiquities, 1995), pp. 430–435.

223 Da Riva, Rocío, 'The Nabonidus Inscription in Sela' (2020), pp. 182–184.

224 Da Riva, 'The Nabonidus Inscription in Sela' (2020), p. 188.

225 Da Riva, 'The Nabonidus Inscription in Sela' (2020), p. 180.

226 Crowell, Bradley L., 'Nabonidus, as-Sila', and the beginning of the end of Edom', in: *Bulletin of the American Society of Overseas Research*, vol. 348 (Chicago: University of Chicago Press, 2007), pp. 84f. Da Riva, 'The Nabonidus Inscription in Sela' (2020), pp. 189f, 193.

227 Lawrence, *Seven Pillars of Wisdom* (1943), pp. 358–363, 402f, 423.

228 *Wadi Rum Protected Area* (Paris: ICOMOS, 2011), p. 41.

229 *Wadi Rum Protected Area* (2011), pp. 40f.

230 Rothenberg, Reno and Glass, Jonathan, 'The Midianite pottery', in: Sawyer, John F.A. and Clines, David J.A., *Midian, Moab and Edom: The History and Archaeology of Late Bronte and Iron Age Jordan and North-West Arabia* (Sheffield: Journal for the Study of the Old Testament, 1983), pp. 65–72, 83, 113–115. Singer-Avitz, Lily, 'Section F: The Qurayyah Painted Ware', in: Ussishkin, D. (ed.), *The Renewed Archaeological Excavations at Lachish (1973–1994)*, vol. 1 (Tel Aviv: Tel Aviv University, 2004), pp. 1280–1287.

231 Tholbecq, Laurent, 'The Nabataeo-Roman site of Wādī Ramm (Iram): A new appraisal', in: *Annual of the Department of Antiquities of Jordan*, vol. 42 (Amman: 1998), p. 252.

232 Lagrange, Marie-Joseph, 'Un sanctuaire d'Allat à Iram', in: *Comptes rendus des séances de l'Académie des Inscriptions et Belles-Lettres*, vol. 76, no. 3 (Paris: Académie des Inscriptions et Belles-Lettres, 1932), p. 226.

233 Glidden, Harold W., 'Koranic Iram, legendary and historical', in: *Bulletin of the American Schools of Oriental Research*, vol. 73 (Chicago: University of Chicago Press, 1939), pp. 13–15.

234 Tholbecq, Laurent, 'Les sanctuaires des Nabatéens. État de la question à la lumière de recherches archéologiques récentes', in: *Topoi. Orient–Occident*, vol. 7, no. 2 (Lyon: MOM, 1997), p. 1095. *Wadi Rum Protected Area* (2011), p. 40.

235 Lawrence, *Seven Pillars of Wisdom* (1943), p. 363.

236 It remains debated whether al-Kutba was a female or male deity; the former interpretation seems more likely. Strugnell, John, 'The Nabataean goddess al-Kutba' and her sanctuaries', in: *Bulletin of the American Society of Overseas Research*, vol. 156 (Chicago: University of Chicago Press, 1959), pp. 29–36.

237 *Wadi Rum Protected Area* (2011), p. 40.

238 Clark, Ian D. and Fontes, Jean-Charles, 'Paleoclimatic reconstruction in Northern Oman based on carbonates from hyperalkaline groundwaters', in: *Quaternary Research*, vol. 33 (Seattle: University of Washington, 1990), pp. 320, 332–335.

239 Garba, Roman and Danielisová, Alžběta, 'Achaeologists unearth unique finds in Oman' (Prague: Institute of Archaeology of the CAS, 2023).

240 Rose, Jeffrey I. et al., 'The Nubian complex of Dhofar, Oman: An African Middle Stone Age industry in Southern Arabia', in: *PLOS ONE*, vol. 6, no. 11 (San Francisco: PLOS, 2011), pp. 1, 15–18. Cleuziou, Serge and Tosi, Maurizio, *In the Shadow of the Ancestors: The Prehistoric Foundations of the Early Arabian Civilization in Oman* (2nd ed., Oxford: Archaeopress, 2020), p. 19. Rose, Jeffrey I., 'On the trail of the first humans in Oman', in: Cleuziou and Tosi, *In the Shadow of the Ancestors* (2020), pp. 34–36.

241 Rose, *An Introduction to Human Prehistory in Arabia* (2022), pp. 201, 215.

242 However, as noted by Jeffrey Rose, 'there was never a land bridge linking Africa and Arabia within the last million years'; but the distances to cross on water were much shorter than today. Rose, *An Introduction to Human Prehistory in Arabia* (2022), p. 136.

243 Groucutt, Huw S., 'Culture and convergence: The curious case of the Nubian complex', in: Groucutt, Huw S. (ed.) *Culture History and Convergent Evolution: Can We Detect Populations in Prehistory?* (Cham: Springer, 2020), pp. 55–86.

244 The following archaeological categorization is mainly based on: Bortolini, Eugenio and Munoz, Olivia, 'Life and death in prehistoric Oman: Insights from late Neolithic and early Bronze Age funerary practices (4th–3rd mill. BC)', in: *The Archaeological Heritage of Oman* (Paris: UNESCO, 2015), pp. 61–80.

245 This classification of rock art is based on the chronology developed by Angelo Fossati. Fossati, Angelo E., *Messages from the Past: Rock Art of al-Hajar Mountains* (Oxford: Archaeopress, 2019), pp. 162–181. 'Rock Art of al-Hajar Mountains: A review and update', in: Cleuziou and Tosi, *In the Shadow of the Ancestors* (2018), pp. 494–499. Classifications based on stylistic criteria are by their nature subject to refinements and corrections over time.

246 Carter, Robert, 'Globalising interactions in the Arabian Neolithic and the Ubaid', in: Boivin, Nicole and Frachetti, Michael, D. (eds), *Globalization in Prehistory: Contact, Exchange, and the 'People without History'* (Cambridge: Cambridge University Press, 2018), p. 43, 47. Dumitru, Iona A. and Harrower, Michael J., 'From rural collectibles to global commodities: Copper from Oman and obsidian from Ethiopia': ibid. (2018), p. 236.

247 Méry, 'The first oases in Eastern Arabia' (2013), pp. 5, 8.

248 It is debated whether the technique of underground channels bringing water from foothills to the plains was developed in Oman or in Iran where the channels are called *qanat (kariz)*. Charbonnier, Julien, 'Human adaptation in Arabia: The role of hydraulic technologies', in: Chiotis, *Climate Changes in the Holocene* (2019), pp. 239f.

249 Dumitru and Harrower, 'From rural collectibles to global commodities' (2018), p. 239.

250 Cleuziou and Tosi, *In the Shadow of the Ancestors* (2020), p. 359. Magee, *The Archaeology of Prehistoric Arabia* (2014), p. 116.

251 Magee, *The Archaeology of Prehistoric Arabia* (2014), pp. 114–116.

252 Cleuziou and Tosi, *In the Shadow of the Ancestors* (2020), pp. 270, 284, 287, 301.

253 Méry, 'The first oases in Eastern Arabia' (2013), p. 11

254 Cleuziou and Tosi, *In the Shadow of the Ancestors* (2020), p. 276.

255 al-Tikriti, *Rock Art in Abu Dhabi Emirate* (2011), pp. 25–28.

256 al-Tikriti, *Rock Art in Abu Dhabi Emirate* (2011), pp. 11–21.

257 Cleuziou and Tosi, *In the Shadow of the Ancestors* (2020), pp. 362–364. Magee, *The Archaeology of Prehistoric Arabia* (2014), p. 112.

258 Dumitru and Harrower, 'From rural collectibles to global commodities' (2018), p. 236.

259 In Dhofar, it is mainly rock paintings that predominate.

260 Fossati, *Messages from the Past* (2019), p. 282. Insall, David, 'The petroglyphs of Shenah', in: *Arabian Archaeology and Epigraphy*, vol. 33 (Oxford: Wiley, 2022), pp. 225–245. Some of the al-Qatarah sites have hundreds of images, others only a few dozen or even fewer.

261 Fossati, *Messages from the Past* (2019), p. 168.

262 Fossati's site al-Qatarah 1 corresponds to Insall's site Qatarah 2, Fossati's no. 2 to Insall's no. 1; Insall's no. 5 is not listed by Fossati.

263 Fossati, *Messages from the Past* (2019), pp. 168, 255. Yule, Paul, 'The Hasat Bani Salt in the al-Zahirah province of the Sultanate of Oman', in: Boehmer, R.M. and Marran J. (eds), *Lux Orientis. Archäologie zwischen Asien und Europa* (Rahden: VML, 2001), pp. 443–450.

264 This rock art site near al-Hamra is not identical with the eponymous mountain village near al-Rustaq.

265 https://en.wikipedia.org/wiki/Jewel_of_Muscat (accessed 2 May 2024).

266 Fossati, *Messages from the Past* (2019), pp. 45, fig. 4.1, 48, fig. 4.5, 210.

267 Like in other narrow wadis, the usually narrow brook can transform into a torrential river after a downpour of rain.

268 Fossati, *Messages from the Past* (2019), p. 64 fig. 4.32.

269 Esposti, Michele Degli et al., 'Rock art survey in the ancient oasis of Salūt (northern Sultanate of Oman): A variegated iconographic record', in: *Arabian Archaeology and Epigraphy*, vol. 31 (Oxford: Wiley, 2020), p. 345.

270 Esposti, 'Rock art survey in the ancient oasis of Salūt' (2020), p. 346.

VIII. Central Sahara

1 Williams, Martin, *When the Sahara was Green: How our Greatest Desert Came to Be* (Princeton: Princeton University Press, 2021), pp. 7, 73.

2 Van Albada, Anne-Michelle and Axel, *La montagne des hommes-chiens. Art rupestre du Messak Libyen* (Paris: Le Seuil, 2000). Barnett, Tertia, *An Engraved Landscape: Rock Carvings in the Wadi al-Ajal, Libya* (2 vols, London: Society for Libyan Studies, 2019).

3 Trost, Franz, *Die Felsbilder des zentralen Ahaggar (Algerische Sahara)* (Graz: Akademische Druck- und Verlagsanstalt, 1981).

4 Soleilhavoup, François, *Art rupestre dans l'Ennedi. Le corps féminin dans l'art préhistorique* (Dijon: Faton, 2018).

5 Menardi Noguera, Alessandro, 'Anoa-1 and the body proportions of the Niola Doa corpulent figures (Ennedi, Chad)', in: Anati, Emmanuel (ed.), *Expression*, no. 29 (Capo di Ponte: Atelier, 2020), pp. 42–56. Simonis, Roberta et al., *Ennedi: Tales on Stone* (Florence: Edizioni All'Insegna del Giglio, 2017), pp. 251–283. Soleilhavoup, *Art rupestre dans l'Ennedi* (2018). 'Réalisme et symbolisme de l'image rupestre de la femme au Sahara', in: Huyge, Dirk and Van Noten F., *What Ever Happened to the People? Humans and Anthropomorphs in the Rock Art of Northern Africa* (Brussels: Académie Royale des Sciences d'Outre-Mer, 2018), pp. 193–217.

6 Kuper, Rudolph (ed.), *Wadi Sura – The Cave of Beasts: A Rock Art Site in the Gilf Kebir (SW Egypt)* (Cologne: Heinrich-Barth-Institut, 2013). Le Quellec, Jean-Loïc and de Flers, Pauline and Philippe, *Peintures et gravures d'avant les pharaons du Sahara au Nil* (Paris: Fayard, 2005).

7 Joussaume, Roger and Cros, Jean-Paul, *Art rupestre dans la Corne de l'Afrique* (Chauvigny: APC, 2020).

8 Huyge, Dirk, 'First evidence of Pleistocene rock art in North Africa: Securing the age of the Qurta petroglyphs (Egypt) through OSL dating', in: *Antiquity*, vol. 85, no. 330 (Cambridge: Cambridge University Press, 2011), pp. 1184–1193. 'The "headless women" of Qurta (Upper Egypt): The earliest anthropomorphic images in Northern-African rock art', in: Huyge and Van Noten, *What Ever Happened to the People?* (2018), pp. 419, 422f.

9 Huyge, Dirk, '"Lascaux along the Nile": The Palaeolithic rock art of Qurta (Upper Egypt)', in: *Bulletin des Séances de l'Académie Royale des Sciences d'Outre-Mer*, no. 54 (Brussels: Académie Royale des Sciences d'Outre-Mer, 2008), 292. 'The "headless women" of Qurta' (2018), pp. 419, 422.

10 Whether there was any cultural exchange between these widely separated regions remains unknown.

11 El-Bialy et al., 'Rock art in Wadi Silwa Baharii, Egypt. Part 1: Occasion of discovery and site content', in: *Sahara*, nr. 23 (www.saharajournal.com, 2012), pp. 59f.

12 Polkowski, Pawel at al., 'Rock art research in the Dakhleh Oasis, Western Desert (Egypt)', in: *Sahara*, nr. 24 (2013), pp. 103, 106.

13 Ikram, Salima, 'Drawing the world: Petroglyphs from Kharga oasis', in: *Archéo-Nil* (Leuven: Peeters, 2009), pp. 67f.

14 Kleinitz, Cornelia, 'Rock art landscapes of the Fourth Nile Cataract: Characterisations and first comparisons', in: Näser, Claudia and Lange, Mathias, *Proceedings of the Second International Conference on the Archaeology of the Fourth Nile Cataract* (Wiesbaden: Harrassowitz, 2007), pp. 215f, 218f, 221, 223f, 227–229.

15 Barth's two companions, James Richardson (1809–1851) and Adolf Overweg (1822–1852) died on the way. The first traveller to have produced a detailed account of his crossing of the Sahara, in 1351–54, was the Berber scholar Ibn Battuta (1304–1368/9).

16 Barth, Heinrich, *Reisen und Entdeckungen in Nord- und Central-Afrika in den Jahren 1849 bis 1855*, vol. 1 (Gotha: Justus Perthes, 1857), pp. 210–214. Herodotus, *The Histories*, IV, 182–184, trans. Aubrey de Sélincourt (London: Penguin, 2003), pp. 303f. For the Garamantes see below, pp. 340, 360.

17 Barth, *Reisen und Entdeckungen in Nord- und Central-Afrika*, vol. 1 (1857), pp. 215–220.

18 It is a matter for debate at what point the Libyco-Berber script turned into Tifinagh in the context of rock art. Therefore, we use the term Tifinagh for all inscriptions associated with rock art.

19 Ruprechtsberger, Erwin M., *Die Garamanten. Geschichte und Kultur eines lybischen Volkes in der Sahara* (Mainz: Philipp von Zabern, 1997), p. 20.

20 Dupuy, Christian, 'Henri Duveyrier et la charrerie antique du Sahara', in: *Le Saharien*, vol. 222 (Paris: L'Harmattan, 2017), pp. 50–57.

21 Frobenius, Leo, 'L'art africain', in: *Cahiers d' Art*, vol. 5, nos 8–9 (Paris: Éditions "Cahiers d' Art", 1935), pp. 395–8, 403. Striedter, Karl-Heinz, *Felsbilder der Sahara* (Munich: Prestel, 1984), p. 32.

22 A craton is a stable part of the continental lithosphere, which consists of the crust and the uppermost mantle of the earth.

23 Williams, *When the Sahara was Green* (2021), p. 30.

24 Baumer, *The History of Central Asia*, vol. 1 (2012), pp. 5, 11.

25 Williams, *When the Sahara was Green* (2021), pp. 23, 31. Villiers, Marq de and Hirtle, Sheila, *Sahara: The Life of the Great Desert* (London: HarperCollins, 2004), p. 42.

26 Williams, *When the Sahara was Green* (2021), pp. 35, 66.

27 Extrapolating from current tectonic trends, Africa will fuse with Europe in 50 million years by which time the Mediterranean Sea will have disappeared.

28 Villiers and Hirtle, *Sahara* (2004), pp. 44f. Williams, *When the Sahara was Green* (2021), pp. 35, 59, 66–71.

29 Benmessaoud, M., 'The Acheulean of the Ahaggar site (Algerian Central Sahara), new research and perspectives', in: *Journal of Historical Archaeology and Anthropological Sciences*, vol. 3, no. 2 (Edmond OK: MedCrave, 2018), pp. 208f.

30 Cunliffe, Barry, *Facing the Sea of Sands: The Sahara and the Peoples of Northern Africa* (Oxford: Oxford University Press, 2023), pp. 42–45, 52.

31 Cunliffe, *Facing the Sea of Sands* (2023), pp. 7f, 52. The start of the African Humid Period is set variously, either – including by the present authors – starting with the Bølling–Allerød interstadial, or beginning with the Holocene.

32 https://www.climate4you.com/ ClimateAndLandscapes.htm#Lake%20Chad. While Lake Chad's surface still measured 25,000 sq km in 1963, by 2007 it had shrunk 95% to 1,350 sq km, mainly due to excessive water drawing for irrigation. See: https://www.grida.no/resources/5593 (both websites accessed 10 May 2024).

33 Williams, *When the Sahara was Green* (2021), pp. 118.

34 Parzinger, *Die Kinder des Prometheus* (2015), p. 304.

35 Chiotis, 'Reconstructing the environment' (2019), p. 16.

36 Parzinger, *Die Kinder des Prometheus* (2015), p. 306.

37 Brooks, Nick et al., 'The climate–environment–society nexus in the Sahara from prehistoric times to the present day', in: *The Journal of North African Studies*, vol. 10, no. 10 (London: Taylor & Francis, 2005), pp. 259f. Parzinger, *Die Kinder des Prometheus* (2015), p. 306.

38 When the eastern Sahara began to desiccate between 5300 and 3500 BCE, its inhabitants retreated southwards or to the Nile Valley. Cunliffe, *Facing the Sea of Sands* (2023), pp. 10, 61.

39 Huysecom, Eric, 'The first emergence of ceramic production in Africa', in: *Oxford Research Encyclopedia of Anthropology* (New York: Oxford University Press, 2020), pp. 1, 4, 9.

40 For Anglo-Saxon scholars, the production of food is the decisive criterion for classifying a culture as Neolithic, whereas for Francophone and Eastern European ones the use of ceramics for storage purposes is sufficient for a classification as Neolithic. Shaw, Ian and Jameson, Robert, *A Dictionary of Archaeology* (Oxford: Blackwell, 2002), p. 423.

41 Di Lernia, Savino, 'From "green" to "brown": The archaeology of the Holocene central Sahara', in: Chiotis, *Climate Changes in the Holocene* (2019), p. 187.

42 Ottoni, Claudio et al., 'Mitochondrial haplogroup H1 in North Africa: An Early Holocene arrival from Iberia', in: *PLOS ONE*, vol. 5, no. 10, art. no. 13378 (San Francisco: PLOS, 2010), pp. 1f, 4, 6. 'Deep into the roots of the Libyan Tuareg: A genetic survey of their paternal heritage', in: *American Journal of Physical Anthropology*,

vol. 145, no. 1 (American Association of Biological Anthropologists; Hoboken: Wiley, 2011), pp. 118f, 122. For Herodotus' description of the Garamantian slave trade see below, p. 340.

43 Cancellieri, Emmanuele and Di Lernia, Savino, 'Re-entering the central Sahara at the onset of the Holocene: A territorial approach to Early Acacus hunter-gatheres (SW Libya)', in: *Quaternary International*, vol. 320 (Amsterdam: Elsevier, 2014), pp. 43, 45, 60. Cremaschi, Mauro and Di Lernia, Savino, 'Holocene climatic changes and cultural dynamics in the Libyan Sahara, in: *African Archaeological Review*, vol. 16, no. 4 (Berlin: Springer, 1999), pp. 228, 233. Di Lernia, Savino, 'Thoughts on the rock art of the Tadrart Acacus Mts, SW Libya', in: *Adoranten* (2012), p. 32.

44 Di Lernia, Savino, ''Earliest herders of the central Sahara (Tadrart Acacus Mountains, Libya): A punctuated model for the emergence of pastoralism in Africa', in: *Journal of World Prehistory*, vol. 34 (Berlin: Springer, 2021), p. 579.

45 Cunliffe, *Facing the Sea of Sands* (2023), pp. 7f, 68, 101. Williams, *When the Sahara was Green* (2021), pp. 46–48.

46 Cherkinsky, Alexander and Di Lernia, Savino, 'Bayesian approach to 14c dates for estimation of long-term archaeological sequences in arid environments: The Holocene site of Takarkori rockshelter, southwest Libya', in: *Radiocarbon*, vol. 55, nos 2–3 (Cambridge: Cambridge University Press, 2013), pp. 771, 773–775. Di Lernia, 'Earliest herders of the central Sahara' (2021), pp. 531, 546, 568, 574f, 577. Guagnin, Maria, 'The rock carvings of the Messak: Monuments in a changing landscape', in: Furholt, Martin et al. (eds), *As Time Goes By'? Monumentality, Landscapes and the Temporal Perspective* (Bonn: Dr. Rudolf Habelt, 2012), p. 98. Soukopova, Jitka, 'Prehistoric colonization of the central Sahara: Hunters versus herders and the evidence from the rock art', in: Anati (ed.), *Expression*, no. 30 (Capo di Ponte: Atelier, 2020), pp. 59f.

47 Whether the spread of caprines and bovines went along with the arrival of a new population remains debated. Cunliffe, *Facing the Sea of Sands* (2023), pp. 66–68, 101. Di Lernia, Savino, 'Dry climatic events and cultural trajectories: Adjusting Middle Holocene pastoral economy of the Libyan Sahara', in: Hassan, Fekri (ed.), *Droughts, Food and Culture: Ecological Change and Food Security in Africa's Later Prehistory* (New York: Kluwer, 2002), p 237. 'Earliest herders of the central Sahara' (2021), p. 537. Le Quellec and de Flers, *Peintures et gravures d'avant les pharaons du Sahara au Nil* (2005), pp. 303, 335.

48 Concerning the date when petroglyphs appeared in the central Sahara see below, pp. 341f.

49 Smith, Andrew B., 'Post-glacial transformations in Africa', in: Cummings et al., *The Oxford Handbook of the Archaeology and Anthropology of Hunter-Gatherers* (2014), p. 481.

50 Cunliffe, *Facing the Sea of Sands* (2023), p. 66. Le Quellec and de Flers, *Peintures et gravures d'avant les pharaons du Sahara au Nil* (2005), pp. 303, 335. Di Lernia, 'Earliest herders of the central Sahara' (2021), p. 533. Williams, *When the Sahara was Green* (2021), pp. 50f, 116f. For the argument that African cattle represent a local domestication of the African wild aurochs see: Van Albada, Anne-Michelle and Axel, 'Quelles informations tirer des représentations humaines dans l'art rupestre du Messak libyen?',

in: Huyge and Van Noten, *What Ever Happened to the People?* (2018), pp. 247, 263. Bradley, Daniel G. et al. 'Mitochondrial diversity and the origins of African and European cattle', in: *Proceedings of the National Academy of Sciences*, vol. 93 (Washington DC: National Academy of Sciences, 1996), pp. 5131, 5135. Brooks, 'The climate–environment–society nexus in the Sahara' (2005), p. 260. Hanotte, Olivier et al., 'African pastoralism: Genetic imprints of origins and migrations', in: *Science*, vol. 296 (Washington DC: AAAS, 2002), pp. 336–339.

51 Di Lernia, Savino et al., 'Inside the "African cattle complex": Animal burials in the Holocene central Sahara', in: *PLOS ONE*, vol. 8, no. 2 (San Francisco: PLOS, 2013), p. 2.

52 Di Lernia, Savino et al., 'Inside the "African cattle complex"' (2013), pp. 2, 4.

53 Di Lernia, Savino and Gallinaro, Marina, 'The date and context of Neolithic rock art in the Sahara: Engravings and ceremonial monuments from Messak Settafet (south-west Libya)', in: *Antiquity*, vol. 84 (Cambridge: Cambridge University Press, 2010), pp. 959, 961f, 972f. Di Lernia, Savino et al., 'Inside the "African Cattle Complex"' (2013), pp. 1, 7. See also: Brooks, 'The Climate–environment–society nexus in the Sahara' (2005), p. 261. Le Quellec, Jean-Loïc, 'Périodisation et chronologie des images rupestres du Sahara central', in: *Préhistoires Méditerranéennes*, vol. 6 (Aix-en-Provence: Maison méditerranéenne des sciences de l'homme, 2013), pp. 21, 24, 30, 32f. Le Quellec and de Flers, *Peintures et gravures d'avant les pharaons du Sahara au Nil* (2005), pp. 306, 313. Ritual cattle burials have also been found in the southern Tassili, albeit without sophisticated above-ground monuments. Hachid, Malika, *Le Tassili des Ajjer. Aux sources de l'Afrique 50 siècles avant les pyramides* (Paris: Éditions Paris-Méditerranée, 2000), pp. 150, 276.

54 Cunliffe, *Facing the Sea of Sands* (2023), p. 69.

55 Cunliffe, *Facing the Sea of Sands* (2023), p. 87. Other pastoralists migrated from the eastern Sahara to the Gilf al-Kebir. Parzinger, *Die Kinder des Prometheus* (2015), pp. 304, 308.

56 Di Lernia, 'From "green" to "brown"' (2019), p. 192.

57 Coulson, David and Campbell, Alec, 'Rock art of the Tassili n Ajjer, Algeria', in: *Adoranten* (2010), pp. 33f.

58 Cunliffe, *Facing the Sea of Sands* (2023), pp. 65, 81, 101. Guagnin, 'The rock carvings of the Messak' (2012), pp. 95, 101f. Smith, 'Post-glacial transformations in Africa' (2014), p. 482.

59 Di Lernia, 'From "green" to "brown"' (2019), p. 194.

60 Brooks, 'The Climate–environment–society nexus in the Sahara' (2005), p. 262.

61 Williams, *When the Sahara was Green* (2021), p. 52.

62 Around 1550 BCE Pharaoh Ahmose I expelled the Hyksos from Lower Egypt and introduced a chariot corps into the Egyptian army.

63 No archaeological remains of a chariot have however been found so far in the Sahara. Muzzolini, Alfred, *Les images rupestres du Sahara* (Castres: istor/published by the author, 1995), p. 175.

64 Cunliffe, Facing the Sea of Sands (2023), pp. 126, 179. Le Quellec and de Flers, *Peintures et gravures d'avant les pharaons du Sahara au Nil* (2005), p. 321.

65 Herodotus, *The Histories*, IV. 183 (2003), p. 301.

66 Le Quellec and de Flers, *Peintures et gravures d'avant les pharaons du Sahara au Nil* (2005), p. 119. Sterry, Martin and Mattingly, David J., 'Introduction to the

themes of sedentarisation', in: eid., *Urbanisation and State Formation in the Ancient Sahara and Beyond* (Cambridge: Cambridge University Press, 2020), p. 26.

67 Gauthier, Yves and Christine. 'Des chars et des Tifinagh: étude aréale et corrélations', in: *Cahiers de l'AARS*, no. 15 (Saint-Benoist-sur-Mer: AARS, 2011), pp. 104f.

68 Barth, *Reisen und Entdeckungen in Nord- und Central-Afrika*, vol. 1 (1857), pp. 215–217.

69 Le Quellec, Jean-Loïc, '"Chasseurs" et "Pasteurs" au Sahara central: les "Chasseurs archaïques" chassé du paradigme', in: *Palethnologie : Archéologie et Sciences humaines*, vol. 4 (Toulouse: CNRS / UMR 5608, 2009), p. 402.

70 *Bubalus antiquus*, formerly also called *Pelorovis antiquus*, which became extinct 4–5,000 years ago, has been mostly classified since 1994 as *Syncerus antiquus*. https://en.wikipedia.org/wiki/Pelorovis; https://scienceblogs.com/tetrapodzoology/2011/04/28/great-bubalus-rock-art (accessed 10 May 2024).

71 Barnett, Tertia and Guagnin, Maria, 'Changing places: Rock art and Holocene landscapes in the Wadi al-Ajal, south-west Libya', in: *Journal of African Archaeology*, vol. 12, no. 2 (Frankfurt a.M.: Africa-Magna, 2014), p. 171. Lhote, Henri, *Die Felsbilder der Sahara. Entdeckung einer 8000jährigen Kultur* (Würzburg: Andreas Zettner, 1958), p. 14. Vérité, Monique, *Henri Lhote. Une aventure scientifique au Sahara* (Paris: Ibis Press, 2010), p. 140.

72 Le Quellec, Jean-Loïc, *Symbolisme et art rupestre au Sahara* (Paris: L'Harmattan, 1993), pp. 33, 38. Vérité, Monique, *Henri Lhote* (2010), p. 263.

73 Striedter, *Felsbilder der Sahara* (1984), pp. 48–61.

74 Lutz, Rüdiger and Gabriele, *Das Geheimnis der Wüste. Die Felskunst des Messak Sattafet und Messak Mellet – Libyen* (Innsbruck: Golf Verlag, 1995), pp. 32–37.

75 Van Albada, *La montagne des hommes-chiens* (2000), pp. 58–61, but see a more nuanced approach in: Van Albada, 'Quelles informations tirer des representations humaines dans l'art rupestre du Messak Libyen?' (2018), pp. 246, 263.

76 Coulson, David and Campbell, Alec, *African Rock Art: Paintings and Engravings in Stone* (New York: Henry N. Abrams, 2001), pp. 155–157. 'Rock Art of the Tassili n Ajjer, Algeria' (2010), p. 30.

77 Le Quellec, Jean-Loïc, '"Chasseurs" et "Pasteurs" au Sahara central' (2000), pp. 406–408. 'Périodisation et chronologie des images rupestres du Sahara central' (2013). Muzzolini, *Les images rupestres du Sahara* (1995), pp. 90–92, 150. However, András Zboray identified pre-Neolithic hunters' rock paintings in the far eastern Sahara, namely in Wadi Sura, located *ca.* 220 km north of the region of the Jabal al-Uweinat, a mountain range in the area of the Egyptian–Libyan–Sudanese tripoint. Zboray dates this rock art of a pre-pastoralist hunting culture to around 6500 BCE. Zboray, András, 'Wadi Sura in the context of regional rock art', in: Kuper, *Wadi Sura – The Cave of Beasts* (2013), pp. 18–23. 'The petroglyphs of Jebel Uweinat: Many questions and a few answers …', in: Kabacinski, J. et al. (eds), *Desert and the Nile: Prehistory of the Nile Basin and the Sahara*, Studies in African Archaeology, vol. 15 (Poznań: Poznań Archaeological Museum, 2018), pp. 657f.

78 'Nulle part au Sahara central on ne connaît de bovinés domestiques avant le cinquième millénaire et les peintures du Bovidien qui représente massivement

ce bétail ne peuvent donc pas être plus anciennes.' Le Quellec, 'Périodisation et chronologie des images rupestres du Sahara central' (2013), p. 21.

79 Biagetti, Stefano and di Lernia, Savino, 'Holocene deposits of Saharan rock shelters: The case of Takarkori and other sites from the Tadrart Acacus Mountains (Southwest Libya)', in: *African Archaeological Review*, vol. 30 (Dordrecht: Springer, 2013), pp. 322f. Di Lernia, Stefano, 'Earliest herders of the central Sahara' (2021), pp. 531, 546f, 568, 574f, 584.

80 Di Lernia, Savino, 'The archaeology of rock art in Northern Africa', in: David and McNiven, *The Oxford Handbook of the Archaeology and Anthropology of Rock Art* (Oxford: Oxford University Press, 2018), p. 109.

81 Di Lernia, 'Thoughts on the rock art of the Tadrart Acacus Mts' (2012), pp. 32f. Gallinaro, Marina, 'Saharan rock art: Local dynamics and wider perspectives', in: *Arts*, vol. 2, no. 4 (Basel: MDPI, 2013), p. 356. Guagnin, 'The rock carvings of the Messak' (2012), pp. 98f. 'Animal engravings in the central Sahara: A proxy of a proxy', in: *Environmental Archaeology*, vol. 20, no. 1 (Leeds: Maney Publishing, 2015), p. 52. Van Albada, 'Quelles informations tirer des représentations humaines dans l'art rupestre du Messak Libyen?' (2018), p. 263.

82 Di Lernia, Savino, 'The archaeology of rock art in Northern Africa' (2018), p. 107. Gallinaro, 'Saharan rock art' (2013), p. 359.

83 Le Quellec and de Flers, *Peintures et gravures d'avant les pharaons du Sahara au Nil* (2005), p. 112. 'Périodisation et chronologie des images rupestres du Sahara central' (2013), pp. 16–18.

84 Mercier, Norbert et al., 'OSL dating of quaternary deposits associated with the parietal art of the Tassili-n-Ajjer plateau (Central Sahara)', in: *Quarternary Geochronology*, vol. 10 (Amsterdam: Elsevier, 2012), pp. 367, 371f. These firm results refute attempts to date the Round Heads to the Late Pleistocene 12,000 years ago as has been attempted by Aïn-Séba. Aïn-Séba, Nagète, 'Saharan rock art: A reflection of climate change in the Sahara', in: *Tabona. Revista de Prehistoria y de Arqueología*, vol. 22 (San Cristóbal de La Laguna: Universidad de La Laguna, 2022), pp. 305, 308.

85 Di Lernia, 'Thoughts on the rock art of the Tadrart Acacus Mts, SW Libya' (2012), p. 34. Di Lernia further asked: 'Why shouldn't late Pleistocene Qurta engravings be considered a possible antecedent of other "wild fauna" styles in the Sahara?' (ibid.). In view of the huge time gap of six millennia between Qurta and the earliest petroglyphs such a transfer is highly improbable.

86 Cremaschi and Di Lernia, 'Holocene climatic changes and cultural dynamics in the Libyan Sahara' (1999), pp. 233f.

87 Main source: Guagnin, Maria, 'The rock carvings of the Messak' (2012), pp. 95–102. 'Patina and environment in the Wadi al-Hayat: Towards a chronology of rock art of the central Sahara', in: *African Archaeological Review*, vol. 31, no. 3 (Berlin: Springer, 2014), pp. 408–413. 'Animal engravings in the central Sahara' (2015), p. 52. Additional sources: Barnett, *An Engraved Landscape*, vol. 1 (2019), pp. 55–57. Di Lernia, 'Thoughts on the rock art of the Tadrart Acacus Mts, SW Libya' (2012), p. 34. Le Quellec, 'Périodisation et chronologie des images rupestres du Sahara central' (2013), p. 33. Muzzolini, *Les images rupestres du Sahara* (1995), pp. 69–71, 97–113, 170f.

88 The geochemical process of the repatination or revarnishing of petroglyphs gives clues as to its duration and to the prevailing climatic conditions. As explained by Maria Guagnin, black and manganese-rich patina developed during the African Wet Period followed by grey manganese patina and, later, by red, iron-rich patina during the arid Late and Final Pastoral Periods. After *ca.* 1000 BCE the repatination is hardly visible. Guagnin, Maria, 'Patina and environment in the Wadi al-Hayat' (2014), pp. 408–410.

89 Guagnin, Maria, 'The rock carvings of the Messak' (2012), pp. 97f.

90 The chariot was introduced in the Sahara around or after 700 BCE, a few centuries later than the horse. Di Lernia, 'The archaeology of rock art in Northern Africa' (2018), p. 112.

91 Due to the unstable situation in Libya since the Revolution of 2011 and the ensuing civil war, the authors were unable to explore the petroglyphs of either Messak or Tadrart Acacus, and concentrated on Wadi Djerat in Algeria.

92 Vérité, Monique, *Henri Lhote* (2010), pp. 133f.

93 Lhote, Henri, *Les gravures rupestres de l'Oued Djerat (Tassili-n Ajjer)* vol. 1 (Algiers: Centre de recherches anthropologiques préhistorique et ethnographiques, 1975), p. 7.

94 Lhote, *Les gravures rupestres* vol.1 (1975), pp. 7, 27. Vérité, *Henri Lhote* (2010), pp. 76f.

95 Lhote, Henri, *Die Felsbilder der Sahara* (1958), p. 44.

96 Hachid, *Le Tassili des Ajjer* (2000), pp. 184–187.

97 Vérité, Monique, *Henri Lhote* (2010), pp. 204–247. Lhote returned to Wadi Djerat in November 1969. Ibid, pp. 262f.

98 Lhote, *Les gravures rupestres* vol. 2 (1975), p. 765. Site numbers higher than Lhote 75 are later finds.

99 About 280 metres west of site Lhote 1 is the shelter 80 where there are a few paintings. Although the meandering wadi continues upstream from here for about 25 km, the makers of petroglyphs did not use this area for their rock art. Lhote's map of Wadi Djerat is in: *Les gravures rupestres* (1975).

100 Berkani, Hayette, Zazzo, Antoine and Paris, François, 'Les tumulus à couloir et enclos de la Tassili du Fadnoun, Tassili Azger (Algérie): Premières datations par la méthode du radiocarbone', in: *Journal of African Archaeology*, vol. 13, no. 1 (Frankfurt a.M.: Africa-Magna, June 2015), pp. 59, 66f.

101 Sites 1 and 75 are 28 km apart as the crow flies. Since the wadi meanders, the walking distance is about 35 km.

102 Hachid, *Le Tassili des Ajjer* (2000), pp. 257, 269f.

103 Translation from the French by the present authors. Hachid, *Le Tassili des Ajjer* (2000), p. 270.

104 At L 28, there is a petroglyph of a hybrid animal consisting of the body of a hippopotamus and the front legs and snout of a crocodile.

105 Petroglyphs of fish are found at L 30 and L 52; they represent *Hemichromis*, which thrive in rivers as well as in lagoons, or *Heterotilapia buttikoferi*, also called *Zebra tilapia*; both fish are native to northern Africa.

106 The isolated petroglyph site of Tin Teghert is situated 112 km south of L 1 in Wadi Djerat. The list is not exhaustive.

107 The stones weighed up to 80 kg. Van Albada, *La montagne des hommes-chiens* (2000), pp. 32, 71 figs 22, 61. Lutz, *Das Geheimnis der Wüste* (1995), pp. 91, 97–99, figs 130–132.

108 In Messak alone there are more than 150 petroglyphs of therianthropes. Van Albada, 'Quelles informations tirer des représentations humaines dans l'art rupestre du Messak Libyen?' (2018), p. 245.

109 Van Albada, *La montagne des hommes-chiens* (2000), p. 24, fig. 15, p. 102.

110 Van Albada, *La montagne des hommes-chiens* (2000), p. 22, fig. 14.

111 Strabo, *Geographica*, XVI. 4.11, trans. A. Korbiger (Wiesbaden: Marix, 2007) p. 1086.

112 Hachid, *Le Tassili des Ajjer* (2000), p. 269.

113 Le Quellec, Jean-Loïc, *Rock Art in Africa: Mythology and Legend* (Paris: Flammarion, 2004), pp. 199f. The present authors are aware of the huge distance today separating the San people from Central Sahara. But it has already been shown that archaic myths could spread over vast distances over the Eurasian continent. Moreover, genetic studies among San people indicate that some of their distant ancestors had not only migrated out of Africa, but migrated about 3,000 years ago back into Africa to their present homeland. The ancestors of the San thus crossed the African continent twice. Hayden, Erika Check, 'African genes tracked back', in: *Nature*, vol. 500 (London: Macmillan, 2013), p. 514.

114 For different opinions on this question, see: Le Quellec, *Symbolisme et art rupestre au Sahara* (1993), pp. 249f, 552.

115 Quite distinct from the Central Saharan petroglyphs of a bull wearing a kind of disc are the petroglyphs in the Atlas Mountains where a ram carries a calabash. Camps, Gabriel, 'Bélier à sphéroïde (Gravure rupestre de l'Afrique du Nord)', in: *Encyclopédie berbère*, vol. 9 (Aix-en-Provence: Edisud, 1991), pp. 1417–1433. Striedter, *Felsbilder der Sahara* (1984), p. 50, figs 53–55.

116 Lecouteux, Claude, 'Les Cynocéphales. Etude d'une tradition tératologique de l'Antiquité au XIIe s', in: *Cahiers de civilisation médiévale*, no. 94 (Poitiers: CESCM, UMR 7302, 1981), p. 117f. Pliny the Elder, *Natural History*, VII.2.23, trans. John Bostock and H.T. Riley (1857), vol. 2, p. 135.

117 Le Quellec, Jean-Loïc, 'Théranthropes du Sahara. L'invention d'une méthode d'étude', in: *Archéologia*, no. 518 (Dijon: Faton, 2014), p. 5. Vachkova, Vesselina, 'Lupus in fabulis et in templo: Les métamorphoses étranges du Saint Christophe dans l'Église orthodoxe', in: Antunes, Gabriela and Reich, Björn (eds), (*De)formierte Körper Die Wahrnehmung und das Andere im Mittelalter* (Göttingen: Universitätsverlag Göttingen, 2012), pp. 172f.

118 Polo, Marco, *The Book of Ser Marco Polo*, vol. 2, book III, chapter 13, trans. Henry Yule (New York: Charles Scribner's sons, 1926), pp. 309–312. However, widespread distribution across space and time of human–animal hybrids, ranging from the Palaeolithic lion-man of Hohlenstein-Stadel to the Elamite lioness-woman figure of Guennol, the petroglyphs of the central Sahara, several Egyptian deities and St Christopher, makes it impossible to ascribe a uniform meaning to this concept. See also: Le Quellec, Jean-Loïc, 'Aréologie, phénétique et art rupestre: l'example des théranthropes du Sahara central', in: *Les Cahiers de l'AARS*, no. 16 (St-Benoist-sur-Mer: AARS, 2013), pp. 155f.

119 Hachid, *Le Tassili des Ajjer* (2000), pp. 266–269. Le Quellec, *Symbolisme et art rupestre au Sahara* (1993), pp. 350, 352, figs 111, 112.

120 D'Huy, Julien, 'Des mythes préhistorique ont-ils pu survivre au dépeuplement du Sahara? Le cas des hommes-chiens', in: *Les Cahiers de l'AARS*, no. 16 (St-Benoist-sur-Mer: AARS, 2013), p. 109.

121 A singular scene and a difficult one to interpret shows dog-headed theriomorphes being harassed by a group of advancing baboons; both groups are armed with bows. The rock painting is in the Tin Tirehart shelter, Tassili n'Ajjer. Smith, Andrew B., 'Masked men, therianthropes, (or charlatans) in Saharan rock art?', in: Huyge and Van Noten, *What Ever Happened to the People?* (2018), p. 543, fig. 8.

122 Hachid, *Le Tassili des Ajjer* (2000), p. 264.

123 Hachid, *Le Tassili des Ajjer* (2000), pp. 264f.

124 Lhote counted 135 spirals in Wadi Djerat. Lhote, *Les gravures rupestres* vol. 2, (1975), p. 802.

125 A lemniscate is a term used in geometry to designate any of several figure-of-eight-shaped or similar curves. https://en.wikipedia.org/wiki/Lemniscate (accessed 11 May 2024).

126 The last crocodile of the Tassili was killed in 1924 at Iherir, less than 90 km from site L 1. Hachid, *Le Tassili des Ajjer* (2000), pp. 71–73.

127 There are no Round Heads or early pastoral rock paintings in Wadi Djerat.

128 The representation of small mammals such as rabbits is rare in Saharan rock art.

129 Holl, Augustin F.C. and Gao Chang, 'Weapons, tools and objects: Material culture systems in African rock art', in: Bettencourt, Ana M.S. et al. (eds), *Weapons and Tools in Rock Art: A World Perspective* (Oxford: Oxbow, 2021), pp. 24, 27.

130 The process of rapid climatic deterioration forces people to either adapt and eventually fight to achieve food security or to migrate elsewhere.

131 Lhote, *Les gravures rupestres*, vol. 2 (1975), pp. 641f, figs 2088–2112.

132 The figure of the warrior holding three javelins could also be interpreted as the driver of a second chariot which is hidden by the first one.

133 This epoch would fall into the Caballine Period according to the older categorization of Saharan rock art.

134 Lajoux, Jean-Dominique, *Tassili n'Ajjer. Art rupestre du Sahara préhistorique* (Paris: Le Chêne, 1977), pp. 134f.

135 Mouchet, Annie, 'Sur les traces de Charles Brenans avec Bernard Fouilleux, à la Tasile-n-Ažžar', in: *Cahiers de l'AARS*, no. 24 (Saint-Benoist-sur-Mer: AARS, 2023), p. 198, figs 53–54. For further painted battle scenes in the central Sahara and Jabal al-Uweinat see: Le Quellec and de Flers, *Peintures et gravures d'avant les pharaons du Sahara au Nil* (2005), pp. 63, 65, figs 110, 111.

136 Barnett, *An engraved Landscape,* vol. 2 (2019), p. 146.

137 Gauthier, 'Des chars et des Tifinagh' (2011), p. 112. 'Nouvelles figurations de chars sahariens: technicité et positionnement chronologique relativement au style de Tazina', in: *Cahiers de l'AARS*, no. 18 (Saint-Benoist-sur-Mer: AARS, 2015), pp. 5–70. 'Images rupestres du nord-est du plateau des Ajjer', in: *Cahiers de l'AARS*, no. 24 (Saint-Benoist-sur-Mer: AARS, 2023), p. 72.

138 Gauthier, 'Des chars et des Tifinagh' (2011), p. 96. There are also paintings of horsemen in a flying gallop, for example at Terkey-Bowdé III in the Ennedi Plateau, Chad, *ca.* 1,650 km south-east of Wadi Djerat. Civrac, Marie-Anne, 'Quelques peintures du site de Terkey-Bowdé III (Ennedi, Tchad)', in: *Cahiers de l'AARS*, no. 16 (Saint-Benoist-sur-Mer: AARS, 2013), pp. 62–64, figs 12–18. Soleilhavoup, *Art rupestre dans l'Ennedi* (2018), p. 46, figs 49f.

139 L 21 is a highly interesting site. Besides the chariots, there are petroglyphs of a small, running therianthrope with a bull's head holding a javelin, a man touching the backside of a hippopotamus, three rhinoceroses, an archer shooting at a lion, several giraffes, a horseman holding a large flag, and the above-mentioned bull with a disc between its horns.

140 Ritual chariot races were held at the burials of famous warriors among Mycenaean Greeks (see book XXIII of Homer's *Iliad*) and Thracians.

141 Egyptian light battle chariots were suitable for use on desert ground provided there was neither deep sand nor large pebbles. Gauthier, 'Des chars et des Tifinagh' (2011), p. 112.

142 Gauthier, 'Des chars et des Tifinagh' (2011), p. 106. Muzzolini, *Les images rupestres du Sahara* (1995), p. 178.

143 Muzzolini, *Les images rupestres du Sahara* (1995), pp. 179, 382.

144 Gauthier, 'Des chars et des Tifinagh' (2011), p. 114.

Part 3. The Influence of Rock Art on Contemporary Art

IX. Transferring the Past into the Future

1 Most of the rock art copies are kept at the Frobenius Institute, Frankfurt am Main, Germany.

2 Frobenius Institute, Frankfurt. https://www.frobeniusinstitut.de/institut/geschichte?view=article&id=30:forschungsreisen-bis-1974&catid=42:das-institut (accessed 1 June 2024).

3 https://www.frobenius-institut.de/veranstaltungen/ausstellungen (accessed 26 May 2024).

4 Translation by Diana Renker. Kohl, Karl-Heinz, et al. (eds), *Kunst der Vorzeit. Felsbilder der Frobenius-Expeditionen; Einleitung* (Munich: Prestel, 2021), p. 15.

5 Translation by Diana Renker. Hildebrandt, Toni, 'Vorahmung und Kosmotechnik – Von der "Geburt des Graphismus" zur Kosmotechnik', in: Blümle, Claudia et al. (eds), *Regards croisés: Leroi-Gourhan*, no. 9 (Ilmtal-Weinstrasse: arts + science, 2019), p. 106.

6 Leroi-Gourhan, *Préhistoire de l'art occidental* (Paris: Mazenod, 1971), pp. 34–42.

7 Anati, Emmanuel, Editorial notes, in: *Expression*, no. 26: *The Role of Women in Prehistoric and Tribal Societies* (2019), p. 2.

8 Hughes, Virginia, 'Were the first artists mostly women?' (2013), in: https://www.nationalgeographic.com/adventure/article/131008-women-handprints-oldest-neolithic-cave-art (accessed 11 May 2024).

9 Hays-Gilpin, Kelley, 'Engendering rock art', in: McDonald and Veth, *Companion to Rock Art* (2012), p. 203.

10 Hays-Gilpin, 'Engendering rock art', (2012), p. 203.

11 The famous Bayeux Tapestry from *ca.* 1070 CE shows that women can very well illustrate so-called 'masculine' subjects.

12 https://fr.wikipedia.org/wiki/Main_n%C3%A9gative (accessed 2 June 2024).

13 Baumer, Christoph, 'Saudi Arabian Rock Art, Part I', unpublished travelogue (2020), p. 26.

14 Lorblanchet, Michel and Bahn, Paul, *The First Artists* (New York: Thames & Hudson, 2017), p. 8.

15 The author in conversation with Muhammad al-Mustaneer, Bir Hima, Saudi Arabia, 27 March 2020.

16 Barr curated the exhibition together with Dorothy Miller and Iris Barry. See below, p. 398 for the 1937 exhibition.

17 John Kay Clegg was a professor at the University of Sydney, Australia.

18 Huntley, Jillian and Nash, George (eds), *Aesthetics, Applications, Artistry and Anarchy: Essays in Prehistoric and Contemporary Art. A Festschrift in Honour of John Kay Clegg*, p. iii.

19 *documenta 14*, Kassel, Germany. Dale, Harding, *Composite Wall Panel: Reckitt's Blue* (2017). Screen prints, each *ca.* 177 × 456 cm.

20 Bieri, Susanne, *Swiss Artists' Books* (Cologne: Walther und Franz König, 2022), p. 31.

21 One of the few exceptions is the cave of Cussac in the Dordogne in south-west France. In the year 2000, large petroglyph palimpsests with human and animal depictions were discovered on the cave walls. In addition to more than 800 engravings, burial sites of Palaeolithic 'inhabitants' were found in the cave. Scratch marks from bears indicate that such animals hibernated in the cave. See also p. 3.

22 Hilfeling's field notebook is kept in the Antikvarisk-topografiska arkivet of the Swedish National Heritage Board in Stockholm. Bertilsson, Ulf, 'From folk oddities and remarkable relics to scientific substratum: 135 years of changing perceptions on the rock art carvings in Tanum, northern Bohuslän, Sweden', in: Skoglund, Ling and Bertilsson, *Picturing the Bronze Age* (2015), p. 7.

23 Nordbladh, Jarl, 'Carl Georg Brunius: An early nineteenth-century pioneer in Swedish petroglyph research', in: Skoglund, Ling and Bertilsson, *Picturing the Bronze Age* (2015), p. 125. The scale used could be as small as millimetres.

24 DStretch is a tool for rock art researchers who wish to enhance images of pictographs. https://dstretch.com/ (accessed 4 June 2024).

25 https://de.wikipedia.org/wiki/Frottage (accessed 1 June 2024).

26 Berger, John, *Ways of Seeing* (London: Penguin, 2008), pp. 7–8.

27 Translation by Diana Renker. Meier, Philippe, 'Der Mann, der aus dem Dunkeln kam: Pierre Soulages wird hundert Jahre alt', *Neue Zürcher Zeitung* (Zurich: NZZ), 24 December 2019, p. 35.

28 Lorblanchet and Bahn, *The First Artists* (2017), p. 7.

29 Lucy R. Lippard (b. 1937) is an American art critic, curator, writer and activist. In her book *Overlay: Contemporary Art and the Art of Prehistory* (New York: The New Press, 1983), she demonstrates how prehistoric images are transferred to contemporary art by today's artists. Lippard was also an early advocate of feminist art.

30 Obrist, Hans Ulrich, *A Brief History of Curating* (Geneva: JRP-Éditions, 2021), p. 233.

31 The oldest known paper was found in a grave behind a bronze mirror, from the time of the Han emperor Wu Di (140–87 BCE). The roughly structured paper measured 10 × 10 cm. Cai Lun (*ca.* 62–121) did not invent paper, for which he is traditionally credited, but he did refine its production. Weber, Therese, *The Language of Paper: A History of 2000 Years* (Bangkok: Orchid Press, 2007), p. 26.

32 The oldest known papyrus sheet comes from the grave of the high Egyptian official Hemaka, keeper of the seal of Hor Den, from the First Dynasty (*ca.* 2870–2820 BCE). Weber, *The Language of Paper* (2007), p. 12.

33 Abaca is a fibre material from the banana family (Musaceae), also known as Manila hemp or banana hemp. Paper is made from the hard fibres of the leaves of the banana tree.

34 In the machine known as the Hollander beater, developed by a Dutchman in 1680, plant fibres or fabrics are defibrated and shredded. https://de.wikipedia.org/wiki/Papierholl%C3%A4nder (accessed 16 June 2024). The Naginata machine or Naginata beater is used exclusively to defiber plants such as kozo/mulberry (Broussonetia kazinoki or Broussonetia papyrifera), gampi (Diplomorpha sikokiana or Wikstroemia retusa), mitsumata (Edgeworthia papyrifera or Edgeworthia chrysantha) or bamboo, but not to shred them. It is mainly used for long-fibre material in the eastern tradition of papermaking.

35 Latour, Bruno, *Existenzweisen: Eine Anthropologie der Modernen* (Berlin: Suhrkamp 2014).

36 In the exhibition *Prehistoric Rock Pictures in Europe and Africa* around 160 copies and photographs of rock art from Africa as well as Norway, Italy and France were on display; most of them came from the expeditions of Leo Frobenius and his team.

37 V. Walter Goetz, Hans Frener et al. (eds), *Propyläen-Weltgeschichte. Der Werdegang der Menschheit in Gesellschaft und Staat, Wirtschaft und Geistesleben*, vol. 1: *Das Erwachen der Menschheit* (Berlin: Propyläen-Verlag 1931), p. 147. Quoted from: Eggelhöfer, Fabienne, 'Auf den Spuren von Paul Klees Reisen in die Vorzeit', in: Seemann, E. A., *Urknall der Kunst*, 2023, p. 34.

38 Eggelhöfer, 'Auf den Spuren von Paul Klees Reisen in die Vorzeit' (2023), pp. 30–39.

39 *Cahiers d'Art*, vol. 5, nos 8–9 (Paris: Éditions 'Cahiers d'Art': 1930).

40 The journal *Documents: doctrines, archéologie, beaux-arts, ethnographie* was founded in 1929 by Georges Henri Rivière and Geoges Bataille. It contains the essay by Leo Frobenius, 'Dessin rupestres du Sud de la Rhodésie': vol. 2, no. 4 (1930), pp. 185–189. Source of information: Eggelhöfer, 'Auf den Spuren von Paul Klees Reisen in die Vorzeit' (2023), p. 35.

41 Translation from the German by Diana Renker. Source: Eggelhöfer, 'Auf den Spuren von Paul Klees Reisen in die Vorzeit' (2023), p. 37

42 Translation from the German by Diana Renker: Delot, Sébastien and Eggelhöfer, Fabienne (eds), *Paul Klee, Ich will nichts Wissen* (Paris, Bern: Flammarion, LaM, Zentrum Paul Klee, 2021), p. 15.

43 In children's drawings, 'X-ray images' are used as a pictorial system to emphasize and visualize a particular concern. For example, a bag is pictured transparently to show its contents, or the façade of a building is missing to show the view of the floors of the house and the people inside.

44 Paul Klee, *Muttertier* (Mother Animal), oil paint on primer on paper on carton, 20.9 × 32.8 cm, 1937, Zentrum Paul Klee, Bern, in: Luckhardt, Ulrich and Zimmer, Nina (eds), *Paul Klee-Tierisches. Internationale Tage Ingelheim*. Kunstforum Ingelheim & Zentrum Paul Klee (Munich: Hirmer, 2020), p. 67.

45 Therese Weber, 'Saudi Arabien, Oman' (2024), unpublished travel journal.

46 Klee taught in the textile workshop at the Bauhaus in Weimar, so he was familiar with the techniques and methods of weaving and working on the loom. This expertise could also be connected to his use of fabric backgrounds with a wide variety of textures made from different raw fibres.

47 Email to the author dated 27 May 2024.

48 The Misk Institute of Art, al-Riyadh. https://miskartinstitute.org/Artists/Details?q=aWQ9NTc%3D (accessed 3 June 2024).

49 Al-Fassam, Ibrahim, *Correlation: The Seventh Art Exhibition for Ibrahim N. Al-Fassam* (Riyadh: Gallery-Edition, 2022).

50 The petroglyph sites mentioned here are discussed on pp. 263, 280f.

51 Translation from the German by Diana Renker. Quote taken from: Schmidt, Aurel, 'Swiss–Libyan Art Project'. https://swiss-libyan-art-project.info/deutsch/rhman.php?m=mm5 (accessed 4 Dec. 2024).

52 The spray-painted work consists of 18 metal panels, each 120 x 260 cm, totalling 120 x 4680 cm. Part of it was last shown at Art Basel, Switzerland (2024). The frieze was originally installed in New York City along a fence on Franklin D. Roosevelt East River Drive (1984) and comprised approximately 30 panels.

53 https://smarthistory.org/keith-haring-subway-drawings/ (accessed 10 July 2024).

54 https://www.swiss-libyan-art-project.info/deutsch/index.php?m=mm1 (accessed 18 June 2024). The rubbings are preserved in several archives in Aosta, Italy and by the Association 'arte e segni'. https://www.arte-segni.ch/wp/ (accessed 31 July 2024).

55 Jörg Mollet, in conversation with the author at the Atelier Mollet, Solothurn, Switzerland, 22 January 2022.

56 Mollet, Jörg, *Carneval des Animaux* (2005), object, acrylic and pigment print on Japanese Shoji paper mounted on a wooden frame, 26 × 42 cm.

57 Film projection, Fondation Louis Vuitton, Open Space # 10, Galerie 8, Paris 7 October 2022–23 January 2023. https://www.fondationlouisvuitton.fr/en/events/open-space-10-lydia-ourahmane (accessed 7 July 2024).

58 https://www.sculpture-center.org/exhibitions/13458/lydia-ourahmane-tassili (accessed 7 July 2024).

59 Exhibition text for Lydia Ourahmane, *Tassili*, Fondation Louis Vuitton, Open Space # 10, Galerie 8, Paris 7 October 2022–23 January 2023.

60 Email to the author dated 29 May 2024.

61 See above, pp. 112–119.

62 Akanaev, Timur, *Caravanserai*, mixed media on hardboard (2011), 30 × 60 cm. https://artnow.ru/en/artists/3/15264/picture/0/547652.html (accessed 14 July 2024).

63 Rozwadowski, Andrzej, 'Rock art as a source of history in Central Asia', in: Kouamé, Nathalie, Meyer, Éric P. and Viguier, Anne, *Encyclopédie des historiographies: Afriques, Amériques, Asies* (Paris: Presses de l'Inalco, 2020), pp. 1520–1535.

64 https://ulturgashev.ru/index.php?view=article&id=1:aleksej-ulturgashev-khakasskij-khudozhnik-mirovogo-urovnya-maina-chebodaeva&catid=2 (accessed 3 August 2024).

65 Rozwadowski, Andrzej and Boniec, Magdalena, 'Face to face with ancestors: Indigenous codes in the contemporary Art of Siberia', in: Rozwadowski and Hampson, *Visual Culture, Heritage and Identity* (2021), fig. 10.

66 Rozwadowski and Boniec, 'Face to face with ancestors' (2021), figs 3, 4.

67 Rozwadowski and Boniec, 'Face to face with ancestors' (2021), pp. 62f.

68 https://en.wikipedia.org/wiki/Colville_Indian_Reservation (accessed 11 July 2024).

69 From a written interview by the author with the artist Joe Feddersen conducted on 27 May 2024. See as well: Oral history interview with Joe Feddersen, 2021. Smithsonian Archives of American Art. https://www.aaa.si.edu/collections/interviews/oral-history-interview-joe-feddersen-22078.

70 Cardinal-Schubert, Joane, *Letters to Emily: Borrowed Power* (1992), 91.4 × 243.8 cm, in two parts. Collage, mixed media on rag paper. MacRae, Alisdair, 'Joane Cardinal-Schubert: Ancient contemporary', in: Rozwadowski and Hampson, *Visual Culture, Heritage and Identity* (2021), pp. 37–50.

71 https://www.thecanadianencyclopedia.ca/en/article/joane-cardinal-schubert (accessed 14 July 2024).

72 A quilt is a multi-layered textile, usually made of cotton fabric, with a fleece layer in the centre. The design of the top of a quilt is created from single-coloured or patterned pieces of fabric, arranged to form a distinctive pattern known as patchwork or appliqué. Finally, the layers are sewn together, usually by hand, with stitches to prevent them from shifting. Quilts are popular as blankets or as decorative wall hangings.

73 One such joint exhibition was: *Dale Harding with Kate Harding: Through a lens of visitation*, at the Chau Chak Wing Museum, University of Sydney, 9 July 2022–February 2023.

74 Harding, Dale, *Composite Wall Panel, Reckitt's Blue* (2017). Three screen prints with mural, prints each approx. 177 × 456 cm. https://universes.art/de/documenta/2017/documenta-14-kassel/03-ottoneum/dale-harding (accessed 13 July 2024).

75 At *documenta 14* (2017) in Kassel, the Carnarvon Gorge was presented as a photographic one-to-one replica. Screen prints were reproduced in monochrome ultramarine blue. These prints represent not only a copy of the murals but also the actual act of copying using stencils. The shades of blue selected for the wall prints refer to a pigment known as 'Reckitt's Blue', which found its way into Indigenous art after initial contact with European missionaries.

76 https://americanart.si.edu/artwork/untitled-silueta-series-34658 (accessed 2 July 2024).

77 Hessel, Katy, *The Story of Art Without Men: Grosse Künstlerinnen und ihre Werke* (München: Piper, 2022), p. 335.

78 Flam, Jack (ed.), *Robert Smithson: The Collected Writings* (Berkeley: University of California Press, 2000), p. 260.

79 Lippard, Lucy R., *Overlay: Contemporary Art and the Art of Prehistory* (New York: The New Press, 1983), p. 138.

80 Schroeter-Bieler, Lisa, *Skandinavien. Der Himmel über Europas Wiege. Gestalten auf nordischen Felsbildern der Bronzezeit. Ein Versuch, sie zu verstehen und zu deuten* (Freiburg im Breisgau: Schillinger Verlag, 1987), p. 2.

81 Translation from the German by Diana Renker. Schroeter-Bieler, *Skandinavien* (1987), p. 108.

82 Schroeter-Bieler, *Skandinavien* (1987), pp. 118, 123.

83 Schroeter-Bieler, *Skandinavien* (1987), p. 2.

84 https://de.wikipedia.org/wiki/Hans_Benesch (accessed June 19, 2024).

85 Zaunschirm, Thomas, 'Im Zoo der Kunst', in:

Kunstforum, no. 174: *Out of Africa* (Cologne: Kunstforum International, 2005), pp. 38–104.

86 Mackert, Gabriele, 'Joseph Beuys im Dialog mit Urbildern', in: Faass and Schmidt, *Urknall der Kunst* (2023), p. 57.

87 Mackert, 'Joseph Beuys im Dialog mit Urbildern' (2023), p. 50.

88 Assmann, Aleida, *Erinnerungsräume: Formen und Wandlungen des kulturellen Gedächtnisses* (Munich: C.H. Beck, 2018), p. 359.

89 Translation from the German by Diana Renker. Penck, A.R., *Mein Denken*, ed. Gallwitz Klaus (Frankfurt am Main: Suhrkamp, 1986), p. 82.

90 Penck, *Mein Denken* (1986), p. v.

91 The exhibition *A.R. Penck Retrospektive* (2008) at the Schirn Kunsthalle in Frankfurt featured 70 notebooks and artist's books.

92 These sculptures were made in collaboration with Frank Breidenbruch. In November 2005, the sculptures were damaged by an excavator during construction work https://www.denkmal-wuppertal.de/2013/04/die-himmlischen-sturze.html (accessed 22 March 2024).

93 Archiv Peter Piller: *Spekulationen (I) Unbestimmte Linien* (2022), in collaboration with Overbeck Gesellschaft, Lübeck. *Spekulationen (II) Zahlreiche Übergangsformen* (2023) and *Spekulationen (III) Begleiter* (2023), in collaboration with Kunsthalle Düsseldorf.

94 Translation from the German by Diana Renker. Schmidt, Sabine Maria, 'Peter Piller. Sie fanden, was sie kannten', in: *Kunstforum*, no. 293: *Parasitäre Paradoxa, Kunst zwischen Anpassung und Widerstand* (Cologne: Kunstforum International, 2023), p. 177.

95 Further linear stone carvings can be found on stone pebbles in the abbey of Laugerie-Basse near Les Eyzies-de-Tayac, Dordogne, France. See: Labrusse, Rémi, *Préhistoire : L'envers du temps* (Vanves: Hazan, 2019), p. 103.

96 Labrusse, Rémi, *Préhistoire : L'envers du temps* (2019), p. 102.

97 Archival pigment prints are photographic images that are printed in the highest quality using inkjet printers and pigment ink on high-quality paper. They have a soft and timeless appearance and are light-fast.

98 For example, there are two replicas of the famous cave of Lascaux located next to the original site, which is closed, as well as an itinerant copy.

99 *Peter Piller – there are a couple of things that bother me*, Kunsthalle Düsseldorf, 11 March–21 May 2023. *Peter Piller – Geduld*, Galerie Capitain Petzel, Berlin, 21 June–3 August 2019.

100 Translation from the German by Diana Renker. Interview between Robin Rhode and Elke Buhr, 'Die Felszeichnungen sind ein Quellcode der Menschheit': https://www.monopol-magazin.de/robin-rhode-interview-die-felszeichnungen-sind-ein-quellcode-der-menschheit (accessed 10 January 2024).

101 Robin Rhode et al., *Rhode Works*, Kunstmuseum Luzern, Switzerland (2014). *African Dream* (2023), Lehmann Maupin Gallery, New York.

102 https://artsafiental.ch/as2018/hiddenpage/circuit-board-for-rock-painting/ (accessed 4 Dec. 2024).

103 'Banksy' is the pseudonym of the artist (probably born 1973 or 1974). His real name as well as his true identity are subject to speculation. There could even be a collective behind the name Banksy. https://de.wikipedia.org/wiki/Banksy (accessed 18 July 2024).

104 Löhndorf, Marion, 'Banksy hat eine rote Nase. Der Street-Artist brachte es zu Weltruhm. Hinter dem Image des Outlaw stecken cleveres Kalkül und Marketing', in: *Neue Zürcher Zeitung* (Zurich: NZZ), 17 December 2021, p. 30.

105 *Arab News* (Riyadh), 2 August 2022. https://www.arabnews.com/node/2133976/saudi-arabia (accessed 13 August 2024).

106 Painted copies of the rock paintings were already exhibited in Paris in 1930 and 1933.

107 Stavrinaki, Maria, 'Die Ausstellung "40,000 years of Modern Art" in London 1948', in: Kohl et al. (eds), *Kunst der Vorzeit: Felsbilder der Frobenius-Expeditionen* (Munich: Prestel, 2021), pp. 204–205.

108 Stavrinaki, 'Die Ausstellung "40,000 Years of Modern Art" in London 1948' (2021), p. 204.

109 12 February–15 March 1953. The exhibition was organized by Jaques A. Mauduit, an early history researcher at the Musée de l'Homme, in collaboration with the Maison des Beaux-Arts and the Musée d'Art Moderne.

110 Brun, Baptiste, '"40 Jahre moderne Kunst" im Musée d'Art Moderne, Paris 1953', in: Kohl et al., *Kunst der Vorzeit, Felsbilder der Frobenius Expedition* (Munich: Prestel, 2021), pp. 206–207.

111 '*Ten Americans after Paul Klee*'. Bern, Zentrum Paul Klee, 15 September 2017–7 January 2018. This exhibition in collaboration with the Phillips Collection, Washington DC, was also shown in Washington from 3 February to 6 May 2018.

112 Duncan Phillips (1886–1966) played a central role in the introduction of modern art in America and was a collector of Paul Klee's works. https://www.phillipscollection.org/press/phillips-presents-ten-americans-after-paul-klee (accessed 18 July 2024).

113 Eggelhöfer, Fabienne, Smithgall, Elsa, et al., *Ten Americans: After Paul Klee* (Munich: Prestel, 2017).

114 Debray, Céline and Labrusse, Rémi (eds), *Préhistoire: Une énigme moderne* (Paris: Edition du Centre Pompidou, 2019).

115 Museum Rietberg, Zürich, 12 March 2021–11 July 2021. The exhibition *Kunst der Vorzeit – Felsbilder der Frobenius-Expeditionen* was first shown in 2016 at the Martin-Gropius-Bau, Berlin, under the title *Kunst der Vorzeit – Felsbilder aus der Sammlung Frobenius*.

116 See the section 'History of Origin', in: Kohl et al., *Kunst der Vorzeit-Felsbilder der Frobenius-Expeditionen* (Munich: Prestel, 2021), pp. 52–101.

117 In addition to scientists, Frobenius' expeditions included artists, the majority of whom were women. They painted the rock paintings true to the original but with their own individual styles. The paintings are not signed, but authorship can be attributed today based on their distinctive styles.

118 Besides Miró, Baumeister and Picasso, the exhibition featured works by Hans Arp (1868–1966), Paul Klee, André Masson (1896–1987) and Joseph Beuys. Faass and Schmidt, *Urknall der Kunst* (2023).

Captions

1 Jaubert, Jacques et al., *Grotte de Cussac -30 000* (Bordeaux: Éditions confluence, 2020), pp. 129–40, 191–194.

2 Bégouën, Robert at al., *La caverne des Trois-Frères. Anthologie d'un exceptionnel sanctuaire préhistorique* (Montesquieu-Avantès: Association Louis Bégouën, 2014), pp. 117–139.

3 Hauptmann, Harald (ed.), *Materialien zur Archäologie der Nordgebiete Pakistans*, vol. 6 (2003), p. 83.

4 Davidson, H.R. Ellis, *Scandinavian Mythology* (1984), pp. 42, 45.

5 *Die Tagebücher des Orientalisten Julius Euting*, Eberhard Karls Universität Tübingen: https://opendigi.ub.uni-tuebingen.de/opendigi/Md676-21#p=198 (accessed 30 July 2024).

Bibliography

Internet

There is a multitude of internet sites with information about local or regional petroglyph sites, while a few supraregional websites also exist, including interactive maps. The overview given below represents only a selection of those sites which were of use to the present authors.

Alta Museum and Alta Rock Art Archive, Norway
https://altamuseum.fotoware.cloud/fotoweb/
https://www.altamuseum.no/en/the-rock-art-of-alta/the-rock-art-archive

Arabian Rock Art Heritage, Sandra L. Olsen et al. (eds)
http://saudi-archaeology.com/overview/

Bradshaw Foundation
https://www.bradshawfoundation.com/

Digital Archive for the Study of Pre-Islamic Inscriptions DASI, Alessandra Avanzini, Michael C.A., Macdonald, and Laïla Nehmé (dir.) http://dasi.cnr.it/.

Don's Maps, webmaster Don Hitchcock
https://www.donsmaps.com/index.html

Fliegel Jezerniczky Expeditions to North African Rock Art
https://fjexpeditions.com/frameset/past.htm

IFRAO. International Federation of Rock Art Organisation
http://www.ifrao.com/ifrao/

Ladakh Archaeology: Petroglyphs & Pictographs
https://ladakharchaeology.com/categories/petro-picto/

Scandinavian Rock Art
http://www.ismoluukkonen.net/kalliotaide/piirros/index.html

Swedish Rock Art Research Archives
https://shfa.dh.gu.se/

TARA. Trust for African Rock Art
https://africanrockart.org/

Ughtasar Rock Art Project, Anna Khechoyan and Tina Walkling (dir.)
http://ughtasarrockartproject.org/index.html.

The Megalithic Portal
https://www.megalithic.co.uk/index.php

Publications

Abadia, Oscar Moro et al. (eds.), *Deep-Time Images in the Age of Globalization: Interdisciplinary Contributions to Archaeology* (Cham: Springer, 2024).

Abdulhamid, Louai A., 'Artistic styles in the engravings of the ancient rock art in Wadi al Baqar (Valley of Cows) in the Sahara Desert in Libya', doctoral thesis (Newcastle, NSW: University of Newcastle, 2015).

Adkins, Lesley, *Empires of the Plain: Henry Rawlinson and the Lost Languages of Babylon* (London: Harper Perennial, 2004).

Adler, Marcus Nathan, *The Itinerary of Benjamin of Tudela* (New York: Philipp Feldheim, Inc.,1907): https://depts.washington.edu/silkroad/texts/tudela.html.

Adoranten (Tanumshede, Sweden: Scandinavian Society for Prehistoric Art, 2008–24).

Aerde, Marike van, 'Routes beyond Gandhara: Buddhist rock carvings in the context of the early Silk Roads', in: Yang et al., *Socio-Environmental Dynamics along the Historical Silk Road* (2019, q.v.), pp. 455–480.

Aerde, Marike van and Khan, Abdul Rani, 'Carvings and community: Inclusive heritage solutions for protecting ancient Karakorum petroglyphs under threat', in: *Journal of Archaeohistorical Studies*, vol. 2, no. 2 (Hochstadt: ASAS, 2021), pp. 77–90.

Aichner, B. et al., 'High-resolution leaf wax carbon and hydrogen isotopic record of the late Holocene paleoclimate in arid Central Asia', in: *Climate of the Past*, vol. 11, no. 4 (Göttingen: Copernicus Publications, 2015), pp. 619–633.

Aïn-Séba, Nagète, 'Saharan rock art: A reflection of climate change in the Sahara', in: *Tabona. Revista de Prehistoria y de Arqueología*, vol. 22 (San Cristóbal de La Laguna: Universidad de La Laguna, 2022), pp. 303–317.

Aksoy, Ömer Can, 'A combat archaeology viewpoint on weapon representations in Northwest Arabian rock art', in: *Mediterranean Archaeology and Archaeometry*, vol. 17, no. 4 (Athens: University of the Aegean, 2017), pp. 1–17.

— 'A sickle boat petroglyph in Wadi Asafir: Possible evidence of Pre-Dynastic Egyptian influence on Northwest Arabia', in: *Antiquity*, vol. 94, art. no. e32 (Cambridge: Cambridge University Press, 2020).

Al-Belushi, Mohammed Ali and ElMahi, Ali Tigani, 'Archaeological investigations in Shenah, Sultanate of Oman', in: *Proceedings of the Seminar for Arabian Studies*, vol. 39 (Oxford: Archaeopress, 2009), pp. 31–42.

Alexander, Craig et al., 'Rules of ordering and grouping in the *Pitoti*, the later prehistoric rock engravings of Valcamonica (BS), Italy', in: Davidson and Nowell, *Making Scenes* (2021, q.v.), pp. 259–276.

Alexev, V., 'The physical specificities of Paleolithic Hominids in Siberia', in: Derev'anko et al., *The Palaeolithic of Siberia* (1998, q.v.), pp. 329–335.

Al-Fassam, Ibrahim, *Correlation: The Seventh Art Exhibition for Ibrahim N. Al-Fassam* (Riyadh: Gallery-Edition, 2022).

Al-Ghabban, Ali Ibrahim et al., (eds), *Roads of Arabia: Archaeology and History of the Kingdom of Saudi Arabia* (Paris: Musée du Louvre, 2010).

Al-Hasan, Husayn bin Ali Abu, 'The Kingdom of Lihyan', in: Al-Ghabban et al., *Roads of Arabia* (2010, q.v.), pp. 270–285.

Al-Jallad, Ahmad, 'What is Ancient North Arabian?', in: Birnstiel, Daniel and Pat-El, Na'ama (eds), *Re-Engaging Comparative Semitic and Arabic Studies* (Wiesbaden: Harrassowitz, 2018), pp. 1–43.

Al-Jallad, Ahmad and Sidky, Hythem, 'A paleo-Arabic inscription on a route north of Tā'if', in: *Arabian Archaeology and Epigraphy*, vol. 33 (Oxford: Wiley, 2022), pp. 202–215.

Allard-Huard, Léone, *Nil–Sahara. Dialogues rupestres*, vol. 1: *Les chasseurs*; vol. 2: *L'homme innovateur* (Divajeu/Crest: self-published, 1993, 2001).

— 'Les secteurs rupestres du sous-continent saharien et du Nil', in: *Art rupestre du Sahara. Dossiers d'Archéologie*, no. 197 (1994, q.v.), pp. 70–83.

Allard-Huard, Léone and Huard, Paul, *Le cheval, le fer et le chameau sur le Nil et au Sahara* (Paris: Éditions et publication des pères Jésuites en Égypte, 1985).

Allchin, F. Raymond et al. (eds), *Gandharan Art in Context: East–West Exchanges at the Crossroads of Asia* (New Delhi: Regency Publications, 1997).

Allentoft, Morten E. et al., 'Population genomics of Bronze Age Eurasia', in: *Nature*, vol. 522 (London: Macmillan, 2015), pp.167–183.

— 'Population genomics of post-glacial western Eurasia', in: *Nature*, vol. 625 (London: Macmillan, 2024), pp. 301–311.

Almgren, Oscar, *Hällristningar och kultbruk* (Stockholm: Wahlström & Widstrand, 1926–7).

— *Nördliche Felszeichnungen als religiöse Urkunden* (Frankfurt a.M.: Moritz Diesterweg 1934).

Alok, Ersin, *Petroglyphs of Gobustan* (Baku: Azerinşaat, 2011).

Al-Said, Said F., 'Dedan (al-Ula)', in: Al-Ghabban et al., *Roads of Arabia* (2010, q.v.), pp. 262–270.

Al-Tikriti, Walid Yasin, *Rock Art in the Abu Dhabi Emirate* (Al-Ain: Abu Dhabi Cultural Heritage, 2011).

Altuntas, Leman, 'Orta Asya'da ilk defa bir Boğa Jeoglifi Keşfedildi = A bull geoglyph discovered for the first time in Central Asia', in: *Arkeonews* (29 September 2021): https://arkeonews.com/orta-asyada-ilk-defa-bir-boga-jeoglifi-kesfedildi/.

Amanbaeva, Bakyt et al., 'Rock Art in Kyrgyzstan', in: Clottes, *Rock Art in Central Asia* (2011, q.v.), pp. 43–72.

Anati, Emmanuel, *Rock-Art in Central Arabia* (4 vols, Louvain: Institut Orientaliste, 1968–1974).

— 'The way of life recorded in the rock art of Valcamonica', in: *Adoranten* (q.v., 2008), pp. 13–35.

— *World Rock Art: The Primordial Language* (Oxford: Archaeopress, 2011).

— (ed.), *Expression: Quarterly E-Journal* (Capo di Ponte: Atelier, 2013–).

— *Decoding Prehistoric Art and the Origins of Writing* (Capo di Ponte: Atelier, 2015).

— *The Rock Art of Azerbaijan* (Capo di Ponte: Atelier, 2015).

— *The Rock Art of Valcamonica* (Capo di Ponte: Atelier, 2015).

— 'Male and female variability in the rock art of Azerbaijan', in: *Expression*, no. 26, December 2019 (Capo di Ponte: Atelier), pp. 9–19.

— *The Origins of Religion: A Study in Conceptual Anthropology* (Capo di Ponte: Atelier, 2020).

— *Cult Sites and Art* (Capo di Ponte: Atelier, 2021).

— *Cultural Changes* (Capo di Ponte: Atelier, 2021).

— *The Function of Art* (Capo di Ponte: Atelier, 2021).

— *The Role of Women in Prehistoric and Tribal Societies* (Capo di Ponte: Atelier, 2021).

The Ancient Walled Oases of Northern Arabia, World Heritage Site Nomination Document (Riyadh: Permanent Delegation of Saudi Arabia to UNESCO, 2022): https://whc.unesco.org/en/tentativelists/6575/.

Andreae, Meinrat O. et al., 'Archaeometric studies on the petroglyphs and rock varnish at Khilwa and Sakaka, northern Saudi Arabia', in: *Arabian Archaeology and Epigraphy*, vol. 31 (Oxford: Wiley, 2020). pp. 219–244.

— 'Iconographic and archaeometric studies on the rock art at Musayqira, Al-Quwaiyah governorate, central Saudi Arabia', in: *Arabian Archaeology and Epigraphy*, vol. 32, suppl. 1 (Oxford: Wiley, 2020). pp. 153–182.

Anthony, David W., *The Horse, the Wheel and Language: How Bronze Age Riders from the Eurasian Steppes Shaped the Modern World* (Princeton: Princeton University Press, 2007).

Arbach, Mounir, Charloux, Guillaume et al, 'Results of four seasons of survey in the province of Najrān (Saudi Arabia), 2007–2019', in: Gerlach, Iris (ed.), *South Arabia and its Neighbours: Phenomena of Intercultural Contacts* (Wiesbaden: Reichert, 2015), pp. 11–46.

Arbach, Mounir, Christian, Robin et al., 'Projet Himà', in: *Centre Français de Recherche de la Péninsule Arabique* (Paris: 2015, 2018), n.p., https://cefas.cnrs.fr/spip.php?article133&lang=fr (link expired).

Arbach, Mounir and Prioletta, Alessia, 'Les inscriptions royales rupestres de la péninsule arabique', in: *L'art rupestre en Arabie. Dossiers d'Archéologie*, no. 407 (2021, q.v.), pp. 60–61.

Arcà, Andrea, 'The topographic engravings of Alpine rock-art: Fields, settlements and agricultural landscapes', in: Chippindale and Nash, *The Figured Landscapes of Rock-Art* (2004, q.v.), pp. 318–349.

Arslanov, Kh. A. et al., 'On the age of the Khvalynian deposits of the Caspian Sea coasts according to ^{14}C and ^{230}Th/^{234}U methods', in: *Quaternary International*, vol. 409, part A, 21 July 2016 (Amsterdam: Elsevier), pp. 81–87.

Art paléolithique. Nouvelles découvertes. Dossiers d'Archéologie, no. 417 (Dijon: Faton, 2023).

L'art rupestre en Arabie. Une histoire oubliée des peuples du désert. Dossiers d'Archéologie, no. 407 (Dijon: Faton, 2021)

Art rupestre du Sahara. Dossiers d'Archéologie, no. 197 (Dijon: Faton, 1994).

Aruz, Joan et al. (eds), *The Golden Deer of Eurasia: Perspectives on the Steppe Nomads of the Ancient World* (New York: The Metropolitan Museum of Art, 2000).

Assmann, Aleida, *Erinnerungsräume: Formen und Wandlungen des kulturellen Gedächtnisses* (Munich: C.H. Beck, 2018).

Assmann, Jan, *Achsenzeit: Eine Archäologie der Moderne* (Munich: C.H. Beck, 2018).

— *Das kulturelle Gedächtnis: Schrift, Erinnerung und politische Identität in frühen Hochkulturen* (Munich: C.H. Beck, 2018).

Atlal: The Journal of Saudi Arabian Archaeology, vol. 1 (Riyadh: Ministry of Education, AH 1397/1977).

Aubarbier, Jean-Luc and Binet, Michel, *Sites préhistoriques en Périgord* (Rennes: Ouest-France, 1984).

Aubekerov, R.J., Sala R. and Nigmatova, S.A., 'Late Holocene paleoclimate and paleogeography in the Tien Shan–Balkhash region', in: *PAGES News*, vol. 11, nos 2–3 (Bern: University of Bern, 2003), pp. 24–26.

Aubert, Maxime et al., 'Pleistocene cave art from Sulawesi, Indonesia', in: *Nature*, vol. 514 (London: Macmillan, 2014), pp. 223–227.

— 'Earliest hunting scene in prehistoric art', in: *Nature*, vol. 576 (London: Macmillan, 2019), pp. 442–445.

Aubry, Thierry and Balbin-Behrmann, Rodrigo de, 'Le plein air, un espace d'expression', in: *Art paléolithique. Dossiers d'Archéologie*, no. 417 (2023, q.v.), pp. 56–59.

Aumassip, Ginette, *Préhistoire du Sahara et de ses abords* (2 vols, Paris: Maisonneuve & Larose, 2004, 2019).

Avesta. Die heiligen Schriften der Parsen, trans. Friedrich Spiegel (1863; Reprint: Paris: Adamant, 2006).

Azandaryani, Esmail Hemati, 'Azandaryan: Newfound petroglyphs in Hamadan, Western Iran', in: *Rock Art Research*, vol. 32, no. 2 (Darwin: International Federation of Rock Art Organizations, IFRAO, 2015), pp. 202–206.

Babayev, Rafael (ed.), *The Encyclopaedia of Nakhchivan Monuments* (Nakhchivan: National Academy of Sciences, 2009).

Bahn, Paul G., *The Cambridge Illustrated History of Prehistoric Art* (Cambridge: Cambridge University Press, 1998).

— *Cave Art: A Guide to the Decorated Caves of Europe* (London: Frances Lincoln, 2007).

— *Prehistoric Rock Art: Polemics and Progress* (Cambridge: Cambridge University Press, 2010).

— 'Bow and errors', in: Stebergløkken et al., *Ritual Landscape and Borders within Rock Art Research* (2015, q.v.), pp. 59–65.

Bahn, Paul G. et al., *Rock Art Studies: News of the World* (6 vols, Oxford: Oxbow, 1996, 2004, 2008, 2012, 2016, 2021).

Bailloud, Gérard, *Art rupestre en Ennedi* (Saint-Maur: Éditions Sépia, 1997).

Baipakov, Karl and Maryashev, Alexey N., *Петроглифы в горах Кулжабасы / Petroglyphs of the Kuljabasy Mountains* (Almaty: Margulan Archaeological Institute, 2004).

— *Петроглифы Баян-Журека / Petroglyphs of Bayan Zhurek* (Almaty: Credos, 2008).

— *Петроглифы Ак-Кайнара / Petroglyphs of Ak-Kainar* (Almaty: Credos, 2009).

— *Петроглифы Малого Каратау и западной оконечности Киргизского Алатау = Petroglyphs of the Lesser Karatau and the Western End of the Kyrgyz Alatau* (Almaty: Archaeological Expertise, 2013).

Baipakov, Karl, Maryashev, Alexey N. et al., *Петроглифы в горах Ешкиольмес / The Eshkiolmes Rock's Petroglyphs* (Almaty: OST-XXI Vek, 2005).

Baipakov, Karl, Maryashev, Alexey and Potapov, S.A., *Петроглифы Тамгалы / Petroglyphs of Tamgaly* (Almaty: Margulan Archaeological Institute, 2006).

Bal, Mieke, et al., *Kulturanalyse* (Frankfurt am Main: Suhrkamp, 2006).

Balzer, Isabel and Baumer, Christoph (eds), *Therese Weber – Topographien der Räume / Therese Weber – Topographies of Spaces* (Berlin: Hatje Cantz, 2023).

Barfield, Lawrence and Chippindale, Christopher, 'Meaning in the later prehistoric rock-engravings of Mont Bégo, Alpes-Maritimes, France', in: *Proceedings of the Prehistoric Society*, vol. 63 (London: The Prehistoric Society, 1997), pp. 103–128.

Barnett, Tertia, 'Patterns on the rocks: Report on recent work to survey rock art sites in the Wadi al-Hayat, Fezzan', in: *Libyan Studies*, 36 (London: Society for Libyan Studies, 2005), pp. 127–140.

— 'Back to life: British rock art in the Iron Age', in: Dodd and Meijer, *Giving the Past a Future* (2018, q.v.), pp. 255–269.

— *An Engraved Landscape: Rock Carvings in the Wadi al-Ajal, Libya* (2 vols, London: Society for Libyan Studies, 2019).

— 'The power of Saharan rock art: Creating images in a changing world', in: *Current World Archaeology*, vol. 97 (London: Current Publishing, 2019), pp. 16–21.

— *Prehistoric Rock Art in Scotland* (Edinburgh: Historic Environment Scotland, 2021).

Barnett, Tertia and Guagnin, Maria, 'Changing places: Rock art and Holocene landscapes in the Wadi al-Ajal, south-west Libya', in: *Journal of African Archaeology*, vol. 12, no. 2 (Frankfurt a.M.: Africa-Magna, 2014), pp. 165–182.

Barth, Heinrich, *Reisen und Entdeckungen in Nord- und Central-Afrika in den Jahren 1849 bis 1855* (5 vols, Gotha: Justus Perthes, 1857–58).

Bataille, Georges, *La peinture préhistorique. Lascaux ou la naissance de l'art* (Geneva: Albert Skira, 1980).

Bätschmann, Oskar and Helfenstein, Josef (eds), *Paul Klee: Kunst und Karriere. Beiträge des Internationalen Symposiums in Bern* (Bern: Stämpfli 2000).

Battiss, Walter, *The Artists of the Rocks* (Pretoria: The Red Fawn Press, 1948).

Baumer, Christoph, *Die Südliche Seidenstrasse. Inseln im Sandmeer. Versunkene Kulturen der Wüste Taklamakan* (Mainz: Philipp von Zabern, 2002).

— *Tibet's Ancient Religion, Bön* (Bangkok: Orchid Press, 2002).

— *The History of Central Asia*, vol. 1: *The Age of the Steppe Warriors* (London: I.B. Tauris, 2012).

— *The History of Central Asia*, vol. 2: *The Age of the Silk Roads* (London: I.B. Tauris, 2014).

— *The Church of the East: An Illustrated History of Assyrian Christianity* (London: I.B. Tauris, 2016).

— *The History of Central Asia*, vol. 4: *The Age of Decline and Revival* (London: I.B. Tauris, 2018).

— *History of the Caucasus*, vol. 1: *At the Crossroads of Empires* (London: I.B. Tauris/Bloomsbury, 2021).

— 'Rock art in Saudi Arabia: A general introduction and new findings', in: *Adoranten* (q.v., 2022), pp. 5–29.

— *History of the Caucasus*, vol. 2: In the Shadow of Great Powers (London: I.B. Tauris/Bloomsbury, 2023).

Baumer, Christoph, Schmidt, Aurel and Weber, Therese, *Durch die Wüste Taklamakan: Auf den Spuren des Sven Hedin und Sir Aurel Stein* (Oppenheim: Nünnerich-Asmus, 2013).

Baumer, Christoph, Novák, Mirko and Rutishauser, Susanne (eds), *Cultures in Contact: Central Asia as Focus of Trade, Cultural Exchange and Knowledge Transmission* (Wiesbaden: Harrassowitz, 2022).

Baumer, Christoph and Weber, Therese, *Eastern Tibet: Bridging Tibet and China* (Bangkok: Orchid Press, 2005).

Bausi, Alessandro, 'The massacre of Najrān: The Ethiopic sources', in: Beaucamp et al., *Juifs et Chrétiens en Arabie aux Vème et VIème siècles* (2010, q.v.), pp. 241–254.

Baytanaev, B.A. (ed.), *The Rock Art of Kulzhabasy Range* (Almaty: Žambyl' baspasy, 2017).

Beaucamp, Joëlle et al., *Juifs et chrétiens en Arabie aux Vème et VIème siècles. Regards croisés sur les sources. Le massacre de Najrân*, vol. 2 (Paris: ACHCByz, 2010).

Beaulieu, Paul-Alain, *The Reign of Nabonidus, King of Babylon 556–539 BC* (New Haven: Yale University Press, 1989).

Beckwith, Christopher I., *The Tibetan Empire in Central Asia: A History of the Struggle for Great Power among Tibetans, Turks, Arabs, and Chinese during the Early Middle Ages* (Princeton: Princeton University Press, 1987).

Bednarik, Robert G., 'To be or not to be palaeolothic, that is the question', in: *Rock Art Research*, vol. 26 (Darwin: International Federation of Rock Art Organizations, IFRAO, 2009), pp. 165–177).

— 'Pleistocene rock art in Central Europe?', in: *International Newsletter on Rock Art*, no. 45 (Foix: INORA, 2006), pp. 27–30.

— 'Cupules', in: *Rock Art Research*, vol. 2, no. 1 (Darwin: International Federation of Rock Art Organizations, IFRAO, 2008), pp. 61–100.

— 'Scientific investigations into Saudi Arabian rock art: A review', in: *Mediterranean Archaeology and Archaeometry*, vol. 17, no.4 (Athens: University of the Aegean, 2017), pp. 43–56.

Bednarik, Robert G. and Khan, Majeed, 'Scientific studies of Saudi Arabian rock art', in: *Rock Art Research*, vol. 22, no. 1 (Darwin: International Federation of Rock Art Organizations, IFRAO, 2005), pp. 49–81.

— 'New Rock Art Complex in Saudi Arabia', in: *Rock Art Research*, vol. 34, no. 2 (Darwin: International Federation of Rock Art Organizations, IFRAO, 2017), pp.179–188.

Bégouën, Robert at al., 'Parietal art and archaeological context: Activities of the Magdalenians in the cave of Tuc d'Audoubert, France', in: McDonald and Veth, *Companion to Rock Art* (2012, q.v.), pp. 364–380.

— *La caverne des Trois-Frères. Anthologie d'un exceptionnel sanctuaire préhistorique* (Montesquieu-Avantès: Association Louis Bégouën, 2014).

Beier, Hans-Jürgen and Hinze, Hans-Peter (eds), *Botschaften in Stein – Dokumentiert, interpretiert und experimentiert* (Langenweissbach: Beier & Beran, 2015).

Belenizki, A.M., *Mittelasien. Kunst der Sogden* (Leipzig: VEB E.A. Seemann, 1980).

Bellezza, John Vincent, *Divine Dyads: The Ancient Civilization of Tibet* (Dharamsala: Library of Tibetan Works and Archives, 1997).

— *Flight of the Khyung*, monthly newsletter (2006–19): https://www.tibetarchaeology.com/newsletter-archive/.

— *Zhang Zhung. Foundations of Civilization in Tibet: A Historical and Ethnoarchaeological Study of the Monuments, Rock Art, Texts, and Oral Tradition of the Ancient Tibetan Upland* (Vienna: Verlag der Österreichischen Akademie der Wissenschaften, 2008).

— 'The origins of the Tibetan people', in: *Flight of the Khyung* (q.v., May 2013)

— *Antiquities of Zhang Zhung: A Comprehensive Inventory of Pre-Buddhist Archaeological Monuments in the Tibetan Upland* (2 vols, Sarnath, Varanasi: Central University of Tibetan Studies, 2014).

— *A Comprehensive Survey of Rock Art in Upper Tibet*, vol. 1: *Eastern Byang thang* (Oxford: Archaeopress, 2023).

— *A Comprehensive Survey of Rock Art in Upper Tibet*, vol. 2: *Central and Western Byang thang* (Oxford: Archaeopress, 2023).

Belli, Oktay, *Kırgızistan'da Taş Balbal ve İnsan Biçimli Heykeller / Stone Balbals and Statues in Human Form in Kirghizistan* (Istanbul: Arkeoloji ve Sanat Yayınları, 2003).

Belting, Hans, *Bild-Anthropologie: Entwürfe für eine Bildwissenschaft* (Paderborn: Fink, 2011).

Beltrán, Antonio et al., *Altamira* (Sigmaringen: Thorbecke, 1998).

Bengtsson, Boel, *Sailing Rock Art Boats: A Reassessment of Seafaring Abilities in Bronze Age Scandinavia and the Introduction of the Sail in the North* (Oxford: BAR, 2017).

Benmessaoud, M., 'The Acheulean of the Ahaggar site (Algerian Central Sahara), new research and perspectives', in: *Journal of Historical Archaeology and Anthropological Sciences*, vol. 3, no. 2 (Edmond OK: MedCrave, 2018), pp. 208–213.

Berezkin, Yuri, 'The cosmic hunt: Variants of a Siberian–North American myth', in: *Folklore* (Tartu: Folklore Electronic Journal, 2005), pp. 79–100.

Berger, John, *Ways of Seeing* (London: Penguin, 2008).

Berkani, Hayette, Zazzo, Antoine and Paris, François, 'Les tumulus à couloir et enclos de la Tassili du Fadnoun, Tassili Azger (Algérie) : Premières datations par la méthode du radiocarbone', in: *Journal of African Archaeology*, vol. 13, no. 1 (Frankfurt a.M.: Africa-Magna, June 2015), pp. 59–70.

Bertilsson, Ulf, *The Rock Carvings of Northern Bohuslän: Spatial Structures and Social Symbols* (Stockholm: University of Stockholm, 1987).

— 'Boundless rock art: Symbols, contexts and times in prehistoric imagery of Fennoscandia', in: Stebergløkken, *Ritual Landscape and Borders within Rock Art Research* (2015, q.v.), pp. 79 97.

— 'From folk oddities and remarkable relics to scientific substratum: 135 years of changing perceptions on the rock art carvings in Tanum, northern Bohuslän, Sweden', in: Skoglund, Ling and Bertilsson, *Picturing the Bronze Age* (2015, q.v.), pp. 5–20.

— 'Nämforsen – A northern rock art metropolis with southern pretences', in: Skoglund, Ling and Bertilsson, *North Meets South* (2017, q.v.), pp. 87–112.

— 'The Spear: Digital documentation sheds new light on Early Bronze Age spear carvings from Sweden – An analysis with some comparative examples from Valcamonica, Italy', in: *Adoranten* (q.v., 2017), pp. 64–83.

— 'New 3D documentation reveals carved Stone Age and Bronze Age axes at Nämforsen, in Ångermanland, Sweden', in: *Adoranten* (q.v., 2018), pp. 72–91.

— '3D-models of Neolithic and Bronze Age axe images at Nämforsen, Sweden, reveals long-distance contacts and new implications for chronology and cultural context', in: *Adoranten* (q.v., 2021), pp. 110–126.

— 'Warriors and weapons: Engraved motifs in the Early Bronze Age rock art in Sweden', in: Bettencourt et al., *Weapons and Tools in Rock Art* (2021, q.v.), pp. 69–83.

Bertilsson, Ulf et al., 'The Kivik tomb: Bredarör enters into the digital arena – documented with OLS, SfM and RTI', in: Bergerbrant, Sophie and Wessman, Anna (eds), *New Perspectives on the Bronze Age* (Oxford: Archaeopress, 2017), pp. 289–305.

— 'Scandinavia and Northern Europe', in: Bahn et al., *Rock Art Studies: News of the World*, vol. 6 (2021, q.v.), pp. 18–30.

Bettencourt, Ana M.S. et al. (eds) *Weapons and Tools in Rock Art: A World Perspective* (Oxford: Oxbow, 2021).

Bevan, Lynne, 'Hyper-masculinity and the construction of gender identities in the Bronze Age rock carvings of Southern Sweden', in: Skoglund, Ling and Bertilsson, *Picturing the Bronze Age* (2015, q.v.), pp. 21–36.

Biagetti, Stefano and di Lernia, Savino, 'Holocene deposits of Saharan rock shelters: The case of Takarkori and other sites from the Tadrart Acacus Mountains (Southwest Libya)', in: *African Archaeological Review*, vol. 30 (Dordrecht: Springer, 2013), pp. 305–338.

Bibby, Geoffrey, *Looking for Dilmun* (London: Stacey International, 1996).

Bieri, Susanne, *Swiss Artists' Books* (Cologne: Walther und Franz König, 2022).

Bignasca, Andrea, 'Vergessene nabatäische Felsbilder auf dem Umm al-Biyara', in: Schmid, Stephan G., *Petra* (Basel: Schwabe, 2012), pp. 262–265.

Blundell, Geoffrey et al. (eds) *Seeing and Knowing: Understanding Rock Art with and without Ethnography* (Johannesburg: Wits University Press, 2010).

Blundell, Valda and Woolagoodja, Donny, 'Rock art, aboriginal culture, and identity: The Wanjina paintings of Northwest Australia', in: McDonald and Veth, *Companion to Rock Art* (2012, q.v.), pp. 472–487.

Blunt, Lady Anne, *A Pilgrimage to Nejd* (2 vols, London: John Murray, 1881).

Bobomulloev, Bobomullo, 'Rock art in Tajikistan', in: Clottes, *Rock Art in Central Asia: A Thematic Study* (2011, q.v.), pp. 73–92.

— 'Петроглифы Сой Сабаг в Верховье Зеравшана = Soi Sabag Petroglyphs in Upper Zeravshan', in: *Учёные записки музея-заповедника "Томская Писаница" = Scientific Notes of the Museum-Reserve 'Tomskaya Pisanitsa'*, no. 12 (Pisanaya: 2020), pp. 22–34.

— 'Discovery of inscriptions in the Almosi Gorge, Tajikistan', in: *Central Asian Archaeological Landscapes* (November 2023): https://uclcaal.org/2022/11/16/discovery-of-inscriptions-in-the-almosi-gorge-tajikistan/.

Boehm, Gottfried and Burioni, Matteo (eds), *Der Grund: Das Feld des Sichtbaren* (Paderborn: Fink, 2012).

Boivin, Nicole and Frachetti, Michael, D. (eds), *Globalization in Prehistory: Contact, Exchange, and the 'People without History'* (Cambridge: Cambridge University Press, 2018).

Bonmann, Svenja et al., 'A partial decipherment of the unknown Kushan script', in: *Transactions of the Philological Society*, vol. 121, no. 2 (London: The Philological Society, 2023), pp. 293–329.

Boomer, Ian et al., 'The palaeolimnology of the Aral Sea: A review', *Quaternary Science Reviews*, vol. 19 (Amsterdam: Elsevier, 2000), pp. 1259–1278.

Bortolini, Eugenio and Munoz, Olivia, 'Life and death in prehistoric Oman: Insights from Late Neolithic and Early Bronze Age funerary practices (4th–3rd mill. BC)', in: *The Archaeological Heritage of Oman* (Paris: UNESCO, 2015), pp. 61–80.

Bosinski, Gerhard, d'Errico, Francesco and Schiller, Petra, *Die gravierten Frauendarstellungen von Gönnersdorf* (Stuttgart: Franz-Steiner Verlag, 2001).

Boulton, G.S. et al., 'Evidence of European ice sheet fluctuation during the last glacial cycle', in: *Developments in Quaternary Sciences*, vol. 2, part 1 (Amsterdam: Elsevier, 2004), pp. 441–460.

Bovagne, Marilyne et al., 'Bellegarde. Un voyage à travers les âges', in: *Archéologia*, no. 627 (Dijon: Faton, 2024), pp. 46–53.

Boyes, Benjamin M., et al., 'The last Fennoscandian Ice Sheet glaciation on the Kola Peninsula and Russian Lapland (Part 1): Ice flow configuration', in: *Quaternary Science Reviews*, vol. 300, art. no. 107871 (Amsterdam: Elsevier, 2023).

— 'The last Fennoscandian Ice Sheet glaciation on the Kola Peninsula and Russian Lapland (Part 2): Ice sheet margin positions, evolution, and dynamics', in: *Quaternary Science Reviews*, vol. 300, art. no. 107872 (Amsterdam: Elsevier, 2023).

Bradley, Daniel G. et al. 'Mitochondrial diversity and the origins of African and European cattle', in: *Proceedings of the National Academy of Sciences*, vol. 93, no. 10 (Washington DC: National Academy of Sciences, 1996), pp. 5131–5135.

— 'Daggers drawn: Depictions of Bronze Age weapons in Atlantic Europe', in: Chippindale and Taçon, *The Archaeology of Rock-Art* (1998, q.v.), pp. 130–145.

Bradley, Richard, *The Past in Prehistoric Societies* (London: Routledge, 2002).

— *Image and Audience: Rethinking Prehistoric Art* (Oxford: Oxford University Press, 2009).

— 'Mixed media, mixed messages: Religious transmission in Bronze Age Scandinavia', in: Skoglund, Ling and Bertilsson, *Picturing the Bronze Age* (2015, q.v.), pp. 37–46.

Bradley, Richard et al., 'Imaginary vessels in the Late Bronze Age of Gotland and South Scandinavia', in: *Current Swedish Archaeology*, vol. 18 (Uddevalla: Svenska Arkeologiska Samfundet, 2010), pp. 79–103.

Brajer, Isabelle et al., 'The removal of aged acrylic coatings from wall paintings using microemulsions': *ICOM-CC 17th Triennial Conference 2014 Preprints* (Paris: The International Council of Museums, 2014).

Bräker, Annette and Geerken, Horst H., *The Karakoram Highway and the Hunza Valley, 1998* (Norderstedt: Bukit Cinta, 2017).

Bramanti, B. et al., 'Genetic discontinuity between local hunter-gatherers and Central Europe's first farmers', in: *Science*, vol. 326 (Washington DC: AAAS, 2009), pp. 137–140.

Bray, N., *A Paladin of Arabia: The Biography of Brevet Lieut.-Colonel G.E. Leachman* (London: John Heritage, The Unicorn Press, 1936).

Breeze, Paul S. et al., 'Palaeohydrological corridors for hominin dispersals in the Middle East ~250–70,000 years ago', in: *Quaternary Science Review* (Amsterdam: Elsevier, 2016), pp. 155–185.

— 'Prehistory and palaeoenvironments of the western Nefud Desert, Saudi Arabia', in: *Archaeological Research in Asia*, vol. 10 (Amsterdam: Elsevier: 2017), pp. 1–16.

Brentjes, Burchard, 'Frühe Steinstelen Sibiriens und der Mongolei', in: *Central Asiatic Journal*, vol. 40 (Wiesbaden: Harrassowitz, 1996), pp. 21–55.

Brentjes, Burchard and Vasilievsky R., *Schamanenkrone und Weltenbaum. Kunst der Nomaden Nordasiens* (Leipzig: Verlag Seemann, 1989).

Breteau, Emmanuel, *Roches de mémoire. 5,000 ans d'art rupestre dans les Alpes* (Paris: Errance, 2010).

Breuil, Henri, 'L'Afrique préhistorique', in: *Cahiers d' Art*, vol. 5, no. 8–9 (Paris: Éditions 'Cahiers d'Art', 1935), pp. 449–500.

— 'L'évolution de l'art pariétal dans les cavernes et abris ornés de France', in: *Compte rendu de la onzième session, Congrès préhistorique de France, Périgueux, 1934* (Paris: Société Préhistorique française, 1935), pp. 102–118.

— *Beyond the Bounds of History: Scenes from the Old Stone Age* (London: P.R. Gawthorn, 1949).

— *Quatre cents siècles d'art pariétal. Les cavernes ornées de l'âge du renne* (Montignac: Centre d'études et de documentations préhistoriques, 1952).

— *Les roches peintes du Tassili-n-Ajjer* (Paris: Arts et Métiers Graphiques, 1954).

Bronowski, J., *The Ascent of Man* (London: BBC, 1973).

Brooks, Nick et al., 'The climate–environment–society nexus in the Sahara from prehistoric times to the present day', in: *The Journal of North African Studies*, vol. 10, no. 10 (London: Taylor & Francis, 2005), pp. 253–292.

Brotherton, Paul et al., 'Neolithic mitochondrial haplogroup H genomes and the genetic origins of Europeans', in: *Nature Communications*, vol. 4, art. no. 1764 (London: Macmillan, 2013).

Brumm, Adam et al., 'Oldest cave art found in Sulawesi', in: *Science Advances*, vol. 7, no. 3 (Washington DC: AAAS, 2022).

— 'Some Implications of Pleistocene Figurative Rock Art in Indonesia and Australia', in: Abadia et al., *Deep-Time Images in the Age of Globalization* (2024, q.v.), pp. 31–44.

Brun, Baptiste, '"40 Jahre moderne Kunst" im Musée d'Art Moderne, Paris 1953', in: Kohl et al., *Kunst der Vorzeit* (2021, q.v.), pp. 206–207.

Bruneau, Laurianne, 'Étude thématique et stylistique des pétroglyphes du Ladakh (Jammu et Cachemire, Inde)', in: *Eurasia Antiqua. Zeitschrift für Archäologie Eurasiens*, vol. 18 (Bonn: Rudolf Habelt, 2012), pp. 69–88.

— 'L'art rupestre du Ladakh (Jammu et Cachemire, Inde): ses liens avec l'Asie centrale', in: *Cahiers d'Asie centrale*, vols 21–22 (Paris: De Boccard, 2013), pp. 487–498.

— 'The rock art of Ladakh: A historiographic and thematic study', in: Kumar, Ajit (ed.), *Rock Art: Recent Researches and New Perspectives* (Delhi: New Bharatiya Book Corp., 2015), pp. 79–99.

Bruneau, Laurianne et al., 'Rock art research in Murgi Tokpo, Nubra Valley in Ladakh', in: *Purakala*, vols. 20–21 (Agra: Rock Art Society of India, 2010–11), pp. 91–97.

Bruneau, Laurianne and Bellezza, John Vincent, 'The rock art of Upper Tibet and Ladakh', in: *Revue d'Études Tibétaines*, no. 28 (Paris: UMR 8155 (CRCAO) of CNR, 2013), pp. 5–161.

Bruneau, Laurianne and Vernier, Martin, 'Animal style of the steppes in Ladakh: A presentation of newly discovered petroglyphs', in: Olivieri, *Pictures in Transformation* (2010, q.v.), pp. 27–36.

Brusgaard, Nathalie Østerled and Akkermans, Keshia A.N., 'Hunting and havoc: Narrative scenes in the Black Desert rock art of Jebel Qurna, Jordan', in: Davidson and Nowell, *Making Scenes* (2021, q.v.), pp. 134–149.

Bruxelles, Laurent et al., 'Biocorrosion et art pariétal : une exclusion mutuelle à l'origine de vides archéologiques : Méthodologie, premiers résultats et nouvelles perspectives de recherche', in: *Hiatus, lacunes et absences : identifier et interpréter les vides archéologiques. Actes du 29e Congrès préhistorique de France, 31 mai–4 juin 2021* (Paris: Société préhistorique française, 2024), pp. 85–104.

Bubnova, M. A., *Археологическая карта Горно-Бадахшанской автономной области: Западный Памир: памятники каменного века – ХХ в. = Archaeological Map of Gorno-Badakhshan Autonomous Oblast: Western Pamir: Stone Age Monuments – 20th Century* (Dushanbe: Donish Institute, 2008).

— *Археологическая карта Горно-Бадахшанской автономной области: Восточной Памир = Archaeological Map of Gorno-Badakhshan Autonomous Oblast: Eastern Pamir* (Dushanbe: Donish Institute, 2015).

Buhr, Elke, 'Die Felszeichnungen sind ein Quellcode der Menschheit – Interview Robin Rhode', in: *Monopol* (Berlin: Res Publica, 2023). https://www.monopol-magazin.de/robin-rhode-interview-die-felszeichnungen-sind-ein-quellcode-der-menschheit.

Buis, Alan, 'The atmosphere: Getting a handle on carbon dioxide, part 2' (Pasadena: NASA's Jet Propulsion Laboratory, California Institute of Technology, 2019): https://climate.nasa.gov/news/2915/the-atmosphere-getting-a-handle-on-carbon-dioxide.

Bunker, Emma C., *Nomadic Art of the Eastern Eurasian Steppes* (New York: The Metropolitan Museum, 2002).

Bunnefeld, Jan-Heinrich, 'The chief and his sword? Some thoughts on the swordbearer's rank in the early Nordic Bronze Age', in: Horn and Kristiansen, *Warfare in Bronze Age Society* (2018, q.v.), pp. 198–212.

Camps, Gabriel, 'Bélier à sphéroïde (Gravure rupestre de l'Afrique du Nord)', in: *Encyclopédie berbère*, vol. 9 (Aix-en-Provence: Edisud, 1991), p. 1417–1433.

Cancellieri, Emmanuele, Cremaschi, Mauro, et al., 'Climate, Environment, and Population Dynamics', in Pleistocene Sahara', in: Sacha C. Jones and Brian A. Stewart (eds), *Africa from MIS 6-2: Population Dynamics and Paleoenvironments* (Dordrecht: Springer, 2016), pp. 123–145.

Cancellieri, Emmanuele and Di Lernia, Savino, 'Re-entering the central Sahara at the onset of the Holocene: A territorial approach to *Early Acacus* hunter-gatherers (SW Libya)', in: *Quaternary International*, vol. 320 (Amsterdam: Elsevier, 2014), pp. 43–62.

Capelle, Torsten, *Bilderwelten der Bronzezeit. Felsbilder in Norddeutschland und Skandinavien* (Mainz: Philipp von Zabern, 2008).

Carter, Robert, 'Globalising interactions in the Arabian Neolithic and the Ubaid', in: Boivin and Frachetti, *Globalization in Prehistory* (2018, q.v.), pp. 43–79.

Casini, Stefania, 'The Valtellina and Valcamonica statue-menhirs: Their characters, chronology and contexts', in: Hansen, S. and Molodin, V.I. (eds) *The Bronze Age Art: Proceedings of International Symposium, April 15–19, 2013, Stralsund, Germany* (Novosibirsk: National Research University and Berlin: German Archaeological Institute, 2015), pp. 94–114.

Casini, Stefania and De Marinis, Raffaele C., 'Des pierres et des dieux. L'art rupestre de la Valteline et du Valcamonica', in: *Le Globe*, vol. 149 (Geneva: University of Geneva, 2009), pp. 61–92.

Casini, Stefania, De Marinis, Raffaele C. and Fossati, Angelo, 'Die Stelen der Gruppe Valcamonica/Valtellina', in: Schweizerisches Landesmuseum, *Menschen in Stein gemeisselt* (Basel: Christoph Merian Verlag, 2021), pp. 52–61.

Casoli, Antonella, 'Research on the organic binders in archaeological wall paintings', in: *Applied Sciences*, vol. 11, no. 19, art. no. 9179 (Basel: MDPI, 2021).

Caspari, Gino et al., 'New evidence for a Bronze Age date of chariot depictions in the Eurasian steppe', in: *Rock Art Research*, vol. 37, no. 1 (Darwin: International Federation of Rock Art Organizations, IFRAO, 2020), pp. 53–58.

Cavazzini, Emma (ed.), *Dei di pietra. La grande statuaria antropomorfa nell' Europa del III millennio a.C. / Dieux de pierre. La grande statuaire anthropomorphe en Europe au IIIe millénaire avant J.C.* (Milan: Skira, 1998).

Cerný, Viktor and Pereira, Luisa, 'Archaeogenetics of Africa and of the African hunter-gatherers', in: Cummings et al., *The Oxford Handbook of the Archaeology and Anthropology of Hunter-Gatherers* (2014, q.v.), pp. 1143–1162.

Cèvèèndorzˇ[=Tseveendorj], Damdinsürèngijn et al., *Aral Tolgojn chadny zurag = Petroglyphs of Aral Tolgoi* (Ulaan Baatar: Mongol Uls, 2005).

Chacon, Richard et al., 'Understanding Bronze Age Scandinavian rock art: The value of interdisciplinary approaches', in: *Adoranten* (q.v., 2020), pp. 74–95.

Chalmin, Emilie and Huntley, Jillian, 'Characterizing rock art pigments', in: David and McNiven, *The Oxford Handbook of the Archaeology and Anthropology of Rock Art* (2018, q.v.), pp. 885–909.

Chaoyin, Zhang, *Stone Carving Art of the Tibetans in China* (Beijing: China Tibetology Publishing House, 1995).

Charbonnier, Julien, 'Human adaptation in Arabia: The role of hydraulic technologies', in: Chiotis, *Climate Changes in the Holocene* (2019, q.v.), pp. 221–245.

Charloux, Guillaume et al., 'The art of rock relief in ancient Arabia: New evidence from the Jawf province', in: *Antiquity*, vol. 92, no. 361 (Cambridge: Cambridge University Press, 2018), pp. 165–182.

— 'Large-sized camel depictions in western Arabia: A characterization across time and space', in: *Proceedings of the Seminar for Arabian Studies*, vol. 50 (Oxford: Archaeopress, 2020), pp. 85–108.

— 'Les dromadaires gravés en grandes dimensions. Un art rupestre monumental méconnu', in: *L'art rupestre en Arabie. Dossiers d'Archéologie*, no. 407 (2021, q.v.), pp. 46–51.

— 'The "walled oases" phenomenon: A study of the ramparts in Dūmat al-Jandal and other pre-Islamic sites in north-western Arabia', in: *Arabian Archaeology and Epigraphy*, vol. 32, no. 1 (Oxford: Wiley, 2021), pp. 1–35.

— 'A rock art tradition of life-sized, naturalistic engravings of camels in Northern Arabia', in: *Antiquity*, vol. 96, no. 389 (Cambridge: Cambridge University Press, 2022), pp. 1301–1309.

— 'The protohistoric and antique landscape of Qaryat al-Faw', in: *Proceedings of the Seminar for Arabian Studies*, vol. 52 (Oxford: Archaeopress, 2023), pp. 45–70.

— 'The ramparts of Khaybar: Multiproxy investigation for reconstructing a Bronze Age walled oasis in Northwest Arabia', in: *Journal of Archaeological Science: Reports*, vol. 53, art. no. 104355 (Amsterdam: Elsevier, 2024).

Charpentier, Vincent, 'Avec les premiers chasseurs-collecteurs maritimes d'Arabie', in: *Archéologia*, no. 601 (Dijon: Faton, 2021), pp. 64–69.

Chauvet, Jean-Marie et al., *La Grotte Chauvet* (Paris: Le Seuil, 1995).

Chayet, Anne, *Art et archéologie du Tibet* (Paris: Picard, 1994).

Chemayeva, Nataliya, '"Deer" image as a possible differentiator of social groups on the basis of Saimaly-Tash petroglyphs', bachelor thesis (Bishkek: American University of Central Asia, 2010).

Chen Zhao Fu, *China. Prähistorische Felsbilder* (Zurich: U. Bär, 1989).

— *The Rock Arts of China* (Hangzhou: Zhejiang Photographic Art Press, 1989).

Cheremisin, D.V., 'The meaning of representations in the Animal Style and their relevance for the reconstruction of Pazyryk ideology', in: *Archaeology, Ethnology and Anthropology of Eurasia*, vol. 31 (Novosibirsk: Russian Academy of Sciences, 2007), pp. 87–102.

— 'On the semantics of animal style ornithomorphic images in Pazyryk ritual artefacts', in: *Archaeology, Ethnology and Anthropology of Eurasia*, vol. 37, no. 1 (Novosibirsk: Russian Academy of Sciences, 2009), pp. 85–94.

Cherkinsky, Alexander and di Lernia, Savino, 'Bayesian approach to [14]c dates for estimation of long-term archaeological sequences in arid environments: The Holocene site of Takarkori rockshelter, southwest Libya', in: *Radiocarbon*, vol. 55, nos 2–3 (Cambridge: Cambridge University Press, 2013), pp. 771–782.

Chiotis, Eustathios (ed.), *Climate Changes in the Holocene: Impacts and Human Adaptation* (Boca Raton FL: CRS Press, 2019).

— 'Reconstructing the environment as a scenery of human history and civilization', in: Chiotis, *Climate Changes in the Holocene* (2019, q.v.), pp. 3–41.

Chippindale, Christopher, 'Theory and meaning of prehistoric European rock art: "Informed methods", "formal methods" and questions of uniformitarianism', in: Helskog, *Theoretical Perspectives in Rock Art Research* (2001, q.v.), pp. 68–98.

Chippindale, Christopher and Nash, George (eds), *The Figured Landscapes of Rock-Art: Looking at Pictures in Place* (Cambridge: Cambridge University Press, 2004).

Chippindale, Christopher and Taçon, Paul S.C. (eds), *The Archaeology of Rock-Art* (Cambridge: Cambridge University Press, 1998).

Cicolani, Veronica and Zamboni, Lorenzo, 'Alpine connections and Iron Age mobility in the Po valley and the Circum-Alpine regions', in: Fernández-Götz et al., *Rethinking Migrations in Late Prehistoric Eurasia* (2023, q.v.), pp. 258–279.

Civrac, Marie-Anne, 'Quelques peintures du site de Terkey-Bowdé III (Ennedi, Tchad)', in: *Cahiers de l'AARS*, no. 16 (Saint-Benoist-sur-Mer: AARS, 2013), pp. 62–64, figs 12–18.

Clark, Ian D. and Fontes, Jean-Charles, 'Paleoclimatic reconstruction in Northern Oman based on carbonates from hyperalkaline groundwaters', in: *Quaternary Research*, vol. 33 (Seattle: University of Washington, 1990), pp. 320–336.

Cleuziou, Serge and Tosi, Maurizio, *In the Shadow of the Ancestors: The Prehistoric Foundations of the Early Arabian Civilization in Oman* (2nd ed., Oxford: Archaeopress, 2020).

Clottes, Jean (ed.), *International Newsletter on Rock Art (INORA)* (Foix: ICOMOS, 1992–2021).

— *Les cavernes de Niaux. Art préhistorique en Ariège* (Le Seuil, 1995).

— *World Rock Art* (Los Angeles: Getty Publications, 2002).

— *Rock Art in Central Asia: A Thematic Study* (Paris: ICOMOS, 2011).

Clottes, Jean and Lewis-Williams, David, *Les Chamanes de la préhistoire. Transe et magie dans les grottes ornées* (Paris: Le Seuil, 1996).

Coles, John, *Images of the Past: A Guide to the Rock Carvings and Other Ancient Monuments of Northern Bohuslän* (Vitlycke: Hällristningsmuseet Vitlycke, 1990).

— *Shadows of a Northern Past: Rock Carvings of Bohuslän and Østfold* (Oxford: Oxbow, 2005).

Conkey, Margaret W., 'Interpretative frameworks and the study of the rock arts', in: David and McNiven, *The Oxford Handbook of the Archaeology and Anthropology of Rock Art* (2018, q.v.), pp. 25–49.

Conrad, Nicholas J. and Floss, Harald, 'Early Figurative Art and Musical Instruments from the Swabian Jura of Southwestern Germany and their Implications for Human Evolution', in: Sachs-Hombach and Schirra, *Origins of Pictures* (2013, q.v.), pp. 172–200.

Conrad, Nicholas J. and Kind, Claus-Joachim, *Als der Mensch die Kunst erfand. Eiszeithöhlen der Schwäbischen Alb* (Darmstadt: Teiss/WBG, 2017).

Corboud, Pierre and Curdy, Philippe (eds), *Stèles préhistoriques. La nécropole néolithique du Petit-Chasseur à Sion / Prähistorische Stelen. Die neolithische Nekropole Petit-Chasseur in Sitten* (Sion: Musées cantonaux de Valais, 2009).

Coulson, David and Campbell, Alec, *African Rock Art: Paintings and Engravings in Stone* (New York: Henry N. Abrams, 2001).

— 'Rock Art of the Tassili n Ajjer, Algeria', in: *Adoranten* (q.v., 2010), pp. 24–38.

Cox, J. Halley and Stasack, Edward, *Hawaiian Petroglyphs* (Honolulu: Bernice Pauahi Bishop Museum, 1970).

Crassard, Rémy et al., 'Middle Palaeolithic and Neolithic occupations around Mundafan palaeolake, Saudi Arabia: Implications for climate change and human dispersals', in: *PLOS ONE*, vol. 8, no. 7, art. no. 69665 (San Francisco: PLOS, 2013).

— 'Middle Palaeolithic occupations in central Saudi Arabia during MIS 5 and MIS 7: New insights on the origins of the peopling of Arabia', in: *Archaeological and Anthropological Sciences*, vol. 11 (Cham: Springer Nature, 2018), pp. 3101–3120.

— 'The oldest plan to scale humanmade mega-structures', in: *PLOS ONE*, vol. 18, no. 5, art. no. 0277927 (San Francisco: PLOS, 2023).

— 'Les cerfs-volants du désert dévoilent peu à peu leurs mystères', in: *Archéologia*, no. 628 (Dijon: Faton, 2024), pp. 34–45.

Cremaschi, Mauro, 'Le paléo-environnement du Tertiaire tardif à l'Holocène', in: *Art rupestre du Sahara. Dossiers d'Archéologie*, no. 197 (1994, q.v.), pp. 4–13.

Cremaschi, Mauro and Di Lernia, Savino, 'Holocene climatic changes and cultural dynamics in the Libyan Sahara', in: *African Archaeological Review*, vol. 16, no. 4 (Berlin: Springer, 1999), pp. 211–238.

— *Wadi Teshuinat: Palaeoenvironment and Prehistory in South-Western Fezzan (Libyan Sahara)* (Florence: Edizioni All'Insegna del Giglio, 1999).

Cremaschi, Mauro et al., 'Takarkori rock shelter (SW Libya): An archive of Holocene climate and environmental changes in the central Sahara', in: *Quaternary Science Reviews*, vol. 101 (Amsterdam: Elsevier, 2014), pp. 36–60.

Cribb, Joe, 'A Kushan royal inscription among the Almosi rock inscriptions recently discovered in Tajikistan', in: *Journal of the Royal Asiatic Society*, vol. 34, no. 2 (London: Royal Asiatic Society, 2024), pp. 361–375.

Crowell, Bradley L., 'Nabonidus, as-Sila`, and the beginning of the end of Edom', in: *Bulletin of the American Society of Overseas Research*, vol. 348 (Chicago: University of Chicago Press, 2007), pp. 75–88.

Crucifix, Michel, 'Pleistocene glaciations', in: Chiotis, *Climate Changes in the Holocene* (2019, q.v.), pp. 77–106.

Cummings, Vicki et al., (eds), *The Oxford Handbook of the Archaeology and Anthropology of Hunter-Gatherers* (Oxford: Oxford University Press, 2014).

— 'Hunter-gatherers in the post-glacial world', in: Cummings et al., *The Oxford Handbook of the Archaeology and Anthropology of Hunter-Gatherers* (2014, q.v.), pp. 437–455.

Cunliffe, Barry, *Facing the Sea of Sand: The Sahara and the Peoples of Northern Africa* (Oxford: Oxford University Press, 2023).

Curry, Andrew, 'Ancient DNA from the Near East probes a cradle of civilization', in *Science*, vol. 377, no. 6609 (Washington DC: AAAS, 2022), pp. 908–909.

Curtis, Gregory, *The Cave Painters: Probing the Mysteries of the World's First Artists* (New York: Alfred A. Knopf, 2006).

Damm, Charlotte, 'Spiritual landscapes: Diversity in practices and perceptions in Northern Fennoscandia', in: Gjerde and Arntzen, *Perspectives on Differences in Rock Art* (2021, q.v.), pp. 76–96.

Damm, Charlotte and Forsberg, Lars, 'Forager–farmer contacts in Northern Fennoscandia', in: Cummings et al., *The Oxford Handbook of the Archaeology and Anthropology of Hunter-Gatherers* (2014, q.v.), pp. 838–856.

Da Riva, Rocío, 'The Nabonidus inscription in Sela (Jordan): Epigraphic study and historical meaning', in: *Zeitschrift für Assyriologie*, vol. 110, no. 2 (Berlin: De Gruyter, 2020), pp. 176–195.

Dauvillier, Jean, *Mélanges offerts au R.P. Ferdinand Cavallera* (Toulouse: Bibliothèque de l'Institut Catholique, 1948). pp. 260–316.

David, Bruno, *Cave Art* (London: Thames & Hudson, 2017).

David, Bruno and McNiven, Ian (eds), *The Oxford Handbook of the Archaeology and Anthropology of Rock Art* (Oxford: Oxford University Press, 2018).

— 'Towards an archaeology and anthropology of rock art', in: David and McNiven, *The Oxford Handbook of the Archaeology and Anthropology of Rock Art* (2018, q.v.), pp. 1–21.

Davidson, H.R. Ellis, *Scandinavian Mythology* (Feltham: Newnes Books, 1984).

Davidson, Iain, 'Variations in early paintings and engravings', in: McDonald and Veth, *Companion to Rock Art* (2012, q.v.), pp. 51–68.

— 'Origins of pictures: An argument for transformation of signs', in: Sachs-Hombach and Schirra, *Origins of Pictures* (2013, q.v.), pp. 16–46.

— 'Images of animals in rock art: Not just "good to think"', in: David and McNiven, *The Oxford Handbook of the Archaeology and Anthropology of Rock Art* (2018, q.v.), pp. 435–467.

Davidson, Iain and Nowell, April, *Making Scenes: Global Perspectives on Scenes on Rock Art* (Oxford: Berghahn Books, 2021).

de Barros Damgaard, Peter et al., '137 ancient human genomes from across Eurasian steppe', in: *Nature*, vol. 557 (London: Macmillan, 2018), pp. 369–374.

— 'The first horse herders and the impact of early bronze age steppe expansions into Asia', in: *Science*, vol. 360, no. 6396 (Washington DC: AAAS, 2018).

Debray, Céline and Labrusse, Rémi (eds), *Préhistoire: Une énigme moderne* (Paris: Edition du Centre Pompidou, 2019).

Deeg, Max, *Das Gaoseng-Faxian-Zhuan als religionsge-schichtliche Quelle* (Wiesbaden: Harrassowitz, 2005).

Defrasne, Claudia and Fedele, Francesco, 'Contextualiser l'imagerie préhistorique : Les figures circulaires et la figure "a bandoliera" des monolithes chalcolithiques centre-alpins', in: *Bulletin de la Société préhistorique française*, vol. 112, no. 3 (Paris: Société Préhistorique Française, 2015), pp. 543–564.

Degli Esposti, Michele et al., 'Rock art survey in the ancient oasis of Salūt (northern Sultanate of Oman): A variegated iconographic record', in: *Arabian Archaeology and Epigraphy*, vol. 31 (Oxford: Wiley, 2020), pp. 327–351.

Delot, Sébastien and Eggelhöfer, Fabienne (eds), *Paul Klee, Ich will nichts Wissen* (Paris, Bern: Flammarion, LaM, Zentrum Paul Klee, 2021).

Denwood, Philip, 'The Tibetans in the Western Himalayas and Karakoram, seventh–eleventh centuries: Rock art and inscriptions', in *Journal of Inner Asian Art and Archaeology*, vol. 2 (Turnhout: Brepols, 2007), pp. 49–59.

— 'The Tibetans in the West: Parts I–II', in *Journal of Inner Asian Art and Archaeology*, vol. 3 (Turnhout: Brepols, 2008), pp. 7–22; vol. 4 (2009), pp. 149–160.

Derev'anko, Anatoliy P. et al. (eds), *The Palaeolithic of Siberia: New Discoveries and Interpretations* (Novosibirsk: Institute of Archaeology and Ethnography, 1998).

d'Errico, Francesco et al., 'A 36,200-year-old carving from Grotte des Gorges, Amange, Jura, France', in: *Scientific Reports*, vol. 13, art. no. 12895 (London: Nature Portfolio, August 2023).

Devers, Quentin et al., 'A review of rock art discoveries in Ladakh over the last fourteen decades', in: Bellezza, *Flight of the Khyung* (q.v., September 2017).

Devlet, Ekaterina and Marianna, 'Siberian shamanistic rock art', in: Rozwadowski and Kośko, *Spirits and Stones* (2002, q.v.), pp. 120–136.

— *Myths in Stone: World of Rock Art in Russia* (Moscow: Aletheia, 2005).

— 'Rock art studies in Northern Russia and the Far East, 2000–2004', in: Bahn et al., *Rock Art Studies: News of the World*, vol. 3 (2008, q.v.), pp. 120–137.

Devlet, Marianna, 'Felsbilder von Aldy-Mozag, Tuva', in: *Eurasia Antiqua. Zeitschrift für Archäologie Eurasiens*, vol. 5 (Mainz: Philipp von Zabern, 1999), pp. 595–651.

D'Huy, Julien, 'A cosmic hunt in the Berber sky: A phylogenetic reconstruction of a Palaeolithic mythology', in: *Les Cahiers de l'AARS*, no. 16 (St-Benoist-sur-Mer: AARS, 2013), pp. 93–106.

— 'Des mythes préhistorique ont-ils pu survivre au dépeuplement du Sahara ? Le cas des hommes-chiens', in: *Les Cahiers de l'AARS*, no. 16 (St-Benoist-sur-Mer: AARS, 2013), pp. 107–112.

— 'The evolution of myths', in: *Scientific American*, vol. 315, no. 6 (New York: Springer Nature, 2016), pp. 64–69.

Di Lernia, Savino, 'Dry climatic events and cultural trajectories: Adjusting Middle Holocene pastoral economy of the Libyan Sahara', in: Hassan, Fekri (ed.), *Droughts, Food and Culture: Ecological Change and Food Security in Africa's Later Prehistory* (New York: Kluwer, 2002), pp. 225–250.

— 'Thoughts on the rock art of the Tadrart Acacus Mts, SW Libya', in: *Adoranten* (q.v., 2012), pp. 19–37.

— 'The emergence and spread of herding in Northern Africa: A critical reappraisal', in: Mitchell, Peter and Lane, Paul J. (eds), *The Oxford Handbook of African Archaeology* (Oxford: Oxford University Press, 2013), pp. 526–540.

— 'The archaeology of rock art in Northern Africa', in: David and McNiven, *The Oxford Handbook of the Archaeology and Anthropology of Rock Art* (2018, q.v.), pp. 95–121.

— 'From "green" to "brown": The archaeology of the Holocene central Sahara', in: Chiotis, *Climate Changes in the Holocene* (2019, q.v.), pp. 183–200.

— 'Earliest herders of the central Sahara (Tadrart Acacus Mountains, Libya): A punctuated model for the emergence of pastoralism in Africa', in: *Journal of World Prehistory*, vol. 34 (Berlin: Springer, 2021), pp. 531–594.

Di Lernia, Savino et al., 'Inside the "African Cattle Complex": Animal burials in the Holocene central Sahara', in: *PLOS ONE*, vol. 8, no. 2, art. no. 56879 (San Francisco: PLOS, 2013).

Di Lernia, Savino and Gallinaro, Marina, 'The date and context of Neolithic rock art in the Sahara: Engravings and ceremonial monuments from Messak Settafet (south-west Libya)', in: *Antiquity*, vol. 84 (Cambridge: Cambridge University Press, 2010), pp. 954–975.

Díaz-Andreu, Margarita and Mattioli, Tommaso, 'Rock art, music, and acoustics', in: David and McNiven, *The Oxford Handbook of the Archaeology and Anthropology of Rock Art* (2018, q.v.), pp. 503–528.

Diodorus Siculus, *Library of Histories*, 12 vols (London and Cambridge MA: Heinemann / Harvard University Press, 1933–67). https://penelope.uchicago.edu/Thayer/E/Roman/Texts/Diodorus_Siculus/home.html.

Dobženko, Nadija et al., *Давня скульптура i пластика України = Ancient Sculptures of Ukraine* (Kyiv: Rodovid, 2009).

Dodd, James, 'Ships on stone: A study in the chronology of Bronze Age and Pre-Roman Iron Age ship carvings in Hordaland, Western Norway', in: *Adoranten* (q.v., 2010), pp. 110–121.

Dodd, James and Meijer, Ellen (eds), *Giving the Past a Future: Essays in Archaeology and Rock Art Studies in Honour of Dr. Phil. h.c. Gerhard Milstreu* (Oxford: Archaeopress, 2018).

Dodd, James and Milstreu, Gerhard, 'Find of the (last) decade! The first ships discovered on vertical surface on Bornholm', in: *Adoranten* (q.v., 2019), pp. 45–53.

Dorjay, Phuntsog, 'Penetration of Buddhist ideology in Ladakh: A study through rock sculptures', in: Olivieri, *Pictures in Transformation* (2010, q.v.), pp. 43–58.

Dorn, Ronald, 'Experimental approaches to dating petroglyphs and geoglyphs with rock varnish in the California deserts: Current status and future directions', in: Allen, Mark W. and Reed, Judyth, *The Human Journey and Ancient Life in California's Deserts* (Ridgecrest, CA: Maturango Museum, 2004), pp. 211–224.

Dorn, Ronald et al., 'Revisiting Alexander von Humboldt's initiation of rock coating research', in: *The Journal of Geology*, vol. 120, no. 1 (Chicago: Chicago University Press, 2012), pp. 1–14.

— 'Rock varnish', in: Nash, D.J. and McLaren, S.J. (eds), *Geochemical Sediments and Landscapes* (Malden: Blackwell, 2007), pp. 246–297.

Dosymbaeva, Aiman, *Западный Тюркский каганат. Культурное наследие казахской степи = The Western Turkic Khaganate: The Cultural Succession of the Kazakh Steppe* (Almaty: Türki Mūrasy, 2006).

Dougherty, Raymond Philip, *Nabonidus and Belshazzar: A Study of the Closing Events of the Neo-Babylonian Empire* (1928; repr. Eugene OR: Wipf & Stock, 2008).

Doughty, Charles M., *Travels in Arabia Deserta*, introduction by T.E. Lawrence (2 vols, London: Jonathan Cape, 1936).

Dupuy, Christian, 'Henri Duveyrier et la charrerie antique du Sahara', in: *Le Saharien*, vol. 222 (Paris : L'Harmattan, 2017), pp. 50–71.

Duquesnoy, Frédérique, 'Pour en finir avec le Bovidien', in: *Cahiers de l'AARS*, no. 20 (Saint-Benoist-sur-Mer: AARS, 2018), pp. 27–36.

Earle, Timothy and Kolb, Michael J., 'Regional Settlement Patterns', in: Earle and Kristiansen, *Organizing Bronze Age Societies* (2010, q.v.), pp. 57–86.

Earle, Timothy and Kristiansen, Kristian (eds), *Organizing Bronze Age Societies* (Cambridge: Cambridge University Press, 2010).

— 'Organizing Bronze Age societies: Concluding thoughts', in: Earle and Kristiansen, *Organizing Bronze Age Societies* (2010, q.v.), pp. 218–256.

Eggelhöfer, Fabienne, 'Auf den Spuren von Paul Klees Reisen in die Vorzeit', in: Faass and Schmidt, *Urknall der Kunst* (2023, q.v.), pp. 30–39.

Eggelhöfer, Fabienne, Smithgall, Elsa, et al., *Ten Americans: After Paul Klee* (Munich: Prestel, 2017).

Eimert, Dorothea and Harutyunyan, Sona (eds), *Therese Weber: Hand und Geist: Erzählungen in der Kunst / Therese Weber: Hand and Mind: Narrations in Art* (Cologne: Wienand, 2017).

Ekdahl, Sven, 'Bronzezeitliche Petroglyphen mit Waffendarstellungen in Schweden', in: *Acta Universitatis Lodziensis. Folia Archaeologica*, vol. 29 (Łódź: Łódź University, 2012), pp. 14–37.

El-Bialy et al., 'Rock art in Wadi Silwa Baharii, Egypt. Part 1: Occasion of discovery and site content', in: *Sahara*, no. 23 (www.saharajournal.com, 2012), pp. 57–68.

Eliade, Mircea, *Shamanism: Archaic Techniques of Ecstasy* (Princeton: Princeton University Press, 1964).

Eliade, Mircea (editor in chief), *The Encyclopedia of Religion*, 16 vols (New York: Simon & Schuster Macmillan, 1993).

Engelstad, Ericka, 'Desire and body maps: All the women are pregnant, all the men are virile, but …', in: Helskog, *Theoretical Perspectives in Rock Art Research* (2001, q.v.), pp. 263–289.

Erdenebaatar D., 'Burial materials related to the history of the Bronze Age in the territory of Mongolia', in: Linduff, Katheryn M. (ed.), *Metallurgy in Ancient Eastern Eurasia from the Urals to the Yellow River* (Lampeter: Edwin Mellen, 2004), pp. 189–222.

Eriksen, Palle and Andersen, Niels H., *Dolmens in Denmark: Architecture and Function* (Højbjerg: Jutland Archaeological Society, 2016).

Ernits, Enn, 'On the cosmic hunt in Northern Eurasian rock art', in: *Folklore*, vol. 44 (Tartu: Folkloristenserver Haldjas, 2010), pp. 61–76.

Esin, Yury N. et al., 'Les peintures dans l'art pariétal de la culture Okuniev', in: *Bulletin Musée d'Anthropologique préhistorique de Monaco*, vol. 54 (Monaco: MAP, 2014), pp. 163–183.

— 'Paint on deer stones of Mongolia', in: *Archaeology, Ethnology and Anthropology of Eurasia*, vol. 45 (Novosibirsk: Russian Academy of Sciences, 2017), pp. 79–89.

— 'Images of camels on a mammoth tusk from West Siberia', in: *Archaeological Research in Asia*, vol. 2, art. no. 100180 (Amsterdam: Elsevier, 2020).

Euting, Julius, *Tagebuch einer Reise durch Inner-Arabien* (Leiden: E.J. Brill, 1896).

— *Die Tagebücher des Orientalisten Julius Euting*, in: Digitale Bestände der Universität Tübingen (Tübingen): https://uni-tuebingen.de/forschung/forschungsinfrastruktur/digital-humanities-center/projekte/julius eutingstagebuecher/.

Evers, Dietrich, *Felsbilder. Botschaften der Vorzeit* (Leipzig: Urania, 1991).

— *The Magic of the Image* (Warmsroth: Pulsar-Verlag, 1994).

— *Berge und Boote* (Langenweissbach: Beier & Beran, 2002).

Faas, Martin and Schmidt, Jessica, *Urknall der Kunst. Moderne trifft Vorzeit* (Leipzig: E.A. Seemann Verlag, 2023).

Facey, William, *Charles Huber: France's Greatest Arabian Explorer. With a Translation of Huber's First Journey in Central Arabia, 1880–1881* (Cowes: Arabian Publishing, 2022).

Fagan, Brian, *The Long Summer: How Climate Changed Civilization* (London: Granta Books, 2004).

Faradzhev, Arsen, *To See the Invisible: Karelian Rock Art* (Oxford: Archaeopress: 2015).

Farajova, Malahat, 'Gobustan rock art cultural landscape', in: *Adoranten* (q.v., 2011), pp. 41–66.

— 'Cultural landscape of archaeological complex of Gobustan', in: Taylor, Paul Michael (ed.), *Pipelines to Cultural Heritage* (Washington DC: Smithsonian Institution, 2011), pp. 25–37.

Farajova, Malahat et al., *Petroglyphs Gobustan* (Baku: Cultural Heritage of Azerbaijan, 2012).

— *Cultural Heritage of Azerbaijan: Petroglyphs* (Baku: Heydar Aliyev Foundation, 2014).

Farès-Drappeau, Saba, 'Wadi Iram : un lieu du culte et de rassemblement des tribus arabes dans l'antiquité', in: *ARAM Periodical*, vol. 8 (Oxford: Society for Syro-Mesopotamian Studies,1996), pp. 269–283.

Faxian, *A Record of Buddhistic Kingdoms: Being an Account by the Chinese Monk Fâ-Hsien of his Travels in India and Ceylon (AD 319–414) in Search of the Buddhist Books of Discipline*, trans. James Legge (Oxford: Clarendon Press, 1886; repr., n.d.).

Felding, Louise, 'A View beyond Bornholm: New perspectives on Danish rock carvings', in: *Adoranten* (q.v., 2010), pp. 81–89.

Fernández-Götz, Manuel et al. (eds), *Rethinking Migrations in Late Prehistoric Eurasia* (London: The British Academy, 2023).

Ferngård Svensson, Ann-Louise, *Das Grab von Kivik. Bredarör, das Königsgrab* (Kivik: Asmiroca Kulturarvsupplevelser, 2017).

Ferrandi, Marco, 'Rock art in Afghanistan and Hindukush: An Overview', in: Olivieri, *Pictures in Transformation* (2010, q.v.), pp. 59–67.

Finch, Damien et al., 'Ages for Australia's oldest rock paintings', in: *Nature Human Behaviour*, vol. 5 (London: Macmillan, 2021), pp. 310–323.

Findeklee, Antje (ed.), *Frühe Kunst. Was Höhlenmalereien und Felszeichnungen verraten. Spektrum Kompakt*, 19 Oct. 2021 (Heidelberg: Spektrum der Wissenschaft).

Fisher, Greg (ed.), *Arabs and Empires before Islam* (Oxford: Oxford University Press, 2015).

Fitzhugh, William, 'The Mongolian deer stone–khirigsuur complex: Dating and organization of a late Bronze Age menagerie', in: Bemmann, Jan et al., *Current Archaeological Research in Mongolia* (Bonn: R.F.W.-Universität, 2009), pp. 183–199.

— 'Stone shamans and flying deer of northern Mongolia: Deer goddess of Siberia or chimera of the steppe?', in: *Arctic Anthropology*, vol. 46, nos 1–2 (Madison: University of Wisconsin, 2009), pp. 72–88.

Fitzhugh, William and Kortum, Richard, 'Conjuring Mongolian deer stones', in: *Current World Archaeology*, vol. 117 (London: Current Publishing, 2023), pp. 32–38.

Fitzpatrick, Andrew P., 'Bell Beaker mobility: Marriage, migration and mortality', in: Fernández-Götz et al., *Rethinking Migrations in Late Prehistoric Eurasia* (2023, q.v.), pp. 63–88.

Flam, Jack (ed.), *Robert Smithson: The Collected Writings* (Berkeley: University of California Press, 2000).

Forrest, Susanna, *The Age of the Horse: An Equine Journey through Human History* (London: Atlantic Books, 2016).

Fossati, Angelo E., 'Morfologia, litotipi e funzionei delle statue stele del gruppo Valcamonica-Valtellina', in: *Bulletin d'études préhistoriques et archaéologiques alpines* (Aosta: Société Valdôtaine de Préhistoire et d'Archéologie, 2007), pp. 77–90.

— 'The rock art tradition of Valcamonica–Valtellina, Northern Italy: A World Heritage view', in: Nash, George et al. (eds), *Landscape Enquiries: The Proceedings of the Clifton Antiquarian Club*, vol. 8 (Bristol: Clifton Antiquarian Club, 2007), pp. 139–155.

— 'Rock art in Jebel Akhdar, Sultanate of Oman: An overview', in: *American Indian Rock Art*, vol. 41 (American Rock Art Association, 2015), pp. 1–8.

— 'The motif of the boat in Valcamonica rock art: Problems of chronology and interpretation', in: Stebergløkken et al., *Ritual Landscape and Borders within Rock Art Research* (2015, q.v.), pp. 119–139.

— 'Current finds in rock art research of Oman: A review and update', in: *Mediterranean Archaeology and Archaeometry*, vol. 17, no. 4 (Athens: University of the Aegean, 2017), pp. 85–98.

— *Messages from the Past: Rock Art of Al-Hajar Mountains* (Oxford: Archaeopress, 2019).

— 'Rock art of al-Hajar Mountains: A review and update', in: Cleuziou and Tosi, *In the Shadow of the Ancestors* (2020, q.v.), pp. 494–499.

Foucault, Michel, *Archäologie des Wissens*, trans. Ulrich Köppen (Frankfurt am Main: Suhrkamp, 2020).

Foucault, Michel, *Die Ordnung der Dinge: Eine Archäologie der Humanwissenschaften*, trans. Ulrich Köppen (Frankfurt am Main: Suhrkamp, 2020).

Frachetti, Michael and Chippindale, Christopher, 'Alpine imagery, Alpine space, Alpine time; and prehistoric human experience', in: Nash and Chippindale, *European Landscapes of Rock Art* (2012, q.v.), pp. 116–143.

Francfort, Henri-Paul, 'Les pétroglyphes de Tamgaly', in: *Bulletin of the Asia Institute*, vol. 9 (1995) (Bloomfield Hills MI: The Asia Institute, 1997), pp. 167–208.

— Central Asian petroglyphs: Between Indo-Iranian and shamanistic interpretations', in: Chippindale and Taçon, *The Archaeology of Rock-Art* (1998, q.v.), pp. 302–318.

— 'De l'art des steppes au sud du Taklamakan', in: *Bulletin of the Asia Institute*, vol. 12 (Bloomfield Hills MI: Asia Institute, 1998), pp. 45–58.

— 'Art, archaeology and the prehistories of shamanism in Central Asia', in: Francfort, Hamayon and Bahn, *The Concept of Shamanism* (2001, q.v.).

— 'Images du combat contre le sanglier en Asie centrale (3ème au 1er millénaire av. J.-C.)', in: *Bulletin of the Asia Institute*, vol. 16 (Bloomfield Hills MI: Asia Institute, 2002), pp. 117–142.

Francfort, Henri-Paul et al., 'Pétroglyphes archaïques du Ladakh et du Zanskar', in: *Arts Asiatiques*, vol. 45 (Paris: Musée national d'art asiatique Guimet, 1990), pp. 5–27.

Francfort, Henri-Paul, Hamayon, Roberte N. and Bahn, Paul G. (eds), *The Concept of Shamanism: Uses and Abuses* (Budapest: Akadémiai Kiadó, 2001).

Francke, A.H., 'Historische Dokumente von Khalatse in West-Tibet (Ladakh)', in: *Zeitschrift der Deutschen Morgenländischen Gesellschaft*, vol. 61 (1907), pp. 583–614 (repr. Ulm: Fabri, 2012).

— *Antiquities of Indian Tibet* (2 vols, 1914; New Delhi: Asian Educational Services, 1992).

Frankopan, Peter, *The Earth Transformed: An Untold History* (London: Bloomsbury, 2023).

Fredell, Åsa, 'Bridging images: Pictorial communication of ideology and cosmology in the southern Scandinavian Bronze Age and the Pre-Roman Iron Age', doctoral thesis (Göteborg: Göteborg Universitet, 2003).

— 'A Mo(ve)ment in time: A comparative study of a rock-picture theme in Galicia and Bohuslän', in: Fredell et al., *Representations and Communications* (2010, q.v.), pp. 52–74.

Fredell, Åsa et al., *Representations and Communications: Creating an Archaeological Matrix of Late Prehistoric Rock Art* (Oxford: Oxbow, 2010).

Fredsjö, Åke et al., *Hällristningar, Kville härad i Bohuslän, Kville socken = Rock Carvings, Kville County in Bohuslän, Kville Parish* (Göteborg: Fornminnesforeningen, 1981).

Frobenius, Leo, *Das unbekannte Afrika: Aufhellung der Schicksale eines Erdteils* (Munich: Beck, 1923).

— 'L'art africain', in: *Cahiers d'Art*, vol. 5, nos 8–9 (Paris: Éditions 'Cahiers d'Art', 1935), pp. 395–430.

— *Kulturgeschichte Afrikas. Prolegomena zu einer historischen Gestaltlehre* (1933; Wuppertal: Peter Hammer, 1993).

Frobenius, Leo and Fox, Douglas C., *Prehistoric Rock Pictures in Europe and Africa* (New York: The Museum of Modern Art, 1937).

Frye, Richard N., *The Heritage of Central Asia: From Antiquity to the Turkish Expansion* (Princeton: Markus Wiener Publishers, 1996).

Fu, Qiaomei et al., 'The genetic history of Ice Age Europe', in: *Nature*, vol. 534, no. 7606 (London: Macmillan 2016), pp. 200–205.

Fuglestvedt, Ingrid, 'The mind in the wild: On "Motemic" Variation in Late Mesolithic Scandinavian Rock Art', in: Gjerde and Arntzen, *Perspectives on Differences in Rock Art* (Sheffield: Equinox, 2021), pp. 163–174.

Fussman, Gérard, 'Dašt-e Nāwor', in: *Encyclopaedia Iranica*, vol. 7, fasc. 1 (1994), p. 96.

Gai Shanlin and Lou Yudong, *Rock Arts of China* (Beijing: Wenwu chubanshe, 1993).

Galbiati, Alberto, *Naquane: National Park of Rock Engravings* (Capo di Ponte: Libreria del parco, n.d.).

Gallay, Alain, *Autour du Petit-Chasseur. L'archéologie aux sources du Rhône 1941–2011* (Paris: Errance, 2011).

Gallinaro, Marina, 'Saharan rock art: Local dynamics and wider perspectives', in: *Arts*, vol. 2, no. 4 (Basel: MDPI, 2013), pp. 350–382.

Gaponenko, V.M., 'Naskalnie izobrazheniya Talasskoï doliny', in: *Arkheologitscheskie pamyatniki Talasskoï doliny* = 'Rock art in the TalasValley', in: *Archaeological monuments of the Talas Valley* (Frunze: 1963), pp. 101–110.

Garba, Roman and Danielisová, Alžběta, 'Achaeologists unearth unique finds in Oman' (Prague: Institute of Archaeology of the CAS, 2023): https://www.avcr.cz/export/sites/avcr.cz/.content/galerie-souboru/tiskove-zpravy/2023/ARU_Oman-finds_PR.pdf.

Garni, René and Neukom-Tschudi, Jolantha, *Peintures rupestres du Sahara, Tassili-n-Ajjer* (Bern: Hallwag, 1960).

Garrow, Duncan and Wilkin, Neil, *The World of Stonehenge* (London: British Museum Press, 2022).

Garvey, Raven and Bettinger, Robert L., 'Adaptive and ecological approaches to the study of hunter-gatherers', in: Cummings et al., *The Oxford Handbook of the Archaeology and Anthropology of Hunter-Gatherers* (2014, q.v.), pp. 69–91.

Gaussen, Jean, *La grotte ornée de Gabillou* (Bordeaux: Éditions confluence, 2019).

Gauthier, Yves and Christine, 'Les lacs de Têh-n-beka: Contribution des gravures à la connaissance de climat à l'Holocène', *Cahiers de l'AARS*, no. 15 (Saint-Benoist-sur-Mer: AARS, 2011), pp. 47–86.

— 'Des chars et des Tifinagh: Étude aréale et corrélations', in: *Cahiers de l'AARS*, no. 15 (Saint-Benoist-sur-Mer: AARS, 2011), pp. 91–118.

— 'Nouvelles figurations de chars sahariens: Technicité et positionnement chronologique relativement au style de Tazina', in: *Cahiers de l'AARS*, no. 18 (Saint-Benoist-sur-Mer: AARS, 2015), pp. 5–70.

— 'Petit manuel d'attelage: Gravures et peintures de chars sahariens', in: *Cahiers de l'AARS*, no. 20 (Saint-Benoist-sur-Mer: AARS, 2018), pp. 37–88.

— 'Images rupestres du nord-est du plateau des Ajjer', in: *Cahiers de l'AARS*, no. 24 (Saint-Benoist-sur-Mer: AARS, 2023), pp. 59–80.

Gebel, H.G. and Wellbrock, Kai, 'Hydraulic cultures and hydrology under climate change: North Arabian Mid-Holocene pastoral and proto-oasis land use', in: Chiotis, *Climate Changes in the Holocene* (2019, q.v.), pp. 247–269.

Gelling, Peter and Davidson, Hilda Ellis, *The Chariot of the Sun and Other Rites and Symbols of the Northern Bronze Age* (London: J.M. Dent & Sons, 1969).

Georget, Jean-Louis et al. (eds), *L'avant et l'ailleurs. Comparatisme, ethnologie et préhistoire* (Paris: Le Cerf, 2019).

Georgievsky, Igor and Lobanova, Nadezhda, *Каменная книга Севера: путеводитель по Беломорским петроглифам* = *Stone Book of the North: A Guide to the White Sea Petroglyphs* (Petrozavodsk: PetroPress, 2012).

Gilman, Ian and Klimkeit, Hans-Joachim, *Christians in Asia before 1500* (Chicago: University of Michigan Press, 1999).

Gjerde, Jan Magne, 'Rock art and landscapes: Studies of Stone Age rock art from northern Fennoscandia', doctoral thesis (Tromsø: University of Tromsø, 2010).

— 'Stone-Age rock art and beluga landscapes at River Vyg, North-Western Russia', in: *Fennoscandia Archaeologica*, vol. 30 (Helsinki: Helsinki University, 2013), pp. 37–54.

— 'A Stone Age rock art map at Nämforsen, Northern Sweden', in: *Adoranten* (q.v., 2015), pp. 74–91.

— 'A boat journey in rock art "from the Bronze Age to the Stone Age – from the Stone Age to the Bronze Age" in northernmost Europe', in: Skoglund, Ling and Bertilsson, *North Meets South* (2017, q.v.), pp. 113–143.

— 'Marine mammals in the rock art of Alta, Norway, northernmost Europe', in: *Whale on the Rock*, vol. 2 (Ulsan, S. Korea: Petroglyph Museum, 2018), pp. 193–208.

— 'An overview of Stone Age rock art in northernmost Europe – what, where and when?', in: 해가 지지 않는 땅. 백해의 암각화 = *Land where the Sun Never Sets: Rock Art of the White Sea* (Ulsan: Ulsan Petroglyph Museum, 2019), pp. 204–222; https://www.ancientportsantiques.com/wp-content/uploads/Documents/ETUDESarchivees/Navires/Documents/Gjerde2018-ScandinavianRockArt.pdf.

— 'Snowscapes of rock art: Seasons and seasonality of Stone Age rock art in Northernmost Europe', in: Gjerde and Arntzen, *Perspectives on Differences in Rock Art* (2021, q.v.), pp. 97–112.

— 'The earliest boat depiction in northern Europe: Newly discovered early Mesolithic rock art at Valle, northern Norway', in: *Oxford Journal of Archaeology*, vol. 40, no. 2 (Hoboken: Wiley, 2021), pp. 136–152.

Gjerde, Jan Magne and Arntzen, Mari Strifeldt (eds), *Perspectives on Differences in Rock Art* (Sheffield: Equinox, 2021).

Glidden, Harold W., 'Koranic Iram, legendary and historical', in: *Bulletin of the American Schools of Oriental Research*, vol. 73 (Chicago: University of Chicago Press, 1939), pp. 13–15.

Glob, P.V., *Denmark: An Archaeological History from the Stone Age to the Vikings* (Ithaca: Cornell University Press, 1971).

Gobustan Rock Art Cultural Landscape: World Heritage Site Nomination Document (Baku: Azerbaijani National Commission for UNESCO, 2006).

'Gobustan Rock Art Cultural Landscape', in: *World Heritage Review*, no. 92: *Special Issue: World Heritage in Azerbaijan* (Paris: UNESCO, 2019), pp. 40–56.

Goldberg, Amy et al., 'Ancient X chromosomes reveal contrasting sex bias in Neolithic and Bronze Age Eurasian migrations', in: *Proceedings of the National Academy of Sciences*, vol. 114, no. 10 (Washington DC: National Academy of Sciences, 2017), pp. 2657–2662.

Goldhahn, Joakim, 'Rock art for the dead and un-dead: Reflections of the significance of hand stones in late Bronze Age Scandinavia', in: *Adoranten* (q.v., 2009), pp. 95–103.

— 'Bredarör on Kivik: A monumental cairn and the history of its interpretation', in: *Antiquity*, vol. 83 (Cambridge: Cambridge University Press, 2009), pp. 359–371.

— *Bredarör på Kivik, en arkeologisk odysse* = *Bredarör on Kivik: An Archaeological Odyssey* (Simrishamn: Artes Liberales AB, 2013).

— *Sagaholm: North European Bronze Age Rock Art and Burial Ritual* (Oxford: Oxbow, 2016).

— North European rock art: A long-term perspective', in: David and McNiven, *The Oxford Handbook of the Archaeology and Anthropology of Rock Art* (2018, q.v.), pp. 51–72.

— 'To let mute stones speak: On the becoming of archaeology', in: Dodd and Meijer, *Giving the Past a Future* (2018, q.v.), pp. 28–36.

— 'On the chronology and use of hunter-gatherer rock painting sites in Northern Europe', in: Gjerde and Arntzen, *Perspectives on Differences in Rock Art* (2021, q.v.), pp. 7–42.

Goldhahn, Joakim and Fuglestvedt, Ingrid, 'Engendering North European rock art: Bodies and cosmologies in Stone and Bronze Age imagery', in: McDonald and Veth, *Companion to Rock Art* (2012, q.v.), pp. 237–260.

Goryachev, A.A. and Mariyashev, A.N., *Petroglyphs of Semirechye* (1999): http://tourkz.com/eng/articles/petrog1e_1.html.

Graichen, Gisela and Hesse, Alexander, *Die Bernsteinstrasse* (Reinbeck: Rowohlt, 2012).

Grenet, Frantz, 'An archaeologist's approach to Avestan geography', in: Curtis, Vesta Sarkhosh and Stewart, Sarah (eds), *The Idea of Iran*, vol. 1: *Birth of the Persian Empire* (London: I.B. Tauris, 2005), pp. 29–51.

Grohmann, Adolf, *Göttersymbole und Symboltiere auf südarabischen Denkmälern* (Vienna: Alfred Hölder, 1915; repr. London: Forgotten Books, 2017).

Grosos, Philippe, *La première image. L'Art préhistorique* (Rennes: Presse universitaires de Rennes, 2023).

Groucutt, Huw S. et al., 'An Arabian perspective on the dispersal of *Homo sapiens* out of Africa', in: Denell, Robin (ed.), *Southern Asia, Australia and the Search for Human Origins* (Cambridge: Cambridge University Press, 2015), pp. 51–63.

— 'Human occupation of the Arabian Empty Quarter during MIS 5: Evidence from Mundafan Al-Buhayrah, Saudi Arabia', in: *Quaternary Science Reviews*, vol. 119 (Amsterdam: Elsevier, 2015), pp. 116–136.

— 'Rethinking the dispersal of Homo sapiens out of Africa', in: *Evolutionary Anthropology*, vol. 24 (Hoboken: Wiley, 2015), pp. 149–164.

— 'First Arabians: Revealing the Stone Age prehistory of Saudi Arabia', in: *Current World Archaeology*, vol. 75 (London: Current Publishing, 2016), pp. 26–30.

— 'Homo sapiens in Arabia by 85,000 years ago', in: *Nature, Ecology and Evolution*, vol. 2 (London: Springer Nature, 2018), pp. 800–809.

— 'Culture and convergence: The curious case of the Nubian complex', in: Groucutt, Huw S. (ed.) *Culture History and Convergent Evolution: Can We Detect Populations in Prehistory?* (Cham: Springer, 2020), pp. 55–86.

— 'Multiple hominin dispersals into Southwest Asia over the past 400,000 years', in: *Nature*, vol. 597 (London: Macmillan, 2021), pp. 376–380.

Grünig, Günther, *Val Camonica. Felsbildkunst in den Alpen* (Weinstadt: B.A. Greiner, 2012).

Guagnin, Maria, 'The rock carvings of the Messak: Monuments in a changing landscape', in: Furholt, Martin et al. (eds), *'As Time Goes By'? Monumentality, Landscapes and the Temporal Perspective* (Bonn: Dr. Rudolf Habelt, 2012), pp. 95–104.

— 'Animal engravings in the central Sahara: A proxy of a proxy', in: *Environmental Archaeology*, vol. 20, no. 1 (Leeds: Maney Publishing, 2015), pp. 52–65.

— 'Patina and environment in the Wadi al-Hayat: Towards a chronology of rock art of the central Sahara', in: *African Archaeological Review*, vol. 31, no. 3 (Berlin: Springer, 2014), pp. 407–423.

Guagnin, Maria et al., 'Rock art imagery as a *proxy* for Holocene environmental change: A view from. Shuwaymis, NW Saudi Arabia', in: *The Holocene*, vol. 26, no. 11 (Thousand Oaks CA: Sage Publishing, 2016), pp. 1822–1834.

— 'An illustrated prehistory of the Jubbah oasis: Reconstructing Holocene occupation patterns in north-western Saudi Arabia from rock art and inscriptions', in: *Arabian Archaeology and Epigraphy*, vol. 28 (Oxford: Wiley, 2017), pp. 138–152.

— 'The Neolithic site of Jebel Oraf 2, northern Saudi Arabia: First report of a directly dated site with faunal remains', in: *Archaeological Research in Asia*, vol. 9 (Amsterdam: Elsevier, 2017), pp. 63–67.

— 'Pre-Neolithic evidence for dog-assisted hunting strategies in Arabia', in: *Journal of Anthropological Archaeology*, vol. 49 (Amsterdam: Elsevier, 2018), pp. 225–254.

— 'Rock art provides new evidence on the biogeography of kudu (*Tragelaphus imberbis*), wild dromedary, aurochs (*Bos primigenius*) and African wild ass (*Equus africanus*) in the early and middle Holocene of north-western Arabia', in: *Journal of Biogeography*, vol. 45, no. 4 (Hoboken: Wiley, 2018), pp. 727–749.

— 'The hunters and herders of Shuwaymis: New evidence for the population dynamics of the Neolithic transition in Saudi Arabia', in: Huyge and Van Noten, *What Ever Happened to the People?* (2018, q.v.), pp. 231–241.

— 'The Holocene humid period in the Nefud Desert: Hunters and herders in the Jebel Oraf palaeolake basin, Saudi Arabia', in: *Journal of Arid Environments*, vol. 178, art. no. 104146 (Amsterdam: Elsevier, 2020).

— 'Life-sized Neolithic camel sculptures in Arabia: A scientific assessment of the craftsmanship and age of the Camel Site relief', in: *Journal of Archaeological Science: Reports*, vol. 42, art. no. 103165 (Amsterdam: Elsevier, 2021).

— 'Before the Holocene humid period: Life-sized camel engravings and early occupations on the southern edge of the Nefud desert', in: *Archaeological Research in Asia*, vol. 36, art. no. 100483 (Amsterdam: Elsevier, 2023).

Guber, Sonja, *Die Bildsteine Gotlands der Völkerwanderungs- und Vendelzeit als Spiegel frühgeschichtlicher Lebenswelten* (Oxford: BAR, 2011).

Günther, Torsten et al., 'Population genomics of Mesolithic Scandinavia: Investigating early postglacial migration routes and high-latitude adaptation', in: *PLOS Biology*, vol. 16, no. 1, art. no. 2003703 (San Francisco: PLOS, 2018).

Gurina, Nina Nikolaevna, *The Petroglyphs at Calmn-Varre on the Kola Peninsula: Analysis and Analogies* (Trondheim: Tapir Academic Press, 2005).

Haak, Wolfgang et al., 'Massive migration from the steppe was a source for Indo-European languages in Europe', in: *Nature*, vol. 522 (London: Macmillan, 2015), pp. 207–211.

Haak, Wolfgang, Krause, Johannes et al., 'Palaeogenomics of Upper Palaeolithic to Neolithic European hunter-gatherers', *Nature*, vol. 615 (London: Macmillan, 2023), pp. 117–140.

Hachid, Malika, *Le Tassili des Ajjer. Aux sources de l'Afrique 50 siècles avant les pyramides* (Paris: Éditions Paris-Méditerranée, 2000).

Hachid, Malika et al., 'Premiers résultats du projet algéro-français de datation directe et indirecte des images rupestres dans le Tassili-n-Ajjer', in: *Sahara*, no. 21 (www.saharajournal.com, 2010), pp. 27–60.

Hachid, Malika and Chentir, Farid, 'Des Noirs dans l'archéologie rupestre de l'Atlas saharien (Algérie), du Maroc présaharien et de l'Ouest saharien', in: Huyge and Van Noten, *What Ever Happened to the People?* (2018, q.v.), pp. 119–154.

Halbertsma, Tjalling and Omirbek, Bikhumar, 'Petroglyphs of Khöltsöötiin Gol Valley (Mongolia)', *International Newsletter on Rock Art*, no. 60 (Foix: INORA, 2016), pp. 1–8.

Hallier, Ulrich and Brigitte, *The People of Iheren and Tahilahi* (2012): http://www.rockart-sahara-hallier.de/media/39_2012.pdf.

— 'Anthropomorphs of the Djado Mountains: Ancestors of the Tassili-n-Ajjer Roundheads?', in: *Cahiers de l'AARS*, no. 20 (Saint-Benoist-sur-Mer: AARS, 2018), pp. 89–102.

— 'Petroglyphs and pictographs of the Djado region (Niger) and of other regions of the Southern Central Sahara. Round Head homeland?', in: *Cahiers de l'AARS*, no. 23 (Saint-Benoist-sur-Mer: AARS, 2021), pp. 9–109.

Hallström, Gustav, *Monumental Art of Northern Sweden from the Stone Age* (2 vols, Stockholm: Almqvist & Wiksell and Malmö: Malmö Ljustryckanstalt, 1960).

Hamilton, James, *Sinai, the Hedjaz and Sudan: Wanderings around the Birth-Place of the Prophet and across the Aethiopian Desert, from Sawakin to Chartoum* (London: Richard Bentley, 1857).

Handa, Omacanda, *Buddhist Western Himalaya*, part 1: *A Politico-Religious History* (New Delhi: Indus Publishing, 2001).

Hanotte, Olivier et al., 'African pastoralism: Genetic imprints of origins and migrations', in: *Science*, vol. 296 (Washington DC: AAAS, 2002), pp. 336–339.

Harding, Anthony, 'Bronze Age encounters: Violent or peaceful?', in: Horn and Kristiansen, *Warfare in Bronze Age Society* (2018, q.v.), pp. 16–22.

Harry, Karen G., 'Cation-ratio dating of varnished artifacts: Testing the assumptions', in: *American Antiquity*, vol. 60, no. 1 (Cambridge: Cambridge University Press, 1995), pp. 118–130.

Hauptmann, Harald (ed.), *Materialien zur Archäologie der Nordgebiete Pakistans*, 11 vols (Mainz: Philipp von Zabern, 1994–2013):

vol. 1: *Die Felsbildstation Oshibat* (1994).

vol. 2: *Die Felsbildstation Shatial* (1997).

vol. 3: *Die Felsbildstation Hodar* (1999).

vol. 4: *Die Felsbildstationen Shing Nala und Gichi Nala* (2001).

vol. 5: *Die Felsbildstation Dadam Das* (2005).

vol. 6: *Die Felsbildstation Thalpan – 1. Kataloge Chilas-Brücke und Thalpan (Steine 1–30)* (2003).

vol. 7: *Die Felsbildstation Thalpan – 2. Katalog Thalpan (Steine 31–195)* (2005).

vol. 8: *Die Felsbildstation Thalpan – 3. Katalog Thalpan (Steine 196–450)* (2007).

vol. 9: *Die Felsbildstation Thalpan – 4. Katalog Thalpan (Steine 451–811)* (2009).

vol. 10: *Die Felsbildstation Thalpan – 5. Kataloge Ziyarat, Thakot, Komar Das, Gichoi Das, Dardarbati Das* (2011).

vol. 11: *Die Felsbildstation Thalpan – 6. Kataloge Ba Das, Ba Das Ost, Gali, Gukona, Mostar Nala, Ke Ges, Ame Ges und Drang Das* (2013).

— *The Indus: Cradle and Crossroads of Civilizations* (Islamabad: Embassy of the Federal Republic of Germany, 1997).

— 'Felsbildkunst am Oberen Indus', in: Luczanits, Christian (ed.), *Gandhara – Das buddhistische Erbe Pakistans. Legenden, Klöster und Paradiese* (Mainz: Philipp von Zabern, 2009), pp. 352–357.

Hausleiter, Arnulf, 'The oasis of Tayma', in: al-Ghabban et al., *Roads of Arabia* (2010, q.v.), pp. 219–261.

— 'North Arabian Kingdoms', in: D.T. Potts (ed.), *A Companion to the Archaeology of the Ancient Near East*, vol. 2 (Hoboken: Blackwell, 2012), pp. 816–832.

Hausleiter, Arnulf and Schaudig, Hanspeter, 'Rock relief and cuneiform inscription of King Nabonidus at al-Ḥāʾiṭ (Province of Ḥāʾil, Saudi Arabia), Ancient Padakku', in: *Zeitschrift für Orient-Archäologie*, vol. 9 (Tübingen: Ernst Wasmuth, 2016), pp. 224–240.

Hayden, Erika Check, 'African genes tracked back', in: *Nature*, vol. 500 (London: Macmillan, 2013), p. 514.

Hays-Gilpin, Kelley, 'Engendering rock art', in: McDonald and Veth, *Companion to Rock Art* (2012, q.v.), pp. 199–213.

Heath, Julian, *Exploring Megalithic Europe* (Lanham: Rowman & Littlefield, 2019).

Hebeisen, Kurt Beat, *Spurensuche nach dem Ursprung der Kunst. Von den Zeichen der Natur zu den Zeichen der Kunst* (Bern: Haupt, 2009).

Hedin, Sven, *Scientific Results of a Journey in Central Asia, 1899–1902*, vol. 3: *North and East Tibet* (Stockholm: Lithographic Institute of the General Staff of the Swedish Army, 1905).

Hegel, Georg Wilhelm Friedrich, *Introductory Lectures on Aesthetics*, trans. Bernard Bosanquet ([1886] London: Penguin, 2004).

Helskog, Knut, 'Selective depictions: A study of 3,500 years of rock carvings from Arctic Norway and their relationship to the Sami drums', in: Hodder, Ian, *Archaeology as Long-Term History* (New York: Press Syndicate of the University of Cambridge, 1987), pp. 17–30.

— 'The shore connection: Cognitive landscape and communications with rock carvings in northernmost Europe', in: *Norwegian Archaeological Review*, vol. 32, no. 2 (Abingdon: Routledge, 1999), pp. 73–94.

— *Theoretical Perspectives in Rock Art Research* (Oslo: Institute for Comparative Research in Human Culture, 2001).

— 'Landscapes in rock-art: Rock-carving and ritual in the old European North', in: Chippindale and Nash, *The Figured Landscapes of Rock-Art* (2004), pp. 265–288.

— 'From the tyranny of the figures to the interrelationship between myths, rock art and their surfaces', in: Blundell et al., *Seeing and Knowing* (2010, q.v.), pp. 168–88.

— *Communicating with the World of Beings: The World Heritage Rock Art Sites in Alta, Arctic Norway* (Oxford: Oxbow, 2014).

— 'Snowshoes and skis in North European rock art', in: Dodd and Meijer, *Giving the Past a Future* (2018, q.v.), pp. 239–251.

— 'Changing settlements, shores and boats through 5,000 years: Dating and connecting petroglyphs to the general archaeological record – a case from northernmost Norway', in: Gjerde and Arntzen, *Perspectives on Differences in Rock Art* (2021, q.v.), pp. 43–75.

Hermann, Luc, 'Rock art of Tamgaly, Kazakhstan', in: *Adoranten* (q.v., 2011), pp. 26–40.

— 'Ship engravings in Armenia?' in: *Adoranten* (q.v., 2011), pp. 93f.

— 'Nouvelles découvertes à Kulzhabasy au Kazakhstan (Otar, Oblys de Djamboul)', in: *International Newsletter on Rock Art*, no. 65 (Foix: INORA, 2013), pp. 1–6.

— 'La sexualité dans l'art rupestre d'Asie centrale', in: *Notae Prehistoricae*, vol. 35 (Liège: Studia praehistorica belgica, 2015), pp. 55–75.

— 'L'évolution thématique de l'art rupestre au Kazakhstan', in: Delnoy, David (ed.), *Bulletin de l'Association Scientifique Liégeoise pour la Recherche Archéologique*, vol. 18 (2013–15) (Liège : ASLiRA, 2016), pp. 95–122.

— 'The rock art site of Akterek in Kazakhstan (Almaty Oblast)', in: *International Newsletter on Rock Art*, no. 76 (Foix: INORA, 2016), pp. 14–21.

— 'Les cultes du soleil et du taureau dans l'art rupestre de l'âge du Bronze en Asie centrale (Kazakhstan et Kirghizstan)', in: *Praehistoria*, vol. 1–2 (11–12), (Miskolc: University of Miskolc, 2019–2020), pp. 303–327.

— 'Dogs on a leash in rock art from Saimaluu-Tash in Kyrgyzstan', in: *Adoranten* (q.v., 2020), pp. 115–122.

— 'Repertory of the tamgas in the Talas region (Kyrgyzstan)', in: Jacobson-Tepfer, E. and Novozhenov, V.A., *Rock Art Chronicles of Golden Steppe*, vol. 2: *From Karatau to Altai* (Almaty: UNESCO Centre for the Rapprochement of Cultures, 2020), pp. 185–211.

— 'Vulture and bird-head anthropomorphs in Saimaluu-Tash, Kyrgyzstan', in: Anati (ed.), *Expression*, no. 39 (q.v., 2023), pp. 33–44.

Hermann, Luc and Bazylkhan, N., 'Kazakh ethnographic petroglyphs and an Arabic inscription in Eshkiolmes (South-Eastern Kazakhstan)', in: Қазақстан археологиясы = *Archaeology of Kazakhstan*, no. 20 (Almaty: Margulan Institute of Archaeology, 2023), pp. 222–231.

Hermann, Luc and Tishin, Vladimir V., 'Two new runic inscriptions in Tchatchikei (the Kenkol Valley in Kyrgyzstan', in: *Oriental Epigraphy*, vol. 37 (Moscow: Institute of Oriental Studies, 2023), pp. 204–214.

Hermann, Luc and Zheleznyakov, B., 'Tamga petroglyphs from Akkainar (Almaty Region) in Kazakhstan', in: Қазақстан археологиясы = *Archaeology of Kazakhstan*, no. 22 (Almaty: Margulan Institute of Archaeology, 2023), pp. 140–154.

Herodotus, *The Histories*, trans. Aubrey de Sélincourt (London: Penguin, 2003).

Herva, Vesa-Pekka and Lahelma, Antti, *Northern Archaeology and Cosmology: A Relational View* (Abingdon: Routledge, 2020).

Hessel, Katy, *The Story of Art Without Men: Grosse Künstlerinnen und ihre Werke* (Munich: Piper, 2022).

Heyd, Thomas, 'Rock "art" and art: Why aesthetics should matter', in: McDonald and Veth, *Companion to Rock Art* (2012, q.v.), pp. 276–293.

— 'Rock art and aesthetics', in: David and McNiven, *The Oxford Handbook of the Archaeology and Anthropology of Rock Art* (2018, q.v.), pp. 717–739.

Heyd, Volker, 'The mobility and migration revolution in 3rd millennium BC Europe', in: Fernández-Götz, Manuel et al. (eds), *Rethinking Migrations in Late Prehistoric Eurasia* (London: The British Academy, 2023), pp. 41–62.

Hilbert, Yamandú et al., 'Epipalaeolothic occupation and palaeoenvironments of the southern Nefud Desert, Saudi Arabia, during the Terminal Pleistocene and Early Holocene', in: *Journal of Archaeological Science*, vol. 50 (Amsterdam: Elsevier, 2014), pp. 460–474.

Hildebrandt, Toni, 'Vorahmung und Kosmotechnik – Von der "Geburt des Graphismus" zur Kosmotechnik', in: Blümle, Claudia et al. (eds), *Regards croisés: Leroi-Gourhan*, no. 9 (Ilmtal-Weinstrasse: arts + science, 2019), pp. 101–13.

Hill, Austin Chad et al. 'Inscribed landscapes in the Black Desert: Petroglyphs and kites at Wisad Pools, Jordan', in: *Arabian Archaeology and Epigraphy*, vol. 30 (Oxford: Wiley, 2020), pp. 245–262.

Hinüber, Oskar von, *Die Palola Sāhis, ihre Steininschriften, Inschriften auf Bronzen, Handschriftenkolophone und Schutzzauber. Materialien zur Geschichte von Gilgit und Chilas* (Mainz: Philipp von Zaben, 2004).

Hirschochs, Christina, *Was ist Kunst?* (Norderstedt: Grin Verlag, 2006).

Hisham ibn al-Kalbi, *The Book of Idols: Being a Translation from the Arabic of the Kitām Al-Aṣnām*, trans. Nabith Amin Faris (Princeton: Princeton University Press, 1952).

Hoffmann, D.L. et al., 'U–Th dating of carbonate crusts reveals Neandertal origin of Iberian cave art', in: *Science*, vol. 359, no. 6378 (Washington DC: AAAS, 2018), pp. 912–915.

Holl, Augustin F.C. and Gao Chang, 'Weapons, tools and objects: Material culture systems in African rock art', in: Bettencourt et al., *Weapons and Tools in Rock Art* (2021, q.v.), pp. 23–36.

Homer, *The Iliad*, trans. A.T. Murray (1924): https://www.theoi.com/Text/HomerIliad1.html.

Hommel, Peter, 'Ceramic technology', in: Cummings et al., *The Oxford Handbook of the Archaeology and Anthropology of Hunter-Gatherers* (2014, q.v.), pp. 663–693.

Hörisch, Jochen, *Hände: Eine Kulturgeschichte* (Munich: Carl Hanser, 2021).

Horn, Christian, 'Cupmarks', in: *Adoranten* (q.v., 2015), pp. 29–43.

— 'Warfare vs. exchange? Thoughts on an integrative approach', in: Horn and Kristiansen, *Warfare in Bronze Age Society* (2018, q.v.), pp. 61–80.

Horn, Christian and Kristiansen, Kristian (eds), *Warfare in Bronze Age Society* (Cambridge: Cambridge University Press, 2018).

Horsfield, George, Horsfield, Agnes and Glueck, Nelson, 'Prehistoric rock-drawings in Transjordan', in: *American Journal of Archaeology*, vol. 38, no. 3 (Boston: Archaeological Institute of America, 1933), pp. 381–386 and plates.

Huard, Paul and Leclant, Jean, 'Les témoignages d'un Sahara fertile gravé sur la pierre il y a 8000 ans', in: *Archéologia*, no. 115 (Dijon: Faton, 1978), pp. 6–17.

Huber, Charles, *Journal d'un voyage en Arabie (1883–1884)* (Paris: Société asiatique et Société de géographie, 1891).

Hublin, Jean-Jacques et al., 'New fossils from Jebel Irhoud, Morocco and the pan-African origin of Homo sapiens', in: *Nature*, vol. 546 (London: Macmillan, 2017), pp. 289–292.

Hudūd al-'Ālam: The Regions of the World, a Persian Geography 372 A.H./982 A.D., trans. V. Minorsky, ed. C.E. Bosworth (repr. Cambridge: Cambridge University Press, 1982).

Hughes, Virginia, 'Were the First Artists Mostly Women?' in: *National Geographic* (Washington DC: NG Media, 2013): https://www.nationalgeographic.com/adventure/article/131008-women-handprints-oldest-neolithic-cave-art.

Hunter, Erica, 'The Church of the East in Central Asia', in: Coakley, J.F. and Parry, K. (eds), *The Church of the East: Life and Thought. The Bulletin of the John Rylands Library*, vol. 78, no. 3 (Manchester: The John Rylands Library, 1996), pp. 129–142.

Huntley, Jillian and Nash, George (eds), *Aesthetics, Applications, Artistry and Anarchy: Essays in Prehistoric and Contemporary Art. A Festschrift in Honour of John Kay Clegg* (Oxford: Archaeopress Publishing Ltd., 2019).

Hunziker-Rodewald, Régine, 'La redécouverte de l'art rupestre' in: *L'art rupestre en Arabie. Dossiers d'Archéologie*, no. 407 (2021, q.v.), pp. 22–25.

Ḥuraysh Āl Mustanīr, Ahmad, حمى -- معزوفة التاريخ : دراسة ميدانية للنقوش والرسوم الصخرية في موقع حمى بمنطقة بنجران / *Ḥimá – ma'zūfat al-tārīkh : dirāsah maydānīyah lil-nuqūsh wa-al-rusūm al-ṣakhrīyah fī mawqi' Ḥimá bi-minṭaqah bi-Najrān = Hima – The Music of History: A Field Study of the Inscriptions and Rock Paintings at the Hima Site in the Najran Region* (Beirut: Mu'assasat al-Riḥāb al-Ḥadīthah lil-Ṭibā'ah, 2019).

Huyge, Dirk, '"Lascaux along the Nile": The Palaeolithic rock art of Qurta (Upper Egypt)', in: *Bulletin des Séances de l'Académie Royale des Sciences d'Outre-Mer*, no. 54 (Brussels: Académie Royale des Sciences d'Outre-Mer, 2008), pp. 281–296.

— 'The "headless women" of Qurta (Upper Egypt): The earliest anthropomorphic images in Northern-African rock art', in: Huyge and Van Noten, *What Ever Happened to the People?* (2018, q.v.), pp. 419–430.

Huyge, Dirk et al., 'First evidence of Pleistocene rock art in North Africa: Securing the age of the Qurta petroglyphs (Egypt) through OSL dating', in: *Antiquity*, vol. 85, no. 330 (Cambridge: Cambridge University Press, 2011), pp. 1184–1193.

Huyge, Dirk and Van Noten, Francis (eds), *What Ever Happened to the People? Humans and Anthropomorphs in the Rock Art of Northern Africa* (Brussels: Académie Royale des Sciences d'Outre-Mer, 2018).

Huysecom, Eric, 'The first emergence of ceramic production in Africa', in: *Oxford Research Encyclopedia of Anthropology* (New York: Oxford University Press, 2020): https://doi.org/10.1093/acrefore/9780190854584.013.66.

Hygen, Anne-Sophie and Bengtsson, Lasse, *Felsbilder im Grenzgebiet. Bohuslän und Östfold* (Sävedalen: Warne Förlag, 2000).

Hykkerud, Martin, 'The management of the Kåfjord Rock Art Site', in: Gjerde and Arntzen, *Perspectives on Differences in Rock Art* (2021, q.v.), pp. 129–144.

Ibhi, Abderrahmane et al., 'Rock art and archaeoastronomy in Morocco: Preliminary observations', in: *Archaeoastronomy and Ancient Technologies*, vol. 6, no. 2 (Rostov-on-Don: Cultural Heritage and Modern Technologies, 2018), pp. 44–52.

Ikram, Salima, 'Drawing the world: Petroglyphs from Kharga oasis', in: *Archéo-Nil* (Leuven: Peeters, 2009), pp. 67–82.

Inizan, Marie-Louise, 'The prehistoric populations', in: Al-Ghabban et al., *Roads of Arabia* (2010, q.v.), pp. 139–157.

Insall, David, 'The petroglyphs of Shenah', in: *Arabian Archaeology and Epigraphy*, vol. 33 (Oxford: Wiley, 2022), pp. 225–245.

Inselmann, Leif et al., 'Warriors from the south? Arrowheads from the Tollense Valley and Central Europe', in: *Antiquity*, vol. 98, no. 401 (Cambridge: Cambridge University Press, 2021), pp. 1252–1270.

Irving-Pease, Evan K. et al., 'The selection landscape and genetic legacy of ancient Eurasians', in: *Nature*, vol. 625 (London: Macmillan, 2024), pp. 312–321.

Jacobs, Bruno and Macdonald, Michael C. A., 'Felszeichnung eines Reiters aus der Umgebung von Taymā', in: *Zeitschrift für Orient-Archäologie*, vol. 2 (Berlin: Walter de Gruyter, 2009), pp. 364–376.

Jacobson, Esther, *The Deer Goddess of Ancient Siberia: A Study in the Ecology of Belief* (Leiden: Brill, 1993).

Jacobson-Tepfer, Esther, 'Cultural riddles: Stylized deer and deer stones on the Mongolian Altai', in: *Bulletin of the Asia Institute*, vol. 15 (Bloomfield Hills MI: Asia Institute, 2001), pp. 31–56.

— 'The rock art of Mongolia', in: *The Silk Road*, vol. 4, no. 1 (Berkeley: The Silkroad House, 2006), pp. 5–13.

— 'Rock art research in Mongolia, 2005–9', in: Bahn et al., *Rock Art Studies: News of the World*, vol. 4 (2012, q.v.), pp. 164–195.

— 'Late Pleistocene and Early Holocene rock art from the Mongolian Altai: The material and its cultural implication', in: *Arts*, vol. 2, no. 3 (Basel: MDPI, 2013), pp.151–181.

— *The Hunter, the Stag, and the Mother of Animals: Image, Monument, and Landscape in Ancient North Asia* (Oxford: Oxford University Press, 2015).

— *The Life of Two Valleys in the Bronze Age: Rock Art in the Altai Mountains of Mongolia* (Eugene OR: Luminare Press, 2019).

— *The Anatomy of Deep Time: Rock Art and Landscape in the Altai Mountains of Mongolia* (Cambridge: Cambridge University Press, 2020).

— *Monumental Archaeology in the Mongolian Altai: Intention, Memory, Myth* (Leiden: Brill, 2023).

— 'Between realms of being: Signs of liminality in ancient Altai stone monuments', in: Laneri and Perdibon, *Sacred Nature* (2023, q.v.), pp. 33–54.

Jacobson-Tepfer, Esther and Meacham, James E., *Archaeology and Landscape in the Mongolian Altai: An Atlas* (Redlands CA: ESRI Press, 2010).

Jacobson-Tepfer, E. and Novozhenov, V.A. (eds), *Rock Art Chronicles of Golden Steppe*, vol. 2: *From Karatau to Altai* (Almaty: UNESCO Centre for the Rapprochement of Cultures, 2020).

Jang Seog-Ho and Chargynov, Temirlan, 키르기스스탄 남부 지역의 암각화 = *Petroglyphs in Southern Kyrgyzstan* (Seoul: Northeast Asian History Foundation, 2012).

Janik, Liliana, 'The development and periodisation of White Sea rock carvings', in: *Acta Archaeologica*, vol. 81, no. 1 (Leiden: Brill, 2010), pp. 84–94.

— 'Prehistoric deep-sea exploitation: Visual clues in the rock art of the White Sea and Alta', in: Gjerde and Arntzen, *Perspectives on Differences in Rock Art* (2021, q.v.), pp. 218–228.

Jasiewicz, Zbigniew and Rozwadowski, Andrzej, 'Rock paintings – Wall paintings: New light on art tradition in Central Asia', in: *Rock Art Research*, vol. 18, no. 1 (Darwin: International Federation of Rock Art Organizations, 2001), pp. 3–14.

Jaubert, Jacques et al., *Grotte de Cussac -30 000* (Bordeaux: Éditions confluence, 2020).

Jaussen, Antonin and Savignac, Raphaël, *Mission archéologique en Arabie, 1907, 1909–10* (6 vols, Paris: Ernst Leroux/Roth-Hotz Reprise, vol. 1, 1909; Paul Geuthner, vols 2–3 (Texte et Atlas), 1914; vol. 4 (Supplément), 1920; vols 5–6 (Les châteaux forts: Texte et Atlas) 1922).

Jelinek, Jan, 'Étude historique du Messak Settafet', *Art rupestre du Sahara. Dossiers d'Archéologie*, no. 197 (1994, q.v.), pp. 14–21.

Jennings, Richard P, 'Rock art landscapes beside the Jubbah palaeolake, Saudi Arabia', in: *Antiquity*, vol. 87 (Cambridge: University Press, 2013), pp. 666–683.

Jensen, Jørgen, *The Prehistory of Denmark* (Abingdon: Routledge, 2015).

Jensen, Jørgen and Kruse, Petra (eds), *Gods and Heroes of the Bronze Age: Europe at the Time of Ulysses* (London: Thames and Hudson, 1999).

Jettmar, Karl, *Zwischen Gandhāra und den Seidenstrassen. Felsbilder am Karakorum Highway* (Mainz: Philipp von Zabern, 1985).

— 'Symbolic systems in collision: Rock art in the Upper Indus valley', in: Allchin, Raymond et al. (eds), *Gandharan Art in Context: East–West Exchanges at the Crossroads of Asia* (New Delhi: Regency Publications, 1997), pp. 55–69.

Jiang Zhenming, *Timeless History: The Rock Art of China* (Beijing: New World Press, 1991).

Johannsen, Jens Winther, 'Carts and wagons on Scandinavian rock carving sites', in: *Adoranten* (q.v., 2011), pp. 95–107.

— 'The Villfara Monument: Rock carvings, death, cosmology and rituals in early Bronze Age Scania', in: *Lund Archaeological Review*, vol. 19 (Lund: Lund University, 2013), pp. 19–34.

Joger, Ulrich and Moldrzyk, Uwe (eds), *Die Wüste* (Darmstadt: Hessisches Landesmuseum, 2002).

Johnson, Berit, *The Cosmic Wedding: A New Interpretation of Southern Scandinavian Rock Carvings, Stonehenge and other Manifestations of Bronze Age Religion* (Copenhagen: Frydenlund, 2005).

Jones, Eppie R. et al, 'Upper Palaeolithic genomes reveal deep roots of modern Eurasians', in: *Nature Communications*, vol. 6, art. no. 8912 (London: Macmillan, 2015).

Jordan, Peter and Cummings, Vicki, 'Prehistoric hunter-gatherer innovations', in: Cummings et al., *The Oxford Handbook of the Archaeology and Anthropology of Hunter-Gatherers* (2014, q.v.), pp. 585–606.

Joussaume, Roger and Cros, Jean-Paul, *Art rupestre dans la Corne de l'Afrique* (Chauvigny : APC, 2020).

Jürgens, Ekkehard, 'Pictures – What for? Seven hypotheses on the origin of art', in: Sachs-Hombach and Schirra, *Origins of Pictures* (2013, q.v.), pp. 521–550.

Kadyrov, Victor, *Masterpieces of Primeval Art* (Bishkek: Rarity, 2014).

Kakroodi, A.A. et al., 'Late Pleistocene and Holocene sea-level change and coastal paleoenvironment evolution along the Caspian shore', *Marine Geology*, vol. 361 (Amsterdam: Elsevier, 2015), pp. 111–125.

Kant, Immanuel, *Kritik der Urteilskraft* (1790): https://gutenberg.org/cache/epub/55925/pg55925-images.html#Pg204.

Kardulias, P. Nick, 'Migration of *Homo sapiens* out of Africa', in: Chiotis, *Climate Changes in the Holocene* (2019, q.v.), pp. 143–156.

Kashchey, O.A. and Nedashkovsky, L.F., 'Хронология наскальных изображений Каракиясая II = Chronology of the Karakiyasay II rock art', in: *Вестник археологии, антропологии и этнографии = Bulletin of Archaeology, Anthropology and Ethnography*, 2023, vol. 61, no. 2 (Tyumen: Tyumen Scientific Centre of Siberian Branch of the Russian Academy of Sciences: 2023), pp. 69–79.

Kashina, Ekaterina and Zhulnikov, Alexandr, 'Rods with elk's heads: Symbol in ritual context', in: *Estonian Journal of Archaeology*, vol. 15, no. 1 (Talinn: Estonian Academic Publishers, 2011), pp. 18–31.

Kaul, Flemming, *Ships on Bronzes: A Study in Bronze Age Religion and Iconography* (2 vols, Copenhagen: The National Museum, 1998).

— 'The Gundestrup Cauldron: Thracian art, Celtic motifs', in: *Études Celtiques*, vol. 37 (Paris: CNRS Éditions, 2011), pp. 81–110.

— 'The Chariot of the Sun and other sun horses of the Nordic Bronze Age – including some interesting anatomical details', in: Dodd and Meijer, *Giving the Past a Future* (2018, q.v.), pp. 58–69.

Kaul, Flemming et al., 'To deposit a fire – during the Bronze Age and in the present', in: *Adoranten* (q.v., 2022), pp. 35–56.

Kaul, Flemming and Rønne, Preben, 'Bronzes, farms and rock art: The agrarian expansion of North Norway', in: *Adoranten* (q.v., 2013), pp. 25–56.

Keenan, Jeremy (ed.), *The Sahara: Past, Present and Future* (London: Taylor & Francis, 2017).

Keller, Dominik and Schorta, Regula, *Fabulous Creatures from the Desert Sands: Central Asian Woolen Textiles from the Second Century BC to the Second Century AD* (Riggisberg: Abegg-Stiftung, 2001).

Kenk, Roman, *Früh- und hochmittelalterliche Gräber von Kudyrge im Altai* (Munich: C.H. Beck, 1982).

Kennedy, Melissa et al., 'Cult, herding, and "pilgrimage" in the Late Neolithic of north-west Arabia: Excavations at a mustatil east of AlUla', in: *PLOS ONE*, vol. 18, no. 3, art. no. 0281904 (San Francisco: PLOS, 2023).

Kęsik, Jacek et al., 'Documenting archaeological petroglyph sites with the use of 3D terrestrial laser scanners: A case study of petroglyphs in Kyrgyzstan', in: Milosz, Marek and Kęsik, Jacek (eds), *Applied Sciences*, vol. 12, no. 20 (special issue: *3D Information Technologies for Tangible and Intangible Cultural Heritage*), art. no. 10521 (Basel: MDPI, 2022).

Khan, Majeed, *Prehistoric Rock Art of Northern Saudi Arabia* (Riyadh: Ministry of Education, 1993).

— 'Rock art of Saudi Arabia', in: *Arts*, vol. 2, no. 4 (Basel: MDPI, 2013), pp. 447–475.

— *An Introduction to the Rock Art of Saudi Arabia* (Riyadh: Saudi Commission for Tourism and National Heritage, 2017).

— 'Deities and gods: A perspective on prehistoric religions in Arabia', in: Anati, *Cultural Changes* (2021, q.v.), pp. 79–91.

— 'Women in prehistoric and tribal societies of Arabia', in: Anati, *The Role of Women in Prehistoric and Tribal Societies* (2021, q.v.), pp. 85–92.

Khechoyan, Anna, 'The rock art of the Mt. Aragats system', in: *Rock Art in the Frame of the Cultural Heritage of Humankind: Papers of the XXII Valcamonica Symposium 2007* (Capo di Ponte: CCSP, 2007), pp. 247–252.

Khechoyan, Anna and Gasparyan, Boris, 'Rock painting phenomenon in the Republic of Armenia', in: Gasparyan, Boris and Arimura, Makoto (eds), *Stone Age of Armenia: A Guide-Book to the Stone Age Archaeology in the Republic of Armenia* (Kanazawa: Center for Cultural Resource Studies, Kanazawa University, 2014).

Khujanazarov, M., 'Petroglyphs of Uzbekistan', in: Tashbayeva et al., *Petroglyphs of Central Asia* (Bishkek: International Institute for Central Asian Studies, 2001), pp. 80–121.

— 'Rock sites in Uzbekistan', in: Clottes, Jean (ed.), *Rock Art in Central Asia: A Thematic Study* (2011, q.v.), pp. 99–112.

Kleinitz, Cornelia, 'Rock art landscapes of the Fourth Nile Cataract: Characterisations and first comparisons', in: Näser, Claudia and Lange, Mathias, *Proceedings of the Second International Conference on the Archaeology of the Fourth Nile Cataract* (Wiesbaden: Harrassowitz, 2007), pp. 213–238.

Klinge, Michael and Sauer, Daniela, 'Spatial pattern of Late Glacial and Holocene climatic and environmental development in Western Mongolia: A critical review and synthesis', in: *Quarternary Science Reviews*, vol. 210 (Amsterdam: Elsevier, 2019), pp. 26–50.

Knoll, Franziska, 'Petroglyphs in the Syunik Highlands (Armenia): Mapping (pre-)historic traces', in: *Adoranten* (q.v., 2016), pp. 73–83.

Knoll, Franziska et al., 'Die Felsbilder im Hochland von Syunik', in: *Archäologie in Armenien*, vol. 2 (Halle: Landesamt für Denkmalpflege und Archäologie Sachsen-Anhalt, 2013), pp. 209–234.

Knutsson, Helena (ed.), *Pioneer Settlements and Colonization Processes in the Barents Region* (Vuollerim, Sweden: Vuollerim 6000 år, 2003).

Koch, John T., 'Rock art and Celto-Germanic vocabulary: Shared iconography and words as reflections of Bronze Age contact', in: *Adoranten* (q.v., 2019), pp. 80–95.

Koenig, Gerd G., 'Skythen in Tibet?', in: Müller, Claudius C. and Raunig, Walter (eds), *Der Weg zum Dach der Welt* (Innsbruck: Pinguin-Verlag, 1982), pp. 318–320.

Kohl, Karl-Heinz et al. (eds), *Kunst der Vorzeit. Texte zu den Felsbildern der Sammlung Frobenius* (Frankfurt am Main: Frobenius-Institut, 2016).

— *Kunst der Vorzeit. Felsbilder der Frobenius-Expeditionen* (Munich: Prestel, 2021).

Kohl-Larsen, Ludwig, *Die Bilderstrasse Ostafrikas. Felsbilder in Tanganyika* (Kassel: Erich Röth-Verlag, 1958).

Kolpakov, Eugen M., 'Land hunting in the rock art of northern Fennoscandia', in: Gjerde and Arntzen, *Perspectives on Differences in Rock Art* (2021, q.v.), pp. 193–201.

Kolpakov, Eugen M. and Shumkin, Vladimir Ya., *Rock Carvings of Kanozero* (St Petersburg: Russian Academy of Sciences, 2012).

Konstantinov, Nikita et al., 'Battle and hunting scenes in Turkic rock art of the early Middle Ages in Altai', in: *Rock Art Research*, vol. 33, no. 1 (Darwin: International Federation of Rock Art Organizations, 2016), pp. 8–18.

Kootstra, Fokelien, 'The language of the Taymanitic inscriptions and its classification', in: *Arabian Epigraphic Notes*, vol. 2 (Leiden: Leiden Center for the Study of Ancient Arabia, 2016): pp. 67–140.

Kortum, Richard, 'Sacred imagery and ritual landscape: New discoveries at the Biluut petroglyph complex in the Mongolian Altai', in: Lami, Martina Revello and Fernandez, Mónica Palmero (eds), *Time and Mind*, vol. 7, No. 4 (Abingdon: Routledge, 2014), pp. 329–384.

— *Ceremony in Stone: The Biluut Petroglyph Complex, Prehistoric Rock Art in the Mongolian Altai* (Ulaan Baatar: Nepko, 2018).

— 'Altai rock art: Visions of the past in Mongolia', in: *Current World Archaeology*, vol. 106 (London: Current Publishing, 2021), pp. 16–22.

Kostianoy, Andrey G., 'Interannual variability of water level in two largest lakes of Europe', in: *Remote Sensing*, vol. 14, no. 3, art. no. 659 (Basel: MDPI, 2022).

Kovalev, Alexey A., 'Überlegungen zur Herkunft der Skythen aufgrund archäologischer Daten', in: *Eurasia Antiqua. Zeitschrift für Archäologie Eurasiens*, vol. 4 (Mainz: Philipp von Zabern, 1998), pp. 247–271.

— *Древнейшие европейцы в сердце Азии: чемурчекский культурный феномен*, vol. 2: *Результаты исследований в центральной части Монгольского Алтая и в истоках Кобдо; памятники Синьцзяна и окраинных земель = Earliest Europeans in the Heart of Asia: The Chemurchek Cultural Phenomenon*, vol. 2: *Excavations in the Central Mongolian Altai and in the Headwaters of the Khovd River; Sites and Finds in Xinjiang and in Outlying Regions* (St Petersburg: MISR, 2015).

— 'The Chemurchek (Qie'muerqieke) cultural phenomenon as a result of Western European migration to Dzungaria and the Mongolian Altai', in: Baumer, Novák and Rutishauser (eds), *Cultures in Contact* (2022, q.v.), pp. 531–554.

Kovalev, Alexey A. et al., 'A ritual complex with deer stones at Uushigiin Uvur, Mongolia: Composition and construction stages', in: *Archaeology, Ethnology and Anthropology of Eurasia*, vol. 44 (Novosibirsk: Russian Academy of Sciences, 2016), pp. 82–92.

Kovalev, Alexey A. and Munkhbayar, Ch., 'Петроглифы на чемурчекских ритуальных оградах в высокогорье Монгольского Алтая (3 тыс до н.э.): репертуар образов = Petroglyphs of the Chemurchek ritual fences in the highlands of the Mongolian Altai (3rd millennium BC): Repertoire of images', in: Batbold, N., *Төв Азийн эртний нүүдэлчдийн хадны зураг = Petroglyphs of Ancient Nomads from Central Asia* (Ulaan Baatar: Nuhus, 2022), pp. 84–101.

Kovalev, Alexey A. and Solodovnikov, K N. et al., 'Палеоантропологическое изучение черепа погребенного в захоронении на чемурчекском святилище Хулагаш (Баян-Ульгийский аймак Монголии) = 'Paleoanthropological study of a skull from a burial at the Chemurchek sanctuary Hulagash (Bayan-Ulgii aimag, Mongolia)', in: *Вестник археологии, антропологии и этнографии = Bulletin of Archaeology, Anthropology and Ethnography*, vol. 48, no. 1 (Novosibirsk: Institute of Archaeology and Ethnography, 2020), pp. 78–95.

Kristiansen, Kristian, 'Rock art and religion: The sun journey in Indo-European mythology and Bronze Age rock art', in: Fredell, Åsa et al., *Representations and Communications* (2010, q.v.), pp. 93–115; also in: *Adoranten* (q.v., 2012), pp. 69–86.

— 'The winged triad in Bronze Age symbolism: Birds and their feet', in: Dodd and Meijer, *Giving the Past a Future* (2018, q.v.), pp. 70–83.

— 'Warfare and the political economy: Europe 1500–1100 BC', in: Horn and Kristiansen, *Warfare in Bronze Age Society* (2018, q.v.), pp. 23–46.

— 'Bronze Age travellers', in: Fernández-Götz et al., *Rethinking Migrations in Late Prehistoric Eurasia* (2023, q.v.), pp. 89–109.

Kristiansen, Kristian and Larsson, Thomas B., *The Rise of Bronze Age Society: Travels, Transmissions and Transformations* (Cambridge: Cambridge University Press, 2005).

Krivora, Natalie, 'Solar irradiance variability and Earth's climate', in: Chiotis, *Climate Changes in the Holocene* (2019, q.v.), pp. 107–120.

Krüger, Werner and Pehnt, Wolfgang, *Documenta – Documente. Künstler im Gespräch* (Cologne: Artemedia, 1984).

Kšica, Miroslav, *Vom Urbild zur Schrift. Vom Naturbild zur Kunst* (Brno: s.n., 1994).

Kšica, Miroslav and Kšicová, Olga, *Felsbilder zwischen Schwarzem Meer und Beringstrasse* (Brno: PREH-ART-EXPO, 1994).

Kubarev, Gleb V., *Alttürkische Gräber des Altaj* (Bonn: Habelt, 2017).

Kubarev, Vladimir D., *Древние росписи Каракола = Old Paintings of Karakol* (Novosibirsk: Nauka Publishing House, 1988).

— 'Skythische Kurgane aus den Gräberfeldern Bike I und III am mittleren Katun', Sibirien', in: *Eurasia Antiqua. Zeitschrift für Archäologie Eurasiens*, vol.7 (Mainz: Philipp von Zabern, 2001), pp. 133–167.

— 'Traces of shamanic motives in the petroglyphs and burial paintings', in: Rozwadowski and Kośko, *Spirits and Stones* (2002, q.v.), pp. 99–119.

— 'Biluut-Tolgoi: A new rock art site in Mongolia', in: *The Silk Road*, vol. 4, no. 1 (Berkeley: The Silkroad House, 2006), pp. 63–68.

— 'Aral Tolgoi: New rock art site in Mongolia', in: *Archaeology, Ethnology and Anthropology of Eurasia*, vol. 29 (Novosibirsk: Russian Academy of Sciences, 2007), pp. 111–126.

— 'Biluut-Tolgoi: A new rock art site in Mongolia', in: *Archaeology, Ethnology and Anthropology of Eurasia*, vol. 31 (Elsevier, Amsterdam 2007) pp. 63–68.

— 'Results and prospects of studying ancient art monuments in Mongolia', in: Bemmann, Jan et al., *Current Archaeological Research in Mongolia* (Bonn: Friedrich-Wilhelms-Universität 2009), pp. 67–81.

Kubarev, Vladimir and Larichev, V.E., *Древние росписи Каракола = The Ancient Painting of Karakol* (Novosibirsk: Nauka Publishing House, Siberian Branch, 1988).

Kubarev, Vladimir and Zevendorz D., 'Steinstelen aus der Westmongolei', in: *Eurasia Antiqua. Zeitschrift für Archäologie Eurasiens*, vol.3 (1997) (Mainz: Philipp von Zabern 1998), pp. 571–580.

Kühn, Herbert, *Wenn Steinen reden. Die Sprache der Felsbilder* (Wiesbaden: F.A. Brockhaus, 1966).

Kuper, Rudolph (ed.), *Wadi Sura – The Cave of Beasts: A Rock Art Site in the Gilf Kebir (SW Egypt)* (Cologne: Heinrich-Barth-Institut, 2013).

Kurochkin, Evgeny N. et al., 'The timing of ostrich existence in Central Asia: AMS ^{14}C age of eggshells from Mongolia and southern Siberia (a pilot study)', in: *Nuclear Instruments and Methods in Physics Research Section B: Beam Interactions with Materials and Atoms*, vol. 268, nos 7–8 (Amsterdam: Elsevier, 2010), pp. 1091–1093.

Kuz'mina, Elena, *The Origins of the Indo-Iranians*, ed. J. P. Mallory (Leiden: Brill, 2007).

Kynällä, Joutsenen, *Rock Art from Lake Onega 4000–2000 BC: Swansongs* (Tartu: Estonian Society of Prehistoric Art, 1990).

Labrusse, Remi, *Préhistoire : L'envers du temps* (Vanves: Hazan, 2019).

Lachaud, Gérard and Suzanne, 'L'arc composite et le Sahara', in: *Cahiers de l'AARS*, no.15 (Saint-Benoist-sur-Mer: AARS, 2011), pp. 153–158.

— 'La pierre sonore de Ti-Duneĝ (Tadrart, Algérie) et quelques grands lithophones sahariens', in: *Cahiers de l'AARS*, no. 24 (Saint-Benoist-sur-Mer: AARS, 2023), pp. 91–101.

Lagrange, Marie-Joseph, 'Un sanctuaire d'Allat à Iram', in: *Comptes rendus des séances de l'Académie des Inscriptions et Belles-Lettres*, vol. 76, no. 3 (Paris: Académie des Inscriptions et Belles-Lettres, 1932), pp. 225–227.

Lahelma, Antti, 'Strange swans and odd ducks: Interpreting the ambiguous waterfowl imagery of Lake Onega', in: Cochrane, Andrew and Meirion Jones, Andrew (eds), *Visualising the Neolithic* (Oxford: Oxbow, 2012), pp. 15–33.

— 'The circumpolar context of the "sun ship" motif in south Scandinavian rock art', in: Skoglund, Ling and Bertilsson, *North Meets South* (2017, q.v.), pp. 144–171.

Lajoux, Jean-Dominique, *Tassili n'Ajjer. Art rupestre du Sahara préhistorique* (Paris: Le Chêne, 1977).

— *Murs d'images. Art rupestre du Sahara préhistorique* (Paris: Errance, 2012).

Lami, Martina Revello and Fernandez, Mónica Palmero (eds), *Time and Mind*, vol. 7, no. 4 (Abingdon: Routledge, 2014).

Laneri, Nicola and Perdibon, Anna (eds), *Sacred Nature: Animism and Materiality in Ancient Religions* (Oxford: Oxbow, 2023).

Larsson, Thomas B. and Broström, Sven-Gunnar, *Nämforsens Hällristningar / The Rock Art of Nämforsen* (Nämforsen: Nämforsens Hällristningsmuseum, 2018).

Lasheras, José Antonio, 'The cave of Altamira: 22,000 years of history', in: *Adoranten* (q.v., 2009), pp. 5–33.

Latour, Bruno, *Existenzweisen: Eine Anthropologie der Modernen* (Berlin: Suhrkamp, 2014).

Lawrence, T.E., *Seven Pillars of Wisdom: A Triumph* (London: Jonathan Cape, 1943).

Laziridis, Iosif et al., 'Ancient human genomes suggest three ancestral populations for present-day Europeans', in: *Nature*, vol. 513 (London: Macmillan, 2014), pp. 409–413.

Lazaridis, Iosif, Alpaslan-Roodenberg, Songül et al., 'The genetic history of the Southern Arc: A bridge between West Asia and Europe', in *Science*, vol. 377, art. no. 6609 (Washington DC: AAAS, 2022).

Lecouteux, Claude, 'Les Cynocéphales. Étude d'une tradition tératologique de l'Antiquité au XIIe s', in: *Cahiers de civilisation médiévale*, vol. 94 (Poitiers: CESCM, UMR 7302, 1981), pp. 117–128.

Lee, Jane J. and Wang, Andrew, 'Tonga eruption blasted unprecedented amount of water into stratosphere' (Pasadena: Jet Propulsion Laboratory, California Institute of Technology, 2 August, 2022): https://www.jpl.nasa.gov/news/tonga-eruption-blasted-unprecedented-amount-of-water-into-stratosphere.

Leont'ev, Nikolaj V. and Kapel'ko, Vladimir F., *Steinstelen der Okunev-Kultur* (Mainz: Philipp von Zabern, 2002).

Lepetz S. et al., *Occupations et espaces sacrés dans l'Altaï mongol : les sites archéologiques de Burgast et Ikh Khatuu (1100 a.C.–1100 p.C.), résultats des fouilles (2014–2016) de la mission archéologique franco-mongole dirigée par Sébastien Lepetz et Tsagaan Turbat* (Drémil-Lafage: Editions Mergoil, 2022).

— 'Customs, rites, and sacrifices relating to a mortuary complex in Late Bronze Age Mongolia (Tsatsyn Ereg, Arkhangai)', in: Lepetz et al., *Occupations et espaces sacrés dans l'Altaï mongol* (2022, q.v.), pp. 151–177.

— 'Cheval et pensée symbolique', in: *Archéologia*, no. 632 (Dijon: Faton, 2024), pp. 36f.

Le Quellec, Jean-Loïc, *Symbolisme et art rupestre au Sahara* (Paris: L'Harmattan, 1993).

— 'L'art rupestre de style dit "arabo-éthiopien" et l'école de Chabbè-Galma', in: *Afrique : Archéologie et Arts*, vol. 2 (Paris: UMR, 2002–3), pp. 47–68.

— *Rock Art in Africa: Mythology and Legend* (Paris: Flammarion, 2004).

— 'Chamanes et martiens: même combat ! Les lectures chamaniques des arts rupestres du Sahara', in: Lorblanchet, Michel et al., *Chamanismes et arts préhistoriques* (2006, q.v.), pp. 244–260.

— 'Can one "read" rock art? An Egyptian example', in: Taylor, Paul (ed.), *Iconography without Texts* (London: The Warburg Institute, 2008), pp. 25–42.

— '"Chasseurs" et "Pasteurs" au Sahara central: les "Chasseurs archaïques" chassé du paradigme', in: *Palethnologie: Archéologie et Sciences humaines*, vol. 4 (Toulouse: CNRS / UMR 5608, 2009), pp. 401–409.

— 'Rock art, scripts and proto-scripts in Africa: The Libyco-Berber Example', in: Delmas, Adrien and Penn, Nigel (eds), *Written Culture in a Colonial Context: Africa and the Americas 1500–1900* (Leiden: Brill, 2011), pp. 1–29.

— 'Aréologie, phénétique et art rupestre: l'example des théranthropes du Sahara central', in: *Les Cahiers de l'AARS*, no. 16 (St-Benoist-sur-Mer: AARS, 2013), pp. 155–715.

— 'Théranthropes du Sahara. L'invention d'une méthode d'étude', in: *Archéologia*, no. 518 (Dijon: Faton, 2014), pp. 46–51.

— 'Périodisation et chronologie des images rupestres du Sahara central', in: *Préhistoires Méditerranéennes*, vol. 4 (Aix-en-Provence: Maison méditerranéenne des sciences de l'homme, 2013).

— 'Peut-on retrouver les mythes préhistoriques? L'example des récits anthropogoniques', in: *Comptes rendus des séances de l'Académie des Inscriptions et Belles-Lettres (CRAI)*, vol. 1 (Paris, Institut de France: 2015), pp. 235–268.

— '"La religion" et "le fait religieux" : deux notions obsolètes', in: Le Quellec, Jean-Loïc (ed.), *L'Anthropologie pour tous* (Saint-Benoist-sur-Mer: Traces, 2015), pp. 19–32.

— 'The rock art of sub-Saharan Africa', in: David and McNiven, *The Oxford Handbook of the Archaeology and Anthropology of Rock Art* (2018, q.v.), pp. 123–150.

— 'Égypte, Afrique, Sahara: arts rupestres et mythologies', in: *Archéo-Nil*, no. 29 (Paris: Société pour l'étude des cultures prépharaoniques de la vallée du Nil, 2019), pp. 81–100.

— *Avant nous le Déluge ! L'humanité et ses mythes* (Paris: Éditions du Détour, 2021).

— 'What's new in the Sahara? (2015–2020)', in: Bahn et al., *Rock Art Studies: News of the World*, vol. 6 (2021, q.v.), pp. 63–78.

— *La caverne originelle. Art, mythes et premières humanités* (Paris: La Découverte, 2022).

— 'Fezzaniana 3: I-n-Ălobbu (Ăkukas, Libye). Style d'Ihəren et chasse à l'éléphant', in: *Cahiers de l'AARS*, no. 24 (Saint-Benoist-sur-Mer: AARS, 2023), pp. 103–146.

Le Quellec, Jean-Loïc et al., *Art rupestre et patrimoine mondial en Afrique subsaharienne* (Paris: Hémisphères Éditions, 2001).

— *Ithyphalliques, traditions orales, monuments lithiques et art rupestre au Sahara* (Saint-Lizier: AARS, 2002).

Le Quellec, Jean-Loïc and de Flers, Pauline and Philippe, *Peintures et gravures d'avant les pharaons du Sahara au Nil* (Paris: Fayard, 2005).

Le Quellec, Jean-Loïc and Sergent, Bernard, *Dictionnaire critique de mythologie* (Paris: CNRS Éditions, 2017).

Leroi-Gourhan, André, *Les religions de la préhistoire (Paléolithique)* (Paris: Presse Universitaire de France PUF, 1964).

— *Préhistoire de l'art occidental* (Paris: Mazenod, 1971).

— *Hand und Wort: Die Evolution von Technik, Sprache und Kunst* (Frankfurt am Main: Suhrkamp, 2009).

Lévi-Strauss, Claude, *La pensée sauvage* (Paris: Plon, 1962).

— *Anthropologie structurale* (Paris: Plon, 1958).

— *Structural Anthropology*, trans. Claire Jacobson and Brooke Grundfest Schoepf (New York: Anchor Books, 1967).

Lewis-Williams, J. David, *Believing and Seeing: Symbolic Meanings in Southern San Rock Paintings* (London: Academic Press, 1981).

— *The Rock Art of Southern Africa* (Cambridge: Cambridge University Press, 1983).

— 'Monolithism and polysemy: Scylla and Charybdis in rock art research', in: Helskog, *Theoretical Perspectives in Rock Art Research* (2001, q.v.), pp. 23–39.

— *The Mind in the Cave* (London: Thames & Hudson, 2002).

— 'Rock art and shamanism', in: McDonald and Veth, *Companion to Rock Art* (2012, q.v.), pp. 17–33.

— 'Art for the living', in: Cummings et al., *The Oxford Handbook of the Archaeology and Anthropology of Hunter-Gatherers* (2014, q.v.), pp. 635–642.

Lézine, Anne-Marie et al., 'Climate change and human occupation in the Southern Arabian lowlands during the last deglaciation and the Holocene', in: *Global and Planetary Change*, vol. 72 (Amsterdam: Elsevier, 2010), pp. 412–428.

Lhote, Henri, 'Comparaison avec d'autres sites peints d'Afrique septentrionale', in: Breuil, Henri, *Les roches peintes du Tassili-n-Ajjer* (Paris: Arts et Métiers Graphiques, 1954), pp. 65–86.

— *Die Felsbilder der Sahara. Entdeckung einer 8000jährigen Kultur* (Würzburg: Andreas Zettner, 1958).

— *Les gravures rupestres de l'Oued Djerat (Tassili-n-Ajjer)* (2 vols, Algiers: Centre de recherches anthropologiques, préhistoriques et ethnographiques, 1975).

— *Les chars rupestres sahariens: des Syrtes au Niger, par le pays des Garamantes et des* Atlantes (Paris: Editions des Hespérides, 1982).

Lhuillier, Johanna, 'Intercultural interactions of the Sine Sepulchro cultural community (Handmade Painted Ware cultures) of the Early Iron Age with the neighbouring cultures of Asia and the Near East', in: Baumer, Novák and Rutishauser, *Cultures in Contact* (2022, q.v.), pp. 135–152.

Likhachev, Vadim, *Рисунки Канозера. Открытие, изучение, сочранение = Rock Art of Kanozero: Discovery, Research, Preservation* (Apatity: IIMK RAN, 2011).

— 'Bow elk hunt: Composition of the Kanozero petroglyph complex', in: *Adoranten* (q.v., 2017), pp. 76–84.

— 'Kanozero petroglyphs: History of discovery and investigation', in: *Adoranten* (q.v., 2018), pp. 48–71.

— 'New motives and compositions of the Kanozero petroglyphs', in: *Adoranten* (q.v., 2021), pp. 72–87.

Lima, Pedro and Psaïla, Philippe, *La grotte Cosquer révélée. Les secrets du sanctuaire préhistorique englouti* (Montélimar: Synops, 2021).

Limerov, Pavel, 'Forest myths: A brief overview of ideologies before St. Stefan', in: *Folklore*, vol. 30 (Tartu: Institute of the Estonian Language, 2005), pp. 29–134.

Lindgaard, Eva, 'Subsistence in central Norway elucidated through rock art excavation and documentation', in: Stebergløkken et al., *Ritual Landscape and Borders within Rock Art Research* (2015, q.v.), pp. 99–110.

Lindgren, Britta, *Hällbilder i Norr* (Umeå: Umeå Universitet, 2004).

Ling, Johan, 'Beyond transgressive lands and forgotten seas: Towards a maritime understanding of rock art in Bohuslän', in: *Current Swedish Archaeology*, vol. 12 (Uddevalla: Svenska Arkeologiska Samfundet, 2004), pp. 121–140.

— 'Elevated rock art: Maritime images and situations', in: Fredell et al., *Representations and Communications* (2010, q.v.), pp. 31–51.

— *Rock Art and Seascapes in Uppland* (Oxford: Oxbow, 2013).

— *Elevated Rock Art: Towards a Maritime Understanding of Rock Art in Northern Bohuslän, Sweden* (Oxford: Oxbow, 2014).

Ling, Johan and Bertilsson, Ulf, 'Biography of the Fossum Panel', in: *Adoranten* (q.v., 2016), pp. 58–72.

Ling, Johan and Chacon, Richard and Yamilette, 'Rock Art, secret societies, long-distance exchange and warfare in Bronze Age Scandinavia', in: Dolfini A. et al. (eds), *Prehistoric Warfare and Violence* (Berlin: Springer, 2018), pp. 149–174.

— 'Rock art and nautical routes to social complexity: Comparing Haida and Scandinavian Bronze Age societies', in: *Adoranten* (q.v., 2020), pp. 5–23.

Ling, John and Koch, John, 'A sea beyond Europe to the north and west', in: Dodd and Meijer, *Giving the Past a Future* (2018, q.v.), pp. 96–111.

Ling, Johan and Rowlands, Michael, 'The "Stranger King" (bull) and rock art', in: Skoglund, Ling and Bertilsson, *Picturing the Bronze Age* (2015, q.v.), pp. 89–104.

Ling, Johan and Toreld, Andreas, 'Maritime warfare in Scandinavian rock art', in: Horn and Kristiansen, *Warfare in Bronze Age Society* (2018, q.v.), pp. 61–80.

Ling, Johan and Uhnér, Claes, 'Rock art and metal trade', in: *Adoranten* (q.v., 2021), pp. 72–87.

Linge, Trond Eilev, 'Seasons and landscape in North European hunter-gatherer rock art: The case of salmon at Honnhammar, central Norway', in: Gjerde and Arntzen, *Perspectives on Differences in Rock Art* (2021, q.v.), pp. 145–162.

Linstädter, Jörg and Kröpelin, Stefan, 'Wadi Bakht revisited: Holocene climate change and prehistoric occupation in the Gilf Kebir region of the Eastern Sahara, SW Egypt', in: *Geoarchaeology*, vol. 19, no. 8 (Hoboken: Wiley, 2004), pp. 753–778.

Lippard, Lucy, R., *The Lure of the Local: Senses of Place in a Multicentered Society* (New York: New Press, 1998).

— *Overlay: Contemporary Art and the Art of Prehistory* (New York: The New Press, 2010).

Lippens, Philippe, *Expédition en Arabie centrale* (Paris: Adrien Maisonneuve, 1956).

Lischi, Silvia et al., 'First results of the 2020 and 2021 seasons of Saudi–French Archaeological and Epigraphic Mission to Najrān in the area of Himā (Najrān, Saudi Arabia)', in: *Proceedings of the Seminar for Arabian Studies*, vol. 52 (Oxford: Archaeopress, 2023), pp. 237–252.

Lobanova, N.V., 'New data on the chronology of Lake Onega and the White Sea area petroglyphs', in: Gjerde and Arntzen, *Perspectives on Differences in Rock Art* (2021, q.v.), pp. 202–217.

Lobell, Jarret A., 'Which island is it anyway? Unidentified island, English Channel', in: *Archaeology*, vol. 77, no. 3 (Long Island City: Archaeological Institute of America, 2024), pp. 30–39.

Lødøen, Trond Klungseth, 'The method and physical processes behind the making of hunters' rock art in Western Norway: The experimental production of images', in: Stebergløkken et al., *Ritual Landscape and Borders within Rock Art Research* (2015, q.v.), pp. 67–77.

Lødøen, Trond and Mandt, Gro, *The Rock Art of Norway* (Oxford: Windgather Press, 2010).

Lohmann, Polly, 'Antike und historische Graffiti als Forschungsgegenstand', in: *Antike Welt*, vol. 21, no. 2 (Darmstadt: WBG, 2021), pp. 8–15.

Löhndorf, Marion, 'Bansky hat eine rote Nase. Der Street-Artist brachte es zu Weltruhm. Hinter dem Image des Outlaw stecken cleveres Kalkül und Marketing', in: *Neue Zürcher Zeitung* (Zurich: NZZ, 17 December 2021), p. 30.

Lorblanchet, Michel (ed.), *Rock Art in the Old World* (New Delhi: Indira Gandhi National Centre for the Arts, 1992).

Lorblanchet, Michel et al. (eds), *Chamanismes et arts préhistoriques. Vision critique* (Paris: Errance, 2006).

Lorblanchet, Michel and Bahn, Paul, *The First Artists* (New York: Thames & Hudson, 2017).

Lozachmeur H. and Briquel-Chatonnet F., 'Charles Huber und Julius Euting in Arabien nach französischen, auch heute nicht veröffentlichten Dokumenten', in: *Anabases*, vol. 12 (Toulouse: De Boccard, 2010), pp. 195–200.

Lu, Dongsheng et al., 'Ancestral origins and genetic history of Tibetan highlanders', in: *The American Journal of Human Genetics*, vol. 99 (Birmingham AL: AJHG, 2016), pp. 580–594.

Luckhardt, Ulrich and Zimmer, Nina (eds), *Paul Klee-Tierisches. Internationale Tage Ingelheim.* Kunstforum Ingelheim & Zentrum Paul Klee (Munich: Hirmer, 2020).

Lumley, Henry de, *Le mont Bego. Vallées des Merveilles et de Fontanalba* (Paris: Éditions du patrimoine, 2003).

Lumley, Henry de and Clergue, Lucien, *Fascinant Mont Bego* (Aix-en-Provence: Edisud, 2002).

Lutz, Rüdiger and Gabriele, *Das Geheimnis der Wüste. Die Felskunst des Messak Sattafet und Messak Mellet – Libyen* (Innsbruck: Golf Verlag, 1995).

Lymer, Kenneth, 'The petroglyphs of Terekty Aulie in central Kazakhstan', in: Anati (ed.), *Expression*, no. 8 (q.v., 2015), pp. 96–101.

Macdonald, M.C.A., 'Wheels in a land of camels: Another look at the chariot in Arabia', in: *Arabian Archaeology and Epigraphy*, vol. 20 (Oxford: Wiley, 2009), pp. 156–184.

— 'The development of Arabic as a written language', in: *Supplement to the Proceedings of the Seminar for Arabian Studies*, vol. 40 (Oxford: Archaeopress, 2010), pp. 5–28.

— 'Goddesses, dancing girls or cheerleaders?', in: Sachet et al., *Dieux et déesses d'Arabie* (2012, q.v.), pp. 261–297.

Macholdt, Dorothea S. et al., 'Growth of desert varnish on petroglyphs from Jubbah and Shuwaymis, Ha'il region, Saudi Arabia', in: *The Holocene*, vol. 28, no. 9 (Thousand Oaks CA: SAGE Publications, 2018), pp. 1495–1511.

— 'Rock varnish on petroglyphs from the Hima region, southwestern Saudi Arabia: Chemical composition, growth rates, and tentative ages', in: *The Holocene*, vol. 29, no. 8 (Thousand Oaks CA: SAGE Publications, 2019), pp. 1377–1395.

Mackert, Gabriele, 'Joseph Beuys im Dialog mit Urbildern', in: Faass and Schmidt, *Urknall der Kunst* (2023, q.v.), pp. 50–59.

MacRae, Alisdair, 'Joane Cardinal-Schubert: Ancient contemporary', in: Rozwadowski and Hampson, *Visual Culture, Heritage and Identity* (2021, q.v.), pp. 37–50.

Maestrucci, Fabio and Gianelli, Gianna, 'Tikadiouine: Integrazione grafica, nuova analisi ed interpretazione. L'approvvigionamento alimentare nel periodo pastorale', in: *Cahiers de l'AARS*, no. 15 (Saint-Benoist-sur-Mer: AARS, 2011), pp. 241–273.

Magail, Jérôme et al., 'Bronze Age and Iron Age decorated megaliths and funerary complexes in Mongolia and Southern Siberia', in: Laporte, Luc and Large, Jean-Marie (eds), *Megaliths of the World*, vol. 2 (Oxford: Archaeopress, 2022), pp. 747–766.

Magee, Peter, *The Archaeology of Prehistoric Arabia* (Cambridge: Cambridge University Press, 2014).

— 'When was the dromedary domesticated in the Ancient Near East?', in: *Zeitschrift für Orient-Archäologie*, vol. 8 (Berlin: Deutsches Archäologisches Institut, 2015), pp. 253–277.

Maher, Lisa, A, 'The Late Pleistocene of Arabia in relation to the Levant', in: Petraglia and Rose, *The Evolution of Human Populations in Arabia* (2009, q.v.), pp. 187–202.

Maier, Andreas, 'Population and settlement dynamics from the Gravettian to the Magdalenian', in: *Mitteilungen der Gesellschaft für Urgeschichte*, vol. 26 (Tübingen: MGFU, 2017), pp. 83–101.

Mallory J.P., *In Search of the Indo-Europeans: Language, Archaeology and Myth* (London: Thames & Hudson, 1989).

Mallory J.P. and Adams D.Q. (eds), *Encyclopedia of Indo-European Culture* (London: Fitzroy Dearborn, 1997).

— *The Oxford Introduction to Proto-Indo-European and the Proto-Indo-European World* (Oxford: Oxford University Press, 2006).

Mamedov, A.V., 'The Late Pleistocene–Holocene history of the Caspian Sea', *Quaternary International*, vols 41–42 (Amsterdam: Elsevier, 1997), pp. 161–166.

Manco, Jean, *Ancestral Journeys: The Peopling of Europe from the First Venturers to the Vikings* (London: Thames and Hudson, 2021).

Manninen, Mikael A., et al., 'First encounters in the north: Cultural diversity and gene flow in early Mesolithic Scandinavia', in: *Antiquity*, vol. 95, no. 380 (Cambridge: Cambridge University Press, 2021), pp. 310–328.

Maraqten, Mohammed, 'The Aramaic pantheon of Taymā', in: *Arabian Archaeology and Epigraphy*, vol. 7 (Oxford: Wiley, 1996), pp. 17–31.

Marquet, Jean-Claude et al., 'The earliest unambiguous Neanderthal engravings on cave walls: La Roche-Cotard, Loire Valley, France', in: *PLOS ONE*, vol. 18, no. 6, art no. 0286568 (San Francisco: PLOS, 2023).

Marretta, Alberto, 'Digging the past: One hundred years of research on Valcamonica rock art', in: *Adoranten* (q.v., 2008), pp. 36–54.

— *Valcamonica Rock Art Parks* (Capo di Ponte: Edizione del Centro, 2011).

— 'When it all begun: The Copper Age roots of Valcamonica rock art', in: *Adoranten* (q.v., 2012), pp. 52–67.

— 'Age of the heroes: A brief overview of Valcamonica rock-art during the Iron Age (I millennium BC)', in: *Adoranten* (q.v., 2013), pp. 75–88.

— 'Trading images: Exchange, transformation and identity in rock art from Valcamonica between the Bronze Age and the Iron Age', in: Skoglund, Ling and Bertilsson, *Picturing the Bronze Age* (2015, q.v.), pp. 105–119.

— 'Enlightening a rock art masterpiece: New research on Seraldina I Rock 12 (Valcamonica)' in: *Adoranten* (q.v., 2016), pp. 110–125.

— 'The duel in place: Morphological, structural and spatial variability of a basic scene among Valcamonica Iron Age rock art', in: Dodd and Meijer, *Giving the Past a Future* (2018, q.v.), pp. 153–174.

— 'From the core to the periphery: Notes on recent research in western rock art areas of Central Valcamonica', in: *Adoranten* (q.v., 2020), pp. 85–102.

Marretta, Alberto and Cittadini, Tiziana (eds), *Valcamonica Rock Art Parks* (Capo di Ponte: Centro Camuno die Studi Preistorici, 2011).

Martel, Álvaro Rodrigo, 'Semiotics and Meaning of Rock Art', in: Smith, Claire (ed.), *Encyclopedia of Global Archaeology* (New York: Springer, 2019), pp. 1–8.

Martin, Nils, 'A solemn praise to a West-Tibetan councillor at Kharul, Purik', in: *Zentralasiatische Studien*, vol. 46 (Bonn: ZAS, 2018), pp. 189–232.

Martirosyan,H.A.,Գեղամալեռներիհժայռապատկերները = *Petroglyphs of the Gegham Mountains* (Yerevan: Haykakan SSR G.A. Hratarakchutyun, 1981).

Martynov, A.J., Mariachev, A.N. and Abetekov, A.K., *Gravures rupestres de Saimaly-Tach*, ed. Karl Baipakov (Almaty: Ministère de l'instruction publique, 1992).

Mar'yashev, A.N., *Petroglyphs of South Kazakhstan and Semirechye* (Almaty: Margulan Institute of Archaeology, 1994).

Masov, Rahim et al. (eds), *National Museum of Antiquities of Tajikistan* (Dushanbe: Donish Institute, 2005).

Masson, V.M. and Ploskich, V.M., *По следам памятников истории и культуры Киргизстана = On the Track of Memorials to the History and Culture of Kyrgyzstan* (Frunze: Ilim, 1982).

Masson Mourey, Jules, 'De l'ancienneté du "Christ", dans la vallée des Merveilles', in: *Préhistoires Méditerranéennes*, vol. 6 (Aix-en-Provence: Maison Méditerranéenne des Sciences de l'Homme, 2018).

Mastrucci, Fabio and Gianelli, Gianna, 'Tikadiouine. Integrazione grafica, nuova analisi ed interpretazione. L'approvvigionamento alimentare nel periodo alimentare pastorale', in: *Cahiers de l'AARS*, no. 15 (Saint-Benoist-sur-Mer: AARS, 2011), pp. 241–273.

Mattet, Laurence (ed.), *Arts de l'Antiquité de l'Europe au Sud-Est asiatique* (Paris: Hazan, 2008).

Mattingly, David J., 'Garamantian oasis settlements in Fazzan', in: Sterry and Mattingly, *Urbanisation and State Formation in the Ancient Sahara and Beyond* (2020, q.v.), pp. 54–111.

Mazzena, Franco, 'Les stèles anthropomorphes en Europe', in: Cavazzini, *Dei di pietra / Dieux de pierre* (1998, q.v.), pp. 15–89.

— 'Les stèles anthropomorphes de l'aire mégalithique d'Aoste', in: Cavazzini, *Dei di pietra / Dieux de pierre* (1998, q.v.), pp. 91–127.

McCarthy, M.C, 'Lichenometry', in: *Earth Systems and Environmental Sciences: Encyclopedia of Quaternary Science* (2nd ed., Amsterdam: Elsevier, 2013), pp. 565–572.

McCorriston, Joy, *Persistant Pastoralism: Monuments and Settlements in the Archaeology of Dhofar* (Oxford: Archaeopress, 2023).

McDonald, Jo and Veth, Peter A. (eds), *A Companion to Rock Art* (Chichester: Blackwell, 2012).

McKinley, Jacqueline I. et al., 'Dead-Sea connections: A Bronze Age and Iron Age ritual scene on the Isle of Thanet', in: Koch, John T. and Cunliffe, Barry, *Celtic from the West*, vol. 2: *Rethinking the Bronze Age and the Arrival of Indo-European in Atlantic Europe* (Oxford: Oxbow, 2013), pp. 157–184.

Medina-Alcaide, María Ángeles et al., '35,000 years of recurrent visits inside Nerja cave (Andalusia, Spain) based on charcoals and soot micro-layers analyses', in: *Scientific Reports*, vol. 13, art. no. 5901 (London: Macmillan, 2023).

Meier, Philippe, 'Der Mann, der aus dem Dunkeln kam: Pierre Soulages wird hundert Jahre alt', in: *Neue Zürcher Zeitung* (Zurich: NZZ, 24 December 2019), p. 35.

Melheim, Lene, 'An epos carved in stone: Three heroes, one giant and a cosmic task', in: Bergerbrant, Sophie and Sabatini, Serena, *Counterpoint: Essays in Archaeology and Heritage Studies in Honour of Professor Kristian Kristiansen* (Oxford: Archaeopress, 2013), pp. 273–282.

Melheim, Lene and Ling, Johan, 'Taking the stranger on board: The two maritime legacies of bronze age rock art', in: Skoglund, Ling and Bertilsson, *North Meets South* (2017, q.v.), pp. 59–86.

Meller, Harald (ed.), *Der geschmiedete Himmel. Die weite Welt im Herzen Europas vor 3600 Jahren* (Stuttgart: Theiss, 2004).

— 'Das Wissen um Zeit und Raum. Himmelsdarstellungen in der Bronzezeit', in: Wemhoff, Matthias and Rind, Michael M. (eds), *Bewegte Zeiten. Archäologie in Deutschland* (Petersberg: Michael Imhof, 2019), pp. 351–359.

Meller, Harald, Knoll, Franziska and Dresely, Veit, 'Die Felsbilder von Ughtasar, Provinz Sjunik', in: *Archäologie in Armenien* (Halle: Landesamt für Denkmalpflege und Archäologie Sachsen-Anhalt, 2011), pp. 131–142.

Menardi Noguera, Alessandro, 'Anoa-1 and the body proportions of the Niola Doa corpulent figures (Ennedi, Chad)', in: Anati (ed.), *Expression*, no. 29 (q.v., 2020), pp. 42–56.

Menghin, Wilfried et al. (eds) *Im Zeichen des goldenen Greifen. Königsgräber der Skythen* (Munich: Prestel, 2007).

Mercier, Norbert et al., 'OSL dating of quaternary deposits associated with the parietal art of the Tassili-n-Ajjer plateau (Central Sahara)', in: *Quarternary Geochronology*, vol. 10 (Amsterdam: Elsevier, 2012), pp. 367–373.

Méry, Sophie, 'The first oases in Eastern Arabia: Society and craft technology, in the 3rd millennium BC at Hili, United Arab Emirates', in: *Revue d'Éthnoécologie*, vol. 4 (Paris: Open Edition, 2013), pp. 63–79.

Messili, Lamia et al. 'Direct ^{14}C dating of early and mid-Holocene Saharan pottery', in: *Radiocarbon*, vol. 55 (Tucson: University of Arizona, 2013), pp. 1391–1402.

Meyering, Lisa-Elen, 'Fleshing out the stickman: A hypothesis about the long-legged anthropomorphs in Scandinavian rock art', in: Dodd and Meijer, *Giving the Past a Future* (2018, q.v.), pp. 136–152.

Mikkel, Christian and Hansen, Dam, 'Interpreting a Bronze Age motif: Revisiting the hand signs of southern Scandinavia', in: *Adoranten* (2020, q.v.), pp. 57–73.

Miklashevich, Elena, 'Rock art research in Siberia and Central Asia, 2000–2004', in: Bahn et al., *Rock Art Studies: News of the World*, vol. 3 (2008, q.v.), pp. 138–178.

Milstreu, Gerhard, 'Updating rock art: Re-cut rock art images (with a special emphasis on ship carvings)', in: *Adoranten* (q.v., 2017), pp. 37–47.

Milstreu, Gerhard and Dodd, James, 'The cup-mark: The smallest, most frequent, cosmopolitan and most complicated symbol', in: *Adoranten* (q.v., 2018), pp. 5–29.

Milstreu, Gerhard and Prøhl, Henning, *Dokumentation och registrering av hällristninggar i Tanum / Documentation and Registration of Rock Art*, vols 1–4 (Tanumshede, Sweden: Hällristnings Museum, 1966, 1999, 2009, 2020).

Mineta, Katsuhiko et al., 'Population structure of indigenous inhabitants of Arabia', in: *PLOS Genetics* (San Francisco: PLOS, 2021), p. 1–18.

Mission archéologique franco-saoudienne dans la région de Najrān, 2007–2012, 5 reports (Paris : Orient & Méditerranée, UMR 8167, 2007–2012).

Moawiyah, M. Ibrahim and Strachan, Laura M., *The Tangible and Intangible Cultural Landscape of Wadi Bani Kharus: Investigations in the Sultanate of Oman* (Oxford: Archaeopress, 2020).

Moberg, Carl-Axel, *Kiviks graven* (Stockholm: Riksantikvarieämbetet, 1975).

— *The Kivik Grave* (Stockholm: Central Board of National Antiquities, 1992).

Mock, John, 'New discoveries of rock art in Afghanistan's Wakhan Corridor and Pamir: A preliminary study', in: *The Silk Road*, vol. 11 (Berkeley: The Silkroad House, 2013), pp. 36–55.

Mohammad, Ghulam, 'Festivals and folklore of Gilgit', in: *Memoirs of the Asiatic Society of Bengal*, vol. 1, no. 7 (Calcutta: Asiatic Society of Bengal, 1905), pp. 93–127.

Mohns, Alexander D.L., 'Buddha on the rocks: Analyzing the anthropomorphic Buddhist rock carvings on the Silk Roads along the Upper Indus', bachelor thesis (Leiden: University of Leiden, 2018).

Mollet, Jörg and Schmidt, Aurel (eds), *Swiss-Libyan Art Project*, https://www.swiss-libyan-art-project.info/deutsch/index.php?m=mm1.

Molodin, Vjačeslav I. et al., 'Das skythenzeitliche Kriegergrab aus Olin-Kurin-Gol. Neue Entdeckungen in der Permafrostzone des mongolischen Altaj', in: *Eurasia Antiqua. Zeitschrift für Archäologie Eurasiens*, vol. 14 (2008) (Mainz: Philipp von Zabern, 2009), pp. 241–265.

Molodin, Vyacheslav I. and Cheremissin [Cheremisin], D.V., 'Pétroglyphes de l'âge du bronze du plateau d'Ukok. A propos des représentations de personnages avec une coiffure fongiforme', in: *Arts Asiatiques*, vol. 54 (Paris: Musée national d'art asiatique Guimet, 1999), pp. 148–152.

— 'Petroglyphs of the Ukok Plateau', in: *Archaeology, Ethnology and Anthropology of Eurasia*, vol. 32 (Novosibirsk: Archaeological Institute and Academy of Sciences, 2007), pp. 91–101.

— 'The "Kalgutsinsky" style in the rock art of Central Asia', in: *Archaeology, Ethnology and Anthropology of Eurasia*, vol. 47 (Novosibirsk: Archaeological Institute and Academy of Sciences, 2019), pp. 12–26.

Molodin, V.I., Cheremisin, D.V. et al., 'Chronology of rock art of the Russian and Mongolian Altai: From the Paleolithic to the late Middle Ages', in: *Archaeology, Ethnology and Anthropology of Eurasia*, vol. 51, no. 4 (Novosibirsk: Russian Academy of Sciences, 2023), pp. 65–77.

Moorcroft, William and Trebeck, George, *Travels in the Himalayan Provinces of Hindustan and the Panjab; in Ladakh and Kashmir; in Peshawar, Kabul, Kunduz, and Bokhara, from 1819 to 1825* (2 vols, London: John Murray, 1841).

Morgan, Christopher et al., 'Paleolakes, archaeology, and Late Quarternary palaeoenvironments in northwestern Mongolia', in: *Quarternary Research*, vol. 109 (Cambridge: Cambridge University Press, 2022).

Mörner, Nils-Axel and Lind, Bob G., 'Long-distance travel and trading in the Bronze Age: The East Mediterranean–Scandinavia Case', in: *Archaeological Discovery*, vol. 3, no. 4 (Wuhan: Scientific Research Publishing, 2015), pp. 129–139.

Morphy, Howard, 'Recursive and iterative process in Australian rock art: An anthropological perspective', in: McDonald and Veth, *Companion to Rock Art* (2012, q.v.), pp. 294–305.

Morrissey, Alan, 'Shuwaymis: Painting tales of an intriguing past', in: *Saudi Voyager Online* (2018): www.saudiarabiatourismguide.com/shuwaymis/.

Mortensen, Karl, *A Handbook of Norse Mythology* (Garden City NY: Dover Publications, 2021).

Morup, Tashi, 'Pre-Tibetan Buddhist rock art of Ladakh' (2021): https://www.sahapedia.org/pre-tibetan-buddhist-rock-art-ladakh.

Mouchet, Annie, 'Sur les traces de Charles Brenans avec Bernard Fouilleux, à la Tasile-n-Ažžar', in: *Cahiers de l'AARS*, no. 24 (Saint-Benoist-sur-Mer: AARS, 2023), pp. 187–208.

Mowaljarlai, David and Malnic, Jutta, *Yorro Yorro: Everything Standing up Alive. Spirit of the Kimberley* (Broome: Magabala Books, 1993).

Mukhareva, A.N., 'Camel scenes in the rock art of the Minusinsk Basin', in: *Archaeology, Ethnology and Anthropology of Eurasia*, vol. 31 (Novosibirsk: Russian Academy of Sciences, 2007), pp. 102–109.

Müller, D.H., *Epigraphische Denkmäler aus Arabien. Nach Abklatschen und Copien des Herrn Professor Dr. Julius Euting in Strasburg* (Vienna: Denkschriften der kaiserlichen Akademie der Wissenschaften, 1889).

Muzzolini, Alfred, *Les images rupestres du Sahara* (Castres: istor/published by the author, 1995).

Mykhailova, Nataliia, 'Shaman – Hunter – Deer', in: *Adoranten* (q.v., 2012), pp. 84–98.

— '"Celestial Deer": The flight from the Stone Age to the Middle Ages', in: Anati, *The Function of Art* (q.v., 2021), pp. 97–104.

Nagler, Anatoli. *Kurgane der Mozdok-Steppe in Nordkaukasien.* (Marie Leidorf, Espelkamp 1996).

— 'О стилизованных изображениях оленей на оленных камнях Центральной Азии = Concerning the stilistic representation of deer on deer stones of Central Asia': in *Terra Scythika: Материалы международного симпозиума 'Terra Scythika' = Materials of the International Symposium 'Terra Scythika'* (Novosibirsk: Archaeological Institute and Academy of Sciences, 2011), advance copy.

Napolskikh V. V., 'Earth-Diver Myth (A812) in northern Eurasia and North America: Twenty years later', in: Frog, Anna-Leena Siikala and Stepanova, Eila, *Mythic Discourses: Studies in Uralic Traditions* (Helsinki: Studia Fennica Folkloristica, 2012), pp. 120–140.

Nash, George H., 'Megalithic rock art of the Mediterranean and Atlantic seaboard Europe', in: McDonald and Veth, *Companion to Rock Art* (2012, q.v.), pp. 127–142.

— 'Art and environment: How can rock art inform on past environments?' in: David and McNiven, *The Oxford Handbook of the Archaeology and Anthropology of Rock Art* (2018, q.v.), pp. 411–433.

Nash, George and Chippindale, Christopher (eds), *European Landscapes of Rock-Art* (Abingdon: Routledge, 2012).

Nash, George H. et al., 'Unlocking a hidden landscape: Preliminary fieldwork at Qarn Bint Sa'ud, Abu Dhabi', in: *Current World Archaeology*, vol. 116 (London: Current Publishing, 2022), pp. 32–38.

Nash Briggs, Daphne, 'Reading the images on Iron Age coins: 1. The sun-boat and its passengers. 2. Horses of the day and night. 3. Some cosmic wolves' (n.d.): https://oxford.academia.edu/DaphneNashBriggs.

Natuniewicz-Sekula, Magdalena and Rein Seehusen, Christina, 'Baltic connections: Some remarks about studies of boat-graves from the Roman Iron Age. Finds from the Slusegård and Weklice cemeteries', in: Lund Hansen, Ulla and Bitner-Wróblewska, Anna, *Worlds Apart? Contacts Across the Baltic Sea in the Iron Age: Network Denmark–Poland, 2005–2008* (Copenhagen: Kongelige Nordiske Oldkriftselskab, 2010), pp. 287–313.

Naudinot, Nicholas et al., 'Divergence in the evolution of Paleolithic symbolic and technological systems: The shining bull and engraved tablets of Rocher de l'Impératrice', *PLOS ONE*, vol. 12, no. 3 (San Francisco: PLOS, 2017).

Nayeem, Muhammed Abdul, *The Rock Art of Arabia* (Hyderabad: Hyderabad Publishers, 2000).

Neelis, Jason, 'Overland shortcuts for the transmission of Buddhism', in: Alcock, Susan et al. (eds), *Highways, Byways and Road Systems in the Pre-Modern World* (Malden: Wiley Blackwell, 2012), pp. 12–32.

Nehmé, Laïla, 'Nouvelles gravures rupestres à Petra: Techniques, religion, épigraphie', in: *Studies in the History and Archaeology of Jordan*, vol. 5 (Amman: Department of Antiquities, 1995), pp. 427–435.

— *Archéologie au pays des Nabatéens d'Arabie* (Paris: Hémisphères, 2019).

Nehmé, Laïla and Alsuhaibani, Abdulrahman (eds), *AlUla. Merveille d'Arabie* (Paris: Gallimard, 2019).

Neubauer, Simon et al., 'The evolution of modern human brain shape', in: *Science Advances*, vol. 4, no. 1 (Washington DC: AAAS, 2018).

Neugebauer, Ina et al., 'The unexpectedly short Holocene Humid Period in northern Arabia', in: *Communications Earth and Environment*, vol. 3, art. no. 47 (London: Macmillan, 2022).

Newton, Iris, *Die Bilderwelt von Lascaux* (Berlin: Palm Verlag, 2015).

Nicoll, Kathleen, 'Radiocarbon chronologies for prehistoric human occupation and hydroclimatic change in Egypt and northern Sudan', in: *Geoarchaeology*, vol. 16, no. 1 (Hoboken: Wiley, 2001), pp. 47–64.

Nielsen, Jesper et al., 'Seductive similarities: A comment on Gerum, Trans-Atlantic contacts, and analogies', in: *Adoranten* (q.v., 2009), pp. 71–80.

Nielsen, Poul Otto, *National Museum of Denmark: Danish Prehistory* (Copenhagen: The National Museum, 2016).

Nielsen, Svend, 'The Gundestrup Cauldron: New scientific and technical investigations', in: *Acta Archaeologica*, vol. 76, no. 2 (Hoboken: Wiley, 2005), pp. 1–58.

Nielsson, Per, 'New discoveries of rock carvings and settlements at Himmelstalund', in: *Adoranten* (q.v., 2007), pp. 20–28.

— 'A Life Aquatic? Looking at the relationships between settlements, rock art and sea levels in the Himmelstalund region of eastern Sweden', in: Fredell et al., *Representations and Communications* (2010, q.v.), pp. 1–15.

— 'The Beauty is in the Act of the Beholder: South Scandinavian Rock Art from a Uses of the Past-Perspective', in: Back Danielsson, Ing-Marie, Fahlander, Fredrik and Sjöstrand, Ylva (eds), *Encountering Imagery: Materialities, Perceptions, Relations* (Stockholm: Stockholm University, 2012), pp. 77–110.

Nimura, Courtney, *Prehistoric Rock Art in Scandinavia: Agency and Environmental Change* (Oxford: Oxbow, 2016).

Noguera, Alessandro Menardi, 'The Duellers' Shelter, Ennedi (Chad)', in: *Cahiers de l'AARS*, no. 22 (Saint-Benoist-sur-Mer: AARS, 2021), pp. 183–204.

Nordbladh, Jarl, 'Carl Georg Brunius: An early nineteenth-century pioneer in Swedish petroglyph research', in: Skoglund, Ling and Bertilsson, *Picturing the Bronze Age* (2015, q.v.), pp. 121–127.

Norris, Jérôme, 'Les inscriptions préislamiques associées à l'art rupestre de l'Arabie du Nord-Ouest', in: *L'art rupestre en Arabie. Dossiers d'Archéologie*, no. 407 (2021, q.v.), pp. 56–59.

Norsted, Terje, 'The cave paintings of Norway', in: *Adoranten* (q.v., 2013), pp. 5–24.

Noujaim, Souraya and Daucé, Noëmi (eds), *Routes d'Arabie. Trésors archéologiques de l'Arabie Saoudite* (Beirut: Kaph Books, 2018).

Novozhenov, Victor A., *Communications and the Earliest Wheeled Transport of Eurasia*, ed. E.E. Kuzmina (Moscow: TAUS Publishing, 2012).

— *Rock Art Chronicles of Golden Steppe*, vol. 1: *Model of Communication in Antiquity and Early Middle Ages* (Almaty: UNESCO Centre for the Rapprochement of Cultures, 2020).

Nowgorodowa, Eleonora, *Alte Kunst der Mongolei* (Leipzig: VEB E.A. Seemann, 1979).

Nylén, Erik and Lamm, Jan Peder, *Stones, Ships and Symbols: The Picture Stones of Gotland from the Viking Age and Before* (Stockholm: Gidlunds Bokförlag, 1988).

Obrist, Hans Ulrich, *A Brief History of Curating* (Geneva: JRP-Éditions, 2021).

Oeschger, Ernesto, 'Sahara Algeria: Rock art in Oued Djerat and the Tefedest region', in: *Adoranten* (q.v., 2004), pp. 5–19.

Ofer, Bar-Josef, 'The Natufian Culture in the Levant, threshold to the origins of agriculture', in: *Evolutionary Anthropology*, vol. 6, no. 5 (Hoboken: Wiley, 1998), pp. 159–177.

O'Hara, Kieran D., *Cave Art and Climate Change* (Bloomington: Archway, 2014).

Okladnikow, Aleksej Pawlowitsch, *Der Hirsch mit dem goldenen Geweih. Vorgeschichtliche Felsbilder Sibiriens* (Wiesbaden: F.A. Brockhaus), 1972.

Oktaviana, Adhi Agus et al., 'Narrative cave art in Indonesia by 51,200 years ago', in: *Nature*, vol. 631 (London: Macmillan, 2024), pp. 814–818.

Olivieri, Luca Maria et al. (eds), *Pictures in Transformation: Rock Art Research between Central Asia and the Subcontinent* (Oxford: BAR, 2010).

Olsen Sandra L. and Bryant, Richard T., *Stories in the Rock: Exploring Saudi Arabian Rock Art* (Pittsburgh: Carnegie Museum of Natural History, 2013).

Online Corpus of the Inscriptions of Ancient North Arabia (Oxford: University of Oxford, 2012–): https://krc.web.ox.ac.uk/article/ociana.

Oosterwijk, Barbara, 'Caught in a net: An analysis of net-figures in the rock art of Bohuslän and southern Sweden', in: *Adoranten* (q.v., 2020), pp. 96–114.

Orchard, Andy, *Dictionary of Norse Myth and Legend* (London: Weidenfeld & Nicolson, 2022).

Ottoni, Claudio et al., 'Mitochondrial haplogroup H1 in North Africa: An Early Holocene arrival from Iberia', in: *PLOS ONE*, vol. 5, no. 10, art. no. 13378 (San Francisco: PLOS, 2010).

— 'Deep into the roots of the Libyan Tuareg: A Genetic Survey of Their Paternal Heritage', in: *American Journal of Physical Anthropology*, vol. 145, no. 1 (Hoboken: Wiley, 2011), pp. 118–124.

Outram, Alan K., 'Animal domestications', in: Cummings et al., *The Oxford Handbook of the Archaeology and Anthropology of Hunter-Gatherers* (2014, q.v.), pp. 749–763.

Ouzman, Sven, 'Towards a mindscape of landscape: Rock-art as expression of world-understanding', in: Chippindale and Taçon, *The Archaeology of Rock-Art* (1998, q.v.), pp. 30–41.

Pace, Davide, *Petroglifi dei colli di Grosio* (Grosio: Istituto archeologico valtellinese and Pro Loco Grosio, 1977).

Paillet, Patrick and Robert, Éric (eds), *Arts et préhistoire* (Paris: Museum national d'histoire naturelle, 2022).

Pakhunov, Alexander et al., 'The camel in the cave: Ice Age art in the Ural Mountains', in: *Current World Archaeology*, vol. 87 (London: Current Publishing, 2018), pp. 10–11.

Parker, Adrian et al., 'The Early to Mid-Holocene moist period in Arabia: Some recent evidence from lacustrine sequences in eastern and south-western Arabia', in: *Proceedings of the Seminar for Arabian Studies*, vol. 36 (Oxford: Archaeopress, 2006), pp. 243–255.

— 'A record of Holocene climate change from lake geochemical analyses in southeastern Arabia', in: *Quaternary Research*, vol. 60 (Amsterdam: Elsevier, 2006), pp. 465–476.

— 'Pleistocene climate change in Arabia: Developing a framework for hominin dispersal over the last 350 ka', in: Petraglia and Rose, *The Evolution of Human Populations in Arabia* (2009, q.v.), pp. 39–49.

Parzinger, Hermann, *Die frühen Völker Eurasiens. Vom Neolithikum bis zum Mittelalter* (Munich: C.H. Beck, 2006).

— *Die Kinder des Prometheus. Eine Geschichte der Menschheit vor der Erfindung der Schrift* (Darmstadt: WBG, 2015).

Paula, Wilhelm, 'Wagendarstellungen in der Sahara und ihre Beziehungen zu Alt-Europa', in: *Almogaren*, vols 24–5 (Korb: Institutum Canarium, 1994), pp. 375–387.

Pearson, Kristen, 'Chasing the shaman's steed: The horse in myth from Central Asia to Scandinavia', in: Mair, Victor H. (ed.), *Sino-Platonic Papers*, no. 269 (Philadelphia: University of Pennsylvania, 2017), pp. 1–21.

Peissel, Michel, *Zanskar. Royaume oublié aux confins du Tibet* (Paris: Robert Laffont, 1979).

Penck, A.R., *Mein Denken*, ed. Klaus Gallwitz (Frankfurt am Main: Suhrkamp, 1986).

Petchey, Fiona, 'Radiocarbon dating in rock art research', in: David and McNiven, *The Oxford Handbook of the Archaeology and Anthropology of Rock Art* (2018, q.v.), pp. 927–943.

Petech, Luciano, *The Kingdom of Ladakh, c. 950–1842 A.D.* (Rome: ISMEO, 1977).

Petraglia, Michael D. et al., 'Acheulean landscapes and large cutting tools assemblages in the Arabian Peninsula,' in: Petraglia and Rose, *The Evolution of Human Populations in Arabia* (2009, q.v.), pp. 103–116.

Petraglia, Michael D., and Rose, Jeffrey I. (eds), *The Evolution of Human Populations in Arabia: Palaeoenvironments, Prehistory and Genetics* (Dordrecht: Springer, 2009).

Pettitt, Paul, 'The European Upper Palaeolithic', in: Cummings et al., *The Oxford Handbook of the Archaeology and Anthropology of Hunter-Gatherers* (2014, q.v.), pp. 279–309.

Pfisterer, Ulrich, 'Altamira – oder: Die Anfänge von Kunst und Kunstwissenschaft', in: Mosebach, Martin (ed.), *Die Gärten von Capri* (Berlin: Akademischer Verlag, 2007), pp. 13–80.

Philby, H. St J. B., *The Heart of Arabia: A Record of Travel and Exploration* (2 vols, London: Constable, 1922).

— *The Empty Quarter: Being a Description of the Great South Desert of Arabia Known as Rub' al Khali* (London: Constable, 1933).

— *Sheba's Daughters: Being a Record of Travel in Southern Arabia* (London: Methuen, 1939).

— 'The lost ruins of Quraiya', in: *Geographical Journal*, vol. 117, no. 4 (London: Royal Geographical Society, 1952), pp. 448–458.

Pike, Alistair W.G., 'Uranium–thorium dating of cave art', in: David and McNiven, *The Oxford Handbook of the Archaeology and Anthropology of Rock Art* (2018, q.v.), pp. 953–967.

Pike, Alistair W.G. et al., 'U-series dating of paleolithic art in 11 caves in Spain', in: *Science*, vol. 336, no. 6087 (Washington DC: AAAS, 2011), pp. 1409–1414.

Pim, Joám Evans et al. (eds), *Traditional Marking Systems: A Preliminary Survey* (London and Dover: Dunkling Books, 2010).

Plato, *The Republic*, trans. Benjamin Jowett (1888): https://classics.mit.edu/Plato/republic.html.

Pliny the Elder [C. Plinius Secundus], *The Natural History*, trans. John Bostock and H.T. Riley (1857): www.gutenberg.org/ebooks/author/50041.

Poggiani Keller, Raffaela et al., *The Megalithic Area Saint-Martin-de-Corléans Archaeological Park and Museum* (Aosta: Assessorato Instruzione e Cultura, 2016).

Pohle, Perdita, 'Felsbilder in Zentralasien. Quellen zur Kultur- und Landschaftsgeschichte', in: *Geographische Rundschau*, vol. 49 (Braunschweig: Westermann, 1997), pp. 287–292.

Poikalainen, Väino, 'Some statistics about rock carvings at Lake Onega', in: *Folklore*, vol. 11 (Tartu: Institute of the Estonian Language, 1999).

Poikalainen, Väino and Ernits, Enn, *Rock Carvings of Lake Onega*, vol. 1: *The Vodla Region* (Tartu: Estonian Society of Prehistoric Art, 1998).

— *Rock Carvings of Lake Onega*, vol. 2: *The Besov Nos Region: Karetski and Peri Localities* (Tartu: Estonian Society of Prehistoric Art, 2019).

— *Rock Carvings of Lake Onega*, vol. 3: *The Besov Nos Region: Besov Nos, Kladovets, Gazhi and Guri Localities* (Tartu: Estonian Society of Prehistoric Art, 2021).

Polkowski, Paweł, 'The Life of Petroglyphs: A Biographical Approach to Rock Art in the Dakhleh Oasis, Egypt', in: *American Indian Rock Art*, vol. 41 (American Rock Art Research Association, 2015, pp. 43-55.

Polkowski, Paweł et al., 'Rock art research in the Dakhleh Oasis, Western Desert (Egypt)', in: *Sahara*, no. 24 (www.saharajournal.com, 2013), pp. 101–118.

Polo, Marco, *The Book of Ser Marco Polo*, trans. Henry Yule (2 vols, New York: Charles Scribner's sons, 1926).

Polzer, Brita, 'Art Safiental: Horizontal-Vertikal', in: *Kunst Bulletin*, 9 (Zurich: Schweizerischer Kunstverein, 2018), pp. 118–119.

Pommereau, Claude (ed.), *Préhistomania. Trésors mondiaux de l'art rupestre* (Paris: Beaux Arts & Cie, 2023).

Potts, Daniel T., 'Bactrian camels and Bactrian dromedary hybrids', in: *The Silk Road*, vol. 3, no. 1 (Berkeley: The Silkroad House, 2005), pp. 49–57.

— 'The Arabian Peninsula, 600 BCE to 600 CE', in: Huth, Martin and Van Alfen, Peter, *Coinage of the Caravan Kingdoms* (New York: The American Numismatic Society, 2010), pp. 27–64.

— 'The story of the origins', in: Al-Ghabban et al., *Roads of Arabia* (2010, q.v.), pp. 70–79.

Powell, Eric A., 'Breaking the code of the Kushan kings', in: *Archaeology*, March/April 2024 (Boston: Archaeological Institute of America), pp. 50–55.

— 'Europe's lost Bronze Age civilization', in: *Archaeology*, November/December 2024 (Boston: Archaeological Institute of America), pp. 34–37.

Price, T. Douglas, *Ancient Scandinavia: An Archaeological History from the First Humans to the Vikings* (Oxford: Oxford University Press, 2015).

Priuli, Ausilio, *Valcamonica: Valley of Prehistory* (Capo di Ponte: Priuli Edizione, n.d.).

Procopius, *History of the Wars*, books 1–2, trans. H.B. Dewing (1924; Cambridge MA and London: Harvard University Press, 2006).

Putkinen, Niko, 'Late Weichselian deglaciation chronology and palaeoenvironments in northern Karelia, NW Russia', doctoral thesis, Geological Survey of Finland (Espoo: University of Oulu, 2011).

Quiles, Anita et al., 'A high-precision chronological model for the decorated Upper Paleolithic cave of Chauvet-Pont d'Arc, Ardèche, France', in: *Proceedings of the National Academy of Sciences*, vol. 113, no. 17 (Washington: National Academy of Sciences, 2016), pp. 4670–4675.

Radloff, Wilhelm, *Aus Sibirien* (2 vols, Leipzig: Weigel Nachfolger, 1893).

Radula, Malgorzata et al., 'Palaeoclimate has a major effect on the diversity of endemic species in the hotspot of mountain biodiversity in Tajikistan', in: *Scientific Reports*, vol. 11, art. no. 18684 (London: Macmillan, 2021).

Ramirez, Primitiva Bueno and Behrmann, Rodrigo de Balbin, 'Holocene rock art of the Iberian Peninsula, 2005–2008', in: Bahn et al., *Rock Art Studies: News of the World*, vol. 4 (2012, q.v.), pp. 45–64.

Ramqvist, Per, 'Rock-art and settlement: Issues of spatial order in the prehistoric rock-art of Fenno-Scandia', in: Nash and Chippindale, *European Landscapes of Rock-Art* (2012, q.v.), pp. 144–157.

Ramskou, Thorkild, *Prehistoric Denmark* (Copenhagen: The National Museum, 1966).

Rankama, Tuija and Kankaanpää, Jarmo, 'Eastern arrivals in post-glacial Lapland: The Sujala site 10,000 cal. BP', in: *Antiquity*, vol. 82 (Cambridge: Cambridge University Press, 2008), pp. 884–899.

Ranov, Vadim, 'L'exploration archéologique du Pamir', in: *Bulletin de l'École française de d'Extrême Orient*, vol. 73 (Paris: EFEO, 1984), pp. 67–97.

— 'Petroglyphs of Tajikistan', in: Tashbayeva et al., *Petroglyphs of Central Asia* (2001, q.v.), pp. 122–150.

Ranov, Vadim and Veber, Cecile, *Guide to the Principal Archaeological Sites of the Eastern Pamirs (Tajikistan)* (Khorog: ACTED, n.d.): https://www.marcovasta.net/viaggi/PamirOrientale/Documenti/Archaeology-brochure.pdf.

Ranta, Michael et al., 'Levels of narrativity in Scandinavian Bronze Age petroglyphs', in: *Cambridge Archaeological Journal*, vol. 29, no. 3 (Cambridge: McDonald Institute, 2019), pp. 497–516.

— 'Hunting stories in Scandinavian rock art: Aspects of "tellability" in the North versus the South', in: *Oxford Journal of Archaeology*, vol. 39, no. 3 (Hoboken: Wiley, 2020), pp. 2282–2246.

Rasmussen, S.O. et al., 'A new Greenland ice core chronology for the last glacial termination', in: *Journal for Geophysical Research: Atmospheres*, vol. 111, no. D6 (Washington DC: AGU, 2006), pp. 1–16.

Raswan, Carl R., *Black Tents of Arabia* (Boston: Little, Brown and Co., 1935).

Reckel, Johannes, *Saimaluu Tash. Antike Felsbilder in den Hochgebirgen Kirgistans / Ancient Rock Art in the High Mountains of Kyrgyzstan* (Göttingen: Göttinger Verlag der Kunst, 2024).

Reckel, Johannes and Schatz, Merle, *Fliegende Hirsche und Sonnengötter. Prähistorische Gesellschaften in Felsbildern Zentralasiens* (Oppenheim am Rhein: Nünnerich-Asmus, 2022).

Reichle, Ingeborg, 'Die Entdeckung prähistorischer Kunst und "Buschmannmalereien" vor dem Ersten Weltkrieg', in: Kohl, Karl-Heinz et al., *Kunst der Vorzeit. Texte zu den Felsbildern der Sammlung Frobenius* (Frankfurt a.M.: Frobenius-Institut, 2016), pp. 23–31.

Renfrew, Colin, *Archaeology and Language: The Puzzle of Indo-European Origins* (London: Jonathan Cape, 1987).

Reutova, M.A., *Petroglyphs in Sarmishsay: The Methodological Recommendations for Conservation* (Samarkand: International Institute for Central Asian Studies, 2009).

Rhie, Marylin Martin, *Early Buddhist Art of China and Central Asia* (3 vols, Leiden: Brill, 1999, 2002, 2010).

Riede, Felix, 'The resettlement of Northern Europe', in: Cummings et al., *The Oxford Handbook of the Archaeology and Anthropology of Hunter-Gatherers* (2014, q.v.), pp. 556–581.

Rifkin, Riaan F. et al., 'Characterising pigments on 30,000-year-old portable art from Apollo 11 Cave, Karas Region, southern Namibia', in: *Journal of Archaeological Science: Reports*, vol. 5 (Amsterdam: Elsevier, 2016), pp. 336–347.

Rig Veda, ed. Peter Michel (1923; 2 vols, Wiesbaden: Marix, 2008).

— *The Hymns of the Rig Veda* [vol. 1, trans. Ralph T.H. Griffith (Benares: 1889)]. https://archive.org/details/hymnsrigveda02grifgoog/page/n28/mode/2up.

Riris, Philip et al., 'Monumental snake engravings of the Orinoco River', in: *Antiquity*, vol. 98 (Cambridge: Cambridge University Press, 2024), pp. 724–742.

Rivero, Olivia and Ruiz, Juan F., 'The rock art of sub-Scandinavian Europe', in: David and McNiven, *The Oxford Handbook of the Archaeology and Anthropology of Rock Art* (2018, q.v.), pp. 73–94.

Roberts, Richard G., 'Optical dating of rock art', in: David and McNiven, *The Oxford Handbook of the Archaeology and Anthropology of Rock Art* (2018, q.v.), pp. 945–952.

Robin, Christian Julien, 'Le royaume Hujride dit "Royaume de Kinda", entre Himyar et Byzance', in: *Comptes rendus des séances de l'Académie des Inscriptions et Belles-Lettres (CRAI)*, vol. 2 (Paris: Institut de France, 1996), pp. 665–714.

— 'Joseph, dernier roi des Himyar (de 522 à 525, ou une des années suivantes)', in: *Jerusalem Studies in Arabic and Islam*, vol. 34 (Jerusalem: Hebrew University, 2008), pp. 1–124.

— 'Nagrān vers l'époque du massacre : notes sur l'histoire politique, économique et institutionnelle et sur l'introduction du christianisme', in: Beaucamp, et al., *Juifs et Chrétiens en Arabie aux Vème et VIème siècles* (Paris: ACHCByz, 2010), pp. 39–107.

— 'Antiquity', in: Al-Ghabban et al., *Roads of Arabia* (2010, q.v.), pp. 81–99.

— 'L'Arabie à la veille de l'islam. La campagne d'Abraha contre La Mecque, ou la guerre des pèlerinages', in: de La Genière, Juliette et al. (eds), *Les sanctuaires et leur rayonnement dans le monde méditerranéen de l'antiquité à l'époque moderne. Actes du 20ème colloque de la Villa Kérylos à Beaulieu-sur-Mer les 9 et 10 octobre 2009*. Publications de l'Académie des Inscriptions et Belles-Lettres, vol. 21 (Paris: Institut de France, 2010), pp. 213–242.

— 'Languages and scripts', in: Al-Ghabban et al., *Roads of Arabia* (2010, q.v.), pp. 119–131.

— 'Images divines', in: Sachet et al., *Dieux et déesses d'Arabie* (2012, q.v.), pp. 5–118.

— 'Abraha et la reconquête de l'Arabie déserte: un réexamen de l'inscription Ryckmans 506 = Murayghan 1', in: *Jerusalem Studies in Arabic and Islam*, vol. 39 (Jerusalem: Hebrew University, 2012), pp. 11–31.

— 'Un sanctuaire rupestre au dieu dhu-Samawi à an-Halkan', in: Sachet et al., *Dieux et déesses d'Arabie* (2012, q.v.), pp. 119–128.

— 'Le roi Himyarite Tha'ran Yuhan'im (avant 325–vers 375). Stabilisation politique et réforme religieuse', in: *Jerusalem Studies in Arabic and Islam*, vol. 41 (Jerusalem: Hebrew University, 2014), pp. 1–95.

— 'Les expéditions militaires du roi Abraha dans l'Arabie désertique dans les années 548–565 de l'ère chrétienne', in: *Comptes rendus des séances de l'Académie des Inscriptions et Belles-Lettres (CRAI)*, no. 3 (Paris: Institut de France, 2018), pp. 1313–1376.

— 'La faune de l'Arabie heureuse: Les textes et les images rupestres de Himà', in: Jouanna, Jacques et al. (eds) *Vie et climat d'Hésiode à Montesquieu* (Paris: De Boccard, 2018), pp. 319–84.

— 'Art rupestre et inscriptions de la région de Himà', in: *L'art rupestre en Arabie. Dossiers d'Archéologie*, no. 407 (2021, q.v.), pp. 62–67.

— 'Les gravures d'une nécropole Chrétienne à Himà', in: *L'art rupestre en Arabie. Dossiers d'Archéologie*, no. 407 (2021, q.v.), pp. 68–71.

— 'Le Guèze maquillé en saba'ique des inscriptions royales aksūmites (Éthiopie antique)', in : *Hiéroglossie*, vol. 3 (Paris: Collège de France, 2022), pp. 171–205.

Robin, Christian Julien et al., 'Inscriptions antiques de la région de Najran (Arabie séoudite méridionale) : nouveaux jalons pour l'histoire de l'écriture, de la langue et du calendrier arabe' in: *Comptes rendus des séances de l'Académie des Inscriptions et Belles-Lettres (CRAI)*, no. 3 (Paris: Institut de France, 2014), pp. 1033–1127.

— *A Stopover in the Steppe: The Rock Carvings of 'Ān Jamal near Himà (Region of Najrān, Saudi Arabia)* (Paris: Académie des Inscriptions et Belles Lettres, 2022).

Robin, Christian Julien and Antonini de Maigret, Sabina, 'Le cheval dans l'Arabie méridionale antique', in: *Arabian Humanities*, vol. 8 (Paris: Centre français de recherche de la péninsule Arabique, 2017).

Robin, Christian Julien and Tayran, Salim, 'Soixante-dix ans avant l'Islam: l'Arabie toute entière dominée par un roi chrétien', in: *Comptes rendus des séances de l'Académie des Inscriptions et Belles-Lettres (CRAI)*, no. 1 (Paris: Institut de France, 2012), pp. 525–553.

Rock Art in the Hail Region of Saudi Arabia. Submitted by the Saudi Commission for Tourism and Antiquities as a proposal for inclusion in the UNESCO World Heritage List (Riyadh: 2013–14).

Rodrigue, Alain, 'Note sur le signe cruciforme dans l'art rupestre du Maroc', in: *Cahiers de l'AARS*, no. 15, (Saint-Benoist-sur-Mer: AARS, 2011), pp. 295–299.

Rogozhinsky, Alexey E. (ed.), *Rock Art Sites of Central Asia: Documentation, Conservation, Management, Community Participation* (Almaty: Kazakhstan Ministry of Culture, 2004).

— 'Petroglyph sites of Kazakhstan and Western Central Asia as part of the archaeological landscape: New challenges', in: *Archaeology, Ethnology and Anthropology of Eurasia*, vol. 36 (Amsterdam: Elsevier, 2008), pp. 83–94.

— *Petroglyphs within the Archaeological Landscape of Tamgaly* (Almaty: Margulan Institute of Archaeology, 2011).

— 'Rock art sites in Kazakhstan', in: Clottes, *Rock Art in Central Asia: A Thematic Study* (2011, q.v.), pp. 9–42.

— 'Medieval Petroglyph Tamgas of Southern Kazakhstan and Semirechie', in: Voyakin and Iskanderova, *Tamgas of Pre-Islamic Central Asia* (q.v. 2019), pp. 249–295.

— 'Shatyrtas: Discovery of rock paintings', in: Jacobson-Tepfer and Novozhenov, *Rock Art Chronicles of Golden Steppe*, vol. 2 (2020, q.v.), pp. 110–129.

— 'Rock art in western Central Asia (2015–2019)', in: Bahn et al., *Rock Art Studies: News of the World*, vol. 6 (2021, q.v.), pp. 113–125.

Rogozhinsky, Alexey and Novozhenov, Viktor, Культурные ландшафты с петроглифами центральной Азии в вопросах и ответах: *Central Asia Cultural and Rock Art Landscapes: Frequently Asked Questions* (Samarkand: International Institute for Central Asian Studies, 2018).

Rogozhinsky, Alexey E. and Yatsenko, Sergey A., 'The ancient Tamga-signs of Southeast Kazakhstan and their owners', in: *The Silk Road*, vol. 13 (Berkeley: The Silkroad House, 2013), pp. 109–125.

Rollefson, Gary O. et al., 'Images of the environment: Rock art and the exploitation of the Jordanian Badiah', in: *Journal of Epigraphy and Rock Drawings*, vol. 2 (Amman: Department of Antiquities of Jordan, 2008), pp. 17–51.

Rose, Jeffrey I., 'New light on human prehistory in the Arabo-Persian Gulf oasis', in: *Current Anthropology* vol. 51, no. 6 (Chicago: Chicago Press Journals, 2010), pp. 849–883.

— *An Introduction to Human Prehistory in Arabia* (Cham: Springer Nature, 2022).

Rose, Jeffrey I. and Petraglia, Michael D., 'Tracking the origin and evolution of human populations in Arabia', in: Petraglia and Rose, *The Evolution of Human Populations in Arabia* (2009, q.v.), pp. 1–12.

— 'The search for the earliest humans in Oman: On the trail of the first humans in Oman', in: Cleuziou and Tosi, *In the Shadow of the Ancestors* (2020, q.v.), pp. 19–36.

Rose, Jeffrey I. et al., 'The Nubian Complex of Dhofar, Oman: An African Middle Stone Age industry in Southern Arabia', in: *PLOS ONE*, vol. 6, no. 11, art. no. 28239 (San Francisco: PLOS, 2011).

— *The First Peoples of Oman: Palaeolithic Archaeology of the Nejd Plateau* (Oxford: Archaeopress, 2019).

Rosenberg, Thomas M. et al., 'Middle and Late Pleistocene humid periods recorded in palaeolake deposits of the Nafud desert, Saudi Arabia', in: *Quaternary Science Reviews*, vol. 70 (Amsterdam: Elsevier, 2013), pp. 109–123.

Rothenberg, Reno and Glass, Jonathan, 'The Midianite pottery', in: Sawyer and Clines, *Midian, Moab and Edom* (1983, q.v.), pp. 65–124.

Rovira, James (ed.), *Women in Rock, Women in Romanticism* (Abingdon: Routledge, 2023).

Rowan, Yorke M. and Hill, Austin Chad, 'Pecking at basalt: Photogrammetric documentation of petroglyphs in the Black Desert, Jordan', in: Finlayson, W. and Makarewicz C. (eds), *Settlement, Survey, and Stone: Essays on Near Eastern Prehistory in Honour of Gary Rollefson* (Ahrensfelde-Lindenberg: Ex Oriente, 2014), pp. 209–217.

Rozwadowski, Andrzej, 'From semiotics to phenomenology: Central Asian petroglyphs and the Indo-Iranian mythology', in: Helskog, *Theoretical Perspectives in Rock Art Research* (2001, q.v.), pp. 155–174.

— 'Sun gods or shamans? Interpreting the "solar-headed" petroglyphs of Central Asia', in: Price, Neil (ed.), *The Archaeology of Shamanism* (Abingdon: Routledge, 2001), pp. 65–86.

— 'Disappearing into the rock: Shamanistic aspects of Indo-Iranian mythology as a context for interpreting Central Asian petroglyphs', in: Rozwadowski and Kośko, *Spirits and Stones* (2002, q.v.), pp. 49–78.

— *Indoirańczycy – sztuka i mitologia: petroglify Azji Środkowej* (Poznań: Adam Mickiewicz University, 2003).

— *Symbols through Time: Interpreting the Rock Art of Central Asia* (Poznań: Adam Mickiewicz University, 2004).

— 'Did shamans always play the drum? Tracking down prehistoric shamanism in Central Asia', in: *Documenta Praehistorica*, vol.39 (Ljubljana: University of Ljubljana Press, 2012), pp. 277–286.

— 'Shamanism in indigenous context: Understanding Siberian rock art', in: McDonald and Veth, *Companion to Rock Art* (2012, q.v.), pp. 454–471.

— *Rocks, Cracks and Drums* (Budapest: Molnar & Kelemen, 2017).

— 'Travelling through the rock to the Otherworld: The shamanic "grammar of mind" within the rock art of Siberia', in: *Cambridge Archaeological Journal*, vol. 27, no. 3 (Cambridge: McDonald Institute, 2017), pp. 413–432.

— 'Rock art of Northern, Central and Western Asia', in: David and McNiven, *The Oxford Handbook of the Archaeology and Anthropology of Rock Art* (2018, q.v.), pp. 151–176.

— 'Sacred holes: Portals to the world of spirits in Siberian shamanism', in: Pásztor, Emilia (ed.), *Shamanism and Nature Worship: Past and Present* (Baja, Hungary: Türr István Múzeum, 2019), pp. 175–203.

— 'Rock art as a source of history in Central Asia', in: Kouamé, Nathalie, Meyer, Éric P. and Viguier, Anne, *Encyclopédie des historiographies: Afriques, Amériques, Asies* (Paris: Inalco Presses, 2020), pp. 1520–1535.

— 'Rock art as a source of contemporary cultural identity: a Siberian–Canadian comparative study', in: Żurkiewicz, *Treasures of Time* (2021, q.v.), pp. 432–450.

Rozwadowski, Andrzej and Boniec, Magdalena, 'Face to face with ancestors: Indigenous codes in the contemporary art of Siberia', in: Rozwadowski and Hampson, *Visual Culture, Heritage and Identity* (2021, q.v.), pp. 51–70.

Rozwadowski, Andrzej and Hampson, Jamie (eds), *Visual Culture, Heritage and Identity: Using Rock Art to Reconnect Past and Present* (Oxford: Archaeopress, 2021).

Rozwadowski, Andrzej and Kośko, Maria M. (eds), *Spirits and Stones: Shamanism and Rock Art in Central Asia and Siberia* (Poznań: Instytut Wschodni UAM, 2002).

Rozwadowski, Andrzej and Lymer, Kenneth, 'Rock art in Central Asia: History, recent developments and new directions', in: Bahn et al., *Rock Art Studies: News of the World*, vol. 4 (2012, q.v.), pp. 149–163.

Rudenko, Sergei, *Frozen Tombs of Siberia: The Pazyryk Burials of Iron-Age Horsemen* (London: Dent & Sons, 1970).

Rudenko, Sergey I. and Glukhov, Alexey N., 'Kudyrge burial ground in Altai', in: *Materials on Ethnography*, vol. 3, no. 2 (Leningrad: State Publisher of Russian Museums, 1927), pp. 37–52.

Ruiz-Redondo, Altor, 'Out of Franco-Cantabria: The globalization of Pleistocene rock art', in: Abadia et al., *Deep-Time Images in the Age of Globalization* (2024, q.v.), pp. 19–29.

Ruprechtsberger, Erwin M., *Die Garamanten. Geschichte und Kultur eines lybischen Volkes in der Sahara* (Mainz: Philipp von Zabern, 1997).

Ruspoli, Mario, *Die Höhlenmalerei von Lascaux. Auf den Spuren der frühen Menschen* (Augsburg: Weltbild Verlag, 1998).

Ryckmans, Gonzague, *Les religions arabes préislamiques* (Louvain: Publications universitaires, 1951).

Ryckmans, Jacques, 'Al-Ukhdud. The Philby–Rickmans–Lippens Expedition of 1951', in: *Proceedings of the Seminar for Arabian Studies*, vol. 11 (1980) (Oxford: Archaeopress, 1981), pp. 55–63.

Sachet, Isabelle et al. (eds), *Dieux et déesses d'Arabie: images et représentations* (Paris: de Bocard, 2012).

Sachs-Hombach, Klaus and Schirra, Jörg (eds), *Origins of Pictures: Anthropological Discourses in Image Science* (Cologne: Herbert von Halem, 2013).

Sadier, Benjamin et al., 'Further constraints on the Chauvet cave artwork elaboration', in: *Proceedings of the National Academy of Sciences*, vol. 109, no. 21 (Washington: National Academy of Sciences, 2012), pp. 8002–8006.

Saduakasuly A., Zheleznyakov, B.A. and Hermann, L., *Құлжабасы сілемінің жартас өнері / Наскальное искусство хребта Кулжабасы = The Rock Art of the Kulzhabasy Range* (Almaty: Zhambyl, 2017).

Sagona, Antonio, *The Archaeology of the Caucasus: From Earliest Settlements to the Iron Age* (Cambridge: Cambridge University Press, 2018).

Sala, Renato, 'Interaction of climate, environment and humans in North and Central Asia during the Late Glacial and Holocene', in: Chiotis, *Climate Changes in the Holocene* (2019, q.v.), pp. 327–359.

Sala, Renato and Deom, Jean-Marc, *Petroglyphs of South Kazakhstan* (Almaty: Laboratory of Geoarchaeology, 2005).

Salmivuori, Seppo, 'Female agency in Bronze Age Scandinavia as represented in rock art: Rethinking the mourning woman in Vitlycke, Tanum' (*Academia Letters*, 2021), article 1161; https://independentresearcher. academia.edu/SeppoSalmivuori.

Salo, Unto, *The Gundestrup Cauldron: Cultural-Historical and Social-Historical Perspectives* (Washington DC: Institute for the Study of Man, 2018).

Samashev, Zainolla, *Petroglyphs of the East Kazakhstan as a Historical Sources* (Almaty: Rakurs, 1993).

— 'Petroglyphs of Kazakhstan', in: Tashbayeva et al., *Petroglyphs of Central Asia* (2001, q.v.), pp. 151–219.

— *Петроглифы Казахстана = Petroglyphs of Kazakhstan* (Almaty: Öner, 2006).

— *The History of Kazakhstan Fine Art: Ancient Time and Middle Ages* (Astana: Margulan Institute of Archaeology et al., 2013).

Samashev, Zainolla et al., 'Le kourgane de Berel dans l'Altaï kazakhstanais', in: *Arts asiatiques*, vol. 55 (Paris: Musée national des Arts asiatiques-Guimet, 2000), pp. 5–20.

— 'Les gravures rupestres de Terekty Aulie, Kazakhstan central,' in: *International Newsletter on Rock Art*, no. 25 (Foix: 2000), pp. 4–8.

— *Treasures from the Ustyurt Plateau* (Almaty: Aktau State University, 2007).

Sanlaville, Paul, 'Geographic introduction to the Arabian Peninsula', in: Al-Ghabban et al., *Roads of Arabia* (2010, q.v.), pp. 54–69.

Sansoni, Umberto, 'Alpine and Scandinavian rock art in the Bronze Age: A common cultural matrix in a web of continental influences', in: Skoglund, Ling and Bertilsson, *Picturing the Bronze Age* (2015, q.v.), pp. 129–141.

Sapwell, Mark and Janik, Liliana, 'Making community: Rock art and the creative acts of accumulation', in: Stebergløkken et al., *Ritual Landscape and Borders within Rock Art Research* (2015, q.v.), pp. 47–58.

Sauvet, Georges, 'In search of lost time. Dating methods for prehistoric art: The example of Aurignacian sites', in: *Palethnologie: Archéologie et Sciences humaines*, vol. 7 (Toulouse: CNRS/UMR 5608, 2015).

Sauvet, Georges and Ruiz-Lopez, Juan Francisco, 'Du Paléolithique au Néolithique. Art mésolithique et art du Levant espagnol', in: *Art paléolithique. Dossiers d'Archéologie*, no. 417 (2023, q.v.), pp. 66–69.

Sawwatejew, Juri, *Karelische Felsbilder* (Leipzig: VEB E.A. Seemann Verlag, 1984).

Sawyer, John F.A. and Clines, David J.A., *Midian, Moab and Edom: The History and Archaeology of Late Bronze and Iron Age Jordan and North-West Arabia* (Sheffield: Journal for the Study of the Old Testament, 1983).

Ščelinskij, Vjačeslav E. et al., *Höhlenmalerei im Ural. Kapova und Ignatievka. Die altsteinzeitlichen Bilderhöhlen im südlichen Ural* (Sigmaringen: Jan Thorbecke, 1999).

Scerri, Eleanor M.L. et al., 'The expansion of Acheulan hominins into the Nefud Desert of Arabia', in: *Scientific Reports* vol. 11, no. 1, article 10111 (London: Macmillan, 2021).

Schiettecatte, Jérémie, 'L'antique Najrān: confrontation des données archéologiques et des sources écrites', in: Beaucamp et al., *Juifs et Chrétiens en Arabie aux Vème et VIème siècles* (2010, q.v.), pp. 11–37.

Schiettecatte, Jérémie, and Zouache, Abbès, 'The horse in Arabia and the Arabian Horse: Origins, myths and realities', in: *Arabian Humanities*, vol. 8 (Open Edition Journals, 2017).

Schiltz, Véronique, *Die Skythen und andere Steppenvölker* (Munich: C.H. Beck, 1994).

Schmidt, Isabell and Zimmermann, Andreas, 'Population dynamics and socio-spatial organization of the Aurignacian: Scalable quantitative demographic data for western and central Europe', in: *PLOS ONE*, vol. 14, no. 2, art. no. 0211562 (San Francisco: PLOS, 2019).

Schmidt, Sabine Maria, 'Peter Piller. Sie fanden, was sie kannten', in: *Kunstforum*, no. 293: *Parasitäre Paradoxa, Kunst zwischen Anpassung und Widerstand* (Cologne: Kunstforum International, 2023), pp. 168–179.

Schneider, Joan S. and Bierman, Paul R., 'Surface dating using rock varnish', in: Taylor, R.E. and Aitken, M.J., *Chronometric Dating in Archaeology* (New York: Plenum Press, 1997), pp. 357–388.

Schroeder, Ulrich von, *Buddhist Sculptures in Tibet* (2 vols, Hong Kong: Visual Dharma, 2001).

Schroeter-Bieler, Lisa, *Skandinavien. Der Himmel über Europas Wiege. Gestalten auf nordischen Felsbildern der Bronzezeit. Ein Versuch, sie zu verstehen und zu deuten* (Freiburg im Breisgau: Schillinger, 1987).

Schwegler, Urs, 'Felsbilder der Alpen', in: Beier and Hinze, *Botschaften in Stein* (2015, q.v.), pp. 105–129.

Schweizerisches Landesmuseum, *Menschen in Stein gemeisselt* (Basel: Christoph Merian Verlag, 2021).

Seibert, Elke, *Prehistoric Pictures and American Modernism: Abstract Art at MoMA 1937–1939* (London: Bloomsbury, 2023).

Seibert, Elke et al., *Discovering/Uncovering the Modernity of Prehistory* (Heidelberg: arthistoricum.net, 2020).

Sellito, Pasquale et al., 'The unexpected radiative impact of the Hunga Tonga eruption of 15th January 2022', in: *Communications Earth and Environment*, vol. 3, no. 1, art. no. 288 (London: Macmillan, 2022).

Semenenko, Aleksandr, 'бычье-эквидные упряжки двухколёсных повозок в древности и современности = Two-wheeled ox-drawn carriages in antiquity and modern times' (Voronezh: 2021): https://dzen.ru/media/rakshasendra/bycheekvidnye-upriajki-dvuhkolesnyh-povozok-v-drevnosti-i-sovremennosti-618031aa23a98576ed66167f.

Shakabpa, Tsepon W.D., *Tibet: A Political History* (New York: Potala Publications, 1984).

Sharman, Lindsey (ed), *The Writing on the Wall: The Work of Joane Cardinal-Schubert* (Calgary: University of Calgary Press, 2017).

Shaw, Ian and Jameson, Robert, *A Dictionary of Archaeology* (Oxford: Blackwell, 2002).

Sher, Jakov, 'Interpretation of scenes on some petroglyphs of Saymaly Tash', in: Lukonin, V.G. (ed.), *Культура Востока: Древность и раннее средневековье = Culture of the East: Antiquity and Early Middle Ages* (Leningrad: Aurora, 1978), pp. 163–79.

— *Петроглифы Средней и Центральной Азии = Petroglyphs of Middle and Central Asia* (Moscow: NAUK, 1980).

Sher, Jakov and Francfort, Henri-Paul (eds.), *Répertoire des Pétroglyphes d'Asie centrale* (Paris: De Boccard, 1994–2006).

    fasc. 1: Sher, Jakov, *Sibérie du Sud, 1: Oglakhty I–III (Russie, Khakassie)* (1994).

    fasc. 2: Francfort, Henri-Paul and Sher, Jakov, *Sibérie du Sud, 2: Tepsej I–III, Ust'Tuba I–VI (Russie, Khakassie)* (1995).

    fasc. 3: Kubarev, Vladimir and Jacobson, Esther, *Sibérie du Sud, 3: Kalbak–Tash I (République de l'Altai)* (1996).

    fasc. 4: Sher, Jakov and Savinov, Dimitri, *Sibérie du Sud, 4: Cheremushny Log, Ust-Kulog. Stèle de Khakassie* (1999).

    fasc. 5: Mar'yashev, A.N., Goryashev, A.A. and Potapov, S.A., *Kazakhstan, 1: Choix de Pétroglyphes du Semirech'e* (1998).

    fasc. 6: Jacobson, Esther, Kubarev, Vladimir, and Tseevendorj, Damdinsurenjin, *Mongolie du nord-ouest. Tsagaan Salaa/Baga Oigor, 1: texte et figures*; vol. 2: *planches* (2001).

    fasc. 7: Jacobson-Tepfer, Esther, Kubarev, Vladimir, and Tseevendorj, Damdinsurenjin, *Mongolie du nord-ouest, haut Tsagaan Gol, 1–2* (2006).

Sher, Jakov and Garyaeva, Olga, 'The rock art of Northern Eurasia', in: Bahn et al., *Rock Art Studies: News of the World*, vol. 1 (1996, q.v.), pp. 105–125.

Shipton, Ceri et al., 'Large Flake Acheulean in the Nefud Desert of northern Arabia', in: *Paleoanthropology* (Paleoanthropology Society, 2014), pp. 446–462.

— 'Acheulean technology and landscape use at Dawadmi, central Arabia', in: *PLOS ONE*, vol. 13, no. 7, art. no. 0200497 (San Francisco: PLOS, 2018).

Shnaider, Svetlana, 'Occupation of highland Central Asia: New evidence from Kurteke rockshelter, Eastern Pamir', in: *Archaeological Research in Asia*, vol. 34, art. no. 100443 (Amsterdam: Elsevier June 2023).

Shvets, Irina, 'Kazakh petroglyphs in the light of recently discovered stations and their dating', in: Olivieri, *Pictures in Transformation* (2010, q.v.), pp. 77–81.

— *Studien zur Felsbildkunst Kasachstans* (Darmstadt: Philipp von Zabern, 2012).

Sigari, Dario, 'Palaeolithic rock art in Gobustan, Azerbaijan: The rock 44 of Böyük Daş, Gobustan', in: *Iranian Archaeology*, vol. 4 (Tehran: Wahesht Mina International Institute, 2013), pp. 15–22.

— 'Gobustan Rock Art Cultural Landscape (Azerbaijan)', in: Smith, Claire (ed.), *Encyclopedia of Global Archaeology* (New York: Springer Nature, 2019).

— *Palaeolithic Rock Art of the Italian Peninsula* (Capo di Ponte: Centro Camuno die Studi Preistorici, 2022).

Simonis, Roberta et al., *Ennedi: Tales on Stone* (Florence: Edizioni All'Insegna del Giglio, 2017).

— *Ouri: Images in Wonderland* (Milan: Ulrico Hoepli, 2021).

Sims-Williams, Nicholas, 'The Sogdian inscription in Ladakh', in: Jettmar, Karl (ed.), *Antiquities of Northern Pakistan: Reports and Studies*, vol. 2 (Mainz: Philipp von Zabern, 1993), pp. 151–163.

Singer-Avitz, Lily, 'Section F: The Qurayyah Painted Ware', in: Ussishkin, D. (ed.), *The Renewed Archaeological Excavations at Lachish (1973–1994)*, vol. 1 (Tel Aviv: Tel Aviv University, 2004), pp. 1280–1287.

Sjöstrand, Ylva, 'Memory and destruction: Pictorial practices surrounding red ochre paintings in late Neolithic northern Sweden', in: Stebergløkken et al., *Ritual Landscape and Borders within Rock Art Research* (2015, q.v.), pp. 167–180.

Skånberg, Torbjörn, 'The Fossum Panel: A calendar?' in: *Adoranten* (q.v., 2012), pp. 103–111.

Skandfer, Marianne, 'The appreciation of reindeer: Rock carvings and Sámi reindeer knowledge', in: Gjerde and Arntzen, *Perspectives on Differences in Rock Art* (2021, q.v.), pp. 113–128.

Skoglund, Peter, 'Rock art as history: Representations of human images from an historical perspective', in: Skoglund, Ling and Bertilsson, *Picturing the Bronze Age* (2015, q.v.), pp. 155–165.

— *Rock Art Through Time: Scanian Rock Carvings in the Bronze Age and Earliest Iron Age* (Oxford: Oxbow, 2016).

— 'Axes and long-distance trade: Scania and Wessex in the early second millennium BC', in: Skoglund, Ling and Bertilsson, *North Meets South* (2017, q.v.), pp. 199–213.

— 'The wild boar in Scandinavian rock art', in: Dodd and Meijer, *Giving the Past a Future* (2018, q.v.), pp. 112–120.

Skoglund, Peter, Ling, Johan and Bertilsson, Ulf (eds), *Picturing the Bronze Age* (Oxford: Oxbow, 2015).

— *North Meets South: Theoretical Aspects on the Northern and Southern Rock Art Traditions in Scandinavia* (Oxford: Oxbow, 2017).

Skoglund, Pontus et al., 'Origins and genetic legacy of Neolithic farmers and hunter-gatherers in Europe', in: *Science*, vol. 336, no. 6080 (Washington DC: AAAS, 2012), pp. 466–469.

Slimak, Ludovic, 'The three waves: Rethinking the structure of the first Upper Paleolithic in Western Europe', in: *PLOS ONE*, vol. 18, no. 5, art. no 0277444 (San Francisco: PLOS, 2023).

Slimak, Ludovic et al., 'Modern human incursion into Neanderthal territories 54,000 years ago at Mandrin, France', in: *Science Advances*, vol. 8, no. 6 (Washington DC: AAAS, 2022).

Smith, Andrew B., 'Post-glacial transformations in Africa', in: Cummings et al., *The Oxford Handbook of the Archaeology and Anthropology of Hunter-Gatherers* (2014, q.v.), pp. 479–506.

— 'Masked men, therianthropes, (or charlatans) in Saharan rock art?', in: Huyge and Van Noten, *What Ever Happened to the People?* (2018, q.v.), pp. 541–549.

Snellgrove, David L. and Skorupski, Tadeusz, *The Cultural Heritage of Ladakh* (2 vols, New Delhi: Vikas Publishing, 1977; Warminster: Aris & Phillips, 1980).

Snorri Sturluson, *The Prose Edda*, trans. Arthur Gilchrist Brodeur (1916): https://archive.org/details/proseedda00snor/page/n11/mode/2up.

Sognnes, Kalle, 'Symbols in a changing world: Rock-art and the transition from hunting to farming in mid Norway', in: Chippindale and Taçon, *The Archaeology of Rock-Art* (1998, q.v.), pp. 146–159.

— 'Land of elks – sea of whales: Landscapes of the Stone Age rock-art in central Scandinavia', in: Nash and Chippindale, *European Landscapes of Rock-Art* (Abingdon: Routledge, 2012), pp. 195–212.

— 'Blowing the horn: Lure images in rock art in *Trøndelag, Norway*', in: *Adoranten* (q.v., 2012), pp. 24–36.

Solano, Serena, 'Places of worship in Valcamonica from Prehistory to the Christianization of the area', in: *Adoranten* (q.v., 2010), pp. 104–109.

Soleilhavoup, François, 'Rock art investigations in the Fezzan, south-west Libya', in: *International Newsletter on Rock Art*, no. 45 (Foix: INORA, 2006), pp. 1–9.

— 'Niola Doa. Un site exceptionnel d'art rupestre au Sahara préhistorique', in: *Archéologia*, no. 535 (Dijon: Faton, 2015), pp. 54–61.

— *Art rupestre dans l'Ennedi. Le corps féminin dans l'art préhistorique* (Dijon: Faton, 2018).

— 'Réalisme et symbolisme de l'image rupestre de la femme au Sahara', in: Huyge and Van Noten, *What Ever Happened to the People?* (2018, q.v.), pp. 193–217.

Solomon, Anne, 'Rock arts, shamans, and grand theories', in: David and McNiven, *The Oxford Handbook of the Archaeology and Anthropology of Rock Art* (2018, q.v.), pp. 565–585.

Sonnabend, Holger, *Höhlenmalerei. Glanzlichter der frühzeitlichen Kunst* (Berlin: BeBra Verlag, 2024).

Sørensen, Mikkel et al., 'The first eastern migrations of people and knowledge into Scandinavia: Evidence from studies in Mesolithic technology, 9th–8th Millennium BC', in: *Norwegian Archaeological Review*, vol. 46, no. 1 (Abingdon: Routledge, 2013), pp. 19–56.

Soukopova, Jitka, *Round Heads: The Earliest Rock Paintings in the Sahara* (Newcastle upon Tyne: Cambridge Scholars Publishing, 2012).

— 'Similarities between Round-Head paintings and Kel Essuf engravings', in: Huyge and Van Noten, *What Ever Happened to the People?* (2018, q.v.), pp. 173–188.

— 'Prehistoric colonization of the central Sahara: Hunters versus herders and the evidence from the rock art', in: Anati (ed.), *Expression*, no. 30 (2020, q.v.), pp. 58–73.

— 'Rain animals in Central Saharan Round Head rock art: An ethnographic approach', in: Anati (ed.), *Expression*, no. 44 (2024, q.v.), pp. 67–84.

Sperveslage, Gunnar and Eichmann, Ricardo, 'Egyptian cultural impact on north-west Arabia in the second and first millennia BC', in: *Proceedings of the Seminar for Arabian Studies*, vol. 42 (Oxford: Archaeopress, 2012), pp. 371–384.

— 'Ägyptische Einflüsse auf der Arabischen Halbinsel in vorislamischer Zeit am Beispiel der Oase von Tayma', in: *Zeitschrift für Orient-Archäologie*, vol. 6 (Tübingen: Ernst Wasmuth, 2013), pp. 234–254.

Stark, Sören et al. (eds), *Nomads and Networks: The Ancient Art and Culture of Kazakhstan* (Princeton: Princeton University Press, 2012).

Stavrinaki, Maria, 'Die Ausstellung "40,000 years of Modern Art" in London 1948', in: Kohl et al., *Kunst der Vorzeit* (2021, q.v.), pp. 200–205.

Stebergløkken, Heidrun et al. (eds) *Ritual Landscape and Borders within Rock Art Research* (Oxford: Archaeopress, 2015).

Steelman, Karen L. and Rowe, Marvin W., 'Radiocarbon dating of rock paintings: Incorporating pictographs into the archaeological record', in: McDonald and Veth, *Companion to Rock Art* (2012), pp. 565–582.

Stein, Marc Aurel, 'A Chinese expedition across the Pamirs and Hindukush, A.D. 747', in *The Geographical Journal*, vol. 59, no. 2 (London: RGS, February 1922), pp. 112–130.

— *Innermost Asia*, vol. 1 (Oxford: Clarendon, 1928).

— 'Archaeological notes from the Hindukush region', in: *The Journal of the Royal Asiatic Society of Great Britain and Ireland*, vol. 1 (London: The Royal Asiatic Society, 1944), pp. 5–24.

Sterry, Martin and Mattingly, David J. (eds), *Urbanisation and State Formation in the Ancient Sahara and Beyond* (Cambridge: Cambridge University Press, 2020).

— 'Introduction to the themes of sedentarisation', in: Sterry and Mattingly, *Urbanisation and State Formation* (2020, q.v.). pp. 3–50.

Stewart, Mathew, 'A taphonomic and zooarchaeological study of Pleistocene fossil assemblages from the western Nefud Desert, Saudi Arabia', doctoral thesis (Sydney: University of New South Wales, 2019).

Stockhammer, Philipp W. and Massy, Ken, 'Mobility at the onset of the Bronze Age: A bioarchaeologicaal perspective', in: Fernández-Götz et al., *Rethinking Migrations in Late Prehistoric Eurasia* (2023, q.v.), pp. 142–169.

Stöllner, Thomas et al., 'Andronovo mobility revisited: New research on Bronze Age mining and metallurgical communities in Central Asia', in: Fernández-Götz et al., *Rethinking Migrations in Late Prehistoric Eurasia* (2023, q.v.), pp. 110–131.

Strabo, *Geographica*, trans. A. Korbiger (Wiesbaden: Marix, 2007).

Strachan, Laura and al-Mustaneer, Mohammad, 'Alia: The many manifestations of southern Saudi-Arabia's alleged goddess', preprint received 10 March 2024 based on the lecture given at the Conference of the GCC Society for History and Archaeology on 9 February 2023 in Najran, Saudi Arabia.

Strahlenberg, Philipp Johann von, *Das Nord- und Östliche Theil von Europa und Asia, in so weit solches das gantze russische Reich mit Siberien und der grossen Tartarey in sich begreiffet* (Stockholm: published by the author, 1730).

Striedter, Karl-Heinz, *Felsbilder der Sahara* (Munich: Prestel, 1984).

Stroeven, Arjen P, et al., 'Deglaciation of Fennoscandia', in: *Quaternary Science Reviews*, vol. 147 (Amsterdam: Elsevier, 2016), pp. 91–121.

Strugnell, John, 'The Nabataean goddess al-Kutba' and her sanctuaries', in: *Bulletin of the American Society of Overseas Research*, vol. 156 (Chicago: University of Chicago Press, 1959), pp. 29–36.

Sveen, Arvid, *Felsbilder. Jiepmaluokta Hjemmeluft, Alta* (Tromsø: Sveen, 1996).

Svensson, Ann-Louise, *A Guide to the Rock Carvings of South-East Scania* (Simrishamn, Sweden: Simrishamne kommun, 2013).

Symonds, Matthew, 'Cova Dones: A surprising palaeolithic cave-art site', in: *Current World Archaeology*, vol. 123 (London: Current Publishing, 2024), pp. 16–21.

Tacitus, C. Cornelius, *Die Germania* [*De Origine et Situ Germanorum*, trans. Adolf Bacmeister (1868)]: https://www.projekt-gutenberg.org/tacitus/germania/.

Taçon, Paul S.C., 'The rock art of South and East Asia', in: David and McNiven, *The Oxford Handbook of the Archaeology and Anthropology of Rock Art* (2018, q.v.), pp. 177–196.

Taçon, Paul S.C. and Chippindale, Christopher, 'An archaeology of rock art through informed methods and formal methods', in: Chippindale and Taçon, *The Archaeology of Rock-Art* (1998, q.v.), pp. 1–10.

Takahama, Shu et al., 'Preliminary report of the archaeological investigations in Ulaan Uushig I (Uushigiin Övör) in Mongolia', in: 金沢大学考古学紀要 = *Kanazawa University Archeology Bulletin*, vol. 28 (Kanazawa: The University of Kanazawa, 2006), pp. 61–102.

Tansem, Karin and Johansen, Heidi, 'The World Heritage rock art in Alta', in: *Adoranten* (q.v., 2008), pp. 65–97.

Tansem, Karin and Storemyr, Per, 'Red-coated rocks at the seashore: The aesthetics and geology of prehistoric rock art in Alta, Arctic Norway', in: *Geoarchaeology*, vol. 36 (Hoboken: Wiley, 2021), pp. 314–334.

Tashbayeva, K., 'Petroglyphs of Kyrgyzstan', in: Tashbayeva et al., *Petroglyphs of Central Asia* (2001, q.v.), pp. 9–79.

Tashbayeva K. et al., *Petroglyphs of Central Asia* (Bishkek: International Institute for Central Asian Studies, 2001).

Tashbaeva K. and Francfort, Henri-Paul, 'Studies in the Jaltyrak-Tash petroglyphs', in: *Bulletin of IICAS*, vol. 1 (Samarkand: International Institute for Central Asian Studies, 2005), pp. 14–19.

Tatiev, E.E., et al., 'Semiotic analysis of petroglyph "Ancient Turks and the Mother Goddess Umay/Umai"', in: *Rupkatha Journal on Interdisciplinary Studies in Humanities*, vol. 13, no. 3 (Murshidabad, India: 2021).

Taylor, Luke, 'Bodies revealed: X-ray art in Western Arnhem Land', in: David and McNiven, *The Oxford Handbook of the Archaeology and Anthropology of Rock Art* (2018, q.v.), pp. 695–716.

Taylor, William T.T. et al., 'Early pastoral economies and herding transitions in eastern Eurasia', in: *Scientific Reports*, vol. 10, art. no. 1001 (London: Macmillan, 2020).

Thangspa, Tashi Ldawa, 'Petroglyphs of Ladakh', in: *Sahapedia* (2021): https://www.sahapedia.org/petroglyphs-ladakh.

Tholbecq, Laurent, 'Les sanctuaires des Nabatéens. État de la question à la lumière de recherches archéologiques récentes', in: *Topoi. Orient–Occident*, vol. 7, no. 2 (Lyon: MOM, 1997), pp. 1069–1095.

— 'The Nabataeo-Roman site of Wādī Ramm (Iram): A new appraisal' in: *Annual of the Department of Antiquities of Jordan*, vol. 42 (Amman: 1998), pp. 241–254.

Tilley, Christopher, *Thinking Through Images: Narratives. Rhythm, Embodiment and Landscape in the Nordic Bronze Age* (Oxford: Oxbow, 2021).

Tokhatyan, K.S., 'Rock carving in Armenia', trans. G.D. Vardumyan, in: *Fundamental Armenology*, no. 2 (Yerevan: Armenian National Academy of Sciences, 2015), pp. 184–205.

— 'Petroglyphs in Armenian Highland', in: Harutyunyan, Khachik (ed.), *Historical and Cultural Heritage of Armenia* (Yerevan: Armenpress, 2022), pp. 21–31.

Tokmagambetov, Erkebolat (ed.), *Nomination of Cultural Property for Inscription on the World Heritage List: Petroglyphs within the Archaeological Landscape of Tamgaly* (Astana: Ministry of Culture, 2003): https://whc.unesco.org/uploads/nominations/1145.pdf.

Tomasello, Michael, *Die kulturelle Entwicklung des menschlichen Denkens: Zur Evolution der Kognition* (Frankfurt am Main: Suhrkamp, 2015).

— *Die Ursprünge der menschlichen Kommunikation* (Frankfurt a.M.: Suhrkamp, 2022).

Toreld, Andreas, 'Sword-wielders and manslaughter: Recently discovered images of rock carvings of Brastad, western Sweden', in: Skoglund, Ling and Bertilsson, *Picturing the Bronze Age* (2015, q.v.), pp. 167–176.

Toreld, Andreas and Andersson, Tommy, 'Ny documentation av Kiviksgravens hällbilder', in: *Fornvännen. Journal of Swedish Antiquarian Research*, vol. 110, no. 1 (Stockholm: Vitterhetsakademien and the Swedish National Historical Museums, 2015), pp. 10–26.

— *Rock Carvings at Vitlycke* (Tanum: Vitlycke Museum, 2018).

Troncoso, Andrés et al., 'Rock art in Central and South America', in: David and McNiven, *The Oxford Handbook of the Archaeology and Anthropology of Rock Art* (2018, q.v.), pp. 273–314.

Trost, Franz, *Die Felsbilder des zentralen Ahaggar (Algerische Sahara)* (Graz: Akademische Druck- und Verlagsanstalt, 1981).

Trousset, P. et al., 'Fezzân', in: *Encyclopédie berbère*, vol. 18 (Saint-Rémy-de-Provence: Édisud, 1997), pp. 2777–2817.

Tschudin, Peter F., *Megalithische Welten. Eine Spurensuche* (Basel: Schwabe, 2016).

Tseveendorj, D., Kubarev, V.D. and Jacobson, E., *Арал Толгойн хадны зураг = Петроглифы Арал Толгой (Монголия) = Petroglyphs of Aral Tolgoi (Mongolia)* (Ulaan Baatar: Mongolian Academy of Sciences, 2005).

Ujfalvy de Mezőkövesd, Károly Jenő (Karl Eugen) *Aus dem westlichen Himalaya: Erlebnisse und Forschungen* (Leipzig: Brockhaus, 1884; facsimile edition, 2011).

Uray, Géza, 'Tibet's connections with Nestorianism and Manicheism in the 8th–10th centuries', in: Steinkellner, Ernst and Tauscher Helmut (eds), *Contributions on Tibetan Language, History and Culture*, vol. 1 (Vienna: University of Vienna, 1983), pp. 399–429.

Vachkova, Vesselina, '*Lupus in fabulis et in templo*: Les métamorphoses étranges du Saint Christophe dans l'Église orthodoxe', in: Antunes, Gabriela and Reich, Björn (eds), (*De*)*formierte Körper Die Wahrnehmung und das Andere im Mittelalter* (Göttingen: Universitätsverlag Göttingen, 2012), pp. 171–190.

Van Albada, Anne-Michelle and Axel, 'De nombreux "centres culturels"', in: *Art rupestre du Sahara. Dossiers d'Archéologie*, no. 197 (1994, q.v.), pp. 22–33.

— 'Les représentations humaines', in: *Art rupestre du Sahara. Dossiers d'Archéologie*, no. 197 (1994, q.v.), pp. 46–59.

— 'Un riche bestiaire néolithique', in: *Art rupestre du Sahara. Dossiers d'Archéologie*, no. 197 (1994, q.v.), pp. 34–45.

— 'L'univers imaginaire. Une population de lycanthropes aux activités multiples', in: *Art rupestre du Sahara. Dossiers d'Archéologie*, no. 197 (1994, q.v.), pp. 6–69.

— 'La femme, le chat, l'aurochs et le rhinocéros dans le néolithique Saharien', in: *Anthropologie*, vol. 33, no. 3 (Brno: Moravian Museum Anthropos Institute, 1995), pp. 145–170.

— *La montagne des hommes-chiens. Art rupestre du Messak Libyen* (Paris: Le Seuil, 2000).

— 'Quelles informations tirer des représentations humaines dans l'art rupestre du Messak libyen?', in: Huyge and Van Noten, *What Ever Happened to the People?* (2018, q.v.), pp. 243–63.

Van Baak, Christiaan G.C. et al., 'A magnetostratigraphic time frame for Plio-Pleistocene transgressions in the South Caspian Basin, Azerbaijan', in: *Global and Planetary Change*, vol. 103 (Amsterdam: Elsevier, 2013), pp. 119–134.

Vandkilde, Helle, 'Breakthrough of the Nordic Bronze Age: Transcultural warriorhood and a Carpathian crossroad in the sixteenth century BC', in: *European Journal of Archaeology*, vol. 17, no. 4 (Cambridge: Cambridge University Press, 2014), pp. 602–633.

Vandkilde, Helle et al., 'Anthropomorphised warlike beings with horned helmets: Bronze Age Scandinavia, Sardinia, and Iberia compared', in: *Prähistorische Zeitschrift*, vol. 97, no. 1 (Berlin: De Gruyter, 2022), pp. 130–158.

Varberg, Jeanette, Kaul, Flemming and Gratuze, Bernard, 'Bronze Age glass and amber: Evidence of Bronze Age long distance exchange', in: *Adoranten* (q.v., 2019), pp. 5–29.

Vérité, Monique, *Henri Lhote. Une aventure scientifique au Sahara* (Paris: Ibis Press, 2010).

Vernier, Martin, 'Zamthang, epicentre of Zanskar's rock heritage', in: *Revue d'Études Tibétaines*, vol. 35 (Paris: UMR 8155 (CRCAO) of CNR, 2016), pp. 53–105.

Vialou, Denis, *Au Coeur de la Préhistoire* (Paris: Gallimard, 1996).

Vieira, Vincent, 'A context analysis of Neolithic *Cygnus* petroglyphs at Lake Onega', in: *Cambridge Archaeological Journal*, vol. 20, no. 2 (Cambridge: McDonald Institute, 2010), pp. 255–261.

Villiers, Marq de and Hirtle, Sheila, *Sahara: The Life of the Great Desert* (London: HarperCollins, 2004).

Vogt, David, 'Continuity and discontinuity in South Scandinavian Bronze Age rock art research', in: Helskog, *Theoretical Perspectives in Rock Art Research* (2001), pp. 99–109.

Voyakin, Dimitri A., Iskanderova, A.D., et al. (eds), *Tamgas of Pre-Islamic Central Asia* (Samarkand: International Institute for Central Asian Studies, 2019).

Wadi Rum Protected Area. Report and documentation submitted to the World Heritage Centre on 1 February 2010 (Paris: ICOMOS, 2011): https://whc.unesco.org/en/list/1377/documents/.

Wagner, Sebastian and Zorita, Eduardo, 'High resolution climate reconstruction of the last 2,000 years', in: Chiotis, *Climate Changes in the Holocene* (2019, q.v.), pp. 121–140.

Walderhaug, Eva M., 'Changing art in a changing society: The hunters' rock-art of western Norway', in: Chippindale and Taçon, *The Archaeology of Rock-Art* (1998, q.v.), pp. 302–318.

Wallin, Georg August, *Skrifter*, vol. 4: *Färderna till Mekka och Jerusalem 1845–1847*, ed. Kaj Öhrnberg and Patricia Berg (Helsinki: Svenska litteratursällskapet i Finland; Stockholm: Atlantis, 2013).

Wang, Bo, 'Hirschsteine in Xinjiang', in: *Eurasia Antiqua. Zeitschrift für Archäologie Eurasiens*, vol. 7 (Mainz: Philipp von Zabern, 2001), pp. 105–132.

Wang, Chuan-Chao et al., 'Ancient human genome-wide data from a 3000-year interval in the Caucasus corresponds with eco-geographic regions', in: *Nature Communications*, vol. 10, art. no. 590 (London: Macmillan, 2019).

Warren, Graeme, 'Transformations? The Mesolithic of North-West Europe', in: Cummings et al., *The Oxford Handbook of the Archaeology and Anthropology of Hunter-Gatherers* (2014, q.v.), pp. 537–555.

Weber, Therese, *The Language of Paper: A History of 2000 Years* (Bangkok: Orchid Press, 2007).

Wehrberger, Kurt (ed.), *Die Rückkehr des Löwenmenschen. Geschichte, Mythos Magie* (Ostfildern: Jan Thorbecke, 2013).

Weihreter, Hans, *Ladakh. Vergessene Feste. Botschaften im Fels* (Graz: ADEVA, 2010).

Weisgerber, Gerd, 'Trade and the beginnings of seafaring in the Indian Ocean: Copper from Magan for the Mesopotamian Cities', in: Cleuziou and Tosi, *In the Shadow of the Ancestors* (2020, q.v.), pp. 269–302.

Werner, Louis, 'Libya's forgotten desert kingdom', in: *Aramco World*, vol. 55, no. 3 (Houston: Aramco Services, 2004), pp. 8–13.

Westerdahl, Christer, 'Contrasts of the maritime environment: Possible implications in prehistory', in: Stebergløkken et al., *Ritual Landscape and Borders within Rock Art Research* (2015, q.v.), pp. 141–154.

Whalen, Norman M. and Fritz, Glen A., 'The Oldowan in Arabia,' in: *Adumatu*, no. 9 (Riyadh: Al-Sudairy Foundation, 2004), pp. 7–18.

White, Randall, *Prehistoric Art: The Symbolic Journey of Humankind* (New York: Henry N. Abrams, 2003).

White, Randall et al., 'Still no archaeological evidence that Neanderthals created Iberian cave art', in: *Journal of Human Evolution*, vol. 144, art. no. 102640 (Amsterdam: Elsevier July 2020).

Whitley, David S. (ed.), *Handbook of Rock Art Research* (Walnut Creek: Altamira Press, 2001).

— *Cave Paintings and the Human Spirit: The Origin of Creativity and Belief* (Amherst: Prometheus Books, 2008).

— 'In suspect terrain: Dating rock engravings', in: McDonald and Veth, *Companion to Rock Art* (2012, q.v.), pp. 605–624.

— 'Hunter-gatherer religion and ritual', in: Cummings et al., *The Oxford Handbook of the Archaeology and Anthropology of Hunter-Gatherers* (2014, q.v.), pp. 1221–1242.

Wickham-Jones, C.R., 'Coastal adaptations', in: Cummings et al., *The Oxford Handbook of the Archaeology and Anthropology of Hunter-Gatherers* (q.v., 2014), pp. 694–711.

Widmer, Jean-Pierre, *Ces fascinantes gravures de l'art rupestre du Val Camonica* (Weinstadt : Bernhard-Albert Greiner, 2013).

Williams, James, 'The Tahilt region: A preliminary archaeological survey of the Tahilt surroundings to contextualize the Tahilt cemeteries', in: *The Silk Road*, vol. 5, no. 2 (Berkeley: The Silkroad House, 2005), pp. 42–47.

Williams, Martin, *When the Sahara was Green: How our Greatest Desert Came to Be* (Princeton: Princeton University Press, 2021).

Widgren, M. and Pedersen, E.A., 'Agriculture in Sweden: 800 BC–AD 1000', in: Myrdal, Janken and Morell, Mats (eds), *The Agrarian History of Sweden: From 4000 BC to AD 2000* (Lund: Nordic Academic Press, 2000), pp. 46–71.

Winter, Li, 'Rock art, landscape and interaction: Examples from Bronze Age Bohuslän', in: Estévez, Manuel Santos and Meléndez, Andrés Troncoso (eds), *Reflexiones sobre Arte Rupestre, paisaje, forma y contenido* (Xunta de Galicia: Instituto de Estudos Galegos Padre Sarmiento, 2005), pp. 123–138.

Wirth, Stefan, 'Sonnenbarke und zyklisches Weltbild. Überlegungen zum Verständnis der spätbronzezeitlichen Ikonographie in Mitteleuropa', in: *Der Griff nach den Sternen. Wie Europas Eliten zu Macht und Reichtum kamen*: Tagungen des Landesmuseums für Vorgeschichte Halle, vol. 5 (Halle: Landesamt für Denkmalpflege und Archäologie Sachsen-Anhalt, 2011), pp. 501–515.

Wrigglesworth, Melanie, 'Between land and water: The ship in Bronze Age West Norway', in: Stebergløkken et al. (eds), *Ritual Landscape and Borders within Rock Art Research* (2015, q.v.), pp. 111–118.

Wright, Aaron M., *Religion on the Rocks: Hohokam Rock Art, Ritual Practice and Social Transformation* (Salt Lake City: University of Utah Press, 2014).

Wright, Joshua and Janz, Lisa, 'The Younger Dryas in arid Northeast Asia', in: Eren, Metin I. (ed.), *Hunter-Gatherer Behavior: Human Response during the Younger Dryas* (New York: Routledge, 2012), pp. 231–247.

Xuanzang, *Si-yu-ki: Buddhist Records of the Western World*, trans. Samuel Beal (1906, repr. New Delhi: Manoharlal, 2004).

Yang, Liang Emlyn et al. (eds), *Socio-Environmental Dynamics along the Historical Silk Road* (Cham: Springer Nature Switzerland, 2019): https://link.springer.com/book/10.1007/978-3-030-00728-7.

Yanina, Tamara A., 'Correlation of the Late Pleistocene paleographical events of the Caspian Sea and Russian Plain', *Quaternary International*, vol. 271 (Amsterdam: Elsevier, 2012), pp. 120–129.

Yanko-Hombach, Valentina et al., 'Controversy over the great flood hypotheses in the Black Sea in light of geological, paleontological and archaeological evidence', *Quaternary International*, vols 167–8 (Amsterdam: Elsevier, 2007), pp. 91–113.

Yatsenko, Sergey, 'Marks of the Ancient and medieval Iranian-speaking peoples of Iran, Eastern Europe, Transoxiana and South Siberia', in: Pim et al., *Traditional Marking Systems* (2010, q.v.), pp. 133–154.

— 'Signs of the Early Nomads on the Ustyurt Plateau', in: Voyakin and Iskanderova, *Tamgas of Pre-Islamic Central Asia* (q.v. 2019), pp. 58–88.

— 'General and Special Use of Tamgas by the Ancient People of Central Asia', in: Voyakin and Iskanderova, *Tamgas of Pre-Islamic Central Asia* (q.v. 2019), pp. 387–417.

Yatsenko, Sergey and Ilyasov, Jangar, 'Tamgas/Nishan and socio-political history', in: Voyakin and Iskanderova, *Tamgas of Pre-Islamic Central Asia* (2019, q.v.), pp. 296–363.

Yatsenko, Sergey and Rogozhinsky A.E., 'Introduction', in: Voyakin and Iskanderova, *Tamgas of Pre-Islamic Central Asia* (q.v. 2019), pp. 8–42.

Yule, Paul, 'The Hasat Bani Salt in the al-Zahirah Province of the Sultanate of Oman', in: Boehmer, R.M. and Marran J. (eds), *Lux Orientis. Archäologie zwischen Asien und Europa* (Rahden: VML, 2001), pp. 443–450.

— 'Pre-Arabic inscriptions from Wādī Saḥtan, Wilāyat al-Rustāq, Governorate of the South al-Bāṭinah region, Sultanate of Oman', in: Kuty, Renaud, Seeger Ulrich and Talay, Shabo (eds), *Nicht nur mit Engelszungen. Beiträge zur semitischen Dialektologie Festschrift für Werner Arnold zum 60. Geburtstag* (Wiesbaden: Harrassowitz, 2013), pp. 399–402.

Yusuf, Suhail, 'Threatened rock carvings of Pakistan', in: *Dawn*, 18 May 2011 (Karachi: Dawn, 2011): https://www.dawn.com/news/629659/basha-dam-threatens-thousands-of-ancient-rock-carvings.

Zaunschirm, Thomas, 'Im Zoo der Kunst', in: *Kunstforum*, no. 174: *Out of Africa* (Cologne: Kunstforum International, 2005), pp. 38–104.

Zayadine, Fawzi, 'Le relief néo-babylonien à Sela' près de Tafileh: Interprétation historique', in: *Syria*, vol. 76 (Beirut: Institut français du Proche-Orient, 1999), pp. 83–90.

Zazzo, Antoine et al., 'High-precision dating of ceremonial activity around a large ritual complex in Late Bronze Age Mongolia', in: Lepetz S. et al., *Occupations et espaces sacrés dans l'Altaï mongol* (2022, q.v.), pp. 80–98.

Zboray, András, 'Wadi Sura in the context of regional rock art', in: Kuper, *Wadi Sura* (2013, q.v.), pp. 18–23.

— 'Four elephant hunt scenes among the Iheren style paintings of Tagelahin, Aharhar Tasset and Tamrit (Tasïli-n-Ajjer)', in: *Cahiers de l'AARS*, no. 19 (Saint-Benoist-sur-Mer: AARS, 2016–17), pp. 275–282.

— 'The petroglyphs of Jebel Uweinat: Many questions and a few answers …', in: Kabacinski, J. et al. (eds), *Desert and the Nile: Prehistory of the Nile Basin and the Sahara*, Studies in African Archaeology, vol. 15 (Poznań: Poznań Archaeological Museum, 2018), pp. 657–683.

Zhelezniakov, V.A., *Танбалы: памятник наскального искусства, природа, окрестности, музей = Tanbaly: Rock Art Monument, Nature, Surroundings, Museum* (Almaty: BPKA, 2016).

Zilhão, João, 'The Neanderthals: Evolution, palaeoecology and extinction', in: Cummings et al., *The Oxford Handbook of the Archaeology and Anthropology of Hunter-Gatherers* (2014, q.v.), pp. 191–213.

Ziolkowski, Michele C., 'A study of the petroglyphs from Wadi al-Hayl, Fujairah, United Arab Emirates', in: *Arabian Archaeology and Epigraphy*, vol. 9 (Oxford: Wiley, 1998), pp. 13–89.

— 'Rock on art: petroglyph sites in the United Arab Emirates', in: *Arabian Archaeology and Epigraphy*, vol. 18, no. 2 (Oxford: Wiley, 2007), pp. 208–238.

Zotkina, Lydia, Bobomulloev, Bobomullo et al., 'Новые данные о наскальном искусстве Восточного Памира / New data on the rock paintings of Eastern Pamir', in: *Вестник НГУ. Серия: История, филология / Vestnik NSU Series History and Philology*, vol. 21, no. 3 (Novosibirsk: 2022), pp. 60 72.

Zotkina, Lydia and Sayfulloev, Nuritdin, 'Изображения Навеса Куртеке (Восточный Памир) = Imagery of the Kurteke Rock-Shelter (Eastern Pamir)', in: *Теория и практика археологических исследований = Theory and Practice of Archaeological Research*, vol. 34, no. 4 (Novosibirsk: Institute of Archaeology and Ethnography, 2022), pp. 148–162.

Zuev, Yu. A., 'The strongest tribe: Ezgil', in: *Historical and Cultural Relations Between Iran and Dasht-i Kipchak in the 13–18th c.c.: Materials of International Round Table, Almaty, 2004* (Almaty: R.B. Suleymenov Institute of Oriental Studies, 2004): http://s155239215.onlinehome.us/turkic/29Huns/Zuev/ZuevStrongTribeEn.htm.

Żurkiewicz, Danuta (ed.), *Treasures of Time: Research of the Faculty of Archaeology of Adam Mickiewicz University in Poznań* (Poznań: Adam Mickiewicz University, 2021).

List of Maps

Map 1. The major groups of petroglyph sites in Eurasia, Arabia and northern Africa (pp. 14–15).

Map 2. The last two Glacial Periods in Europe (p. 19). Adapted from: https://en.wikipedia.org/wiki/Saale_glaciation and https://www.iro.umontreal.ca/~vaucher/History/ Evolution/IceAges.html

Map 3. Major petroglyph sites of Mongolia, southern Russia, Xinjiang and Kazakhstan (pp. 38–39).

Map 4. Major petroglyph sites of Kyrgyzstan, Tajikistan and Uzbekistan (p. 84).

Map 5. Major petroglyph sites in the Himalaya, Transhimalaya and Karakoram (p. 125).

Map 6. Major petroglyph sites in the southern Caucasus (p. 151).

Map 7. Major petroglyph sites of Europe (p. 163).

Map 8. Major petroglyph sites of Arabia (p. 253).

Map 9. Major petroglyph sites of northern Africa (pp. 332–33).

Map 10 (fig. 299). Petroglyph sites in Wadi Djerat, Algeria (p. 345). Compiled and assembled from: Lhote, Henry, *Les gravures rupestres de l'Oued Djerat (Tassili-n-Ajjer)* (1975).

Photo Credits

All photos are by Christoph Baumer with the exception of the following:

Al-Fassam, Ibrahim, Riyadh, Saudi Arabia: fig. 332.

Arab News, Jeddah, Saudi Arabia: fig. 340.

Abegg-Stiftung, CH-3132 Riggisberg, Switzerland 2001 (Photo: Christoph von Viràg): fig. 40.

Akanaev, Timur, Almaty, Kazakhstan: fig. 335.

Alamy Ltd, Abingdon, Great Britain: figs 4, 5, 9, 49, 108–110, 112, 116–119, 189, 208, 287, 290, 291, 293.

Archivio Museo Alto Garda, Italy. Photo Gardaphoto: fig. 212.

Association Louis Bégouën, Montesquieu-Avantès, France: fig. 2.

Autonomous Region of Valle d'Aosta, Aosta, Italy. Photo: D. Cesare : fig. 213.

Bégouën, Éric / Association Louis Bégouën, Montesquieu-Avantès, France: fig. 10.

Berig, via https://commons.wikimedia.org/wiki/File:Hammars_(I).JPG. Licensed under the Creative Commons Attribution-Share Alike 3.0 Unported license: fig. 186.

Bobomulloev, Bobomullo, Dushanbe, Tajikistan: fig. 92.

Breteau, Emmanuel, Saint-Sébastien, France: figs 216, 217, 297, 307.

British Museum, London, Great Britain: fig. 111.

Centre National de la Préhistoire, Périgueux, France. Ministère de la Culture; Direction générale des patrimoines et de l'architecture; Service du patrimoine; Sous-direction de l'archéologie: fig. 3.

Choriyev, Behzod Nuriallaevich, Navoiy, Uzbekistan: fig. 334.

Dunand, Maurice and Ryckmans, Gonzague (ed.), *Corpus Inscriptionum Semiticarum. Pars V, Inscriptiones Saracenicas Continens*, vol. 1 : *Inscriptiones Safaiticae* (Paris: Imprimerie nationale, 1950–51), pl. 70, siglum C 1658 (= Dunand 388): fig. 268.

Emch, Martin, Germany via https://commons.wikimedia.org/wiki/File:Garamanten.jpg. Licensed under the Creative Commons Attribution-Share Alike 4.0 International license: fig. 286.

Estate of Joane Cardinal-Schubert & The Alberta Foundation for the Arts, Edmonton, Canada: fig. 337.

Felsbild-Archiv, Heidelberg Academy of Sciences and Humanities, Heidelberg, Germany: fig. 113.

Fouilles Nicholas Naudinot, 2013. Rennes, France. RAC-SRA Bretagne, propriété CD Finistère, 317: fig. 6.

Gold, Anne, Aachen, Germany: fig. 339.

Hanafusa, Takayuki, Osaka, Japan: fig. 285.

Jordan National Museum, Amman, Jordan: fig. 267.

Kamzam, Sepahi, Pakistan, via https://commons.wikimedia.org/wiki/File:Manthal_Rock_(Buddhist_inscriptions),_Skardu. JPG Licensed under the Creative Commons Attribution-Share Alike 4.0 International license: fig. 114.

Kilunovskaya, Marina, Saint Petersburg, Russian Federation: fig. 24.

Kubarev, Vladimir D. (†), permission Esther Jacobson-Tepfer, University of Oregon, Eugene, USA: fig. 26.

Leus, Pavel, Berlin, Germany: figs 22, 41.

Likhachev, Vadim, Rovaniemi, Finland: figs 130, 131.

Ling, Johan, Gothenburg, Sweden: fig. 160.

Minusinsk Regional Museum for Local Heritage named after N.M. Martyanov, Minusinsk, Russian Federation: fig. 336.

Mollet, Jörg, Solothurn, Switzerland: figs 303–306, 333.

Museum Ulm, Ulm, Germany: fig. 4.

National Museum of Denmark, CC BY-SA, Roberto Fortuna & Kira Ursem, Copenhagen, Denmark: figs 178, 183, 211.

National Museum of Denmark, CC BY-SA, John Lee, Copenhagen, Denmark: fig. 182.

National Museum of Prehistory, Val Camonica, Italy: figs 204, 205.

Pangritz, Stefan, Kandern, Germany: figs 99, 120, 327.

Pro Litteris, Zürich, Switzerland: p. 338.

Rappmann, Rainer, Achberg, Germany: fig. 338.

Reckel, Johannes, Göttingen, Germany: fig. 44.

Rogozhinsky, Alexey E., Almaty, Kazakhstan: figs 50, 60, 62.

Spinnler, Dieter, Wisen, Switzerland: figs 1, 7, 11, 180, 284, 317, 319, 320, 321, 326, 328, endpapers.

State Hermitage Museum, Saint Petersburg, Russian Federation: figs 12, 39, 54.

Tansem Karin / World Heritage Rock Art Centre – Alta Museum, Norway: fig. 143.

Todd, Donna, Drummond, Australia: fig. 29.

Weber, Therese, Arlesheim and Hergiswil, Switzerland: figs 86, 87, 95, 97, 128, 223, 252, 270, 315, 318, 322, 323, 325, 329, 341.

Widmer, Jean-Pierre (†), permission Claudia Greiner, BAG-Verlag, Grenzach-Wyhlen, Germany: fig. 210.

Zentrum Paul Klee, Bern, Switzerland: fig. 331.

All efforts have been made to name or identify copyright holders. We will endeavour to rectify any unintended omissions in future editions of this work, upon receipt of evidence of relevant intellectual property rights.

Rubbings

All rubbings were made by Therese Weber with the exception of the followings: Rogozhinsky, Alexey E., Almaty, Kazakhstan: figs 50, 62.

Acknowledgements

This book is the result of nineteen expeditions and journeys made between 1998 and 2024. The research owes its success to countless kind people in Algeria, Armenia, Azerbaijan, China, India, Italy, Jordan, Kazakhstan, Kyrgyzstan, Mongolia, Norway, Oman, Pakistan, Russia, Saudi Arabia, Sweden, Switzerland, Tajikistan and Uzbekistan; to all of them we remain grateful. Most of these helpful persons wish to remain anonymous; others are briefly acknowledged here, in alphabetical order.

Muhammad Abu Ahmad, Buraydah, who guided the authors in 2020 and 2022 to various petroglyph sites of northern and central Saudi Arabia and translated several Thamudic inscriptions.

The Alta Museum for the permission to make rubbings at the Alta rock art sites.

The Bredarör Grave Museum for the permission to photograph inside the Bredarör burial mound.

The Fujimori family and the team of the **Awagami Factory** in Tokushima, Japan, for the precious collaboration during the Artist in Residency of Therese Weber, from 25 April – 18 May, 2023.

Maria Guagnin, Jena, who gave valuable references to the literature on Saudi Arabian petroglyphs and the measurement of desert varnish.

Luc Hermann, Belgium, who in 2017 joined the team researching the petroglyphs of Saimaluu Tash, Kyrgyzstan.

Thomas Koblet and **Matthias Schenker,** Zurich, who in 2017 joined the team researching the petroglyphs of Saimaluu Tash, Kyrgyzstan, and produced a GIS-based interactive map.

Vadim Likhachev, Revda (Murmanskaya oblast), who welcomed the authors in 2019 on the island of Kanozero and explained its rock art.

Dimitry Luzhansky, Bishkek, who guided the authors in 2017 to the petroglyph sites of Saimaluu Tash, Zhaltyrak Tash, Issyk-Kul and several other sites in Kyrgyzstan.

Gerhard Milstreu, Copenhagen and Tanumshede, who provided highly valuable information on rock art in Bohuslän, Sweden. The authors remember with pleasure their ten days' stay in 2021 at Gerhard Milstreu's Rock Art Museum Underslös in Tanumshede.

Jörg Mollet, Solothurn, who opened for the authors his rich archive documenting the petroglyphs of Messak Settafet and Messak Mellet.

Muhammad al-Mustaneer, Najran, who guided the authors in 2020 and 2022 to rock art sites in southern Saudi Arabia.

Ningji, Ulaan Baatar, who accompanied the authors in 2001 and 2002 on two expeditions researching rock art in Mongolia.

Radiy Nurmametov, Cholpon-Ata, who guided the authors in 2004 to the rock art sites at Lake Issyk-Kul.

Stefan Pangritz, Kanders, for the digital processing of selected images.

Christian Robin and **Jérôme Norris,** France, who gave valuable information on pre-Islamic inscriptions from Saudi Arabia and Syria.

Alexey E. Rogozhinsky, Almaty, who showed the unknown site of Kogaly Bastal and shared images of petroglyphs from Khulzhabasy.

Andrzej Rozwadowski, Poznań, who shared valuable information on the petroglyphs of Saimaluu Tash, Kyrgyzstan.

The Saudi Heritage Commission for its permission to conduct fieldwork in the Kingdom of Saudi Arabia.

The Tanum Hällristningsmuseum Underslös for its permission to make the large rubbing of the Fossum panel.

Ingvild Telle, Alta, who in 2022 accompanied the authors at the various sites in Alta, Norway.

Dimitri Voyakin, Almaty and Samarkand, who provided literature on rock art in Central Asia unavailable in Western Europe.

András Zboray, Budapest, and the Tuareg **Kli-Kli,** Illizi, who guided the authors in 2023 to the rock art of Wadi Djerat, Algeria.

Indexes

Index: Concepts

Page locators in *italic* refer to figures, captions, and maps; locators in **bold** refer to tables and boxes; 'n' after a locator indicates the endnote number.

Index: People

Index: Places

Page locators in *italic* refer to figures, captions and maps; locators in **bold** refer to tables and boxes; 'n' after a locator indicates the endnote number.

T

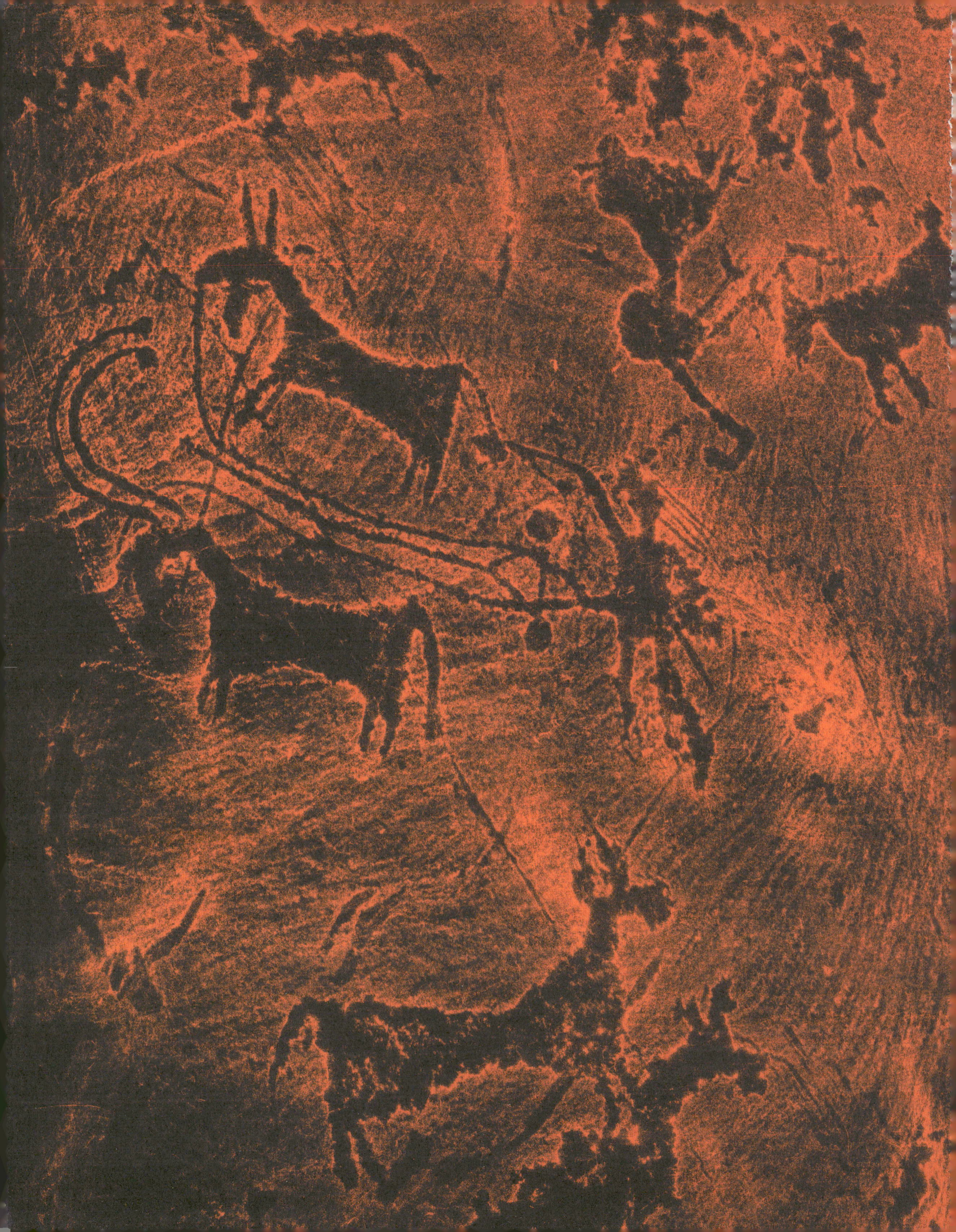